THE EMPEROR IN THE ROMAN WORLD

The Emperor
in the Roman World

(31 BC – AD *337)*

Fergus Millar

Professor of Ancient History
in the University of London

Duckworth

First published in 1977 by
Gerald Duckworth & Co. Ltd.
The Old Piano Factory
43 Gloucester Crescent, London NW1

Second impression 1983

ISBN 0 7156 0951 3

Printed in Great Britain by
Ebenezer Baylis and Son Ltd.
The Trinity Press, Worcester, and London

TO SUSANNA

Contents

vii

Part Four

EPILOGUE

Preface

This book is intended as an essay in historical interpretation. It is not a work of reference, but a guide whose aim is to map out certain essential elements in the structure and functioning of the Roman Empire. While it depends by its very nature on the presentation of a wide range of evidence, it does not set out to provide the complete evidence on any point. Inevitably, furthermore, it will in innumerable places have touched on complex topics whose full nature and significance the author, through ignorance, haste or lack of perception, has failed to bring out. Moreover, an analytical work tends to break up into their component parts sequences of actions and patterns of human relations which would ideally be presented in the full context in which they appeared to those who participated in them.

It must be emphasized that the work is essentially based upon, and springs from, individual items of ancient evidence. While due reference is made in the footnotes to those modern works which have been used, the book does not, either as a whole or in any of its parts, set out to give the 'bibliography of the question' or to take deliberate account of other views. What it presents is essentially its author's conception of certain basic features of the working of the Roman empire. It is impossible for an author himself to appreciate the contemporary influences which have affected his work and his outlook. But it can at least be affirmed that this book had a perfectly simple and concrete origin, namely in the reading of Josephus' *Jewish War* and the latter part of his *Antiquities* in the late summer of 1961, and in the observation that, in the events there described, the population of Judaea repeatedly applied to the emperor in person for decisions in their affairs but never received any spontaneous communications from him.

The work has developed from that point and embodies a number of conscious principles. The first is that any social system must be analysed primarily in terms of the specific patterns of action recorded of its members; the emperor 'was' what the emperor did. The second is that in government the most significant form of action is communication between persons; this book is largely a map of who said or wrote what to whom. The third is that, in interpreting the patterns which are thereby revealed, it is essential not merely to attend to the penumbras of attitudes and expectations expressed in those ancient sources which provide our evidence, but, so far as is possible, to base our conceptions solely on those attitudes and expectations. That is why far more use is made in this book of direct quotations in translation from ancient sources than is usually done, and why I have constantly indicated in the main text the source from which an item of evidence comes. For, however irritating it may be to a reader accustomed to different conventions, it is essential to the logic of the book to indicate the angle of vision of the more important sources of evidence, and also to express as directly as possible the vocabulary, the tone and the associations which each source brings to describing each individual event.

In preparing the work I have rigidly avoided reading sociological works on kingship or related topics, or studies of monarchic institutions in societies other than those of Greece and Rome. I am perfectly conscious that this will have involved considerable losses in percipience, and unawareness of whole ranges of questions which I could have asked. None the less, I am confident that the loss in the opposite case would have been far greater. For to have come to the subject with an array of concepts derived from the study of other societies would merely have made even more unattainable the proper objective of a historian, to subordinate himself to the evidence and to the conceptual world of a society in the past. Moreover, to have contaminated the presentation of the evidence from the Roman empire with conceptions drawn from wider sociological studies would precisely have destroyed whatever value this book may have for the comparative study of societies and institutions. I do indeed hope that the book may be of some interest to people other than students of the Roman empire, and for that reason I have confined quotations in Greek and Latin entirely to the footnotes.

The book touches on or traverses many substantial areas of knowledge, from the ideology of monarchy in the ancient world to Roman law, the government and finance of the empire, the institutions of the cities and the history of the church. It cannot therefore be too strongly emphasized that its actual subject is none of these; it aims to tell the whole truth neither about any one of them, nor still less about the empire as a whole. Nor, indeed, does it set out to deal with all aspects of the role played by the emperor; in particular it does not deal with the still neglected topic of his relations with client kings, or his diplomatic contacts with kings and peoples beyond the empire; nor with his role as general, and his relations with the army and with individual soldiers. Its subject-matter is certain patterns of contact between the inhabitants of the empire and the emperor in person, and its object is to suggest that these patterns are of fundamental importance in understanding what the Roman empire was.

The work for this book was begun while I was a Fellow of All Souls College, Oxford, and has continued through twelve years as a Fellow of The Queen's College. The fact that it will be published when I have moved to the University of London gives me all the better occasion to look back with profound gratitude on the privilege of having belonged to these two colleges. In particular, I owe a debt to Queen's for two periods of leave, during one of which I spent a term at the Institute for Advanced Study in Princeton, which has proved in retrospect to have been the vital formative stage in the evolution of the book.

Almost every word of it, however, has been written in another institution, the Haverfield Library in the Ashmolean Museum at Oxford. From lack of experience, it would perhaps be rash on my part to assert that it is the best library for ancient history and archaeology in the world. But, as built up by the devoted work of Mr R. F. Ovenell, Librarian from 1947 to 1972, vigorously continued by his successor, Mr Clifford Currie, both of them supported by a staff of exceptional helpfulness, courtesy and knowledge, it can have few rivals anywhere as a place of study.

What such an institution contributes is something much more than the mere convenience of access to books. But it was also of vital practical help that the entire manuscript could be typed stage by stage within the walls of the Ashmolean by Mrs G. R. Benfield and Mrs S. Guppy, who displayed not only remarkable skill but an equanimity almost incredible in persons confronted daily with my handwriting over a period of sixteen months.

There are debts which one cannot measure, and I can make only a bare acknowledgement here of all that I have learned from Professor Sir Ronald Syme, Professor A. D. Momigliano, Mr P. M. Fraser, Professor P. R. L. Brown, Dr J. F. Matthews, and Professor T. D. Barnes. To the latter two and to Professor P. A. Brunt, I am also much indebted for detailed comments on the typescript, which have saved me from a host of errors. In the course of the work I have also been greatly helped by receiving advance copies of the *Tabula Banasitana* from Professor W. Seston and of various important Oxyrhynchus papyri from Mr P. J. Parsons; by continuing discussion with Professor A. M. Honoré, and by a text of his fundamental article on imperial rescripts; by the unpublished Oxford thesis of Dr W. Williams of Keele University, 'Imperial Edicts, Epistulae and Rescripts: Authorship, Composition and Function'; and above all by permission from Miss J. M. Reynolds to make use of a preliminary text of the extremely important dossier of Imperial letters from the theatre at Aphrodisias, revealed by the excavations by Professor K. T. Erim. The dossier will be published shortly by Miss Reynolds; in the meantime one may refer to her paper, 'Aphrodisias: A Free and Federate City', *Akten VI. Int. Kong. f. Gr. u. Lat. Epigraphik, München 1972* (1973), 115.

I cannot undertake to express here all that I owe to my wife, both intellectually and in every other way. So the dedication must speak for itself.

The Queen's College,   F.M.
Oxford
30. 6. 75

Abbreviations

I have not listed all the alphabetic abbreviations for periodicals, collections of documents and reference works, which are given in the conventional forms. But it may be useful to give the full titles of some frequently cited works which appear in shortened form in the footnotes:

Abbott and Johnson, *Municipal Administration* = F. F. Abbott and A. C. Johnson, *Municipal Administration in the Roman Empire* (1926).

Barbieri, *Albo senatorio* = G. Barbieri, *L'albo senatorio da Settimio Severo a Carino (193–285)* (1952).

Coll. = *Mosaicarum et Romanarum Legum Collatio* (*FIRA*[2] I, 541–89).

Consultatio = *Consultatio Veteris Cuiusdam Iurisconsulti* (*FIRA*[2] I, 591–621).

FIRA[2] = S. Riccobono, J. Baviera, C. Ferrini, J. Furlani, V. Arangio-Ruiz, *Fontes Iuris Romani Anteiustiniani*[2] I–III (1940–3).

Hirschfeld, *Verwaltungsbeamten*[2] = O. Hirschfeld, *Die kaiserlichen Verwaltungsbeamten bis auf Diocletian*[2] (1905).

Jones, *Later Roman Empire* = A. H. M. Jones, *The Later Roman Empire* I–III (1964).

Mitteis, *Chrestomathie* = L. Mitteis and U. Wilcken, *Grundzüge und Chrestomathie der Papyruskunde* II: *Juristischer Teil* (1912).

Musurillo, *Acts of the Pagan Martyrs* = H. A. Musurillo, *The Acts of the Pagan Martyrs (Acta Alexandrinorum)* (1954).

Pflaum, *Carrières* = H.-G. Pflaum, *Les carrières procuratoriennes équestres* (1960–1).

PLRE = *The Prosopography of the Later Roman Empire* I: *A.D. 260–395*, ed. A. H. M. Jones, J. R. Martindale, J. Morris (1971).

Rostovtzeff, *SEHRE*[2] = M. Rostovtzeff, *Social and Economic History of the Roman Empire*[2], ed. P. M. Fraser (1957).

Schürer, *Jewish People* I = E. Schürer, *History of the Jewish People in the Age of Jesus Christ (175 BC–AD 135)* I, ed. G. Vermes and F. Millar (1973).

Seeck, *Regesten* = O. Seeck, *Regesten der Kaiser und Päpste für die Jahre 311 bis 476 n. Chr.* (1919).

Sherk, *Roman Documents* = R. K. Sherk, *Roman Documents from the Greek East* (Senatus Consulta *and* Epistulae *to the Age of Augustus*) (1969).

Wilcken, *Chrestomathie* = L. Mitteis and U. Wilcken, *Grundzüge und Chrestomathie der Papyruskunde* I: *Historischer Teil* (1912).

As regards texts, the *Panegyrici Latini* are cited with the numbering given in the Budé edition by E. Galletier, *Panégyriques Latines* I–II (1949–52); the subdivisions of chapters in Plutarch's *Lives*, Suetonius' *Lives* and Tacitus are those of the Teubner editions; and the figures in brackets following some references to Books LX–LXXX of Cassius Dio's *Roman History* are to pages in vol. III (1901) of the edition by U. P. Boissevain.

PART ONE

Prologue

I

Marcus Aurelius at Sirmium

'Reflect continually,' Marcus Aurelius advised himself, 'on the fact that all such things as happen now, also happened before, and on the fact that they will happen again. The whole dramas and the comparable scenes which you know from your own experience or from the history of the past, place these before your eyes, such as the whole court of Hadrian, the whole court of Antoninus, and the whole court of Philip, Alexander, Croesus. All these were similar, only the actors were different.'[1] This private moral reflection cannot be taken as a considered historical judgment. The court of the Roman emperors, developing out of a senatorial household, was long shaped by conceptions wholly alien to the Macedonian monarchy; and furthermore it was to evolve continually under the pressure of circumstances until its establishment as a Christian court in the new Greek city of Constantinople. Yet, none the less, Marcus' words reveal the consciousness of a real continuity; for, just as the memory of Alexander exercised an enduring influence on the military role of the emperor, so there persisted long-established conceptions of what a 'king' should be which did indeed help to transform a Roman *princeps* into a descendant of the Hellenistic kings.

One of these conceptions, and indeed the most central and effective of all, is reflected in an anecdote told by Cassius Dio about Hadrian. When the emperor was on a journey, so the story runs, a woman approached him and asked for his attention. Hadrian replied that he had no time, at which the woman shouted, 'Then do not be a king!' So he turned round and gave her leave to speak.[2] It is easy, and not wholly misleading, to quote this anecdote as evidence for the role required of the Roman emperors, and accepted by them.[3] But this is not the whole truth, nor the whole problem. For almost identical stories are told twice by Plutarch, once of Philip II and once of Demetrius Poliorcetes,[4] and again by a writer called Serenus about Antipater.[5] Plutarch's story about Demetrius relates to his reception of written petitions: we shall see how the answering of such *libelli* became one of the primary functions of the emperor. Moreover, Plutarch concludes with some observations on kingship and the giving of justice:

[1] *Med.* x, 27.
[2] LIX, 6, 3.
[3] Quoted by myself in *JRS* LVII (1967), 9. Professors J. Béranger, J. F. Gilliam and Chr. Habich were each independently kind enough to point out to me the parallel references which follow.
[4] *Mor.* 179 C–D; *Demetr.* 42, 7. The translation which follows is that of the Loeb ed.
[5] In Stobaeus, *Flor.* III, 13, 48.

And surely nothing so befits a king as the work of justice. For 'Ares is tyrant', in the words of Timotheus, but 'Law is the King of all things' according to Pindar; and Homer speaks of kings as receiving from Zeus for protection and safe-keeping not bronze-beaked ships, but 'ordinances of justice'; and he calls a disciple and 'confidant' of Zeus not the most warlike or unjust of murderous of kings, but the most just.

So we are left to wonder whether the incident of Hadrian and the woman petitioner, set at about the time of Plutarch's death, is fact or fiction. In either case we should beware of dismissing as irrelevant literary affectation either the display of classical quotations by Plutarch or the expectations about the conduct of a king which he derives from them. Not only do quotations from Homer and other classical Greek writers appear from time to time in the works of the Roman jurists themselves,[6] but the conceptions clothed in Plutarch's mannered compositions imposed themselves firmly and concretely on the real life and routine of the emperor.

There were other demands, of which the conduct of wars assumed an ever-growing importance. But it is a fact of fundamental significance that when an emperor on campaign had leisure from actual fighting it was precisely to the giving of justice that he returned. This is shown with perfect clarity in Dio's description of the conduct of civil affairs by Marcus Aurelius during the five years from 169/70 onwards which he spent conducting the Danubian wars:[7] 'But the emperor, whenever he had leisure from the war, gave judgment. He ordered that ample time should be allotted on the water-clock to the advocates, and engaged in most extensive enquiries and interrogations, so that the just solution could be determined by all possible means. In this way he often spent eleven and even twelve days on a case, sometimes even judging at night.'[8]

A long story in Philostratus' *Lives of the Sophists* supports this generalization with a vivid portrayal of Marcus in the role of judge in Pannonia.[9] The occasion arose from a notorious dispute in Athens, in which the people accused the millionaire Herodes Atticus of tyranny. When he in turn accused his opponents before the proconsul, they made their way to Sirmium, which Marcus was using as his base for the Marcommanic war. There they lodged near the imperial residence (*basileia*) and were granted upkeep by the emperor. When the case came on, Herodes was distraught by a personal loss, and spoke wildly: 'This is my reward for hospitality to Lucius, though it was you who sent him to me.' The reference was to Lucius Verus, who as co-emperor in 162 had visited Athens on his way to the Parthian war, and had stayed with Herodes; then too he had sacrificed in the city and had been initiated into the Eleusinian mysteries.[10] Herodes' outburst was answered by

[6] Homer: e.g. *Digest* XVIII, 1, 1, 1; XXXII, 65, 4; XLVIII, 5, 14, 1; XLVIII, 19, 16, 8; L, 16, 236. Solon: X, 1, 13; XLVII, 22, 4; XLVIII, 5, 24 (and Draco). Xenophon: L, 16, 233. Plato: L, 11, 2. Demosthenes: 1, 3, 2; XLVIII, 19, 16, 6. Theophrastus: V, 4, 3. Chrysippus: 1, 3, 2.

[7] See A. R. Birley, *Marcus Aurelius* (1966), 222 f.

[8] LXXI, 6, 1 (256–7).

[9] Philostratus, *VS* II, 1 (559–63).

[10] Jerome, *Chron.* ed. Helm, p. 204; *Syll.*[3] 869 (= *IG* II[2] 3592); 872 (= *IG* II[2] 3620); see T. D. Barnes, *JRS* LVII (1967), 71; E. Kapetanopoulos, 'Flavius Hierophantes Paianieus and Lucius Verus', *RÉG* LXXXIII (1970), 63.

a threat from 'Bassaeus, who was entrusted with the sword', that is the
praetorian prefect, M. Bassaeus Rufus;[11] whereupon Herodes left the court
leaving much of his allotted time to run. Marcus then asked the Athenian
opponents of Herodes to make their defence, in the course of which they
went over to accusation, reciting a bitterly-worded decree of the Athenian
people, which caused the emperor to burst into tears. The speech of one of
these Athenian opponents, Demostratus, was preserved, and Philostratus
comments later on its integrated yet varied style.

In the event Marcus laid a mild penalty on the freedmen of Herodes, and
punished Herodes himself only with a temporary displeasure. For a period,
Herodes remained at odds with the Athenians, and stayed in Epirus. But
even then Marcus is found, in a long inscription of his judicial decisions
discovered at Athens, expressing his anxiety that they should be reconciled.[12]
Finally, Herodes returned to Athens, an event elegantly celebrated in an
epigram from an inscription there.[13] From Athens he wrote to Marcus to
complain that the emperor no longer wrote to him; previously he had
written so frequently that three letter-carriers might arrive in a single day.
Marcus replied from his winter-quarters in Syria in 175/6, propitiating him
and recalling that he too intended to visit Athens to be initiated in the
Eleusinian mysteries.[14]

This complex story need not be pursued further here. But it raises a
number of issues and questions whose appreciation is essential to any
understanding of the Roman empire.

The first point is the location of the emperor's headquarters. It is far from
a pure accident that roughly halfway in time between Augustus and
Constantine we find Marcus working for several years from a base on the
great route which ran from Rome to Northern Italy, and then through
Pannonia and Thrace to Byzantium, Asia Minor and the Euphrates frontier.
We shall see that military necessities made Sirmium one of the centres of
Imperial activity long before the tetrarchic period.[15] If, however, we try to
examine the emperor's establishment there more closely, the picture is confused. What were the *basileia* there which the emperor occupied—a *hospitium*
provided by the city, the governor's *praetorium*, or a private possession
acquired in some way by the emperor? The question of imperial property
and wealth confronts us again in this story, in the form of the supplies
granted by way of largesse to Herodes' opponents. The varied pattern of
ways in which the imperial wealth was acquired, institutionalized and used
provides us with one of the most important, and certainly the most difficult,
aspects of the manner in which a monarch came to relate to the *res publica* of
Rome and to the population of the empire.

In playing his part in those relations, what advisers and assistants did the
emperor have? We note the presence in court with Marcus of the praetorian

[11] *PIR*² B 69; Pflaum, *Carrières*, no. 162.
[12] Published by J. H. Oliver, *Marcus Aurelius: Aspects of Civic and Cultural Policy in the East*,
Hesperia Supp. XIII (1970), Plaque E, lines 87–91.
[13] *IG* II² 3606. See *Hesperia* Supp. XIII, 34.
[14] pp. 36; 502–3.
[15] pp. 47–8.

prefect. No other individual is named, but abundant evidence will make clear that imperial 'friends', of the senatorial and equestrian orders, will have been there too.[16] So too will an *ab epistulis*, in charge of letters; Philostratus happens to record elsewhere that Marcus summoned to Pannonia a sophist from Seleucia, Alexander 'the Clay-Plato', to be *ab epistulis Graecis*.[17] That is no accident either, for abundant evidence illustrates the constant flow of letters to and from the emperor wherever he happened to be.[18] The same is true of judicial cases, whether heard in person by the emperor or presented for his decision by letter or *libellus*. It is to be noted that the *basileia* at Sirmium had a *dikastêrion*, or court-room, which a Latin source would have called *auditorium*. The implication that it was to judicial business that the emperor had to turn when the war allowed is confirmed by Marcus' own words in one of the decisions inscribed in Athens: he rejects one case 'in order that after so long he shall not have to wait for the opportune moments in which it will be possible for me to judge the cases which need a decision precisely at the time of our military activity'.[19]

The emperor was what the emperor did. The emperor's role in the 'government' of the empire must have been such that it could be carried on while he spent years (like Hadrian) travelling through the provinces or (like Marcus) on campaign, assisted by his prefect, his *amici* and his 'secretaries'. This study will suggest that the apparent impossibility of such a pattern of government is an illusion, for the emperor's role in relation to his subjects was essentially that of listening to requests, and of hearing disputes. If we follow our evidence, we might almost come to believe that the primary role of the emperor was to listen to speeches in Greek. The great Herodes Atticus himself, so his enemies recalled, had in his youth broken down in a speech before an emperor in Pannonia;[20] and Philostratus in person heard Heliodorus from Arabia score a brilliant triumph before Caracalla in Gaul.[21]

It is the essential passivity of the role expected of the emperor both by himself and by others which explains the very limited and simple 'governmental' apparatus which he needed. A very large proportion of his contacts with his subjects fell into a pattern which may be called 'petition-and-response'. This will cover not merely the interminable embassies from cities, mainly Greek, but also the vast mass of imperial rescripts which we know from the *Codex* of Justinian and the legal writings collected in the *Digest*. Documentary evidence now confirms how substantial a part of an emperor's daily work the answering of petitions represented.[22] Many of them were of the most minor local or personal importance; that they were considered at all by the ruler of the Roman empire can be explained only by the fact that in the ancient world this role was essential to the conception of what monarchy should be. This conception was shared also by the Christian

---

[16] pp. 119–22.
[17] Philostratus, *VS* II, 5. See further p. 91
[18] See esp. pp. 27–8, 38–9, 46–51, 211.
[19] *Hesperia* Supp. XIII, Plaque II, lines 26–7. Trans. Oliver.
[20] Philostratus, *VS* II, 1.
[21] *VS* II, 32; cf. pp. 234, 281.
[22] pp. 244–5.

church; and thus it is again no accident that, for instance, the Donatist schism was first put as an issue before Constantine in the form of *libelli*, sent to him not by the Catholic but by the schismatic party in the African church.[23]

If an emperor was what he did, so a whole social system can be defined in terms of the precise form of contacts between individuals and groups. We can, and must, grant the acceptance, from the very beginning, by the emperor as well as by his subjects, of the assumption that he was there to listen to requests and grant favours. For in 30 BC, only a year after his victory at Actium, Octavian wrote to the city of Rhosus in Syria, 'I recommend this man [his former admiral, Seleucus] to you. For such men render one's benevolence more ready towards their native cities as well. So, granted that I shall gladly do whatever I can for you for the sake of Seleucus, have confidence and send to me for whatever you want.'[24] The questions remain of exactly how a city or a private individual approached the emperor; of what rules or conventions governed the sending of an embassy; and of what court officials or bureaucrats stood in their way. Above all, how was an emperor actually addressed, in speech or writing? We may recall that Philostratus thought Demostratus' speech before Marcus particularly impressive. But there was more to it than individual taste, and an orator of the late third or early fourth century could lay down precise rules for speeches made on embassies to the emperor.[25]

Philostratus' story shows Marcus hearing the case of Herodes himself, reacting philosophically or emotionally to its development, and giving a verdict himself. It similarly shows him later writing personally to Herodes, while the inscription of his decisions shows him writing in equally personal terms to the city of Athens:[26]

> I think that I have shown through my pronouncements that I have made every effort to ensure, by my concern rather than my power, that in future Herodes should be able to join gladly with the Athenians in their religious and secular celebrations with his well known concern for education and culture; and that the Athenians, recalling the generosity which the excellent Herodes had already displayed to them, should renew their warm mutual friendship for him, on account of which they do not require me as mediator.

Abundant evidence makes clear that the emperors heard cases and embassies themselves, issued verdicts and decisions and favours themselves, and composed, though only occasionally wrote with their own hand, letters, answers and edicts.[27] But we would still wish to know how copies were made and (perhaps) filed, and how they were published, transmitted to their

[23] pp. 584 f.

[24] *IGLS* III, 718, lines 91–3; quoted in *JRS* LXIII (1973), 58.

[25] Spengel, *Rhetores Graeci* III, 422–4. On the complex question of the authorship of the works going under the name of Menander, see C. Bursian, 'Der Rhetor Menandros und seine Schriften', *Abh. Bay. Akad.* XVI. 3 (1882).

[26] *Hesperia* Supp. XIII, Plaque E, lines 87–91. For a revised text of these lines see C. P. Jones, *ZPE* VIII (1971), 181–2.

[27] See esp. ch. v.

addressees, and preserved at their destination. For these practical questions too will affect how we visualize the currency of the emperor's word among his subjects.

But in dealing with the transmission of words between the emperor and the population we have to avoid ignoring the words themselves. For the enormous mass of available evidence enables us to go beyond the formal transmission of communications up and down the extremely simple and personal power-structure, to the values and motives which informed the system, and determined the decisions made, the preferences felt and the favours granted within it. It cannot be emphasized too strongly that these values were themselves the product of the traditional literary and rhetorical education which was the common heritage of the ruling classes of the empire, including the emperor himself. Moreover it was, for the vast majority of them, the only education they received, and consequently the most important factor in guiding their decisions. These priorities affected equally the emperor and his subjects. It is once again not an accident that all the individual cases so far presented of matters brought before an emperor have come from within the Greek world. This study will present the hypothesis that the overwhelming bias towards the Greek provinces (and, to a lesser extent, the civilized Latin provinces of the Mediterranean) in the evidence relating to contacts between subject and emperor is not just the reflection of chance, of the survival of literary and documentary records; but that on the contrary it was precisely considerations of cultural and historical status which gave cities, and individuals from them, the confidence to approach the emperor. These themes are made quite explicit in the work on rhetoric mentioned earlier:[28]

> When you have spoken of his courage in war and the blessings of peace, you will draw his attention to the city for which you are ambassador. Here you should develop two themes. One is that of amplification by means of contrast, as for instance that Ilium was once a fine city, the most famous of all under the sun, and long ago resisted invasion from Europe. Then you turn to description and set out its present fate, that it has fallen into ruins; and you should especially mention those buildings which are for public use and public life, and for which emperors usually take thought, for instance that the baths have collapsed, the aqueducts are destroyed and the whole appearance of the city disfigured . . .

The question of a city's historical role and associations was of real significance. It is not merely the accident of thorough excavation in these two places which has meant that we have so many imperial letters on inscriptions from Athens and Delphi. The fact reflects a real and important aspect of the values in terms of which the government of the Roman empire was conducted. The claims which could be made on the attention of Marcus Aurelius by Athens (and by a famous sophist, and ex-consul, Herodes Atticus) were only the high points on a scale of claims which could be made by innumerable cities throughout the Mediterranean—and could not be

---

[28] [Menander], περὶ πρεσβευτικοῦ, Spengel, o.c., 423.

made, and, it will be suggested, were not made, by cities and communities in Gaul or Britain or Noricum or Pannonia. Once again the values at work do not have to be deduced by argument, but are explicitly attested from the very beginning of the empire. When Octavian took Alexandria in 30 BC, the people saw him enter the city in a carriage accompanied by his tutor, their fellow-citizen Areus. Octavian ascended a tribunal erected for him in the gymnasium and, addressing the terrified people in Greek, told them that he would spare them, for three reasons: first the memory of Alexander, second the size and beauty of the city, and third as a favour to his friend Areus.[29]

The incident, like the letter of the same year to Rhosus, illustrates another essential feature of the working of the empire as a political system, namely the immensely complex network of relationships which bound the emperor to the educated bourgeoisie of the cities. Here again, cultural factors were of all-embracing, though not exclusive, importance. It was the rhetoricians, the poets, grammarians and philosophers of the provincial cities who, after his senatorial 'friends', had the easiest access to the emperor—far quicker and easier than that eventually afforded by military service or the long climb up the equestrian career. As we shall see, it was from these educated provincials that, apart from a brief moment of glory for the imperial freedmen, the emperor's assistants and secretaries were drawn; and it was they who were most successful in channelling benefits to their protégés and native cities. The eventual detachment of the emperor from the social context of the city of Rome meant on the one hand his closer attachment to the army, but on the other his capture by the educated provincials, mainly Greek, who now staffed his court. It is perhaps not an accident that the 'great' persecution of Diocletian took place a few years after the imperial court first became firmly established in a Greek city, and was more than ever before exposed to the influence of pagan Greek intellectuals.

The personal favour, openly and deliberately advertised in the case of Areus, had from the beginning had a darker side to it. However consistent and comprehensible were the attitudes and priorities which informed the system, there remained an essential element of arbitrariness on the part of the emperors, of fear, sycophancy and uncertainty on the part of their subjects. Only a man of Herodes' standing could have escaped the threat of death made to him by Bassaeus Rufus at Sirmium. For others the fear of death was never entirely absent. The fear which watched the emperor's every gesture and expression is vividly reflected in an incident before Augustus in Syria in 20 BC: a delegation from Gadara accused Herod of malpractices, saw that the emperor's friendly bearing towards the king remained unaltered—and committed suicide to a man.[30] By contrast we see a real and significant aspect of imperial life in Suetonius' report that at dinner Tiberius would put questions from his day's reading in the classics to a circle of learned men; but, for trying to find out from the servants what Tiberius had been reading, Seleucus of Alexandria was forced to commit

[29] Plutarch, *Ant.* 80, 1–3; *Mor.* 207 A–B; cf. Dio LI, 16, 3–4. On Areus cf. p. 85.
[30] Josephus, *Ant.* XV, 10, 3 (354–9).

suicide.[31] Three hundred years later it was a truly historic moment when, as Eusebius records, Christian bishops dined with Constantine, passing without fear between the drawn swords of the soldiers.[32]

That arbitrary exercise of power and favour on the one side, and that ever-present fear and uncertainty on the other have to be remembered when we look at a system which was in many ways, by its very passivity, remarkably open, responsive to pressures, and humane. Jurisdiction and the receipt of city and provincial embassies must have exposed the emperor each year to the presence of literally thousands of men from the dominant classes; and in a provincial city the possibility of an appeal or petition or embassy to the emperor was never formally precluded, however hazardous the outcome might be. It was open not only to prominent citizens of Athens, but also, on many occasions, to the Jews of first-century Judaea,[33] to a remote community in Mauretania under Antoninus Pius,[34] and in the third century to the churches of Egypt and Antioch.[35] Yet, again, a favourable verdict for one group or individual inevitably meant a rejection or a penalty for another. Only Constantine tried to bring together the two conceptions of the emperor, as judge and as dispenser of benefits, by granting properties and land to those who lost cases before him—so that no one should leave his presence dejected and sorrowful.[36] Even the endlessly repeated gifts of cash or land made by emperors were very largely favours which simply transferred wealth from one group or individual to another. This emerges most clearly perhaps in the pattern by which *bona damnatorum*, the property of persons condemned on criminal charges, first became (it will be argued) the property of the emperor, and were certainly at his free disposal, and by the end of the period had become a category of goods to be petitioned for directly by those in imperial favour.[37] Imperial generosity was creative only in that sense in which the civilization in which it operated was most widely creative, namely the attachment to and preservation of the amenities of urban life. Marcus, who burst into tears when the ambassadors from Athens spoke before him, was to weep again when he read the letter of Aelius Aristides on the destruction of Smyrna by an earthquake—and he then had the city restored.[38]

The evidence does on occasion show emperors receiving petitions from obscure village communities in Thrace and Asia, and from common soldiers, freedmen and even slaves.[39] But it would be futile to deny that, just as the social and cultural values of ancient society meant that the intricate pattern of relations between the emperor and his subjects which this study describes affected only the more civilized areas, so these same values meant that the

[31] *Tib.* 56. On Seleucus see the Suda s.v. Σέλευκος 'Αλεξανδρεύς, and *FGrH* 341.

[32] *VC* III, 15, 2.

[33] pp. 376–9.

[34] pp. 380–1.

[35] Eusebius, *HE* VII, 13; 30. See below, pp. 571–3.

[36] Eusebius, *VC* IV, 4.

[37] pp. 163–74.

[38] Philostratus, *VS* II, 9. The letter is Aristides, *Or.* XIX Keil. See below, pp. 423–4; and for Smyrna, the earthquake and the reconstruction see C. J. Cadoux, *Ancient Smyrna* (1938), 279–83,

[39] On petitions from slaves note the article by A. Piganiol, 'Les Empereurs parlent aux esclaves', *Romanitas* I (1958), 7 = *Scripta Varia* III (1973), 202; see further pp. 476, 489–90 below.

social range of these contacts was generally limited to the upper classes. It was only in the mass, predominantly at the games and shows of Rome, sometimes in provincial cities and at last in Constantinople, that the emperor was regularly faced with the demands and aspirations of wider groups in society.[40]

None the less, the determination of the precise verbal and written forms of communication between the emperor and his subjects is a matter of fundamental importance for the understanding not only of what 'government' was in the ancient world, but also of the nature and values of ancient society as a whole. Society demanded from the emperor military protection, and if possible resounding victories over foreign enemies. But when he had leisure from that, it demanded not a programme of change but a willingness to listen; a willingness to respond to demands, to grant gifts and privileges, to give justice, to issue legal rulings. In short, from the very beginning of the empire, there was a demand that the emperor should behave as a *basileus* who heard the petitions of his subjects and answered them with verbal or written pronouncements which were themselves effective and legal acts. As we have seen, as early as 30 BC Octavian was already consciously and explicitly playing this role; the type of pressure which created it is visible in Strabo's report of how in the following year he met a fisherman from the Aegean island of Gyarus on his way to petition Octavian for remission of tribute for his native city.[41]

This whole conception of course ran directly counter to that of the emperor as the holder of a number of limited and constitutional powers of republican origin, as an office-holder dependent on the senate and people of Rome. It will be necessary to observe how far the continued existence of republican institutions, the senate in particular, directed or determined the nature of his activities. At the same time, we shall see how the emergence of monarchy to some extent transformed those very republican institutions themselves into instruments of patronage: so the 'public horse', membership of the jury-panels, entry to the senate or appointment to a wide range of senatorial offices became things to be petitioned for, and to be granted as a favour by the emperor; while, beside these ranks and posts, there evolved the whole pattern of equestrian office-holding which was from the beginning entirely dependent on imperial patronage, and which by the end of the period represented the major part of the administration of the empire.[42] Thus, just as Bassaeus owed the praetorian prefecture which he held at Sirmium, so Herodes Atticus owed the consulate which he had held in 143 to imperial appointment. Roman ranks, titles and posts themselves became benefits which emperors could bestow, and thereby became both directly and indirectly an element in the communications between the emperor and his subjects. Under Antoninus Pius the town council of Tergeste was to flatter itself that a native of the town had sought senatorial rank with the prime object of defending its interests in cases before the emperor.[43]

[40] pp. 54, 368–75.
[41] Strabo x, 5, 3 (485).
[42] Cf. pp. 279–313 below.
[43] *ILS* 6680; cf. pp. 420, 433–4.

Marcus Aurelius at Sirmium thought of himself as no more than temporarily and fortuitously absent from Rome. In a famous phrase from the *Meditations*, some at least of which was written at Carnuntum in Pannonia, he said: 'My city and fatherland is, as Antoninus, Rome: as a man, the Universe.'[44] Yet both his presence and his role at Sirmium may symbolize for us a crucial evolution in the place and the function of the emperor in the Roman world. The circumstances which brought him there were military, just as were those which were to take Constantine along the same route first to Serdica, which he at one time called 'my Rome', and then further east.[45] But if military pressures provoked this evolution, it was that conception of the emperor's personal role which this study examines which both made it possible at all and fundamentally influenced the nature of the new Christian monarchy which established itself at Constantinople. Philostratus' emphasis on the philosophic quality of Aurelius' judgments at Sirmium had been forestalled by Athenagoras,[46] who had addressed his defence of Christianity to 'the Emperors Marcus Aurelius Antoninus and Lucius Aurelius Commodus, Armenian Victors, Sarmatian Victors and above all Philosophers'—and had given the work the title 'Embassy'.

---

[44] *Med.* VI, 44.
[45] Petrus Patricius, frag. 190 in Dio, ed. Boissevain, III, p. 748; *FHG* IV, 199.
[46] Athenagoras, *Legatio* I, I. The wording gives a mere approximation to the official titulature of the emperors. See T. D. Barnes in *JThSt* XXVI (1975), III, and cf. pp. 564–5.

PART TWO

The Emperor: Setting, Resources and Function

II

From Rome to Constantinople

1. *Introduction*

'For just as the heavens are the home of gods, so is Italy that of kings,' wrote Artemidorus of Daldis in the second century, confidently applying this accepted truth in the interpretation of a dream.[1] That conception indeed still mirrored the facts. The imperial residences were still situated in Rome and the more fashionable areas of Italy, very much as the houses and villas of Cicero and his contemporaries had been. To Rome the emperor returned from wars or travels, to attend the senate, to give and attend games and shows, to address the people and distribute largesse to them. When Marcus Aurelius returned to Rome in 176, Dio writes, 'He made a speech to the people. When he mentioned in the course of it among other things the fact that he had been abroad for many years, they shouted "eight" and indicated this with their hands also, so that they should receive this number of gold pieces for a banquet.'[2]

To the very end of our period, as we can see from Constantine's return there to celebrate his *vicennalia* in 326, Rome retained its role as the setting for the major rituals and celebrations of the imperial regime. But precisely that fact presents us with a whole series of problems about the social character of the office of emperor, and its evolution over three and a half centuries. How much did the role and function of emperor owe to the functions and the setting of the republican magistracies from which it developed? And, outside the sphere of the actual performance of public duties, how much to the social patterns of late republican senatorial life in Rome? For example, it is one of the most distinctive features of republican public life that the holders of annual magistracies had no public buildings specific to themselves in which to carry out their functions. Their duties were conducted in public, in the senate, the Forum or the Campus Martius; it was in their own houses that they held *salutationes* in the morning, and from and to their own houses that they were escorted each day by large crowds.[3] More than that, embassies from Greek cities could call at the houses of individual senators and urge their support, as Diodorus describes a

---

[1] *Oneirocritica* II, 68.
[2] LXXI, 32, 1 (272).
[3] The essential illustrative evidence is neatly collected by W. Kroll, *Die Kultur der ciceronischen Zeit* II (1933), ch. 8, 'Umgangsformen und Etikette'.

Cretan embassy doing in about 69 BC,[4] and as a famous inscription shows some Teans doing a century earlier.[5] It is therefore impossible to exaggerate the importance of the fact that a significant part of the imperial functions necessarily developed within the context of what was in origin a private household. But how far did the typical architecture and social structure of a senatorial household serve to retard the emergence of a setting which was distinctively imperial?

The life of a Roman senator conventionally included substantial periods on his villas, supervising, however distantly, the management of his estates, hunting, or enjoying the aesthetic pleasures of gardens elegantly laid out and adorned with statuary looted or bought from the Greek east. The richest senators, indeed, could afford to move from villa to villa of their own in Latium or Campania. This pattern of life persisted on the part of the emperors through the first three centuries, so long as they remained rooted in Italy; and though it is significantly less apparent there, there are some traces of it in the new context of Nicomedia and Constantinople at the end of our period. But the imperial villas were more than just choice items of social or architectural history. They were indeed both, and even functioned in a small way as tourist centres: at Antium, for instance, the visitor could see a book by Pythagoras, and letters of Apollonius of Tyana, and at Baiae a cloak and jewellery given to Tiberius as a child by the wife of Sextus Pompey.[6] Their significance for the nature of the Empire lies rather in the fact that the emperors did spend substantial periods at their villas, and while there continued to hold jurisdiction, write letters and issue edicts. This pattern too persisted at least until the early third century: Herodian records that Severus in the period 205–8, 'spent most of his time in the imperial villas outside Rome and on the coast of Campania, giving judgment and seeing to political affairs'.[7] So, whatever the duties and functions of an emperor were, they must have been such that they could be performed for substantial periods in Italian villas.

The same is true of the extensive journeys of many emperors through the provinces or on campaigns. What is more, it had been in his government of a province that a republican senator had entered a manner of life which most closely foreshadowed that of the emperors. In his province, accompanied by a few slaves and freedmen, scribes and personal friends, he commanded an army, exercised jurisdiction (delivering the verdicts himself on the advice of his *consilium*), received embassies and negotiated with kings. Especially in the Greek world he could not fail to feel the influence of some of the functions and roles of kings and dynasts in the past or still in power. Verres, for instance, used the former royal palace in Syracuse, and entertained a

---

[4] Diodorus XL, 1, 1: οὗτοι δὲ κατ' ἰδίαν περιπορευόμενοι τὰς οἰκίας τῶν συγκλητικῶν καὶ πᾶσαν δεητικὴν προϊέμενοι φωνήν.

[5] *Syll.*[3] 656, ll. 21–2: ἐντυγχάνοντες μὲν τοῖ[ς πρώτοι]ς 'Ρωμαίων καὶ ἐξομηρευόμενοι διὰ τῆς καθ' ἡμέρα[ν προσκυν]ήσεως (or [ἀπαντ]ήσεως), L. Robert, *RÉA* LXII (1960), 327, n. 2. On either reading this should be a reference to the daily *salutationes*.

[6] Philostratus, *Vit. Ap. Ty.* VIII, 20; Suetonius, *Tib.* 6, 3.

[7] III, 13, 1.

Seleucid prince on his way from Rome to Syria.[8] More important is the fact that the Greek cities approached a Roman *imperator* in precisely the same style as they did a king. Thus an inscription from Dionysopolis of the early 40s BC honours a citizen who had protected the interests of the city both before Burebista the king of Thrace and before Pompey when he was encamped near Heraclea Lyncestis.[9] Moreover the actions of Tryphon, the leader of the Sicilian slave revolt in 103 BC, show a perfect fusion between the popular concepts of a king and of a Roman governor:[10]

> He also constructed a royal residence and a market-place (*forum*?) large enough to accommodate a crowd of men. He selected sufficient men of exceptional judgment whom he named as counsellors, and used as advisers in jurisdiction. When giving audience he put on a toga with a purple border and a tunic with a wide border; he had lictors with axes to march before him, and arranged all the other things which make up and adorn kingship.

It was thus his almost untrammelled power as a provincial governor, and also the very personal context in which he exercised it, that of all the elements in the experience of a republican senator provided the most detailed preparation for the exercise of a true monarchy. Indeed the evolution of monarchy in Rome could be described, in part at least, as the importation into the city of the attributes and functions of a supreme and permanent provincial governor. If the most obvious and simple of these attributes is the appearance there of praetorian cohorts, discussed below, there was also that steady isolation of the emperor and detachment from the collective institutions of Rome without which the eventual transference to Constantinople would not have been possible. The dictatorship of Julius Caesar provided a short-lived foretaste of these effects, which did not pass unnoticed by contemporaries. This fact is vividly illustrated in an anecdote preserved by Macrobius:[11] Cicero, on being greeted by Andron of Laodicea, and finding that he had come to Rome on an embassy to seek the freedom of his city from Caesar, replied in Greek, 'If you are successful, intercede as ambassador for us too.'

So before we can understand fully the nature of the emperor's role, we must examine its various physical and social settings, in Rome, Italy and the provinces, concentrating on those aspects which directly affected his contacts with his subjects.

[8] Cicero, *Verr.* II. iv, 24/54; 27/61 f.

[9] *IGBulg.* I, 13 (with references to earlier publications, notably *IGR* I 662 and *Syll.*³ 762); cf. *SEG* XVIII, 286.

[10] Diodorus XXXVI, 7, 3–4.

[11] *Sat.* II, 3, 12: 'quippe ab Androne quodam Laodiceno salutatus, cum causam adventus requisisset comperissetque—nam ille se legatum de libertate patriae ad Caesarem venisse respondit —ita expressit publicam servitutem ἐὰν ἐπιτύχῃς, καὶ περὶ ἡμῶν πρέσβευσον'. Cf. Cicero, *Ad fam.* XIII, 67.

2

2. *The Emperor's Residences in Rome*

Since a Roman senator's house was where a significant part of his public role was played it was clearly of significance both where it was and what sort of house it was. Cicero, for instance, relates that C. Octavius was helped to the consulate of 165 BC by building a magnificent house on the Palatine. He goes on, however:[1]

> *Dignitas* may be increased by a house, but should not be sought entirely from a house. It is not the house which does honour to the master, but the reverse. And, just as in other matters account has to be taken not only of oneself but of others, thus in the house of a prominent man in which many guests must be received and a large number of all sorts admitted, attention must be paid to a certain amplitude.

Vitruvius, writing his work on architecture in the early part of the reign of Augustus, goes further, and in the course of setting out the appropriate type of house for persons of different social ranks, both expresses the close relation between social function and design and scale, and gives the most vivid surviving description of the house of a prominent Roman office-holder.[2]

> But for *nobiles*, who must perform their duties to their fellow-citizens by holding offices and magistracies, lofty regal vestibules must be built, expensive atriums and peristyle courts, with extensive groves and strolling-places in a style to add lustre to their importance; moreover libraries, picture-galleries and basilicas, made with a magnificence no less than that of public buildings, because their houses are often the setting for counsels on public affairs and also private suits and arbitrations.

Where a senator's house was situated was naturally also of significance. Marius, according to Plutarch, bought a house near the Forum specifically because it would be easy of access for *salutationes*.[3] He says the same of Cicero's purchase of a house on the Palatine,[4] which was always the most favoured area. This was indeed on the very site where Livius Drusus, the tribune of 91 BC, had built his, ordering the architect to make it open to public view so that all his actions would be known to the people. It was later owned by Crassus, who sold it to Cicero in 62 BC for 3,500,000 *sesterces*,[5] and after his death by L. Marcius Censorinus, consul of 39 BC, and then by Statilius Sisenna, the consul of 16 BC.[6] Grand private houses lasted on the Palatine at least down to the great fire of 64, after which the last survivors were almost certainly absorbed within the area of the 'Golden House' of

---

[1] *De off.* I, 39/138-9.
[2] *De arch.* VI, 5, 2.
[3] *Mar.* 32, 1.
[4] *Cic.* 8, 6.
[5] Cicero, *Ad fam.* V, 6, 2.
[6] Velleius II, 14, 3.

Nero. One case which is clear is a house belonging to the orator Crassus, censor of 92 BC, and later to Caecina Largus, who was consul with Claudius in 42. The fire of 64 destroyed, along with the house, the six famous nettle-trees in the garden, already well established in the time of Crassus, and carefully tended ever since.[7]

It was precisely in this context, a nexus of grand town houses with gardens covering the Palatine hill,[8] that the main and typical imperial residence was established. It might have been otherwise, for Julius Caesar, as Pontifex Maximus since 63 BC, had benefited from one of the few official residences of a Roman office-holder, the Domus Publica on the Sacra Via.[9] But though the position of Pontifex Maximus was integral to that of emperor throughout our period from Augustus onwards, Augustus was not elected to it until 12 BC, after the death of Lepidus; and by that time the imperial identity of the Palatine was already well established. Rather than move to the Domus Publica, Augustus granted it to the Vestal Virgins, and had part of his own house on the Palatine made public property.[10]

That procedure marked another step in the remarkably rapid definition of a distinctive imperial 'palace'. Augustus had been born as C. Octavius in a house in the area of the Palatine called *ad Capita bubula*, as Suetonius describes it, mentioning that after his death a shrine was established there; the area cannot now be identified.[11] Subsequently he lived near the Forum, in a house previously owned by the orator Calvus. By 36 BC he had moved to the house on the Palatine which had belonged to another orator, Hortensius. It was relatively modest by later imperial standards,[12] but still prominent enough to have been marked out for himself, along with Caesar's gardens and villa at Baiae, by the consul of 49 BC, had a victory been gained by the Pompeians.[13] It was here, after the victory over Sextus Pompey in 36 BC, that 'C. Iulius Divi filius', as he then was, bought up some neighbouring houses, declaring that they would be for public use, and promised to build a temple of Apollo and surrounding porticoes.[14] The temple was completed in 28 BC, with the promised porticoes, and also a library which was soon used for a variety of public functions. It was there that in his old age Augustus checked the lists of equestrian jurors, and that the Senate often met, as it continued to do in later reigns.[15] In the library of the temple a papyrus shows Augustus taking his seat with his 'friends' and other leading Romans to hear an embassy from Alexandria in AD 13[16]; it was probably outside the temple that he had heard the rival delegations which presented claims and proposals

[7] Asconius, *In Scaurianam* 27C; Pliny, *NH* XVII, 1/1–6.

[8] For a recent survey of houses there see B. Tamm, *Auditorium and Palatium* (1963), ch. iii.

[9] Suetonius, *Jul.* 46.

[10] Dio LIV, 27, 2–3.

[11] *Aug.* 5.

[12] ib. 72.

[13] Cicero, *ad Att.* XI, 6, 6.

[14] Velleius II, 81, 3–4; cf. Dio XLIX, 15, 5.

[15] Suetonius, *Aug.* 29; for later examples Dio LVIII, 9, 4; Tacitus, *Ann.* XIII, 5, 1. For the expression in the *Tabula Hebana*, l. 1: 'in Palatio in porticu quae est ad Apollonis in eo templo in quo senatus haberi sole[t]', see H. M. Last, 'The *Tabula Hebana* and Propertius II, 31', *JRS* XLIII (1953), 27.

[16] *P. Oxy.* 2435 *verso.* See further p. 120.

for Judaea after the death of Herod in 4 BC; Josephus' narrative states that the hearing was actually in the temple itself, but a crowd of several thousands was present.[17] The new temple was thus both integral to the 'palace', and the setting for a range of imperial functions. Both aspects are reflected in Virgil's vision in the *Aeneid* of Augustus seated before the threshold of the temple receiving the gifts of the peoples of the empire.[18]

The house itself was also soon marked out as an imperial residence. In 27 BC he was voted, along with the name 'Augustus', the honour of laurel wreaths affixed to the door-posts of his house and a 'civic crown' of oak leaves over the door.[19] In 2 BC when the senate, equestrian order and people voted that he should be called 'Pater Patriae', and inscription to record this was placed in the vestibule of his house.[20] Commenting on the first of these votes, Cassius Dio says, 'The royal residence is called "Palatium", not because it was ever decided that this should be so, but because the emperor lives on the Palatium and has his headquarters there. His house also gained to some extent in prestige from the hill itself, because Romulus had previously dwelt there. For this reason, if the emperor resides anywhere else, his stopping-place receives the name of "Palatium".'[21] The subsequent stages of this development will be noted later.[22] What must be emphasized here is that the crucial shift from 'Palatium', meaning the hill itself, to 'Palatium' or 'Palatia', meaning the imperial residence, is already visible in the poetry of the reign of Augustus himself.[23] For instance, Ovid in the *Metamorphoses* portrays Jupiter calling a meeting of his council: 'This is the place which, if courage is granted to my words, I would not be afraid to call the *Palatia* of the wide heavens.'[24] It was indeed in the Palatium that Augustus continued, even in old age, to perform his judicial and other functions, seated on a tribunal which was placed there.[25]

Thus already in the reign of Augustus the Palatine hill was established as a new focus for the public life of Rome. But it is significant of the nature of the imperial role that it became a focus for intellectual life also. C. Julius Hyginus, a freedman of Augustus, was in charge of the Palatine library,[26] and a grammarian, Verrius Flaccus, transferred to the Palatium *cum tota schola* and taught, at a salary of 100,000 *sesterces*, in the atrium of the Catulina Domus there.[27]

That reference already hints at how complex and extensive imperial

[17] *Ant.* XVII, 11, 1 (301): Καίσαρός τε συνέδριον φίλων τε τῶν αὐτοῦ καὶ Ῥωμαίων τῶν πρώτων συναγαγόντος ἐν ἱερῷ Ἀπόλλωνος μεγάλοις τέλεσιν ὑπ' αὐτοῦ ἱδρυμένῳ. For further references and discussion see pp. 230, 376.

[18] *Aen.* VIII, 720–2: 'ipse sedens niveo candentis limine Phoebi / dona recognoscit populorum aptatque superbis / postibus'.

[19] *RG* 34, 2. For other references see Tamm, o.c., 47.

[20] *RG* 35.

[21] LIII, 16, 5–6.

[22] pp. 41–2.

[23] See S. Viarre, 'Palatium "Palais" ', *Rev. Phil.* XXXV (1961), 241.

[24] I, 175–6: cf. *Ars Amat.* III, 119, and *Tristia* III, 31 f.

[25] Dio LV, 33, 5.

[26] Suetonius, *De gram. et rhet.* 20.

[27] ib. 17.

ownership on the Palatine was. It is indicated further by Josephus' report of the temporary escape of the assassins of Gaius in 41:[28]

> They took another route, and came to the house of Germanicus, the father of the Gaius whom they had just killed, which was contiguous with the palace of Gaius. For the palace, although a single edifice, had been enlarged part by part, and this occasioned the naming of the additions for members of the ruling family who had completed or else started some part of the structure.

Gaius himself had converted the temple of Castor and Pollux to serve as a vestibule for the palace facing on to the Forum[29]—only for it to be re-converted by Claudius.[30] There followed the great fire of 64, and the construction of Nero's Golden House—in effect a park with gardens, lakes and palaces—which covered the Palatine, and stretched across the centre of Rome to the Caelian. This development too was reversed by Vespasian. The immense and enigmatic (and remarkably little studied) remains of this, and of its successor, the great palace of Domitian on the Palatine, give us evidence of a major revolution in Roman architecture,[31] but yield very few clues to the social functions performed there. Domitian's palace contains side by side two large halls, described by modern scholars as the 'basilica' and the 'aula regia'; and it may well be, as is often supposed,[32] that in the apses which figure in both halls the emperor took his seat to give audience or receive embassies. But this remains entirely a hypothesis.

It is clear that there was at all times a regular entrance to the Palatium at the corner nearest to the Forum, and in Domitian's time a series of ramp corridors was built leading up the hill at this point.[33] It is probable, but cannot be certain, that it is to this point that Pliny refers, in speaking of a crowd of embassies besieging the emperor's gates.[34] The same entrance-point may also be indicated in the two passages in Aulus Gellius' *Noctes Atticae*, in which he describes learned persons conversing while waiting, either in the *vestibulum* of the Palatine or *in area Palatina*, to attend the *salutatio* of the emperor.[35] At least it is clear that the custom of the *salutatio* continued in the second century, and that there was a definite entrance to the palace at which the people would wait. The fact of the continuance is of some importance, for this takes us into the period when abundant evidence illustrates the consultation of the emperor by means of *libelli*; and a few early

[28] Josephus, *Ant.* XIX, 1, 15 (117), Loeb trans.

[29] Suetonius, *Cal.* 22, 2; Dio LIX, 28, 5.

[30] Dio LX, 6, 8.

[31] See for example J. Ward Perkins, 'Nero's Golden House', *Antiquity* XXX (1956), 209; A. Boëthius, *The Golden House of Nero* (1960), ch. iii; Tamm, o.c., ch. v; W. L. MacDonald, *The Architecture of the Roman Empire* I (1965), chs. ii–iii. For photographs and plans of parts of Domitian's palace see H. Finsen, *Domus Flavia sur le Palatin; Aula Regia—Basilica* (1962); *La résidence de Domitien sur le Palatin* (1969).

[32] See e.g. MacDonald, o.c., 53.

[33] See Tamm, o.c., 79 f.

[34] *Pan.* 79, 7.

[35] *NA* IV, 1, 1: 'in vestibulo aedium Palatinarum omnium fere ordinum multitudo opperientes salutationem Caesaris constiterant'; XX, 1, 2: 'forte in area Palatina, cum salutationem Caesaris opperiremur'. Cf. also XIX, 13, 1: 'stabant forte una in vestibulo Palatii fabulantes'.

references indicate that *libelli* were commonly presented precisely at *salutationes*.[36]

There does not seem to be evidence of extensive imperial re-building on the Palatine after the end of the first century. So, without being able to envisage any details clearly, we can accept that from then on the main imperial 'palace' was a network of buildings of varying periods, within which an emperor could choose his own favoured dwelling-place and manner of life. In the Antonine period, for instance, one part of it, the Domus Tiberiana, whose existence is known from the first century, was used by Marcus Aurelius when he was the 'Caesar' of Antoninus Pius; and there he would greet the leading citizens with deliberate informality, not wearing his toga, and in the room in which he had slept.[37]

Further concrete details are lacking, and we are left with passing indications that the Palatium contained stores of cash and valuables, and archives of documents relating to the empire,[38] or a reference in Dio to the building in the Palatium in which Septimius Severus usually dispensed justice—on the ceiling of which he had represented the stars under which he had been born.[39] We have to accept that we cannot gain any clear conception of how the functions of the emperor and the architecture of the Palatine complex affected each other. Indeed there are some reasons to think that such mutual effects cannot have been profound. For among the immense and varied range of properties which fell to the emperor by gift or inheritance or confiscation,[40] there early appeared houses and gardens (*horti*) in Rome itself, and in these too emperors are found discharging their functions, or even taking up permanent residence. When Philo and a delegation from the Alexandrian Jewish community arrived in Rome in 40, they were first greeted by Gaius as he was coming out of the gardens of his mother Agrippina on the right bank of the Tiber.[41] It was there also, while walking in the colonnaded wrestling-ground (*xystus*) which lay between a portico and the bank of the river, that Gaius would watch executions of prominent Romans.[42] Near the gardens, and possibly within them, lay the site of the Circus Vaticanus built by Gaius and Nero; at any rate Tacitus mentions in a single sentence that Nero offered his gardens for the executions of the Christians in 64, and also gave circus games.[43]

When Philo and his embassy finally gained an audience with Gaius, it was when he was spending three or four days in the gardens of Lamia and Maecenas which lay near each other on the Esquiline hill.[44] The hearing was

[36] See pp. 240–2 below.
[37] Dio LXXI, 35, 4 (278). Cf. Tacitus, *Hist.* I, 27, 2; Suetonius, *Vit.* 15, 3; *HA, Ant. Pius* 10, 4; *Marc. Ant.* 6, 3; *Ver.* 2, 4.
[38] See pp. 144–50, 259–64 below.
[39] Dio LXXVI, 11, 1.
[40] Ch. iv.
[41] Philo, *Leg.* 28/181.
[42] Seneca, *De ira* III, 18, 4.
[43] See Pliny, *NH* XXXVI, 15/74; XVI, 76/201; Tacitus, *Ann.* XIV, 14, 2; XV, 44, 5. It is now clear that Constantine's basilica of St. Peter was not built on the site of this circus. See J. M. C. Toynbee and J. B. Ward Perkins, *The Shrine of St. Peter and the Vatican Excavations* (1956), ch. i.
[44] Philo, *Leg.* 44/351–45/367. See Platner-Ashby, *Topographical Dictionary of Ancient Rome* (1929), 267–9.

interrupted by the emperor going round the various luxurious buildings which stood there, inspecting their fittings and ordering improvements. This well-known episode is of course cited by Philo as an outrage; but it is none the less merely an extreme instance of the fact that the work of an emperor was fitted into the framework of the leisured existence of an upper-class Roman. In the same way one of the papyrus texts known as the 'Acts of the Pagan Martyrs' shows Claudius with his senatorial advisers hearing a case in an imperial garden in Rome.[45] Only the end of the name survives, but it is probable that this was the Horti Lucullani on the Mons Pincius, laid out by Lucullus in about 60 BC, and later acquired by a senator, Valerius Asiaticus, who was judicially murdered in 47 specifically for them, so Tacitus and Dio report.[46] In Plutarch's time they were counted among the most luxurious of imperial gardens.[47]

The best-attested, and perhaps the most used, of all the imperial gardens, were the Horti Sallustiani which lay on the side of the Mons Pincius near the Via Salaria, and were probably inherited by Tiberius from his adviser Sallustius Crispus, who died in 20.[48] Nero is found going to them on one occasion,[49] but it was Vespasian who used them extensively, as part of a demonstration of a more modest and open way of life than that of the Julio-Claudian dynasty:[50]

> He dwelt little in the Palatium, but for the most part lived in the Horti Sallustiani, and there received anyone who wished it, not just of the senators but also of the others. To his actual friends he was accessible before dawn while still lying in his bedroom, and others were able to greet him on the road. The doors of the imperial residences were open all day, and no guard was placed at them.

Nerva evidently used them also, for it was there that he died.[51] Later, the *Historia Augusta* reports of Aurelian, much as Dio had of Vespasian, that he disliked living in the Palatium and preferred the Horti of Sallust or Domitia; in the gardens of Sallust he built a portico where he rode daily.[52] From this source, the report could easily be a mere fabrication, an imitation of an earlier report like that of Dio. But the continuing use of these gardens is attested by the anonymous Panegyric of Constantine delivered in 313: Maxentius, the author says, had been so lazy that he regarded going to the Horti Sallustiani as a journey and expedition.[53]

Thus, even within Rome, an emperor had a choice, either from day to day

---

[45] Musurillo, *Acts of the Pagan Martyrs*, no. IV, Text A, col. ii, ll. 4–5, [ἐν τοῖς . . .]λιανοῖς κήποις. Cf. B, col. i, l. 1.

[46] Tacitus, *Ann.* XI, 1, 1; Dio LX, 31, 5. The most likely alternative is the Horti Serviliani, first attested under Nero; Tacitus, *Ann.* XV, 55, 1; Suetonius, *Nero* 47, 1. Cf. Tacitus, *Hist.* III, 38, 1. See Platner-Ashby, o.c. 272.

[47] *Luc.* 39, 2.

[48] Platner-Ashby, o.c. 271–2.

[49] Tacitus, *Ann.* XIII, 47, 2.

[50] Dio LXVI, 10, 4–5 (144).

[51] Jerome, *Chron.* ed. Helm, p. 193.

[52] *HA, Aurel.* 49, 1–2. On the Horti of Domitia, either an aunt of Nero or the wife of Domitian, see Platner-Ashby, o.c. 267.

[53] *Pan.* IX (12), 14, 4.

or for a settled mode of life, of a range of different imperial dwellings with different associations and different architectural and social characters. All of them, even the range of houses on the Palatine hill, which was very quickly marked out by overt symbols of the imperial presence, had as their origins, and largely retained, the character of luxurious town houses of the Roman upper classes.

3. *The Emperor in Italy*

Before they finally had their fruitless audience with Gaius, Philo and his embassy had experienced yet another facet of imperial life: 'We had travelled from Rome to Dicaearchia in attendance on Gaius; he had gone down to the sea and was staying by the bay, going from one to another of his numerous luxuriously appointed country-houses.'[1] The bay was the bay of Naples, the favoured resort of rich Romans for some two centuries before.[2] Cicero had owned, in all, three villas in this area, at Pompeii, Cumae and Dicaearchia (Puteoli) itself.[3] In the late republic and early empire luxurious villas, senatorial and imperial, are attested mainly here, in Campania, in Latium immediately to the south of Rome, and inland from Rome especially at Tibur. In the second century they appear also west and north of Rome, at Centumcellae, Lorium and Alsium. Their use by the emperors followed no plan or decision, though they did serve at particular moments as convenient points or retreat, either in the immediate neighbourhood of Rome or more distant. On the contrary, like the imperial residences in Rome, they reflected an established pattern of life into which the functions of the emperor were fitted. It is only this aspect which concerns us here, the extent to which these villas provided the setting for the emperor's contacts with his subjects, either in person or by written pronouncement.[4] We may postpone for the moment various questions that concern the wider patterns of imperial landholding: the means of acquisition, by inheritance, gift, confiscation or purchase; their role as sources of income or as stores of wealth; and their functions as potential gifts to favoured individuals or eventually to the church.[5] In all of these contexts the history of any individual site or villa is exceptionally difficult to trace. We cannot tell, for instance, whether the site of the luxurious villa on Lake Nemi, which Julius Caesar built and then pulled down,[6] was or was not the same as the 'massa Nemus' providing an income of 280 *solidi*, which Constantine donated to the basilica of John the Baptist in Alba.[7]

[1] Philo, *Leg.* 29/185, trans. Smallwood.

[2] See J. H. D'Arms, *Romans on the Bay of Naples: a Social and Cultural Study of the Villas and their Owners from 150 BC to AD 400* (1970).

[3] D'Arms, o.c., 189–200.

[4] A full collection of the evidence for the imperial villas would be both laborious and of no great aid to historical understanding; and in detail it could not go significantly beyond the masterly work of O. Hirschfeld, 'Der Grundbesitz der römischen Kaiser in den ersten drei Jahrhunderten', *Kleine Schriften* (1913), 516.

[5] See ch. iv.

[6] Suetonius, *Jul.* 46.

[7] *Liber Pontificalis* XXXIV, 30, 14; ed. Duchesne I, 185.

The continuity of imperial villa-ownership with that of the Roman upper classes of the late Republic can be immediately illustrated from the actions of the young Octavian in 44 BC. Setting off to gain the support of Caesar's veterans in Campania, he deceived his mother Atia with the excuse that he was going to sell up his inherited possessions there so as to have enough ready cash to carry out Caesar's bequests.[8] One of these properties can in fact be identified; for he was to die fifty-eight years later in the same bedroom at Nola as had his father Octavius.[9] Thereafter we find that, as Augustus, he had villas in the traditional areas. One was the villa 'ad Gallinas' on the Via Flaminia outside Rome, where after a portent in 38 BC the augurs ordered a laurel branch to be planted; for at least a century it remained the custom that emperors celebrating triumphs should take their laurel wreath from the tree which grew from it.[10] More generally, Suetonius records of Augustus: 'Of his retreats, he especially used the coast and islands of Campania, or the towns nearest to the city, Lanuvium, Praeneste and Tibur, where he also very often gave justice in the porticoes of the temple of Hercules.'[11] Of the islands, the most famous was of course Capri, which Augustus acquired from the city of Neapolis,[12] and where Tiberius lived permanently for the last ten years of his reign. This, the extreme case of an imperial withdrawal, did indeed lead to a neglect of some functions which the emperor had to perform.[13] None the less, he continued from there to keep control of the major crisis, such as the 'conspiracy' of Sejanus in 31 or the question of the eastern frontier. He could also of course carry out trials and executions; in Suetonius' time the place was still pointed out where he would have his victims thrown into the sea.[14] Lanuvium and Praeneste are not attested again as the sites of imperial villas until the Antonine period. But at Tibur Claudius too gave judgment in the summer months before the temple of Hercules.[15] At Tibur also Hadrian built his immense villa, in effect a chain of buildings stretching over acres of parkland.[16] Here again there is no hint that any of the buildings were designed for the performance of the emperor's duties; but it was from here, none the less, that he replied to an embassy from Delphi in September 125.[17]

Suetonius' list omits two much-used imperial retreats, Alba and Antium, both well-attested from Augustus into the early second century. It was to his

---

[8] Nicolaus of Damascus, *FGrH* 90 F. 130, xxxi (134).

[9] Suetonius, *Aug.* 100, 1; the house became a shrine, Dio LVI, 46, 3.

[10] Pliny, *NH* XV, 40/136–7; Suetonius, *Galba* 1; Dio XLVIII, 52, 3–4.

[11] Suetonius, *Aug.* 72, 2.

[12] Strabo, V, 4, 9 (248); Suetonius, *Aug.* 92, 2; 98, 4; Dio LII, 43, 2.

[13] Suetonius, *Tib.* 41: 'regressus in insulam rei p. quidem curam usque adeo abiecit, ut postea non decurias equitum umquam supplerit, non tribunos militum praefectosque, non provinciarum praesides ullos mutaverit.'

[14] ib. 62, 2.

[15] This depends on a very probable restoration in Seneca, *Apoc.* 7, 4. Claudius is represented as saying to Hercules: 'ego eram qui Tiburi [for tibi] ante templum tuum ius dicebam totis diebus mense Iulio et Augusto.'

[16] See esp. H. Kähler, *Hadrian und seine Villa bei Tivoli* (1950); S. Aurigemma, *Villa Adriana* (1961).

[17] See E. Bourguet, *De rebus Delphicis* (1900), 82; cf. A. Plassart, *Fouilles de Delphes* III. 4 (1970), 82–3. In l. 34 we have [ἀπὸ οἰκίας Τιβου]ρτείνης.

2*

Alban villa that Augustus retired on renouncing the consulate in 23 BC, and Tiberius, Gaius and Nero all used it.[18] So did Domitian before the beginning of his reign,[19] and it was he who temporarily made it into his regular seat of government. Juvenal, looking back on Domitian's reign, describes in the fourth satire first the crowd, including senators, awaiting admission at the door of the Alban villa, and then a meeting of Domitian's council there.[20] It was within the 'arx Albana', (the 'Alban citadel') that until near the end of the reign the voice of Messalinus, Domitian's cruel adviser, was confined;[21] and there that an inscription of 82 shows Domitian meeting with his advisers to hear a case.[22] Domitian even summoned his fellow *pontifices* there, and not to the Regia in Rome, in order to decide the case of a Vestal Virgin who had broken her vows.[23]

The Alban villa certainly remained in imperial possession in the second century[24] but seems to have been little used. The associations with Domitian were no doubt too strong.[25] It appears, naturally enough, in a reference to some typical imperial resorts by Martial, namely Alba, Nemus, Antium, Caieta or Circeii, and Anxur,[26] but not in the otherwise rather traditional list of places whose climate Marcus Aurelius compares in a letter with that of Neapolis, where he is staying: Laurentum, Lanuvium, Algidus, Tusculum, Puteoli, Tibur.[27]

The coasts of Latium and Campania thus remained favoured imperial retreats. It had been to Antium that the Roman *plebs* had sent an embassy to offer Augustus the title of 'Pater Patriae' in 2 BC, and Tiberius and Nero had also used it.[28] Moreover, an inscription from Pessinus shows Trajan writing to a friend named Claudianus from there,[29] as he did also in reply to an embassy from Delphi in November 99.[30] Again the evidence is less clear for the second century, except for the remark of Philostratus mentioned earlier, that Hadrian liked it, and that a volume of Pythagoras and letters of Apollonius could still be seen there. Baiae remained in use longer, and it may even be that one of the villas there was the same one which had been in the possession of Julius Caesar in 48 BC. Augustus and Gaius had villas there,[31]

[18] Dio LIII, 32, 3; LVIII, 24, 1; Seneca, *Ad Polyb.* 17, 4; Suetonius, *Nero* 25, 1.

[19] Dio LXVI, 9, 4.

[20] *Sat.* IV, 62–4: 'obstitit intranti miratrix turba parumper. / ut cessit, facili patuerunt cardine valvae; / exclusi spectant admissa obsonia patres.' On the council, see ll. 72–149, esp. 144–9; cf. p. 130 below.

[21] Tacitus, *Agricola* 45, 1.

[22] *CIL* IX 5420 = *FIRA*² I, no. 75: 'd(atum) XI Kal. Aug. in Albano'. See p. 120 below.

[23] Pliny, *Ep.* IV, 11, 6; cf. p. 359.

[24] *CIL* XIV 2307. The reference in a 'letter' of Faustina in *HA, Av. Cass.* 9, 8 is not evidence.

[25] Whether the establishment of the legion II Parthica at Alba by Septimius Severus—the first and only legion stationed in Italy under the empire—owed anything to the existence of an imperial residence there, remains obscure.

[26] Martial, *Epig.* V, 1; cf. XI, 7, 3–4: 'Caesar in Albanum iussit me mane venire, / Caesar Circeios'.

[27] Fronto, *ad M. Caes.* II, 6, 3.

[28] Suetonius, *Aug.* 58, 1; *Tib.* 38; *Nero* 25; Tacitus, *Ann.* XIV, 3, 1. Cf. *Ann.* XV, 23, where, after the birth of a daughter to Poppaea at Antium in 63, the whole senate goes there to offer congratulations.

[29] W. H. Buckler, 'Les lettres impériales de Pessinonte', *Rev. Phil.* n.s. XI (1937), 105, Text A.

[30] Plassart, *Fouilles de Delphes* III. 4 (1970), no. 288.

[31] Suetonius, *Aug.* 64, 2; Josephus, *Ant.* XVIII, 7, 2 (248–9).

and it was 'at Baiae in the praetorium', that Claudius posted up his edict about various North Italian matters in March of 46.[32] It was there, according to the *Historia Augusta*, that Hadrian died,[33] and that Severus Alexander built a *palatium* named after his mother Mammaea.[34] As always with the *Historia Augusta*, these references may be mere imitation; but it is certain at least that Marcus Aurelius as 'Caesar' stayed at Baiae on occasion.[35] In this period, however, various places north of the Tiber came to be frequented and were used like the others for carrying out official duties. One of our most detailed accounts of an emperor dispensing justice with his *amici* is Pliny's report of his own participation in such a council at Trajan's villa at Centumcellae in 107.[36] He makes particularly clear how the business of judging cases was fitted into the framework of an elegant, but not improperly luxurious, country life. The advisers attended a dinner each night, modest by imperial standards, after which they sometimes heard an entertainment and sometimes passed the evening in conversation. On departure on the last day they each received gifts.

At Alsium, on the coast between Centumcellae and the Tiber, Marcus Aurelius is found, according to a letter of Fronto, supposedly relaxing and studying, but in reality devoting day and night to judicial business. In reproach, Fronto goes into a set of elaborate conceits:[37]

> If no one had stolen fire from heaven, would not the sun suffice you for your judicial duties? Do realise in your conscience that you are tied to a daily falsehood, for when you say that you 'appoint the day' for trial of cases, and yet try by night, then you are bound to be untruthful, whether you condemn or acquit. If you condemn anyone you say *there appears to have been gross negligence*; where indeed, but for the lights, nothing could appear at all.

At Lorium, on the Via Aurelia between Rome and the coast, Antoninus Pius was brought up; he built a *palatium* there later, and it was there that he died.[38] Repeated references in the correspondence of Marcus Aurelius and Fronto show it as the favourite resort of the family;[39] and from there Marcus Aurelius, as 'Caesar' in 147, wrote in reply to a decree by the synod of 'Briseus Dionysus' at Smyrna, congratulating him on the birth of a son.[40]

---

[32] *CIL* v 5050 = *ILS* 206 = *FIRA*[2] I, 71. See pp. 254–6 below. The occasional use of the expression *praetorium*, 'headquarters' or literally a place associated with a praetor, for imperial villas aptly illustrates the fusion of public and private functions. See e.g. Suetonius, *Aug.* 72, 3; *Tib.* 39 (Terracina); *Cal.* 37, 2; *CIL* x 6667 (Antium); Phlegon, *FGrH* 257 F. 37 (iv): Φαῦστος Καίσαρου δοῦλος, ἐκ Σαβίνων, ἀπὸ πραιτωρίου Παλλαντιανοῦ. Cf. Statius, *Silv.* I, 3, 25, 'alternas servant praetoria ripas', where the reference is not specifically to imperial villas. Note also *ILS* 1554 (Placentia); 1582 (Ostia); 1583 (Caieta), and esp. 9024–5: 'proc. praetori Fidenatium et Rubrensium et Gallinaru[m Alba]rum sacrum, quae praestu est usibus Caesaris'. By comparison, in *ILS* 7741 *praetorium* relates to Hadrian's entourage on the move.

[33] *HA, Had.* 25, 6; *Ant. Pius* 5, 1; *M. Ant.* 6, 1.

[34] *HA, Sev. Alex.* 26, 9.

[35] Fronto, *ad M. Caes.* I, 4, 2.

[36] *Ep.* VI, 31. Cf. pp. 525–6.

[37] *De feriis Alsiensibus*, Loeb trans.

[38] *HA, Ant. Pius* I, 8; 12, 6; Eutrop. VIII, 8, 4; Jerome, *Chron.* ed. Helm, 204.

[39] *ad M. Caes.* III, 20; v, 7; *De feriis Alsiensibus* I; 3, 2; *Ad Ant. imp.* I, 1; I, 3.

[40] *Syll.*[2] 851 = *IGR* IV 1399.

The use of this area, however, seems to have been a passing phase of the Antonine period. Campania remained the most favoured region: Antoninus Pius wrote to an association in Pergamon from Capua in 140–6,[41] as did Severus and Caracalla to Delphi in 197.[42] This pattern is further reflected in Cassius Dio's report that before going home to Bithynia after his second consulship, held with Severus Alexander in 229, he spent a few days with the emperor in Rome and in Campania.[43] Yet it is perhaps in the case of Vespasian, who retained a deep attachment to the relatively unfashionable area where he had been born, Reate in Etruria, that we see most clearly the continuance of the emperors' business in their country retreats, and also gain the clearest conception of what that business was. In 79, while in Campania, he felt a touch of fever, and returned to Rome, and thence to his estates near Reate and the waters of Cutiliae nearby. When his illness got worse, 'he none the less carried out his imperial functions according to his custom, even receiving embassies while lying in bed'. When a sudden attack of diarrhoea caused him almost to faint, he proclaimed that 'an emperor should die standing', and died while trying to get up.[44]

The imperial villas of Italy disappear from our view in the third century, partly because of the failure of our evidence but partly because the pattern of the emperor's activities entered a new phase, in which the necessities of wars and civil wars forced them to spend more time than before in the provinces and on the frontiers. But that pattern of life itself had its origins in the imperial journeys of the first two centuries, and beyond that in the sphere of action of a republican governor.

4. *Imperial Journeys*

The nature of a republican provincial governor's duties was such that when he was not marching with an army he was travelling from city to city in his province dispensing justice.[1] Not only his journeys within his province, but his travels to and from it, involved for the provincials on the one hand a burden of organizing supplies and stopping-places, and elaborate rituals of greeting, entertainment and farewell, and on the other the possibilities of gaining favour, and for the leading men, of establishing personal links which would be valuable for the future. Such a journey thus involved complex and potentially important choices on both sides. A city or an individual might incur serious risks by misjudging the warmth of welcome to which a Roman governor felt himself entitled, while the governor would have open to him an unpredictable set of choices as to what he would demand or how he would treat those who came before him.

On his departure from Rome an office-holder would expect to be escorted,

[41] *IGR* IV 357.
[42] A. Plassart, *Fouilles de Delphes* III. 4 (1970), no. 329, correcting the dating in E. Bourguet, *De rebus Delphicis*, 90, to the 15th *trib. pot.*, so 207, to the 5th, giving 197.
[43] Dio LXXX, 5, 1.
[44] Suetonius, *Vesp.* 24.
[1] This is illustrated most vividly by Cicero's activities as governor of Cilicia in 51–50 BC; see A. J. Marshall, 'Governors on the Move', *Phoenix* XX (1966), 231.

and when approaching on his return to be greeted by large crowds, among whom any individuals who needed his support would take care to be prominent.[2] He would similarly expect a ceremonial welcome at towns along his route. In delicate political situations the extent of this might be an important indication of a man's real support.[3] A similar reception might be prepared for a prominent senator when travelling privately, or even, as Cato the Younger found at Antioch, for an important freedman; 'As he was walking into Antioch, he saw at the gate outside a multitude of people drawn up on either side of the road, among whom stood, in one group, young men with military cloaks, and in another, boys with gala robes, while some had white rainment and crowns, being priests or magistrates.' Cato was angry at first, thinking that the welcome had been prepared, against his wishes, for himself; but in fact it was for Demetrius, a freedman of Pompey.[4]

The expectation of a ceremonial welcome went hand in hand with demands, occasionally restrained by laws passed in Rome, for elaborate practical provisions. Both the established practice and the extension of demands are illustrated in Livy's report of events in 173 BC. The consul Postumius, 'angered with the people of Praeneste because, when he had gone there as a private person to make a sacrifice in the temple of Fortuna there, he had received no honorific attentions from them either publicly or privately, sent a letter to the town before he left Rome, ordering the magistrates to come to meet him, a place for him to stay to be prepared at public expense, and beasts of burden to be ready for his departure'. Previously, Livy notes, magistrates had been content with the travelling equipment issued to them in Rome, and had accepted private hospitality in the towns, offering their hosts the hospitality of their own houses in Rome in exchange.[5]

The various forms of relationship here referred to, which by their very indeterminacy constituted a sensitive area in the contact between subject and governor in the provinces, persisted through the later republic and into the empire. Cicero solemnly advises his brother Quintus, as proconsul of Asia in 60/59, not to terrify men by his journeys, to drain their resources by expenditure on him, or to alarm them by his arrival.[6] A law passed by Julius Caesar as consul in 59 laid down strict rules as to what provisions might be demanded.[7] But the development of an official transport service under the empire, and the vastly increased number of official travellers, right down to common soldiers and imperial slaves, made this a source of tension throughout the period.[8]

[2] e.g. Livy XXVIII, 9, 5–6; XLV, 35, 3; Cicero, *Pro Sestio* 31/68; *Ad Att.* XIII, 50, 3–4; *Phil.* II, 32/78; *Pro Mur.* 33/68 (arrival); Livy XLII, 49; XLIV, 22, 17; Cicero, *Ad Fam.* III, 10, 8; *Phil.* IX, 9 (departure).

[3] See e.g. Cicero, *Ad Att.* VIII, 16, 2; XVI, 11, 6; *Phil.* II, 41/106.

[4] Plutarch, *Cato Min.* 13, 1, Loeb trans.

[5] XLII, 1, 7–12.

[6] *Ad Q.f.* I, 1, 9.

[7] G. Rotondi, *Leges Publicae Populi Romani* (1912), 389–91.

[8] See, for example, Rostovtzeff, *SEHRE*[2], ch. viii, nn. 35, 37; H.-G. Pflaum, 'Essai sur le cursus publicus sous le Haut-Empire romain', *Mém. prés. à l'Acad. des Ins.* XIV (1940), 189; W. H. C. Frend, 'A Third-Century Inscription relating to *Angareia* in Phrygia', *JRS* XLVI (1956), 46; I. Stoian, 'De nouveau sur la plainte des paysans du territoire d'Histria', *Dacia* III (1959), 369; cf. T. Pekáry, *Untersuchungen zu den römischen Reichsstrassen* (1968), 173–5.

An office-holder travelling through a province might stay the night either at an official residence (*praetorium*?),[9] or at a public guest-house, provided by the city, or at the house of a prominent citizen. What types of establishment the former typically were is not easy to grasp, but scattered items of evidence make clear that they did exist, under various names, at least in the cities of the Greek half of the empire;[10] an engaging anecdote in Pliny's *Natural History* shows the triumvir Lepidus being conducted to a *hospitium* by the magistrates of a town, but upbraiding them in the morning because he had been kept awake by birds in the grove which surrounded it.[11] This may have been a public guest-house, but was perhaps more probably a private house allotted to him. Reception by private *hospites* was indeed probably the most common pattern. The tensions engendered were rarely as sharp as when Verres and some companions arrived at Lampsacus, and their outrages led to a full-scale riot; more typical is the indication in the story that Roman visitors would be distributed among the most prominent citizens in proportion to their rank.[12] It might be a mark of favour to stay with a particular provincial, as when Julius Caesar continued to use the house of Catullus' father in Verona, even after the son's opprobrious verses.[13] The host was expected to keep up a high standard of hospitality; Caesar had to restrain his companions from protesting when his host at Milan served asparagus dressed with myrrh instead of olive-oil.[14] In a similar situation Augustus was not to be so mild, crushing his host with the parting remark, 'I did not think that I was so close a friend of yours.'[15]

In his province a governor would hold daily *salutationes* just as at Rome. Thus Plutarch reports of Cicero in Cilicia, 'his residence had no doorkeeper, nor was he ever seen lying in bed by anyone, but in the morning he received those who came to greet him, either standing or while walking outside his bedchamber.'[16] A governor would also be met by embassies on his travels, such as the large number that appeared before Cicero in Samos and Ephesus before he had even reached his province,[17] or the envoys from Tragurion who met Julius Caesar at Aquileia on 2 March 56 BC.[18] Perhaps the extreme case of the attachment of a provincial ambassador to a Roman

---

[9] Note the *quaestorium* in which Cicero was accommodated in Thessalonica, Cicero, *Pro Plancio* 41/99. The term *praetorium* is more common, see *Excavations at Dura-Europos, Ninth Season* III (1952), 83 f.; and especially R. Egger, 'Das Praetorium als Amtssitz und Quartier römischer Spitzenfunktionäre', *Öst. Ak. Wien*, Phil.-hist. Kl. S-b. 250 (1966), no. 4; and for *praetoria* placed on major routes, Pekáry, o.c., 164–7.

[10] In the Greek cities we hear of such guest-houses called κατάλυμα, see Diodorus, xxxvii, 27, 1, and A. H. M. Jones, *The Greek City* (1940), 328, n. 90, or ξένων (*OGIS* 609 = *IGR* III 1119). I can not find a case in Latin, on the other hand, where *hospitium* certainly means this rather than a private house placed at the disposal of the official visitor, see *Thes. Ling. Lat.* cols. 3040–41.

[11] xxxv, 38/121.

[12] Cicero, *Verr.* II/1, 24/63–27/69.

[13] Suetonius, *Jul.* 73.

[14] Plutarch, *Caesar* 17, 9–10.

[15] Macrobius, *Sat.* II, 4, 13.

[16] Plutarch, *Cic.* 36. Compare Cicero's own rather allusive reference to the same topic, *Ad Att.* vi, 2, 5: 'aditus ad me minime provinciales; nihil per cubicularium; ante lucem inambulabam domi ut olim candidatus.'

[17] *Ad Att.* v, 13, 1; cf. v, 20, 1, and *Ad fam.* III, 8, 4.

[18] Sherk, *Roman Documents*, no. 24.

governor on his travels is that recorded by Memnon of Heraclea of his fellow-citizen Brithagoras. He travelled to Julius Caesar to obtain freedom for his city, but could not win it at once, as Caesar was in the provinces; so he stayed in his train and travelled about with him for twelve years (so Memnon records) only to die just before Caesar returned to Rome.[19]

As Memnon explicitly says, Brithagoras acted thus because the empire was already inclining towards the rule of one man. When monarchy was established, all these social and political aspects of a governor's journey reappeared on a larger scale, and are richly illustrated in our evidence. It was on a journey that the emperor was most readily exposed to the petitions of individual subjects; it was then alone that his existence imposed itself on a whole population obligatorily and without initiative by them; and it was the mobility of the court which was the essential precondition for the creation of the new imperial centres of the tetrarchic period and then of Constantinople itself. All these factors demand that this aspect of the imperial role be treated in considerable detail.

An emperor passing by could not fail to make an immense impact on a provincial population; it was not for nothing that the Rabbis laid down that the rule forbidding a *cohen* to have contact with a corpse did not apply to one who went through a cemetery in order to appear before Diocletian on his visit to Tyre.[20] The ritual of *profectio* and *adventus*, best attested for Rome itself, was repeated in some form in each town through which the emperor travelled.[21] On the arch of Galerius at Thessalonica there is an admirable representation, in somewhat foreshortened style, of an emperor leaving one town and making his *adventus* at the next, being hailed outside the gates by the leading citizens.[22] There was of course an element of compulsion in this, a fact which is the setting for a story, possibly itself fictional, about the poet Oppian. When Septimius Severus arrived at Anazarbus, all the citizens had to meet him; but Oppian, being concerned with the philosophic life, did not—and was exiled.[23]

Our best accounts of popular reactions to imperial visits come from the Latin panegyrics of the tetrarchic period. Mamertinus recounts in the following terms the journey of Diocletian and Maximian to meet at Milan in the winter of 290/1: 'All the fields were filled with crowds not only of men rushing to see, but with herds of beasts leaving their remote pastures and woods; the peasants vied with each other in reporting what they had seen to all the villages. Altars were lit, incense thrown on, libations poured,

---

[19] Memnon, *FGrH* 434 F. 1 (40).

[20] *Jerusalem Talmud, Berachoth* 3, 1 (trans. Schwabe, 1871, p. 58).

[21] For the form of the ceremonial see for example A. Alföldi, *Die monarchische Repräsentation im römischen Kaiserreiche* (1970), 79f.; R. Brilliant, *Gesture and Rank in Roman Art* (1963), 173f.; G. Koeppel, 'Profectio und Adventus', *Bonn. Jahrb.* CLXIX (1969), 130; S. MacCormack, 'Change and Continuity in Late Antiquity: the Ceremony of *Adventus*', *Historia* XXI (1972), 721. For literary descriptions of *adventus* in Rome see e.g. Josephus, *BJ* VII, 4, 1 (68–74); Herodian I, 7, 3. For Constantine's entry to Milan, *Pan.* IX (12), 7, 15.

[22] K.-F. Kinch, *L'arc de triomphe de Salonique* (1890), Pl. vi, top panel.

[23] On the two *vitae* of Oppian, printed by A. Westermann, ΒΙΟΓΡΑΦΟΙ (1845), 63f., see the Introduction to the Loeb *Oppian, Colluthus and Tryphiodorus* by A. W. Mair (1928).

sacrificial victims slain.'[24] One may recall the altars and sacrifices with which Spanish cities had greeted the visit of Metellus Pius in the early 70s BC.[25]

Even more vivid is the description in a later panegyric of the reception of Constantine in Autun in 311, when local enthusiasm was further sharpened by the expectation of relief from crushing taxation. Once again, men rushed from all the surrounding fields. Inside the city the streets leading to the *palatium*[26] were lined with the banners of the *collegia*, with images of the local gods and with bands, which were apparently in short supply, as they had to play at several successive points on the route. The emperor, so the panegyrist says, was conspicuously ready to allow the citizens access to him and to hear their requests.[27]

Behind these receptions lay months, sometimes a year or more, of preparations, some of which came to nothing, as the emperor never in fact arrived; we may think of the unfortunate prefect of Egypt, Caecina Tuscus, who was exiled for using a bath in Alexandria, prepared for a visit by Nero which never took place.[28] An imperial visit might be an opportunity, as it was for Herod, who in 30 BC richly entertained the future Augustus and his whole army at Akko-Ptolemais, provided water and wine for their journey to Egypt and back across the desert, and escorted him on his return as far as Antioch.[29] More often it was simply a burden, as Constantius recognizes in a letter of 339: 'For what evils are inflicted on the provincials [by excessive demands by other officials] can be gathered from the fact, that for our journeys, which are impelled by public necessities, by great and strenuous exertions scarcely twenty pack-animals each can be provided.'[30]

The advance preparations for an imperial journey are reflected in Suetonius' report that almost every year Tiberius made abortive arrangements, 'with *vehicula* collected and supplies placed in the *coloniae* and *municipia*'.[31] We also have what *may* be a valid indication of the form of the advance announcement of an imperial journey in the notoriously unreliable *Vita* of Severus Alexander.[32] An *edictum* was posted up two months in advance, stating that on a certain day at a certain hour he would leave the city and, if the gods so willed, would spend the night at the first stopping-place (*mansio*). He would then indicate in order the stopping-places, camping-stations and where supplies were to be received along the entire route up to the frontier. The existence of regular *mansiones* is well attested,[33] and

[24] *Pan.* III (11), 10, 5.

[25] Plutarch, *Sert.* 22, 2.

[26] For a discussion of the names and types of buildings for the reception of emperors see pp. 41–3 below.

[27] *Pan.* VIII (5), 8, 1–9, 1.

[28] Suetonius, *Nero* 35, 5. The incident quite closely parallels the one at Teanum Sidicinum which Gaius Gracchus gave as an instance of the maltreatment of the Italians by Roman magistrates, Aulus Gellius, *NA*, x, 3, 2–3 = Malcovati, *Or. Rom. Frag.*[3], 191–2.

[29] Josephus, *BJ* I, 20, 3 (394–5); *Ant.* XV, 6, 7 (196–201); 7, 4 (218).

[30] *CTh* VIII, 5, 3 (*CJ* XII, 50, 2).

[31] Suetonius, *Tib.* 38. Cf. Tacitus, *Ann.* I, 47, 3.

[32] *HA, Sev. Alex.* 45, 2; see D. van Berchem, 'L'annone militaire dans l'Empire romain du IIIᵉ siècle', *Mem. Soc. Nat. Ant. France* VIIIᵉ. ser., x (1937), 117–201, on p. 176.

[33] See e.g. Suetonius, *Tit.* 10, 1: 'deinde ad primam statim mansionem febrim nanctus'; Lactantius, *De mort. pers.* 24, 5: 'sublatisque per mansiones multas omnibus equis publicis'; *Pan.* VII (6), 16, 1: 'consumptis copiis mansionum'. Cf. van Berchem, o.c., 181f.

the Greek form of the word (*monê*) now appears on an inscription from Apamea in Syria probably relating to Caracalla's journey in 215,[34] and repeatedly in a papyrus from Panopolis relating to a visit to Egypt by Diocletian in 298. It contains three references to the delivery of various supplies to individual *mansiones* for the expected visit.[35]

The journeys of Caracalla produce vigorous complaints from Cassius Dio, a well-placed witness who was with the emperor at Nicomedia over the winter of 214/15:[36]

> But apart from all these burdens, we were also compelled to build at our own expense all sorts of houses for him whenever he set out from Rome, and costly lodgings in the middle of even the very shortest journeys; yet he not only never lived in them, but in some cases was not destined even to see them. Moreover we constructed amphitheatres and race-courses wherever he spent the winter or expected to spend it, all without receiving any contribution from him.

But our best evidence for the impact of a prospective imperial journey—and again one which did not in fact take place—is what Philo says about Petronius, the *legatus* of Syria under Gaius. The emperor intended to travel to Egypt, coasting along Asia Minor and Syria and going ashore each night:[37]

> In that case it would be necessary to provide fodder for the animals and generous supplies of food in all the Syrian cities, particularly those on the coast. For a vast crowd would arrive by land and sea, not only people who had travelled from Rome itself and Italy, but also people from the line of provinces right to Syria who had joined Gaius' train; there would be a crowd of officials, another of soldiers—infantry, cavalry and marines—and sailors, and another of household retainers, who would be quite as numerous. Supplies would be needed, calculated to provide not only essentials but the extravagant abundance which Gaius demanded.

Documentary evidence supports these general accounts in literature. For instance an inscription from Palmyra records a man named Males who was clerk (*grammateus*) of the city during the visit of Hadrian in 130, and who provided food for the citizens and strangers and saw to the reception of the army.[38] An emperor never travelled without some military escort, but when he was on a regular military expedition this naturally multiplied the problem, especially but not only for those communities which were situated immediately on the route. The cities of Bithynia, for instance, lay directly on the normal path of emperors and armies travelling from Italy or the Danube to the Euphrates frontier. So a whole group of inscriptions from Prusias honours men who saw to the provisioning of the Severan emperors and their

[34] *IGLS* IV 1346, a dedication for the safety of Caracalla, ending with the words ἀπαρχουμ(ένου) ἐν [α]ὐτῇ ἀπὸ μον(ῆς) τῆς γο΄ (203).

[35] T. C. Skeat, *Papyri from Panopolis* (1964), 1, ll. 223, 262, 263. For literary uses of μόνη see Athanasius, *Apol. c. Arianos* 29, 3; *Vita Ant.* 86.

[36] LXXVII, 9, 5–7 (382–3), Loeb trans.

[37] *Leg.* 33/252–3, trans. Smallwood.

[38] *IGR* III 1054 = C. Dunant, *Le sanctuaire de Baalshamin à Palmyre III: les inscriptions* (1971), no. 44.

forces on their way to the east.[39] But the demands of an imperial expedition stretched much more widely than that, and inscriptions from Cilicia now show men who went on formal embassies to the emperor, accompanying supplies sent to the army in Syria.[40]

Much more revealing are the papyri, which in some form or other reflect every visit of an emperor or member of the imperial family which is known from literature, and inevitably reveal much more precisely what these visits involved for a provincial population. From the visit of Germanicus in 19, for instance, we have his edict restraining the forcible requisitioning of animals and billeting on private persons, except in accordance with the orders of Baebius, 'my friend and secretary', who would also make the appropriate payments.[41]

Then, just over a century later, Hadrian arrived in Alexandria in August 130. It is striking to find that as early as 19 December of the previous year we have a letter from a village secretary to the *stratêgos* of the Oxyrhynchite district listing provisions stored 'for the presence of the greatest Emperor Hadrian': they included barley, hay, sucking-pigs, dates, full-grown pigs, sheep, oil, chaff and olives.[42] Similarly, from 5 November 199, during the visit of Severus and Caracalla to Egypt, we have a letter from the *epistratêgos* to the *stratêgoi* of the Arsinoite district asking for a record of the amounts of wine, cattle, hay and so forth produced 'for the supplying of our lords', and of the sums paid by the 'Sacred Treasury' for various types of provisions.[43]

More vivid and personal is the report of camels made in 216/17 to the *stratêgos* of Arsinoe and the *basilico-grammateus* by a woman in Socnopaiou Nesos: in the previous year two camels had been requisitioned for the visit of Caracalla, and subsequently returned; one was now unfit for service and the other had been requisitioned again, this time for the army in Syria.[44] Another papyrus appears to show that Caracalla had intended to return to Egypt in 216, for it announces the restoration of camels requisitioned for the return of the emperor;[45] in a third, one fisherman gives a guarantee that another will provide fish-sauce, fish and salt-fish 'for the most auspicious visit of our lord [Caracalla]'.[46]

These isolated papyri, however, pale in comparison with the papyrus from Panopolis mentioned earlier,[47] which contains the correspondence of

---

[39] See Rostovtzeff, *SEHRE*², ch. ix, n. 46. Note especially *IGR* III 60, honouring a local magistrate, M. Aurelius Philippianus Jason, παραπέμψαντα τὸν κύριο[ν ἡμῶ]ν αὐτοκράτορα Μ. Αὐρήλιο[ν Ἀν]τωνε[ῖνο]ν [κ]αὶ Θεῖον Λ. Σεπτιμίο[ν] Σεουῆρ[ο]ν καὶ [τ]ὰ [ἱε]ρὰ αὐτῶν στρατεύματ[α] ἐν τῷ τῆ[ς] ἀρχῆς καιρῷ ἐπὶ τὴν ἀνατολή[ν]. Cf. *IGR* III 62; 66; 68.

[40] G. E. Bean, T. B. Mitford, *Journeys in Rough Cilicia 1964–8* (1970), nos. 19, 20, 21 (= *AE* 1972 626–8).

[41] *SB* 3924; see D. G. Weingärtner, *Die Ägyptenreise des Germanicus* (1969), 122f.

[42] B. A. van Groningen, 'Preparatives to Hadrian's Visit to Egypt', *Studi in onore di Aristide Calderini e Roberto Paribeni* II (1957), 253; cf. P. J. Sijpesteijn, 'A New Document concerning Hadrian's Visit to Egypt', *Historia* XVIII (1969), 109.

[43] *PSI* 683. See U. Wilcken, *Arch. f. Papyrusforschung* VII (1924), 84; K. Hannestad, 'Septimius Severus in Egypt', *Classica et Mediaevalia* VI (1944), 194.

[44] *BGU* 266.

[45] *P. Strasbourg* 245; see J. Schwartz, 'Note sur le séjour de Caracalla en Égypte', *Chron. d'Ég.* XXXIV (1959), 120. Cf. now *P. Oxy.* 3090–1.

[46] *P. Gothembourg* 3.

[47] p. 33.

the *stratêgos* of the Panopolite district in September 298 relating to the impending visit by Diocletian, accompanied by a military force. The unhappy *stratêgos* stands between the procurator of the lower Thebaid and the city-officials, notably the President of the council of Panopolis. On the one hand, he writes repeatedly to the President urging the city to appoint officials to see to the different commodities; on the other, he writes continually to the procurator to report that these orders have not been carried out. Among other things he has to see to the provision of ships for Diocletian's voyage up the Nile. The letter which he writes to the procurator about these ships is perhaps the best illustration of his situation:[48]

> To the Procurator. Upon your orders, my lord, that the ships of the Treasury requisitioned from the Upper Thebaid should be repaired from Treasury funds for the service of the auspiciously impending visit of our ruler the Emperor Diocletian, the ever-victorious senior Augustus, I have commanded the President of the city, Aurelius Plutogenes also called Rhodinus, to select a surveyor, so that the supervision of the aforesaid ships may be carried out honestly and for the profit of the Sacred Treasury; and also to select an overseer of the same ships, to receive the money from the public bank and account for the expenditure incurred, so that by all means the true amount incurred should be made known to your Diligence. But he, in contempt for his most honourable duty, had the audacity to reply that the city ought not to be troubled.

The movement of an emperor was thus a social and economic event of significant proportions. Just how much of a burden it was, and what type of social experiences would be associated with it, depended, like so many things, on the character of the emperor himself. One extreme was reached with Vitellius' leisurely and luxurious progress to Rome after his proclamation in 69. The leading men of the towns through which he passed were ruined by the provision of enormous banquets; luxuriously-equipped boats were provided for the crossing of rivers. The armies of his generals, Caecina and Valens, were hard at work in advance, building amphitheatres and bringing the equipment from Rome for gladiatorial shows at Cremona and Bononia.[49] On the other hand, Antoninus Pius declined to travel at all through the provinces, saying that the train of an emperor was a burden on the provincials, however sparing he was.[50] It is also significant that one of the contrasts between Trajan and Domitian that Pliny makes in the *Panegyric* is precisely in the character of their journeys. With Trajan there was 'no disturbance in requisitioning vehicles, no fastidiousness about *hospitia*; he has the same supplies as others'. How different from the journeys of a recent emperor! If indeed they were journeys rather than devastations![51]

Depending on the circumstances and also on the nature and standing of the city, a number of different rituals or social events might accompany the

[48] *P. Beatty Panop.* 1, ll. 167f., trans. Skeat. The ships are called τὰ πλοῖα τὰ ταμιακά, 'Treasury (or Fiscal) Ships', an expression for which there does not seem to be any parallel. Cf. p. 199 below.

[49] Tacitus, *Hist.* II, 62, 1; 67, 2; 70–1; Suetonius, *Vit.* 10, 2.

[50] *HA, Ant. Pius* 7, 11.

[51] *Pan.* 20.

emperor's presence. The carrying out of sacrifices was probably a regular matter; at any rate among the orders mentioned in the papyrus from Panopolis is one for the provision of beasts at certain places 'for the sacrifices which will take place'.[52] He might also either give or attend shows and contests. After the destruction of Jerusalem in 70 Titus used some of his captives for massive gladiatorial shows in Caesarea Philippi, Berytus and the cities of Syria;[53] while Gaius gave games in Syracuse and in Lugdunum, where he also put on a contest in Greek and Latin rhetoric.[54] Alternatively the city put on performances for him. Hadrian heard the local ephebes sing a hymn to him in the theatre at Ephesus,[55] and similarly at Ephesus, a prominent citizen, P. Vedius Antoninus, as *gymnasiarch* during the visit of Lucius Verus in 162, evidently gave magnificent games.[56] In the great cities of the Greek world (to which most of our evidence relates) emperors might attend the oratorical displays of the famous sophists who taught there; on his way back from the East in 176, Marcus Aurelius heard both Aelius Aristides in Smyrna and Hadrianus of Tyre in Athens.[57] In Alexandria Hadrian debated with the scholars in the Museum, and granted maintenance there to a local poet, Pancrates, who presented him with a poem on his killing of a lion in Cyrenaica.[58] Shortly after, in November 130, Hadrian and his entourage visited the colossus of Memnon at Thebes, and heard the sound which the statue emitted at dawn.[59] Given all these associations of an imperial visit, it is not surprising to find that cities sometimes either dated from the moment of the imperial 'presence'[60] or held some form of festival on the anniversary of it.[61] The prestige conferred by being a place in which the emperor stayed is nowhere better expressed than in an elaborate simile by Athanasius in his *On the Incarnation of the Word*:[62]

> As when a great king arrives in a great city and takes up his residence in one of the houses in it, such a city is thought worthy in every way of great honour; and no longer does any enemy or bandit come to ravage it, but it is felt to be worthy of every consideration because one house in it is occupied by a king.

But a visit by an emperor could have a practical importance beyond mere questions of prestige, an importance affecting both communities and individuals and at least compensating for the burdens imposed. For, in the first place, on a journey an emperor was relatively exposed to individual

[52] *P. Beatty Panop.* I, ll. 381–3. So the mention in *P. Oxy.* 1626 of beasts being sent to Babylon in Egypt for an impending imperial visit in 325 (which almost certainly did not take place) *may* have been intended for sacrifice.

[53] Josephus, *BJ* VII, 2, 1 (23–4); 5, 1 (96).

[54] Suetonius, *Cal.* 20.

[55] *SEG* XVII 504.

[56] *JÖAI* XLIV (1959), Beibl., 257f., no. 3, corrected in *BE* 1959, no. 381.

[57] Smyrna: Philostratus, *VS* II, 9, cf. Aristides, *Or.* XLII K, 14. Athens: Philostratus, *VS* II, 19.

[58] p. 504.

[59] For the inscriptions in verse left by members of his entourage, see A. and E. Bernard, *Les inscriptions grecques et latines du colosse de Memnon* (1960), nos. 28–33.

[60] For example *IG* II² 3190 (Athens); *IG* v.2, 50; 52 (Tegea); *IG* IV² 384 = *Syll.*³ 842 (Epidaurus).

[61] For example *P. Oxy.* 2553 (Oxyrhynchus); *Ins. Didyma* I, 254 (Didyma); cf. *Fouilles de Delphes* III. 4 (1970), no. 307, col. iii.

[62] *De Incarnatione Verbi* 9, 3.

petitions. To avoid this Tiberius, when leaving for Capri, issued an edict that no one should petition him, and had the whole route cleared of people who might approach him.[63] Similarly, Vespasian once had occasion to interrogate one of his muleteers as to whether he had been bribed to get down and shoe the mules, in order to give time for a litigant to approach.[64] Prominent individuals could hope for an increase in their public honours when an emperor came. Inscriptions relating to Caracalla's eastern journey in 214/15 record that a woman in Pergamon, the holder of several city priesthoods, was 'three times honourably received' by the emperor;[65] and that, when his city was honoured by the emperor, M. Aurelius Asclepiodotianus Asclepiades of Prusias 'asked from him [the right to wear] the purple robe, and obtained it'.[66] More important, however, were the collective benefits, in terms of privileges or actual cash, which a city could hope for from an imperial visit. It is not merely that such benefits are in fact attested—as when Jerome records under the year 125, 'Hadrian after being initated in the Eleusinian mysteries grants many gifts to the Athenians';[67] but rather that people would expect to use the opportunity to present their requests. So when Titus came to Antioch in 70 after the destruction of Jerusalem, the people first greeted him several miles outside the gates, accompanying their greetings with a petition for the removal of the Jews; later, when he returned there from the Euphrates, the council and people invited him to hear the requests of the whole population in the theatre. On this occasion, however, the petition was not successful, and Titus refused to cancel the rights of the Jews in the city.[68] A source which is essentially fictional, Philostratus' *Life of Apollonius of Tyana*, represents Titus shortly after this as carrying out sacrifices at Tarsus in Cilicia, and being petitioned by the whole population for important privileges. When he said that he would intercede with his father Vespasian on their behalf, Apollonius reproached him for prevaricating, whereupon he granted the privileges on the spot.[69]

Not only might the occasion of the imperial presence be taken to present requests and gain privileges, but this could be openly anticipated in addressing an emperor. So an orator speaking before Constantine in 310 invites him to visit Autun:[70]

You will make gifts there also, and establish privileges; in short you will restore my native city with the veneration due to it. The ancient nobility of this

---

[63] Suetonius, *Tib.* 40: 'urbe egrediens ne quis se interpellaret edixerat, ac toto itinere adeuntis submoverat.'

[64] Suetonius, *Vesp.* 23, 2.

[65] *OGIS* 513.

[66] *IGR* III 1422. The reference is not, as supposed in *A Study of Cassius Dio* (1964), 221, to the *latus clavus*, i.e. senatorial status (see pp. 291–3 below), but to the purple robe of a president of provincial games. See the parallel inscription in *Forschungen im Ephesos* III (1923), 152, no. 70, with commentary. As such it is therefore an example of the remarkable range of local institutions within which the emperor's right of granting privileges operated.

[67] Jerome, *Chron.* ed. Helm, p. 199.

[68] Josephus, *BJ* VII, 5, 2 (100–11); cf. *Ant.* XII, 3, 1 (121).

[69] Philostratus, *Vit. Ap. Ty.* VI, 34.

[70] *Pan.* VII (6), 22, 3–4. The opening phrase, 'dabis et illic munera', *could* mean 'you will give shows there', in which case it would be a further example of the pattern mentioned above, p. 36.

city, once honoured by the name of ally of the Roman people, awaits the aid of your majesty, so that there too the public places and the most beautiful temples may be repaired by your liberality . . .

It is indisputable that cities which lay on an emperor's route had an increased chance of benefits from him, and that interested parties from the locality might be able to bring before him personally issues which would have been unlikely to reach him otherwise. One very clear example is the case heard by Caracalla at Antioch in May 216, an accusation brought by the Goharieni against a man who had usurped the priesthood of a temple at Dmeir east of Damascus; it is evident from the exchanges recorded on the inscription that they had seized the opportunity of bringing the matter straight to him rather than to the governor.[71] Another is the now substantial list of *subscriptiones* of Severus and Caracalla posted up in Alexandria while they were there in 200.[72] But what is perhaps more striking and ultimately more important about imperial journeys is the volume of evidence indicating that embassies, and to a lesser extent individual petitioners, came to him not just from the general region where he was but from all over the empire. Some embassies must (one presumes) have been deterred by the difficulty of travel to distant provinces or frontiers; though no instance can be put forward of a potential embassy which turned back, or failed to start, for this reason. On the contrary, just as client kings made a point of paying their respects to Augustus daily, without regard to whether he was in Rome or travelling through the provinces,[73] so it was laid down by Severus and Caracalla that a city ambassador gained a two-year immunity, whether he had been to the emperor in Rome or in some province.[74] So we have to imagine the emperor on his journeys being followed by embassies from within and outside the empire, and by private litigants and petitioners. When in Tarraco, for instance, in the 20s BC, Augustus was joined by the exiled king of Armenia, Tiridates, 'with a large band of friends', followed by an embassy from Phraates of Parthia to counter his complaints;[75] but there too he heard an embassy from Tralles, which had been struck by an earthquake.[76] He is found there also, in an anecdote related by the elder Seneca, judging a succession of apparently private suits.[77]

In consequence it is not surprising to find Dio remarking of the earthquake which struck Antioch when Trajan was there in 114/115, that the whole Empire suffered because people had gathered there from all parts, for cases, embassies, trade or out of curiosity.[78] For examples of this pattern,

[71] *SEG* XVII, 759; cf. pp. 121, 233, 455, 535.

[72] pp. 244–5.

[73] Suetonius, *Div. Aug.* 60: 'ac saepe regnis relictis non Romae modo sed et provincias peragranti cotidiana officia togati et sine regio insigni more clientium praestiterunt.'

[74] *Dig.* L, 7, 9(8), 1.

[75] Justin, *Epitoma Pompei Trogi* XLII, 5, 6–8, cf. Dio LIII, 33, 1–2.

[76] Agathias II, 17. See *JRS* LVI (1966), 163.

[77] *Controv.* X, 14; cf. p. 529.

[78] Dio LXVIII, 24, 1–2; cf. pp. 375, 469. Compare the expectation ascribed to Helicon, the *cubicularius* of Gaius, by Philo, *Leg.* 27/173, that if he visited Alexandria, his native city, with Gaius he would be honoured not only by his fellow-citizens but by the cream of all the cities of the empire.

we may think of the embassy from Aezani in Asia to which Tiberius replied from Boulogne in AD 4,[79] or that from Pergamum to which Hadrian replied from Iuliopolis in 117.[80] Embassies from Asia Minor and Greece went to congratulate Aelius Caesar in Pannonia in 136–8 upon his adoption by Hadrian,[81] and from Athens to Britain, almost certainly when Severus was there in 208–11.[82] In the opposite direction, Constantine wrote to the Lusitanians from Savaria in 322.[38] Three other items from the *Codex Justinianus*, all dating to the decade 310–20, give a particularly vivid picture of one aspect of the traffic between the provinces and the temporary residences of the emperor; one answer to a letter from an office-holder was given in Trier in early November 314, and received in Hadrumetum in the middle of February 315; one at Arles in the middle of August 316, and received in Theveste in mid-October; and one at Serdica in December 317, received at Corduba in March 318.[84]

It is not necessary to illustrate further the evident fact that the emperor functioned as a sort of moving capital of the empire in himself. After the first century, when imperial journeys, except within Italy, were relatively infrequent, the peregrinatory character of the imperial court becomes progressively more pronounced. The pattern is clear, and is reflected in a curious passage of the jurist Callistratus, written in the early third century and preserved in the *Digest*: 'A man who is relegated cannot live in Rome, even if that is not explicitly stated in his sentence, because it is our common native city (*communis patria*): nor in any city where the emperor is residing, or through which he is passing. For only those are permitted to look on the emperor who may enter Rome, for the emperor is *Pater Patriae*.'[85] The passage corresponds, with the addition of some academic colour, to the bare statement in Ulpian that soldiers dismissed with ignominy may not reside either in Rome, or anywhere else where the emperor is in residence.[86] It further reflects the assumption by jurists of this period of the peripatetic nature of the imperial court: as Papinian put it, the honour conferred on a jurist of being a member of the emperor's *consilium* was one which had no certain limits of time or place.[87]

That raises another problem which will be considered later, namely what entourage of advisers, secretaries or humbler assistants an emperor took with him on his journeys to sustain the burden of his extensive communications with cities and individuals throughout the empire.[88] But for the moment we may turn to two different and interrelated issues: the question of

---

[79] *IGR* IV 1693; cf. Robert, *BE* 1949, no. 181.

[80] *IGR* IV 349.

[81] p. 415.

[82] *IG* II² 3707.

[83] *CJ* I, 23, 4.

[84] XII, 61, 1; I, 21, 3; III, 24, 1.

[85] *Dig.* XLVIII, 22, 18 *pr.* The textual attestation of the passage is not good (it is missing from the main MSS. of the Digest, and is supplied from the *Basilica*) but it clearly reflects notions current in the period. See the discussion by V. Nutton, 'Two Notes on Immunities: *Digest* 27, 1, 6, 10 and 11', *JRS* LXI (1971), 52, on pp. 56–61.

[86] *Dig.* III, 2, 2, 4.

[87] *Dig.* XXVII, 1, 30 *pr.*; cf. p. 95.

[88] chs. iii and v passim.

the existence of distinctive imperial residences outside Italy, and the emergence, culminating in the tetrarchic period, of a group of North Italian and provincial cities as secondary imperial 'capitals'.

5. *Imperial Residences in Northern Italy and the Provinces: the Tetrarchic 'Capitals'*

In his last letter to Libanius the emperor Julian describes his journey through Syria in 363 to the Euphrates.[1] At Litarbae in the territory of Chalcis he received a large embassy from the council of Antioch. At Beroea he visited the acropolis, sacrificed a bull to Zeus and addressed the council. At Batnae, where the inhabitants overdid their zeal in sacrificing to demonstrate their paganism to him, he stayed in a 'royal residence' (*basileia*), a remarkably modest structure made of wood and clay, and surrounded by a small garden and a grove of cypresses. At Hierapolis the inhabitants came out to greet him, and he was the guest of a friend named Sopater.

The letter reveals to us not only more indications of the social context of an imperial journey, but something of the range of physical settings, of forms of accommodation, in which he might find himself. It is clear, first, that the custom of the reception of the emperor by prominent individuals continued through and beyond our period. We may note an inscription of a man who had been a *hospes* of Tiberius,[2] and another of a *hospes* of Hadrian from Camerinum; he was appointed to military posts and procuratorships by Hadrian, and is honoured by some villagers for gaining some privileges for them from Antoninus Pius.[3] Similarly, Herodes Atticus received Lucius Verus in Athens,[4] and the inscription of a local magnate in Thyatira records that he received Caracalla when he passed through there in 215.[5] That part of the pattern is relatively clear; the reception of the emperor by prominent Italians or provincials is furthermore an aspect of the complex set of links which bound him to the educated bourgeoisie of the cities.

During a campaign in the field, on the other hand, the emperor inevitably occupied accommodation in the camp comparable to, though more luxurious than, that of other officers. Velleius records that Tiberius during the German and Pannonian wars of AD 4–9 gave to those who needed it the use of his *vehiculum* and litter, his private doctors and his kitchen equipment and portable baths.[6] Fronto similarly writes a glowing, if not necessarily literally accurate, account of Lucius Verus on campaign in the east, sharing every detail of camp life with the troops.[7] The emperor's establishment in a legionary camp is clearly indicated by what remains of Hyginus' work *De munitionibus castrorum*, which describes the camp of an actual legion in

---

[1] *Ep.* 98 Bidez.
[2] *ILS* 7358.
[3] *ILS* 2735. Cf. p. 433.
[4] Philostratus, *VS* II, 1. See p. 4 above.
[5] *IGR* IV 1247 = *OGIS* 516.
[6] Velleius, II, 114, 2.
[7] Fronto, *Principia Historiae* 13.

the Marcomannic war of Marcus Aurelius.[8] The text does not mention
the quarters of the emperor himself, but does refer to the placing within the
legionary camp of the praetorian cohorts, the *equites singulares*, the *officiales*
and the *comites* of the emperor. It is consonant with this that we find
Caracalla living in a tent in the course of the British expedition of Severus,[9]
or Constantine entering the *principia* (the headquarters of a camp) and being
hailed by the *tribuni, praefecti* and *viri eminentissimi*.[10]

So one possible context of the emperors' activity is clear, at least in outline. What remains obscure is what was the typical context of their life and
work while staying in a provincial city. It is clearly possible to suppose that
they used the *praetoria* of the provincial governors. If proved, this would raise
a further intriguing possibility, for in certain cases governors used the actual
palaces of the kings who had preceded them. Just as Verres could use the
royal palace in Syracuse,[11] so the governor of Judaea used what *Acts* actually
calls 'the *praetorium* of Herod' in Caesarea[12] and the royal fortresses in
Jerusalem (of which the Gospels also use 'praetorium').[13] Similarly, Josephus
reports that Quinctilius Varus, as *legatus* of Syria, established himself in
Antioch, because that was the *basileion*, the royal capital, of the country.[14]

But it does not seem possible to show in any instance that the building an
emperor is found using is the normal headquarters of the provincial governor.
Indeed, precisely in the case of Antioch the narrative of Ammianus Marcellinus for the year 354 shows that then at any rate the *palatium* and the
praetorium were quite separate buildings.[15] In this case the *palatium* is
clearly the palace created by Diocletian, which will be discussed below.[16] But
it has to be noted that buildings described as *palatia*, or in Greek *basileia*,
appear also with some frequency in places which were not normal imperial
residences. It may be recalled that Dio says both that *palatium* was used of
any place where the emperor stayed, and that Caracalla had buildings constructed for his accommodation even in places which he was never likely to
visit.[17] It seems likely, therefore, that *palatium* came to be used for any
official stopping-place, as *basileia* is of the wood-and-clay building where
Julian stayed. This would explain how the jurist Arcadius Charisius, writing
probably under Diocletian,[18] can refer to city officials, 'for building or repairing public buildings, whether intended as *palatia* or dockyards or *mansiones*'.[19]

---

[8] *Hygini Gromatici liber de munitionibus castrorum*, ed. A. von Domaszewski (1887); cf. Pflaum,
Carrières I, 482.

[9] Dio LXXVI, 14, 1 (368).

[10] *CTh* VII, 20, 2 = *CJ* XII, 46, 1.

[11] p. 16.

[12] *Acts* 23, 35.

[13] See Schürer, *Jewish People* I, 361.

[14] *Ant.* XVII, 5, 7 (132).

[15] Ammianus XIV, 7, 10: 'praestrictis palatii ianuis, contempto Caesare quem videri decuerat,
ad praetorium cum pompa sollemni perrexit.'

[16] p. 50.

[17] pp. 20 and 33.

[18] See Jones, *Later Roman Empire*, ch. ii, n. 1.

[19] *Dig.* L, 4, 18, 10. For a *palatium* in Carthage in 295 see *Acta Maximiliani* 3, 4. Cf. *CTh* VII,
10, 1 (405) and 2 (407), firstly attempting to prevent the use of *palatia* by officials, and then allowing
it in the case of remote cities where there were no *praetoria*. Cf. *CTh* XV, 1, 35, and *HA, Sev. Alex.*
60, 4, Alexander represented as staying 'in palatio . . . civitatis'.

It is perhaps such *palatia* which are referred to when Eusebius says that
statues of Constantine in a posture of prayer were placed in the *basileia* of
some cities.[20] *Palatia* are found in quite remote places in Egypt, at Arsinoe in
the third century and Hermopolis in the fourth.[21] They could, if the event
ever occurred, actually be used for the accommodation of an emperor or
his entourage: one of the many vivid details in the great papyrus from
Panopolis is a letter to a man who had been 'selected for the superintendence
of bedding of the palace in the Tripheion (the sanctuary of the goddess
Triphis) for the auspiciously impending visit of our ruler the Emperor
Diocletian'.[22] It was similarly to the *palatium* at Autun that Constantine was
escorted on his visit in 311, and at the entrance to it that he formally received
the councillors of the city.[23]

The *basileia* at York, where his father Constantius had died five years
before, were perhaps a building of a similar type and purpose.[24] But we
cannot be sure, and must be still less sure as to how soon such a network of
distinctively (or at least primarily)[25] imperial stopping-places came into
existence. It *may* even be that it was in the same building, or a similar one,
that a *subscriptio* of Severus and Caracalla in reply to a female petitioner was
posted up in York in May 210.[26] There is however no clear and positive
evidence that chains of buildings distinct from mere *mansiones*, and designed
essentially for imperial use, existed in the second or third centuries. The
possibility is suggested only by the fact that the case which Caracalla heard
in Antioch in May 216 was held in a room described as an *auditorium*;[27] and
also, as we have seen,[28] it was in a room with the equivalent Greek name,
dikastêrion, in the *basileia* at Sirmium, that Marcus Aurelius heard the case
between Herodes Atticus and his Athenian enemies.

It may also be significant that both of these cities were to be regular seats
of government in the tetrarchic period. But before we look at the evidence
for the imperial presence there and in the other main centres, we may note
that by the early fourth century, although *palatium* was still very occasionally
used, as Dio had indicated, to mean the emperor's headquarters wherever
he happened to be,[29] it normally meant now an actual imperial building,
whether occupied by the emperor or not. The word which came to mean the
imperial headquarters had a quite different origin, namely *comitatus*,

[20] *VC* IV, 15.

[21] *BGU* 1087, i, 12; iii, 4; *Stud. Pal.* xx, no. 230 (this too contained statues).

[22] *P. Beatty Panop.* I, ll. 259–61, trans. Skeat.

[23] *Pan.* VIII (5), 8, 4; 1, 3.

[24] Eusebius, *VC* I, 21, 2.

[25] It is puzzling to read that Constantine's letter addressed to Arius and his followers in 333,
Gelasius, *HE* III, 19 = Opitz, *Athanasius' Werke* III.1, no. 34, was read out in the *palatium* in
Alexandria—ἀνεγνώσθη ἐν τῷ παλατίῳ. Nor is it clear why the Bordeaux Pilgrim (581, 6) uses
the expression 'ad palatium Dafne' for the famous grove outside Antioch, but not at any other point
(*Corp. Christ. Lat.* clxxv, p. 11).

[26] *CJ* III, 32, 1.

[27] See p. 6 above and 49, 121, 233 below. For the nature of an *auditorium* see B. Tamm,
Auditorium and Palatium (1963).

[28] p. 6 above. Philostratus, *VS* II, 1.

[29] From, or rather referring to, this period I know only Optatus, *Contra Parmenianum Donatistam*
I, 17: 'rescriptum venit, ut, si Mensurius Felicem diaconum non reddidisset, ad palatium
dirigeretur'. See p. 578.

derived from *comes*, a travelling-companion. In its original use it is a collective term for persons accompanying or escorting someone, and in its earlier uses relating to the emperor it still has this meaning.[30] It is perhaps beginning to have a more impersonal sense in the legal writings of the early third century, when Papinian discusses the situation of a *filius familiae* with a post *in comitatu*, and Macer states that a soldier dismissed with ignominy can remain neither in Rome nor 'in the sacred *comitatus*'.[31] The same transitional sense might be present in the *subscriptio* of Diocletian and Maximian of 286, in reply to a doctor whose duties prevented him from 'departing from our *comitatus*' to attend to his property.[32] But the impersonal sense is already absolutely clear in the edict of Constantius and Galerius of 305/6 ordering records of fiscal debts to be sent 'to our *comitatus*'; what is more, the Greek text of the same edict uses a phrase meaning literally 'to our camp'.[33] These two terms, used as equivalents, reflect with remarkable clarity the travels of the imperial court in the third century and the largely military environment in which they were conducted. Indeed they both continue to be used of the movement or despatch of persons or things to the imperial court up to and including the time after 330 when it was firmly based in Constantinople. When, for instance, Constantine ordered the council of Tyre to transfer to Constantinople in 335, his instruction was that they should come 'to the camp of our Clemency'.[34]

Few people in the first two centuries of the Roman empire could have expected seriously that the headquarters of the emperor would ever be established permanently in a city other than Rome. When such thoughts appear in our sources, they are the products of scandal, rumour or propaganda. It was rumoured, for instance, that Julius Caesar would move his capital to Egypt or to Troy;[35] in 32 BC that Antony would transfer the centre of power to Egypt, and shortly before Caligula's death that he would move to Alexandria.[36] Herodian reports, what is again no doubt pure rumour, that after the death of Severus in 211 Caracalla and Geta planned to divide the empire: Geta, so he says, declared that he would establish himself either in Antioch or Alexandria.[37]

The repeated references to Egypt in this context reflect the prestige of

[30] *Thes. Ling. Lat.* cols. 1793–6. Note *AE* 1949 38, a centurion '[adl]ecto in comitatu Imp. [Com]modi'.

[31] *Dig.* XXIX, 1, 43; XLIX, 16, 13, 3.

[32] *CJ* VII, 35, 2.

[33] *CIL* III 12134 (Tlos, Lycia); *IG* II² 1121 (Athens), 39: εἰς τὸ ἡμέτερον στρατόπαιδον [sic] εὐθέως ἀποσταλῶσιν.

[34] The letter is quoted in Athanasius, *Apol. c. Arianos* 86: εἰς τὸ στρατόπεδον τῆς ἡμετέρας ἡμεροτήτος. Cf. p. 605 below. For an earlier use, largely retaining the original meaning, see Philostratus, *VS* II, 32 (Heliodorus going 'to the camp' of Caracalla in Gaul or Germany in 213). Compare, for Latin texts, Optatus, App. II: 'ad comitatum sacrum' (*CSEL* XXVI, 199); V: 'ad comitatum meum' (p. 210); Augustine, *Ep.* 88, 4 = *C. Cresc.* III, 70, 81: 'ad comitatum meum'; *CTh* XI, 30, 5 (316); I, 16, 2 (317); XI, 30, 8 (319); XII, 1, 9 = *CJ* X, 32, 16 (324). Texts in Greek: Socrates, *HE* I, 25: ἐς τὸ ἐμὸν στρατόπεδον, and Athanasius, *Apol. c. Arianos* 70, 2, and cf. Epiphanius, *Pan.* 68, 5. Note also *P. Abinn.* I, l. 9, 'remeandoque [ad sa]crum comitatum vestrum', from a draft petition and referring to the year 340/1.

[35] Nicolaus, *FGrH* 90 F. 130 (XX) (68); Suetonius, *Jul.* 79, 5.

[36] Dio L, 4, 1; Suetonius, *Cal.* 49, 2.

[37] IV, 3, 5–7.

Alexandria in the Graeco-Roman world. The gradual shift from Rome, when it came, answered however to other factors, which find some reflection in the mention of Antioch in Herodian. For it was the military necessities of the empire which progressively caused imperial activities to shift primarily to the route from northern Italy to Sirmium, the Danube, through Thrace to Byzantium, and then from Bithynia through Asia Minor to Antioch;[38] less frequently, they found themselves in Gaul and on the Rhine frontier, and occasionally in Britain.

It is within this framework that we can see the emergence of certain cities as typical imperial centres, some of which become the 'capitals' of the tetrarchic period. It is striking that several of these cities are marked out in the heading of that section of the *Itinerarium Antonini* which actually seems to indicate the route of Caracalla to the east in 214/15: 'ab Urbe, Mediolanum . . . Aquileia . . . Sirmium . . . Nicomedia . . . Antiocia [*sic*] . . . Alexandria.'[39] But even more vivid is the record on an inscription of the embassies to the emperors carried out by a prominent Ephesian between about 202 and 218.[40] He went to defend successfully the precedences and other rights of Ephesus before Severus and Caracalla, several times to Rome (presumably in 202–8), to Britain (208–11), Upper Germany and the shrine of Granius Apollo (213), Sirmium (214), Nicomedia (214/15), Antioch (215/16) and 'as far as Mesopotamia', that is on Caracalla's last campaign in 216/17.

Of the places mentioned in these two sources, the North Italian cities appear as imperial centres in a small way as early as Augustus: Suetonius mentions that his later wars, after 13 BC, were conducted by his *legati*, but that he would sometimes come as far as Ravenna, Mediolanum or Aquileia to keep in touch with the fighting.[41] These places do not however reappear as the setting of imperial activity until the barbarian onslaughts of the mid-third century, except that we find Marcus Aurelius and Lucius Verus, at the time of a similar invasion, wintering at Aquileia in 168/9.[42] Quintillus, however, was killed there in 270, and Aurelian is found there on his way to Pannonia, probably later in the same year.[43] More significant than these scattered references is the fact that there was a *palatium* in Aquileia in the early fourth century, the dining-room of which contained a painting symbolizing the betrothal of the young Constantine to Fausta, the daughter of

---

[38] For the importance of this route in the empire see above all E. Gren, *Kleinasien und der Ostbalkan in der wirtschaftlichen Entwicklung der römischen Kaiserzeit* (1941).

[39] *Itin. Antonini* 123, 8–124, 5. See D. van Berchem, *L'annone militaire* (1937), 177, and idem in *CRAI* 1973, 123.

[40] J. Keil, 'Ein ephesischer Anwalt des 3. Jahrhunderts durchreist das Imperium Romanum', *Sitz-Ber. Bay. Ak. Wiss.* 1956, 3; *SEG* XVII 505. See A. Piganiol, *REG* LXX (1957), 108; R. Duval, *REA* LX (1958), 381–2; L. Robert, *BE* 1958, no. 422.

[41] *Aug.* 20. According to Josephus, *Ant.* XVI, 4, 1 (91), Herod followed Augustus to Aquileia in 12 BC to make accusations against his sons. In *Ant.* XVI, 4, 3 (106) and *BJ* I, 23, 3 (452) the incident appears to be described as occurring in Rome. Note also Val. Max. V, 5, 3, Tiberius, fresh from a victorious war, meeting Augustus and Livia at Ticinum.

[42] Galen XIV Kühn, 649–50.

[43] *Chron. ann. 354* (Mommsen, *Chron. Min.* I, 148); Jerome, *Chron.* ed. Helm, 222; Zosimus I, 48.

Maximian.[44] A tetrarchic *subscriptio* was given there in 296, and Constantine also issued various letters from there, notably in 318.[45] At Ravenna Petrus Patricius represents Aurelian summoning a council of eminent Romans early in his reign, and Diocletian entered on the consulate of 304,[46] but otherwise nothing is recorded of it at this period. Gallienus was killed outside Milan in 268,[47] and there too a *palatium* existed in the late third century. In his address to Maximian in 291 Mamertinus describes the meeting of Diocletian and Maximian there in the previous winter. 'What a spectacle your piety provided, when you were seen together in the *palatium* at Milan by those admitted to adore your sacred countenances.' The *palatium* was evidently in the centre of the city, as the orator's ecstatic description of the emperors' departure shows.[48]

We know of *subscriptiones* posted in Milan in 286 and 295,[49] and it was there that Maximian announced his retirement in 305,[50] and that Constantine and Licinius met in the winter of 312/13, after which Licinius issued at Nicomedia the document which we know conventionally, if inaccurately, as the 'Edict of Milan'.[51] In 315 we find Constantine ordering the various parties in the accusation by the Donatists against Caecilian, the Catholic bishop of Carthage, to follow him to Milan, where he finally heard the case.[52]

Milan and the other north Italian cities therefore provide some illustration of the way in which the setting of imperial activity responded to the necessity of the emperor being closer to the main military areas than Rome was. But they were not (except, in rather different circumstances, Ravenna) to be of major importance in this role. None the less it is in relation to Milan in 290/1 that we first hear, in affected and rhetorical forms, the theme of another city acting as a rival 'capital' to Rome. Mamertinus imagines Rome trying to catch a glimpse, from the seven hills, of the emperors in Milan: 'Indeed she sent the luminaries of her senate, gladly sharing with Milan, a blessed city in those days, the appearance of her own majesty; in consequence the capital of the empire appeared to be there, where the two emperors had met.'[53]

Similar sentiments, but in a much more vivid and explicit form, appear in the panegyric of Constantine delivered at Trier in 310. 'I see that a Circus Maximus, the rival, I believe, of that in Rome, I see the basilicas and a Forum, royal works, and a seat of justice are being raised to such a height that they promise to be worthy neighbours of the sky and the stars. All these are

[44] *Pan.* VI (7), 6–7.
[45] *Frag. Vat.* 313. Constantine: Seeck, *Regesten*, 166–7.
[46] Petrus Patricius, *FHG* IV, p. 197 = Dio, ed. Boissevain III, p. 745, frag. 173. Diocletian: Lactantius, *de mort. pers.* 17, 3.
[47] *Chron. ann. 354* (Mommsen, *Chron. Min.* I, p. 148); Jerome, *Chron.* ed. Helm, 221.
[48] *Pan.* III (11), 11. Note Ammianus XV, 1, 2, Constantius in the *regia* in Milan in 354/5.
[49] *Frag. Vat.* 282; V, 7. *CJ* IV, 23, 9, of 293, is also attributed to Milan. Krueger asserts firmly 'in loco error inest', but if it is a *subscriptio* of Maximian it could be correct.
[50] Eutropius IX, 27, 2; Jerome, *Chron.* ed. Helm, 228; Zonaras, XII, 32.
[51] Lactantius, *De mort. pers.* 45, 1; 48; Eusebius, *HE*, X, 5, 1–14. See pp. 580–2 below.
[52] Augustine, *Ep.* 43, 7/20 (cf. *Frag. Vat.* 273 given at Milan on 1 November 315); see further p. 588.
[53] *Pan.* III (11), 12.

assuredly the gifts of your presence.'[54] In this case the orator's words are strongly confirmed by archaeological evidence, notably the great basilica which still stands in Trier. Beneath it are the foundations of an earlier basilica, perhaps of the mid-third century, but it itself was under construction in 305–12.[55] Connected with it are traces of what may have been an imperial palace; a second bath building on a magnificent scale, the so-called Imperial Baths, also belongs to the tetrarchic period; and a large Christian church, in double-basilica form, was built towards the end of Constantine's reign.[56]

Trier was an exception among the tetrarchic centres in that there is no indication of imperial use of it before that time,[57] but its role as the main seat of Constantine up to 312 is clearly attested: an orator in 312 refers to the presence there of the whole company of the emperor's friends, all the accoutrements of Empire and men from every city either on public embassies or as private petitioners.[58] He continued to use it on occasion in the following few years: various letters and *subscriptiones* of his were issued from there in 313–16.[59] Through the fourth century it was clearly established as the 'noted seat of emperors'.[60] It was to Trier that Constantine was to banish Athanasius in 335, and from there that immediately after his death his son Constantine wrote to restore Athanasius to the see of Alexandria.[61]

Trier was however essentially an outpost, to which only a division of the empire, as in the tetrarchic system, could have given a real role as an imperial centre. It was different with those areas which lay closer to the nodal point where the straits divided Europe and Asia: that is the Danube and Balkans on the one side and Syria, essentially Antioch, on the other. On the route to the Danube frontier and through Moesia and Thrace to the Bosporus at Byzantium there are few significant places where emperors are not found at some point between the middle of the second century and the first part of the fourth. It was at Carnuntum, further north, that Marcus Aurelius, according to Jerome, had his *stativa castra* for three years (177–180),[62] although he died in 180 either at Vindobona (Vienna), or at

---

[54] *Pan.* VII (6), 22, 5: 'video circum maximum aemulum, credo, Romano, video basilicas et forum, opera regia, sedemque iustitiae in tantam altitudinem suscitari ut se sideribus et caelo digna et vicina promittant. Quae certe omnia sunt praesentiae tuae munera.' Note also that in *Pan.* II (10), 14, 3, delivered in 289 and probably in Trier, the orator also uses the motif of the jealousy of Rome at seeing the emperor celebrating his *natalis dies* there.

[55] See esp. W. Reusch, 'L'Aula Palatina de Trèves et le palais preconstantinien qui l'a precedée', *Bull. Soc. Nat. Ant. fr.* 1954/5, 127; idem, 'Die Aula Palatina in Trier (die sogenannte Basilika)', *Germania* XXXIII (1955), 180; T. K. Kempf, W. Reusch, *Frühchristliche Zeugnisse im Einzugsgebiet von Rhein und Mosel* (1965), 144f. Cf. R. Krautheimer, 'The Constantinian Basilica', *DOP* XXI (1967), 115.

[56] The evidence is discussed with salutary caution by E. M. Wightman, *Roman Trier and the Treveri* (1970), 98–113.

[57] There are, however, very slight indications that it was used as a second 'capital' to Cologne by the Gallic emperors; see Wightman, o.c., 52–4.

[58] *Pan.* VIII (5), 2, 1: 'totus tibi amicorum tuorum comitatus et omnis imperii apparatus assistit et cum omnes homines omnium fere civitatum aut publice missi aut pro se tibi supplices assunt.'

[59] Seeck, *Regesten*, 161–2, 164.

[60] Ammianus XV, 11, 9: 'domicilium principum clarum.'

[61] Athanasius, *Apol. c. Arian.* 87, 4–7; see pp. 604–5.

[62] Jerome, *Chron.* ed. Helm, 207; Eutropius VIII, 13, 1.

Sirmium.[63] One can only speculate as to whether the second-century 'palace' excavated in Carnuntum was ever used by an emperor.[64]

From Viminacium on the Danube in Moesia Superior Marcus wrote at least two and possibly three letters to Delphi, of which fragments survive on inscriptions.[65] The evidence of headings in the *Codex Justinianus* shows that Diocletian spent some time at Viminacium in the summer of 293. These headings cannot be regarded as reliable in every case. But when those of this period are reassembled in chronological order from the different sections of the work,[66] they show a perfectly convincing progress in 293, from Byzantium in April to Heraclea (Perinthus), Hadrianopolis, Beroea, Philippopolis (Plovdiv), and then to Viminacium in August and September, and Sirmium over the winter of 293/4 and through to August. He then went back, stopping first at Singidunum (Belgrade), Viminacium and other places, to reach Nicomedia in November.

It is not necessary to collect all the scattered evidence of imperial activity along this route; but two places stand out, and demand a brief mention, Sirmium on the R. Save in Pannonia Inferior, and Serdica in Thrace. At Sirmium emperors do not appear earlier than Marcus Aurelius, whom the story in Philostratus shows established in his *basileia* there.[67] By the later fourth century it certainly contained what Ammianus calls alternatively a *regia* and a *palatium*.[68] The remains of what is thought to be the fourth-century palace have recently come to light, and are reported to include a large room with an apse, and leading from it a long corridor to the imperial box in the hippodrome.[69] We have seen the Ephesian ambassador follow Caracalla there in 214;[70] later Maximinus, who never came to Rome as emperor, had his main seat there,[71] a Thessalian embassy went to Gallienus,[72] Claudius died in 270, and Probus was killed in 282.[73] The earliest *subscriptio* from there in the *Codex Justinianus* is one from Probus, dating to May 277.[74] Thereafter imperial pronouncements issued from Sirmium are common through the tetrarchic and Constantinian periods, as they are also later.[75] One may note especially Diocletian's stay in 293–4, and the fact that Licinius seems to have used it as one of his main centres until pushed back

[63] Sirmium: Tertullian, *Apol.* 25, 5. Vindobona: Aurelius Victor, *Caes.* 16, 12; *Epit.* 16, 12.

[64] See E. Swoboda, *Carnuntum*⁴ (1964), 146f. Plan opposite p. 144. The building contains what appears to be an audience-hall with an apse, which *could* have been used by an emperor; but of course not only, or necessarily, by an emperor.

[65] A. Plassart, *Fouilles de Delphes* III. 4 (1970), nos. 332, 324, 326.

[66] See *Codex Justinianus* ed. Krueger, 495–7.

[67] pp. 4–5.

[68] XXI, 10, 1; XXX, 5, 16.

[69] See E. L. Ochsenschlager, V. Popović, 'Excavations at Sirmium, Yugoslavia', *Archaeology* XXVI (1973), 85 (a general preliminary report); cf. V. Popović (ed.), *Sirmium* I–II (1971); see also *MEFAR* LXXXVI (1974), 597.

[70] p. 44.

[71] Herodian VII, 2, 9.

[72] Ἐφ. Ἀρχ. 1945/7, 106 (Larisa); cf. *BE* 1951, no. 124.

[73] Claudius: *Chron. ann. 354* (Mommsen, *Chron. Min.* I, p. 148; Jerome, *Chron.* ed. Helm, 222); Zonaras XII, 26. Probus: *Chron. ann. 354*, loc. cit.; Jerome, o.c., 224; Eutropius IX, 17, 3.

[74] *CJ* VIII, 55, 2.

[75] See, for the period up to 337, *Codex Justinianus* ed. Krueger, 494–9; cf. Seeck, *Regesten*, 159–84.

to Asia Minor by Constantine in 316/17. *Thermae Licinianae* were built there, and it was from Sirmium that he hastily collected his family and stores (*thesauri*) after his defeat.[76]

Between 316 and 323 Constantine is found most frequently either in Sirmium or Serdica,[77] and it must have been at this time that he described Serdica as 'my Rome'.[78] It had been used before in the tetrarchic period—apart from the legal evidence, there is the inscribed letter of Constantine and Licinius on the privileges of soldiers and veterans, issued by the latter at Serdica in June 311.[79] Constantine was also there on occasion after his final defeat of Licinius in 324; in February 330 he wrote from Serdica simultaneously to the *consularis* of Numidia and to the Catholic church of Cirta about harassments by schismatic Christians.[80] At least by 343/4, the city contained a *palatium*, which accommodated some of the bishops at the Council of Serdica.[81]

The imperial presence in Antioch is attested much earlier and more fully than at any of the east European cities; it begins indeed with the visit of the future Augustus in 30 BC, to which Ioannes Malalas, writing his *Chronicle* in the sixth century, attaches a fictional account of building there by Agrippa. Ten years later it was probably at Antioch that Augustus heard and rejected the accusations of Zenodorus and the people of Gadara against Herod.[82] Thereafter until the early third century, if we except the visits of Titus in 70, Trajan in 114/15,[83] and Lucius Verus in the 160s, Antioch was more notable as the seat of usurpers, a fact which itself indicates its importance. In 69 Vespasian spoke in Greek to the people assembled in the theatre, and established a mint there.[84] Of the revolt of Avidius Cassius in 175 we know only that he was supported by the citizens of Antioch.[85] But when Pescennius Niger, the *legatus* of Syria, was proclaimed emperor in Antioch in 193, the soldiers and the population 'put the purple cloak of an emperor on him and provided him with all the other tokens of imperial dignity made out of makeshift materials, including the carrying of fire before him in processions. After conducting him to the temples of Antioch, they installed him ceremoniously in his own house, which was now regarded as the imperial court and no longer as a private house. Outside it was decorated with all the insignia of office.'[86] It is interesting to observe both how easy it was to give a private house the appearance of a court, and also that there

---

[76] See Minkovic, in V. Popović, *Sirmium* I (1971), 37–8. On *thesauri* see pp. 151–2.

[77] *Codex Justinianus* ed. Krueger, 498; Seeck, *Regesten*, 165–72.

[78] p. 12.

[79] *FIRA*² I, no. 93. See further p. 222.

[80] *CTh* XVI, 2, 7; Optatus, App. X. See p. 590 below.

[81] Athanasius, *Hist. Arian.* 15, 4.

[82] The visit of 30 BC is securely attested by Josephus, *Ant.* XV, 7, 4 (218). See Malalas, *Chron.* 222; and for Antioch in general G. Downey, *A History of Antioch in Syria from Seleucus to the Arab Conquest* (1961). The hearing in 20 BC certainly took place in Syria (Josephus, *Ant.* XV, 10, 3 (354)), but Antioch is mentioned specifically only in connection with the death of Zenodorus (359), which took place before Herod returned home, after escorting Augustus to the sea (363).

[83] pp. 37, 375.

[84] Tacitus, *Hist.* II, 80, 2; 82, 1.

[85] *HA, Marc. Ant.* 25, 8–12; *Avid. Cass.* 9, 1.

[86] Herodian II, 8, 6, Loeb trans.

was clearly no imperial *palatium* there to be taken over. As soon as the news of the proclamation spread, embassies came to Niger from all the provinces of Asia Minor 'as to the acknowledged emperor'.[87] Antioch was the natural centre for a usurper in the east. When Caracalla was murdered in April 217 on the road between Edessa and Carrhae, and the Praetorian Prefect, Opellius Macrinus, was proclaimed emperor, it was Antioch which he made his main residence,[88] hastening there as soon as he had concluded peace with the Parthians.[89] Herodian describes him delaying in Antioch, answering those who presented themselves before him in a low voice and ponderous manner which was supposed to recall Marcus Aurelius.[90] When he was overthrown by the young Elagabal (properly Varius Avitus, the great-nephew of Julia Domna, the wife of Septimius Severus), the new emperor stayed in Antioch for several months before setting out for Rome.[91]

We cannot estimate the effects of these episodes in Antioch any more than we can those of the brief regimes there of Macrianus and Quietus in the early 260s or of Vabalathus and Zenobia, the Palmyrenes, a decade later. More significant is its use as a base, or a source of luxurious pleasures, by Lucius Verus in the Parthian war of 162–6.[92] It was there also, in the winter of 201/2, that Septimius Severus bestowed the *toga virilis* on Caracalla and entered on his second consulate with him (a rare and remarkable honour for a provincial city).[93] More typical is its use once again as the base for eastern campaigns. Caracalla was there in 215 and 216, and inscriptions reveal not only the Ephesian embassy and the case of the Goharieni which he heard there, but also, perhaps, a letter written from there in reply to an embassy from Apollonia in Caria.[94] Moreover, while he was on his last campaign in Mesopotamia in 217, his mother Julia Domna, to whom he had entrusted the handling of routine *libelli* and *epistulae*, was at Antioch dealing with his correspondence.[95] Antioch was also used by Severus Alexander as a base for his campaign against the newly-restored Persian empire in 231–3,[96] and by Valerian in the 250s. The dates of Valerian's presence there are disputed,[97] but one fixed point is provided by a letter given in reply to an

[87] ibid. II, 8, 7.

[88] Ammianus XXVI, 6, 20: 'sic Antiochiae Macrino imperatore agente.' Cf. Dio LXXVIII, 34, 5 (443); 39, 1–2 (447–8); *HA, Op. Mac.* 10, 1.

[89] Herodian IV, 15, 9; V, 1, 1.

[90] V, 2, 3–4; cf. 4, 1. The anonymous Ephesian ambassador (p. 44) also went to Macrinus and his son Diadumenianus, probably in Antioch.

[91] Dio LXXX, 3, 1 (455–6).

[92] Dio LXXI, 2, 2 (246); Eutropius VIII, 10, 2; *HA, Verus* 7, 1–3.

[93] *HA, Sept. Sev.* 16, 8.

[94] See L. and J. Robert, *La Carie II: le plateau de Tabai et ses environs* (1954), 274, no. 149. The period late 213–17 is indicated by the third imperatorial acclamation in l. 7, and the name of Antioch can be fitted easily into ll. 24–5: [Πρὸ .] καλανδῶν Ἰανουαρίων ἀ[π' ᾿Αντι/οχεία]ς. But the restoration of course remains conjectural.

[95] See Dio LXXVII, 18, 2 (397), where βιβλιδίων (*libelli*) should possibly be read for βιβλίων (but cf. p. 210), and for Julia's presence at Antioch, LXXVIII, 4, 2–3 (406–7).

[96] Herodian VI, 4, 3; 6, 2–6. It will have been at this time that the emperor's mother sent an escort of soldiers to bring Origen from Caesarea to Antioch for her to hear him, see Eusebius, *HE* VI, 21, 3–4.

[97] See Downey, o.c., 259, and especially T. Pekáry, 'Bemerkungen zur Chronologie des Jahrzehnts 250–60 n. Chr.', *Historia* XI (1962), 123.

3

embassy from Philadelphia in Lydia, and dated from Antioch on 18 January 255.[98] Zosimus reports that Valerian began to rebuild Antioch after it had been ravaged by the Persians, while Malalas claims that when Diocletian began to build his *palatium* there, he discovered foundations laid by 'Gallienus Licinianus'—which, if not entirely fictional is more likely to refer to Licinius Valerianus than his son Gallienus, who never came to Antioch.[99]

It was indeed in the period of the tetrarchy that Antioch became a true imperial capital.[100] As the *Expositio totius mundi*, written soon after the middle of the fourth century, puts it: 'You have Antioch, abounding indeed in all delights, but especially in circus games. But why? Because the emperor takes up his residence there, all things are required because of him.'[101] As we have seen, Malalas states that Diocletian built a *palatium* there, probably correctly, for half a century later a statue of his co-emperor Maximian stood in the *vestibulum* of the *regia* there.[102] Nothing remains of it, and we have to rely for a description of the *palatium* on the *Oration* XI of Libanius, delivered in 360.[103] A palace certainly existed by about 303, for a passage in the same oration describes a usurper named Eugenius entering the *basileion* at Antioch then, and seizing the accoutrements of the emperors.[104]

None the less Antioch was clearly a residence of secondary importance in Diocletian's reign. According to Malalas he remained there during the Persian campaign of Galerius. The date is probably 299:[105] one *subscriptio* possibly of 299 and a few of 300–1 also show Diocletian there.[106] Similarly occasional items of evidence show emperors at Antioch through the period of persecutions, 303–13. Romanus, a deacon at Caesarea, was tried and tortured there before an emperor, probably Galerius, in 303,[107] while at the end of this phase Licinius is found arriving in Antioch in 313, and putting to death the leading pagans.[108]

By this time, however, although even in Constantine's time prominent members of the imperial family are found in residence in Antioch,[109] the centre of imperial activity in the east had shifted decisively to the area of the Bosporus. In so doing it was moving, as we have seen, to the focal point of an established route. In the early second century, when Pliny was governing

---

[98] J. Keil, F. Gschnitzer, 'Neue Inschriften aus Lydien', *Anz. Ost. Ak. Wien*, Ph.-hist. Kl. XCIII (1956), 219, no. 8; *BE* 1958, no. 438; *SEG* XVII 528. See further, p. 390. The *subscriptio* (or *epistula*) of April or May 258, *CJ* V, 3, 5 = IX, 9, 18 *may* indicate Valerian's presence in Antioch at that time. But see p. 570.

[99] Zosimus I, 32, 2; Malalas 306, 21f. See Downey, o.c., 259–60.

[100] On Antioch in the later fourth century see now J. H. W. G. Liebeschuetz, *Antioch: City and Imperial Administration in the Later Roman Empire* (1972).

[101] *Expositio totius mundi et gentium* (ed. Rougé, 1966), 32.

[102] Ammianus XXV, 10, 2. As noted above (p. 41), what is evidently the same building is called *palatium* (and *regia*) in Ammianus XIV, 7, 9–11.

[103] See Downey, o.c., 318f.

[104] Libanius, *Or.* XI, 161.

[105] Malalas 306, 15f. Lactantius, *De mort. pers.* 9, 6, relates merely that he stayed behind in the east. For the date see T. C. Skeat, *Papyri from Panopolis* (1964), xiiif.

[106] *Codex Justinianus* ed. Krueger, p. 497.

[107] Eusebius, *Mart. Pal.* 2.

[108] Eusebius, *HE* IX, 11, 6.

[109] Dalmatius: Athanasius, *Apol. c. Arian.* 65 (see p. 602); Socrates, *HE* I, 27/64. Constantius: Sozomenus, *HE* III, 5; Zonaras XIII, 4.

Bithynia, a legionary centurion was posted at Byzantium to control traffic, and the question arose of having another at Juliopolis near the eastern border of the province on the road to Ancyra.[110] In 202 we find Severus and Caracalla, accompanied by Julia Domna and the praetorian prefect, Fulvius Plautianus, travelling back to Rome from Antioch through Asia Minor, stopping at Tyana and Nicaea. Dio's narrative reveals that Severus was judging cases at his stopping-places along the way, and that Plautianus had more luxurious accommodation, and more lavish supplies than the emperor.[111] Nicaea might well have become a major imperial centre, and in the early fourth century there was indeed a palace there, in which the Council of Nicaea was held in 325:[112] Constantine was present in person, and also wrote a letter to the *praefectus urbi* from there on 23 May.[113]

But already in the Severan period the preference was clearly given to the neighbouring city of Nicomedia. When the Ephesian ambassador followed Caracalla there, it will have been when he was established for the winter of 214/15.[114] Cassius Dio, who was present, describes him training his Macedonian 'phalanx' there, holding gladiatorial games, giving a dinner to celebrate the Saturnalia, and also giving judgment—or rather keeping his advisers, of whom Dio was one, waiting all day for the cases to begin, while he ate and drank with his soldiers.[115]

Four years later, Elagabal, on his way to Rome, spent the winter of 218/19 at Nicomedia, where he entered on the consulate of 219, and carried out various executions.[116] Thereafter we do not hear of emperors at Nicomedia until, after the murder of Numerianus on the march back from the east, Diocletian was proclaimed by the soldiers there, or possibly at Chalcedon, in 284.[117] The *subscriptiones* and *epistulae* from the *Codex Justinianus* show him there in the spring of 286 and again in the winter of 294.[118] It was while there in 286, that on the first of April he proclaimed Maximian as joint Augustus.[119] By the winter of 302/3, when he was joined there by Galerius, it is clear that there was a *palatium* in the city; a fire, accidental or otherwise, by which it was damaged, added impetus to the Great Persecution.[120] Before he comes to this, Lactantius rhetorically alludes to rather than describes the massive rebuilding which followed the establishment of Diocletian in Nicomedia: 'Here there were basilicas, here a circus, a mint, an arms factory, a house for his wife and one for his daughter. Suddenly a whole section of the city was destroyed, and all the people were

---

[110] Pliny, *Ep.* x, 77–8.

[111] Dio LXXV, 15, 3–6 (354).

[112] Eusebius, *VC* III, 10; Sozomenus, *HE* I, 19. For the Council see pp. 595–8 below. For later references to the palace, Ammianus XXVI, 10, 1; Procopius, *De aedif.* V, 3, 3.

[113] *CTh* I, 2, 5 = *CJ* I, 19, 2.

[114] See in the *Acta Fratrum Arvalium* for 214 (*CIL* VI, 2103) a sacrifice carried out because Caracalla 'felicissime ad (h)iberna Nicomediae ing[ressus sit]'.

[115] LXXVII, 17, 1–18, 1 (396–7); 19, 3 (399); LXXVIII, 8, 4 (411).

[116] Dio LXXVIII, 35, 3 (444); LXXIX, 6, 1; 7, 3; 8, 3 (460–1); Herodian V, 5, 3.

[117] Zosimus I, 73, 2, gives Nicomedia, see Paschoud ad loc.; cf. Jo. Ant., Fr. 163 (*FHG* IV, 601); Chalcedon is given by the *Chronicon Paschale* (Mommsen, *Chron. Min.* I, 229).

[118] *Codex Justinianus* ed. Krueger, 494, 497.

[119] *Chron. Pasch.* (Mommsen, *Chron. Min.* I, 229–30). Cf. *RE* s.v. 'Valerius' (142), 2427.

[120] Lactantius *De mort. pers.* 12; 14; Eusebius, *HE* VIII, 6, 6; Constantine, *Oratio* 25, 2.

in flight with their wives and children as if from a captured town. Such was his incessant mania for making Nicomedia the equal of Rome.'[121] Here again the perception that the tetrarchic centres genuinely rivalled the status and function of Rome was quite conscious in the mind of a contemporary.

Nicomedia remained the 'capital' of the eastern part of the empire up to and even beyond the defeat of Licinius by Constantine in 324. The edict of toleration of Galerius was posted there on 30 April 311, shortly before his death at Serdica, which became known there in the middle of May.[122] Maximin hastened there, probably from Antioch, forestalling Licinius' advance from the Balkans, and implicitly emphasizing the now central importance of the city. The period of toleration only lasted a few months, and Maximin himself describes in a letter written in 312 how the people of Nicomedia, among others, petitioned him later in the year against the Christians, presenting themselves on the occasion of his arrival to take up residence in the city.[123] In the persecution under Maximin, the presbyter Lucian of Antioch was brought to Nicomedia and tried before the emperor himself.[124] In the next year war broke out between Licinius and Maximin, and after his defeat Maximin collected his family and *comites* from Nicomedia and fled eastwards.[125] Under the agreement reached between Constantine and Licinius at Milan in the winter of 312/13 persecution was ended: the primary document for this is the letter to the *praeses* (of Bithynia) which Licinius posted up in Nicomedia on 15 June 313.[126]

Of Licinius as emperor there our sources tell us very little. But the significance of Nicomedia had its reflection even on the church. For the bishop Eusebius of Berytus saw his chance of political power and moved to the see of Nicomedia; the fact and the motive are both attested in a letter of Alexander, bishop of Alexandria, written in about 319.[127] We catch glimpses of the life of the court there in reactions to the brief period of persecution which began about 321. Sozomenus relates the engaging tale of Arsacius, a soldier who had charge of the imperial lions; he was a *confessor* under Licinius and left the service to meditate in a tower at Nicomedia.[128] More revealing still is the story of Auxentius, the future bishop of Mopsuestia, which is preserved in the Suda. In one of the courtyards of the palace there was a fountain, with a statue of Dionysus beside it, and a vine which shaded the whole spot. There Licinius came to relax, accompanied by a large retinue including Auxentius, who was then a *notarius* in his service. The emperor ordered Auxentius to cut a bunch of grapes, which he did; but then ordered him to lay it at the feet of the statue, which he refused to do, and retired from the emperor's service.[129]

---

[121] o.c., 7, 9–10.

[122] Lactantius, o.c., 33, 1. For the place of Galerius' death, *Origo Constantini Imperatoris* (= *Anon. Valesianus* I) 3, 8.

[123] Eusebius, *HE* IX, 9a, 4. See further pp. 445 and 580.

[124] p. 580.

[125] Lactantius, *De mort. pers.* 47, 5.

[126] o.c., 48; Eusebius, *HE* X, 5. See further pp. 580–3.

[127] Socrates, *HE* I, 6; Opitz, *Urk. z. Gesch. des arian. Streites*, no. 4b.

[128] Sozomenus, *HE* IV, 16, 6.

[129] Suda, ed. Adler, s.v. Αὐξέντιος.

Thus an imperial court had been settled in a Greek city near the Bosporus for some three decades before the victory of Constantine over Licinius. At the same time, however, Rome had remained the seat of Maxentius in 306–312, and then to a much lesser extent of Constantine, who moved mainly between Milan, Trier, Sirmium and Serdica, and later Thessalonica.[130] With hindsight one can see a long foreshadowing of the decisive step which Constantine was soon to take. But it could not have been taken at all, and would not have assumed the form which it did, but for his victory on 18 September 324, at Chrysopolis opposite the ancient Greek city of Byzantium.

6. *Constantinople*

The foundation of Constantinople was thus the culmination of a long process. It had been a characteristic of the empire from the beginning that the emperor could conduct his business for substantial periods away from Rome; many emperors, from taste or necessity, had in fact done so. Similarly, the focus of imperial activity had already shifted to the Bosporus area. So the ultimate choice of Byzantium might seem almost to have been inevitable. The magnificence of its site had been appreciated ever since the classical period of Greece, and the strength of its walls, even before Constantine's extension, demonstrated in its resistance to the three-year siege by Severus' generals in 193–6. As it lay directly on the established route from the Danube to the Euphrates, it is not surprising that occasional *subscriptiones* are dated from there,[1] and in particular a whole group from April 293.[2]

None the less, later writers relate that several other sites were considered first, and in some cases that building was actually begun there. The most common tale, which takes us back to the rumour once current about Julius Caesar,[3] is that Constantine intended to rebuild Troy.[4] Cedrenus describes him spending two years in Thessalonica, and adorning it with splendid buildings, and then moving to Chalcedon and beginning to rebuild it, until eagles appeared and carried the foundation-stones to Byzantium.[5] Zonaras makes Constantine settle first at Serdica, then Sigeum (Troy in effect) and then Chalcedon, with the same portent of the eagles.[6] An anonymous fourth-century Latin history of Constantine, the so-called *Origo Constantini Imperatoris*, refers neither to those tales nor to the strategic significance of the site, but regards the new foundation simply as a memorial to the victory

---

[130] Zosimus II, 22, 1, notes that Constantine used Thessalonica as a base for his final operations against Licinius; cf. also *Origo Const. Imp.* 21. *Epistulae* are dated from there in spring 323 and 324, Seeck, *Regesten*, 172–3.
  [1] *CJ* v, 72, 2 (Aurelian); *Frag. Vat.* 281 (286); *CJ* II, 4, 13 (290); II, 4, 31; VIII, 27, 20 (294).
  [2] *Codex Justinianus* ed. Krueger, p. 495.
  [3] p. 43.
  [4] Zosimus II, 30, 1; Sozomenus, *HE* II, 3, 2. For a discussion of possible sites and possible Constantinian remains reported in the area at various times, see J. M. Cook, *The Troad: an Archaeological and Topographical Study* (1973), 158–9.
  [5] *Chron.* I, pp. 495–6 Bonn.
  [6] Zonaras XIII, 3.

at Chrysopolis.[7] This explanation may well be correct, and there cannot in any case have been much time for abortive projects elsewhere; for the building of the new city seems to have begun immediately at the end of 324.[8]

In the meantime, it seems clear, Nicomedia remained Constantine's main centre. He rebuilt the basilica there and also had a magnificent church constructed.[9] His *vicennalia* were celebrated there in 325—and in Rome in the following year.[10] Some letters of 325, 327 and 328 are dated from Nicomedia, though this was a period when he was frequently on the move, even as far as Trier in 328.[11] It will have been about this time that a delegation from the schismatic Meletian church in Egypt made its way to the *comitatus* and waited about in Nicomedia and Constantinople for an opportunity to gain access to the emperor; we shall return to their story later.[12]

Though a few letters and *subscriptiones* are dated from Constantinople even in the 320s, it is clear that it was in 330, when the new city was dedicated that the court established itself there. We need not discuss all that is reported in literary sources, many of them very late, of the vast series of buildings constructed in the city at this time;[13] of all the buildings of this period, only the hippodrome, with some of the monuments brought from elsewhere and set up in it, survives for archaeological investigation. What is more important is to observe some of the social effects of the quite novel presumptions which were applied in the re-foundation.

These effects are most vividly described in the hostile account by Eunapius:[14]

> For Constantinople, originally called Byzantium, in distant times used to furnish the Athenians with a regular supply of corn, and an enormous quantity was imported thence. But in our times neither the great fleet of merchant vessels from Egypt and from all Asia, nor the abundance of corn that is contributed from Syria and Phoenicia and the other nations as the payment of tribute, can suffice to satisfy the intoxicated multitude which Constantine transported to Byzantium by emptying other cities, and established near him because he loved to be applauded in the theatres by men so drunk that they could not hold their liquor. For he desired to be praised by the unstable populace, and that his name should be in their mouths, though so stupid were they that they could hardly pronounce the word.

[7] 29–30: 'Constantinus autem ex se Byzantium Constantinopolim nuncupavit ob insignis victoriae [memoriam].'

[8] The most precise evidence is Themistius, *Or.* IV, 58b: πυνθάνομαι γὰρ ὡς καὶ ἡμφίασεν ὁμοῦ ὁ γεννήτωρ (Constantine) τό τε ἄστυ τῷ κύκλῳ καὶ τὸν υἱέα (Constantinus II) τῇ ἀλουργίδι. See A. Alföldi, 'On the Foundation of Constantinople: a Few Notes', *JRS* xxxvii (1947), 10, on p. 11.

[9] *Expositio totius mundi*, 42; Eusebius, *VC* III, 50; *Or. ad Tric.* 9, 14.

[10] Jerome, *Chron.* ed. Helm, 213: 'Vicennalia Constantini Nicomediae acta et sequenti anno Romae edita.'

[11] Seeck, *Regesten*, 174–80.

[12] Epiphanius, *Pan.* 68, 6: καὶ ἐν τούτῳ συμβέβηκε χρονοτριβῆσαι τοὺς περὶ Παφνούτιον καὶ Ἰωάννην καὶ λοιποὺς ἐπὶ τὰ μέρη τῆς Κωνσταντινουπόλεως καὶ Νικομηδείας. See pp. 600–1.

[13] See R. Janin, *Constantinople Byzantine*[2] (1964), and now also G. Dagron, *Naissance d'une capitale: Constantinople et ses institutions de 330 à 451* (1974).

[14] *VS* 462, Loeb trans.

The transfer of a substantial population is a fact[15] as is the diversion of the tribute-corn to feed it; as we shall see, the change that finally sent Athanasius into exile in 335 was that of having threatened to hold up in Alexandria the corn-ships due for Constantinople.[16]

The bread-distribution in Constantinople, confirmed by Zosimus, began according to the *Chronicon Paschale* in 332;[17] under the year 328 the same source gives a detailed description of the imperial box at the hippodrome, in which the emperor made his appearance directly from a corridor leading from the *palatium*.[18] This is a feature which may have been present in the main 'capitals' of the tetrarchic period.[19] But, even if so, it should not obscure the immense difference in the scale of innovation applied to Constantinople. There is not only the change of name, the diversion of corn, and the bread distributions, but most significantly the creation of a new senate whose members had, in this period, a status second to that of the Roman senators, *clari* rather than *clarissimi*.[20] Not unnaturally, later literary sources readily attribute to Constantine the conscious desire to establish a rival capital to Rome.[21] The motive can be accepted,[22] even though we cannot document it from Constantine's own words, any more than we can the expression 'New Rome' or 'Second Rome', which is very rare in other fourth-century sources also.[23] Orators of the later fourth century do, however, begin to apply to Constantinople the expressions 'royal city' or 'reigning city' which had previously been commonly applied to Rome.[24] But when Julian composed his encomium of Constantius in 356, he kept the term, 'reigning city' for Rome, and expressed the eminence of Constantinople by saying that it surpassed all other cities by as much as it was surpassed by Rome.[25]

So the foundation of Constantinople, though it represented an immense change in relation to the past, as against the wanderings of the court in the past centuries and even as against the relatively settled 'capitals' of the

---

[15] Cf. *Origo Constantini Imperatoris* 30.

[16] Athanasius, *Apol. c. Arian.* 87, 1–2; Socrates, *HE* I, 35, 2; cf. p. 605.

[17] Zosimus II, 32, 1; *Chron. Pasch.* (Mommsen, *Chron. Min.* 1, 234). Cf. Philostorgius, *HE* II, 9.

[18] *Chron. Pasch.* ib., 233. The author alleges that this was copied from a similar feature in Rome, which, though topographically possible, is not directly attested.

[19] For such a feature reported from Sirmium see p. 47 above, and for the probable conjunction of *palatium* and hippodrome in other tetrarchic centres see M. Vickers, 'The Hippodrome at Thessaloniki', *JRS* LXII (1972), 25. The historical evidence for imperial use of Thessalonica in the tetrarchic period is very slight, as is that for the regular conjunction of hippodrome and palace in this period.

[20] *Origo Constantini Imperatoris* 30.

[21] ibid.: 'quam velut patriam cultu decoravit et Romae desideravit aequari'; Eutropius X, 8, 1: 'primusque urbem nominis sui ad tantum fastigium evehere molitus est, ut Romae aemulam faceret'; Zosimus II, 30, 1: πόλιν ἀντίρροπον τῆς Ῥώμης ἐζήτει, καθ' ἣν αὐτὸν ἔδει βασίλεια καταστήσασθαι; Sozomenus, *HE* II, 3, 1: ἐπὶ τῆς Βυζαντίων πόλεως, ἣν ἴσα Ῥώμη κρατεῖν καὶ κοινωνεῖν αὐτῇ τῆς ἀρχῆς κατεστήσατο.

[22] For an illuminating discussion, see A. Alföldi, *The Conversion of Constantine and Pagan Rome* (1948; repr. 1971), ch. ix.

[23] 'Altera Roma' is used of Constantinople in Publilius Optatianus Porfyrius, *Carm.* IV, 6. For later examples, Socrates, *HE* I, 16; Sozomenus, *HE* II, 3, 5; *Chron. Pasch.* (Mommsen, *Chron. Min.* 1, 234). See F. J. Dölger, 'Rom in der Gedankenwelt der Byzantiner', *Zeitschr. f. Kirchengesch.* LVI (1937), 1, on pp. 13–17.

[24] For the latest survey see M. Wörrle, 'Ägyptisches Getreide für Ephesos', *Chiron* I (1971), 325, on pp. 329–31.

[25] Julian, *Or.* I (Bidez), 4 (Rome is ἡ μὲν βασιλεύουσα τῶν ἀπάντων πόλις) and 6.

tetrarchy, still did not mean a sudden break, a sudden transference of all the associations of Rome. But in practical terms it was now the capital. After his visit in 326 Constantine never returned to Rome: and from 330 onwards, though he still travelled in eastern Europe (for instance to Singidunum, Viminacium and Naissus in July and August of 334), he was essentially settled in Constantinople. It was there that his subjects came to find him, and from there that he most often wrote. One letter is dated already to 16 July 330;[26] and on 30 June 331 he and his sons wrote from there in reply to a petition from the inhabitants of Orcistus on the borders of Galatia and Asia.[27] But the most vivid impression of the concentration of imperial business there is provided by the complex affairs of the church in these years.[28] For instance we find Constantine writing to Eusebius of Caesarea to have fifty bibles prepared for the Christian congregations of 'the city named after us', and brought 'to our sight' on two wagons of the *cursus publicus*.[29] More often, the Christians applied to him, as did a monk named Eutychianus, who made his way to Constantinople from his retreat in Bithynia, and successfully petitioned the emperor for the life of one of his escort, who had been condemned to death.[30] Similarly it was at Psammathia outside Nicomedia that Constantine heard accusations by the Arians and Meletians against Athanasius in 332[31] (it is interesting to note the appearance in this area of the use of imperial villas for business which is so well attested in the vicinity of Rome); and it was to Constantinople that Athanasius fled from the council of Tyre in 335, to petition the emperor.[32] Constantinople had become the focal point of church politics. So when Athanasius was soon banished to Trier, and Arius was restored to communion with the church in Alexandria, only to be rejected there, it was to Constantinople that he returned. There, supported by the party of Eusebius, bishop of Nicomedia, he was about to be accepted under compulsion, and with the support of the emperor, when he died suddenly in a public lavatory in the city.[33]

One might take as a symbol of the new order the death of Constantine in 337 in a suburb of Nicomedia, and his burial in the Church of the Apostles in Constantinople; or possibly the second transference of the bishop Eusebius to the seat of power, this time in 338 from Nicomedia to the See of Constantinople.[34] But we might also look to the impact of Constantine's foundation on a much longer-established mode of life, that of the great orators of the Greek world, and consider what Eunapius reports of Libanius' movements in 340: 'As he gained confidence in his eloquence and convinced himself that he could rival any that prided themselves on theirs, he resolved not to bury himself in a small town and sink in the esteem of the

[26] *Frag. Vat.* 248.
[27] *MAMA* VII, 305. See p. 410.
[28] See further pp. 600–11.
[29] Eusebius, *VC* IV, 36.
[30] Socrates, *HE* I, 13.
[31] See p. 602.
[32] Athanasius, *Apol. c. Arian.* 86, 6. See p. 604.
[33] Sozomenus, *HE* II, 29–30, quoting Athanasius, *Ep.* 54.
[34] Athanasius, *Apol. c. Arian.* 6, 6–7 (a letter of the Synod of Alexandria, 338).

world to that city's level. Therefore he crossed over to Constantinople, a city which had recently attained to greatness, and, being at the height of her prosperity, needed both deeds and words to adorn her as she deserved.'[35] Even twenty years before, who could have imagined a Libanius leaving, of all places, Athens for the modest city of Byzantium? But when a Roman emperor finally established himself in a Greek city, and identified it with himself, it necessarily became the chief focus for the culture of the Greek world and the object of the ambitions of the most prominent orators and intellectuals, just as the emperor himself had always been.

---

[35] Eunapius, *VS* 495, Loeb trans.

3*

III

Entourage, Assistants and Advisers

1. *Introduction*

'For those who approach the rulers', wrote the author of a third- or fourth-century homily, 'since they know that on the one side those who practise in the courts surround them, and on the other the lictors make a clamour, while before them heralds make their proclamation, and the ruler himself rides on a high carriage and has his mind on many things—for all these reasons the petitioner is forced to shout to gain a hearing.'[1] The preacher may be thinking of provincial governors as well as, or even rather than, the emperor. But the passage none the less illustrates a popular conception of the nature of contacts between subjects and ruler, and emphasizes the particular aspect with which we shall now be concerned. What types of persons surrounded the emperor, and either actively intervened in the contacts between his subjects and himself, or significantly affected by their presence or their influence the form and atmosphere of such contacts? Here we shall be concerned with the persons themselves, not with the listing of names for its own sake, but with an assessment of the social character, background and standing of those who made up the entourage, and with the nature of the qualifications which brought them there.

The subject is of all the more significance because, when a sole ruler emerged, the *res publica*, just as it provided no official residence or still less public 'office' for him, also provided almost no publicly employed persons to assist or escort him. Such persons were in fact limited to the soldiers of the praetorian cohorts (Dio notes with some acerbity that they were voted double the pay of the other soldiers immediately after the formal vote of his powers to Augustus in 27 BC),[2] and the attendants (*apparitores*) and lictors, who accompanied the emperor, as they did the city magistrates of Rome, and the provincial governors.

Even these attendants, though public officials, were sometimes freedmen from the imperial household, and it is natural to suppose that, being without

---

[1] [Asterius Sophista], *Hom.* x, 4, see *Symb. Osl.*, Supp. XVI (1956), 70–5: οἱ γὰρ ὧδε τοῖς ἄρχουσι προσερχόμενοι, ἐπειδὴ οἴδασιν ὅτι ἔνθεν μὲν οἱ ἐν ταῖς ἀγοραῖς περιηχοῦσιν, ἑτέρωθεν δὲ οἱ ῥαβδοῦχοι θορυβοῦσιν, ἔμπροσθεν οἱ κήρυκες κράζουσιν, αὐτὸς ὁ ἄρχων ἐπὶ ὑψηλοῦ ὀχήματος φέρεται καὶ περὶ πολλὰ ἔχει τὴν διάνοιαν — καὶ διὰ ταῦτα πάντα ὁ ἱκέτης ἀναγκάζεται μετὰ κραυγῆς ποιεῖσθαι τὴν πρόσοδον. I owe this reference to the kindness of Dr H. Chadwick.

[2] LIII, 11, 5.

publicly-appointed assistants, the emperor would turn to his own freedmen. Such was of course the case, and the power and influence of the freedman, by cutting across the conventions of Roman society, was a major source of tension in the early empire. It has not been sufficiently emphasized, however, how brief and transient a phase this was, confined essentially to a few decades in the middle of the first century AD. Freedmen retained some major 'secretarial' functions until the early second century (and subordinate ones thereafter), and occasionally *cubicularii* exercised a real influence right through the period. But in historical importance the influence of the freedmen is far outweighed by that of men who came into the emperor's service from outside. It is crucial to the whole nature of the imperial function, and by implication also to the values of the societies from which it grew, that the qualifications of these men were, typically, first a social eminence in their native cities, and second a prominence in literature or rhetoric. Their attraction to the side of the emperor began earlier than, and was never wholly superseded by, that of another group which cannot be clearly distinguished from them, and which came from the same level of society; namely men who rose through the equestrian military and civilian 'career' which developed in the course of the first century AD. The various paths by which individuals from the upper classes of the Italian and provincial cities came into the immediate service of the emperor themselves represent one of the most important patterns of communication between emperor and subjects.

Since jurisdiction was so large a part of what an emperor did, it is, if anything, surprising that it is only in the second century that we can trace the emergence of men with primarily legal qualifications in the emperor's service. It is not an accident that Marcus Aurelius, in speaking of what he had learned from Antoninus Pius about an emperor's proper relationship to his advisers, explicitly singles out rhetorical and legal abilities: 'especially to give away without resentment to those possessed of some special skill, whether in verbal expression or in knowledge of the law or of customs or of some other matters.'[3] The appearance in the second and third centuries of known legal writers both in actual posts in the emperor's service and among his advisers is certainly important. But its precise significance has to be assessed in the light of the fact that the legal writing of the period was much more academic, more close at times to scholarly antiquarianism than has often been realized. Ulpian, Papinian and Paul have yet to be given their place in the literary culture of the Roman empire.

With these names we begin to move from the level of employees of the emperor to the much less easily definable circle of his friends (*amici*) and advisers, who belonged to the equestrian and senatorial orders. Here too we may postpone for the moment the evidence for actual discussions and decision-making conducted by the emperor, and concentrate on the friends and advisers themselves and the social framework within which their relations with the emperor took place. At this level only the post of praetorian prefect (*Praefectus praetorio*) formally indicated that a man performed his duties at the emperor's side. Even here we see in the

[3] *Med.* I, 16, 6.

tetrarchic period a multiplication of *praefecti*, and below them deputies (*vicarii*), and their partial detachment from the emperor and attachment to the overall control of different areas of the empire. A rather similar development occurred with the term *comes*, which began as a simple designation of the fact that a man had accompanied the emperor on a journey or journeys, and became in the fourth century the name of a post or rank (the origin of the title 'Count'), with duties again detached from the emperor's person. To quite a significant extent the administrative structure of the late empire emerged out of the relatively small, loosely defined and slowly developing entourage of the emperor in the first three centuries.

2. *Military Escorts and Bodyguards*

No conception of the emperor's relation to his subjects would be complete without taking into account the fact that he was almost always escorted by armed soldiers. The selection of a *praetoria cohors* of picked soldiers by a Roman *imperator* was something which went back to Scipio Africanus (whether the elder or younger is not clear).[1] It was a crucial development of this practice when Antonius and Octavian after Philippi divided 8,000 veterans between them as praetorian cohorts,[2] for this meant that after Octavian's return such cohorts were for the first time regularly stationed in Rome and Italy. As Lucius Antonius, the consul of 41, was to point out, this constituted a fundamental distinction between Octavian and himself.[3] Thereafter they continued in his service as Augustus, though no more than three cohorts were stationed in Rome, and these without a regular camp, while the others were divided among the neighbouring towns.[4] Nor were *Praefecti praetorio* appointed until 2 BC.[5] As is well known, the nine cohorts which existed under Tiberius were established in the *castra praetoria* on the Viminal by the then sole *praefectus*, Aelius Sejanus.[6] But when Augustus died and Tiberius became emperor in 14, the practice was already established of one cohort keeping guard at the *palatium* each night, and of the Emperor having an escort of soldiers in Rome and even in the Senate-house.[7] The subsequent evidence need not be set out. But we may note that soldiers accompanied the emperor on all journeys even in Italy. Some were present for instance when the roof of Tiberius' grotto at Sperlonga collapsed in 26;[8] Suetonius relates that Tiberius executed a praetorian soldier for stealing a pheasant from one of his game-parks, and had a centurion flogged

[1] Festus, *De verborum significatione*, p. 223 Mueller/249 Lindsay: 'praetoria cohors est dicta quod a praetore non discedebat. Scipio enim Africanus primus fortissimum quemque delegit, qui ab eo in bello non discederent et cetero munere militiae vacarent et sesquiplex stipendium acciperent.' See the two standard works, M. Durry, *Les cohortes prétoriennes* (1938); A. Passerini, *Le coorti pretorie* (1939).

[2] Appian, *BC* v, 3/13.

[3] ibid., v, 21/82. See F. Millar, 'Triumvirate and Principate', *JRS* LXIII (1973), 50, on p. 59.

[4] Suetonius, *Aug.* 49, 1.

[5] Dio LV, 10, 10.

[6] Tacitus, *Ann.* IV, 2, 1.

[7] ibid., I, 7, 5.

[8] ibid., IV, 59, 2.

to death for failing to have his route cleared of brambles.[9] Some praetorian cohorts, for instance, were sent with Tiberius' son Drusus to Pannonia in 14,[10] or accompanied Nero on his tour of Greece in 66/7.[11] They naturally went on all campaigns at which the emperor was present, and from the Flavian period onwards took part in regular fighting, and were not confined to escort duty.

Between the reigns of Claudius and that of Vespasian the duty of the personal protection of the emperor extended even to his dining with his friends; it was for instance while Galba as emperor was dining with Otho that the latter was able to bribe the praetorians on escort duty.[12] Suetonius' description of Claudius dining out shows him surrounded by *speculatores* with lances, while other soldiers replaced the slaves who served the meal.[13] *Speculatores* were promoted praetorians on special duties, such as carrying Gaius' messages from his Gallic campaign of 39 to the Senate[14] or escorting the emperor.[15] The significance of having a guard of praetorians appeared clearly in 55, when Nero withdrew it from his mother Agrippina,[16] or conversely in 217 when Julia Domna retained hers after the murder of her son Caracalla.[17]

By contrast with the praetorian cohorts, who were regular Roman soldiers, Augustus inherited from Julius Caesar, but not only from him, the custom of having a private guard of barbarians. In Gaul Caesar had had a guard of 400 German cavalry,[18] and later in Rome Spanish guards, whom he dismissed shortly before his murder;[19] while Antonius, as consul in 44, had a guard of Ituraean archers.[20] This custom was paralleled by client kings: Juba of Mauretania had Gallic and Spanish cavalry as a guard,[21] and Cleopatra had 400 Gauls, whom Octavian presented to Herod the Great in 30 BC.[22]

Suetonius indeed alleges that Augustus dismissed a guard of Spaniards from Calagurris after Actium, and of Germans after the defeat of Varus in AD 9.[23] But some *Germani custodes* certainly remained, and are well attested in inscriptions and literature up to 69.[24] Some of these too accompanied Drusus in 14, and were withdrawn from Agrippina in 55. Although their presence must have had an appreciable effect on the atmosphere of the court, they are rarely attested as playing an active role in events. One such

---

[9] *Tib.* 60.
[10] Tacitus, *Ann.* I, 24, 1.
[11] Tacitus, *Hist.* I, 23; Suetonius, *Nero* 19, 2.
[12] Tacitus, *Hist.* I, 24, 1; Suetonius, *Otho* 4, 2; Plutarch, *Galba* 20, 7.
[13] *Claud.* 35, 1.
[14] Suetonius, *Cal.* 44, 2.
[15] Tacitus, *Hist.* II, 11, 3.
[16] Tacitus, *Ann.* XIII, 18, 3; Suetonius, *Nero* 34, 1; Dio LXI, 8, 4.
[17] Dio LXXVIII, 23, 2 (429).
[18] Caesar, *BG* VII, 13, 1.
[19] Suetonius, *Jul.* 86; Appian, *BC* II, 109/455.
[20] Cicero, *Phil.* II, 44/112. Cf. v, 6/17–18.
[21] Caesar, *BC* II, 40, 1.
[22] Josephus, *Ant.* XV, 7, 3 (217).
[23] *Aug.* 49.
[24] See Th. Mommsen, 'Die germanischen Leibwächter der römischen Kaiser', *Ges. Schr.* VI (1910), 17; *ILS* 1717–32; cf. *Notizie degli Scavi* 1950, 86–90; *Epigraphica* XXIX (1967), 62–4.

occasion was in 41 when they reacted violently to the murder of Gaius, to whom they were devoted, and slew several of the conspirators before they left the *palatium*.[25]

This corps was dismissed by Galba in 68/9, on the grounds of their inclination towards Dolabella, next to whose gardens they were stationed (although Dio describes Vitellius in 69 as protected by German guards).[26] Thereafter we hear in passing of a Moorish escort of Trajan,[27] but have no consistent evidence of a barbarian guard again until those employed by Caracalla, whom Dio calls Scythians and Celts, and Herodian calls Germans. They were with him at the time of his murder in Mesopotamia in 217, and cut down his murderer before he could escape.[28]

Such barbarian guards were, one must presume, privately recruited (or, if slaves, owned) by the emperor. Somewhere between them and the regular praetorian cohorts (but nearer the latter) one must place the *equites singulares Augusti*, a unit of 1,000 cavalry attested in the second and third centuries and individually recruited, mainly from auxiliary units on the Rhine and Danube.[29] They had their own barracks in Rome, forming a mounted complement to the praetorian cohorts, and like them accompanied the emperor on journeys and expeditions. So we have an inscription of the *equites singulares* of Hadrian wintering at Gerasa, evidently during Hadrian's visit to Syria in 129/30,[30] or Hyginus' account in the *De munitionibus castrorum*, almost certainly relating to a legionary camp of the 170s, of them encamped alongside the praetorian cohorts.[31] It is also probably they who are the 'royal cavalrymen' whom Herodian describes cutting down a mob who went to a suburban villa of Commodus in 190 to demand the death of Cleander;[32] and the 'cavalry' who might have protected Pertinax from his murder in the *palatium* in 193 were also probably *equites singulares*.[33]

It is best to admit, however, that we cannot in general do more than state that the imperial presence always had a military aspect; the precise functions of the different units which accompanied him cannot be clearly stated. Nor can we always tell from which unit the soldiers came whom we find from time to time being sent to carry out executions, to bring persons to the emperor, or to carry letters from him.[34] The distinctions are rarely even as

[25] Josephus, *Ant.* XIX, 1, 15 (119–26); Suetonius, *Cal.* 58, 3.

[26] Suetonius, *Galba* 12, 2; Dio LXV, 17, 2.

[27] Martial, *Epig.* X, 6, 7–8.

[28] Dio LXXVIII, 5,5–6,1; cf. 7, 2–3 (408–10); Herodian IV, 7, 3; 13, 6. Note also the *Germani* who escorted Maximus and Balbinus according to *HA, Max. et Balb.* 15, 5; 14, 2–8, and a rhetorical reference to what is apparently a Sarmatian guard of Maximin in 311/12, Lactantius, *De mort. pers.* 38, 6–7.

[29] See M. Speidel, *Die Equites Singulares Augusti: Begleittruppe der römischen Kaiser des zweiten und dritten Jahrhunderts* (1965); cf. F. Grosso, 'Equites Singulares Augusti', *Latomus* XXV (1966), 900.

[30] C. H. Kraeling, *Gerasa* (1938), 390, no. 30.

[31] p. 41.

[32] Herodian I, 12, 5–9; see Whittaker, Loeb ed., ad loc.

[33] Dio LXXIII, 9, 3.

[34] Executions: e.g. Suetonius, *Cal.* 32, 1; Tacitus, *Ann.* XIV, 58–9; Philo, *Leg.* 5/30–1 (by implication); Dio LIX, 22, 7; Musurillo, *Acts of the Alexandrian Martyrs* (1954), no. xi. Persons being brought to the emperor: e.g. Galen XIV Kühn, 648–9; Eusebius, *HE*, VI, 21, 4. Carrying letter: see Plutarch, *Mor.* 522E.

clear as in Tacitus' account of arrests after the conspiracy of 65, when 'footsoldiers and cavalry (evidently praetorians), mingled with the Germans, whom the emperor trusted as being foreigners' rushed around the city and its vicinity.[35]

We cannot doubt, however, that the constant presence of armed soldiers had an important influence on what it meant to appear before the emperor, and lent an increased immediacy and force to any sign of imperial displeasure. Even without such a sign, their presence must have added to the fear felt before the emperor; so for instance a senator who inadvertently caused Tiberius to fall by clasping his knees in supplication was 'nearly killed by the soldiers';[36] while Philostratus records that the sophist Heraclides of Lycia once broke down in an extempore oration before Septimius Severus, 'fearing the court and the guards'.[37] The presence of soldiers might affect also the emperor's own entourage; as we have noted, Dio describes Caracalla at Nicomedia in 214/15 keeping his advisers waiting, sometimes all day, at the door while he drank with his soldiers within.[38]

None the less it must be emphasized that the amount of direct evidence which we have for the presence of the emperor's escort and its role in relations between emperor and subjects is not large. Its presence appears normally to have been taken for granted by contemporaries, as it has to be by us. Moreover, if we except those notorious occasions such as the accession of Claudius in 41, Nero in 54, Otho in 69 or Didius Julianus in 193, when the praetorian cohorts played an important role in ensuring who should be the next emperor, the attested influence of the members of the imperial escort on decisions is remarkably small. The praetorian prefect himself is of course quite another matter; but even the tribunes, who were of equestrian rank, who were often destined for distinguished careers, and who on occasion appear by name in narrative sources, are not attested as exerting any influence either for themselves or others. This is the more surprising, as for instance even a legionary centurion is honoured by his native town in Umbria for interceding on its behalf with Antoninus Pius.[39] For the influence of persons serving in the Praetorian cohorts we can point to one indirect case, when Claudius says that he was favourably influenced in confirming the dubious possession of citizenship by some Alpine tribes by learning that some of their men had served in his *praetorium* and even held the rank of centurion there.[40] The only clear and certain case where a soldier in the praetorian cohort acted as the intermediary in a petition from his native community to the emperor is that of the village of Scaptopara in Thrace to Gordian in 238—and here the *subscriptio* in reply was no more than an instruction to take the matter to the provincial governor.[41]

The paucity of this evidence is surprising, and all the more so because

---

[35] Tacitus, *Ann.* xv, 58, 2.
[36] ibid., I, 13, 6.
[37] Philostratus, *VS* II, 26.
[38] Dio LXXVII, 17, 4 (396), cf. p. 51.
[39] *ILS* 2666, 2666a; cf. p. 427.
[40] *ILS* 206; cf. pp. 254, 256.
[41] pp. 247, 543-4.

service in the praetorian cohorts was itself a privilege. We have for instance
a case of a man petitioning Hadrian to be allowed to serve there—and being
told to enter the urban cohorts first and earn a transfer later.[42] The praetorians, as is notorious, had both higher pay and higher donatives than the
legionaries. On discharge they and soldiers from the urban cohorts received
from the emperor, while the legionaries did not, certificates (*diplomata*)
granting the right to legally recognized marriage (*conubium*) with non-
citizen women, with citizenship for any children and descendants.[43] The
wording of the *diplomata*, which remains effectively constant from the reign
of Vespasian to the tetrarchy, is that of a personal grant of rights from the
emperor himself.[44]

The *equites singulares* are not securely attested after the middle of the third
century, and the praetorian cohorts were disbanded by Constantine after
his victory over Maxentius in 312.[45] From the mid-third century onwards it
is difficult to specify what categories of soldiers escorted and guarded the
emperor in person, all the more so because continual wars and civil wars
meant that emperors spent a large part of their time in a wider military
context. Without going into details, we may note that documents of this
period speak of men serving as soldiers in the *comitatus*: a proconsul of
Africa in 295 remarks that there are Christian soldiers in the *comitatus* of the
four emperors;[46] a grammarian questioned by a later proconsul of Africa in
320 explains that his grandfather 'had served as a soldier in the *comitatus*';[47]
and an inscription of around the same time shows a legionary soldier who was
'chosen as a lancer (*lanciarius*) in the sacred *comitatus*'.[48] This man went on
to be a *protector*; in spite of the implications of the name, however, the
protectores of the later third and early fourth centuries were not bodyguards, but officers of centurion or equestrian rank, who sometimes, but not
invariably, attended the emperor in person.[49] A category of person who do
seem to have been imperial guards appears, however, in what Lactantius says
of the career of Maximin—'first a *scutarius* (shield-bearer), next a *protector*,

---

[42] *Divi Hadriani sententiae et epistulae, Corp. Gloss. Lat.* III, p. 31, l. 24 (Latin text): 'petente
quodam ut militaret, Adrianus dixit, "Ubi vis militare?" illo dicente, "in pretorio", Adrianus
interrogavit quam staturam habet. "quinque pedes et semis." Adrianus dixit, "interim in
urbanam milita, et si bonus miles fueris tertio stipendio poteris in pretorium transire".'

[43] On praetorian pay and *donativa* see Durry, o.c., 264f.; Passerini, o.c., 100f.

[44] Praetorian *diplomata* are listed in *CIL* XVI, p. 156, with no. 189, and now *AE* 1972 503 (236).
For a clear example of the categories of privileged troops concerned we may take XVI 21 of AD 76:
'nomina speculatorum qui in praetorio meo militaverunt, item militum qui in cohortibus novem
praetoriis et quattuor urbanis, subieci [Vespasian], quibus fortiter et pie militia functis ius tribuo
conubi . . .'

[45] Aurelius Victor, *Caes.* 40, 24–5; Zosimus II, 17, 2.

[46] *Acta Maximiliani* 2, 9; Knopf-Krüger-Ruhbach, *Ausgewählte Martyrakten*[4] (1965), no. 19.

[47] Optatus, App. I (*CSEL* XXVI, 185).

[48] *CIL* III 6194 = *ILS* 2781.

[49] See R. I. Frank, *Scholae Palatinae: the Palace Guards of the Later Roman Empire* (1969), 33f.
The collection of evidence here is unfortunately very incomplete. Add for instance the inscription
of Marcianus, whose first post was *protector* of Gallienus, published by B. Gerov, 'La carriera
militare di Marciano, generale di Gallieno', *Athenaeum* XLIII (1965), 333; *CIL* III 3529 and the
new inscription published by T. Nagy, 'Die Inschrift des Legionspräfekten P. Ael. Aelianus aus
Ulcisia castra', *Klio* XLVI (1965), 339, both relating to another *protector* of Gallienus, see Pflaum,
Carrières, no. 357; also *ILS* 5695 (AD 280). The inscription of Traianus Mucianus is now
IGBulg. 1570.

soon a *tribunus* and next day a Caesar'.[50] Beyond that, we do not have clear and certainly datable evidence for the categories of imperial guards in the earlier fourth century.[51] Half a century later, for instance, Valentinian mentions that it was claimed that Constantine had granted free bread distribution in Constantinople to the *scholae* of *scutarii* and *scutarii clibanarii* (mail-clad shield-bearers);[52] but the *scholae palatinae*, the corps of palace guards, are not formally attested before 353.[53]

But if we cannot determine how far the military entourage of the emperor had developed towards its later fourth-century form, it is clear enough that the presence of soldiers remained a significant element in the imperial court. Constantine obliged his escort to be Christians and to observe Sunday, while the elevation of his sons to be 'Caesars' was marked by the appointment to each of military guards and escort troops.[54] It was a crucial gesture on his part, that when he took his seat with the bishops at Nicaea he did so with some trusted friends but without a bodyguard.[55] However, when the bishops were subsequently invited to dinner, 'bodyguards and armed men, with their swords unsheathed stood in a circle guarding the vestibule of the palace; between them the men of God passed without fear and entered the inner parts of the royal residence'.[56] What Eusebius says is not mere empty flattery; the bishops entered where many had certainly been excluded, and where many who entered had not looked without fear on the swords of the soldiers.

3. *Public Attendants*

The importance of the public attendants whom the emperor had was, first, that they *were* public, that they were visibly comparable to, and as persons were sometimes identical with, the attendants of the magistrates in Rome and of proconsuls and quaestors in the provinces. They were indeed, along with the soldiers of the praetorian cohorts, the only persons whom the *res publica* supplied to assist the emperor. Secondly, at least some of them actually accompanied the emperor wherever he went, and thus formed a constituent part of the image which he presented to his subjects, and played a certain role in his communications with them. Thirdly, many of them, and in the case of the *accensi* it seems all, were in fact freedmen of the emperor. So, just as the freedmen of republican office-holders had done,[1] they

---

[50] Lactantius, *De mort. pers.* 19, 6.

[51] Much earlier work, e.g. D. van Berchem, *L'armée de Dioclétien et la réforme constantinienne* (1952), 106f., will need revision in the light of the evidence of *P. Beatty Panop.* 2, ll. 260, 286, 301, that *lanciarii* were attached to legions as well as serving in the *comitatus*. The evidence cited by Frank, o.c., 33–49, is presented without consideration of questions of dating. The best treatment is (of course) that of Jones, *The Later Roman Empire* I, 53–4 and notes; see now H.-J. Diesner, *RE* Supp. XI (1968), 1113f. s.v. 'protectores (domestici)'.

[52] *CTh* XIV, 17, 9 (389); cf. 10 (392).

[53] See Ammianus XIV, 7, 9 and 12. *CIL* VI 32965 cannot be securely dated; nor can III 371 = *ILS* 2783, which also depends solely on an eighteenth-century copy.

[54] Eusebius, *VC* IV, 18, 1; 51, 3.

[55] ibid., III, 10, 2; cf. I, 44, 2.

[56] ibid., III, 15, 2.

[1] See S. Treggiari, *Roman Freedmen during the Late Republic* (1969), 153–9.

straddled the borderline between private service and the service of the state.[2]

The panels (*decuriae*) of attendants, whose social rank stretched from freedmen to the lower border of the equestrian order, continued to exist right through and beyond our period;[3] in 335 we find Constantine giving a favourable answer to the petition of the panels of scribes, *librarii* and consular lictors that they should continue their traditional role in legal proceedings.[4] Their functions in connection with the emperor are clearly attested from the beginning; how long they continued is not so easy to determine.

The victory at Actium had been won while Octavian (or properly 'Imperator Caesar Divi filius') was consul, as he continued to be until 23; he will therefore have had the twelve *fasces* borne before him by twelve lictors (possibly twenty-four up to the settlement of 27 BC).[5] Precisely the same right was restored to him after a short interval, when he was given consular *imperium* for life in 19 BC.[6] Later emperors may or may not have continued the right which Domitian was voted, of having twenty-four; they more certainly did not imitate him in having Roman *equites*, robed and carrying military spears, 'precede him among the lictors and *apparitores*'.[7] Neither such extensions of the right to *fasces*, nor the fact that the imperial *fasces* were permanently wreathed in laurel as a symbol of victory, could entirely obscure the republican associations of the custom. One inscription at any rate describes a man as a 'lictor of the three *decuriae* which attend Caesar and the magistrates'.[8] The lictors are not, however, attested as performing for the emperor their traditional functions of clearing his path, keeping order and compelling respect for the office-holder; nor do our sources attribute to any individual imperial lictor the influence which for instance Cicero ascribes to a lictor of Verres in Sicily.[9] We might, however, presume such an influence on the part of M. Ulpius Phaedimus, a freedman of Trajan who rose from being *a potione* (in charge of the emperor's drinking-cup) to being *lictor proximus* (the one who walked last, nearest to the emperor), and in charge of the records of *beneficia*, privileges granted by the emperor. He died at Selinus in August 117 a few days after the emperor died there.[10] But any influence he may have exercised will have been, like the position of *lictor proximus* itself, a product of his role as a favoured freedman.

[2] For the evidence for imperial *liberti* in these positions see G. Boulvert, *Esclaves et affranchis impériaux sous le Haut-Empire romain: rôle politique et administratif* (1970), 43f.

[3] See A. H. M. Jones, 'The Roman Civil Service (Clerical and Sub-Clerical Grades)', *JRS* XXXIX (1949), 38 = *Studies in Roman Government and Law* (1960), 151.

[4] *CTh* VIII, 9, 1: 'ordines decuriarum scribarum librariorum et lictoriae consularis oblatis precibus meruerunt, ut in civilibus causis et editionibus libellorum officiorum sollemnitate fungantur . . .'

[5] Dio LIII, 1, 1. See Mommsen, *Staatsrecht*[3] I, 387.

[6] Dio LIV, 10, 5. I cannot follow the argument of E. S. Staveley, 'The *Fasces* and *Imperium Maius*', *Historia* XII (1963), 458, on p. 483, that the grant of *imperium maius* to Augustus in 23 BC will necessarily have given him 24 *fasces*.

[7] Dio LXVII, 4, 3; Suetonius, *Dom.* 14.

[8] *ILS* 1911; cf. *AE* 1907 225.

[9] Cicero, *Verr.* II/v, 45/118f.

[10] *ILS* 1792.

There does not seem to be clear evidence of lictors attending the emperor later than this, although they probably did so.[11] Their presence is implied by an orator addressing Maximin, probably in 289, who includes among the outward signs of imperial glory the consular *fasces*.[12] *Viatores* (messengers) are attested only until 138, when those who attended the emperor, consuls and praetors made a dedication to Antoninus Pius.[13] The emperor was similarly attended by a herald (*praeco*); an inscription records one who attended Augustus, and who belonged to 'the three *decuriae* which by custom attend the consuls, censors and praetors'.[14] There was clearly a role for a herald whenever the emperor faced mass demands from the crowds assembled in the circus or the theatre, or made a speech to the people. But in fact it was taken as an indication of exceptional arrogance and reserve when Domitian answered demands for the restoration of a senator solely by having his *praeco* order the crowd to be silent;[15] he was once imitated in the same situation by Hadrian, whose herald had only raised his hand when the crowd fell silent.[16] It was more normal for the emperor to answer in person, vocally or by gestures.[17] Once again we cannot attest the role of *praecones* beyond the second century.

With the *accensi* (personal attendants who originally took the place of lictors if an office-holder had none, and later were in addition to them) we in effect cross the blurred line between the public service and the household of the emperor. Even in the republic the position of *accensus* had been one in the personal gift of an annual office-holder, and was normally granted to one of his own freedmen.[18] The same is true of the emperor's household. One of them rose (it seems) from lower posts as *apparitor* to be *accensus* of Vespasian, and later *ab epistulis* (concerned with imperial letters).[19] Though imperial freedmen, they could as an honour be 'reported' to the public treasury (*aerarium*) as public office-holders; this was done by Augustus for one Antemus, who was later *a rationibus*, concerned with accounts, under Tiberius.[20] The one partial exception is an *accensus velatus* of free birth who attended the consuls from 27 onwards, Claudius as consul and censor, and Nero as consul.[21] It is clear that the position was normally one of honour for

[11] Herodian VII, 6, 2, followed by *HA, Max.* 14, 4, describing Gordian I having his *fasces* (as proconsul of Africa) laurelled as a sign of his proclamation as emperor, is strongly suggestive. Mommsen, *Staatsrecht*[3] I, 388, quotes *CIL* VI 1876 for a possibly post-Diocletianic *fascalis Aug.* The text, and description of the *fasces* and axes engraved on the stone, depend on a seventeenth/eighteenth-century MS.

[12] *Pan.* II (10), 3, 2: 'trabeae vestrae triumphales et fasces consulares et sellae curules et haec obsequiorum stipatio et fulgor.' The date is not certain. If Galletier is correct in suggesting 289, neither Augustus was then holding the consulate.

[13] *ILS* 331. For earlier imperial *viatores* see *ILS* 1920 (Tiberius); *CIL* VI 1921 (Claudius).

[14] *CIL* VI 1945.

[15] Suetonius, *Dom.* 13, 1.

[16] Dio LXIX, 6, 1–2. Note also LXXI, 29, 4 (269), Marcus Aurelius causing it to be announced (κηρυχθῆναι) that he would not free the trainer of a man-eating lion.

[17] pp. 371–5.

[18] Treggiari, o.c., 154–6.

[19] *ILS* 1944; cf. 1942–3 and Boulvert, o.c., 46–8.

[20] *CIL* VI 8409; see Boulvert, o.c. 47.

[21] *CIL* XIV 4012–14, revised and supplemented with a new fragment by A. Ferrua in *Epigraphica* XXIV (1962), 113–18 = *AE* 1964 115.

an imperial freedman, but there is no evidence that its holders, who are attested only by inscriptions, ever exercised even the degree of influence wielded by their predecessors in the republic.[22] To say that is merely to emphasize that although these *apparitores* formed a significant link between republican and imperial office-holding, they were immediately obscured in importance by other persons from both within and outside the imperial household, who came to form the entourage of the emperor.

4. Imperial Freedmen

The appearance among the friends and confidants of Roman office-holders of provincial dignitaries and literary men, especially from the Greek east, was already a clearly established pattern before the emergence of monarchy.[1] But what aroused attention and resentment in the early empire was the personal influence, power, wealth and status which the elevation of a monarch gave to some of his *liberti*, freed slaves from his household. Their prominence was a profound shock to Roman sentiment. Pliny the Elder, for instance, after noting that Crassus, with landed property worth 200,000,000 *sesterces*, had been the richest Roman after Sulla, goes on to say: 'We have seen subsequently many men freed from slavery who were richer, and not long ago three simultaneously in the reign of Claudius, namely Callistus, Pallas and Narcissus.'[2] The few prominent imperial freedmen with whom we shall be concerned, those who worked personally with the emperor, and influenced his decisions and his relations with his subjects, were of course only a tiny privileged minority among the thousands of imperial slaves and freedmen who served in the imperial palaces and villas or were attached to estates and properties in Italy or the provinces.[3] Even these men, however, were now able to attain a local honour and influence; so, out of many examples, we may note the inscription which shows the town council of Veii in AD 26 honouring a freedman of the Deified Augustus, C. Julius Gelos, 'who has not only constantly aided the *municipium* by his advice and influence (*gratia*) but has been willing to add to its distinction both at his own expense and that of his son'; he was given the honorary rank of *Augustalis*, and a seat among the *Augustales* at public shows, and among the town-councillors at public dinners.[4] Alternatively, we find the prefect of Egypt in 38, accompanied by the commander of a legion, dining at the house of an imperial freedman in Alexandria.[5] Special circumstances might give an even more public role to a freedman in the provinces. Tacitus notes that

---

[22] Treggiari, o.c., 158–9.

[1] For the East see G. W. Bowersock, *Augustus and the Greek World* (1965), ch. i; cf. pp. 83–4.

[2] Pliny, *NH* XXXIII, 47/134.

[3] See most fully G. Boulvert, *Esclaves et affranchis impériaux sous le Haut-Empire romain: rôle politique et administratif* (1970); also P. R. C. Weaver, *Familia Caesaris: a Social Study of the Emperor's Freedmen and Slaves* (1972). For those serving in the *palatium* see E. Fairon, 'L'organisation du palais impérial à Rome', *Mus. Belge* IV (1900), 5. See now also G. Boulvert, *Domestique et fonctionnaire sous le Haut-Empire romain* (1974).

[4] *ILS* 6579.

[5] Philo, *In Flacc.* 13/112.

Crescens, a freedman of Nero, gave a public dinner in Carthage to celebrate the accession of Vespasian; 'in troubled times these too make themselves part of the *res publica*'.[6] We shall see later, in connection with the development of imperial property, some instances where his freedmen in the provinces impinged on relations between emperor and subjects.[7] But essentially the members of the widely-spread imperial *familia* were no closer to the emperor than the rest of the population, and their contacts with him might be rare or non-existent. An anecdote retailed by the poet Phaedrus, himself an imperial *libertus* under Tiberius, vividly illuminates this situation. When Tiberius visited his villa at Misenum, one of the house-slaves (*atrienses*) there tried to use his fleeting opportunity to gain manumission. Seeing the emperor strolling in the grounds, he began to water the ground before him in order to lay the dust; all he received was a passing witticism.[8]

So what concerns us here is not the imperial *familia* as a whole or even the staff of the palaces, but only that narrow group which was in the immediate service of the emperor. That with the emergence of a monarch the freedmen of his household should exercise a real influence was an inevitable product of features discussed earlier, the domestic setting of the exercise of power by Roman office-holders, and the exiguous nature of the staff supplied to them by the *res publica*. Both the fact of a freedman's influence on a late-republican office-holder and a typical senatorial reaction to it are reflected, for instance, in one of Cicero's letters to his brother Quintus as proconsul of Asia: 'the very appearance of a freedman or slave with such influence must be devoid of *dignitas*'.[9] It was of course when a senator found himself as an effective monarch in his province that the patterns of the future were most clearly foreshadowed, all the more so with the major commands of the late republic. Thus Josephus can record that it was in order to gratify his freedman Demetrius, a native of the place, that Pompey rebuilt Gadara in 63 BC.[10] This will not be the last occasion on which we see a former slave retaining connections with his native city which are not significantly different from those of free men with theirs. Demetrius gained an exceptionally prominent position. It was he whom, as we saw earlier,[11] a civic reception was awaiting when Cato the Younger arrived in Antioch; Plutarch also records him dining with Pompey, owning villas outside Rome, and dying worth 40,000 talents.[12] Even more striking, and more offensive to general sentiment, were the activities in Rome and Italy of Sulla's freedman Chrysogonus, who made a fortune in the proscriptions and could assume the outward role in public life of a Roman noble.[13]

On the other hand the dictatorship of Julius Caesar reveals less of the influence or public functions of freedmen than might have been expected

[6] Tacitus, *Hist.* I, 76, 3.
[7] pp. 180–4.
[8] Phaedrus, *Fab.* II, 5.
[9] Cicero, *Ad Qu. f.* I, 2, 3.
[10] Josephus, *BJ* I, 7, 7 (155).
[11] p. 29.
[12] *Pomp.* 2, 9; 40, 4–8. Cf. Treggiari, *Roman Freedmen*, 184–5.
[13] See Treggiari, o.c., 183–4.

(though the two *cubicularii* captured with the young Caesar by the pirates are the earliest attested in Roman history; the role was to have a long history).[14] At this period too it was when the Roman office-holder was in an exposed position outside Rome that the *familia* assumed a greater importance: a slave hairdresser revealed a plot against Caesar in Alexandria in the winter of 48/7 BC;[15] and the three legions which he left there were under the command of the son of one of his freedmen. But of the regime in Rome itself only an isolated reference in Suetonius asserts that he placed his household slaves in charge of the mint and the public revenues.[16] The underlying importance of Caesar's *familia* comes out more clearly after his death. In April 44 BC Cicero heard rumours of a conspiracy by the freedmen of Caesar;[17] and Appian believed that the acquisition of the rich *liberti* of Caesar was one of the prime motives of Octavian's struggle to achieve ratification of his adoption by Caesar.[18] One of these freedmen—not necessarily rich or influential by this time—was Licinus, a striking example of the fluidity possible within the generally status-conscious society of Rome; a fluidity which was to be greatly increased by the untrammelled exercise of will by the emperors, and the relatively wide range of social groups with whom their activities brought them into contact. Licinus had been captured in Caesar's Gallic war, retained by him as a slave and then freed, apparently to act as his *dispensator*.[19] Subsequently we find him as one of the most honoured freedmen of Augustus, a notorious procurator of the Three Gauls (whom Dio describes personally exhibiting to the emperor the vast piles of gold and silver which he had extorted as tribute), and a prominent example of the wealth of imperial freedmen. He made contributions of money for the public works carried out by Augustus, and ran a luxurious household; his marble tomb on the Via Salaria was later a well-known landmark.[20]

In the following period various freedmen of the triumvirs and of Sextus Pompeius played prominent roles as agents, intermediaries and especially as the commanders of fleets.[21] The most important of them was Menas or Menodorus, a freedman of Sextus Pompeius, who in 38 BC brought over to Octavian Corsica and Sardinia with 60 ships and three legions. Octavian recompensed him by the award of the right to wear a gold ring and by the status of *eques*; Cassius Dio, reporting these events, adds a comment on the contemporary practice of emperors awarding the gold ring to those of their

---

[14] Suetonius, *Jul.* 4; cf. J. E. Dunlap, 'The Office of the Grand Chamberlain in the Late Roman and Byzantine Empires', *Univ. Mich. Stud. Hum. Sc.* XIV (1924), 161.

[15] Plutarch, *Caes.* 49, 4.

[16] *Jul.* 76, 3.

[17] *Ad Att.* XIV, 5, 1.

[18] *BC* III, 94/391.

[19] On *dispensatores* see p. 136

[20] See *PIR*² I 381. Note also another freedman of Caesar, Demetrius, placed in charge of Cyprus by Antonius in 39 BC, Dio XLVIII, 40, 6.

[21] e.g. Plutarch, *Ant.* 67, 9–10. Theophilus, apparently a slave of Antonius, *dioikêtês* at Corinth, and his son Hipparchus, the first of his freedmen to desert to Octavian (cf. 73, 4); Dio LI, 8, 6, Thyrsus, a freedman of Octavian, sent to Menodorus (or Menas, see below), Pompeius' commander of Corsica and Sardinia.

freedmen whom they favoured.[22] Suetonius notes that Menas was the only freedman whom Augustus would invite to dinner—but he had been proclaimed of free birth after his betrayal of Pompeius.[23]

It is not an accident that this exception came to be recorded, for Augustus was careful to avoid open affronts to public sentiment by allowing his freedmen too prominent a social position; when one of them committed adultery with a Roman matron, he was compelled to commit suicide.[24] None the less, his freedmen included wealthy men whose houses near the Circus Maximus would be visited by Augustus, as they were by Tiberius;[25] the suburban villa of one of his freedmen was one of Augustus' customary retreats.[26] The influence of the freedmen, though still relatively modest and not publicly displayed, was no secret to any one who had an intimate connection with the imperial household. It was certainly clear to Herod, who left some 500 talents to the 'wife, children, friends and freedmen' of Augustus.[27] Herod should have known; if he needed reminding, he had ample recent evidence from a complex intrigue involving his own household and Acme, a Jewish freedwoman of Livia, later executed by Augustus.[28] The links between the two households were close. Shortly after Herod's death there arose an impersonator of his son Alexander, who had been executed some three years earlier. The man who aided Augustus to unmask the impostor was his freedman Celadus, who had known the sons of Herod during their education in Rome some years before. As Suetonius records, Celadus was one of the most honoured freedmen of Augustus.[29]

A multitude of different circumstances already placed the freedmen in an influential position beside the emperor. So Pliny the Elder records a freedman of Augustus tasting the local wines provided by his host for the emperor's dinner and remarking coldly, 'The flavour of this wine is new to me, and it is not of a fine quality, but Caesar will not refuse it.'[30] An even more public position was occupied by Antonius Musa, evidently a freedman of Antonius who had joined the household of Augustus. After he had cured Augustus of a dangerous illness in 23 BC, he was granted the gold ring by Augustus, money from both Augustus and the senate, and immunity from taxation for himself and his descendants.[31]

The intimate relationship in which the emperor worked with his freedmen was vividly revealed on the death of Augustus in AD 14, when the Vestal Virgins produced his will which had been written in the previous year. It was contained in two *codices*, partly in his own hand and partly in those of his freedmen, Polybius and Hilarion, and was read out in the senate

---

[22] XLVIII, 45, 5–9. Cf. Plutarch, *Ant.* 32, and Appian, *BC* V, 78/330f., where the same man is called Menodorus. Cf. *RE* s.v. 'Menas' (3).

[23] *Aug.* 74.

[24] ibid., 67, 2.

[25] ibid., 45; Dio LVII, 11, 4–5.

[26] ibid., 72.

[27] Josephus, *BJ* I, 32, 7 (646); *Ant.* XVII, 6, 1 (146).

[28] *BJ* I, 32, 6–7 (641–5); *Ant.* XVII, 5, 7–8 (134–45); 7, 1 (182).

[29] *BJ* II, 7, 2 (106–10); *Ant.* XVII, 12, 2 (332); Suetonius, *Aug.* 67, 1, cf. *PIR²* C 616.

[30] Pliny, *NH* XIV, 8/72. Contrast the anecdote recorded on p. 30.

[31] See Dio LIII, 30, 3, and p. 491.

by Polybius. At the same time the *breviarium* of the finances of the empire which he left contained the names of the freedmen and slaves from whom an account could be demanded.[32] It is here that we see the first clear evidence of the semi-official, 'secretarial' functions henceforward performed by the freedmen; there is as yet very little evidence of the characteristic, and grammatically puzzling titles by which they came to be designated—*a rationibus* (literally 'from the accounts'), *ab epistulis* and so forth.[33]

With the reign of Tiberius we are still in the period before the great days of the freedmen. But some power and influence was theirs. Before AD 22 Julius Agrippa, later king of Judaea, had wasted his fortune at court, mainly by gifts to the freedmen in the hope of their favour; later he was to borrow 1,000,000 *sesterces* from a Samaritan freedman of Tiberius to pay his debts to Antonia.[34] Another wealthy freedman of this period was one Nomius, recorded in passing by Pliny the Elder as the owner of a massive citruswood table, finer than the best owned by the emperor himself.[35] Such were the pressures of existence in the orbit of the emperor that even mere slaves could confer favours on important men, which might lead to a lifetime of benefit for themselves. So Agrippa, imprisoned for a rash remark while at Capri in the last year of Tiberius, begged a drink from a slave named Thaumastus, and promised him his freedom in return. When freed by Gaius, he redeemed his promise, and took Thaumastus as the procurator of his estates, a position he still held under Agrippa II and Berenice. Josephus, who records this, also notes that it was Euodus, 'the most honoured of his freedmen', who brought Tiberius' relatives to his deathbed in 37.[36]

The same period saw the beginning of the imperial service of a man whose long career is known from the *consolatio* addressed by Statius to his son, Claudius Etruscus, on his death in 92/3.[37] Born in Smyrna in AD 2/3, he passed (either by birth in the imperial *familia*, or more probably by sale after exposure) into the imperial household in Rome. As always, propinquity was a vital factor in advancement: 'To you it was given always to take your course near the divinities, always to attend the side of the emperor, and to be close to the sacred mysteries of the gods.'[38] Freed by Tiberius, he was

---

[32] Suetonius, *Aug.* 101; Dio LVI, 32, 1.

[33] (a) Suetonius, *Aug.* 67, 2, records that Augustus punished Thallus *a manu*, 'pro epistula prodita'. *a manu* is the only one of the terms with this grammatical form which is recorded for the republic: Suetonius, *Jul.* 74, 1: 'Philemonem a manu servum'. See *Thes. Ling. Lat.* 22–3.

(b) *a rationibus* appears once as the title of a freedman of Tiberius, *CIL* VI 8409c.

(c) *a memoria* may be attested in Suetonius, *Aug.* 79, 'Iulius Marathus libertus et a memoria (etiam memoriam).' But see Hirschfeld, *Kaiserliche Verwaltungsbeamten*², 334, n. 6.

(d) *ab epistulis* does not appear in literary sources relating Augustus and Tiberius, but is attested in the titles of two minor figures apparently of this period, *CIL* VI 8596 and 8613; 4249. See Hirschfeld, o.c., 319.

(e) The title *acceptor a subscr(iptionibus)* attested for a freedman of Tiberius, *CIL* VI 5181, *may* be an earlier form of *a libellis*, as asserted by Hirschfeld, o.c., 327, n. 2.

[34] Josephus, *Ant.* XVIII, 6, 1 (145); 6, 4 (167).

[35] *NH* XIII, 29/93–4.

[36] *Ant.* XVIII, 6, 6 (192–4); 6, 8 (205). Perhaps the same Euodus as in Tacitus, *Ann.* XI, 37, 2.

[37] Statius, *Silv.* III, 3. For a full discussion see P. R. C. Weaver, 'The Father of Claudius Etruscus: Statius, *Silvae* 3, 3', *CQ* n.s. XV (1965), 145 = *Familia Caesaris* (1972), ch. 22.

[38] ibid., ll. 64–66: 'semperque gradi prope numina semper / Caesareum coluisse latus sacrisque deorum / arcanis haerere datum.' For other examples of cult-terms metaphorically applied to the emperors see pp. 79, 98, 100, 468, 539.

part of Gaius' entourage on the expedition of 39, promoted by Claudius, and finally raised to be *a rationibus* by Vespasian. In Claudius' reign he had married a free woman of good birth; his two sons reached equestrian rank, and he was then granted it also, along with the gold ring, by Vespasian. Under Domitian he was suddenly banished, and ten years later recalled shortly before his death. His career illustrates both the opportunities and the essential uncertainty, the background of fear, which attended all imperial service. In this case all ended well, and Claudius Etruscus himself remained a rich and prominent man, with both Statius and Martial to celebrate the luxurious baths which he built.[39]

The few years from the latter part of Tiberius' reign to that of Claudius saw the rise of the freedmen to a relatively brief but sensational period of extravagant and scandalous power and influence. By the reign of Trajan the imperial court had already reached a period of conscious reaction. From then on the influence of men from within the household, while always present, came to the fore only in isolated episodes (as in the reign of Commodus), and was quite outbalanced by that of men drawn from outside.

Our conception of the period of domination by freedmen is illustrated at its beginning by the exceptionally vivid testimony of Philo, recounting his embassy to Gaius in 40.[40] His account of Helicon, the chief *cubicularius* of Gaius and main opponent of the Alexandrian Jewish embassy, is a classic formulation of the social patterns of court life. Helicon had been a slave from Egypt, educated by his former master and presented to Tiberius as a gift. But it was in Gaius' reign that his opportunity came: 'For he played ball with Gaius, exercised with him, bathed with him, had meals with him and was with him when he was going to bed.'[41] As is evident in other cases, slave or freedman status did not necessarily break the ties of local origin. Helicon shared the prejudices of the Alexandrian Greeks among whom he had been born, and was duly approached by the Greek embassy both with bribes and with promises of public honours when Gaius paid his intended visit to the city. He and Apelles, an actor from Ascalon, are also said by Philo to have supported Gaius' plan to place a statue of himself in the Temple.

These two men illustrate the uncertainty of the life of an imperial favourite: Apelles was put to the torture by Gaius, and Helicon was executed by Claudius.[42] The same fate befell Protogenes who used to carry Gaius' documents with the names of those due for execution, and once, merely by greeting a senator with hostile words as he entered the *curia*, caused him to be killed on the spot by his fellow-senators; he too was killed at the beginning of Claudius' reign.[43] Other men survived, to reach their greatest influence under Claudius. Pallas appears first as a slave, carrying a crucial message from Antonia, the mother of Claudius, to Tiberius about Sejanus in 31. By 37 he had been manumitted by her, hence his full name, M.

[39] *PIR*[2] c 860.

[40] Philo, *Legatio*, ed. E. M. Smallwood, ed. 2 (1969). For the date see Schürer, *Jewish People* I, 392–3.

[41] 27/175 trans. Smallwood.

[42] 30/206.

[43] Dio LIX, 26, 1–2; LX, 4, 5; cf. Suetonius, *Calig.* 28.

Antonius Pallas, and is attested as the owner of an estate in Egypt.[44] Under Claudius he was *a rationibus*, and deeply involved in the intrigues of the court. He is found discussing Messalina's affair with Silius in 48, and later that year successfully supported the claims of Agrippina to be the next wife of Claudius. In 52 came the most striking demonstration of his influence and of the extent to which the established norms of society could be overturned by it. Claudius put forward the *senatus consultum Claudianum*, on the punishment of women who had affairs with slaves, and named Pallas as the author of its terms. Barea Soranus, consul designate, proposed that he should be awarded praetorian *insignia* and an immense cash reward. Cornelius Scipio added that he should be publicly thanked for not letting his descent from Arcadian kings stand in the way of imperial service. Claudius replied that Pallas was content with his present poverty.[45] To Pliny the Younger, who happened in about 106 to came across Pallas' monument on the Via Tiburtina, with an inscription relating the honour and the refusal of the money, the whole affair seemed already an absurd but shameful historical curiosity. He was moved to look up the text of the *senatus consultum* in honour of Pallas, and could hardly believe that it was not ironical: 'What a pleasure not to have coincided with those times, which fill me with as much shame as if I had lived in them.'[46]

The same scene is referred to also in Suetonius' chapter on the honours which Claudius awarded to his freedmen, which exhibits with remarkable accuracy the various forms of offence which their prominence caused:[47]

> Of his freedmen he especially honoured Posides the eunuch, to whom he even awarded the *hasta pura* among the military men at his British triumph; and equally Felix, the husband of three queens, whom he placed over *cohortes* and *alae* and the province of Judaea; and Harpocras, to whom he gave the right to be carried through the city in a litter and to give public shows; and beyond these Polybius *a studiis*, who often walked between the two consuls. But above all Narcissus *ab epistulis* and Pallas *a rationibus*, whom he readily allowed to be granted by the senate not only huge cash rewards but quaestorian and praetorian privileges. Moreover, they collected so much money by corrupt means that when Claudius was once complaining of the poverty of the *fiscus*, it was aptly said that he would have plenty of money if his two freedmen took him into partnership.

Callistus too had risen to power before the reign of Claudius. Josephus describes his influence under Gaius, the wealth he gained from bribes, and the fact that this very wealth made him fear Gaius and intrigue with Claudius.[48] In the reign of Claudius he was duly *a libellis*. In a classic status-reversal typical of this period of the empire, Seneca saw the former master of

---

[44] For the evidence on Pallas see *PIR*[2] A 858, and S. I. Oost, 'The Career of M. Antonius Pallas', *AJPh* LXXIX (1958), 113.

[45] Tacitus, *Ann.* XII, 53.

[46] *Ep.* VII, 29; VIII, 6.

[47] *Claud.* 28.

[48] *Ant.* XIX, 1, 10 (64–9). Dio LIX, 19, 5–6, shows that Callistus was influential enough to protect an ex-consul, Domitius Afer.

Callistus waiting at his door while others were admitted.[49] Pliny the Elder notes that he had seen the dining-room built by Callistus, adorned with thirty pillars of onyx marble; in 13 BC a mere four small columns in the theatre built by Cornelius Balbus had caused a sensation.[50] It was to Callistus that Scribonius Largus, an imperial doctor, dedicated his *Compositiones*; its familiar and peaceable tone, with casual references to cures of members of the imperial family, betrays nothing of the sinister reputation which Callistus gained. But that in itself reflects an important truth relevant to the activities of the freedmen, as it is to all the other aspects of the exercise of power in the ambience of the emperor: namely that it was conducted within the framework of the leisured existence of the Roman upper classes, with its semi-rural background and devotion to traditional literary pursuits.[51]

So too the activities of Polybius had included the translation of Homer into Latin and of the *Aeneid* into Greek. This we learn from Seneca's *Ad Polybium de consolatione*, addressed to him from exile in 43; in the course of it he urges Polybius to write both a history of Claudius and fables in the manner of Aesop.[52] The work ends with an extended plea for the *clementia* of Claudius, that is the restoration of the writer. Few works exhibit more clearly both the power of the freedmen under Claudius and the culture which they shared with the Roman aristocracy.

Of the major freedmen, there remains Narcissus, of whom we learn little detail beyond a long list of intrigues and judicial murders.[53] Dio sums up his position with two essential points: he possessed millions, and received supplications from cities and kings.[54] Perhaps no single detail reveals the prominence of the freedmen more vividly than the fact which Suetonius records, that the obsequious consular, Lucius Vitellius, placed golden images of Narcissus and Pallas among his *lares*.[55]

The great period of the freedmen was very brief. Polybius was killed at Messalina's command in 47.[56] Callistus died in about 52,[57] and Narcissus was killed immediately after the murder of Claudius in 54, while curing his gout in Campania.[58] Only Pallas survived into Nero's reign, and he was dismissed in 55.[59] When he was accused in this year of joining a conspiracy, his own freedmen gave evidence that he never communicated with them except by nodding, by gesture, or in writing (a fine example of the adoption of the

---

[49] Seneca, *Ep.* 47, 9.

[50] Pliny, *NH* XXXVI, 12/60.

[51] We may note that it was Claudius' freedman, Optatus, prefect of the fleet at Misenum, who first brought the fish called wrasse from the Troad, and bred it off the Campanian coast (Pliny, *NH* IX, 29/62); and another imperial freedman, Thessalicus, who had transferred from the *familia* of Marcellus Aeserninus to that of Claudius, who first transplanted plane trees from Crete to Italy, growing them on his suburban estate (XII, 5/12). The emulation of aristocratic life-styles extended even to imperial slaves; under Claudius an imperial *dispensator* of Tarraconensis possessed a silver dish weighing 800 lb., with eight side-dishes of 250 lb. each (XXXIII, 52/145).

[52] 8, 2–3; 11, 5.

[53] *PIR*[1] N 18.

[54] LX, 34, 4.

[55] *Vit.* 2, 5.

[56] Dio LX, 31, 2.

[57] Dio LX, 33, 3a (12).

[58] Tacitus, *Ann.* XIII, 1, 3: Dio LX, 34, 4–5.

[59] *Ann.* XIII, 14, 1.

aristocratic ethos).[60] Yet still towards the year 60 he was able by an appeal to Nero to save his brother Felix from punishment for misconduct as procurator of Judaea;[61] and when he died in 62 he was generally believed to have been killed for the sake of his wealth.[62]

Already immediately after Claudius' death the power and independence of the freedmen was a reproach to his memory: 'You would have thought that all were his freedmen, so little attention did anyone pay him', as Seneca wrote in the *Apocolocyntosis*.[63] And although there is evidence for the power of freedmen under Nero, it has nothing like the coherence and extent of that relating to Claudius' reign. So for instance Tacitus portrays Vitellius speaking early in 69 about corruption by a freedman of Galba: 'It is seven months since Nero's death, and already Icelus has acquired more than Polyclitus, Vatinius and (?)Tigellinus.'[64] The phrase is re-echoed by Tacitus, speaking in his own person of a freedman of Vitellius: 'It was less than three months since the victory, and Vitellius' freedman Asiaticus was rivalling Polyclitus and Patrobius and the hated names of the old regime.'[65] Polyclitus became a byword. It is again Pliny the Younger who illustrates for us the period of reaction, in describing Trajan's response to the discovery that some of the parties to a case before him had deserted the case through *reverentia* for their opponent, an imperial *libertus* named Eurythmus: 'He is not Polyclitus, nor I Nero.'[66] We have indeed a brief reference to Polyclitus collaborating with another freedman, Helius, to ravage Rome in Nero's absence.[67] But otherwise all we know of him is his mission to Britain in 61 to report to Nero on the aftermath of the great revolt; as Tacitus writes, 'Polyclitus did not fail to burden Italy and Gaul with his massive train, and after crossing the sea to inspire fear in our soldiers also. But it was a source of derision to our enemies, among whom liberty still flourished and the power of *libertini* was not yet known.'[68]

In fact, however, even the holders of the main 'secretarial' posts at the emperor's side are far less fully attested under Nero than under Claudius. Doryphorus was probably *a libellis*, but is attested only as receiving a large gift of money from Nero, assisting his debaucheries, and being executed in 62 on the pretext of his having opposed Nero's marriage to Poppaea; his wealth is reflected in papyri referring to his estate in Egypt.[69] Phaon, on whose suburban estate Nero committed suicide in 68, was apparently *a rationibus*— though the fact depends on a single amphora-stamp from Carnuntum.[70] He, Sporus and Epaphroditus were the men who remained with Nero till his death. Epaphroditus at this time was *a libellis*. He appears in a significant

---

[60] *Ann.* XIII, 23.
[61] Josephus, *Ant.* XX, 8, 9 (182); cf. p. 378.
[62] Tacitus, *Ann.* XIV, 65, 1; Dio LXII, 14, 3; cf. Suetonius, *Nero* 35, 5.
[63] 6, 2.
[64] Tacitus, *Hist.* I, 37, 5. The text relating to the last name is not secure.
[65] *Hist.* II, 95, 4.
[66] *Ep.* VI, 31, 9.
[67] Dio LXII, 12, 3 (78).
[68] *Ann.* XIV, 39, 1–2.
[69] Dio LXI, 5, 4 (24): τῷ τὰ τῆς ἀρχῆς αὐτοῦ βιβλία διέποντι. Cf. *PIR²* D 194.
[70] *CIL* III 14112.2: 'Phaon Aug. lib. a rat'. See *RE* s.v. 'Phaon' (2).

role earlier, for when the informer of the Pisonian conspiracy in 65 went to the Horti Serviliani, he was taken by the door-keepers there first to Epaphroditus and then to Nero.[71] Surprisingly he survived the death of Nero, and remained safe, and possibly even in office, until relegated by Domitian, and in 95 executed by him.[72] Of him we happen to know a little more than of the others because one of his freedmen was Epictetus, who provides some invaluable information, limited in extent but from a unique viewpoint, on the imperial court and the overshadowing influence of the imperial power.[73] He too is a voice of the reaction, though of a quite different sort. His testimony comes from the dialogues which Arrian recorded as his pupil in Nicopolis in about 107/8.[74] Epictetus' experience of Rome may have begun under Nero, and continued until Domitian's expulsion of philosophers in the early 90s. For his teaching about the unimportance of worldly suffering or rewards, and the treacherous and double-edged nature of worldly success and favour, the imperial court, among other spheres, provided a fund of examples. Three anecdotes concern Epaphroditus: one shows a senator actually daring to reply to him, 'If I want anything I will speak to your master.' Another, more typical of the Neronian period, describes a man clinging to Epaphroditus' knees and proclaiming that he has only 1,500,000 *sesterces* left in the world; he was almost certainly a senator begging for a capital subvention to keep him within the senatorial census-qualification.[75] The third shows another status-reversal, when Epaphroditus, probably now out of office, had himself to pay court to a former slave of his who had become the emperor's cobbler.[76]

The rapid changes of emperor in the years 68–9 introduce the period when the main posts at the emperor's side began to pass definitively to men of equestrian status; the process was to be effectively completed under Hadrian.[77] But 68–9 also provides classic illustrations of the workings of power as they affected freedmen who rose to a sudden eminence with their masters, exercised an arbitrary power, were exposed to popular favour or disfavour, and were rapidly doomed when their master fell.[78] Even on the victorious Flavian side there was Hormus, a freedman of Vespasian, who was one of the leaders of the campaign in Italy, and was voted equestrian rank by the senate.[79] This was not prophetic of the nature of Vespasian's

---

[71] Suetonius, *Nero* 49; Tacitus, *Ann.* xv, 55, 1.

[72] Dio LXVII, 14, 4–5. He was possibly the Epaphroditus who encouraged Josephus to write his *Antiquities*, completed in 93/4. See *PIR²* E 69, and Th. Frankfort, 'La date de l'autobiographie de Flavius Josèphe et des oeuvres de Justus de Tibériade', *Rev. Belge de Phil. et d'Hist.* XXXIX (1961), 52.

[73] See F. Millar, 'Epictetus and the Imperial Court', *JRS* LV (1965), 141.

[74] The date hangs on the identification of the Maximus in III, 7 with the Maximus of Pliny, *Ep.* VIII, 24. See Millar, o.c., 142, and for a more precise date, A. N. Sherwin-White, *The Letters of Pliny* (1966), 38–9.

[75] p. 298.

[76] *Diss.* I, 1, 20; I, 26, 11–12; I, 19, 20–1. See Millar, o.c., 143–4.

[77] p. 89.

[78] Note for example Icelus, a freedman of Galba, *PIR²* I 16; Asiaticus a freedman of Vitellius, *PIR²* A 1216; and Coenus, a freedman of Nero who survived to serve Otho and be executed by Vitellius, Tacitus, *Hist.* II, 54.

[79] *Hist.* III, 12, 3; 27–8; IV, 39, 1.

regime, for what little our sources tell us of his freedmen mostly concerns his firm treatment of them.[80] The single partial exception is an exotic product of the Julio-Claudian era, Antonia Caenis, once the slave, then the freedwoman and *a manu* of Antonia, the mother of Claudius; Vespasian's mistress earlier, she was recalled after the death of his wife.[81] What Dio tells us of her neatly illustrates the opportunities open to an imperial favourite, and the ways in which these might vary in accordance with the character of the ruler himself: 'For she received vast sums from many sources, sometimes selling governorships, sometimes procuratorships, generalships and priesthoods, and in some cases even imperial decisions. For although Vespasian killed no one on account of his money, he did spare the lives of many who gave it; and while it was Caenis who received the money, people suspected that Vespasian willingly allowed her to do as she did.'[82]

The poems of Martial and Statius show us the freedmen of the Flavian house in quite a different light. If our only evidence for the regime of Domitian were the poems written during it, we should see the imperial court as a benign centre of patronage, literary as well as official, and the scene of a civilized existence carried on against a background of elegant houses and suburban estates. One of the murderers of Domitian was Entellus, apparently his *a libellis*;[83] three years before, Martial had addressed to him an epigram celebrating the elegant and fruitful gardens of his house in Rome.[84] Another was Parthenius, a *cubicularius*.[85] Martial addresses a number of epigrams to him, for instance on his son's birthday in 88, thanking him for the gift of a fine toga in 93, asking him to present some poems to Domitian in 89.[86] When the Praetorian guard rose against the murderers in 97, they cut off Parthenius' testicles, stuffed them in his mouth, and strangled him.[87]

Statius addresses a poem to Abascantus, *ab epistulis*, an elegy for his deceased wife Priscilla.[88] In his prefatory address he refers to his habit of cultivating the imperial household: 'Moreover I always try, from my modest position, to deserve well of the attendants of the divine house: for he who truly worships a god, also loves the priests.' He goes on to refer to the manifold duties of the *ab epistulis*, and to his arduous travels with Domitian to Rhine and Danube; then to the death of Priscilla, her elaborate funeral and her tomb on the Via Appia decorated with bronze and marble statues.

These poems indicate the centrality in Roman society of the imperial court, and the forms of both political and literary patronage. The freedmen and freedwomen took their place within this society and entered on its lifestyle; even Phyllis, the nurse (*nutrix*) of Domitian, had a suburban villa,

---

[80] See the instances in Suetonius, *Vesp.* 23.
[81] *PIR*² A 888.
[82] LXVI, 14, 3–4, Loeb trans.
[83] Dio LXVII, 15, 1 (182): ὁ τὰ τῆς ἀρχῆς βιβλία διέπων, see *PIR*² E 66.
[84] *Epig.* VIII, 68.
[85] Suetonius, *Dom.* 16–17; Dio LXVII, 15, 1 (182).
[86] *Epig.* IV, 45; V, 6; VIII, 28.
[87] *Epit. de Caes.* 12, 8.
[88] *Silvae* V, 1.

where she buried him after his murder.[89] But in spite of the universal
hostility of the accounts of Domitian written after his death we learn little
of the political influence of freedmen. Tacitus mentions a freedman 'from
among the more intimate assistants' sent to entice Agricola from his command in Britain: and when he claims that public opinion demanded
Agricola's appointment to another major command assumes that the
emperor's decision will have been influenced by his freedmen; 'while all
the best of the freedmen used their devotion and loyalty, and the worst their
malevolence and hostility, to influence the emperor, who inclined to the
worse.'[90] But on our evidence, Pliny should not have been referring specifically to Domitian when he summed up one aspect of the contrast between
Trajan and earlier emperors in his *Panegyric*:[91]

> Most emperors, while they were the masters of the citizens, were the slaves of
> their freedmen; by the advice of these, by their nod, they were ruled; by their
> agency they both listened and made pronouncements. By their agency they
> awarded praetorships, priesthoods and consulates—which were even petitioned
> for from them. *You* keep your freedmen in the highest honour, but such as
> befits freedmen, and believe it entirely sufficient for them if they gain a reputa-
> tion for honesty and frugality. For you know that the chief sign of an insignificant
> emperor is great freedmen.

The passage may reasonably be taken to mark the end of an era. From
this time on it was relatively unusual for persons from within the *familia* to
achieve any recognized personal influence with the emperor. When they did
so, it was not as the holders of the main 'secretarial' posts, but usually as
cubicularii, attendants of the bedchamber. Towards the end of the period
indeed it becomes difficult to identify which if any of the personal attendants
of the emperor were former slaves from the *familia*; the only category which
certainly consisted of ex-slaves were the eunuchs, whose influence at court is
emphasized, and generally regarded as sinister, in fourth-century sources.[92]
The *familia* itself of course remained, both scattered through the provinces
and in Rome. Various imperial freedmen of the second century were known
as authors,[93] the most prominent being Phlegon of Tralles, the historian and
antiquarian. It is noteworthy that one of his numerous works, the *Olympic
Chronicle*, was dedicated to Alcibiades, 'one of those appointed to guard the
emperor', that is a *cubicularius*.[94] This will have been P. Aelius Alcibiades
from Nysa in Caria, whom various tribes there honoured as 'lover and
benefactor of his city'.[95] He was not the only *cubicularius* to be honoured by

---

[89] Suetonius, *Dom.* 17, 3.

[90] *Agric.* 40, 2; 41, 4.

[91] 88, 1–2.

[92] See M. K. Hopkins, 'Eunuchs in Politics in the Later Roman Empire', *PCPhS* n.s. IX (1963),
62.

[93] For instance Aristomenes of Athens, a learned freedman of Hadrian, who was an actor of
Old Comedy and the author of three books *On Ceremonials*, Athenaeus, *Deipn.* 115 a–b; or the
chronicler Chryserus, a freedman and *nomenclator* of Marcus Aurelius, Theophilus, *Ad Autolycum*
III, 27, cf. Jacoby, *FGrH* 96.

[94] Photius, *Bib.* 97 = Jacoby, *FGrH* 257 T. 3.

[95] See *PIR*² A 134; *ILS* 8857 (Nysa); see L. Robert, *Études épigraphiques et philologiques* (1938),
45f.

public inscriptions.[96] Moreover, it is important to emphasize that he too, though a *libertus*, retained his connections with his native city, and could confer benefits on it; and also that *cubicularii* could share the literary culture common both to Roman society and to the vast majority of the provincial dignitaries who appeared before the emperor.

Like their predecessors, the freedmen of the second century could be wealthy, and well-placed in Roman society. Galen's first contact with the imperial court was when he cured a slave of the *cubicularius* Charilampes— 'none of the court doctors being able to do this'.[97] Charilampes is perhaps to be identified with the 'Charilas', a freedman of Marcus Aurelius, to whom even Fronto himself wrote to ask whether the time was opportune before calling on Aurelius and Lucius Verus.[98] A few men, even in this period, emerged from these positions of essentially domestic influence to more public roles. An *a cubiculo* of L. Aelius Caesar, probably called Nicomedes, was later *nutritor* of Lucius Verus and was then raised to the rank of *eques* by Antoninus Pius, had an equestrian career and returned to court as a high financial official, *procurator summarum rationum*.[99]

He was merely the forerunner of two much more striking figures in the reign of Commodus (as Pliny had said, great freedmen were a sign—to Roman society almost a definition—of weak emperors), namely Saoterus and M. Aurelius Cleander. Saoterus came from Nicomedia, and was Commodus' *cubicularius* and favourite—a fact advertised by his sharing the emperor's chariot in the triumph of 180. Dio and the *Historia Augusta* agree on his great influence. The only instance given is a significant one, that it was through him that the senate voted Nicomedia permission to establish an athletic contest and build a temple to Commodus. According to the *Historia Augusta*, he was killed by the praetorian prefects, pretending to escort him to his suburban villa.[100] Much more is known of Cleander, whose biography is one of the most revealing of the imperial period. Born in Phrygia, he seems to have been brought to Rome with a group of slave porters, was sold into the imperial household, and became the *nutritor* of Commodus. He is referred to in a letter written by Commodus to Athens as 'my *nutritor* entrusted with the care of my bedroom and my person'.[101] Here he apparently comes second in a list of advisers, preceded by an ex-consul and followed by the *ab epistulis Graecis* and *a rationibus*. Dio gives the fullest account of his period of power—granting and selling places in the senate, army commands, praetorships and prefectures. Some men gave over their whole property to be made senators. One year he had twenty-five consuls appointed, among them Septimius Severus. He gathered a greater fortune than any other

[96] See e.g. *IGR* III 75 (Claudiopolis), and now *JÖAI* XLIX (1968–71), Beiblatt, 19, no. 3 (a former *a cubiculo* of Titus).

[97] Galen XIV, 624–5 Kühn.

[98] Fronto, *ad Verum* 1, 3, 2. See *PIR²* C 713.

[99] *ILS* 1740; *HA, Verus* 2, 8; see Pflaum, *Carrières*, no. 163.

[100] Dio LXXII, 12, 2 (294); *HA, Com.* 4, 5. See *PIR¹* S 137 and F. Grosso, *La lotta politica al tempo di Commodo* (1964), 113–16.

[101] *AE* 1952 6: [Αὐρήλιος Κ]λέανδρος ὁ τροφεύς μου καὶ ἐπὶ [τὴν τοῦ θαλάμου καὶ τ]οῦ σώματος τοῦ ἐμοῦ πίστιν ἐπιτε[ταγμένος]. See Pflaum, *Carrières*, no. 180 bis and *Add.*; Grosso, o.c., 116f., 217f.

4

cubicularius, and gave much of it to Commodus and his concubines, one of whom he married. But he also, Dio says, gave substantial sums to cities and individuals for the construction of houses and baths and other useful objects.[102]

Dio does not mention what the *Historia Augusta* records, and an inscription confirms, that Cleander gained the title *a pugione*, making him in effect a freedman colleague of the two praetorian prefects.[103] The rise of such a figure to public prominence inevitably led to a reaction, and a riot over a corn shortage in 190 led to his execution on the orders of Commodus.[104]

It is not necessary to pursue the scattered evidence from the Severan period which shows *cubicularii* attending the emperor in Rome and elsewhere, sometimes having also the (unknown) functions of *a memoria*, engaging in court intrigues, and on occasion meeting the sudden end which threatened all who played any role in the court;[105] nor the group of favourites who made their brief appearances in the reigns of Caracalla and Elagabal. The essential point is clear, namely that through the third century an imperial *familia* of slaves and ex-slaves persisted, and undoubtedly still provided the domestic setting of imperial activity; while some members, eunuchs in particular by the early fourth century, served as the immediate domestic attendants of the emperor. In major crises they are occasionally exposed to the view of our sources, as in the persecution of 303, when rumour accused the Christians of having conspired to set fire to the imperial palace in Nicomedia. The investigation made little progress, 'since no one would put to the torture the *familia* of Caesar'. But after a second fire there were executions even of the most powerful eunuchs, who had previously controlled the palace.[106] Meanwhile Constantius in the west gave Christians in his household, from slaves upwards it seems, the choice of sacrificing or leaving his service; those who chose the more honourable path were rewarded, so Eusebius claims, with positions close to his person.[107]

Even where what they actually report cannot be relied upon, the assumptions of our sources when they retail events in the court are of some significance. So for instance Rufinus reports that in 337 the eunuchs at court for a time suppressed the news of the death of Constantine because they favoured his son Constantius.[108] Socrates names the *praepositus sacri*

---

[102] LXXII, 12, 3–5 (294).

[103] See L. Moretti, *Riv. di filol.* XXXVIII (1960), 68 = *AE* 1961 280; *HA, Com.* 6,12–7,1.

[104] Herodian I, 12,3–13,6, with Whittaker's notes in the Loeb ed.

[105] Of *cubicularii* note Castor under Severus, who ἐπεπίστευτο τήν τε μνήμην αὐτοῦ καὶ τὸν κοιτῶνα, Dio LXXVI, 14, 2, cf. 14, 5 (368–9) and LXXVII, 1, 2 (373). He went on the British expedition with Severus and his sons, and was later killed by Caracalla; Festus, *a cubiculo et a memoria*, who died at Ilium when Caracalla was there in 214 (*Ins. Ital.* IV. 1, 180; Dio LXXIII, 32, 4 (441); Herodian IV, 8, 4). It was surely his former estate ('massa Festi praepositi sacri cubiculi') near Praeneste which Constantine was to grant to the Lateran Bapistery. See Duchesne, *Liber Pontificalis* I (repr. 1955), 174. Also M. Aurelius Prosenes, a Christian *a cubiculo* who died on his way back to Rome 'from the expeditions' in 217, *ILS* 1738, see H. U. Instinsky, *Marcus Aurelius Prosenes—Freigelassener und Christ am Kaiserhof*, Abh. Ak. Wiss. Mainz III, 1964.

[106] Lactantius, *De mort. pers.* 14–15.

[107] Eusebius, *VC* I, 15–16. Both the categories of employees referred to, and the posts awarded them, remain obscure.

[108] Rufinus, *HE* X, 12.

cubiculi at the time as Eusebius, an Arian: while Photius goes into more detail, and portrays this Eusebius and others as keeping Constantine's will from his son Constantine and passing it to Constantius.[109] One element in the court had remained relatively constant since the day more than three centuries before when the *cubicularii* had overheard Augustus' parting comment when Tiberius left his deathbed after their last interview.[110]

These rumours about intrigues in 337 may well be false, but the eunuch *cubicularii* themselves were a reality. We can see this for instance in Ammianus' brief sketch of the life-history of Eutherius, one of the most powerful eunuchs of the mid-fourth century.[111] He was born in Armenia of free parents, kidnapped by hostile tribesmen, castrated, sold to some Roman traders and brought by them to the palace of Constantine. There he 'received such training in letters as was adequate to his circumstances', and was eventually *praepositus cubiculi* of Julian.

It is interesting to note that the imperial *familia* was still acquiring new members by purchase, but more important to emphasize that the training which even a *cubicularius* received was in *litterae*. Such a training was even more clearly the hallmark of those persons from outside the *familia* who for more than two centuries had usurped the earlier functions of the freedmen in the emperor's service, and significantly affected the tone of his communications with his subjects.

5. *The Equestrian 'Secretaries': Intellectuals, Orators and Jurists*

The attraction to the immediate service of the emperor of men whose qualifications were essentially intellectual, literary or scholastic was in itself only a part of the immensely complex and richly documented relations between the emperor and the educated upper classes of Italy and the provinces. Beyond the limited group who were called to his side, there were innumerable others who addressed poems or learned works to him, received *beneficia* in the form of money or privileges, acted as doctors or astrologers, taught the children of the imperial household, or (the largest number of all) appeared on embassies before him.[1] Here we shall be concerned only with those who did not rise through any recognizable career but came directly into the imperial entourage, either holding some specific 'secretarial' post or at least passing some significant period with the emperor and being able to exercise some influence on him.

Of the many men from the Greek cities who established close links with leading senators in the late republic, few are attested as holding specific positions or as executing an influence on decisions. The most notable exception is Theophanes of Mytilene, the friend and confidant of Pompey; he accompanied him on his campaigns and wrote a history of them, and also

---

[109] Socrates, *HE* II, 2, 5–6; Photius, *Bib.* 256 (473a Bekker). See *PLRE* Eusebius II.
[110] Suetonius, *Tib.* 21, 2.
[111] Ammianus XVI, 7, 4–7; cf. *PLRE* Eutherius I.
   [1] See pp. 494–506.

secured from him the freedom of his city, which duly awarded him divine honours.[2] In the campaign leading up to Pharsalus he had the rank of *praefectus fabrum* on Pompey's staff.[3] After Pharsalus, Julius Caesar similarly gave freedom to Cnidus as a favour to his friend Theopompus, the author of a collection of myths; it was probably his son Artemidorus who was to warn Caesar in vain on the Ides of March. Both father and son are referred to in an inscription containing a treaty between Rome and Cnidus.[4]

It was not only among the *litterateurs* of the Greek east that such links were forged. The best-known case from the west is that of Balbus from Gades, who was awarded the citizenship by Pompey for his services in the civil war in Spain in the 70s, and was *praefectus fabrum* of Caesar in Lusitania in 61–0, securing many benefits for his native city, and again in Gaul in 58–50. Then and afterwards he achieved a central role in Roman society, culminating in the consulship of 40 BC.[5] But the clearest and most concrete instance in the late republic comes from Gaul, in the account given by the historian Pompeius Trogus of his family's services to Rome.[6] Trogus' grandfather, from the Vocontii of Narbonensis, fought with Pompey against Sertorius, and was also given the citizenship by him; and his uncle commanded a cavalry unit in Pompey's campaigns against Mithridates. His father served under Julius Caesar and had 'the care of his letters and embassies, and at the same time his ring'. We cannot specify what exactly was entailed by these functions at this time; but Trogus' father may possibly be identified with the Cn. Pompeius whom Caesar mentions as his interpreter in Gaul in 54.[7] Caesar had other confidants from the 'province', such as his trusted friend, C. Valerius Troncillus, with whom he interrogated Diviciacus in 58.[8] Again he still had with him on the campaign of Pharsalus in 48 two brothers from the Allobroges, leading men in their tribe, who had assisted him throughout the conquest of Gaul. In return he had given them major magistracies in the tribe, enrolled them irregularly in its 'senate', and given them money and large stretches of land in Gaul.[9]

These particular contacts were the product of circumstances, of the geography of the campaigns which Pompey and Caesar fought. But, as we shall see, the majority of the persons from the provinces who exercised a direct influence with the emperor were Greeks, who did so as a product of the overwhelming prestige of Greek culture. Near the end of the period, however, when several centuries of largely undisturbed peace had had their effects, and when the tetrarchic system established an emperor in Gaul, it is from the Gallic panegyrists of the late third and early fourth century that we

---

[2] See Jacoby, *FGrH* 188, and now L. Robert, 'Théophane de Mytilène à Constantinople', *CRAI* 1969, 42.

[3] Plutarch, *Cic.* 38, 4; for his role as adviser see Caesar, *BC* III, 18, 3.

[4] See Plutarch, *Caesar*, 48, 1; 65; Appian, *BC* II, 116/486 (cf. p. 240); Strabo XIV, 2, 15 (656); *IBM* 787, 792, 801; A. Jardé, 'Un traité entre Cnide et Rome', *Mél. Cagnat* (1912), 51.

[5] See *RE* s.v. 'Cornelius' (69). On his initiative in securing benefits for Gades, Cicero, *Pro Balbo* 18–19/43.

[6] Justinus, *Epit. Pompei Trogi Philippicarum* XLIII, 5, 11–12, cf. p. 213.

[7] Caesar, *BG* V, 36, 1.

[8] I, 19, 3.

[9] Caesar *BC* III, 59, 1–2.

have the clearest of all expressions of the link between rhetorical culture and employment with the emperor.[10]

The exercise of a personal influence by persons in the confidence of the emperor was not something which had to be artfully concealed, to be deduced by observers or historians. On the contrary, as we have seen, it was deliberately advertised at the very beginning of the principate, when Octavian drove into Alexandria in 30 BC with his tutor Areus, and told the people that he had spared them because of the memory of Alexander, the beauty of the city—and as a favour to Areus.[11] One essential function which Areus performed is revealed by a passage of Suetonius about Augustus: 'He gained a varied erudition from the company of Areus the philosopher and his sons Dionysius and Nicanor; not however to the extent of speaking [Greek] fluently or writing anything in it. If the occasion demanded, he wrote in Latin and had it translated by others.'[12] Areus occupied no actual post at court, though he was offered, and declined, one in Egypt, perhaps that of Idios Logos; he did however serve as Augustus' procurator in Sicily.[13]

Another former teacher of Augustus was the Stoic philosopher, Athenodorus of Tarsus, who was already in Rome in 44 BC, and who stayed many years with the emperor as a trusted and privileged adviser. Nothing is known of his role vis-à-vis the outside world until he returned to Tarsus, with powers given by Augustus, to eject a local tyrant. In his position there he was succeeded by Nestor, previously the teacher of Marcellus, who, in Strabo's words, died 'honoured by the governors and the city'.[14]

The role played by such men did not as yet involve any specific post or even any specific function with the emperor. It was however to a definite function, though not so far as we know to a named post, that Augustus tried to attract Horace. The *vita* of Horace records, 'Augustus offered also the *officium epistularum*, as he indicates in this letter to Maecenas: "Previously I could cope myself with my letters to my friends. Now I am very busy and not well, and wish to take our friend Horace away from you. So he will come from that 'parasitic' table of yours to this 'royal' one and help me with my correspondence.' '[15] The fact that Augustus was thinking primarily of his correspondence with friends does not, however, show that the *officium* offered by Horace had no connection with the later post *ab epistulis*,[16] many of whose holders had qualifications very similar to those of Horace.

It is, however, not until the reign of Claudius that we can trace significant further developments. The clearest evidence relates to Stertinius Xenophon

[10] See pp. 98–9.

[11] See p. 9.

[12] Suetonius, *Aug.* 89, 1.

[13] Julian, *Ep. ad Themist*, p. 343 Hertlein; see G. W. Bowersock, *Augustus and the Greek World* (1965), 33.

[14] See Strabo XIV, 5, 14 (674–5). For Athenodorus *PIR*² A 1288; P. Grimal, 'Auguste et Athénodore', *RÉA* XLVII (1945), 261; XLVIII (1946), 62.

[15] Suetonius, *Vita Horatii*, p. 45 Reifferscheid; Rostagni, *Suetonio 'de poetis'*, pp. 113–14. The terms 'parasitica' and 'regia' come from the vocabulary of comedy, see E. Fraenkel, *Horace* (1957), 18. There remains all the same a play of words relating to Augustus' monarchical position.

[16] As asserted by Fraenkel, o.c., 17. Nor is there evidence at any time for a specifically 'literary', as opposed to official, *ab epistulis*, as presumed by A. N. Sherwin-White, *The Letters of Pliny* (1966), 125. See further pp. 219–28 below.

from Cos, who exhibits all the main characteristics of the class of men we are concerned with: eminence in a branch of learning, a personal attachment to the court, a secretarial function there, public honours in Rome, and an unbroken role in his native city.[17] He is perhaps first attested as an ambassador from Cos in AD 23, when the rights of asylum of the temples in many Greek cities were defended in Rome. Later he was in practice as a doctor in Rome. When Claudius, possibly before he became emperor, wished to appoint him as his own doctor, he rejected the normal salary of 250,000 *sesterces*, saying that he earned 600,000 in private practice (which he proved by pointing to his houses in the city). So Claudius appointed both himself and his brother at 500,000. The appointment must at the latest have come early in the reign, for Xenophon accompanied Claudius on the British expedition of 43/4. His honours and functions rapidly extended. An inscription from Calymnus on Cos honours him as Chief Doctor (*archiatros*) of the Divine Emperors, and in charge of *apokrimata* (legal decisions?) in Greek, tribune, *praefectus fabrum*, as having received military decorations at the British triumph—and also as benefactor (*euergetês*) of his city, High Priest of the Gods, High Priest of the Emperor for life, and of Asclepius, Hygia and Epione; another inscription from Cos lengthens the list of priesthoods.[18] By now he was a prominent public figure. In 53 Claudius made a speech in the senate asking for a grant of immunity from taxation for Cos: 'It should be granted to Xenophon's entreaties that the people of Cos, free of all tribute, should devote themselves to their island, sacred and in the service of their god [Asclepius] alone.'[19] Claudius' patronage was ill-rewarded, for in the following year Xenophon is said to have assisted in poisoning him.[20]

A position such as that of Xenophon naturally did not go unexploited by his fellow-citizens. An inscription from Cos records his brother, Ti. Claudius Cleonymus, a former local office-holder and tribune of the twenty-second legion Primigenia 'who has been on many embassies for the city to the emperors'.[21]

A man who *may* have been closely comparable to Stertinius Xenophon was Ti. Claudius Balbillus, whom a damaged inscription from Ephesus, describes as *ad legationes et res[ponsa—or rescripta—Graeca?]* of Claudius, tribune of the twentieth legion, *praefectus fabrum* and decorated in the British triumph.[22] The twentieth legion took part in the invasion, and the parallel with Xenophon allows us to assume that all these posts were held concurrently. *Praefectus fabrum* was a post which could be a sinecure,[23] and it may be suggested that both these tribunates were sinecures too. The inscription also, however, fragmentarily records a number of posts in Egypt,

---

[17] See R. Herzog, 'Nikias und Xenophon von Kos', *Hist. Zeitschr.* cxxv (1921–2), 189, on pp. 216f.; see Pflaum, *Carrières*, no. 16.

[18] *Syll.*[3] 804; Herzog, o.c., p. 236, n. 1.

[19] Tacitus, *Ann.* xii, 61.

[20] xii, 67, 2.

[21] *Syll.*[3] 805.

[22] See Pflaum, *Carrières*, no. 15.

[23] See B. Dobson, 'The Praefectus Fabrum in the Early Principate', *Britain and Rome: Essays presented to Eric Birley*, ed. Jarrett and Dobson (1966), 61, esp. 72–3.

to do with the temple of Augustus, sacred groves, the Museum in Alexandria and the library, and (probably) a high priesthood. We know from Strabo that the emperors, following the Ptolemies, appointed the head of the Museum from the beginning.[24] But the other posts mentioned cannot be paralleled; so it remains obscure whether they preceded or followed those with Claudius. It may be suggested that they in fact preceded them, and that what we have is another case of a Greek intellectual proceeding straight from the Museum, with some extra duties, to the service of the emperor.

Such a man could easily be identified with the Claudius Balbillus who in 55 became prefect of Egypt and whom Seneca knew as 'the best of men and most exceptionally skilled in all branches of literature'.[25] The same man could very easily be the Ti. Claudius Balbillus, who had been a member of an Alexandria delegation to Claudius in 41 and is specifically acknowledged by the emperor as his friend at the end of his letter.[26] On this reconstruction (which is far from being the only possible one), Claudius Balbillus or Barbillus was an Alexandrian who was appointed to various offices there by the emperor, then came into his immediate service, and later went back as prefect of Egypt.

However obscure the details, and however uncertain it may be as to whether the men mentioned in these various items of evidence are the same, the inscription from Ephesus does reveal a connection between the Museum in Alexandria and the imperial court. Other aspects of that important and significant connection will be discussed later,[27] but for the moment we may note some other examples of individuals who formed such a link in themselves. One was another member of the Alexandrian embassy of 41, Chaeremon, whose extensive literary output included a history of Egypt with a marked anti-Jewish bias. He too, it seems, was head of the Museum, and also at some time the teacher of Nero.[28] Nothing is known of any influence exerted by him, but his pupil and successor at the Museum, Dionysius of Alexandria, was (subsequently?) in charge of libraries, apparently in Rome, and 'in charge of letters, embassies and verdicts(?)'.[29] According to the Suda, his life covered the period from Nero to Trajan, but nothing more precise is known of the dates of these appointments. We do however know from an inscription preserved only in manuscript of a successor of Chaeremon and Dionysius in the first half of the second

[24] Strabo XVII, 1, 8 (794).

[25] Tacitus, *Ann.* XIII, 22 (appointment to Egypt); Seneca, *QN* IV, 2, 13: 'virorum optimus, perfectusque in omni litterarum genere rarissime.'

[26] The famous letter of Claudius to the Alexandrines is best cited as *Corp. Pap. Jud.*, no. 153. Claudius' reference runs (ll. 105–7): Βαρβίλλωι τῶι ἐμωι ἑτέρωι (sic) μαρτυρῶι ἀεὶ πρόνοια[ν] ⟨ὑ⟩μῶν παρ' ἐμοὶ ποιουμένωι, ὃς καὶ νῦν πάσηι φιλοτειμείᾳ περὶ τ⟨ὸ⟩ν ἀγ⟨ῶ⟩να τὸνὑπὲρ ὑμῶν κέχρ[ητε]. The question of the identity of the various persons named 'Claudius Barbillus' or 'Balbillus' has often been discussed. For a clear statement, taking a different view from that expressed here, see Pflaum, *Carrières*, no. 15.

[27] pp. 504f.

[28] *PIR*² C 706; see Jacoby, *FGrH* 618. That he was head of the Museum is an implication from the wording of the Suda 1173 s.v. Διονύσιος : μαθητὴς δὲ Χαιρήμονος τοῦ φιλοσόφου, ὃν καὶ διεδέξατο ἐν 'Αλεξανδρείᾳ.

[29] Suda, loc. cit.: ὅστις ἀπὸ Νέρωνος συνῆν καὶ τοῖς μεχρὶ Τραϊανοῦ καὶ τῶν βιβλιοθηκῶν προῦστη καὶ ἐπὶ τῶν ἐπιστολῶν καὶ πρεσβειῶν ἐγένετο καὶ ἀποκριμάτων.

century. This was Julius Vestinus, high priest of Alexandria and all Egypt, head of the Museum, in charge of the Greek and Latin libraries in Rome, *a studiis* and *ab epistulis* of Hadrian.[30] The Suda records that he was a sophist and wrote a number of learned works, including selections of words from Demosthenes, Thucydides and Isocrates.[31] Such pursuits were not purely academic exercises, but important aids towards what counted as correct vocabulary for a sophist or orator in the second century.

Two other orators were *ab epistulis Graecis* under Hadrian. One was Avidius Heliodorus, of whom Cassius Dio says baldly that he rose to be prefect of Egypt (that is subsequently, in 138–40) 'in virtue of his rhetorical skill'.[32] Not all of his own contemporaries took so favourable a view of his abilities. A sophist named Dionysius was said to have said to him while he was *ab epistulis*, 'The emperor can give you money and honour, but he cannot make you an orator.'[33] Dionysius had other enemies, one of whom was Celer, the author of a work entitled *Araspes the Lover of Panthea*, which some attributed to Dionysius himself. Philostratus knew better:[34]

> This work is not by Dionysius, but by Celer the writer on rhetoric; and Celer, though he was a good imperial secretary, lacked skill in declamation, and was on unfriendly terms with Dionysius throughout his life.

This passage, which so casually illustrates the relation of the position of *ab epistulis Graecis* to the rhetoric and culture of the Greek world, also brings us to the period when the lives of some holders of the position are illuminated by Philostratus in the *Lives of the Sophists*.[35] But before we come to his evidence, we may turn back for a moment to Secundus, 'the orator', who appears briefly in Plutarch accompanying Otho on campaign in 69 and acting as his *ab epistulis*. He was a product of a closely comparable rhetorical tradition, that of the orators of southern Gaul in the first century. A nephew of Julius Florus, *princeps eloquentiae Galliarum*, he probably came from Bordeaux. Moreover he was a friend of Quintilian, was heard by Tacitus, who gives him a role in his *Dialogus*, and was the author of a life of Julius Africanus, a famous Gallic orator of a generation earlier.[36]

Secundus was a senator by the time of his death, and was almost certainly an *eques* in 69. But it is in relation to Otho's rival and eventual successor, Vitellius, in the same year, that Tacitus mentions that he 'gave out to *equites Romani* the posts in the emperor's service which had continuously

[30] The inscription is *IG* xiv 1085 = *IGR* i 136 = *OGIS* 679: Ἀρχιερεῖ Ἀλεξανδρείας καὶ Αἰγύπτου πάσης Λευκίωι Ἰουλίωι Οὐηστίνωι καὶ ἐπιστάτηι τοῦ Μουσείου καὶ ἐπὶ τῶν ἐν Ῥώμηι βιβλιοθηκῶν Ῥωμαϊκῶν τε καὶ Ἑλληνικῶν καὶ ἐπὶ τῆς παιδείας Ἀδριανοῦ, ἐπιστολεῖ τοῦ αὐτοῦ αὐτοκράτορος. See Pflaum, *Carrières*, no. 105, and *PIR*² i 623. What the functions of an *a studiis* were is discussed below, p. 205.

[31] Suda s.v. Οὐστῖνος, Ἰούλιος χρηματίσας (ed. Adler iii, p. 581).

[32] Dio LXXI, 22, 2 (264).

[33] LXIX, 3, 5. For Avidius Heliodorus' career see *PIR*² A 1405; Pflaum, *Carrières*, no. 106.

[34] *VS* i, 22, Loeb trans. Celer is also referred to as *ab epistulis* in Aristides, *Or* L. Keil, 57, see *PIR*² c 388.

[35] See G. W. Bowersock, *Greek Sophists in the Roman Empire* (1969).

[36] Plutarch, *Otho* 9, 3. See *PIR*² i 559, and C. P. Jones, 'Julius Naso and Julius Secundus', *HSCPh* LXXII (1967), 279.

been held by freedmen'.[37] It is not clear exactly to what posts Tacitus means to refer; as we have seen, some 'secretarial' posts with the emperor had been held by Greeks of equestrian rank as early as Claudius' reign. So this step does not seem to mark as clear a break with the past as Tacitus' words might imply. Moreover the only beneficiary of it whom our evidence attests is Sextus Caesius Propertianus, who happened to be a tribune of the fourth legion at Mainz, and was therefore on the spot when Vitellius was proclaimed by the Rhine army on 1 January 69. In the hasty arrangements made by Vitellius he found himself, without any intervening civilian posts, made procurator of the *patrimonium* and inheritances[38] and *a libellis*. It is significant in relation to him, as to so many equestrian office-holders, that our knowledge of him comes from an inscription from his native town, Mevania in Umbria, where he was a local office-holder, and of which he was *patronus*.[39]

Thus, insofar as there was an innovation here, it was a mere expedient, a product of circumstances. None the less, it was part of a significant change, which Suetonius further marks by saying that Domitian 'shared certain of the chief *officia* between *libertini* and *equites Romani*';[40] while the *Historia Augusta* states (incorrectly) that Hadrian was the first emperor to have *equites Romani* as *ab epistulis* and *a libellis*.[41] It is important to emphasize that the change to which these sources allude (even if in not very clear and satisfactory terms) meant essentially the gradual replacement of the *liberti* not in the first instance by equestrian 'civil servants', but by intellectuals from the Latin world who are closely comparable to the Greeks whom we have already encountered.

Two of the clearest cases are provided by the letters of Pliny. One of the central figures in his circle was Titinius Capito, whom we meet first petitioning Nerva for permission to erect in the Forum a statue of L. Silanus (who had been executed under Nero); Pliny also mentions that Capito kept in his house *imagines* of Brutus, Cassius and Cato. Later, Pliny writes to him to answer his urgings that he should take up writing history; and later still we hear of him arranging recitations of literary works at his house, acting as a patron of literature, and himself writing on *The Deaths of Famous Men*.[42] Nothing could be clearer than his established role in cultivated Roman society. Pliny, however, gives no hint of what we learn from two inscriptions, that Cn. Octavius Titinius Capito had been prefect of a cohort and tribune of a legion, and had then moved straight (like Sextus Caesius Propertianus) into the service of an emperor who is carefully not named, but is certainly Domitian.[43] Even if the two military ranks were not sinecures (it is noticeable that no units are named) Capito had no 'career' before becoming *ab epistulis* and *a patrimonio* of Domitian, continuing as *ab epistulis* under Nerva (on

---

[37] *Hist.* I, 58, 1.
[38] See pp. 153–8, 625–7.
[39] *ILS* 1447; see Pflaum, *Carrières*, no. 37.
[40] *Dom.* 7, 2.
[41] *Had.* 22, 8.
[42] *Ep.* I, 17; V, 8; VIII, 12.
[43] *ILS* 1448; *AE* 1934 154; cf. Pflaum, *Carrières*, no. 60.

4*

whose motion he was awarded praetorian *insignia* by the senate) and again
under Trajan. We cannot be certain, but everything suggests that his role as
an imperial secretary was the product, not the source, of his prominence in
Roman literary circles.

The same is more clearly true of another friend of Pliny who also became
an *ab epistulis*, namely Suetonius.[44] Born in about 70, the son of a military
tribune, Suetonius appears first in an early letter of Pliny written under
Nerva, when he is seeking the purchase of a modest estate near Rome as a
suitable background for the life of a *scholasticus*.[45] About 102 he made an
abortive start on equestrian military service, for we find Pliny writing to him
in answer to his request that a tribunate which Pliny had gained for him
from Neratius Marcellus should be transferred to someone else.[46] In about
105/6 Pliny writes to Suetonius about the publication of some verses of his
own, and urges him to publish his *libelli*, which are awaited; and a couple of
years later discusses his abilities in recitation.[47] In about 111 he appears to
have been in Bithynia with Pliny, who writes to Trajan to ask, successfully,
for the privilege of the *ius trium liberorum* for him. The terms of his recommendation are of some interest: 'Suetonius Tranquillus, the most honourable, respectable and learned of men, whose character and studies I had
followed even before, I have taken on to my staff, and have came to appreciate him more now that I have seen him at closer quarters.'[48] In other words,
up to the point where Pliny's correspondence stops, we can see Suetonius as
an established literary figure, who is a protégé of Pliny and is successfully
recommended as such to the emperor.

The fragmentary inscription of Suetonius from Hippo seems to show that
Trajan gave him the further honour of adlection *inter selectos*, that is to the
juries of *equites* who sat in Rome.[49] It may also in the original have mentioned other posts; but what is visible is *a studiis* and *a bibliothecis*, in charge
of libraries, both of which he *may* have held under Trajan, and then *ab
epistulis* of Hadrian.[50] It is noteworthy that exactly the same three posts were
held by Julius Vestinus, the former head of the Museum in Alexandria.[51]
Suetonius' post as *ab epistulis* had long been known from the reference in the
Historia Augusta to his dismissal along with the praetorian prefect Septicius
Clarus, the dedicatee of Suetonius' *Lives of the Caesars*.[52] The reason is given
as excessive familiarity with Hadrian's wife Sabina, and the setting was, it
seems, Britain during the emperor's visit in 121/2. This is not improbable,

---

[44] For recent discussion of the evidence relating to him see R. Syme, *Tacitus* (1958), App. 76;
G. B. Townend, 'The Hippo Inscription and the Career of Suetonius', *Historia* x (1961), 99;
Pflaum, *Carrières*, no. 96; *JRS* LIII (1963), 199; G. W. Bowersock, 'Suetonius and Trajan',
Mélanges Renard I (1969), 118.

[45] *Ep.* I, 18.

[46] III, 8.

[47] V, 10; IX, 34.

[48] X, 94; 'nunc propius inspexi' rather than 'hunc' or 'tunc' is clearly required by the sense,
see Syme, loc. cit.

[49] On *adlectio inter selectos* see further pp. 282–4.

[50] *AE* 1953, 73. The key words are: '[adlecto] int[er selectos a di]vo Tr[aiano Parthico, p]on[t]
Volca[nali] . . . [a] studiis, a byblio[thecis, ab e]pistulis [Imp. Caes. Tra]iani Hadr[i]an[i Aug.].'

[51] p.88.

[52] *Had.* 11, 3.

for the prefect and the *ab epistulis* are the officials most frequently attested as accompanying the emperor on journeys or campaigns.[53]

The chronology of the writing of the long list of Suetonius' scholarly, antiquarian and biographical works, of which nearly all except the *Caesars* is lost, remains entirely obscure. But it is evident that he was known as a scholar long before his rapid rise at the age of about 50 into imperial posts, and it must be concluded that his scholarly reputation was his main recommendation. We can see the antiquarian and the courtier neatly combined in his own report of how he acquired a small bronze statue of the future Augustus as a boy, and presented it to the emperor.[54]

Thus far we can see from the combination of scattered items of evidence the emergence of men of fairly similar types from both the Greek and Latin worlds who passed directly into the service of the emperor. With Philostratus we reach an area of incomparably more coherent evidence, for of the rhetors of the second and early third centuries whose lives he recounts, four became *ab epistulis Graecis*. The earliest is Alexander, the 'Clay-Plato', from Seleucia.[55] Before his appointment his only direct contact with the court was an embassy from Seleucia to Antoninus Pius, with whom he had a famous altercation.[56] For most of his life he seems to have travelled, to Antioch, Rome, Tarsus and Egypt. It was while he was somewhere in the eastern Mediterranean that he received a summons to join Marcus Aurelius as his *ab epistulis* in Pannonia, so in 169/70 to 175.[57] On his way he reached Athens, and took the occasion to deliver an oration on a theme neatly relevant to his destination: 'Recalling the Scythians to their former nomadic life, since they fall ill through living in cities.' A nicely-chosen compliment to the oration delivered in return by Herodes Atticus enabled him to proceed on his way to the frontier enriched by ten pack-animals, ten horses, ten cup-bearers, ten shorthand writers, twenty talents of gold, a mass of silver and two lisping children from the deme Collytus.

The career of Hadrian of Tyre illustrates even more fully the complex of relationships which linked the emperors with the cultivated circles and the intellectual life of the Greek provinces.[58] Hadrian left Tyre at about eighteen, attended the school of Herodes Atticus at Athens and was later appointed to the chair of rhetoric there (opening his first oration with the famous sentence 'Once again letters have come from Phoenicia'). While there he was the object of great popular enthusiasm and lived in considerable ostentation, riding to his lectures in a carriage with silver-mounted bridles. The crowning point of this stage in his career came when Marcus Aurelius visited Athens in 176 to be initiated in the Eleusinian mysteries. He wished to hear Hadrian, whom he had appointed on the basis of his reputation, and gave him as the theme for his oration, 'Hyperides heeds only the argument of Demosthenes, while Philip is at Elatea'. Marcus' response to Hadrian's successful oration

[53] pp. 6, 79, 90–3, 127–8.
[54] *Aug.* 7, 1.
[55] *VS* II, 5.
[56] p. 234.
[57] p. 6.
[58] *VS* II, 10. See now C. P. Jones, 'Two Enemies of Lucian', *GRBS* XIII (1972), 475, on pp. 478f.

provides a classic case of the range of privileges and gifts at imperial disposal—public upkeep (in Athens), precedence at games, immunities,
priesthoods, gold, silver, horses and slaves.

Hadrian was then promoted either by Marcus or Commodus to 'the
higher chair', that of Rome, winning such popularity that even those who
knew no Greek rushed to hear him declaim. It was now, when he was
actually on his deathbed, that Commodus sent him the nomination as *ab
epistulis*, apologizing for not doing so earlier. At this time Hadrian was about
80, and it may be that the nomination was a mere compliment. But that very
fact would show the function of the post of *ab epistulis Graecis* as one of the
chief rewards open to a Greek sophist. So Phrynichus writes, addressing
another *ab epistulis* of a few years earlier, Cornelianus, the dedicatee of his
work on words in Attic Greek: 'You, having the greatest reputation of all for
learning, have for this reason been chosen by the kings, in preference to
other distinguished men, as their *ab epistulis*.'[59]

With Aelius Antipater of Hierapolis in Phrygia,[60] we come to an area
which was central to the Greek renaissance. His grandfather, P. Aelius
Zeuxidemus Cassianus, was an Asiarch, high priest of the provincial council
of Asia. His father, P. Aelius Zeuxidemus Aristus Zeno, was *advocatus fisci*
first in Phrygia, then in all of Asia.[61] As Philostratus says, Hierapolis was one
of the most flourishing cities in Asia, and Zeuxidemus one of its most
distinguished citizens. Antipater studied under Hadrian of Tyre, probably
in Athens, and under Pollux, whom Commodus appointed to the chair in
Athens. It is not clear how or where he gained the reputation which caused
Severus to appoint him *ab epistulis Graecis* and also tutor to his sons
Caracalla and Geta; but Philostratus, who heard him in this period, records
that his audience would acclaim him as 'Teacher of the Gods'. We also see
him through the eyes of Galen, who reports that Severus and Caracalla had
medicines provided for him from the imperial stores; here he is 'Antipater
who had the task of composing their Greek letters, and who was greatly
honoured by them for the weightiness of his character and the perfection of
his skill in rhetoric'.[62] Caracalla himself, writing to Ephesus at some time
before 205, calls him 'my friend and teacher who is entrusted with the
composition [or arrangement?] of the Greek letters'.[63]

Antipater's competitors naturally took a less favourable view. Heraclides
of Lycia broke down in the course of an extempore oration before Severus,
and was said to have been put off, not only by the presence of the guards,[64]
but also by feeling the malice of Antipater, who will have been in atten-

[59] Phrynichus, *Eclogue*, p. 418 Lobeck, CCCXCIII Rutherford. I have slightly paraphrased. The
original is πρώτιστον (?) μὲν ἐν παιδείᾳ μέγιστον ἀξίωμα ἁπάντων ἔχοντα σὲ καὶ διὰ τοῦτο ἐκ
προκρίτων ἀποφανθέντα ὑπὸ τῶν βασιλέων ἐπιστολέα αὐτῶν. For Phrynichus' other remarks
on the office of *ab epistulis*, see p. 227.
[60] *VS* II, 24. See *PIR*² A 137, and Pflaum, *Carrières*, no. 230.
[61] *PIR*² A 281.
[62] Galen XIV Kühn, 218.
[63] *Forschungen in Ephesos* II, 125, no. 26: ὁ φίλος μου καὶ διδάσκαλος κ[αὶ τὴν σύντα?]ξιν τῶν
Ἑλλη[νι]κῶν ἐπιστολῶν ἐπιτετραμμένος. Cf. p. 226.
[64] p. 64.

dance.[65] Hermocrates of Phocaea resisted a plan for him to marry Antipater's unattractive daughter (though his family urged the wealth and prominence of Antipater), and only gave in when Severus summoned him to the east, where Antipater and his daughter were evidently in his entourage.[66]

Antipater composed written works as well as extempore orations, and left Olympic and Panathenaic orations, and a history of Septimius Severus. Unusually, he was awarded senatorial rank and governed Bithynia, being removed for excessive harshness. He was said to have starved himself to death after writing to Caracalla to reproach him for the murder of Geta.

Finally, Aspasius, though born in Ravenna, was also known as a Greek orator, a pupil of Pausanias of Cappadocia, who held the chair in Rome, and of Hippodromus, who taught for a time in Athens. Aspasius himself held the chair in Rome, and was still teaching there when Philostratus concluded his *Lives*, at some date not far from 230.[67] He was also, concurrently or previously, *ab epistulis*, and as such accompanied the emperor to various parts of the earth. He too had a well-known opponent, Philostratus of Lemnos, the nephew of the biographer.[68] What the latter says of aspects of their disagreement is of crucial importance for the conceptions prevailing in the period:

> The epistle composed by Philostratus called *How to Write Letters* is aimed at Aspasius, who on being appointed imperial secretary wrote certain letters in a style more controversial than is suitable; and others he wrote in obscure language, though neither of these qualities is becoming to an emperor. For an emperor when he writes a letter ought not to use rhetorical syllogisms or trains of reasoning, but ought to express only his own will; nor again should he be obscure, since he is the voice of the law, and lucidity is the interpreter of the law.

It will be necessary to return later to the difficult question of the role of these learned and self-confident rhetoricians in the composition of imperial letters.[69] For the moment the mention of the emperor's role as the expositor of the law may lead us to the exponents of that other branch of learning so typical of the second and third centuries. It will be recalled that Marcus Aurelius links precisely these two forms of expertise as entitling a man to be listened to by the emperor.[70]

The conjunction is not misleading in its second-century context, however much it may seem so in the light of the immense achievement, and immense importance in subsequent history, of the writings of the major Roman

---

[65] *VS* II, 26.

[66] II, 25.

[67] See Bowersock, o.c., ch. 1.

[68] On him see *RE* s.v. 'Philostratos' (11). For Aspasius, and Philostratus' comments, *VS* II, 33, Loeb trans.

[69] pp. 226–8. The connection is not confined to the Greek world. Note the inscription from Verona, *ILS* 1453, honouring their fellow-citizen and patronus, C. Calvisius Statianus (*PIR*² c 356; Pflaum, *Carrières*, no. 166) as 'populi advocato, ab epistulis Latinis Augustor(um)'. No other posts are recorded, and the reference to him as *populi advocatus* may suggest that he attracted imperial notice on an embassy or law-suit.

[70] p. 60.

jurists. As a glance at the *Noctes Atticae* of Aulus Gellius will show, there were no clear boundaries in the philosophical, philological, antiquarian, historical and legal learning which characterizes the world of scholars writing in Greek or Latin in the second century. The works of the classical jurists of this period, which were later to be excerpted and collated for the *Digest* of Justinian, were not written as 'law codes' but as private scholarly works.[71] Their authors, as we have seen, occasionally quote classical Greek writers,[72] and were significantly influenced by the didactic and systematizing tendencies of Greek culture.[73] On the other side some of their work has the character of antiquarian or historical scholarship.[74] A notable example of this is the discussion of the origins of the office of *praefectus praetorio* by Aurelius Arcadius Charisius, who was *magister libellorum* (the new form of the title) in the late third or early fourth century.[75]

The persons who in the second and third centuries entered the emperor's service as jurists did so in fact either as *a libellis* or as *consiliarii*, advisers on the *consilium*. The appearance of legally-qualified *a libellis* in particular is a sign of the volume of legal business which came to the emperor, essentially in the form of written requests for legal rulings (*libelli*); the development of this system and the roles of the emperor and his secretaries within it will be discussed later.[76]

The first man whom we know of who began his career directly as an imperial *consiliarius* was M. Aurelius Papirius Dionysius, whom the people of Antium in a dedication to him describe as *iuris peritus*; it is a paradox typical of this period of imperial history that there is every reason to think that he was of Greek origin.[77] His first position, probably under Marcus Aurelius, was that of being taken into the *consilium* at 60,000 *sesterces*; later he returned at 100,000, and after a couple of other posts he was *a libellis* and *a cognitionibus* (in charge of the emperor's court of law). Later he was prefect of the *annona* and prefect of Egypt; but it is evident that the origin and source of his career was his standing as a lawyer.

By the Severan period it is clear that it was regular for *iurisperiti* to be co-opted directly into the *consilium*. Papinian writes: 'Our best and greatest emperors (Severus and Caracalla) have laid down that *iurisperiti* should be excused from *tutelae* which they have begun to undertake, when co-opted

[71] I know of no really illuminating study of the works of the classical jurists considered as scholarly literature of the period. For a good survey see O. Schulz, *Roman Legal Science* (1946), ch. iv.

[72] p. 4.

[73] See F. Wieacker, 'Uber das Verhältniss der römischen Fachjurisprudenz zur griechisch-hellenistischen Theorie', *Iura* xx (1969), 448.

[74] An obvious case is the *Enchiridium* of Pomponius (*Dig.* 1, 2, 2), which is a brief history of Roman law; note also Ulpian, *De officio quaestoris*, quoted in *Dig.* 1, 13.

[75] *Dig.* 1, 11. On the date of his tenure see Jones, *Later Roman Empire*, ch. ii, n. 1; *PLRE* Charisius 2. From his name it is likely that he was of Greek origin.

[76] pp. 240–52.

[77] *PIR*² A 1567; W. Kunkel, *Herkunft und soziale Stellung der römischen Juristen*² (1969), no. 55; Pflaum, *Carrières*. no. 181. His Greek origin is suggested by his name, by a dedication to him at Sagalassus in Pisidia and by an inscription to someone who was 'Latinae linguae facundissimo in causis' put up in Rome by a man who is evidently a relative, M. Aurelius Papirius Socrates. See *CIL* vi 1357 and *PIR*² A 1568.

into the imperial *consilium*, since they are serving at the side of the emperors, and the post awarded to them has no limits of time or space.'[78] Elsewhere he gives a specific case: *tutelae* could only be given up by those abroad on public business or in the immediate service of the emperor, 'as was allowed in the case of the *consiliarius*, Arrius Menander'.[79] Menander was the author of four books *De re militari*; his name also is Greek.[80]

Legal learning was in all probability the source of the position at the emperor's side held by other men for whom no earlier career is positively attested; but as the lawyers, unlike the sophists, had no collective biographer, we can never prove that they did not rise through more junior posts. The *Historia Augusta*, for instance, reports that Marcus Aurelius 'kept beside him his (praetorian) prefects, on whose authority and responsibility he gave judgment. But he also relied on Scaevola, an outstanding jurist.'[81] This is confirmed by a passage in the *Digest*, where Ulpian quotes Scaevola's own report of a judgment by Marcus *in auditorio*.[82] Cervidius Scaevola is not attested as holding any office until 175, when he was *praefectus vigilum*;[83] but his extensive legal works—*Digesta*, *Responsa* and *Quaestiones*—were themselves written later than this.[84] The position is very similar with P. Taruttienus Paternus, who wrote a legal work *De re militari* and is first attested serving as *ab epistulis Latinis* with Marcus in about 171. The *Tabula Banasitana* now shows him among the advisers of Marcus in 177; he was perhaps already praetorian prefect, which he certainly was by 179.[85] In both cases we may suggest, but cannot prove, that legal knowledge brought them directly to the emperor's service.

The evidence is not much clearer, and is in some ways more contentious, when we come to the three great jurists of the Severan period, Papinian, Ulpian and Paul. Aemilius Papinianus[86] is reliably attested in his own report of having persuaded the praetorian prefects of a legal point, evidently as a member of their *consilium*; but his first known post is that of *a libellis* in the early part of Severus' reign.[87] A recent study of verbal similarities between his legal works and the rescripts of this period suggests that he was in office from 194 to 202[88]. His 37 books of *Quaestiones* seem to have been written after 193 and before Caracalla joined his father as Augustus in 198, and his 19 books of *Responsa* during their joint rule (198–211). In the latter part of this period, 205–11, he was praetorian prefect, and as such

---

[78] *Dig.* XXVII, 1, 30 *pr.* Cf. p. 39.

[79] *Dig.* IV, 4, 11, 2.

[80] *PIR*² A 1100. See Kunkel, *Herkunft*, no. 59.

[81] *Marc. Ant.* 11, 10.

[82] XXXVI, 1, 23 *pr.*

[83] *PIR*² C 681.

[84] Schanz-Hosius-Krüger, *Gesch. röm. Lit.*³ III (1922), 199.

[85] See Kunkel, *Herkunft*, no. 54; for the *Tabula Banasitana*, W. Seston, M. Euzennat, *CRAI* 1971, 468, and p. 130 below. It is this which supplies the correct form of his name.

[86] *PIR*² A 388; Kunkel, *Herkunft*, no. 56. For a critical appraisal of the evidence of Aurelius Victor, Eutropius and the *Historia Augusta* relating to these jurists see R. Syme, 'Three Jurists', *Historia-Augusta Colloquium, Bonn 1968/9* (1970), 309.

[87] *Dig.* XXII, 1, 3, 3; *Dig.* XX, 5, 12 *pr.*: 'rescriptum est ab Imperatore libellos agente Papiniano.'

[88] See A. M. Honoré, 'Private Rescripts and their Authors, 193–290 A.D.', to appear in *Aufstieg und Niedergang*, ed. H. Temporini.

accompanied Severus and his sons to Britain in 208–11.[89] It is probably as praetorian prefect that he appears along with Tryphoninus, another legal writer, arguing a point on the *consilium* in the third book of *Decreta* by Paulus.[90] In this case it seems quite clear that he was an established legal expert at least as early as the earliest post reliably attested for him.

Of Domitius Ulpianus[91] we know from his own statement that he came from Tyre—'the most splendid colony of the Tyrians, from which my *origo* is, in a noble setting, of the most remote antiquity, powerful in arms, most loyal to the treaty which it struck with Rome'.[92] We might be listening to the praises of an ancient city as composed by a sophist; and indeed the persons who converse in Athenaeus' *Deipnosophistae* include an Ulpian, a learned sophist from Tyre, who must surely be a relative.[93] What is more, as Ulpian states later in the same passage, the title of *colonia* was conferred by Severus and Caracalla in about 198; the city from which Ulpian had come had been purely Greek.[94]

It appears to be relatively early in Ulpian's career that we find him acting as *assessor* to a praetor in Rome, who receives a rescript from 'our emperor', evidently Severus in 193–8.[95] Late and unreliable sources record that he served as *assessor* to Papinian as *praefectus praetorio*, and was also at some stage *a libellis*.[96] These vague and contradictory reports have no independent weight; but none the less it can be shown that there are correspondences between the style of Ulpian and of the *subscriptiones* of the period 202–9.[97] Ulpian's own works, whose remains occupy more than a third of the *Digest*, seem to have been written between the sole reign of Severus in 193–8 and that of Caracalla (211–17). Thereafter, we can be certain only that he was *praefectus annonae* on 31 March 222, and briefly until his death in 223 a much-honoured *praefectus praetorio* under Severus Alexander.[98]

With the third great jurist of the period, Julius Paulus, no actual post is reliably attested.[99] Instead we have a number of anecdotes of his activities from his own writings. One shows him acting as *advocatus* in a case before the *praetor fideicommissarius* in Rome, which he lost, and subsequently reading the seven books on *fideicommissaria* by Alburnius Valens, a jurist

---

[89] The evidence is best discussed by L. L. Howe, *The Pretorian Prefect from Commodus to Diocletian (A.D. 180–305)* (1942), 71–2.

[90] *Dig.* XLIX, 14, 50.

[91] *PIR²* D 169; Kunkel, *Herkunft*, no. 68; cf. Syme, o.c.

[92] *Dig.* L, 15, 1: 'splendidissima Tyriorum colonia, unde mihi origo est, nobilis regionibus, serie saeculorum antiquissima, armipotens, foederis quod cum Romanis percussit tenacissima.'

[93] References collected in Athenaeus ed. Kaibel III, 564.

[94] See M. Chéhab, 'Tyr à l'époque romaine', *Mél. Univ. St. Joseph* XXXVIII (1962), 11.

[95] *Dig.* IV, 2, 9, 3.

[96] *HA, Pesc. Nig.* 7, 4; *Ant. Hel.* 16, 4; *Sev. Alex.* 26, 5–6; Eutropius VIII, 23; Festus, *Brev.* 22. The details and dates vary considerably. For the unreliability of the reports see Syme, o.c.

[97] See Honoré, o.c. (p. 95).

[98] *CJ* VIII, 37, 4: 'secundum responsum Domitii Ulpiani, Praefecti annonae, iuris consulti, amici mei' (March, 222); IV, 65, 4, 1: 'Domitium Ulpianum, Praefectum Praetorio et parentem meum' (December, 222). For the significance of *P. Oxy.* 2565 in establishing that Ulpian was killed in 223, see J. Modrzejewski, T. Zawadzki, 'La date de la mort d'Ulpien et la Préfecture du Prétoire au début du règne d'Alexandre Sévère', *Rev. Hist. du Droit* XLV (1967), 565.

[99] See Kunkel, *Herkunft*, no. 67; *PIR²* I 453 (over credulous); cf. Syme, o.c.

of a century earlier.[100] Later he recalls giving his opinion as *assessor* in the *auditorium* of Papinian as *praefectus praetorio* (thus confirming a statement given twice in even more than usually unreliable parts of the *Historia Augusta*).[101] Moreover, a series of passages from his writings, composed over the reigns from Severus and Caracalla to Severus Alexander, relate discussions on the imperial *consilium* in which he took part.[102] He is thus highly important for the nature of the discussions between the emperor and his legal advisers. But we do not know even if he was formally called a *consiliarius*; nor is there any confirmation of the statement in the same two passages of the *Historia Augusta*, that he became praetorian prefect under Severus Alexander.[103]

Thereafter the role of identifiable legal writers at the emperor's side ceases,[104] until we come to Aurelius Arcadius Charisius, *magister libellorum* at some time about 300.[105] Their prominence is of course a reflection of two established patterns of imperial activity of primary importance, the giving of judgment and the answering of *libelli*. But the fact that it manifested itself precisely in the second and third centuries is a product of the place of legal studies in the culture of the period. As Gregorius, later called Thaumaturgus, from Neocaesarea in Cappadocia, was to admit, the Roman laws were 'wise, precise, varied and admirable, and, in a word, extremely Greek'; unfortunately they were in Latin, a language 'appropriate to the royal power, but none the less arduous for me'.[106] As we have seen, some men from a Greek background were not similarly deterred. The role which they, like men trained in other disciplines, played at the emperor's side is also an important aspect of the capture of the emperor by the ruling circles of the provincial cities.

Occasional inscriptions allow us to discern this pattern persisting through the third century. For instance a local magnate and office-holder from Sufetula in Africa went directly, after equestrian military posts, to be *ab epistulis Latinis*, perhaps in the reign of Severus Alexander.[107] Almost exactly similarly, M. Aurelius Hermogenes, a *patronus* of Ostia and holder of a priesthood there, went after equestrian military service to be *proc(urator) a studi(i)s Aug(usti) n(ostri)*, first at 60,000 and then at 100,000 *sesterces*, in the middle of the third century. It is interesting to note that he was rewarded

---

[100] *Dig.* XXXII, 78, 6.

[101] *Dig.* XII, 1, 40; cf. *Pesc. Nig.* 7, 4; *Sev. Alex.* 26, 5–6. However the statement of the former passage that he was *a memoria* can be discounted, for its known holders at this period were *liberti*. See p. 82, and Syme, o.c., 314.

[102] *Dig.* IV, 4, 38 *pr.*; XIV, 5, 8; XXXII, 27, 1; XXXVI, 1, 76, 1. See G. Gualandi, *Legislazione imperiale e giurisprudenza* II (1963), 129, n. 25; cf. pp. 238–9, 533.

[103] See Howe, *Pretorian Prefect*, 105–6, and Syme, o.c., 316–17.

[104] Though note that Honoré, o.c., proposes on linguistic grounds to identify the *a libellis* in office in 223–6 as Herennius Modestinus (*PIR*² H 112; Kunkel, *Herkunft*, no. 72). It is noteworthy that he, almost alone of the jurists of this period, wrote a work in Greek, παραίτησις ἐπιτροπῆς καὶ κουρατορίας, addressed to a friend, Egnatius Dexter, see Lenel, *Palingenesia* I, 707f.

[105] p. 94.

[106] Gregorius, *Address to Origen* 1, 7, ed. H. Crouzel, *Grégoire le Thaumaturge, Remerciement à Origène, Sources Chrétiennes* 148 (1969).

[107] *CIL* VIII 11340, see Pflaum, *Carrières*, no. 319. The engraver inscribed 'ab studiis Lat(inis)' and then erased it, clearly having made a mistake for 'ab epistulis Latinis'.

with the immunity from taxation attached to membership of the Museum in Alexandria.[108] It is more striking to find as an imperial *consiliarius* in the late third century, with a salary of 200,000 *sesterces*, a man all of whose other offices belonged to the city life of Ancyra, of which he was also *patronus*, and to the provincial council of Galatia, of which he was high priest. Significantly, Caecilius Hermianus is described as the father and grandfather of senators.[109]

Less surprising, but still significant of the pattern, is the third-century *patronus* of Aquileia who was *a consiliis* and *a studiis* of the emperor, perhaps concurrently, and then *magister sacrarum cognitionum*.[110] He leads up to C. Caelius Saturninus, who had a long equestrian career in the early fourth century, ending by being a *comes* of Constantine, adlected into the senate with the rank of ex-consul, and praetorian prefect, perhaps in Gaul in the 330s. He began, however, as *advocatus fisci* in Italy, and then held seven 'secretarial' posts at court, which are carefully differentiated on his inscription in a way for which no earlier evidence prepares us.[111] But it is also significant that his only visible preparation for these posts was forensic, as *advocatus* for the *fiscus*. For it is precisely in this period that we have the fullest and most explicit evidence for the relevance of rhetorical training to service in the immediate entourage of the emperor, namely in the Gallic panegyrics of the late third and early fourth century.

First we have the anonymous orator who delivered his speech before Constantius, probably on 1 March 297. He had been a teacher of rhetoric, and had then been called to the palace, apparently after catching the attention of Maximian in a speech before him,[112] and had later been allowed to retire. He does not make clear the nature of the post, only referring to it to apologise for his recent lack of practice in rhetoric—'but since the time when from my former career I was brought into the innermost sanctuary of the Palace by the needs of a different, confidential form of discourse . . .';[113] but it certainly involved accompanying the emperor on campaign.[114]

From the following year we have the speech delivered at Autun before the governor of Lugdunensis to celebrate the re-opening by the emperor of the school of rhetoric there (the *scholae Maenianae*). The orator himself, Eumenius, had been appointed to the chair from being *magister memoriae* of Constantius. He too says little of his functions, and also resorts to metaphors drawn from the vocabulary of pagan cults: Constantius had transferred 'my voice which, modest as it is in view of my lack of natural brilliance, had pronounced the celestial words and divine thoughts of the emperor, from the

---

[108] *CIL* xiv 5340, see Pflaum, *Carrières*, no. 352; cf. p. 506.

[109] *OGIS* 549 = *IGR* iii, 179; cf. *PIR*² c 48.

[110] Q . Axilius Urbicus, *ILS* 1459; cf. Pflaum, *Carrières*, no. 340.

[111] *ILS* 1214, 1215. See *PLRE* Saturninus 9. The posts are, in ascending order of seniority, *sexagenarius studiorum adiutor*; *sexagenarius a consiliis sacris*; *ducenarius a consiliis*; *magister libellorum*; *magister studiorum*; *vicarius a consiliis sacris*; *magister censu(u)m*. See J. A. Crook, *Consilium Principis* (1955), 98.

[112] *Pan.* iv (8), 1, 5: 'praesertim cum favente numine tuo ipse ille iam pridem mihi, qui me in lucem primus eduxit, divinarum patris tui aurium aditus evenerit.'

[113] 1, 4.

[114] 2, 1.

recesses of the imperial sanctuary to the private temple of the Muses'.[115] More significant even than his own career is what Eumenius says about the motivation of the emperors in appointing him to the chair of rhetoric:[116]

> Just as if they had to consider whom it would be best to place in command of a squadron of cavalry or a praetorian cohort, so they thought it a matter for their judgment [to appoint a professor of rhetoric], lest those who ought to look forward to advocacy before all the various tribunals, or on occasion to the service of the imperial law-courts, or perhaps to the very imperial secretariats themselves, should, as if caught in a sudden mist amidst the waves of youth, have no reliable chart for attaining eloquence.

Precisely as in the Greek east, the training of which the imperial *officia* were the goal was above all a training in rhetoric.

So we find another orator from Autun, addressing Constantine at Trier in 310, referring to his voice which had been employed both in private life (probably in teaching rhetoric) and in the palace. The connection was a routine one, which needed no elaboration. Furthermore, he concludes by recommending for imperial service both his own five sons and his pupils: 'I commend to you my sons, and especially the one who is already acting as *advocatus fisci* . . . But when I speak of "all my sons", emperor, my ambition is vast. For beside those five whom I have fathered, I count as my own all those whom I have brought up to public advocacy, to service in the Palace.'[117] It now becomes easy to see how an *advocatus fisci per Italiam* could have moved directly to the imperial *consilium*.

It is thus abundantly clear that in this period some at least of the persons who served in the immediate entourage of the emperor came there directly from an established political or intellectual function in their native areas— in virtue of which function they might appear to speak before the emperor, move into his service, and later perhaps return to their original setting. We can dimly discern such a person from the Greek world at around this period in Innocentius, the member of a leading family in Sardis; we know of him only from a brief mention in Eunapius' biography of his grandson, the philosopher Chrysanthius. Innocentius gained wealth and reputation from being 'entrusted with a law-making power by the emperors'; he also wrote books on the Latin language and on (the history of?) Greece.[118]

A man of whom Eunapius tells us more is Sopater, a philosopher from Syria who was a pupil of Iamblichus. 'Because of his lofty nature and greatness of soul . . . [he] would not condescend to associate with ordinary men, and went in haste to the imperial court, hoping to dominate and convert by his arguments the purpose and headlong policy of Constantine. And he attained to such wisdom and power that the emperor was captivated by him and publicly made him his assessor, giving him a seat at his right

[115] *Pan.* v (9), 6, 2.

[116] 5, 4; cf. p. 503.

[117] *Pan.* VII (6), 23, 1–2.

[118] Eunapius, *VS* 500; cf. *PLRE* Innocentius 1. The language is of some obscurity—ὅς γε νομοθετικὴν εἶχε δύναμιν παρὰ τῶν τότε βασιλευόντων ἐπιτετραμμένος. καὶ βιβλία γε αὐτοῦ διασώζεται, τὰ μὲν εἰς τὴν Ῥωμαίων γλῶσσαν, τὰ δὲ εἰς τὴν Ἑλλάδα φέροντα.

hand, a thing incredible to hear and see.' This naturally excited jealousy, and other persons at court persuaded Constantine that Sopater had used his magical powers to 'fetter the winds' and delay the corn-ships due for Constantinople. So Sopater was executed.[119]

Sopater was a pagan, which did not prevent his rise at the court of Constantine, though it may have contributed to his fall.[120] A pagan who survived the vicissitudes of court life in this period was Hermogenes, whose career is retailed with remarkable obscurity in the oration which Himerius delivered before him later when he was proconsul of Achaea. After a passing reference to the literary and philosophical education of Hermogenes (who came from Pontus),[121] Himerius passes to the functions which he performed while still young at the court of an emperor who is probably Licinius:

> Established in the imperial court in early youth, he earned such trust that he alone was considered a worthy guardian of the secrets. On the one hand he advised the 'gods' [the emperors] concerning them, while on the other he conveyed the divine pronouncements to whoever had sent for them. He was the interpreter of the laws and the best customs, always trying to mollify the mind of the ruler, as they say Pythagoras the Samian did when he was with Phalaris in Sicily.

How Hermogenes is said to have influenced the tyrant is of some interest: 'by retailing ancient myths and examples from poetry and history; for he was already, before his study of philosophy, a man of great learning.'[122]

Hermogenes then left the court (on the fall of Licinius?) and betook himself to a long course of study in philosophy, astronomy and geography, and travelled round seeing the world. Finally he added a political education, 'acquiring rhetorical skill in Greek and Latin, as two guards and aids, so to speak, for this course of life'. Thus armed, he went to Constantinople, and was welcomed into his service by the emperor, apparently Constantine. Once there, he exercised, so Himerius says, the decisive influence at court:[123]

> What humane laws were not issued through him? What men in danger did not escape through him? What men worthy of honours did not gain them through him? What men with petitions to make did not resort to him? He stood between the emperor and those he ruled, conveying to him the requests of his subjects and to them the commands of the emperor.

Amid the grandiloquence of the language we still do not know what the post actually was—possibly that of *quaestor sacri Palati*, which according to

---

[119] Eunapius, *VS* 462, Loeb trans.

[120] Eunapius, loc. cit., and Zosimus II, 40, 3, record that the Praetorian Prefect, Ablabius (who was a Christian) was responsible for his fall. The Suda, Σ 845, states directly that he was killed because he was a pagan.

[121] See *RE* s.v. 'Hermogenes' (16); O. Seeck, *Die Briefe des Libanius* (1906) s.v. 'Hermogenes' IV.

[122] Himerius, *Or.* XIV, 18. The use of vocabulary drawn from pagan cults, already familiar from several examples (pp. 73, 79, 98), has misled some commentators into thinking that Hermogenes actually was some sort of religious adviser. So Seeck, loc. cit.; A. Alföldi, *The Conversion of Constantine and Pagan Rome* (1948), 57, 99; *PLRE* Hermogenes 9.

[123] 28–30.

Zosimus was created by Constantine.[124] What is more important is that Himerius, in spite of—or even in virtue of—the floridity and rotundity of his style, catches the essence of so many features of the imperial court; and above all the relevance of the traditional literary education of the Graeco-Roman world to the personal service of the emperor.

6. *The Imperial Secretaries: Men Promoted from an Equestrian Career*

No clear or definite barrier separates the intellectuals of various types who moved directly into the emperor's immediate service, and the men who arrived there after some recognizable career in posts of equestrian status. In the first place we may happen to be ignorant of posts which the intellectuals discussed above had in fact held, or of intellectual qualifications which the office-holders possessed. It is more important to stress that all *equites* had to have property worth at least 400,000 *sesterces*, which we may assume, though cannot prove, was normally in land; Pliny the Elder, for instance, twice refers to the effects of an earthquake in 68 on the fields and olive-groves near Teate belonging to Vettius Marcellus, a procurator under Nero.[1] Moreover, an inscription from Teate records the construction of a building there at their own expense by Marcellus and his wife.[2] This is a very small and slight example of the essential fact that if we are to see these men in the right perspective we must consider them first, exactly as with the intellectuals, in their local context. Indeed in the vast majority of cases our knowledge of their careers in equestrian posts comes from inscriptions set up in their home towns; inscriptions which would not have been set up unless they had played some role there, as *patroni* or benefactors, or as the holders of local offices or priesthoods. When, for instance, we come across the same Vettius Marcellus on inscriptions from Thrace and Thasos as procurator of Thrace under Claudius or Nero, we *may* be seeing what is in reality a relatively brief episode in the life of an Italian landowner.[3]

This will not be so in all cases, for our evidence includes cases of long successions of posts which must represent the best part of an adult lifetime spent in different parts of the empire. But even here the evidence of inscriptions will not tell us what qualities gained a man his posts or in what spirit they were held. If we may believe Seneca, his friend Lucilius owed his equestrian career to 'the vigour of his mind, the elegance of his writing, and the fame and nobility of his friends'.[4] After he had toured the island as procurator of Sicily, Seneca asks him for information on Scylla and Charybdis, requests him to climb Mt. Etna to examine the volcano, and expects that he will be composing a poem on it.[5] Similarly, items of evidence

---

[124] Zosimus v, 32. See Jones, *Later Roman Empire*, ch. xii, n. 3.

[1] Pliny, *NH* II, 85/199; XVII, 38/245.

[2] *ILS* 1377.

[3] *SEG* XVI 415 (Paradisos, Thrace); C. Dunant, J. Pouilloux, *Recherches sur l'histoire et les cultes de Thasos* II (1958), nos. 182–3.

[4] Seneca, *Ep.* 19, 3.

[5] *Ep.* 79. Cf. Pflaum, *Carrières*, no. 30, and *PIR*² L 388.

collected in various provinces during an equestrian career—Germany, Spain and Africa at least—were used by Pliny the Elder in his *Natural History*.[6] Nor did even the longest and most distinguished of careers necessarily cause a man to lose contact with his home town and its interests. The classic case is C. Minicius Italus from Aquilea, who was *quattuorvir iure dicundo* there before entering on equestrian military posts and a long career culminating in the prefectures of the *annona* and of Egypt, which he held in 101–3. We know the details solely from the inscription in which in 105 the town council of Aquileia recorded its decision to erect a bronze statue of him; the occasion was that at his request Trajan had ruled that *incolae* (inhabitants of the city who were not citizens of it) should be liable to local obligations (*munera*) along with the citizens.[7]

Thus all the persons with whom we are concerned here were property-owners of some standing, who may be presumed to have had the usual literary education of the Graeco-Roman upper classes. Their normal 'career' consisted of three military posts, followed by procuratorial positions in Italy, or more often in the provinces, and in some cases by 'secretarial' posts with the emperor, or (like Minicius Italus) by one or more major prefectures.[8]

An equestrian 'career', in some ways analogous to the senatorial *cursus*, evolved only gradually in the course of the first century. None the less, and even taking into account the erratic nature of our evidence, it remains surprising that we cannot find a single *eques* promoted from regular pro-curatorial posts into a secretarial position proper until we come to the reign of Trajan or Hadrian. A man who is in all probability T. Haterius Nepos, prefect of Egypt from 119 to 124, is honoured on an inscription from Fulginiae in Umbria, which shows that after military posts he was *censitor*, procurator of the province of Armenia Minor (which existed only in 114–17), and then of the *ludus magnus* in Rome (a training-school for gladiators), simultaneously procurator of the *hereditates* and *a censibus*, and then *a libellis* before becoming prefect. If the identification is correct, his tenure cannot have been very long.[9]

We can discern only a little more about a contemporary, Valerius Eudaemon. He began with the ill-attested post of *procurator ad dioecesin* in Alexandria, became (like his other contemporaries, Suetonius and Julius Vestinus)[10] procurator of the Greek and Latin libraries in Rome, and was then *ab epistulis Graecis*. For reasons which cannot be guessed, he moved on to a series of procuratorial posts in Asia Minor and Syria before being prefect of Egypt in 142.[11] He must therefore be classified as an office-holder in the equestrian career. But his posts before being *ab epistulis* are minimal, and do not serve to distinguish him fully from a Suetonius or a Claudius Balbillus.[12] There is no specific evidence that he was a literary man; but he

[6] See R. Syme, 'Pliny the Procurator', *HSCPh* LXXIII (1969), 201.
[7] *ILS* 1374; cf. Pflaum, *Carrières*, no. 59.
[8] On the equestrian 'career' see further, pp. 284–90.
[9] See Pflaum, *Carrières*, no. 95; *PIR*[2] H 29.
[10] See pp. 88, 90–1.
[11] See Pflaum, *Carrières*, no. 110.
[12] pp. 86–7, 90–1.

could well be the Eudaemon whom Marcus Aurelius mentions, along with
an unknown Demetrius and Charax (the historian and senator from
Pergamum) as brilliant men who have passed away.[13]

A marginal case in a quite different sense is L. Domitius Rogatus, who
was *ab epistulis* of Hadrian's intended successor, L. Aelius Caesar, in
Pannonia in 136–7. Aelius was adopted by Hadrian while governing the two
Pannonias, and Domitius Rogatus' previous post was that of prefect of an
ala stationed in Pannonia Superior. A secretarial staff was clearly needed, for
even our fragmentary evidence includes several inscriptions from Greek
cities which sent embassies to Aelius Caesar at this time.[14] Rogatus continued afterwards to an unremarkable procuratorial career.[15]

When Aelius Caesar died in 138 and Hadrian adopted the future
Antoninus Pius, the latter's *a libellis* was L. Volusius Maecianus, who was
both a career *eques* and a jurisconsult.[16] The *Historia Augusta* asserts that he
instructed the young Marcus Aurelius in law, and was one of the *iurisperiti*
consulted by Antoninus Pius.[17] Better evidence is the fact that Aurelius and
Verus refer to his opinion in a rescript: 'Volusius Maecianus, our *amicus*,
was led, over and above his long-established and well-grounded knowledge of
the law, by the reverence due to our rescript, to affirm in our presence that
he did not think it was correct to give a different response.'[18] Maecianus was
the author of sixteen books on *fideicommissa*, written under Antoninus Pius,
and a work on the Rhodian Sea Law in Greek. He also composed a book on
the multifarious means of division of the small coin called an *as*, probably
addressed to Marcus Aurelius: 'I have often noticed, Caesar, that you were
embarrassed by not knowing the subdivisions of the *as*, which are essential
in the establishment of heirs and many other matters . . .'[19]

Maecianus could thus be considered simply as one of the learned jurists of
the period. But it is to the fact that he was *patronus* of Ostia that we owe our
knowledge that he also had an equestrian career. Inscriptions from there
show that after being *praefectus fabrum* and prefect of a cohort he was
adiutor (assistant) of public works and then *a libellis* of Antoninus Pius in
138. Once again the previous 'career' is minimal, and it can be assumed that
he was already known as a lawyer. However, he went on to be *praefectus
vehiculorum* before returning to be concurrently *a studiis* and procurator of
libraries, and then *a libellis* and *a censibus* of Antoninus Pius. He was subsequently prefect of the *annona* and in 160/1 prefect of Egypt. In the next
reign, when we meet him advising Aurelius and Verus, he was adlected to
the senate and held the suffect consulate. We cannot doubt that it was his
reputation as a jurist which determined the pattern of his career.

A man who may have been somewhat similar is Sextus Caecilius Crescens

---

[13] *Med.* VIII, 25. The passage opens with the deaths of various members of the imperial family
and household in the period of Hadrian and Antoninus Pius.

[14] p. 415.

[15] *ILS* 1450; cf. Pflaum, *Carrières*, no. 140.

[16] Pflaum, *Carrières*, no. 141; Kunkel, *Herkunft*, no. 42.

[17] *HA, Marc. Ant.* 3, 6; *Ant. Pius* 12, 1.

[18] *Dig.* XXXVII, 14, 17 *pr.* See further p. 249.

[19] F. Hultsch, *Metrologiorum Scriptorum Reliquiae* IV (1866), 61. Cf. Schanz-Hosius, *Gesch.
röm. Lit.*³ III (1922), 191–2.

Volusianus, who also began as *praefectus fabrum*, but was then *advocatus fisci* in Rome, held one procuratorship and was then *ab epistulis* first of Antoninus Pius and subsequently of Aurelius and Verus. Again, we know the details of his posts because he was *patronus* of Thuburbo Minus in Africa, where his inscription was found; he was probably a native of the place.[20] His part as *advocatus fisci* shows that he had practised in the courts, which is more certainly evidence of rhetorical than of legal training. It is quite probable, but not certain, that he was the brother of Sextus Caecilius Africanus, who was a well-known jurist towards the middle of the second century.[21]

Even if that connection cannot be proved, Caecilius Volusianus can still be seen as an educated provincial making his way, with an ease characteristic of second-century Rome, through a minimal 'career' to the side of the emperor. Indeed what is not so easy to attest is cases of men who did go through any substantial career before occupying one of the secretarial positions proper. One case is Julius Celsus from Amiternum in the Sabine country, where he owned a house. One inscription of his career comes from there and one from Lugdunum, evidently put up while he was procurator of Lugdunensis and Aquitania and immediately before he returned to Rome as *a libellis* and *a censibus*. He was clearly in favour, for the same inscription records that his son had been adlected by Antoninus Pius to the senate at the age of four. But, unlike most of the men we have discussed before, he had earned his favour by a succession of six posts, in Gaul, Egypt and Rome, before his major procuratorship in Lugdunensis. A very mutilated inscription from Portugal seems to indicate that he too was later adlected into the senate.[22]

Julius Celsus, however, does not seem to have served in any equestrian military posts, and of all the 'secretaries' of this period the only one who can be shown to have gone through the full range of military and civilian posts which made up the equestrian 'career' is T. Varius Clemens from Celeia in Noricum.[23] A long succession of military posts was followed by a series of provincial procuratorships, including the governorship of Mauretania in the early 150s, and culminating in the procuratorship of Belgica and the two Germanies. From there he became *ab epistulis* of the *Augusti*, evidently Marcus Aurelius and Verus. Whether this represents the appointment of a military man with conscious reference to the outbreak of the Parthian war in 161,[24] is a matter of speculation. But it may be accepted that the comparison of his background with that of other *ab epistulis* is very striking.

As regards both those 'secretaries' who had and those who had not passed through something resembling a career, we can see a loose nexus linking posts at the libraries in Rome, and those of *a libellis*, *a censibus*, *a studiis*, and *ab epistulis*. Apart from the post of *a censibus*, on whose functions we have absolutely no evidence, it is clear that the concerns of the others were essentially verbal, whether they related to the giving of advice or the preparation of various forms of imperial pronouncement, oral or written. It is of course that which accounts in part for the predominance of literary men in these positions.

A quite different picture emerges if we consider the post of *a rationibus*. With one possible exception, no literary men or jurists are attested, and instead we have a substantial series of men with full military and civilian equestrian careers. Some even rose from below the equestrian order, from the rank of senior centurion;[25] and, for reasons which remain obscure, many held procuratorships in Gaul immediately before being *a rationibus*.[26] Moreover, there is very little interconnection between the two groups; almost the only instance is Ti. Claudius Vibianus Tertullus, known from inscriptions at Ephesus and Pergamum, who was *ab epistulis Graecis* in about 173–5 and *a rationibus* some time in 177–80 before being *praefectus vigilum*; nothing is known of his background or earlier career if any.[27] This pattern is very close to that of T. Aius Sanctus, who was *ab epistulis Graecis* a little earlier, and was subsequently procurator of the *ratio privata*,[28] and then *a rationibus*, before being prefect of Egypt, probably in 179/80; under Commodus he was adlected to the senate. As a man whose earliest attested post is that of *ab epistulis Graecis*, he could well be identical with the Ateus (or Attius) Sanctus whom the *Historia Augusta* records as the teacher in rhetoric of Commodus.[29]

The explanation for the generally different background of the *a rationibus* and the degree of separation between them and the secretaries proper may well be that the post was not one which involved attendance on the emperor in the same way as theirs did. It is not necessarily indicative that the *Historia Augusta* gives only *ab epistulis* and *a libellis* as the posts to which Hadrian appointed *equites*.[30] But there is much more significance in the advice which Cassius Dio puts into the mouth of Maecenas addressing Augustus, and which certainly relates to the early third century:[31]

Moreover as regards legal cases, letters and decrees of the cities, petitions of individuals and whatever else concerns the administration of the empire, you should have helpers and assistants from the *equites*.

[25] On this distinctive form of career see A. von Domaszewski, *Die Rangordnung des romischen Heeres*, ed. B. Dobson (1967), xxixf., 112f. The cases are Cn. Pompeius Homullus Aelius Gracilis Cassianus Longinus (Pflaum, *Carrières*, no. 89); Ti. Claudius Secundinus L. Statius Macedo (109); and M. Bassaeus Rufus (162).

[26] For the list see Pflaum, *Carrières*, 1019.

[27] *ILS* 1344 (Ephesus); see Pflaum, *Carrières*, no. 252, and for the best account, Chr. Habicht, *Alt. von Pergamon VIII.3: die Inschriften des Asklepieions* (1969), no. 28. Note also the [. . .]ilius who appears from a fragmentary inscription from Rome (*ILS* 1452) to have been at various times *ab epistulis Latinis, procurator summarum rationum* and *ab epistulis [Graecis?]*; cf. Pflaum, *Carrières*, no. 178. Also M. Aurelius Julianus, *a rationibus et a memoria* (Pflaum, *Carrières*, no. 354) apparently in the third century.

[28] See App. 3.

[29] See L. Moretti, 'Due iscrizioni latine inedite di Roma', *Riv. di filol.* xxxviii (1960), 68; *AE* 1961 280. Cf. Pflaum, *Carrières*, no. 178 *bis* (pp. 1002–7).

[30] *Had.* 22, 8.

[31] LII, 33, 5. On the speech of Maecenas see F. Millar, *A Study of Cassius Dio* (1964), 102–18. The precise date for the composition of the speech suggested there is not certain.

It is these functions which Dio envisages as being performed by the emperor personally. His assumptions are indeed very close to those of Constantine a century later—'those who have served in our *scrinia*, that is those of the *memoria*, the *epistulae* and the *libelli*'.[32]

Individual items of evidence tend to support the view that the *a rationibus* did not work closely with the emperor. After the Julio–Claudian period none is attested as attending the emperor in person, or travelling with him.[33] Nor does any appear as the adviser of the emperor; the sole exception is in the letter of Commodus to Athens in 186 in which Julius Candidus, 'my friend and in charge of the *rationes*', is listed along with Cleander and others, apparently as a member of the *consilium*.[34] The acutely confusing terminology relating to financial officials from the later second century onwards makes all certainty impossible; but it is at least clear that persons concerned with *rationes* or finance operated independently of the emperor and at a distance from him.[35] We have no clear example of any of them exercising an influence on imperial decisions.[36]

Our evidence about imperial secretaries from the late second century onwards is very slight and scattered. There is a small concentration of evidence only in relation to the post of *a cognitionibus*, whose first known equestrian holder was M. Aurelius Papirius Dionysius under Commodus.[37] It is clear that this was a post whose holder personally attended the emperor, and accompanied him on his journeys. We find one with Severus in Asia Minor in 202, and with Caracalla in both Rome and Gaul or Germany;[38]

[32] *CTh* VI, 35, 1 = *CJ* XII, 28, 1: 'illis qui in scriniis nostris, id est memoriae epistularum libellorumque, versati sunt.'

[33] It is noticeable that Statius attests the *ab epistulis* Abascantus travelling with the emperor (p. 79), but not the father of Claudius Etruscus, as *a rationibus* (p. 74).

[34] *AE* 1952 6, ll. 18–19: Ἰουλίος Κάνδιδ[ος ὁ φίλος μου καὶ ἐπὶ τ]ὴν τῶν καθόλου λόγω[ν] προστασίαν ἐπ[ιτετραμμένος ..]. For references and discussion see F. Grosso, *La lotta politica al tempo di Commodo* (1964), 217–21.

[35] A few examples will suffice. In *CIL* IX 2438 = *FIRA*² I, no. 61, the *a rationibus* receives and sends letters on his own account, as do the *rationales* in *ILS* 5920. Marcus Aurelius writes from Pannonia to a καθολικός (*rationalis*) in Rome, Galen XIV, 4 Kühn. Severus and Caracalla (*CJ* IX, 8, 6, 4), Severus Alexander (X, 5, 1) and Diocletian and Maximian (X, 10, 1) send *litterae* to *rationales*. An imperial edict of the early fourth century refers to consequential instructions being issued to 'our prefects, the *rationalis*, the *magister privatae* and the provincial governors', *FIRA*² I, no. 94. When Gallienus concludes his letter, or *subscriptio*, on church property addressed to some Egyptian bishops (see p. 571 below), Αὐρήλιος Κυρίνιος, ὁ τοῦ μεγίστου πράγματος προστατεύων, τὸν διατυπόν τὸν ὑπ' ἐμοῦ δοθέντα διαφυλάξει (Eusebius., *HE* VII, 13), this may be either 'the' *rationalis* or the *rationalis* of Egypt. Cf. P. J. Parsons, 'Philippus Arabs and Egypt', *JRS* LVII (1967), 134, esp. 138–9.

[36] Dionysius of Alexandria *ap.* Eusebius, *HE* VII, 10, 5, implies that Macrianus, πρότερον μὲν ἐπὶ τῶν καθόλου λόγων λεγόμενος εἶναι βασιλέως had a role in instigating the persecution under Valerian. But he may have been *rationalis* in Egypt, see *PIR*² F 549 and cf. Parsons, o.c. But Pflaum, *Carrières*, no. 350, would translate *a rationibus Augusti*. Eusebius, *HE* IX, 11, 4, implies that Peucetius, τῶν καθόλου λόγων ἔπαρχος (*praefectus summae rei*?), had been influential in the persecution under Maximin in 312/13.

[37] p. 94. The existence of such a post, presumably then held by a freedman, is implied by Seneca, *Apoc.* 15, 2, cf. p. 77. For freedmen connected with the post, note *CIL* VI 8634 = *ILS* 1697; VI 8628; 8630–1; *ILS* 1680; *AE* 1935 20: 'Aurelio, Augg. lib. Alexandro v.e. praep(osito) sacr(arum) cogn(itionum)'.

[38] Dio LXXV, 15, 5 (354); Philostratus, *VS* II, 30; 32. Cf. Hirschfeld, *Verwaltungsbeamten*², 331, n. 2. Note also *ILS* 1681: 'Delicatus Augg. adiut. a cognitionib. dominicis, obiit in expeditione Germanica' (213?).

while Cledonius, the *a cognitionibus* of Valerian, was with him when he was captured by Shapur.[39] Those *a cognitionibus* from the Severan period of whom we know something, seem to have had normal equestrian careers.[40] For contrast, we have a brief and hostile biographical sketch by Cassius Dio of Marcius Agrippa, an *advocatus fisci* of low birth exiled by Severus, recalled by Caracalla, who made him *a cognitionibus* and *ab epistulis*, and later adlected him to the senate.[41] Almost the same cumulation of offices appears in the fragmentary inscription from Ephesus of someone who was *a cognitionibus* and *ab epistulis Latinis* of Macrinus during his brief reign, entirely passed in Syria, in 217/18.[42]

Through the rest of the third century we have no significant information on the careers of men who gained positions in the emperor's immediate service. In the tetrarchic period we can see a few developments, in the first place the emergence of the *memoria*, previously held by freedmen,[43] as a post open to free men from outside the *familia*; a clear example is Eumenius, the orator from Autun.[44] Another is presumably the Sicorius Probus who was sent by Diocletian and Galerius in 298 to lead an embassy to Narses the king of Persia; the narrative shows him making a speech before Narses and then negotiating with him.[45] In the same period we see the first uses of the term *magister* for the chief imperial secretaries; its earliest appearances in documents are *magister cognitionum* in the inscription of Q. Axilius Urbicus, and *magister libellorum, studiorum* and *censu(u)m* in that of C. Caelius Saturninus.[46] But *sacrae memoriae magister* and also the general term *ipsa Palatii magisteria* are used in the oration of Eumenius spoken in 298.[47]

By the 320s this development had culminated in the appointment of a single *magister officiorum*. Pronouncements of Constantine from December 320, when he was in Serdica, and from 323, mention two men, Heraclianus and Proculeianus, each described as *tribunus et magister officiorum*.[48] Contemporaneously, Licinius had a *magister officiorum*, Martinianus, whom he eventually made emperor with himself.[49] According to Joannes Lydus, Constantine subsequently had as his *magister* one Palladius, who had previously acted as ambassador to Persia.[50] Nothing more is known of the background of any of these men.

In the same period we first find as imperial secretaries men described as *notarii*. The term is attested earlier for a shorthand writer in private

[39] Petrus Patricius, *FHG* IV, p. 193; Cassius Dio ed. Boissevain III, p. 742, Fr. 159.

[40] E.g. (probably) P. Aelius Peregrinus Rogatus (Pflaum, *Carrières*, no. 233) and certainly L. Cominius Vipsanius Salutaris (235), and L. Didius Marinus (295).

[41] Dio LXXVIII, 13, 2–4 (416–17).

[42] *JÖAI* XLV (1960), Beibl. 95, no. 24 = *AE* 1966 431: ἐπίτρο[π]ον καὶ ἐπὶ διαγνώσεων [καὶ] τῶν Ῥωμαικῶν [ἐπ]ιστολῶν.

[43] p. 82.

[44] p. 98.

[45] Petrus Patricius, Fr. 14, *FHG* IV, 189. His office is given as ἀντιγραφεὺς τῆς μνήμης.

[46] p. 98.

[47] pp. 98–9.

[48] *CTh* XVI, 10, 1; XI, 9, 1.

[49] Literary sources record him as 'Caesar' only: *Epit. de Caes.* 41, 6; Zosimus II, 25, 2; *PLRE* Martinianus 2. On coins he appears as 'Augustus', P. Bruun, *RIC* VII, 25.

[50] *De mag.* II, 25.

employment, who took down matter dictated by his master,[51] and it is in precisely this role that a *notarius* first appears in an imperial context. Lactantius describes Licinius calling a *notarius* and dictating to him a monotheist prayer for use by his soldiers in the battle of Tzirallum in 313.[52] The relatively humble nature of the function itself, combined with the scorn expressed by Libanius for the cultural level of later *notarii*, has tended to give a misleading impression of their real social status.[53] In fact it is likely that they came from the same educated bourgeoisie which supplied the other officials of the court. The earliest *notarius* whom we know by name, Auxentius, whom we find serving at the court of Licinius in Nicomedia,[54] had a brother, Theodore, who had been educated in Athens, and who was later bishop of Tarsus; he himself became bishop of Mopsuestia. It is therefore not surprising that in the latter part of Constantine's reign *notarii* began their important later role as personal emissaries of the emperor.[55] It was a notarius named Marianus who came to Tyre in 335 to summon the synod of bishops there to Jerusalem for the dedication of the Church of the Holy Sepulchre; during the celebrations he entertained the bishops to sumptuous dinners and made distributions to the poor in the name of the emperor.[56]

Their relatively high status is reflected a couple of decades later in the title *tribunus et notarius*. But the title in itself, with its military overtones, raises a problem which is already suggested by the Suda's narrative about Auxentius. His position is described as 'military service' (*strateia*) and when he is allowed to leave it he 'looses his belt' and quits the palace. In what sense was the imperial court by this time a military institution? The question is a real one, for we have seen already that the emperor was invariably accompanied by a military escort, and we know that the *officia* of the praetorian prefects and of provincial governors were essentially staffed by soldiers.[57] It is by no means impossible *a priori* that the soldiers who escorted the emperor could have come to perform a significant part of the clerical functions which he required; and it has indeed been suggested that the *princeps praetorii* was the head of the *officium* of the emperor himself.[58]

But there is in fact no evidence that soldiers played such a role in the service of the emperor. On the contrary the evidence for the 'militarization' of the court in the first part of the fourth century shows precisely that the

[51] Most clearly in Pliny, *Ep.* IX, 36, 2: 'notarium voco et . . . quae formaveram dicto.' Cf. ibid., III, 5, 15; Quintilian, *Inst.* VII, 2, 24; Jerome, *De vir. ill.* 53; 61 (*notarii* of Cyprian and Origen).

[52] Lactantius, *De mort. pers.* 46, 5.

[53] See Jones, *Later Roman Empire*, 572. Cf. M. K. Hopkins, 'Eunuchs in Politics in the Later Roman Empire', *PCPhS* n.s. IX (1963), 62, on p. 75.

[54] Suda s.v. Αὐξέντιος. Cf. p. 52.

[55] See Jones, loc. cit.

[56] Eusebius, *VC* IV, 43–5. His name and title do not appear here but in the chapter-heading (44) at the beginning of the book—περὶ τῆς διὰ Μαριανοῦ τοῦ νοταρίου δεξιώσεως αὐτῶν. The name and title (βασιλικὸς ταχυγράφος) are also in Sozomenus, *HE* II, 26, 1. Cf. p. 603.

[57] See A. H. M. Jones, 'The Roman Civil Service (Clerical and Sub-Clerical Grades)', *JRS* XXXIX (1949), 38 = *Studies in Roman Government and Law* (1960), 151. Cf. A. von Domaszewski, *Die Rangordnung des römischen Heeres*², ed. B. Dobson (1967), and now the inscription in honour of M. Gavius Bassus, *praefectus orae Ponticae maritimae*, by his military staff—two *stratores*, three *cornicularii*, two *optiones* and a *tesserarius*, D. Knibbe, *JÖAI* XLIX (1968–71), Beiblatt, 15, no. 2.

[58] See Domaszewski, o.c., 101; M. Durry, *Les cohortes prétoriennes* (1938), 127–8.

staff were civilians, who received as a privilege certain rights which had previously been restricted to soldiers.[59] Moreover these privileges represent only a part of a series of privileges granted to the *Palatini* by Constantine, all of which show them against the same social background; for they are designed to protect them from burdens which normally fell on the rich men of the cities. So in October 314 Constantine wrote from Trier a letter to the *Palatini* laying down that they—both those who had performed duties in his service and those who had served in his *scrinia*, that is the *memoria*, the *epistulae* and the *libelli*—should be free of all 'calumnies' and *nominationes* (to local office); that this privilege should extend to their sons and grandsons; and that they should be free of all *munera* (burdens) *sordida et personalia*, along with their movable property and household slaves.[60] The context is that of the obligations imposed by the cities of the Roman empire on their richer citizens.[61] The letter thus reflects precisely the pattern which it has been suggested was typical, that the men who worked in the emperor's immediate service came from the upper classes of the cities and normally returned to their cities after their service. Thus Constantine wrote subsequently to the proconsul of Africa to say that even if former *memoriales* or *Palatini* were raised to any responsibility or office, they should at least be free from the duty of providing horses (for the *cursus publicus*);[62] the context is again the same.

Then a complex document, issued perhaps by Constantius II, and preserved in variant forms by the *Codex Theodosianus* and *Codex Justinianus*,[63] lays down the privileges of those who have retired from the *cubicula* (apparently not freedmen?), from Palatine duties, from the *scrinia* of the *memoria*, *libelli* and *epistulae* and other posts. All these, and their sons and grandsons were, among other things, to be exempt from membership of *curiae* (town councils) and from city offices or obligations. Moreover, the version preserved in the *Codex Theodosianus* adds that neither their sons nor slaves acquired as part of their *castrense peculium*—a soldier's property which as a specific privilege was exempt from the normal rule of *patria potestas*— should be included in local census lists, and thus seems to indicate at least that the *Palatini* and others were considered as if they were soldiers. How this convention arose, we do not know.[64] It is not in fact explicitly affirmed until a letter of Constantine to the prefect of Rome, dating probably to 326.[65] The very fact that the document justifies the right of *castrense peculium* on the part of the *Palatini* by setting out how they shared the toils of the camp shows quite clearly that the *Palatini* were civilians. But its significance goes far beyond that; for perhaps no surviving document

[59] See Jones, *Studies*, 164–5.
[60] *CTh* VI, 35, 1 = *CJ* XII, 28, 1. The essence of these provisions is repeated in *CTh* VI, 35, 4, addressed to the *Vicarius Italiae* in 321, and VI, 35, 5, to the *Palatini* again, in 328.
[61] For the terms see e.g. Rostovtzeff, *SEHRE*², 714, n. 18.
[62] *CTh* VI, 35, 2.
[63] *CTh* VI, 35, 3; *CJ* XII, 28, 2 (XII, 1, 3); see *PLRE* Rufinus 25.
[64] We may however note that Papinian a century earlier had laid down (*Dig.* XXIX, 1, 43) that a *filius familias*, 'equestri militia exornatus et in comitatu principum retentus . . . confestim testamentum de castrensi facere potest.'
[65] *CTh* VI, 36, 1; *CJ* XII, 30, 1.

reflects so many aspects of the conditions of work of those in the immediate service of the emperor, or expresses in such unambiguous terms the scholastic nature of their occupations:

> If any of the *Palatini*, who are already endowed with distinct privileges under our edict, have during their service in our *palatium* acquired anything either by their own savings or by our gift, we order that they should have it as *castrense peculium*. For what is so germane to the camp (*castra*) as what is gained with our knowledge and in our sight? But nor are they strangers to the dust and toil of the camp who follow our standards, who are constantly in attendance in our business, and who are distracted by lengthy journeys and arduous expeditions as they bend their minds to their learned studies.

7. *Friends and Advisers*

If we may believe Diogenes Laertius, the instability of life as the friend of a monarch had already been observed by Solon:[1]

> He used to say that those who had influence with tyrants were like the pebbles employed in calculations; for as each of the pebbles represented now a large and now a small number, so the tyrants would treat each one of those about them at one time as great and famous, at another as of no account.

The same image is applied by Polybius in commenting on the sudden rejection by Philip V of his adviser Apelles in 218.[2] Such reversals of fortune clearly became a commonplace, which is reflected in Christian writing in Hippolytus' *Commentary on Daniel*:[3]

> Many men who have gained honour and gifts from a king and been placed in positions of power and dignity have later found that these very facts brought them into danger, either when they were revealed as conspirators, or were destroyed by others because they were friends of the king. What gain to them was a king's friendship?

Yet because the emperor was in fact accompanied everywhere by some of his friends, appeared with them in public, received embassies with them, and had them as his advisers in giving judgment, their prominent role could not fail to have an effect on the imagination of his subjects. So Dionysius, bishop of Alexandria, writing in the 250s to Fabius, bishop of Antioch, speaks of 'these holy martyrs from among us who are now the assessors of Christ, participants in his kingship, sharers of his judgment and giving justice along with him'.[4]

---

[1] *Vit. Phil.* I, 59.

[2] v, 26, 12–13; cf. Walbank, ad. loc.

[3] III, 6, 5–6.

[4] Eusebius, *HE* VI, 42, 5. The vocabulary is in part precisely that used in Greek sources of the court of an emperor or governor—οἱ νῦν τοῦ Χριστοῦ πάρεδροι καὶ τῆς βασιλείας αὐτοῦ κοινωνοὶ καὶ μέτοχοι τῆς κρίσεως αὐτοῦ καὶ συνδικάζοντες αὐτῷ. The reference is not in fact to deceased martyrs, but to those who had survived, and arrogated to themselves a special place in the church.

These passages reflect certain important aspects of the position of the *amici* of the Roman emperors. The term has no precise or definable connotation; *amicitia*, as used in senatorial circles in the late republic, could refer to a wide variety of relationships, from political alliance to ordinary private friendship.[5] When one member of these circles emerged as an emperor the relationship retained much of its indefinite quality; but, as we shall see, the term *amicus* could appear in official letters of the emperor, and the emperor could also formally and abruptly terminate his friendship. There is nothing, however, to show that it could always have been clearly stated whether a man was an *amicus* of the emperor or not; as Ovid wrote, who, if known to the Caesars, does not pretend to be their friend?[6] Nor is it entirely clear whether Augustus or later emperors followed the custom which Seneca says was first instituted in Rome by Gaius Gracchus and Livius Drusus, in imitation of the (Hellenistic) kings, of dividing their *amici* into three categories; first those admitted into private audience, then those admitted with a larger, but still restricted, number, and finally those let in without distinction.[7] Seneca does, however, say elsewhere that Augustus enrolled his whole *cohors primae admissionis* from the ranks of his adversaries.[8] The expression would not necessarily indicate a formal division of his *amici* into categories. To support the possibility of such a division, we have one inscription, known only from sixteenth-century copies, of an *eques* under Augustus or Tiberius who was *ex prima admissione*;[9] and another of a senator who had the *salutatio secunda* of Antoninus Pius.[10]

How definite or persistent these distinctions were therefore remains uncertain. Claudius, however, did introduce a rigid distinction by issuing to favoured persons gold rings with his portrait on them, which allowed *admissio* at will; the custom is said to have given much scope for accusations (presumably of forgery), and was abolished by Vespasian.[11] Alternatively, the expression *cohors amicorum* which appears in a number of first-century contexts[12] might recall the *syntagma*, or unit, of friends which had appeared in procession with Antiochus Epiphanes in 166 BC.[13] There is indeed one quite close parallel to that, when Gaius was accompanied as he drove across his bridge of boats from Baiae to Puteoli by a column of praetorians, and his *cohors amicorum* in chariots.[14]

More important is the fact that 'friendship' with the emperor involved a complex of undefined relationships, with privileges and dangers which were

[5] So P. A. Brunt, ' "Amicitia" in the Late Republic', *PCPhS* XI (1965), 1 = R. Seager (ed.), *The Crisis of the Roman Republic* (1969), 199. For what follows, see also J. A. Crook, *Consilium Principis* (1955), ch. iii.

[6] *Ep. ex Ponto* I, 7, 21.

[7] *De ben.* VI, 34, 1–2. For the 'friends', 'first friends' and 'honoured friends' of the Seleucids see E. Bikerman, *Institutions des Séleucides* (1938), 40–2.

[8] *De clem.* I, 10, 1.

[9] *ILS* 1320.

[10] *ILS* 1078.

[11] Pliny, *NH* XXXIII, 12/41.

[12] E.g. Suetonius, *Nero* 5, 1; *Galba* 7, 1; Tacitus, *Ann.* VI, 9, 2.

[13] Bikerman, o.c., 40.

[14] Suetonius, *Cal.* 19.

both essentially dependent on the character or passing whim of the emperor himself. In the early period we can still see some traces of the pattern of mutual obligations which characterized *amicitia* in Roman society. So, for instance, Tarius, when judging his son under the rights of *patria potestas*, was able to call Augustus to his *consilium*; the emperor came to his house because, as Seneca says, if the case had been held in his house it would have been his *cognitio* not Tarius'.[15]

On rare occasions Augustus would also make an appearance to support his friends in court.[16] The performance of mutual social duties (*officia*), which Augustus kept up until his old age,[17] became subsequently a matter of condescension, and was limited to relatively trivial gestures such as visiting *amici* when they were ill.[18] But Augustus himself was particularly insistent that his *amici* should leave him something in their wills; in this case as in others, something which was a feature of the mutual obligations of Roman society was to become a one-sided imposition which pressed particularly hard on the *amici*, but also extended to wider areas of society.[19] The extent to which the customary forms of social exchange themselves became double-edged obligations is illustrated by the example of invitations to dinner by the emperor. As praetor in 39, Vespasian formally thanked Gaius in the senate for an invitation to dinner;[20] but on the other hand Marcus Aurelius includes among the things which he had learnt from Antoninus Pius to allow his friends not to dine with him, and not to compel them to accompany him on journeys.[21] If he intended to reduce the pressure on the *amici*, he hardly succeeded; for we have the best of witnesses, Galen, to the fact that in his time they all wore their hair short in imitation of him, while those of Lucius Verus had theirs long.[22]

As always, however, our most detailed evidence for the pressures of court life comes from Epictetus.[23] In depicting the insecurity and humiliation of the life of an imperial *amicus* he could clearly draw on long-established common-places concerning the friends of kings. But what he says is much more concrete and specific than that. In the beginning of the fourth book of the *Dissertations* he returns repeatedly to the situation of an *amicus* of the emperor. Using the metaphor of a traveller fearing attack by robbers, he represents a man saying to himself, 'What shall I do? I shall become a

---

[15] *De clem.* I, 15, 3.

[16] Suetonius, *Aug.* 56; Dio LIV, 30, 4.

[17] Suetonius, *Aug.* 53: 'officia cum multis mutuo exercuit, nec prius dies cuiusque solemnes frequentare desiit, quam grandior iam natu et in turba quondam sponsaliorum die vexatus.' On the *officia* of Tiberius to his friends see Dio LVII, 11, 7.

[18] This particular gesture is quite often mentioned; see Dio, loc. cit. (along with other *officia* by Tiberius); Suetonius, *Claud.* 35, 1; Eutropius, *Brev.* 8, 4; Dio LXIX, 7, 4; LXXI, 35, 4 (278). Cf. *HA, Had.* 9, 7; 23, 4.

[19] Suetonius, *Aug.* 66, 4; cf. pp. 153–8.

[20] Suetonius, *Vesp.* 2, 3.

[21] *Med.* I, 16, 2.

[22] Galen XVII. 2, 150 Kühn. Compare his remark, XIV, 24 Kühn, that during Aurelius' lifetime all the richest Romans took the *thêriakê* prepared for him, but ceased to do so after his death— θαυμαστὸν γὰρ ὅπως οἱ πλούσιοι τὰ τῶν αὐτοκρατόρων ζηλοῦσιν, ἢ βούλονταί γε φαίνεσθαι ζηλοῦντες.

[23] p. 78.

friend of Caesar. While I am his companion, no one will injure me. But before I can become famous, how much must I suffer and endure, how often must I be robbed by how many! And if I do become his friend, he too is mortal.' A little earlier he has discussed the delusions of a man who believes that misfortune consists in not being a friend of Caesar, and constructs an imaginary dialogue in refutation, making a friend of Caesar his witness:[24]

'You do not know what I suffer. I hardly get to sleep before one person or another comes to say that he (Caesar) is already awake, is already coming forth. Then there is uproar and anxiety.' 'Come, when did you dine more pleasantly, now or previously?' Listen to what he says about this. That if he is not invited, he is mortified; if he is, he dines like a slave with his master, constantly avoiding some *faux pas* in word or deed. And what do you think he fears? A beating, like a slave? How could he hope for such good treatment? As befits a man of such standing, a friend of Caesar, he fears to lose his head.

For the emperor's displeasure to result in the death of one of his *amici* he did not need actually to execute him. Plutarch records the story of a friend of Augustus in his old age, whose imprudent remark on the question of the succession was reported to the emperor. When the man attended the emperor, as he was accustomed, in the morning,[25] his greeting was returned with 'Farewell'. He returned home and committed suicide.[26] His very prominence exposed any friend of an emperor to rumour and accusation. Not all emperors would react as Trajan did when rumour assailed his friend Licinius Sura; going to Sura's house, he had his eyes anointed by Sura's doctor and was shaved by his barber.[27]

That the gesture was sufficient in itself, both at the time and as retailed by Dio a century later, is an adequate illustration of the latent fear and suspicion which underlay the relations of an emperor with his *amici*. It was always a sign of exceptional trust if he visited anyone without his military escort.[28] But, short of an actual assassination, the power was all on the emperor's side, and his friendship could be renounced at his whim at any moment.[29]

This acute instability of their position has to be recalled while we consider the influence exerted by individual friends, or even more their collective role as advisers, in court and elsewhere. None of the men who advised the emperor had a secure base from which to do so, and none represented even in an informal way, any sectional interest which he would fear to offend. In spite of this, however, it was of course the case that the emperor's friends, while in favour, could secure benefits for themselves and their protégés and do corresponding damage to their enemies. So, in a passage which is remarkably indicative of the values of Roman society, Epictetus says to a senator

[24] IV, 1, 95; 45–8.
[25] pp. 209–10
[26] Plutarch, *Mor.* 508A–B. The identity of the man is not certain; Plutarch calls him Φούλβιος, but Tacitus, *Ann.* I, 5, tells a similar story, more briefly, of Fabius Maximus, and is not certain that he died by his own hand; see *PIR*² F 47.
[27] Dio LXVIII, 15, 3²–16, 1ᵃ. On Sura see now C. P. Jones, 'Sura and Senecio', *JRS* LX (1970), 98.
[28] On the escort see pp. 61–6, and for visits without them Dio LVII, 11, 7 (Tiberius); Tacitus, *Ann.* XV, 52, 1 (Nero); Dio LXVIII, 7, 3 (Trajan).
[29] See R. S. Rogers, 'The Emperor's Displeasure—*amicitiam renuntiare*', *TAPhA* XC (1959), 224.

who visits him, 'What could anyone imagine you to want? You are rich, you have children, a wife and many slaves; Caesar knows you, you have many friends in Rome, you can perform your duties and know how to return kindness with kindness and injury with injury.'[30] The effects of the influence of Caesar's friends could be felt in distant provinces. Dio of Prusa openly advises his fellow-citizens to have regard for him because of his familiarity with the emperor, and his friendship with many other powerful Romans.[31] In Egypt in 213 a man who is apparently *epistratêgus Heptanomiae* writes to the *stratêgoi* of Arsinoe: 'No one is unaware that [. . .] lius Titanianus, *vir egregius*, is highly honoured by our Lord the unconquered Emperor Antoninus. So I advise you to behave with circumspection towards his relatives . . .'[32] The same forces were felt in Rome; Pliny the Younger records the trepidation he felt as a young man in taking a case against 'the most powerful men in the state and even friends of Caesar'.[33]

An influence whether real or merely presumed by others, on the part of his intimates, was an inevitable corollary of the emergence of a monarch. Even Cicero, who disapproved violently of Julius Caesar's associates, had none the less congratulated himself on several occasions for being in favour with them.[34] Nepos emphasizes that while Atticus could have increased his possessions by the favour (*gratia*) of Antony, he made no use of it except to intercede for friends who were in danger or difficulty.[35] The influence of an *amicus* could sometimes be advertised openly, as when Otho brought an ex-consul into the senate to express his gratitude for his restoration after being condemned for peculation, even before actually interceding for the man with Nero.[36] More often it was exerted in a whole range of smaller ways, privately and as part of the normal functions of government. This comes out perhaps most clearly in the earlier correspondence of Pliny with Trajan; Pliny was certainly an *amicus* of the emperor, but equally certainly not an intimate friend in our sense. So the substance of his communications to Trajan should not be untypical of that of reasonably well-placed senators as a whole.

Indeed Pliny had earlier been the subject of a petition to Trajan by a full intimate of the emperor, Julius Servianus, who had gained the *ius trium liberorum* for him.[37] But thereafter we see him, for instance, asking for adlection to the senate for his friend Voconius Romanus; for Roman citizenship for his doctor, who was the freedman of an Egyptian woman of non-citizen status, and also full citizen rights for the freedman of a woman named Antonia Maximilla; and then for the relations of another doctor who

---

[30] *Diss.* II, 14, 18.

[31] *Or.* XLVII, 22.

[32] *P. Gen.* I. In spite of his *nomen* ending apparently in '. . lius' the man is probably Valerius Titanianus, who four years later was *Praefectus Vigilum*. See J. F. Gilliam, 'Valerius Titanianus', *Mnem.* XVII (1964), 293, and *Mélanges Seston* (1974), 217. *AE* 1966 474 (Side) now shows that he had been *ab epistulis Graecis* under Caracalla.

[33] *Ep.* I, 18, 3.

[34] e.g. *Ad fam.* IX, 6; 16; VI, 8, 1 shows him interceding with Balbus and Oppius on behalf of Aulus Caecina.

[35] *V. Att.* 12, 2.

[36] Suetonius, *Otho* 2, 2.

[37] *Ep.* X, 2. On L. Julius Ursus Servianus see R. Syme, *Tacitus* (1958), esp. App. 7; *PIR*² I 631.

had attended him.[38] The letters provide an exceptionally clear example of how benefits spread down from any point of contact with the emperor.

Finally Pliny asks for a vacant praetorship to be given to a senator named Accius Sura, and beseeches him for appointment for himself to one of the priestly colleges in Rome, as an *augur* or *septemvir*; as another letter shows, he was in fact granted the augurate by Trajan.[39]

Some fairly similar recommendations and requests, although not on his own behalf, appear in the correspondence of Fronto, who was an intimate friend of Marcus Aurelius, and an *amicus*, but not quite so close a one, of Antoninus Pius and Lucius Verus. To Verus indeed he writes in rather elaborate terms to acknowledge the personal marks of favour which the emperor had shown him, and which had aroused the jealousy of others, such as greeting him with a kiss, supporting him when he felt unwell and conversing with him freely and at length; as Fronto says, the minutest features of the emperor's conduct to those about them were scrutinized with all the care devoted to omens.[40] To Antoninus Pius Fronto recommends Aridelus, who in fact was an imperial freedman, for a procuratorship,[41] and the historian Appian for (it seems) the title of 'procurator' without either the duties or the salary.[42] To Verus he recommends Gavius Clarus, an impoverished senator, who had already received one subvention from Antoninus Pius, and evidently needed another.[43]

Such were some of the types of benefit which the status of *amicus* of the emperor might allow a man to confer. The status itself is quite frequently advertised by the emperors in their letters, when they refer to provincial governors or other officials involved. This may often be no more than a courtesy to the person referred to, but may in certain cases be intended precisely to demonstrate the emperor's confidence and lend the man authority in dealing with the matter in hand.[44] Occasionally letters of emperors addressed to private individuals and containing expressions of personal friendship were preserved on inscriptions. Indeed the one Caracalla wrote to Aurelius Julianus of Philadelphia, which ended with the greeting 'Be well, Julianus, most honoured and loved by us', had previously been read out in the theatre there.[45]

---

[38] Pliny, *Ep.* X, 4; 5–7, and 10; 11. Only summary details are given here, as specimens of the types of request made and influence exerted. For a full discussion see Sherwin-White, ad. loc., and pp. 279, 483, 487.

[39] X, 12; 13, and IV, 8. See further pp. 306 (praetorship), 278.

[40] *Ad Verum imp.* II, 8.

[41] *Ad M. Caes.* V, 52.

[42] Fronto, *Ad Ant. Pium* 9; see pp. 286–7.

[43] Fronto, *Ad Verum imp.* II, 7; see p. 299.

[44] For examples from imperial letters, *Syll.*³ 780, Augustus to Cnidus, referring to Asinius Gallus, τῶι ἐμῶι φίλωι (see p. 443); 801D = *Fouilles de Delphes* III. 4 (1970), no. 286, Claudius to Delphi, referring to Junius Gallio; *FIRA*² I, no. 72; *AE* 1962 288; *P. Oxy.* 3022 (Trajan to Alexandria in 98, referring to Pompeius Planta, τῷ φίλῳ μου καὶ ἐπάρχῳ); *IGR* IV 1399 = *Syll.*³ 851; *IGBulg.* 659; *AE* 1969/70 599; *Frag. Vat.* 271, 41; Eusebius, *VC* III, 31, 2; III, 52, 2: πρὸς Ἀκάκιον τὸν διασημότατον κόμητα καὶ φίλον ἡμέτερον. There are two examples in the new dossier from Aphrodisias (see p. xiii), Trajan to Smyrna, referring to Julius Balbus, his friend and proconsul of Asia, and Commodus to Aphrodisias, referring to Ulpius Marcellus.

[45] *IGR* IV 1619b = *Syll.*³ 883; cf. *CIL* III 412 = *IGR* IV 1404, Valerian and Gallienus to Julius Apellas of Smyrna, and pp. 469–72 below.

That a man was a 'friend of Caesar', was likely to be a publicly known and significant fact about him. Thus an *eques* is honoured by his son, Crepereius Fronto, at Attalea in Pamphylia as 'friend and procurator of the Augusti',[46] while Eusebius can record of Astyrius, who dared to give burial to a Christian martyr in Palestine in about 260, that he was 'a Roman senator, a friend of the emperors, and known to all for his noble birth and wealth'.[47] In the case of a governor the fact might even on occasion be used to bring pressure on him. We find Epictetus reproving a procurator of Epirus for his unrestrained conduct in the theatre; if the people, he says, see their governor, the *amicus* and procurator of the emperor, showing his feelings so crudely, they will follow suit.[48] We may contrast with this the scene in the Gospel of St. John— whose Passion-narrative has more claims to historicity than some have supposed—where the crowd shouts to Pilate, 'If you release him you are no friend of Caesar!'[49] If a friend of Caesar fell, the pleasure for his enemies was all the greater—as we see for instance in Eusebius' account of the sudden trial and execution by Maximin of Urbanus, the *praeses* of Palestine, 'the dearest companion and table-fellow of the tyrant'.[50]

The role of *amicus* of the emperor thus on the one hand conferred a real public honour and privilege, and the ability to distribute benefits to others, and on the other was acutely unstable, and exposed a man to pressures and suspicions both from the emperor himself, and from other persons at court and from society at large. As for the persons who counted as *amici*, it is not necessary to consider them individually, as with the *liberti* and *equites* who held secretarial posts. The evidence is readily accessible,[51] and we can take it that at any one time the *amici* constituted a roughly identifiable group drawn from the senatorial and equestrian orders. It is more important to look at their role at the side of the emperor: first at the function of the term *comes*, literally, as we have seen, 'travelling-companion', which develops markedly at the end of the period, and then at those items of evidence—now rapidly increasing—which show the *amici* as a group advising the emperor, or sitting with him in receiving embassies or giving judgment.

The term *amicus* hardly appears on inscriptions other than those of imperial letters and is not used as a formal public designation; no doubt there were dangers in claiming publicly a status which the emperor could revoke so easily; it is only on the part of a few notables from Greek cities that we find a comparable expression, *sebastognôstos*, 'known to the

[46] *IGR* III 777; see Pflaum, *Carrières*, no. 147, and cf. B. Levick and S. Jameson, 'C. Crepereius Gallus and his *Gens*', *JRS* LIV (1964), 98.

[47] Eusebius, *HE* VII, 16. That the scene was Palestine is not directly stated but is made probable by the context in chs. 15–18.

[48] *Diss.* III, 4, 2. For a possible identification of the procurator see *JRS* LV (1965), 147.

[49] Jn. 19, 12. It is one of the few weaknesses of the book by P. Winter, *On the Trial of Jesus*[2] (1974), that he assumes (esp. 129–30) that this scene must be unhistorical. For arguments relating to the historicity of John's narrative see C. H. Dodd, *Historical Tradition in the Fourth Gospel* (1963), 82f., and J. B. Segal, *The Hebrew Passover* (1963), 34–7.

[50] *Mart. Pal.* 7, 7.

[51] For a prosopographical survey see J. A. Crook, *Consilium Principis* (1955), passim in chs. iv–vii, and esp. 148–90. See also R. Syme, 'Some Friends of the Caesars', *AJPh* LXXVII (1956), 264.

emperor'.[52] By contrast, *comes* is quite frequently used on the inscriptions of men of senatorial and equestrian rank, for it could be, and originally was, a reference to a specific journey or expedition in the past, during which a man was in the emperor's entourage; so for instance L. Fabius Cilo is described on one inscription as '*comes* of Imperator Caesar L. Septimius Severus Pertinax Augustus on the eastern expedition'.[53] Though the evidence is in itself very slight, it *may* be significant that *comes* is not linked to any specific expedition on any inscriptions of later than the beginning of the third century. For in the first half of the fourth century it became a rank or title, which could be bestowed as an honour or used of an actual emissary, not a 'companion', of the emperor; and also it came to be used along with the name of an area or function in the genitive (*comes Orientis*, *comes sacrarum largitiarum*) to designate various posts. We cannot discern the sequence in which these developments occurred, but all are first attested in the reign of Constantine. Legal evidence reveals a whole series of *comites* of particular areas in office from as early as 316 onwards.[54] Legal evidence apart, the Constantinian period reveals only the resplendent figure of Q. Flavius Maesius Egnatius Lollianus, whom a number of inscriptions name as *comes Orientis* in the 330s; it was after this that Julius Firmicus Maternus dedicated to him his work on astrology entitled *Mathesis*—'the severe and revered judgments of our lord and emperor Constantinus Augustus had entrusted to you the reins of the whole Orient'.[55]

Various inscriptions also name him as being previously to this *comes Flavialis* (Flavius being the *nomen* of Constantine) or '*comes* within the *Palatium*', a striking example of how quickly *comes* had lost its original sense. Equally significant is that he is described as having become subsequently *comes primi ordinis*, '*comes* of the first rank'. This is one case where the origin and motivation of a change is explicitly stated; for Eusebius, in listing the immense range of *beneficia* distributed by Constantine, concludes by saying that of the *comites* some gained the first rank, some the second and some the third, while the perfectissimate and many other honours were shared by large numbers. For the emperor thought up different honours in order to reward more men.[56]

Inscriptions confirm the division of *comites* into different ranks. L. Aradius Valerius Proculus, for instance, was *comes* of the second rank, then of the first and later '*comes* again of the first rank within the Palace' before

[52] p. 472.

[53] *AE* 1926 79. For a list of occurrences of *comes* on inscriptions of the first three centuries see H.-G. Pflaum, *Bayerische Vorgeschichtesblätter* XXVII (1962), 90–1. Add now *AE* 1964 223 (L. Caesonius Ovinius Manlius Rufinianus Bassus, *comes Augg.* in the late third century). For inscriptions of senatorial *comites* of Constantine see *ILS* 1213; 1216–18.

[54] *CTh* IX, 1, 1 = *CJ* III, 24, 1; *CTh* XII, 1, 4, Octavianus, *comes Hispaniarum*, 316–17; *CTh* XII, 5, 1, Tiberianus, *comes per Afric(am)*, 325 or 326, *PLRE* Tiberianus 4; *CTh* XI, 3, 2, Acacius, *comes Macedoniae*, 327; *CTh* II, 26, 1 = *CJ* III, 39, 3, Tertullianus, *v.p. comes dioceseos Asianae*, 330; *CJ* VI, 1, 6, Tiberianus, *comes Hispaniarum*, 322 (the same man as above); probably *CJ* XI, 68, 2, Januarius, *comes Orientis* under Constantine, see *PLRE* Ianuarius 2. General references in *CTh* I, 16, 6 = *CJ* I, 40, 3, and *CTh* XI, 30, 16, both 331.

[55] *Math.* I, *pr.* 7. For the full evidence see *PLRE* Lollianus 5. Malalas 319 Bonn also records a *comes Orientis* named Felicianus at Antioch in 335. His evidence is not necessarily reliable.

[56] *VC* IV, 1, 2.

being *praefectus urbi* in 337.[57] But the new functions of the *comitiva* as a rank granted by the emperor, and the benefits which it conferred on the recipient, are best illustrated in the career of Joseph of Tiberias. He was a prominent member of the Jewish community, in close relations with the patriarchal dynasty, who converted to Christianity in the reign of Constantine. Presenting himself to the emperor, he retailed his sufferings at the hands of the Jews, and was rewarded with the rank of *comes* and the right to ask for whatever he wished. So he requested and obtained the right to build churches in the main Jewish centres, Tiberias, Diocaesarea, Sepphoris, Nazareth and Capernaum. He returned home armed with his title of *comes*, letters from the emperor and an income granted by him. Later it was only his status as *comes* which protected him from persecution by the Arian bishop of Scythopolis.[58]

In Constantine's reign *comites* played a role as emissaries of the emperor in the central issues in the history of the church. When a complex set of disputes disturbed the church of Antioch towards 330, Constantine sent two *comites* to reconcile the parties and report to him.[59] One of them, Acacius, had earlier been instructed by Constantine to eradicate the pagan cults found at Mambre.[60] The other, Strategius, is more fully known from a paragraph in Ammianus relating to his appointment as Praetorian Prefect of the Orient in 354: he was famous for his eloquence in both languages and had been selected by Constantine to assist him in enquiring into various religious sects, such as the Manichees; his command of this subject earned him the nick-name 'Musonianus' from the emperor (after the first-century Stoic, Musonius Rufus), and a distinguished career.[61]

At the council of Tyre in 335 another *comes*, Flavius Dionysius, actually presided. He appears most clearly in a passage of the *Autobiography* of Libanius relating to 341: on his arrival 'there was in Constantinople a Sicilian named Dionysius who was great and influential because of his successes in the courts, his reputation in office, his ready hospitality and his ability to bring to heel any who fell foul of him'.[62]

The brief glimpses which our sources afford us of these educated provincials of Constantine's time, whose learning or rhetorical skill brought them into the confidence and favour of the emperor, may remind us of the very similar qualities typical of the 'secretaries' throughout the period. But they also recall the striking analysis which Tacitus makes in the *Dialogus* of the position of Eprius Marcellus and Vibius Crispus as *amici* of Vespasian; they were both Italians of undistinguished birth, who owed to their oratorical powers their immense wealth, their success in the courts, and their

[57] See A. Chastagnol, *Les fastes de la Préfecture de Rome au Bas-Empire* (1962), 96–102; *PLRE* Proculus 11. Cf. M. Maecius Memmius Furius Baburius Caecilianus Placidus, *comes ordinis primi*, and then *comes Orientis, Aegypti et Mesopotamiae*, both soon after 337, see *PLRE* Placidus 2.

[58] Epiphanius, *Panarion* 30, 4–12, esp. 4–5, 11–12.

[59] Eusebius, *VC* III, 59, 3; 62, 1. See p. 600.

[60] III, 53, 2, from Constantine's letter to the bishops of Palestine. It is possible that in both these contexts Acacius' role is that of *comes Orientis* rather than an immediate imperial emissary.

[61] XV, 13, 1–2. See *PLRE* Musonianus.

[62] *Or.* I, 36 trans. Norman (1965). For the full evidence see *PLRE* Dionysius 11; for the council of Tyre, pp. 603–5.

leading position and relative independence among the emperor's friends; for while all the others owed everything to the friendship of the emperor, they brought to it something, their eloquence, which he could not confer.[63] The role of *comites* as provincial officials and as imperial emissaries is only an extension of that of the *amici* at the emperor's side; and the gradual predominance of the term *comes* for an imperial adviser is yet another reflection of the peripatetic nature of the court in the third and early fourth centuries. The distinction is no more than that, and the two expressions appear together in the words of the orator who addressed Constantine at Trier in 312: 'So now when in this city . . . the whole *comitatus* of your *amici* is at your side, and when men from almost every city are here, either on public embassies or as supplicants on their own behalf . . .'[64]

In the eyes of the subject the essential role of the *amici* was to be visibly present with the emperor in receiving delegations or petitions or, above all, in giving judgment. This is set out explicitly by Philo in laying down how Gaius ought to have conducted himself, and did not, in hearing the rival Jewish and Greek embassies from Alexandria in 40:[65]

> For the duties of a judge were as follows: to sit with assessors chosen on their merits . . . to let the opposing parties stand on either side of him; to listen first to the accusation and then to the defence for the allotted time; and finally to retire and discuss with his assessors what would be the fairest judgment to pronounce.[65]

All through the empire we find in literary evidence accounts in varying degrees of detail of the emperor consulting his *amici* in private, in Rome or in the provinces, on all matters up to the conduct of major wars.[66] The majority do not contribute much to the various problems, which will be discussed later,[67] relating to how decisions in the immediate entourage of the emperor were actually made. We are, however, inevitably better informed about the composition and function of the emperor's *consilium* of friends when we turn to those public or semi-public sessions which are recounted in literary sources, or referred to in imperial letters, or of which the protocols survive in legal sources, and now increasingly on papyri. Here as in so many other respects what we can know is what the subjects of the emperor saw.

An anecdote in Suetonius shows that Augustus, at least on occasion,

[63] *Dial.* 8. See *PIR*[1] V 379; *PIR*[2] E 84.
[64] *Pan.* VIII(5), 2, 1.
[65] Philo, *Leg.* 44/350, trans. Smallwood. The passage is rightly emphasized by W. Kunkel, 'Die Funktion des Konsiliums in der magistratischen Strafjustiz und im Kaisergericht II', *ZSS* LXXXV (1968), 253 on p. 255 = *Kleine Schriften* (1974), 180. It does, however, tend to refute his objection to Crook, *Consilium Principis*, stated ibid., 253, n. 1 = *Kl. Schr.* 179, that it does not distinguish between the political and the judicial functions of the *amici*; precisely such a fusion of roles is visible in the context and vocabulary of this passage, see further pp. 235–6.
[66] For example, Philo, *Leg.* 4/26; Dio LXIII, 26, 4 (91); Tacitus, *Hist.* II, 31–3; Juvenal, *Sat.* IV, 72–149 (the satire on a discussion in the *consilium* of Domitian); Macrobius, *Sat.* I, 23, 14 (Trajan on the Parthian campaign); Dio LXIX, 20; Herodian I, 4, 1–7, cf. *HA, Marc. Ant.* 28, 4–6; Lactantius, *De mort. pers.* 11, 4–6 (Diocletian); 25, 2 (Galerius); *Pan.* IX(12), 2, 4; Eusebius, *VC* I, 30 (Constantine); II, 5 (Licinius).
[67] ch. v passim.

would give judgment in Rome in public seated on a tribunal with his *consilium*, and surrounded by a crowd of bystanders.[68] Similarly, when a number of parties and delegations arrived to dispute the future of Judaea after the death of Herod in 4 BC, Augustus 'summoned a *consilium* of Roman office-holders and *amici*' in the temple of Apollo on the Palatine, or rather in its *area*, as a large crowd of Jews from Rome was present.[69] It was only a slightly less public matter when in AD 13, as a papyrus records, 'Augustus took his seat in the temple of Apollo, in the Roman library', to hear an embassy from Alexandria. His *assessores* were Tiberius and his son Drusus, Valerius Messalinus Corvinus, an ex-consul, and apparently about five other men, probably senators. If the list, which is fragmentary, originally included all the members of the *consilium*, it is surprisingly short.[70]

Tiberius, according to Dio, gave judgment from a tribunal in the Forum, scrupulously consulting his *assessores*, who were granted complete freedom to express their opinions; his son Drusus gave his opinion on an equal footing with the others, and there were even occasions when the advisers prevailed against Tiberius' original view. Claudius also, Dio says, gave judgment from a tribunal, sometimes in the Forum and sometimes elsewhere, and renewed the consultation of advisers which had lapsed since Tiberius retired to Capri.[71] From his reign, either at the beginning or near the end, we have papyri of the type now classified as *Acta Alexandrinorum*, which describe a dispute between an Alexandrian embassy and King Agrippa of Judaea (I or II) before the emperor.[72] Claudius takes his seat in some *horti* in Rome whose name is lost,[73] assisted by twenty senatorial *assessores* and also sixteen consulars, and some Roman matrons.

When in July 82 Domitian heard a case over disputed land between embassies from two Italian communities, Falerii and Firmum, he did so in his Alban residence,[74] 'with distinguished men from both orders (senate and *equites*) called as assessors'.[75] Although there can be no doubt that individual *equites* sat with the emperor previously, the conjunction of the two orders in this way is significant; and all the more so because almost precisely the same phrase now appears, in Greek, in a papyrus containing a decision by Antoninus Pius.[76]

[68] *Aug.* 93: 'namque Athenis initiatus, cum postea Romae pro tribunali de privilegio sacerdotum Atticae Cereris cognosceret et quaedam secretiora proponerentur, dimisso consilio et corona circumstantium solus audiit disceptantes.' Cf. also Dio LV, 7, 2.

[69] Josephus, *BJ* II, 6, 1 (81); *Ant.* XVII, 11, 1 (301). See pp. 19–20, 230, 376.

[70] *P. Oxy.* 2435 verso.

[71] Dio LVII, 7, 2–5; LX, 4, 3.

[72] Musurillo, *Acts of the Pagan Martyrs*, no. iv (arguing for AD 53); Tcherikover and Fuks, *Corp. Pap. Jud.*, no. 156 (arguing for 41). The question of the authenticity, or fictional character, of these narratives is not crucial here, because we are concerned with the vision of the emperor and his advisers as the subjects saw it. But it should be noted that we have now more papyri (e.g. *P. Oxy.* 3019; 3020) of hearings before the emperor, which are clearly documentary, and that there is abundant evidence that scenes comparable to those in the *Acta* did occur before emperors; a good example is Philostratus, *VS* II, 30.

[73] p. 23.

[74] p. 26.

[75] *CIL* IX 5420 = *FIRA*² I, no. 75: 'adhibitis utriusque ordinis splendidis viris.'

[76] J. David Thomas, 'An Imperial *Constitutio* on Papyrus', *Bull. Inst. Class. Stud.* XIX (1972), 103. The phrase, evidently translated from Latin, as the use of the dative as an ablative absolute

A rather different formula appears in another new papyrus which contains the protocol of the reception of an Egyptian embassy by Septimius Severus in Alexandria on 9 March 200: 'Caesar, having taken his seat in the *dikastêrion* with his *amici* and those called to the *consilium*, gave orders to call in ambassadors who were bringing the common requests of the Egyptians.'[77] We may note that here, as elsewhere on his travels, the emperor had the use of a regular court-room (*dikastêrion*).[78] The *amici* are clearly the group of senators and *equites* who were the emperor's *comites* on this journey; 'those called to the *consilium*' may have been *consiliarii*,[79] or officers of the praetorian cohorts or perhaps prominent men from Alexandria.[80] The central role of the *amici* is clear, just as it is in Herodian's report of Severus in Britain in 208–11 leaving Geta with some senior *assessores* from among his friends to carry on jurisdiction and administration in the settled part of the island, while he and Caracalla conducted a campaign on the frontier.[81]

The position of the *amici* is relatively less prominent in the two well-known protocols from the reign of Caracalla. The first, from the *Codex Justinianus*, has no indication of date or place: 'The Emperor Antoninus Augustus, when he had been saluted by Oclatinus Adventus and Opellius Macrinus, the praetorian prefects, also by his *amici* and the *principales officiorum* and men of both orders...'[82] The second is precisely dated to May 216 in Antioch, but is otherwise essentially very similar: 'When (the emperor), having been saluted by the praetorian prefects, e(minentissimi) v(iri), also by the *amici* and the *princ(ipes) officior(um)*, had taken his seat in the *auditorium*'.[83] The role of the praetorian prefects at the side of the emperor was already long established,[84] but it is still significant that both they and the 'chiefs of the bureaux' are so formally indicated in both cases.

According to Herodian, and possibly to Dio also, advisers were formally chosen for the young Severus Alexander from the senate; and according to Herodian they were with him at the time of his murder near Mainz in 235.[85] The constant campaigns on which emperors engaged in the third century must however have tended to limit their immediate entourage to actual office-holders; and this is indeed implied in Dexippus' description of

---

[77] *P. Oxy.* 3019, ll. 5–13: Καῖσαρ κατίσας/ ἐν τῷ δικαστηρίῳ με/τὰ τῶν φίλων καὶ τῶν/ εἰς τὸ συμβούλειον κε/κλημένων ἐκέλευ/σεν εἰσκληθῆναι πρέσ/βεις Αἰγυπτίων τὰς/ κοινὰς ἀξιώσεις προφέροντας.

indicates, runs (ll. 11–13): παραλημφθεῖσιν Μάρκῳ Αὐληρί[ῳ Οὐήρῳ Καίσαρι]/ καὶ Λουκ[ίῳ Α]ὐρηλ[ί]ῳ Κομόδῳ υἱοῖς [μοῦ καὶ?]/ ἐξ ἑκατ[έ]ρας τάξεως ἀνδράσιν ἐπι[σημοῖς or —σημοτατοῖς].

[78] pp. 6, 42.

[79] pp. 94–5.

[80] Compare *Acts* 25, 23, Festus and Agrippa hearing Paul σύν τε χιλιάρχοις καὶ ἀνδράσιν τοῖς κατ' ἐξοχὴν τῆς πόλεως.

[81] Herodian III, 14, 9.

[82] *CJ* IX, 51, 1: 'Imp. Antoninus A. cum salutatus (esset) ab Oclatinio Advento et Opellio Macrino praefectis praetorio clarissimis viris, item amicis et principalibus officiorum et utriusque ordinis viris...' As the following protocol shows, 'clarissimis' must be a mistake for 'eminentissimis'.

[83] *SEG* XVII 759. Cf. pp. 38, 233, 455, 535.

[84] See pp. 127–8.

[85] Herodian VI, 1, 2; cf. 2, 3 and 7, 4, and VII, 1, 3. For the passage of Zonaras, which may derive from Dio, see Boissevain III, p. 477.

5*

Aurelian receiving an embassy from the Juthungi in 270/1: 'He placed beside him those men of authority to whom some command had been entrusted, all on horseback.'[86] But, for what it is worth, an anecdote from Petrus Patricius shows Aurelian assembling a *consilium* of prominent men at Ravenna, among them at least one senator.[87] Another anecdote from the same source is perhaps more typical of the times, in describing a council held by Probus, at which a *tribunus*, presumably of the praetorian cohorts, is the only man to speak.[88] So also, when Lactantius gives his malicious account of Diocletian deliberately consulting his *amici* about the persecution of the Christians in order to spread the blame, he says specifically 'therefore a few *iudices* (governors) and a few military commanders were admitted in order of rank, and asked their opinion.'[89]

We also see Constantine with what appears to be a wholly military entourage in a protocol of 320: 'Imperator Constantinus Augustus, when he had entered the *principia* [the headquarters-building of a camp] and had been saluted by the Prefects and tribunes and *viri eminentissimi* [distinguished *equites*].'[90] In this case, however, we cannot tell how far the character of the proceedings had been determined by the fact that the emperor was within a camp. It may none the less be suggested that we can observe a general tendency for the entourage of the emperor to be made up increasingly of persons holding specific offices, whether this was a matter of the appointment of *consiliarii*, the increasing role of officers attached to the emperor, or the development of the old informal role of *amicus* into the rank, or ranks, of *comes*. But with all these developments it remained the case throughout the empire that any subject or group of subjects who came before the emperor found him attended by a substantial group of friends and advisers, on whose advice he was supposed in principle to rely. The tenuous nature of their position was no doubt often more apparent to the emperor's subjects on subsequent reflection than at the moment of audience.

To complete the picture of the entourage it is necessary to look finally at an element in it which depended from the beginning on the tenure of a specific office, though equally revocable at the emperor's whim, namely the praetorian prefecture. This too, like the position of *comes*, developed at the end of our period functions which partially removed it from its traditional role at the side of the emperor.

8. *The Praetorian Prefects and the Emperor*

When Herodes Atticus appeared before Marcus Aurelius at Sirmium in the 170s, and found himself threatened with death by the praetorian prefect, Bassaeus Rufus, he encountered one of the fundamental elements of the

---

[86] *FGrH* 100 F. 6 (2). See *JRS* LIX (1969), 25, and LXI (1971), 15–16.

[87] *FHG* IV, p. 197; Dio ed. Boissevain III, p. 745, Fr. 173.

[88] *FHG* IV, p. 198; Boissevain III, p. 747, Fr. 179.

[89] Lactantius, *De mort. pers.* 11, 6.

[90] *CTh* VII, 20, 2 = *CJ* XII, 46, 1. The date is 1 March 320. The place is given as 'in civitate Velovocorum' which has not been identified, but cannot be very far from Serdica, where Constantine was on 31 January and 19 May, see Seeck, *Regesten*, 169–70.

imperial entourage.[1] Rufus is described by Philostratus as 'the man entrusted with the sword',[2] which is sufficient to identify his rank without further question. For the praetorian prefects, alone of the higher officials at the side of the emperor, were armed, and 'the sword' was the essential symbol of their office.[3] Various sources recall the famous remark of Trajan as he handed the sword to Sextus Attius Suburanus on his appointment: 'Take this sword and use it for me if I rule well, and against me if I rule badly.'[4] The sword indicated not only that the praetorian prefects, from the first appointment of two in 2 BC, commanded the praetorian cohorts, of which some accompanied the emperor everywhere, but also that they monopolized the use of force in the immediate vicinity of the emperor. So we find Q. Naevius Sutorius Macro, prefect in 31–7, conducting investigations under torture, and first bringing the future Agrippa I of Judaea to Tiberius at Tusculum in 36 and then having him chained at the emperor's request.[5] Conversely, Seneca shows us Afranius Burrus asking Nero for his *subscriptio* as authority for the execution of two bandits; he places the document before the emperor with his own hand.[6] Similarly, Ofonius Tigellinus is found persuading Nero to order the execution of Rubellius Plautus and Cornelius Sulla, or personally supervising the torture of *ancillae* of Octavia;[7] while Rufrius Crispinus was sent to Baiae in 47 to arrest Valerius Asiaticus.[8]

It is a small extension of functions of this sort when we find emperors directing that prisoners from the provinces should be sent under guard to the praetorian prefects; Trajan sends such an instruction to Pliny in Bithynia,[9] and Gordian writes, apparently to a Greek city, to say that a *decurio* who has failed in his promise to produce a bandit whom he undertook to capture, should be sent either to the praetorian prefects or the provincial governor.[10] The third-century legal work entitled *Sententiae Pauli* lays down as a general rule that *officiales* guilty of extortion 'are sent to the praetorian prefect for punishment'.[11] It is yet another extension of their role when we find an emperor commissioning a praetorian prefect to examine a matter which had initially come before himself; so Hadrian replied to a

---

[1] The praetorian prefecture has been very fully discussed elsewhere, and only certain essential data will be used here. See M. Durry, *Les cohortes prétoriennes* (1938), ch. vi; A. Passerini, *Le coorti pretorie* (1939), 205–356; L. L. Howe, *The Pretorian Prefect from Commodus to Diocletian (AD 180–305)* (1942); W. Ensslin, 'Praefectus Praetorio', *RE* XXII. 2 (1954), cols. 2391–502; Jones, *Later Roman Empire*, 448–62, 586–92; A. Chastagnol, 'Les préfets du prétoire de Constantin', *REA* LXX (1968), 321; 'L'Histoire Auguste et le rang des Préfets du Prétoire', *Recherches sur l'Histoire Auguste* (1970), 39; note the list of prefects from 202 to 326 on pp. 63–8.

[2] Philostratus, *VS* II, 1; p. 5.

[3] Plutarch, *Galba* 8, 3; Philostratus, *V. Ap. Ty.* IV, 42; VII, 16.

[4] Dio LXVIII, 16, 12, is the best source for the words, but does not name the prefect. The name Suburanus is given by Aurelius Victor, *Caes.* 13, 9; cf. Pliny, *Pan.* 67, 8. See Pflaum, *Carrières*, no. 56.

[5] Tacitus, *Ann.* VI, 47, 1; Dio LVIII, 21, 3; 24, 2. Josephus, *Ant.* XVIII, 6, 6 (186–90). For Macro's full name, *AE* 1957 250.

[6] *De clem.* II, 1, 2; cf. Suetonius, *Nero* 10, 2.

[7] Tacitus, *Ann.* XIV, 57; XIV, 60, and Dio LXII, 13, 4.

[8] *Ann.* XI, 1, 3.

[9] *Ep.* X, 57, 2: 'vinctus mitti ad praefectos praetorii mei debet.

[10] *CJ* VIII, 40, 13.

[11] V, 12, 6.

petitioner who complained of unjust usury, 'the *eminentissimus vir*, my *praefectus*, will judge this and report to me in a *libellus*'.[12] Among the *apokrimata* of Severus in Egypt in 200 contained in a papyrus is one which runs: 'To Isidorus son of Deios. The outrages committed by Komon will be examined by Fulvius Plautianus, the most eminent Prefect of the Camps and our relative.'[13] They might also be called in to act as a court of appeal, as when Gordian tells a man who has been condemned in his absence by a provincial governor to approach the praetorian prefects, who will correct any injustice.[14] In quite different circumstances Diocletian (and notionally Maximian) at Nicomedia in 286 reply to a doctor in the imperial *comitatus*: 'Since you assert that those of whom you complain have in your absence invaded property which belongs to you, and since it is clear that because of your medical duties you cannot leave the *comitatus*, the praetorian prefect will summon those concerned in the case and judge between you.'[15]

It may well be that it was individual commissions of this sort which led to the development of an independent jurisdiction by the praetorian prefects. Legal sources do not reflect the existence of such a jurisdiction before the beginning of the third century. But even before this the well-known inscription from Saepinum shows an *a rationibus* writing to the praetorian prefects, Bassaeus Rufus and Macrinius Vindex, in 169–72 to complain of interference with imperial flocks in the Abruzzi; they in turn write to the magistrates of Saepinum ordering them to cease interference 'lest it should be necessary to examine the case and exact punishment for what has been done, if it is so'.[16] In the early third century there appears the principle that cases within a hundred miles of Rome went to the *praefectus urbi*, and those beyond to the praetorian prefects;[17] and it is no doubt in the context of maintaining public order that we find Papinian personally examining a bandit named Felix Bulla in about 207.[18] But it is not clear that the fairly wide range of jurisdiction attested for them at this period only related to Italy.[19] We do not know to which island the sophist Heliodorus had been relegated when he was acquitted by the praetorian prefects on a charge of murder, and also released from his relegation.[20]

Moreover, in 222 Severus Alexander tells a petitioner to approach the provincial governor, who on proof, if the matter requires a more serious punishment, 'will take care to send the accused persons to Domitius Ulpianus, my praetorian prefect and parent'.[21] The matter is therefore certainly a provincial one. There does not however seem to have been

[12] *Corp. Gloss. Lat.* III, 32; 387–8.

[13] *SB* 9526, *Apokrima* 11; see p. 244.

[14] *CJ* IX, 2, 6, 1 (243).

[15] *CJ* VII, 35, 2; cf. I, 19, 1 (290).

[16] *CIL* IX 2438; *FIRA*[2] I, no. 61; cf. Passerini, o.c., 251f. Cf. pp. 187–8.

[17] *Coll.* XIV, 3, 2 (Ulpian); cf. *Dig.* I, 12, 1, 4 (Ulpian).

[18] Dio LXXVI, 10, 7 (365).

[19] *Dig.* III, 2, 21 (*iniuria*); XII, 1, 40 (a *cautio* read in the *auditorium* of Papinian as praetorian prefect); XXII, 1, 3, 3 (*fideicommissa*); XXIX, 2, 97 (Papinian's judgment in an inheritance case); XXXII, 1, 4 (persons *deportati* by the prefects); XLIX, 3, 1 (appeal from *iudex datus* by one *praefectus* to his successor); *CJ* I, 26, 1 (*libellus* given to *praefectus*); I, 26, 2 (*forma* given by *praefectus*).

[20] Philostratus, *VS* II, 32. The date will be not far from 220.

[21] *CJ* IV, 65, 4, 1.

subsequent to this a regular system of transferring cases, on appeal or otherwise, from provincial governors to the prefect. But it was debated in the tetrarchic period whether there could be an appeal (to the emperor) from the praetorian prefect.[22] Constantine himself had no doubts: 'We do not permit appeals to be made from the praetorian prefects, who alone should be described as judging in the divine stead (*vice sacra*), lest the veneration due to us should seem to be impugned.'[23]

All these wider juridical functions should be seen as extensions of the essential role of the praetorian prefects as the protectors of the emperor and commander of the cohorts: 'that guardian of the sacred side and of the togaed Mars, to whom the camp of the supreme *dux* has been entrusted', as Martial puts it, addressing the prefect, Cornelius Fuscus.[24] Since this meant, as we can see in the case of Herodes Atticus before Marcus, an actual personal attendance on the emperor, it is important to emphasize how different was the background of many praetorian prefects from those of the other persons who formed the immediate entourage. The difference is most clearly documented in the second century, and nowhere more clearly than in the case of M. Bassaeus Rufus himself. Dio's remark that he was in other respects a good man, but uneducated owing to his rusticity, is explained by the long inscription of his career set up in Rome.[25] It is indeed the classic instance of the career open to a senior centurion in this period, from *primus pilus*, tribune successively in the three units in Rome (*vigiles*, *cohortes urbanae*, praetorian cohorts), *primus pilus* of another legion, and then a series of procuratorships up to *procurator a rationibus*. Finally there are three prefectures, of the *vigiles*, Egypt and the praetorian cohorts. Although even in this period few careers are as fully documented as this, it can be said that from the later first century to the middle of the third it was not uncommon for the prefecture to be gained by men on the basis of a long military and procuratorial career, culminating in the post of *a rationibus* and prefectures of the *vigiles*, the *annona* or of Egypt; a clear case of just this is T. Furius Victorinus, *praefectus* in 160–3.[26] In the Julio-Claudian period the 'career' itself was only beginning to develop and coalesce, and the appointees seem often to have been essentially confidants of the emperor.[27] But even in this period Macro had been *praefectus vigilum* before becoming praetorian

[22] See *Dig.* I, 11, 1, 1 (Arcadius Charisius); cf. IV, 4, 17 (Hermogenianus).

[23] *CTh* XI, 30, 16 (331); cf. *CJ* VII, 62, 19, omitting most of the sentence quoted. On persons who judged *vice sacra* see pp. 514–15.

[24] *Epig.* VI, 76, 1–3.

[25] Dio LXXI, 5, 2–3 (256); *ILS* 1326, cf. Pflaum, *Carrières*, no. 162.

[26] *PIR²* F 584; Pflaum, *Carrières*, no. 139; for praetorian prefects of this period with substantial earlier careers, see Sex. Attius Suburanus Aemilianus, Pflaum, *Carrières*, no. 56; Ser. Sulpicius Similis, once a centurion and later prefect of Egypt and then *annona*, Passerini, o.c., 297; Q. Marcius Turbo, R. Syme, *JRS* LII (1962), 187; possibly M. Gavius Maximus, Pflaum, no. 105 *bis*, and M. Petronius Mamertinus, *RE* s.v. 'Petronius' (44); C. Tattius Maximus, Pflaum, no. 138; L. Julius Vehilius Gratus Julianus, Pflaum, no. 180; *PIR²* I 615; Q. Maecius Laetus, Pflaum, no. 219; Cn. Marcius Rustius Rufinus, Pflaum, no. 234. The latter two are particularly good examples. There are also several cases of very full third-century careers, e.g. C. Furius Sabinius Aquila Timesitheus (Pflaum, no. 317), the father-in-law of Gordian III; C. Julius Priscus (Pflaum, nos. 324–324a; *PIR²* I 488), brother of M. Julius Philippus, the future emperor; C. Attius Alcimus Felicianus (Pflaum, no. 327); L. Petronius Taurus Volusianus (Pflaum, no. 347).

[27] See the classic discussion by A. N. Sherwin-White, 'Procurator Augusti', *PBSR* XV (1939), 1.

prefect in 31; Afranius Burrus had been a military tribune, and procurator of Livia, Tiberius and Claudius before his appointment in 51; and Faenius Rufus *praefectus annonae* when elevated in 62.[28] Even Ofonius Tigellinus, the prime case of a corrupt imperial favourite, had been *praefectus vigilum* before his appointment with Faenius Rufus—'gaining the prefectures of the *vigiles* and the *praetorium*, the rewards of virtue, by his vices, since this was quicker', as Tacitus puts it.[29]

But even in the period of greatest regularity, the second century, when we can see the praetorian prefecture as the summit of a long career open to *equites* and *primi pili*, it remained essentially a personal appointment by the emperor, who could make it on any basis he chose. This personal element had been very clear, for instance, in the letter of appointment (*codicilli*) sent by Domitian to Laberius Maximus, prefect of Egypt, nominating him as praetorian prefect in 83;[30] or conversely in Pliny the Younger's somewhat sentimental description of Trajan bidding farewell to a praetorian prefect who had insisted on retiring.[31] The patterns of personal contact and influence which might lie behind what we would otherwise see simply as a 'career' are brought out by Dio in describing the rise of Opellius Macrinus; originating from Caesarea in Mauretania, he became known to the praetorian prefect, Plautianus, through acting as *advocatus* in a law-suit, and was subsequently his procurator. When Plautianus fell in 205, Macrinus was saved by the intercession of a prominent senatorial friend of Severus, L. Fabius Cilo; after this he received equestrian posts from both Severus and then Caracalla, who soon made him praetorian prefect.[32]

The very prominence of the praetorian prefect, his military role at the side of the emperor and the particular imperial favour which his position implied led some to dangerous ambitions, and exposed them all to suspicions on the part both of the emperor himself and of others. A large number of praetorian prefects met sudden and violent deaths; it is one of the clearest signs of the relative stability of the imperial regime in the middle of the period that none is recorded as having done so between 97 and the reign of Commodus. The suspicions which might at any time arise in the mind of the emperor—perhaps most clearly described by Philo in relation to Gaius and Macro[33]—were not of course always unjustified. Praetorian prefects played a crucial role in the downfall of Nero, and in the murders of Domitian, Commodus, Caracalla, Gordian III, Gallienus and Numerianus.[34] In the

---

[28] Afranius Burrus, Pflaum, *Carrières*, no. 13; Faenius Rufus, Tacitus, *Ann.* XIV, 51, 2. But in all three cases personal factors were involved, Macro's role as *praefectus vigilum* in the fall of Sejanus; Agrippina's support for Burrus (*Ann.* XII, 42, 1); and Rufus' popularity with the people.

[29] Tacitus, *Hist.* I, 72. See *RE* s.v. 'Ofonius Tigellinus'.

[30] *P. Berl.* 8334; *Corp. Pap. Lat.* 238, with bibliography. Cf. R. Syme, *Tacitus* (1958), App. 7. On *codicilli* see further pp. 288–90, 296, 305–11.

[31] *Pan.* 86.

[32] LXXVIII, 11, 1–3 (413). Cf. Pflaum, *Carrières*, no. 248.

[33] *Leg.* 8/52–61.

[34] Nero: Tacitus, *Hist.* I, 72, 1; Plutarch, *Galba* 2, 8; Josephus, *BJ* IV, 9, 2 (492–3). Domitian: Dio LXVII, 15, 2, cf. Eutropius, *Brev.* VIII, 1, 1. Commodus: Dio LXXII, 22 (303–4); Herodian I, 16,5–17,12; *HA, Com.* 17, 1–2. Caracalla—see n. 35 below. Gordian—see n. 36 below. Gallienus: *HA, Gall.* 14; Zosimus I, 40, 2–3; Zonaras XII, 25. Numerianus: Aurelius Victor, *Caes.* 38, 6; *HA, Car.* 12, 1; Zonaras XII, 31.

case of Caracalla, it was precisely Macrinus' knowledge of accusations being made against him which led to the murder of the emperor, and the first proclamation as emperor of a praetorian prefect. This event, which took place in Mesopotamia during Caracalla's eastern campaign in 217,[35] was closely mirrored in 244, when Gordian III was murdered and the praetorian prefect M. Julius Philippus assumed power.[36]

These incidents were a reflection and a product of the essential role of the praetorian prefects up to the early fourth century, namely that of accompanying the emperor everywhere, and commanding the praetorian cohorts, at least some of which did likewise.[37] This is almost the earliest role in which we find a praetorian prefect, when Sejanus, with some praetorian cohorts, goes with Drusus to Pannonia in AD 14.[38] Thereafter, to take only some instances, Macro was with Tiberius at Misenum in 37 and was thought to have hastened his death;[39] Rufrius Pollio accompanied Claudius on the British expedition of 43/4;[40] and Ofonius Tigellinus went with Nero on his tour of Greece in 66/7.[41] Later, Claudius Livianus was with Trajan in the first Dacian War, and was sent by him on an embassy to Decebalus,[42] while Acilius Attianus was with Trajan at his death at Selinus in Cilicia in 117.[43] Septicius Clarus was apparently in Britain with Hadrian in 121/2, when he and Suetonius were dismissed.[44] Macrinius Vindex died in about 171, while with Marcus Aurelius in the Marcomannic campaign.[45]

Fulvius Plautianus appears not only with Severus in Alexandria in 200, but also in two anecdotes in Dio relating to Severus' journey from Antioch through Asia Minor in 202. At Tyana when Plautianus was ill and Severus came to visit him, his attendants would not let the emperor's entourage accompany him into the room; his accommodation and supplies along the route were more luxurious than those of the emperor, and at Nicaea Severus had to ask Plautianus to let him have a mullet from the lake.[46] When Severus made his expedition to Britain in 208/11, Papinian is found with him.[47] From the following reigns we have already seen Macrinus and Oclatinius Adventus with Caracalla, and Julius Philippus with Gordian.[48] Later in the third century, Successianus, on appointment as *praefectus*, joined Valerian at Antioch in the 250s, and may have been the *praefectus* who was captured with him by Shapur.[49] Gallienus was murdered in 268 by his *praefectus*,

[35] Dio LXXIX, 4,1–6,4; Herodian IV, 12,5–13,8.

[36] *HA, Gord.* 29–30; Zosimus I, 19, 1. Cf. S. I. Oost, 'The Death of the Emperor Gordian III', *CPh* LIII (1958), 106.

[37] pp. 61–2.

[38] Tacitus, *Ann.* I, 24.

[39] VI, 50.

[40] Dio LX, 23, 2.

[41] LXIII, 12, 3 (78).

[42] LXVIII, 9, 2.

[43] LXIX, 1, 2.

[44] *HA, Had.* 11, 3 (cf. 11, 2 and 12, 1). Cf. p. 90.

[45] Dio LXXI, 3, 5 (255).

[46] LXXV, 15, 3–5 (354); cf. p. 51.

[47] LXXVII, 14, 6 (369).

[48] See above and p. 121.

[49] Zosimus, I, 32, 2; cf. A. Maricq, 'Res Gestae Divi Saporis', *Syria* XXXV (1958), 295; l. 25 of the Greek text.

Heraclianus, en route between the Danube and Milan, and Numerianus by his *praefectus*, Aper, on the way back from the eastern frontier through Asia Minor in 282/3.[50]

In the tetrarchic period it is not possible to follow in any detail the movements of *praefecti praetorio*, or even to state with any confidence how the creation of two *Augusti* and two *Caesares*, let alone the multiplication from 306 onwards, affected the office. Julius Asclepiodotus certainly took part in the campaign of the 'Caesar', Constantius, against Allectus in 197, possibly in part in an independent command.[51] Maxentius sent one prefect, C. Ceionius Rufius Volusianus, to recover Africa from Domitius Alexander in about 310,[52] and another, Ruricius Pompeianus, to oppose Constantine at Verona in 312.[53] In 311 Sabinus, the *praefectus praetorio* of Maximin, issued on his behalf a letter to provincial governors ordering the cessation of the harassment of Christians. The intention was to fall in with, without subscribing to, the proclamation of toleration of Galerius, Constantine and Licinius. Sabinus was clearly acting on the immediate orders of the emperor.[54] A letter instructing the *vicarius* of Africa to see to the safe return of some bishops on their way back from Trier was issued from Trier in April 315, apparently jointly, by Petronius Annianus and (Julius) Julianus, whom we know to have been *praefecti praetorio* in this period.[55] The former at least was evidently at Trier with Constantine;[56] but Julius Julianus, the grandfather of Julian the Apostate, had been prefect of Egypt in 314 and was subsequently *praefectus* of Licinius in the east, surviving Constantine's victory to be made consul by him in 325.[57] It seems more than likely that Julianus' name was added as a formality to Annianus' letter, just as the names of emperors are in their pronouncements of this period.

It thus seems clear that the fact that Constantine in 312 abolished the praetorian cohorts in Rome—which had fought for Maxentius—and pulled down their camp,[58] did not of itself end the role of praetorian prefects. On the contrary it is evident that the reign of Constantine saw the beginnings of a development which Zosimus attributes to him,[59] namely regional prefectures not attached to the person of an emperor or 'Caesar'.[60] It is certain, none the less, that, as we have seen in part, a prefect could still be found at the emperor's side. It is to his functions in this role, which were continuous from the moment when the post was created, that we finally turn.

[50] p. 126, n. 34.

[51] Aurelius Victor, *Caes.* 39, 42; Eutropius, *Brev.* IX, 22, 2. Cf. *PLRE* Asclepiodotus 3.

[52] *Caes.* 40, 18; Zosimus II, 14, 2.

[53] *Pan.* IX(12), 8, 1; X(4), 25; *PLRE* Pompeianus 8.

[54] Eusebius, *HE* IX, 1, 1–7, not in the final version of the *HE*. Sabinus is described (1, 2) as ὁ γοῦν παρ' αὐτοῖς τῷ τῶν ἐξοχωτάτων ἐπάρχων ἀξιώματι τετιμημένος, and the text given (3–6) is that of a letter addressed to one governor. Cf. pp. 579–80.

[55] Optatus, App. VIII. For the date and the offices of the two men see *PLRE* Annianus 2.

[56] pp. 587–8.

[57] See *PLRE* Iulianus 35.

[58] p. 65.

[59] Zosimus II, 33, 1–2.

[60] The clearest statement is that of Jones, *Later Roman Empire*, 101–3 and notes. Cf. Chastagnol in *RÉA* LXX (1968), 321.

There is nothing to suggest that the prefect remained permanently in the emperor's presence, but it is clear that he might share more than that fairly restricted part of the day which was devoted to official business.[61] For instance, Sejanus earned added trust and credit by saving Tiberius' life in 26 when the roof of the emperor's ornamental grotto at Sperlonga collapsed while they were dining there.[62] In contexts which bore more directly on the relations of the Emperor and his subjects, we have seen already the prefect's role in the custody of prisoners and the examination and torture of suspects. It is this role and the closely related one of assisting the emperor in court of which Philostratus makes use in his historical novel *The Life of Apollonius of Tyana*.[63] Here he relates how when Apollonius is due to be tried before Domitian, the prefect Aelian first tries to influence the emperor in his favour and then has Apollonius arrested and brought to him, in order to give him the details of the charges to be made against him. When Apollonius, after being returned to custody on Aelian's orders, is finally brought for an interview with the emperor, Aelian is in attendance. In this case the account of the trial itself, which follows, contains no reference to the prefect; but we can assume that it was at least common and, probably almost invariable, for the prefect to be one of the emperor's *assessores*. This established role may explain how, when in 55 accusations were made against Afranius Burrus and Pallas of promoting a rival candidate as emperor, Burrus himself appeared in the role of *assessor* at the trial of Pallas.[64] It is probably to the same context, though possibly to the independent jurisdiction of the prefect, that we should relate Dio's account of the conscientiousness of Marcius Turbo under Hadrian.[65] He spent all day at the *palatium*, and often went to it before the middle of the night. When the orator Cornelius Fronto was returning late from a dinner one night, he was told that Turbo was already 'judging': he went straight to court to represent a client and greeted the prefect as if it were morning rather than late at night. The reference to the *palatium* and the story of Hadrian encouraging Turbo to rest, which follows immediately in Xiphilinus' epitome of Dio, both suggest that we are actually concerned with Turbo as *assessor* of Hadrian. If on the contrary it is his own court, it is striking that it was situated within the *palatium* itself.

A later anecdote in Dio shows Fulvius Plautianus, like Bassaeus Rufus with Marcus Aurelius, or Macrinus and Adventus with Caracalla, with an integral part in Severus' juridical activity. According to Dio, on one occasion when Severus told his *a cognitionibus* to bring on a particular case, the man replied, 'I cannot, because Plautianus has not given me instructions.'[66]

It cannot be doubted that the praetorian prefects were as a general rule to

[61] For the daily routine of emperors see pp. 209–11.

[62] Tacitus, *Ann.* IV, 59, 1–2. For the archaeological remains see G. Jacopi, *L'antro di Tiberio a Sperlonga* (1963).

[63] VII, 16–32.

[64] Tacitus, *Ann.* XIII, 23. The actual words used are 'Burrus, quamvis reus inter iudices sententiam dixit', and there is no specific mention of Nero. But it must be that this is an imperial trial and that *iudex* is used, with typically Tacitean perversity, instead of *assessor*. This meaning is rightly assumed by Crook, *Consilium Principis*, 47.

[65] LXIX, 18.

[66] LXXVI, 15, 5 (354).

be found at the emperor's side when he gave justice to his subjects. It can equally be assumed that they normally had a prominent role among the emperor's *amici* when decisions were taken in private. In Juvenal's famous satire representing a meeting of Domitian's *amici* summoned to Alba in 83 to discuss a huge turbot which had been presented to the emperor, there appear, along with eight others who all appear to be senators, Cornelius Fuscus, who was certainly *Praefectus* by this time, and one Crispinus who may have been also.[67] In the *Tabula Banasitana* which records the grant of citizenship by Marcus Aurelius and Commodus to the family of a Maureta-nian chief in 177, the document concludes with the names of twelve witnesses drawn from the emperor's *amici*; the seventh and eighth names are M. Bassaeus Rufus, who may still have been praetorian prefect, and Tarrutienus Paternus, who is known to have been in office not later than 179.[68]

These two names may remind us that while the prefecture was unique among the positions closest to the emperor in being frequently, and perhaps normally the culmination of a long military and administrative career, it could also be open to men whose only known qualification was their legal learning. There is no reason to suppose that most praetorian prefects did not share the common literary culture,[69] but it is conspicuous that none is stated to have owed his rise to his skill in rhetoric. The different route by which they arrived there and their continuing military command, sym-bolized by their wearing of a sword, must both have made them an extraneous element among those who attended the emperor, and have prepared the way for the independent administrative role which they began to assume at the end of the period. But while they remained at the emperor's side their position and role, essentially dependent on his favour, cannot have been wholly distinct from that of the other courtiers.

Many of these different facets of the role of the praetorian prefects are reflected in the career and activities of Flavius Ablabius, prefect in 329–37. To Libanius he was an example of how far one could rise from humble beginnings: Ablabius had once served the *praeses* of Crete, his homeland, in some humble capacity, and was later very rich, and a senator.[70] Eunapius too emphasizes his low birth, and tells the story of an Egyptian astrologer who foretold the child's fate at the moment of birth: 'So, woman, tell the mother that she has given birth to one only second to an emperor.' He enters Eunapius' *Lives of the Sophists* because he was responsible for the death of Constantine's adviser Sopater:[71] 'He even put Sopater to death, after bring-ing against him a charge more foolish even than that against Socrates, swaying the then emperor as if he were an unstable crowd.' But when Constantius came to the throne, Eunapius relates, Ablabius was dismissed, retired to his luxurious estate in Bithynia, and was later executed on the

---

[67] Juvenal, *Sat.* IV, 37–149. But see Syme, *Tacitus* (1958), 636.
[68] For the text W. Seston, M. Euzennat, 'Un dossier de la chancellerie romaine: la *Tabula Banasitana*, étude de diplomatique', *CRAI* 1971, 468. See pp. 223, 261–2.
[69] Jerome, *Chron. ad* 336 (ed. Helm, p. 233) has 'Tiberianus vir disertus praefectus praetorio Gallias regit'. Possibly with Constantinus Caesar at Trier?
[70] Libanius, *Or.* XLII, 23; for full details *PLRE* Ablabius 4.
[71] p. 100.

emperor's orders.[72] Few biographies show more clearly the opportunities opened by the existence of a court, the mutual tensions there, and the latent dangers which accompanied all marks of imperial favour. Neither writer mentions the intermediate stages of the career through which Ablabius rose to his prefecture, and other evidence provides only one, the vicariate of Asiana in 324–6. On a long Latin inscription from Orcistus on the border of Galatia and Phrygia he appears as interceding on behalf of the inhabitants with Constantine, and receiving from him a letter couched in warm and personal terms (ending 'Farewell, Ablabius, dearest and most agreeable to us'). Furthermore, Constantine writes that the culminating factor which predisposed him in favour of the Orcistans' request for the status of a city was that they were all said to be Christians.[73] For Ablabius too was a Christian, a fact which no doubt helped his rise, and was to be relevant to one of the numerous experiences of Athanasius at the court of Constantine.[74] In 332, when the time came for Athanasius to write the Festal letter which he issued to the congregation in Alexandria each Easter, he was at the court in Constantinople to answer accusations brought by his enemies. But he was able to send his letter all the same, though belatedly: 'We have sent this letter from the court by the hand of an *officialis*, to whom it was given by Ablabius, the prefect of the *praetorium*, who fears God in truth.'[75] His intervention neatly illustrates another aspect of the long-standing functions of the praetorian prefect, and the new considerations which might govern their exercise towards those who came to be judged by the emperor.

[72] *VS* 463–4. Loeb trans. with amendments. Cf. Zosimus II, 40, 3.
[73] *MAMA* VII, 305. Cf. pp. 410, 544.
[74] p. 602.
[75] For the Festal letters of this period we depend on a Syriac text. For an English translation of this letter (IV) see A. Robertson, *Select Writings and Letters of Athanasius, Bishop of Alexandria* (1892), 515–17. We may confidently substitute 'officialis' for the 'officilius' which results from a straight transliteration from the Syriac. The same man is referred to in the heading of the letter as a 'soldier'. This will be correct, see p. 63.

IV

The Imperial Wealth: Gifts and Exactions

1. Introduction

When Augustus was coming down from the Palatium, he was regularly accosted by a Greek poet, who tried to offer him a flattering epigram. But one day, when the emperor saw him about to make yet another vain attempt, he quickly scribbled a Greek epigram of his own, and handed it to the man as he approached. By the time Augustus was seated in his litter, the poet had recovered; reaching into his purse for a few coins, he gave them to the emperor, saying in Greek, 'By your Fortune, Augustus, if I had had more I would have given it to you.' Amid the laughter of those present Augustus, realising that he had been outdone, called a *dispensator* and ordered him to pay out 100,000 *sesterces* to the Greek.[1]

We may contrast with this anecdote part of a letter which Constantine wrote to some Catholic bishops in Numidia in 330, after their basilica in Cirta (by now re-named Constantina) had been occupied by schismatics:[2]

> You, however, as imitators of the patience of the most high God, have peacefully left to their malevolence the property which is yours, and instead request for yourselves another site in its place, that is a fiscal one. This petition I have in my accustomed manner gladly embraced, and have immediately sent letters of authority to the *rationalis*, instructing him to transfer a house belonging to us into the full legal ownership of the catholic church; this I have granted with prompt liberality (*liberalitas*), and have ordered to be handed over to you at once. On this site I have ordered a basilica to be built at fiscal expense (*sumptu fiscali*), and have also ordered a letter to be written to the *consularis* of Numidia, to instruct him to aid Your Sanctimony in every way in the construction of this basilica.

These two episodes more than three centuries apart exemplify two extremes of a single pattern of activity. All the way from the *Cyropaedia* of Xenophon, which was read by both Scipio Africanus and Julius Caesar, we can trace the integral part played by 'liberality' in the conception of what a monarch was, and what 'kingly' conduct should be.[3] Nor was the continuity of outlook and practice merely something which we are now able to discern.

[1] Macrobius, *Sat.* II, 4, 31.
[2] Optatus, App. x (*CSEL* XXVI, p. 215). For the date and circumstances, see p. 590.
[3] See the excellent and illuminating study by H. Kloft, *Liberalitas Principis, Herkunft und Bedeutung: Studien zur Prinzipatsideologie* (1970). For the *Cyropaedia* and its use by Scipio Africanus (Cicero, *Ad Q. f.* I, 1, 23) and Caesar (Suetonius, *Jul.* 87) see ibid. pp. 20–2.

The link was perfectly conscious and explicit. 'Artaxerxes, the King of the Persians,' wrote Plutarch addressing a work to Trajan, 'thought it no less kingly and benevolent to accept small gifts than to give great ones.'[4] The gifts which monarchs were expected to distribute were not of course confined to money, objects or land, but extended to a whole range of benefits and privileges. As the epitaph on the grave of Sulla had succinctly expressed it, 'None of his friends ever surpassed him in conferring benefits or his enemies in doing harm'.[5]

But it was precisely the transference of property from its lawful owners to other beneficiaries on the part of Sulla and Julius Caesar that caused Cicero to lay down that such conferments, not even being just, could not be true liberality.[6] That takes us back to an essential aspect of the contrast between the incident of Augustus and the poet, and the letter of Constantine to the bishops. Both indeed rest on assumptions by both ruler and ruled about the liberality of the monarch. But the first is a simple gift of cash, disbursed on the spot by an attendant of the emperor. The second shows an act of what is explicitly called *liberalitas*, which involves not only instructions to two highly-placed officials in a province, but the transference of substantial property which apparently belongs to the emperor and is certainly at his free disposition. It therefore takes us further back to a whole range of problems which are essential to our understanding of the nature and functions of the emperor. From whom and by what processes were the imperial properties acquired? Within what legal and constitutional framework are we to understand the acquisition of wealth by the emperor, and its distribution to those whom he favoured? These problems will be touched upon, but it must be confessed in advance that they cannot be satisfactorily answered. Even the commonest terms which appear in this context, such as *fiscus* and *fiscalis*, resist any generally agreed definition. So it will be necessary to concentrate not so much on the definition of terms as on the social relations involved in the acquisition of wealth by the emperors, their eventual ownership (or control) of immense ranges of property, and the deployment of that wealth and property in their dealings with their subjects. It will be seen that one of the most crucial of these relations involved precisely the acquisition by the emperor of the property of condemned persons (*bona damnatorum*), and on occasions the granting of this to others.[7]

It must also be emphasized that both the poet and the Numidian bishops took the initiative in approaching the emperor to obtain the money or land that they wanted. That is a feature which runs through the whole range of relations between the emperor and individual subjects, cities and institutions, including the church. But for the moment we may turn to the distribution of money and goods by the emperor in person, before continuing to the question of the stores of money and valuables at his disposal, and from there to the much wider question of the sources and role of his wealth.

[4] *Mor.* 172 B.
[5] Plutarch, *Sulla* 38, 6. For this and what follows see Kloft, o.c., 57.
[6] *De off.* 1, 14/43.
[7] pp. 163–74.

2. *Gifts of Money and Goods by the Emperor in Person*

We have already encountered Pliny the Younger and other *amici* of the emperor assisting Trajan in jurisdiction at Centumcellae, and departing each with gifts.[1] Such distributions had from the beginning an integral part in the relations of the emperor and his intimates. Another anecdote in Macrobius shows Julius Caesar giving a hundred *sesterces* each to some people with whom he was playing ball, but only fifty to L. Caecilius—who exclaimed, 'Why do I play with one hand?'[2] But the clearest indication of the role of gifts is the story told by Seneca of a senator who went to Augustus, again as he was 'descending' from the Palatium, to ask forgiveness for a treasonable remark. On receiving it, he continued, 'No one will believe that I have been restored to your favour unless you have given me something' —and named a substantial sum.[3] Fabius Maximus similarly made a witticism about the exiguity of the gifts (*congiaria*) which Augustus made to his friends.[4] On our evidence, such an accusation was hardly justified. At the Saturnalia and other occasions he made gifts of clothing, gold and silver, and sometimes coins of all denominations including 'ancient royal and foreign ones' (presumably of Hellenistic kings); and Nonius Asprenas was given a gold torque after being injured by a fall in the *lusus Troiae* (thus earning the *cognomen* 'Torquatus'). Shortly before his death, pleased by the acclamations of some Alexandrian sailors, he gave forty *aurei* each to his *comites*, with instructions to spend the money on Alexandrian goods. A few days later he distributed (as well as other gifts) togas to his Greek companions and Greek cloaks (*pallia*) to his Roman ones.[5]

As in all things, the form and occasion of gifts were at the whim of the emperor. But an indefinite range of occasions presented themselves, on which the distribution of large or small sums of money was appropriate, or even openly requested. For instance, a soldier who caught an owl which disturbed Augustus' sleep at one of his villas was offered 1,000 *sesterces*.[6] Augustus usually distributed money to choirs of singers who entertained him at dinner, but on occasion gave corn instead; when he next asked at dinner for the same choir, their owner replied, 'They are at the mill'. The hint was clear, just as it had been when he returned after Actium, and among the crowds who came out to greet him[7] was a man with a crow trained to say, 'Hail, Caesar victor Imperator!' It was only after he had paid 20,000 *sesterces* for it that the man's partner, who had not shared the *liberalitas*, revealed that he had another crow which said, 'Hail, victor Imperator Antonius!'[8]

[1] *Ep.* VI, 31, 4; cf. p. 27.
[2] *Sat.* II, 6, 5.
[3] *De ben.* III, 27, 2–3.
[4] Quintilian, *Inst.* VI, 3, 52: 'ut Fabius Maximus, incusans Augusti congiariorum quae amicis dabantur exiguitatem, heminaria esse dixit (nam congiarium commune liberalitatis atque mensurae).'
[5] Suetonius, *Aug.* 75; 43, 2; 98, 2–3.
[6] Macrobius, *Sat.* II, 4, 26. The man in fact insisted on releasing the bird instead. He will of course have been a member of the *cohortes praetoriae*, cf. p. 61.
[7] Cf. p. 29.
[8] Macrobius, *Sat.* II, 4, 28–9.

The maintenance of the emperor's role demanded not only a constant outflow of gifts, but the giving of them in a magnanimous and dignified manner. It was remembered to Galba's discredit that he had rewarded a flute-player with a mere five *denarii*, which the emperor brought out with his own hand from his purse.[9] But normally, as the story of Augustus and the poet indicates, the actual payment was made by a *dispensator*. Tiberius, according to Dio, insisted that all payments promised by him should be made at once before his eyes; for under Augustus the *dispensatores* had pocketed large sums, and he was determined that this should not happen under him.[10]

With such opportunities for profit, combined with the normal rewards open to those near the emperor, it is not surprising that the post of *dispensator* was eagerly sought after. Suetonius records one of his freedmen petitioning Vespasian for it for his brother,[11] and Otho taking 1,000,000 *sesterces* from a slave of Galba's for having gained the post from the emperor for him.[12] A slave of Nero, soon after acting as *dispensator* for the Parthian War, was able to pay 13,000,000 *sesterces* for his freedom; 'but this was the price of the war, not the man', Pliny the Elder comments, apparently meaning that the man had thus had exceptional opportunities for profit.[13] A famous inscription shows a slave *dispensator ad fiscum Gallicum* who had sixteen slave attendants of his own when he died in Rome under Tiberius.[14]

Dispensatores were also supposed to keep accounts of payments made on the Emperor's orders. Suetonius mentions one presenting a record of accounts (*breviarium rationum*) to Galba (and receiving a dish of beans as a reward), and another asking Vespasian in what form an entry should be made in the *rationes*.[15] But our clearest evidence of the visible functions of *dispensatores* comes from coins representing the periodic distributions of cash to the people of Rome (*congiaria* or *liberalitates*). There are variations in the form of the coins, but nearly all show the emperor seated on a tribunal, while a *dispensator* makes the actual payments to the citizens, who approach individually to receive their share.[16] The representation on these coins of the emperor as personally present at the *congiaria* is not merely symbolic; an anecdote shows a woman petitioning Hadrian while he was 'giving a *congiarium*'.[17]

[9] Suetonius, *Galba* 12, 3; Plutarch, *Galba* 16, 2; cf. Dio LXIV, 2, 1 (100).

[10] LVII, 10, 4.

[11] *Vesp.* 23.

[12] *Otho* 5, 2.

[13] *NH* VII, 39/129.

[14] *ILS* 1514.

[15] *Galba* 12, 3; *Vesp.* 22. Vespasian's answer, 'Vespasiano adamato', gives some idea of the form in which entries were usually made.

[16] See D. van Berchem, *Les distributions de blé et d'argent à la plèbe romaine sous l'Empire* (1939), 164f.; R. Brilliant, *Gesture and Rank in Roman Art* (1963), 77, 106, 132–3, 151, 170–3. This practical detail is however lost in the representation of a *liberalitas* on the Arch of Constantine (Brilliant, p. 172), where the emperor alone occupies the central place.

[17] *Corp. Gloss. Lat.* III, 36; 389: 'Hadriano congiarium dante, mulier quaedam exclamavit.' Cf. also *HA, Com.* 2, 1: 'adhuc in praetexta puerili congiarium dedit atque ipse in Basilica Traiani praesedit.' If this location was regular, then the 'arcarii Caesariani qui in foro Traiani habent stationes', mentioned by Ulpian in *Frag. Vat.* 134, may have been concerned with storing the coin for *congiaria*. So van Berchem, o.c., 165.

Gaius, however, went beyond this, and himself threw coins to the people from the roof of the Basilica Iulia, spending several days doing so. Josephus notes that his eventual murderer, Cassius Chaerea, escorting him as a praetorian tribune, could easily have pushed him over the edge. Dio repeats the story of the distribution, adding that some said that pieces of iron were mixed with the gold and silver.[18]

Such an action on the part of Gaius was of course an eccentric variant in the usual pattern of liberality. But he was followed by at least some other emperors in the practice, which he introduced,[19] of distributing *missilia*, tokens which entitled the persons who caught them to a range of different goods. The 'scattering' of these *missilia* always seems to have taken place when the people were assembled at games or shows. Suetonius says of the *ludi* given by Nero: '*Missilia* for all sorts of things were scattered to the people on all the days of the games: for a thousand birds of all breeds on every day, all types of foods, tickets for corn-distributions, clothes, gold, silver, gems, pearls, pictures, slaves, cattle and even trained wild animals, and finally ships, blocks of apartments, and land.'[20] There is nothing here to indicate that the *missilia* were thrown by the emperor with his own hand. But when Dio describes a similar distribution by Titus he does seem to imply this: 'He would throw down into the theatre from above small wooden balls with various marks, one indicating some foodstuff, others clothing, silver or gold ornaments, horses, beasts of burden, cattle or slaves. Those who caught them had to take them to the *dispensatores*, and receive whatever was marked.'[21]

Similar actions are recorded, in less detail, of Domitian,[22] Hadrian[23] and Elagabal,[24] but not of any other emperors. So this too, though more frequent, was still an eccentricity. But the action was still an expression, however crude, of the deeply-ingrained notion of the liberality of the monarch. Moreover it offers a hint of the immense range of valuables and possessions which were at the disposal of the emperors even in the first century. As we shall see,[25] the imperial treasures and ornaments had various significant functions in the activities of the emperor.

Of all the gifts of cash or goods or land made by the emperor to individual subjects or groups, only a small minority are concretely attested as being made in his presence. But these, like the full range of imperial gifts, affected all the classes of persons with whom he had contact. So we find Gaius giving a dinner for senators and *equites* with their wives and children, and distributing togas to the men, and scarves of purple and scarlet to the women and children.[26] The members of successful embassies could also expect gifts—the oration of Scopelianus which persuaded Domitian to revoke his

[18] Suetonius, *Cal.* 37, 1; Josephus, *Ant.* XIX, 1, 11 (71); Dio LIX, 25, 5.
[19] Suetonius, *Cal.* 18, 2: 'sparsit et missilia variarum rerum'; cf. Dio LIX, 9, 6–7.
[20] *Nero* 11–12; cf. Dio LXI, 18, 1–2.
[21] LXVI, 25, 5.
[22] Suetonius, *Dom.* 4, 5; Dio LXVII, 4, 4.
[23] Dio LXIX, 8, 2.
[24] Herodian V, 6, 9; *HA, Heliog.* 8, 3.
[25] pp. 144–53.
[26] Suetonius, *Cal.* 17, 2.

edict on vines won him, among other things, 'the gifts which are customary in the presence of the emperor'.[27] Like every act of imperial favour, gifts could excite jealousies and suspicions, and we find Dio of Prusa trying to combat the rumour among his fellow citizens that Trajan had given vast presents to an embassy from Smyrna, and had sent the city untold riches along with some images of the Nemeseis.[28] The substantially fictional lives of the third-century emperors in the *Historia Augusta* contain a lot of details, not necessarily false but unreliable and unusable, which reflect the ideology of imperial gifts as it continued even after our period.[29] But if that material has to be left aside, we may still note the story in Petrus Patricius of Claudius Gothicus at dinner after the defeat of the Heruli:[30]

> When the emperor was celebrating at dinner after his victory over the Scythians, Andannoballus (a Herulian renegade) entered in the presence of the whole company and said, 'I wish to ask a favour of you.' The emperor, thinking that he would ask for something substantial, gave him permission to make his request. Andannobalus said, 'Give me good wine, so that I may summon my household and celebrate with them.' The emperor laughed and ordered the wine to be given to him; but he also gave him many other gifts.

What might appear at first light to be a purely fictional element, a man requesting permission to ask for a 'boon', can in fact be shown to be a recurrent element in the relations of the emperor with his subjects.[31] It is typical that the liberality takes place in the context of a social occasion, and not wholly surprising that a man should ask for a commodity such as wine; we shall see later that there is evidence of precious or rare commodities being in the emperor's possession.[32]

Such informal gifts were certainly the most frequent form of imperial liberality, interspered with the formal and public *congiaria* to the people of Rome. It was undoubtedly an exception to such regular public distributions when, for instance, during a fire at Rome Claudius encouraged the people to combat it by addressing them with bags (*fisci*) of money placed before him, and offering rewards in proportion to their exertions.[33] But the notion that the reception of gifts was something which resulted especially, but not only, from personal contact with the emperor remained essential to men's conception of his role, and was easily clad in a Christian garb by Eusebius. In describing the gifts of money, clothing and land made by Constantine in Rome after his conquest in 312, he uses a novel simile: 'In short, as the sun, when he rises upon the earth, liberally imparts his rays of light to all, so did Constantine, proceeding at early dawn from the imperial palace, and

---

[27] Philostratus, *VS* I, 21.
[28] Dio Prus., *Or.* XL, 14.
[29] See R. MacMullen, 'The Emperor's Largesses', *Latomus* XXI (1962), 159, n. 2.
[30] Petrus Patricius, *FHG* IV, 196; Dio ed. Boissevain III, p. 745, Fr. 172. For the Herulian invasion see F. Millar, 'P. Herennius Dexippus: the Greek World and the Third-Century Invasions', *JRS* LIX (1969), 12.
[31] pp. 467–8.
[32] pp. 144–5.
[33] Suetonius, *Claud.* 18, 1.

rising as it were with the heavenly luminary, impart the rays of his own beneficence to all who came into his presence.'[34] When he comes to Constantine's practice in the celebration of Easter in the latter part of his reign, a clearly Christian tone enters his description of imperial liberality: 'When dawn broke, imitating the benevolent acts of the Saviour, he stretched out his beneficent hand to all nations, races and peoples, granting unlimited riches to them all.'[35] Behind the high-flown language there clearly lies an established pattern of activity, the emperor's celebration of a festival by the distribution of especially lavish gifts to those from all over the empire who attended his morning audience.

3. *Gifts to the Emperor: Contributions, Curiosities and Valuables*

The distribution of gifts by the emperor was not a one-sided process. For gifts were made continually to him from both within and outside the empire. Eusebius himself had on occasion seen crowds of barbarians at the door of the palace in Constantinople bearing gifts to Constantine:[1]

> All these in due succession, like some painted pageant, presented to the emperor those gifts which their own nation held in most esteem; some offering crowns of gold, others diadems set with precious stones; some bringing fair-haired boys, others barbaric vestments embroidered with gold and flowers; some appeared with horses, others with shields and long spears, with arrows and bows, thereby offering their services and alliance for the emperor's acceptance. These presents he separately received and carefully laid aside, acknowledging them in so munificent a manner as at once to enrich those who bore them.

This pattern was not new. An embassy from the Cimbri had brought Augustus a sacred cauldron as a gift when they requested his friendship,[2] and Nicolaus of Damascus met at Antioch an Indian embassy to Augustus, with gifts borne by eight attendants, naked except for perfumed loin-cloths. The gifts included a variety of exotic wild animals, and a boy with no arms or shoulders who could do everything with his feet.[3]

The exchange of gifts played an essential role in the external diplomacy of the emperors, as is shown by various incidents before and during Trajan's Parthian War.[4] But the emperor's subjects also presented him with gifts on a variety of occasions, some of a regular and formalized kind, others purely

---

[34] *VC* I, 43, trans. Richardson, *Nicene and Post-Nicene Fathers*, Ser. 2. 1 (1890).

[35] *VC* IV, 22, 2: διαλαβούσης δὲ τῆς ἕω, τὰς σωτηρίους εὐεργεσίας μιμούμενος πᾶσιν ἔθνεσι λαοῖς τε καὶ δήμοις τὴν εὐεργετικὴν ἐξῆπλου δεξιάν, πλούσια πάντα τοῖς πᾶσι δωρούμενος.

[1] *VC* IV, 7, trans. Richardson.

[2] Strabo VII, 2, 1 (293).

[3] idem, XV, 1, 73 (719–20); see Dio LIV, 9, 8–10, and Florus II, 34.

[4] See e.g. Dio LXVIII, 17, 2–3; 18, 2; 19, 2; 21, 1. The diplomacy of the Roman emperors in relation to foreign kings and peoples is a neglected topic which falls outside the scope of this study. For some indications see J. Gagé, 'L'empereur romain et les rois: politique et protocole', *Rev. Hist.* CCXXI (1959), 221; cf. also M. Lemosse, *Le régime des relations internationales dans le Haut-Empire romain* (1967).

incidental. The most surprising, if also least important in economic terms, of these gifts from both kings and subjects are a number of freaks and curiosities, human, animal and inanimate, which were brought to various emperors, and afterwards shown by them at games, or put on permanent display at imperial residences. So for instance a king of Arabia (Nabatea?) sent a 'hippocentaur' to Claudius. When the creature died en route, it was embalmed by the prefect of Egypt and sent on. It was first displayed in the palace, where Pliny the Elder saw it; and when Phlegon of Tralles was writing in the first half of the second century, it lay in the imperial storehouses (*horrea*).[5] Similarly, the bones of two persons of Augustus' time who were more than nine feet tall were preserved, according to Pliny, in a tomb in the Horti Sallustiani.[6] The very tall Jew, whom Columella saw in the procession (*pompa*) of the circus games, was presumably the same Eleazar whom Artabanus of Parthia had sent among other gifts to Tiberius.[7] Individual subjects also might make gifts; the presentation of a giant turbot to Domitian by the fisherman who caught it forms the occasion of Juvenal's fourth satire, and has parallels in actual events from the reign of Tiberius.[8] The team of hermaphrodite mares found in the territory of Trier, which Nero put on show, were presumably a gift;[9] for the custom of putting rare gifts on show in front of the *Palatium* was sufficiently established and well known to be reflected even in rabbinic writings.[10]

Such gifts are significant for the tone of the exercise of monarchy in the empire, but not of course for its economic basis. It was different with gifts which represented a real store of value in themselves, such as the gold torque weighing 100 lbs. which the Gauls, evidently on an embassy, presented to Augustus.[11] For such objects could if necessary be put to uses quite different from those of mere ornament. The most regular and extensive gifts of this type which an emperor received were the gold crowns which were offered on a variety of occasions, notably on his accession and after victories.[12] This custom was inherited from the Hellenistic kings,[13] and had established

---

[5] Pliny, *NH* VII, 3/35; Phlegon, *FGrH* 257 F. 36 (xxxiv–v), concluding ἀπόκειται γὰρ ἐν τοῖς ὀ⟨ρ⟩ρίοις τοῦ αὐτοκράτορος τεταριχευμένος.

[6] VII, 16/74–5, followed by Solinus, *Coll. rer. mem.* I, 88–9, both mentioning also a very tall man brought (*advectus*) from Arabia in the time of Claudius. For other freaks brought to emperors, see Phlegon, F. 36 (vi), a hermaphrodite brought from Antioch on the Maeander to Claudius; 36 (xx), a four-headed boy brought to Nero; and 36 (xxix), an Alexandrian woman and her quintuplets to whom Trajan granted upkeep. It is apparently the same woman whom Gaius (*Dig.* XXXIV, 5, 7 *pr.*) mentions as being *perducta* to Hadrian, and whom Julianus (*Dig.* XLVI, 3, 36) refers to as being in Rome. Cf. also Phlegon's report, F. 37 (iv), of seeing a man of over 130 ἐπιδειχθέντα to Hadrian.

[7] Columella III, 8, 2; Josephus, *Ant.* XVIII, 4, 5 (103).

[8] Suetonius, *Tib.* 60; Seneca, *Ep.* 95, 42.

[9] Pliny, *NH* XI, 109/262.

[10] See I. Ziegler, *Die Königsgleichnisse des Midrasch beleuchtet durch die römische Kaiserzeit* (1903), 52–3.

[11] Quintilian, *Inst.* VI, 3, 79.

[12] See Th. Klauser, 'Aurum Coronarium', *Röm. Mitt.* LIX (1944), 129. The 'corona', or (invariably) in Greek στέφανος, would be more accurately described as a wreath made of solid gold.

[13] On the offering of gold crowns to victors and monarchs in the Greek and Hellenistic world see U. Wilcken, *Griechische Ostraka* I (1899), 295f.; E. Bikerman, *Institutions des Séleucides* (1938), 111–12; C. Préaux, *L'économie politique des Lagides* (1939), 294–5; Klauser, o.c., 134–7.

itself in Rome as soon as major victories were won by Roman generals in the Greek east; for the Greek cities naturally made to these victors the same offerings which they were accustomed to make to victorious kings. So, for instance, 'forty-five gold crowns, the gifts of the allied cities', were carried in the triumph of M.' Acilius Glabrio in 190;[14] and after the victory of Magnesia embassies from cities and peoples in Asia came to Cn. Manlius, not only to congratulate him but to bring gold crowns, each according to their means.[15] Again, in the triumph of Aemilius Paullus over Perseus, 'there were carried four hundred gold crowns, which embassies from the cities had brought to Aemilius as the rewards of victory'.[16] As we shall see, the offering of gold crowns retained its formal and diplomatic character under the empire. But, as figures such as those relating to Aemilius Paullus show, these offerings had long involved significant quantities of bullion which could have substantial uses; so Dio can mention the gold crowns given by dynasts and kings among the extra sources of revenue which Caesar acquired in 47 BC, and which he badly needed for his numerous projects.[17]

When Augustus celebrated his triple triumph in 29 BC, the *coloniae* and *municipia* of Italy itself also offered him gold crowns, weighing a total of 35,000 lbs.; but these he states that he declined to accept.[18] It is significant that the custom was now evidently universal, for it can be presumed that cities outside Italy offered crowns, which were not remitted; Rhosus in Syria had already sent an embassy with a crown to meet him in Ephesus at the end of 31.[19] Moreover, the very fact of his remission as a favour shows the strong element of obligation which had entered the custom. It had certainly spread to the western provinces by the reign of Claudius, for in his triumph after the invasion of Britain in 43 he indicated on placards the weight of the gold crowns presented by Gallia Comata and Hispania Citerior.[20] Here too we can presume that embassies came bringing crowns from all over the empire; a papyrus preserves Claudius' letter in answer to one of them, sent not by a city but by a *synodos* of athletes. They were evidently none too prompt in despatching it, for the emperor's letter dates to 46; he writes, 'The gold crown sent by you for the British victory I have gladly accepted as a sign of your loyalty towards me', and concludes with the names of the three ambassadors.[21] It is important to stress that in spite of the element of obligation the offering of gold crowns retained the outward form of a spontaneous gift, brought by an embassy from a city or other body, and handed over to the accompaniment of a suitable oration delivered before the emperor in person. A Greek rhetorician, probably of the late third century, gives the rules for the appropriate form of oration in presenting a crown to the emperor. He ends, 'Then you will ask for the decree (of the

[14] Livy XXXVII, 46, 4.
[15] XXXVIII, 37, 4; cf. XXXIX, 7, 1.
[16] Plutarch, *Aem.* 34, 5.
[17] XLII, 49, 3.
[18] *RG* 21, 3; cf. Dio LI, 21, 4.
[19] pp. 410–11.
[20] Pliny, *NH* XXXIII, 16/54.
[21] Wilcken, *Chrestomathie* I, no. 156. On the history of the *synodos* and its relations with the emperors see pp. 456–8.

city) to be read. Let your speech be of not more than 150 or 200 words.'[22]

Formal embassies presenting gold crowns to the emperor in person continued right through and beyond our period; Eunapius describes such embassies going to Julian on his proclamation in 361, and taking the opportunity to make requests of him.[23] So when we find the town council of Oxyrhynchus under Aurelian discussing payment for a gold crown, made by craftsmen, which is destined for the emperor,[24] we can assume that it was intended to be delivered by an embassy. But while actual gold crowns, or sums in lieu of them, continued to be voted on special occasions, the 'crown gold' was also a regular tax levied in addition to these. In the edict of Severus Alexander preserved on papyrus it is now clear that he is remitting the payments in respect of gold crowns for his accession but (with some embarrassment) not the regular payments.[25]

It is however only the gold crowns themselves with which we are concerned here, partly because their presentation by embassies was itself a central part of the relations between subjects and emperor, and partly because that presentation added to the reserves of bullion at the emperor's immediate disposition. As regards the uses to which it might have been put, we can rarely distinguish bullion from this source from other bullion; but we may note that Galba melted down a gold crown, supposedly weighing 15 lbs., presented by the province of Tarraconensis—and exacted the few ounces which were found to be lacking.[26] It is also significant that in 198, when two typical occasions for the offering of crowns arose, a victory of Severus in the east and the elevation of Caracalla as 'Augustus', the city of Nicopolis in Moesia Inferior sent instead a large sum of money, for which the emperor duly thanks them in a letter inscribed there.[27]

The *populus Romanus* itself naturally never offered gold crowns to the emperor. But there were occasions on which at least individual members of it made gifts, which might sometimes be in reality forced exactions. From Augustus to Claudius the emperor received individual gifts of money from the people on 1 January, in accordance with the custom of making gifts at New Year. Augustus used the money to purchase statues, which were placed in the various quarters (*vici*) of Rome, and also made larger gifts in return; if he were away the gifts were presented on the Capitol in his absence.[28] Tiberius objected to the expense involved in returning the gifts

---

[22] [Menander], περὶ στεφανωτικοῦ, Spengel, *Rhet. Gr.* III, 422–3. Cf. p. 8.

[23] *FHG* IV, p. 21, F. 15.

[24] *P. Oxy.* 1413. See A. K. Bowman, *The Town Councils of Roman Egypt* (1971), 151–3.

[25] *P. Fay.* 20; see A. K. Bowman, 'The Crown-Tax in Roman Egypt', *Bull. Am. Soc. Pap.* IV (1967), 59. The distinction between the two forms of exaction is expressed very clearly by Dio LXXVII, 9, 2 (382), relating to Caracalla's practice. For other remissions see e.g. *HA, Had.* 6, 5; *Ant. Pius* 4, 10; *Prob.* 15, 4. Cf. *P. Oxy.* 3121, a gold crown for Licinius, *c.* 316–18.

[26] Suetonius, *Galba* 12.

[27] *IGBulg.* 659, ll. 33–5: τὴν συντέλειαν τῶν χρημάτων τὰς ἑβδομήκοντα μυριάδας ὡς παρὰ ἀνδρῶν εὔνων προσηκά[μ]εθα The diplomatic tone is again clear. Unfortunately the emperor does not indicate of what currency the '700,000' consisted.

[28] Suetonius, *Aug.* 57, 1; Dio LIV, 35, 2. Cf. *ILS* 99: 'Laribus publicis sacrum imp. Caesar Augustus pontifex maximus, tribunic. potestat. XVIIII, ex stipe, quam populus ei contulit K. Ianuar. apsenti, C. Calvisio Sabino, L. Passieno Rufo cos'. (4 BC). See M. Meslin, *La fête des kalendes de janvier dans l'empire romain* (1970), esp. 31f.

fourfold, as was apparently customary for the emperor, and also to being troubled throughout the whole of January by people who had been unable to approach him on the 1st. So he ordered that the custom should be confined to that day, and also tried to be out of Rome then; in 17, when some people brought money to him, he refused, and published an edict about it.[29] Gaius, however, announced by edict that he was reviving the practice, and received contributions on each January 1, seated in the *vestibulum* of a temple. This was probably the temple of Jupiter on the Capitol, for when Gaius was absent at the beginning of 40, the senate solemnly presented money to his chair which stood there.[30]

This custom was abolished by Claudius,[31] and does not seem to have been revived. It was more significant, again, for the form of personal contacts between emperor and people than as a source of revenue; for (at least in principle) the emperor returned more than he received. But, apart from this formalized exchange of gifts, we do have some instances of contributions for particular needs or occasions by private individuals or communities. About AD 3, for instance, the Palatium was damaged by fire, and many cities and individuals offered contributions for restoring it; but Augustus accepted only an *aureus* from each community and a *denarius* from each individual.[32] When he set up the *aerarium militare* in AD 6 he accepted contributions from client kings and communities, but none from individuals.[33] Dio doubts whether the offers from individuals were truly voluntary, just as he does when Gaius, while in Gaul in 39, received gifts from individuals and communities.[34] He takes the same view of the allegedly voluntary contributions made to Nero by cities and private persons after the fire of Rome in 64[35]—not surprisingly, as they were linked with forays by imperial agents to seize treasures and cult-statues from the temples of provincial cities.[36] As Suetonius puts it, contributions (*conlationes*) were 'not only accepted but demanded'.[37] We can specify only one case, the 4,000,000 *sesterces* which Lugdunum contributed; the same sum was given back by Nero two years later, apparently to restore the city after a fire there.[38]

It was apparently the implied element of compulsion which made Titus refuse offers of contribution from kings, communities and private persons after the eruption of Vesuvius.[39] The line between exaction and gift could indeed never be clear. For instance, Dio records of Severus that he exacted fourfold any contributions made by peoples or individuals to his rival Pescennius Niger, whether this had been voluntarily or under compulsion;

---

[29] Suetonius, *Tib.* 34, 2; Dio LVII, 8, 6; 17, 1.
[30] Suetonius, *Cal.* 42; Dio LIX, 6, 4; 24, 4.
[31] Dio LX, 6, 3.
[32] Suetonius, *Aug.* 57, 2; Dio LV, 12, 4.
[33] Dio, LV, 25, 3.
[34] LIX, 21, 4.
[35] LXII, 18, 5 (57).
[36] Tacitus, *Ann.* XV, 45; XVI, 23; Dio of Prusa, *Or.* XXXI, 147–50. For imperial exactions of statues and other works of art see also pp. 145–6.
[37] *Nero* 38, 3.
[38] Tacitus, *Ann.* XVI, 13, 3.
[39] Dio LXVI, 24, 4 (159).

and he lists among the revenues of Caracalla the 'gifts' which he demanded from persons and cities.[40] All these brief items of evidence are sufficient to indicate another significant element in the relations between emperor and subjects, but tell us nothing of the form in which the contributions or gifts were made, whether they involved any ceremonial presentation to the emperor, or where they were placed on receipt. We can, however, make rather more of what Eusebius relates of Constantine's father, Constantius, as 'Caesar' in the west in 293–305;[41] the apparent absurdity of the tale may seem less certain in the light of the evidence just discussed and of what will be said below of the 'treasures' stored by the emperors.

According to Eusebius' story, Constantius was too mild and beneficent to exact sufficient money from his subjects, and was reproached by messengers from Diocletian for the empty state of his treasury. Asking Diocletian's messengers to wait, he summoned the wealthiest men from his territory and informed them that he needed money, and that now was the time for each to show his spontaneous goodwill towards their own emperor. So they gladly consented to fill his treasures with gold and silver and other money. After the messengers had been ordered to inspect the overflowing treasures, they were sent home. It is said, Eusebius continues, that Constantius then summoned the contributors and restored their wealth to them.

4. *The Imperial 'Treasures': Valuables, Bullion and Coin*

Eusebius' story implies both that rich private individuals could, when pressed, call on substantial quantities of coin, and that an emperor should normally have even larger stores of coin in his immediate vicinity. Moreover, the evidence of gifts both from and to the emperor implies the presence at his immediate disposition, not only of coin, but of large quantities of precious metals and of valuables of other kinds. On a wider view, we tend greatly to underestimate the role played in the economy of the ancient world by stores of wealth, in the form of ornaments, bullion or coin, reposing in temples, public buildings or private houses; stores which were for the most part static, but which could be put to use if the occasion arose. Even such things as articles of clothing could serve not only, as we have seen, as gifts,[1] but as stores of value. It is far from an insignificant fact that the will of Augustus mentioned 'my woollen cloths, and blankets, purple and multi-coloured'.[2]

Wine too could be granted by an emperor as a gift.[3] So also could cinnamon for use in medicines, which, as Galen records, the *amici* could obtain by petitioning the emperor.[4] Galen himself was able to select from quantities

---

[40] LXXV, 8, 4 (333); LXXVIII, 9, 3 (382).

[41] *VC* I, 14.

[1] pp. 135, 137. Note also Tacitus, *Ann.* XIII, 13, 4, Nero in 55 inspecting the stores of imperial clothing, and selecting some garments and jewels to send as a gift to his mother; and Lactantius, *De mort. pers.* 37, 5, of Maximin: 'cum satellites universos . . . pretiosis vestibus et aureis nummis expungeret.'

[2] Charisius, *Ars Gram.* I, 104 Keil; p. 132 Barwich: 'gausapes, lodices purpureas et colorias meas.' Note that Nero paid 4,000,000 *sesterces* for *tricliniaria Babylonica*, Pliny, *NH* VIII, 74/196.

[3] p. 138.

[4] Galen XIV, 71 Kühn.

of Hymettus honey laid up 'in the imperial repositories',[5] and also saw there large amounts of cinnamon stored in wooden containers, some laid down in the time of Trajan, some under Hadrian and some under Antoninus Pius. It seems to have been there too that he was able to taste a selection of Falernian wines stored in jars with the vintage inscribed on them, some being more than 120 years old.[6]

Apart from such commodities for consumption, it is clear that the imperial palaces contained immense treasures in statues, ornaments, furniture and tableware. Of these the most prominent individual items were statues and works of art by the great masters of classical and Hellenistic Greece. To take only a few examples, when Pliny was writing his *Natural History*, the 'Astragalizontes' of Polyclitus stood in the atrium of Titus' house, which also contained the famous Laocoon by three Rhodian sculptors of the first century BC.[7] Three statues by Praxiteles stood in the Horti Serviliani.[8] The acquisition of such works of art had followed varied patterns, from direct exaction in war or civil war to simple purchase, in all of which the emperors succeeded to the Hellenizing tastes of later republican society. More often than not, however, the statues were then placed in some temple or public place in Rome. After the victory of Actium for instance, Augustus took from Tegea the ivory statue of Athena Alea, and the tusks of the Calydonian boar. When Pausanias was writing towards the end of the second century, these statues stood in the Forum of Augustus: 'As to the boar's tusks, the keepers of the curiosities say that one of them is broken; but the remaining one is preserved in the imperial gardens, in a sanctuary of Dionysus, and is just half a fathom long.'[9] Augustus restored to Samos the 'Athena' and 'Hercules' of Myron which Antonius had taken, but kept the 'Zeus' and made a shrine for it on the Capitol.[10] Again the painting called 'Hyacinthus' by Nicias, which Augustus brought back from Alexandria after its capture, was dedicated by Tiberius in the temple of Augustus;[11] just as Augustus himself dedicated in the temple of Caesar Apelles' painting of 'Venus Rising from the Waves' from the Asclepieum at Cos, in return for which he is said to have allowed the Coans 100 talents remission of tribute each year.[12]

[5] ibid., 26: τοῦ δ' Ὑμηττίου μέλιτος ἐν ταῖς αὐτοκρατορικαῖς ἀποθήκαις ὄντος πολλοῦ, τοῦ διετοῦς γευομένου, ἐκλέγων ἐξ αὐτοῦ πάλιν τὸ γλυκύτατον καὶ δριμύτατον . . . ἐπεὶ δ' οὐ μόνοις τοῖς βασιλικὴν ἀφθονίαν ἔχουσι . . . For the cinnamon see 64: Ἀντωνίνῳ γοῦν σκευάζων τὴν θηριακὴν ἐθεασάμην ἀγγεῖα πολλὰ ξύλινα, τὰ μὲν ἐπὶ Τραϊανοῦ ταῖς ἀποθήκαις ἐγκαθέντα μετὰ κινναμώμου, τὰ δὲ ἐπ' Ἀδριανοῦ, τὰ δὲ ἐπ' Ἀντωνίνου τοῦ μετὰ τὸν Ἀδριανὸν ἄρξαντος.

[6] ibid., 25: κομιζομένων γὰρ τοῖς βασιλεῦσι τῶν ἀρίστων ἁπανταχόθεν, ἐξ αὐτῶν πάλιν τούτων τὸ κάλλιστον αἱρήσεται, ἔγωγέ τοι τῶν οἴνων τῶν Φαλερίνων ἑκάστου τὴν ἡλικίαν ἀναγινώσκων ἐπιγεγραμμένην τοῖς κεραμίοις, εὐχόμην τῆς γεύσεως.

[7] XXXIV, 19/55; XXXVI, 5/37. For all these references see K. Jex-Blake, E. Sellers, *The Elder Pliny's Chapters on the History of Art* (1896), ad locc.

[8] XXXVI, 4/23.

[9] Pausanias VIII, 46, trans. Frazer. The keepers are described as οἱ ἐπὶ τοῖς θαύμασιν. For examples of other curiosities on show at imperial residences see pp. 16, 140. Two statues by Apelles were also placed by Augustus in his Forum, Pliny, *NH* XXXV, 36/93–4.

[10] Strabo XIV, 1, 14 (637). He also restored the 'Apollo' of Myron to Ephesus, though only after being warned to do so in a dream, Pliny, *NH* XXXIV, 19/58.

[11] Pliny, *NH* XXXV, 40/131.

[12] Strabo XIV, 2, 19 (657); Pliny, *NH* XXXV, 36/91.

6

The seizure of works of art continued intermittently later; Pliny concludes a long list of classical sculptures by saying that the best of them were taken by Nero and placed in the 'Golden House', and subsequently dedicated in the temple of Pax by Vespasian.[13] After the capture of Seleucia on the Tigris, Lucius Verus dedicated the statue of Apollo Comaeus from there in the temple of Apollo on the Palatine.[14] But it was not until the foundation of Constantinople that the Greek world experienced a wholesale seizure of works of art and cult-objects which surpassed those of the late republic or of Nero.[15] It can be assumed that an important motive on the part of Constantine was simply the traditional one of adorning his new capital with the finest examples of antique art. But Eusebius manages to imply a strictly Christian motivation, namely that of robbing cult-statues of their religious setting and exposing them to the public view, 'so that here a Pythian and there a Sminthian Apollo excited the contempt of the beholder: while the Delphic tripods were deposited in the Hippodrome and the Muses of Helicon in the palace'.[16] Firmicus Maternus, however, addressing the sons of Constantine a few years later with all the fervour of a convert, introduces quite a different aspect of this process: 'Remove, remove without fear, most sacred emperors, the ornaments of the temples. Let the flame of the mint or the mines melt those gods. Transfer those offerings, one and all, to your service and control.'[17] Eusebius confirms in passing that some of the precious metal of the statues was melted down;[18] and the anonymous author of the later fourth-century treatise *De rebus bellicis* attributes Constantine's introduction of the gold *solidus* as common currency directly to his putting into circulation vast quantities of precious metal from the pagan temples.[19]

If some significant part of the gold from the temple treasures was indeed minted by Constantine he would have been following a long-attested practice. For instance Herodian, in describing the exactions of Maximinus a century earlier, says 'temple dedications, statues of the gods, honorary presentations to the heroes, any ornamentation on public buildings or city decorations, or material that could be turned into coin was all melted down'.[20] Three centuries before that, in 86 BC, a *senatus consultum* had authorized the melting down and minting of gold and silver ornaments in the temples, so that the soldiers could be paid.[21] Dio's report that Augustus coined the silver gained from melting down statues of himself seems to rest on a misunderstanding;[22]

---

[13] Pliny, *NH* XXXIV, 19/84. For works in the temple of Pax see e.g. XXXV, 36/74 and 109. They were joined there by the Table of Shewbread and the seven-branched candlestick from the temple in Jerusalem. See Schürer, *Jewish People* I, 510.

[14] Ammianus XXIII, 6, 24.

[15] See most recently C. Mango, 'Antique Statuary and the Byzantine Beholder', *DOP* XVII (1963), 53. Cf. pp. 619–20.

[16] *VC* III, 54, 1–2, trans. Mango, o.c., 56.

[17] *De errore profanarum religionum* 28, 6: 'tollite, tollite securi, sacratissimi imperatores, ornamenta templorum, deos istos aut monetae ignis aut metallorum coquat flamma, donaria universa ad utilitatem vestrem dominiumque transferte.'

[18] *VC* III, 54, 6.

[19] *De rebus bellicis* 2, 1; see E. A. Thompson, *A Roman Reformer and Inventor* (1952), 26–34.

[20] VII, 3, 5, Loeb trans.

[21] Valerius Maximus VII, 6, 4.

[22] LIII, 22, 3, compared with *RG* 24 and Suetonius, *Aug.* 52.

but there seems no reason to disbelieve his statement that a lot of coin was made from melting down statues of Domitian after his assassination in 96.[23]

What was true of the precious metal of statues, was true potentially also of the domestic ornaments of the imperial palace. We find Herod of Judaea, during the famine in about 24 BC, melting down the gold and silver ornaments in his palace, including those of artistic value, to mint coin which was sent to the prefect of Egypt for the purchase of corn.[24] But more clearly still, Plutarch reports that when Galba was proclaimed in Tarraconensis in 68, Otho, who was then *legatus* of Lusitania, joined him, and 'bringing all the gold and silver that he had in the shape of drinking-cups and tables, he gave it to him for conversion into coin'.[25]

It is therefore not a naive misconception on Philo's part when he writes, in describing the hopeful beginnings of the reign of Gaius, that he inherited 'a mass of goods ready accumulated, numerous treasuries of money, gold and silver, some in bullion and some in coin, and some in the form of ornamental drinking-cups and other artistic products made for display'.[26] Ornaments were readily convertible to coin, as indeed was coin to ornaments (for Petrus Patricius records that Licinius melted down and converted to 'other uses' gold coins with the head of Constantine on them).[27] But unlike valuables looted or exacted from elsewhere, the existing stock of imperial treasures or ornaments is never actually attested as being coined in times of crisis. That did not mean, however, that it had no functions other than purely decorative ones. The importance attached to the imperial valuables is suggested (if no more than that) by the titles of freedmen in charge of the different categories of them,[28] and more clearly indicated by Dio's report that Messalina gave her lover Silius one of the imperial residences, and transferred to it all the most valuable of the ornaments of Claudius.[29] Such ornaments, it seems, were seen as an essential accompaniment of the imperial role; indeed Herodian twice refers to the imperial ornaments being carried in procession in Rome.[30] They could also be used as gifts, like the two drinking-cups made by Calamis in the fifth century BC which Germanicus gave to his teacher, Cassius Salanus.[31] Individual items might also be sent as dedications to temples. The Temple of Jerusalem contained gold bowls, cups and other vessels sent by Livia and Augustus;[32] more than three centuries later, Constantine not merely ordered the construction of the Church of the Holy Sepulchre, but sent a personal offering of twelve silver bowls, which

[23] LXVIII, 1, 1.

[24] Josephus, *Ant.* XV, 9, 2 (306–7). For the date and circumstances see Schürer, *Jewish People* I, 290–1.

[25] *Galba* 20, 3, Loeb trans. (20, 2).

[26] *Leg.* 2/9.

[27] *FHG* IV, 198; Dio ed. Boissevain III, 748, Fr. 187.

[28] A few examples in A. M. Duff, *Freedmen in the Early Roman Empire* (1928), 144–5.

[29] LXI, 31, 3.

[30] I, 10, 5; V, 6, 8.

[31] Pliny, *NH* XXXIV, 18/47.

[32] Philo, *Leg.* 40/319, cf. 23/157; Josephus, *BJ* V, 13, 6 (561)—their being melted down by John of Gischala in 70.

surmounted the twelve pillars round the altar.[33] Sozomenus describes the bishops at Jerusalem in 335 dedicating 'the ornaments and offerings sent from the emperor, which are still to be found in the church, and cause amazement to those who see them by their luxury and size'.[34]

In moments of financial need, whether in a serious crisis or merely as the result of extravagance, emperors normally resorted to selling rather than coining the ornaments and treasures of the palace. If that were the only occasion of such a sale, we could afford to disregard, as another eccentricity on the part of Gaius, Suetonius' story of the auction in Gaul at which the emperor personally presided, and for which wagons and animals were requisitioned to bring the treasures of the palace from Rome.[35] Dio repeats this, adding that Gaius would comment on the individual items, saying, for instance, 'This Egyptian object was Antonius's, a prize of victory for Augustus.'[36]

When Nerva was short of money, Dio records, one of the steps which he took was to sell clothing, gold and silver vessels, and other equipment both from his own house and the imperial possessions, as well as estates and houses, winning favour by not being too particular over the price.[37] Various sources decribe the occasion on which Marcus Aurelius held an auction of the treasures of the palace in order to gain money for paying the troops;[38] according to the *Historia Augusta*, the sale took place in the Forum of Trajan, lasted two months, and included silk robes, gold ornaments, jewels and paintings by famous artists. When the war was over, those who had made purchases were allowed, but not compelled, to return them and reclaim their money. In very different circumstances, Pertinax, proclaimed after the murder of Commodus, paid the praetorian cohorts what he had promised them by selling statues, weapons, horses, slave-boys and other items which Commodus had collected either for his gladiatorial pursuits or for pleasure; in this case there were the extra motives of exhibiting the way of life of his predecessor, and observing who wished to buy the objects.[39]

The wealth stored in imperial objects of luxury was clearly put into circulation only at exceptional moments. But at all times the maintenance of the imperial household, and of the emperor's individual role, must have necessitated a constant outflow of payments in coin. Even ignoring for the moment both the more general question of what rights the emperor had to what sources of revenue, and also the more particular question of how substantial quantities of coin were physically transported to him, there remains a real difficulty in envisaging what stores of coin he possessed, and where. The difficulties are considerable even in relation to Rome, but are

[33] Eusebius, *VC* III, 38: κρατῆρσι μεγίστοις ἐξ ἀργύρου πεποιημένοις τὰς κορυφὰς κοσμού-μενοι, οὓς δὴ βασιλεὺς αὐτὸς ἀνάθημα κάλλιστον ἐδωρεῖτο τῷ αὐτοῦ θεῷ.
[34] *HE* II, 26, 3.
[35] *Cal.* 39.
[36] LIX, 22, 5–6.
[37] LXVIII, 2, 2. The frequent supposition that a step such as this could only be of trivial importance rests on anachronistic assumptions about the balance of private (or imperial) and public resources.
[38] Dio ed. Boissevain III, 280–1; *HA, Marc. Ant.* 17, 4–5; 21, 9; Eutropius, *Brev.* VIII, 13, 2.
[39] Dio LXXIV, 5, 3–5 (310); cf. *HA, Pert.* 7, 8–8, 7.

much greater when we take into account the amount of time spent by emperors at their villas in Italy, or travelling in the provinces.

Although even the richest of Roman landowners might on occasion be vulnerable to a shortage of actual cash in coin,[40] there are conversely indications that they might keep substantial quantities of coin stored in their houses. One man is said to have survived the triumviral proscriptions by being hidden in an iron chest in his house, which was used for keeping money or books.[41] Plutarch relates how when Marcus Antonius promised 250,000 *denarii* to a friend, his procurator piled up the whole sum before him to show him how excessive it was—so Antonius doubled it.[42] The significance of the story for our purposes is perhaps increased rather than decreased by the fact that Dio tells it of Nero, with Agrippina playing the role of the procurator, and the sum increased tenfold.[43] Antonius himself is reported to have found 4,000 talents in the house of Julius Caesar after the Ides of March, and to have kept it for himself;[44] other private cash of Caesar's had been sent east for the intended Parthian war, and was retained by Octavian when it was brought back.[45]

That the emperors normally had large quantities of coin available in Rome seems clear enough. Apart from normal needs, large quantities were distributed at one moment in a *congiarium*.[46] Similarly, in his will Augustus left many millions of *sesterces* to the Roman people, the praetorian cohorts and the legions 'which sum he ordered to be paid out, for he had always had it in store and set aside'.[47] The money was certainly in Rome, but nothing is clear beyond that. In 33 Tiberius was able to put out for loan without interest 100,000,000 *sesterces* to meet a shortage of currency in Rome.[48] Tiberius himself was not in Rome, and no source indicates from where the coin was produced. We cannot locate any specific place or places, whether in the Palatium or elsewhere, where imperial cash was stored. The difficulty is first of all verbal, in that Dio, for instance, quite frequently indicates that at a certain time there was a certain sum in the *basilikon*; we can translate this as 'the Imperial Treasury', while still being uncertain as to whether the term is concrete, and refers to a specific place, or abstract.[49] He and others also talk on occasion of the imperial 'treasures' or 'treasuries'—*thesauri*—and

---

[40] See M. W. Frederiksen, 'Caesar, Cicero and the Problem of Debt', *JRS* LVI (1966), 128.

[41] Appian, *BC* IV, 44/187.

[42] *Ant.* 4, 7–9.

[43] LXI, 5, 4.

[44] Plutarch, *Ant.* 15, 1.

[45] Nicolaus of Damascus, *FGrH* 90 F. 130 (XVIII) (55).

[46] Cf. pp. 136–7, and note Herodian VII 3, 5: Maximinus εἴ τινα ἦν χρήματα πολιτικὰ εἰς εὐθηνίας ἢ νομὰς τῶν δημοτῶν ἀθροιζόμενα εἴτε θεάτροις ἢ πανηγύρεσιν ἀνακείμενα, ἐς ἑαυτὸν μετῆγε. But it is not certain that this refers to Rome rather than to provincial towns.

[47] Suetonius, *Aug.* 101, 2: 'quam summam repraesentari iussit, nam et confiscatum semper repositamque habuerat.'

[48] Tacitus, *Ann.* VI, 17; Suetonius, *Tib.* 48; Dio LVIII, 21, 5. Both the latter indicate that money represented a private munificence by Tiberius, and therefore did not come from the *aerarium*.

[49] e.g. LXI, 5, 5 (24–5): τοὺς ἐν τῷ βασιλικῷ θησαυροὺς (see below) ἐξήντλησε (Nero). Cf. LXXIII, 5, 4 (310), where βασίλειον appears to be used in the same sense; LXXIX, 12, 2² (463): ὅτι χρήματα πολλὰ ὁ Μακρῖνος ἐν τῷ βασιλικῷ εὑρὼν διεσπάθησεν (it is at least clear that this is not an actual place in Rome, to which Macrinus never came as emperor).

leave us with precisely the same problem.[50] It *may* be significant that when Dio describes a fire which caused extensive damage to the Palatium in 192, he mentions that 'almost all the documents relating to the government' were destroyed, but says nothing about stocks of cash.[51] We have seen that there were repositories of good belonging to the emperor (though their location is obscure),[52] but with cash we are quite in the dark, unless we place more weight than is justified on the very slight indications that the emperors, like private persons, may have deposited money in temples in Rome.[53] Herodian indeed speaks of Severus showing Caracalla and Geta the treasuries (*thesauri*) and temples (apparently in Rome) overflowing with money, and later describes Caracalla ordering the soldiers to take money from the temples and treasuries.[54] But his grasp on reality is always weak and unreliable.

Our evidence as to what cash or bullion was available to the emperor outside Rome, and how, is, if possible, even more unsatisfactory. It is clear enough that substantial quantities *could* have been carried with him. Plutarch records that Clodius incensed the soldiers on service in the east in the early 60s BC by pointing to the 'waggons and camels of Lucullus laden with golden beakers set with precious stones', which they had to escort.[55] On his flight from Actium, Antonius tried to divide among his friends the contents of a transport-ship in his fleet, which was loaded with coined money and many royal utensils of gold and silver.[56] Earlier, Octavian had set out to raise troops in Campania in 44 BC with large sums of money loaded on pack-animals;[57] and the private money of Germanicus, kept in bags (*fisci*), was seized by his mutinous soldiers near Ara Ubii in AD 14.[58] We hear also on occasion of valuable objects which emperors took with them, such as the statue of an Amazon by the fifth-century sculptor Strongylion, which was carried around in the *comitatus* of Nero;[59] or the golden bowls and gilded ox-horn, both spoils from the Dacian war, which Trajan evidently took with him on the Parthian war, and dedicated in the temple of Zeus on Mt. Casius near Antioch.[60]

Throughout, however, the evidence concerning coined money or valuables

[50] Dio LIX, 10, 7: οἵ τε γὰρ θησαυροὶ ἐξανάλωντο καὶ οὐδὲν αὐτῷ (Gaius) ἐξήρκει. Cf. LXXVII, 3, 2 (375) and Eusebius, *VC* I, 55, 2; II, 45, 2; III, 1, 4. A few inscriptions indicate actual imperial *thesauri* in Rome in the earlier period, Hirschfeld, *Verwaltungsbeanten*[2], 307 n. 3, but we have no idea of their nature or function.

[51] LXXII, 24, 2–3 (305): εἴς τε τὸ παλάτιον μετεωρισθὲν ἐσῆλθε καὶ πολλὰ πάνυ αὐτοῦ κατέκαυσεν, ὥστε καὶ τὰ γράμματα τὰ τῇ ἀρχῇ προσήκοντα ὀλίγου δεῖν πάντα φθαρῆναι.

[52] If the ἀποθήκας τῶν τε Αἰγυπτίων καὶ τῶν Ἀραβίων φορτίων, which Dio mentions just previously in his account of the fire, were identical with the imperial ἀποθηκαί which Galen used (p. 145), then these lay between the temple of Pax and the Palatium. Note also the claim of *HA, Marc. Ant.* 17, 4 that Marcus found a large number of gems 'in repositorio sanctiore Hadriani'. Dio LXXVIII, 6, 4 (409) claims that poisons were found ἐν τῷ βασιλικῷ after the death of Caracalla. τὸ βασιλικόν here must at least be a definite place (or receptacle).

[53] See Hirschfeld, *Verwaltungsbeanten*[2], 4–5.

[54] III, 13, 4; IV, 4, 7.

[55] *Luc.* 34, 4.

[56] Plutarch, *Ant.* 67, 8.

[57] Nicolaus of Damascus, *FGrH* 90 F. 130 (XXXI) (133). Compare Suetonius, *Galba* 8, 1: Galba, as a rich *privatus* in disfavour with Nero, was accompanied everywhere by a *vehiculum* loaded ready with 1,000,000 *sesterces* in gold.

[58] Tacitus, *Ann.* I, 37.

[59] Pliny, *NH* XXXIV, 19/82.

[60] Arrian, *Parthica*, F. *36 Roos.

with the emperor on journeys or campaigns is extremely sparse. We may note that before his suicide at Bedriacum in 69 Otho distributed money 'from the supply which was to hand' to his domestic slaves;[61] and we have seen that when Marcus Aurelius was pleased by the oration of Hadrian of Tyre in Athens in 176 he could give him gold, silver, horses and slaves.[62] Similarly we find Helena, the mother of Constantine, when touring the east in the late 320s, making distributions of money in cities and to army units, giving cash and clothing to the poor and placing dedications in churches.[63]

We are hampered here by lack of evidence not only on the specific problem of what money from what source was to hand when the emperor travelled, but on the relation of this question to much wider problems, which are even more insoluble, on the movement of bullion and coin in the empire, the relative dependence of minting on either the mining of new ore on the one hand or the coining or recoining of bullion or old coins on the other,[64] and the physical distribution of coin to the army.[65] In other words we have no clear conception of what provincial centres existed or developed for the collection and storage of tribute or other revenues, and how such centres might have related to mints in the provinces, to the availability of cash to the emperors while on their travels, or to the imperial centres which we have seen developing in the provinces.[66] It is indeed in the period of the tetrarchy and Constantine that we can see some indications of these elements coinciding. The story of the 'voluntary' contributions to Constantius involves, as we saw, the existence of a treasury where the emperor was.[67] The place, perhaps Trier, is not specified. Nor is an actual place named in Lactantius' account of Maximian's attempted coup against Constantine in 307; but Lactantius does say that Maximian 'suddenly seized the purple, invaded the *thesauri* and made lavish donations, as was his custom'.[68] However, a description of the flight of Licinius in 316/7 shows him hastening to Sirmium, collecting his wife, and son and the *thesauri* and making his way with them to Chalcedon.[69] If we may trust Eusebius, the palace at Constantinople

[61] Suetonius, *Otho* 10: 'divisit et pecunias domesticis ex copia praesenti.'

[62] Philostratus, *VS* II, 10; p. 92.

[63] Eusebius, *VC* III, 44–5.

[64] To the evidence on the role of existing bullion as potential coin mentioned above, we can add for instance Plutarch, *Luc.* 4, 1—when Sulla fined the cities of Asia 2,000 talents in 84, προσταχθὲν αὐτῷ (Lucullus) τά τε χρήματα ταῦτα πρᾶξαι καὶ νόμισμα κόψαι. Cf. Appian, *BC* IV, 75/320, Brutus in 43/2 BC gets possession of the treasures of a minor king in Thrace καὶ τοῦτο μὲν ἔκοπτε καὶ νόμισμα ἐποίει. Theories which discuss Roman coinage on the assumption of a direct relationship between mining and minting rest on a very insecure foundation, at least as regards any short-term effects. For a longer-term view (whose validity I am not qualified to assess), C. C. Patterson, 'Silver Stocks and Losses in Ancient and Medieval Times', *Econ. Hist. Rev.* XXV (1972), 205, esp. 225–8.

[65] There is strikingly little evidence on this. Some such evidence is for instance Tacitus, *Hist.* IV, 36, a *donativum* from Vitellius arriving at Vetera; Arrian, *Periplus* 6, 1–2; 10, 3; cf. T. C. Skeat. *Papyri from Panopolis* (1964), no. 2, ll. 37–42, 57–60, 161–75, 180–208, 259–70, 291–304 (delivery of payments for auxiliary units); these last few lines seem to envisage the transport of the money in a waggon drawn by four mules.

[66] pp. 40–53.

[67] p. 144.

[68] *De mort. pers.* 29, 5. The place may be Arelate.

[69] *Exc. Val.* I (*Origo Constantini Imperatoris*), 16–17. On the date of this conflict with Constantine see now T. D. Barnes, 'Lactantius and Constantine', *JRS* LXIII (1973), 29, on p. 38.

contained actual treasuries, into which Constantine would retire to pray in private.[70]

Minting in this period was not confined to identifiable tetrarchic centres, but the location of mints was certainly heavily influenced by them. The connection is clearest in the case of Nicomedia, where Lactantius includes a mint among the building-projects initiated by Diocletian.[71] The coins themselves indicate that minting began there in 294/5. Other mints which were active in the period include Trier, Aquileia, Serdica, Thessalonica, Heraclea (Perinthus) and Antioch,[72] which are all attested in other evidence as established imperial centres, or at least as frequent stopping-places. It may even be that we can see developing in this period, and becoming clearer in that of Constantine, a pattern whereby minting regularly followed the emperor from one to another of his main centres; but for that to be accepted, we should require more separate and non-interdependent evidence for the imperial presence and minting coinciding in particular cities than we at present possess.[73]

What we do know is that in the tetrarchic period purchases of gold were made from the population of Egypt; the earliest evidence comes from the year 300, and shows that monthly payments were required, at a fixed maximum price. The element of compulsion is quite clear[74] (though a document of about this time relating to silver states that the emperors have forbidden compulsion).[75] The direct link with the emperor's residence is provided by a papyrus from Oxyrhynchus, a letter perhaps from the prefect and addressed to the council and *logistēs* of Oxyrhynchus in 304 or soon after;[76] the city was to provide 38 lb. of gold (to be paid for by the 'most sacred treasury' at 100,000 *denarii* per lb.), which should be delivered in Alexandria in time for it to reach Nicomedia by 1 September.

It is typical of our evidence on the financial sub-structure of the imperial regime that we cannot be certain what degree of benefit the 'most sacred treasury' expected from these transactions, whether it was simply the acquisition of the most valuable metals themselves which mattered, or to what use they would be put.[77] As always, while we can to some extent map the relations of emperor and subjects, in which exaction and benefaction maintained a rough and precarious balance, whenever we ask more precise

---

[70] *VC* IV, 22, 1; cf. *Or. in Tric.* 9, 11.

[71] *De mort. pers.* 7, 9.

[72] See C. H. V. Sutherland, *RIC* VI: *From Diocletian's Reform (AD 294) to the Death of Maximinus (AD 313)* (1967), 4–7. For other factors relevant to the positioning of mints in this period see M. Hendy, 'Mint and Fiscal Administration under Diocletian, his Colleagues and his Successors', *JRS* LXII (1971), 75.

[73] See Sutherland, o.c., 54–5; P. Bruun, *Studies in Constantinian Chronology* (1961), 23f.; M. R. Alföldi, *Die Constantinische Goldprägung* (1963), 12–20; Bruun, *RIC* VII: *Constantine and Licinius AD 313–337* (1966), 13–18; Hendy, o.c., 81.

[74] *P. Beatty Panop.* 2, ll. 215–21.

[75] *SB* 9253.

[76] *P. Oxy.* 2106. For arguments on the precise date see A. Segré, 'On the Date and Circumstances of the Prefect's Letter: P. Oxy. 2106', *JEA* XXVI (1940), 114, and now J. Rea, 'P.S.I. IV 310 and imperial bullion purchases', *Chron. d'Ég.* XLIX (1974), 163. As the gold was supposed to be paid for, it was not, as Segré believed, *aurum coronarium*.

[77] There is nothing to indicate any significant emission of *aurei* from Nicomedia at or near this time, see Sutherland, o.c., 543–52.

questions about the exchange of wealth involved, no answer can be found. We are fortunate even to have the glimpse which Galen offers us of the imperial stores of cinnamon, honey and wine as they were in the second century; but we cannot follow Constantine into the treasuries of his palace in Constantinople.

5. *Inheritances and Legacies*

When Herod the Great died in 4 BC he left in his will substantial sums to Augustus: 'To Caesar he left ten million pieces of coined silver besides vessels of gold and of silver and some very valuable garments, while to Caesar's wife Julia and some others he left five million pieces.' Josephus' report of this shows once again the importance of valuables in precious metal or other materials;[1] but it also indicates Herod's adherence to a custom of considerable financial and social significance in the early empire. In the event Augustus gave the bulk of this sum to Herod's sons and daughters, 'and chose for himself only a few of the vessels that had been given him as a gift. This he did not so much because of their great value as because they were regarded by him as memorials of the king.'[2] Here, almost more than in any other area, the actual workings of what can be regarded as an important form of imperial income were subject to the vagaries of individual emperors, the conventions of society and the constant pressure for the exhibition of liberality.

The importance of the steady flow of legacies and inheritances to the emperor is reflected in a curious passage in the sixth-century *Chronicle* of John Malalas, who relates that Antoninus Pius burnt the documents in the *aerarium* recording a vote of the senate passed on the order of Julius Caesar, and forbidding any senator to make a will for the benefit of his family without making the current emperor heir to half his property.[3] The report is fictional, but in practice we can find examples of almost exactly this actually occurring: for instance Tacitus records that when his father-in-law Agricola died in 93 he named Domitian as co-heir with his wife and daughter.[4] We shall also see later that emperors and jurists in the second and third centuries did attempt to solve some of the legal problems which arose from the custom.[5] But we can be quite certain that there never was any such *senatus consultum*, and that what we are seeing is once again the application to the emperor of a custom already prevalent in senatorial circles in Rome.[6] The custom of making one's friends or allies either partial heirs or legatees

[1] *Ant.* XVII, 8, 1 (190), Loeb trans.; cf. *BJ* 1, 32, 7 (646).

[2] *Ant.* XVII, 11, 5 (322–3), Loeb trans. It is not clear whether Augustus' grants amounted to more or less than the legacies of Herod.

[3] Malalas, p. 280, 11–17 (Dio ed. Boissevain III, 281); see A. Schenk Graf von Stauffenberg, *Die römische Kaisergeschichte bei Malalas* (1931), 318–20.

[4] *Agric.* 43, 4.

[5] p. 157.

[6] See in general R. S. Rogers, 'The Roman Emperors as Heirs and Legatees', *TAPhA* LXXVIII (1947), 140; J. Gaudemet, ' "Testamenta Ingrata et pietas Augusti": contribution à l'étude du sentiment impérial', *Studi Arangio-Ruiz* III (1953), 115.

6*

in one's will was continuous from the later republic into the empire, and was important in the financial position of both Cicero[7] and Pliny the Younger.[8]

It is consonant with this that in the first century of the empire the emperor is often attested as part-heir or legatee along with other friends from outside a man's family. So, according to the *Vita* by Donatus, Vergil named his half-brother as heir to half his property, Augustus to a quarter, and Maecenas a twelfth, and divided the rest between L. Varius and Plotius Tucca;[9] and Tiberius was part heir to the estate of an *eques* named Patuleius, but gave up his share to someone who had been named in an earlier will.[10] When Domitius Ahenobarbus died in 38, his three-month-old son (the future Emperor Nero) and the current emperor, Gaius, were both heirs to part of his property, but the whole estate was seized by Gaius, to be restored subsequently by Claudius.[11]

The element of obligation on the part of the subject, and of the threat of exaction on that of the emperor, was present from the beginning, varying sharply with the character of the successive emperors. Cicero mentions in a letter of 45 BC a man who inherited a third of a property, while Caesar got a twelfth, and was afraid that he would not be able to keep it;[12] and in the *Second Philippic* he explicitly contrasts the genuine inheritances which he himself received with those which Antonius took by pretending to be the heir.[13] In Augustus' reign it was a matter for comment if protégés of the emperor did *not* mention him in their wills.[14] As we have noted above,[15] Augustus himself, though he would not take inheritances or legacies from men who were unknown to him, eagerly scanned the wills of his *amici* in the expectation of their remembering him.[16] It is important to stress that his concern was not merely sentimental; for in his own will, which was written in 13, he stated that over the twenty previous years he had received 1,400,000,000 *sesterces* in the wills of his friends, and had spent nearly all of it on the needs of the state.[17] For the significance of this sum we may note that Suetonius supposed that the annual revenues of the provinces of Gaul when conquered by Julius Caesar were about 40,000,000 *sesterces*, and that Velleius thought that the revenues of Egypt under Augustus were slightly

[7] Rogers, o.c., 141.

[8] See R. Duncan-Jones, 'The Finances of the Younger Pliny', *PBSR* XXXIII, n.s. XX (1965), 177, esp. 180–1, 183–4, revised in *The Economy of the Roman Empire: Quantitative Studies* (1974), 17f.

[9] *Vita Vergilii* (Suetonius ed. Reifferscheid, p. 63; OCT, *Vitae Vergilianae*, p. 14).

[10] Tacitus, *Ann.* II, 48, 1.

[11] Suetonius, *Nero* 6, 3.

[12] *Ad Att.* XIII, 48, 1 (Shackleton-Bailey, no. 345).

[13] *Phil.* II, 16/40–2.

[14] See Valerius Maximus VII, 8, 6 (T. Marius Urbinas, a military man honoured and enriched by Augustus who even on the day before his death had said that Augustus was his heir, but whose will contained no mention of him); Suetonius, *Vita Horatii*, ed. Reifferscheid, 48; cf. E. Fraenkel, *Horace* (1957), 23.

[15] p. 112.

[16] Suetonius, *Aug.* 66, 4: 'nam quamvis minime appeteret hereditates, ut qui numquam ex ignoti testamento capere quicquam sustinuerit, amicorum tamen suprema iudicia morosissime pensitavit, neque dolore dissimulato, si parcius aut citra honorem verborum, neque gaudio, si grate pieque quis se prosecutus fuisset.'

[17] ibid., 101.

less;[18] if such figures are not wholly misleading, then these two rich provinces between them produced annually only something rather more than half what Augustus received in legacies and inheritances.

These figures make it clear that Augustus' benefits from the wills of his friends went far beyond the cases such as Maecenas, L. Sempronius Atratinus and Cn. Cornelius Cinna Magnus (the grandson of Pompey) where we know that he was sole heir.[19] The presumption that he would normally benefit is very clear in the case of his *amicus* Tarius, whose *consilium* he joined to judge his son; to demonstrate his disinterest, he swore that he would not accept an inheritance from Tarius.[20]

Under Tiberius also it appears to have been assumed that prominent persons would leave something to the emperor. So it was a matter of widespread comment among the people that when Junia (the widow of Cassius and sister of Brutus) died in 22, her will named nearly all the leading men, but omitted the emperor.[21] It was clearly an established form of income, and we know for instance of a freedman of Tiberius 'in charge of inheritances'.[22] But the flow of inheritances and legacies of the emperor was subject to contrasting pressures typical of the social forces related to the emperor. On the one hand, Tacitus attests that in the early part of his reign Tiberius took no inheritances except from *amici*, and rejected those from persons unknown to him, or who had made him their heir out of spite towards others.[23] On the other hand, Dio records both that when a senator was accused of *maiestas* in 30 he displayed his will in the senate to demonstrate that Tiberius was co-heir with his children; and that Tiberius was not only the sole heir of Sejanus, but received something from almost all those forced to suicide—as both he and Sejanus had done before the latter's fall.[24] Suetonius asserts in the case of Cn. Lentulus Augurinus that Tiberius forced him both to commit suicide and to leave him as his sole heir.[25]

The pressure to mention the emperor in one's will had, however, already spread far beyond the circle of leading senators, so that Gaius could declare invalid the wills of top-ranking centurions (*primipilares*) who had made neither Tiberius not himself their heirs. He did the same, so Suetonius claims, with the will of anyone who was said to have intended to make the emperor his heir, and urged to suicide any from whom he was due to inherit.[26] While we cannot be certain of the truth of every assertion of this kind, it is clear that from the beginning there was here, as in so many other fields, an area of indeterminacy where the emperor could choose either to extend his claims (or allow others

[18] *Jul.* 25; Velleius II, 39, 2.

[19] Maecenas: Dio LV, 7, 5; Atratinus: Suetonius, *De orat.* IX, 65* (ed. Reifferscheid, 84), cf. Jerome, *Chron.* ed. Helm, p. 165; Cinna: Seneca, *De clem.* I, 9, 12.

[20] Seneca, *De clem.* I, 15, 4.

[21] Tacitus, *Ann.* III, 76, 1.

[22] Scribonius Largus, *Compositiones* 162: 'Anteros Tiberii libertus supra hereditates.' For other imperial freedmen concerned with *hereditates* or *legata* see *ILS* 1520, 1523-7.

[23] *Ann.* II, 48, 2; cf. Dio LVII, 17, 8.

[24] LVIII, 4, 5; 16, 2. Tiberius had probably also inherited from Sejanus' father, Seius Strabo, Pliny, *NH* XXXVI, 67/197, though the reading of the name is not quite certain.

[25] *Tib.* 49.

[26] *Cal.* 38, 2.

to do so for him) and thereby increase his revenues, or retract them, and gain the credit for so doing. So Claudius forbade people who had relatives to make him their heir, and repressed accusations against new citizens for either not taking the name Claudius or not leaving him anything in their wills.[27] None the less, Pliny found that a former citizen of Prusa had not only been named Claudius Polyaenus, but had left as a legacy to Claudius a house on whose site a temple to the emperor was to be built.[28] The fact does not seem to surprise Pliny, and is accepted without comment by Trajan; just as Petronius in the *Satyricon* makes Trimalchio say of his *patronus*, 'He made me his co-heir with Caesar, and I gained a senator's fortune.'[29] This practice was clearly in many cases precautionary, though not always effectively so. Tacitus mentions that Prasutagus, king of the Iceni in Britain, had made Nero joint heir with his two daughters in the vain hope of protecting his kingdom and house.[30] Similarly, L. Vetus, when compelled to suicide in 65, was urged by his friends to protect the remaining inheritance of his grandsons by making Nero heir to a large part of his estate; and an *eques* being led to execution on Vitellius' orders shouted out, 'You are my heir.'[31]

Nero, according to Suetonius, took for the *fiscus* the estates of those who proved 'ungrateful' to the emperor and threatened punishment for lawyers who drafted such wills;[32] and a very similar position was reached in the end by Domitian. Of the early part of his reign Suetonius says that he too would not accept inheritances from men who had children;[33] but we have seen that in the case of Agricola who died in 93 he did just this; what is more, Tacitus adds that he was delighted by this supposed mark of esteem, 'for his mind was so blinded and depraved by constant flattery, that he did not know that only a bad emperor is made heir by a good father'.[34] This is consonant with what Suetonius says of his later period, that 'the inheritances of the most complete strangers were pocketed (*confiscabantur*), if even one man came forward to say that he had heard the deceased say that the emperor would be his heir'.[35]

All the forms of ambivalence, and the conflicting pressures and conventions, which mark this means of acquisition of wealth by the emperor come together in what Pliny says addressing Trajan in the *Panegyric*, and implicitly contrasting him with Domitian:[36]

In the same class should be placed the fact that our wills are safe, and there is not one heir of everyone, either because named as heir or because not named ... You are named as heir not because another has caused offence, but because you

[27] Dio LX, 6, 3; 17, 7.
[28] Pliny, *Ep.* X, 70-1.
[29] *Sat.* 76: 'coheredem me Caesari fecit, et accepi patrimonium laticlavium.'
[30] *Ann.* XIV, 31, 1.
[31] ibid., XVI, 11; Suetonius, *Vit.* 14, 3.
[32] *Nero* 32: 'deinde, ut ingratorum in principem testamenta ad fiscum pertinerent, ac ne impune esset studiosis iuris, qui scripsissent vel dictassent ea.'
[33] *Dom.* 9, 2.
[34] *Agric.* 43, 4; p. 153.
[35] *Dom.* 12, 2.
[36] *Pan.* 43, 1-3.

have deserved it. You are named by friends and passed over by strangers, and there is no difference between you as a *privatus* and as *princeps* except that you are now the *amicus* of more men, because you make more your *amici*. Hold to this course, Caesar, and it will be proved by experiment whether it is more productive and fruitful not only for the reputation but also for the funds of the emperor, if men wish, rather than are forced, to die with him as heir.

Thereafter our evidence on inheritance and legacies going to the emperor is very much less. But the practice certainly continued, for, even apart from various passages in the *Historia Augusta* mentioning exactly those forms of self-restraint as exercised by second-century emperors which we have seen in the first century,[37] we have Dio's evidence that Caracalla confiscated the property of those who had mentioned his brother Geta in their wills.[38] Much more important is the fact that legal sources of the second and third centuries offer opinions, or quote imperial rulings, on the applicability of the laws to inheritances and legacies left to an emperor. So for instance Severus Alexander refers in a *subscriptio* of 222 to Hadrian's ruling a century earlier that the *Lex Falcidia* applied also to legacies to the emperor.[39] Hadrian and Antoninus Pius both ruled that legacies to the wife of the emperor lapsed if she died before the testator; but Pius laid down that one due to an emperor who died first was legally due to his successor.[40] Ulpian and Paulus refer to aspects of the acquisition, or non-acceptance, of inheritances by the emperor,[41] while the *Sententiae* of Paulus (now considered to be a later third-century compilation) several times lays down that various general rules apply also to legacies or inheritances to the emperor: for instance the author states (as does Severus Alexander in a *subscriptio* of 232)[42] that not even the emperor can claim an inheritance on the basis of an incomplete will, 'for it is proper for a Majesty so great to obey those laws, from which he is considered to have been freed'.[43] He similarly lays down that a legacy or *fideicommissum* can be sought from an emperor named as heir of a property, and that a will naming the emperor as heir can be argued to be invalid, 'for it is proper that he who makes the laws should with unimpaired majesty yield to the laws'.[44] There seems to be no evidence for the continuance of this custom beyond the third century; and even in the period before this we cannot tell whether it still retained the immense importance in strictly financial terms which it undoubtedly had for Augustus. But even though the twenty years before Augustus wrote his will are the only ones for which we know how much came to the emperor in this form, it is still extremely significant as another social custom of the late republic which hardened into something approaching an

---

[37] *Had.* 18, 5; *Ant. Pius* 8, 5; *Marc. Ant.* 7, 1; *Pert.* 7, 3.

[38] LXXVII, 12, 5 (387); cf. Herodian VI, 1, 8: οὐσίας τινῶν καὶ κληρονομίας ἐξ ἐπηρείας ὑφαρπάσης ἐκείνης.

[39] *CJ* VI, 50, 4.

[40] *Dig.* XXXI, 57 (Mauricianus, *Ad legem Iuliam et Papiam* II); 56 (Gaius, *Ad legem Iuliam et Papiam* XIV).

[41] *Dig.* I, 19, 1–2; XXVIII, 1, 31.

[42] *CJ* VI, 23, 3.

[43] *Dig.* XXXII, 23 (Paulus, *Sententiae* V). For the date see p. 509.

[44] *Sent.* IV, 1, 3; 5, 3: 'eum enim qui leges facit pari maiestate legibus obtemperare convenit.'

obligation under the empire, and lasted as such for at least three centuries. Moreover, it owed that significance to an aspect of the ancient world which was of much wider importance, namely the relatively static nature of wealth. It is not an accident that so large a proportion of Roman legal writing concerns wills and inheritances; for wealth could be exchanged or divided, but not easily increased or multiplied. The same limitation applied to the emperor himself, for whom there was no better way of acquiring extra capital than if someone, willingly or otherwise, left it to him. But the process by which the emperor laid a claim to the property of his subjects was not likely to stop there; and that is why through all the legal works on inheritance there run the twin streams of the claims of the *fiscus* to *bona vacantia* or *caduca* (property to which there was no heir, or for which the disposition by will was in some way invalid) and *bona damnatorum*, the goods of persons condemned on criminal charges. Both played an essential part in imperial revenues and the steady acquisition of imperial property; and both played a central role in the relations between emperor and subject.

6. Bona Caduca *and* Bona Vacantia

That the majority of the institutions of the empire were developments of institutions or customs of the late republic is beyond all dispute. But in certain areas it has to be conceded that the precedents lie not there but in the practices of the cities and kingdoms of the Hellenistic world; and, while proof is impossible, it seems probable that one of these cases is the reception by the emperor (or the *fiscus*) of properties of which the ownership had lapsed (*vacantia*), or for which the testamentary dispositions were legally invalid (*caduca*). The continuity is particularly clear in Egypt both because of the rich documentation available from the Ptolemaic and Roman periods, and because the country passed in 30 BC directly from the rule of the Ptolemies to that of the future Augustus.

The financial apparatus of the Ptolemies in the second century BC included a 'Private Account' (*idios logos*) in which were deposited the proceeds of sales of government property, of confiscated property, newly-occupied land and ownerless parcels of land (*adespota*).[1] By the first century BC it had become a department which administered such properties and was under the control of a high official, called simply 'the man in charge of the *idios logos*'.[2] It is significant of this development that the earlier documents talk of land being confiscated (literally 'taken up'—*analambanesthai*) to the *basilikon*, the royal estate, and the later ones of it being similarly 'taken up' to the *idios logos*. We shall see that precisely these terms are used—of both *caduca* and the property of condemned persons—in Greek sources and documents of the Roman period.[3] What is more, the empire shows a re-

---

[1] For this and what follows see the invaluable study by P. R. Swarney, *The Ptolemaic and Roman Idios Logos* (1970), which does, however, seem to me to exaggerate the provable differences between the various successive periods of the *idios logos*.

[2] ὁ πρὸς τῷ ἰδίῳ λόγῳ.

[3] pp. 162 and esp. 165–6.

markably similar development, in the emergence in the second century of the *ratio privata* ('private account'), which appears primarily as the destination of confiscated property.[4]

The immediate link to Roman practice is provided by the account of Egypt given by Strabo, who visited the province only a few years after the conquest, and travelled up the Nile with the prefect Aelius Gallus.[5] Listing the Roman officials in Egypt he gives in third place 'the one called *idios logos*, who is the auditor of the *adespota* and of the properties which by law fall to Caesar'.[6] To be pedantically correct, he should still have said 'the man in charge of the *idios logos*', the expression used in papyri of this period; but essentially what he says is fully confirmed by papyri from as early as the reign of Augustus itself. In AD 13 we find a man purchasing from the *idios logos* some pieces of wood which were 'dry and ownerless' (*adespota*) and due to be 'taken up to the *idios logos* in accordance with the *gnomon*'.[7] The *gnomon* was a handbook governing the dealings of the *idios logos* issued by Augustus. It is referred to for instance by the prefect of Egypt in 68, Tiberius Julius Alexander, in the edict by which he attempted to correct financial abuses by officials there: 'and overall I shall order the *gnomon* of the *idios logos* to stand, having corrected the innovations contrary to the indulgences granted by Augustus.'[8] Some of the actual provisions of the *gnomon* are known, primarily from the famous second-century Greek papyrus, whose author collects for a friend the headings 'of the *gnomon* which the deified Augustus issued to the administration of the *idios logos*' with later modifications.[9]

Rather than pursue here either the complex history of the *idios logos* in the empire or the detailed provisions of the *gnomon* (to some of which we will return), it is important to stress that there was an essential continuity with Ptolemaic practice, that Strabo, a well-placed and extremely well-informed observer, thought of the properties taken by the *idios logos* as going 'to Caesar', and that the rules governing this process were believed later to have been laid down by Augustus in person. Whether this was on his only visit to Egypt, at the moment of the conquest in 30 BC, or later, is not known. But we cannot escape the conclusion that the perpetuation of a right of the Ptolemaic 'private account' did not just happen by inertia but was known to, and directed by, the emperor.

Nor was this the only context in which the issue confronted him, for we know from a letter which Trajan wrote to Pliny that the Nicaeans claimed

<hr/>

[4] pp. 171–4 and App. 3.

[5] See G. W. Bowersock, *Augustus and the Greek World* (1965), 126–9.

[6] XVII, 1, 12 (797): ὁ προσαγορευόμενος ἴδιος λόγος, ὃς τῶν ἀδεσπότων καὶ τῶν εἰς Καίσαρα πίπτειν ὀφειλόντων ἐξεταστής ἐστι.

[7] *P. Oxy.* 1188, ll. 4, 10, 15–16, 19–20. See also *P. Oxy.* 2277 (AD 13), and Mitteis, *Chrestomathie*, no. 68 (AD 14/15), a man complaining of the delation of his property by someone else βουλόμενος ὠνήσασθαι αὐτοὺς [ἐκ τ]οῦ ἰδίου λόγου ὡς ὄντας ἀδεσπότους. On this highly complex affair see Swarney, o.c., 43f.

[8] *OGIS* 669, ll. 43–4; I use the text of G. Chalon, *L'Édit de Tiberius Julius Alexander* (1964), and follow his restoration [κεῖσθ]αι in l. 44, rather than [φανῆν]αι as proposed by Swarney, o.c., 62.

[9] Text, translation and commentary by S. Riccobono, *Il Gnomon dell'Idios Logos* (1950). But note that a partial text (of paras. 35–41) is now available in a papyrus of the mid-first century, *P. Oxy.* 3014.

that Augustus had granted their city the right to claim the goods of its citizens who died intestate.[10] This right also is attested, though rarely, on the part of cities in the Hellenistic period,[11] so the background of the Nicaeans' claim to Augustus is sufficiently clear. Moreover we find the same right being successfully claimed from Claudius by an embassy from the *municipium* of Volubilis in Mauretania.[12] What remains entirely obscure is what the alternative was, and to whom these properties would have gone if not to the city. Two and a half centuries later, however, there was no doubt. Diocletian and Maximian wrote to a *rationalis* named Scyrio in 292:[13]

> Your Gravity must be aware that the property of intestate persons who have died without a legal heir must be claimed for the accounts of our *fiscus*. Nor should you give ear to the cities which pretend to the right of claiming those properties as if by permission. And henceforward, whatever properties of intestate persons you discover to have been taken over by the cities under the pretext of their privileges, do not hesitate to regain the same for our service.

Once again it is evident that the fate of *bona vacantia* depended directly on rulings issued by the emperors in person. But how had the situation been reached in which 'our *fiscus*' made an automatic claim to such goods? The general principle is already expressed in the *gnomon* in the middle of the second century: 'The goods of those who die intestate, and who have no other legal heir, are adjudged to the *fiscus*.'[14] Unfortunately, there is no means of telling when this provision was incorporated in the *gnomon*. It may have been there quite early, for Tacitus records under AD 17 how Tiberius exhibited a welcome *liberalitas* by assigning to a man who appeared to be her relative the goods of a rich woman who died intestate, and which were 'claimed for the *fiscus*'.[15] Tacitus' language suggests that the claims of the *fiscus* were routine, and also makes clear that the property was at Tiberius' free disposal and could be granted as a personal act of liberality. But if we look further back, the situation is quite unclear. It is probable, but not certain, that a parchment from Dura-Europos shows a general rule by which property to which there were no heirs became 'royal';[16] the terms of the document are presumed to be Seleucid, but the parchment itself was copied in the Roman period. But, suggestive as it is, it is clearly too slight a basis for any general

---

[10] Pliny, *Ep.* x, 84.

[11] See S. von Bolla, 'Zum römischen Heimfallsrecht', *Zeitschr. Sav. Stift., Röm. Abt.* LIX (1939), 546, on pp. 548–9. Add Michel, *Recueil*, no. 546, from A. H. M. Jones, *The Greek City* (1940), ch. xvii, n. 67.

[12] *FIRA*² I, no. 70; *Ins. Lat. Maroc.* 116: 'bona civium bello interfectorum, quorum heredes non extabant, suis impetravit.'

[13] *CJ* x, 10, 1.

[14] *Gnomon* (cf. n. 9 above), para. 4: [τ]ῶν [τ]ελευτώ[ν⟨των⟩] ἀδιαθέτω[ν] οἷς οὐδείς ἐστιν ἄλλος κατὰ νόμους κληρονόμο[[υ]]ς τὰ ὑπάρχοντα τῷ φίσκῳ προσκρείνεται.

[15] Tacitus, *Ann.* II, 48: 'haud minus grata liberalitate, quod bona Aemiliae Musae, locupletis intestatae, petita in fiscum, Aemilio Lepido cuius e domo videbatur... tradidit.'

[16] *P. Dura.* 12, ll. 14–16: ἐὰν δὲ μηθὶς τούτων (relatives) ὑπάρχῃ, βασιλικὴ ἡ οὐσία ἔστω. For the argument that this is a general Seleucid rule, and not confined to the resumption of *cleroi* in a military *apoikia*, see J. Modrzejewski, 'La dévolution à l'État des successions en déshérence dans le droit hellénistique', *RIDA* VIII (1961), 79; 'La dévolution au fisc des biens vacants d'après le Gnomon de l'Idiologue (BGU 1210, §4)', *Studi Volterra* VI (1971), 91.

theory. As regards the Roman republican practice, there appears to be no specific evidence as to what happened to *bona vacantia*. If we presume, as we probably should, that they were sold for the benefit of the public treasury (*aerarium*), it can be on no better basis than the hesitant statement of the Augustan jurist, Labeo, that no one can inherit from an intestate Vestal Virgin, 'but they say that her property reverts to the public funds'.[17]

The best reason for supposing that this is likely is that this was certainly the effect of the various laws of the Augustan period and earlier, which limited the capacity of various types of persons either to make wills or to benefit from them, and thereby created the closely comparable category of *bona caduca*[18] discussed below. But in the empire, from the first century onwards, *bona vacantia* always appear to be at the free disposition of the emperor (as when after the eruption of Vesuvius Titus contributed, among other funds, 'the money of those who had died without heirs'),[19] and in legal sources as going to the *fiscus*.[20] In 326 however we find Constantine ordering that the *bona vacantia* of a *navicularius* should go, not to the *fiscus*, but to the corporation of *navicularii* to which he belonged.[21] The process of concession was carried further by Constantius, who ordered in 352 that the property of an intestate town-councillor should go to the council of his city 'with no provision being granted for petitioning for these goods as being *vacantia* from Our Clemency'.[22] It would be interesting to know how long the custom of petitioning the emperor for *bona vacantia* had existed. But it is noticeable that the section of the Theodosian Code on *bona vacantia* begins with three letters of Constantine designed to protect the right of ownership on the part of persons to whom the emperor had granted property.[23]

Two Republican laws, the *Lex Voconia* of 160 and the *Lex Falcidia* of 40, had restricted the legal rights of making wills or leaving legacies.[24] But it was the two Augustan marriage laws, the *Lex Julia de maritandis ordinibus* and the *Lex Papia Poppaea* which in effect created the category of *bona caduca*. Ulpian indeed refers in a careless moment to the '*Lex Julia caducaria*' —'and if there is no one who is entitled to the ownership of the goods, or there is someone, but he had lost his right, the goods are reported to the *populus* under the *Lex Julia caducaria*.'[25] It was clearly the intention of these

---

[17] Aulus Gellius, *NA* I, 12, 18.

[18] It is not clear whether the terms were always distinguished by ancient writers. But in order to keep separate two analogous, but in social terms significantly different, situations, I confine *vacantia* to those cases where no heir or owner appears at all, and *caduca* to those where actual or potential claimants are banned by some legal disability.

[19] Dio LXVI, 24, 3 (159).

[20] e.g. *Dig.* XL, 5, 51 *pr.* (Marcianus); XLI, 3, 18 (Modestinus), cf. *Inst.* II, 6, 9; *CJ* V, 16, 1 (Caracalla, 212); VI, 21, 13 (Valerian and Gallienus, 254); VII, 72, 5 (Diocletian and Maximian, 293); VII, 37, 1 (Constantine). One case where the text is dubious is *Dig.* XL, 4, 50 *pr.* (Papinian): 'vacantibus fisco vindicatis', as compared with Papinian, *Lib. IX responsorum fragmenta* V, 13: 'vacantibus populo vindicatis' in the same passage.

[21] *CJ* VI, 61, 1.

[22] *CTh* V, 2, 1. For the date of 352 rather than 319 as indicated in the protocol see *PLRE* Rufinus 25.

[23] *CTh* X, 8, 1–3.

[24] For a general treatment see B. Biondi, *Successione testamentaria e donazioni*[2] (1955); A. Watson, *The Law of Succession in the Later Roman Republic* (1971).

[25] Ulpian, *Fr.* XXVIII, 7 (*FIRA*[2] II, 299); cf. Gaius, *Inst.* II, 150.

laws that the *res publica* should succeed to goods which were now made *caduca*. Tacitus says that the *Lex Papia Poppaea* was brought in 'for the increase of the *aerarium*', and that its effects were 'that the *populus*, as if the parent of all, should take possession of *vacantia*';[26] and Gaius says of a further item of legislation passed under Vespasian that under it *fideicommissa* made to orphans would fall to the *populus*.[27]

But Pliny in the *Panegyric*, apparently speaking of both *bona caduca* and *bona damnatorum*, says: 'Both the *aerarium* and the *fiscus* were enriched, not so much by the *Leges Voconia* and *Julia*, as by the special and particular charge of *maiestas*.'[28] His words seem to indicate both a clear distinction between the two 'treasuries', and some division of the proceeds of *caduca* between them. Moreover, a number of passages in legal sources, often assumed to be interpolated, do in fact yield a possible and intelligible view of the relation between *aerarium* and *fiscus* in this area: namely that the actual reporting (*delatio*) of *bona caduca* was made (in Rome) to the *aerarium*, whose *praefecti* also maintained jurisdiction in the relevant cases, and even took in the goods, but that the ultimate beneficiary was the *fiscus*. These passages relate specifically to an *edictum* of Trajan, extended by a *senatus consultum* under Hadrian, by which those who spontaneously reported to the *aerarium* that goods left to them were legally *caduca*, were allowed to share them half-and-half with the *fiscus*.[29] Exactly the same provision appears in a clause of the *gnomon*, which records that Vespasian 'took up' *fideicommissa* between Greeks and Romans, 'but those who have reported them have received half'.[30] The rule allowing division under these circumstances survived throughout the period, for in 317 we find Constantine writing to the *rationales* in Spain about the case of an improper will: 'If she . . . whom the deceased wished to be his heir [spontaneously] made known the will, let her receive a reward such that from the whole property she receives half and carries out a division of it with our *fiscus*, also having the privilege of choosing her share first.'[31]

We cannot state how long the *aerarium* continued to receive either all *caduca* or a share, or how long the *praefecti* had some role in receiving reports of *caduca*; they are last attested in this area when Marcus Aurelius sent a case to them.[32] But whatever their role was, it can hardly have been applicable outside Rome, or at the most Italy. In the *gnomon* the numerous references to the taking up of *caduca* never mention any destination other than the *fiscus*.[33] In the second century Artemidorus can mention without comment

---

[26] *Ann.* III, 25; 28. For the lack of clear distinction of these terms see n. 18 above.

[27] *Inst.* II, 286a; cf. III, 62.

[28] *Pan.* 42, 1.

[29] *Dig.* XLIX, 14, 13; 15, 3–6; 16; 42.

[30] *Gnomon* 18.

[31] *CTh* X, 11, 1 = *CJ* X, 13, 1 (317).

[32] *Dig.* XXXIV, 9, 12. Ulpian, however, refers to them in the present tense in *Dig.* II, 15, 8, 19.

[33] *Gnomon* 9: θυγατέρες δὲ ἢ ἄλλος τις οὐ κληρονομήσουσι ἀλλὰ ὁ φίσκος. 24: τὴν διδομένην προοῖκα ὑπὸ γυναικὸς Ῥωμαίας ὑπὲρ πεντήκοντα ἔτη γεγονυ[ί]ας ἀνδρὶ Ῥωμαίῳ ἐντὸς ἑξήκοντα ἐτῶν γεγονότι μετὰ θάνατον ὁ φίσκος ἀναλαμβάνει. Cf. also 45. The characteristic verb ἀναλαμβανεῖν (see p. 158) is also used in this context without φίσκος in paras. 16, 17, 19, 20, 22, 23, 25, 26, 27, 30, 33, 50. Cf. Mitteis, *Chrestomathie*, no. 372, col. VI (*P. Cattaoui* v), where the *Idios Logos* adjudges *bona caduca* [ε]ἰς τὸν κυριακὸν λόγον.

the occasion when the meaning of a dream was made clear when a man died when away from home, his property was taken by the *fiscus*, and his wife had to institute proceedings to recover it.[34] If the large number of the passages in the *Digest* and other legal sources which reflect similar situations is any guide,[35] the reception of *caduca* by the *fiscus* was of major social significance, and must have contributed substantially to imperial property and revenue. We may assume that such cases in the provinces will have involved the imperial procurators in investigations or legal proceedings,[36] as they did the *rationales* of Constantine. So it is not surprising that legal sources came to speak of the *delatio* itself as being made to the *fiscus*.[37] On occasion the emperor might be involved directly in such a case, as when in 166 two *advocati fisci* pleaded before Marcus Aurelius the case of a man who had added extra names of heirs in his will, in consequence of which 'his property was claimed for the *fiscus* as *caduca*'. Marcellus, who was present in the *consilium*, describes how Marcus concluded after debate that a manumission allowed for in the will could stand.[38]

With rare exceptions, of which this and Constantine's letter to the *rationales* are the clearest, the evidence on *bona vacantia* and *caduca* does not have the concreteness and immediacy which make themselves felt in other aspects of the imperial acquisition and distribution of wealth. Instead we have very specific evidence of how the emperors inherited a right enjoyed by the Ptolemies, and perhaps by other Hellenistic kings, a right which seems steadily to have overborne the provisions of the Augustan marriage laws. The importance of this right in the form which it had in the second century and after is clear, as is the involvement of the emperor in ruling on how it should be exercised, and (it seems) in disposing of the proceeds. But we cannot pretend to understand how or by what steps it developed as it did.

7. *Condemnation and Confiscation*

Of all the processes by which wealth passed from subject to emperor, to be kept or expended by him, or granted to favourites, the most crucial, the most loaded with social and political overtones and legal ambiguities, was the acquisition of *bona damnatorum*, the property of persons condemned on criminal charges. The process had its roots in the early republic, when the property of condemned men, or at least those condemned for offences against the state, was sold by auction. A condemnation was thus in part a

---

[34] *Oneirocritica* IV, 59.

[35] e.g. Gaius II, 285; *Dig.* V, 3 passim; XXIX, 5, 8–9; XXXVIII, 9 passim; XL, 5, 4, 17–20; *Frag. de iure fisci* I, 3; Paulus, *Sent.* III, 5, 12a; *CJ* VI, 35, 4 (Severus Alexander, 223). Cf. also *HA*, *Pert.* 7, 2.

[36] e.g. *CJ* VI, 35, 3 (Severus Alexander, 222): 'hereditas a fisco vindicatur et ideo agi causa apud procuratorem meum debet'; cf. III, 28, 10 (223); VI, 35, 6 (229). Note also the expanded judicial powers of the head of the *idios logos* in the second century, Swarney, o.c., ch. iii.

[37] e.g. *Dig.* XXXVI, 1, 6, 3 (Ulpian). Compare XXXVIII, 9, 1 *pr.* (Ulpian) and 2 (Papinian) referring to the *delatio* to the *fiscus* of *vacantia*, where it is strictly a question of no heirs being to hand, not of an invalid succession.

[38] *Dig.* XXVIII, 4, 3. Cf. pp. 237–8.

process, wide open to profiteering and corruption, of transferring wealth from one individual to others. This aspect was enormously exaggerated by the Sullan and triumviral proscriptions, when the sales of property were often at nominal prices, and in numerous cases men were killed specifically in order that someone else should secure their property. In the early empire the question of condemnation and confiscation was central to the strained and insecure relations of the emperor and the upper classes. By the second century, as we can see from legal sources, the acquisition of a man's property by the *fiscus* was the automatic accompaniment of the penalty of trans-portation (*deportatio*), and thus affected potentially persons in all areas of the empire. In the third and early fourth centuries we find martyrs and eventually the churches themselves having their property seized by the *fiscus*, only for it to be restored in a complex process of disbursement by Constantine.

From the earliest days of the republic we have reports of the consecration to various gods of the goods of the condemned.[1] From the middle republic we have ample evidence of *publicatio bonorum* as the accompaniment of condemnation for crimes against the state; it can be regarded as the extension to internal 'public enemies' of the treatment of defeated enemies in war. So, for instance, Cassius Dio writes of the condemnation of Capitolinus in 384 BC, 'The people condemned Capitolinus to death, his house was pulled down, his property made public, his name and any statues of him erased and destroyed. Even now, all these things, except the pulling-down of the house, are done in the case of those who plot against the state.'[2] The continuity which Dio indicates is real, but hard to document in the later republic until we reach the period of the proscriptions. Indeed Suetonius, reporting a measure of Julius Caesar, by which parricides lost all and other criminals half their property, states that previously rich persons when condemned had gone into exile with their property intact.[3]

On the other hand various features of the handling of *bona damnatorum* in the empire appear very clearly in the proscriptions under Sulla. Some men found themselves on the list because of their property;[4] Sulla himself presided at the sales,[5] and properties were made over to persons who were in favour for either a nominal price or as an outright gift.[6] Julius Caesar, though he conducted no regular proscription, none the less sold up the property of his enemies: Servilia gained substantial estates at a minimal price from the sales, but others were aggrieved to find that they were made to pay the full price.[7] Among the properties sold was the house of Pompey, with all its contents; it went to Antonius, who alone dared to bid for it.[8]

[1] *RE* s.v. 'Publicatio bonorum', XXIII, 2484f.

[2] Fr. 26, 1.

[3] *Jul.* 42.

[4] e.g. Cicero, *pro Rosc. Amer.* 7/20–8/21; Plutarch, *Sulla* 31, 10. See P. A. Brunt, *Italian Man-power 225 BC–AD 14* (1971), 301–5.

[5] Cicero, *De leg. ag.* II, 21/56; Plutarch, *Sulla* 33, 3.

[6] e.g. Cicero, *Pro Roscio* 2/6; Sallust, *Hist.* I, 55, Fr. 17 Maurenbrecher (*oratio Lepidi*); Cicero, *Verr.* II, I, 15/38.

[7] Suetonius, *Jul.* 50, 2; Dio XLII, 50, 5.

[8] Cicero, *Phil.* II, 26/64–28/68; Plutarch, *Ant.* 10, 3; 21, 2–3; Appian, *BC* V, 79/336.

In Africa in 46 Caesar regularly sold off the property of Romans captured while on the other side.[9] The selling-up of goods was now an established procedure, and we find Caesar before his death issuing rules to limit its effects, giving the wives a right to their dowries, and a portion of the property to the children.[10]

By now the prospect of a large-scale transfer of property was a significant element in any civil conflict. Cicero describes in horrific terms the expectations of Antonius' followers early in 43 BC, marking out for themselves *horti* in Rome and villas at Alba and Tusculum.[11] These expectations were more than amply fulfilled in the triumviral proscriptions, where again men were listed specifically for their wealth,[12] and large amounts of property were sold.[13] In this case some of the properties, or the proceeds of the sales, were given directly to the soldiers, in response to their outright demands.[14] Similarly those who were executed after the capture of Perusia in 41 BC had their property seized, and used to pay a donative to Octavian's veterans; this is in fact the earliest event to which the term 'confiscate' is applied in Latin literature.[15]

The new factor under the empire was to be the extension of the confiscation of property to all major criminal convictions, and the large-scale retention, rather than sale, of the property by the ruler. Neither process took place at once. The former is only one aspect of the steady increase in the range and severity of penalties applied under the empire.[16] It is important, and characteristic of the empire, that this process is reflected in language which expresses the personal character of the emperor's rule. Thus for instance Plutarch, in his *On Brotherly Love*, written early in the second century, mentions the case of two brothers in Greece in his own time who quarrelled and caused such disturbances that they were exiled and 'deprived of everything by the despot', probably Nero.[17] More significantly, he refers back in the same work to an incident which apparently took place before his own birth in about 50, when a Greek was condemned for rape or kidnapping, and lost his property which was 'taken up into the treasury of Caesar'.[18] As we have noted in passing before,[19] the same terminology is used in Greek documents and literary sources of the Hellenistic period to refer to property confiscated,

---

[9] *Bell. Afr.* 90, 1; 97, 1–2; 98, 2.

[10] Dio XLIII, 50, 2. Cf. XLVII, 14, 1, the triumviral ruling preserving dowries for wives, plus a tenth for male children and a twentieth for female.

[11] Cicero, *Phil.* VIII, 3/9.

[12] e.g. Appian, *BC* IV, 25/102, 29/124–5; or Pliny's story of the senator who was proscribed by Antonius for an opal ring worth 2,000,000 *sesterces*, *NH* XXXVII, 21/81–2.

[13] e.g. Plutarch, *Ant.* 21, 4; Appian, *BC* IV, 29/127, 31/133; Dio XLVII, 14, 5; 16, 2–3.

[14] Appian, *BC* IV, 35/147; V, 20/79, 22/87; Dio XLVII, 14, 4.

[15] Suetonius, *Aug.* 15: 'ut... devictisque iis et confiscatis promissa veteranis praemia solverentur.'

[16] See P. Garnsey, *Social Status and Legal Privilege in the Roman Empire* (1970), esp. ch. iv; idem, 'Why penalties become harsher: the Roman case, late Republic to fourth-century Empire', *Natural Law Forum* XIII (1968), 141.

[17] *Mor.* 487F–8A. See C. P. Jones, 'Towards a Chronology of Plutarch's Works', *JRS* LVI (1966), 61, esp. 70.

[18] 484A: τέλος δ' ἁρπάσας γυναῖκα καὶ καταδικασθεὶς ἀπώλεσε τὴν οὐσίαν, εἰς τὸ Καίσαρος ταμιεῖον ἀναληφθεῖσαν.

[19] p. 158.

or 'taken up', for the royal treasury (*basilikon*).[20] It might of course be argued that in using such terminology Plutarch has misconceived the real character of confiscation in this period; if so, the misconception is striking, given that he was a Roman citizen with many friends who were prominent members of the senate.[21] We cannot really escape from the fact that by the middle of the first century AD a provincial condemned for a non-political crime found his property appropriated by the *fiscus*.

How that stage was reached, and within what legal framework if any, we cannot say. It is possible that the device of fictitious sales was used, as apparently in the proscriptions; and it may well be also that Hellenistic precedents, including the continuing functions of the *idios logos*, had some influence. The new papyrus fragment of the *gnomon* of the *idios logos*, dating from the middle of the first century, reveals that the clause about the 'taking-up' of the property of those condemned for murder or other serious crimes was already in force then.[22] The earliest concrete instances of confiscation, however, give no help. In about 26 BC, for instance, the senate voted that the prefect of Egypt, Cornelius Gallus, should be condemned in the courts, and his property taken and granted to Augustus.[23] We could regard as a similarly 'political' matter the fact that when Herod's son Archelaus was deposed and exiled by Augustus in AD 6 his property was 'awarded to the treasuries of Caesar'.[24] But three items of evidence suggest that Augustus, like later emperors, had the effective disposition of the goods of condemned men. The *Life* of Virgil records that Augustus offered him the property of someone in exile, which he refused.[25] Suetonius states that when there was an excess of money 'from the goods of the condemned', he allowed the use of it without interest to those who could give surety for double the amount; and Ovid, speaking of his own exile, says 'nor was my fortune conceded to others.'[26]

That is all the evidence which we have for the reign of Augustus. When he begins his account of Tiberius, however, Dio soon brings in one of the most frequently recurring themes of imperial history, saying that he neither

[20] For Ptolemaic precedents see Swarney, *Idios Logos*, 23–6; for Seleucid examplex see 2 Macc. III, 13: ἔλεγεν εἰς τὸ βασιλικὸν ἀναλημπτέα ταῦτα εἶναι; Diodorus XXXIII, 4, 3: Demetrius II Nicator εἰς τὸ βασιλικὸν ταμεῖον τὰς οὐσίας ἀνέλαβε. See E. Bikerman, *Institutions des Séleucides* (1938), 121. Diodorus also uses it of Orophernes of Cappadocia, XXXI, 32, and of Fimbria in Cyzicus in 85, XXXVIII/IX, 8, 3, executing two men καὶ τὰς οὐσίας αὐτῶν ἀναλαβών. Cf. also Diogenes Laertius VII, 181 (of Chrysippus) and *OGIS* 338, ll. 24–5 (concerning the testament of Attalus III, 133 BC).

[21] See C. P. Jones, *Plutarch and Rome* (1971), esp. 48–64.

[22] *P. Oxy.* 3014. Previous to this, there had been no specific evidence from the Julio-Claudian, as opposed to both the Ptolemaic and the later period, of the *idios logos* handling confiscated property, see Swarney, *Idios logos*, 71–3.

[23] Dio LIII, 23, 7; cf. Suetonius, *Aug.* 66. If the reference to 'provinciis suis' (sc. Augustus) here is not misleading, the fall of Gallus cannot be earlier than 27, *pace* S. Jameson, *JRS* LVIII (1968), 71 on p. 79.

[24] Josephus, *BJ* II, 7, 3 (111): ἡ οὐσία δ' αὐτοῦ τοῖς Καίσαρος θησαυροῖς ἐγκατασταστάσσεται. Cf. *Ant.* XVII, 13, 2 (344), and *JRS* LIII (1963), 36.

[25] Suetonius, ed. Reifferscheid, p. 57; OCT, *Vitae Vergilianae*, p. 9: 'bona autem cuiusdam exulantis offerente Augusto non sustinuit accipere.'

[26] Suetonius, *Aug.* 41, 1; Ovid, *Trist.* V, 2, 57 (2b, 13).

killed anyone for his wealth nor took anyone's property.[27] Then under AD 23 he places the beginning of one of the essential characteristics of penal practice in the empire; 'Tiberius forbade those under *aquae et ignis inter-dictio* to make wills; this provision is still in force'.[28] If Dio is correct, this is the beginning of the penalty which we know accompanied *deportatio* in the second century, the loss of all civil rights and all property.[29]

The effect of this provision must have been to increase the volume of property lost by confiscation. Dio, however, says nothing of the ultimate fate of such property, and we have so far no other evidence either which indicates whether it was still, in theory or in practice, sold for the benefit of the *aerarium*. But immediately after this there begins a series of brief and enigmatic references in Tacitus to confiscations under Tiberius, which do suggest a usurpation by the emperor, or the *fiscus*, of the rights of the *aerarium*. In the case of Silius, condemned in 24, 'the liberality of the emperor was withdrawn, and the claims of the *fiscus* were added up one by one';[30] in 31, the goods of Sejanus were taken away from the *aerarium* to be brought by compulsion into the *fiscus*, so far as that made any difference;[31] in 33 we have, 'so many men having been condemned and their goods sold up, the coined silver was kept by the *fiscus* or the *aerarium*';[32] and finally under the same year Tacitus records the condemnation of the richest man in Spain, Sextus Marius; 'Tiberius, in case there should be any doubt that the extent of his wealth had caused his misfortune, kept for himself his gold and silver mines although they were made public property.'[33]

These references, however cursory and uninformative, do imply both that there were continuing rights on the part of the public treasury, and that, in Tacitus' view, the intrusion of the *fiscus* was a usurpation. We *may* have a reflection of just such conflicting claims in what Philo says of the condemnation of Flaccus, the prefect of Egypt, under Gaius: 'A clear proof of this [the excellence of his possessions] is that while a vast number of properties belonging to condemned persons were sold by public auction, that of Flaccus alone was reserved for the emperor, a few articles alone being excepted so as not to run counter to the law enacted about persons convicted on these grounds.'[34] These exceptions were quite probably for the benefit of the *aerarium*;[35] but they may alternatively have been for the condemned persons themselves.[36] What is clear at least is the notion of reserving specially

[27] LVII, 10, 5.
[28] LVII, 22, 5; cf. *RE* XXIII, 2499–500.
[29] See Gaius in *Dig.* XXVIII, 1, 8, comparing those under *aquae et ignis interdictio* with *deportati* and *qui ad ferrum aut ad bestias aut in metallum damnantur*—all of whom lost all their property and the right to make a will—and contrasting them with *relegati in insulam*, who kept both.
[30] *Ann.* IV, 20, 1.
[31] VI, 2, 1: 'bona Seiani ablata aerario ut in fiscum cogerentur, tam⟨quam⟩ referret.' This latter expression refers to the unimportance of this from the point of view of the victims at the time (hence the past tense), and cannot be used to show that the distinction itself was unimportant to Tacitus.
[32] VI, 17, 1.
[33] VI, 19, 1. The text of the description of the mines is conjectural.
[34] *In Flaccum*, 18/150, Loeb trans.
[35] So Hirschfeld, *Verwaltungsbeanten*², 46, n. 2; *RE* XXIII, 2510; Millar, *JRS* LIII (1963), 37.
[36] So P. A. Brunt, 'The Development of the Fiscus', *JRS* LVI (1966), 75, on p. 88.

valuable items of *bona damnatorum* for the emperor; the other side of the
coin is the story of how Petronius, when forced to commit suicide, broke
a myrrhine dipper worth 300,000 *sesterces* in order to deprive Nero of
it.[37]

The fatal attractiveness of private wealth appears already in Suetonius'
report that under Tiberius the leading men of Gaul, Spain, Syria and Greece
were *confiscati*, some merely on the charge of having some of their wealth in
cash.[38] The theme naturally returns in exaggerated form under Gaius;
according to Dio, when he was in Gaul in 39 he would have charges of
rebellion or conspiracy brought against the richest inhabitants, and made a
fortune from selling up their properties.[39] According to Suetonius, he once
left a game of dice, went outside, saw two *equites* walking past, ordered them
to be arrested and *confiscati*, and returned to the game to boast of his
winnings.[40]

We do not have to assume the literal truth of every anecdote in our
sources in order to accept that an emperor enjoyed, in the short run, an
untrammelled freedom in condemnation and confiscation, as he did also in
disposing of the proceeds. So, for instance, Claudius returned the property.
of those condemned under Tiberius or Gaius either to the survivors or to
their children, and Vitellius and Nerva did likewise.[41] Trajan evolved an
original variant on this theme, which neatly combined the granting of
beneficia with the retention of the relevant profits, for he sold back the splendid houses of the rich which had been occupied as *bona damnatorum* by
Domitian and earlier emperors, and allowed to fall into ruin; Pliny paints an
engaging picture of the gratitude of the noble families who re-occupied, at a
price, the luxurious homes and *horti* which had been lost to the *patrimonium*
of the emperors. Some, but evidently a minority, even received such houses
as gifts.[42]

It is clear that property which came to the emperor as *bona damnatorum*
could be disposed of by him as freely as that acquired in other ways. For
instance Octavia, when divorced from Nero in 62, received as gifts from him
the house of Burrus, which was probably inherited by the emperor on
Burrus' death earlier that year, and the estates of Rubellius Plautius, who
had just been executed while in forced retirement on his ancestral properties
in Asia; his property will certainly have been confiscated.[43] Though, as we

[37] Pliny, *NH* XXXVII, 7/20; cf. Tacitus, *Ann.* XVI, 17–20, which makes clear that Petronius was
forced to commit suicide, and left Nero nothing in his will. Note the story immediately preceding
(7/19), of how Nero took away from the children of an ex-consul his whole collection of myrrhine
ware, and placed it on display in his *theatrum peculiare trans Tiberim in hortis* (for other rarities
and oddities on display in imperial properties see pp. 16, 140, 145).

[38] *Tib.* 49, 2.

[39] LIX, 21, 4–5. Note also Philo, *Leg.* 14/105–8, and the legend in Malalas, *Chron.* X, 245, 9f.;
see G. Downey, *History of Antioch in Syria* (1961), 192f.

[40] *Cal.* 41, 2.

[41] Dio LX, 6, 3; LXV, 6, 2 (120); LXVIII, 2, 1 (188).

[42] *Pan.* 50. The expression *bona damnatorum* is not used, but the context is clear—'non enim
exturbatis prioribus dominis' (50, 1); '. . . tum exitialis erat apud principem huic laxior domus,
illi amoenior villa' (50, 6). That the houses belonged to the *patrimonium* of the emperor is indicated
twice in 50, 2.

[43] Tacitus, *Ann.* XIV, 60, 4; cf. 22, 3 and 57–9.

shall see, a substantial body of legal rules about *bona damnatorum* eventually came into existence, nothing seriously hampered the emperor's freedom of choice in the matter. Thus there is no real parallel for the procedure which Dio describes Nero as following in Greece in 67. Many people were executed, but in order to avoid the imputation of having executed them for their wealth, he allowed them to leave their property to their families or freedmen, but forced these in their turn to leave half their property to himself or his praetorian prefect, Tigellinus; if not enough was left to him, the wills were set aside. Later, he took all the property of the condemned, executed men who were already in exile and seized the property of others who were still alive.[44]

Much of our evidence from this period relates to political charges, and here too the emperor's freedom of choice is evident. Immediately after the proclamation of Galba in 68 Nero declared him a *hostis*, and confiscated his property.[45] But Vitellius did not take the property even of those followers of Otho whom he executed.[46] Vespasian, ever resourceful in financial matters, was believed to promote procurators with the specific intention of condemning them when their wealth had reached its height.[47] In his reign a proconsul of Cyrene executed 3,000 wealthy Jews 'which he thought that he could do safely, as he took up their properties into the revenues of Caesar'.[48] *Bona damnatorum* undoubtedly represented a significant form of acquisition of wealth for the emperor; the disadvantage of its exceptional invidiousness was balanced by the ease and flexibility with which it could be applied. It is not an accident that Martial writes in 80 under Titus, 'The accuser is exiled, and flees from Rome; you may put that down to the expenses of the emperor.'[49] The checking of the accusations of the rich, which became common again under Domitian,[50] meant a real financial loss. For what was taken, by whatever means, by the emperor with one hand, was also available for him to give out with the other. It is significant that Dio says of Trajan that he spent what was needed on war, peace, roads, harbours and public building, but 'shed no one's blood for any of these'.[51] Pliny in the *Panegyric* puts the same point in more colourful language: 'You give a *congiarium* from money that is rightfully yours, and *alimenta* too; and the children of citizens are not fed by you like troops of beasts on the blood of slaughtered men.'[52]

By this time the experience of execution and confiscation was a commonplace in the provinces also. Dio of Prusa can use in his *Euboicus* the case of a rich man who was executed and had his property confiscated—'they say

---

[44] Dio, LXIII, 11, 1–3 (76–7).
[45] Plutarch, *Galba* 5, 5–6.
[46] Dio LXV, 6, 2–3 (120).
[47] Suetonius, *Vesp.* 16, 2.
[48] Josephus, *BJ* VII, 11, 2 (446): ὅτι τὰς οὐσίας αὐτῶν εἰς τὰς τοῦ Καίσαρος προσόδους ἀνελάμβανεν.
[49] *Epig.* 1, 4, 5–6: 'exulat Ausonia profugus delator ab urbe: / haec licet impensis principis adnumeres.'
[50] Pliny, *Pan.* 42; Dio·LXVII, 4, 5 (169).
[51] LXVIII, 7, 1 (192); cf. Eutropius, *Brev.* VIII, 4.
[52] *Pan.* 27, 3.

that he was killed by the emperor for his money'.[53] The practice of confiscation tended to become more extensive, and by Trajan's time had spread improperly to the goods of those who had been sentenced to be *relegati* but not *deportati*.[54] So Trajan wrote to Didius Secundus, in all probability a provincial governor, 'I know that by the avarice of previous periods the goods of *relegati* have been claimed for the *fiscus*. But a different procedure is in accordance with my clemency . . .'[55] But at the same time it appears that the range of crimes for which property was confiscated steadily increased. Ulpian quotes in his *On the Office of Proconsul* a rescript of Hadrian evidently addressed to a provincial governor: 'It is laid down, in order that persons should not be made eunuchs, that those convicted on this charge should be subject to the penalty of the *Lex Cornelia*, and their goods should be deservedly claimed for my *fiscus*.'[56] A rough indication of the range of criminal offences which involved total confiscation is given by a clause of the *gnomon*, not only as it stood under Antoninus Pius, but also as it appears in the new text dating to the first century:[57]

> Those who have been condemned for murder or more serious crimes, or have chosen exile when faced with such charges, have their goods confiscated. A tenth is allowed to their children, and dowries in silver to the wives. These latter have also been granted a twelfth by the Emperor Antoninus Caesar.

The last two sentences recall similar concessions which are attested on the part of Julius Caesar, of the triumvirs, in the edict of Tiberius Julius Alexander in Egypt in 68, and by Constantine.[58] Confiscation was thus an established part of penal practice in the provinces, and applied far outside the range of political offences.[59] Under Severus we come to the first attested case of a Christian, the father of Origen, who was martyred in Alexandria and whose property was 'taken up for the imperial treasuries'.[60]

With these extensions of the practice of confiscation, it was inevitable that

---

[53] *Or.* VII, 12.

[54] See n. 29.

[55] *Dig.* XLVIII, 22, 1 (cf. p. 324). With a similar intention, *Dig.* XLVIII, 20, 6, a rescript of Hadrian ending the practice of transmitting to the *fiscus* the proceeds of selling *pannicularia*.

[56] *Dig.* XLVIII, 8, 4, 2: 'eorumque bona merito fisco meo vindicari'. The possessive is significant. The passage also disposes of *HA, Had.* 7, 7: 'damnatorum bona in fiscum privatum redigi vetuit, omni summa in aerario publico recepta.'

[57] *Gnomon*, para. 36. The expression is (again) τὰ ὑπάρχοντα ἀναλαμβάνεται. The new text, *P. Oxy.* 3014, attributes the concession of a twelfth to some authority, evidently an emperor, whose name is lost. Cf. also para. 22 (incest).

[58] Caesar and triumvirs: p. 165; edict of Tiberius Julius Alexander: *OGIS* 669, cf. Chalon, *L'Édit* (1964), l. 25 (Chalon, ad loc. takes this to refer to debtors to the *fiscus*, but these parallels make it likely that condemned persons were at least understood to be included in the provision); Constantine: *CJ* v, 16, 24 (321), ending 'fisco nostro ad easdem res nullam in posterum communionem habituro'.

[59] Note the anecdote in Philostratus, *VS* II, 26, of Heraclides the Lycian who had a large part of his property confiscated (δημευθῆναι τὸ πολὺ τῆς οὐσίας) for cutting down sacred cedars. As his parody of *Odyssey* IV, 498, εἰς δή που λοιπὸς κατερύκεται εὐρέϊ 'φίσκῳ', indicates, his property went to the *fiscus*.

[60] Eusebius, *HE* VI, 2, 13: τῆς γε μὴν τοῦ πατρὸς περιουσίας τοῖς βασιλικοῖς ταμείοις ἀναληφθείσης. Cf. Jerome, *De vir. ill.* 54, cf. p. 566.

the jurists of the second and third centuries should give a lot of attention to the problems which arose.[61] We need not consider the complex details involved, except to note that the charge of treason (*maiestas*) still occupied a special place. A charge of *maiestas* could be laid even after the death of the man concerned, and his property in consequence could be claimed for the *fiscus*. This was specifically ordered by Marcus Aurelius in the case of a senator who had supported the proclamation of Avidius Cassius in 175.[62] Ulpian formulates the general rule that whereas in other cases the natural death of a man under accusation extinguished the charge, in the case of treason his estate was confiscated unless his heirs could prove his innocence.[63] Modestinus repeats this and adds *repetundae* as a charge to which this rule applied.[64]

The reign of Severus, which saw two civil wars against his rival pretenders, Pescennius Niger and Clodius Albinus, gave ample scope for the application of these principles. So we may reasonably believe the report of the *Historia Augusta* that widespread executions were followed by *publicatio bonorum*. In particular many of the leading men of Spain and Gaul, supporters of Albinus, were killed; and in consequence Severus left his sons 'immense riches', since he had made a large part of the gold throughout the Gallic and Spanish provinces and Italy imperial property.[65] Herodian also reports that Severus executed the followers of Clodius Albinus, and confiscated their property, and adds that he granted the property of condemned men to his notorious praetorian prefect, Plautianus.[66] Such property was not, however, lost to the emperor for good, for after the prefect's downfall in 205 we find a special procurator 'for the goods of Plautianus'.[67] In spite of all this Dio manages to say of Severus, as of Trajan, that he made all the necessary expenditures, but killed no one for their money.[68]

The *Historia Augusta* does, however, seem to be essentially correct in dating a major relevant development to the reign of Severus. Immediately after speaking of Severus' confiscations, the author continues: 'then for the first time the *procuratio* of the *res privatae* was established.'[69] The *ratio privata* is attested earlier, under Commodus, but it is indeed under Severus

[61] e.g. *Dig.* XXIV, 3, 31 *pr.*; XXXVI, 1, 18, 5; XXXVIII, 16, 1, 3; XLVIII, 17, 5 *pr.*; 20, 7, 1 and 5; 20, 8, and 10; 21, 3; 22, 15; 23, 3. Cf. Paulus, *Sent.* V, 12, 12; *CJ* IX, 50, 1 *pr.* (Caracalla, 212).

[62] *CJ* IX, 8, 6 *pr.* This evidence from Paulus, *de iudiciis publicis*, disposes of *HA, Avid. Cass.* 7, 6, cf. *Marc. Ant.* 24, 9, which states that the *bona* of Avidius were proscribed by the senate, refused by Marcus for the *fiscus* ('privatum aerarium') and taken for the *aerarium. Avid. Cass.* 9, 2 and 12, 7, also claims that Marcus returned half of Avidius' property to his sons.

[63] *Dig.* XLVIII, 4, 11. In the case of a man's suicide under accusation on a charge which if proved would have meant confiscation, the property was confiscated unless either it could be shown that he killed himself 'taedio vitae vel impatientia doloris', or if the heirs were prepared to defend him posthumously, in which case the charge had to be proved, *Dig.* XLVIII, 21, 3.

[64] *Dig.* XLVIII, 2, 20. The sole rights left to the sons of persons condemned for *maiestas* were to a share of the property of *liberti* of the condemned, *Dig.* XLVIII, 4, 9 (Hermogenianus).

[65] *Sept. Sev.* 12, 1 and 3. It was presumably also *bona damnatorum* which were the concern of the *procurator ad bona cogenda*, a unique office attested (for Africa) at this time by *ILS* 1421, see Pflaum, *Carrières*, no. 222.

[66] III, 8, 2; 10, 6.

[67] *ILS* 1370, *proc. ad bona Plautiani*; cf. Pflaum, *Carrières*, no. 257.

[68] LXXVI, 16, 2 (371).

[69] *Sept. Sev.* 12, 4: 'tuncque primum privatarum rerum procuratio constituta est.'

that local officials of it appear.[70] Moreover, the weak implication of the passage that the *privata* was in some way connected with confiscated property is fully borne out by papyri of the tetrarchic period.[71]

From Herodian we have a vivid general account of a reign of terror under Maximinus, with endless accusations and condemnations of the rich—'such was the avarice of the tyrant under the pretext of the constant necessity of providing money for the soldiers'. He also asserts, what does not seem to be attested elsewhere, that the despoliation of the rich might be greeted not merely with indifference but with positive pleasure by the poor.[72] Herodian's view, however illuminating, remains a rhetorical generalization. But the persecutions under Decius and Valerian, to which we shall return in more detail later,[73] offer specific and concrete evidence of the practice of confiscation. For instance, Cyprian writes in a letter of 257:[74]

> Know that Xystus (bishop of Rome) was executed in a cemetery on the sixth of August, and four deacons with him. Moreover the Prefects in the city press on daily with the persecution, so whoever is brought before them is executed and their goods claimed for the *fiscus*.

From about this time we can specify an actual property in Rome which was taken by the *fiscus*, for among the endowments granted to the basilica of Laurentius by Constantine was 'the property of a certain Cyriace, a devout woman, which the *fiscus* had occupied in a time of persecution'.[75] It is highly significant that property acquired by the *fiscus* as *bona damnatorum* could be granted by Constantine to the Church just like any that had come into his disposition by other means, for instance as a gift.[76] Once again we see the balance between the endlessly resented acquisition of property by the emperor on the one hand, and his distribution of benefits on the other.

In the period up to Constantine it is, as usual, the acquisition which receives the most emphasis in our sources. Ammianus recalls that, in the lamentable state of the empire after Gallienus, Aurelian fell 'like a torrent' on the rich.[77] Lactantius, who emphasises the rapacity of the state even more than most other writers, asserts that whenever Diocletian saw an especially well cultivated field or fine building, a charge and capital penalty were ready for the owner; and says of Maximian that his 'most cruel *fiscus* overflowed with ill-gotten gains'.[78] Eusebius similarly claims that Maximin in the east robbed the rich of their ancestral possessions, and heaped wealth

---

[70] See App. 3.

[71] pp. 173–4 and App. 3.

[72] VII, 3, 2–5.

[73] pp. 566–71.

[74] Cyprian, *Ep.* 80, 4: 'animadvertantur et bona eorum fisco vindicentur.'

[75] Duchesne, *Liber Pontificalis* I, p. 182: 'possessio cuiusdam Cyriacae religiosae feminae quod fiscus occupaverat tempore persecutionis.' Cf. p. 155 (xxv).

[76] For donations which originated in gifts to the emperor see, for example, Duchesne, I, p. 177: 'possessio Sybilles, donata Augusto'; 'possessio Timialica, donata Augusto Constantino ab Ambrosio'; p. 178: 'possessio Agapi, quod donavit Augusto Constantino'.

[77] xxx, 8, 8. For quite unreliable evidence to the contrary see the spurious letter in *HA*, *Aurel.* 24. 5,

[78] *De mort. pers.* 7, 12; 8, 4.

on the flatterers who surrounded him.[79] On the other hand Libanius and
Eutropius contrast the consideration of Constantius for the property of the
rich with the unbridled rapacity of his tetrarchic colleagues.[80]

But while at one level the pattern of confiscation was directly influenced
by the character, attitudes and needs of the individual emperors, we can see
it at another as an established, and probably increasing, part of the exercise
of jurisdiction in the provinces. For instance, a long series of enactments by
Constantine extended the range of offences punishable by confiscation.[81]
Perhaps more important, a series of papyri from the tetrarchic period
illustrate the handling of confiscated property, and show that it fell under the
control of the *magister privatae*. We can only speculate about whether there
was in fact any continuity between the *idios logos* ('private account'), which
handled confiscated property among other things, and whose chief official
is last attested in the first half of the third century,[82] and the *ratio privata*
('private account'), which begins to operate on a local basis in the early third
century.[83] Its role in relation to confiscated property is, however, attested for
the first time in Egypt in the correspondence of the *stratēgos* of the Panopolite
nome in 298, which includes for instance the following entry:[84]

Public Notice. Immediately after I received the letters of my lord the most
eminent *Magister privatae* Pomponius Domnus, enquiring the amount of wine
included in the confiscations of goods accruing of the Treasury, together with
the expected produce of the vintage, I accordingly made public proclamation
that each of the secretaries of the Treasury estates should report to my office
the amount already in store and that being produced from the vintage.

Perhaps even clearer is the report of two property registrars sent in
305/6 to the officials of the city of Oxyrhynchus:[85]

You have written informing us that Aurelius Athanasius, *procurator privatae* in
Egypt, has given orders by a letter written in accordance with a divine edict
of our masters the Emperors and Caesars and in conformity with letters directed
to him from Neratius Apollonides [the *magister privatae*] that the property of

[79] *HE* VIII, 14, 10. Cf. Lactantius, *De mort. pers.* 37, 3.

[80] Libanius, *Or.* LIX, 15; Eutropius, *Brev.* X, 1, 12. Cf. *Pan.* X(4), 33, 7, Nazarius addressing
Constantine in 321 and referring to his victory over Maxentius in 312: 'praeterea privatim reddita
omnibus patrimonia quos illa monstrosa labes extorres domo fecerat.' It is very probable, but not
perhaps certain, that such *patrimonia* would have counted as *bona damnatorum*. If they did, the
use of 'privatim' is of some significance. For general references to condemnations and confiscation
by Maxentius see *Pan.* IX(12), 3, 6; Eusebius, *VC* I, 35; 41.

[81] See for example *CTh* IX, 1, 2 = *CJ* IX, 40, 2 (319); *CTh* XII, 1, 6 = *CJ* V, 5, 3, 3 (319); *CTh* IX,
21, 2-4, with *CJ* VII, 13, 2, and IX, 24, 1-2 (penalties for counterfeiters); *CTh* IX, 8, 1 = *CJ* IX,
10, 1 (326); *CTh* XV, 2, 1 = *CJ* XI, 43, 1 (330); *CTh* I, 5, 3 (331); *CTh* XI, 34, 1 (331); *CJ* V, 27,
1 (336).

[82] See Swarney, *Idios Logos*, 127–30, and *P. Oxy.* 2133 (AD 239), with commentary.

[83] See App. 3.

[84] *P. Beatty Panop.* 1, ll. 205–8 trans. Skeat, with the substitution of the translation *magister
privatae* for *magister rei privatae*, for μάγιστρος τῆς πριουάτης. The attestation of the term *res
privata* is in fact remarkably weak, see App. 3. Cf. also ll. 337–46 for references to confiscation
and the *magister privatae*.

[85] *P. Oxy.* 2665, trans. Rea (with the same emendation as in previous note). Cf. Mitteis,
Chrestomathie, no. 196. For Neratius Apollonides as *magister privatae* see *P. Oxy.* 2673 (p. 575).

Paul from the Oxyrhynchite nome, who has been laid under sentence by the most illustrious *praeses* of the Thebaid, Satrius Arrianus, should be adjudged to the accounts of the Treasury.

Even this item of local procedure had its origins, as is stated, in an imperial edict. The widespread local reflections of changes in the imperial will are nowhere better attested than in the religious conflicts of this period. So, first, when the tetrarchs wrote a letter in perhaps about 300–3 to Julianus, the proconsul of Africa, on the suppression of Manicheeism, they ordered that the followers of the sect should be executed, or if of high rank sent to hard labour, 'and their property claimed for our *fiscus*'.[86] How far this was carried out we do not know, but in the Great Persecution we have substantial evidence of the loss of church property, which was then restored in the proclamations of 313. It is indeed precisely this positive element, the restoration of property, which distinguished these pronouncements from the proclamation of mere toleration issued by Galerius, Licinius and Constantine in 311.[87] So for instance we find Maximin in his edict of 313 ordering the restoration of houses and land which had formerly belonged to the church and had fallen into the ownership of the *fiscus*, been taken by a city, sold up, or, significantly, 'given to anyone as a favour'.[88] The victory of Constantine over Licinius in 324 brought a further transfer of property in the eastern provinces. Eusebius writes: 'He ordered that the property of the holy martyrs of god . . . should be restored to their relatives, and if there were none such, that the church should inherit. Furthermore the proclamation of his gift laid down that goods which had formerly been disposed of by the *fiscus* (*tameion*) to others by sale or gift, and those remaining in its possession, should be restored to their proper owners.'[89]

Of course it was always possible to take a less benevolent view of the disbursement of *bona damnatorum* by the emperor, and Ammianus asserts that it was Constantine himself who first caused the jaws of his intimates to open and engulf the property of the condemned, and the favourites of Constantius who stimulated civil war with an eye to the property of their neighbours, and were the first to feast on the marrow of the provinces.[90] He could hardly have committed a more profound historical error; for it was precisely the circumstances of civil war in the late republic that had created the possibility of irregular acquisition of the goods of the condemned, and had opened the way for an institution belonging to the Hellenistic kingdoms to become under the emperors an established part of criminal justice. As such, it was furthermore one of the primary sources of the reserves of land and property which the emperors acquired.

---

[86] *Coll.* xv, 3, 6: 'et eorum bona fisco nostro vindicari sancimus', and in 7: 'eorum patrimonia fisco nostro adsociari facies'. On the possible date see *PLRE* Iulianus 23. Cf. p. 314.

[87] pp. 578–83.

[88] Eusebius, *HE* IX, 10, 11: εἰς τὸ δίκαιον μετέπεσεν τοῦ φίσκου ἢ ὑπό τινος κατελήφθη πόλεως, εἴτε διάπρασις τούτων γεγένηται εἴτε εἰς χάρισμα δέδοταί τινι.

[89] *VC* II, 21; see pp. 592–3.

[90] xvi, 8, 11–12. Cf. *CTh* x, 8, 4 (Constantius in 346): 'quamvis plurimis petentibus facultates eorum, qui sub hoste publico egerunt adque in proelio poenas debitas pependerunt liberalitas nostra largita sit . . .'

8. *The Imperial Properties: Character, Exploitation and Social Significance*

A history of the properties of the Roman emperors cannot be written. It is not merely that the evidence, if collected, would be disparate in time, local setting and character, nor even that a large proportion of the individual items of such evidence would themselves prove to be fragmentary, allusive or enigmatic. It is more that we are hopelessly ignorant of the patterns of private ownership and exploitation of land, of mines or quarries, or of manufacturing establishments, which prevailed in the different regions of the empire; and even if we ignore such local aspects of the problem, we still cannot state with any certainty what was the juridical character of those properties which were in some sense in the possession of the emperor. It is only a modest consolation to know that similar doubts were clearly felt by Ulpian:[1]

> I do not think that this interdict (ensuring right of way in public places) applies to those places which are in the *patrimonium* of the *fiscus* . . . for fiscal properties are, as it were, the private property of the Emperor.

A few aspects of the problem are clear in rough outline. It is evident from what has been said above that substantial quantities of property passed by inheritance, by its ownership lapsing, or by confiscation, into the possession of the emperor. Furthermore, there is no doubt that property which was owned by one emperor passed into the hands of his successor on the throne, irrespective of whether there was a family connection or not. Thus for example the Horti Sallustiani, in Rome, probably left to Tiberius by his friend and adviser Sallustius Crispus in 20, remained imperial property through and beyond the period.[2] Thirdly, such properties could be granted or sold by the emperor at will; and indeed the conferring of properties was among the principal forms of benefaction which he had at his disposal.

But even here, while the fact is clear enough, the legal and administrative contexts can be alluded to in our sources in a bewildering variety of terms. For instance Constantine writes to the *rationalis* of Africa in 319: 'We have granted certain persons properties and slaves withdrawn from the *patrimonium* of the *fiscus*. We wish these to be held in full and perpetual ownership without any risk of question, laying down a penalty for *rationales*, *magistri* of the *privata res* or *officiales* who make any attempt to contravene it.'[3] But in the very next year, when Constantine issues an edict about the status of the free wives of imperial slaves and of their children, he employs a different set of terms: 'We wish this law to be observed in the case of fiscal slaves, of those who originate from the patrimonial estates, [who are attached to]

---

[1] *Dig.* XLIII, 8, 2, 4; cf. *JRS* LIII (1963), 42.

[2] See Hirschfeld, *Kleine Schriften* (1913), 528f.; Platner-Ashby, *Topographical Dictionary of Ancient Rome*, 271f. Cf. p. 23.

[3] *CTh* X, 1, 2. Cf. *CTh* IV, 11, 1 (316) referring to the gift of a *rem ad fiscum pertinentem*.

emphyteutic estates and who are concerned with properties which form part of our *res privatae*.'[4]

Emphyteutic estates were those leased out on a long-term basis in return for a rent in kind; the term does not appear in connection with imperial estates before the fourth century.[5] The terms *patrimonium* and *privata* have a long and complex history which need not be discussed here; but it is evident that from the early third century imperial properties could be distinguished as being attached to one or the other; from the late third century onwards the *ratio privata*, with its *magistri* and *procuratores*, *seems* to have been the agency which controlled all imperial properties; but some of them none the less retained the label 'patrimonial'.[6] It is typical of our difficulties that when Constantine writes to the bishop of Carthage in 313 to announce a subvention for the Catholic priesthood, and says that any extra money may be obtained from 'Heraclides the procurator of our properties', we have no clear notion as to how these terms, transmitted by Eusebius in Greek, should be translated into Latin.[7] But what is clear is, once again, the role of the estates in providing a store of value on which the emperor could draw at will in conferring benefits on his subjects.

If we look back earlier than the fourth century, whose rich documentation is made less helpful than it might be by the variability of the technical terms employed, we still find ourselves faced with acute difficulties over the formal categories of land in imperial possession, as is visible in another passage of Ulpian:[8]

> But if anyone left as a legacy the Horti Sallustiani which are [the property] of the emperor, or the Alban estate, which serves imperial uses, the act of including such legacies in a will would be a sign of insanity. Similarly it is agreed that the Campus Martius, the Forum Romanum or a sacred temple cannot be left as a legacy. But, in the case of those estates of the emperor which have been placed in the category of the *patrimonium* under the *procurator patrimonii*, if any are left as a legacy, an *aestimatio* should not be carried out, since they are not sold except by the command of the emperor and it is not customary to break them up.

Ulpian's discussion clearly distinguishes imperial properties from those of the *res publica* of Rome, and also places in a special category those imperial properties which were used personally by the emperor. But we remain in the dark as to whether he is deliberately excluding property under the newly-formed *ratio privata*, whether all imperial properties were now either 'patrimonial' or attached to the *ratio privata*, whether there was a wider category of 'fiscal' properties, and whether he intends to exclude this also.

---

[4] *CTh* IV, 12, 3: 'quod ius et in fiscalibus servis et in patrimoniorum fundorum originariis et ad emphyteuticaria praedia et qui ad privatarum rerum nostrarum corpora pertinent servari volumus.'

[5] See Jones, *Later Roman Empire*, 417f.

[6] See App. 3.

[7] Eusebius, *HE* x, 6, 3: παρὰ Ἡρακλείδα τοῦ ἐπιτρόπου τῶν ἡμετέρων κτημάτων. Cf. p. 583 below.

[8] *Dig.* xxx, 39, 8–10.

At all events, what is clear is that only the fact that they were the property of the emperor, and the custom of retaining and not disposing of them, distinguished 'patrimonial' properties from those of private persons.

If we ignore for the moment the insoluble problem of the juridical status of imperial property in the established empire, and go further back, to its origins, it is important to stress the roots of imperial property-holding in the normal social and economic patterns of life of the Roman upper classes. Just as the actual residences of the emperors developed out of a set of houses and villas typical of any well-placed senator,[9] so his ownership of land had the same origins. Octavian had been the heir both of his real father, C. Octavius, and of Julius Caesar, who adopted him in his will.[10] As is well known, the position of a Roman senator depended essentially on the possession of landed estates; from the late republic onwards senators are found owning estates not only in Italy but also in the provinces. The estates provided the census valuation without which, from Augustus' time onwards, a man could not remain a senator; but even before that they provided the basis of his income and a store of value which could be drawn on in emergency. As we have noted earlier, Octavian deceived his mother in the summer of 44 with the claim that he was going to Campania to sell the estates which he had inherited there in order to fulfil the bequests of Caesar.[11] Thereafter our evidence on the estates of Augustus relates almost entirely to those which he used on occasion as residences. But it is certain, for instance, that he owned land in Africa, from where his procurator sent him nearly 400 shoots of corn grown from a single grain, while a successor sent 360 to Nero. This passing reference in Pliny's *Natural History*[12] introduces a difficult problem, to which we shall return later: did imperial properties serve as sources solely of revenue in cash (from rents) or did they also supply produce, for imperial use or for distribution? The latter would be clear from Pliny if only his reference did not leave open the possibility that what the procurator sent was merely a specimen, rather than part of a shipment.

We can however be reasonably sure that, in any public province governed by a proconsul, where Augustus had a procurator he owned property in some form; the attested cases are Africa, Sicily, Achaea, Crete and Asia,[13] a fairly extensive list for this period, especially considering that inscriptional evidence is still very slight. As to the nature or source of the property we have hardly any evidence; but we owe to Dio the note that M. Agrippa had somehow acquired the Chersonese as his private property, and bequeathed it to Augustus on his death in 12 BC.[14] There was a *familia* of imperial slaves

---

[9] pp. 18–28.

[10] In his own will he referred to what he had spent 'ex duobus paternis patrimoniis', Suetonius, *Aug.* 101, 3. He certainly inherited a house at Nola from C. Octavius, ibid., 98, see p. 25. For the background see now I. Shatzman, *Senatorial Wealth and Roman Politics* (1975).

[11] p. 25.

[12] XVIII, 21/94–5.

[13] See Pflaum, *Carrières*, 1044, 1070–2, 1092.

[14] LIV, 29, 5. It is possible that Agrippa had acquired it through his first marriage, to Attica the daughter of Atticus, see T. R. S. Broughton, 'Roman Landholding in Asia Minor', *TAPhA* LXV (1934), 207, on 219–20.

7

there in 55, and a procurator of the *regio* of the Chersonese is attested early in the second century.[15] Then, by a more indirect route, the emperors acquired the region of Jamnia in Judaea. Towards the end of the reign of Augustus, Salome the sister of Herod died and left to Livia the town of Jamnia with its toparchy, along with Phasaelis and Archelais, which produced a rich crop of dates.[16] These areas had been left to her by Herod, and this provision of his will had been confirmed by Augustus, who added the 'royal dwelling' in Ascalon, the whole producing an annual revenue of sixty talents.[17] It is evident that on Livia's death in 29 this property came into the possession of Tiberius and then of Gaius, for Herennius Capito, procurator of Jamnia under Tiberius, is described on an inscription as procurator of all three persons in succession.[18] In Josephus' narrative of the adventurous earlier history of the future Agrippa I of Judaea, Capito is found sending soldiers to arrest Agrippa at Anthedon and exact from him a large sum which he owed to 'the treasury of Caesar in Rome'.[19]

In this case the progression of events is clear, as is the fact that what was involved was a revenue in cash. But, as with similar grants made by the Seleucids,[20] it remains entirely unclear what was the juridical status of the granting of individuals of areas which included cities. It is a prime instance of the fact that even where our evidence is relatively good we cannot fully understand the legal nature of imperial property for lack of a clear conception of the background.

Elsewhere, however, there is good evidence of estates belonging in an ordinary, private-law sense to the emperor—'the estates of Caesar were (still) rare in Italy' writes Tacitus, recording the better aspects of Tiberius' reign.[21] What is more, it is clear that the same assumptions could be applied to them as to other private estates. For instance Claudius asked the consuls for permission to establish a fair on his private estates; exactly the same requests on the part of senators were later discussed by the senate under Trajan and in 138.[22] On the other hand Claudius relegated a senator who as aedile had fined inhabitants of his estates for contravening the regulation forbidding the sale of cooked food, and had flogged a *vilicus* who intervened.[23]

It lay in the nature of the situation that the role of the emperor as one landowner among others could not be fully maintained indefinitely. But

[15] *ILS* 5682, 1419; cf. Pflaum, *Carrières*, no. 64. It is presumably this *regio* which two Greek inscriptions refer to as an ἐπαρχεία, *AE* 1924 82, cf. Pflaum, *Carrières*, no. 145; *IGR* I 822.

[16] Josephus, *Ant.* XVIII, 2, 2 (31); cf. *BJ* II, 9, 1 (167).

[17] *Ant.* XVII, 8, 1 (189); 11, 5 (321).

[18] See Pflaum, *Carrières*, no. 9. In Philo, *Leg.* 30/199, φόρων ἐκλογεὺς ὁ Καπίτων ἐστὶ τῶν τῆς Ἰουδαίας, the correct reading is probably Ἰαμνείας, as suggested by Smallwood, ad loc. Note also *AE* 1948 141 (Jamnia): 'Ti. Julius Aug. l. Mellon proc.'

[19] *Ant.* XVIII, 6, 3 (158). This was presumably among the extensive private debts which he had contracted while living previously in Rome, see XVIII, 6, 1–2 (143–7).

[20] See E. Bikerman, *Institutions des Séleucides* (1938), 176f.

[21] *Ann.* IV, 6, 4.

[22] Suetonius, *Claud.* 12, 2: cf. p. 350. For the economic significance of fairs, and the problem of public order posed by them, see R. MacMullen, 'Market-Days in the Roman Empire', *Phoenix* XXIV (1970), 333.

[23] ibid., 38, 2. Since the senator was by now an ex-praetor, the incident *may* have occurred before Claudius became emperor.

in a list of properties, for instance, registered in the territory of the Ligures Baebiani near Beneventum as guaranteeing the capital and income for Trajan's alimentary scheme, 'Caesar noster' (our emperor) is recorded as neighbour no less than seven times.[24] From various parts of the empire we have boundary-stones marking off imperial properties, where the current emperor is given as the owner, with his name in the genitive.[25] The same is true for instance of markings on lead pipes from Antium,[26] or on the bricks and tiles (among the few semi-industrial products of the estates of upper-class Romans) produced on various properties which successively fell into imperial ownership.[27]

More important and revealing are the references to the major estates (*saltus*) of private persons and the emperor in the work of Frontinus, *On Disputes over Land*. Writing towards the end of the first century, he states for instance that disputes often arise in the provinces between cities and private persons, 'especially in Africa where private persons have estates no smaller than the territories of cities'. The estates contained substantial populations and villages attached to the villas which resembled towns. Disputes arose over the rights of cities to exact services from within such estates: 'they have such disputes not only with private persons but also very frequently with Caesar, who possesses not a little in the province.'[28] This evidence is extremely important in indicating how the ownership of major stretches of land by the emperor was merely an aspect of similar ownership by private persons. Indeed it was directly a product of it, for the well-known sentence in Pliny the Elder, 'Six owners possessed half of Africa, when Nero killed them',[29] must be meant to imply that their estates were confiscated. There is moreover extensive evidence, which will not be discussed here, for imperial estates (*saltus* or *regiones*) in Africa, run by procurators and with a central office (*tabularium*) in Carthage.[30]

The passage also suggests the existence of substantial continuous stretches of land under either private or, increasingly, imperial ownership, and the inscriptions of Africa confirm this. It remains the case, however, that even here, let alone elsewhere, we cannot map the boundaries of a single imperial

[24] *CIL* IX 1455, col. II, 35, 49, 54, 70; III, 5, 17, 25. It does not of course follow that there were seven separate imperial properties in this area, though they are listed as bordering properties in four or five different *pagi*, see P. Veyne, 'La table des Ligures Baebiani', *MÉFR* LXX (1958), 177, on p. 206. In the Table of Veleia, *CIL* XI 1147, 'Imp(erator) n(oster)' is listed four times: col. IV, 60, 76; VI, 2, 37.

[25] e.g. from Sagallassus (Galatia), *CIL* III 6872: 'finis Caesaris noster'; *OGIS* 538 = *IGR* III 335, re-edited by G. E. Bean, *Anat. Stud.* IX (1959), 84, no. 30 = *SEG* XIX 765. Cf. *ILAlg.* I, 2988, a boundary established on the orders of Trajan *inter Aug. et Musal(amios)*; *CIL* VIII 25944, 25988, 25893b. From Mauretania Caesariensis, VIII, 10567.

[26] *CIL* XV 7790–3; 7815 = XIV 2226; 7816 (L. Nemi). The list could be considerably extended.

[27] See H. Bloch, *I bolli laterizi e la storia edilizia romana* (1938–9); 'The Roman Brick-Stamps', *HSCPh* LVI–VII (1947), 1, and 'Indices to Roman Brick-Stamps', LVIII–IX (1948), 1, on 77–82.

[28] Julius Frontinus, *de controversiis agrorum* in *Corp. agrim. rom.* ed. Thulin, 45–6; cf. also 36.

[29] *NH* XVIII, 7/35.

[30] See for example J. J. Van Nostrand, *The Imperial Domains of Africa Proconsularis: an epigraphical Study* (1925); R. M. Haywood in *Economic Survey of Ancient Rome*, ed. Tenney Frank, IV (1938), 83–102; Ch. Saumagne, 'Circonscriptions domaniales dans l'Afrique romaine', *Rev. Tun.* XLI–IV (1940), 231; J. Kolendo, 'Sur la législation relative aux grands domaines de l'Afrique romaine', *REA* LXV (1963), 80.

property, and cannot exclude the possibility that both private and imperial holdings were often made up of small separate lots.[31] None the less, for the position of the emperor within the state and the effects of his existence on society, we may still ask whether there is any evidence of his control of any significant areas, whether agricultural or otherwise, which were thereby withdrawn from local institutions and placed under imperial agents. As the passage of Frontinus indicates, such a withdrawal would only have exacerbated conflicts already present in the case of private estates.[32]

Marcus Aurelius, for instance, laid down in an oration which he delivered in the senate that people had the right of entering the estates of both the emperor, and of senators and country-people in order to search for fugitive slaves.[33] Conversely, Antoninus Pius had ruled that although procurators of the emperor did not have the right of deportation, they were entitled to exclude from imperial estates (*praedia Caesariana*) anyone who caused disturbance or injury to the *coloni* of the emperor.[34] As the passage of Frontinus implies, there was clearly a standing issue as to whether the *coloni* or *conductores* of imperial estates were liable to the obligations imposed by neighbouring cities, and on this point our sources contradict each other. Callistratus, writing in the early third century, states that 'the *coloni* of Caesar are freed from obligations, so that they may be kept more serviceable for the fiscal estates (*praedia fiscalia*)'.[35] But Aurelius and Verus had laid down that *coloni* of the *praedia fisci* must carry out such obligations 'without loss to the *fiscus*';[36] and Severus Alexander similarly wrote in 225: '*coloni* (that is *conductores*) of *praedia* pertaining to the *fiscus* do not thereby gain relief from civil obligations, and so must perform *tutelae* which are imposed on them.'[37] But this again is partially contradicted by Herennius Modestinus, who says that men must complete their obligations as *tutores* or *curatores* before becoming tenants of the lands of Caesar, and that failure to reveal such obligations is a criminal offence; this latter he attributes to a ruling by Severus.[38]

This was, therefore, an area of debate, and the uncertainty clearly implies that there was no definite line between imperial tenants and others. But documents do provide some further indications of the control exercised within imperial possessions by the procurators. In the estates which lay in Bagradas valley in Africa the procurators issued regulations (*leges*) governing the obligations, in cash, kind or labour, of the tenants (*coloni*) to the

[31] Compare Jones, *Later Roman Empire*, 781f.

[32] The question of procuratorial jurisdiction within the bounds of imperial properties was attempted, in rather rough fashion, in *Historia* XIII (1964), 180, and XIV (1965), 362; cf. P. A. Brunt, 'Procuratorial Jurisdiction', *Latomus* XXV (1966), 461, esp. 483f.

[33] *Dig.* XI, 4, 3; cf. Paulus, *Sent.* I, 6a, 5.

[34] *Dig.* I, 19, 3; Severus and Caracalla added that the procurators could not subsequently permit such a person to return.

[35] *Dig.* L, 6, 6, 10–11.

[36] *Dig.* L, 1, 38, 1.

[37] *CJ* v, 62, 8.

[38] *Dig.* XIX, 2, 49: οἱ ἐπίτροποι γενόμενοι ἢ κουράτορες πρὶν ἐκτίσαι τὰ τῆς κηδεμονίας μισθωταὶ Καίσαρος γενέσθαι κωλύονται. It is not clear what distinction Modestinus implies when he goes on to say that such persons also cannot μισθοῦσθαι καὶ παρὰ τοῦ ταμείου χωρία. ταμιεῖον can refer either to the *fiscus* or the *aerarium*.

lessees (*conductores*).[39] In one well-known inscription a group of these *coloni* appeal to Commodus against non-observance of these rules as a result of collusion between the procurator and the *conductores*, 'to the detriment of your accounts'. Their complaints had been answered only by the procurator sending soldiers to beat them. So they appeal for a restoration of the proper rules, 'so that by the kindliness of your majesty we, your rural workers, born and raised on your estates, may no longer be harassed by the lessors of the imperial estates'.[40]

Both of these aspects of the situation of imperial tenants are reflected in the appeal to early third-century emperors (Severus and Caracalla?) by the villagers from an estate in Lydia, who complain both of oppression by the procurators and of being troubled by persons trying to impose on them liturgies and offices (in neighbouring cities). They state that they are prevented from making their due payments to 'the imperial account' and threaten to leave the imperial land which contained their houses and ancestral tombs, and migrate to private land.[41] As we shall see,[42] it was not unknown for other villagers to petition the emperor, but it is clear that both these groups could attempt at least to claim a special attention as his own tenants.

The types of imperial possessions which were most clearly marked off from the rest of society were, however, not agricultural estates, but mines and quarries (*metalla*), and eventually other industrial establishments, such as dye-works and cloth-works. The clearest and best-known case of what appears to be a whole community living under rules issued by an imperial procurator is provided by the inscription from the mines at Vipasca in Lusitania. All leases and sales within the boundaries of the mining area were controlled by the procurator, who could also exact fines which were payable to the *fiscus*. Some imperial slaves and freedmen were in his employment, but the mines and other services in the area were contracted out to free lessors. A second lengthy document, in the form of a letter and possibly addressed to the procurator, makes clear that half the ore from each mine was reserved to the *fiscus*, unless commuted for a lump sum. Among the most significant provisions of this document are the procedures to be followed by the procurator in punishing those who either robbed or damaged the mines: slaves were to be beaten and sold, and free men to have their property confiscated; and both were to be banished from the mines and their territories.[43]

---

[39] *CIL* VIII 25902, 25943, 26416; cf. n. 30 above.

[40] *CIL* VIII 10570, trans. Haywood: 'ut beneficio maiestatis tuae rustici tui vernulae et alumni saltu(u)m tuorum n(on) ultra a conductorib(us) agror(um) fiscalium inquietem[ur].' Cf. pp. 246 and 542.

[41] J. Keil, A. von Premerstein, *Bericht über eine Dritte Reise in Lydien* (1914), 37, no. 55; Abbott and Johnson, *Municipal Administration*, no. 142. The significant phrases are (28f.) μηδὲ ταῖς δε/[σ]ποτικαῖς ἐπακούειν ἀποφοραῖς καὶ ψήφοις, (38f.) τῷ πάντα τὰ ἡμέτερα ἐκ προγόνων προϋπε[ύ]/θυνα εἶναι τῷ ἱερωτάτῳ ταμείῳ τῷ τῆς γεωργί[ας]/ δικαίῳ and (51) φυγάδας ⟨τε⟩ γενέσθαι τῶν δεσποτικῶν χωρίων.

[42] pp. 541f.

[43] *FIRA*[2] I, no. 105 = *ILS* 6891; *FIRA*[2] I, no. 104. See J. J. Van Nostrand in *Economic Survey of Ancient Rome*, ed. Tenney Frank, III (1937), 167–74.

These rules apparently conflict with the evidence of the *Digest*, that Antoninus Pius ruled that those who stole gold or silver from imperial mines (*metalla Caesariana*) should be condemned to exile or *metallum* (hard labour in a mine or quarry).[44] But there is no real conflict, for the procurator at Vipasca is concerned with removing troublesome persons from his own area, while Pius' regulation brings us to one of the penalties, new to Roman law, which appear in the imperial period, and affect the whole range of criminal offences.[45] For the present purposes an important question arises—did the appearance of such penalties depend on the acquisition by the emperor of the relevant properties? If so, this would add a new dimension of significance to the variety of patterns by which properties passed into the hands of the emperor.

The development cannot be securely grasped on the basis of the existing evidence, but a few relevant points can be established. It is clear, firstly, that under the republic there were mines in Italy and the provinces which were let out to *publicani* by the censors.[46] A couple of passages of Pliny the Elder even seem to indicate that the public leasing of some mines in Baetica continued in his time.[47] On the other hand there is no evidence from the republic of the use of mines (or any other establishments) for hard labour by condemned criminals; but such a system was certainly employed in Ptolemaic Egypt.[48] It is also demonstrable that some mines, like estates, tile- and brick-works and granaries and store-houses (*horrea*) in Rome,[49] passed from private into imperial possession by the processes discussed above, principally inheritance and confiscation.[50]

Finally, we have occasional evidence of imperial properties other than semi-industrial establishments being used as places of imprisonment. For instance Gaius destroyed the villa at Herculaneum in which his mother Agrippina had been imprisoned by Tiberius,[51] and Commodus imprisoned his wife and sister on Capri.[52] More generally, a letter of Cyprian shows that Valerian ordered imperial freedmen who confessed to Christianity to

---

[44] *Dig.* XLVIII, 13, 8, 2; cf. 19, 38 *pr.* = Paulus, *Sent.* V, 21a, 1.

[45] See Garnsey, o.c. (p. 165, n. 16).

[46] See Polybius XXXIV, 9, 8–11, and Strabo III, 2, 10 (147–8) (Carthagena); IV, 6, 7 (205) (gold mines of the Salassi); Pliny, *NH* XXXIII, 21/78: 'extat lex Censoria Victimularum auri-fodinae in Vercellensi agro, quo cavebatur, ne plus quinque milia hominum in opere publicani haberent.'

[47] *NH* XXXIV, 49/165, and XXXIII, 40/118: 'celeberrimo Sisaponensi regione in Baetica miniario metallo vectigalibus populi Romani.' The same passage refers, in the present tense, to the *societas* (of *publicani*) of the mines, confirmed by *CIL* X 3964. See Daremberg, Saglio, *Dict. Ant.* s.v. 'metalla', 1870–1; Hirschfeld, *Verwaltungsbeanten²*, 150–2. By whom the leasing was carried out, and what was the later fate of such mines, is only part of the larger problem of the surviving *ager publicus populi Romani*, see App. 1.

[48] See the famous description in Diodorus III, 12–14; cf. C. Préaux, *L'économie royale des Lagides* (1939), 246, 256–60.

[49] See G. E. Rickman, *Roman Granaries and Store Buildings* (1971), 164–72.

[50] pp. 153f., 163f., and *JRS* LIII (1963), 31, 37.

[51] Seneca, *De ira* III, 21, 5.

[52] Dio LXXII, 4, 6. In the Julio-Claudian period the islands of Pandateria and Pontia were used on several occasions for banishing members of the imperial house. The inscriptions of imperial *liberti* there suggest, but do not quite prove, that they and the extensive villas on them were imperial property. See J. H. D'Arms, *Romans on the Bay of Naples* (1970), 77–8.

have their property confiscated and be sent in chains 'to the properties of Caesar.'[53]

This provision follows orders relating to the punishment of other persons who confessed to being Christians, and must be seen not just as an administrative measure but as a criminal penalty. There is no indication whether Cyprian is referring specifically to *metalla*, but his evidence still raises the question of whether the *metalla* to which criminals were sent were in fact typically, or invariably, imperial properties. If they were, it would explain why the legal writers have to emphasize that a man so condemned did not actually become a slave of Caesar, or of the *fiscus*, but a *servus poenae*, 'slave of the penalty'.[54] But a slave who was condemned to *metallum*, and then freed by the *indulgentia* of the emperor, ceased to be a *servus poenae* and became a *servus fisci*, not reverting to his former master.[55] Similarly, if a person condemned to *metallum* or salt-works were captured by bandits and sold as a slave, he reverted to the *poena*, but the purchaser was repaid by the *fiscus*.[56] It is hardly surprising therefore that this fine distinction was eventually lost to view. In the first half of the fourth century we find that dye-works and weaving establishments (*gynaecia*), controlled by the *privata*, were also used for hard labour by the condemned;[57] and in this context, after his victory in 324, Constantine proclaimed the release of those Christians who 'deprived by force of the privileges of superior birth had suffered a judicial penalty, such as to be thrown into *gynaecia* or linen-weaveries and endure unwonted wretched toil, or be considered slaves of the *fiscus*'.[58]

The ample evidence on the sentences to hard labour endured by Christians all relates however to *metalla*.[59] 'We are condemned to the mines, whence your gods have their origin,' wrote Tertullian, alluding to the artificial nature of pagan cult-objects; and later in the same work, 'these very materials come from the *metalla* of the Caesars, and whole temples depend on the nod of Caesar.'[60] There are some indications that private ownership of *metalla* did not entirely disappear.[61] But Tertullian's words imply that it was common, and perhaps typical, to think of mines and quarries as being 'of the emperors', and make it more than probable that it was to such imperial *metalla* that condemned prisoners, branded and with their heads shaven, were sent.

If that is so, it is not easy to see how the system of convict labour related

---

[53] *Ep.* 80, 2: 'Caesariani ... confiscentur et vincti in Caesarianas possessiones descripti mittantur.'

[54] *Dig.* XXXIV, 8, 3, and XLVIII, 19, 17 *pr.* (both Marcianus); XXIX, 2, 25, 2–3 (Ulpian). Both authors refer to a rescript of Pius laying down that a *servus fisci* could, but a *condemnatus* as a *servus poenae* could not, receive an inheritance.

[55] *Dig.* XL, 5, 23, 5 (Ulpian); *CJ* IX, 49, 4 (Gordian); 51, 8 (Valerian and Gallienus); his possessions also became the property of the *fiscus*.

[56] *Dig.* XLIX, 15, 6; 15, 12, 17.

[57] Condemnation, see *CTh* IV, 6, 3 = *CJ* V, 27, 1 (336). *Privata*: *CTh* I, 32, 1 = *CJ* XI, 8, 2 (333), and see Jones, *Later Roman Empire*, 836.

[58] Eusebius, *VC* II, 34; cf. Sozomenus, *HE* I, 7, 3.

[59] It is collected by J. G. Davies, 'Condemnation to the Mines: a Neglected Chapter in the History of the Persecutions', *Univ. Birmingham Hist. Journ.* VI (1957/8), 29.

[60] *Apol.* 12, 5; 29, 2.

[61] *RE* IIIA, 2278.

to the system of leasing-out separate mine-shafts to private contractors, attested in the Lusitanian mines, as it is in the mines in Dacia which were worked in the middle of the second century by *conductores* employing free labour on contract.[62] It is a matter of mere guesswork whether the one system replaced the other, or whether they were operated simultaneously in different areas. But the question is linked to another of equal significance, namely the extent to which imperial properties of all types were either rented out, and therefore produced a cash revenue, or were exploited directly and were a source of products which could be employed by the emperor or his household, applied to public purposes, sold, or used as gifts.

This latter function is illustrated by an inscription from Smyrna which indicates among other things the privileges and gifts obtained for the city from Hadrian by the great rhetor Antonius Polemo:[63] the gifts were 72 pillars of marble from Synnada, 20 'Numidian' pillars and seven of porphyrite. A mass of inscriptions illustrates the working of the imperial quarries at Synnada in Phrygia, managed by imperial freedmen with various functions.[64] The same is true of the quarries at Henschir Schemtu in Numidia, certainly the source of the 20 Numidian pillars.[65] In these two cases we have no evidence on the nature of the work-force, any more than we have for instance in the case of the quarries of Paros and Karystos, which were certainly under direct imperial control.[66] But of the Mons Porphyritis in the Egyptian desert Aelius Aristides states that, like other quarries, it was worked by condemned convicts.[67]

It therefore seems likely that at least some products of imperial quarries were handled by direct labour, and were available for use or disposal by the emperor; Synnadic and Numidian marble was used in imperial palaces, and in public buildings constructed by the emperors, but also elsewhere, though whether by sale or gift we do not know.[68] Even in the Lusitanian mines, as we have seen, half the product of the workings leased to contractors was reserved to the *fiscus*, unless commuted for a lump sum.[69] But as to the subsequent fate of such ore, and whether for instance it was intended to be used directly in minting, we have no evidence. By contrast Galen's detailed

---

[62] See *CIL* III, pp. 948f.

[63] *IGR* IV 1431; cf. p. 421.

[64] See C. Dubois, *Étude sur l'administration et l'exploitation des carrières, marbres, porphyres, granit etc. dans le monde romain* (1908), 79f.; W. M. Ramsay, *The Social Basis of Roman Power in Asia Minor* (1941), 266–81; L. Robert in *Journal des Savants* (1962), 13–43; for the inscription from Smyrna see ibid., 15.

[65] See e.g. Dubois, o.c., 31f.; J. Ward Perkins, 'Tripolitania and the Marble Trade', *JRS* XLI (1951), 89, on 96–7. Note that *HA, Tac.* 10, 5, alleges that Tacitus 'columnas centum Numidicas ... Ostiensibus donavit de proprio'.

[66] See Dubois, o.c., 109f.

[67] *Or.* XXXVI Keil, 67: ἔν γε τῇ Ἀραβικῇ καὶ ἡ περιβόητος αὕτη λιθοτομία ἡ πορφυρῖτίς ἐστιν· ἐργάζονται δ' αὐτὴν ὥσπερ καὶ τὰς ἄλλας δήπου κατάδικοι. Cf. K. Fitzler, *Steinbrüche und Bergwerke im ptolemäischen und römischen Ägypten* (1910), 119–21, noting also Josephus, *BJ* VI, 9, 2 (418), Jewish prisoners in 70 sent to the 'works' in Egypt, and Eusebius, *MP* 8, 1; 9, 1; *HE* VIII, 9, 1.

[68] See Ward-Perkins, o.c. The notion of an emperor (Antoninus Pius) providing ἐκ τῶν ἰδίων ἀγαθῶν λίθους ἀπὸ Θηβαΐδος for paving the streets of a city (Antioch) is given by Malalas, *Chron.*, p. 280, 20f.

[69] p. 181.

report of his visit to the copper mines near Soli in Cyprus makes clear that the imperial procurator there had direct control of the workings, and allowed him to collect specimens from the slag-heaps and the shaft itself.[70] Some at least of the workers whom he saw there were fettered, and so were certainly of slave status, and probably condemned persons, like the Christians sent there in 309/10 on the orders of Maximin from the copper mines of Palestine.[71]

If we turn to the question of agricultural produce, it is again Galen who reports that the emperor supported herb-growers in Crete, who despatched their produce in baskets 'not only to Caesar but to all the city of Rome'. They were used for making up medicines for the emperor, but were also bought and re-sold by herb-dealers in Rome.[72] Such a pattern of production and distribution may perhaps lie behind the lead seals from Egypt marked '*aromatikê* of the lord Caesars',[73] or Pausanias' enigmatic remark about the excellent olive-oil of Tithorea, 'they send the oil to Caesar'.[74] It may also explain some aspects of Pliny the Elder's report that the *fiscus* now cultivated the balsam plantations near Jericho and sold the produce. But the legal character and the origins of the *fiscus*' role remain obscure.[75]

This evidence, however, concerns rare and highly-priced specialities, which there would be good reason to retain, or to put on sale in Rome. These apart, it is probable that the ordinary agricultural properties in imperial possession were leased out to tenants. This is clear at least in the case of the large number of imperial estates (*ousiai*) in Egypt, which were farmed by lessees (*misthôtai*).[76] It is probable, but not certain, that they paid a rent in cash—not always successfully, as appears from a letter of 199 ordering the seizure of the property of a former lessee of an *ousia*, now a debtor to the *fiscus*.[77] A *misthôtês* of imperial properties is also attested at Nacolea in Phrygia.[78] But the very fact that it is necessary to resort to such isolated and fragmentary evidence shows how uncertain all generalization on this topic

---

[70] XII, 214–41 Kühn; XIV, 7. These mines were already at the disposition of Augustus by 12 BC, Josephus, *Ant.* XVI, 4, 5 (128), by what process, it is not known.

[71] Eusebius, *MP* 13, 1–2. It was to the *metalla* of Phaeno and Proconnesus that the tetrarchs ordered Manichees to be sent from Africa, *Coll.* XV, 3, 7, cf. p. 174.

[72] XIV 9 Kühn; 79 (used for the emperor's antidote); 10, 30, 53 (purchase and re-sale).

[73] *IGR* I 1375; cf. 1376: ἀρωματικῆς 'Αντωνίνου Καίσαρος, and 1377, a wooden seal marked Τραιανοῦ (*SB* 8843–5).

[74] X, 32, 11/19.

[75] *NH* XII, 54/111–13, 123. 54/111 shows that both plantations were once *horti regii*, and also that specimens were exhibited in the triumph of 71. 'Servit nunc haec ac tributa pendit cum sua gente' (112) may refer back to Pompey's conquest, mentioned just above, or to the war of 66–70, mentioned immediately below. For references on the balsam plantations see Schürer, *Jewish People* I, 298, n. 36. I would not press the explanation for the *fiscus*' possession of these plantations offered in *JRS* LIII (1963), 30, but also cannot follow that of P. Baldacci, '*Patrimonium e ager publicus* al tempo dei Flavi', *Parola del Passato* XXIV (1969), 349.

[76] For the οὐσίαι, which cannot be discussed here, see e.g. M. Rostovtzeff, *Studien zur Geschichte des römischen Kolonates* (1910), 119f.; *SEHRE*², ch. vii, n. 45; A. Tomsin, 'Notes sur les *ousiai* de l'époque romaine', *Studi Calderini-Paribeni* II (1957), 221; 'Le recrutement de la main d'oeuvre dans les domaines privés de l'Égypte romaine', *Studien zur Papyrologie und antiken Wirtschaftsgeschichte Friedrich Oertel . . . gewidmet* (1964), 81. For more recent documents see esp. *P. Oxy.* 2837. See now H.-Chr. Kuhnke, Οὐσιακὴ γῆ (Diss. Köln, 1971).

[77] Wilcken, *Chrestomathie* I, no. 174.

[78] *IGR* IV 592, see *MAMA* V, p. xxviii.

7*

must be. Even as regards the African estates, while we have fairly extensive
evidence concerning the payments in cash, kind and labour by the *coloni*
to the *conductores*, there is no positive indication of the type of payment
made by the *conductores* to the procurator. The story of Augustus' procurator
suggests, but, as we have seen, does not prove, that he received some payments in produce. Moreover, we have to allow both for basic differences of
practice in different areas and for changes of practice in each area over the
three and a half centuries concerned. But Constantine indicates, in writing
to the proconsul of Africa, probably in 318, that the *patrimoniales fundi* there
paid both gold and corn.[79] That some payments were made in cash is
strongly suggested by Constantine's letter of 313 telling the bishop of
Carthage to draw extra funds, if needed, from the 'procurator of our
properties'.[80]

A mixed system of payments in cash and kind is the most likely. If so, it
may be that the 'corn of Caesar', which was stored in the villages of upper
Galilee when John of Gischala demanded it from Josephus in 67, was in
fact the produce of imperial estates.[81] It is also easy to suppose that the fragments of wine jars from the *patrimonium* of Baetica and Tarraconensis
found (along with millions of others) in the Monte Testaccio in Rome, had
carried the produce of imperial estates[82]—or at least, to use Ulpian's wording,
of 'those estates of Caesar which have been placed in the category of the
patrimonium under the procurator *patrimonii*'.[83] It may be significant that
these jars lack the marks visible on others, which have been interpreted as
showing the rate of duty payable on them;[84] for according to the *Sententiae*
of Paulus, the *fiscus* was free of all indirect taxes or duties, but this did not
apply to merchants who traded with *fundi fiscales*.[85] This reference itself,
however, implies that it was common for some of the produce of imperial
estates to be sold locally.

It need hardly be emphasized again that the evidence on the economic
role of imperial properties, the extent to which they either yielded a cash
revenue or sent products in kind to the emperor, is acutely scanty and
disparate. So it is hardly surprising that we are not well placed to offer
convincing interpretations when we are suddenly presented by the *Liber
Pontificalis* with a mass of data from the second and third decades of the
fourth century relating to the properties with which Constantine endowed
a number of churches in Rome.[86] Some aspects of this complex evidence
are clear. First, as we have seen, the properties included some which had

[79] *CTh* XI, 16, 1 = *CJ* XI, 65, 2. For the date see *PLRE* Catullinus 2. *CTh* XI, 16, 2 (323) extends
the ruling to *fundi patrimoniales et enfyteuticarii per Italiam nostram.*

[80] p. 176.

[81] Josephus, *Vita* 13/71. For this view see Rostovtzeff, *SEHRE*[2], ch. vii, n. 32. The alternative
is to suppose that it was tribute corn, loosely described as being 'of Caesar' (cf. p. 199), or corn
requisitioned for the army.

[82] *CIL* XV, nos. 4102, 4111, 4114, 4124–36. 4102 (only) is dated to 217. They are inscribed
FISCI RATIONIS PATRIMONI PROVINC(IAE) BAETICAE or TARRACONE.

[83] p. 176.

[84] Tenney Frank, 'On the Export Tax of Spanish Harbours', *AJPh* LVII (1936).87.

[85] V, 1ᵃ, 9 = *Dig.* XXXIX, 4, 9, 8.

[86] Duchesne, *Le Liber Pontificalis* I, pp. 170–87.

been given to Constantine, and at least one which had been confiscated in an earlier reign.[87] Secondly, each of the properties is listed as providing a fixed revenue in cash; whether the properties lay in Rome, Italy or the provinces, it must in the nature of the case have been intended that the revenues from them should be remitted annually to Rome. The earlier endowments, to the (later) Church of St Sylvester, the Lateran basilica, the Lateran baptistery and also to other later foundations are all of this type. But the endowments to St. Peter's and St. Paul's include estates in Syria and Egypt which are listed as also making payments in kind—in spices, oil, balsam, saffron, linen, or papyrus rolls.[88] It seems clear that these items—which are not entirely unlike the valuable foodstuffs which Galen had found in the imperial stores in Rome—were not products of the estates themselves. They might well have been things which could more certainly be acquired in Egypt and Syria; and it may even be that their function was to be that of a store of value, suitable for putting on the market in Rome.[89] But many of them seem to have a liturgical use, and this possibility perhaps receives some confirmation from the fact that as well as the immense gifts of gold and silver ornaments which Constantine made to the Roman churches, as he did also to the Church of the Holy Sepulchre,[90] he also made one of them an annual gift of incense 'before the altars', and to another oil, balsam and 'spice for the incense for the holy martyrs'.[91]

So it remains dubious whether these widely scattered imperial properties had previously sent any items in kind to the emperor. They must, however, have provided the stated revenues in cash; and in spite of all the remaining obscurities the *Liber Pontificalis* remains the most impressive testimony which we have of the role of the imperial properties as a store of benefits which the emperor could confer on his subjects.

In Italy, at least in the earlier period, it is clear that the emperor, like the class from which he emerged, depended partly on rents in cash from his estates and partly on produce from them. In the well-known inscription of about 170 from Saepinum, for instance, we find flocks owned by the emperor (*greges dominicae*) in transhumance along the mountain paths. In the same way those owned by Terentius Varro two centuries before had moved between the mountains of Reate and the plains of Apulia, while he mentions others which travelled between Apulia and Samnium.[92] In this case the imperial flocks were let out to contractors (*conductores*), on what conditions

---

[87] p. 172.

[88] For a representative entry, Duchesne, I, p. 178, from Egypt: 'possessio Passinopolimse, praest. sol. DCCC, charta decadas CCCC, piper medemnos L, crocum lib. C, storace lib. CL, aromata cassia lib. CC, oleu nardinu lib. CCC, balsamu lib. C, linu saccus C, cariophylu lib. CL, oleu Cypriu lib. C, papyru racanas mundas I.'

[89] For these points see Duchesne, o.c., p. cl.

[90] pp. 147–8.

[91] o.c., p. 174: 'donum aromaticum ante altaria annis singulis lib. CL'. p. 183: 'annis singulis oleum nardinum pisticum lib. DCCCC, balsamum lib. C, aromata in incensum sanctis martyribus suprascriptis, beato Marcellino et Petro, lib. C.'

[92] *CIL* IX 2438; Riccobono, *FIRA*² I, no. 61. See the revised text and valuable discussion by U. Laffi, *Studi Classici e Orientali* XIV (1965), 177. For Varro's flocks see *de re rustica* II, 2, 9, and for other flocks moving between Apulia and Sammium, II, 1, 16–17.

we do not know, and it was they who complained to the freedman *a rationibus* of harassment by the magistrates of Saepinum and Bovianum in searching for fugitive slaves and stolen sheep. In the resulting tumult some sheep strayed, and the *fiscus* (or *res dominica*) suffered loss. It is more than unlikely that private flocks also were not still driven along these trails. What distinguished the *conductores* of the imperial flocks was their ability to complain to the *a rationibus*, and have a threatening letter written by the praetorian prefects to the local magistrates.

Similar conflicts must have arisen in innumerable other circumstances. But what is essential is that whatever legal or practical advantages accrued to the imperial properties did so by a process of development from a situation in which the emperor was a property-owner like others. This will be true generally of the imperial estates in Italy, though most of our scanty information relates to those properties whose productive role was combined with a function as imperial residences. In the case of those villas which the emperor visited personally, regularly or on rare occasions, we cannot clearly distinguish their agricultural role proper from their use in providing that aesthetic or recreational background essential to the still strongly rural traditions of the Roman upper class.[93] Hence, for instance the emperor, like the great landowners of the late republic, owned fish-ponds (*piscinae* or *vivaria*); one of Martial's epigrams describes the 'sacred fish' in the lake at Baiae, which nibble the hand of their all-powerful owner,[94] while Juvenal's satire on the imperial *consilium* starts from the presentation to Domitian of a mullet so large that it was assumed to have escaped from the *vivaria* of Caesar.[95] One of the 'fish-ponds of Caesar' was that at Pausilypon in Campania, inherited by Augustus from Vedius Pollio. Pliny the Elder quotes Seneca for the statement that one of the fish introduced by Pollio died sixty years later, and was survived by two others.[96]

The imperial villas clearly provided food for consumption by the emperor and his household, such as the cucumbers of which Tiberius was so fond that his kitchen-gardeners (*olitores*) grew them on movable beds which could be moved into the sun or drawn back into covered greenhouses.[97] They could also provide the emperor with a little gardening or farming on his own part, as with the figs, apparently at Nola, which Augustus would pluck with his own hand, and which Livia was alleged to have poisoned.[98] Much more clearly, the correspondence of Fronto reveals Antoninus Pius, with Marcus Aurelius in attendance, working on the vintage at one of his

---

[93] For Pliny the Younger's aesthetic appreciation of his estates see P. Malat, 'Pline le Jeune, propriétaire foncier', *Hommages à L. Herrmann* (1960), 522; for wider aspects J. Aymard, *Essai sur les chasses romaines des origines à la fin du siècle des Antonins (Cynegetica)* (1951); P. Grimal, *Les jardins romains*[2] (1969).

[94] *Epig.* IV, 30; cf. Pliny, *NH* X, 89/193.

[95] *Sat.* IV, 50: 'non dubitaturi fugitivum dicere piscem / depastumque diu vivaria Caesaris . . .'; 54: 'quidquid conspicuum pulchrumque est aequore toto, / res fisci est, ubicumque natat. donabitur ergo, / ne pereat.' For a good collection of evidence on *vivaria* see Mayor ad loc.

[96] *NH* IX, 78/167. For Augustus' inheritance of this property from Pollio, Dio LIV, 23, 5. See J. H. D'Arms, *Romans on the Bay of Naples* (1970), 76–7, 111–12.

[97] Columella, *de re rustica* XI, 3, 52–3; Pliny, *NH* XIX, 23/64.

[98] Dio LVI, 30, 2.

villas, and afterwards joining the labourers at supper in the oil-press room. The *Life* of Pius also records this custom of his;[99] and it is this work alone which refers to his custom, which its author regards as an honourable exception, of having his table supplied by his own slaves, fowlers, fishermen and hunters.[100]

It is not possible to define closely the legal character of those properties which in some sense belonged to the emperor, or still less to discern the nature of the different categories into which they were at various times divided. Nor can we come anywhere near measuring their extent at any time, the importance of their economic role in the life of the empire, or even their significance in providing for the emperor and his household. All that can be done is to pick up a few hints as to the effects of imperial ownership of land, the functions and management of the different types of property and the uses to which their revenues and products might be put by the emperor. These limitations will be felt all the more clearly when we look briefly at the wider question of the role of the imperial wealth within the empire.

9. *Imperial Wealth and Public Wealth*

At some time in the reign of Constantine the city of Reims put on record in an inscription an example of the emperor's generosity: he 'began from the foundations and completed the construction of the baths at the expense of his *fiscus*, and granted them to his *civitas* of the Remi with his accustomed liberality'.[1] The action seems simple enough, and can indeed be paralleled by many other similar documents from the preceding three centuries. But if we ask what 'his *fiscus*' was, whether there existed at that period any other 'treasuries' or sources of funds, and whether it would mean anything to say that the benefaction is represented as coming from the private funds of the emperor on the one hand or from 'public' funds on the other, considerable difficulties appear.

By this period, even though the ancient republican treasury (*aerarium*) in the temple of Saturn in Rome still existed and even had *praefecti* attached to it,[2] nothing suggests either that public revenues were still physically transported to it,[3] or even that in an abstract sense the revenues of the provinces were still conceived as public rather than imperial property. A century earlier, however, Cassius Dio makes quite clear that a distinction between imperial and public funds continued to exist in principle, even if it could not always be discerned in practice. Under 27 BC he relates how

---

[99] *Ad. M. Caes.* IV, 6; cf. II, 6; 3. Cf. also *HA, Ant. Pius* II, 2: 'piscando se et venando multum oblectavit et deambulatione cum amicis atque sermone. vindemias privati modo cum amicis agebat'; cf. *Elag.* 11, 2–6.

[100] *Ant. Pius* 7, 5.

[1] *ILS* 703. The text depends on a copy made in the fifteenth century.

[2] See F. Millar, 'The *Aerarium* and its Officials under the Empire', *JRS* LIV (1964), 33.

[3] As noted on p. 151, the physical transport of money is in all contexts remarkably poorly attested. But according to Velleius Paterculus II, 62, 3, Brutus and Cassius in 44 BC, seized 'pecunias etiam, quae ex transmarinis provinciis Romam ab quaestoribus deportabantur'.

Augustus repaired the Via Flaminia at his own expense, and tried to induce various senators to do the same for other roads:[4]

> The other roads were repaired later either from the public treasury, since none of the senators was eager to make the expenditure, or, if one prefers, by Augustus. For I cannot distinguish their respective treasuries (even though Augustus coined certain gold and silver statues of himself dedicated by friends and communities in order to appear to spend from his own pocket as much as he said he did). So I do not intend to indicate whether whoever was in power at any time took any money from public funds, or gave it himself.

Over wide areas both of revenue and of expenditure Dio's perplexity is our own; even though both he, here and elsewhere, and documents and sources of his time continue to reflect a distinction between imperial and public funds,[5] we cannot state where the boundary between them was thought to lie. Moreover, it is undisputed that from Augustus himself onwards the emperors in effect disposed as they wished even of those funds which were clearly public.[6] None the less Dio's comment implies that in theory some expenditures by the emperor were supposed to be from 'his own' funds; just as does his remark about Vespasian, that he was mocked for saying each time he made any expenditure, 'I am paying for this out of my own money'.[7]

Augustus' role in the repair of roads, and his encouragement to other senators to do likewise, reflects the growth of immense personal fortunes in the late republic, some but not all derived directly from the profits of conquest. These in their turn enabled men to offer land or money to soldiers,[8] to maintain large *familiae* of slaves, which might perform semi-public functions, to put up at their own expense temples and other buildings for public use,[9] and to provide gladiators and beasts for shows offered to the populace. When a monarch emerged in the person of Augustus, he was already well equipped to fulfil the role demanded of a true 'king' in Greek thought, in dispensing gifts.

[4] LIII, 22, 1–4. The Via Flaminia at any rate was repaired by Augustus, *RG* 20, 5, and App. 3. On the reference to coinage, cf. p. 146.

[5] LXIX, 8, 1², Hadrian remitted debts τῷ τε βασιλικῷ καὶ τῷ δημοσίῳ τῷ τῶν Ῥωμαίων. Cf. LXXI, 32, 2 (272), of Marcus Aurelius, and LXXVIII, 18, 5 (422). Cf. *CIL* VIII 17639 = Abbott and Johnson, *Municipal Administration*, no. 152, l. 10, '[—]uam populi vel fisci debiti' (from a letter of Severus Alexander, cf. p. 393. See now W. Seston, M. Euzennat, 'La *Tabula Banasitana*', *CRAI* 1971, 468, ll. 37–8: 'sine diminutione tributorum et vect[i]gali/um populi et fisci' (177). Cf. also Paulus, *Sent.* V, 12, 'de iure fisci et populi'; *Dig.* III, 6, 1, 3; XVIII, 1, 72, 1. For earlier references distinguishing *aerarium* and *fiscus* see pp. 162, 167, 193; Suetonius, *Vesp.* 16, 3; Tacitus, *Ann.* II, 47, 2.

[6] Imperial control and disposition of public funds in the early empire is best discussed by P. A. Brunt, 'The "Fiscus" and its Development', *JRS* LVI (1966), 75, on pp. 86–91.

[7] LXV, 10, 3a (144).

[8] Caesar, *BC* I, 17, 4 (Domitius Ahenobarbus at Corfinium in 49 BC): 'militibus in contione agros ex suis possessionibus pollicetur, XL in singulos iugera et pro rata parte centurionibus evocatisque'. Cf. e.g. *Bell. Hisp.* 26, 1; Suetonius, *Jul.* 33; 38, 1; 70; Dio XLII, 54, 1; Appian, *BC* II, 94/395. Cf. P. A. Brunt, 'The Army and the Land in the Roman Revolution', *JRS* LII (1962), 69, esp. 77–9.

[9] See D. E. Strong, 'The Administration of Public Building in Rome during the Late Republic and Early Empire', *Bull. Inst. Class. Stud.* XV (1968), 97.

The disbalance between imperial and public wealth and the framework within which the emperor's disbursement of cash was seen are expressed most clearly and fully in the *Res Gestae* of Augustus, in whose heading the 'expenditures which he made on the *res publica* and *populus Romanus*' becomes, in the Greek translation, simply *dôreai*, gifts. It is consonant with this that the references to finance in the *Res Gestae* are not to the regular income and expenditure of the Roman state, but entirely to voluntary and non-routine payments by Augustus himself out of funds which were in some sense his own.[10] In the *Res Gestae* Augustus lists individual expenditures—on distributions of money to the people, grants of land or money to veterans, subventions to the *aerarium*, the building of temples and the placing of offerings within them, and the giving of shows—which total well over 1,000,000,000 *sesterces*. The summary at the end, given in the third person, provides an even higher figure, 2,400,000,000 *sesterces* on the *aerarium*, the *plebs Romana* and veterans alone, repeats a list of temples and public works, and then concludes: 'Expenditures made on theatrical shows, gladiatorial games, athletes, wild-beast hunts, and the (mock) naval battle; and money given to *coloniae*, *municipia*, and towns destroyed by earthquake or fire, or granted personally to *amici* or senators to restore their census-rating: incalculable.'

These expenditures will include the 1,400,000,000 *sesterces* which Augustus had received in legacies and inheritances in the twenty years up to AD 13, and spent on the needs of the state,[11] but not, of course, the approximately 240,000,000 which he left to his heirs and legatees, to the *populus* and to the soldiers.[12] These figures may be compared with the public revenues going to the *aerarium*, which may have been somewhere in the region of 500,000,000 *sesterces* annually.[13]

Among his personal expenditures, Augustus includes payments made from *manubiae*, the spoils of war; 400 *sesterces* each to the *plebs* in 29 BC, in connection with his return to Rome and his triumph, and 1,000 each on the same occasion to veterans settled in colonies; from the same source he built the temple of Mars Ultor and the Forum Augustum, and placed dedications worth 100,000,000 *sesterces* in four temples.[14] In using *manubiae* for temples and public buildings he was following a long tradition,[15] which was to be

[10] This was established in the classic article by U. Wilcken, 'Zu den Impensae der Res Gestae Divi Augusti', *S-B. Preuss. Ak. Wiss.* XXVII (1931), 772. Cf. also J. Gagé, *Res Gestae*² (1952), 26f.

[11] p. 154.

[12] Suetonius, *Aug.* 101, 2–3.

[13] See the calculations by Tenney Frank, *Economic Survey of the Roman Empire* V (1940), 6–7. Naturally all such figures are hypothetical; the basis available for them is the 340,000,000 *sesterces* stated by Plutarch, *Pomp.* 45, 4, to have been the revenue in 61 BC, and the statements of Suetonius, *Jul.* 25, 1 that the tribute of Gaul was 40,000,000, and of Velleius II, 39, 2, that that of Egypt was approximately the same.

[14] *RG* 15, 1 and 3; 21, 2. These *manubiae* must essentially have come from the vast spoils of Egypt, see Suetonius, *Aug.* 41, 1.

[15] For examples see Strong, o.c., n. 9. The legal status of the *manubiae* disposed of by a victorious general has been much disputed, but it cannot be proved that it was not his own property, or that more than a strong convention compelled him to expend it, or some of it, on public buildings. See F. Bona, 'Sul concetto di "Manubiae" e sulla responsibilità del magistrato in ordine alla preda', *Stud. et Doc. Hist. et Iur.* XXVI (1960), 105; I. Shatzman, 'The Roman General's Authority over Booty', *Historia* XXI (1972), 177.

continued by later emperors on the rare occasions when sufficiently large quantities were available. The capture of the treasures of Decebalus, including gold, silver and ornaments, at the end of the Dacian war allowed Trajan to bring immense quantities of valuables back to Rome.[16] Some of it was expended on the building of the vast Forum Traianum, along the roofs of whose colonnades were placed gilded statues of horses and representations of military standards, with underneath them the words *ex manubiis*.[17]

Augustus does not otherwise indicate the source of the funds on which he could draw, but he does speak of a distribution of money made in 24 BC 'from my *patrimonium*', and similarly of the 170,000,000 *sesterces* with which he established the *aerarium militare* in AD 6.[18] Elsewhere he uses less specific expressions, such as 'with my money' (*pecunia mea*) for the four subventions, totalling 150,000,000 *sesterces*, which he made to the *aerarium*.[19]

Throughout the period we can find, in Rome, Italy and the provinces examples of temples, public buildings, walls, aqueducts, bridges, and occasionally roads, constructed or repaired 'with his own money' by the emperor.[20] In all these cases it is more than probable, and in the case of roads can be demonstrated,[21] that such payments did not represent a regular responsibility of the emperor, but occasional benefactions conferred by him as demonstrations of liberality, or as a response to immediate needs or requests. We shall see later examples of such requests, along with many others, made by cities of the emperor.[22]

In one area of building, the aqueducts of Rome, the imperial role was more than occasional; and it is in this area, which by virtue of Frontinus'

---

[16] Dio LXVIII, 14, 4; see Joannes Lydus, *De mag.* II, 28, quoting an eye-witness, Statilius Criton, the doctor and historian of Trajan (Jacoby, *FGrH* 200, F. 1). See J. Carcopino, *Points de vue sur l'impérialisme romain* (1924), 73f., esp. 80f.

[17] Aulus Gellius, *NA* XIII, 25, 1.

[18] *RG* 15, 1; 17, 2. On his grant to the *aerarium militare* also Dio LV, 25, 5.

[19] *RG* 17, 1. Note 5, 2: a corn shortage in 22 BC dealt with '[impensa et] cura mea' / ταῖς ἐμαῖς δαπάναις. 15, 1: 'duodecim frumentationes frumento pr[i]vatim coempto emensus sum' (23 BC). 18: (shortfall of *vectigalia* in or after 18 BC) ἄλλοτε μὲν δέκα μυριάσιν ἄλ[λοτε δὲ πλείοσιν σει]τικὰς καὶ ἀργυρικὰς συντάξεις ἐκ τῆς ἐμῆς ὑπάρξεως [ἔδωκα]. The Latin text of this section can only be restored by conjecture.

[20] Temples: e.g. *ILS* 3813 (Vespasian restores *sua impensa* an *aedes Victoriae* in the Sabine territory); *Syll.*³ 821 = *ILS* 8905 (Domitian restores temple of Apollo at Delphi *sua impensa*). Public buildings: Pliny, *Ep.* VIII, 8, 6 (a bath given *dono* by Augustus to Hispellum); *IG* V.2, 457 = *CIL* III 13691 (Domitian pays for portico at Megalopolis); *ILS* 334 (Hadrian and Antoninus Pius pay for baths at Ostia); *ILS* 613 (Diocletian rebuilds baths at Nicomedia *sua pecunia*). Walls: e.g. *ILS* 5337 = *IGR* I 712 (Marcus Aurelius pays for walls of Philippopolis); *IGR* III 1287 (walls of Adraa, Arabia, built ἐκ δωρεᾶς τοῦ Σεβ., 262/3). Aqueducts: e.g. *ILS* 218 (Aqua Claudia—Claudius, Vespasian and Titus); cf. *CIL* XI 3309 'impensa fisci s[ui]' (Forum Clodi); 290 (Aqua Traiana); 424 (Severus and Caracalla 'arcus Caelemontanos . . . sua pecunia restituerunt)'; 702 (Aqua Virgo restored *sua pecunia* by Constantine). For bridges and other constructions related to roads see following note. See in general R. MacMullen, 'Roman Imperial Building in the Provinces', *HSCPh* LXIV (1959), 207.

[21] See the thorough discussion by T. Pekáry, *Untersuchungen zu den römischen Reichsstrassen* (1968), esp. ch. iii. Examples of roads built *sua pecunia* by the emperor outside Rome are in effect confined to the works of Trajan, and to a lesser extent Hadrian, in Italy, see *ibid.*, pp. 91–3. But e.g. *ILS* 293 shows a bridge built *sua pecunia* by Trajan on the Carthage–Hippo road, and *AE* 1961 318 *stabula* on the Philippololis–Oescus road rebuilt *sua pecunia* by Marcus Aurelius; also *ILS* 479, a bridge on the Via Latina rebuilt *sua pecunia* by Severus Alexander.

[22] pp. 420–4.

handbook *De aquae ductu* we know better than any other aspect of the government of Rome, that we can see most clearly how the imperial private wealth supported permanent functions within the public system. In the republic the building of aqueducts had been carried out with public money by censors or other magistrates, who let out the work to private contractors. But either when or after Agrippa constructed the Aqua Julia et Tepula as aedile in 33 BC, and the Aqua Virgo as consul in 27 BC, he formed his own gang (*familia*) of slaves, about 240 strong, for work on the aqueducts. On his death in 12 BC he left it, along with the rest of his estate, to Augustus, who made it the property of the *res publica*.[23] It was this *familia* which a *senatus consultum* of the following year placed under the control of two senatorial *curatores aquarum*; their upkeep was to be supplied by the *aerarium*. But the text of the *s.c.* itself refers to a promise by Augustus to repair the aqueducts 'at his own expense'. Later the imperial role increased again; for when Claudius built the Aqua Claudia at his own expense he established a second *familia*, 460 strong, which at the end of the century was still 'Caesar's', and received its pay from the *fiscus*.[24] Moreover, though the office of *curator* had been established by a *senatus consultum*, the holders were appointed by the emperor; and from Claudius' time an imperial freedman served under them as *procurator aquarum*. Beyond that, from 11 BC onwards the right to tap the aqueducts was a privilege (*beneficium*) conferred by the emperor, to whom a petition had to be made.[25] The revenue of nearly 250,000 *sesterces* received (apparently) from such beneficiaries belonged to the *populus*, but had at some time been lost by neglect, and more recently appropriated by Domitian; but Nerva had restored it to the *populus*.[26]

The arrangements for the aqueducts of Rome thus bore, for as long as we can trace them, the clear imprint of the great fortunes and extended households of late republican senators. The same is true in a different way with the human and animal material for games and shows. The established *ludi* of the republican period had been put on by office-holders using public funds, and later contributing also funds of their own. Hence it became, as is well known, a matter of record as to how many pairs of gladiators or what hitherto unknown species of animals a man could produce.[27] The *gladiatores* and *venatores* were normally slaves, who had to be bought and maintained by the person concerned. For instance gladiators of Julius Caesar were in barracks at Capua in 49 BC;[28] others owned by Antonius were in training at Cyzicus in 31–30 BC.[29] The animals also had to be acquired by purchase or gift. Augustus is fulfilling a well-established republican tradition when he writes

[23] Frontinus, *De aquae ductu* 98, 116. For Augustus as Agrippa's heir see p. 177.

[24] See Frontinus, o.c., 96–125 passim.

[25] ibid., 99; cf. *praef.* 3, and 88, 103, 105, 111. Note esp. 105: 'qui aquam in usus privatos deducere volet, impetrare eam debebit et a principe epistulam ad curatorem adferre; curator deinde beneficio Caesaris praestare maturitatem . . .'

[26] ibid., 118.

[27] On the *ludi* in general see *Dict. Ant.* s.v. For animals see G. Jennison, *Animals for Show and Pleasure in Ancient Rome* (1937); J. M. C. Toynbee, *Animals in Roman Life and Art* (1973). On gladiators, *Dict. Ant.* s.v.

[28] Caesar, *BC* I, 14, 4; Cicero, *Ad Att.* VII, 14, 2.

[29] Dio LI, 7, 2–7.

in the *Res Gestae* that, at various gladiatorial shows given by him in his own name or in the names of his adopted sons and grandsons, some 10,000 gladiators fought; and that at various hunts (*venationes*) of African beasts about 3,500 animals were slaughtered; he also put on a naval battle in a lake created for the occasion (and used by later emperors).[30] It is not possible to follow here the complex details of the shows which continued to be given both by office-holders and emperors in Rome, and by local dignitaries in Italy and the provinces. But it is important to stress that this role on the part of the emperor led to his possession of permanent 'schools' of imperial gladiators in Rome, Italy and the provinces, controlled by procurators.[31] Domitian, for instance, when attending the games given by quaestors, which he had re-started, would allow the *populus* to ask him for two pairs of gladiators 'from his school', and would produce them 'in the finest Court equipment'.[32] Epictetus uses as an example the fact that 'among the gladiators of Caesar' there were some who prayed to the gods and begged the procurators to be put on to fight.[33]

Just as some condemned persons were sent to *metalla*,[34] so others were sent 'to the beasts', to be killed directly, while others were condemned to a gladiatorial *ludus*, and might hope eventually to regain their freedom.[35] The execution of the condemned at public spectacles, which is attested from the middle of the first century AD, may have owed something to the custom of using captives (who had the status of slaves) in this way. Josephus describes how Titus in 70 gave spectacles at Caesarea Panias, at which some Jewish prisoners were thrown to the beasts and others made to fight each other as gladiators, as he did later at Berytus and elsewhere in Syria.[36] Similarly Constantine celebrated a victory in 313 by holding games at Trier at which a multitude of German captives were thrown to the beasts.[37]

Condemnation to the beasts or a *ludus* owed something to such celebrations by victorious generals or emperors and no doubt something to the need of the emperors for a ready supply of victims. Modestinus lays down that a provincial governor should not free such persons as a favour to the *populus*; but if they are of sufficient strength or skill to be worthy of exhibition to the people of Rome, he should consult the emperor.[38] But, just as with *metalla*, we must ask, but cannot clearly answer, the question as to what was the relationship between such penalties and the emperor's ownership of schools of gladiators. Or to put it more clearly, if a man were condemned to a *ludus*, was that *ludus* always imperial property? In one case the connection is perfectly clear. In

[30] *RG* 22, and Gagé ad loc.
[31] See Mommsen, *Staatsrecht*[3], II, 1070–2; Hirschfeld, *Verwaltungsbeamten*[2], 285–97; Pflaum, *Carrières*, p. 1027 (*procurator ludi magni*); 1028 (*procurator ludi matutini*); 1036 (procurators of *familiae gladiatoriae* in Italy); 1047 (one known procurator of *fam. glad.* in Gaul, Britain, Spain, Germany and Raetia); 1061 (one attested for the Pannonias and Dalmatia); 1073 (for provinces in Asia Minor, and Cyprus); 1088 (one attested for Egypt).
[32] Suetonius, *Dom.* 4, 1.
[33] *Diss.* I, 29, 37.
[34] pp. 182–4.
[35] See most clearly *Coll.* XI, 7, 4.
[36] *BJ* VII, 2, 1 (23–4); 3, 1 (37–8, 40); 5, 1 (96).
[37] *Pan.* IX(12), 23, 3.
[38] *Dig.* XLVIII, 19, 31.

about 307 a number of Christians in Palestine were condemned, some to fight as gladiators, some to the beasts, some to the mines. Those condemned to be gladiators refused either to train or to take the upkeep provided by the 'royal treasury' (*basilikon tameion*), and maintained this determination not before mere procurators or governors but before Maximin himself.[39]

If, as is possible but not certain, those condemned were normally kept in imperial *ludi*, they were certainly not reserved solely for imperial shows. An illuminating story in Cassius Dio shows a bandit chief in Italy rescuing two of his men who had been condemned to be given to the beasts, by pretending to be a local magistrate who needed them (for a show it is implied).[40] It is certain that the emperors had no monopoly of gladiators, but it may well be that one of the functions of the *familiae* of imperial gladiators in the province was to act as a source of supply for others. The well-known *senatus consultum* of 177–80, on the price of gladiators for games given by city magistrates and high priests of provincial councils, explicitly mentions the price of a *damnatus ad gladium* supplied by an imperial procurator,[41] as well as the prices charged by trainers (*lanistae*) and by the high priests handing over gladiators to their successors. So it may well be that the incomes (*vectigalia*), of which the emperors are said to have deprived the *fiscus*, reflect not, as is often supposed, the removal of a tax on sales of gladiators, but a drastic reduction of the permitted price, affecting both the *fiscus* and the dealers.[42]

As usual, it is when a part of the imperial household or property develops beyond its original setting, and becomes diffused into the life of the provinces, that we cease to have a clear conception of its nature and functions. In Rome at least it is clear that gladiatorial and other games and shows continued to be things which the emperor 'gave';[43] as were also, in the nature of the case, the *congiaria* at which he would normally preside in person.[44] So also were the *donativa* paid on accessions and other occasions to the soldiers; Dio for instance describes in one place the *congiarium* and the *donativum* paid by Severus on his *decennalia* in 202, and says that he spent 200,000,000, *sesterces* on this 'gift'.[45] This sum may even have come from funds which were identifiably imperial rather than public, though neither that nor the contrary can be proved. But in a long papyrus from Panopolis dating to 300 we find that the *donativum* is a regular recurrent payment on various imperial

[39] Eusebius, *Mart. Pal.* VII, 4; VIII, 2–3. Cf. L. Robert, *Hellenica* III (1946), 120f.

[40] LXXVI, 10, 3 (364–5).

[41] *FIRA*[2] I, no. 49; for a revised text see J. H. Oliver, R. E. A. Palmer, 'Minutes of an Act of the Roman Senate', *Hesperia* XXIV (1955), 320. See also the text and discussion by Mommsen in *Eph. Epig.* VII, 388f. Ll. 57–8 of the Italica text have: 'cum maximi pr[in]cipes oratione sua praedixerint fore ut damnatum a ⟨d⟩ gladium / procurator eorum non plure quam sex aureis lanistis pra[ebea]t.' Cf. Sardis text, ll. 16–17.

[42] See ll. 1–10 of the Italica text, which seem to be susceptible of either interpretation.

[43] The clearest and most formal record of this is the *Fasti Ostienses*, see A. Degrassi, *Inscriptiones Italiae* XIII. 1 (1947), 173f.; for instance under 109 (pp. 199–201), (Trajan) 'thermas suas dedicavit et publicavit, VIII K. Iul. aquam suo nomine tota urbe salientem dedicavit. K. Nov. imp. Traianus munus suum consummavit diebus CXVII, gladiatorum (parium quattuor milibus) DCCCCXLI s(emis) . . .'

[44] p. 136.

[45] LXXVI, 1, 1 (357): ἐδωρήσατο τῷ τε ὁμίλῳ παντὶ τῷ σιτοδουμένῳ καὶ τοῖς στρατιώταις τοῖς δορυφόροις ἰσαρίθμους τοῖς τῆς ἡγεμονίας ἔτεσι χρυσοῦς . . . ἐς γὰρ τὴν δωρεὰν ταύτην πεντακισχίλιαι μυριάδες δραχμῶν ἀναλώθησαν.

aniversaries, the order for which is given in exactly the same way as for the regular pay (*stipendium*).[46]

In this case we can safely conclude that a payment which had once been a personal gift was now simply a standing element in the pay-structure—and significantly larger than the *stipendium* itself. The survival of the vocabulary of gifts is still an important pointer to the pattern of transformation between early and late empire.[47]

Before we touch briefly on some wider questions, we may note that another form of personal grant from emperor to soldiers was extremely important in the early decades of the empire, but ceased to be of major significance before the end of the reign of Augustus. As early as the winter of 31/30 BC we find him giving land to soldiers in Italy, and either resettling those dispossessed in provincial colonies or promising them payment in cash. His attempt to raise the cash by selling his own estates and those of his friends failed because no buyers dared to come forward, but Dio says that he was later able to pay out of the spoils of Egypt.[48] On Augustus' own account in the *Res Gestae*, he paid about 600,000,000 *sesterces* for the land allotted to soldiers in *coloniae* in Italy, and about 260,000,000 for land in the provinces in 30 and 14 BC; and afterwards, down to 2 BC, paid about 400,000,000 in cash to discharged soldiers.[49] This came to an end with the establishment of the *aerarium militare* in AD 6; but even to this treasury, which was subsequently to be fed by indirect taxes, Augustus gave a capital sum of 170,000,000 *sesterces*.[50] This distribution at his own expense by Augustus was perhaps the basis of the claim by Vespasian who took 'to himself' the unallotted land (*subseciva*) of *coloniae* in Italy (of which the vast majority were Augustan), and made a substantial sum for the *fiscus* by selling these lots. A wave of appeals from embassies caused him to halt the process, Titus to continue it slowly, and Domitian to abandon it by a single edict.[51]

By this time actual grants of land by the emperor to veterans had become less common—though Hyginus records such a grant in Pannonia 'by the will and *liberalitas*' of Trajan.[52] But it is of fundamental importance that many of the most characteristic features of the Augustan settlement had depended for their fulfilment on the deployment by the emperor of private funds. When Lucan writes 'and then for the first time Rome was poorer

---

[46] *P. Beatty Panop.* 2. Compare ll. 161–207 on the payment of *donativa* to various units, and e.g. 57–60 on the payment of *stipendium*. For the pay (in cash and kind) of the army in the fourth century, and the role of *donativa*, see further Jones, *Later Roman Empire*, 623f.

[47] Cf. p. 201.

[48] LI, 4, 5–8.

[49] *RG* 16. For a full discussion of the settlement of soldiers by Augustus see P. A. Brunt, *Italian Manpower 225 BC–AD 14* (1971), 332–42.

[50] p. 192.

[51] *Corpus Agrimensorum Romanorum*, ed. Thulin, I, 41: 'non enim fieri poterat, ut solum illud, quod nemini erat adsignatum, alterius esse posset quam qui poterat adsignare. non enim exiguum pecuniae fisco contulit venditis subsicvis'; cf. 96–7: 'cum divus Vespasianus subsiciva omnia, quae non vendidissent aut aliquibus personis concessa essent, sibi vindicasse⟨n⟩t . . .' This explanation of Vespasian's claim seems simpler and more acceptable than that previously advanced in *JRS* LIII (1963), 35–6. Note the apparent equation of ownership by the emperor as such, and by the *fiscus*. Cf. p. 444.

[52] *Corpus Agrimensorum Romanorum* I, 84.

than Caesar',[53] it is evident that he is not referring solely to Julius Caesar's removal of money from the *aerarium* in 49 BC. In Lucan's own time Nero claimed that he gave 60,000,000 *sesterces* per year to the *res publica*.[54]

We cannot, however, draw up a balance sheet of imperial and public finance at this or any other period in the empire. Nor can we even state confidently how these two elements, which were undoubtedly considered as in some sense separate up to the earlier third century, were in theory distinguished at successive periods; and still less be confident that such a theory was observed in practice. None the less, it is possible to distinguish certain broad features, which are of basic importance for the manner of operation of the Roman emperors.

The first is the immense scale of private, and *a fortiori* of imperial wealth, in relation to that of the *res publica*. When Seneca writes of Gaius that he 'spent 100,000,000 *sesterces* on a single dinner, and though aided by the ingenuity of all scarcely found the means to use the tribute of three provinces for one dinner',[55] we cannot tell whether in fact any tribute went to pay for his dinner; but we can accept, on comparative figures, that three provinces might well have produced only that sum.[56]

Secondly, the main bulk of the evidence which we have seen for the means of acquisition, and means of control and disposition, of wealth by the emperors—whether it is inheritance or gift, *aurum coronarium*, or the character of estates and properties—is most readily intelligible if seen as a development of patterns visible in the wealth of leading Romans of the late republic. By contrast, there is almost no significant evidence that the emperor (for instance in his notional capacity as proconsul of his provinces) received formal grants of public money.[57] Nor is there the least likelihood that from the beginning the tribute of the imperial provinces was considered to be the property of the emperor;[58] Velleius Paterculus, writing as a senator under Tiberius, refers to the tribute of Egypt as going to the *aerarium*.[59]

Without the support of these two theories, it becomes all the more improbable that when the word *fiscus* came to be used distinctively in connection with the emperor, its usage embraced either tribute-revenues going to him, or public funds voted to him as proconsul,[60] or entrusted to him in some other

---

[53] *Pharsalia* III, 168: 'pauperiorque fuit tum primum Caesare Roma'.

[54] Tacitus, *Ann.* XV, 18, 3. *Ann.* XIII, 31, 2, however, notes as something significant that he put 40,000,000 into the *aerarium* in 56 'ad retinendam populi fidem'.

[55] *ad Helviam matrem de consolatione* 10, 4.

[56] Cf. p. 191.

[57] For the notion of regular sums voted to the emperor by the senate we are reduced to the testimony of Orosius VII, 7, 8, and Jerome, *Chron.*, ed. Helm, p. 184, that Nero had the senate vote him 10,000,000 *sesterces* p.a. 'ad expensas'. See further *JRS* LIV (1964), 37; LVI (1966), 156.

[58] This notion, stated by Mommsen, *Staatsrecht*[3] II. 2, 1004, depends on the further notion of the emperor's 'Bodeneigenthum' in these provinces. But that depends on isolated propositions by Gaius, *Inst.* II, 7 and 21, which can be shown to make distinctions (e.g. between *praedia tributaria* and *praedia stipendiaria*) which are purely academic, and have no roots in the current usage of the empire; see the excellent discussion by F. Grelle, *Stipendium vel Tributum* (1963), 1–21.

[59] Velleius II, 39, 2.

[60] There is in fact only one text where *fiscus* is certainly used of the public funds held by a proconsul, *Verr.* II.3, 85/197, where Cicero represents Verres as saying 'Quaternos HS, quos mihi senatus decrevit et ex aerario dedit, ego habebo et in cistam transferam de fisco'.

way. Particularly in the latter case, it would have been an inexplicable confusion on the part of Seneca to have chosen precisely this word to use in illustrating two distinct meanings of the word *habere*: 'Caesar "has" everything, his *fiscus* only his own private property; and all things are in his *imperium*, in the *patrimonium* (only) his personal property.'[61] The implied equivalence between *fiscus* and *patrimonium* is perfectly clear.

We have already seen many cases where *fiscus* is used in contexts which most naturally imply that it refers to cash or properties owned by the emperor; not least significant are those cases where emperors speak of 'my' or 'our' *fiscus*, and others of 'your' or 'his' *fiscus*.[62] But the situation naturally could not remain one of purely 'private' ownership. First, even as a property-owner, the emperor inevitably assumed a more and more privileged position vis à vis private persons. The development is most succinctly described by Cassius Dio in dicussing the case of Tiberius' procurator in Asia who was condemned in 23 for acting violently and giving orders to troops, though the emperor affirmed that his orders related only to the imperial slaves and money.[63] Dio writes, 'It was not permitted then to those in charge of the imperial funds to do any more than collect the accustomed revenues; and, as regards any disputes, to be judged in the Forum and in accordance with the laws on a level with private persons.'[64]

This passage offers an adequate basis for interpreting the large number of passages in legal works which refer to the private-law position of the *fiscus* as a party to contracts or sales, or as a debtor or creditor;[65] on the assumption that the *fiscus* occupied in origin the position of a private 'person', which it in some respects retained, and in others gradually exceeded, this evidence becomes essentially clear.

Concurrent with that, however, went another process whereby, first, the emperor began to claim for the *fiscus* some sources of revenue, such as *bona damnatorum* and *bona caduca* and *vacantia*, which would otherwise have become public. Our earliest relatively explicit evidence for these processes is that of Tacitus, who regards the claims to *bona damnatorum* as usurpations;[66] there is no need to disbelieve his view. It was perhaps as an extension of this that, as legal and documentary sources of the second and third centuries show, cash penalties or fines (*poenae*) were paid to the *fiscus*. Such *poenae* included ones spontaneously inserted in contracts or deeds by private parties; we may note for instance a document of the mid-second century from Narbonensis, where funds, if misused, were to go 'to the *fiscus* of the greatest emperor'.[67] Here too we may be seeing the influence of legal practice in the late-Hellenistic kingdoms. Indeed the continuity is perfectly clear in two cases: contracts from Dura-Europus from both the Parthian

[61] *De ben.* VII, 6, 3: 'Caesar omnia habet, fiscus eius privata tantum ac sua; et universa in imperio eius sunt, in patrimonio propria.'
[62] esp. pp. 160, 162, 170, 174. Note also *CJ* II, 17, 2 (Gordian, 241).
[63] Tacitus, *Ann.* IV, 15, 2.
[64] LVII, 23, 5.
[65] For some examples see *JRS* LIII (1963), 31–4.
[66] p. 167.
[67] *CIL* XII 4393, ll. 15f.

period (where penalties go to the *basilikon*) and then the Roman (where they go to the *fiscus* or 'the most sacred *tameion*');[68] and in the Nabataean documents from the Judaean Desert, where penalties are payable 'to the King' both before and after the Roman conquest in 106.[69]

Such expressions clearly represent the development of a conception which saw the emperor as being the state, or, more precisely, simply as being a king. Whatever their status as historical narratives, it is significant that the Gospels represent persons in Jerusalem as saying both 'We have no king but Caesar' and, of tribute money, 'Render unto Caesar that which is Caesar's'.[70] So it is not surprising that, from the later first century onwards, we begin to find documents, literary sources and legal works on occasion apparently reflecting the payment of extra-ordinary taxes, indirect taxes or even tribute to the *fiscus*. In most of these cases, however, it is very difficult to say exactly what the nature of the payment is; and overall we cannot tell whether we are witnessing genuine further steps of usurpation by the emperor, or the extension of an 'imperial' terminology to areas of public revenue where it still (properly speaking) did not belong.[71]

Our confusion can be illustrated by a story from Philostratus about Herodes Atticus and Hadrian. Herodes was acting as *curator* of the free cities of Asia, and wrote to Hadrian to ask him to give 12,000,000 *sesterces* to pay for a water-supply for Ilium. The emperor agreed, but when the expenditure had reached 28,000,000 the procurators of Asia complained, saying that the tribute of 500 cities (the whole province, that is) was being wasted on a single spring. So Herodes' father paid the excess himself.[72] The story illustrates again the disbalance between private and public wealth, and between public income and the costs of construction. But it leaves us in the dark as to whether the emperor's procurators (as opposed to the senatorial quaestor of the province) now actually collected the tribute, and whether the emperor's gift was being made out of it—or whether, alternatively, they merely referred to this figure for comparison and rhetorical effect.

From towards the middle of the third century at any rate, our sources cease to reflect any consciousness of a division between imperial and public revenues; *fiscus* and cognate expressions are applied to all the revenues and possessions of the state[73]—except, that is, insofar as imperial properties came under the *ratio privata* or were 'patrimonial'. (The 'private' connotations of these terms are clear, but both the distinction between them and their

---

[68] For details, *JRS* LIII (1963), 37–8.

[69] See *IEJ* XII (1962), 241, a penalty to Rabel, 'and to our lord Rabel the King likewise'; 246, a bill of sale of AD 122 with the clause, 'and to our lord the Emperor likewise'.

[70] pp. 552–3.

[71] See App. 2.

[72] Philostratus, *VS* II, 1.

[73] For early fourth-century evidence implying that regular taxes went to the *fiscus* see *Dig.* L, 4, 18, 26 (Arcadius Charisius); *CTh* XII, 1, 14; XI, 3, 1 = *CJ* IV, 47, 2; VII, 20, 2, 1 = *CJ* XII, 46, 1; XI, 7, 4 = *CJ* X, 21, 1; *Frag. Vat.* 35 — (in part) *CTh* III, 1, 2; cf. *P. Cair. Isidor.* 69, ll. 16–18. Note also e.g. *pecunia fiscalis* (Arcadius Charisius, *Dig.* L, 4, 18, 3); *onera* and *frumenta fiscalia*, S. Lauffer, *Diokletians Preisedikt* (1971), 204–5; *fiscales copiae* in *horrea*, 326, *CTh* XV, 1, 4; cf. the *cupae fisci* (containing vinegar) reposing in the temple of Sarapis at Cirta in 303, *CSEL* XXVI, 193, 196; *mulae fiscales* in *CJ* XI, 55, 1 (ταμιακοὶ ἵπποι in *P. Karanis* 548); πλοῖα ταμιακά in *P. Beatty Panop.* 1 passim (298).

relation to the *fiscus* are remarkably obscure.)[74] None the less, emperors still speak of 'our *fiscus*', as do the tetrarchs in their newly-discovered edict of 301 ordering a re-tariffing of the coinage, which elsewhere makes clear that all debts were either 'fiscal' or private.[75]

Thus, though we cannot trace the detailed evolution, we can safely say that by the last part of the period all the formerly public revenues were thought of as going to the emperor's *fiscus*. A similar process *may* have taken place with the former *ager publicus* of the *res publica* but the evidence here is even more inadequate.[76] By contrast, if we return to the earlier period, when the distinction still survived, almost all the evidence for 'imperial' expenditure relates to acts of liberality, some recurrent, like *congiaria*, others *ad hoc*. When Augustus relieved the cities of Asia of tribute after an earthquake in 12 BC he paid the equivalent himself into the *aerarium*;[77] but there is no sign that this was the practice on the innumerable later occasions when emperors gave comparable *beneficia* to cities or individuals.[78] Almost the only attested large-scale expenditure undertaken by the emperor and designed to have long-term effects is Trajan's alimentary scheme for the support of children in the towns of Italy; this involved the putting-out of very large sums, perhaps of the order of 1,000,000,000 *sesterces*, of what was certainly at least represented as imperial funds; inscriptions speak of the *indulgentia*, *liberalitas* and *munificentia* of the emperor.[79]

When, however, we ask whether there was any range of semi-public purposes for which, even in principle, the imperial funds paid on a permanent basis, we have almost no evidence. We may presume that such funds paid the imperial freedmen who performed a wide variety of public or semi-public functions throughout the empire,[80] and also probably the emperor's procurators of equestrian rank. Certainly Vitruvius, addressing Augustus in his preface, regards the *commoda* which he received as a personal *beneficium* which the emperor had confirmed on the recommendation of his sister.[81] Thereafter we have no formal evidence of the source of the pay which procurators received; but *advocati fisci* received a *salarium* from the *fiscus*, and it may be relevant that Lucian, acting as secretary to a prefect of Egypt,

[74] See App. 3.

[75] See K. T. Erim, J. Reynolds, M. Crawford, 'Diocletian's Currency Reform: a New Inscription', *JRS* LXI (1971), 171; Frag. b (1), l. 2: ['cui?]us legis observantiae etiam fiscum no[st]rum subiectum...', and l. 5: 'super his autem debitoribus qui ante Kal. Septemb. diem vel in fiscalibus debitis deprehendendum vel in privatis contractibus monstrantur obnoxii.'

[76] See App. 1.

[77] Dio LIV, 30, 3.

[78] See ch. vii–viii passim.

[79] For what is still the fullest account see *Dig. Epig.* s.v. 'alimenta'. *Indulgentia*: *CIL* XI, 1147; *liberalitas*: *CIL* VI 1492; *munificentia*: *CIL* IX 5825. Note also Dio LXVIII, 5, 4: ὡς καὶ ταῖς πόλεσι ταῖς ἐν Ἰταλίᾳ πρὸς τὴν τῶν παίδων τροφὴν πολλὰ χαρίσασθαι. Cf. R. Duncan-Jones, 'The Purpose and Organisation of the Alimenta', *PBSR* XXXII, n.s. XIX (1964), 123, revised in *The Economy of the Roman Empire: Quantitative Aspects* (1974), 288. Compare *CTh* XI, 27, 1, where Constantine orders pronouncements throughout Italy that children whom their parents cannot support can be supplied by *fiscus noster* or the *res privata*.

[80] See now G. Boulvert, *Esclaves et affranchis impériaux sous le Haut-Empire romain: rôle politique et administratif* (1970).

[81] *De arch.* I, *pr.* 2.

prides himself on receiving pay which was 'not private but from the emperor'.[82]

Thus over the whole question of pay provided from imperial funds we have no significant evidence; and our hopes of clarification are not increased by the second-century papyrus letter from a recruit in the fleet at Misenum who writes to his father in Egypt that he has received as travelling-expenses (*viaticum*) 'three gold pieces from Caesar'.[83] For the expenses of the army were surely borne in principle by the standing public revenues. So again it is clear that even before the distinction between public and imperial funds ceases to be visible in our sources, we cannot draw a clear boundary between them with regard to either income or expenditure.

These difficulties do not alter the fact that the possession of private wealth by the emperor, the various means which he deployed to increase it at the expense of some of his subjects, and the endless stream of gifts and liberalities in cash and kind which he conferred on others, were all fundamental elements in the nature of his regime, and were basic to the setting and style of his life, and to the pattern of his relations with his subjects. The processes of the acquisition of wealth by the emperor fundamentally affected the property-rights of his subjects, and are reflected in detail in the legal writings of the second and third centuries. Beyond that, the financial structure of the early fourth century was permeated by terms which reflected, directly or indirectly, the origins of the system in the private wealth of a Roman magnate—(our) *fiscus*, *ratio privata*, *patrimoniales fundi*, *procurator*, *donativum*, and later *largitiones*. Something much more than a mere similarity links the temples which Augustus built in Rome, and the *dona* worth 100,000,000 *sesterces* which he dedicated in those of Divus Julius, Apollo, Vesta and Mars Ultor, to the churches which Constantine built there, and the ornaments in gold and silver which he placed within them.

---

[82] *Frag. de iure fisci* 16–17; Lucian, *Apol.* 12.
[83] *BGU* 423 = Hunt and Edgar, *Select Papyri* II, no. 112.

V

The Emperor at Work: Imperial Functions and their Social Setting

1. *Introduction*

In a long letter addressed to Marcus Aurelius, Cornelius Fronto makes one of the few attempts which survive in the literature of the empire to define some of the duties and functions of the emperor:[1]

> Therefore consider whether in this second category of duties the study of eloquence should be included. For the duties of emperors are: to urge necessary steps in the senate; to address the people on very many matters in public meetings; to correct the injustices of the law; to send letters to all parts of the globe; to bring compulson to bear on kings of foreign nations; to repress by their edicts the faults of the provincials, give praise to good actions, quell the seditious and terrify the fierce ones. All these are assuredly things to be achieved by words and letters. Will you therefore not practise a skill which you can see will be of great service to you on so many and such important occasions?

A large number of points arise from this passage. The first is that *eloquentia* is seen as something practised by the emperor himself, and applicable firstly to his speeches and secondly to *litterae* and *edicta* issued by him. The same assumption appears elsewhere in what Fronto writes to Aurelius: 'In short you too, when you have had to speak in the senate or an assembly of the people (*in contione populi*) have never used a relatively obscure word, or a difficult or unusual metaphor. For you know that the eloquence of a Caesar should resemble the sound of a trumpet not of a flute, which has less body and less clarity.'[2] On the other hand he writes of the emperors from Gaius to Vitellius: 'Which of them could address the people or the senate in a speech of his own, or compose an edict or a letter in his own words?'[3] The assumption that an emperor's *eloquentia* was, or should be, his own, and that it provided an important indication by which to judge him, is shared by earlier sources. Tacitus, commenting on the fact that Nero was the first emperor to need another's eloquence, notes that Julius Caesar had been the equal of the greatest orators; Augustus had the readiness and fluency which befitted the eloquence of an emperor; Tiberius was skilled in weighing his words, whether he intended to be clear or obscure; even Gaius'

[1] Fronto, *Ad M. Antoninum de eloquentia* 2, 7; a less detailed portrayal in *Pan.* II(10), 3, 3–4.
[2] *Ad M. Caes.* III, 1.
[3] *Ad Verum imp.* II, 1, 9.

madness had not robbed him of the art of speaking, and Claudius was not short of eloquence, provided that his speech was prepared.[4] Suetonius confirms that Augustus had trained himself laboriously in *eloquentia* and *studia liberalia*, reading, writing and practising declamation every day, even during the war of Mutina in 43 BC. He carefully prepared his speeches before senate, people or army, and would read them out to avoid a failure of memory or waste of time in learning them. When giving a speech in Greek (as at Alexandria in 30 BC), he would write it in Latin first and have it translated.[5]

What Tacitus says confirms what Josephus had written of Gaius: 'He was, moreover, a first-rate orator, deeply versed in the Greek and Latin languages. He knew how to reply impromptu to speeches which others had composed after long preparation, and to show himself instantly more persuasive than anyone else, even where the greatest matters were debated.'[6]

It was thus a matter of comment that Nero should have had his speech written by Seneca, even though he was only seventeen on succeeding Claudius. Seneca is also, however, said to have written the letter which Nero sent to the senate after the murder of Agrippina five years later.[7] But even Nero kept up the convention of the oration as a personal art, proclaiming the freedom of Greece in an oration which he delivered at Corinth in 67.[8] After his forced suicide in 68 the text of a speech appealing to the populace for support was found in his chest for papers (*scrinium*); it is probable, if not certain, that he had written it himself.[9]

From this time on our sources do begin to imply with some greater regularity that the speeches of emperors were written by others. So when Suetonius sums up in paragraph the poverty of Domitian's literary culture he includes the statement that he 'composed (*formabat*) letters, speeches and edicts by the mind of others',[10] while Tacitus says that it was believed that Otho's speeches were written by Galerius Trachalus, and Julian reports that Trajan had his composed by Licinius Sura.[11] This is consonant with the statement of the *Historia Augusta* that after Sura's death Hadrian grew closer to Trajan, in particular because of the speeches which he dictated for him.[12] As emperor himself, Hadrian dictated his own speeches, and even published a book containing twelve of them.[13] According to the *Historia*

---

[4] *Ann.* XIII, 3, 2; cf. Dio LXI, 3, 1.

[5] *Aug.* 84; 89, 1; cf. 86. Cf. p. 9.

[6] *Ant.* XIX, 2, 5 (208), Loeb trans.

[7] For the speech written by Seneca see Tacitus and Dio in n. 4 above. For the letter, Quintilian, *Inst.* VIII, 5, 18, and Tacitus, *Ann.* XIV, 10, 3–11, 3.

[8] The exact site is disputed: Suetonius, *Nero* 24, 2: 'quae beneficia e medio stadio Isthmiorum die sua ipse voce pronuntiavit'; Plutarch, *Flam.* 12, 13: αὐτὸς ἐπὶ τῆς ἀγορᾶς ἀπὸ βήματος ἐν τῷ πλήθει δημηγορήσας. Plutarch is more likely to be correct. The protocol of the speech itself (*Syll.*[3] 814) gives simply συνελθόντων τῶν ὄχλων ἐν ἐκκλησίᾳ προσεφώνησεν τὰ ὑπογεγραμμένα. Cf. p. 430.

[9] Suetonius, *Nero* 47, 2.

[10] *Dom.* 20.

[11] Tacitus, *Hist.* I, 90, 2; Julian, *Caes.* 327 A–B.

[12] *Had.* 3, 11.

[13] ibid., 20, 7; Charisius, *Ars Grammatica*, p. 287 Barwick, *Gram. Lat.* I, ed. Keil, p. 222: 'valdissime: divus Hadrianus orationum XII libro, "a vobis P.C. peto et impetratum valdissime cupio, ut proxime imaginem Augusti argenteum potius clupeum sicut Augusto ponatis".' Cf.

Augusta, again, it was disputed whether the surviving orations by Aelius Caesar and Antoninus Pius were their own compositions.[14]

It was clearly a significant factor in an emperor's standing and subsequent reputation if he could both write his own speeches, and other pronouncements, and deliver them in a creditable way. This need not have excluded some assistance more regular than that provided by senatorial advisers and friends such as Seneca or Licinius Sura; and it may be suggested (though there is no direct evidence) that this was the function of the post *a studiis*, which is attested from Claudius to Constantine (in this period *magister a studiis* or *studiorum*).[15] *Studia* meant in effect the training and polite learning which went to make an orator—Pliny the Younger, in describing the large crowd which awaited him when he came to speak in the centumviral court, says complacently—'honour for *studia* still endures'.[16] But even if some now indefinable role was played in relation to imperial rhetoric by learned men such as Claudius' freedman, Polybius, or later Julius Vestinus, Suetonius or Volusius Maecianus,[17] the tradition of rhetorical training of emperors, as of senators, continued. It was not only Marcus Aurelius who continued as an adult to steep himself in rhetorical and philosophical learning;[18] Dio records also that Severus engaged in daily discourse in Greek and Latin.[19]

From the third century we have little direct evidence beyond Herodian's remark that Maximinus read out to his troops a speech written for him by some of his friends.[20] But for Constantine we have abundant evidence not only that he was brought up in the normal literary and rhetorical culture of the upper classes,[21] but, from Eusebius, that he wrote his speeches himself. The evidence comes from his *Life of Constantine*, perhaps our most valuable source for the activities of any emperor. Eusebius writes: 'The emperor was in the habit of composing his orations in Latin, from which they were translated into Greek by interpreters appointed for this special purpose.'[22] The orations of which Eusebius is speaking were characteristically

---

P. J. Alexander, 'Letters and Speeches of the Emperor Hadrian', *HSCPh* XLIX (1938), 141, which does not however mention this item.

[14] *Ael.* 4, 7: 'orationem pulcherrimam, quae hodieque legitur, sive per se seu per scriniorum aut dicendi magistros parasset' (*magistri scriniorum* is of course the vocabulary of the fourth not the second century); *Ant. Pius* 11, 3: 'orationes plerique alienas esse dixerunt, quae sub eius nomine feruntur; Marius Maximus eius proprias fuisse dicit.'

[15] See e.g. *RE* IVA (1931), 397–8; E. van't Dack, 'A studiis, a bybliothecis', *Historia* XII (1963), 177.

[16] *Ep.* IV, 16, 1. Note that it is apparently the post of *a studiis* which is translated in *IG* XIV 1085 = *OGIS* 679 = *IGR* I 136 (known only from a MS) as ἐπὶ τῆς παιδείας. Cf. p. 88.

[17] pp. 75–6, 88, 90, 103.

[18] Dio LXXI, 35, 6; cf. 35, 1 (277–8).

[19] LXXVI, 17, 2 (372); cf. p. 209.

[20] VII, 8, 3.

[21] Some statements to this effect are questionable in themselves, as having a panegyrical character. So Eusebius, *VC* I, 19, 2: παιδεύσει λόγων . . . διαφερόντως ἐκπρέπων, and cf. Praxagoras, *FGrH* 219, Constantine at Nicomedia παιδευθησόμενον. But note Eutropius x, 7, 2: 'civilibus artibus et studiis liberalibus deditus'; *Epit. de Caes.* 41, 14: 'nutrire artes bonas, praecipue studia litterarum, legere ipse scribere meditari audire legationes et querimonias provinciarum.' The only formal statement to the contrary is that of *Anon. Vales.* 1 (*Origo Constantini Imperatoris*), 2/2: 'litteris minus instructus, obses apud Diocletianum et Galerium.'

[22] *VC* IV, 32.

theological discourses which Constantine would deliver himself in public, on which occasions 'vast multitudes attended, to hear an emperor play the role of a philosopher'.[23] It is not clear from this whether, like Augustus, he delivered the Greek text translated for him, or whether, as he did to the bishops at Nicaea, he spoke in Latin and had his speech translated by an interpreter.[24] But unless we are to reject all the evidence of Eusebius, it is clear that Constantine's orations were his own compositions, just as was the long letter on the errors of polytheism, which Eusebius says was translated from the Latin original in the emperor's own hand.[25]

It was a direct product of the established education and culture of the upper classes in the ancient world that an emperor would be judged partly on his ability to compose and deliver orations; that not all emperors approached the distinction of Julius Caesar, and that some received assistance in composition, is less important than the expectation itself, which continued through and beyond our period.[26] Moreover, whatever assistance could be given in composition could not, in the nature of the case, apply to delivery. In the emperor's absence from Rome his *orationes* could be read in the senate by his quaestor; but otherwise, whether in the senate or before the people of Rome, very frequently to the praetorian cohorts, when on campaign to the army, and on occasion in provincial cities, the emperor fulfilled his role in part by making speeches.

It is vital to remember this irreducibly personal activity of oratory, the frequency with which it was required and its significance to the audience as an indication of the emperor's personal culture, or lack of it, when we consider his written pronouncements, and the emperor's role in formulating them. These took various forms. Fronto mentions letters and edicts, but does not explicitly refer to *subscriptiones*, which he perhaps presumes under the correction of the injustices of the law. Nor indeed does Gaius, writing in the same period, in listing the forms in which the emperor could create law: 'an imperial *constitutio* is whatever the emperor lays down (*constituit*) by *decretum* or *edictum* or *epistula*.'[27] A rather more detailed list is given a few decades later by Ulpian: 'Therefore whatever the emperor has laid down by *epistula* and *subscriptio*, or has determined in giving justice (*cognoscens decrevit*), or has given extrajudicially as a provisional judgment or has ordered by *edictum*, is agreed to be a law.'[28] Some of these forms of pronouncement, such as formal utterances by the emperor or his verdicts in giving judgment, were by their nature personal acts; though even here it will be necessary to ask what evidence we have for the role either of the emperor himself or of friends or advisers in formulating the content or wording of such pronouncements. In the case of the emperor's extensive judicial activity, the presence of a *consilium* of *assessores* was a standard

---

[23] IV, 29, 2.

[24] III, 13, 1.

[25] II, 47: αὐτόγραφον οὖσαν αὐτοῦ, μεταληφθεῖσαν δ᾽ ἐκ τῆς Ῥωμαίων φωνῆς. Text in II, 48–60.

[26] Note for instance Ammianus XVI, 5, 7, on the culture and rhetorical ability of Julian.

[27] *Inst.* I, 5.

Dig. I, 4, 1, 1.

element; their opinions were certainly asked by the emperor, and it is still occasionally argued that in certain types of case at least he was bound by their majority opinion.[29]

With written pronouncements our evidence is very different, for with occasional exceptions their preparation did not take place in public. But it may be noted that the wording and construction of edicts, as of speeches, could be treated as an indication of the culture of the emperor who issued them. Dio tells an anecdote of Tiberius issuing an edict containing a non-Latin word, being troubled by having done so, and the following day consulting scholars on the point. One, the lawyer Ateius Capito, sycophantically pronounced that the emperor's use of it itself made the word respectable; but Pomponius Marcellus replied, 'You, Caesar, can confer the Roman citizenship upon men, but not upon words.'[30] Similarly, Fronto reproaches Marcus Aurelius with using obscure and affected terminology in an edict concerned with Italian towns.[31]

When we consider edicts in more detail, it will be apparent how little external evidence we have of their composition, and how far we have to rely on uncertain criteria drawn from the texts of the edicts themselves; there is also the remarkable fact that there is no trace of any assistants, whether of freedmen or equestrian status, whose titles indicate that they were concerned with edicts.[32] The case is, as we have seen, very different with letters, where it is indisputable that at least by the second century, an *ab epistulis* did play, or at least could play, a significant part in the actual composition of the letters.[33] The same is apparently true of the *a libellis* in relation to *subscriptiones*, the brief answers written under *libelli* (petitions).[34] When Ulpian writes of the emperor making a pronouncement *per epistulam et subscriptionem* it is not clear whether he is referring to these two quite distinct processes, or to the different sense of 'subscription' in which the emperor wrote with his own hand a greeting at the end of a letter. The same ambiguity is present when an orator in 321 affects to imagine that the hand of Constantine's son (then aged five) already rejoiced in 'bountiful subscription'.[35]

Because Fronto is concerned with imperial pronouncements and with the relevance of *eloquentia* to them, he does not say anything of the circumstances under which these various types of pronouncement were made. Part of the deficiency is made good in the oration *On Rome* of Fronto's contemporary Aelius Aristides:[36]

And if the governors [of the provinces] should have even some slight doubt

---

[29] pp. 237–9.

[30] LVII, 17, 1–3; cf. Suetonius, *De gram. et rhet.* 22, where the word is described as being *ex oratione Tiberi.* For Tiberius' use of the hitherto unknown word *colum* in an edict see Pliny, *NH* XXVI, 6/9, and for his normally purist attitude Suetonius, *Tib.* 71.

[31] *Ad Antoninum de orationibus* 17.

[32] pp. 252–9.

[33] pp. 92–3, 224–8.

[34] pp. 96, 248–52.

[35] *Pan.* x(4), 37, 5; cf. *HA, v. Tac.* 6, 5, and *v. Car.* 16, 8.

[36] Εἰς Ῥώμην 32, trans. J. H. Oliver, *The Ruling Power* (1953), 899.

whether certain claims are valid in connection with either public or private lawsuits and petitions from the governed, they straightaway send to him [the emperor] with a request for instructions what to do, and they wait until he renders a reply, like a chorus waiting for its trainer.

The correspondence between provincial governors and the emperor, and in particular the developing pattern whereby governors of all types regularly consulted the emperor by letter, especially on judicial matters, was indeed one of the crucial elements of the role of the emperor.[37] The overwhelming mass of such correspondence was, as Aristides implies, initiated by the governors themselves; and it is this characteristic which it shares with the much wider and more complex pattern of contacts between his subjects, individual and collective, and the emperor. But whereas letters from and to governors were normally delivered by messengers, even written communications from subjects, invariably in the case of decrees of cities, and sometimes in that of the *libelli* of individuals, were presented in person by embassies or interested parties, and the presentation necessarily involved formal or informal verbal exchanges with the emperor himself. So here too an ability to make impromptu speeches, or to make replies which exhibited wit without falling into eccentricity or indignity, was a desirable characteristic of an emperor, though one less easily achieved than the ability to deliver a prepared oration. It is precisely this variety of personal contacts between subjects and emperor, of which we have already seen a number of examples, which will later be our central concern.

Though the emperors of the first century or so tended to make a practice of giving justice in public, normally from a tribunal in the Forum, the absence of any 'office' or public place of work meant, as we have seen, that they largely conducted their business within the context of private residences or temporary stopping-places; and also, partly in consequence of this, within the framework of the relatively leisurely patterns of life of the Roman upper classes.

It is merely an extreme aspect of this pattern when our sources describe Nero, on receiving the news of the final defection of his armies while he was at dinner, as tearing up the letter handed to him, overturning the table, and smashing two rock-crystal cups engraved with scenes from Homer;[38] just as it is with Gaius receiving the Greek and Jewish delegations from Alexandria in the Horti Lamiani, or, more respectably, Marcus giving judgment day and night in his villa at Alsium.[39] Even apart from such extreme cases, we can be certain that the physical setting of the exercise of his functions by the emperor was determined not by the public life of the late republic, but by the social and architectural character of the houses of Roman nobles. Some external accoutrements and some forms of activity were certainly inherited from republican public life: the emperors were, like the consuls, accompanied by lictors and other *apparitores*, and sat between the consuls on their bench; they held occasional censorships, and from Domitian permanently

[37] pp. 321–36.
[38] Pliny, *NH* XXXVII, 10/29; Suetonius, *Nero* 47, 1; cf. Plutarch, *Galba* 5, 3.
[39] pp. 22, 27.

absorbed the functions of that office; they issued *edicta* like republican magistrates, and in the first century occasionally exercised the rights conferred by their *tribunicia potestas*. As an example of this, Suetonius records Tiberius, when abused during his retirement on Rhodes, reappearing with his *apparitores*, having the offender summoned by his herald, and summarily ordering the man to prison.[40]

This is indeed a remarkable case of a power which the annual tribunes of the republic could exercise only within the *pomerium* of Rome being deployed in a Greek city. But in general the very fact that from the beginning the emperors spent so much time out of Rome, either in their villas in Italy, on journeys through the provinces or on campaign, must have reinforced the tendency for their functions to be performed in relative privacy and informality, and with the aid of their own *familia* and personally-chosen assistants and advisers.

These conclusions are borne out by the very few accounts which we have of how an emperor actually spent his day; in spite of their brief and anecdotal character, these descriptions are still of fundamental importance in assessing the tone and character of the imperial household, and the nature and limits of the functions actually performed by the emperors. The earliest is Suetonius' description of Vespasian's manner of life:[41]

> As Emperor he always arose early, and even when it was still night. Then, having read the letters and the *breviaria* [reports?] of all the *officia*, he would admit his friends, and while they were greeting him would put on his own shoes and clothes. After whatever matters came to his notice had been decided, he devoted himself to riding and then to a rest, accompanied by one of his concubines, of whom he had established a considerable number in place of Caenis, who had died. From his private room he would transfer to the bath and then the dining-room. There was no time when he is said to have been easier or more indulgent, and his domestics did their utmost to seize these moments to make requests of him.

The second is Dio's account from personal observation of how Severus passed the day when in Rome; it therefore relates to the period 202–8:[42]

> He was always at work before dawn, and after that would stroll about, speaking and listening on matters concerned with the government. Then he would give judgment, unless there were a major festival. This indeed he did in the most proper manner, for he allowed sufficient time by the water-clock to those being judged, and gave full freedom of expression to those of us who were acting as his *assessores*. He gave judgment until mid-day, and then rode as far as he could. Then he did some gymnastic exercises, and had a bath. He took a substantial lunch either alone or with his sons. Then he usually had a sleep, and when he got up saw to whatever matters were left over, and engaged in discourse in Greek and Latin while walking about. Then towards evening he bathed again, and had dinner with his household.

We could add to these two accounts of an emperor's day in Rome the less

[40] *Tib.* 11, 3.
[41] *Vesp.* 21.
[42] LXXVI, 17, 1–3 (371–2).

formal and less useful description, also by Dio, of Caracalla's way of life at Nicomedia over the winter of 214/15; less useful because it is written explicitly as a protest against the impropriety of the emperor's conduct. There too Dio was an *assessor*, and he relates how Caracalla would announce that he was going to give judgment or carry out some other public business soon after dawn, but would then keep his *amici* waiting at the door through most or all of the day, while he amused himself or feasted—and sometimes would finally give justice. Dio also mentions later that Caracalla allowed his mother, Julia Domna, who was with him on his eastern journey, to look after the *libelli* and *epistulae*, except for the most important ones.[43]

These passages naturally do not offer a complete profile of an emperor's activities, which certainly varied greatly not only from reign to reign, but in accordance with circumstances and with his location at any one time. One has only to point to the successive reigns of Trajan, Hadrian and Antoninus Pius to see how large a scope was left for the emperor's own inclinations in how he fulfilled his role. But, none the less, certain consistent patterns emerge. The emperor's formal business is conducted by himself in private in his own residence of the time, and with the assistance of *amici* summoned at his choice, who come to greet him (*salutare*) in the morning. The business begins (or is supposed to begin) early in the morning, and occupies only a limited part of the day. Of that business, the only element which is clearly identified in Dio's accounts is the emperor's sitting as a judge; this agrees with what he says of Marcus Aurelius' civilian business during the Marcomannic War, and with what Marcus himself says in his communication to Athens from the same period.[44] This element, however, is missing from Suetonius' account of Vespasian, unless it is included in the general phrase 'after whatever matters came to his notice had been decided' ('postque decisa quaecumque obvenissent'). On the other hand, Suetonius mentions the emperor personally reading his *epistulae* and the *breviaria* of all the *officia*; it is not impossible that some may have related to finance or the dispositions of troops, and have borne some resemblance on a smaller scale to the *breviarium* of the whole empire which Augustus had left at his death.[45] But the question of what records and documents were kept by, or were available to, the emperors is always one of acute difficulty.[46]

That the *epistulae* were read personally by the emperor is clear enough in Suetonius' account, as it is (in principle) in what Dio says of Caracalla; Dio later says that in accordance with Caracalla's instructions Julia Domna read

---

[43] LXXVII, 17, 3–4; 18, 2 (396–7): καίτοι καὶ τὴν τῶν βιβλίων τῶν τε ἐπιστολῶν ἑκατέρων, πλὴν τῶν πάνυ ἀναγκαίων, διοίκησιν αὐτῇ ἐπιτρέψας. The translation of βιβλία as *libelli* is virtually certain (though we might expect rather the more literal βιβλίδια), and is formally attested by the *Sententiae et Epistulae Hadriani Imperatoris, Corp. Gloss. Lat.* III, 388: 'renuntiabit mihi per libellum' / ἀπαγγέλλει μοι διὰ βιβλίου. But cf. ibid., 34 and 388: 'per libellum / διὰ βιβλιδίου. Both terms are in common use on papyri with this meaning, see Preisigke, *Wörterbuch*, s.vv.

[44] pp. 4–6.

[45] Suetonius, *Aug.* 101, 4: 'breviarium totius imperii, quantum militum sub signis ubique esset, quantum pecuniae in aerario et fiscis et vectigaliorum residuis. adiecit et libertorum servorumque nomina a quibus ratio exigi posset.' Cf. *Galba* 12, 3: 'ordinario quidem dispensatori breviarium rationum offerenti...'

[46] pp. 259–68.

all the letters which arrived for him at Antioch.[47] Dio adds the *libelli* as documents requiring the attention of the emperor, just as Julian does in writing to Libanius from his last journey in 363: 'As for all the letters and *libelli* to which I have put my subscription—for these travel around with me everywhere, following me like shadows—why should I now take the trouble to enumerate them?'[48]

Perhaps the most surprising feature of these passages is the absence of any explicit mention of the reception of embassies (even though we cannot draw a clear distinction between this and judicial business); for Vespasian himself, as we saw, regarded this as a prime imperial duty, which he continued up to the moment of his death.[49] It may be, though there is no evidence, that only a certain limited number of days were set aside for the reception of embassies, of which unquestionably very large numbers presented themselves every year. The papyrus evidence on the other hand shows incontrovertibly that, at least at certain periods, some *libelli* were answered every day.[50]

What is also noticeable is that the only reference to a public appearance which might interrupt the emperor's normal business is that implied in Dio's statement that Severus gave judgment unless there were a major festival. It is indeed clear that the emperor, if in Rome, was expected to make appearances at some at least of the ever-growing list of festivals, though it is not possible to determine which were the most important for this purpose. But they undoubtedly provided the main context for his direct contacts with the population of Rome.[51] By contrast, neither Suetonius nor Dio mentions in this connection the possibility of the emperor attending the senate. The explanation is probably that while emperors undoubtedly did so on occasion —and, if holding the consulate, presided there—they were not expected to attend regularly; moreover, routine meetings of the senate took place only twice a month in the imperial period.[52]

These public roles performed by the emperor in Rome, either in the senate or before the people, will however be considered in more detail in the wider context of the relations of subject and emperor.[53] What remains to be discussed here is the question of the functions of the emperor and his entourage as the focus of government: the respective roles of the emperor and his assistants and advisers in the reception and hearing of individuals or embassies which came before him; the handling of written material—decrees passed by cities, letters and *libelli*—sent or presented to him; the preparation of his pronouncements in the form of *edicta*, *epistulae* and *subscriptiones*, and the extent to which records of these were kept by the imperial household.

---

[47] LXXVIII, 4, 2–3 (406–7); cf. *JRS* LIII (1963), 11.

[48] Julian, *Ep.* 98 Bidez, 402 b: ἐπιστολαῖς δὲ ὅσαις ὑπέγραψα καὶ βίβλοις [βιβλίοις] (ἑπόμενα ὥσπερ σκιά μοι καὶ ταῦτα συμπερινοστεῖ πανταχοῦ) τί δεῖ νῦν πράγματα ἔχειν ἀπαριθμούμενον; I owe this reference to the kindness of Professor Chr. Habicht. For the translation of βιβλία as *libelli* see n. 43 above. It is made more or less certain here by the indication that both types of document are to be subscribed (ὑπογραφεῖν).

[49] p. 28.

[50] pp. 244–5.

[51] pp. 368–75.

[52] *RE* Supp. VI, col. 766.

[53] pp. 341–55, 368–75.

What has been said so far about the physical contexts in which the emperor worked, the social and educational background of the persons attracted into his immediate service, and the strong tradition by which his verbal and written pronouncements were judged as indications of his level of culture, learning and *eloquentia*, may afford certain presumptions upon which to approach these difficult and sometimes insoluble questions. Some of the activities of the emperor with which we shall be concerned took place, if not fully in public, at least at sessions of a semi-formal character, whose partici- pants could leave some record of what took place. But the nearer we approach to the handling of written material by, or in the service of, the emperor, and still more with the filing or storage of such material, the more we are left to the hazard of making deductions from the titles of attested posts or from partial, enigmatic and possibly unreliable anecdotes. None the less, it is essential to our understanding of the whole nature and limits of govern- ment as conducted by the emperor, to do what we can to envisage as con- cretely as possible the actual processes by which written material was handled by him, his advisers and his staff, and the relations between them which this involved.

To illustrate both the immediacy and the limits of some of the material available to us we cannot do better than conclude this preliminary sketch with a remarkable anecdote in Galen, which is curiously enough the only mention he makes of Hadrian in his extensive and immensely illuminating writings:[54]

> The emperor Hadrian, so they say, struck one of his attendants in the eye with a pen. When he realised that as a result of this blow the man had become one- eyed, he summoned him and in recompense for his loss gave him permission to ask for gifts. When the victim remained silent, Hadrian again invited him to ask for whatever he wished. But the man affirmed that he wanted nothing other than an eye.

The anecdote illustrates, as do several other items of evidence, how the conception of an emperor as the source of gifts and benefits gave rise to the typically monarchic custom of specially favoured persons being given an open invitation to request whatever they wished.[55] The conception and the custom naturally had their place within as well as outside the imperial household. But, more important for our purposes, it also allows us to envisage the emperor writing with his own hand, and with at least one slave or freedman in close attendance. But what the precise role of the attendant was, why he should have suffered from an outburst of rage from his imperial master, what other witnesses were present to retail the story, and whether Hadrian was engaged on literary composition, on a private letter or on official business—all these points entirely escape us. We will not always be able to do much better when we ask how the emperor's edicts were com- posed, his correspondence digested and letters written, his verdicts reached and his answers to petitioners formulated and recorded.

[54] v, 17–18 Kühn.
[55] pp. 467–8.

2. *Imperial Correspondence*

The famous saying attributed by Plutarch to Seleucus, 'If the people knew how laborious was the mere writing and reading of so many letters they would not pick up a diadem which had been thrown away',[1] would have applied with equal or greater force to the Roman emperors. Moreover, we are confronted here not with a mere resemblance of function between kings and emperors, but with a direct and visible historical continuity. Both the earliest literary references to letters written to cities by Roman magistrates and pro-magistrates and the earliest inscribed examples of them belong to the early second century BC, when Rome first became essentially involved in the Hellenistic world. The custom whereby ambassadors from a city would appear before a king, accompany their presentation of a decree (*psêphisma*) of the city with a suitable speech, hear his answer and expect a letter to the city in reply, was immediately applied not only to the senate in Rome but also to individual generals in the field.[2]

In consequence the reception of embassies and the handling of correspondence were closely linked. The father of Pompeius Trogus served as a soldier under Julius Caesar and had 'the care of his letters and embassies and at the same time his ring'.[3] As such he could well be compared to the officials of free birth who had charge of the ring or of correspondence in the Hellenistic monarchies.[4] But the precedent was abortive, though not because the use of an official imperial ring did not become established in the empire. For Augustus first used a ring (or rather two rings, the second of which was employed by his friends in his absence) with a *signum* representing a sphinx, then one with a representation of Alexander the Great, and finally one of himself, which continued, with rare exceptions, to be used by later emperors.[5] The *signum* was used, according to Pliny, for *epistulae* and *edicta*; Suetonius mentions *diplomata*, *libelli* and *epistulae*.[6] *Diplomata* will be considered later;[7] with *epistulae*, only the *acta* of the priestly college of the *Fratres Arvales* are sufficiently formal in character to record that an emperor's letter recommending a senator for co-optation was 'marked with the *signum* which represents the head of Augustus'.[8] Similarly, only one

---

[1] *Mor.* 790A.

[2] For the Hellenistic background, C. B. Welles, *Royal Correspondence in the Hellenistic Period* (1934); for the texts of letters of Roman office-holders, R. K. Sherk, *Roman Documents from the Greek East* (Senatus Consulta *and* Epistulae *to the Age of Augustus*) (1969). For this pattern note no. 34 (the praetor, tribunes and senate to Teos, 193 BC) and 35 (the brothers Scipio to Heraclea ad Latmum, 190 BC).

[3] Justin, *Epit. Pompei Trogi Philippicarum* XLIII, 5, 12. Cf. p. 84. Rostovtzeff in *RE* s.v. 'ab epistulis' notes the relevance of Hellenistic precedents to this post.

[4] See e.g. H. U. Instinsky, *Die Siegel des Kaisers Augustus* (1962), 18f.; E. Bikerman, *Institutions des Séleucides* (1938), 33. For the Ptolemaeus who had charge of Herod's ring, see Schürer, *Jewish People* I, 311.

[5] Instinsky, o.c., 10f.

[6] *NH* XXXVII, 4/10; *Aug.* 50, see Dio LI, 3, 4–7.

[7] pp. 327–8.

[8] *CIL* VI 2071, ii, l. 10 (101); 2078 = 32374 i, ll. 30–2 (118); 2080, ll. 24–5 (120); see Instinsky, o.c., 41, and for the emperor's role as a member of priestly colleges, pp. 355–61.

record of a *subscriptio* to a *libellus* indicates unambiguously that the imperial *signum* was placed on it.[9]

The father of Pompeius Trogus remains a puzzling, though significant, exception, because the handling of the correspondence of the emperors, though its occasions and outward form largely followed Hellenistic patterns, developed much more essentially from that conducted within senatorial households; or to express the same point in a different way, from the private, though often 'political', correspondence of late-republican senators. Their letters were either written with their own hand, or dictated. Suetonius refers to hostile popular reactions to the fact that Julius Caesar could be observed passing the time at public spectacles by reading and replying to *epistulae* and *libelli*;[10] while Plutarch says that, as proconsul of Gaul, Caesar would have one or two, or even more, slaves ride with him to take down letters from dictation.[11] There is abundant evidence that Cicero often wrote in his own hand both private letters and ones on official business, such as that which he sent from Corcyra to his predecessor as proconsul of Cilicia, Appius Claudius Pulcher.[12] If he used dictation in a private letter, it was because he was at dinner, or (like Caesar) travelling in a carriage, or was suffering from inflammation of the eyes, or for reasons of security.[13] We also find for instance Atticus and Decimus Brutus writing with their own hand to Cicero,[14] or Pompey in the critical situation of February 49 BC adding a sentence in his own hand to a letter to him.[15]

The pattern is thus fairly clear. A Roman senator, whether holding office or not, composed his letters himself, writing or dictating them as circumstances required, and had them carried by slave messengers (*tabellarii*) owned by himself or others, or by a freedman; Cicero refers to a freedman of Caesar, Diochares, bringing letters from Alexandria at the end of 48 BC.[16] If Suetonius is correct, republican office-holders had normally written on papyrus rolls, Caesar being the first to send to the senate letters on separate pages bound in *codex* form.[17] With the much greater pressure of correspondence of various kinds on the emperor, it was inevitable that there should be some development of these very simple procedures. But they none the less persisted, especially in certain contexts, to a much greater extent than might be expected.

[9] p. 247. Note also Gelasius, *HE* VI, 8, 5–6.

[10] *Aug.* 45, 1.

[11] *Caes.* 17, 7. Note the more elaborate claim of Pliny, *NH* VII, 25/91: 'scribere aut legere, simul dictare aut audire solitum accepimus, epistulas vero tantarum rerum quaternas pariter dictare +librariis aut si nihil aliud ageret, septenas.+' (some MSS omit these words).

[12] To Appius Claudius Pulcher: *Ad fam.* III, 6, 2; other letters written 'mea manu', *Ad Att.* V, 19, 1; X, 3a, 1; XII, 31, 3 (32, 1); XIII, 28, 4 (29, 1); cf. esp. II, 23, 1: 'numquam ante arbitror te epistulam mea legisse nisi mea manu scriptam'.

[13] See *Ad Qu.* III, 1, 19: 'hoc inter cenam Tironi dictavi, ne mirere alia manu esse', cf. *Ad Att.* XIV, 21, 4; V, 17, 1: 'hanc epistulam dictavi sedens in raeda cum in castra proficiscerer'. Inflammation: VII, 13a, 3: VIII, 12, 1; 13, 1; cf. XVI, 15, 1. Security: XI, 2, 4.

[14] Atticus: *Ad Att.* VI, 9, 1; VII, 2, 3; Decimus Brutus, *Ad fam.* XI, 23.

[15] Seë *Ad Att.* VIII, 1, 1; the letter is VIII, 11 A.

[16] *Ad Att.* XI, 6, 7; for *tabellarii*, e.g. V, 19, 1; XI, 2, 4.

[17] *Jul.* 56, 6: 'epistulae quoque eius ad senatum extant, quas primum videtur ad paginas et formam memorialis libelli convertisse, cum antea consules et duces non nisi transversa charta scriptas mitterent.'

For an emperor to write a complete letter with his own hand it had either to belong in the context of entirely private correspondence, to be a deliberate indication of special goodwill or favour, or a formal diplomatic act. The second, for instance, is already clear in Nepos' report that Antonius during the triumviral proscriptions wrote with his own hand to Atticus to assure him that he would not be harmed.[18] Of the first there is particularly clear evidence in the case of Augustus, who carried on an extensive private correspondence, with particular attention to questions of literature, grammar and orthography. Quintilian notes that 'heri' not 'here' appears for 'yesterday'—'as is found in those letters of Augustus which he wrote or emended with his own hand'; and describes him reproaching Gaius Caesar for writing 'calidus' rather than 'caldus'.[19] Suetonius quotes an autograph letter of Augustus to Tiberius, and discusses in detail the style and orthography of other autograph letters of his which survived.[20] How common such a practice was on the part of later emperors is not at all clear; Dio makes a special point of mentioning that Marcus Aurelius wrote most of his letters to his closest friends with his own hand.[21] It is clear that not all private letters would be written so, as indeed is shown by Quintilian's reference to Augustus 'emending' a letter, that is checking a dictated copy. It is almost certainly to private letters that Marcus Aurelius refers in telling Fronto that he has exhausted his breath by dictating nearly thirty letters in the past three days.[22]

The background of private social and literary correspondence has to be remembered when we consider the official correspondence of emperors. Nor indeed can any clear line be drawn between the two. For official correspondence was conducted either with office-holders, primarily provincial governors, many of whom would be known personally to the emperor, and with regard to all of whom conventions of a certain social equality prevailed; or with cities, associations and provincial councils, of which the major Greek ones at least would do their best to be represented by leading orators or others who might also be known in person or by reputation to him.

The wider questions of imperial correspondence with senatorial and equestrian office-holders will be considered later.[23] For the moment it is necessary to stress that their letters to the emperor were carried by messengers, probably soldiers, as were those of the emperor himself.[24] Our only clear descriptions of letters from provincial governors or officials reaching the emperor come from Philo and Josephus (both of whom had personal

[18] *v. Att.* 10, 4.

[19] *Inst.* I, 7, 22; 6, 19. For the full evidence on Augustus' private correspondence see E. Malcovati, *Imperatoris Caesaris Augusti Operum Fragmenta*⁵ (1969), 6–28.

[20] *Aug.* 71, 87.

[21] LXXI, 36, 2 (278–9). For the concept, cf. *HA, Clod. Alb.* 2, 2 (a supposed letter of Commodus): 'alias ad te . . . misi, sed hanc familiarem et domesticam, omnem, ut vides, mea manu scriptam.' Note also the reference in Eunapius, *VS* 477 to a private letter written with his own hand by Julian.

[22] Fronto, *Ad M. Caes.* IV, 7.

[23] pp. 313–41.

[24] See Apuleius, *Met.* X, 13, 1: 'miles ille . . . tribuni sui praecepto debitum sustinens obsequium, litteras ad magnum scriptas principem Romam versus perlaturus.' Note Plutarch, *Galba* 8, 5, Nymphidius Sabinus, as Praetorian Prefect, demanding that soldiers, not public slaves, should carry decrees of the senate to Galba; and Tacitus, *Ann.* IV, 41, 2.

experience of the court). Josephus describes Tiberius at Capri receiving a letter from Herennius Capito, the procurator of Jamnia, and being pained by the contents, and Philo shows Gaius reading a letter from the same source.[25] More clearly still, Philo reports how Petronius, the *legatus* of Syria, sent off messengers with a letter advising the emperor to delay his plan for placing a statue of himself in the Temple: 'When they arrived, they delivered the letter. Gaius got red in the face before he had finished reading, and was filled with anger as he noted each point.'[26] This evidence supports the implications of Suetonius' statement that Augustus relieved a consular legate of his post because he saw that the man had written 'ixi' instead of 'ipsi'; Suetonius' reference makes explicit the fact that the man had written with his own hand what must have been a letter to the emperor, and clearly implies that Augustus read it himself.[27]

All this evidence comes from the early period, and we happen not to have comparable descriptions of letters from office-holders reaching the emperor in later centuries.[28] But for what they are worth, they imply that the messengers came direct to the emperor himself, who read the letters personally. There is no evidence to suggest that the letters were delivered first to any lower officials, and then passed up to the emperor. So when an emperor writes, as Marcus Aurelius and Commodus do in their remarkably detailed letter to Scapula Tertullus about the treatment of a lunatic of good social standing, 'But since we have learned from your letter . . .,'[29] we should take it that this is a reference to at least one of them actually having read Tertullus' letter. Emperors occasionally speak even more explicitly of having read petitions (*libelli*) from private persons which provincial governors attached to their letters. So for instance Trajan replies to Pliny in Bithynia, 'I have read the *libellus* of P. Accius Aquila, centurion of the *cohors sexta equestris*, which you sent to me; moved by its appeals, I have granted his daughter the Roman citizenship.'[30] In exactly the same way, the *Tabula Banasitana* shows first Marcus Aurelius and Verus and then Marcus and Commodus saying that they have read *libelli* petitioning for citizenship, sent on with letters from two procurators of Mauretania Tingitana.[31] That they had also read the covering letters from the governors went without saying.

If persons who were not senators or equestrian officials could write letters

---

[25] Josephus, *Ant.* XVIII, 6, 4 (163–4); Philo, *Leg.* 30/203.

[26] *Leg.* 34/254, trans. Smallwood. Cf. his description of Gaius reading a letter from Agrippa I, 42/331, and Josephus, *Ant.* XVIII, 7, 2 (249–52) on Gaius at Puteoli reading an earlier letter from Agrippa, and questioning Herod Antipas about it; also XVII, 9, 5 (229), Augustus reading letters from Archelaus, Varus (legate of Syria) and Sabinus (procurator of Syria).

[27] *Aug.* 88; cf. Dio ed. Boissevain II, 557.

[28] One may note certain novelistic descriptions in Herodian: III, 5, 4, messengers bringing letters from Severus to his rival emperor, Clodius Albinus, with instructions to hand them over publicly and then ask for a private interview; IV, 12, 6, messengers from Maternianus, an official in Rome, delivering letters to Caracalla as he is about to mount a racing-chariot, see *JRS* LVII (1967), 11.

[29] *Dig.* I, 18, 14.

[30] Pliny, *Ep.* X, 107; cf. 60, 2: 'libellos Furiae Primae acusatricis, item ipsius Archippi, quos alteri tuae epistulae iunxeras, legi.'

[31] See W. Seston, M. Euzennat, *CRAI* 1971, 468, l.3: 'li⟨i⟩bellum Iuliani Zegrensis litteris tuis iunctum legimus'; cf. l. 14.

to the emperors or receive letters from them, that was a rare and signal honour, which they would often advertise either verbally or on inscriptions;[32] it is not for nothing that Eusebius marks the change created by the conversion of Constantine by saying 'and bishops received letters from the emperor, and honours and gifts of money'.[33]

The delivery by messenger of letters from office-holders or privileged private persons was (we must presume) a relatively private and informal affair on which we can not expect to have much evidence. Letters from cities or other corporate bodies might also on occasion be sent on by provincial governors;[34] but this was an exception and alternative to the normal practice of their formal and public presentation by embassies. The two processes of the receipt of embassies and the receipt and despatch of letters were closely linked; so for instance Dio illustrates the prominence of Agrippina as the wife of Claudius by saying that she took part in receiving embassies, and wrote letters to communities, governors and kings.[35]

Once an embassy had gained a hearing before the emperor, which might involve considerable delays and frustrations, the essential was that one chosen member of it should make a suitable oration, which accompanied the actual handing-over of the letter or decree of the city or other body. So Augustus wrote to Cnidus in 6 BC, 'Your ambassadors . . . presented themselves to me in Rome and, having handed over the decree, made their accusation . . .'[36] The same procedure was followed on less contentious occasions: in the following year, when Gaius Caesar assumed the *toga virilis*, the council and people of Sardis voted 'to send ambassadors from among the most distinguished men to offer greetings from the city, to hand over to him [Gaius] a copy of this decree, sealed with the public seal, and to address Augustus on matters of common interest to Asia and to the city'.[37] The emperor was expected to make a brief speech, or at least some suitable remarks, in reply. We do not have the text of any such speech, and our sources tend to preserve only passing examples of notable remarks, such as Tiberius' reply to an embassy from Ilium which arrived somewhat belatedly to console him for the death of his son Drusus: 'I too am grieved by your misfortune in losing your outstanding citizen, Hector.'[38]

In the case of an embassy which was essentially formal, or at any rate was making requests which were not disputed by any other embassy or individual, the speech and the handing over of the letter or decree concluded the public business. Documentary and other evidence, primarily the

---

[32] pp. 469–72.

[33] *HE* x, 2, 2.

[34] For a governor deciding to send on the decree of a city rather than let an embassy take it, see Pliny, *Ep.* x, 43–4; a similar situation in Philo, *Flacc.* 12/97–103 (except that Flaccus withholds it for his own purposes), and in *Leg.* 38/301–4, except that it is not explicitly mentioned that the letter was sent on by Pilatus. For inscriptional references to decrees or letters sent on by governors or procurators see e.g. Abbott and Johnson, *Municipal Administration*, nos. 100, 101; *IGBulg.* 659; *IGR* III 739 = *TAM* II. 3, 905 (the Opramoas dossier) passim.

[35] LXI, 3, 2 (21).

[36] *Syll.*³ 780 = Sherk, *Roman Documents*, no. 67, ll. 5–8: οἱ πρέσβεις ὑμῶν . . . ἐνέτυχον ἐν Ῥώμῃ μοι καὶ τὸ ψήφισμα ἀποδόντες κατηγόρησαν . . . See further p. 443.

[37] *Sardis* VII, 1, no. 8, para. 1, ll. 17–20; cf. pp. 385–6.

[38] Suetonius, *Tib.* 52, 2.

8*

imperial letters which regularly followed, frequently refers to this public presentation of the decree; the rhetor 'Menander' concludes his advice on the model speech of an ambassador by saying 'then you will request him to agree to accept the decree'.[39] Alternatively the decree might be presented first, as when Claudius writes to Alexandria, 'Your ambassadors presented me with the decree and spoke at length about the city.'[40] More important, the emperors themselves quite frequently refer to their reading the decree or other document which had been given to them.[41] At what stage they would do so is not clear, though a fragmentary papyrus *appears* to show an emperor (Trajan or Hadrian) in the course of dealing with an embassy reading a letter in public, and then summoning his advisers and one of the ambassadors.[42] At any rate it is clear that at some stage subsequent to the initial public reception an imperial reply in the form of a letter would be written, and would be taken back by the same embassy. The letter (if favourable) would often be recorded on an inscription at its destination; the inscriptions occasionally refer also to the formal reception of the letter, as when an ambassador sent by Stratonicea-Hadrianopolis in Mysia received a letter from Hadrian in Rome on 1 March 127, and presented it to the magistrate of the city in an assembly on 12 May.[43]

If on the other hand some matter was in dispute between two or more embassies, or between an embassy, representing a city, and an individual, then the hearing took on a form not significantly different from that of the emperor's legal hearings (*cognitiones*). Decrees might still be presented by one or more parties, speeches would be made on either side, and there might be exchanges and arguments between them and the emperor. He would then consult his *assessores* and announce his decision or verdict. We may consider these procedures more closely later, in the context of the emperor's legal and semi-legal hearings (that is those which did, and those which did not, involve points of Roman law as such).[44] For the moment the essential fact is that the spoken verdict or decision of the emperor was followed by letters to the parties concerned. These two elements are very clearly marked in the letter of Domitian to the magistrates and council of Falerii.[45] A dispute had arisen over the occupation of land between them and

---

[39] Spengel, *Rhet. Graec.* III, 423–4. For documentary examples *ILS* 140 (Pisa); *P. Oxy* 2435, ll. 40–1, 44; *IGR* IV 1042 (Tiberius to Cos); *AE* 1929 100 = *SEG* XI 922 (Tiberius to Gytheum); Dunant, Pouilloux, *Rech. sur l'hist. et les cultes de Thasos* II, no. 179 (Claudius to Thasos); *IGR* IV 1124 = *Syll.*³ 810 = *ILS* 8793 (Nero to Rhodes); *IGR* IV 1033 (Hadrian to Astypalaea); *Forsch. in Ephesos* II, pp. 125–6, no. 26 (Caracalla to Ephesus).

[40] *Corp. Pap. Jud.* 153, col. II, l. 20.

[41] *IG* VII 2711 = *ILS* 8792 (Gaius to Panhellenes): ἀναγνοὺς [τὸ δο]θέ[ν] μοι ὑπὸ τῶν ὑμετέρων πρεσβευτῶν ψήφισμα. Cf. e.g. *Syll.*³ 831 = *IGR* IV 349 (Hadrian to the *synodos* of *neoi* in Pergamum); *Syll.*³ 832 (Hadrian to Astypalaea); *Syll.*³ 837, see Robert, *Hellenica* VI, 80–4 (Hadrian to Stratonicea-Hadrianopolis); *Syll.*³ 850 (Antoninus Pius to Ephesus); unpublished letter of Commodus from the theatre at Aphrodisias.

[42] *P. Oxy* 2177 = Musurillo, *Acts of the Pagan Martyrs* X, ll. 59f. The phrase ὁ δὲ Καῖσαρ ἀναγνο[ὺς] τὴν γραφεῖσαν ἐπιστο[λήν] *might* however show him reading not a letter from the city (Alexandria or Athens), but one which had been composed for him or dictated by him.

[43] *Syll.*³ 837; revised text in L. Robert, *Hellenica* VI, 80–4.

[44] pp. 228–40.

[45] *CIL* IX 5420 = *FIRA*² I, no. 75; cf. pp. 435–6.

the neighbouring *colonia* of Firmum, and had been heard by Domitian and
his *consilium* at his Alban villa in 82. His letter, brought back by the ambassadors who conducted the case, incorporates the verdict which he had
pronounced (*pronuntiavi*); the verdict itself briefly reviews the background
and ends firmly 'for which reason I confirm the rights of the possessors'. It is
also very clear in Josephus' account of the issue over the custody of the
high-priestly robes which arose in 44/5 between the Jewish authorities and
the procurator, Cuspius Fadus.[46] Claudius informed the ambassadors
verbally that he granted their request, and gave them a letter to confirm this,
which they took to Judaea. It concludes, 'I have also written about these
matters to my procurator, Cuspius Fadus. The bearers of this letter are
Cornelius son of Ceron, Tryphon son of Theudion, Dorotheus son of
Nathaniel and Joannes son of Joannes.'

These, in broad outline, were the typical circumstances which gave rise to
the reception of letters by the emperors and the despatch of replies by them.
It has been necessary to treat these circumstances separately, because their
social contexts were very different. But it may be concluded that there is no
evidence to contradict the universal assumption of our sources that all
forms of letter addressed to the emperor normally reached him personally
without being considered previously by any person in his service, and were
then read by him.

If that much is clear, there remain very real difficulties on the other side,
the writing of the emperor's own letters. The difficulties have to be faced,
for once again they are fundamental to the nature of imperial government.
There are three questions, which cannot, and need not, always be clearly
separated: the determination of the content of an imperial letter, the
composition of the text (in Latin or Greek), and the preparation of actual
copies.

As we have seen, it was the convention, at least into the later second
century, that emperors ought at least to be able to compose their own letters
and edicts, as they should their own speeches. Moreover, it is clear that
through the same period emperors still conducted private correspondence,
which they sometimes wrote with their own hand, and probably more often
dictated.

We should have to regard as a borderline case between private and official
correspondence the confidential letters which Tiberius used to write from
Capri to Cossus Cornelius Lentulus, *Praefectus urbi* in 33–6: 'To him,
however, Tiberius wrote many things with his own hand which he judged
should not be confided even to his assistants.'[47] So perhaps is the letter
which Nerva wrote with his own hand to Trajan to announce that he was
adopting him. But with the letter which Trajan wrote with his own hand to
the senate on his accession,[48] we clearly move into the area of public correspondence. This, however, was clearly intended as an exceptional mark of
deference. Equally exceptional, in a very different way, was the autograph

[46] *Ant.* XX, 1, 1–2 (6–14); cf. XV, 11, 4 (406–7); cf. pp. 377–8.
[47] Seneca, *Ep.* 83, 15.
[48] Dio LXVIII, 3, 4; 5, 2.

letter which Constantine sent to Shapur II to demand the protection of Christians in the Sassanid empire.[49]

All these references make quite clear that it was not the normal practice for an emperor to write complete official letters in his own hand. Dictation by them, however, does seem to have been normal, at least (again) into the later second century. Suetonius describes Titus taking over most of the *officiorum cura* from Vespasian and dictating letters and composing edicts in his name,[50] and Domitian dictating a general letter for issue in the name of his procurators.[51] Similarly, Philo describes how Gaius, after reading the letter from Petronius the governor of Syria, dictated his answer to 'one of those concerned with the letters'.[52]

That seems to be all the clear and reliable evidence which is available for the *verbatim* dictation of a letter by the emperor,[53] though the *Historia Augusta* refers to Maximinus dictating a letter to the senate,[54] and Lactantius describes Licinius in 313 dictating a monotheist prayer to a *notarius*.[55] But it is probable that it was a common, if not necessarily universal, means of producing imperial letters, at least for the greater part of the period; and even later we find Ammianus referring to Constantius II dictating, or writing with his own hand, what appear to be official pronouncements.[56] It is, however, clear that there could have been a very easy development towards a procedure where the emperor merely indicated the main points of a letter, leaving the actual text to be composed by others. That possibility will be discussed below in connection with the functions of the *ab epistulis*.

Either procedure, however, still left open the possibility of some further intervention by the emperor. For instance Philo describes Gaius ordering a letter to be written to Petronius (*perhaps* an example of the latter procedure) and then 'writing on' a sentence in threatening terms.[57] In just the same way Dio describes Macrinus 'writing on' a couple of sentences of a

---

[49] Eusebius, *VC* IV, 8: φέρεται μὲν οὖν ʿΡωμαίᾳ γλώττῃ παρ' αὐτοῖς ἡμῖν καὶ τοῦτο τὸ βασιλέως ἰδιόγραφον γράμμα, μεταβληθὲν δ' ἐπὶ τὴν ʿΕλλήνων φωνήν. Text in IV, 9–13; cf. Sozomenus, *HE* II, 15, 1–5, and Theodoret, *HE* I, 24, 13–25, 11. On the question of its authenticity, which has often been questioned, see H. Dörries, *Das Selbstzeugnis Kaiser Konstantins* (1954), 125f.

[50] *Tit.* 6, 1: 'receptaque ad se prope omne officiorum cura, cum patris nomine et epistolas ipse dictaret et edicta conscriberet orationesque in senatu recitaret etiam quaestoris vice.'

[51] *Dom.* 13, 2: 'pari arrogantia, cum procuratorum suorum nomine formalem dictaret epistulam, sic coepit "dominus et deus noster hoc fieri iubet".'

[52] *Leg.* 34/258–60: τίνι τῶν πρὸς ταῖς ἐπιστολαῖς ὑπέβαλε τὰς πρὸς Πετρώνιον ἀποκρίσεις. In the context it seems clear that 'dictated' (Smallwood) is correct as against 'gave one of his secretaries instructions about answering Petronius' (Loeb). Cf. Isocrates, *Or.* XII, 231: οὐ πρότερον ἐπαυσάμην, πρὶν ὑπέβαλον τῷ παιδὶ τὸν λόγον, ὃν ὀλίγῳ μὲν πρότερον μεθ' ἡδονῆς διῆλθον.

[53] The use made in *JRS* LVII (1967), 13, and *The Roman Empire and its Neighbours* (1967), 80, of *Dig.* 1, 18, 8 (Salvius Julianus) to illustrate both dictation by the emperor and the presence of legal advisers at the time, unfortunately resulted from an over-hasty reading of the passage, which reads in full: 'Saepe audivi Caesarem nostrum dicentem hac rescriptione "eum qui provinciae praeest adire potes" non imponi necessitatem proconsuli vel legato eius vel praesidi provinciae suscipiendae cognitionis, sed eum aestimare debere, ipse cognoscere an iudicem dare debeat.' Julianus therefore heard the emperor *interpreting* the significance of a common form of *subscriptio*, *not* dictating such a thing.

[54] *Max.* 12, 5.

[55] *De mort. pers.* 46, 5.

[56] XV, 1, 3.

[57] *Leg.* 42/333–4. The expressions are κελεύει γραφῆναι and προσγράφει.

very personal tone at the end of a letter to the senate.[58] It is not clear whether either writer means to imply that the emperors concerned made these additions with their own hand; but if they did, it would give some weight to a detailed description of the handling of correspondence in the highly unreliable *Life of Severus Alexander*:[59]

> He always gave up the afternoon hours to subscribing and reading letters, with the *ab epistulis*, ⟨*a*⟩ *libellis* and *a memoria* always in attendance . . . the *librarii* and those in charge of the *scrinium* reading back everything, so that Alexander could add whatever was necessary in his own hand, but always on the basis of the opinion of whoever was regarded as the more learned.

This passage again raises the question which will be discussed later, of the role of various assistants and advisers in preparing the emperor's written pronouncements.[60] But while it may be evidence that emperors sometimes added substantial points with their own hand, it is much more certainly a reference to the established custom of 'subscribing' a letter by adding at the bottom not a signature but a greeting. Indeed it is precisely the presence of a formula of address at the beginning and of the greeting at the end which distinguishes a letter proper among imperial *rescripta* from a mere *sub-scriptio* in answer to a *libellus*.[61] Like the letters of Hellenistic kings or of republican or imperial provincial governors, a typical imperial letter would open with an address in the form 'The emperor (name and titles) to the magistrates, council and people of (name of place) *salutem dicit* (*chairein*)', and end, originally, with a greeting in a single word, *valete* (*eutucheite* or *errôsthe*).

The essential fact is that the 'subscribing' of such a greeting seems to have been by convention something which should be done with the emperor's own hand.[62] Plutarch for instance describes Caesar subscribing letters while at dinner with Lepidus on the night before the Ides of March.[63] Thereafter our external evidence for the process is slight. Dio claims that Plotina subscribed the early letters of Hadrian to the senate, and the *Historia Augusta* that Marcus Aurelius would pass the time at public spectacles by reading or listening to something or subscribing.[64] It is probable that this latter reference concerns letters rather than *libelli*, as it is also in the very clear and definite statement of Diocletian and Maximian in 292: 'We lay down that authentic and original *rescripta* themselves, sub-scribed by our hand, and not copies of them, should be placed in official

---

[58] LXXVIII, 36, 5: ἔπειτα καὶ τοιόνδε τι προσενέγραψεν.

[59] *HA, Sev. Alex.* 31, 1.

[60] pp. 223–8, 248–52.

[61] This was shown in the classic article by U. Wilcken, 'Zu den Kaiserreskripten', *Hermes* LV (1920), 1, on which all subsequent discussions, including this one, depend.

[62] There is also some evidence, all relatively late, of the same convention in official letters by other persons: e.g. *ILS* 4175, a letter of the *XVviri sacris faciundis* of 289 ending: 'Optamus vos bene valere. Pontius Gavius Maximus promagist⟨er⟩ suscripsi'; *CSEL* LXV, 172–3, a letter of Liberius, bishop of Rome, of 357 ending: 'et manu ipsius, "Deus te incolumem custodiat".' Note also *ILS* 7259 of AD 149.

[63] *Caesar* 63, 7: ἔτυχε μὲν ἐπιστολαῖς ὑπογράφων, ὥσπερ εἰώθει, κατακείμενος.

[64] Dio LXIX, 1, 4; *HA, Marc. Ant.* 15, 1.

files.'[65] From a little later we have the quite explicit evidence of the letter of Licinius and Constantine to Dalmatius in 311, on the privileges of soldiers and veterans: sent from Serdica, it will certainly in fact have been a letter by Licinius, and it will be his hand which is referred to in the closing formula, 'and in the divine hand: "Farewell Dalmatius, dearest to us".'[66]

In the long series of imperial letters in Eusebius' *Life* of Constantine there is only one explicit reference to a subscription in the emperor's own hand. Before giving the vast letter of 324, of which copies were addressed to all the eastern provinces, Eusebius says of his text: 'It is taken from the authentic royal law preserved among us, of which the subscription in his own hand is like a seal guaranteeing the trustworthiness of his words.' In fact the only subscription to this letter is not a greeting but an instruction, 'Let it be posted up in our eastern regions.'[67] A general letter such as this in fact performed more the functions of an edict.[68] But the large number of Constantine's letters to specific addressees preserved by Eusebius and other sources characteristically end, as do other Christian letters of the period, with an extended greeting formula.[69] In one case the text carries the closing formula, 'and in another hand: "God will preserve you, beloved brothers" ';[70] we can be reasonably certain that 'another hand' refers to that of the emperor. This extension of the greeting formula, first apparent in imperial letters to individuals from the second and early third centuries,[71] may explain why the *Historia Augusta* regards it as a sign of laziness on the part of Commodus that his subscriptions often consisted only of 'Vale'; that would in fact still have been quite normal.[72]

It is thus quite clear that the emperor was both in principle and in practice personally involved in the production of imperial letters. When Philostratus in his novel on Apollonius of Tyana makes his hero come at dawn to Vespasian's residence in Alexandria in 69/70, and hear that the emperor has been long since awake and 'at the letters', that is entirely appropriate to the reality of the emperor's business.[73] The production of the letters also

---

[65] *CJ* I, 23, 3: 'sancimus, ut authentica ipsa et originalia rescripta et nostra (ex nostra or ex nostra etiam, MSS) manu subscripta, non exempla eorum, insinuentur.' The meaning of 'insinuare' in this context is uncertain. The translation offered here is derived from the letter of Anullinus, proconsul of Africa, to Constantine in Augustine, *Ep.* 88, 2: 'scripta caelestia maiestatis vestrae ... devotio mea apud acta parvitatis meae insinuare curavit.'

[66] *FIRA²* I, no. 93: 'et manu divina: "vale, Dalmati carissime nobis".'

[67] *VC* II, 23: τῆς αὐτοῦ δεξιᾶς ἔγγραφος ὑποσημείωσις; text 24–42, ending προτεθήτω ἐν τοῖς ἡμετέροις ἀνατολικοῖς μέρεσιν.

[68] See pp. 319–20.

[69] Compare for example Cyprian, *Ep.* 9, 2, 2: 'opto vos, fratres carissimi, semper bene valere', with Constantine's letter in Optatus, App. IX: 'valete voto communi per saecula iubente deo, fratres carissimi.'

[70] Gelasius, *HE* III, 19, 43 = Opitz, *Athanasius Werke* III.1, doc. 34. Cf. Athanasius, *Ad Episc. Aeg.* 23, ἄλλη χειρί, followed by greeting, in a letter of Constantius II of 356; cf. also *CJ* I, 1, 8, 39.

[71] e.g. Caracalla's letter to Aurelius Julianus of Philadelphia, *IGR* IV 1619b = *Syll.*³ 883, cf. p. 115; for an extended formula in a codicil of appointment of a procurator by Marcus Aurelius, cf. p. 288.

[72] *Com.* 13, 7; for this interpretation see *JRS* LVII (1967), 14. We find just ἔρρωσθε for instance on Commodus' letter to the Eumolpidae, *Syll.*³ 873, see A. E. Raubitschek, *Hesperia* Supp. VIII (1949), 285. The simple εὐτυχεῖτε still appears in the letter of Decius and Herennius to Aphrodisias of 250, *MAMA* VIII 424.

[73] *V. Ap. Ty.* V, 31.

depended on him; a little earlier, according to Suetonius, Nero responded to the news of the revolt of Vindex by issuing no rescripts or orders for eight days.[74]

The question cannot rest there, for the emperor did not work in isolation, and those who surrounded him cannot but have had some influence on the content and composition of his letters. But to specify the precise roles of such advisers or assistants in relation to imperial letters is remarkably difficult. As regards his equestrian and senatorial *consilium*, almost all our evidence on their role relates to the judicial work of the emperor. But at least in the case of letters arising from disputes between embassies, which, as has been mentioned, were heard in a form not materially different from that for legal cases proper, we can be reasonably sure that some *amici* normally attended the emperor, and that their opinions will have been heard before a letter was written. But any more precise relationship of any *amici* to these or other letters is very hard to document.

It is noticeable for instance that Suetonius describes Vespasian having his friends admitted *after* he had read the letters and *breviaria*;[75] it remains quite obscure whether he consulted them about letters to be written by him. It is possible to attest some marginal cases where the *amici* are concerned with written pronouncements or missives of the emperor; none is perhaps more marginal than the engaging tale in Macrobius of how the *amici* who accompanied Trajan persuaded him to consult the oracle at Heliopolis in Syria before invading Parthia; the god received consultations in sealed *diplomata* or *codicilli*, which were duly sent.[76] We shall also see one case which *may* show an emperor's legal advisers discussing the answer (*sub-scriptio*) to a *libellus*.[77] As regards the reception of letters by the emperor, Juvenal, in his satire on Domitian's *consilium*, implies that they would properly have been summoned if for instance an urgent letter had arrived from a distant province.[78] Only one document containing written imperial decisions has attached to it what is certainly a list of *amici*;[79] this is the *Tabula Banasitana*, where the explicit role of the twelve persons named is that of having witnessed (*signaverunt*) an official copy from the *commentarius* (record) of grants of Roman citizenship.[80] This necessarily implies that the senators and *equites* concerned had been physically present at some stage in the preparation of the dossier; but it leaves quite obscure the question as to whether they had dealt collectively with the preceding correspondence (an *epistula* with a *libellus* attached), or had had any influence on the emperor's decision.

[74] *Nero* 40, 4.

[75] p. 209. The same sequence in *HA, Sev. Alex.* 31, 1–2 (p. 221).

[76] *Sat.* I, 23, 14–16, cf. p. 468.

[77] pp. 248–9.

[78] *Sat.* IV, 148–9: 'tamquam ex diversis partibus orbis anxia praecipiti venisset epistula pinna.'

[79] Two imperial letters mention a number of imperial *employees*; first a letter of Commodus to Athens, see A. E. Raubitschek, *Hesperia*, Supp. VIII (1949), 287f. = *AE* 1952 6; J. H. Oliver, *AJPh* LXXI (1950), 177f.; F. Grosso, *La lotta politica al tempo di Commodo* (1964), 217f.; and the letter of Caracalla to Ephesus, *Forsch. in Eph.* II, pp. 125–6, no. 26. The former also mentions Acilius Glabrio, but whether *qua* consul (i.e. for dating purposes) or as an *amicus*, remains obscure in the fragmentary state of the text.

[80] pp. 261–2.

We have to accept that our wholly inadequate evidence does not reveal any immediate and positive role of the *amici* in the production of imperial letters. Our situation is not markedly better when we turn to the 'secretarial' posts of *ab epistulis* and later *magister epistularum*. But some points are clear. First, as we saw earlier, a large proportion of the holders of these posts, especially that of *ab epistulis Graecis*, had qualifications which were essentially literary, whether predominantly scholarly or rhetorical.[81] Secondly, there is even clearer evidence for the *ab epistulis* than for other imperial 'secretaries' personally accompanying the emperor on his travels and campaigns.[82] This was a natural consequence of the fact that embassies continued to approach the emperor, and his letters continued to be written, wherever he happened to be.

Indeed, from the father of Pompeius Trogus onwards, the titulature of imperial 'secretaries' continues intermittently to show a link between embassies and letters,[83] right down to the Late Roman *Notitia Dignitatum*, or List of Offices.[84] Here, in the section on the *magistri scriniorum*,[85] we find clear statements about the functions of these officials, of a sort entirely lacking in our period:

> *Magister memoriae:* dictates and gives out all *adnotationes*, and replies to petitions (*preces*).
> *Magister epistolarum:* deals with embassies from cities, enquiries (*consultationes*) and *preces*.
> *Magister libellorum:* deals with *cognitiones* (judicial hearings) and *preces*.
> *Magister epistolarum graecarum:* those letters which are customarily given out in Greek, he either dictates himself or, if dictated in Latin, translates into Greek.

Confining ourselves for the moment to the *epistulae*, it may be convenient to work back from this probably early fifth-century source to see how far any such positive functions are attested in our period. Then too, the problem will necessarily be significantly different with regard to letters in Greek. First, as regards the role of the *ab epistulis* proper, we have already seen some indications of the volume of correspondence generated by embassies from the cities; an anecdote in Dio shows Narcissus, who was *ab epistulis*, at Claudius' side while he heard an embassy from Bithynia.[86] Secondly, if there was any real continuity of function, the *consultationes* which the *Notitia* mentions are likely to have been letters from provincial governors asking for advice or rulings from the emperor, often on legal points. It is relevant here that when Statius gives his sketch of the duties of Domitian's *ab epistulis*, Abascantus,

---

[81] pp. 85–94.
[82] pp. 6, 79, 90–3.
[83] e.g. Ti. Claudius Balbillus, *ad legationes et res[ponsa]*—or *re[scripta—Graeca]*, Pflaum, *Carrières*, no. 15, see p. 86; Dionysius, ἐπὶ τῶν ἐπιστολῶν καὶ πρεσβειῶν καὶ ἀποκριμάτων, Pflaum, no. 46, see p. 87.
[84] O. Seeck, *Notitia Dignitatum* (1876). For the date see Jones, *Later Roman Empire*, 1417f.; G. Clemente, *La Notitia Dignitatum* (1968).
[85] *Or.* XIX (Seeck, pp. 43–4); less fully in *Oc.* XVII (pp. 161–2).
[86] LX, 33, 5.

he concentrates on the nature and subject-matter of the letters themselves, and almost all of what he says implies that the correspondence is with governors—he mentions the sending of *mandata*, military news, recommendations for promotion and so forth.[87]

But in spite of all that Statius says, he gives no indication of the precise role played by Abascantus in relation to this correspondence; nor is there any clearer indication in Suetonius' report that Augustus punished his *a manu* Thallus for 'betraying' a letter[88]—presumably he showed it to some unauthorized person. The episode may suggest that the role of the *ab epistulis* was more essentially concerned with the custody or despatch of imperial correspondence than its composition. Such a theory might be supported by Dio's report that Narcissus, in virtue of being *ab epistulis*, had charge of secret letters of Claudius against Agrippina and others, which he burnt after the emperor's death.[89] By contrast when Manilius, the *ab epistulis Latinis* of the pretender Avidius Cassius, was traced after many years, Commodus burned the letters which he offered to reveal.[90]

Such a function might explain why, even though the emperor essentially composed his own letters, we find imperial slaves and freedmen continuing into the second century to have positions entitled *ab epistulis*, or later *proximus ab epistulis Latinis* and *adiutor ab epistulis Latinis*.[91] Such a hypothesis—and it cannot be more, since not one of these inscriptions illustrates the functions of the man concerned—would still fail to explain how learned men of equestrian rank came to occupy the position of *ab epistulis* (*Latinis*). Horace, as we saw, was unsuccessfully invited by Augustus specifically to assist (in what way is not clear) with his personal correspondence.[92] The functions of the equestrian *ab epistulis* of the later first century onwards can hardly have been so limited. But the fact remains that we have no positive evidence to show them composing imperial letters in Latin to set against the convention that the emperor should write his own. Their role may have been advisory, or supervisory or even essentially honorific, and thereby an indication of the value placed on literary culture by all, the emperor included. But we do not know.

Indeed even the *Notitia* does not represent the *magister epistolarum* as actually composing or dictating imperial letters, and in this it offers a clear contrast with the *magister epistolarum graecarum*, who either dictated the actual text of the Greek letters or translated a Latin text. For in this case the question of the composition of the text was one of quite a different order.

---

[87] *Silvae* V, 1, 86–100.

[88] *Aug.* 67, 2.

[89] LX, 34, 5: τὰ γὰρ γράμματα τοῦ Κλαυδίου, ὅσα ἀπόρρητα κατά τε τῆς Ἀγριππίνης καὶ κατὰ ἄλλων τινῶν, οἷα τὰς ἐπιστολὰς αὐτοῦ διοικῶν, πάντα προκατέκαυσεν.

[90] LXXI, 7, 4 (288).

[91] e.g. *CIL* VI 8596: 'Ianuarius Caesaris Aug. ab epistulis'; VI 8597 (age 16); 8598–601; 8603 = *ILS* 1670; 8604 = *ILS* 1519; 8605; *ILS* 1944 (two Flavian *ab ep.*); VI 8610: 'Flavio Alexandro Aug. lib. ab epistulis Latinis'; 8611; XIV 2840; *ILS* 1667: 'M. Ulpio Aug. lib. Vernae ab epistulis Latinis'; VI 8609: *ILS* 1669: 'prox(imus) ab epistul(is) Lat(inis)'; VI 8612–13 (age 19): 'adiutor ab epistulis Lat(inis)'; *ILS* 1671: 'scriniarius ab epistulis'; note also VI 4249: 'Ti. Iuli Agat(h)opodis stator(is) a epis[t]'.

[92] p. 85.

The problem was not one of a simple ignorance of Greek; virtually all the emperors of the period were familiar with Greek literature and could converse in Greek, and some, like Marcus Aurelius, could compose in it *in extenso*. Rather it was, exactly as with imperial speeches in Greek, the necessity of producing a text which would live up to the exacting standards of grammar and vocabulary expected of public pronouncements in the Greek world. Thus, as we saw, even Augustus, who was a highly literate man, would write in Latin a speech for delivery in Greek and have it translated.[93] Similarly Eusebius, immediately after describing how Constantine made a speech in Latin at Nicaea, with an interpreter repeating it in Greek, emphasizes that he could and did subsequently converse with the bishops in Greek.[94]

We do not hear of imperial 'secretaries' of free birth concerned with pronouncements in Greek until the reign of Claudius; and in neither of the two cases is the man's title entirely clear. Ti. Claudius Balbillus was concerned with embassies and either *res[ponsa]* or *res[cripta]* in Greek, depending on how the fragmentary inscription is restored;[95] the latter is more likely. Stertinius Xenophon was concerned with *apokrimata* in Greek, which later meant specifically *subscriptiones*. We cannot state with any confidence what form of imperial pronouncement an *apokrima* was in this early period.[96]

In the reign of Nero we at last come upon an *ab epistulis Graecis* at work, concerned, as we might expect, with embassies. In the course of a long dispute over their respective rights, embassies from the Greek and Jewish communities in Caesarea were sent by the procurator Felix to Nero; while they were in Rome the Greek embassy bribed Beryllus, the former *paedogus* of Nero and 'entrusted with the *taxis* in relation to the Greek letters', to ask Nero for a letter invalidating the rights of the Jews. Beryllus petitioned the emperor and gained his request that the letter should be written.[97] It is clear that the whole episode takes place within Nero's household, for, as a former *paedagogus*, Beryllus was almost certainly a freedman. The decision about the contents of the letter is Nero's; but it is perhaps implied that it itself could then be written by Beryllus. None the less the expression *taxis* used of his role, which reappears again in a letter of Commodus in relation to Greek letters, and possibly also in one of Caracalla,[98] probably does not imply this so much as 'arrangement' or 'ordering'. *Syntaxis*, which may be the correct reading in Caracalla's letter, would on the other hand mean 'composition'.

[93] p. 204.

[94] *VC* III, 13, 1-2.

[95] p. 86.

[96] See p. 86; on *apokrimata / subscriptiones* see p. 243.

[97] Details on p. 378. The crucial passage is *Ant.* xx, 8, 9 (183-4): καὶ τῶν ἐν Καισαρείᾳ δὲ οἱ πρῶτοι Σύρων Βήρυλλον, παιδαγωγὸς δ᾽ ἦν οὗτος τοῦ Νέρωνος τάξιν τὴν ἐπὶ τῶν Ἑλληνικῶν ἐπιστολῶν πεπιστευμένος, πείθουσι πολλοῖς χρήμασιν αἰτήσασθαι παρὰ τοῦ Νέρωνος αὐτοῖς ἐπιστολὴν ἀκυροῦσαν τὴν Ἰουδαίων πρὸς αὐτοὺς ἰσοπολιτείαν. καὶ Βήρυλλος τὸν αὐτοκράτορα παρακαλέσας ἐπέτυχε γραφῆναι τὴν ἐπιστολήν.

[98] See p. 223. In Commodus' letter we have, ll. 16-17: [Αὐρήλιο]ς Λάριχος, ὁ φίλος μου καὶ τὴν τάξιν τῶ[ν Ἑλληνικῶν ἐπισ]τολῶν πεπιστευμένος. In Caracalla's, ll. 18-19: Αἴλ. Ἀντίπατρος, ὁ φίλος μου καὶ διδάσκαλος κ[αὶ τὴν σύντα?]ξιν τῶν Ἑλλη[νι]κῶν ἐπιστολῶν ἐπιτετραμμένος.

The man to whom Caracalla refers, Aelius Antipater, was a well-known sophist, and as we have seen it is beyond doubt that he and other representatives of the Second Sophistic were given the position of *ab epistulis Graecis* in virtue of their oratorical powers.[99] In the second and early third centuries our sources also make quite clear that these Greek sophists actually composed at least some imperial letters in Greek. So for instance Philostratus writes of Antipater:[100]

> For my part let me here openly express my opinion that, though there were many men who both declaimed and wrote historical narrative better than Antipater, yet no one composed letters better than he, but like a brilliant tragic actor who has a thorough knowledge of his profession, his utterances were always in keeping with the imperial rôle. For what he said was always clear, the sentiments were elevated, the style was always well adapted to the occasion, and he secured a pleasing effect by the use of asyndeton, a device that, in a letter above all, enhances the brilliance of the style.

The close connection of letter-writing with rhetoric, the importance of a correct classical vocabulary in both, and the fact that it could be claimed that the influence of an *ab epistulis Graecis* went beyond words to the substance of imperial decisions, are all evident in what Phrynichus says to Cornelianus, to whom he dedicated his work on Attic vocabulary, and who was an *ab epistulis* either of Marcus and Verus or Marcus and Commodus. After describing how Cornelianus as an orator had so 'Hellenised and Atticised' the imperial court-room that even the other speakers had not dared to use inappropriate words, he continues: 'Therefore the kings of the Romans thought you worthy of the highest honours, and set you to manage all the affairs of the Greeks, placing you beside them as a guardian, in theory appointing you as *ab epistulis*, but in reality choosing you as a partner in their kingship.'[101]

Once again we cannot discern the precise details of procedure, which were no doubt variable from reign to reign and even from moment to moment. But the *ab epistulis Graecis* clearly formed part of the immediate entourage of the emperor, and some of them may well have exerted a personal influence. As for their precise functions, we can do no better than the alternatives presented by the *Notitia Dignitatum*—dictating Greek letters (to express an imperial decision) or translating letters already written in Latin.

Legal sources occasionally indicate that imperial letters to Greek cities or provincial councils were written in Greek,[102] or quote from rescripts in Greek.[103] Though a universal rule cannot be proved, we should assume that the scores of imperial letters inscribed in Greek in Greek cities were sent in

[99] pp. 91–3; note also the reference in Philostratus, *V. Ap. Ty.* I, 12, to Maximus of Aegae, ἠξιώθη δὲ καὶ βασιλείων ἐπιστολῶν οὗτος εὐδοκιμῶν τὴν φωνήν.

[100] *VS* II, 24, Loeb trans.

[101] Phrynichus, *Ecolga*, p. 379 Lobeck; CCCLVI Rutherford. The chronological sequence here was not appreciated in *JRS* LVII (1967), 16. For other references in this work to Cornelianus as *ab epistulis*, see p. 225 Lobeck/CCIII Rutherford and p. 92.

[102] e.g. *Dig.* V, 1, 37; XVI, 1, 2, 3 (addressee not specified); XLVIII, 3, 3.

[103] e.g. *Dig.* I, 16, 4, 5; XLIX, 1, 1, 1; XLIX, 1, 25 = *P. Oxy.* 2104 (Severus Alexander to the *koinon* of Bithynia).

that language, and not translated at their destination; for one imperial letter, addressed to an individual, is inscribed in Latin with a Greek translation,[104] while other dossiers visibly preserve letters in their original language, whether Latin or Greek.[105] So, in view of the constant pressure of Greek embassies, the imperial letters in Greek must have represented a considerable and continuous volume of work. Moreover we must imagine that copies were taken and kept; Constantine, for instance, writing to the synod of Antioch, says that he is appending a copy of a letter which he had written to the congregation there.[106] In view of these facts the inscriptional evidence for freedmen *ab epistulis Graecis* is extraordinarily slight.[107]

In the course of the third century we also lose sight of individual *ab epistulis*, or *magistri epistularum*. But the pronouncements of Constantine show clearly that the three main *scrinia* in his *comitatus* were those of the *memoria*, the *epistulae* and the *libelli*;[108] and we catch occasional hints of the *scrinium epistularum* at work, as when Constantine writes to the bishops at Tyre that he has 'gladly ordered this to be written to you'.[109] The letter itself, with its description of Athanasius' petition to him outside Constantinople, and his remarks on his role in spreading Christianity among the barbarians, could hardly be more personal, and must in some sense have been composed by the emperor. But it will certainly, like his orations, have been translated at court, and sent out in Greek. The function was a crucial one; when Eunapius writes of a sophist who was put in charge of the Greek letters by Julian that the 'royal tongue' was entrusted to him, it is something more than a mere metaphor.[110] But we must rest content to be clearer about the importance of the position, and the honour it conferred on its learned holders, than about the precise manner in which its functions were performed. So indeed was Firmicus Maternus when he wrote his work on astrology at the end of Constantine's reign: a certain position of the stars 'will produce learned secretaries of kings, or men to whom the task of dictation is entrusted, prominent for their great rank and honour'.[111]

3. *Imperial Hearings: Verbal Decisions and Verdicts*

From the very beginning the giving of justice was an essential element in the role played by the emperors. That it was essentially a matter of routine, and not of decisions on major cases of exceptional interest, was involuntarily demonstrated by Claudius, who was liable to fall asleep in the process,

---

[104] *CIL* III 412 = *IGR* IV 1404 (Smyrna).

[105] e.g. *CIL* III 12283 = *IG* II² 1099 (Hadrian and Plotina on the rules for the Epicurean school in Athens, see p. 504); *IGR* IV 571 = *OGIS* 502 etc., re-edited by U. Laffi, *Athenaeum* XLIX (1971), 3 (Hadrian's ruling on the lands of Zeus at Aezani, see pp. 328–9).

[106] Eusebius, *VC* III, 62, 1.

[107] *CIL* VI 8606 = *ILS* 1668; 8607–8.

[108] *CJ* XII, 28, 1–2; cf. p. 109.

[109] Athanasius, *Apol. c. Arian.* 86, 9: ἀσμένως ταῦτα γραφῆναι πρὸς ὑμᾶς προσέταξα. See p. 605.

[110] *VS* 497.

[111] *Math.* VIII, 25, 6: 'faciet litteratos scribas regum, vel quibus dictandi committatur officium, magno nobilitatis honore perspicuos.'

causing the *advocati* to raise their voices to wake him. On one occasion, while giving justice in the Forum of Augustus, he was attracted by the smell of lunch being prepared for the Salian priests in the nearby temple of Mars, descended from his tribunal, and joined them at the meal.[1]

When our sources refer to the continuance of imperial business in periods of mourning or festivity, or during campaigns, they almost always make a specific mention of jurisdiction.[2] In Rome many of the emperors up to Hadrian gave judgment in public from a tribunal, often in the Forum; it is quite clear that this was a deliberate procedure to evoke popular favour, and avert rumour.[3] It was while Claudius was giving judgment (*iura reddentem*) in the Forum in 51 that an angry mob assailed him to complain of corn prices, so that only his escort of soldiers enabled him to escape through the door into the Palatium.[4] Outside Rome, on journeys or campaigns, emperors continued to give judgment or receive embassies, seated on tribunals erected in the open. Suetonius records that while Vitellius was giving judgment on his tribunal at Vienne after his proclamation in 69, a cock settled on his shoulder and then on his head;[5] while Dexippus shows us Aurelian seated on his tribunal to receive an embassy from the Juthungi in Pannonia in 270.[6] Such tribunals must usually have been temporary structures, though in the late fourth century a tribunal used by Trajan was still preserved at Ozogardana in Persia.[7]

Alternatively, we find Claudius in a dangerous crisis, trying his wife's lover, C. Silius, from a tribunal in the praetorian camp.[8] More significant was the tendency which we have seen for the emperor's jurisdiction to be withdrawn within the Palatium, or other residences in Rome or Italy, and eventually within the 'palaces' which developed elsewhere.[9] This process clearly aroused suspicion and resentment in the first century. Tacitus even shows us the trial of Valerius Asiaticus in 47 taking place 'within the bedroom' of Claudius,[10] and records Nero's speech promising that he 'would not be the judge of all cases, and thus swell the power of a few by shutting accusers and accused into a single house'.[11] By the second century it is clear

---

[1] Suetonius, *Claud*. 33.

[2] See e.g. ibid., 14; Dio LX, 5, 7 and 25, 8 (Claudius); LXXVI, 7, 3 (362), Severus during an illness of Caracalla; Herodian III, 14, 9, Geta left in the province of Britain δικάσοντά τε καὶ τὰ πολιτικὰ τῆς ἀρχῆς διοικήσοντα while Severus and Caracalla were on campaign there. For Marcus Aurelius see pp. 4–6.

[3] e.g. Suetonius, *Aug*. 93: 'cum postea ... pro tribunali ... cognosceret'; Dio LVII, 7, 2–5 (Tiberius in the Forum); LX, 4, 3 (Claudius, in the Forum and elsewhere); LXVI, 10, 5 (Vespasian, in the Forum); Suetonius, *Dom*. 8, 1: 'ius diligenter et industrie dixit, plerumque et in foro pro tribunali extra ordinem'; Dio LXVIII, 10, 2 (Trajan, in the Forum of Augustus, the Porticus Liviae or elsewhere, from a tribunal). The motive is quite explicit in what Dio says of Hadrian, LXIX, 7, 1, his judging in the Palatium, Forum or Pantheon and elsewhere from a tribunal, ὥστε δημοσιεύεσθαι τὰ γιγνόμενα.

[4] Tacitus, *Ann*. XII, 43, 1; Suetonius, *Claud*. 18, 2.

[5] *Vit*. 9.

[6] Jacoby, *FGrH* 100 F. 6 (2)–(3).

[7] Ammianus XXIV, 2, 3. For Trajan acting from a tribunal during the Parthian campaigns see e.g. Dio LXVIII, 19, 3; 30, 3.

[8] Tacitus, *Ann*. XI, 35, 2.

[9] ch. ii.

[10] *Ann*. XI, 2–3; cf. Dio LX, 29, 4–6. This is the only attested instance of a trial *intra cubiculum*.

[11] XIII, 4.

that there was a regular *auditorium* in the palace, where the emperors gave justice; and similar *auditoria* are attested at least at Sirmium and Antioch.[12] However, even from the beginning, hearings within the palace, or any other residence, were not necessarily sinister and secretive affairs, but could be formal sessions of a semi-public nature.

We can see what is already a significant step towards such a pattern in the second session which Augustus held to decide the future of Judaea after Herod's death in 4 BC; it was held at the temple of Apollo which, as we saw, had been built by Augustus in close association with his Palatine house.[13] At the hearing Augustus was attended by a *consilium* of 'his own friends and the most prominent Romans'; before him there appeared a Jewish delegation of fifty persons, with a large crowd of supporters from the local Jewish community, and a delegation or delegations from the Greek cities, seeking liberation from Herodian rule.[14] In Josephus' account there was first a speech against Herod and his sons from a member of the Jewish embassy and then one in defence of them by Nicolaus of Damascus. Augustus is then described as dismissing the session, and announcing a few days later the decision to divide the kingdom.

This account has features which will prove to be characteristic of the way imperial business was done. The hearing has a formal and semi-public character, and takes the form of a contest between the conflicting parties, in the shape of orations by their representatives. Though this is not explicit here, it will be shown that such speeches were always directed to the emperor himself, and that if there were any verbal exchanges in addition they were invariably between him and the parties concerned. A *consilium* was always present, but the threatening remarks of Bassaeus Rufus to Herodes Atticus in the case at Sirmium before Marcus Aurelius[15] appear to provide the only instance where a person in attendance on the emperor intervenes publicly and addresses himself to one of the parties in a case. We must presume however that the *consilium* was subsequently consulted, though this too is not explicit; the decision is announced by the emperor individually as his own. We do have some brief indications of how the emperor collected the opinions (*sententiae*) of his advisers in legal cases, and from later juristic sources some invaluable accounts of the content and nature of such discussions; but these show quite clearly that the role of the *consilium* was essentially advisory. The verdict or decision was in fact as well as in form that of the emperor himself.[16]

It is impossible to make a clear distinction between contested hearings between embassies on the one hand and legal cases on the other, if only because there is abundant evidence of issues over rights or duties where an

---

[12] pp. 6, 121.

[13] On the temple, pp. 19–20. For the session, Josephus, *BJ* II, 6, 1–2 (80–92), and more fully in *Ant.* XVII, 11, 1–4 (300–23).

[14] Josephus omits this essential item, which we know from the account of Nicolaus of Damascus, *FGrH* 90 F. 136 (8)–(11), and which explains Augustus' action in detaching Gaza, Gadara, and Hippus and attaching them to Syria, *Ant.* XVII, 11, 4 (320).

[15] Philostratus, *VS* II, 1; pp. 5, 122.

[16] pp. 237–9.

individual, whether a king, a Roman official or a private person, confronted an embassy from a community. This is quite clear for instance in Augustus' reference in his second Cyrene edict to the fact that an embassy from Cyrene had accused someone of removing public statues of the emperor; the investigation which Augustus says he will make must have involved a hearing with both sides present.[17] So we may consider together the various types of contested or accusatory hearings conducted by the emperor; but also consider separately at the end the limited but invaluable evidence for the subsequent private sessions at which the emperor heard the opinions of his advisers.

As we have seen, our very slight evidence suggests that it was normal for emperors to conduct their hearings in the morning,[18] and Dio supports this in relating how Domitian rose from the court-room (*dikastêrion*) and lay down to rest for the afternoon 'as was his custom'.[19] Equally slight evidence seems to make clear that an order of hearings was established in advance, though acutely subject, like everything else, to imperial whims. Suetonius notes that when embassies arrived from Greek cities bringing Nero crowns for his notional victories in musical contests, they were not only admitted first but invited to dinner.[20] It is clear that there were very frequently, and perhaps almost at any moment, embassies waiting to be heard. This was the situation for instance when Philo's delegation came to Gaius in 40. They greeted him on arrival just as he was proceeding out of the gardens of Agrippina in Rome, and he sent one Homilus, 'in charge of embassies' to tell them that he would hear their case when he was free. Philo rightly doubted the sincerity of the promise, since embassies had arrived 'from almost every land'.[21]

We have remarkably little evidence specifically showing the emperor appointing a day when a particular hearing would take place. But we do find occasional reflections of events in a waiting period between the arrival of the parties and the moment of the hearing itself. Both appear in a complex issue in 52 involving the Jews, Samaritans and the procurator Cumanus. They 'received a day' from Claudius when the dispute would be heard, but in the meantime the emperor's friends and freedmen inclined him towards Cumanus and the Samaritans, and only the influence of Agrippa II with Agrippina led Claudius in the event to give a fair hearing.[22] In the same way, a few years earlier, Agrippa had influenced Claudius, before the formal hearing, to grant the request of a Jewish embassy for custody of the high-priestly robes.[23] Similarly, Philostratus shows a Thessalian sophist named Philiscus travelling to Rome in 212/13 to defend himself against a claim that

[17] *FIRA*² I, no. 68, ii. Augustus writes ἕως ἂν περὶ τούτου τοῦ πράγματος διαγνῶ, the normal equivalent for *cognoscere*.
[18] pp. 209–10.
[19] LXVII, 17, 1.
[20] *Nero* 22, 3.
[21] *Leg.* 28/181–3. Compare the very fragmentary papyrus, 'The Gerousia Acta', Musurillo, *Acts of the Pagan Martyrs*, no. iii, col. ii, ll. 7–8, where a delegation seems to be greeted by a *cubicularius* of Tiberius. For a further section of this text *ZPE* xv (1974), 1.
[22] Josephus, *Ant.* xx, 6, 2–3 (131–6); cf. *BJ* II, 12, 6–7 (242–6). See p. 378.
[23] *Ant.* xx, 1, 1–2 (8–14).

he was liable to liturgies in his home city, and using the interval to acquire influence with Caracalla's mother, Julia Domna, and thence the chair of rhetoric at Athens. Here too the emperor was aware of the case in advance, and ordered 'the man in charge of cases' (*a cognitionibus*) to inform Philiscus that he must speak in his own defence.[24] Again, Philostratus himself was present with Caracalla in Gaul later in 213, when Heliodorus 'the Arab', as ambassador for his native city, was called in to present his case earlier than he expected and found that 'the official who called in the cases' (presumably the *a cognitionibus* again) would allow no delay.[25]

Philostratus' experience of the imperial court may afford us some justification for using his account of the trial of Apollonius of Tyana before Domitian, which, though entirely fictional in itself, should not be misleading in its framework and assumptions. Here too a day is appointed, in this case some five days in advance. Apollonius, who has been in prison, is brought to the court-room in the palace by an imperial 'secretary' (*grammateus*), as soon as the sun has risen and the leading men of Rome are admitted. The emperor has prepared himself by reading the documents of the case, while Apollonius has composed an oration which he intends to deliver by the water-clock which was customarily used; but in the event the trial proceeds by the emperor interrogating Apollonius point by point. When Apollonius astounds all present by vanishing, the emperor is left to try to collect his wits and deal with the next case—convincingly represented as a suit brought by a city against an individual in connection with a will—and cannot remember either the names of the parties or the nature of the issue; it is clear that he is supposed to have had some advance information on both.[26]

Philostratus' stories represent almost all the evidence which we possess on the duties of the *a cognitionibus*, except for Dio's anecdote, mentioned earlier, of Severus instructing an *a cognitionibus* to call the next case, and the man replying that he cannot do so without the orders of Plautianus, the praetorian prefect.[27] The anecdote possibly relates, like others retailed along with it, to Severus' journey from the east in 200–2, for it is clear that staff concerned with *cognitiones* accompanied the emperor everywhere.[28] The few inscriptions recording imperial freedmen concerned with *cognitiones* reveal nothing further about their functions. The titles of equestrain *a cognitionibus* of the late second and early third centuries show a conjunction between *cognitiones* and *libelli*, or *cognitiones* and *epistulae Latinae*. Much the same appears in the case of Marcius Claudius Agrippa, who was made *a cognitionibus* and *ab epistulis* by Caracalla. But any hope of the insight for which we usually have to depend on literary sources is baffled by Dio's remark that he was removed, by promotion to the senate, for admitting immature boys into the army.[29]

While such puzzles remain, we can be certain that the *a cognitionibus* will

[24] *VS* II, 30; cf. p. 439.
[25] II, 32; cf. *JRS* LIX (1969), 12–13.
[26] *V. Ap. Ty.* VII, 40–1; VIII, 1–6 (the 'trial'); 7 (Apollonius' 'oration'); 9 (the following case).
[27] Dio LXXV, 15, 5 (354). Cf. p. 129.
[28] For this and what follows cf. pp. 106–7.
[29] LXXVIII, 13, 4 (417).

have been among the 'chiefs of the *officia*' who attended Caracalla in the one imperial hearing of which an authentic and reasonably extensive record remains, the case of the Goharieni heard at Antioch at the end of May 216. The record begins:[30]

> In the consulship of Sabinus and Anulinus, on the [sixth?] day before the Kalends of June at Antioch, when Imp. Caesar M. Aurelius Pius Felix Augustus Parthicus Maximus Britannicus Maximus Ge[rmanicus] Maximus, having been saluted by the praetorian prefects, *e*(*minentissimi*) *v*(*iri*), also by the *amici* and the *princ*(*ipes*) *officior*(*um*), had taken his seat in the *auditorium*, he ordered to be admitted Aurelius Carzeus son of Sergius the *defensor* of the Goharieni acting against Avidius Hadrianus the contractor, which *cognitio* the emperor deigned to undertake . . .

There follows a verbal exchange conducted in Greek between the *advocati* of the two sides and the emperor. Its relevance to the question of how cases reached the emperor will have to be considered later,[31] but for the moment we may emphasize that, while the emperor is attended by officials and *amici*, it is he alone whom the *advocati* address, and he alone who conducts the exchanges with them in the public hearing. The same pattern appears in less detail in the papyrus record of Severus' hearing of an Egyptian embassy in Alexandria on 9 March 200.[32] The fact that the emperor takes his seat in the *dikastêrion*, or court-room, is a significant further indication that the legal and non-legal hearings of the emperor were conducted in the same context. Severus is accompanied by 'his friends and those called to the *consilium*',[33] but when the ambassadors have made their oration presenting the requests of the Egyptians, it is the emperor who replies. The same pattern can be attested virtually throughout the period. Another papyrus contains both a letter of Augustus to Alexandria written in 10/9 BC—'the ambassadors whom you sent having come to me in Gaul'— and the opening of their speech, beginning with the words 'Caesar, unconquered hero'.[34] Similarly the so-called '*Boulê*-papyrus' contains the speech of an Alexandrian ambassador to one of the early emperors, with what survives of his reply—'About this I shall make a decision.'[35]

From the period of the tetrarchy the *Codex Justinianus* preserves the remains of the protocol of the hearing of an embassy from Antioch by Diocletian:[36]

> Part of the *acta* of the Augusti Diocletian and Maximian, Ides of February . . . When Firminus and Apollinarius had been brought in, with other leading citizens of Antioch in attendance, Sabinus said . . . [fragmentary traces of speech in Greek].

[30] *AE* 1947 182 = *SEG* XVII 759; see also p. 121.
[31] p. 535.
[32] *P. Oxy.* 3019.
[33] p. 121.
[34] *P. Oxy.* 3020.
[35] Musurillo, *Acts of the Pagan Martyrs*, no. i = *Corp. Pap. Jud.*, no. 150.
[36] *CJ* x, 48, 2.

Diocletian: To the holders of certain ranks we have granted an exception (*indulgentia*) from city and personal obligations, that is to those who are ex-*protectores* or ex-*praepositi*. Those therefore will not be summoned to perform personal or city obligations.

Even the relatively formal type of hearing associated with the appearance of embassies was subject to many vagaries depending, like everything else, on the character and attitudes of the emperor himself. The famous scene when Philo's embassy finally appeared before Gaius in 40 is only the extreme case. Here Gaius answered their greeting with a contemptuous reference to their disbelief in his divinity, causing the rival Alexandrian embassy to dance with joy and shower divine titles on the emperor, and its leader Isidorus to interject an accusation of their not having sacrificed for Gaius' recovery from illness. The rest of the hearing, as Philo describes it, was an erratic verbal exchange conducted while Gaius was inspecting the buildings in his gardens.[37]

Philostratus' *Lives of the Sophists* provides several cases where the course of the hearing was materially affected by the personal predilections or antipathies aroused in emperors by orators who came before them. Alexander, 'the Clay-Plato', from Seleucia, went so far as to say to Antoninus Pius, 'Pay attention to me, Caesar', only to be answered with 'I am paying attention, and I know you well. You are the fellow who is always arranging his hair, cleaning his teeth and polishing his nails, and always smells of myrrh.'[38] Similarly, when Philiscus made his appearance before Caracalla, his manner and dress gave offence to the emperor, who kept on interrupting in the time allotted to him by the water-clock, and making rude observations about him. Philiscus lost his case for exemption from city obligations.[39] By contrast Heliodorus, 'the Arab', won immediate favour from Caracalla by his ready reaction to being called in earlier than he expected, and without his colleague; he was granted an equestrian dignity on the spot by the emperor and then took advantage of the moment to give a display of impromptu oratory. Caracalla gave him the theme, 'Demosthenes after breaking down before Philip defends himself on the charge of cowardice'; the emperor, moreover, 'not only showed himself in a friendly mood, but also secured applause from the others present by looking sternly at those who failed to applaud'.[40]

Our evidence on imperial hearings includes, potentially at least, the papyri which we call collectively the 'Acts of the Pagan Martyrs', the texts of which exhibit again these same features, the emperor attended by a *consilium* of *amici*, and the actual proceedings being conducted in the form of verbal exchanges, sometimes of an abusive and disorderly sort, between the parties and the emperor.[41] But even if the narratives in these papyri are partly or

[37] *Leg.* 44–5/351–67.
[38] *VS* II, 5, Loeb trans.
[39] II, 30; more fully on p. 439.
[40] II, 32, Loeb trans.; cf. p. 281.
[41] Musurillo, *Acts of the Pagan Martyrs*, esp. nos. iv ('Acta Isidori'); viii ('Acta Hermaisci'); ix ('Acta Pauli et Antonini'); x ('Acta Athenodori'); xviii ('Acta Heracliti').

wholly fictional, the pseudo-documentary form in which they are cast tends to imply that formal records of imperial hearings and *cognitiones* were in fact kept; an implication which is surely confirmed by the more sober papyrus records of Alexandrian embassies before emperors, as it is by the inscriptional record of the case of the Goharieni and by the *acta* of Diocletian and Maximian. If the parallel evidence for hearings in Egypt is any guide, records of proceedings using direct speech began to be kept in the first century, and full verbatim records based on shorthand notes perhaps in the time of Diocletian.[42]

In fact we have almost no evidence about the recording of imperial hearings. But we may note that when an embassy from Cnidus put a particularly complex case before Augustus in 6 BC, he referred the examination of some slaves to his *amicus*, Asinius Gallus, and then said in his letter to the city, 'I have sent you also (a copy of) the interrogations themselves.'[43] It was certainly possible, as we should expect, to have copies made of documents brought by embassies; Hadrian, for instance, writes to the *gerousia* of Ephesus that he has sent a copy of their decree to the proconsul.[44] It may well be that the copying of documents and recording of hearings formed a significant part of the responsibilities of the 'secretaries' concerned with *cognitiones* and the hearing of embassies; but we do not know.

As we saw, the hearing of embassies seems normally to have ended with a verbal pronouncement by the emperor, followed later by the preparation of letters which the embassies took back with them. But though it was normal for a *consilium* of *amici* to be present at the public hearings, it is not at all clear at what stage they normally gave their advice. Indeed, even on difficult matters, emperors are found writing as if no *consilium* were involved at all: 'As regards the request which you have sought to gain from me I decide thus,' Claudius writes to the Alexandrines, '. . . But about the council, as to what was customary under the ancient kings, I cannot say.' Instead, he will write to the prefect of Egypt for information.[45] Moreover, although Philo, for instance, lays down categorically that it was Gaius' duty to retire and consider with his *consilium* the issue at stake between the Greeks and the Jews of Alexandria,[46] we do not in fact have a single narrative description of this being done in relation to issues posed by rival embassies. But when Vespasian writes in 78 to the magistrates and council of Sabora in Spain that he cannot decide about their request to raise new revenues, *nullo respondente*, this surely means 'as no one is able to give [me] authoritative advice'. This inscription also reveals what is evidently an exceptionally rapid completion of the business of the embassy—'I received your decree on the eighth day

---

[42] See R. A. Coles, *Reports of Proceedings in Papyri* (1966).

[43] *Syll.*³ 780 = Sherk, *Roman Documents*, no. 67, ll. 27–8: πέπονφα δὲ ὑμεῖν καὶ α[ὐτ]ὰς τὰς ἀνακρίσεις. I would now be more inclined than in *JRS* LVI (1966), 163–4, to accept Sherk's argument in *GRBS* VII (1966), 57, and loc. cit., that Asinius Gallus was currently in Rome, and was not until later proconsul of Asia.

[44] *Syll.*³ 833 = J. H. Oliver, *The Sacred Gerusia*; *Hesperia* Supp. VI (1941), no. 7.

[45] *Corp. Pap. Jud.*, no. 153, ll. 52–72.

[46] *Leg.* 44/350. As noted above, p. 119, this passage shows precisely those considerations relevant to how a judge should behave being applied to an issue which was *not* one of Roman law.

before the Kalends of August and dismissed the ambassadors on the fourth.'[47]

It may indeed be that the attendance of the emperor's *amici* at the hearing of embassies was essentially a formality, in that neither the emperor's immediate response nor the subsequent composition of the letters to the cities or other bodies involved depended on any significant consultation with them. If so, this marks a certain contrast with legal cases proper, where such consultation is attested in some detail. Dio makes a point of mentioning that the *assessores* who sat with Tiberius when he gave judgment in the Forum were free to express their own opinions;[48] a judgment of Philip the Arabian, more than two centuries later, is prefaced in the *Codex Justinianus* with 'The Emperor Philippus Augustus, having conferred with his *consilium*, said'.[49]

None the less, here too the hearing itself would be conducted by the emperor, and would involve not only speeches on either side, but verbal exchanges between himself and the parties. The procedure in a *cognitio* (literally 'enquiry') of this sort was not bound by any rules, and could be varied according to the views, or whims, of the emperor. So Quintilian mentions that mutual accusations by the two sides in a case could be admitted in a *cognitio* of the emperor or senate (but were not permissible in the public courts of Rome).[50] Nero preferred to deal separately in turn with each matter involved in a case rather than hear formal speeches (*actiones*); and precisely this procedure is found in one of the *cognitiones* of Trajan at which Pliny acted as *assessor*.[51] Hadrian held very firmly that he, and others, should rely not on written evidence (*testimonia*), but on the interrogation of witnesses: 'In that Alexander laid charges before me against Aper, and neither proved them nor produced witnesses, but wished to employ *testimonia*, for which there is no place before me (for it is my custom to interrogate the persons themselves), I have referred him back to the provincial governor . . .'[52]

The evidence which survives from these imperial hearings consists largely of notable remarks by either an emperor or one of the parties: for instance Augustus trying to prevent a man confessing to parricide (which would have meant his execution in an antique and barbarous form) by interrogating him with the words 'Surely you did not kill your father?'; a high-born Spartan, acting as the accuser of the local dynast Eurycles, rudely reminding Augustus of Thucydides' *History*, in which his ancestor Brasidas played a notable part; or the exasperated Greek litigant who in the middle of an exchange with Claudius was heard to exclaim, 'You too are an old fool!'[53] From the second century we have some apparently verbatim reports of parts

---

[47] *ILS* 6092 = Abbott and Johnson, *Municipal Administration*, no. 61 = *FIRA²* I, no. 74.

[48] LVII, 7, 2–5.

[49] *CJ* VII, 26, 6.

[50] *Inst.* VII, 2, 20. He uses the Greek term ἀντικατηγορία.

[51] Suetonius, *Nero* 15, 1; Pliny, *Ep.* VI, 22, 2: 'egit uterque pro se, egit autem carptim et κατὰ κεφάλαιον.

[52] *Dig.* XXII, 5, 3, 3; cf. ibid., 3, 1–2.

[53] Suetonius, *Aug.* 33, 1; Plutarch, *Mor.* 207 F (cf. G. W. Bowersock, *JRS* LI (1961), 115–16); Suetonius, *Claud.* 15.

of hearings; for instance the *Sententiae et Epistulae divi Hadriani* contains two brief exchanges involving a party to a suit, an *advocatus* and the emperor.[54] Cassius Dio gives in direct speech the oration of a senator tried before Severus for having supported his rival Pescennius; typically, it is addressed to the emperor, in the second person singular, and refers to the *amici* acting as *assessores* in court in the third person.[55]

Our fullest verbatim report from this period comes from the *Digesta* of the jurist Marcellus, and concerns a case heard by Marcus Aurelius in 166 at which he himself was evidently acting as adviser. Whether he relied on his own recollection or notes, or on an official transcript, is not clear. The report runs in part as follows:[56]

> Vibius Zeno said: I beg you, lord emperor, to hear me patiently; what will you decide about the legacies?
> Antoninus Caesar said: Do you think that the testator wished his will to be valid when he erased the names of the heirs?
> Cornelius Priscianus, the advocate of Leo, said: It was the names (only) of the heirs he erased.

The custom that hearings should be conducted personally by the emperor continued into the fourth century, though our evidence from the later period is much more sparse. The *Codex Theodosianus* however contains a dialogue between Constantine, speaking in Latin, and a female litigant, speaking in Greek. The case concerned something which the woman had bought from someone who was alleged to have acquired it illegally, because he was holding office at the time:[57]

> Agrippina said: He is not in office in that place.
> Constantinus Augustus said: But it is laid down by law that no one established in office may acquire anything, and whence makes no difference, whether in his own district or another, since it is laid down that he has acquired it in a way which is against the law;
> and he added: Are you unaware that whatever persons in office have acquired is made fiscal property?
> Agrippina said: He was not *praepositus* of that place. I made the purchase from his brother. Here are the deeds of sale.
> Constantinus Augustus said: Codia and Agrippina will recover the appropriate price from the vendor.

In this instance Constantine gives his verdict apparently without consulting a *consilium*. But in earlier centuries at least such consultation is very well attested; its precise form, once again, depended on the emperor. On occasion the *consilium* went through procedures which sound very like those of a regular jury reaching a majority verdict. Augustus, for instance, in

[54] *Corp. Gloss. Lat.* III, p. 33, ll. 37f.; p. 34, ll. 48f.
[55] LXXIV, 9 (333–4).
[56] *Dig.* XXVIII, 4, 3, trans. P. A. Brunt, *JRS* LVI (1966), 80–1; the case is also referred to in *Dig.* XXXIV, 9, 12. Cf. also pp. 163, 533.
[57] *CTh* VIII, 15, 1.

judging a case in which a will had been falsified 'gave those who were judging with him not only two *tabellae*, of condemnation or acquittal, but a third, by which a pardon might be given to those who were proved to have been led to sign by fraud or misunderstanding'.[58] There is no subsequent reference to the issuing of tablets with different verdicts, which the *assessores* were to give in according to their opinion. But Josephus speaks of Claudius 'giving the vote' to his *amici* on what should be done with Cassius Chaerea, the murderer of Gaius (though it is not at all clear that this was in the context of anything resembling a trial).[59] Alternatively, Nero would not conduct a verbal discussion among his *amici*, 'but had each of them give his opinion in written form; these he read silently and in private and then gave a verdict according to his own inclination, as if it were the view of the majority'.[60] Under such a procedure it is clear that Nero neither was nor could be bound by the opinion of the majority; but it leaves open the question of whether he ought in principle to have been so bound.

The same indeterminacy is present in Pliny's descriptions of the more normal procedure of Trajan, by which at the conclusion of a *cognitio* he asked the opinions (*sententiae*) of his *consilium* verbally, and then announced his decision *ex consilii sententia*.[61] But the evidence of jurists who served on the imperial *consilium* in the second and early third centuries makes quite clear that their role was purely advisory. The emperor might or might not be persuaded by their arguments, but the verdict was his. Indeed in the case from 166 recorded by Marcellus Marcus Aurelius had all parties withdraw (*remotis omnibus*), and after he had deliberated had them readmitted to hear him pronounce his verdict: 'The present case seems to admit of the more humane interpretation . . .'[62]

Paulus mentions in some detail three cases where he argued for a particular interpretation, but where the emperor (Severus) preferred a different view, and so ruled (*pronuntiavit*),[63] and one where his own view seems to have prevailed: 'But our emperor was moved by the consideration of fairness and by the words of the will . . . (but) when I put forward considerations

---

[58] Suetonius, *Aug.* 33, 2: 'non tantum duas tabellas, damnatoriam et absolutoriam, simul cognoscentibus dedit, sed tertiam quoque, qua ignosceretur iis, quos fraude ad signandum vel errore inductos constitisset.' This is regarded by J. M. Kelly, *Princeps Iudex* (1957), 12–13, and J. Bleicken, *Senatsgericht und Kaisergericht* (1962), 71, as an example of Augustus taking part in a regular *quaestio*. But the role of the emperor and the context in Suetonius' *Vita* show that this was his own *cognitio*.

[59] Josephus, *Ant.* XIX, 4, 5 (268): συναγαγὼν τοὺς ἑταίρους ψῆφον ἀνεδίδου περὶ Χαιρέου. This and the other passages relating to the emperor's *consilium* are given by W. Kunkel, 'Die Funktion des Konsiliums in der magistratischen Strafjustiz und im Kaisergericht II', *Zeitschr. Sav.-St.* LXXXV (1968), 253, on pp. 304–7 = *Kleine Schriften* (1974), 178f. His no. 2, Josephus, *Ant.* XVI, 6, 2 (163), should be omitted, as it comes from an *edictum* issued after an embassy (see p. 257).

[60] Suetonius, *Nero* 15, Loeb trans. The same method is proposed in the 'speech of Maecenas' in Dio LII, 33, 4.

[61] *Ep.* IV, 22, 3: 'cum sententiae perrogarentur, dixit Junius Mauricus . . .'; in VI, 31, 12 the decision announced *ex consilii sententia* after consultation of the *amici* is not an actual verdict, but a ruling that the *heredes* should either pursue the case or face charges of *calumnia*.

[62] *Dig.* XXVIII, 4, 3, cf. p. 237.

[63] *Dig.* IV, 4, 38 *pr.*; XIV, 5, 8 ('sententiam conservavit imperator'); XXXII, 27, 1. The last two passages, but not the first, are given by Kunkel, o.c., 305–6.

from the *lex Aelia Sentia* and certain other points, he ruled (*pronuntiavit*) against the petitioner.'[64] In another case the emperor gives a verdict in a will case which differs from both of the two contrary opinions given by Papinian and Paulus.[65]

Paulus' evidence comes from his three books of 'Decreta' or imperial verdicts; for 'decretum' was the normal term for the verdict pronounced verbally by the emperor at the conclusion of a case. The term, and its Greek equivalent *epikrima*, could also be used of individual decisions in non-legal matters.[66] So for instance Valerius Maximus says that Augustus concluded a case by ordering in his *decretum* that a man could take possession of his paternal property.[67] Though *decreta* were in the first instance verbal, they were naturally recorded in writing; both aspects appear in Callistratus' report, copied twice in the *Digest*, of a *decretum* of Marcus Aurelius which was still in existence (*exstat*); when it was pronounced, the losing party blurted out 'I have committed no violence', to be answered by the emperor with, 'Do you think that it is violence only when men are wounded? . . .'[68] *Decreta*, like letters, might also be translated into Greek at court for despatch to the interested parties. In the document (perhaps an edict rather than a letter) containing his judicial decisions, which was inscribed in Athens, Marcus Aurelius adds a postscript, saying 'It occurred to me, when all this material concerned with what had been judicially decided had been put together in the Greek language . . .'[69]

A *decretum* was thus a personal pronouncement by the emperor, and could bear a highly individual character. Aulus Gellius read the *decretum* in which Hadrian ruled that a child born to a woman in the eleventh month after her husband's death could be legitimate—'in that *decretum* Hadrian says that he has ruled so after seeking out the opinions of ancient philosophers and doctors'.[70]

Thus our sources do not mislead us in regarding all verdicts reached in the emperor's court as being essentially actions of the emperor himself; a notable category of such verdicts was, as we have seen, those condemnations believed to have been made for the sake of the property of the condemned.[71] The same applied to all aspects of the handling of the cases; Augustus for instance recorded in his *Autobiography* (which covered only the period down

---

[64] XXXVI, 1, 76, 1.

[65] XXIX, 2, 97; Kunkel, o.c., 306.

[66] See *RE* s.v. 'decretum'; L. Wenger, *Die Quellen des römischen Rechts* (1953), 415. For some republican examples see Aulus Gellius, *NA* VI, 19, 4–8. For the uses of ἐπίκριμα see L. Robert in *Ant. Class.* XXXV (1966), 406–7. For its use in one of the unpublished triumviral documents from Aphrodisias see *JRS* LXIII (1973), 57.

[67] Valerius Maximus VII, 7, 3; cf. also *Dig.* XXXVI, 1, 23 *pr.*: 'decrevisse igitur divum Marcum refert (Scaevola).'

[68] *Dig.* IV, 2, 13 = XLVIII, 7, 7. In *Coll.* XV, 2, 4, however, a *rescriptum* of Marcus Aurelius to a provincial governor is described as a *decretum*.

[69] J. H. Oliver, *Marcus Aurelius: Aspects of Civic and Cultural Policy in the East, Hesperia* Supp. XIII (1970), Plaque E, ll. 94–5. Cf. C. P. Jones, *ZPE* VIII (1971), 161, on pp. 182–3. See now the valuable paper by W. Williams, 'Formal and Historical Aspects of Two New Documents of Marcus Aurelius', *ZPE* XVII (1975), 37.

[70] *NA* III, 16, 12.

[71] pp. 163–74. Note Pliny to Trajan, *Pan.* 80, 1: 'non tu locupletando fisco operatus sedes, nec aliud tibi sententiae tuae pretium quam bene iudicasse' and cf. ibid., 36.

to 24 BC) that it had not been his practice to deny to their families the bodies of those condemned to death.[72]

The main significance of the imperial jurisdiction, however, does not lie in the executions of political enemies, or even of rich men for their wealth, but in its routine nature and often insignificant subject-matter, whose very unimportance reflects his subjects' conception of him as a source of law and justice. Such a conception appears with equal clarity in the similarly routine duty imposed on him of answering the *libelli* which they presented to him.

4. *Answers to Written Petitions:* Libelli *and* Subscriptiones

When Julius Caesar was assassinated in the senate on the Ides of March 44 BC, he was holding in his hand a *libellus* giving information on the conspiracy. A man, whom Plutarch names as the philosopher Artemidorus of Cnidus, had presented it to him on his way through Rome to the senate-house; but not having time to read it, he arrived still holding it, along with others which he had received. Plutarch adds the circumstance that Caesar handed the *libelli* to his attendants, but, urged by Artemidorus, kept this one and would have read it but for the crowd of persons petitioning him.[1]

Any small written document or even literary work could be called a *libellus*, and it is only in the sense of a document presented to an office-holder for his attention that it came to have the more limited sense of written petition or request.[2] The *libellus* which Artemidorus presented to Caesar contained information, and perhaps accusations of the conspirators; and warnings and accusations continued to be given in this form to the emperors. Gaius on one occasion refused to accept a *libellus* offered to him with information concerning his safety, proclaiming that he had done nothing for which he could be hated by anyone.[3] Domitian took a different view, and was actually murdered by an imperial freedman, while he was reading a supposed *libellus* about a conspiracy which the man had just handed to him.[4] Such documents could also, in normal circumstances, be stored up for later use; Pliny the Younger was later to claim that a *libellus* accusing him had been found in Domitian's *scrinium* after his murder.[5]

But already in the late republic we see the presentation of *libelli* becoming a characteristic means of approaching office-holders for favours or benefits. In 48 BC Q. Cassius Longinus, when governor of Spain, was murdered as he

[72] *Dig.* XLVIII, 24, 1 (Ulpian) = Malcovati, *Caesaris Augusti Operum Fragmenta*[5] (1969), 95, no. xviii.

[1] See Nicolaus of Damascus, *FGrH* 90 F. 130 (xix) (66), where the story is given from hearsay (φασὶ δέ τινες), and the document is called a γραμματίδιον; Suetonius, *Jul.* 81, 4: 'libellumque insidiarum indicem ab obvio quodam porrectum libellis ceteris, quos sinistra manu tenebat, quasi mox lecturus commiscuit'; Plutarch, *Caes.* 65, who calls it a βιβλίδιον. Cf. Appian, *BC* II, 116/486–7, where Artemidorus attempts to warn Caesar, but is not the man who gives him the βιβλίον, and Dio XLIV, 18, 3. On Artemidorus cf. p. 84.

[2] For an excellent survey see G. Samonati in *Diz. Epig.* s.v. 'libellus'.

[3] Suetonius, *Cal.* 15, 4.

[4] *Dom.* 17, 1.

[5] *Ep.* VII, 27, 14.

entered the basilica at Corduba by some conspirators, one of whom pretended to be a soldier presenting him with a *libellus* containing a request.[6] Moreover, writing later in 44 BC, Cicero recalls in some detail how Atticus had composed a *libellus* asking Caesar for protection for his lands at Buthrotum, which Cicero gave to Caesar while dining with him. Caesar wrote a favourable letter to Atticus in reply, and later Cicero spoke formally before him on behalf of the Buthrotians, and obtained a *decretum* witnessed by a number of leading senators.[7]

In spite of their varying details, the accounts of what happened on the Ides of March make clear that the presentation of *libelli* to Caesar was by now an established custom. Its origins are not easy to trace, for no source seems to show later Hellenistic monarchs imitating Demetrius Poliorcetes, whom Plutarch describes receiving 'written requests' from his subjects, which he folded in his cloak—and subsequently threw, unread, into a river.[8] We cannot tell whether the formalized *enteuxeis*, or petitions, with opening and closing formulae resembling those of letters, which were addressed to the Ptolemies, and sometimes personally received by them,[9] had any parallels outside Egypt. There is certainly no visible continuity of form between the Ptolemaic *enteuxeis* preserved on papyri, and *libelli* addressed to the Emperor; nor do the brief instructions sometimes found written on *enteuxeis* resemble the imperial *subscriptiones* addressed to the petitioners, or offer any indication that they were, even in theory, the work of the king's own hand.

It was this which was the essential feature of the handling of *libelli*; as we saw before, Julius Caesar earned some popular disfavour by being seen to pass the time at public shows by reading and replying to letters and *libelli*;[10] and as we saw also, both Trajan and Marcus Aurelius are found stating that they had read and been persuaded by *libelli* from private persons sent on by provincial governors.[11]

Evidence from the early empire suggests that it was common, if not necessarily the rule, for *libelli* to be presented to the emperor in person at his *salutationes*. Suetonius relates how an intending litigant used such an occasion to get rid of his opponent: just as the other man was presenting Claudius with a *libellus*, he drew the emperor aside and informed him that the man was an assassin; he was immediately seized and executed.[12] The crowd of persons whom Martial mentions pressing *libelli* of complaint on Domitian were probably doing so at a *salutatio*, as was the man to whom he addresses an epigram, who had come from his native city to ask for the *ius trium liberorum*.[13] We cannot, however, always be certain of the context. Suetonius, for instance, places in the setting of Augustus' *salutationes* the

---

[6] *Bell. Alex.* 52, 2.

[7] *Ad Att.* XVI 16A, 2–3; 16C, 2; 16E, 1 (ed. Shackleton-Bailey, nos. 407A, C, E).

[8] Plutarch, *Dem.* 42, 4–5; cf. p. 2. Note, however, Plutarch, *Cleom.* 13, 3

[9] See P. Collomp, *Recherches sur la chancellerie et la diplomatique des Lagides* (1926), chs. ii–iv; cf. also A. Di Bitonto, 'Le petizioni al re', *Aegyptus* XLVII (1967), 5.

[10] p. 214.

[11] p. 216.

[12] *Claud.* 37, 1.

[13] *Epig.* VIII, 82 and 31.

9

anecdote of his saying to a man who offered his _libellus_ with apparent timidity, that he was as dubious about giving it as if he were giving a present to an elephant; but Quintilian, writing a little earlier, describes the man as a soldier, and does not associate the exchange with a _salutatio_.[14]

It is at least clear, however, that the petitioner, if not the contents of his _libellus_, was greeted verbally by the emperor. Three brief and enigmatic anecdotes in the _Sententiae et Epistulae Divi Hadriani_ show something more than this, the emperor responding verbally to the actual substance of _libelli_ presented in person by the petitioners; but the brevity of the accounts makes it unclear whether the petitioners had accompanied the presentation of their _libelli_ with a verbal explanation (as ambassadors did when presenting the decree of a city) or whether, as is less likely, the emperor had looked at the _libelli_ on the spot.[15] Philostratus' novel on Apollonius of Tyana does however represent Vespasian as putting the philosopher Euphrates to shame by reading our aloud his written petition (described as a letter) asking for money for himself and others; but the point of the episode is that Euphrates had expected the emperor to keep it to read in private.[16]

Essentially, however, a _libellus_, as a written document addressed to the emperor, received a written reply. We shall look more closely later at the form and content of _libelli_, in the context of the approaches made by private persons to the emperor.[17] It will suffice to say here that while _libelli_ could be of considerable length they lacked the formal characteristics of letters: they began just with 'To (name of emperor) from (petitioner or petitioners)', with no formula of address such as 'salutem (dicit)', and with no closing formula. The emperors' answers (of which many more examples survive), called _subscriptiones_ because they were, at least in principle, written under the petitions themselves, were frequently very brief and were correspondingly informal, beginning simply '(name of emperor) to (petitioner)'; and were equally devoid of any closing formula of greeting.

As a general rule it is clear that while cities, provincial assemblies, Roman officials and important private persons addressed the emperor in letters, village communities and all less important individuals did so by _libelli_.[18] But almost all our evidence about the _libellus-subscriptio_ procedure belongs to the second century and after, and we cannot tell to what extent it was common before that. Apart from the one general statement of Suetonius that Augustus used his _signum_ for _libelli_ (which in the light of the documents from Smyrna and, less certainly, Scaptopara suggests that he did subscribe the

---

[14] _Aug._ 53, 2; _Inst._ VI, 3, 59; and cf. Macrobius, _Sat._ II, 4, 3.

[15] _Corp. Gloss. Lat._ III, p. 31, ll. 45f.: 'per libellum petente quodam ... Adrianus dixit ...'; 32, ll. 33f.: 'codicellos aliquis ⟨qui⟩ Adriano tradidit ... Adrianus dixit ...'; 34, ll. 6f.: 'per libellum dicente quodam patrem suum confiscatum esse ... Adrianus inquisivit ...' From the context it is clear that the _codicelli_ mentioned in the second episode were _libelli_; we do not know whether petitions were normally written in small folded codices.

[16] _V. Ap. Ty._ v, 38.

[17] pp. 541–4.

[18] The _libellus_ of the city of Apamea which Pliny sent on to Trajan is not a true exception, since it was at his request that they had set down their requests in _libellus_ form, _Ep._ x, 47–8; but those from Nicaea, x, 83–4 and Amisus, 92–3, do seem to have been composed by the cities spontaneously.

libelli),[19] we have until recently had only one rather enigmatic example of this being done by any of the early emperors. Plutarch retails the anecdote of a man who gave Augustus a *libellus* with the question 'Is Theodorus of Tarsus a baldhead(?) or a thief. What do you think?' The emperor read it and wrote underneath 'I think so'.[20] What the allusion, or witticism, is here remains obscure; but it is clear that the exchange takes the form of the subscription of a *libellus* by the emperor.

But now, quite unexpectedly, we have from Aphrodisias an inscription which quotes verbatim the unfavourable reply which Augustus 'wrote under' a petition from Samos; it was inscribed at Aphrodisias precisely because it explicitly preserved the uniqueness of the grant of immunity to that city.[21] As noted above, a petition and reply in this form between a city and the emperor is unusual; but rigid distinctions are not to be expected, especially at this early stage.

Thereafter, it is only with the reign of Trajan that we begin to see the system more clearly. Trajan replies to Pliny that he has read the *libellus* of a centurion, and, moved by his petition (*preces*), has granted the citizenship to his daughter: 'I have sent you the *libellum rescriptum* for you to return it to him.' If this wording is correct,[22] it should mean that an answer had been written on the *libellus* itself before its return. It is however only with the reign of Hadrian that we find the term *subscriptio* coming into regular use for this type of imperial reply. Antoninus Pius speaks of a '*subscriptio* of my father', and both his contemporary Gaius and the *Institutes* of Justinian refer to *subscriptiones* of Hadrian;[23] while a papyrus preserves the documents of a property-case heard under Hadrian and including a reply of his to an individual, which is described as an *apokrima*; on later parallels this is almost certainly a *subscriptio*.[24] The literal Greek translation of *subscriptio*, *hypographê*, appears in another papyrus, in the text of what itself is evidently a *subscriptio* of an emperor named Antoninus, probably Antoninus Pius:[25]

The emperor Antoninus to Usenophis son of [. . . . .]: I have ordered to be appended a copy of the *libellus* given to me by Valerius Zoilus, and of my *subscriptio*, being moved not only by the name of the man who presented it but also by the precedent . . .

[19] p. 247.
[20] *Mor.* 207B: ἐπιδόντος δέ τινος αὐτῷ βιβλίον, ἐν ᾧ γεγραμμένον ἦν 'φαλακρὸς ἢ κλέπτης Θεόδωρος ὁ Ταρσεύς· τί σοι δοκεῖ;' ἀναγνοὺς Καῖσαρ ὑπέγραψε 'δοκεῖ'. The text is probably corrupt.
[21] Unpublished inscription from the theatre at Aphrodisias (see p. xiii). Quoted in translation on pp. 431–2
[22] *Ep.* X, 107. 'Libellum rescriptum' is a correction for 'libellum rescripti', but is justified by comparison with *IGBulg.* 2236, l.3: '[e]x [li]bro (?) [li]bellorum rescript[o]rum' (see p. 247). See Sherwin-White, *The Letters of Pliny*, ad loc.
[23] *CJ* VII, 43, 1; Gaius, *Inst.* I, 94; Justinian, *Inst.* II, 12 *pr.*
[24] *P. Tebt.* 286 = Mitteis, *Chrestomathie*, no. 83 = *FIRA*² III, no. 100. Cf. p. 226. *ILS* 8860 distinguishes ἀποκρίματα from letters; contrast *Sardis* VII. 1, 8 (Augustan), which identifies them.
[25] *P. Rendel Harris* 67, col. ii, ll. 12f.: αὐτοκράτωρ Ἀντωνεῖνος Οὐσενώφει . . . ἀντίγραφον βιβλιδίου δοθέντος μοι ὑπὸ Οὐαλερίου Ζωίλου ὁμοίως καὶ τῆς ὑπογραφῆς μ[ο]ῦ ὑποταγῆναι ἐκέλευσα, κεινηθεὶς οὐ μόνον τῷ τοῦ ἐπιδόντος ὀνόματι ἀλλὰ καὶ πρὸς αὐτὸ τὸ παράδειγμα . . .

If our evidence is not misleading, it was thus in the first half of the second century that the subscribing of *libelli*, often but not always on points of law, became one of the primary means by which the emperor gave responses to his subjects. Certain aspects at least of this procedure are exceptionally well illustrated by legal sources, inscriptions and papyri. The legal evidence is most significant for a question which will be discussed shortly, the composition and authorship of the *subscriptiones*.[26] But it also gives some hints of the formal procedures involved. From the years 150 and 155 we have in the *Codex Justinianus* the earliest indications ('pp', short for 'proposita') of the posting up of a *subscriptio* at the emperor's current residence; in these cases the place-name has not survived.[27] It appears first in 162, under a *subscriptio* of Marcus Aurelius and Verus.[28] Thereafter such indications have survived erratically, and when they do appear are not always correct; but the papyri confirm that they are the traces of a regular practice. The indications of place become incomparably more regular in the tetrarchic period and in some years can be used to trace in detail the movements of the emperors.[29] This is particularly true of 293–4 when, for reasons which are quite obscure, the formula 'Subscripta' replaces 'P(ro)p(osita)' in referring to the place of issue of *subscriptiones*;[30] the latter is found again later.[31]

These indications gain immediately in relevance when contrasted with those which survive on papyri relating to the presence of Severus and Caracalla in Alexandria in 200.[32] A number of these give precise dates, so that we can establish a sequence over several months. Thus we have on separate papyri: '(posted) in Alexandria year 8, Mecheir 27 (22 February)'; 'posted in Alexandria year 8, Phamenoth 18, and 24 (14 and 20 March)'; another from 19 March, and two more from the month Pharmouthi (March–April).[33] Much more significant even than these, however, is the single papyrus headed 'In Alexandria, copies of the *apokrimata* posted in the stoa

---

[26] pp. 249–51.

[27] *CJ* II, 12, 1: 'PP IIII Id. Oct. Gallicano et Vetere conss.' (150); II, 1, 1 (155); note also the variant form 'accepta' in *CJ* II, 12, 2 (161).

[28] *CJ* V, 25, 3: 'PP XIII K. Mart. Romae Rustico et Aquilino conss.' For later examples, *Frag. Vat.* 267 (Rome, 205); *CJ* V, 52, 2 (Emesa, 284); and without place name *Consultatio* I, 7 (213); IX, 8 (215); *Coll.* I, 9, 1 (222); X, 8 (234).

[29] p. 47.

[30] Texts with 'subscripta' from 293 and 294: 293—*CJ* VII, 75, 4; VIII, 1, 3; 8, 2; 17, 7; *Coll.* X, 3, 1; *Frag. Vat.* 42. 294—*CJ* III, 33, 11; IV, 34, 10 = *Coll.* X, 6; VIII, 6, 1; 27, 18; *Frag. Vat.* 43; 270. For the attribution of *subscriptiones* with 'Augg. cos.' to 293 and 'Caes. cos.' to 294 see Th. Mommsen, 'Über die Zeitfolge der Verordnungen Diocletians und seiner Mitregenten', *Ges. Schr.* II, 195f., on pp. 273f. *Frag. Vat.* 34, which has 'subscripta', is dated to 313, but its address reads 'Augg. et Caess. Flaviae Aprillae', so it will more probably belong to the tetrarchs. For two cases of 'scripta' at this time, *Corp. Hermog.* I, 1; II, 1 (*FIRA*[2] II, 665).

[31] e.g. *Frag. Vat.* 32 (312); 33 (313); *CTh* I, 2, 4 (319), which is probably a *subscriptio* to a *libellus* from a private person rather than a letter to an official. In *CTh* the latter usually have the indication 'data', and the place of issue.

[32] See the full treatment of these papyri by W. Williams, 'The *Libellus* Procedure and the Severan Papyri', *JRS* LIV (1974), 86.

[33] *P. Flor.* 382, ll. 1–4 (cf. ll. 17–23, apparently the same as *P. Mich.* 529 verso, ll. 39–53, also from Mecheir of year 8; note l. 25: [ἐξ ἀπ]οκριμάτων θεῶν Σεουήρου κ[αὶ 'Αντωνίνου]); *P. Amherst* 63 = Mitteis, *Chrestomathie*, no. 376; the date 19 March is given on *P. Strasb.* I, 22 = Mitteis, *Chrestomathie*, no. 374 = Meyer, *Juristische Papyri*, no. 54; but the same *subscriptio* appears with the date 29 December 199 in *BGU* 267; *P. Oxy.* 1405; *BGU* 473 = Mitteis, *Chrestomathie*, no. 375(noi ndication of place).

of the gymnasium, year 8, Phamenoth 18 (14 March)'. Five *subscriptiones* are then given verbatim, followed by 'likewise on the 19th (15 March), posted in the same stoa', and four *subscriptiones*; finally there appears 'on the 20th (16 March) likewise', and another four.[34] The primary significance of the papyrus lies in the fact that it gives an indication of the scale of the work involved in answering *libelli*. Since there is no visible connection either in subject-matter or in the addressees, we can only suppose that the list represents all the *subscriptiones* posted on these three days. The other papyri seem to suggest that the giving of such responses went on fairly steadily, if not necessarily every day, through the first few months of 200. What was true of a period when the court was temporarily established in a major Greek city cannot of course be assumed for a period of travel or campaigning. But if emperors typically gave *subscriptiones* at a rate of four or five per day—as they did on these three successive days—even on less than one day in two, this will still have meant that they answered several hundred *libelli* per year.

We owe the survival of those *subscriptiones* to the accident of Severus and Caracalla having stayed for some time in Egypt.[35] There is no reason to suppose that imperial responses were not given in exactly the same form elsewhere. One such is indeed perfectly preserved on papyrus, a *subscriptio* given in 239 by Gordian III, who is not known to have left Rome in this year:[36]

> [The divine] Gordian Augustus to Nero Pudens. The omission of the registration of children neither makes these illegitimate if they are legitimate, nor if persons are outside the family, can registration introduce them into it. July 8, in the consulship of Gordian and Aviola.

The *subscriptiones* preserved on papyrus are either private copies made for unknown purposes, or are quoted in records of legal proceedings. An example of the latter is the response of Constantine and his sons addressed in 326–33 to a town councillor named Agrippinus (one of relatively few *subscriptiones* to private persons surviving from the period after 305), which is quoted in the course of a case held in 340.[37] They are thus excellent evidence for the verbal form of *subscriptiones*, and their typical brevity (the thirteen answers from 14–16 March 200 run to either one or two sentences each);

[34] *P. Columbia* 123, published by W. L. Westermann and A. A. Schiller, *Apokrimata: Decisions of Septimius Severus on legal Matters* (1954); text revised by H. C. Youtie and A. A. Schiller, 'Second Thoughts on the Columbia Apokrimata (P. Col. 123)', *Chron. d'Eg.* xxx (1955), 327, whence (without a reference) *SB* 9526.

[35] There are other *subscriptiones* of theirs which are less precisely dated, e.g. the two in *P. Oxy.* 1020 = Meyer, *Juristische Papyri*, no. 17; see for other possible cases Westermann and Schiller, o.c., 27–30. See also now N. Lewis, 'A Fragment of a Severan Constitution', *Bull. Am. Soc. Pap.* vi (1969), 17, ll. 6–8, and *P. Oxy.* 3018.

[36] *P. Tebt.* 285 = Mitteis, *Chrestomathie*, no. 379. The appearance of θεός shows that this copy was made after Gordian's death. I translate the document slightly differently from the editors of *P. Tebt.* They draw attention to the closely similar *subscriptio* preserved in *CJ* vii, 16, 15 (from 293).

[37] *FIRA*² iii, no. 101 = *SB* 8246; published by C. J. Kraemer and N. Lewis, 'A Referee's Hearing on Ownership', *TAPhA* lxviii (1937), 357, who unfortunately take βουλ(ευτῆι) to mean 'Roman senator', and therefore both mistake the social level of the petitioner and deduce that the original must have been in Latin.

and they also confirm beyond question the custom of 'posting up' the answers in public in the emperor's current city of residence. The question of the original language of the *subscriptiones* is less clear, as of course are all details about the actual handling of the *libelli* and composition of the *subscriptiones* in the immediate vicinity of the emperor. All the papyrus copies of *subscriptiones* mentioned so far are in Greek, but one of them is explicitly described as a translation from the Latin;[38] that such replies *could* be originally in Greek is perhaps suggested by Callistratus' quotation in the *Digest* of a Greek *subscriptio* of Pertinax.[39]

Rather more light is thrown on these questions by the few well-known inscribed texts of *libelli* and *subscriptiones*; but many problems remain, not least because the original stones of two of the most important texts have disappeared since they were copied. These difficulties at least do not arise in the clearest of these texts, the long inscription from the province of Africa, most of which is taken up with the *libellus* of the *coloni* of an imperial estate (the *saltus Burunitanus*) concerning the wrongdoings of the procurators, and addressed to Commodus.[40] They had indeed already received one imperial *subscriptio*, evidently from Marcus and Commodus (*vestramq[ue] divinam subscriptionem*), which the procurator had ignored. In answer to their long exposition Commodus gives the following answer, which is immediately afterwards referred to as 'the *sacra subscriptio* of our lord, the most sacred emperor, which, when it had been given to his *libellus*, Lurius Lucullus' [text breaks off]:[41]

> Imperator Caesar M. Aurelius Commodus Antoninus Augustus Sarmaticus Germanicus Maximus to Lurius Lucullus and others. The procurators, having regard to my rules and customs, will see to it that nothing is wrongly exacted from you in contravention of the standing regulations. [and in another hand] I have written it. I have checked it.

Commodus' reply was thus very brief, and confined to an unhelpful restatement of an established rule. Moreover it is clear that two persons were involved in the actual writing-down of the *subscriptio*. Certainty is impossible, but it seems most likely that the one-sentence reply was dictated, and that whoever dictated it then read it through, and wrote *scripsi, recognovi* as an authentication. The same two words appear in the much-damaged inscription apparently containing a *subscriptio* of Caracalla in Latin to a *libellus* in Greek from the college of Paeanistae in Rome, which itself quotes an earlier Latin *subscriptio* of Severus.[42]

[38] *P. Rendel Harris* 67, see p. 243 above. Col. ii, l. 11 has ὁμ(οίως) ἑρμηνεία ʽΡωμα[ϊ]κῶν κατὰ τὸ δυνατόν.

[39] *Dig.* L, 6, 6, 2. Pertinax refers explicitly to the man's *libellus* —διὰ τοῦ βιβλίου ἐδήλωσας. Note also the *subscriptio* addressed to a Jewish congregation some time between 213 and 315, and quoted in Greek in *CJ* I, 9, 2. The texts could, however, have been derived from private copies in Greek.

[40] *CIL* VIII 10570 and 14464 = *ILS* 6870 = *FIRA*² I, no. 103. Cf. pp. 181, 542.

[41] This translation assumes the correctness of the general view that the words 'ne plus quam ter binas operas' which appear ungrammatically in the inscribed text were inserted by the recipients in an attempt to give some definition to Commodus' reply.

[42] *CIL* VI 3770 = 31330 = Moretti, *IGUR* I 35.

A slightly different formula seems to have been used on an inscription from Smyrna copied several times in the seventeenth century, and now lost.[43] The text begins with the end of what is evidently a *libellus* in Greek asking permission to take a copy of a judgment of Hadrian: Antoninus Pius replies in Latin:

Imperator Caesar T. Aelius Hadrianus Antoninus Augustus Pius to Sextilius Acutianus. The judgment (*sententia*) of my divine father, if he pronounced anything as a judgment, I permit you to copy. *Rescripsi. Recogn(ovi)*.

After the word 'nineteenth' (*undevicensimus*), whose significance is unknown, we have the date (8 April 139) in Latin, and then in Greek 'it was sealed in Rome on 5 May in the presence of (names of seven witnesses)'. Finally, as the text stands, we have an instruction in Latin, 'Stasimus, Daphnus, issue the *sententia* or *constitutio* in the regulation form.' It cannot be pretended that everything is clear, even if we could be sure that the text was copied correctly. But it does give a hint, however obscure, of a complex filing system for imperial decisions.

The response of Gordian III in 238 to the villagers of Scaptopara in Thrace, also part of a longer dossier and also from an inscription which is now lost,[44] exhibits something different, the copying of the text from the version posted up in public in Rome: it was 'copied down and checked from the *liber* (?) of *libelli* answered by our Lord Imperator Caesar M. Antonius Gordianus, and posted up in Rome in the portico of the baths of Trajan'. From this it is quite clear that the reference is not to a filed copy but to the public one.[45] Here again the emperor answers the lengthy Greek petition (*deêsis*) of the villagers with a single sentence in Latin, telling them to approach the governor. Once again there follow the words *rescripsi, recognovi*, and in this case a fragmentary word apparently indicating that it has been sealed.[46]

The same essential features appear in the exchange a few years later between Philip and the villagers of Aragua in Pisidia, a long petition in Greek answered by a brief *subscriptio* in Latin.[47] Taken together, these four examples of petitions in Greek with *subscriptiones* in Latin make it reasonable to assume that Latin was normally used, without regard to the language of the petition. *Subscriptiones* could, it seems, be given in Greek, but the diplomatic considerations which made it advisable to prepare letters in Greek for despatch to Greek cities and provincial assemblies did not apply

[43] For the full text *CIL* III 411; partial texts in *ILS* 338; *FIRA*² I, no. 82.

[44] *CIL* III 12336 = *Syll.*³ 888 = *IGR* I 674 and now re-edited with extensive commentary by G. Mihailov, *IGBulg.* 2236. All the current texts depend on extensive emendation; for what was actually visible on the stone see A. E. Kontoleon and Th. Mommsen in *Ath. Mitt.* XVI (1891), 267–82.

[45] It is common to quote this inscription as proving the existence of an imperial file (*liber*) of *libelli rescripti*. But (a) what was originally reported on the stone was FXIIBROUBELLORUM-RESCRIPTURUM; (b) the reference is to the publicly posted copies, and also only to those of Gordian (in the first year of his reign).

[46] What appeared on the last line of the stone was SIG A.

[47] *CIL* III 14191 = *OGIS* 519 = *IGR* IV 598.

to most individuals, or to groups of villagers; there was no *a libellis* (or *a subscriptionibus*) *Graecis* to match the grand and prominent post of *ab epistulis Graecis*.

That reference raises the question of who decided the content of *sub-scriptiones*, who actually dictated or wrote them, and whose was the 'other hand'—formally attested only on the *subscriptio* to the African *coloni*—which wrote (*re*)*scripsi, recognovi*. An 'other hand' could, as we saw, appear in relation to the other sort of 'subscription', namely the greeting formula placed with his own hand by the emperor at the end of letters.[48] The evidence surely suggests—but does not prove—that the emperor normally wrote at least these two words of authentication; and where the indication of 'another hand' is missing—as it is elsewhere—we cannot formally exclude the possibility that he wrote the very brief replies himself.

All interpretations of these documents must remain speculative. But what is clear is that our sources continue to speak of the issuing of *subscriptiones* as an activity of the emperor himself; the same is indeed true of the sub-scribing of *libelli* by provincial governors and other officials.[49] So Callistratus speaks of Hadrian being 'approached *per libellum*' by someone, and writing a letter on the matter to the governor enclosing a copy of it;[50] and Paulus states that Caracalla 'subscribed' a *libellus*.[51] Moreover the emperors them-selves also write as if their replies to *libelli* were a personal matter: 'Tell that Valerius Antonius of yours to give me a *libellus*', Lucius Verus writes to Fronto, 'so that our favourable view may be expressed also in a *rescriptio*'.[52] Similarly, Antoninus Pius writes to a provincial governor 'I have ordered to be attached a copy of the *libellus* given to me by Domitius Silvanus . . . moved by his complaint, in which he indicated . . .'[53]

Moreover emperors can express in such contexts not merely their feelings but their own views on legal points: 'The intention of the deceased woman I interpret as having been this . . .' Pius writes in a *subscriptio* to the *liberti* of a woman named Sextia Basilia.[54] Much more significant than this, however, is what Marcus and Verus say in the course of what appears to be an *epistula*,

---

[48] pp. 221–2.

[49] This is clearest in *CJ* I, 51, 2, a letter of Constantine of 320: 'Praesides non per adsessores, sed per se subscribant libellis'; cf. VII, 57, 5 (Gordian, 241): 'subscriptionem ad libellum datam' (by a *iudex*); cf. also *Frag. Vat.* 163: 'si sessionem invenerit pro tribunali (litteras) reddere praetori, ut subnotet sua manu quod volet.' For the *libellus* of some veterans with the *subscriptio* of the *legatus* of Syria Palaestina in 150 (copied from one posted publicly with others in a portico) see *PSI* 1026 = Cavenaille, *Corp. Pap. Lat.*, no. 117. For a βυ[β]λε[ί]διον addressed to a *legatus*, and his *subscriptio*/ ὑπογραφή see I. Stoian, *Dacia* III (1969), 369. Note also *Dig.* XXXIX, 4, 4 (a different sense of *libellus*), and Pliny, *Ep.* I, 10, 9: 'subnoto libellos' (as *Praefectus aerarii Saturni*). Cf. also *Corp. Gloss. Lat.* III, p. 227, ll. 32–3: 'ex subscriptione praesidis provinciae' / ἐξ ὑπογραφῆς τοῦ διέποντος τὴν ἐπαρχίαν. For recently published papyrus examples of one-sentence *sub-scriptiones* to *libelli* see *BGU* 2012; *P. Mich.* 530.

[50] *Dig.* XLII, 1, 33: 'exemplum libelli dati mihi a Iulio Tarentino . . .'

[51] *Dig.* IV, 8, 32, 14: 'libello cuiusdam id querentis Imperator Antoninus subscribsit'; cf. XXXIII, 2, 23: 'et hoc nuper Imperator Antoninus ad libellum rescripsit' (Junius Mauricianus, of Antoninus Pius); *Coll.* III, 3, 5–6: 'item divus Pius ad libellum Alfi Iuli rescripsit in haec verba.' Note also *HA, Com.* 13, 7: 'in subscribendo tardus et neglegens, ita ut libellis una forma multis subscriberet.'

[52] Fronto, *Ad Verum imp.* I, 1, 1.

[53] *Dig.* XLVIII, 6, 6.

[54] XXXIV, 1, 13, 1.

perhaps to a provincial governor. They refer to the question of whether under certain circumstances a man could bring an action for possession of the property of a freedman of his grandfather:

> We have learned . . . also that Proculus, a jurist of no small weight, was of this opinion, that in such a case the grandson should not be granted *bonorum possessio*. We also followed his ruling when we replied to the *libellus* of Caesidia Longina. But also our *amicus* Volusius Maecianus . . . was led by the reverence due to our *rescriptum* to affirm in our presence that he did not think it was correct to give a different response.

But afterwards, they continue, in the course of a fuller discussion among the *amici* and jurists, the opposite opinion prevailed.[55] The precise sequence of events is not beyond doubt, but it seems that in answering the *libellus* the emperors (or more probably Marcus himself) had followed what they took to be the received opinion of previous juristic writers; that it was the reverence (*religio*) due to a *subscriptio* which had already been issued, which moved Volusius Maecianus to his display of pusillanimity; and that it was in some later context, perhaps a question raised in a letter to which this one was the reply, that the fuller discussion took place.[56] This is not the only occasion on which imperial replies refer explicitly to the views of legal writers;[57] specifically in *subscriptiones*, Gordian refers to a response of the '*vir prudentissimus*, Paulus', and Diocletian and Maximian to a decision by Marcus and a view expressed by Ulpian in his *Publicae Disputationes*.'[58] But the significant thing in this case is that it seems that Marcus and Verus had composed their answer to the original *libellus* themselves, and apparently without consultation at that particular moment.

No general rule can be given on the basis of one instance; nor can we be certain that the formulae of the *subscriptio* had not become ossified, and applied to a process in which the emperor no longer really had so immediate and personal a part. But the fact remains that the evidence considered so far—whether inscriptions, references to the subscribing of *libelli* in literary or legal sources, or the words of the emperors themselves—all follows the common assumption that a *subscriptio* was precisely such a personal act; it is ambiguous only on the question of whether the emperor wrote the *subscriptio* with his own hand, or simply *rescripsi, recognovi*, or neither.

In the light of this conception shared by our sources we are left with the question of what role was actually played by the *a libellis*. The statement of the *Notitia Dignitatum* that the *magister libellorum* 'deals with *cognitiones* and *preces*'[59] is less than helpful in this instance, and the evidence from our period is persistently elusive. Volusius Maecianus, for instance, had been *a libellis et a censibus* of Antoninus Pius, but was no longer in this position under

[55] XXXVII, 14, 17 *pr.*

[56] Cf. pp. 103, 223.

[57] On this whole question see the invaluable collection of evidence and discussion by G. Gualandi, *Legislazione imperiale e giurisprudenza* (1963), esp. II, 107f.

[58] *CJ* V, 4, 6; IX, 41, 11. Cf. VI, 42, 16 (Carus, Carinus and Numerianus referring to Papinian).

[59] p. 224.

9*

Marcus and Verus.[60] Similarly, we can only speculate about the functions of various imperial freedmen concerned with *libelli*, whose titles appear on inscriptions: the single *acceptor a subscr(iptionibus?)* attested in the early period[61] is perhaps relevant (might the emperor for instance have handed the subscribed *libelli* to him?), but we actually know no more of his functions than of those of a *custos, scriniarius* or *adiutor a libellis*;[62] the title of *scriniarius* naturally recalls the *scrinium* of Domitian in which Pliny claims that a *libellus* against himself was found.[63]

The freedmen *a libellis* who are attested up to the end of the Flavian period were evidently powerful and prominent figures in personal contact with the emperor.[64] But in this period only one literary text describes the functions of a freedman in relation to *libelli*—and this relates to Polybius, whom Suetonius describes not as *a libellis* but as the *a studiis* of Claudius.[65] Seneca, addressing Polybius, says:[66]

> So many thousands of people have to be given audience, so many *libelli* to be dealt with (*disponendi*); such a crush of matters coming together from the whole world has to be sorted out, so that it can be submitted in due order to the mind of the most eminent Princeps. To you, I say, it is not permitted to weep: in order that you may hear the many who weep, and may attend to the tears of those who are struggling and longing to reach the mercy of the most gentle Caesar, your tears must be dried.

For all its exaggerated tone, the passage is a genuine and vivid reflection of the conception of the emperor as the object of petitions, and the source of money and benefits. It also clearly implies that Polybius was involved in the audiences at which, in this period, *libelli* were typically presented. Beyond that, the details are obscure; but it would not be incompatible with the pattern suggested by Plutarch's account of the Ides of March, namely that the emperor, on receiving *libelli*, handed them to an attendant, to have them re-submitted for his attention in private.

From the early second century onwards, when the *a libellis*, and later *magister libellorum*, was of equestrian rank, their titles not infrequently show a conjunction of *libelli* and *census*;[67] and once only the conjunction suggested

---

[60] p. 103. There is no evidence on the functions of the *a censibus*.

[61] *CIL* vi 5181.

[62] *CIL* vi 8616 (*custos*); 8617 = 1675; x 527 = *ILS* 1671 (*scriniarii*); 8615, 33741 (*adiutores*); also *ILS* 3703 (*proximus a libellis*).

[63] p. 240.

[64] The title, surprisingly, does not appear in Suetonius, *Claud.* 28 (see p. 75) on the prominence of Claudius' freedmen. But Dio LX, 6b (5) lists as the three most powerful freedmen Callistus, ὃς ἐπὶ ταῖς βίβλοις τῶν ἀξιώσεων ἐτέτακτο, with Narcissus and Pallas. Note also LXI, 5, 4 (24), Nero's gift of cash to Doryphorus τῷ τὰ τῆς ἀρχῆς αὐτοῦ βιβλία διέποντι (cf. p. 149), and the importance under Domitian of Entellus ὁ τὰ τῆς ἀρχῆς βιβλία διέπων, LXVII, 15, 1; his *domus* and *horti* in Martial, *Epig.* VIII, 68, cf. *PIR²* E 66. Cf. also *ILS* 1674 (a Flavian, or slightly post-Flavian, *Aug. lib. a libellis*).

[65] *Claud.* 28.

[66] *Ad Polyb.* 6, 5.

[67] T. Haterius Nepos, Pflaum, *Carrières*, no. 95 (under Hadrian); L. Volusius Maecianus, Pflaum, no. 141; C. Julius Celsus, Pflaum, no. 106 *bis* (both under Antoninus Pius); *CIL* iii 299 = *IGR* iii 193 (second to third century); Priscus, *magister a libellis, magister a censibus*, Pflaum, no. 338.

by the *Notitia Dignitatum*, when M. Aurelius Papirius Dionysius is described as *a libellis* and *a cognitionibus* under Commodus.[68] But although, as we have seen, the question of expressing *subscriptiones* in Greek did not normally arise, we must still ask whether the literate *equites*, some of them the authors of major legal works, who typically occupied the post in this period, would not have had at least some real influence on the content or composition of the *subscriptiones*. Something of the sort may seem to be implied by the description of Aelius Coeranus in a letter of Caracalla as 'entrusted with the interpretation(?) of the petitions'.[69] The same is perhaps true of the mention by the contemporary jurist Tryphoninus of a rescript which the emperor (Severus) sent 'while Papinian was in charge of the *libelli*';[70] there is no obvious reason why he should have mentioned this unless it were relevant to the nature of the rescript.

The external evidence takes us no further, and Papinian is indeed the only one of early third-century legal writers who is firmly attested by a good source as having held the post of *a libellis*.[71] In this case it has recently been shown that there is an undeniable similarity between the style and vocabulary of his writings, and those of the imperial *subscriptiones* of the period 194 to 202. If it is a valid inference that it was then that he was *a libellis*, then the argument can be pushed further to suggest that the *a libellis* of 202–9 was Ulpian, of 212–13 perhaps Arrius Menander, and of 223–6 Herennius Modestinus.[72] Very much as with the question of the *ab epistulis Graecis* in the same period, we must attempt to reconcile the general assumption of our sources that the emperor was personally responsible for his pronouncements, with the evident influence of the 'secretaries' on their style and content. Purely as a hypothesis, we may surmise again that emperors now tended to decide the main tenor of a *subscriptio*, perhaps after consultation, and to leave its precise wording to be composed by the *a libellis*. But it is not at all clear whether such a notion should be extended, even as a hypothesis, to the relatively brief and curt *subscriptiones* surviving in papyri and inscriptions. It must be supposed that Papinian, if he was then *a libellis*, was with Severus in Alexandria in 200; but we may perhaps doubt whether he was needed, for instance, to write Severus' *subscriptio* of 15 March: 'To Aurelius Sarapion— we have already forbidden that priesthoods should be held by descent on the mother's side.'[73]

That example may remind us that the subject-matter of *libelli* and

---

[68] Moretti, *IGUR* I, 59: ἐπὶ βιβλειδίω[ν] καὶ διαγνώσεων τοῦ Σεβαστοῦ; Pflaum, *Carrières*, no. 181 and cf. p. 94.

[69] *Forschungen in Ephesos* II, 125, no. 26, ll. 19–20: Αἴλ. Κοίραν[ος, ὁ κράτιστος / φίλος μ]ου καὶ τὴν ἐξή[γησιν] τ[ῶ]ν [ἀ]ξ[ιω]μάτ[ω]ν πεπισ[τευμένος]. See G. Barbieri, *L'albo senatorio da Severo a Carino* (1952), no. 6.

[70] *Dig.* XX, 5, 12: 'libellos agente Papiniano.' An extract from the *Decreta* of Paulus (*Dig.* XLIX, 14, 50) shows Tryphoninus, Messius and Papinian arguing a point on the imperial *consilium* (necessarily before the death of Papinian in 212). Cf. p. 96.

[71] pp. 95–6.

[72] For these arguments, which are also of fundamental importance for the transmission of Roman legal texts, and will require further consideration by all who are interested in the history of Roman Law, see A. M. Honoré, 'Private Rescripts and their Authors, 193–280 AD', to appear in *Aufstieg und Niedergang*, ed. H. Temporini.

[73] *SB* 9526, ll. 25–7, cf. pp. 244–5.

subscriptiones extended far outside the area of Roman law proper, to any kind of request, for privileges or exceptions, and to complaints or accusations. Lactantius even implies that the barbarian guards of Maximin gained high-born brides by the expedient of presenting petitions for them, which the emperor would subscribe.[74] But far more important than such exchanges within the court was the role of the submission of *libelli* by private persons, and the reception of answers in the form of *subscriptiones*, as one of the primary forms of communication between emperor and subject; moreover it is precisely the insignificance of much of the subject-matter which confirms that it took place because it was integral to the conception of the emperor's role which his subjects had.

The fact that this function could still, at the end of our period, involve the personal reception of *libelli* by the emperor in public is clearly demonstrated by what ecclesiastical historians report from the Council of Nicaea. When the bishops were gathered, various disputes broke out amongst them, and Constantine was frequently approached by individual bishops proffering *libelli* with mutual accusations. So he appointed a special day for receiving them: 'When he had taken his seat, he received *libelli* from each separately. Holding all the *libelli* in his lap, and not revealing what was in them', he addressed words of reproof to the bishops—and afterwards ordered that the *libelli* should be burnt.[75] The story makes an interesting contrast with that of Demetrius Poliorcetes,[76] who more than six hundred years before had kept the 'written requests' of his subjects in his cloak before throwing them into a river.

5. *Imperial Edicts*

'Do you not also daily ... reduce and cut down that whole ancient and sordid thicket of laws with the new axes of imperial rescripts and edicts?' wrote Tertullian, at the end of the second century, reflecting in his best rhetorical style the fact which the lawyers had already recognized, that imperial pronouncements had the force of law.[1] The emperors, like both the magistrates of the city of Rome and the governors of the provinces, could issue statements or orders in the form of *edicta*; as the word implies, *edicta* must once have been 'spoken out' verbally, but from the late republic onwards were written documents posted up in public.[2] Imperial edicts sometimes referred solely to, or gave instructions for, certain immediate circumstances; but, insofar as they laid down general rules, they remained in force even after

---

[74] *De mort. pers.* 38, 5: 'primariae (filiae), quae rapi non poterant, in beneficiis petebantur, nec recusare licebat subscribente imperatore.' It is possible that the use of 'subscribente' is metaphorical.

[75] Rufinus, *HE* x, 2; repeated by Socrates, *HE* I, 8, 18–19; Sozomenus, *HE* I, 16, 3–5; Theodoret, *HE* I, 11, 4–5, and Gelasius, *HE* II, 8, 1–4.

[76] p. 241.

[1] *Apol.* 4, 7. For the formal statements of this principle see p. 206. That Tertullian must be seen as having been by training a rhetor, and in no sense as a lawyer (and still less as identical with the jurist Tertullianus), is demonstrated by T. D. Barnes, *Tertullian: a Historical and Literary Study* (1971), esp. ch. iv.

[2] For a summary account of the background see *RE* s.v. 'edictum'.

the death of their author, unless they were specifically superseded.[3] Thus for instance, Paulus can quote the edict on the use of torture to obtain evidence from slaves which Augustus had posted up (*proposuit*) in AD 8.[4]

Unlike all the forms of imperial pronouncement which we have considered so far—letters to governors or communities, verdicts in court (*decreta* or *sententiae*), and *subscriptiones*—an *edictum* had in principle no specific addressee; it began simply with the name of the emperor or emperors and 'dicit' or 'dicunt' (in Greek *legei* or *legousi*). Moreover, all these other forms of pronouncement were almost without exception responses to initiatives from others, which put before the emperor information, requests for guidance, demands, petitions or accusations; and in very many cases (as, for instance, with all *subscriptiones*) they were explicitly responses in form.

In certain cases, as we shall see, we find emperors issuing edicts also in response to specific initiatives from below, and even addressing the persons concerned in the second person in the course of them.[5] By contrast, we also find Constantine, after his victory in 324, issuing what Eusebius calls letters to the churches or to the provincials, which in some ways more resemble edicts.[6] But in spite of the fact that the lines could be blurred on occasion, there remains a genuine distinction between the other pronouncements and *edicta*. Moreover, Tertullian's rhetorical reference to the daily issue of imperial rescripts and edicts, blurs another essential distinction; for while *rescripta* (which could refer equally to *epistulae* and *subscriptiones*) really were issued daily if circumstances allowed, there is every reason to suppose that *edicta* were very much less frequent. Not only do they play no part in such descriptions of emperors at their duties as we possess,[7] but there is no trace at all of imperial 'secretaries', whether of freedman or equestrian status, concerned with edicts. Given the immense volume of known inscriptions, this can hardly now be an accident. Nor is it an accident that they are absent from the speech which Dio puts into the mouth of Maecenas addressing Augustus, which in reality applies to his own time and which advises him to have equestrian secretaries 'for legal cases, letters and decrees of the cities, the petitions of individuals, and whatever else concerns the administration of the empire'.[8] The imperial functions which are mentioned individually correspond exactly to those which we have already discussed; if edicts are included at all, it is only implicitly, in the wider category of other relevant duties.

If the issuing of edicts did not require a secretary and his assistants devoted to it, this was not because it was not an activity conducted

---

[3] See R. Orestano, *Gli editti imperiali: contributo alla teoria della loro validità ed efficacia nel diritto romano classico* (1937).

[4] *Dig.* XLVIII, 18, 8 *pr.* Cf. XXVIII, 2, 26: 'iam sublato edicto divi Augusti.'

[5] p. 256.

[6] The pronouncement in Eusebius, *VC* II, 24–42 is described as an ἐπιστολή, but it does not have the usual χαιρεῖν after the address ἐπαρχιώταις Παλαιστίνης. And what Eusebius calls the ὑποσημείωσις (cf. p. 222), namely προτεθήτω ἐν τοῖς ἡμετέροις ἀνατολικοῖς μέρεσιν, would better fit an edict (cf. n. 10 below). II, 48–60, is similarly described as an ἐπιστολή, but also lacks χαιρεῖν and has no final formula.

[7] pp. 209–10.

[8] LII, 33, 5; cf. p. 105.

personally by the emperor. For, as we have seen, Pliny the Elder at least records that *edicta*, like *epistulae*, were sealed with the emperor's own signet-ring; and the wording of edicts, as of letters, was regarded as an indication of the emperor's personal level of culture.[9] There is also evidence that emperors might add a *subscriptio* to an edict, in the sense of an instruction for its publication.[10]

It is clear that the initial publication itself consisted of the posting-up of the edict at the emperor's current place of residence. So, for instance, the edict of Claudius concerning the status of lands in Northern Italy and the rights of some Alpine tribes 'was posted at Baiae in the *praetorium*' in 46;[11] or that of Caracalla on the right of a man to hold public office after temporary relegation posted at Rome in July 212.[12] In rare instances we can follow the diffusion of the edict in space and time from that point. An edict of Caracalla confirming certain points in his original edict restoring exiles was posted up in Rome on the eleventh of the same month, July 212, was copied in the office of the prefect of Egypt in Alexandria on 29 January 213 (so more than six months later), and finally posted there on 10 February.[13] The first edict of the great persecution was posted at Nicomedia, where Diocletian and Galerius were, on 24 February 303, in the cities of the Palestine region in about March, and at a town in Africa on 5 June,[14] just over three months later.

The edict of persecution was torn down by an indignant Christian when it was put up, which seems to imply that it was written on something relatively fragile and impermanent; and there is one indication that emperors continued, as republican magistrates had, to have their edicts written on a white-painted wooden board (*album*) with headings written in red (hence 'rubrics').[15] Such a temporary form would have sufficed for edicts issued in response to immediate local circumstances, such as that of Augustus stating that on the following day women should not attend the *ludi pontificales* before the fifth hour (to prevent their seeing a pair of naked boxers), those of Tiberius in response to popular complaints about the 1 per cent sales tax or

[9] *NH* xxxvii, 4/10; cf. pp. 203–7 and 213.

[10] This is clear only in the edict of Vespasian on the privileges of doctors and others, partially preserved on an inscription from Pergamum. See R. Herzog, *S.-B. Preuss. Akad. Wiss.* xxxii (1935), 967 (with very conjectural restorations), and *FIRA²* I, no. 73. In ll. 17–19 we have Αὐτοκρά/[τωρ Καῖσαρ Οὐεσπα]σιανὸς ὑπέγραψα (*subscripsi*) καὶ ἐκέλευσα/[προτεθῆναι ἐν λε]υκώματι (*in albo*). It *may* be to such a subscription of an edict that Eusebius intends to refer in *HE* vii, 30, 21, describing Aurelian as μέλλοντα δὲ ἤδη καὶ σχεδὸν εἰπεῖν τοῖς καθ' ἡμῶν γράμμασιν ὑποσημειούμενον (or to *epistulae* to governors).

[11] *ILS* 206 = *FIRA²* I, no. 71. For *praetorium* see p. 27, and cf. p. 41. For a good discussion of the publication of imperial edicts, F. von Schwind, *Zur Frage der Publikation im römischen Recht* (1940), 157f.

[12] *CJ* x, 61, 1; cf. *Dig.* L, 2, 3, 1.

[13] *P. Giss.* 40, col. ii, ll. 1–15; a fragmentary second text in *P. Oxy.* 2755. Both of these will be copies made, directly or indirectly, from that posted in Alexandria.

[14] The date of the initial *propositio* is given by Lactantius, *De mort. pers.* 12–13, and the place by Eusebius, *HE* viii, 5. For the posting (ἥπλωτο πανταχόσε) in his own region Eusebius gives the month Dystrus (Feb.–March) in *HE* viii, 2, 4, and Xanthicus (March–April) in *Mart. Pal.* i, 1. For the place in Africa, *Acta Felicis* 1, 2 (Knopf-Krüger-Ruhbach, *Ausgewählte Martyrakten*, no. 22); see now R. P. Duncan-Jones, *JThS* xxv (1974), 106.

[15] See *RE* s.v. 'edictum', col. 1941. The one indication is the use of λεύκωμα in the edict of Vespasian (no. 10 above).

to excuse his non-appearance in public,[16] or of Nero and Galba repressing popular disorders in Rome.[17] But even for those edicts whose provisions, whether legal or administrative, were intended to be of indefinite application, we have no record of their being recorded in any permanent public form in Rome. So far as we know, the references which we have to imperial edicts as sources of law depend on copies taken down at the time and then passing into literary circulation.[18] The papyri also supply us with texts of edicts, which are presumably private copies taken down for private use or record;[19] occasionally such copies appear in an intelligible context, as when part of an edict of Hadrian is preserved within a long document of the late third century on the affairs of the synod of the artists of Dionysus.[20]

In certain cases, however, the emperors are found giving orders for the display of their edicts all over the empire. The classic instance is the general edict of Claudius protecting the rights of the Jewish communities of the Diaspora:[21]

> This edict of mine I wish the magistrates of the cities and *coloniae* and *municipia* of Italy and outside, and also kings and dynasts through their own representatives, to have written up, and to keep it on display for not less than thirty days in a position where it can easily be read from the ground.

Almost identical provisions, but without the explicit limitation of time, appear in the edict of Severus Alexander remitting payment of *aurum coronarium* at the beginning of his reign:[22]

> Let the magistrates of each city take care to display the copies of this edict of mine as publicly as possible, so that they are visible to the readers.

From Claudius' reference to a period of thirty days it seems probable that in the provinces also imperial edicts were displayed in the first instance in non-permanent form. The same conclusion is suggested by the fact that before the tetrarchic period, when there is a significant change, copies of general edicts inscribed on stone or bronze are remarkably rare. One such, which does not survive, was 'the bronze tablet which is fixed in the great Caesareum (in Alexandria), as you go up the second stairs under the right-hand portico beside the marble temple of Venus', from which a veteran of the legion X Fretensis testified in 94 that he had copied the text of Domitian's

---

[16] Suetonius, *Aug.* 44, 3; Tacitus, *Ann.* I, 78; Pliny, *NH* XXVI, 6/9.

[17] Tacitus, *Ann.* XIV, 45; Suetonius, *Galba* 15, cf. Plutarch, *Galba* 17, 5.

[18] See p. 245, and e.g. *Dig.* XVI, 1, 2 *pr.* (Augustus and Claudius); *Dig.* XLVIII, 10, 14, 2; 15 *pr.*; *CJ* IX, 23, 3 (Claudius on *testamenta*); *Dig.* L, 7, 5, 6 (Vespasian on size of provincial embassies); XL, 15, 4 (Nerva, limiting enquiries on a person's status to the five years after their death), etc. For literary transmission note esp. Hyginus in *Corp. agrim. rom.* (Teubner, p. 97): 'cuius edicti verba itemque constitutiones quasdam aliorum principum . . . in uno libello contulimus.'

[19] This is presumably the nature of the text of two edicts of Caracalla, plus (probably) a letter of his to the prefect of Egypt (so Hunt and Edgar, *Select Papyri* II, no. 215) in *P. Giss.* 40. Similarly *BGU* 628, with on the *recto* an edict on appeals to the emperor, probably of the late second or early third century (see pp. 512–13); and on the *verso* a record also in Latin of the recitation of an edict of Octavian on the privileges of veterans (see Cavenaile, *Corp. Pap. Lat.*, no. 103). Also an edict of Caracalla, *P. Oxy.* 1406 = *FIRA²* I, no. 89.

[20] *P. Oxy.* 2476, ll. 4–7; cf. pp. 460–1.

[21] Josephus, *Ant.* XIX, 5, 3 (291).

[22] *P. Fayum* 20 = Hunt and Edgar, *Select Papyri* II, no. 216. Cf. p. 142.

edict on the privileges of veterans.[23] But otherwise the only actual surviving examples of general edicts preserved on inscriptions before the tetrarchic period are the edict of Vespasian inscribed at Pergamum, that of Claudius on abuses over the provision of *vehicula* found at Tegea[24]—and the 'edict of Caesar' on a stone possibly from Nazareth and now in Paris.[25]

The explanation is quite clear. Imperial pronouncements of whatever kind, if they survive on inscriptions, do so because cities (or private persons) had them inscribed; and they had the pronouncements inscribed if and only if they were of direct interest or advantage to themselves. There is a striking contrast between the rare cases of inscribed general edicts and the scores of surviving inscriptions of imperial letters addressed to cities.

This explanation is supported by the fact that those edicts which are found on inscriptions are predominantly those which are not general, but arise from and relate to the affairs of particular communities. It is precisely in these cases that the edict is performing a function more like that of an *epistula* or even a *decretum*. Perhaps the extreme case is the pronouncement of Caracalla found at Banasa in Mauretania which is cast in edict form (beginning with 'dicit'), but uses the second person throughout, and is the emperor's favourable reply to an appeal from the town about the payment of certain taxes, an issue on which they were engaged in legal proceedings, presumably before the governor. In this case it is mentioned explicitly that the inscription was put up by the *duumviri* of the town.[26]

Similarly, the edict of a second-century emperor inscribed in Pisidia uses the second person, and is evidently in effect a reply to a city;[27] while Nero's edict issued in Greece in 67 is an announcement of his speech giving freedom to the province—and both are in any case inscribed along with honours to a local magnate.[28] Claudius' edict issued from Baiae relates primarily to an enquiry about the ownership of certain lands, which had been continuing spasmodically since the reign of Tiberius; but in the course of it certain information had been put forward about the dubious status of certain Alpine tribes, the Anauni, Tulliasses and Sinduni, on which Claudius gives a favourable ruling. Not surprisingly, it was in the territory of the Anauni that the edict was inscribed.[29] Similarly, it was naturally at Venafrum that there was inscribed the edict of Augustus laying down detailed regulations for the aqueduct there.[30]

---

[23] *ILS* 9059 = *FIRA*² i, no. 76.

[24] *ILS* 214 = Abbott and Johnson, *Municipal Administration*, no. 51.

[25] *FIRA*² i, no. 69.

[26] *AE* 1948 109.

[27] Published by G. E. Bean, *Anat. Stud.* x (1960), p. 71 no. 124 = *SEG* xix 854; cf. Robert, *BE* 1961, no. 750.

[28] *Syll.*³ 814. For the whole set of inscriptions see J. H. Oliver, 'Epaminondas of Acraephia', *GRBS* xii (1971), 221; cf. p. 388.

[29] p. 254. For a detailed discussion of the inscription see U. Schillinger-Häfele, 'Das Edikt des Claudius *CIL* v 5050', *Hermes* xcv (1967), 353.

[30] *CIL* x 4842 = *ILS* 5743 = *FIRA*² i, no. 67, with fragments of a second text from the sources of the Volturnus by A. Pantoni, 'L'editto augusteo sull'acquedotto di Venafro e una sua replica alle fonti del Volturno', *Rend. Pont. Acc. rom. arch.* xxxiii (1960–1), 155. All that survives of the heading is '[Ed]ict[um im]p. Ca[esaris Augusti?]', and it is only the related *cippi* (*ILS* 5744; cf. *AE* 1962 91) with 'iussu Caesaris Aug.' which make the attribution probable.

If the occasion demanded, an edict rather than a letter might be promulgated in response to a provincial embassy. This was the case when embassies from the Jewish communities of Asia and Cyrene came to Augustus in 12 BC to ask for protection for their traditional rights; as well as writing to various governors, Augustus issued a general edict in their favour; he ordered it, and their honorific decree for himself and Cn. Marcius Censorinus, 'to be put up in the most prominent place dedicated to me by the council of Asia'. His words do not indicate whether he means a temporary notice or permanent inscription; but Josephus notes that 'it was inscribed on a pillar in the temple of Caesar', which confirms the latter.[31]

Of the five edicts of Augustus issued a few years later, between 7/6 and 4 BC, and inscribed at Cyrene, the first four all refer explicitly to Cyrenaican affairs, and the first two specifically to the sending of embassies; while the second mentions also the despatch of prisoners for examination by the emperor. The third and fourth ones make no concrete reference to the circumstances which inspired them, but can be seen to give rulings on questions of citizen status and judicial liability, which are bound up with the issues between Roman citizens and non-citizens in the province which are concerned in the first two. The fifth is in any case a unique document, since *qua* edict it is simply the introduction to a *senatus consultum* on the procedure for accusations of governors for illegal acquisitions.[32]

From the whole of the two centuries between the Flavian period and the tetrarchy we have no examples of general imperial edicts recorded on inscriptions, and must conclude that edicts were not the form of imperial pronouncement of most interest to the communities of the empire. Since it is precisely those aspects of an emperor's activity which did interest his subjects about which we are likely to have evidence, we can only surmise, but cannot firmly conclude, that general edicts were in fact a relatively minor part of imperial business.

From the tetrarchic period, however, we suddenly find a whole series of lengthy and detailed imperial edicts on inscriptions, sometimes on copies from different parts of the empire. The edicts of this period reflect a quite new degree of innovation and intended impact on the population. So, for instance, in his own edict of 297 referring to a tetrarchic edict on taxation reform, the prefect of Egypt writes:[33]

Thus it is possible for all to know the amount levied on each *aroura* in accordance with the character of the land, and the amount levied on each head of the rural population, and the minimum and maximum ages of liability, from the imperial edict which has been put up, and the schedule (*brevium*) attached thereto, the copies of which I have placed before this edict of mine.

He later gives orders for city magistrates to despatch copies of both

[31] Josephus, *Ant.* XVI, 6, 1–2 (160–5). For the date see G. W. Bowersock, *HSCPh* LXVIII (1964), 207, and cf. *JRS* LVI (1966), 161.

[32] *SEG* IX, 8 = *FIRA*² I, no. 68; for the *s.c.* see p. 345.

[33] *P. Cairo Isidor.* I, trans. Boak and Youtie, with emendations, see Crawford and Reynolds, *JRS* LXV (1975), 161–2.

edits to every village or inhabited place, 'in order that the munificence (*megalodôria*) of our emperors and Caesars may come to the notice of all.' The classic instance is, however, the great price-edict of 301, with its lengthy preface justifying the measure and its vast list (also called a *brevis*) of goods and services with permitted prices, of which fragments are known from Egypt, Greece, Asia Minor, Crete, Samos, Cyrenaica and Italy.[34] We may compare the long edict of Constantius and Galerius of 305/6 checking accusations for the benefit of the *fiscus*, of which a Latin text is known from Tlos in Lycia and a Greek one from Athens.[35] Apart from minor fragments of other edicts of this period,[36] we also have what is probably an edict of Constantine, similarly on accusations, which is known from partial texts in the *Codex Theodosianus* and *Codex Justinianus*, and from inscriptions found at Tlos, Padua, Lyttos in Crete and Sinope;[37] while yet another long edict, apparently of the same period is also inscribed at Lyttos.[38]

In this period edicts could apparently still be directed to particular areas, for a pronouncement of Constantine about the excesses of *stationarii* is described in the *Codex Justinianus* as being 'in his edict to the Africans', and as having been put up in Carthage in 315.[39] But what is unquestionably a novelty in terms of our evidence is both the length and detail of the edicts, and the wide distribution of copies of them inscribed for permanent record. It would not be unreasonable to see this as suggesting a real change in the nature and ambitions of government. But if it was, the striking fact remains that we cannot trace even in this period any officials or secretaries in the imperial entourage who were specifically concerned with edicts, even though both the original composition of them and the making of large numbers of copies must have involved considerable labour. Still less do we know whether the edicts were sent out invariably in Latin, or whether Greek texts might be prepared at court.

We know from Cicero that while still in Rome he composed himself the edict which he was due to issue as governor of Cilicia in 51;[40] and, as we should expect, emperors normally use in their edicts language which implies that these are essentially personal decisions and pronouncements. So, for instance, Claudius writes in his edict defending the privileges of Jewish communities, 'Kings Agrippa and Herod, my dearest friends, having petitioned me to permit the same privileges to be maintained for the Jews

---

[34] See the full collection, edition and commentary by S. Lauffer, *Domitians Preisedikt* (1971). The rough list of locations given above naturally affords no indication of the number or extent of the fragments found in different places. See now M. H. Crawford and J. Reynolds, 'The Publication of the Prices Edict: a new Inscription from Aezani', *JRS* LXV (1975), 160.

[35] For the Latin text, *CIL* III 12134; Greek, *IG* II² 1121.

[36] *CIL* III 578 (Corcyra); III 6979 = *ILS* 660 (Sinope).

[37] *CIL* III 12133 (Tlos); V 2781 (Padua); III 12034 = *Ins. Cret.* I. xviii, 188 (Lyttos); cf. J. Moreau, 'Fragment, découvert à Sinope, de l'édit de Constantin *de accusationibus*', *Historia* V (1956), 254. None of these indicates the author, but the Lyttos text has *exemplum sacri edicti*. The two extracts in the *Codices*, *CTh* IX, 5 and *CJ* IX, 8, 3, both attribute the edict to Constantine, but give the address 'ad Maximum P(raefectum) U(rbis)' and the date 'PP. Kal. Ian(uar). Volusiano et Anniano conss.' (314). But Valerius Maximus (*PLRE* Maximus 48) was *Praef. Urb.* in 319–23.

[38] *Ins. Cret.* I. xviii, 189.

[39] XII, 57, 1.

[40] *Ad fam.* III, 8, 4.

throughout the Empire under the Romans as those in Alexandria enjoy, I very gladly consented . . .';[41] while Hadrian, in remitting taxes in Egypt, speaks of his having learnt that the Nile inundation had been smaller than normal.[42] On a single occasion, Augustus' edict on Jewish privileges, an emperor states explicitly, 'it was decided by myself and my *consilium*, under oath'.[43] Similarly, Tacitus describes some persons who seem to be Nero's *consilium* dissuading the emperor from responding to popular clamour against the *publicani* by abolishing indirect taxes altogether. As a result, Nero issued instead an edict intended to control their activities.[44] Later, Lactantius claims that Diocletian and Galerius consulted their advisers before issuing the first edict of persecution in 303, precisely in order to spread the blame for an invidious measure.[45]

It is not improbable that the *consilium* of the emperor—or those *amici* who happened to be with him if he were away from Rome—were normally consulted before an edict was issued. But an edict, as we have seen, though it could in practice be a response to an initiative from below, was not so in principle; and for that very reason we not only have relatively few documentary texts of edicts, but also lack narrative accounts of how they came to be composed. These limitations on our knowledge will appear all the more clearly when we attempt briefly to set the issuing of the emperors' pronouncements in the wider pattern of their functions, resources and manner of life.

6. *Information and Decision*

An inscription from Rome records an imperial freedman, Ti. Aelius Titianus, *proximus a libris sacerdotalibus*, who died at Carnuntum on the Danube at the age of forty-two. The occasion was probably the three-year stay there by Marcus Aurelius in the early 170s.[1] The mention of this function, which is attested only here, may serve to remind us of the strict limits of our understanding; for it is impossible to offer more than a guess as to what the *libri sacerdotales* were—they probably have some relation to the emperor's role as a member of the four major priestly colleges in Rome.[2] But it also gives rise to wider questions. On what stores of information or archives could an emperor draw in performing his various functions? And if such existed and were necessary to him, how was their use affected by the very frequent

[41] Josephus, *Ant.* XIX, 5, 3 (288), Loeb trans.; cf. p. 255.

[42] *SB* 6944 = *FIRA*² I, no. 81.

[43] Josephus, *Ant.* XVI, 6, 2 (163): ἔδοξέ μοι καὶ τῶι ἐμῷ συμβουλίῳ, μετὰ ὁρκωμοσίας. It is not clear what is the significance of the words which follow, γνώμη δήμου Ῥωμαίων. Cf. p. 268.

[44] *Ann.* XIII, 50–1 (AD 58). The text reads 'impetum eius . . . attinuere senatores', but it is generally agreed that the reference is not to a debate in the senate but to persuasion by individuals, and that 'seniores' might be a less unsatisfactory reading. See e.g. J. A. Crook, *Consilium Principis* (1955), 46.

[45] *De mort. pers.* II, 5–6.

[1] *ILS* 1685. See p. 46, and P. R. C. Weaver, *Familia Caesaris* (1972), 252–3.

[2] Cf. pp. 355–61, and cf. G. Wissowa, *Religion und Kultus der Römer*² (1912), 497, n. 2.

movements of the emperor either within Italy or outside it, on journeys or campaigns? We can go from there to ask similar questions about the other resource on which the emperor could draw in making decisions, namely his staff and advisers. Both need to be discussed before we can assess the true significance of the patterns of contact between subject and emperor which our sources reveal in operation with remarkable stability through the best part of four centuries.

The word most commonly used in referring to imperial archives is *commentarii*, which tells us little or nothing in itself, for the term could be used of any sort of record, notebook or manual of instructions, or even of certain literary works.[3] That it could refer to household matters is clear from Cicero's reference to his making a note of a debt due to him with his own hand in his *commentarii*.[4] After the assassination of Caesar in 44 the word appears in a context which was to be regular for it under the empire, that of *beneficia* granted to communities or individuals. For, once the senate had voted to uphold the *acta* of the dictator, Antonius—or so both Cicero and later historians believed—was able to distribute benefits and gifts on the basis of spurious personal documents allegedly left by him; they are described variously as *chirographa* (autographs), *commentarii* (or *commentarioli*) and *libelli*.[5] Plutarch seems to imply that it was from Caesar's house that Antonius received 'the documents of Caesar, in which were written the records (*hypomnêmata*) of his judgments and decisions', before forging others.[6] *Hypomnêmata* was the normal Greek translation for the 'commentarii' of the emperors.

In the first century *commentarii* appear quite frequently as records of trials, kept in imperial possession. Caligula is found solemnly burning the *commentarii* relating to the trials of his mother and brothers under Tiberius.[7] Nero quashed one charge made against a senator early in his reign, 'saying that he had discovered from the *commentarii* of his father [Claudius] that no accusation of anyone had been compelled by him';[8] and in 70 it was abortively suggested in the Senate that the imperial *commentarii* should be made available, so that the names of accusers should be known.[9] From the context it is clear that all parties are concerned with 'political' trials, mainly of senators. But in the more settled circumstances of the second century it is clear that the *commentarii* embraced also more routine cases; for we find in

---

[3] See *RE* s.v. 'commentarii'. For more general treatments of the imperial archives see e.g. M. Memelsdorff, *De archivis Imperatorum Romanorum, qualia fuerint usque ad Diocletiani aetatem* (Diss. Halle, 1896); G. Cencetti, 'Tabularium Principis', *Studi . . . in onore di Cesare Manaresi* (1953), 131.

[4] *Ad Att.* VII, 3, 7.

[5] Cicero, *Ad Att.* XIV, 13, 6; *Ad fam.* XII, 1; *Phil.* I, 1/3, and esp. 7/16–17 ('in commentariolis et chirographis et libellis'), and note the indication in 7/17 that the contents were *beneficia*); V, 4/11–12; cf. Dio XLIV, 53, 2.

[6] *Ant.* 15, 1–2: ἔλαβε δὲ καὶ τὰ βιβλία τοῦ Καίσαρος, ἐν οἷς ὑπομνήματα τῶν κεκριμένων καὶ δεδογμένων ἦν ἀναγεγραμμένα.

[7] Suetonius, *Cal.* 15, 1; cf. Dio LIX, 4, 3; 10, 8; 16, 3. Other documents containing accusations, which he claimed to have burnt were, so Dio says, found after his death, LX, 4, 5 (presumably identical with the *libelli* found 'in secretis eius', Suetonius, *Cal.* 49, 3).

[8] Tacitus, *Ann.* XIII, 43, 3.

[9] Tacitus, *Hist.* IV, 40, 3.

the *Sententiae et Epistulae Divi Hadriani* a man petitioning for the release of his father from exile, and the emperor replying, 'Let me look up the *commentarii*, while you make it your business to approach me again.'[10]

Unless our evidence is entirely misleading, such *commentarii* were directly under the control of the emperor. A slightly more distant and formalized system can be discerned in relation to the wider class of *commentarii* of imperial decisions, pronouncements and *beneficia*, as is revealed in the correspondence of Pliny and Trajan. When for instance some persons, apparently in the course of legal proceedings, recited before Pliny an edict of Augustus and various imperial *epistulae*, he consulted the emperor on the issue concerned, but did not send copies, 'both because they were not adequately corrected—and some did not seem certainly genuine—and because I believe that there were true and corrected copies in your *scrinia*'. In reply Trajan confirmed the genuineness of two of the letters mentioned (while saying nothing of the other three, or the edict), but also stated that 'nothing relevant is found in the *commentarii* of those emperors who have preceded me'.[11] There is no indication here that he had looked up the *commentarii* himself.

That impression is confirmed by the exchanges relating to Pliny's requests for grants of citizenship or other benefits to various protégés. In one instance, from before his governorship of Bithynia, Pliny refers to Trajan's instruction in a missing letter to send a note of the age and census-rating of a beneficiary 'to those of your *liberti* whom you indicated'.[12] During the governorship Trajan replies to Pliny, 'I have subscribed (*subscripsi*) to your request, and have ordered that it should be recorded in my *commentarii* that I have given the *ius trium liberorum* to Suetonius Tranquillus, on my usual conditions'; almost exactly the same instruction is mentioned soon after in connection with a grant of citizenship.[13]

The regular system for the recording of imperial grants which these passing references imply is now fully confirmed in documentary form by the *Tabula Banasitana*.[14] Two documents in the dossier are relevant. First, Marcus Aurelius and Commodus reply in an *epistula* to the procurator of Mauretania, saying that they have granted citizenship to the wife and children of the chief of a tribe called the Zegrenses, and conclude 'in order that it may be recorded in our *commentarii*, find out what the age of each is, and write to us'. There then follows the extract from the *commentarii* themselves (the only actual extract from any form of imperial *commentarii* in our entire evidence). It is preceded in formal style by the authentication 'copied down and checked (*descriptum et recognitum*) from the *commentarius* of persons

---

[10] *Corp. Gloss. Lat.* III, p. 33, ll. 26f.: 'Adrianus dixit, "Sine videam commentarios (ὄψομαι τὰ ὑπομνήματα), tu tamen cura reverti ad me".'

[11] *Ep.* X, 65–6.

[12] X, 6.

[13] X, 95; 105.

[14] W. Seston, M. Euzennat, 'Un dossier de la chancellerie romaine: la *Tabula Banasitana*', *CRAI* 1971, 468; cf. A. N. Sherwin-White, 'The *Tabula* of Banasa and the *Constitutio Antoniniana*', *JRS* LXIII (1973), 86. See now W. Williams, 'Formal and Historical Aspects of Two New Documents of Marcus Aurelius', *ZPE* XVII (1975), 37, on pp. 56f.

granted Roman citizenship'—by Augustus, Tiberius, Gaius, Claudius, Nero, Galba, Vespasian, Titus, Domitian, Nerva, Trajan, Hadrian, Antoninus Pius, Verus, Marcus Aurelius and Commodus—'which Asclepiodotus, *libertus*, produced, as it is written below'.

In view of its unique character, it is worth looking at the extract in full:

> In the consulship of Imperator Caesar L. Aurelius Commodus Aug. and M. Plautius Quintillus, on the day before the nones of July, at Rome (6 July 177).
>
> Faggura, wife of Julianus, *princeps* of the tribe Zegrenses, age 22, Juliana age 8, Maxima age 4, Julianus age 3, Diogenia age 2, children of Julianus mentioned above:
>
> At the request *per libellum* of Aurelius Julianus, *princeps* of the Zegrenses, supported by Vallius Maximianus by letter (*suffragante . . . per epistulam*), to these we have given the Roman citizenship, without prejudice to the law of the tribe, and without diminution of the *tributa* and *vectigalia* of the *populus* and the *fiscus*.

This is followed by 'Carried out on the same day, in the same place, under the same consuls, Asclepiodotus, *libertus*, I have checked (*recognovi*),' and the names of twelve imperial *amici* as witnesses.[15]

It is thus clear that an entry in the *commentarius* listing persons granted Roman citizenship was a document of considerable length and formality. Moreover, as we shall see, in the first two-and-a-half centuries of the empire petitions for the citizenship were among the most common of personal requests directed to the emperor,[16] and the *commentarius* (if properly kept) will eventually have contained many thousands of entries. But that very fact raises problems of its own. The particular transaction took place at Rome, where the emperors happened to be (and as Trajan was during Pliny's governorship); but what happened during journeys or campaigns, or from the mid-third century onwards, when emperors were rarely in Rome at all? For instance, were the *commentarii* carried with Caracalla when he left Rome in 214, taken over by Macrinus after Caracalla's murder in Syria in 217 and finally brought back by Elagabal in 219? We do not know whether the *commentarii* were kept in *codex* form, or, like those of officials in Egypt, on papyrus rolls;[17] in either case, if the full imperial archives were taken, the bulk will have been very considerable, and the likelihood of loss, damage or disorganization very high. But if they were not taken, we can ask how significant they were for the fulfilment of the imperial role. We have, however, to confess ignorance; the only hint of files passing

---

[15] For *libelli* sent on by governors see p. 473; for the relevance of the expression *sine deminutione tributorum et vect[i]galium populi et fisci* see p. 190; for the role of the *amici*, p. 223. Note that the use of *suffragante* is a perfect example of the development of 'suffragium' and its cognates as set out by G. E. M. de Ste Croix, ' "Suffragium": from Vote to Patronage', *Brit. Journ. Sociology* v (1954), 33.

[16] pp. 479–85.

[17] Documents, other than *leges*, in the *aerarium* seem in the republic to have been kept on waxed wooden tablets (from which the codex descended); see M. W. Frederiksen in *JRS* LV (1965), 186; for a *codex ansatus* of the governors of Sardinia, see the inscription mentioned in n. 23 below; for the files of officials in Roman Egypt see the brief account by E. G. Turner, *Greek Papyri* (1968), 138f.

from Caracalla to Macrinus, for instance, is Dio's report that Macrinus, writing from Syria, informed the senate he had found no documents of accusations in the *basilikon*, for Caracalla had destroyed them or returned them to their authors.[18] It was natural that the emperor would be expected to have with him such recent correspondence; and we may compare the fact that Otho before his suicide at Bedriacum in 69 destroyed *epistulae* and *libelli* which would compromise their authors before Vitellius.[19] Bulky long-term records were another matter. None the less, the presence of these *may* be implied by the fact that a freedman, and evidently a favourite, of Trajan, who was a *commentar(iis) beneficiorum*, was with him at Selinus in 117.[20]

Other imperial *commentarii* which certainly existed up to the end of the first century were those relating to the aqueducts of Rome, which Augustus inherited from Agrippa, along with the *familia* of slaves who worked there. But whereas the slaves were made public by him,[21] the *commentarii* remained imperial. Their chief function in fact seems to have been, once again, the recording of *beneficia*, grants of permission to tap water from the aqueducts for private use; the right was gained by personal petition to the emperor.[22] Here too we have no evidence as to the later fate of these *commentarii*.

In their origins, contents and function they cannot have been entirely unlike the records of land assigned in colonies by the emperors, or otherwise given as a *beneficium*, which were kept in the '*tabularium* (or *sanctuarium*) of Caesar'. Indeed the *tabularium* seems to have embodied records of decisions and assignments made even by office-holders in the republic. According to the inscription of a verdict by the proconsul of Sardinia in 69, one community in the dispute about boundaries based its claim on a bronze tablet with the decisions of M. Metellus, proconsul in 114 BC; but the other side promised to produce a *tabula* 'from the *tabularium* of the *princeps*'. At the time of the verdict this document, also described as a *forma* (plan?), had not yet arrived.[23] But the reference does give a concrete meaning to the mention in an inscription from Capua of Vespasian restoring 'from the *forma* of Divus Augustus' the boundaries of land dedicated by Sulla to Diana Tifatina.[24]

The two together, moreover, lend some weight to the references to such an imperial archive in the writings of the Roman land-surveyors

---

[18] LXXVIII, 21, 1–2 (425–6). Exactly what is referred to as τὸ βασιλικόν is quite obscure.

[19] Tacitus, *Hist.* II, 48, 1; cf. Suetonius, *Otho* 10, 2, mentioning *epistulae* only. Note also Plutarch, *Ant.* 78, 3, recording that Octavian had letters from Antonius with him at Alexandria in 30 BC.

[20] *ILS* 1792 (cf. p. 67, the same man as *lictor proximus*); the same post in *CIL* VI 8626, and a *custos a com[mentariis] beneficioru[m]*, 8627 (both also freedmen of Trajan); an *adiutor a comm. b(eneficiorum)*, *ILS* 9030; *a commentariis*, *CIL* VI 8623–5; *AE* 1959, 305.

[21] pp. 192–3.

[22] See Frontinus, *De aquae ductu* 99: 'Augustus quoque edicto complexus est, quo iure uterentur qui ex commentariis Agrippae aquas haberent, tota re in sua beneficia translata'; for the imperial *commentarii* listing the volume of water due to flow either to public places or private establishments, see 74–86; for the imperial *beneficia* also 86 and for the procedure in petitioning 103, 105, 110–11. Note *ILS* 1609, an imperial freedman *a commentari(i)s aquarum*.

[23] *CIL* X 7852 = *ILS* 5947 = *FIRA*² I, no. 59.

[24] *CIL* X 3828 = *ILS* 251.

(*agrimensores*).[25] Hyginus, writing in the early second century, says in the context of the foundation of a colony:[26]

> The books of the bronze [record] and a plan of the whole area assigned, copied out with boundary lines in accordance with the delimitations made, and with the names of neighbours recorded, we shall place in the *tabularium* of Caesar. And if any lands are conceded or assigned to the *colonia* by way of *beneficium*, whether in the neighbourhood or in the territory of other *civitates*, we shall list them in the *liber beneficiorum*. And as regards any other records of the *mensores*, not only the *colonia* but the *tabularium* of Caesar must retain them, subscribed by the hand of the founder.

The founder of a colony in this period was invariably the emperor, so we see yet another form of document to which the emperor put his subscription with his own hand. The same archive is referred to by Siculus Flaccus, writing apparently a little later about land divided or assigned: 'If there is any dispute, it is customary to have recourse to the *sanctuarium* of Caesar. For the emperor has in his *sanctuarium* plans (*formae*) of all lands, both divided and assigned, and records (*commentarii*) of the divisions (and assignments?)'.[27] Once again, the function of the *commentarii* and other documents in the *tabularium* was to serve as a record of imperial acts, essentially seen as grants or *beneficia*, which would serve as a check in the case of future disputes.

We have no evidence as to whether the imperial *tabularium* was a specific building in Rome, or whether the *commentarii* were lodged, as they easily could have been, somewhere in the network of imperial residences on the Palatine. That possibility is indeed suggested by Dio's passing reference to a fire in 192, whose flames 'were carried up into the Palatium and burned a large part of it, so that almost all the documents relating to the government were destroyed'.[28] Whether this fire was the decisive factor or not, it is the case with records of grants of land, as of most other types of *commentarii*, that we hear nothing of them after the second century, and have no hint of their fate. The single exception from the third century is the statement of the lawyer Modestinus that the category of persons 'absent on public business' included tribunes and others, 'who have been reported to the *aerarium*, or listed in the *commentarius principis*'. As in the late republic and early empire, such a step will again have had the character of a *beneficium*.[29]

Our evidence for the nature, or even the existence, of imperial records

[25] F. Blume, K. Lachmann, A. Rudorff, *Die Schriften der römischen Feldmesser* I–II (1848–52); Teubner ed. by C. Thulin, *Corpus Agrimensorum Romanorum* I. 1 (1913). For Hyginus and Siculus Flaccus see Schanz-Hosius, *Gesch. d. röm. Lit.*[4] II (1935), 801–3; M. Fuhrmann, *Das systematische Lehrbuch* (1960), 102f. The valuable work of O. A. W. Dilke, *The Roman Land Surveyors* (1971), does not give a clear conception of the individual authors.

[26] Hyginus, *De limitibus constituendis*, pp. 202–3 Lachmann; pp. 165–6 Thulin.

[27] Siculus Flaccus, *De condicionibus agrorum*, pp. 154–5 Lachmann; pp. 118–30 Thulin. It is not possible to make use of the reference in the *Liber coloniarum* (p. 239 Lachmann) to the *libri* of Augustus, Nero and 'Balbi mensoris, qui temporibus Augusti omnium provinciarum et formas civitatium et mensuras compertas in commentariis contulit'. See Schanz-Hosius, o.c., 803.

[28] LXXII, 24, 2–3 (305); cf. p. 150.

[29] *Dig.* IV, 6, 32, reading 'qui ad aerarium delati aut in commentarium principis relati (rather than 'delati') sunt', as confirmed by the *Tabula Banasitana* and Pliny X, 95 above. For men 'delati ad aerarium' as a *beneficium* see *JRS* LIV (1964), 37–8.

after the middle of the second century is very poor[30]—although, as we saw, it is likely that verbatim records of imperial hearings continued to be kept subsequently.[31] In the later period there may even have been some devolution of the handling of documents to the praetorian prefecture; for when in 314 Constantine lays down that records of all hearings by *praesides* should be sent in, it is to the *scrinia* of the praetorian prefecture that they are to go in the first instance.[32]

Nor are officials concerned with the *commentarii* attested after this period. On the other hand we do see the emergence of officials of the imperial *memoria*, a word which inevitably suggests some connection with records.[33] A few freedmen officials of the *memoria* are attested in the second and third centuries;[34] one was *a memoria* and *a cubiculo*, as was also Festus, the freedman favourite of Caracalla who accompanied him on his eastern journey and was buried at Troy, and Castor a freedman of Severus who went with the emperors on the British expedition.[35] That the office brought a man close to the emperor is further implied by two fragmentary imperial letters to a *proximus a memoria*, one of which speaks of his long service 'at the side of emperors';[36] and perhaps by the inscription of an *exceptor* in the *officium memoriae* who died at Nicomedia, presumably in the tetrarchic period.[37] That the function had to do with recording or copying down, is further suggested by the term *antigrapheus*, which a late source applies to Sicorius Probus, who served with Diocletian.[38]

By this time the head of the *memoria* was an *eques*, with the title *magister*; but even the speech of Eumenius, a retiring *magister memoria*, tells us, as we saw, no more about the precise functions of the office than that it had some relation to imperial pronouncements—'[my] voice . . . which had pronounced the celestial words and divine thoughts of the emperors'.[39] Similarly, although it is quite explicit from Constantine's pronouncements that the three main *officia* which accompanied him were those of the *memoria*, the *epistulae* and the *libelli*,[40] it is not until the *Notitia Dignitatum* that we find any positive evidence of the duties of the *magister*: 'dictates and gives out all *adnotationes*, and responds to petitions (*preces*).'[41] The *magistri epistolarum*

---

[30] We may note in passing that there is evidence of a record of his decisions kept by Marcus Aurelius (only), and called *semestria*; see *Dig.* II, 14, 46 (cf. *CJ* VI, 54, 2); XVIII, 7, 10; *Inst.* I, 25, 1; cf. L. Wenger, *Die Quellen des römischen Rechts* (1953), 439. Nothing more is known of its form or character.

[31] pp. 235–7.

[32] *CTh* I, 16, 3 = *CJ* VII, 49, 2; cf. 16, 6 = *CJ* I, 40, 3 (331), a demand for the reporting of *acclamationes* of governors by the provincials ('si verae voces sunt nec ad libidinem per clientelas effusae').

[33] See O. Seeck in *RE* s.v. 'scrinium', cols. 897–8; Fluss, ibid., s.v. 'a memoria', XV, cols. 655–7.

[34] *CIL* VI 8620–1; X 1727 = *ILS* 1678: *officiali veteri a memoria et a diplomatibus*; XIII 1800: *proximus a memoria*; XIV 4062: *adlectus* (?) *a memoria*; *AE* 1929 152.

[35] See p. 82.

[36] *CIL* VI 8619.

[37] *AE* 1961 308.

[38] See p. 107.

[39] *Pan.* V(9), 6, 2; cf. p. 98.

[40] p. 109.

[41] p. 224. Note also the references in *HA* to the role of the *a memoria* (*Sev. Alex.* 31, 1, see p. 221), *magister memoriae* (*Claud.* 7, 2), and 'Iulius Calpurnius, qui ad memoriam dictabat' (*Car.* 8, 4).

and *libellorum* are also described as 'handling' *preces*, so that will not mark any distinct function of the *memoria* (though it does serve to emphasize the continued importance of petitions). The *adnotatio*, as a new form of imperial document, is however attested in the tetrarchic and Constantinian period. In 290 Diocletian and Maximian reply to a slave who has given information about the murder of his or her owner that they have entrusted the praetorian prefect, 'along with the *decretum* of our *adnotatio*', to investigate the matter;[42] in March 313 Constantine explains to a *rationalis* the force of an *adnotatio* granting property as a gift; but in December 314 he writes to the *praefectus vigilum* in Rome to state that 'our *annotationes*', as opposed to *rescripta* or *epistulae*, should be regarded as having no legal force.[43] Finally, in the Constantinian dossier of the petition of the Orcistani to be granted the status of a city, there is a letter of Constantine to Ablabius (probably as *vicarius* of Asiana in 324–6), in the course of which he says: 'Since they petition that our Clemency should grant them their former right and name of *civitas*, as the attached copies of our *adnotatio* with the *preces* attest, we have given a decision in this sense.'[44]

The nature of an *adnotatio* is thus far from clear, but it seems to have been a memorandum, normally (or always?) evoked by a petition, embodying some interim imperial decision, and directed to an official.[45] If that is correct, then here too those imperial documents whose existence we can trace relate by and large to responses to matters initiated by their subjects. This is not the case with the records of the original arrangements made in the early empire for the aqueducts of Rome or the settlement of *coloniae*, though in fact Augustan colonial settlements were *beneficia* paid for by himself; but it is true of the use made subsequently of those documents, namely for reference in granting petitions or solving disputes. Moreover it applies without qualification to the best-attested form of imperial archives, the *commentarii* of grants of citizenship, and other privileges, and to the keeping of copies of the records of hearings, of *decreta* or *sententiae*, and of *epistulae*. If copies of *edicta* were also kept, as Pliny appears to have assumed, though Trajan's reply to him does not specifically confirm it,[46] that would in most cases be another exception to the rule.

Thus the archives and stores of information which were at the immediate disposal of an emperor related essentially to the acts and pronouncements of himself and his predecessors; and none of the evidence on such archives which we have seen so far goes against the hypothesis that the emperor's role was typically passive, and that he normally made his pronouncements in response to initiatives from below. Nor are there more than a few scattered

[42] *CJ* I, 19, 1 ('Firminae'; but cf. VII, 13, 1, part of the same *subscriptio*, addressed 'Firmino'); from the same year, IX, 16, 4 = *Coll.* I, 10, 1 (cf. p. 335).

[43] *CJ* X, 10, 2; *CTh* I, 2, 1.

[44] *MAMA* VII 305, Panel i, ll. 42–7. On the date see *PLRE* Ablabius 4; cf. pp. 131, 410.

[45] For a discussion see L. Wenger, *Die Quellen des römischen Rechts* (1953), 432–3. Note that the term *adnotationes* is used in the edict of Constantius and Galerius (p. 258); in the Greek text, *IG* II² 1121, ll. 17, 28, 38, the word παρασημειώσεις appears, and in the Latin (*CIL* III 12134), at the point equivalent to the last of these, l. 22, *adnotationes* is used. But it remains obscure whether these *adnotationes* are imperial.

[46] *Ep.* X, 65–6, see p. 261.

indications that emperors actively sought information from any other source. The fact that the learned equestrian secretaries of the second century quite frequently combined the posts of *a studiis*, or *ab epistulis*, and *a bibliothecis* (or *procurator bibliothecarum*),[47] has sometimes led to the view that the imperial libraries served as an active tool of research for the secretariat. But when emperors refer to legal works in giving their replies, or Hadrian mentions the opinions of ancient medical writers and philosophers on the possibility of an eleven-month pregnancy,[48]—or Trajan rules that a man with one testicle may serve in the army, for 'both Sulla and Cotta are recorded to have been in this condition'[49]—all it shows is that the emperors, like their contemporaries, drew their responses to current situations from the inherited corpus of literature and learning.

Moreover, while both provincial governors and communities on occasion reported to an emperor odd or remarkable events,[50] the evidence on the spontaneous despatch by the emperors of persons sent to bring information to them is slight, and relates entirely to the fringes of the empire.[51] The major exception to this pattern of apparent passivity on the part of the emperors is again confined to the early empire,[52] and concerns the collection of financial and military records. Of the *rationarium* of the empire which Augustus handed over in 23 BC, when he thought himself near death, we know only that it listed the existing forces and public revenues;[53] but what Suetonius calls the '*breviarium* of the whole empire' which Augustus left on his death in AD 14, Tacitus describes as a *libellus*, and says that it contained 'the public wealth, the number of citizens and non-citizens under arms, of fleets, provinces, tribute and indirect taxes, essential payments and ex gratia gifts (*largitiones*); all of which Augustus had written out with his own hand'.[54] Though Suetonius goes on to mention that Augustus added the names of his freedmen and slaves from whom an account could be demanded, Tacitus' reference to Augustus writing out the *libellus* with his own hand clearly indicates the essentially domestic context from which this document emerged. Moreover, although it is recorded that Tiberius allowed to lapse, and Gaius revived, the 'accounts of the empire' which had been 'put up' ('proponi', as with *edicta* or *subscriptiones*) by Augustus,[55] and literary

---

[47] pp. 88–90, 102–3. The evidence is collected by E. van't Dack, 'A Studiis, a bybliothecis', *Historia* XII (1963), 177.

[48] pp. 239, 249.

[49] *Dig.* XLIX, 16, 4 *pr.*

[50] pp. 322, 418.

[51] Pliny, *NH* VI, 31/141, Dionysius of Charax sent to the east 'ad commentanda omnia' by Augustus before the campaign of Gaius; 35/181, some praetorians sent to explore Nubia by Nero; Plutarch, *Mor.* 410A, 419E, Demetrius of Tarsus going to the islands off Britain, ἱστορίας καὶ θέας ἕνεκα πομπῇ τοῦ βασιλέως (Domitian); see R. M. Ogilvie, *Phoenix* XXI (1967), 112–15.

[52] Ignoring the claim of *HA, Sev. Alex.* 21, 6–8, that the emperor kept detailed records of the army in his bedroom.

[53] Suetonius, *Aug.* 28, 1; Dio LIII, 30, 2: τῷ μὲν Πίσωνι τάς τε δυνάμεις καὶ τὰς προσόδους τὰς κοινὰς ἐς βιβλίον ἐσγράψας ἔδωκε. The βιβλίον was perhaps not unlike the *libellus* allegedly containing 'thesaurorum rationes' which Gaius Caesar was given by a supposed traitor, Florus II, 32; Festus, *Brev.* 19, but cf. Velleius II, 102, 2.

[54] Suetonius, *Aug.* 101, 4; Tacitus, *Ann.* I, 11, 4; cf. Dio LVI, 33, 2.

[55] Suetonius, *Cal.* 16, 1.

authorities occasionally record the sums left by emperors,[56] there is no sign later of any comparable effort either to collect or to publish full accounts of the resources of the empire. The most specific evidence we have is the familiar passage of Statius, addressed to Abascantus, *a rationibus* under Domitian, which does imply that his duties included balancing revenues (whether public or imperial) against public expenditures.[57]

In short, the positive activity which marks the reign of Augustus, for instance in finance, in re-organization in Rome and in the foundation of colonies, and which had its reflection in the nature and extent of the documentation collected at that time in the imperial household, was not necessarily typical of other periods of the empire, at least until the tetrarchy. After Augustus' reign our evidence suggests that the majority of the documentation kept by the emperor's entourage—and possibly carried around with him on his travels—simply recorded previous responses, in various forms, to requests and disputes put before the emperors by their subjects.

We can see an analogous development in the history of the imperial *consilium*. Augustus began, at what precise date is unknown, with an elaborate plan by which he used as his advisers over each period of six months the consuls (or the other consul, if he were consul himself), one from each of other magistracies, and fifteen other senators chosen by lot; the function of this body was explicitly to consider matters before they were brought before the senate.[58] This system can in fact be observed in operation in precisely one document, the fifth Cyrene edict, where the *senatus consultum* begins with the words, 'On those matters on which the consuls . . . brought forward a motion, concerning which Imperator Caesar Augustus, our Princeps, on the advice of the *consilium* which he has by lot from among the senate . . .'[59] Such a system could operate in full only when the emperor was in Rome or near it, as Augustus was not between 27 and 24 BC, between the latter part of 23 and 19, between 16 and 13 BC, and on occasion thereafter.[60] But in any case even before the end of Augustus' reign, Dio reports a change in AD 13 which removed the selection by lot, added members of the imperial family and allowed the emperor to choose further members; moreover decisions of this body were supposed to have the force of *senatus consulta*.[61] Thereafter, a single passing reference in Suetonius (the purpose of which is to emphasize how few of them survived the reign) to the twenty leading men, for whom Tiberius 'asked'—presumably from the senate—as

[56] e.g. Suetonius, *Cal.* 37, 3 (2,700,000,000 *sesterces* left by Tiberius); cf. Dio LIX, 2, 6. Dio (quoting an oration by Pertinax) gives exactly the same sum as left (by Antoninus Pius) to Marcus Aurelius and Verus, LXXIII, 8, 3 (312).

[57] *Silv.* III, 3, 85f.; for the most recent discussion, P. A. Brunt, *JRS* LVI (1966), 89f. Vespasian's pronouncement about the vast sum needed at the beginning of his reign (Suetonius, *Vesp.* 16, 3) may also imply some general accounts.

[58] Suetonius, *Aug.* 35, 3; Dio LIII, 21, 4–5 (that it appears in Dio's general account of the Augustan constitution under 27 BC indicates nothing about its actual date); see J. A. Crook, *Consilium Principis* (1955), ch. ii.

[59] *SEG* IX, 8, v; Sherk, *Roman Documents*, no. 31.

[60] e.g. in Lugdunum in 10 BC, Dio LIV, 36, 4; to N. Italy on occasion to keep in contact with the northern wars, Suetonius, *Aug.* 20 (cf. p. 44); in Capri and Campania in 14 before his death, *Aug.* 97–100.

[61] LVI, 28, 2–3; see Crook, o.c., 14–15.

advisers in addition to his own friends,[62] represents the last significant trace
of anything beyond that essentially informal consultation of *amici* which we
have already seen in operation.[63] Thus, here too, an innovation of a positive
character in the Augustan period relapsed very rapidly into something of a
more passive and informal nature. In this case it was essentially a reversion
to reliance on a *consilium* very similar to that of a provincial governor, with
the difference only that those summoned to it frequently found themselves
in the essentially private context of the imperial residences in Rome and
Italy.

Again, just as with the *consilium* of a governor, the matters on which our
evidence shows the *amici* of the emperor deliberating were very largely
judicial—and it is in this context that the regular *consiliarii* of the later
second century and after appear. For if we set aside firstly the occasions on
which the emperor's advisers are attested discussing military matters or
foreign relations,[64] which lie outside our scope, and secondly immediate
crises relating to conspiracies, or the question of the succession,[65] then there
remains very little evidence for their embarking on any deliberation which
was neither the hearing of an accusation, the settlement of a legal or semi-
legal dispute, nor a response to an embassy, complaint or petition.

From the middle of the first century it is clear that the emperor was
regularly attended and assisted by his freedmen 'secretaries', whose influence
on him could rival or surpass that of the *amici*; Josephus can note without
comment that Claudius did not appoint Agrippa II to succeed his father as
king of Judaea because he was dissuaded by his freedmen and friends.[66] The
brief power of the freedmen in this period could be felt in areas which had no
connection with the specific functions entrusted to them; the classic instance
is the dispute between Pallas, Callistus and Narcissus over the choice of a
wife for Claudius.[67] But the emergence of the secretarial posts themselves,
with their distinctive titles, had a significance of its own, clearly indicated by
the fact that Torquatus Silanus was accused in 64 'of having among his
freedmen those whom he called *ab epistulis*, *a libellis* and *a rationibus*,

[62] *Tib.* 55.

[63] Note, however, that if we may believe Herodian VI, 1, 2 and VII, 1, 3, sixteen senators were
chosen by the senate as advisers to the young Severus Alexander, and were with him at his death
at Moguntiacum in 235. On the allegations of the *HA* about Alexander's *consilium* see Crook,
o.c., 89–90.

[64] e.g. Tacitus, *Ann.* XV, 25 (Nero on war with Parthia); *Hist.* II, 31–3 (Otho in 69); Juvenal,
Sat. IV, 144 (*amici* expecting to be consulted on a letter about the Sygambri, or reporting some
other disturbance); Macrobius, *Sat.* I, 23, 14–16 (Trajan in Syria before the Parthian War); *HA*,
Marc. Ant. 22, 3 (Marcus Aurelius in the Marcommannic War); Herodian VI, 2, 3; 7, 4 (Severus
Alexander on an embassy to Artaxerxes, and on fear of German invasion); Petrus Patricius, *FHG*
IV, p. 198, Fr. 11 = Dio ed. Boissevain, p. 747, Fr. 179 (Probus on resisting Carus); *Pan.* IX(12),
2, 4; 11, 4; cf. Eusebius, *VC* I, 30 (Constantine on the campaign of 312); *VC* II, 5 (Licinius con-
templating war with Constantine).

[65] e.g. Seneca, *De clem.* I, 9, 3 (Augustus intending to call a *consilium amicorum* over the conspiracy
of Cn. Cornelius Cinna Magnus); Philo, *Leg.* 4/26–7 (Tiberius addressing τοὺς ἐν τέλει on the
succession); Tacitus, *Ann.* XI, 31, 1 (Claudius on Messalina and Silius); *Hist.* I, 13 (Galba on the
adoption of a successor); Dio LXIX, 20 (Hadrian addressing leading men on adoption of Antoninus);
Herodian I, 4 (Marcus addressing his *amici* to recommend Commodus as successor).

[66] *Ant.* XIX, 9, 2 (362).

[67] Tacitus, *Ann.* XII, 1–3.

deliberately chosen names of the highest offices', while his nephew was killed in the following year for the same offence.[68] The charges may well have been false, especially in the second case; but the fact that they could be brought at all makes clear that the new titles were confined to the imperial entourage.[69]

As we have seen, the process by which these posts became open to men of free birth and equestrian rank had already begun in the Julio–Claudian period, and was complete by the reign of Hadrian. As such, they carried prestige and influence not only because their holders were in immediate and continuous attendance on the emperor, but as a prize for oratorical ability or legal knowledge, or as stages near the top of the evolving equestrian career. But once again the functions in connection with which we find these *equites* assisting the emperor, primarily embassies, *epistulae*, *cognitiones* and *libelli*, were all ones which involved responses, whether these were decisions between disputing parties, or answers to delegations or individuals. The various forms of written reply seem, so far as we can judge from our in-adequate evidence, to have involved the 'secretaries' more closely than they did the looser body of *amici*. But even the secretaries had functions which were essentially subordinate in relation to the personal decisions of the emperor himself: that is to say, they admitted litigants or embassies, attended the emperor at hearings, took down pronouncements from dictation, and, it seems, progressively took over the task of expressing some or all of his written replies in appropriate language. Perhaps not much less important, though less public, was the role of those freedmen who took and preserved texts of imperial hearings, verdicts and replies, and 'produced' them from the archives when required.

Any freedman in close attendance on the emperor, or equestrian secretary, or *amicus*, or still more the praetorian prefect, *might* exercise a temporary or continuing influence over an emperor and his decisions. But both in external form and in fact the decisions and pronouncements of the emperor were his own. It is only in the third century that we see some attempt to devolve the emperor's jurisdiction, by appointing some persons to judge *vice sacra*, 'in the place of the emperor';[70] and only at the very end of it that there begins the emergence of the praetorian prefecture in a central administrative role in partial independence of the imperial entourage.[71] Up to that time what the emperor did was limited to what he could do, or chose to do, himself; and it was further limited on the one hand by the conventions of upper-class Roman life, which in effect confined the conduct of business on a normal day to a few hours in the morning; and on the other by the restrictions imposed by frequent imperial journeys, either for pleasure between villas in Italy, or

---

[68] *Ann.* XV, 35; XVI, 8.

[69] For some data on the emergence of 'secretarial' titles with 'a' or 'ab' see p. 73. I have been unable to discern any intelligible grammatical background to the appearance of this form, or even what literal meaning was conveyed by it. Apart from the partially analogous *a manu* it seems to have been entirely confined to the imperial household; note the well-known *ILS* 1514, when an imperial *dispensator* has *vicarii* including three *a manu*, two *ab argento*, two *ab veste* and an *a cubiculo*; and *TAM* II.2 461 (an *a manu* of a *legatus* of Lycia).

[70] See pp. 514–15.

[71] See *RE* XXII 2426f.

for curiosity, business or war in the provinces and on the frontiers. On any such journey the human, monetary and documentary resources available to the emperor for the performance of his role were those which he had with him. Moreover, while he could communicate at a delay of weeks or months in each direction,[72] with any part of the empire, and could similarly send letters to the senate or to office-holders in Rome,[73] there is not the slightest evidence to suggest that he left behind him in the city any central administration of his own with which he could maintain contact.[74]

So the restrictions on what would or could be done by the emperors in ordinary circumstances were very considerable. But in attempting to define the nature and content of his decisions we need not overemphasize such negative conclusions. Nothing said here is meant to deny the obvious fact that from time to time in the empire new laws were put forward, aspects of taxation changed, and new legions raised. All that is argued is that the nature of the emperor's personal activities, and of the physical and social contexts in which they were conducted, was such as to exclude the initiation of change as a normal and expected function.

It is much more important to emphasize by contrast that the conduct of imperial business, and the structure of the entourage, was visibly designed to perform the function of answering consultations from officials, receiving and replying to embassies, responding to petitions and giving decisions on disputes, both legal and non-legal. Furthermore, when we turn from the emperor to his subjects, we shall see that this structure of the entourage was itself a response to widespread expectations and widespread patterns of initiative on the part of the population of the empire. Innumerable cities and associations, undeterred by distance in time and space, did in fact send off representatives as ambassadors to make orations before the emperor; and innumerable individuals did in fact present their often insignificant requests, queries, complaints and accusations to him. And where the established patterns and assumptions of society led, there individual Christians, and eventually the Church itself, followed.

It is crucial to all that has been said, that it was not merely a fact but a general expectation that the emperor would give ear to his subjects, and that the answers they would receive would be in both content and tone in some real sense his own, and would embody the values of that same traditional culture which both they and the emperor shared; the expectation is far more significant than the fact that it was not always fulfilled. It is reflected everywhere in the literature and documents of the empire, but in few places more clearly than in the paragraph which Herodian devotes to Marcus Aurelius at the beginning of his *History*. What he says is of all the greater importance because he is an unoriginal minor writer, who can reasonably

---

[72] For some examples see pp. 39, 218, 254.

[73] pp. 337–41, 353–5.

[74] Note however Helius, left in charge of Rome by Nero in 66/7, writing to urge the emperor's return from Achaea, and receiving a letter in reply, Suetonius, *Vesp.* 23, 1; Dio LXIII, 19, 1. Aurelius wrote from the Danube to his καθολικός, Euphrates, about the preparation of his antidote, XIV, 4 Kühn; Flavius Maternianus (perhaps *vice Praefectorum Praetorio*, *PIR*² F 317), wrote from Rome in 217 to Caracalla in Mesopotamia, Dio LXXVIII, 3, 2 (406).

be taken to represent the general attitudes of educated provincials in the Greek east. For him, Aurelius was the ideal of an emperor:[75]

> He practised every virtue, and was devoted to the literature of the past, to an extent not surpassed by any Roman or Greek; this is shown by speeches and writings of his which have come down to us. He showed himself a merciful and moderate king to his subjects, receiving those who approached him, and preventing the guards who surrounded him from thrusting away petitioners.

[75] Herodian I, 2, 3-4.

PART THREE

Subject and Emperor

VI

The Equestrian Order and the Senate

1. *Introduction*

Alexander of Aphrodisias, who dedicated his work *On Fate* to Severus and Caracalla, and acknowledged that he had gained from them whatever he had requested, could none the less use in his commentary on Aristotle's *Topica* some conventional wisdom on the friendship of kings, and add to it a specific element of his own: 'This passage tends to show that virtue is preferable to honour from kings, for if the object of virtue is well-being, that of honour from kings is to be governor of some province.'[1] His contemporary, Tertullian, also alludes to the patronage of the emperor, and deploys it in the course of a highly specious and rhetorical argument. The pagan traditions themselves, he points out, recorded cases of mortals who achieved immortality; but, if that were so, it necessarily implied the existence of a supreme deity who adlected new gods, just as the emperor adlected men into the senate.[2]

The exercise of patronage had from the beginning been an essential element in the functions of the emperor. All of the slowly-expanding range of posts held by *equites* were filled by direct appointment by the emperor, as were all senatorial posts in the imperial provinces, and many other senatorial appointments outside the central *cursus* of magistracies in Rome. Entry to the senate for those not of senatorial birth was in his gift, and so was the extension of his 'commendation' to some candidates for each of the magistracies proper. In the third century it may be that the emperor's will became entrenched here too, for not long after Alexander and Tertullian were writing Modestinus states flatly that the *Lex Julia* on electoral malpractices 'no longer applies in the city, for the appointment of magistrates is a matter for the consideration of the Princeps, not the favour of the people.'[3]

The steady intrusion of imperial patronage into the complex area of senatorial office-holding, with its background of inherited conventions, with new rules created by the Augustan marriage-legislation, and with the development of new posts and functions in Rome, Italy and the provinces, involves many disputed questions which we need not examine in detail. It is more

[1] *Com. in Topica* 116b 24 (*Com. Gr. in Arist.* II. 2, p. 238). For the dedication see p. 497; for the theme of the friendship of kings, p. 110. This element is introduced by Alexander and is not found in the text of Aristotle.

[2] *Ad Nat.* II, 13, 1–2.

[3] *Dig.* XLVIII, 14, 1 *pr.* Cf. pp. 300f.

important to emphasize that the granting of office, both equestrian and senatorial, was one of the principal forms in which the emperor showed favour to members of the upper classes of the empire (and occasionally, to universal indignation, to others); or, to express it differently, it was one of the principle subjects of communication from him to them. Appian, for instance, ends the preface of his *Roman History* by introducing himself— 'Appian, an Alexandrian, one of the most prominent men in my native city, who has acted as *advocatus* in Rome before the kings, and has now been thought worthy by them to be one of their procurators'.[4]

But we may also ask how far office-holding was also a subject of communication from them to him; how far, in other words, equestrian or senatorial office was not only a favour or honour to be granted, but also, like the innumerable rights, privileges and honours within provincial life which we shall examine later, something to be petitioned for, on behalf of oneself or others. It was certainly so in the case of Appian's procuratorship, which was gained as a result of at least two years' supplication by Cornelius Fronto.[5] Appian is perfectly typical of his age, in that he quite clearly sees his procuratorship as the product firstly of his prominence in a famous city and secondly of his oratorical ability. From what Fronto says in recommending him it may well be that the procuratorship was purely honorific and involved no actual post. If so, that would emphasize even further his resemblance to the many local dignitaries who were honoured with equestrian distinctions by the emperor. Whether the rank of *eques* itself could be granted by the emperor remains curiously unclear; but the two special equestrian distinctions of the 'public horse' (*equus publicus*) and adlection into the jury panels (*decuriae iudicum*) in Rome certainly were.[6]

Such honours themselves formed a significant element in the emperor's links with the upper classes of the cities, who maintained, as we shall see, a remarkable degree of direct contact with him, primarily in the form of embassies. But his decisions relating to provincial matters were also of course channelled and expressed in correspondence with office-holders of both orders, sometimes passing on the requests or complaints of individuals or communities, and sometimes sending him information or consulting him spontaneously. The nature and limits of this correspondence are absolutely essential to any conception of what role the emperor actually played in the government of the empire; for the moment, it may be observed that the vast bulk of it was initiated by individual office-holders, and that it was comparatively rare for general orders to be sent spontaneously to them by the emperor; and further that the frequency of consultation of the emperor *seems* to have increased in the latter part of the period. Quite a number of imperial *rescripta* in the *Digest* and the *Codex Justinianus*, and almost all those of this period in the *Codex Theodosianus*, are in origin *epistulae* to provincial governors and other office-holders, and many of these are replies to individual queries.

[4] *Praef.* 15/62.
[5] pp. 286–7.
[6] pp. 279–84.

When an emperor emerged as ruler of the Roman world, he long remained in principle a member of the senate himself; the evolution of his role there was again a matter of the greatest complexity, which can only be sketched here. Though even in the early empire we can find cases of the senate sending embassies to the emperor very much as the council of a city would do, we have far more evidence of his speaking in the senate as a member of it; indeed, as Fronto makes clear, his *orationes* in the senate were among the principal occasions for the deployment of his *eloquentia*.[7] Fronto himself, for instance, says in another letter to Aurelius: 'At the last sitting of the senate, when you spoke of the serious case of the Cyzicenes, you embellished your speech with a figure which the Greeks call *paraleipsis*, in such a way that, while waiving the point, you yet mentioned it, and, while mentioning it, you yet waived it.'[8] Imperial *orationes* were not mere oratorical displays, however, nor were they confined to immediate issues such as the earthquake in Cyzicus. On the contrary, they served at least until the early third century as their primary vehicle, along with *edicta*, for the promulgation of new legislation.

Even beyond that time, and indeed to the very end of our period, the emperor might on occasion speak in person in the senate, as Constantine did after his victory in 312.[9] But it had long since become common for his *oratio* to be 'recited' by someone else; the very fact of the increasing absence of the emperor from Rome must have tended to make this the rule. In 258 Cyprian can refer to the same communication from Valerian to the senate both as an *oratio* and as an *epistula*.[10] From Augustus onwards we have references to letters of emperors to the senate, especially to announce their accession to power, or to proclaim victories on campaigns. But it is only from the reign of Constantine that we have a couple of texts of such letters, addressed in formal style almost exactly as if to a provincial city— '(Constantine) to the consuls, praetors, tribunes of the people and Senate *salutem dicit*.'[11] We may reasonably see this as a symbol of the long-prepared and now virtually complete separation of the emperor from the senate from which his office had emerged.

None the less, the emperors continued up to this time (as they were to do up to the sixth century) to hold the consulate from time to time, and, when doing so, could (if in Rome) preside in the senate. They also retained in their titulature elements of republican origin, such as 'proconsul', 'tribunicia potestas' or 'Pontifex Maximus'.[12] The latter title may recall that the emperor was not only the head of the priestly college of Pontifices, but also a member of the colleges of Augures, Quindecimviri sacris faciundis, and Septemviri epulonum, of the Fetiales, Sodales Titii, Fratres Arvales, and, with the passage of time, of various *sodalitates* for the cults of deified emperors. In the

---

[7] p. 204.

[8] *Ad Antoninum Imp.* I, 2, 4 (6), Loeb trans.

[9] *Pan.* IX(12), 20.

[10] p. 570.

[11] pp. 341, 353–5; and for the formulae of address of letters to cities, p. 221. There remains the significant difference that the name of Rome does not have to be given.

[12] e.g. *ILS* 697 (Vicetia) with Constantine's titulature as of the 320s.

empire all these colleges and sodalities were open only to senators, and thus formed a limited and privileged group within the senate. In some of them vacancies were filled by a vote in the senate, in others by co-optation; in either case any recommendation by the emperor was decisive. Both aspects are vividly illustrated by the letter in which Pliny writes to Trajan in the most urgent terms to ask for either an augurate or septemvirate:[13]

> Since I know, Lord, that it stands as a witness and credit of my character to be adorned by the judgment of so good a *Princeps*, I beseech you to add to the *dignitas* to which your *indulgentia* has elevated me an augurate or septemvirate, since there are vacancies in both, so that I may pray to the gods for your safety in my public capacity as priest, as I do now with private piety.

It is a matter of some significance that, just as we can see the emperor acting partly as a member of the senate and partly in dissociation from it, so we have evidence at least up to the early third century of his acting as a member of these smaller and more exclusive priestly colleges: carrying out sacrifices and rituals with them, and writing letters to them to put forward a new member or to appoint a day for the conduct of their duties.[14] Once again we cannot tell how the conduct of this important aspect of the imperial role was affected by the steadily more continuous absence of the emperor from Rome from the first half of the third century onwards.

Nor can we do more than speculate as to how much, if at all, the long-established role of the emperor as Pontifex Maximus and a member of the priestly colleges affected the assumptions on which Constantine based his relations with the Christian church. But while it casts no light on this, Eusebius' *Life of Constantine* does serve to emphasize perhaps more explicitly than any other source from the period the importance of office and rank among the *beneficia* distributed by the emperor. Slightly less clearly, Eusebius also reflects the assumption that ranks and honours, like money or land, could be petitioned from the emperor:[15]

> No one could request a favour from the emperor, and fail of obtaining what he sought: no one expected a boon from him, and found that expectation vain. Some received presents of money, others in land; some obtained the praefectural dignities, others senatorial, others again consular rank: many were appointed provincial governors; others were made *comites* of the first, second or third order: in numberless instances the title of *perfectissimus*, and many other distinctions were conferred; for the emperor devised new dignities, that he might invest a larger number with the tokens of his favour.

---

[13] *Ep.* X, 13. He was rewarded with the augurate, IV, 8.
[14] pp. 355–61.
[15] *VC* IV, 1, trans. Richardson (with slight adjustments). For Constantine's creation of three grades of *comites*, see p. 278.

2. *The Equestrian Order: the 'Public Horse',*
the Jury Panels and Equestrian Offices

It was a principle of Roman law that legally valid gifts could not be made between husband and wife. But like every other such principle it was subject to concessions made by the indulgence of the emperor. So, for instance, Gaius, writing in the middle of the second century, mentions that it had been permitted by the *indulgentia* of Antoninus Pius that a wife could make a gift to her husband *honoris causa*: 'For example, if a wife made a gift to her husband in order for him to seek the *latus clavus* [the broad stripe on the toga signifying senatorial rank] or that he should become [or be made?] a member of the *equester ordo* or for the sake of games [which he would be giving]'.[1] Ulpian in the early third century expresses the matter slightly differently: the right had been conceded by imperial *constitutiones*, if the gift were 'in order that the husband should be rewarded by the emperor with the *latus clavus* or the *equus publicus* or a similar honour'.[2]

Both passages clearly illustrate the assumption that such honours would be gained by the initiative of the person concerned, and that of Gaius reflects the background typical of a man with such expectations, namely that of the upper classes of the cities, whose status required the giving of expensive games. Moreover, as we shall see, the seeking of the *latus clavus* from the emperor is well attested.[3] Our difficulties begin when we compare the two references to equestrian status. The relevance to it of such a gift is not in itself in doubt; for it is not disputed that the possession of a census valuation of 400,000 *sesterces* was necessary for equestrian status under the empire. But was a further condition required, namely conferment of the rank by the emperor; and, if so, was this identical with the grant of the 'public horse' to which Ulpian refers?[4]

What Gaius says, 'that he should become [or be made?] a member of the *equestor ordo*', could imply conferment of the rank, presumably by the emperor, but does not state this clearly. At the end of the first century, however, we find Pliny the Younger writing to a friend from Comum to offer him 300,000 *sesterces* 'to make up the wealth required of an *eques*' and speaking of the '*dignitas* given by myself'; the letter is in marked contrast with one which he writes to Trajan to ask for the *latus clavus* for a friend *after* the latter's mother has made over sufficient property to him.[5] Writing

---

[1] *Dig.* XXIV, 1, 42, reading 'ut ecce si uxor viro lati petendi (for 'petenti') gratia donat vel ut equestris ordinis fiat vel ludorum gratia'.

[2] *Tit.* VII, 1 (*FIRA*² II, p. 271): 'ut is ab imperatore lato clavo vel equo publico similive honore honoretur.' Both passages are quoted, for instance, in Mommsen, *Staatsrecht*³ II, 2, 920.

[3] pp. 291–3.

[4] For these long-debated questions see e.g. A. Stein, *Der römische Ritterstand* (1927), 54f.; M. I. Henderson, 'The Establishment of the *Equester Ordo*', *JRS* LIII (1963), 61; C. Nicolet, *L'ordre équestre a l'époque républicaine* I (1966), 177f.; R. P. Duncan-Jones, 'Equestrian Rank in the Cities of the African Provinces under the Principate: an Epigraphic Survey', *PBSR* XXXV, n.s. XXII (1967), 147; T. P. Wiseman, 'The Definition of "Eques Romanus" in the Late Republic and Early Empire', *Historia* XIX (1970), 67.

[5] Pliny, *Ep.* I, 19 (Romatius Firmus); X, 4.

to Romatius Firmus from Comum, Pliny would not have omitted to mention confirment or confirmation of the rank by the emperor if it had been required.

Can we then conclude that the broad class of *equites* in the empire was made up of men who were Roman citizens and possessed the required census, but had not individually received the honour from the emperor, or sought it from him? That is certainly implied by the inscription from Rome which describes a man as 'born an *eques Romanus*',[6] and much more clearly by the very rarity of evidence for the emperors conferring equestrian rank as such. Suetonius reports that Augustus gave *equestris dignitas* to a freedman as a reward for his having concealed his *patronus* in the proscriptions;[7] but such a grant must have carried with it the grant of notional free birth, symbolized in the late republic and the empire by the conferment of a gold ring, which itself is obscurely connected in our sources with equestrian rank.[8] Otherwise, apart from an apparent reference in Juvenal to the emperor himself giving a man the 400,000 *sesterces*,[9] all our evidence for the conferment of equestrian rank by the emperor relates either to the 'public horse' or the panels of jurors (*decuriae iudicum*). The possible exceptions are Dio's and Suetonius' brief reports that Gaius and Vespasian replenished the order of *equites* by summoning suitable men from the provinces and enrolling them;[10] and it may be significant that Claudius could remove the *equestris dignitas* of men who declined promotion to the senate.[11]

The institution of the 'public horse' went back to the role of the equestrian centuries in the remote past as the cavalry of the Roman army. In the late republic the possession of the *equus publicus* was an honour, and the maintenance of the list was a duty carried out every five years by the censors. Augustus revived the ceremonial of an annual parade (*transvectio*) of the *equites*; and Suetonius may not be wrong in representing Augustus as carrying out the censorial function of the examination (*recognitio*) of the *equites* at the parade itself. Augustus heard accusations of unfitness against the participants in person, with ten assistants whom he requested from the senate, and pronounced on the cases there and then; the lightest form of reproof according to Suetonius, was for him to hand over some notes (presumably containing admonitions), which the *eques* was required to read in his presence.[12] It will be from this context that we have anecdotes of exchanges between Augustus and individual *equites*: Quintilian describes a man replying to Augustus' admonition for wasting his property, 'I thought

---

[6] *ILS* 1318.

[7] Suetonius, *Aug.* 27.

[8] Cf. Wiseman, o.c., 73, and for the empire *Dig.* XL, 10 (relating entirely to grants by the emperor to freedmen), see Mommsen, *Staatsrecht*[3] II. 2, 893; and cf. pp. 488–90.

[9] *Sat.* V, 132f.

[10] Dio LIX, 9, 5: τοῦ τε τέλους τοῦ τῶν ἱππέων ὀλιγανδροῦντος, τοὺς πρώτους ἐξ ἁπάσης καὶ τῆς ἔξω ἀρχῆς τοῖς τε γένεσι καὶ ταῖς περιουσίαις μεταπεμψάμενος κατελέξατο. Suetonius, *Vesp.* 9, 2: 'Amplissimos ordines ... purgavit, supplevitque recenso senatu et equite ... honestissimo quoque italicorum et provincialium allecto.' The references *could*, however, be to either the *turmae equitum* or the *decuriae*.

[11] Suetonius, *Claud.* 24, 1 (during his censorship?).

[12] *Aug.* 38–9: 'equitum turmas frequenter recognovit, post longum intercapedinem reducto more travectionis'; *contra*, Wiseman, o.c., 69.

it was my own';[13] while Macrobius reports another refuting the same accusation, producing his wife and three children to show that he had obeyed the marriage laws, and finally saying, 'Caesar, when you make enquiries (*inquiris*) about honest men, entrust the task to honest men.'[14] We have no evidence as to how or to what extent evidence was sought in advance of these public examinations by the emperor in person, but it is clearly this process which is referred to in a later Greek inscription from Bithynia, which describes a local magnate, a relative of senators and consuls, as 'honoured with a public horse by *inquisitio*'.[15]

That expression seems to imply that the emperor's examination could be directed not merely to approving or disapproving a man's retention of the public horse, but to his receiving it in the first place. More clearly still, Ovid addresses Augustus from his exile, 'You used to approve my way of life and character when I rode past on that horse which you had given.'[16] However, the only concrete evidence of a man positively seeking the *equus publicus* from the emperor comes from a not very clear anecdote preserved in two slightly different forms in the *Sententiae* of Hadrian.[17] The man states that he possesses the equestrian census (*facultates*), but when he had sought the *equus publicus*, had been passed over because of a charge against him; Hadrian replies that any man who seeks the *equus publicus* must be of blameless life.

This episode does, however, make quite clear the distinction between possession of the requisite equestrian census-valuation and the grant of the public horse, and also emphasizes the personal role of the emperor; whether the exchange is supposed to take place at the formal parade is not clear. Nor do we know how long the parade itself continued to be held. But Philostratus seems to be referring to this when he describes Caracalla rewarding the Arabian sophist Heliodorus for his successful appearance before him in Gaul in 213, by granting him and his sons the right 'to ride publicly';[18] while inscriptions continue to mention prominent individuals who were 'honoured with the public horse' by one emperor or another, up to Severus Alexander in the third and fourth decades of the third century.[19] Some of

---

[13] *Inst.* VI, 3, 74.

[14] *Sat.* II, 4, 25. Note also Pliny, *NH* XXXIII, 8/33, accusations against supposed *equites* being laid 'apud Claudium Caesarem in censura'.

[15] *AE* 1954 230 (Prusias ad Hypium), Olympius Titius Calpurnianus, ἵππῳ δημοσίῳ τετειμημένον ἐξ ἰνκουισιτιῶνος. It is unfortunate that the title of the valuable article by C. Nicolet, ' "Eques romanus ex inquisitione" à propos d'une inscription de Prousias de l'Hypios', *BCH* XCI (1967), 411, misrepresents the contents of the document. 'Eq. r. ex inquisitione allecto' is attested only in *ILAlg.* I 2145 (Madauros), for a very similar local magnate, M. Cornelius Fronto Gabinianus, and surely also refers to the *equus publicus*. Note also *ILS* 2711 (Tarraco): 'adlecto in equite a T. imp.', which depends on a single sixteenth-century copy.

[16] *Tristia* II, 89–90, cf. 541–2.

[17] *Corp. Gloss. Lat.* III, 33, ll. 1–25; 388, ll. 11–21.

[18] *VS* II, 32: ἱππεύειν αὐτῷ τε δημοσίᾳ ἔδωκε καὶ παισίν, ὁπόσους ἔχοι. Cf. the grant by Hadrian to Dionysius of Miletus, ibid., I, 22: ἐγκατέλεξε δὲ τοῖς δημοσίᾳ ἱππεύουσι.

[19] Q. Rupilius Honoratus is described in *ILS* 1315 (Mactar) as 'in equestres turmas adlecto a divo Alexandro'. Cf. Duncan-Jones, o.c., esp. 151–2. *ILS* 5473 (Rusicade), L. Cornelius Fronto Probianus 'eq. p. orn', is subsequent to the death of Elagabal (222). *AE* 1964 223 shows that the honorific pre-senatorial post of *sevir turmae deducendae* still existed towards the middle of the third century.

10*

these also held equestrian posts in the emperor's service, but others are clear examples of the class of men whose role was essentially based on their own cities or provinces—for instance M. Licinius Pompenna Potitus Urbanus, a decurion, *pontifex*, agonothete and so forth at Heliopolis in Syria, who was 'granted the public horse by the deified Hadrian'.[20]

None of the inscriptions recording the public horse gives any concrete indication of how the honour came to be awarded. All that is clear is that it took its place among the other honours and *beneficia* which the emperors could distribute. For instance, an inscription of 170 from Abella in Campania records a man who had been permitted by the *indulgentia* of the emperor to give a gladiatorial show at his own expense, and whose son had been honoured with the *equus publicus* by Marcus Aurelius and Verus.[21] In such a case the son might possibly have gained it, like Heliodorus, as a result of a successful appearance before the emperors.

That might be true also of a man like M. Gavius Gallicus, a provincial high priest from Attalia in Pamphylia, whose inscription records that he was widely honoured by cities both there and in the province of Asia, and who had 'delivered many speeches on behalf of his own and very many other cities before both the governors and the emperors'; he held the evidently honorific post of *praefectus fabrum*, and was also 'honoured by the emperor with the public horse in Rome' and was 'a chosen judge (*iudex selectus*) of the *decuriae* in Rome'.[22]

The honour of being adlected to the *decuriae* of *iudices* in Rome appears on inscriptions in the same context and over the same period—from the end of the first century to the first part of the third[23]—as do those mentioning the 'public horse'. One of the earliest cases is provided by a new inscription from Ephesus showing that M. Gavius Bassus, who was *praefectus orae Ponticae maritimae* while Pliny was governor of Bithynia in 109–11, had previously been 'adlected into the fifth *decuria* among the *selecti*' between his tribunate of a legion and prefecture of an *ala*.[24] Both these units were stationed in Moesia, and even though Bassus, as the inscription indicates, came from Rome, it may be doubted whether he returned there in the interval. Whether either involved any actual attendance in Rome or not, the two honours were both granted solely by the emperor, and might or might not both be given to the same man. For instance, Q. Voltedius Optatus Aurelianus, who had been a military tribune and otherwise held office only in Carthage (where he gave a show with gladiators and elephants towards the end of Hadrian's reign), had been granted the *equus publicus* by Trajan and

[20] *IGLS* VI 2791.

[21] *ILS* 5058.

[22] *IGR* III 778 = *OGIS* 567, ll. 7–11: τετειμημένον ὑπὸ τοῦ Σεβαστοῦ ἵππῳ δημοσίῳ ἐν Ῥώμῃ, ἐπίλεκτον κριτὴν ἐκ τῶν ἐν Ῥώμῃ δεκουριῶν.

[23] *ILS* 7122 shows a man 'a[dl.] in V dec. inter select.' who was a decurion of the *colonia Septimia Aurelia Antoniniana Carnuntum*, the titles which the town had from the reign of Severus (193–211) onwards. There does not seem to be any example which is provably later than this.

[24] D. Knibbe, 'Neue Inschriften aus Ephesos II', *JÖAI* XLIX (1968–71, pub. 1973), Beiblatt, col. 16, no. 2 = *AE* 1972 573. The inscription is in both Latin and Greek.

entry to the *decuriae* by Hadrian; by contrast a local dignitary from Curulis in Africa received both from Antoninus Pius.[25]

Some men who received this honour went on to equestrian careers, as did Sex. Iulius Possessor who was adlected into the *decuriae* by Marcus Aurelius and Verus;[26] while others remained in their local contexts. One such was L. Septimius Severus, the grandfather of the emperor, who held office only in Lepcis in Tripolitania, except that he 'judged in the *decuriae* and among the *selecti* at Rome'.[27] In this case the wording certainly suggests that he actually was in Rome for a period.[28]

That some men did come from the provinces to Rome to act as *iudices* is made clear by a passage of Pliny the Elder, which further indicates that the selection of the *decuriae* was an aspect of the censorial functions of the emperors:[29]

> But the *decuriae* are examined according to custom by the censorial powers of the emperors, the *inquisitio* invades the home, and to judge about a single coin a man is summoned from Gades and the Pillars of Hercules, while on a question of exile the vote is put to not less than forty-five *electi viri*.

Of Augustus, Suetonius reports that he chose (*adlegit*) *iudices* of age 30 and over;[30] and his statement that Tiberius, after leaving Rome in 26, never again filled up the *decuriae* makes clear that this function depended entirely on the will of the emperor. It is he too who relates that when Livia insisted that a man to whom he had given the citizenship should also be adlected into the *decuriae*, Tiberius said that he would not unless the words 'this was extorted from me by my mother' were written on the *album*.[31] It is clear that, for certain persons at least, a place in the *decuriae* was a *beneficium* to be gained by the intercession of powerful friends. That even in this period it did not necessarily involve any duties is suggested by Suetonius' story of Claudius in his censorship of 47–8 discovering among the *iudices* a man who was the leading figure of a Greek province, but knew no Latin; he lost not only his place on the *album* but his Roman citizenship as well.[32]

Thus in the first two and a half centuries of the empire both the *equus publicus* and a place in the *decuriae* could function as dignities conferred by the emperor, and sometimes petitioned for from him; in both cases it is not clear to what extent they were mere titles, or involved actual duties in Rome. But, though the evidence is far from certain, it is on balance necessary to conclude that imperial patronage did not extend beyond these two specific dignities to the award of equestrian rank itself; but rather that the wider class of *equites* from whom imperial officials and new entrants to the senate

[25] *ILS* 9406–7.
[26] *ILS* 1403; cf. Pflaum, *Carrières*, no. 185.
[27] *IRT* 412 (Lepcis): 'in decuriis et inter selectos Romae iudicavit.'
[28] cf. A. Birley, *Septimius Severus, the African Emperor* (1971), 39.
[29] *NH* xxix, 8/18, emended Loeb trans. For the actual functions performed by the panels of *iudices* see also Suetonius, *Galba* 14, 3. Cf. also *ILS* 206.
[30] *Aug.* 32, 3.
[31] *Tib.* 41; 51, 1.
[32] *Claud.* 16, 2.

were recruited was formed by men of free birth and the necessary census.[33]

While the 'public horse' and the panels of jurors disappear from view after the first part of the third century, equestrian office-holding continued to gain in importance; only Constantine's action in opening a wider range of offices to senators to some degree reversed the trend.[34] So we must ask how the emperor's patronage was exercised, on what assumptions it was based and what pattern of social relations it involved; and in particular how far did men actively seek office from him, and on what did they base their claims?

A few scattered references show that even centurionates might be gained by the exercise of patronage, and sometimes by request to the emperor;[35] and it is, perhaps surprisingly, in connection with the military posts (normally, *praefectus cohortis*, *tribunus militum* or *legionis*, and *praefectus alae*) which formed the first part of the developing equestrian career, that we find the most evidence of requests to the emperor and of patronage by others. For instance Artemidorus of Daldis includes in his book on dreams the case of an *eques* who was 'asking for a military post from the king'; after dreaming that he had been given a crown of olive 'such as the Roman *equites* wear in processions', he believed that he would be successful—but it turned out to have portended his marriage.[36] Pliny's correspondence seems to show that such posts could also be granted directly by imperial *legati*; Pliny asks Sosius Senecio to make a friend of his, Varisidius Nepos, 'more splendid' by granting him a six-month tribunate;[37] and later requests Pompeius Falco to confer a tribunate on Cornelius Minicianus, 'an ornament of my region in both *dignitas* and character'. When he had got to know the man more closely, Falco would feel that he had received a *beneficium* rather than conferred one.[38] In this case it seems clear that as tribune Minicianus would actually join his *legatus*. It is not so certain in the first instance, and still less so where Pliny writes to Suetonius to answer his request that the tribunate which Pliny had gained for him from Neratius Marcellus should be transferred to a relative; the change could still be made, for Suetonius' name had not yet been placed on the list.[39] There is nothing to indicate that the tribunate would have involved either Suetonius or his relative in a journey to Britain.

Pliny's evidence on the right of imperial *legati* to appoint to tribunates remains entirely isolated, except for the letter of a *legatus* of Britannia Inferior of about 220 to a friend and client of his in Gaul, sending him

---

[33] Note Suetonius, *Aug.* 40, Augustus allowed *equites* whose *patrimonia* had declined to sit in the fourteen rows reserved for them at the theatre if 'ipsis parentibusve equester census unquam fuisset'.

[34] p. 296.

[35] e.g. Dio LXXVIII, 5, 3 (408), an *evocatus* who had unsuccessfully requested Caracalla for a centurionate; Pliny, *Ep.* VI, 25, 3, mentions that he had requested (*impetraveram*) a centurionate (from Trajan?) for his *municeps*, Metilius Crispus, who was at the time evidently a civilian; Suetonius, *De gram. et rhet.* 24, M. Valerus Probus from Berytus, 'diu centurionatum petit, donec taedio ad studia se contulit'. Again it is not clear from whom.

[36] *Oneir.* IV, 28: ἱππικὸς ἀνὴρ στρατείαν αἰτῶν παρὰ τοῦ βασιλέως.

[37] *Ep.* IV, 4.

[38] VII, 22; this is evidently during Falco's praetorian governorship of Judaea, see Schürer, *Jewish People* I, 516–17.

[39] III, 8; cf. p. 90.

valuable items of military dress, and promising him a letter of appointment to a *semestris* (*tribunatus*), with a salary of 25,000 *sesterces*, as soon as there was a vacancy.[40] It may well be that *legati* were entitled to fill a limited number of such posts by exercising their own patronage.[41] Otherwise our sources are unanimous in regarding the emperor himself as the source of equestrian military posts. 'If the greatest emperor had granted me the rod, that is the command over a hundred men,' wrote Florus early in the second century, 'I would regard that as an honour of no small moment; and similarly if a prefecture or tribunate, for the honour is the same, except that the pay is greater'—but he still preferred to teach literature.[42] How the names of the persons to be appointed came before the emperor is less clear. Suetonius reports, evidently as a rarity, that Augustus appointed men seeking the *equestris militia* 'even on the official recommendation of the several cities'.[43] From his reign also Macrobius retails the anecdote of a man who was removed from his prefecture of cavalry, but still demanded the pay, saying to Augustus in person, 'It is not for the sake of gain that I ask for it to be given to me, but in order that I may seem to have gained the gift by your choice, and under such circumstances to have laid down my post.' Augustus replied, 'Tell everyone that you received it, and I will not deny it.'[44]

The personal involvement of the emperor is even clearer in an anecdote of Suetonius about Vespasian; on being confronted with a highly-scented young man making a speech of thanks for a prefecture which he had gained by request, he retorted 'I would have preferred it if you had smelt of garlic', and recalled the *litterae* of appointment.[45]

It is evident from this story that appointment to a *praefectura* could be regarded as a *beneficium* conferred by the emperor, for which gratitude was due; there is a comparable implication in Dio's reference to the earlier career of Pertinax: he was acquainted with Claudius Pompeianus (a prominent senator, and son-in-law of Marcus Aurelius), and through him gained a military tribunate.[46] The workings of such patronage are also illustrated in the letter which Pliny wrote to Trajan to ask for promotion for the son of an old friend who was currently on his staff in Bithynia:[47]

For these reasons I count his connections as my own, and above all his son, Nymphidius Lupus, a young man of integrity and energy, most worthy of his excellent father, who will show himself deserving of your *indulgentia*, as you can discern from the earliest trials of him, when as prefect of a cohort he earned

[40] *CIL* XIII 3162; cf. H. G. Pflaum, *Le marbre de Thorigny* (1948).

[41] So Mommsen, *Staatsrecht*[3] II. I, 266.

[42] Florus, *Vergilius orator an poeta* 3, 5 (ed. Malcovati). For imperial appointment cf. *HA, Had.* 10, 6; Eumenius, *Pan.* v(9), 5, 4; patronage by imperial favourites, Juvenal, *Sat.* VII, 88–92; appointments by Mucianus early in 70, Tacitus, *Hist.* IV, 39, 4.

[43] *Aug.* 46.

[44] *Sat.* II, 4, 5.

[45] *Vesp.* 8, 3.

[46] LXXIII, 3, 1 (307).

[47] *Ep.* X, 87, 3. At this time *clarissimus vir* was just becoming the conventional status-appellation for a senator. Ti. Julius Ferox (*PIR*[2] I 306) and Cn. Pedanius Fuscus Salinator, *RE* s.v. 'Pedanius' (5), had both evidently been consular legates, of which provinces is not known.

the strongest testimonials from Julius Ferox and Fuscus Salinator, *clarissimi viri*. You will complete my pleasure and satisfaction, lord, by honouring him.

Pliny thus refers to the *testimonia* which might be sent to the emperor by a man's superiors (or might also be brought by a provincial embassy to attest the virtues of a Roman official),[48] but his own letter is not such a thing, for there is no indication that the young man himself is serving in Bithynia. It is an act of personal friendship and patronage, evidently designed to help Nymphidius Lupus to the next stage after his prefecture of a cohort, presumably a military tribunate. Statius will be referring to letters of all these types when he describes Abascantus, the *ab epistulis* of Domitian, as assisting the emperor in allotting military posts by making known who was fit for a centurionate, the prefecture of a cohort, a military tribunate or the prefecture of an *ala*.[49] In a system where all decisions were made at the centre, the exercise of patronage by sending in letters of recommendation was indeed natural and necessary. But the very multiplicity of such letters could lead to confusion, perfectly illustrated by the petition addressed by an officer named Flavius Abinnaeus to Constantius and Constans in 340/1: 'Your Clemency deigned to promote me *praefectus alae* at Dionysias in the province of Egypt. But when I submitted the *sacrae litterae* to the *comes* Valacius, his *officium* replied that other men had put forward letters of the same sort . . . But since it is evident that they have been promoted by *suffragium*, but I by the true *iudicium sacrum* . . .'[50] Such letters were also an aspect of the exchange of *officia* traditional in Roman society. Fronto, for instance, writes to Avidius Cassius in Syria to say that the tribune who had brought his 'laurelled letter' (announcing a victory) had served his interests well in Rome—'he deserves to be favoured by you and to be adorned by your recommendations (*suffragia*). You will add to your own *gloria*, the more you increase the *dignitas* of your eulogist.'[51]

Similar considerations affected equestrian promotion at all levels. Pliny, for instance, had said in writing to Suetonius about the transference of his tribunate, 'Moreover I realize that it will redound to my *gloria* also, if from your action it becomes known that my *amici* can not only hold tribunates, but give them.'[52] It is precisely the fact that the credit of persons of superior standing was related to their ability to secure posts for their protégés which explains why posts could be gained by recommendation, and then declined by the recipient. So Fronto writes with striking clarity to Antoninus Pius:

At my request you have adorned the *dignitas* of one *eques Romanus*, my former comrade Sextius Calpurnius, by having granted him two procuratorships

[48] p. 419.
[49] *Silvae* V, 1, 94–8: 'praeterea, fidos dominus si dividat enses, / pandere, (1) quis centum valeat frenare, maniplos / inter missus eques, (2) quis praecepisse cohorti, / (3) quem deceat clari praestantior ordo tribuni, / (4) quisnam frenigerae signum dare dignior alae.' The posts are mentioned in ascending order of seniority. (1) will be the case of an *eques* commissioned directly as a centurion, see p. 284, and cf. H. Zwicky, *Zur Verwendung des Militärs in der Verwaltung der römischen Kaiserzeit* (1944), 90f.
[50] *P. Abinn.* 1 (H. I. Bell, V. Martin, E. G. Turner, D. van Berchem, *The Abinnaeus Archive* (1962), no. 1).
[51] *Ad Amicos* I, 6.
[52] *Ep.* III, 8, 3, cf. p. 284.

already. Those two *beneficia* of procuratorships I count four times: twice when you granted them and again twice when you accepted his excuses.

These remarks form the preliminaries to Fronto's request for a procuratorship for Appian, which he says he has already been making over a period of two years. He supports it by claiming that Appian 'wishes to gain this honour in order to adorn his *dignitas* in his old age, not from ambition or desire for the salary of a procurator', and tries to refute gently Antoninus' earlier response that if he granted it, 'a torrent of forensic orators would well up demanding the same thing'.[53]

Personal appointment by the emperor applied to all the civilian posts open to *equites*, from minor *ad hoc* appointments relating to particular towns,[54] to the junior post of *advocatus fisci*, procuratorships and major prefectures, up to the praetorian prefecture itself. According to Dio, Claudius' wife and freedmen would sell not only grants of citizenship, but military posts, procuratorships and governorships; just as Vespasian's concubine Caenis sold offices, procuratorships, military posts and priesthoods.[55] Similarly, Tacitus describes Vespasian distributing prefectures, procuratorships and senatorial rank immediately on his proclamation in Syria in 69.[56]

From the earlier empire we have occasional references to men being appointed *advocatus fisci* by the emperor, including Quirinus a sophist from Nicomedia, and possibly Heliodorus from Arabia.[57] But our clearest evidence comes from the letter of Constantine to the praetorian prefect, written in Singidunum in 334: 'We have ordered . . . that, if several men have earned from us the office of defending the *fiscus*, that one should be preferred to the others who has been proved by experience to be superior in integrity, more powerful in rhetoric and otherwise better endowed, even if it was later than the others that he gained this *beneficium* from our *clementia*.'[58] From the first and second centuries we have little further evidence of how men obtained procuratorial posts, except for Josephus' imputation that Gessius Florus owed his appointment as procurator of Judaea in 66 to his wife's friendship with Poppaea, the wife of Nero;[59] and his much more remarkable statement that the high priest Jonathan had been responsible for requesting Claudius to send Felix as procurator to Judaea in about 52.[60] More generally, Pliny's

---

[53] *Ad Ant. Pium* 9; cf. p. 276.

[54] e.g. *CIL* x 416 (Volcei), a local dignitary, P. Otacilius Rufus, 'flam. perpetuo divi Hadriani, ab eodem equo publ(ico) honorato, curatori kalendari r(ei) p(ublicae) Aeclanensium electo a divo Pio . . .'

[55] LX, 17, 8; cf. 18, 2; LXVI, 14, 3 (149), Caenis, cf. p. 79.

[56] *Hist.* II, 82, 2.

[57] Quirinus, Philostratus, *VS* II, 29: ἐπιστεύθη ἐκ βασιλέως τὴν τοῦ ταμιείου γλῶτταν. Heliodorus, II, 32: προὐστήσατο αὐτὸν τῆς μεγίστης τῶν κατὰ τὴν Ῥώμην συνηγοριῶν. It is not clear what this means, but we do not know of any other body of *advocati* appointed by the emperor. Cf. also *ILS* 6502 (Beneventum), Vesedius Rufinus, 'advocato fisci summe [sic] rei iudicio sacro promoto'.

[58] *CTh* x, 15, 2.

[59] *Ant.* XX, 11, 1 (252).

[60] xx, 8, 5 (162). Felix was an imperial freedman, but the post was one which was normally held by *equites*. The occasion will presumably have been when Jonathan and others were examined in Rome in connection with communal disturbances just previously, *BJ* II, 12, 6–7 (243–6), and the request itself will have been an attempt to gain favour with Claudius.

letters to Trajan suggest that it was a matter of routine to send to the emperor testimonia recommending equestrian officials.[61] But from the third century we have three dedications from Rome by equestrian office-holders to the prominent persons by whose recommendation (*suffragium*) they had obtained their posts.[62]

All the major offices at least were conferred, like senatorial ones, by letters of appointment from the emperor, known as *codicilli*; that they issued directly from him in person is shown by Suetonius' illustration of the mal-practices of the freedmen under Claudius—'his *liberalitates* were recalled, judgments reversed, and *codicilli* granting *officia* substituted or even openly changed'.[63] The implication of the word, that the document would normally be in the form of a small folded *codex*, is confirmed by a pronouncement of Constantine, which mentions the outer inscription and inner writing of the *codicilli*.[64] But the actual text was cast exactly in the form of an *epistula*, as we know from the only complete and certainly attested example which survives. It was addressed by Marcus Aurelius to Q. Domitius Marsianus, to appoint him *procurator patrimonii* of Narbonensis. The text, as inscribed at the home town of Marsianus, Bulla Regia in Africa, runs as follows:[65]

> Caesar Antoninus Aug. to his own Domitius Marsianus, greeting. Having long been eager to promote you to the splendour of a procuratorship at 200,000 *sesterces* I seize the opportunity which now offers. Succeed therefore to Marius Pudens with every hope of my continued favour, so long as you know yourself to retain your integrity, diligence and experience. Farewell, my Marsianus, dearest to me.

The reception of proper *codicilli* from the emperor was normal for all the higher equestrian posts. As Hermogenianus writes at about the turn of the third and fourth centuries, 'Those who administer the property of the emperors by their *indulgentia*, even without *codicilli*, are excused from a *tutela* or *cura* laid upon them during the period of their administration. The same applies to those who hold the prefecture of the *annona* or the *vigiles*'.[66] The higher prefectures also were in the direct gift of the emperor—Domitian was overheard while attending gladiatorial games saying to his favourite dwarf, 'Do you know any reason why I should have decided at the last appointment to put Mettius Rufus in charge of Egypt?'[67] Unfortunately, no answer is recorded, and for something resembling one we have to turn to a damaged Latin papyrus containing what is probably the text of Domitian's *codicilli* promoting Laberius Maximus from prefect of Egypt to praetorian

[61] See Pliny, *Ep.* x, 86a on Gavius Bassus (cf. p. 282), 'voto pariter et suffragio prosequor'; 85 and 86b are also routine letters of recommendation.

[62] *ILS* 1191; 2941; 4928.

[63] *Claud.* 29, 1.

[64] p. 290.

[65] *AE* 1962 183; cf. H.-G. Pflaum, 'Une lettre de promotion de l'empereur Marc Aurèle pour un procurateur ducénaire de Gaule Narbonaise', *Bonn. Jahrb.* CLXXI (1971), 349.

[66] *Dig.* XXVII, 1, 41 *pr.* I take this to be the meaning of the phrase 'licet citra codicillis'.

[67] Suetonius, *Dom.* 4, 2: 'ecquid sciret cur sibi visum esset ordinatione proxima Aegypto praeficere Mettium Rufum.'

prefect in 83; the sense is not fully recoverable but the normal vocabulary is visible, *pietas, dignitas, devotissima fides*.[68] That the praetorian prefects also received *codicilli* from the emperor is attested by Tacitus' account of an episode in 55; accusations were made against the prefect Afranius Burrus, and an earlier historian, Fabius Rusticus, alleged that *codicilli* had already been written, giving the command to Caecina Tuscus, when Seneca's intervention preserved the *dignatio* of Burrus.[69]

From the latter half of the second century, while the praetorian prefects began to have the appellation *vir eminentissimus*, the other major prefects, the imperial secretaries and subsequently, in the course of the third century, some other equestrian officials, came to be called *vir perfectissimus*. Procurators of ducenariate rank (that is those receiving 200,000 *sesterces* per year) had the appellation *vir egregius*.[70] But by the end of the third century the appellation of *egregius* had become a status which could be gained for itself, without holding any office. What is more, this and other higher statuses, began to be claimed as conferring exemption from the burdensome obligations which fell on city councillors. So we find the *advocatus* for a man named Aurelius Plutarchus claiming in the court of the *rationalis* of Egypt in 299 that his client was exempt from nomination as a *dekaprôtos*:[71]

> Plutarchus, *egregius*, who stands before your Virtue, wishing to obtain relief from city liturgies, some time ago petitioned the divine Fortune of our lords the Augusti and Caesars to grant him the dignity of the egregiate, and their divine Fortune agreed and granted it to him, and it is now in him.

Plutarchus' petition might (but need not) have been made when Diocletian was in Egypt in the previous year.[72] Whether his appeal against nomination was ultimately successful we do not know, but it was certainly taken as forming a basis for legal proceedings, though we know of no general rule which would have justified this. But just for this reason it is an excellent example of how people secured statuses for themselves, and then made as much use of them as they could. The same was evidently true of the perfectissimate. Constantine writes to an office-holder of uncertain status to say 'let those make use of *codicilli* of the *perfectissimatus* who have gained it by petition', provided that they are neither of servile status, nor debtors to the *fiscus*, nor debarred by various other circumstances, including 'if they have bought the honour by paying for a *suffragium*'.[73] But this brief text is far surpassed in significance by the letter of Constantine to an office-holder

---

[68] Cavenaille, *Corp. Pap. Lat.* 238; cf. p. 126.

[69] *Ann.* XIII, 20.

[70] See P. Hirschfeld, 'Die Rangtiteln der römischen Kaiserzeit', *Kleine Schriften* (1913), 646, on pp. 652f.; cf. now H.-G. Pflaum, 'Titulature et rang social sous le Haut-Empire', *Recherches sur les structures sociales dans l'antiquité classique*, ed. C. Nicolet (1970), 159, on pp. 177f.

[71] *P. Oxy.* 1204, ll. 13–16: ἀπαλλαγὴν εὕρασθαι πειρώμενος ὁ παρεστὼς τῇ σῇ ἀρετῇ Πλούταρχος ὁ κράτιστος τῶν πολειτικῶν λειτουργιῶν δεδέηται τῆς θείας τύχης ἔτι ἄνωθεν τῶν δεσποτῶν ἡμῶν τῶν Σεβαστῶν καὶ τῶν Καισάρων μεταδοῦναι αὐτῷ τοῦ τῆς κρατιστίας ἀξιώματος, καὶ ἐπένευσεν ἡ θεία τύχη αὐτῶν καὶ μετέδωκεν, καὶ νῦν ἐστιν ἐν αὐτῷ.

[72] p. 35.

[73] *CJ* XII, 32, 1; fragmentary text in *CTh* VI, 38 [37], 1. Undated.

named Severus.[74] Few surviving documents are so rich in implications for the relations of subject and emperor; the eagerness with which men sought actual office or nominal dignities from the emperor; the means which they employed, whether by personal contact or the patronage of others; the use of the higher ranks as a way of escape from the obligations of the lower; the form of the imperial *codicilli* which conferred office or rank; and the tension between the emperor's expected liberality in bestowing distinctions, so complaisantly described by Eusebius,[75] and his efforts to check corruption and ensure that men did not improperly avoid the services required by their native cities—all these are reflected here. As a primary document for the role of honours and distinctions in the communications in both directions between the emperor and his subjects, it deserves to be set out in full:

> If anyone claims that he has acquired *codicilli* by our judgment, and this is confirmed by either the outer inscription or the inner text of the *codicilli*, none the less if it is proved that money was expected for this, he will be deprived (of his rank), and returned to the *plebs*, the more so as he tried to extract himself from it. It shall be permitted for those alone who have held office within the *palatium*, or have performed administrative functions, to be received into *honores*, all the others being excluded, and restored to the town-councils. If however any, by the *suffragium* of good men and without giving any money, or by undertaking a provincial embassy, have been illumined by our regard, let these, if they have gained decemvirates, *curae* or the High-Priesthood of a province, not refuse to undergo the other public obligations. But let those who have bought posts as *procuratores*, and after receiving pay from the *fiscus* have gained retirement, whether they are *perfectissimi* or are placed in the rank and order of *egregii*, be nominated as city-councillors. To these should be added those who have not filled any post, and none the less skulk as *perfectissimi*.

3. *Senatorial Status and the Emperor*

To Tertullian, as we saw, the fact that new senators were recruited by the emperor was an unquestioned assumption,[1] and it is important to stress that he was essentially correct. Of all the men who become members of the senate in the empire only those who were themselves the sons of senators did not owe their entry to the emperor. How far and in what respects the relations of the senate as a body with the emperor can be characterized as those of subject and ruler is a complex issue, which will be touched on later, as will the more straightforward question of the extent and limits of imperial patronage in the promotion of those already members of the senate.[2] But the fact that senatorial rank, virtually confined to Italians at the beginning of the period, was steadily extended to men from all the more civilized provinces in both the Latin west and the Greek east, and thence to their descendants, was

[74] *CTh* VI, 22, I. For the problems about the dating of this letter, and the identification of its addressee and his post, see Seeck, *Regesten*, 62.

[75] p. 278.

[1] p. 275.

[2] pp. 300–13, 341–55.

entirely a function of imperial patronage. So the granting of senatorial status in various forms was, like that of the 'public horse' or the panels of jurors, a constituent element in the emperor's relations with the upper classes of the empire. There remained the significant difference that senatorial status was in practice hereditary, whereas these equestrian honours were not.

But if senatorial status took its place among all the other *beneficia* which could be granted by the emperor, it remains to ask in what form this was done, and how commonly, if at all, the conferment was the response to a request from the recipient, or from others on his behalf. The latter is clearly exemplified by a letter of Pliny the Younger: 'I gained for Sextus the *latus clavus* from our Caesar, and also the quaestorship, and by my *suffragium* he has attained the right to seek the tribunate.' The further stages of Sextus' career will be considered later,[3] but its dependence on requests by Pliny is obvious, as is the object of the initial request, namely the *latus clavus*. The latter was the broad purple stripe on the tunic which distinguished persons of senatorial rank from *equites*, who had a narrow stripe (*angustus clavus*). It would seem natural to see the conferment of it by the emperor as a development from the permission granted by Augustus for the sons of senators to assume the *latus clavus* and attend the senate immediately upon taking the *toga virilis*.[4] But in fact Suetonius can quote a popular song from the dictatorship of Julius Caesar, which associated his introduction of Gauls into the senate with their taking the *latus clavus*;[5] while Seneca mentions a man who refused the *latus clavus* when Caesar offered it.[6] On what Caesar's right to do this was based seems quite obscure.

On the other hand the evidence for the practice in the reigns of Augustus and Tiberius is also very slight. But Suetonius reports that Vespasian, an Italian of non-senatorial birth, 'having taken the *toga virilis*, long spurned the *latus clavus*, although his brother had gained it, and was at last compelled to seek it only by his mother'; the time in question will be the latter part of Tiberius' reign, probably about 30 or soon after.[7] Suetonius seems to have assumed that Vespasian's *latus clavus* was to be sought from the emperor; he also records that Tiberius removed the *latus clavus* from a senator as a punishment.[8] By contrast, Dio follows his report of Gaius summoning men from the provinces to fill the *equester ordo* by saying that he granted some of them permission to wear 'the senatorial dress' before holding any office 'through which we enter the senate', which had, it seemed, been permitted previously only to the sons of senators.[9] If Suetonius is correct, Dio's slight uncertainty

---

[3] *Ep.* II, 9, 2; cf. p. 303.

[4] Suetonius, *Aug.* 38, 2. For what follows, compare now A. Chastagnol, ' "Latus Clavus" et "Adlectio",' *Rev. hist. de droit* LIII (1975), 375.

[5] *Jul.* 80, 2: 'Gallos Caesar in triumphum ducit, idem in curiam: / Galli bracas deposuerunt, latum clavum sumpserunt.'

[6] *Ep.* 98, 13.

[7] *Vesp.* 2. Vespasian was born in AD 9 and will have taken the *toga virilis* in about 27. Before being aedile in 38 (Dio LIX, 12, 3) he had held a military tribunate and quaestorship.

[8] *Tib.* 35, 2.

[9] LIX, 9, 5: καί τισιν αὐτῶν καὶ τῇ ἐσθῆτι τῇ βουλευτικῇ, καὶ πρὶν ἄρξαι τινὰ ἀρχὴν δι' ἧς ἐς τὴν γερουσίαν ἐσερχόμεθα, χρῆσθαι ἐπὶ τῇ τῆς βουλείας ἐλπίδι ἔδωκε· πρότερον γὰρ μόνοις, ὡς ἔοικε, τοῖς ἐκ τοῦ βουλευτικοῦ φύλου γεγενημένοις τοῦτο ποιεῖν ἐξῆν.

was justified; but he makes clear the essential connection between the grant of the *latus clavus* and the intention to seek senatorial office. It is not clear whether Gaius' grants of this right were spontaneous or in response to petitions.

By the reign of Claudius the granting of the *latus clavus* by the emperor was established practice. At the beginning he announced the general principle that he would not choose any one as a senator who was not at least the great-grandson of a citizen, but in fact gave the *latus clavus* to the son of a freedman, on condition that he should be adopted by an *eques*.[10] Thereafter occasional mentions of the grant of the *latus clavus* appear in literature and inscriptions up to the early third century; in the middle of the second century, as we saw, Gaius refers to it, and assumes that it would be requested by the potential recipient. Among the later cases we have Julius Maximus Mucianus, from the *colonia* of Philippi, who was 'honoured with the *latus clavus*' by Pius;[11] and M. Coculnius Quintillianus, a local office-holder at Cirta, who was granted it by Severus and was also *quaestor designatus*.[12] The honour was not always sought by the person concerned, for an inscription shows another local office-holder, from Vienne in Gaul, to whom Hadrian 'offered the *latus clavus* with the quaestorship, and accepted his *excusatio* when he requested it'.[13] The exchange may well have occurred when Hadrian was in Gaul in 121 and 122. We may reasonably suppose, however, that a more usual pattern is represented by the report of the *Historia Augusta* that Septimius Severus came from Lepcis to Rome at the age of seventeen and, with the help of a consular relative, successfully petitioned Marcus Aurelius for the *latus clavus*.[14]

Though certainty is impossible, it is probable that other grants of senatorial status reported in various general terms from the early empire—and earlier on the part of Julius Caesar[15]—were in fact grants of the *latus clavus*. At any rate it is impossible to demonstrate the existence in this period of any other mechanism for giving men senatorial rank, apart from adlection, to which we shall come shortly.[16] If this is correct, then it was the *latus clavus* which the grandfather of Otho gained under Augustus by the *gratia* of Livia, in whose house he was brought up, and which Nero refused to the sons of freedmen.[17]

More important, it will have been this which Tacitus calls the 'right of seeking *honores*' which Fabricius Veiento was condemned in 62 for selling

---

[10] Suetonius, *Claud.* 24, 1.

[11] *PIR²* I 427; his brother, Julius Teres, was High Priest of the province, *PIR²* I 597, cf. Chr. Habicht, *Chiron* II (1972), 133. For Gaius' reference, p. 279, cf. Tacitus, *Dial.* 7, 1; *ILS* 1018 (Nerva).

[12] *ILS* 6857.

[13] *ILS* 6998.

[14] *Sept. Sev.* 1, 5. The probability of the story is greatly increased by the appearance of the consular relative, C. Septimius Severus, as proconsul of Africa in 174 (*AE* 1967 536) and as one of the *consilium* in 177 in the *Tabula*, cf. pp. 223, 262). Severus' own father was not a senator.

[15] Cicero, *Ad fam.* XIII, 5, 2: 'eum Caesar in senatum legit . . . qui Caesaris beneficio senator sit'; *Bell. Afr.* 28, 2: 'quorum patrem Caesar in senatum legerat'; Suetonius, *Jul.* 41; 76, 3; Dio XLVII, 51, 5.

[16] pp. 294–6.

[17] Suetonius, *Otho* I, 1: 'per gratiam Liviae Augustae, in cuius domo creverat, senator est factus', see *PIR¹* s 108; *Nero* 15, 2.

along with other 'gifts of the emperor';[18] and possibly this which the leading men of Gaul sought from Claudius in 48. Tacitus' narrative makes clear at least that the initiative in seeking the right came from the *primores Galliae* themselves, and that the request provoked a debate on the part of the emperor and his advisers; but, as is well known, Claudius then took the issue to the senate, and made a speech there of which part of the original appears in the famous bronze tablet from Lyon. Tacitus concludes his account 'the speech of the emperor was followed by a *senatus consultum*, and the Aedui were the first to gain the right of [being] senators in the city'.[19] In the original of his speech Claudius refers to the censorship which he was then holding, so it remains uncertain whether the point at issue was a censorial adlection or a grant of the *latus clavus*. In either case it was essentially a *beneficium* by the Emperor in response to a petition, and the function of the debate and vote in the senate can only have been political, an attempt to reduce resentment at a step which seemed drastically novel.[20] We see by contrast the reflection of the normal and gradual process of advancement into the senate in the poem in which Statius congratulates Julius Menecrates, an *eques* from Naples, on the birth of a second son; he concludes: 'Assuredly their wealth and origin . . . will permit them as soon as they reach manhood, if only they are assisted by the divine spirit of the unconquered Caesar, which favours good men, to cross the threshold of Romulus' senate.'[21]

The grant of the *latus clavus*, which gave a man no more than the right to stand for senatorial office, disappears from our view in the early third century. As a form of advancement, and a mark of imperial favour, it had long been surpassed by adlection, which conferred a rank within the senate, from ex-quaestor to ex-consul. As such it took up, in a different form and greatly altered context, the custom of the republic up to the reforms of Sulla whereby the censors, holding office every five years, enrolled new senators; they normally included those who had been elected in the interval to public offices such as quaestor or aedile, a step which created an expectation of adlection but did not guarantee it. Augustus never actually held a censorship, and used the censorial powers conferred on him from time to time more to remove than to create senators.[22] But Claudius held the censorship itself in 47–8, and a few inscriptions show him adlecting men into the senate, mainly *inter tribunicios*, that is with the rank of ex-tribune.[23]

A regular imperial censorship was held for the second and last time by Vespasian and Titus in 73/4, and from this occasion we have a substantial

[18] *Ann.* XIV, 50, 1: 'vendita ab eo munera principis et adipiscendorum honorum ius.'

[19] *Ann.* XI, 23,1–25, 1; *ILS* 212.

[20] *Contra*, A. Chastagnol, 'Les modes d'accès au Sénat romain au debut de l'Empire: remarques à propos de la table claudienne de Lyon', *Bull. Soc. Nat. Ant. Fr.* 1971, 282, who returns to the hypothesis that there existed a formal category of provincial citizens without the *ius honorum.*

[21] *Silv.* IV, 8, 59–62.

[22] Suetonius, *Aug.* 35, 54; Dio LII, 42, 1–4; LIV, 13–14. For the clearest treatment of the powers exercised by Augustus and the occasions of their use see A. H. M. Jones, 'The Censorial Powers of Augustus', *Studies in Roman Government and Law* (1960), 21.

[23] *Inter tribunicios*: *ILS* 968; *CIL* x 6520; presumably the same is meant in *AE* 1925 85 (M. Julius Romulus, *PIR*² I 523), 'adlecto [trib. p]lebis a divo Claudi[o]'; cf. also the fragmentary *CIL* VI 1442 (*PIR*² L 171). Cf. Chastagnol, o.c., p. 304, n. 1.

list of *equites* adlected into the senate.[24] Moreover we can observe here a clear instance of the way in which the honours granted by the emperor tended to increase in value (or apparent value); for at least four men are attested who were adlected directly *inter praetorios*, with the rank of ex-praetor,[25] two were adlected *inter tribunicios* and then *inter praetorios*,[26] and one became an *aedilicius*.[27] We have no positive evidence that any of the men promoted at this time petitioned for advancement, and know of one who certainly did not; for Pliny mentions that Minicius Macrinus, a leading *eques* from Brixia, when adlected *inter praetorios* by Vespasian, 'preferred an honourable withdrawal to this *ambitio* and *dignitas* of ours'.[28] It must be presumed that the man presented his *excusatio* to Vespasian.

Another novelty of this censorship was the use of *adlectio* to confer a more elevated rank on men who were already senators. A marginal case is L. Antistius Rusticus who was, or had been, a military tribune of pre-senatorial rank (with the *latus clavus*) when adlected *inter praetorios* by Vespasian and Titus;[29] but two other men are known who had held senatorial office before being adlected to praetorian rank.[30] Such a process is both another example of the deployment of imperial patronage, and, like the perfectissimate and other equestrian ranks, an aspect of the allied tendency to divorce status from function.

Julius Caesar by virtue of a *Lex Cassia*, Augustus by a *Lex Saenia* passed in 30 BC, and Claudius in his censorship are attested as having elevated senators to the status of patrician.[31] We know no individual cases of such elevation by Augustus,[32] and only five from the censorship of Claudius; in the case of one, the father of Otho, Suetonius quotes from a speech in his praise made on the occasion by Claudius, apparently in the senate.[33] From 73/4 however we have a substantial list of senators adlected *inter patricios* by Vespasian and Titus.[34]

After Domitian, who held the censorship in perpetuity from 85 onwards, no emperor held the office or used a reference to it in his titulature; its

[24] For an up-to-date list see W. Eck, *Senatoren von Vespasian bis Hadrian* (1970), 103–5, who unfortunately does not indicate the rank into which each man was adlected.

[25] L. Baebius Avitus (*PIR²* B 12); C. Fulvius Lupus Servilianus (*PIR²* F 548); [. . .]tilius Lol[lianus?] (*CIL* III 335); Q. Aurelius Pactumeius Clemens (*CIL* VIII 7057).

[26] C. Caristanius Fronto (*PIR²* C 423); C. Salvius Liberalis Nonius Bassus (*ILS* 1011).

[27] C. Julius Celsus Polemaeanus (*PIR²* I 260).

[28] *Ep.* I, 14, 5.

[29] *AE* 1925 126, *PIR²* A 765.

[30] C. Julius Cornutus Tertullus (*PIR²* I 273); and now L. Flavius Silva Nonius Bassus, Eck, o.c., 93f.

[31] Julius Caesar: Suetonius, *Jul.* 41, 1; Tacitus, *Ann.* XI, 25; Dio XLIII, 47, 3; Augustus: *RG* 8; Tacitus, loc. cit.; Dio LII, 42, 5; Claudius: Tacitus, loc. cit. See in general H.-H. Pistor, *Prinzeps und Patriziat in der Zeit von Augustus bis Commodus* (Diss. Freiburg in Breisgau, 1965).

[32] See Pistor, o.c., 15–28, for families which can be deduced to have acquired the patriciate in this period.

[33] *Otho* I, 3: 'Claudius adlectum inter patricios conlaudans amplissimis verbis hoc quoque adiecit: "vir, quo meliores liberos habere ne opto quidem".' See also *ILS* 965, P. Plautius Pulcher, 'ab eo censore inter patricios lectus'; M. Helvius Geminus, *ILS* 975; Q. Veranius, *RE* s.v. 'Veranius' (3). I cannot see that *AE* 1953 251 shows that he received the patriciate in 49, after the end of the censorship, rather than in 48. Anon., *AE* 1916 110.

[34] Pistor, o.c., 42–52, with corrections and additions by Eck, o.c., 106–9.

functions, however, became absorbed in those of the emperor as such.[35] In consequence it became established practice for *equites* to be adlected into the senate at various grades, and for senators to be adlected to higher grades or into the patriciate.[36] For instance a recently-published inscription from Ephesus shows an *eques* who was adlected into the senate *inter aedilicios*, probably by Domitian.[37] He was evidently rewarded for his equestrian military career, and went on to hold senatorial office; but for instance a man from Marsala in Sicily received first the *equus publicus*, and then adlection *inter tribunicios* from Commodus, without holding any post, equestrian or senatorial.[38]

Under Commodus also we meet the earliest case of adlection *inter consulares*, when the praetorian prefect, Tarrutienus Paternus, first received this apparent promotion, and was then executed by Commodus.[39] The few examples of this honour from the third century were all senators, notably M. Caecilius Novatillianus, who was honoured by the people of Beneventum, probably in the second half of the century, for having defended their public and private interests as their *patronus*, and is described as 'a famous poet and orator'.[40]

By contrast it is surprising to find two *equites* who were adlected *inter consulares* 'by the judgment of the divine Constantine'. In the case of C. Caelius Saturninus the honour followed a long career at court, in imperial service and as a *comes* of the emperor, and was gained 'by the petition of the senate'.[41] But C. Julius Rufinianus Ablabius Tatianus had risen no further than being *fisci patronus rationum summarum*, that is a mere *advocatus fisci*, when he was adlected among the *consulares* by the *iudicium* of Constantine. The inscription from the statue erected to him at Abellinum in Campania mentions his pagan priesthoods and also refers to his father, Rufinianus 'the orator'—presumably the Julius Rufinianus who has left a short work on the figures of speech used in oratory.[42] The prevailing prestige of oratory may well account for the son's exceptional honour from Constantine. According to the Suda at any rate, a sophist named Theon who taught at Sidon, was granted by Constantine the ranks of ex-consul and *praefectus*.[43]

Eusebius' chapter on the generosity of Constantine in conferring ranks of

[35] See esp. Dio LIII, 18, 4–5.

[36] For examples of adlections of *equites*, H.-G. Pflaum in *Bayerische Vorgeschichtsblätter* XXVII (1962), 86–7; adlections of all types from the late second to the late third century, Barbieri, *Albo senatorio*, pp. 533f., 773–4; *inter patricios* up to Commodus, Pistor, o.c., 52f.

[37] D. Knibbe, *JÖAI* XLIX (1968–71), Beiblatt 6, no. 1, ll. 10–11: '[adlectum im senatori]um ordine[m] / [inter aed]ilicios'; ll. 20–1: καταλελεγμένον εἰς σύνκλητον / ἐν τοῖς ἀγορανομικοῖς.

[38] *ILS* 6770.

[39] Dio LXXII, 5, 1 (286); cf. *HA, Com.* 4, 7: 'per lati clavi honorem a praefecturae administratione summovit.' See p. 130. When Philostratus, *VS* II, 3, says of the Pergamene sophist, Ti. Claudius Aristocles (*PIR*² C 789), ἐτέλει... ἐς ὑπάτους, he *may* mean this, as he may also, II, 24 in saying of Aelius Antipater (pp. 92–3) ὑπάτοις δ' ἐγγραφείς.

[40] Barbieri, *Albo Senatorio*, no. 1493; cf. no. 1966.

[41] *ILS* 1214; see *PLRE* Saturninus 9, and p. 98.

[42] *ILS* 2942; see *PLRE* Tatianus 4. C. Halm, *Rhetores Latini Minores* (1863), 38–47. Tatianus himself may also be the rhetorician referred to by Julius Victor, ibid., 371, 448.

[43] Suda, ed. Adler, θ 208: γενόμενος δὲ ὑπὸ τοῦ βασιλέως Κωνσταντίνου καὶ ἀπὸ ὑπάτων καὶ ὕπαρχος.

honour includes a reference to his granting the status of senator and consul.[44] The conferment of actual senatorial office, especially the consulate, was a commonplace then as earlier.[45] But in what other form or forms senatorial status itself was granted by the emperor in this period is quite obscure. That it was in fact so conferred is clear from the speech of Nazarius in 321 in which he includes among the *beneficia* of Constantine an increase in the number of senators:[46]

> You, Rome, have felt yourself at last to be the citadel of all races and the Queen of all lands, when you claimed for your *curia* the best men from every province, that the dignity of the Senate might be no less illustrious in fact than in name, since it consisted of the flower of the whole world.

There are some possible cases in this period, as there are quite clear ones earlier, of men who began with equestrian posts and then continued with senatorial ones, without any specific mention of the conferment of senatorial rank by the emperor;[47] but there is much better evidence from Constantine's reign for men with senatorial careers coming to occupy prefectures and other posts previously held exclusively by *equites*.[48] It can only be at best a hypothesis that it was possible in the time of Constantine to acquire from the emperor *codicilli* of the *clarissima dignitas* for presentation to the senate, as we know it was from the middle of the fourth century onwards.[49] If such *codicilli* took the form of a letter, as did *codicilli* of appointment (addressed to the beneficiary himself), it would be interesting to know how far they resembled the well-known letter of Hadrian recommending a ship-captain named Erastus as a member of the city council of Ephesus.[50]

It has to be confessed that we do not know by what process or at what rank men from outside the senatorial order normally entered the senate in the first part of the fourth century. The nearest approach we can make is the letter written by Constantine to the senate permitting them to restore to senatorial rank those who had been deprived of it by the 'tyrant' (Maxentius or Licinius), provided that they were suitable in wealth, birth and character; the names were however to be submitted to the emperor for approval.[51] Our ignorance in this respect is merely the reflection of the lack of real evidence at all periods concerning the actual processes by which adlection was granted.

[44] p. 278.
[45] pp. 300–13.
[46] *Pan.* x(4), 35, 2.
[47] See A. Chastagnol, 'Les modes de recrutement du Sénat au IVe siècle après J.-C.', *Recherches sur les structures sociales dans l'antiquité classique*, ed. C. Nicolet (1970), 187. Apart from Caelius Saturninus and C. Julius Rufinianus Ablabius Tatianus (see above) and also Julius Julianus, the Praetorian Prefect of Licinius who received the consulate from Constantine, and Pacatianus, consul and *Praef. Praet.* in 332, who hence fall into a different pattern (p. 309), we are left with two very dubious cases. For some clear second- and third-century examples of such careers, H.-G. Pflaum, *Bayerische Vorgeschichtsblätter* XXVII (1962), 87–8.
[48] Jones, *Later Roman Empire*, 106–7; Chastagnol, o.c., 188.
[49] The system can be discerned in *CTh* XII, I, 42 (354) and subsequently, see Jones, o.c., 531.
[50] *Syll.*[3] 838; see p. 420.
[51] *CTh* XV, 14, 4. The letter is dated 326, which suggests Licinius, but the context seems to imply the senate of Rome, which suggests Maxentius. The former is more probable, cf. Mommsen on XV, 14, 3.

That it could however be an entirely personal act of favour by the emperor is illustrated by Dio's story of how Caracalla, on discovering that an equestrian tribune of Macedonian origin was called Antigonus and was the son of a Philip, instantly promoted the man, and later adlected him *inter praetorios*.[52] In the early empire it could also be a personal favour to restore a man to senatorial status—a fact which gives added significance to Constantine's partial concession. For instance, on becoming emperor in 54, Nero demonstrated his mildness by restoring a man demoted for adultery with Messalina; while some years later Cossutianus Capito regained his senatorial rank, after condemnation, by the *preces* of his father-in-law, Tigellinus, who was soon to become praetorian prefect.[53]

But if our evidence is inadequate to give any real conception of the social patterns typically involved in the grant of senatorial status or rank by the emperor, this does not apply (at least in the early empire) to the opposite situation, the threat of the loss of senatorial status. For one of the consequences of Augustus' establishment of a minimum census valuation for senators (of 1,000,000 or 1,200,000 *sesterces*) was that senators faced loss of their status if their property declined. In this situation they could be saved most easily by the emperor himself, by his either paying their debts, giving them a capital sum, or granting them an annual allowance.[54] The emperor's possession of immense private or semi-private wealth was as fundamental here as it was in all the other relationships in which he was involved. Here too it was clearly common for the emperor's gift to be a response to a request. Macrobius singles out the occasion when Augustus paid the debts of a senator who was especially dear to him without being asked—and received as thanks only a note saying, 'Nothing for myself?' It is implied by Macrobius' language that some more formal act of thanks would have been expected.[55] Similarly, as Seneca relates, Cn. Cornelius Lentulus Augur (the consul of 14 BC) 'owed all the increase of his wealth to Augustus, to whom he had brought his nobility labouring under the weight of poverty'. The words strongly suggest that he had requested Augustus for aid, even though he complained that the gift had (by keeping him in public life) torn him away from the practice of oratory. That he was subsequently forced by Tiberius to make him his heir is a perfect example of the complementary effects of largesse and exaction in the exchange of wealth between the emperor and the upper classes.[56]

[52] LXXVII, 8, 1–2 (381); Barbieri, *Albo senatorio*, no. 33. Cf. LXXVIII, 21, 4–5 (426), Lucilius Priscillianus (*Albo*, no. 337) rewarded by Caracalla with adlection *inter praetorios* for fighting in *venationes* and bringing accusations against senators and *equites*.

[53] Tacitus, *Ann.* XIII, 11, 2; XIV, 48, 1.

[54] For the census, Suetonius, *Aug.* 41, 1, says that he raised it from 800,000 to 1,200,000 *sesterces* (though we have no evidence for the former or any other fixed senatorial census in the republic), and that he 'supplevitque non habentibus'; Dio LIV, 17, 3, under 18 BC, says that he first established it at 400,000 and then raised it to 1,000,000, and made up the deficit in both cases to those who deserved it. But see now C. Nicolet in *JRS* LXVI (1976), 20.

[55] *Sat.* II, 4, 23: 'aes alienum Augustus cuiusdam senatoris cari sibi non rogatus exsolverat numerato quadragies. at ille pro gratiarum actione hoc solum ei scripsit, "mihi nihil?".' I have supplied the question mark, which seems to make better sense.

[56] Seneca, *De ben.* II, 27, 1–2; Suetonius, *Tib.* 49, 1; cf. *PIR*² C 1379. For the emperors as *heredes* see pp. 153–8.

The possession of a famous name itself constituted a *prima facie* claim for assistance from the emperor. Thus M. Hortensius Hortalus, the grandson of the orator Hortensius, was given 1,000,000 *sesterces* by Augustus in order to marry and have children, 'lest a most famous family should be extinguished'. In 16, under Tiberius, he placed the four resultant sons before the threshold of the senate when it was meeting in the Palatium, and, when his turn came to give his *sententia*, took the opportunity to appeal for more. Tiberius reproached him for the impropriety, but yielded to the feeling of the senators present to the extent of granting 200,000 *sesterces* to each of the sons; other senators made speeches of thanks, but Hortalus did not.[57] Requests for such subventions were evidently particularly common under Tiberius, and the emperor obliged the petitioners to justify their claims before the senate.[58] To Seneca this was an example of censorial functions rather than *liberalitas*; just as it was not a true *beneficium* when Tiberius responded to a request by a senator to help him out of debt, by asking for the names of the creditors and then writing to say that he had paid them, adding humiliating admonitions—'he freed him from his creditors, but did not oblige him to himself'.[59] Sometimes Tiberius would hear such requests personally, replying to a senator who confessed that he had wasted a huge *patrimonium* and been reduced to poverty, 'You have woken late.'[60]

Nero seems to have preferred to grant impoverished senators an annual income rather than a capital gift; but again the recipients were typically the descendants of the most noble houses.[61] Such petitions for subsistence were evidently a commonplace, for the plan to murder Nero in 65 was that, when he made a rare appearance in public to attend the *ludi Cereales*, a senator, Plautius Lateranus, should pretend to petition him for a subvention, and by clasping his knees throw him to the ground, allowing others in the entourage to finish the task.[62] In the nature of the case, this procedure could not have been adopted if it had involved anything unusual or suspicious. It is almost certainly in the context of such requests for subvention that we should place Epictetus' report of having seen a man clasping the knees of Epaphroditus, the freedman of Nero, and exclaiming in tears that he had only 1,500,000 *sesterces* left.[63]

Suetonius reports among Vespasian's liberalities that 'he made up the census of senators and supported poor *consulares* with allowances of 500,000 *sesterces* per year',[64] but thereafter we do not have evidence of regular subventions of this sort, except for one report of it on the part of Hadrian.[65] By a typical paradox it was precisely the effort to preserve within the

[57] Tacitus, *Ann.* II, 37–8.
[58] Seneca, *De ben.* II, 8, 1–2; Suetonius, *Tib.* 47; Tacitus, *Ann.* I, 75, 3–4. Cf. Dio LVII, 10, 3–4.
[59] ibid., II, 7, 2–3.
[60] Seneca, *Ep.* 122, 10.
[61] Suetonius, *Nero* 10, 1; Tacitus, *Ann.* XIII, 34, 1.
[62] Tacitus, *Ann.* XV, 53, 1–2.
[63] *Diss.* I, 26, 11–12; see *JRS* LV (1965), 144.
[64] *Vesp.* 17. For a not easily intelligible case of Vespasian granting a *census* to a young man 'honeste natum' see Frontinus, *Strat.* IV, 6, 4.
[65] *HA, Had.* 7, 9; his gifts to senators and *equites*, Dio LXIX, 5, 1. Other possible references, *HA, Marc. Ant.* 23, 2–3; *Sev. Alex.* 40, 2; payment of debts of *amici*, Sept. Sev. 7, 9.

senate of the early empire a visible continuity with that of the republic which principally gave rise to this particularly invidious form of petition and largesse. In the second century and after we hear rather of the emperor assisting senators with the expenses of particular offices. So for instance Fronto recalls to Lucius Verus that Antoninus Pius had paid the expenses of the praetorship of Gavius Clarus; the latter had apparently been ill and out of Rome, for as soon as he returned in good health to the city he had repaid the same to 'your *fiscus*'.[66] Similarly Severus Alexander paid the expenses of the consulship which Cassius Dio held with him in 229.[67]

It is unfortunate for our understanding of a very significant historical process that we have so little information on the actual processes of conferment of senatorial status or rank by the emperor, a form of patronage without which the senate would not have been opened to men from so many parts of the empire. In part it was conscious policy: as Suetonius writes, Vespasian in his censorship replenished the *equestor ordo* and the senate 'adlecting all the most honourable men, both Italians and provincials'.[68] Or, as Claudius reminded the senate, Augustus and Tiberius 'wished to see in this senate-house all the flower of the *coloniae* and *municipia* everywhere, provided that they were good men, and rich'. But this very speech, as we saw, was provoked by an application from the leading men of Gaul.[69] It is moreover an orator from Gaul, M. Aper, who in the *Dialogus* of Tacitus affirms the value which he attached to his major appearances in court by saying that they were even more significant to him than 'the day on which I was offered the *latus clavus*, or on which—as a new man born in a community of the least possible influence—I accepted the quaestorship, tribunate or praetorship'.[70]

The *latus clavus* can only have been offered by the emperor, and the magistracies mentioned may well have been accepted from him also.[71] For the patronage of the emperor was already entrenched here too; in the middle of the first century Seneca can outline the range of expectations with which senators looked to the emperor without even needing to mention him explicitly:[72]

He has given me the praetorship, but I had hoped for the consulship; he has given the twelve *fasces*, but has not made me *consul ordinarius*; he wished the year to be dated by my name, but has failed me with regard to a priesthood; he has co-opted me into a priestly college—but why into only one? He has filled the measure of my *dignitas*, but has contributed nothing to my *patrimonium*. He has given to me what he would have been obliged to give to anyone, but has added nothing of his own volition.

We can see here how important in the early period was the role of cash subventions from the emperor among the benefits which he could grant to

[66] *Ad Verum imp.* II, 7, 5–6. Cf. *HA, Ant. Pius* 8, 4; *Had.* 7, 10.
[67] Dio LXXX, 5, 1 (476); cf. p. 28.
[68] *Vesp.* 9, 2.
[69] *ILS* 212, col. II, ll. 1–4; cf. p. 293.
[70] *Dial.* 7, 1; see Syme, *Tacitus* (1958), App. 91.
[71] pp. 300–13.
[72] *De ira* III, 31, 2.

senators. But his power to grant office was of far greater and longer-lasting significance, and it is to the limits of this power and the manner of its exercise that we must turn next. But it is important to remember that here too, in relation to offices within the senate, we are observing a form of the emperor's patronage which itself formed an aspect of his relations with the cities of the empire, and his response to the aspirations of their leading citizens. 'Yet there are others,' Plutarch writes in the early second century, 'Chians, Galatians or Bithynians, who are not content with whatever portion of either repute or power among their own fellow-countrymen has fallen to their lot, but weep because they do not wear the patrician shoe; yet if they do wear it, they weep because they are not yet Roman praetors; if they are praetors, because they are not consuls; and if consuls because they were proclaimed, not first, but later.'[73]

Of the honours which Plutarch mentions, only the praetorship could be acquired otherwise than by the gift of the emperor; and even the praetorship itself could be conferred by him. That it was in fact to the emperor that men looked for the bestowal of senatorial posts and honours is quite explicit, for instance, in the oration which Aelius Aristides pronounced in Pergamum in 147 to celebrate the birthday of Julius Apellas, a boy who descended from a prominent family there, which had enjoyed senatorial rank through several generations.[74] The orator concludes with a prayer to Asclepius: 'Preserve his house, granting him such honours from the great king as his own ancestors gained from his ancestors . . .'

4. *Senatorial Office*

'No one fears Caesar himself,' Epictetus asserted, 'but death, exile, confiscation of property, imprisonment or loss of rights. Nor does anyone love Caesar, unless he is of especial merit, but we love wealth, a tribunate, a praetorship or a consulate.'[1] No one portrayed more vividly than he the fear and servility engendered by the role of the emperor as judge and benefactor; and abundant evidence illustrates the exercise of imperial patronage in relation to the *cursus* of republican magistracies in Rome. But the precise limits of his patronage at various periods, the forms in which it was exercised and its relation to the wider play of politics, which under Augustus still had a place in genuine popular elections, and thereafter was confined within the senate, are all complex topics. As we shall see, there was at no time any senatorial office for which the emperor could not make recommendations which in effect ensured the post for his beneficiary. But in Epictetus' time,

---

[73] *Mor.* 470c, Loeb trans. The 'patrician shoe' must in fact (in this period) be a reference to the distinctive shoes worn by all members of the senatorial order, see Mommsen, *Staatsrecht*[3] III, 888–92.

[74] Aelius Aristides, *Or.* xxx Keil, 28. See A. Boulanger, *Aelius Aristide* (1923), 333–40; C. A. Behr, *Aelius Aristides and the Sacred Tales* (1968), 57–9. Note also ibid., 12, a reference to his grandfather, Julius Apellas, οὐχ ὅσων ἐθνῶν ἐπῆρξεν, οὐδ' ὅσας τιμὰς ἐκ βασιλέων ἐκαρπώσατο. Cf. p. 471.

[1] *Diss.* IV, 1, 60; cf. *JRS* LV (1965), 144–5.

early in the second century, the posts up to praetor could still be filled by competition among senators. 'He has risen through the quaestorship, tribunate and praetorship with the greatest credit,' wrote Epictetus' contemporary Pliny the Younger, recommending a potential son-in-law to Junius Mauricus, 'and so has already relieved you of the obligation to canvass on his behalf.'[2] The implication that canvassing would not be relevant to the consulship is not misleading, for it had long since been entirely in the gift of the emperor. 'His own standing beckons him to the praetorship and the favour of the Caesars prepares him for the consulate', as Apuleius said to the proconsul of Africa, referring to the man's son.[3]

How long any of the posts in the *cursus* below the consulate continued to be filled by election within the senate is an acutely difficult question, but the reality of the political processes involved in his time is quite clear from Pliny's letters. Outside the *cursus* itself there was on the one hand a range of senatorial posts such as legateships of legions or imperial provinces, curatorships or special commissions in Rome, Italy or the provinces, and what soon became the crown of the senatorial career, the prefecture of the city, which by their nature were from the beginning filled by direct imperial appointment. On the other hand the proconsulates of public provinces, whether held by ex-praetors or ex-consuls, were supposed throughout our period to be determined by the lot; but while this was in fact normal, it will be seen that the imperial will could easily intervene here also.[4]

After Augustus' settlement of 27 BC, Dio says that the *plebs* and *populus* began to meet again for the elections, but that nothing was done which was displeasing to the emperor; he recommended some candidates of his own, and also took care that unsuitable persons were not elected by improper means.[5] His measures to prevent corruption, the occurrence of riots and disorders at some elections, and the occasional candidatures even for the consulate of persons who were hostile to him all show that a considerable area of freedom existed at this time.[6] There was certainly a significant change in AD 8, when Augustus, for reasons of old age, ceased to go round commending verbally the candidates whom he favoured, but put up a list of them instead;[7] for, whether such an effect was intended or not, the act must have tended to formalize the process of imperial commendation. No less important, sources from Seneca in the middle of the first century to the jurist Pomponius in the middle of the second record five cases of Augustus offering or giving the consulate itself. Seneca indeed describes Augustus as granting Cn. Cornelius Cinna Magnus the consulate spontaneously, and complaining that he had not asked for it.[8]

---

[2] *Ep.* I, 14, 7.

[3] Apuleius, *Flor.* IX, 40.

[4] p. 309.

[5] LIII, 21, 6–7. For some problems about the restoration of elections at this time see *JRS* LXIII (1973), 52–3, 63.

[6] For the best treatment see A. H. M. Jones, 'The Elections under Augustus', *JRS* XLV (1955), 9 = *Studies in Roman Government and Law* (1960), 27; cf. also R. Frei-Stolba, *Untersuchungen zu den Wahlen in der römischen Kaiserzeit* (1967), 87–129.

[7] Dio LV, 34, 2.

[8] *De clem.* I, 9, 12: 'post hoc detulit ultro consulatum, questus, quod non auderet petere.'

The change which established the context in which the election of Roman magistrates was conducted for the rest of our period came in AD 14, immediately on the succession of Tiberius, when we know from a brief and obscure reference in Tacitus that the elections were transferred to the senate.[9] What this meant in practice or theory is entirely unclear in Tacitus, but is revealed adequately enough in a passage of Dio relating to the latter part of Tiberius' reign. Having explained that Tiberius appointed the consuls, both the *ordinarii* by whom the year was dated and the *suffecti*, as he wished, and changed the periods over which they held office as it suited him, Dio continues:[10]

> Of the candidates for the other magistracies he would select as many as he wished, and send them to the Senate, some with his recommendation, who were to be elected unanimously, and leaving the others to be decided on by their merits, or by agreement or by the lot. After this the candidates for each office came before the *populus* and *plebs* and were proclaimed, just as they are now, to fulfil the ancient ritual and to give the formal appearance of being elected.

It is thus clear that the change involved no formal abolition of the electoral assemblies (the *comitia centuriata* and *tributa*), which continued, in form at least, until the third century. Seutonius indeed records the unfortunate consequences when the herald at the elections proclaimed a relative of Domitian to the people not as consul but as 'Imperator';[11] and Pliny proudly records that Trajan, holding the consulate *ordinarius* in 100, had presided at the election of himself and Cornutus Tertullus as *suffecti* in the same year, and had been both their '*suffragator* in the senate-house and their *declarator* in the *campus*'—the Campus Martius where the *comitia centuriata* met.[12] What the change did was to withdraw the electoral process *de facto* within the senate, which was to produce a single list of candidates for presentation to the people. In the early period the process occasionally did not work, as in 60 when 'the election of praetors normally conducted by the choice of the senate' led to unresolved rivalries which Nero settled by appointing the three extra competitors to legionary commands.[13] But by the end of the century there was an established day for the elections in the senate, during which formal voting might occur;[14] a century later Dio mentions that Oclatinius Adventus, as consul *ordinarius* in 218, feeling his inadequacy for

---

Petere could in itself apply to being a candidate for election, but the context, and especially the contrast with *ultro*, shows that a request to Augustus is referred to; cf. Tacitus, *Ann.* II, 43, 2 (Cn. Piso, *cos. suff.* 23 BC); III. 75, 1 (Ateius Capito, *cos. suff.* AD 5); Pomponius, *Dig.* I, 2, 2, 45 (offer to Aulus Cascellius); 47 (to Antistius Labeo).

[9] *Ann.* I, 15, 1. I accept the view of P. A. Brunt, 'The Lex Valeria Cornelia', *JRS* LI (1961),71, that the change in electoral procedure in AD 5 attested by the *Tabula Hebana* was not intended to produce some result desired by Augustus, and that it and its extensions under Tiberius were significant mainly for the status conferred on the members of the new *centuriae*.

[10] LVIII, 20, 3–4.

[11] *Dom.* 10, 4.

[12] *Pan.* 92, 3–4.

[13] Tacitus, *Ann.* XIV, 28, 1; Suetonius, *Nero* 15, 2.

[14] Pliny, *Ep.* III, 20; IV, 25; VI, 19; *Pan.* 69–72.

the required verbal exchanges, kept away from the senate on the day of the elections on the pretence of being ill.[15]

At about this time, however, Modestinus appears to claim that all magistrates in Rome were appointed by the emperor.[16] But no other source marks so drastic a change; and, as we shall see, quaestors and praetors are found describing themselves as *candidati* (of the emperor) until the first half of the fourth century. In any case, though we have no direct evidence from the later third century, that of the Constantinian period shows that magistrates below the rank of consul were still nominated by the senate.[17] In that period our evidence tends to suggest that senatorial office in Rome was an expensive burden which men sought to avoid. It was certainly not so earlier, for Pliny's letters illustrate very clearly both the support which he had received in his own career from the *suffragium* of others, and the real anxiety which he felt about the electoral prospects of his own protégés, both for their sake and because of the consequences for his own *dignitas* if they were unsuccessful.[18]

Dio's account of the procedure under Tiberius implies that the emperor not only gave a positive commendation to certain candidates, but also played some formal role in accepting, or rejecting, candidatures. What this function was called, and how it related to that of accepting or rejecting the *professiones* of candidates which had been exercised in the republic by consuls or other presiding magistrates, are matters of debate.[19] But it is clearly reflected, along with other senatorial privileges which could be gained by petition to the emperor, in what Pliny says of the candidature for the tribunate of Sextus Erucius: 'I gained for Sextus the *latus clavus* from our Caesar, and also the quaestorship, and by my *suffragium* he has attained the right to seek the tribunate. If he does not gain it in the senate I am afraid that I shall seem to have deceived Caesar'.[20] It appears that Pliny had achieved a commendation for the quaestorship for Sextus, but had gained only the right to be a candidate in the case of the tribunate; the very fact however that this too was sought by *suffragium* shows that the emperor could have refused it. The same three possibilities, rejection, permission to stand, and commendation, seem to be reflected in Pliny's description of Trajan's handling of the candidates in 100: none (on this occasion) needed consolation, some departed with gladness, and some with hope.[21]

What Pliny says about the career of Sextus Erucius also illustrates how the exercise of influence and the *suffragia* of leading senators had their place not merely in the senate-house, but in relation to the decisions and favours

[15] LXXVIII, 14, 2 (418).

[16] p. 275.

[17] See Jones, *Later Roman Empire*, 540.

[18] *Suffragium* of others for Pliny: II, 1, 8 (Verginius Rufus); IV, 17, 6 (Corellius Rufus); Pliny supporting candidatures: e.g. IV, 15; VI, 6; VIII, 23.

[19] For a thorough discussion see B. M. Levick, 'Imperial Control of the Elections under the Early Principate', *Historia* XVI (1967), 207. Tacitus, *Ann.* I, 14, 4 says that Tacitus 'nominavit' twelve candidates for the praetorship; I, 81 seems to refer, with remarkable obscurity, to both the listing and commending of candidates for the consulate.

[20] *Ep.* II, 9, 2; cf. p. 291.

[21] *Pan.* 69, 1: 'sollicitudini pudorique candidatorum ita consuluisti, ne ullius gaudium alterius tristitia turbaret. alii cum laetitia, alii cum spe recesserunt, multis gratulandum, nemo consolandus fuit.'

of the emperor himself. Some hints of the social relations involved can be gleaned if we follow the successive stages of the senatorial career. First, so far as we know, appointments to the 'pre-senatorial' military posts (almost invariably the tribunate of a legion), and the civil posts of the vigintivirate, were always made by the emperor.[22] At any rate, in celebrating the military tribunate of Crispinus, the sixteen-year-old son of the ex-consul, Vettius Bolanus, Statius makes quite clear that the appointment came from Domitian —who would also in the future give him promotion up to the consulate.[23]

With the quaestorship, held normally at the age of 25, a man entered the senate, and this office was the earliest in the career for which we find the expression 'candidate of Caesar' (*candidatus Caesaris*) in regular use; a man who was *candidatus* naturally tended also to be the *quaestor Caesaris*, who read out the emperor's communications in the senate.[24] A *quaestor* of the emperor is recorded on an inscription as early as the reign of Augustus, while another inscription shows a senator who had been '*quaestor* of the divine Claudius' and '*candidatus* of the Augusti through all his *honores*;'[25] 'quaestor candidatus' becomes regular in the early second century, and is found still in the reign of Constantine.[26] We do not know how many of the twenty quaestors each year were commended by the emperor; and as to how this honour was gained we have only a few items of evidence from the early empire. Seneca, for instance, says that he gained his quaestorship, under Tiberius, by the *gratia* of his aunt; she was the wife of a prefect of Egypt and the *gratia* was almost certainly exercised with the emperor.[27] From the same reign Suetonius retails the anecdote that Tiberius preferred a very obscure candidate for the quaestorship to ones of most noble birth because at a dinner in his presence the man had drunk a whole amphora of wine.[28] He is probably more reliable in quoting, as an example of the emperor's eccentricity, one of the reasons which Claudius gave for his *suffragatio* of a candidate for the quaestorship—that the man's father had opportunely given him a drink of cold water when he was ill.[29] The story is most significant for its implication that the emperor gave either written—or much more probably verbal—reasons in supporting a candidate. It is certainly to such a speech that Pliny refers when he says that Trajan had been the *suffragator* of Cornutus Tertullus and himself in the senate, for he also speaks explicitly of the *testimonium* in their praise which the emperor delivered in the senate.[30]

---

[22] Note Suetonius, *Aug.* 38, Augustus appointing sons of senators to military tribunates and *praefecturae alarum*; Dio LX, 5, 8, Claudius allowing Junius Silanus and Cn. Pompeius Magnus to hold the vigintivirate at once, and other posts five years early.

[23] *Silvae* v, 2, esp. 166f. Note 166–7 on his future prospects: 'idem (Domitian) omnes perferre gradus cingique superbis / fascibus et patrias dabit insedisse curules.'

[24] See the thorough survey by M. Cebeillac, *Les 'quaestores Principis et candidati' aux 1er et 11ème siècles de l'empire* (1972). Ulpian indeed identifies the two categories, *Dig.* I, 13, 1, 4: 'quidam sunt qui candidati principis dicebantur quique epistulas eius in senatu legunt.'

[25] *ILS* 928; 973.

[26] For q.k. in the inscriptions of Q. Flavius Maesius Egnatius Lollianus *signo* Mavortius see *PLRE* Lollianus 5. For third-century examples see Barbieri, *Albo senatorio*, 775, and *AE* 1964 223.

[27] *Ad Helviam* 19, 2; cf. 5, 4. See *PIR²* A 617.

[28] *Tib.* 42, 2.

[29] *Claud.* 40, 2.

[30] Pliny, *Pan.* 91–2; cf. p. 302.

For the elections to the tribunate or the aedileship we have no significant evidence of the emperor's role.[31] Inscriptions record a fair number of *candidati* (*Caesaris*) for the tribunate, but only a single case for the aedileship, a man who was *candidatus* of Hadrian for both this and the praetorship.[32] The praetorship was in fact what mattered, for it gave access to legionary legateships and to governorships of the less important provinces, whether as *legatus Augusti pro praetore* in the imperial provinces, or as proconsul in the public ones. Once again, though inscriptional references to *candidati* for the praetorship continue to the reign of Constantine,[33] all the illuminating evidence in our possession comes from the early empire. From the very moment in AD 14 when the elections were transferred to the senate we have, first, Tacitus' report that Tiberius commended only four candidates (all apparently for the praetorship) who were to be designated for the next year without the possibility of rejection or the need for canvassing.[34] Secondly, and much more important, there is the reference by Velleius Paterculus (a prime example of the worthy Italians whom Augustus and Tiberius wished to see in the senate), to the election of himself and his brother to the praetorship in this year. Tiberius' first task as emperor was the *ordinatio* of the elections, 'which the divine Augustus had left, written out with his own hand'. The document either consisted of, or at least contained, a list of candidates for commendation, for Velleius says that he and his brother were elected along with men of most noble birth and holders of priesthoods: 'as *candidati Caesaris*, having the good fortune that the divine Augustus commended no one after us, nor Caesar Tiberius before us.'[35] This autobiographical report is of considerable importance in establishing conclusively that the term *candidatus Caesaris* refers to the emperor's commendation.

Nomination as praetor could be a spontaneous personal favour by the emperor, as appears in Suetonius' story of Gaius rewarding a senator for the voracity with which he ate at dinner by sending him *codicilli* carrying an extra-ordinary designation as praetor.[36] It is remarkable to find that *codicilli* could be employed in relation to the magistracies of Rome, as they were for both equestrian and senatorial appointments by the emperor.[37] But the use of *codicilli* for such magistracies, and not merely on such irregular occasions as that which Suetonius mentions, does seem to be implied by the words

[31] Note Suetonius, *Aug.* 40, 1, and Dio LVI, 27, 1, Augustus permitting *equites* to stand for the tribunate, and Dio LX, 11, 8, Claudius doing likewise.

[32] *ILS* 1096. *Candidati* for the tribunate, see *ILS* iii. 1, p. 411, Barbieri, *Albo senatorio*, 775; *AE* 1915 77; 1957 135; 1965 244; 1968 474.

[33] *ILS* 1216 (*PLRE* Censorinus 2); *AE* 1969/70 21 (Attius Caecilius Maximilianus—in the 340s?), see A. Chastagnol, 'Les modes de recrutement du Sénat au IVᵉ siècle après J.-C.', *Recherches sur les structures sociales dans l'antiquité classique*, ed. C. Nicolet (1970), 187, on p. 192. A further third-century case, *AE* 1964 223.

[34] *Ann.* I, 15, 1.

[35] II, 124, 3–4: 'primum principalium eius operum fuit ordinatio comitiorum, quam manu sua scriptam divus Augustus reliquerat. quo tempore mihi fratrique meo, candidatis Caesaris, proxime a nobilissimis ac sacerdotablibus viris destinari praetoribus contigit, consecutis, ut neque post nos quemquam divus Augustus, neque ante nos Caesar commendaret Tiberius.' On the background and career of Velleius, see G. V. Summer, 'The Truth about Velleius Paterculus: Prolegomena', *HSCPh* LXXIV (1970), 257.

[36] *Cal.* 18, 2.

[37] pp. 288–90, 310–11.

which Tacitus in the *Dialogus* puts into the mouth of the Gallic orator Aper; when he spoke in court, he says, he felt himself to rise above tribunates and praetorships and consulates, and to possess something 'which is neither given by *codicilli* nor comes through *gratia*'.[38] If the implication is correct, the use of *codicilli* must be taken as an illustration of how the magistracies of Rome themselves became to some extent assimilated to the posts distributed by the emperor.

As such, they could also be gained by the exercise of *gratia*; it was for instance the influence of Agrippina which secured for Seneca both his return from exile and a praetorship in 49.[39] It will similarly have been for reasons of personal favour that Domitian allowed Pliny, who had been his *quaestor Caesaris*, to stand for the praetorship a year early.[40] Pliny himself later attempted, with what success we do not know, to obtain a praetorship from Trajan for a senator named Accius Sura. His brief letter runs as follows:[41]

I know, Lord, that our *preces* lodge in your *memoria*, which is most tenacious in giving benefits (*bene faciendi*). Because moreover you have indulged me in this area also, I advise and urgently ask you to deign to honour (*exornare*) Accius Sura with the praetorship, since a place is vacant. Though a man who is otherwise most unambitious, he is roused to hope for this by the splendour of his birth, the highest integrity which he displays in poverty, and above all by the happiness of the times, which summons and inspires all your citizens of good conscience to make use of your *indulgentia*.

When the emperor extended his *indulgentia* to a candidate for the praetorship, he might also make a speech in his support in the senate. This was done at any rate by Tiberius for a senator of obscure origins named Curtius Rufus, who 'gained a praetorship against noble candidates by the *suffragium* of the emperor, on which occasion Tiberius had drawn a veil over the shame of his birth with the words, "I regard Curtius Rufus as having been born from himself" '.[42]

From the period after the beginning of the second century we lack evidence to illustrate the imperial distribution of praetorships, except Cassius Dio's statement that Pertinax in 193 honoured him in other ways and also appointed him praetor (for the same year or the next).[43] Dio also records that Severus Alexander appointed him as consul *ordinarius* with himself in 229, as well as paying the expenses involved (for giving games), and allowing him to spend the period of the consulate outside Rome to avoid hostility of the praetorian cohorts.[44] We could hardly ask for a better illustration of the process by which

[38] *Dial.* 7, 2.

[39] Tacitus, *Ann.* XII, 8, 2.

[40] *Ep.* VII, 16, 2. Owing to *lacunae* the inscriptions of Pliny's career do not make clear whether he was *candidatus Caesaris* as praetor. He need not have been, cf. *ILS* 1048, an ex-praetor who 'hos honores beneficio optumi princip(is) maturius quam per annos permitti solet gessit', but who was not a *candidatus Caesaris*.

[41] *Ep.* X, 12.

[42] Tacitus, *Ann.* XI, 21, 2.

[43] LXXIII, 12, 2 (316), cf. F. Millar, *A Study of Cassius Dio* (1964), 16.

[44] LXXX, 5, 1 (476); cf. p. 299.

the republican magistracies developed by the fourth century into mere titles, retaining no substantial functions except, in certain cases, that of shouldering the expenses of games. Long before this, in the early second century, Epictetus could pour scorn on the honours which men so eagerly sought: 'If you wish to be consul, you must lose your sleep, run around, kiss hands, rot away at other men's doors, say and do many undignified things, send gifts to many and daily tokens to some. And what is the result? Twelve bundles of rods, sitting three or four times on the *tribunal*, giving circus games, and distributing dinners in baskets.'[45]

The canvassing which Epictetus mentions must relate either to gaining the favour of persons close to the emperor, or to the earlier offices through which a man had to rise before attaining the consulate; for from the reign of Tiberius onwards it is certain that the consulate was in the gift of the emperor, who might arrange the suffect consulships in advance, and then alter them, or leave them open, or dismiss the consuls at will.[46] After Claudius' death in October 54 it was regarded as having been a portent that he had designated no consuls for November and December.[47] The fact that the emperor appointed consuls was openly accepted, as for instance in the last sentence of the inscription of Tiberius Plautius Silvanus Aelianus from his family mausoleum at Tibur: 'This man, in the same prefecture of the city, Caesar Aug. Vespasianus made (*fecit*) consul for the second time.'[48] But nothing shows more clearly that the office was invariably granted by the emperor than precisely the fact that men are never attested on inscriptions as *candidati Caesaris* in relation to the consulate; for what was true of all did not need to be stated.

As a result, so it appears from a letter of Pliny, a consul designate was expected to expatiate on the virtues of the emperor when he next spoke in the senate.[49] More formally still, he would make a solemn speech of thanks to the emperor on entering office: 'The office of consul has laid on me the task of giving thanks to the emperor in the name of the *res publica*', as Pliny writes.[50] Similarly Fronto, as consul in 143, writes to Marcus Aurelius to say that he is putting off his speech in the senate giving thanks to Antoninus Pius until August, in order to prepare it properly. But before that, when he gives his circus games, he will issue an edict beginning, 'On the day on which by the *beneficium* of the greatest emperor I give a show which is most welcome to the people and especially popular, I thought it appropriate to give thanks, so that some day'—here some Ciceronian conclusion would follow.[51]

Pliny's speech—or rather the expanded version which he read on three

---

[45] *Diss.* IV, 10, 20–1; so also Martial, *Epig.* XII, 29 (26).

[46] See e.g. Dio LVIII, 20, 1–2 (cf. p. 302); LIX, 13, 2; 20, 1 and 3; Suetonius, *Nero* 15, 2; Pliny, *Ep.* III, 7, 9 (Silius Italicus—'novissimus a Nerone factus est consul', in 68); Tacitus, *Hist.* I, 77; II, 60; 71; Martial, *Epig.* VIII, 66; IX, 42; Pliny, *Pan.* 63, 2; Appian, *BC* I, 103/479; cf. Mommsen, *Staatsrecht*² II, 925.

[47] Suetonius, *Claud.* 46.

[48] *ILS* 986.

[49] *Ep.* VI, 27; cf. Sherwin-White, ad loc.

[50] III, 18, 1.

[51] *Ad M. Caes.* II, 1, 1. Note that Fronto made a speech both on designation and on entry to office, *Ad Ant.* IV (II, Naber), 2, 3: 'laudes a me in senatu designato et inito consulatu meo dictas.'

successive days to his long-suffering friends—survives as his *Panegyricus*.[52] When Pliny comes towards the end to speak explicitly of Trajan's appointment to the consulate of himself and of his colleague as *praefectus aerarii Saturni*, he describes this repeatedly as a *beneficium*, made even more valuable by his keeping them as colleagues, and giving them the month (September) in which Domitian had been assassinated and Trajan himself born; they would be issuing a special edict, and giving a *spectaculum* to celebrate the anniversary.[53]

The consulate was certainly in the personal gift of the emperor, and may possibly have been conferred, like other magistracies, by imperial *codicilli*; when Claudius, on being granted *consularia ornamenta* by his uncle Tiberius, urgently requested the consulate itself, the emperor did reply in *codicilli*, but only to refer insultingly to a gift of money which he had sent.[54] This incident, which Claudius' relationship to the emperor in any case makes quite exceptional, appears to be the only evidence of a direct request to the emperor for a consulship. Moreover we have almost no references to the exercise of influence to secure consulates for others; Tacitus however states that under Tiberius the consulate could be gained only by the favour of the praetorian prefect, Sejanus.[55] It may well be that the relatively formal and public recommendations and requests which took place in relation both to senatorial status as such and to senatorial magistracies, and which thus find a place in our sources, were not felt to be appropriate for the consulate. But we do not know.

More significant in the long term was the fact that Sejanus himself was given the consulate for 31 by Tiberius, without having held any previous senatorial office.[56] *Ornamenta praetoria* (which Sejanus had received earlier from Tiberius) and *consularia* were quite commonly granted to praetorian prefects;[57] as 'senatorial' distinctions, whose precise content is unclear, but which did not afford actual membership of the senate, such *ornamenta* illustrate once again the divorce of honour or status and function. The divorce appears even wider in those cases where the same *ornamenta* were granted to client kings,[58] or to writers or orators. Nero addressed the senate in 54 to ask for the *consularia insignia* for his tutor, Asconius Labeo.[59] But later emperors seem to have granted the *insignia* or *ornamenta* as their own gift, as did Trajan to Plutarch, or, surprisingly, Maximinus the Thracian to the orator Valerius Apsines.[60]

The consulate itself was of course a more important matter. In the first two centuries no equestrian praetorian prefect after Sejanus held it while retaining his office; but it is probable that L. Julius Ursus was praetorian

[52] See M. Durry, *Pline le Jeune, Panégyrique de Trajan* (1938).
[53] *Pan.* 91–2.
[54] Suetonius, *Claud.* 5; cf. Tacitus, *Dial.* 7, 2 (p. 306).
[55] *Ann.* IV, 68, 2; cf. also Juvenal, *Sat.* X, 90–2.
[56] For details see *PIR*[2] A 255.
[57] See e.g. A. Passerini, *Le coorti pretorie* (1939), 223; *RE* s.v. 'Praefectus Praetorio', XXII. 2, 2398f.
[58] See Mommsen, *Staatsrecht*[3] I, 464.
[59] Tacitus, *Ann.* XIII, 10, 1.
[60] See C. P. Jones, *Plutarch and Rome* (1971), 29; Apsines: *JRS* LIX (1969), 16.

prefect before being made suffect consul in 84 by Domitian, at the request of Julia, the daughter of Titus.[61] But in 203 the exceptionally powerful sole prefect under Severus, C. Fulvius Plautianus, was consul *ordinarius*, notionally for the second time because of his previous *ornamenta consularia*;[62] and in the following two decades several others gained the same honour after him. In the second half of the third century it again became common for men to combine the praetorian prefecture with the consulship, as for instance did Julius Placidianus in 273.[63] The same pattern continues into Constantine's reign, and Flavius Ablabius, for instance, was consul in 331 while praetorian prefect.[64] By comparison Julius Julianus, the grandfather of Julian the Apostate, was praetorian prefect of Licinius up to 324, but was praised by Constantine after his victory, and was consul in 325.[65]

Paradoxically, therefore, the very prominence of the consulate as the crown of the regular senatorial career, and the function of the consulate *ordinarius* in giving a name to the year, meant that it passed rapidly and completely into imperial gift, and could be—though was not normally—dissociated from a senatorial career altogether. As such, it might be regarded as bearing no more resemblance to the other magistracies than to the wide range of senatorial posts outside the *cursus* which were subject to direct imperial appointment exactly as were equestrian posts.

In principle, the positions held by *quaestores* in Rome and the public provinces, and the proconsulates of public provinces held by ex-praetors or ex-consuls, remained exempt from imperial patronage, and were distributed by lot.[66] But even here the emperor is found intervening to prevent men presenting themselves for the distribution by lot, or to make appointments without the use of it.[67] Tacitus reports that Domitian prevented Agricola from gaining the proconsulate of Africa or Asia by sending confidants to warn him off; as a result he had to go through what was evidently a conventional process of addressing *preces* to the emperor to ask for his *excusatio*, being granted it, and then having to offer formal thanks into the bargain. Tacitus further notes that Domitian did not offer the *salarium* of the post, though he had conceded it to others (that is others who had not actually held it), possibly because Agricola had not gone through the accustomed form of petitioning for it.[68]

Especially in the early empire we can find cases where the emperor promoted a motion in the senate in order to have a man appointed to a special

[61] For the complex arguments leading to the reconstruction of this series of events see R. Syme, *Tacitus* (1958), App. 7.

[62] See *PIR*² F 554.

[63] A. Chastagnol, 'L'Histoire Auguste et le rang des Préfets du Prétoire', *Recherches sur l'Histoire Auguste* (1970), 39, on p. 67.

[64] *PLRE* Ablabius 4; see pp. 130–1.

[65] *PLRE* Iulianus 35; see esp. Libanius, *Or.* XVIII, 9.

[66] See e.g. Dio LIII, 13, 2; Suetonius, *Vesp.* 2, 3; 4, 3; Tacitus, *Ann.* XV, 19, 1; Pliny, *Ep.* II, 12, 2; IV, 9, 2: Dio LXXIX, 3, 5 (457); *ILS* 1217: 'proconsuli provinciae Achaiae sortito' (early fourth century).

[67] e.g. Velleius II, 111, 4; Suetonius, *Galba* 3, 4 (Galba's father 'prohibitusque a Tiberio sortiri anno suo proconsulatum'); 7, 1: 'Africam pro consule biennio optinuit extra sortem'; Dio LX, 25, 6.

[68] *Agric.* 42, 1–3; a very similar pattern from the early third century in Dio LXXVIII, 22, 3–5 (427–8).

commission or extra-ordinary governorship;[69] while in the case of the *praefecti aerarii militaris* Dio records that they were for long chosen by lot from ex-praetors, but were now (the early third century) selected by the emperor.[70] But the patronage of the emperor was entrenched from the very beginning, and not merely in relation to the *legati* of imperial provinces and of legions; for instance the *senatus consultum* which established the consular *curatores aquarum* in 11 BC explicitly provided that they should be selected by Augustus, and Frontinus begins his account of the aqueducts with a reference to his appointment by Nerva.[71]

The fact of imperial appointment to a wide range of senatorial posts may be taken for granted; as Onasander wrote, addressing his *Strategemata* to Q. Veranius, the consul of 49, the work was suitable for Romans and especially for senators who were 'adorned with consular and praetorian commands by the judgment of the emperor'.[72] It is only in particular contexts that any emphasis is placed on the fact that an appointment has been made by the emperor. So Pliny, writing to Trajan to ask permission to act as *advocatus* while holding an imperial post, says elaborately, 'When your *indulgentia*, Lord, first promoted me to the prefecture of the *aerarium Saturni* . . .'[73] Alternatively, men referred to the emperor's commission if their post was in any way exceptional; so the inscriptions of Julius Severus from Ancyra record that he had been 'sent as *legatus* in Asia by a letter and *codicilli* of the divine Hadrian'—*legati* in proconsular provinces were normally appointed by the proconsul himself.[74] Similarly the imperial *codicilli* are mentioned in the dialogue between Epictetus and a senator named Maximus who is on his way to Achaia as *corrector* (or *curator*) of the free cities.[75]

'What need have you of philosophical doctrines?' 'But I am judge of the Greeks'. 'Do you know how to judge? What brought you to know that?' 'Caesar wrote a *codicillus* for me' . . . 'But how did you come to be a judge? Whose hand did you kiss—Symphorus' or Numenius'? Before whose bedroom door did you sleep? To whom did you send presents?'

Maximus thus emphasizes in his defence the personal nature of his appointment by Trajan, even implying, if taken literally, that the letter of appointment was written by the emperor himself. Epictetus by contrast points to the influence of other persons, whose names make clear in the context that they are imperial freedmen, and emphasizes the sycophancy to which a senator would be reduced to gain an appointment by their aid. The exercise of such influence, whether by freedmen or *amici*, is an attested fact.

[69] e.g. *ILS* 915, P. Paquius Scaeva, 'procos. iterum extra sortem auctoritate Aug. Caesaris et s.c. misso'; 942; *CIL* v 5262 and xi 5272 (Pliny sent by Trajan to Bithynia *ex. s.c.*); cf. Tacitus, *Ann.* III, 25.

[70] LV, 25, 3.

[71] Frontinus, *De aquae ductu* I, 100.

[72] *Strat.*, pr. 1.

[73] *Ep.* x, 3a, 1; cf. 8, 3.

[74] *IGR* III 174 = *OGIS* 543, ll. 9–11: πρεσβεύσα[ν]|τα ἐν ᾿Ασίᾳ ἐξ ἐπιστολῆς [καὶ]| κωδικίλλων Θεοῦ ῾Αδρια[νοῦ]; cf. 175 and see *PIR*[2] I 573; and for the background H.-G. Pflaum, 'Légats impériaux à l'interieur des provinces sénatoriales', *Hommages Grenier* (1962), 1232.

[75] *Diss.* III, 7, 29–31; note ῾Καῖσάρ μοι κωδίκελλον ἔγραψεν᾿, and cf. *JRS* LV (1965), 145.

Suetonius mentions in passing that Vespasian gained appointment as *legatus* of a legion in Germany (the II Augusta which then took part in the invasion of Britain) by the *gratia* of Narcissus, the *ab epistulis* of Claudius,[76] and that people thought that Vitellius had been appointed by Galba as *legatus* of Germania Inferior through the *suffragium* of the emperor's *amicus*, T. Vinius.[77] Similarly Plutarch reports that Otho, when he fell into disfavour with Nero, was saved by Seneca, who interceded with the emperor and persuaded him to send Otho, though only an ex-quaestor, as *legatus pro praetore* of Lusitania.[78]

It cannot be shown that it was regular for imperial legateships to be gained by direct or indirect petition, but it was certainly common in the early empire. Dio indeed attests that Claudius forbade governors whom he had selected to thank him formally in the senate (saying that he ought to thank them), which may suggest no more than that such an appointment was regarded publicly as a *beneficium*.[79] But Quintilian reports a remark of Domitius Afer to Didius Gallus 'who had petitioned most urgently for a province, and then, when he gained one, complained as if he had been compelled'; the reference could be to one or other of Gallus' consular legateships, in Moesia and Britain.[80] Both patterns were possible (Tiberius complained that he had to resort to *preces* to persuade ex-consuls to take appointments),[81] but petition was certainly a familiar phenomenon; in the *Life of Apollonius of Tyana*, for instance, Philostratus represents his hero, when at the court of Domitian, as seeing a very old man fawning on the emperor in order to obtain a governorship.[82]

Consular governorships also were granted by means of *codicilli* emanating from the emperor. Tacitus records that, as most people believed, Domitian took precautions to ensure that Agricola left his command in Britain by sending one of his trusted freedmen to meet him with *codicilli* nominating him as *legatus* of Syria; but, on finding that Agricola was duly leaving Britain, he returned without transmitting the *codicilli*.[83] Like the *codicilli* addressed to equestrian officials, they could have a highly personal tone. Suetonius reports that Tiberius spent two days and nights dining and drinking with Pomponius Flaccus and L. Calpurnius Piso, and immediately afterwards appointed the former as *legatus* of Syria and the latter as *Praefectus urbi*, 'declaring in the *codicilli* that they were the most agreeable of friends, and at all hours'.[84] There is some chronological confusion here,[85] but the

---

[76] *Vesp.* 4, 1. Cf. *Tit.* 2 for the family's connection with Narcissus.

[77] *Vit.* 7, 1.

[78] *Galba* 20, 1; cf. Suetonius, *Otho* 3, 2 and Tacitus, *Ann.* XIII, 46, 3.

[79] LX, 11, 6–7.

[80] *Inst.* VI, 3, 68: 'qui provinciam ambitiosissime petierat, deinde impetrata ea, tamquam coactus querebatur.' For Gallus' career see *PIR²* D 70. His second legateship, in Britain, began in 52. Afer died in 59, *PIR²* D 126.

[81] Tacitus, *Ann.* VI, 27, 3.

[82] *V. Ap. Ty.* VII, 31.

[83] *Agric.* 40, 2. For imperial *liberti* entitled *a codicillis* see e.g. *ILS* 1529 = *IGR* I 113; 1530; *adiutor a codicillis*, 1531.

[84] *Tib.* 42.

[85] That Piso was both a habitual drunkard and a close confidant of Tiberius when *Praefectus*

anecdote should still imply that the prefects of the city also received *codicilli* of appointment from the emperor. That the post was at all periods in the direct gift of the emperor is certain: 'When we entrusted our city to your *fides*', Severus and Caracalla wrote in their letter to Fabius Cilo.[86] Often associated with the consulate, and particularly with the further distinction of a second consulate as *ordinarius*, this post, which could in the earlier part of the period be held for an indefinite period, marked the true apex of the senatorial career under the empire; it will have performed this function even more clearly from the middle of the third century when a tenure of a year or so became normal.[87] But, as with the consulate, we have no evidence to show that it was sought or gained by petition or patronage.

Our evidence for the conferment of senatorial posts at all levels is much poorer in the last than the first part of the period; and we can hardly go beyond the few inscriptions which mention that such posts had been given by the judgment (*iudicium*) of the emperor,[88] or the elegant address of Firmicus Maternus to Q. Flavius Maesius Egnatius Lollianus Mavortius, *comes Orientis* in the 330s—'when the serene and revered judgments of our emperor Constantinus Augustus had entrusted to you the reins of the whole Orient'.[89]

Eusebius' account of the bestowal of honours and posts by Constantine will suffice to show that these were still sought from the emperor, and given as rewards by him.[90] But we cannot claim to have for any period much evidence on the forms of relationship which this involved; what hints we possess come mainly from the beginning of the second century and earlier. Yet it is necessary to insist on this patronage by the emperor, and the degree to which it was exercised in response to requests by men seeking posts for themselves or others. For it was precisely the fact that Roman ranks, titles and posts, both new and old, could be conferred by the emperor, and in many cases could be and were sought from him by the beneficiaries, which gave a real or symbolic place within the Roman state to an ever-widening range of individuals, to their families and descendants, and in the long run to whole areas of society in the provinces. It is necessary to recall that the consu-

---

Urbi is confirmed by Seneca, *Ep.* 83, 14. His appointment by Tiberius is attested also by Pliny, *NH* xiv, 28/145, who gives the same reason; *contra PIR²* c 289, it is therefore preferable to believe that Tacitus, *Ann.* vi, 11, is mistaken in saying that he had been *Praefectus* for 20 years when he died in 32. But Flaccus was not in any case appointed to Syria until 32, see Schürer, *Jewish People* 1, 262.

[86] *Dig.* 1, 12, 1, 4. Cf. the expression ἐπάρχῳ τῆς πατρίδος τῆς ἐμῆς in the letter of Gordian III to Aurelius Epagathus from Aphrodisias, *AE* 1969/70 599.

[87] See *RE* s.v. 'Praefectus urbi', xxii. 2, 2513f.; G. Vitucci, *Ricerche sulla Praefectura Urbi in età imperiale (sec. I–III)* (1956); A. Chastagnol, *La Préfecture urbaine à Rome sous le Bas-Empire* (1960).

[88] *CIL* x 1655, a dedication to Carinus by (C. Ceionius) Rufus Volusianus, 'v.c. corum iudicio beatissimus iterum corrector', see *PLRE* Volusianus 4; *ILS* 1240, L. Aradius Valerius Proculus, 'iudicio sacro . . . perfuncto officio praefecturae praetorio' in Africa *c.* 330, see *PLRE* Proculus 11; *ILAfr.* 456: 'Acaiae [*sic*], Asiae iterum et Africae IV procos. sacro iudicio Constantini' (perhaps referring only to prolongation in office), *PLRE* Anon. 37.

[89] p. 117.

[90] p. 278.

late had long been granted only by the emperor when we read an inscription carved at Ephesus in the first half of the third century:[91]

> The council and People honoured Claudia Caninia Severa, *clarissima consularis* (*femina*) by descent ... daughter of Tiberius Claudius Severus, first of the Ephesians to have held the consulate, and of Caninia Gargonilla, *consularis* by descent, who had adorned our city with many great works.

5. *Equestrian and Senatorial Office-Holders:*
Imperial Mandata *and* Epistulae

The patronage of the emperor was thus of crucial long-term importance in widening the basis of at least the upper of the two 'orders' of Roman society and in awarding honours, distinctions and offices within these orders to the provincial upper classes. But it had also, of course, an immediate short-term significance, in that the emperor personally appointed all the *equites*, and a substantial proportion of the senators, who held office in Rome, Italy or the provinces. If he were of senatorial birth, a man could rise as far as the praetorship and govern a minor pro-consular province as an ex-praetor, without needing or seeking imperial patronage. But without it he could never command a legion, govern an imperial province, hold the consulate or be prefect of the city. It would not be easy to find many examples of senatorial careers which will not have required some imperial patronage at some stage (even putting aside the less active patronage of being permitted to stand for office); and the rapid entrenchment of such patronage throughout the senatorial career must necessarily have affected the relationship to the emperor even of those magistrates in Rome who owed their current position to election by their fellow-senators, and of proconsuls who owed theirs to the lot.

It is not surprising, therefore, that the period saw a steady reduction of the semi-independent position of proconsuls to the point when, while they were in office, the pattern of their contracts with the emperor was indistinguishable from that of his appointees. By the early second century, for instance, they, like the appointees, received orders (*mandata*) from the emperor; and in about the same period we find them beginning to consult the emperor regularly on a wide range of matters which came before them, just as imperial prefects, procurators and legates had already come to do. As we saw earlier, the exchange of letters with office-holders formed a substantial part of imperial correspondence, and hence was a significant element in what the emperor did.[1] Consultation of the emperor by governors was also an important indirect channel by which individuals and cities and groups

---

[91] D. Knibbe, 'Neue Inschriften aus Ephesos III', *JÖAI* XLIX (1968–71), Beibl., 64, no. 6 = *AE* 1972 587: ['Η βουλὴ καὶ ὁ δῆμος ἐτείμησαν Κλαυδίαν Κανεινίαν] Σεουῆραν τὴν λαμπροτάτην ἐκ προγόνων ὑπατικὴν . . . θυγατέρα Τιβ. Κλ. Σεουήρου, πρώτου ὑπατεύσαντος Ἐφεσίων, καὶ Κανεινίας Γαργωνίλλης ἐκ προγόνων ὑπατικῆς, πολλοῖς καὶ μεγάλοις ἔργοις κοσμοῦσαν τὴν πατρίδα ἡμῶν. For confirmation of the date see Chr. Habicht, *ZPE* XIII (1974), 4–6.

[1] pp. 207–8, 215–16.

11*

in the provinces communicated with him. But beyond that the study of the pattern, occasions and tone of such correspondence is highly significant for assessing to what extent the relations of office-holders and the emperor can themselves be regarded as the relations of subject and monarch.[2]

For all these questions it is essential to emphasize the overwhelming extent to which contacts by letter between office-holders and the emperor were initiated by the former. General imperial orders affecting the whole population were sometimes transmitted—like for instance the orders for the persecutions under Valerian—in the form of letters sent round to all governors. But a large proportion of the surviving documents expressing the imperial will or giving rulings on points of law are in origin replies to individual governors or office-holders. For instance the famous pronouncement of Diocletian and Maximian on the punishment of the devotees of Manicheeism is in fact a letter to the proconsul of Africa in reply to a report sent by him:[3]

> We have heard that the Manichees, about whom your Conscientiousness reported to our Serenity, have most recently, like novel and unexpected prodigies, advanced into our world from the hostile race of the Persians . . . and because all the types of wrongdoing, which your Prudence sets out in your report on their religion . . . In order therefore that this abomination of wickedness may be wholly rooted out from our most blessed age, your Devotion will hasten to obey the orders and regulations of our Tranquillity.

A century and a half of the empire had to pass before it would have been normal for a proconsul of Africa to write for guidance to the emperor, and perhaps another century and a half after that before the tone of obsequious deference on the one side and grandiose self-exhaltation on the other became a common medium of exchange. But in being a reply to one particular report—and the only recorded pronouncement of the tetrarchs on Manicheeism—the letter is absolutely typical of the structure and functioning of the empire from the beginning, and of the role of the emperor within it.

Imperial appointees, whether equestrian or senatorial, all seem to have received instructions (*mandata*, or in Greek *entolai*) from the emperor when they took office. The occasional literary references to such *mandata* in the early empire are not sufficient to determine their scope or contents, but do make clear that they were a matter of routine for senatorial *legati*,[4] as they were probably for the prefect of Egypt[5] and for procurators in proconsular provinces.[6] At least by the end of the first century, the *mandata* which *legati* received had reached a degree of generality and consistency: Frontinus writes, 'There is nothing which the *legati* of the provinces are more accustomed to receive in their *mandata* than that those places which are sacred

---

[2] Many of the themes, and some of the evidence, in this section, were treated in different form in 'The Emperor, the Senate and the Provinces', *JRS* LVI (1966), 156.

[3] *Coll.* XV, 3. Cf. p. 174.

[4] Tacitus, *Ann.* II, 77, 1.

[5] Philo, *In Flaccum* 10/74: διὰ τῶν πρὸς Μάγιον Μάξιμον ἐντολῶν, referring to Augustus' instructions to one prefect on a particular matter. Cf. also *Dig.* I, 17, 1 (Ulpian) on the standing *mandata* of the prefect in the early third century.

[6] Tacitus, *Ann.* IV, 15, 2.

should be preserved as such.'[7] Frontinus also, as *curator aquarum* in 98, refers to and quotes from the *mandata* relating to the aqueducts as they were in his time:[8]

> But this custom is vulnerable to the frauds of those who draw water; how much care has to be exercised in preventing these will be clear from the section of the *mandata* which I have appended: 'I wish no one to draw excess water except those who have the right by the *beneficium* of myself or previous Emperors. For it is necessary that some surplus water should flow from the *castella*, for this is relevant not only to the hygiene of our city but for the function of washing out of drains.'

It is noticeable that these *mandata*, which can hardly have changed significantly from reign to reign, none the less use the first person, and are in form personal instructions from the emperor to the *curator*. The personal element is much more clearly present, however, in the inscription containing an extract in Greek from the *mandata* of Domitian to the procurator of the imperial province of Syria:[9]

> From the *mandata* of Imperator Domitianus Caesar Augustus, son of Augustus, to Claudius Athenodorus, procurator. Among the matters of special importance, and demanding particular care, I know that the privileges of the cities received attention from my divine father, Vespasianus Caesar; bending his mind to which, he ordered that the provinces should be burdened neither by the hiring of beasts of burden nor demands for lodgings . . .

The orders which had been given by Vespasian, and were now repeated, perhaps in more detail, by Domitian, touched on one of the perennial areas of conflict between subjects and officials, the rights of requisitioning transport and lodging for soldiers and travellers on public business. There is no specific reference to Syria in what survives of these *mandata*, and it may well be that they were issued by Domitian to his appointees in all provinces. The same might be true of at least the bulk of the *mandata* which Pliny received from Trajan when he was sent, probably in 109, as *legatus* of Pontus and Bithynia. For the references which are made to the *mandata* in his correspondence with Trajan—which naturally do not give more than a very partial conception of them—show that they covered matters which were common to all provinces: the numbers and recruitment of troops, legal procedures, or rules relating to city funds.[10] It is important to stress that the issuing of such *mandata* could be an indirect means by which the emperor

---

[7] *De controversiis agrorum, Corp. Agrim. Rom.* ed. Thulin, p. 48.

[8] *De aquae ductu* 109–11.

[9] *IGLS* v, 1998; *SEG* XVII 755. For a revised text, and a translation, see N. Lewis, 'Domitian's Order on Requisitioned Transport and Lodgings', *RIDA* XV (1968), 135. The common description of this document as a letter (*epistula*) is incorrect, as the heading is unambiguous: ἐξ ἐντολῶν Αὐτοκράτορος [Δομ]ιτιανοῦ Καίσ[α]ρος Σεβαστοῦ υἱοῦ Σεβαστ[οῦ] πρὸς Κλαύδιον Ἀθηνόδωρον ἐπίτροπον. It is an extract from the *mandata* exactly analogous to that from Frontinus. For the view that Athenodorus will be the procurator of Syria see *JRS* LIII (1963), 199.

[10] *Ep.* X, 22; 30; 56; 110–11; L. Vidman, *Étude sur la correspondance de Pline le jeune avec Trajan* (1960), 45f., and Sherwin-White, *The Letters of Pliny* (1966), esp. 543–4, 547.

communicated with the population of a province; for Pliny mentions that he had incorporated in his edict a provision of Trajan's *mandata* banning private association (*hetaeriae*), and that in accordance with this the Christians had disbanded their congregations.[11]

There is nothing to suggest that the proconsuls whom Pliny, by virtue of his special appointment, succeeded as governor of Pontus and Bithynia, had themselves received *mandata* from the emperor. But from almost the same time as Pliny's governorship, we have a letter to the city of Aezani from the proconsul of Asia in about 111/12, Q. Fabius Postuminus, in which he says, 'At the very beginning of my proconsulate, considering it to be in accordance with the orders (*mandata*?), and necessary for the city, to make a visit to you, I gladly came.'[12] The orders to which he refers can hardly have come from anyone other than the emperor. If so, then this marks a fundamental change in the hitherto essentially independent position of proconsuls. The change appears even more clearly in Marcianus' reference to a section of the *mandata* (*caput mandatorum*) which the future emperor, Antoninus Pius, included in his edict as proconsul of Asia in about 134/5.[13]

According to Ulpian, Trajan finally confirmed the privilege granted to soldiers by some previous emperors, that their wills would be valid even if not made in the strictly correct form, 'and from that time on the following section (*caput*) began to be included in the *mandata*'; the extract which he then quotes—and which appears verbatim in a fragmentary Latin papyrus of the second or third century—is evidently the text as issued by Trajan: 'Since it has been brought to my notice . . . I have thought it right to take account . . .'[14] But Ulpian's words also suggest that the same text was taken over and perpetuated in the *mandata* of subsequent emperors. By his time, as both he, and other legal writers of the early third century, and Cassius Dio all attest, *mandata* were issued as a matter of routine to all governors, both imperial appointees and proconsuls; and it may well be that both the extension to proconsuls and the development of a standard form of *mandata* go back to the reign of Trajan. Ulpian and others refer quite frequently to standing provisions of the *mandata*, as to an established code of law; they include for instance precisely the instructions given to Pliny about the banning of associations. It is also striking, however, that all those sections of the *mandata* which are quoted verbatim are still couched in the second person singular, as if addressed personally by the emperor to each office-holder.[15]

---

[11] x, 96, 7.

[12] *IGR* IV 572, revised by L. Robert, *Études Anatoliennes* (1937), 301–5. The key phrase is ἀκό[λουθ]όν τε ταῖς ἐντολαῖς ἡγησάμενος. See *PIR*² F 54, and for the date W. Eck, *Senatoren von Vespasian bis Hadrian* (1970), 236. But see now the reference to ἐντολαῖς by a proconsul under Claudius, *Parola del Passato* CLX (1975), 102.

[13] *Dig.* XLVIII, 3, 6, 1 (Marcianus, *De iudiciis publicis* II, written in the first half of the third century).

[14] *Dig.* XXIX, 1, 1 *pr.*; Cavenaille, *Corp. Pap. Lat.*, no. 71.

[15] *Dig.* I, 16, 6, 3 (Ulpian, *De officio proconsulis*); XXIV, 1, 3, 1 (Ulpian, *Ad Sabinum*); XLVII, 11, 6 *pr.* (Ulpian, *De officio proconsulis*): 'mandatis denique ita cavetur: "Praeterea debebis custodire, ne dardanarii ullius mercis sint..."'; XLVII, 22, 1 *pr.* (cf. 3, 1) (Marcianus, *Institutiones*): 'mandatis principalibus praecipitur praesidibus provinciarum ne patiantur esse

Both this surviving personal element and an important restriction which the *mandata* now imposed on all categories of governor are clearly visible in the passage of Callistratus' *De cognitionibus*, in which he lays down that governors must consult the emperor before condemning to exile any leading men or councillors of the cities. He then continues:[16]

> In another section of the *mandata* the following provision appears: 'If any of the leading men of any city have been guilty of brigandage or any other crime such that they seem to deserve a capital penalty, you will keep them in chains and write to me, adding details of what each one has done.'

The *mandata* are mentioned in a *subscriptio* of Gordian III dating to 239, and again at the end of the third century by Arcadius Charisius.[17] Constantine also refers, in a letter of 326, to the *mandata* which should be obeyed by the officials of 'our private properties'.[18] Their significance lies firstly in the fact that they came to be addressed by the emperors to proconsuls, as well as to his own appointees, and secondly in that they might represent the only positive communication from the emperor to an office-holder in the entire course of his functions. We shall see shortly the limited occasions and frequency of those communications from the emperor to governors, which were not explicitly replies to letters from them. But their relative rarity gives all the more significance to the fact that the *mandata* themselves, though preserving the verbal style of a personal commission from the emperor to the individual office-holder, in fact ossified into a standard code. It is perhaps precisely in relation to provincial governors that the passivity of the emperor's role, and its substantial (though not complete) limitation to the function of responding to reports, requests and inquiries, is most striking. It is a highly significant fact, which we tend to dwell on too little, that the correspondence of Pliny and Trajan contains not a single example of a letter sent spontaneously by the emperor.

Provincial governors, as we have seen, were sometimes made responsible for copying and posting up imperial edicts in their own areas, though the function is if anything more clearly attested for city authorities.[19] Moreover, all edicts, or other imperial pronouncements which created law, could affect the jurisdiction of a governor, normally in the form of their being quoted by interested parties before him in court. Some edicts, though not many among those attested, also explicitly laid down what course of action should be

---

collegia sodalicia . . .'; XLVIII, 3, 10 (Venuleius Saturninus, *De officio proconsulis*): 'mandatis ita cavetur: "Si quos ex his, qui in civitatibus sunt, celeriter et sine causa solutos a magistratibus cognoveris, vinciri iubebis . . ."'; XLVIII, 19, 35 (Callistratus, *Quaestiones*); *Coll.* XI, 7, 4 (Ulpian, *De officio proconsulis*); cf. Dio LIII, 15, 4 and esp. Lucian, *Pro lapsu* 13.

[16] *Dig.* XLVIII, 19, 27, 1–2. For the background to this provision see P. Garnsey, *Social Status and Legal Privilege in the Roman Empire* (1970), chs. 4–6.

[17] *CJ* V, 4, 6; *Dig.* XXII, 5, 25. Note also *Pan.* II(10), 3, 4: 'accipere innumerabiles undique nuntios, totidem mandata dimittere' (289).

[18] *CTh* X, 4, 1; for the date, Seeck, *Regesters*, 176.

[19] pp. 254–7. Note also *P. Oxy.* 2558, an *edictum* of the Prefect of Egypt in 303–6, Clodius Culcianus, accompanying the publication of an imperial *edictum*.

followed by governors. It may still be suggested, though the text has many obscurities, that an early case of this is the well-known inscription from Cyme in Asia. The text starts with a pronouncement by Augustus and Agrippa as consuls in 27 BC, which seems to order the restoration of sacred properties in every province, and to lay down that the governors should see to this. It is followed by a letter of a proconsul named Vinicius, perhaps in 27/6 BC, informing the city of Cyme that one Apollonides has approached him and informed him that a shrine is in the illegal possession of a private person, and that the cult-association wished to recover it in accordance with the order (*iussum*) of Augustus. Since the relevant verb is missing, we do not know the form of Augustus and Agrippa's pronouncement, but it seems to be it which is referred to as the 'order of Augustus'.[20] Later in his reign we find Augustus saying explicitly in the first of the edicts inscribed at Cyrene, which dates to 7/6 BC: 'It seems to me that those who in the future govern the province of Crete and Cyrene will act well and appropriately'—if they follow certain principles in selecting jurors and handling cases.[21] The province was governed by proconsuls, and the pronouncement is in form advisory; it is not likely that it was treated other than as an order.

This, as we saw, was a relatively rare instance of an *edictum* relating to the affairs of one province as a whole.[22] General edicts also sometimes gave explicit or implicit instructions to governors; so for instance Nero's edict of 58 on abuses by the *publicani* laid down that 'at Rome the praetor, and throughout the provinces the proconsuls and *legati pro praetore*' should give precedence to cases against them.[23] The edicts of Hadrian on the proper gradation of penalties and of Antoninus Pius on the punishments appropriate to thefts from imperial *metalla* must also certainly have constituted at least implicit orders to governors on their procedures in jurisdiction,[24] while Hadrian's edict on the plundering of wrecked ships explicitly instructed governors to return the property and inflict heavy penalties on the guilty.[25] Similarly, Diocletian and Maximian, in an edict of 294, laid down certain rules for the conduct of jurisdiction by governors.[26]

Alternatively, an edict could be accompanied by letters sent individually to governors and office-holders; for instance in what is probably an edict of Constantine on informers, the emperor mentions that he has also sent letters to the prefects, governors, *rationales* and *magister privatae*.[27] Such letters distributed generally to office-holders and expressing some general principles or command may be distiguished from two other categories of correspondence; first, letters sent to one or more governors or office-holders

---

[20] *SEG* XVIII 555; cf. XX 15. The interpretation given here is that in *JRS* LVI (1966), 160–1; for a different view see Sherk, *Roman Documents*, no. 61.

[21] *SEG* IX 8, i = *FIRA*² I, no. 68, ll. 13–14: δοκοῦσί μοι καλῶς καὶ προσηκόντως ποιήσειν οἱ τὴν Κρητικὴν καὶ Κυρηναϊκὴν ἐπαρχήαν καθέξοντες. Cf. ll. 37–8.

[22] p. 257.

[23] Tacitus, *Ann.* XIII, 51, 1; cf. p. 259.

[24] *Dig.* XLVIII, 19, 28, 13 (Hadrian); XLVIII, 13, 8, 1 (Antoninus Pius).

[25] *Dig.* XLVII, 9, 7.

[26] *CJ* III, 3, 2.

[27] *Ins. Cret.* I. xviii, 188 *ad fin.*; for other partial texts and the problem of dating and attribution see p. 258.

which were prompted by initiatives from other persons; and second, (much the most fully attested category) letters sent in reply to information or enquiries from the office-holders themselves. Even these were in many, though not all, cases written in order to transmit the requests or problems of individual subjects or of communities; and not only in those cases, already mentioned, where they enclosed *libelli* for presentation to the emperor.[28] Both of these latter two classes therefore themselves represent aspects of the patterns of communication between subject and emperor.

For most of the period it seems to have been rare for emperors to communicate anything spontaneously to a wide range of office-holders; no other emperor followed the example of Augustus in sending improving excerpts from his reading in Greek and Latin not only to his household, but to the magistrates of Rome and the governors of armies and provinces.[29] Philo claims, however, that after the death of Sejanus, Tiberius wrote to all governors throughout the empire instructing them to reassure the Jewish communities.[30] Hadrian also wrote to governors about the procedure for exempting the private goods of themselves and his procurators from the tolls taken by *publicani*.[30a] It is less clear who were the precise addressees of the *generalis epistula* in which Marcus Aurelius and Commodus gave orders that governors, city magistrates and soldiers manning provincial guard-posts must assist in recovering fugitive slaves.[31]

Specific orders transmitted generally to governors by letter are hardly attested except in relation to the persecutions of the third and early fourth centuries. The persecution of Decius was promulgated by the medium of an *edictum*, but those under Valerian in 257 and 258 by letters to the governors.[32]

The great persecution of 303 and after was again promulgated by means of edicts;[33] but in the proclamation of toleration issued by Galerius in the name of himself, Constantine and Licinius in 311, he adds that he will indicate in a separate letter to the governors (*iudices*) what action they should take.[34] It is indeed just at this time that we begin to find some imperial letters to office-holders coming to have something of the function of edicts, firstly in expressing general orders or rules deliberately promulgated by the emperors, and secondly in containing explicit provisions for publication in a manner very similar to edicts. This is clearly evident in the bronze tablet containing the letter which Constantine and Licinius addressed in 311 to Dalmatius (an important office-holder whose precise rank is unknown), laying down certain privileges for soldiers and veterans: our text owes its existence to their instruction that 'the content of this *indulgentia* of ours

---

[28] p. 216.
[29] Suetonius, *Aug.* 89.
[30] *Leg.* 24/161: καὶ τοῖς πανταχόσε χειροτονουμένοις ὑπάρχοις ἐπέσκηψε παρηγορῆσαι μὲν τοὺς κατὰ πόλεις τῶν ἀπὸ τοῦ ἔθνους.
[30a] *Dig.* XXXIX, 4, 4, 1.
[31] *Dig.* XI, 4, 1, 2.
[32] pp. 566–70.
[33] pp. 254, 574–7.
[34] Lactantius, *De mort. pers.* 34, 5; Eusebius, *HE* VIII, 17, 9; cf. pp. 578–9.

should be inscribed on a bronze tablet and dedicated at the standards in each camp'.[35] Alternatively, when Maximin decided to reinstitute a bare toleration of Christianity in his region towards the end of 312, he did so by sending a letter to this effect to his praetorian prefect, Sabinus, and ordering him to post up an edict containing its substance.[36] The prouncement by which Constantine and Licinius proclaimed the restoration of the church on the following year, often called the 'Edict of Milan', was in fact not an edict, but consisted of letters to provincial governors, which they ordered to be put up (*proponi*) exactly in the manner of an edict. Such letters are the source both of the Greek text in Eusebius and the Latin one in Lactantius. According to both texts the imperial letter was to be accompanied by a *programma* of the governor (in the latter case the *praeses* of Bithynia);[37] precisely the same provision is attached to a long letter of Constantine to the prefect of Rome on the law of gifts (*donationes*).[38] By contrast in his letter on Jewish circumcision, sent to Felix, the praetorian prefect of Africa, in October 335, Constantine requests him in his turn to write to the governors in his diocese; but in fact the imperial letter was *proposita*, like an *edictum*, in Carthage in March 336.[39]

To the letters addressed in this period to provincial governors in order to transmit spontaneous instruction or laying down general principles we can probably add the two sent early in 313, to Anullinus, the proconsul of Africa, ordering the restoration of church property and laying down that the clerics were to be exempt from financial obligations (*munera*) in the cities.[40] It is probable, but not attested, that other governors received similar letters at the same time. But it is almost certainly to the second of them that Anullinus refers when he addresses Constantine in a letter written in a style typical of the period: 'The celestial missive of your Majesty, once it had been accepted and saluted by Caecilian and those who act under him who are called *clerici*, my Devotion took care to file among the records of my Insignificance'.[41]

The apparently intensive use of letters to governors and other office-holders in this period to impose positive orders and novel principles parallels the contemporary use of edicts for the same purposes, and bring into relief the extreme rarity of such things from the earlier part of the period. The only earlier parallel appears to be the letter of Hadrian addressed in 119 to Rammius Martialis, the prefect of Egypt, and concerned with the rights of inheritance of soldiers' children. Hadrian instructs Martialis to make its

---

[35] *FIRA²* I, no. 93 (cf. p. 222); cf. *PLRE* Dalmatius 2.

[36] Eusebius, *HE* IX, 9a, 1–9, *ad fin.*: ἵνα δὲ αὕτη ἡμῶν ἡ κέλευσις εἰς γνῶσιν πάντων τῶν ἐπαρχιωτῶν τῶν ἡμετέρων ἔλθη, διατάγματι ὑπὸ σοῦ προτεθέντι τὸ κελευσμένον ὀφείλεις δηλῶσαι. Cf. p. 581.

[37] Eusebius, *HE* X, 5, 1–14; Lactantius, *De mort. pers.* 48; cf. p. 582.

[38] *Frag. Vat.* 249 (partial texts in *CTh* VIII, 12, 1; *CJ* V, 37, 21; VIII, 53, 25).

[39] *Const. Sirmond.* 4 (partial texts in *CTh* XVI, 8, 5 and 9, 1).

[40] Eusebius, *HE* X, 5, 15–17; X, 7. See further pp. 581–2.

[41] Quoted by Augustine, *Ep.* 88, 2: 'scripta caelestia maiestatis vestrae accepta atque adorata Caeciliano et his, qui sub eodem agunt quique clerici appellantur, devotio mea apud acta parvitatis meae insinuare curavit.' The letter is formally addressed to three Augusti and therefore dates to before the fall of Maximin in May–June 313.

provisions known to the soldiers; and in fact its heading records that it was 'put up' in the camps of the two Egyptian legions.[42] But, that apart, we know of no letters from the earlier period which provably embody positive enactments by the emperor. There are some cases where we do not know whose initiative led to the despatch of imperial letters to office-holders;[43] and it is possible that whenever legal sources indicate that an imperial letter was *proposita* this means that it was designed to promulgate a new general ruling. Before Constantine such cases are very rare, namely a letter of Marcus Aurelius to the proconsul of Africa, C. Serius Augurinus, *proposita* in 170,[44] and one of Diocletian and Maximian to the *praeses* of Numidia in 295;[45] both seem to express general principles. But with the advent of Constantine indications that a letter was *proposita* by the recipient become quite common.[46] In the vast majority of cases from before his reign, however, it is clear from external or internal evidence either that office-holders themselves, governors in particular, initiated correspondence with the emperor, or that other parties did so, and thereby prompted an imperial letter.

The latter pattern is very clearly attested in the case of the Jewish communities of Asia and Cyrene under Augustus. In 12 BC they sent embassies to Augustus to protect both their civic rights and the funds which they sent annually to Jerusalem. Augustus responded favourably not only in the edict mentioned earlier, but also by letters to Norbanus Flaccus, probably proconsul soon after, and (according to a letter of Agrippa which Josephus quotes) to various successive proconsuls of Cyrene. Flaccus writes without qualification to the city of Sardis, 'Caesar has written to me ordering that the Jews . . . should not be prevented from collecting money according to their ancestral custom, and sending it to Jerusalem.' Augustus evidently did not write similarly to Jullus Antonius, proconsul a few years later; but the Jewish communities again took the initiative and brought to his notice the rights confirmed by Augustus and Agrippa.[47]

Similarly a letter from the emperor to one office-holder might be provoked by a letter to him from another—and this in its turn by an initiative from below. So when the Greeks of Jamnia complained to the procurator,

---

[42] *BGU* 140 = Hunt and Edgar, *Select Papyri* II, no. 213.

[43] e.g. the letter from Claudius to Ti. Julius Postuminus, *Praefectus Aegypti c.* 45/7, referred to in the edict of Tiberius Julius Alexander, *OGIS* 669, ll. 26–7; or the letter of Claudius authorizing the establishment of the boundary of what is apparently an imperial estate at Sagalassus in Galatia, *OGIS* 538 = *IGR* III 335, revised by G. E. Bean, *Anat. Stud.* IX (1959), 85, no. 30; or possibly the pronouncement of Caracalla ordering the expulsion of Egyptians from Alexandria, in *P. Giss.* 40, which is probably a letter to the prefect, see Hunt and Edgar, *Select Papyri* II, no. 215. See also n. 62 below

[44] *CJ* III, 31, 1; 'PP VI K. Febr. Claro et Cethego conss.'; see *PIR*¹ s 387; B. E. Thomasson, *Oposc. Rom.* VII (1969), 173.

[45] *CJ* IX, 9, 27: 'PP. K. Iun. Tusco et Anullino conss.'

[46] e.g. *CTh* II, 16, 2 = *CJ* II, 52, 5 (319); II, 8, 1 = *CJ* III, 12, 7 (321); IX, 7, 2 = *CJ* IX, 7, 29 (326); *CJ* IV, 62, 4: 'PP. VII Id. Mart. Carthagine' (addressed to Felix, *Praefectus Praetorio* of Africa 333–6). Many more examples could be given. These letters, unlike *subscriptiones*, were 'put up', like those for which explicit instructions for publication were given, at the place of receipt.

[47] Josephus, *Ant.* XVI, 6, 1–7 (160–73); cf. *JRS* LVI (1966), 161. Orders from Augustus are also mentioned in the letter of Flaccus to Sardis quoted in Philo, *Leg.* 40/315. For the embassy and edict see p. 257.

Herennius Capito, that the Jews there had pulled down an altar which they had constructed, Capito wrote to Gaius, and Gaius responded by writing to Petronius, the *legatus* of Syria, to order the establishment in the Temple of a golden statue of himself as Zeus.[48] Alternatively, an office-holder might find himself receiving a letter from the emperor about an issue which had arisen under one of his predecessors, as when Titus wrote in August 79 to Cornelius Gallicanus, the proconsul of Baetica, about an appeal by the *municipium* of Munigua against an earlier proconsul, Sempronius Tuscus.[49] Or again a community might send a letter, normally by an embassy, direct to the emperor and thus initiate a reply to the governor: for instance, Domitian wrote to the proconsul of Achaea after he had received an embassy from Delphi protesting at changes in the conduct of the Pythian games proposed by the Amphictyony; the proconsul's letter refers explicitly to the order sent to him by the emperor.[50] Trajan also wrote to the proconsul of Achaea and to his procurator there after an embassy from Delphi;[51] and in one of the imperial letters from Aphrodisias Trajan writes to that city about its privileges and about a claim by one of its citizens for exemption from priestly service at Pergamum, and says that he has written also to the proconsul, Julius Balbus.[52]

Such cases as these are therefore only in a formal sense exceptions to the general pattern that the emperor rarely initiated correspondence with office-holders; for in each instance the issue is some specific matter on which the initiative has been taken by an individual or city, or other group, in the area concerned. Up to the early second century, however, it is noticeable that all the examples of office-holders spontaneously sending enquiries or information to the emperor come from his own appointees, whether senatorial or equestrian. Thus for instance Pliny the Elder records that a *legatus* in Gaul wrote to Augustus to inform him that a large number of dead sea-nymphs had appeared on the shore there.[53] Whether this was reported as a prodigy, or as a curiosity of natural history which might be of interest to the emperor, we do not know. The majority of such letters, however, naturally concerned more practical matters. So Varro, the *legatus* of Syria, wrote in about 24 or 23 to Augustus to complain at the request of the neighbouring peoples about the depredations of brigands from Trachonitis.[54] On the death of Herod both the then *legatus* of Syria, Quinctilius Varus, and the procurator, Sabinus, wrote to Augustus to give information or make accusations about the situation in Judaea.[55] In Josephus' subsequent

---

[48] Philo, *Leg.* 30/200f.; cf. p. 377.

[49] *AE* 1962 288; cf. p. 441.

[50] *Syll.*³ 821.

[51] *Fouilles de Delphes* III. 4 (1970), no. 287. The same proconsul and a procurator are also referred to in no. 288, which is also in response to an embassy, but is too fragmentary for the context to be recoverable. Cf. *IG* V. 1 1147, which seems to show an embassy from Gytheum to Hadrian, followed by his instructions to the proconsul.

[52] Unpublished inscription from the theatre at Aphrodisias. Cf. pp. xiii and 438–9.

[53] *NH* IX, 4/9.

[54] Josephus, *Ant.* XV, 10, 1 (345). For the date, and the question of identity of Varro, see Schürer, *Jewish People* I, 246.

[55] *Ant.* XVII, 9, 4–5 (227–9).

narrative, as we shall see later, the various and frequently-repeated forms of recourse to the emperors include several cases where the prefect or procurator of the province and the *legatus* of Syria address letters to them.[56] It will be sufficient to mention here two letters of *legati* of Syria, from Domitius Marsus to Claudius informing him of the rebuilding of the walls of Jerusalem by Agrippa I (41–44), and from Caesennius Paetus to Vespasian about a supposed plot by Antiochus of Commagene.[57]

Procurators might also write to the emperor to give him information, as did Herennius Capito from Jamnia to apprise Tiberius of a debt owed by Agrippa, Julius Classicianus from Britain to Nero on the aftermath of the revolt of Boudicca, or Pompeius Propinquus from Belgica to Galba about the rebellion of Vitellius.[58] So, too, of course, could the prefect of Egypt. Philo describes how Avillius Flaccus falsely promised to send on the decree passed by the Jewish community of Alexandria in honour of Gaius on his accession in 37, and adds that everything sent on by governors received especial attention from the emperor;[59] and in the preface of his edict published in 68 Tiberius Julius Alexander says that he will inform Galba in detail of any abuses which it requires the power and majesty of the emperor to correct.[60]

In this period there are no certain examples of letters sent spontaneously to the emperor by proconsuls (unless, as is not unlikely, on the few known occasions when they sent prisoners for trial by the emperor they sent a letter as well).[61] A letter of Domitian to Lappius Maximus, proconsul of Bithynia, about a petition from a philosopher named Flavius Archippus may be a reply to an enquiry from the proconsul himself, but need not be.[62] Similarly, legal sources record a number of cases where emperors of the first century 'wrote back' (normally 'rescripsit') in reply to persons who are not identified, and who may have been governors of either type—or even private persons.[63] With Trajan our evidence suddenly increases sharply, and we find not only a whole series of references to rescripts whose addressees are not given,[64] but also a number to named individuals who are quite certainly provincial governors. For instance he answers a query from Statilius Severus about the

[56] pp. 376–9.

[57] *Ant.* XIX, 7, 2 (326–7); *BJ* VII, 7, 1 (220–5).

[58] Josephus, *Ant.* XVIII, 6, 4 (163–4); Tacitus, *Ann.* XIV, 38, 3; *Hist.* I, 12, 1. Note also Gavius Bassus, *Praefectus orae Ponticae maritimae*, writing to Trajan, Pliny, *Ep.* X, 21–2.

[59] *In Flaccum*, 12/97–101.

[60] *OGIS* 669, l. 9; cf. G. Chalon, *L'Édit de Tiberius Julius Alexander* (1964).

[61] The possible instances are *SEG* IX 8, i (by Paquius Scaeva, almost certainly the proconsul, from Cyrene in 7/6 BC); Tacitus, *Ann.* XVI, 10, 2; Josephus, *BJ* VII, 11, 3 (499–50) and *Vita* 76/525–5 (here however *BJ*, though not *Vita*, says that the proconsul brought the prisoner to Rome himself); cf. *JRS* LVI (1966), 165.

[62] *Pliny, Ep.* X, 58, 6. See more fully pp. 473–5. The circumstances of that of Nerva to Tullius Justus, 58, 9–10, are unclear, as are those of the letters of Domitian to Avidius Nigrinus and Armenius Brochus, both proconsuls, apparently of Achaea, 65, 3.

[63] *Dig.* XLVIII, 5, 39(38), 10: 'et hoc ita Tiberius Caesar rescripsit'; XL, 15, 4: 'divus Claudius Claudiano rescripsit'; L, 4, 18, 30: 'divus Vespasianus et divus Hadrianus rescripserunt'; XLVIII, 16, 16: 'Domitianus rescripsit'. For this and the further legal evidence which follows see the invaluable collection by G. Gualandi, *Legislazione imperiale e giurisprudenza* I (1963), 3f.

[64] *Dig.* V, 3, 7 *pr.*; XXVII, 1, 17, 6; XXVIII, 5, 1 *pr.*; XXXVI, 1, 31(30), 5; XLVIII, 17, 5, 2; XLIX, 16, 4 *pr.*; 16, 4, 5.

privilege in relation to soldiers' wills which he himself had confirmed and perhaps incorporated in the *mandata*:[65]

> That *privilegium* which has been given to the soldiers, that their wills should be valid irrespective of the form in which they have been made, should be interpreted thus ... Therefore if the soldier, over whose property a question has been raised before you, having called some men together for the purpose of declaring his wishes, spoke so as to indicate ...

The addressee was presumably T. Statilius Maximus Severus Hadrianus, known as praetorian *legatus* of Thrace in 111/12,[66] and it is quite clear that he had consulted the emperor about a case which came before him. Trajan also replies to a man whom the text of the *Digest* calls 'Sernius' Quartus to lay down that a husband's slave may be examined by torture in relation to the murder of his wife; this was certainly P. Stertinius Quartus, suffect consul in 113, and he also had perhaps consulted Trajan when a praetorian *legatus* previous to this. The same passage refers to another rescript of Trajan on the torture of slaves addressed to 'Mummius Lollianus', who cannot be securely identified, but who is surely a provincial governor, as are the unnamed addressees of two further rescripts of Trajan on the same topic.[67] Trajan seems also to be using the tone of an emperor addressing a provincial governor in a rescript to Didius Secundus, 'I know that by the avarice of previous periods the property of *relegati* has been claimed for the *fiscus*. But another course is appropriate to my *clementia* . . .'[68]

It is noticeable that all these rescripts appear to be replies to queries about procedures to be followed in jurisdiction, as are two other rescripts of Trajan to individuals who are named, but cannot be identified.[69] Such problems do not arise in the case of the rescript of Trajan to Minicius Natalis, whose inscriptions show that he was *legatus* of the legion III Augusta in Africa in about 105 (a position almost equivalent to a governorship) and of Pannonia, as a consular, by 116. He was surely in the latter post when Trajan wrote to him: 'The divine Trajan wrote back (*rescripsit*) to Minicius Natalis that holidays give exemption only from juridical business, but that those matters which pertain to military discipline must be carried on even on holidays; among which the inspection of the *custodiae* is included.'[70]

We cannot be certain whether the sudden appearance in legal writers of reference to replies to governors by Trajan marks a genuine development, or merely indicates that the interests or knowledge of those writers did not

---

[65] *Inst.* II, 11, 1 = *Dig.* XXIX, 1, 24.

[66] See G. P. Burton in *JRS* LXII (1972), 183.

[67] *Dig.* XLVIII, 18, 1, 11 ('Sernius' Quartus); 12 ('Mummius Lollianus'); 19; 21. 'Mummius Lollianus' might possibly conceal the name of L. (Hedius Rufus) Lollianus Avitus, suffect consul in 114, see *PIR*² H 39.

[68] *Dig.* XLVIII, 22, 1; see p. 170. Didius Secundus could be identical with the Secundus attested as proconsul of Asia under Trajan, see Burton, loc. cit.

[69] *Dig.* XLVIII, 19, 5 *pr.*, laying down that a man cannot be condemned *absens* or *de suspicionibus*, and addressed to Julius Fronto (unknown, see *PIR*¹ I 323) and 'Adsidius Severus', possibly identical with, or related to, the consular Annidius Severus, *ILS* 7378, see *PIR*² A 107.

[70] *Dig.* II, 12, 9; *ILS* 1029 etc, see Syme, *Tacitus* (1958), esp. 243. It is certain that he governed no province other than Pannonia under Trajan.

extend earlier. But the evidence is sufficient to show that such consultations, at least by imperial *legati*, were common in this reign. It will also show that they commonly consulted the emperor about matters relating to the rights of soldiers and the conduct of jurisdiction, but cannot exclude the possibility of general consultation on other issues.

It is necessary to stress the significance of this legal evidence because, once it is taken into account, we have less reason to believe that Pliny, when *legatus* of Bithynia, was anything other than a normal imperial governor; what distinguished him from the proconsuls who had preceded him was his seniority, as an ex-consul as compared with ex-praetors, and the fact that his appointment was made by the emperor, and thereby marked a change in the status of the province. These aspects of his position are reflected in the fact that the reference to it on his inscriptions is amplified by the phrase 'sent with consular power to that province by Trajan on the basis of a *senatus consultum*'.[71] Trajan himself makes quite clear that Pliny had been chosen in order to restore propriety, including financial propriety, to the conduct of affairs in the province; for in approving Pliny's ban on distributions of cash by prominent citizens on significant private or public occasions he adds, 'But I chose your prudence precisely in order that you might yourself regulate those customs of that province which required reform, and lay down those provisions which will promote its future *quies*.'[72] It would be difficult to show that the actual range of affairs handled by Pliny was different from that dealt with by other governors;[73] and, as we have seen, the fact that Pliny both sent reports to the emperor and consulted him about individual matters which came before him, does not of itself distinguish him from other *legati* of this period. It is noticeable that in one letter he refers explicitly to the fact that the emperor has given him the right to refer to himself when in doubt, and that the subject-matter is juridical, namely the proper treatment of persons condemned to hard labour.[74]

In the event Pliny fulfilled his function, exactly as the proconsuls will have done before him,[75] by going on circuit round the cities to exercise jurisdiction. A significant number of the matters on which he consults Trajan arise from legal issues which were brought before him, from civil or criminal cases to queries about rights and privileges and requests for rulings on them; or are letters of patronage or simple transmissions of requests for communal or individual *beneficia*.[76] If we add questions relating to the

[71] *CIL* v 5262: 'consulari potestate[t(e)] in eam provinciam e[x s.c. missus ab] Imp. Caesar. Nerva Traiano Aug. German[ico Dacico P. P.]'; cf. 5272. His successor, C. Julius Cornutus Tertullus, was also a *legatus*, but with no exceptional features in his titulature. See *PIR*[2] I 273, and cf. W. Eck, *Senatoren von Vespasian bis Hadrian* (1970), 12–13.

[72] *Ep.* x, 117.

[73] See *JRS* LVIII (1968), 223–4; and note the available evidence on his *mandata*, p. 315.

[74] *Ep.* x, 31, 1: 'salva magnitudine tua, domine, descendas oportet ad meas curas, cum ius mihi dederis referendi ad te, de quibus dubito.' Note Trajan's reply (32) to the effect that this was precisely the type of matter which Pliny had been sent to correct.

[75] See G. P. Burton, 'Proconsuls, Assizes and the Administration of Justice under the Empire', *JRS* LXV (1975), 92.

[76] Cases: 56–7; 58–60; 81–2; 96–7; 110–11. Requests for rulings: 47–8; 49–50; 65–6; 68–9; 72–3; 79–80; 108–9; 112–13; 114–15; 116–17; 118–19. Patronage and *beneficia*: 26; 83–4; 85–7; 92–3; 94–5; 104–5; 106–7.

recruitment and disposition of troops,[77] and reports on matters relating to kings beyond the empire,[78] and on the due celebration of imperial anniversaries,[79] only a relatively restricted number of issues are left, involving either active inspection of city accounts, or the approval of building projects. Both might involve for Pliny, as they had for the proconsuls who preceded him, the recovery of city funds illegally held by private persons or of sums promised to the cities, but never paid; and almost all the building projects mentioned involved requests by Pliny to Trajan for the despatch of experts, whether *mensores, libratores* or *architecti*.[80]

It is evident, though nowhere explicitly stated, that public building projects in the cities had to be approved by Pliny, subject to the consent of Trajan. The emperor's permission is seen as an indulgence giving an exception to a general rule: 'If you, lord, will grant this type of work to the health and amenity of a *colonia* which is seriously short of water', as Pliny writes about the proposed aqueduct at Sinope.[81] In one case other overtones are perceptible in Pliny's elaborately obsequious requests for the approval of public works. He conceived the project of a canal linking the lake of Nicomedia with the sea, and found on the site the traces of a canal or ditch begun by a king of Bithynia, but then abandoned:

> But this very fact incites and fires me (you will allow me to be ambitious for your glory) to long for the completion by you of a work which was only begun by the kings.

We shall see later various instances of the way in which the emperors were explicitly regarded as performing specific functions which had previously been those of Hellenistic kings.[82] But Pliny's correspondence with Trajan is significant primarily because it seems to belong just at the moment when consultation of the emperor by his *legati* was developing beyond political or military reports to the routine of their jurisdiction and the problems and demands brought before them by their subjects. Moreover it seems also to have been just at this time that the emperor began to issue *mandata* not only to his own appointees but to proconsuls as well.[83] The way was thus open for the system of incessant and in some aspects obligatory, consultation of the emperor by all provincial governors, which is first clearly attested under Hadrian, and which was to be one of the fundamental features of the government of the empire for the rest of the period. As we saw, Aelius Aristides,

[77] 19–22; 27–8; 29–30; 77–8.

[78] 63–4; 67; 74 (for similar reports from *legati* of Syria, see p. 323).

[79] 35–6; 52–3; 88–9; 100–2.

[80] *Impendia* and *rationes*: 17a; 18 (note 17a, 3: 'multae enim pecuniae variis ex causis a privatis detinentur'); 43–4; 47–8; 54–5 (note 54, 1: 'pecuniae publicae, domine, providentia tua et ministerio nostro et iam exactae sunt et exiguntur'). Building projects: 17b (request for *mensor*); 23–4 (both for Prusa; note 23, 2: 'ea (pecunia) quam revocare a privatis et exigere iam coepi'); 37–8 (request for *aquilex* or *architectus*); 39–40 (recovery of money and request for *architectus*); 41–2, 61–2 (request for *librator* or *architectus*); 90–1 (note 90, 2: 'percunia curantibus nobis non deerit'); 98–9 (note 98, 2: 'curantibus nobis, ne desit quoque pecunia operi tum magno quam necessario'). For this function performed previously by a proconsul of Bithynia, see Dio, *Or.* XLVII, 19.

[81] 90, 2. The verb is 'indulseris'.

[82] 41, 4, and for the inheritance of the kings' functions, pp. 329, 396, 448, 454, 493.

[83] p. 316.

writing his *Roman Oration* under Antoninus Pius, alludes explicitly to the importance and frequency of such consultations by provincial governors.[84] The involvement of the governor in the social and ceremonial life of his province and his domination by the distant presence of the emperor are perfectly reflected in a scene used, precisely because it was typical, in a Greek–Latin translation manual, perhaps in the early third century:[85]

> He [the governor] was at work in the *praetorium*. He was saluted by the magistrates [of the city] and received letters from my lords the emperors, and immediately went up to the temple to sacrifice for their eternity and victory, and came down again. Today he is hearing cases from the first hour.

Before we turn to the developed system of consultation and rescript as it was from Hadrian to Constantine, we may note one other form of imperial missive which Pliny's correspondence seems to show was already sent to all provincial governors. Pliny asks in one letter whether *diplomata* (documents giving an official traveller the right to exact transport and lodging) should be used even if out of date. Trajan replies: '*Diplomata* whose date is past ought not to be in use; so I lay it on myself as one of my primary duties to send out through all provinces new *diplomata* before they can be required.'[86]

The implication that this was a duty discharged personally by the emperor is at first sight surprising, but is supported by Suetonius' report that Augustus used his signet-ring for sealing *diplomata* as well as *libelli* and *epistulae*.[87] They evidently contained some statement of the rights of the holder, issued in the name of the emperor: it was noted that Otho on seizing power first added 'Nero' to his names as given on the *diplomata* used by messengers, and then desisted.[88] The misuse of such *diplomata* once issued was a recurrent problem, explicitly referred to for instance by Domitian in his orders to the procurator of Syria;[89] Julian even went so far at one moment as to lay down that he would issue to *vicarii* only *evectiones* (as they were then called) written with his own hand.[90] But, like all other privileges which emperors might attempt to restrict to properly entitled persons, the use of *diplomata* was also thereby a *beneficium* which they could extend at will to others. So Augustus granted *diplomata*, as a sign of his *clementia*, to the condemned lovers of Julia as they went into exile;[91] and permission to use official transport was one of the principal *beneficia* extended from time to time by Constantine to bishops whom he summoned to his presence, or commanded to meet in council.[92]

---

[84] pp. 207–8

[85] *Corp. Gloss. Lat.* III, 640, para. 9 (the *Colloquium Harleianum*). The διαχρίσεων in the Greek makes it certain that we should read *cognitiones* for *condiciones*. On such bilingual manuals see H. Marrou, *Histoire de l'éducation dans l'Antiquité*[6] (1965), 386f.

[86] *Ep.* X, 45–6.

[87] p. 213. For imperial *liberti* concerned with *diplomata* see e.g. *ILS* 1677–8.

[88] Suetonius, *Otho* 7, 1; Plutarch, *Otho* 3, 2.

[89] p. 315.

[90] *CTh* VIII, 5, 12: 'vicariis denas vel duodenas evectiones mea manu perscribtas ipse permittam.'

[91] Seneca, *De clem.* I, 10, 3 (perhaps more like safe-conducts—'quo tutiores essent').

[92] See Eusebius, *HE* X, 5, 23; *VC* III, 6, 12; Optatus, App. III; VIII; Theodoret, *HE* I, 21, 2; Socrates, *HE* I, 25; Athanasius, *Apol. c. Arian.* 70, 2.

If Trajan meant what his letter implies, then all provincial governors already received their *diplomata* from the emperor. They will thus in this respect also have been placed in dependence on him, and will have had to make requests to him to allow the type of extensions to unqualified persons which Domitian's *mandata* had attempted to prevent. A perfect instance both of such an extension and of a petition to Trajan for retrospective indemnity is provided by Pliny himself, who allowed *diplomata* to his wife, so that she could return to Italy after the death of her aunt:[93]

> I have written this to you, because I would seem to myself to be insufficiently grateful, if I had concealed the fact that among your other *beneficia* I owe this one also to your *indulgentia*, that relying upon it I have as it were deliberately failed to doubt that you would do that which, if I had consulted you, I would have done too late.

Neither Pliny's elaborately worded request nor Trajan's friendly reply excusing his action, the last item in their correspondence, can conceal the fact that a provincial governor now felt obliged to consult the emperor over a wide range of his conduct of affairs, and might depend on his indulgence in a way not wholly different from that of an ordinary subject.

6. *Equestrian and Senatorial Office-Holders: Consultation and Rescript*

If our evidence is not entirely misleading, the reign of Hadrian marks a further significant stage in the patterns of communication within which the emperor functioned. For it is from this time that we have the first unambiguous cases of consultation of him by proconsuls as well as by his own *legati*; inscriptional, legal and Christian evidence can be combined to attest this new pattern. When an inscription from Lamia records the *decretum* read out by Q. Gellius Sentius Augurinus, proconsul (probably of Achaea rather than Macedonia), his words do not quite make clear whether it had been he or some interested party who had consulted Hadrian about a boundary dispute; 'Since the best and greatest *princeps*, Traianus Hadrianus Aug(ustus), has written to me that I should summon *mensores*, hear the case over territories between the peoples of Lamia and Hypata and establish the boundaries . . .'[1] But in the dossier of documents concerning plots of land dedicated to Zeus at Aezani in Asia by two Hellenistic kings the process of consultation is perfectly clear.[2] Avidius Quietus, proconsul of Asia in 125/6, writes to the magistrates, council and people of Aezani:

---

[93] *Ep.* x, 120–1.

[1] *ILS* 5947a. See *PIR*[2] G 135. Wrongly quoted as a clear case of consultation in *JRS* LVI (1966), 164.

[2] *CIL* III 35 = *IGR* IV 571 = *OGIS* 502. Now re-edited by U. Laffi, 'I terreni del tempio di Zeus ad Aizanoi', *Athenaeum*, n.s. XLIX (1971), 3.

The dispute over sacred land dedicated long ago to Zeus, which has dragged on for many years, has reached a conclusion by the forethought of the greatest emperor. For when I wrote to him explaining the whole matter, and asked what should be done . . . uniting justice and indulgence and in accordance with his concern over judicial cases, he solved your longstanding strife and mutual suspicion, as you will learn from the letter which he sent to me, of which I have sent you a copy.

The dossier contains not only this letter of Quietus in Greek, but Hadrian's reply to him in Latin, laying down that the size of the lots of sacred land should be determined by using the typical size of similar lots in neighbouring cities, and that a rent should be paid for them either retrospectively, if due, or from the present.

It is interesting to note that the dossier concludes, after copies of letters between Quietus and the procurator of Asia, with a pronouncement in the first person from Hadrian, dating to 128: 'The territory given to Juppiter Genitor and the city of Aezani by the kings, Attalus and Prusias, I restored by the agency of Septimius Saturninus, *primipilaris*, as King Prusias had established it'. Once again, the inheritance of some of the functions of the Hellenistic kings is perfectly explicit. The one item which the dossier fails to provide is the text of Quietus' letter to Hadrian; but, as was mentioned earlier, Pliny's letters from Bithynia are almost unique in providing both sides of an official's correspondence with the emperor. But this too is preserved in one instance, rather surprisingly, by Ulpian; excerpted in a late source, he quotes *verbatim* both the *consultatio* of Egnatius Taurinus, proconsul of Baetica, and the rescript of Hadrian:[3]

I learnt by enquiry, best of emperors, in the case between Claudius and Euaristus, that while Claudius the son of Lupus was being thrown in a blanket at a dinner, a slip on the part of Manius Euaristus caused him to be caught so unsuccessfully that he died after four days. Though it appeared that there was no enmity between him and Euaristus, none the less I took the view that, as he was guilty of unrestraint, he should be punished, to reform the other young men of the same age. So I banished Manius Euaristus from Rome, Italy and Baetica for five years, and ruled that he should pay two thousand in compensation to the father of Claudius, because his poverty was already manifest. [The words of the rescript] You have fixed the punishment of Euaristus, Taurinus, in accordance with his guilt; for it is relevant in major crimes also, whether the act is regarded as deliberate or accidental.

However exceptional it may be that both sides of the exchange are reported, this text is absolutely typical in relating to a minor local episode, which happened to be thought to require the emperor's attention; such scenes from provincial life recur repeatedly in the rescripts of emperors as the legal sources report them. Such *ad hoc* consultations might of course embody issues of long-term importance, as when the proconsul of Asia in 121/2 wrote to ask for guidance in dealing with accusations of Christians, the reply

[3] *Coll.* I, II, 1–4; referred to in *Dig.* XLVIII, 8, 4, 1.

going to his successor in 122/3, Minicius Fundanus.[4] Hadrian also sent rescripts to various governors, including a proconsul of Macedonia and a *legatus* of Cilicia, about how much weight they should give to witnesses and to written depositions (*testimonia*), and on judicial torture of slaves.[5] The *Digest* mentions rescripts of his, which were explicitly answers to queries about individual cases, addressed to Salvius Carus, proconsul of Crete in about 134,[6] and to Vitruvius Pollio, *legatus* of Lugdunensis;[7] and it also refers to his 'writing back' (as Trajan had done) on the subject of military *custodiae* to a *legatus* of Aquitania and to another *legatus*, perhaps of Cappadocia;[8] to Calpurnius Rufus, proconsul of Achaea, he replied laying down the rule that the proconsul must not let his *legatus* leave the province before he departs himself.[9] The 'Aquilius Bradua' to whom he replied in a long letter on the proper procedure for disposing of the personal property of executed prisoners (*pannicularia*), is almost certainly M. Atilius Appius Bradua, consul *ordinarius* of 108, and now a provincial governor, possibly proconsul of Africa in about 123/4.[10]

The *epistulae* which Hadrian wrote to Claudius Saturninus, *legatus* of Belgica, and to Pompeius Falco, probably as *legatus* of Britain in 118–22[11] may or may not have been replies to consultations by them. But enough has been said to make clear both how firmly established the system of consultation now was, and the fact that it applied equally to *legati* of the emperor and to proconsuls. For subsequent reigns it will not be necessary to set out the evidence in such detail. Instead it will be better to concentrate on the fact that such consultation was not merely an observable fact, but in relation to certain topics was explicitly imposed on governors by imperial enactments. The most important area was that of punishments, especially those of persons of higher social standing. By Callistratus' time, the early third century, the imperial *mandata* laid down that if town-councillors or leading men of the

---

[4] pp. 558–9.

[5] *Dig.* XXII, 5, 3, 3 (to Junius Rufinus, proconsul of Macedonia); 5, 3, 1 (to Vibius Varus, *legatus* of Cilicia *c.* 132/3); Valerius Verus (5, 3, 2) is also presumably a provincial governor, as will be 'Gabinius Maximus' (5, 3, 4) possibly to be identified with Gavius Maximus, *PIR*[2] G 104, procurator of Mauretania Tingitana under Hadrian, and later Praetorian Prefect. On *tormenta servorum* see XLVIII, 18, 1, 1–5: Sennius Sabinus is not otherwise attested; Claudius Quartinus will be Ti. Claudius Quartinus, *PIR*[2] C 990, *cos. suff.* 130. and *legatus* of Lugdunensis, and of Germania Superior (134).

[6] XLVIII, 16, 14; for the date see Eck, *Senatoren*, 210 (from *AE* 1951 122).

[7] XXVII, 1, 15, 17, replying to what was evidently a detailed query about a case: 'Si Clodius Macer, quamvis filius familias sit . . .'; for a similar reply by Hadrian, evidently to a governor, *Coll.* I, 6, 1–4; and to Calpurnius Celerianus, also presumably a governor, *Dig.* XLVIII, 18, 1, 22.

[8] XLVIII, 3, 12 *pr.*: 'Salvio quoque legato Aquitaniae', and 'Statilio Secundo legato'; the latter might be Statorius Secundus, *legatus* of Cappadocia in 126/7, Eck *Senatoren*, 200, or T. Statilius Maximus Severus Hadrianus, who had been a *legatus* in Thrace 111/12, ibid., 174 (or neither). It was presumably as *legatus* of Cappadocia in 130/1–36/7 that Flavius Arrianus (the historian) received the rescript quoted in *Dig.* XLIX, 14, 2, 1.

[9] I, 16, 10.

[10] XLVIII, 20, 6; see *PIR*[2] A 1298, and for the suggestion about the proconsulate of Africa, R. Syme, *REA* LXVII (1965), 344, who also suggests (344–5) that two other addressees of rescripts from Hadrian, Ninnius Hasta (XLVIII, 8, 5), *cos. ord.* 114, and Ti. Julius Secundus (XLVIII, 3, 6), *cos. suff.* 116, were proconsuls of Africa, in 128/9 and 131/2 respectively.

[11] Claudius Saturninus, *Frag. Vat.* 223; Pompeius Falco, *Dig.* XXVIII, 3, 6, 7. For the latest evidence on his career see *JÖAI* XLIX (1968–71), Beibl. 29, no. 6. The letter concerns soldiers' wills, and makes Britain more likely than his proconsulate of Asia in 123/4.

cities had committed an offence deserving of relegation to an island, the governor should write to the emperor, enclosing his verdict; if their offence were capital, they were to be kept in custody while a report was sent to the emperor.[12] Callistratus' contemporary, Ulpian, adds that governors, unlike the *praefectus urbi*, were forbidden to inflict the heavier penalty of *deportatio* (including loss of all property and civil rights) without writing a full report to the emperor, who would decide whether the case deserved it; in consequence, the will of such a person remained valid after the governor's sentence had been passed and until the emperor's answer was received. An *oratio* by Marcus Aurelius had laid down that this applied also where the governor had rejected an appeal by a condemned man (meaning presumably a request to appear before the emperor in person), but had written to the emperor instead; only in an emergency, such as civil disorder, could the governor carry out such a sentence at once—and should then write to the emperor.[13] Similarly, when a man returned from *relegatio* (which was temporary), he could not be restored to the council of his city without imperial permission, as Marcus Aurelius and Verus ruled in a rescript.[14] By contrast, in the altered circumstances of the early fourth century, Constantine ruled that a governor could not release a man from membership of a city council without consulting himself.[15] Naturally, it is not to be imagined that these or any other imperial rulings were ever carried out without exception. The mere effects of distance in space and delay in time, together with the fact that the consultation in each particular instance necessarily depended on the governor himself, must have meant the many condemnations were in fact carried out without the emperor's knowledge. For instance the *Codex Justinianus* records an episode when a former town-councillor, who had been condemned to *deportatio* by a *legatus*, appeared (how, we do not know) before Caracalla, and was granted restoration in his *ordo*, *honores* and entire former standing.[16]

None the less, we have a large number of specific examples from sources of all types, literary, legal and inscriptional, of queries on individual matters, both judicial and otherwise, addressed by provincial governors to the emperor. For instance the *Digest* records that Severus and Caracalla sent a rescript to Ovinius Tertullus, *legatus* of Moesia Inferior, to give a ruling on the citizen rights of a person who had been born in captivity and then returned, and part of the text of the letter survives in the *Codex Justinianus*.[17] Furthermore an inscription put up in Tyra in Moesia Inferior in February 201 contains the end of a letter of Severus and Caracalla to Tertullus, the whole of another of theirs to someone called Heraclitus, probably the procurator of the province, and Tertullus' letter in Greek to the magistrates, council and people of Tyra: 'I have attached to this letter of mine a copy of the divine letters sent to me by our lords, the unconquered and most

[12] *Dig.* XLVIII, 19, 27, 1–2.
[13] XLVIII, 22, 6, 1; XXVIII, 3, 6, 7–8; cf. XLVIII, 21, 2, 1 (Macer).
[14] L, 2, 13 *pr*.
[15] *CTh* XII, 1, 1 = *CJ* X, 32, 14.
[16] *CJ* IX, 51, 1.
[17] XLIX, 15, 9, cf. XXXVIII, 17, 1, 3; *CJ* VIII, 50, 1. See A. Stein, *Die Legaten von Moesien* (1940), 84–6.

fortunate emperors, so that, being aware of their divine generosity towards you, you may rejoice in their great Fortune.'[18] It is not quite clear whether it had been Tertullus or Heraclitus who had in this instance consulted the emperors about the rights of Tyra to enrol new citizens, who would then benefit from the city's immunity from tolls, a matter which had already been the subject of letters from Antoninus Pius and from Marcus Aurelius and Verus. But these were not the only two instances in which the emperors (who in the second case were currently in Egypt) were confronted with the affairs of communities or individuals in Moesia, and transmitted their rulings through Ovinius Tertullus.[19]

So, to take only a few examples, Antoninus Pius is attested as sending rescripts to *legati* of Lugdunensis and Numidia,[20] to proconsuls,[21] and to a number of other named individuals who are clearly senatorial office-holders, though their actual post in not indicated.[22] The most vivid case is his reply to Aelius, or Aurelius, Marcianus, proconsul of Baetica:[23]

> The power of masters over their slaves ought to be inviolate, nor should anyone withdraw their rights from them. But it is in the interests of masters that help against cruelty, starvation or degrading injury should not be denied to those who make a just appeal. Examine therefore the complaints of those from the household of Julius Sabinus who have taken refuge at the statue, and if you discover that they have been treated more harshly than is proper, or have suffered degrading injury, order that they should be sold on the condition that they do not return to the ownership of their master.

Marcianus' letter had evidently described the situation of the slaves in some detail, as far as it was so far known to him, and had asked for the emperor's ruling on the point of principle involved. The fact that Pius begins his reply with a statement of the principle is of some importance. For the many indirect references in legal sources to principles laid down in imperial letters, or the partial quotations of such letters which are the rule in the Theodosian Code, may in many cases conceal the fact that the letter is a response to a particular query.[24]

Such responses were not made only to provincial governors. An inscription from Ephesus, for instance, contains the letter of Marcus Aurelius and Verus

[18] *CIL* III 781 = *IGR* I 598 = *ILS* 423.

[19] See p. 416.

[20] Lugdunensis: *Coll.* XV, 2, 4. Numidia (a post which was still technically that of *legatus* of the legion III Augusta): *Dig.* XXXVII, 5, 7 (described as a *constitutio*). 'Tuscius Fuscianus' is evidently the *legatus* attested by inscriptions for 158–9, L. Matuccius Fuscinus, W. Hüttl, *Antoninus Pius* II (1933), 137–8.

[21] *Dig.* XLII, 1, 31: 'Cassio proconsuli divus Pius in haec verba rescripsit'; L, 6, 6, 1: 'ex litteris divi Pii quas emisit ad Ennium (?) Proculum proconsulem Africae.'

[22] e.g. *Dig.* XLVIII, 2, 7, 3, to Julius Candidus (cf. *PIR*² I 233–41); XXXVI, 3, 1, 11, to Junius Mauricus (cf. *PIR*² I 771–3); XXXVI, I, 17, 17, and XL, 5, 30, 6 to Cassius Dexter, evidently P. Cassius Dexter Augustanus Alpinus Bellicius Sollers, *PIR*² C 490; XX, 3, 1, 2 and L, 7, 5 *pr.*, to Claudius Saturninus (*PIR*² C 1012, *legatus* of Moesia Inferior in 145); IV, 2, 18, to Claudius Frontinus (Ti. Claudius Frontinus Niceratus, *PIR*² C 873); cf. XXXVI, 4, 1, 3; XLVIII, 2, 7, 2; 5, 39, 8; *Frag. Vat.* 223.

[23] *Inst.* I, 8, 2; *Dig.* I, 6, 2; *Coll.* III, 3, 2–3.

[24] See esp. pp. 335–6.

in reply to a query by Ulpius Eurycles who had been appointed *logistês* (accountant) of the *gerousia* at Ephesus by successive proconsuls of Asia; as the emperors make clear, his approach was justified in the first instance by the fact that he had to enquire about what to do with a collection of silver statues of earlier emperors. But he had added a request for procedural guidance on a case of peculation, on which they indicate that the proconsul should judge.[25] The same emperors also replied to the *procuratores heredita-tium* that hostages who had adopted Roman manners should by imperial *beneficium* be allowed to inherit from Roman citizens;[26] and Marcus along with Verus, and later with Commodus, sent rescripts, like earlier emperors, to a wide range of provincial governors.[27] We have a perfect instance of a typical procedure of consultation and rescript in the account preserved in Eusebius of the martyrdoms at Lugdunum in about 177. The *legatus*, having discovered that a Christian named Attalus was a Roman citizen 'ordered that he be put with the others who were in prison, about whom he wrote to Caesar and awaited the reply from him'. After some delay there arrived the emperor's answer, that they should be executed but that those who denied Christianity should be released.[28]

Rescripts to governors and office-holders continue to be attested up to the reign of Severus Alexander. We may note for instance the reply of Severus and Caracalla to M. Valerius Bradua Mauricus, proconsul of Africa, to the effect that, once he had given jurisdiction to his *legati*, it followed that they had jurisdiction in cases over guardians (*tutores*).[29] It was evidently also to a proconsul that the same emperors wrote 'most elegantly', as Ulpian says in his *On the Duties of a Proconsul*, on the subject of *xenia*, gifts from the inhabitants of the province: 'As regards *xenia*, hear what our view is: there is an old proverb, "Neither all, nor on every occasion, nor from all" [quoted in Greek]. For it is most uncivilized to accept gifts from no one, but to take them generally is degrading and to accept all of them a sign of excessive avarice.'[30] Severus also replied to a *legatus* of Britain,[31] he and Caracalla to a *legatus* of Hispania Citerior,[32] and probably Caracalla in 215 to a proconsul of Lycia-

---

[25] R. Heberdey, *Forschungen in Ephesos* II (1912), 119, no. 23; J. H. Oliver, *The Sacred Gerusia, Hesperia* Suppl. VI (1941), 93, no. 11. Cf. *AE* 1960 202, which seems to be a letter of a *curator* of Catane to Marcus Aurelius and Verus.

[26] *Dig.* XLIX, 14, 32.

[27] e.g. *Dig.* L, 2, 3, 2 (Marcus and Verus to Lollianus Avitus, *praeses Bithyniae*, i.e. L. Hedius Rufus Lollianus Avitus, *legatus pro praetore* of Bithynia in 165, *PIR*² H 40); XLVIII, 18, 1, 27, the same to Voconius Saxa, almost certainly a provincial governor ('Prudenter et egregia ratione humanitatis, Saxa carissime...'); *Tabula Banasitana* (*CRAI* 1971, 468, ll. 1–13), the same to Coiedius Maximus, procurator of Mauretania Tingitana; *Dig.* II, 14, 60, Marcus to Avidius Cassius; I, 18, 14, Marcus and Commodus to Scapula Tertullus (evidently P. Julius Scapula Tertullus, *PIR*² I 556, probably then *legatus* of Dalmatia); *Tabula Banasitana*, ll. 14–21, to Vallius Maximianus, procurator of Mauretania Tingitana.

[28] cf. p. 559.

[29] *Dig.* I, 21, 4 *pr.*; cf. XXVI, 10, 1, 4. See *PIR*¹ V 31, and B. E. Thomasson, *Die Statthalter der römischen Provinzen Nordafrikas* I (1960), 107–8.

[30] I, 16, 6, 3.

[31] XXVIII, 6, 2, 4: 'quae sententia rescripto Imperatoris nostri ad Virium Lupum Britanniae praesidem comprobata est.' The date will be 197/8, see A. R. Birley, *Epig. Stud.* IV (1967), 79.

[32] XLVIII, 22, 7, 10: 'Maecio enim Probo praesidi provinciae Hispaniae rescripserunt'; cf. G. Alföldy, *Fasti Hispanienses* (1969), 46.

Pamphylia.[33] Among a number of named individuals whose posts are not attested, but who receive rescripts in this period,[34] is Q. Atrius Clonius, to whom Severus and Caracalla wrote about frauds by guardians. The same man is found as *legatus* of Thrace under Caracalla, and an inscription from Augusta Traiana partially preserves a letter of his referring to a reply of Caracalla to himself, in which the emperor ruled that the previous customs in regard to distributions of cash should continue as before, unless the city decided otherwise.[35] The issue, very similar to one on which Pliny had consulted Trajan a century before, was typical of those sent for the emperor's ruling, as was his entirely passive reply.

Equally typical is the reply by Severus Alexander to Julianus, an otherwise unknown proconsul of Narbonensis.[36] The emperor's letter clearly reflects an enquiry giving the details of a murder case where the verdict and sentence were in doubt:

> If Gracchus, whom Numerius caught in the act of adultery and killed, was in the circumstances in which under the Lex Julia he could be killed with impunity, then the act was legal, and calls for no punishment; and the same applies to his sons, who obeyed their father. But if, even though outside the terms of the law, he killed the adulterer under the effects of grief and without forethought, although the act was homicide, nevertheless because the darkness and his justified grief offer some excuse for his action, he may be sent into exile.

The despatch of enquiries to the emperor was a commonplace, so much so that Ulpian has to state that *legati* of proconsuls should not consult the emperor, but their own proconsul, who would reply to their *consultationes*.[37] It is not likely that such consultations and replies ceased to be sent for several decades in the middle of the third century, but it is the case that we have no certain examples of them in the period from Gordian to Carus and Carinus (238–84). The *Acta* of Acacius, however, represent a governor as sending a transcript of the interrogation of a Christian to Decius, who bursts out laughing on reading it, promotes the governor and frees Acacius.[38] This text is fictional, but we may place more reliance on the *Acta* of Marcellus, which represent a governor in 298 as sending to the tetrarchs a report on a centurion who confessed Christianity;[39] we also have Optatus' account of how a deacon in Africa, when accused, perhaps in about 308–11, of abusing

---

[33] *CJ* IX, 43, 1: 'Imp. Antoninus A. Rutiliano consulari +Lyciae+ (or +Cilicia+).' There was no province of Cilicia, and a proconsul of Lycia-Pamphylia whose fragmentary name appears as Σα . . . . . ἀνοῦ is attested in *TAM* II 620, see Barbieri, *Albo senatorio*, no. 843.

[34] *Epistula* to Celer: *Dig.* V, 3, 20, 12, text in *CJ* VI, 35, 1; dated to 204 and certainly a reply. To Julius Julianus, *Dig.* XLVIII, 21, 2 *pr.* and *Frag. Vat.* 119; he was a senator and governor in this period, see *PIR*² I 367. To Cuspius Rufinus, XXVI, 6, 2, 2, a reply about a particular case; *cos. ord.* in 197, see *PIR*² C 1638.

[35] *Dig.* XXVI, 10, 7, 2; *IGBulg.* 1581. See Barbieri, *Albo senatorio*, no. 62.

[36] *CJ* IX, 9, 4.

[37] *Dig.* I, 16, 6, 2.

[38] Knopf-Krüger-Ruhbach, *Ausgewählte Martyrakten*⁴ (1965), no. 11, 5, 5–6.

[39] ibid., no. 20. The two groups of MSS. give the names and circumstances in rather different terms.

the emperor, took refuge with the bishop, whereupon a report (*relatio*) was sent, and was answered by a *rescriptum* ordering his arrest.[40] The dependence of the provincial governors on such rescripts is very clear in this instance.

The governor's letters to the emperor remained in the tetrarchic period a recognized and familiar channel for the transmission of the requests and complaints of the population. So Eumenius concludes the oration which he delivered in 298 to appeal for the restoration of the rhetorical school at Autun by making a specific request to the governor:[41]

> You have heard, *vir perfectissimus*, the statement of my desire and hope. From you I request that you will not hesitate to send it in a letter of yours to the ears of the emperors, since indeed it is the greatest and almost the only reward of those of good will that their wishes should be brought to the divine knowledge of such great emperors.

One of the letters of this period is of particular importance, for it is preserved in two partial texts which are not equally revealing of its occasion and purpose. The *Codex Justinianus* quotes from the *sacrae litterae* addressed by Diocletian and Maximian in 290 to an official named Agatho, and containing the ruling that a man who had caused the death of another accidentally, by throwing a stone, could be released. If this were our only evidence we would very probably deduce, but could not be quite certain, that the issue arose in relation to a particular case. But the text preserved in a late compilation, the *Mosaicarum et romanarum legum collatio*, makes the situation quite clear:[42]

> Greetings, Agatho, dearest to us. The nature of the appeal (*preces*) of Julius Antoninus has easily moved our *clementia*, in that he asserts that he has committed a homicide not by his own will but by chance, since the occasion of death appears to have been provided by the throwing of a stone.

Thus, it may be that, while on the one hand many of the letters addressed to officials in the tetrarchic and Constantinian period (and occasionally earlier) are clearly spontaneous promulgations of rules or principles, the proportion of the remainder which were in origin responses to particular queries may be larger than appears from those instances where this characteristic is either explicit or can be deduced with reasonable certainty.

On occasion it is quite explicit, as when Constantius and Galerius reply to a governor in 305: 'Since you consult us as to whether the festivals which are to be added by us to celebrate military successes should be taken into account in the same way (as regular ones) in relation to the periods allowed for appeals, dearest Verinus, we are pleased to write back to your Experience . . .'[43] Diocletian and Maximian had replied in comparable style to Crispinus, governor of Phoenicia, in 292,[44] and a number of other

---

[40] Optatus, *Adv. Parmenianum Donatistam* I, 17; cf. p. 578.

[41] *Pan.* V(9), 21, 4.

[42] *CJ* IX, 16, 4; *Coll.* I, 10, I.

[43] *CJ* III, 12, I.

[44] *CJ* IX, 2, 11, 'Have, Crispine, carissime nobis'; the contents make clear that the letter is a reply. See *PLRE* Crispinus 2. The suggestion here, as elsewhere in *PLRE*, that this form of address suggests that a man is a senator, as opposed to an *eques*, is without foundation.

tetrarchic letters can be regarded, with varying degrees of certainty, as replies to queries from office-holders.[45]

Under Constantine, even though, as we have seen, there seems to have been a marked increase in the frequency of positive pronouncements in various forms by the emperor, consultations on individual cases remained an essential feature of government. One of his latest pronouncements, given from Naissus in 337, is a reply to an office-holder named Delmatius, ruling that a woman who had remarried four years after the last news of her husband (evidently a soldier), and after petition to the local *dux*, had not laid herself open to any penalty.[46] Constantine also laid down more precise rules about consultation, writing to Profuturus, *Praefectus annonae*, in 319 to say that any person holding jurisdiction who was in any doubt should proceed no further with the case but consult *nostra scientia*—'but let not anything be sent to us which is lacking in the full details'. A copy of the *consultatio* was also to be posted up, so that the parties could enter objections.[47] Again we have a number of letters of Constantine to office-holders which are either probably or possibly consultations on specific cases or issues,[48] and others which are quite certainly so.

The reply in the names of Constantine and Lucinius to Titianus, *praeses* of Cappadocia, perhaps in 316, about the evidence as to whether a certain Aelius, who claimed to be of city-councillor status, was really a slave, will certainly have emanated from Licinius alone.[49] But we have clear cases of Constantine's replies to letters from governors in his letter of 317 to Catullinus, proconsul of Africa, about a property-case in which mass violence had been employed by both sides,[50] or in the extract of his letter to Felix, *praeses* of Corsica in 319, threatening him that if some petitioners proved that their appeals had been put off by his negligence, they would be compensated from his property.[51] In the same period, however, provincial officials also still performed their previous function of transmitting the petitions of his subjects to the emperor. In 324-6, for instance, the people of Orcistus appealed to Constantine for restoration of city status and were supported by the *intercessio* of Ablabius, *vicarius* of Asiana. The emperor's reply to Ablabius is replete with the traditional formulae, beginning 'Greetings, Ablabius, dearest to us', and ending 'Farewell Ablabius, dearest and most agreeable to us'.[52] But the clearest case of a reply to a consultation is the letter which Constantine addressed to the same Ablabius as praetorian prefect in 333, on

---

[45] *CJ* x, 10, 1 (292), to Scyrio, *rationalis*: 'Scire debet gravitas tua . . .'; vii, 33, 6, *epistula* to Primosus, *praeses Syriae*, probably a reply; ii, 13, 1 (293): 'Aristobulo salutem' (Ti. Cl. Aurelius Aristobulus, proconsul of Africa, 290-4, *PLRE* Aristobulus), almost certainly a reply; iii, 3, 3 (294), *sacrae litterae* to Serapio, evidently a provincial governor: 'Placet, ut iudicibus, si quos gravitas tua disceptatores dederit, insinues . . .'; iii, 28, 26 (304); 'Serapioni suo salutem.'

[46] *CJ* v, 17, 7; this Delmatius may be the half-brother of Constantine, see *PLRE* Dalmatius 6.

[47] *CTh* xi, 29, 2; more fully in *CJ* vii, 61, 1. On the same issue *CTh* xi, 30, 9 = *CJ* vii, 62, 15.

[48] e.g. *CJ* iii, 1, 8 and vii, 22, 3 (314); *CTh* xi, 30, 5 = *CJ* vii, 62, 13 (315/16); *CJ* vi, 56, 3 (318 or 319); cf. *PLRE* Catullinus 2); *CTh* ii, 26, 1 = *CJ* iii, 39, 3 and viii, 4, 5 (330); *CTh* i, 2, 6 = *CJ* i, 22, 4.

[49] *CJ* vii, 16, 41; for the possible date see *PLRE* Titianus 1 and 2.

[50] *CTh* ix, 10, 1 = *CJ* ix, 12, 6.

[51] *CTh* ii, 6, 2.

[52] p. 131.

the subject of episcopal jurisdiction. As we have seen, the praetorian prefects had always performed their functions essentially at the side of the emperor,[53] and the fact that they are found on occasions towards the end of the period receiving imperial letters is itself a sign of their developing independent functions. But the closeness of the relationship is still apparent in the wording of Constantine's intended rebuke:[54]

> Imperator Constantinus to Ablabius, *Praefectus praetorio*. We have been considerably surprised that your *gravitas*, which is filled with justice and the true religion, should have thought fit to enquire of our Clemency as to what our Moderation has laid down previously concerning the judgments of bishops, or what rules we wish to be observed now, Ablabius, dearest and most beloved parent. So since you have expressed the wish to be instructed by us . . .

When the pattern of correspondence between office-holders in the provinces and the emperor is so well attested, it is no surprise to find that emperors wrote also to their equestrian appointees in Rome, such as the prefects of the Vigiles and the Annona.[55] It is more significant that from Hadrian onwards we find imperial replies not only to proconsuls but to magistrates holding office in Rome. Antoninus Pius indeed sent a rescript to the magistrates of Rome collectively to the effect that they must carry out the judgments of arbiters and judges appointed by them.[56] That appears to be a unique case, but even if we postpone consideration of occasions where individuals secured directly from the emperor a ruling that a magistrate should hear a particular case, or appealed to him from a magistrate,[57] there remain a number of instances where emperors replied to praetors or even consuls in Rome. Hadrian, for instance, instructed a praetor, Claudius Proculus, as to how he should handle a case, evidently in response to a consultation by him.[58]

Marcellus, moreover, quotes verbatim from a rescript of Antoninus Pius to a praetor:[59]

> Even if none of the established forms should be readily altered, none the less some relief should be given when equity clearly demands it. So if the man when summoned did not respond, and the due proclamation to this effect was then made, but immediately afterwards he approached you as you were seated on the tribunal, it can be concluded that he failed to appear not by his own fault but

---

[53] pp. 122–31.

[54] *Const. Sirmond.* I. The earliest reasonably certain example of an imperial letter addressed to a praetorian prefect is Eusebius, *HE* IX, 9a, I (cf. IX, I, 2), dating to 312; cf. p. 581. They become regular with the prefecture of Junius Bassus, 318–31, see *PLRE* Bassus 14.

[55] *Praefecti vigilum*: Severus and Caracalla to Junius Rufinus (*PIR*² I 807), *Dig.* I, 15, 5; Constantine to Julius Antiochus, *CTh* I, 2, 1; II, 10, I and 2; XV, 14, 3. *Praefecti annonae*: litterae of Trajan to Sulpicius Similis, *Frag. Vat.* 233; rescripts of Hadrian to Claudius Julianus, and of Caracalla to Marcus Dioca, 235; Marcus and Commodus, *Dig.* XXVII, 1, 26; Constantine to Profuturus (318), *CJ* III, 11, 3; to Mastichianus (326), *CJ* VI, 62, 1; to Cerealis (328), *CTh* XIV, 24, 1.

[56] *Dig.* XLII, 1, 15 *pr.*: 'a divo Pio rescriptum est magistratibus populi Romani . . .'

[57] pp. 513–14, 545–6.

[58] *Dig.* XXXVII, 9, 1, 14.

[59] *Dig.* IV, 1, 7 *pr.*

12

because he had not heard the voice of the herald clearly. He may therefore be restored to his action.

Thereafter we have rescripts to praetors from Marcus Aurelius and Verus,[60] and a whole series from Septimius Severus and Caracalla.[61] In one instance Ulpian narrates the sequence of consultation and reply:[62]

Aetrius Severus, because he was in doubt, referred to the emperor Severus. In response to this *consultatio* he wrote to his successor, Venidius Quietus, that the praetor had no standing in the matter . . .

Though the praetors in Rome continued to exercise some jurisdiction beyond the end of our period,[63] there do not seem to be any later examples of rescripts to them. The evidence on rescripts to consuls covers an even shorter period, the middle of the second century. The *epistula* of Hadrian to Acilius Glabrio, the consul of 124, on the immunity of magistrates from prosecution, may be a special case.[64] But from the reign of Marcus Aurelius there are two, or possibly three, instances of rescripts to pairs of consuls. One of these rescripts explicitly concerns a case which had arisen in the jurisdiction of the courts:[65]

Since Romulus, whose status is in question, is still of age to be a ward, as to the question whether, as his mother Varia Hedo requests with the concurrence of his guardian, Varius Hermes, the case should be postponed until he reaches puberty, it is for your *gravitas* to determine, having regard to the trustworthiness of the persons, what is of advantage to the ward.

Thus for a time in the middle period of the empire the magistrates of Rome also came to turn to the emperor for advice and direction. But both the relative meagreness of the evidence and its limits in time mean that we cannot regard his response to *consultationes* from them, as from governors and other provincial officials, as one of the essential media through which the emperor's rule was exercised. In relation to Rome his communications with the magistrates were in any case eventually overtaken in importance by those between himself and the prefect of the city.

A few passing items of information from the early empire illustrate the communications between the emperor and the *praefectus urbi*, who was of course his appointee: a single isolated rescript from Augustus to Statilius

[60] *Dig.* xxv, 4, 1 *pr.*; *Frag. Vat.* 244.
[61] Severus: *Frag. Vat.* 159 = 246; 191; 208; 211; 215; 247. Caracalla: *Frag. Vat.* 232.
[62] *Dig.* iv, 4, 11, 2.
[63] See e.g. *CTh* ii, 19, 1 (319); vi, 4, 3 (339).
[64] *Dig.* xlviii, 2, 12, 1; cf. *PIR*[2] a 68.
[65] *Dig.* xl, 12, 27 *pr.* (Ulpian, *De officio consulis*): 'Divi fratres Proculo et Munatio rescripserunt.' The pair cannot otherwise be securely identified or dated, see A. Degrassi, *I fasti consolari* (1952), 46. See also *Frag. Vat.* 203: 'idque et divus Marcus Pertinaci et "Aeliano" consulibus rescripsit.' Both the wording and the fact that the pair were not *coss. ord.* excludes the possibility that they are mentioned for dating purposes. The date is 174 or 175, see Degrassi, o.c., 47, and the two are the future emperors, P. Helvius Pertinax (*PIR*[2] h 73) and M. Didius Severus Julianus (*PIR*[2] d 77). Note also *Dig.* xlviii, 5, 30, 5: 'rescripto ad Tertullum et Maximum consules' (undatable).

Taurus, presumably while he was prefect in 16–13 BC; Seneca's reference to the secret *mandata* which Tiberius gave to L. Calpurnius Piso on leaving Rome in AD 26, and the missives in his own hand which he sent (from Capri) to Cossus Cornelius Lentulus; or Josephus' report of the prefect in 36 sending a prisoner to appear before Tiberius in Capri.[66] The absence of Augustus and Tiberius from Rome at the periods concerned seems to have been the circumstance which brought about these exchanges, and we hear nothing more until Ulpian's reference to an *epistula* of Hadrian which gave a ruling on the jurisdiction of the prefect.[67] It is not clear however whether it was actually addressed to a prefect, as was that of Septimius Severus to Fabius Cilo, which is referred to several times in the *Digest*.[68] This does not seem to have been a rescript, but was a formal statement of the powers of the prefect, including that of deportation, and of their geographical limits, which were to extend to all of Italy up to the 100th milestone from Rome.

We can indeed see the distant beginning of the prefect's later role as the head of the entire administration of Rome in the rescript of Antoninus Pius to Erucius Clarus, prefect up to 146, which is referred to by Paulus, *On the Duties of the Praefectus Vigilum*; in it the emperor laid down that when store-houses (*horrea*) were broken into, the slave watchmen could be subjected to examination by torture, even if property of the emperor had been deposited there.[69] We also perhaps see a hint of the later prominence of the prefect in the fact that it was to the incumbent in 218, L. Marius Maximus, rather than to the consuls, that Macrinus wrote from Syria, where he spent all of his brief reign.[70]

From the reign of Severus Alexander we have the first clear instance of an imperial rescript in response to a consultation by a prefect of the city, Claudius Julianus. The style is that familiar from replies to other office-holders:[71]

> If it is clear to you, dearest Julianus, that the grandmother, in order to forestall a claim that the will was improper, has exhausted her property by making gifts to her grandson, reason demands that half of such gifts should be recalled.

The reply clearly reflects a consultation giving the details of the case, as does that of Diocletian and Maximian to Junius Maximus in 287:[72]

> Since you indicate that slaves are being removed from the city by kidnappers, and you write that on occasion free men are being carried off by their criminal act, we decree that the licence shown by these crimes must be checked with greater severity.

---

[66] *Dig.* VIII, 3, 35; cf. p. 465; Seneca, *Ep.* 83, 14–15; Josephus, *Ant.* XVIII, 6, 5 (169).

[67] *Dig.* I, 12, 2.

[68] I, 12, 1; XXXII, 1, 4; XLVIII, 19, 8, 5; 22, 6, 1. For L. Fabius Cilo Septiminus Catinius Acilianus Lepidus Fulcinianus, the friend and confidant of Severus, see *PIR*² F 27.

[69] I, 15, 3, 2; on Erucius Clarus *PIR*² E 96.

[70] Dio LXXVIII, 36, 1 (444); LXXIX, 2, 1 (453). Macrinus also wrote to the senate collectively, but not to the consuls as such.

[71] *Dig.* XXXI, 87, 3.

[72] *CJ* IX, 20, 7; see *PLRE* Maximus 38.

Up to this point the evidence is slight, and only the letter of Severus gives a substantial indication of an overriding rule of the prefect as the emperor's senior appointee in Rome. But from 314 to the end of Constantine's reign, and especially in the case of the incumbents from 314 to 324, we have a significant volume of evidence for the prefects receiving letters from the emperor, some of them whole series of letters. It may be significant that a particularly large number of letters were sent in the period of Constantine's domination in the west before his final victory over Licinius in 324. It is not that Constantine was frequently in Rome in this period, but rather that it was a period of intensive legislation by him; it is noticable that the letters to prefects of the city include a substantial number which were 'posted up' in Rome.[73] Indeed in the period after 312 he is attested as having been in Rome only in 315 and 326; from August 326 we have a letter of his to the prefect, Acilius Severus, which was 'read out' (*recitata*) in the Palatium in Rome.[74] By contrast the prefect of 317–19, Septimius Bassus, was absent for a month in 318 because he had 'gone to the emperor'.[75]

That was a rare exception, the occasion of which we do not know. The emperor's relations with the prefect were by now normally conducted from a distance, by letter. Almost none of Constantine's numerous letters to the prefects of Rome, however, carry any indication of being replies to consultations or reports. The one exception is that addressed to the prefect, Valerius Maximus, written in Serdica in December 320 and received in Rome on 9 March:[76]

> If it is established that any part of our Palatium or the other public buildings has been struck by lightning, in accordance with the ancestral custom of observance let enquiry be made of the *haruspices* as to what this portends, and let the reports be most diligently collected and referred to our *scientia*. Others may be permitted also to observe this custom, provided that they abstain from private sacrifices, which are specifically forbidden. As for the report and interpretation which was written about the striking of the amphitheatre, concerning which you had written to Heraclianus, *tribunus* and *magister officiorum*, you may know that it has been transmitted to us.

Constantine's evidently reluctant concession to traditional beliefs and practices may aptly symbolize the increasing withdrawal of the emperor from his long-established role in the rituals and within the priestly colleges of the city.[77] Such a withdrawal was itself an aspect of his gradual detachment from his place and role within the senate, in which the prefect himself was already acquiring the dominating position. Both developments are visible in

---

[73] For a recent survey see Cl. Dupont, 'Les textes constantiniens et le Préfect de la Ville', *Rev. hist. du droit fr. et étr.* XLVII (1969), 613. On 'proposita' as an indication that a positive enactment is being promulgated see pp. 319–21. Examples are *CTh* V, 8, 1 (314); XI, 36, 2 (315); IV, 11, 1 (316); XI, 30, 8 (319); IV, 9, 1 = *CJ* VII, 10, 7 (319); II, 16, 2 = *CJ* II, 52, 5 (319); IX, 19, 2 = *CJ* IX, 22, 22 (320); *CJ* III, 11, 5 (322); *CTh* II, 17, 1 (324); also II, 18, 3 = *CJ* III, 1, 10 (325); VI, 36, 1 = *CJ* XII, 30, 1 (326); II, 7, 2 = *CJ* II, 52, 6 (327); XI, 30, 18 (329).

[74] *CTh* X, 8, 3.

[75] *Chron. Ann.* 354; Mommsen, *Chronica Minora* I (1892), 67.

[76] *CTh* XVI, 10, 1. On the *magister officiorum* see p. 107.

[77] cf. pp. 355–61.

the latter which Constantine addressed in 315, almost as he might have done to a provincial city: 'Imperator Constantinus Augustus to the consuls, praetors, tribunes of the people, and senate greeting (*salutem dicit*)'; the letter was 'given on 18 July in Aquaviva(?), and read out in the senate on 5 September in the presence of Vettius Rufinus, the prefect of the city.'[78]

7. *Senate and Emperor*

The fact that a man from outside the senate could only enter with the emperor's permission or patronage; that many appointments within it depended directly on him; that of its members only the *praefectus urbi* controlled any troops in Rome; that it met infrequently, only twice in each month as a normal rule; that the emperor was often absent from Rome, and did not necessarily attend its meetings when he was there—all these and many other such considerations might lead to the supposition that the senate quickly lost all significance under the empire. It is notorious, however, that this was not so. The very fact of the extensive use of senatorial rank and senatorial offices as the currency of Imperial patronage tended to give it a status throughout wide areas of provincial society to which it might otherwise have remained irrelevant. The sense of the corporate identity, traditions and the rights of the senate was strongly felt by a first-generation senator from Transpadana such as Pliny the Younger (who must have gained the *latus clavus* from Titus or Domitian), as it was by a Greek from Bithynia, Cassius Dio, a century later. The consciousness of continuity with the senate which had guided the Roman state in the republic was still clearly felt in the fourth century, as is shown perhaps even more clearly by false assertions of descent from republican families than by the one genuine case which can still be attested.[1]

All this would be only marginally relevant to the themes of the role of the emperor and the pattern of his relations with his subjects, if it were not the case that all the emperors of the period were regarded as being at least in principle members of the senate, and all (except those who did not survive long enough) held the consulate at least once (normally occupying it as *ordinarius* in the first year after accession); moreover, up to the proclamation of Macrinus, the praetorian prefect, in Syria in 217, all had actually been senators before their accession. More important still, at least up to the third century matters of imperial policy could still be debated in the senate;

---

[78] *CTh* VIII, 18, 1 = *CJ* VI, 60, 1. On the assumption that the name of the *Praefectus Urbi* would be less easily distorted, it is necessary to amend the consular dates from *Constantino A. V et Licinio C. conss.* (319) to *Constantino A. IV et Licinio C. conss.* (315). See *PLRE* Rufinus 15. Both texts give the place as Aquileia, but see Seeck, *Regesten*, 59. In fact Constantine came to Rome after sending the letter, and was there, though evidently not in the senate, when it was read out.

[1] For real and fictional ancestries of third- and fourth-century senatorial families see e.g. R. Syme, *Ammianus and the Historia Augusta* (1968), ch. xxiv. For some possible cases of genuine continuities from the first century BC or AD see J. Morris, 'Munatius Plancus Paulinus', *Bonn. Jahrb.* CLXV (1965), 88; J. F. Matthews, 'Continuity in a Roman Family: the Rufii Festi of Volsinii', *Historia* XVI (1967), 484; the theme is roughly sketched in M. T. W. Arnheim, *The Senatorial Aristocracy in the Later Roman Empire* (1972), ch. v. The one indubitable case of continuity from the republic to the fourth century is the Acilii Glabriones.

and *senatus consulta*, which in the republic had been in principle merely advisory, came to be quoted as sources of law in themselves. It is here that we touch on a specific aspect of the range of functions performed by the emperor in person. For, as we saw,[2] Fronto regarded the delivery of speeches in the senate as one of the emperor's primary roles. Many such speeches were formal or honorific; the inscription of Ti. Plautius Silvanus Aelianus, for instance, quotes from the rather restrained oration which Vespasian delivered in asking the senate to grant him *triumphalia ornamenta* for his governorship of Moesia under Nero.[3] But the emperor often spoke either about current circumstances or policies, or to propose new legislation in the form of *senatus consulta*. His *oratio* might be delivered by himself or might be read out by the *quaestor Caesaris*. It is a sign of the strength of the senatorial tradition that this means of legislation was used until the early third century; but it is also an indication that this was becoming a mere formality, that legal writers can quote as a source of law not the resultant *senatus consultum* but the *oratio* itself. This is the case with the last attested legislative *oratio* delivered by an emperor in the senate, that which Caracalla gave in 206, while joint Augustus with his father Severus, on the law relating to gifts between husband and wife. Ulpian refers to some of its contents and quotes a few brief extracts, for instance: 'He who made such a gift has indeed the right to repent of it; but for the heir to snatch it away, perhaps against the last wish of the donor, is hard and grasping.'[4]

Senatus consulta passed in the earlier empire and up to the early third century were valid for the whole empire unless they specifically related to particular places; it is quite certain that they did not apply solely to the public, or 'senatorial', provinces ruled by proconsuls.[5] Moreover, even after *senatus consulta* ceased to be a means of passing new legislation, the provisions of previous *senatus consulta* continued, as is evident throughout the *Codes* and the *Digest*, to be quoted as sources of law. They also continued to be regarded as such by the provincials; an inscription from Ephesus, which cannot be earlier than the third century, refers to the ancient precedence of the city, based on 'the laws and the imperial *constitutiones* and decrees of the sacred senate'; the writer recommends the collection of relevant points from enactments in these three forms, as preserved in Ulpian's *De officio proconsulis*.[6]

But even before this we can see in certain specific instances the law-making role of the senate being overshadowed, and finally superseded, by that of the emperor. For example the city of Aphrodisias in Caria gained certain privileges, in particular freedom and immunity from taxation, from

---

[2] p. 203.

[3] *ILS* 986: 'Senatus in praefectura triumphalibus ornamentis honoravit, auctore imp. Caesare Augusto Vespasiano, verbis ex oratione eius q(uae) i(nfra) s(cripta) s(unt): "Moesiae ita praefuit, ut non debuerit in me diferri honor triumphalium eius ornamentorum; nisi quod latior ei contigit mora titulus praefecto urbis".'

[4] *Dig.* XXIV, 1, 32; quotation in 32, 2.

[5] See 'The Emperor, the Senate and the Provinces', *JRS* LVI (1966), 156.

[6] The inscription is published by J. Keil, G. Maresch, *JÖAI* XLV (1960), Beiblatt, 82, no. 8. Comparison with *Dig.* I, 16, 4 shows clearly that ἐν τοῖς Δη ὀφφι[. . . . .]/Οὐλπιανῷ εἰρημένα is a reference to his *De officio proconsulis*.

Julius Caesar, Octavian and Antonius, all of which were confirmed by a
senatus consultum passed in 39 BC, and apparently also by a law of the Roman
people.[7] But in 119/20 Hadrian, in response to an embassy from the city,
writes without further reference to the senate to confirm 'the freedom and
autonomy and other privileges granted by the senate and by the emperors
before me'; while in 250 Decius and Herennius, again in reply to an embassy, write 'we preserve your existing freedom and all the other privileges
which you have gained from the emperors before us'.[8]

For almost a century before this we have no certain evidence of a provincial
embassy appearing in the senate; the latest evidence which can be approximately dated seems to be that of an inscription from Ephesus honouring
P. Vedius Antoninus 'who has been on embassies to the senate and the
emperors about the most important matters and has always been victorious',
and who had also acted as gymnasiarch during the visits of the emperor
Lucius Verus, which took place in the 160s.[9] If it was indeed in the second
half of the second century that provincial embassies ceased to appear before
the senate—and arguments from the silence of our sources can at best be
hypothetical—then this too marks a turning-point hardly less significant
than the ending of senatorial legislation in the form of *senatus consulta*. For
with that there will have ceased a centuries-old element in the business and
procedures of the senate, and one which had been one of the central elements
in its domination of the relations of the Roman republic with its subjects
and allies.[10] As we saw earlier, from an early date such embassies tended also
to approach leading Romans individually in the course of their efforts, and
in the dictatorship of Caesar the fact that some will have come essentially to
appear before him rather than the senate was keenly felt;[11] the transition is
visible for instance in an inscription from the Crimea mentioning a man who
had gone on an embassy to Rome in 46 BC 'to the senate of the Romans and
to Gaius Julius Caesar'.[12]

It is noteworthy, however, that various documents of the triumviral period,
among them the *senatus consultum* relating to Aphrodisias, establish specific
privileges for particular persons or cities as regards future embassies before
the senate.[13] Once the rule of Augustus was established, many embassies

[7] See *JRS* LXIII (1973), 56–7, Docs. 8 and 12–13; cf. J. M. Reynolds, 'Aphrodisias: A Free and
Federate City', *Akten des VI. Internationalen Kongresses für Griechische und Lateinische Epigrafik,
München 1972* (1973), 115.

[8] Hadrian: unpublished document from the excavations by K. T. Erim and J. M. Reynolds in
the theatre at Aphrodisias (see p. xiii); Decius and Herennius: *MAMA* VIII, 424.

[9] *JÖAI* XLIV (1959), Beiblatt, 258, no. 3 = *AE* 1959 13. For the chronological evidence see T. D.
Barnes, *JRS* LVII (1967), 71–2. Cn. Pompeius Hermippus, πρεσβεύσαντα πολλάκις πρὸς τοὺς
Αὐτοκράτορας καὶ τὴν ἱερωτάτην σύνκλητον, *Forsch. in Eph.* II (1912), 178, no. 69, seems to
be no later than this. For Marcus Aurelius' spontaneous referral to the Senate of a matter brought
to him by an embassy from Miletus see the inscription published by P. Herrmann, *Ist. Mitt.* XXV
(1975), 149.

[10] The evidence is most fully collected by G. Iacopi in *Diz. Epig.* IV, 500f. Cf. Th. Büttner-
Wobst, *De legationibus reipublicae liberae temporibus Roman missis* (Diss. Leipzig, 1876).

[11] pp. 15–17.

[12] Latyschev, *IOSPE*² I 691, ll. 7–10: πρεσ[βεύσας μ]έχρι ['Ρ]ώμας ποτὶ τὰν 'Ρωμαίων
σύν[κλητον Κ]αὶ Γαίον 'Ιούλιον Καίσαρα τρὶς ὕπατον [δικτάτορ]ά τε τὸ τρίτον. See M.
Rostovtzeff, 'Caesar and the South of Russia', *JRS* VII (1917), 27.

[13] See *JRS* LXIII (1973), 55–6, Docs. 5, 8; cf. no. 7, *senatus consultum* in reply to an embassy.

came directly to the emperor, as they continued to do throughout the period; the reception of such embassies was one of the primary forms in which the emperor heard the requests and disputes of his subjects.[14] But the senate also functioned as a forum for the reception of embassies, sometimes in collaboration with or as an immediate alternative to, the emperor, and sometimes independently. Such hearings might also provide a stage for the exercise of their rhetorical powers by younger members of the imperial house. Already in the 20s BC the young Tiberius made a speech in the senate in support of an appeal for aid by Laodicea, Thyatira and Chios, which had been struck by an earthquake.[15] In the summer of 25 BC, following *relationes* by Augustus' colleague in the consulship, M. Junius Silanus, the senate passed two *consulta* concerning a formal oath of alliance with Mytilene; the fragmentary inscription recording this seems to suggest that Augustus, then in Spain, was consulted. An embassy from Mytilene must have appeared for the occasion in order to take the oath. It may be also that it included the poet Crinagoras, and that he and perhaps the rest of the embassy also went either before or after this to appear before Augustus in Spain.[16] At any rate it was presumably in connection with this episode that the Mytileneans voted to send an embassy to make a speech of thanks to Augustus before the senate, the Vestal Virgins, Livia and his sister Octavia, and before him to the senate (as well as delivering a large gold crown).[17]

When an embassy from Cyrene came to Rome in 7/6 BC to complain of judicial oppression by the Roman citizens there, they apparently approached Augustus directly, and he issued an edict which was to have effect 'until the senate has debated the matter or I myself have found a better solution'.[18] The further decision is perhaps the fourth edict from Cyrene, which is in fact purely a pronouncement of Augustus. But the implication that in this period the provincials could still look either to the emperor or the senate for decisions is reflected also in two of the other edicts engraved in Cyrene. In the third Augustus refers to 'those to whom by a *lex*, *senatus consultum* or the *decretum* of my father (Julius Caesar) or myself immunity from taxation has been given along with citizenship'.[19] But for the next two centuries grants of citizenship were to be among the most common forms of imperial

---

[14] pp. 375–463 *passim*.

[15] Suetonius, *Tib.* 8. For the chronological problems here see G. W. Bowersock, *Augustus and the Greek World* (1965), 157f.; B. M. Levick, *CQ* n.s. XVI (1971), 478. For other instances of joint responses to cities Dio LIV, 23, 7–8.

[16] *IGR* III 33; see Sherk, *Roman Documents*, no. 26, for a very clear discussion with references to previous literature. Various poems by Crinagoras *may* suggest that he took part in the embassy, as he had to Julius Caesar two decades before: Gow and Page, *The Greek Anthology: the Garland of Philip* I (1968), Crinagoras xxxii concerns preparations for a journey to Italy; xvi commemorates the death of one Seleucus in Spain; xxiii celebrates the milch-goat used on a voyage by 'Caesar', presumably Augustus; xxix concerns baths built by Augustus in the Pyrenees, cf. R. Étienne, *Ann. du Midi* LXIV (1952), 5. But none proves such a journey, and nor does the mention of Tarraco in *IGR* III 38, for cf. the context in which it is mentioned ibid., 39. Note however the embassy from Tralles to Augustus in Spain, pp. 422–3

[17] *IGR* IV 39; see the text and commentary by Dittenberger, *OGIS* 456.

[18] *SEG* IX 8 = *FIRA*² I, no. 68 i, ll. 12–13: ἄχρι ἂν ἡ σύνκλητος βουλεύσηται περὶ τούτου ἢ ἐγὼ αὐτὸς ἄμεινον εὕρω τι. Cf. p. 257.

[19] ibid., iii, ll. 58–9: οἷς κατὰ νόμον ἢ δόγμα συνκλη⟨τοῦ ἢ⟩ τῷ τοῦ πατρός μου ἐπικρίματι ἢ τῷ ἐμῷ ἀνεισφορία σὺν τῇ πολειτήᾳ δέδοται. Cf. pp. 479f.

beneficium, and there is no evidence that they were ever subsequently conferred by anyone else, or by any organ of the *res publica*. Similarly, Dio mentions that the privileges of those with three children had once been conferred by the senate but were now given by the emperor; all the known instances show the latter.[20]

The clearest example of joint action by senate and emperor as it affected the provincials is of course precisely the fifth Cyrene edict. First, its form is that of an edict of Augustus introducing a *senatus consultum*, which is explicitly based on a recommendation by Augustus and his senatorial *consilium*.[21] Secondly, it provides for the appearance before the senate of provincials—presumably in all cases an embassy—who wished to reclaim money improperly acquired by a provincial governor in the course of his duties; it was to be the duty of the senate to establish a panel of its members to decide the case, or at least to assess the amount due to be repaid. It is disputed whether the subsequent full-scale trials in the senate on this and related charges do or do not represent a developed form of this procedure.[22] But, as we shall see, many provincial embassies did in fact appear for this purpose before the senate at least until the early second century.

Under Tiberius it seems from Tacitus' narrative to have been the senate which allowed the request of the imperial province of Tarraconensis to erect a temple to Augustus, and it certainly heard embassies from various Italian *coloniae* and *municipia*.[23] On a similar occasion, when the city of Trebiae requested permission for a legacy left for the building of a theatre to be used for constructing a road, Tiberius was present in the senate and was in favour, but did not carry the majority with him; on another, when a vote took place by division, he found himself on the minority side.[24] He also seems to have been present when his procurator in Asia was accused by the province in 24 of using violence, and asserted that his orders had given the man power only over imperial slaves and cash. In consequence of the condemnation the cities of Asia decreed, and the senate permitted, the construction of a temple there to Tiberius, Livia and the personified senate; to celebrate the occasion the young Nero, the son of Tiberius' nephew and adopted son, Germanicus, made a speech of thanks to emperor and senate.[25] Two years later the senate, with Tiberius again present, was to spend several days hearing the rival claims of eleven of the major Greek cities of Asia, as to which was to be the site of the temple; Aristides was later to recall that Smyrna eventually received 400 votes, and all the other cities only seven.[26] On this occasion it is not recorded that Tiberius spoke; but in 25, when Baetica 'sending ambassadors to the senate asked that following the example of Asia it might erect a shrine to Tiberius and Livia', the emperor delivered

---

[20] Dio LV, 2, 6; cf. p. 496.

[21] p. 268.

[22] For a survey and discussion see P. A. Brunt, 'Charges of Provincial Maladministration under the Early Principate', *Historia* x (1961), 189; on the Fifth Edict itself Sherk, *Roman Documents*, no. 31.

[23] Tacitus, *Ann.* I, 78–9.

[24] Suetonius, *Tib.* 31, 1.

[25] Tacitus, *Ann.* IV, 15.

[26] IV, 55–6; Aristides, *Or.* XIX Keil, 13.

an oration which, as reproduced by Tacitus, represents some of our primary evidence for the ideology of the refusal of divine honours by the early emperors.[27]

Even when embassies came in the first instance to the emperor, they might also apply, or be transferred, to the senate. Suetonius gives as an example of Tiberius' deference to republican sentiment the fact that some ambassadors from the province of Africa could come to the consuls to complain of delays by the emperor, to whom they had been sent.[28] More significant still was Tiberius' action in 22 when he 'provided the senate with the appearance of its ancient dignity' by sending to it the requests on the question of rights of asylum brought by embassies from many Greek cities. An inscription from Miletus honouring a man 'who had been on an embassy to the emperor over the privilege of asylum of Apollo at Didyma and the rights of the city' probably refers to this occasion, and if so confirms that the embassies had gone in the first instance to the emperor.[29] In the event the hearings were conducted by the senate (except that it deputed a preliminary examination to the consuls), and further cases arose in the following year.[30] Just before this Tiberius himself had been the mover of a *senatus consultum* granting Cibyra in Asia and Aegium in Achaea (at this time an imperial province) remission from tribute for five years because of the effects of an earthquake; the senate's vote was in response to petitions (*preces*), which will have been brought before it by embassies.[31]

The holding of such senatorial hearings might of course be at the will of the emperor, and could be used simply as a platform for himself or members of his household. So Suetonius notes that Claudius often answered embassies in the senate with full-scale orations of his own, which may even have been in Greek.[32] Dio reports, as does Suetonius, that Claudius reduced the Lycians, who had previously been free, to provincial status, because they had killed some Roman citizens; but he adds that the emperor 'had the investigation held in the senate and personally cross-examined one of the envoys, removing his citizenship on discovering that he could not understand a question in Latin'.[33] In 53 Claudius delivered an oration in the senate, asking for immunity from tribute for Cos, retailing the salient features of its history and finally dwelling on the services of its Coan doctor, C. Stertinius Xenophon.[34] Tacitus does not say that the issue was raised by an embassy; but an inscription from there mentions a man who held the office of priest of Tiberius and Claudius, and 'had often been on embassies at his own expense

---

[27] IV, 37–8; see most recently Chr. Habicht, 'Die augusteische Zeit und das erste Jahrhundert nach Christi Geburt', in *Le culte des souverains dans l'Empire romain, Entretiens Hardt* XIX (1973), 39.

[28] *Tib.* 31, 2.

[29] *OGIS* 472 = *Ins. von Didyma* 107. Miletos is mentioned in Tacitus, *Ann.* III, 63, 3.

[30] Tacitus, *Ann.* III, 60–3; IV, 14, 1–2.

[31] IV, 13, 1.

[32] *Claud.* 42, 1: 'Nec minore cura Graeca studia secutus est ... ac saepe in senatu legatis perpetua oratione respondit.' The context suggests, but does not prove, that the orations concerned were in Greek.

[33] Dio LX, 17, 3–4; Suetonius, *Claud.* 25, 3.

[34] Tacitus, *Ann.* XII, 61; on Xenophon see pp. 85–6.

on behalf of his city to Rome to the emperors and the senate, and to Asia to the governors'.[35] The request of the Byzantines for a remission of tribute, which came shortly after, was brought by an embassy which delivered an oration in the senate on the history of the city, its past services to Rome— and, significantly in view of the future, the burdens imposed by the passage of armies and generals. Claudius spoke in support, and five years' remission was granted.[36]

When Nero addressed the senate on his accession, he promised among other things 'that Italy and the public provinces could apply to the tribunals of the consuls, who would give access to the senate'; and in fact all the known embassies to the senate in his reign did come from Italy or public provinces (though some from public provinces also went to the emperor).[37] In 58 separate embassies from the council and people of Puteoli came before the senate to make mutual accusations, followed by one from Syracuse asking for permission to increase the number of pairs of gladiators allowed in their games. To Tacitus this was a trivial affair which would not have earned a mention from him if Thrasea Paetus had not spoken in the debate; to us it may seem the more significant in that permission for exactly such an increase was later regularly granted by the emperor.[38]

In 59 the question of a riot between the inhabitants of Nuceria and Pompeii was brought, it is not stated how, before Nero, and referred by him to the senate, by the senate to the consuls and by them back to the senate.[39] Once again it is clear how in this early period a significant range of matters could be decided either by the emperor or the senate. A different aspect of this same intermingling of roles appeared in the course of the trial of a prominent Cretan, Timarchus, in 62. It emerged in the course of the proceedings that he had said that it was within his power to determine whether thanks were decreed to proconsuls of Crete and Cyrene on leaving office. What this meant is made clear by the senate's reaction, a *consultum* passed on the motion of the emperor, that it should be illegal to move a motion in a provincial council that such a speech of thanks to a *legatus pro praetore* or proconsul should be made before the senate, or to serve on an embassy for this purpose.[40] It is thus clear that it was the custom for embassies from both imperial and public provinces to appear in the senate for this reason. The prohibition, if effective, must have applied only to the provincial councils proper. For Pliny lists among the virtues of Trajan's conduct of the elections in 100 precisely the fact that he admitted as evidence in support of candidates

[35] A. Maiuri, *Nuova silloge epigrafica di Rodi e Cos* (1925), no. 462, ll. 13–17: πρεσβεύσαντα πολλάκις δωρεὰν ὑπὲρ τᾶς πατρίδος ἐς Ῥώμαν ποτὶ τὸς Σεβαστὸς καὶ τὰν σύνκλητον καὶ ἐς τὰν Ἀσίαν ποτὶ τὸς ἀγεμόνας. Some at least of the occasions could go back to the issue of asylum under Tiberius. For Cos see Tacitus, *Ann.* IV, 14, 1–2.

[36] *Ann.* XII, 62–3. On the strategic significance of Byzantium and the relevance of this fact to its refoundation as Constantinople see pp. 38, 51.

[37] *Ann.* XIII, 4, 2. For embassies to Nero see pp. 381, 388.

[38] *Ann.* XIII, 48–9. An embassy is not specifically mentioned in the case of Syracuse, but should be assumed. For an extra pair of gladiators being granted by Gordian III to a High Priest of Macedonia in 240 see J. P. Touratsoglou in *Ancient Macedonia*, ed. B. Laourdas (1970), 180; cf. *BE* 1971, no. 400.

[39] *Ann.* XIV, 17.

[40] *Ann.* XV, 20–2.

the decrees and motions of thanks of provincial cities and peoples. But possibly yet another shift of provincial attention to the emperor had already occurred, and these thanks had been expressed to the emperor himself.[41] For in 127 Hadrian replied to an embassy from Stratonicea-Hadrianopolis which had no other purpose than to bring him a testimony to the beneficent conduct of Avidius Quietus, the proconsul of Asia in 125/6.[42]

The counterpart of such embassies bringing expressions of thanks was the laying of accusations, usually related to money improperly acquired, whose restoration was sought (*pecuniae repetundae*), and sometimes to more serious charges. Both *pecuniae repetundae* and *maiestas* (treason) were involved for instance in the accusations brought in AD 15 against Granius Marcellus, the proconsul of Pontus and Bithynia. In this instance Tacitus' narrative names as the accusers the quaestor of the province and another individual Roman, and it remains uncertain whether a provincial embassy was also involved. But the trial for *maiestas* in the senate was notable for raising the essential contradiction between Tiberius' role as emperor and as a member of the senate: for Cn. Piso asked him, 'In what place in the order will you give your opinion, Caesar? If first, I will have something to follow; if after all the others, I fear that I may have committed the imprudence of disagreeing.'[43] A few years later, in 22, the province of Asia, represented by 'the most eloquent men of all Asia chosen to make the accusation', brought an accusation for *repetundae* against the former proconsul, C. Junius Silanus, to which again individual senators added capital charges. In this instance Tiberius was present in the senate and took part in the interrogation, and is also found, as though he were holding the consulate, asking the senators for their opinions in the due order, and then giving his own at the end.[44]

Up to at least the early second century the senate retained the function of acting as a court where the provincials could seek redress against the peculations of governors. From the cases reported by Pliny, in which he himself took part, it is clear that a provincial embassy normally requested by name from the senate a *patronus* who would speak for them;[45] but members of the embassy might also make speeches before the senate.[46] In these cases (as in all the scenes in the senate described by Pliny) Trajan is never present in his capacity as a senator; but in one of them, conducted during his consulship of 100, he presided as consul.[47] He became involved otherwise only when a Bithynian embassy accusing a former proconsul, Varenus Rufus, was dissatisfied with the procedure and complained to him, only to be referred back to the senate; and again when a rival embassy from Bithynia

---

[41] *Pan.* 70. Note 70, 3: 'nec fuit quisquam, quem non haec cogitatio subiret, cum sciret, quidquid a quoque in provinciis bene fieret, omnia te scire.'

[42] *IGR* IV 1156 (revised text by L. Robert, *Hellenica* VI, 80–4), ll. 29–32: τοῖς ἐπισταλεῖσιν ὑφ' ὑμῶν ἐντυχὼν ἔ[μαθ]ον ὅτι χάριν ἠπίστασθε 'Αουιδίδ.ῳ Κυ[ιή]τῳ τῷ κρατίστῳ ὡς εὖ ποιήσαντι ὑμᾶς [κ]ατὰ τὸν τῆς ἀνθυ[π]ατείας χρόνον.

[43] Tacitus, *Ann.* I, 74.

[44] III, 66–9.

[45] *Ep.* II, 11, 2; see X, 3a, 2–3; III, 4, 2–6; V, 20, 1.

[46] IV, 9, 3–5 and 14; V, 20, 4.

[47] II, 11, 10–15. The significant fact that in Pliny's letters it is assumed that Trajan does not attend the senate is noted by Sherwin-White on *Ep.* VI, 13, 2.

sent by the provincial council, brought to him, to some leading senators and to Pliny (as the *advocatus* of Varenus), a decree ordering the abandonment of the prosecution. On this occasion too, one of the new embassy spoke in the senate, and requested that nothing be done to prejudice an enquiry (*cognitio*) by the emperor. On this occasion alone Trajan *may* have appeared in the senate; for Pliny represents him saying at the conclusion of the proceedings, 'Let neither party complain. It will be my concern to discover the intentions of the province.'[48]

With that we lose sight of the procedures for the accusation of governors by the provincials. But occasional documents and literary references show how the senate continued for most of the remainder of the second century to respond, often in conjunction with the emperor, to provincial needs and requests. For instance an extensively damaged inscription from Pergamum dating to the last years of Trajan's reign shows that there was both a *senatus consultum* and a *constitutio* of the emperor in response to a request by the city for permission to establish a second set of quinquennial games. The request was probably brought by an embassy, to which the emperor possibly refers in his concluding letter to the city.[49] Then an inscription from Gaulos in Sicily honours a man who had been on an embassy at his own expense to Hadrian and the senate, possibly to reclaim certain local revenues;[50] and in a letter to the Delphic Amphictyony and to the city of Delphi Hadrian says that a letter to him from there has been brought before the senate.[51] An even more fragmentary inscription from Cyzicus in Asia records that under Antoninus Pius the senate passed a *consultum* at the request (*postulatio*) of the Cyzicenes, confirming their right to have an association of young men (*neoi*); Marcus Aurelius, at this time designated 'Caesar' and the presumptive heir of his adoptive father Antoninus Pius, appears first among the senatorial witnesses of the text of the *s.c.*, and the emperor himself is mentioned as having given a place on the agenda for the motion.[52]

Under Marcus Aurelius and Commodus (177–80) inscriptions from Sardis in Asia and Italica in Baetica record part of a meeting of the senate which debated a proposal by the emperors to take steps to reduce the price of gladiators to the holders of provincial priesthoods (on whom custom imposed the duty of giving games). It is not clear whether the issue had been raised by a provincial embassy, but it is noticeable that there are specific references to High Priests (*sacerdotes*) of the three Gallic provinces, and to gladiators put on display there. The main surviving text consists of the *sententia* of a senator, given in response to the reading in the senate of the imperial *oratio* (of which a small part survives separately). It is significant that the speaker excuses himself for discussing in detail what the *oratio* has

---

[48] VI, 13, 2; VII, 6, 1–7; 10.

[49] *CIL* III 7086 = *IGR* IV 336; full commentary in *Alt. v. Pergamon* VIII.2, no. 269; cf. Abbott and Johnson, *Municipal Administration*, no. 73.

[50] *ILS* 6772: 'item legatione gratuita apud [Divum] Hadrianum et apud amplissimum ordinem de [. . .]ALLIB (vectigalibus?) redhibendis.'

[51] Partially published by E. Bourguet, *De rebus Delphicis* (1902), 82f.; a full reading by C. Vatin, with new restorations, is reported by A. Plassart, *Fouilles de Delphes* III.4 (1970), pp. 82–3, but has not yet been published.

[52] *CIL* III 7060 = *ILS* 7190 = *FIRA*² I, no. 48.

proposed: 'But although some consider that, as regards all matters on which the greatest *principes* have sent a *relatio* to us, one's opinion should be given in a single succint *sententia* . . .'[53] The tendency for the disappearance of any significant public role on the part of the senate is thus clear; and it is not entirely inappropriate that the last occasion on which a provincial city is attested as obtaining a privilege from it is that under Commodus, when the influence of his favourite, Saoterus, meant that the man's native city, Nicomedia, was able to gain from the senate the right to hold games and build a temple of the emperor.[54]

It is thus apparent that, so far as our evidence shows, *senatus consulta* embodying legislation, embassies to the senate and decisions by the senate on the affairs of provincial communities all came to an end in the second half of the second or the first half of the third century. We can see the shift precisely exemplified in the case of requests for permission to hold recurrent fairs or markets (*nundinae*). Claudius actually asked the senate for permission to hold *nundinae* on his estates;[55] and under Trajan and Hadrian senators are found making the same requests in respect of estates in Italy and Africa.[56] But a century later Modestinus assumes that *nundinae* were 'requested from the emperor'.[57] Documentary evidence confirms this: an inscription from Numidia shows Probus sending a rescript approving twice-monthy *nundinae* requested by a land-owner; and another shows Constantine both restoring baths and establishing or permitting *nundinae* at a place in the territory of Poetovio.[58]

So far as the relations of subject and emperor are concerned, we may therefore regard the late second and early third centuries as the period in which the emperor finally emerged from what remained of the senatorial context, and could be seen as an independent monarch. The question of the developing role of the emperor within the senate is a much more complex one, which need not be considered in detail; indeed it hardly can be so considered, given the surprising absence of any full study of the procedures and functions of the imperial senate as a collective body.[59] But we may note that the convention that the emperor could take part in debates as one senator among others hardly survived to the end of the first century. Tiberius is

[53] *FIRA*[2] I, no. 49; see the revised text and discussion by J. H. Oliver, R. E. A. Palmer, 'Minutes of an Act of the Roman Senate', *Hesperia* XXIV (1955), 320. 'Sacerdotes fidelissimarum Galliarum vestrarum', *Aes Ital.*, l. 14; 'in civitatibus splendidissimarum Galliarum', ibid., 56; 'legebatur etiam nunc aput nos oratio', ibid., 13, cf. 28, 46–7. Part of the *oratio* itself see *Marm. Sard.*, l. 16: 'procurator noster p[raebebit . . .].' On the brevity of the normal *sententia*, *Aes Ital.*, ll. 27–8. For the relevance of this document to the *fiscus* see p. 195.

[54] p. 81.

[55] p. 178.

[56] Pliny, *Ep.* v, 4; *CIL* VIII 270 = *FIRA*[2] I, no. 47.

[57] *Dig.* L, 11, 1.

[58] *AE* 1903 243: 'ex rescripto dei Probi, postulante Mun. Flaviano nundinas Emadaucapens(es) immun[e]s V Kal. et III Iduum celebrandas v. p. p(raeses) N(umidiae) Aug. Diogenes beneficium datum sup[l]ere dignatus e[st]'; *ILS* 704.

[59] For the formal aspects of the emperor's dealings with the senate see Mommsen, *Staatsrecht*[3] II. 2, 894–904; cf. O'Brien-Moore, *RE* s.v. 'Senatus', Suppl. VI, 66of., esp. 766–800. I cannot see any reason why the speech from a meeting in the senate, partially preserved on papyrus, *FIRA*[2] I, no. 44 = Cavenaille, *Corp. Pap. Lat.*, no. 236, should be attributed, as is normally assumed, to Claudius, or even, with certainty, to any emperor.

quoted as disagreeing with a previous *sententia*, saying to the senator concerned, 'Pardon me if, as one senator to another, I speak with excessive freedom against your view'.[60] But the convention was already wearing thin when Vitellius, on reaching Rome after his proclamation in 69, made a point of attending senatorial debates even on insignificant matters. For when Helvidius Priscus, as praetor designate for 70, expressed a *sententia* which was contrary to his wish, he first called on the tribunes to exercise their veto, and then, when Helvidius' friends began to implore his mercy, said that there was nothing novel in the fact that two senators had disagreed.[61] Thereafter, there is no evidence of the emperor sitting in the senate as a voting member, and with the possible exception of Trajan's response in affair of the Bithynian embassy[62] all the attested imperial *orationes* seem to have been formal pronouncements (*relationes*) which initiated the proceedings, either spoken by the emperor in person or read out by a quaestor. On very rare occasions his proposals might meet with some resistance, as when Antoninus Pius had to resort to a combination of tears and a threat not to accept the position of emperor, before the senate would agree to deify Hadrian in 138.[63] But essentially the imperial addresses, whether they embodied legislation,[64] or accompanied reports of victories.[65] or, like that made by Severus on his first appearance after his victory over Albinus in 197, were designed to instil terror,[66] were not open to debate.

From the very beginning the emperor's role in the senate, or in relation to it, was marked by an inevitable ambivalence which could only be resolved by his steadily increasing detachment from it. The senate, for instance, took oaths on the first of January to observe not only the measures of all past emperors whose memory had not been condemned, but also the future measures of the current emperor. Dio reports that this custom persisted from the beginning up to his own time, the early third century.[67] Yet however much this can be regarded as a sign of subordination, it still carried with it a residual claim to a role in the legitimation of imperial acts which was quite lacking either in the oaths of loyalty taken throughout the empire on an emperor's accession,[68] or the prayers for his safety taken equally generally on each 1 or 3 January.[69] For it was the senate itself which formally

[60] Suetonius, *Tib.* 29.

[61] Tacitus, *Hist.* II, 91, 3.

[62] p. 349.

[63] Dio LXX, 1, 2–3.

[64] e.g. *Dig.* V, 3, 22. Paulus quotes the *oratio* of Hadrian, 'Dispicite, patres conscripti, numquid sit aequius ...', but derives his statement of the law ('oportet igitur') directly from what is apparently merely suggested there; cf. *Frag. Vat.* 224, an *oratio* of Marcus and Verus; *Dig.* II, 12, 1–2, of Marcus ('eadem oratione divus Marcus in senatu recitata effecit ...'); *Dig.* XXVII, 9, 1, 1–2, of Severus (with a substantial quotation).

[65] e.g. Fronto, *Ad Verum imp.* II, 1, 1–6, on Verus' letter to the senate on his victories, which was accompanied by a speech there by Marcus Aurelius.

[66] The scene is described by Dio LXXV, 8, 1–3 (344–5). He makes clear, incidentally, that Severus read the speech.

[67] LVII, 8, 4–5. There were however exceptions, see Tacitus, *Ann.* I, 72, 1; Dio LX, 10, 1.

[68] See P. Herrmann, *Der römische Kaisereid* (1968).

[69] See Sherwin-White, *The Letters of Pliny* (1966), on *Ep.* X, 35–6 and 100–3.

deified dead emperors or condemned their memory, and thus in principle rescinded their acts; or (as with Tiberius) did neither.

Though our concern is essentially with the role of the emperor once in power and not with the theory or practice of the establishment or legitimation of his rule,[70] we may note that the senate never entirely ceased in our period to claim some role in voting titles to emperors: Lactantius records that in 312 the senate voted that the name of Constantine should stand first in the list of emperors (before those of Maximin and Licinius).[71]

If an emperor assumed power when outside Rome he would write to the senate, either with deliberate deference as in the case of Trajan, who carefully sent a letter written in his own hand,[72] or Hadrian, who formally asked for ratification of his position;[73] or without it, as with Macrinus, whose first letter to the senate in 217 was headed by the imperial titles which Dio says should have been voted by the senate.[74] If we may believe the *Historia Augusta*, in the third century the reading in the senate of letters announcing the proclamation of emperors was normally followed by ritual acclamations of a type which is in fact well attested from the early second century onwards.[75] For its part, the senate might send an embassy to a newly proclaimed emperor. Here too there cannot have failed to be some resemblance between this and the embassies which cities sent on the same occasion;[76] but again the substance could be significantly different, for the question of the powers and titles of the emperor might be involved. So, for instance, Galba in 68 declined to accept the imperial titles until they were conferred by a senatorial embassy which met him at Narbo on his march to Rome.[77] In the following year Vitellius heard at Ticinum the embassy which the senate had sent after voting his titles;[78] and under very similar circumstances a senatorial embassy met Septimius Severus at Interamna as he advanced on Rome in 193.[79]

Once an emperor was in power it was normal for him, as for a republican general, to send to the senate reports from the field.[80] He might also write to the senate after political crises, as Nero did after the murder of Agrippina,[81] or Gaius from Germany after the execution of Lepidus. On this

[70] See e.g. B. Parsi, *Désignation et investiture de l'empereur romain, 1er et 11e siècles après J.-C* (1963).

[71] *De mort. pers.* 44, 11.

[72] Dio LXVIII, 5, 2; see p. 219.

[73] LXIX, 2, 2.

[74] LXXVIII, 16, 2–17, 1 (419–21).

[75] See e.g. *HA, Max.* 16; *Claud.* 4, 2–4; *Prob.* 11–12. For *acclamationes* of emperors attested earlier see Pliny, *Pan.* 71, 4; 73, 4; 74, 1 and 4; 75; Dio LXXVI, 6, 2 (361); LXXVIII, 8, 3 (411). Cf. *HA, Av. Cass.* 13, 1–5; *Sev. Alex.* 6, 2–12, 1; 56 (*oratio* followed by *acclamationes*).

[76] pp. 410–18.

[77] Dio LXIII, 29, 6; Plutarch, *Galba* 11, 1–2.

[78] Tacitus, *Hist.* II, 55, 2; 69, 1.

[79] Herodian II, 12, 6; *HA, Sept. Sev.* 6, 1–2.

[80] Imperial letters from the frontiers on campaign: e.g. Dio LIV, 9, 1 (Augustus from the East in 20 BC); Suetonius, *Cal.* 44, 2 (Gaius from Gaul); Dio LXVIII, 29, 1 (Trajan from Parthia); LXIX, 14, 3 (Hadrian from Judaea); for Verus' letter from the Parthian war see p. 351. A Republican proconsul to 'the consuls, praetors, tribunes and senate', Cicero, *Ad fam.* XV, 1 and 2 (from Cilicia). Note that Tiberius expected his *legati* to write *de rebus gestis* to the senate, Suetonius, *Tib.* 32, 1.

[81] Dio LXI, 14, 3; 15, 2 (the letter being read in the senate). It was composed by Seneca, Quintilian, *Inst.* VIII, 5, 18. For provincial embassies on this occasion see p. 388.

latter occasion the senate voted to send a congratulatory embassy to him; Gaius rejected some members of it, including his uncle Claudius, but later agreed to receive a larger embassy bringing even greater honours.[82] Senatorial embassies might also go to the emperor on significant imperial occasions, as one went to Severus in Germany, and to his son Caracalla in Pannonia when he was *destinatus* as *Imperator*.[83] Perhaps more commonly it was the convention to send a senatorial embassy to an emperor in the provinces to beseech him to hasten his return to Rome,[84] or to greet him as he approached.[85] Such formal embassies are mainly attested in the earlier period, and must be regarded as suggesting the very rapid delimitation of a distinct position of the emperor as monarch. They may have continued throughout, however, if it is an embassy to which an orator refers when he describes Rome as despatching 'the luminaries of the senate' to the meeting of Diocletian and Maximian at Milan in the winter of 290/1.[86]

From the reign of Augustus onwards emperors also addressed letters to the senate.[87] The mere fact that they did so will not of itself show anything, for proconsuls in the republic had done the same. What is more they used the same standard form of address, 'To the consuls, praetors, tribunes and senate', and followed it with the same greeting, which the proconsuls themselves had taken over and adapted from a formula which had been common in private letters in Greek, and was used on occasion in the letters of Hellenistic kings: 'If you are well, it is well. I too am well.' In late-republican usage the last phrase had expanded to read 'I and the army are well,' and it was this form which characterized imperial letters to the senate.[88] Commodus towards the end of his reign used a different formula, more reminiscent of letters to cities: 'To the consuls, praetors, tribunes and Fortunate Commodian Senate, greeting,'[89] Constantine, as we saw, used the same formula, *salutem dicit*, in the letter of 315 which was *recitata* in the senate before the prefect of the city.[90]

It was actually to the prefect himself, probably Anicius Julianus, in office in 326, that Constantine wrote concerning the obligations of persons who had been nominated it their absence, and before the age of sixteen, to serve as

---

[82] Dio LIX, 23, 1–6; cf. Suetonius, *Claud.* 9, 1. Compare Dio LVIII, 13, 2–3, the embassy sent to Tiberius after the death of Sejanus.

[83] *ILS* 1143.

[84] Porphyrio, Σ Horace, *Carm.* IV, 5 (to Augustus in Spain); Suetonius, *Cal.* 49, 1: 'aditus ergo in itinere a legatis amplissimi ordinis ut maturaret orantibus.'

[85] *AE* 1940, 99, P. Cluvius Maximus Paullinus, 'legato misso a Senatu ad Im[p. H]adrian[um] cum ex Africa reverteretur'.

[86] *Pan.* III(11), 12, 1.

[87] cf. p. 277, and e.g. Seneca, *De brev. vit.* 4, 3 (Augustus on his desire for *otium*).

[88] Versions of this formula are present in C. B. Welles, *Royal Correspondence in the Hellenistic Period* (1934), nos. 56 (Eumenes II), 58, 59, 61 (Attalus II), 71 and 72 (Antiochus VIII or IX). For its use in the correspondence of Roman officials in the republic see Sherk, *Roman Documents*, p. 190, showing that the expansion of the phrase to include the army is a Roman innovation. In the first century BC it appears both in letters to cities, Sherk, nos. 26, (54? Julius Caesar), 28, 58, 60 ('Triumvirs), and to the senate (Cicero, *Ad fam.* XV, 1 and 2). It never appears in imperial letters to cities, but Dio LXIX, 14, 3, makes clear that it was normal when writing to the senate.

[89] Dio LXXII, 15, 5 (297): ὑπάτοις στρατηγοῖς δημάρχοις γερουσίᾳ Κομμοδιανῇ εὐτυχεῖ χαίρειν.

[90] p. 341.

quaestors. The wording makes quite clear that this was in response to a request or motion by the senate, perhaps transmitted by the prefect. Both in that and in the nature of its subject-matter it closely resembles scores of replies which emperors had made in the preceding centuries to cities throughout the empire:[91]

> Persuaded by the dutiful voices of the most magnificent Senate, we have decided that quaestors should enjoy the same privileges as consuls and praetors, namely that, if anyone has been nominated in his absence before the age of sixteen, when his games are given he should in no wise be subject to the obligation of supplying corn, since it is appropriate that this privilege should be granted to the age mentioned.

We can also observe a senatorial request to Constantine in the process which let to the erection of a gilded statue of Amnius Manius Caesonius Nicomachus Anicius Paulinus, prefect of the city in 334-5, 'by the request of the people, the *testimonium* of the senate and the *iudicium* of our lords the *triumphator* Augustus and the flourishing Caesars'.[92] Two centuries before, a public statue in Rome would be voted by the senate on the motion of the emperor.[93]

It is perhaps appropriate that the one and only imperial letter to the senate which we have because (like innumerable letters to cities) it was preserved on an inscription erected in a public place, was written in the last year of Constantine's reign, between September or December 336 and his death in May 337.[94] The text, found in the Forum of Trajan, begins with an extensive version of the names and titles of Constantine and of his four sons, the *nobilissimi Caesares*, and continues in traditional style, with one small but significant difference, 'to the consuls, praetors, *tribuni plebis* and their own senate (*senatui suo*), greeting (*salutem dicunt*). If you and your children are well, it is well. We and our armies are well.' The formula is almost exactly that used by Cicero nearly four centuries before—except for the possessive adjective applied by the emperor to the senate.

Of the content of the letter only enough survives of the first sentence to show that it concerned some honour to a senator named Proculus, usually identified as L. Aradius Valerius Proculus, prefect of the city in 337-8. In this case it is not clear whether the initiative had come from emperor or senate:

> To us, as we recall the family of Proculus, *clarissimus vir*, distinguished for its nobility, and observe his own virtues, which are known from the public and

---

[91] *CTh* VI, 4, 1.

[92] *ILS* 1221; cf. *PLRE* Paulinus 14.

[93] e.g. the accephalous *ILS* 1022: 'Huic senatus auctore imp. Traiano Aug. Germanico Dacico triumphalia ornament(a) decrevit statuamq(ue) pecun(ia) public(a) ponend(am) censuit.' See C. P. Jones, 'Sura and Senecio', *JRS* LX (1970), 98.

[94] R. Paribeni, *Not. d. Scavi* 1933, 489, no. 165 and pl. xiv = *AE* 1934 158. Misdescribed simply as an imperial oration in the senate both by A. Chastagnol, *Les fastes de la Préfecture de Rome au Bas-Empire* (1962), 100, and *PLRE* Proculus 11. Its form is that of a letter. It is not clear on what both works base their view that the inscription relates to a statue.

private *officia* which he has performed, it is easy *patres conscripti*, to conceive that Proculus, *clarissimus vir* [. . .] as much glory as he had received from his forefathers . . .

In the manner of its presentation, its reflection of the large, and even increasing, number of public functions still performed by senators, its emphasis on birth and ancestry, and its heavily ceremonious and courteous language, combined with the relative insignificance of what we can assume to have been its contents, this document may reasonably sum up for us the evolution of the complex, greatly changed, but still significant relations of senate and emperor.

8. *The Emperor in the Priestly Colleges*

'From the fact that they are enrolled in all the priesthoods—and moreover are able to grant most of the priesthoods to others—and that one of them, even if two or three emperors are ruling jointly, is Pontifex Maximus, they control all sacred and religious matters.'[1] Dio's summary relates to almost the whole period covered from Augustus to his own time, and would not be wholly inapplicable even to the reign of Constantine. Augustus himself had solemnly recorded in the *Res Gestae* that he was Pontifex Maximus, Augur, Quindecimvir Sacris Faciundis, Septemvir Epulonum, Frater Arvalis, Sodalis Titius and Fetialis.[2] From AD 14 onwards subsequent emperors, and the more prominent members of their families, also joined the *sodalitates* which conducted the worship of their deified predecessors. The emperor performed within these privileged groups many functions analogous to those which he fulfilled in relation to the senate as a whole: the exercise of patronage, the conduct of business along with notionally equal colleagues, and the issuing of decisions which affected individuals or groups in the population at large; moreover, here too we can observe an absorption of collective functions by the emperor himself, and finally a progressive detachment from them.

The priesthoods were from the beginning a significant medium of imperial patronage. Velleius Paterculus, writing under Tiberius, notes indignantly the Jullus Antonius, exiled for adultery with Augustus' daughter Julia, had been honoured by him with a priesthood, a praetorship, a consulship and the government of provinces.[3] Fairly soon, the priesthoods, which were held for life and restricted to relatively small numbers, in principle sixteen each for the pontifices proper, the augurs and (in spite of the name) the quindecim-

---

[1] Dio LIII, 17, 8. For the role of the emperor as Pontifex Maximus and as one of the *sacerdotes publici populi Romani*, see Mommsen, *Staatsrecht*[3] II. 2, 1102f., and more generally G. Wissowa, *Religion und Kultus der Romer*[2] (1912), 479f.; cf. M. W. H. Lewis, *The Official Priests of Rome under the Julio-Claudians* (1955). It goes without saying that all that is attempted here is to pick out a few aspects of this role which relate to the main themes of this work.

[2] *RG* 7, 3.

[3] II. 100, 4: 'quem victo eius patre non tantum incolumitate donaverat, sed sacerdotio, praetura, consulatu, provinciis honoratum, etiam matrimonio sororis suae filiae in artissimam adfinitatem receperat.' See *PIR*[2] A 800.

viri, came to be even more highly regarded than temporary magistracies or posts. So, as we saw, Seneca in the *De ira* represents co-optation into a college of priests, or preferably more than one, as the most which the emperor could offer to complete a man's *dignitas*.[4]

A man could in fact hold more than one priesthood, as did Galba, who after being proconsul of Africa for two years in the 40s, 'received *ornamenta triumphalia* and a triple priesthood, being co-opted among the Quindecimviri, the Sodales Titii and the Sodales Augustales'.[5] But until the early third century no private person could hold more than one of the four major priesthoods; co-optation in the case of these and the less important colleges, the *fratres Arvales* and the various *sodalitates*, meant a relatively simple procedure of effective co-optation by the members themselves.

It is in these cases, particularly that of the Fratres Arvales, an ancient fraternity, revived under Augustus, which was essentially concerned with sacrifices and prayers for the fertility of the land, that we can see most clearly the forms in which imperial patronage was exerted. Indeed it is precisely the extensive inscribed records of the fraternity which preserve the most formal surviving description of an imperial letter. The procedure is clearest in the case of a co-optation carried out on the seventh of February 120:[6]

> In the vestibule of the temple of Concord after a solemn prayer had been uttered by the *magister*, C. Vitorius Hosidius Geta, they co-opted P. Manlius Carbo as a Frater Arvalis in place of Q. Bittius Proculus on the basis of a letter of Imperator Caesar Traianus Hadrianus, son of Divus Traianus Parthicus, grandson of Divus Nerva, and summoned him to the rites; and there were opened there the tablets sealed with the seal which shows the head of Augustus, in which was written:
> Imperator Caesar Traianus Hadrianus Augustus to the Fratres Arvales, his colleagues, greeting. By my vote I co-opt P. Manlius Carbo as a colleague for us in place of Q. Bittius Proculus.

It is clear from the records that the emperor did not always put forward a candidate. But if he chose to do so he was not prevented by absence from Rome. A co-optation had already been made in February 118 on the basis of *litterae* from Hadrian, who at that time had not yet reached Rome from Cilicia, where he was proclaimed in 117.[7] The point is of some significance, for it shows that the emperor's preoccupations elsewhere, while they must have assisted his dissociation from the colleges in Rome, need not have produced this effect directly and immediately. Caracalla had probably already left Rome for his German expedition of 213 when on 5 May one of the *sodalitates* co-opted L. Egnatius Victor Lollianus on the basis of *litterae* from him.[8] In the *sodalitates* also the emperor did not nominate all the candi-

---

[4] p. 299.
[5] Suetonius, *Galba* 8, 1.
[6] *CIL* VI 2080, ll. 22–6; cf. W. Henzen, *Acta Fratrum Arvalium* (1874), 153, for some parallel records from other years. For the *signum* with the head of Augustus see p. 213.
[7] *CIL* VI 2078 = 32374 = *ILS* 5028.
[8] *CIL* VI 2001; on 20 May the Fratres Arvales were already acclaiming the emperor in advance as 'Germanicus', VI 2086.

dates, for an inscription mentions explicitly that one senator was made a Sodalis Flavialis Titialis by the *iudicium* of Septimius Severus.[9]

With the four major colleges the procedure was much more complex, but places within them could still be regarded as being in the emperor's gift. Tacitus records that immediately after his consulate Agricola 'was made governor of Britain, with a priesthood as Pontifex added';[10] and, as we saw, Pliny descends to his most sycophantic in imploring Trajan for an augurate or septemvirate. It was in fact the augurate which he obtained, and in replying to the congratulations of a friend treats it explicitly as a sign ef the favourable judgment (*iudicium*) of the emperor. In the same letter, however, he refers to the fact that on the day of *nominatio* Julius Frontinus had always put him forward for a priesthood, and elsewhere that Verginius Rufus had done the same.[11] The procedure under the empire was that nominations were made by members of the colleges, but that the effective election, like those for magistracies, had been withdrawn in AD 14 from the assembly (or rather seventeen of the tribes chosen by lot) to the senate. A formal election still took place in the assembly,[12] and the process was completed by the ceremony of co-optation into the college. In recording that Claudius always made his nominations in the colleges on oath, Suetonius seems to imply that he would be present in person to do so;[13] but the emperor might also move the granting of priesthoods in the senate.[14] In either case it is clear that his nomination or recommendation was regarded as being itself the award of a priesthood. As with magistracies below the consulate, we cannot tell what proportion of the places was filled by imperial patronage, though Dio implies that the majority were. From his time, the early third century, we find men holding more than one of the major priesthoods,[15] and in the first half of the fourth some men held as many as three.[16] There is no further evidence from within the period for the emperors making nominations to these priesthoods; but the fact that Constantius did so in 357, strongly suggests that the practice continued unbroken.[16a]

All these priesthoods involved the emperor, if present, in performing various rituals along with his colleagues. Two of them furthermore, those as Pontifex Maximus and as Quindecimvir Sacris Facundis, involved decisions and pronouncements which might affect the public at large. The primary duty of the Quindecimviri was the consultation of the Sibylline books, which from Augustus' time onwards were kept in the temple of Apollo on the

---

[9] *ILS* 1143. Cf. the *acta* of an unidentified priesthood, in *CIL* VI 2004, where one cooptation is made *ex litteris* (evidently of the emperor) and three previous ones (in 190, 198 and 200) without.

[10] *Agric.* 9, 6.

[11] Pliny, *Ep.* X, 13; cf. p. 278; IV, 8; II, 1, 8.

[12] e.g. *CIL* VI 2051, l. 70 = *ILS* 241, a sacrifice 'ob comitia sacerdotior(um) Imp. O[t]honis Aug.' on 5 March 69. Galba had been killed on 15 January. The *comitia* for his Pontificatus Maximus followed on 9 March, ibid., l. 74.

[13] *Claud.* 22: 'in cooptandis per collegia sacerdotibus neminem nisi iuratus nominavit.'

[14] e.g. Tacitus, *Ann.* III, 19, 1.

[15] The earliest case is C. Octavius Appius Suetrius Sabinus, consul in 214, who was Pontifex and Augur, *ILS* 1159, see Barbieri, *Albo senatorio*, no. 387.

[16] *ILS* 1231; 1240 (L. Aradius Valerius Proculus, cf. p. 354).

[16a] Symmachus, *Rel.* III, 7.

Palatine. It was presumably they who were the 'certain senators' whom Lactantius describes Maxentius summoning and ordering to consult the books, as
Constantine's army drew near in 312.[17] As a by-product of this duty, they
had the function of declaring from time to time that Secular Games should
be held, and of making arrangements for them. The inscribed *commentarii*
of the *ludi saeculares* in 17 BC begin with the fragments of what is evidently
a letter of Augustus to the other Quindecimviri, followed by their edict, and
then the remains of a complete record of the proceedings, including several
further edicts. Where the members of the college are listed, Augustus and
Agrippa come first, but are not otherwise distinguished from their
colleagues.[18]

The surviving records of the Secular Games held in 204 under Septimius
Severus (supposedly the seventh in the series) begin with the text of a short
oration read by the *magister* of the college and containing frequent references
to Severus and Caracalla,[19] and also reproduce the text of two brief imperial
letters about the arrangements addressed to 'the Quindecimviri, their
colleagues' (and ending in a version of the now conventional style 'Farewell,
colleagues, dearest to us'). Severus and Caracalla were present with their
colleagues when lots were drawn to see at what points in the city *suffimenta*
(incense) should be distributed to the populace. The edict was however
issued in the names of Severus and Caracalla (and possibly Geta), though
the phrase 'with the other Quindecimviri' may have appeared also. From a
further fragment it is clear that the emperors and their colleagues sacrificed
together, as indeed Zosimus indicates that they did in his excursus on the
Secular Games.[20]

The functions of the Quindecimviri could however extend beyond ritual
and also outside Rome itself. An inscription found at Circeii, and perhaps
originally from Terracina, shows the *promagister* restoring an altar of Circe
'on the authority' of Caracalla and 'by the decree of the college of the
XV sac(ris) fac(iundis)'; at the moment of the dedication, 15 June 213,
Caracalla was certainly absent on his German campaign, but he might have
been in Rome when the decision was taken.[21] In 289, however, an inscription
from Baiae shows the college acting quite independently of the emperors
(Diocletian was currently fighting the Sarmatians, and Maximian was in
Gaul). The *promagister* of the college gives his *subscriptio* to a letter of the
Quindecimviri permitting the magistrates of Cumae to allow a newly elected
priest of the Mother of the Gods to wear an armlet and crown, provided that
it was within the territory of the city.[22] We have no means of knowing how
common such decisions or consultations were, whether they extended

---

[17] *De mort. pers.* 44, 8; Zosimus II, 16, 1. Lactantius knew that the duty was confined to the
Quindecimviri, *Inst.* 1, 6, 13.

[18] *CIL* VI 32323; cf. G. B. Pighi, *De ludis saecularibus* (1941), 107f.; for the letter of Augustus
see also H. Malcovati, *Imperatoris Caesaris Augusti Operum Fragmenta*[5] (1969), *Ep.* LXXI.

[19] *CIL* VI 32326–35; cf. Pighi, o.c., 137f. The letters of Severus and Caracalla are in 32327,
ll. 1–6.

[20] VI 32329, l. 8; Zosimus II, 5, 3.

[21] *ILS* 4037.

[22] *ILS* 4175.

outside the cities of Latium and Campania, or to what degree they at any time involved the emperor.

As Pontifex Maximus, the emperor was necessarily engaged in a significantly wider range of decisions; for the solution of points of sacred law, relating to rituals, temples or sacred places, had always been a primary function of the Pontifices—who are presumed, though there is no direct evidence, to have met under the presidency of the Pontifex Maximus. The emperor could also, if he chose, address himself to the people in his capacity as Pontifex Maximus, as when Claudius conducted from the rostra the supplication necessary after the sighting of a bird of ill-omen;[23] he could also issue edicts, as did Vitellius on assuming the office—but he thereby showed his ignorance by giving as the day for the formal ceremony of election the anniversary of two famous disasters in the early republic.[24] He might also appear as the spokesman of his colleagues, as when Tiberius read out in the senate the *decretum* of the Pontifices concerning a question which had been raised about the restrictions imposed on the Flamen Dialis.[25]

It was the custom for the emperor to summon his pontifical colleagues for consultation at the Regia, the 'royal house' on the Via Sacra, traditionally supposed to have been built by King Numa, and throughout the republic the official place of business of the Pontifex Maximus. This is clear from Pliny's reference to Domitian's procedure in condemning a Vestal Virgin to be buried alive for breaking her vow of chastity: 'By the rights of the Pontifex Maximus, or rather the cruelty of a tyrant, the licence of a master, he called together the other Pontifices not to the Regia but to the Alban villa.'[26] This is the only occasion attested in the empire when the Pontifices carried out a condemnation and sentence (though both Pliny and Suetonius treat it as in reality an action of the emperor himself).[27] But the fact that it was the custom to consult them on matters of sacral law is expressly stated by Pliny in writing to Trajan. His letter is noteworthy in relating to an area where we can trace the simultaneous extension of the principles of Roman law and of the personal role of the emperor:

> As certain persons are petitioning me that I should follow the example of the proconsuls and permit them to move the remains of relatives of theirs, either because of damage caused by decay, the inflow of a river or other such reasons, because I knew that in the City it is the custom in such a case to approach the college of Pontifices, I thought that I should consult you, lord, as Pontifex Maximus, as to what rule you wish me to follow.

[23] Suetonius, *Claud.* 22.

[24] Tacitus, *Hist.* II, 91, 1; Suetonius, *Vit.* 11, 2. In the first century the date of formal election as Pontifex Maximus was separate from, and later than, the *dies imperii*. See Mommsen, *Staatsrecht*[3] II. 2, 1107.

[25] Tacitus, *Ann.* III, 71, 2; for the question, III, 58,1–59,1. It is not clear whether the further speech of Tiberius on this question, IV, 16, was or was not based on consultation of the other Pontifices.

[26] *Ep.* IV, 11, 6. On the Regia see Platner-Ashby, *Topographical Dictionary of Ancient Rome* (1927), 440–3; on the Alban villa, see p. 26.

[27] cf. *Dom.* 8, 4.

Trajan replies, not entirely to the point, that it would be harsh to impose on provincials the need to consult the Pontifices, and says that local custom should be followed.[28] By Roman law any places in Italy where bodies were buried became not *sacra* (which applied only to places sanctified by a law or *senatus consultum*), but *religiosa*, and could not be disturbed for transference of the bodies, or even for repair, without recourse to the Pontifices and the carrying out of a sacrifice of expiation (*piaculum*). It is indeed precisely in the context of the making or preservation of tombs that the activity of the Pontifices is best attested in the imperial period, primarily by inscriptions of the second or third century from Rome.[29] One substantial inscription of 155 contains a letter of a Pontifex, Velius Fidus, to the *promagister* of the *collegium*, Juventius Celsus, enclosing the *libellus* in which an imperial freedman petitions (evidently to Velius Fidus in the first instance) for permission to move the bodies of his wife and son from a clay sarcophagus to a marble one which he has just bought. Permission was decreed, and the *libellus* 'subscribed' by the *promagister*.[30]

On occasion the same role of the Pontifices is reflected on inscriptions from Italian cities.[31] It might also apply when a person's remains were brought from a province to Rome. Thirteen years after his death, just after that of the emperor, at Selinus in Cilicia, the bones of M. Ulpius Phaedimus, the freedman and favourite of Trajan, were transferred to Rome by permission of the college of Pontifices.[32] Those of another freedman of Trajan were brought from Ampelum in Dacia, but this time 'by the *indulgentia* of our Augustus'.[33] Similarly, the bones of the imperial freedman *proximus a libris sacerdotalibus* who died at Carnuntum, presumably while Marcus Aurelius was there, were taken by his wife to Rome by permission of the emperor.[34]

According to Gaius, writing in the middle of the second century, provincial land could not be *religiosum*, but even so was now regarded as *pro religioso*, that is subject in practice to the same rules.[35] We find this notion reflected in the inscription from Thubursicu Numidarum of a young man who died, perhaps in the third century, as a student in Carthage, and whose remains were brought home 'by permission of the governor'.[36]

In the early third century Ulpian still says on one occasion that it was the duty of the Pontifices to determine how far repairs could be carried out in a *locus religiosus*, but on another that it was a disputed question whether the owner of a property had the right to dig up a body placed there by someone

---

[28] *Ep.* x, 68–9; cf. Sherwin-White ad loc.

[29] e.g. *CIL* vi 8875 (a freedman of Trajan and others); *AE* 1909 92 (petition to Pontifices for permission to repair a tomb); *ILS* 8382–3; *AE* 1926 48; cases to be brought before the Pontifices, and in some cases fines payable to them, *ILS* 7947; 8226–9; 8282; 8386; 8392.

[30] *ILS* 8380. It is often deduced from the use of the expression 'domine' in the text of the *libellus* that it was addressed to the emperor. But the context suggests strongly that it had been directed to Velius Fidus.

[31] *ILS* 8110 (Beneventum); 8381 (Tarracina); 8390 (Sabine territory).

[32] *ILS* 1792; cf. pp. 67, 263.

[33] *ILS* 1593.

[34] *ILS* 1685. Cf. p. 259.

[35] *Inst.* II, 7.

[36] *ILS* 7742a. Cf. A. Merlin, *MEFR* XXIII (1903), 117.

else, unless he had a *decretum* of the Pontifices or an order from the emperor.[37] We cannot tell how long the Pontifices continued to give rulings on questions of sacred law; they may well have done so beyond the end of our period. But what is made quite clear by various *subscriptiones* of the third century is that by then the emperor in person was giving answers on such questions to individuals, including individuals living in the provinces. Caracalla, for instance, replies to a woman named Dionysia in 213: 'If the remains of your son are being disturbed by the force of a river, or some other proper and necessary cause has intervened, you may by the judgment of the governor of the province transfer them to another place.'[38] Similarly, various third-century emperors issued *subscriptiones* addressed to individuals, to the effect that tombs could not be the subject of normal legal claims and transactions.[39] On a different aspect of religious law, Diocletian and Maximian gave a less strict interpretation than had prevailed in the past on the moving of corpses: in a *subscriptio* of 287, in reply to a woman named Aquilina, they wrote: 'If the body has not yet been committed to its permanent tomb, you are not prohibited from transferring it.'[40]

Such *subscriptiones* offer a clear illustration of how the emperor emerged from his role within a corporate institution of the *res publica* to perform, in the area of sacred law as in so many others, the very different role of answering the individual queries and petitions of his subjects. In the process he thus detached himself from the body of Pontifices (a fact which is perhaps already reflected in two letters addressed to the Pontifices by Antoninus Pius, and giving rulings on legal points)[41] and also came to respond to needs on the part of individuals which may seem at first sight insignificant to us, but were clearly not so to them.

It was thus in this instance the collective institutions of the Republic which constituted the setting from which the emperor came to give responses on a range of matters which we would not necessarily expect to have required the personal attention of a head of state. The fact is of some significance for how the Roman emperor came to be what he was. But we should not exaggerate the importance of this particular function and its specifically Roman background. For, as we shall see, it was precisely in the related areas of petitions and requests concerning the rights and privileges of temples and priests, of religious and artistic festivals and associations, that we have the most specific testimony to the inheritance by the emperor of roles performed by the Hellenistic kings.

---

[37] *Dig.* XI, 8, 5, 1; XI, 7, 8 *pr.* (For a *subscriptio* of Caracalla on precisely this point, see *CJ* III, 44, 2.) Compare Papinian's view in *Dig.* V, 3, 50, 1, that heirs were not bound *stricto iure* to erect a tomb if so instructed by the testator—'tamen principali vel pontificali auctoritate compelluntur ad obsequium supremae voluntatis.' For Severus Alexander doing exactly this in a *subscriptio*, see *CJ* III, 44, 5.

[38] *CJ* III, 44, 1.

[39] *CJ* VIII, 16, 3 (Caracalla, 215); III, 44, 4 and 6 (Severus Alexander, 223 and 224); 44, 8–9 (Philip, 244, 245); 44, 13 (Diocletian and Maximian, 294).

[40] III, 44, 10.

[41] Gaius, *Inst.* I, 102: ex epistula . . . imperatoris Antonini, quam scripsit pontificibus' (on adoption); *Dig.* XXXVIII, 16, 3, 12 (Ulpian): 'de eo autem, qui centesimo octogesimo secundo die natus est, Hippocrates scripsit et divus Pius pontificibus rescripsit iusto tempore videri natum.'

VII

Cities, Provincial Councils and Associations

1. *Introduction*

In his *Responsa*, written in the first half of the third century, the jurist Herennius Modestinus preserves an attractive example of the type of legal problem which might arise in the empire:[1]

> Titius, who was in Rome for the sake of his studies, was sent a letter by the magistrates of his native city, in order that he should hand to the emperor the decree of the city, which was sent with it. But the man who had undertaken to deliver the letter acted in collusion with Lucius Titius, who was also in Rome on his own business, and gave it to him; and he, removing the name of Titius, to whom the decree had been sent for delivery to the emperor, substituted his own name and thus gave it to the emperor in accordance with the instructions of the city. My question is, who was entitled to reclaim his travelling-expenses (*viaticum*) from the city?

These precise circumstances, which seem to represent an imaginary example designed to raise problems in relation to existing law and custom, clearly constitute a variant on the standard procedure, by which a formal embassy would have travelled to Rome to present the decree. As we shall see, the question of who was entitled to the *viaticum* of an ambassador, or had promised to go at his own expense, finds innumerable reflections in the legal and inscriptional evidence from the empire; and so too, in legal works, does the question of the protection of *legati*, from the imposition of obligations or the bringing of civil or criminal actions during their absence.

The significance of the legal evidence is precisely that it represents absence on an embassy as a normal, or at least a common and recurrent, state of affairs. The despatch of embassies was in part a product of the fact that, unless the decree of a city (like the *libellus* of an individual) was sent on by a provincial governor,[2] there was no alternative to its being brought by the representatives of the city themselves. Even in Modestinus' case, where for some reason an actual embassy is avoided, it is quite clear that none of the three persons involved is a mere employee of the city. On the contrary, they are clearly persons of standing, who may go to Rome for study or for their own business, and thus act in place of an embassy proper. The student

[1] *Dig.* L, I, 36.
[2] See p. 217.

himself can only have been a young man who had gone to Rome to study law, or to hear one or other of the holders of the chairs of Greek or Latin oratory established by Vespasian;[3] and it could not have been expected that he would hand over the decree without at least a brief accompanying oration.

It is a fact which is so obvious that it is not normally taken sufficiently into account, that no information or request could reach the emperor unless either a written missive were physically brought to him or he were addressed verbally (or, as in many cases, both). Letters sent by provincial governors, other officials, or exceptionally privileged private persons could be carried by messengers, but otherwise any form of communication to the emperor necessitated a journey by the interested parties to wherever he currently was. The process thus involved journeys of anything up to a couple of thousand miles, and delays in time which could amount to weeks or months. None the less, precisely because it is a commonplace in modern writing about the ancient world that travel was slow, arduous and hazardous, it is important to emphasize not merely that such journeys to the emperor were in fact frequently undertaken, but that they were, in a number of different contexts, a standard and accepted part of the way the empire worked.

Moreover, although inscriptions reveal occasional instances of men who died in Rome in the course of embassies,[4] and the two well-known cases of Josephus and Paul show men enduring shipwreck while either going on a mission, or being sent, to the emperor,[5] our extensive evidence contains remarkably few allusions to the rigours of the journeys involved. On the contrary, what is emphasized is either the expense, whether to the city or the individual, or the strain incurred by having to address oneself to the emperor in person.[6]

Travel, however arduous, was a fundamental feature of ancient society, and in this period above all travel to Rome itself. The presence there at any one time of large numbers of persons from other parts of the empire and even beyond it, both on embassies and on their own private business, was a literary commonplace, particularly in the first century, As Seneca wrote in trying to console his mother over his exile, many of the immense crowd of persons in Rome were away from their native cities:[7]

They have gathered from their *municipia* and *coloniae*, in short from all over the globe. Some have been brought by ambition, others by the requirements of some public office, others by an embassy imposed on them, others by self-indulgence seeking a ready and fertile field for vice, others by the pursuit of liberal studies, others by the shows.

---

[3] For students of law in Rome see *Frag. Vat.* 204; for the chairs of oratory, pp. 502–3; and for students of *litterae*, *Epit. Cod. Greg. Wisig.* III, 10 (from 230).

[4] *ILS* 7026, a decurion of Lugdunum 'Romae in legatione defuncto'; 7115, a decurion of Virunum (Noricum) 'defuncto Romae in legatione'.

[5] Josephus, *Vita* 3/14–16; *Acts* 27,1–28,16.

[6] pp. 382–5; *CIL* VIII 20758, on a man from Mauretania who died while attempting to gain relief from tribute for his native community, does refer to the toils of the journey.

[7] *Ad Helviam matrem de consolatione* 6, 2.

Tacitus turns the commonplace to account in describing the reactions to Nero's theatrical performances on the part of those 'who from remote *municipia* in Italy which still retained its severe and ancient ways, or who in their distant provinces were unaccustomed to licence, had been brought by the duties of embassies or by private advantage'.[8] That the crowds which attended the shows and spectacles of Rome were made up partly of persons who had come from other parts of the empire is clear enough. The performing elephants put on by Germanicus at his consular games in AD 12 achieved a lasting fame; for instance the main speaker in Philo's dialogue *Alexander* mentions them, and also records beast-fights which he saw when he went to Rome on an embassy, evidently from Alexandria.[9] Similarly, the seventh eclogue of Calpurnius Siculus, dating from Nero's reign, is a dialogue between two countrymen, one of whom gives an ecstatic description of attending the shows in Rome, ending with a mention of having seen the emperor from afar;[10] and again Florus' essay, *Vergil, orator or poet?*, is a dialogue between some persons returning to Baetica from the *certamen Capitolinum* held in Rome before Domitian, and Florus himself who had been a victor in the contest, and whom they meet when blown off course to Africa; one of the Baeticans attests that the crown for poetry would have been awarded to Florus by the applause of the crowd, but for the emperor's reluctance.[11]

It is important to stress that the shows and contests of various types in Rome were not only an attraction in themselves, but provided the most clearly-established type of occasion actually to see the emperor, even if from some distance, and if necessary to make demands of him. Herodian, for instance, records that heralds were sent throughout Italy summoning people to Septimius Severus' Secular Games in 204.[12] But in fact people came from further than that, and an epitaph from Rome commemorates a man who died there after coming from Tripolis in Asia 'to see the contest presided over by the emperor Severus'.[13]

Thus not only could the vast imperial expenditure on buildings in Rome and on shows there be enjoyed by visitors as well as the inhabitants of the city, but these same visitors could, like the inhabitants, use the opportunity of the emperor's public appearances there—most obviously, but not only, at the circus or the theatre—to press demands and complaints on him. That may explain in part why, as we shall see, the demands which the populace

[8] *Ann.* XVI, 5, 1.

[9] Philo, *Ad Lysimachum: de animalibus adversus Alexandrum* (Latin trans. from Armenian by J. B. Aucher, 1822), p. 137 (elephants), 152 (embassy). See E. G. Turner on *P. Oxy.* 2435, l. 41. For other references to Germanicus' elephants, Pliny, *NH* VIII, 2/4–5; Aelian, *De natura anim.* II, 11.

[10] *Ecl.* VII, esp. 82–5: 'utcumque tamen conspeximus ipsum / longius; ac, nisi me visus decepit, in uno / et Martis vultus et Apollinis esse putatur.'

[11] *Vergilius, orator an poeta* 1, 1–9.

[12] III, 8, 9–10. Cf. Suetonius, *Claud.* 17, 3, Claudius permitting even provincial governors and exiles to come to his triumphal games in 44; and Herodian I, 15, 1, people coming from Italy and neighbouring provinces to see Commodus perform as a gladiator.

[13] *CIG* 5921–2 = Kaibel, *Epig.* 920 = *IG* XIV 1092–3 = *IGR* I 167–8. See L. Robert, *Hellenica* XI/XII (1960), 11–14: προλιπὼν Ἀσίας Τρίπολιν πατρίδαν πόλιν ἁγνήν, ἔνθαδε ἦλθα ἀγῶνα ἰδεῖν προκαθεζομένου βασιλεύοντι Σεβήρῳ [sic].

voiced in the mass in Rome sometimes related to wider issues which affected the whole population of the empire.

In origin, of course, the role of the Roman people had been something far beyond what was conferred by the fact that their physical presence gave them a direct relationship to the emperor which was only available rarely and by chance to city populations elsewhere. For in the beginning the popular assemblies, in which in principle all citizens could take part, still passed laws and elected magistrates and priests: Augustus records that when he was elected Pontifex Maximus in 12 BC such a crowd gathered from Italy for the electoral assembly as had never been known before.[14] But while electoral assemblies continued in form at least up to the third century,[15] the technical term *lex*, implying a law passed by the people, is not used of any measure passed after the end of the first[16]—and it is far from clear whether genuine legislative assemblies lasted even as long as that.

None the less, so long as the emperor remained in principle based in Rome, and in fact returned there when not required elsewhere, it was a significant part of his role to appear before the people there, to respond to the demands which they voiced in the mass, and to address speeches to them. It is in this area perhaps more clearly than in any other that we can observe the primary importance of purely verbal exchanges in the pattern of contacts between the emperor and his subjects.

Before the end of our period, however, the emperors had ceased to make more than occasional visits to Rome; one such visit was that made by Diocletian in 303 to celebrate his *vicennalia*, and Lactantius says that he left immediately after the conclusion of the ceremonies because he could not support the *libertas* of the Roman people.[17] Maxentius, between 306 and 312, was the last emperor to reside continuously in Rome, but Lactantius reports that he too, when giving circus games to celebrate his birthday in 312, was confronted with the shouts of the people that Constantine could not be defeated.[18] When games were given after the victory, so an orator addressing Constantine in 313 avers, the people could not take their eyes from the emperor, and were pleased by the performances only because they were given in his presence.[19]

From the beginning of the empire the travels of the emperors through the provinces meant that a similarly direct relationship could on occasion arise between the population of a provincial city and an emperor who was staying there. Shows might be given either by or in the presence of the emperor when he visited a city,[20] and on occasion he might address the people in person, as Octavian did in Alexandria in 30 BC, and Germanicus in AD 19; a papyrus records the text of part of his speech, punctuated by the acclamations of the

[14] *RG* 10, 2.
[15] p. 302.
[16] The latest measure of which it is used is the *Lex agraria* passed by Nerva, referred to only in *Dig.* XLVII, 21, 3, 1.
[17] *De mort. pers.* 17, 1–3.
[18] ibid., 44, 7.
[19] *Pan.* IX(12), 19, 6.
[20] p. 36.

people.[21] In 67 Nero addressed the assembled people of Greece at the Isthmus of Corinth, and granted them their freedom,[22] and in 69, when Vespasian was proclaimed, almost his first action was to make a speech in Greek to the people of Antioch assembled in the theatre.[23] In the following year, as we saw earlier, the Antiochenes petitioned Titus for the removal of the rights of the Jewish community there, and his reply refusing the request was again made verbally in the theatre.[24]

Such public exchanges may have become more common when certain provincial cities gradually became marked out as imperial centres; but specific evidence seems to be lacking, unless we include a confused story in Malalas of how the populace of Antioch abused an emperor of the tetrarchic period in the hippodrome because he had not made a distribution of cash in recognition of having been proclaimed there; in consequence, so it is said, he turned the soldiers on them, and two thousand were killed.[25] Less public hearings, when leading citizens of a city where the emperor was in residence presented formal requests to him, as to Constantine at Autun in 311 or to Maximin at Nicomedia in the same year,[26] are better considered along with embassies proper. For the emperor's presence in the city, though it facilitated such requests, was not absolutely essential to them, as it was for a confrontation with the people in the mass.

Such occasional confrontations and imperial orations to city populations in the provinces do not compare in importance with his complex relationship to the populace of Rome, a relationship which served both as one quite significant channel for the expression to the emperor of popular wishes, and as a vehicle for the display of the emperor's character and attitudes. As soon, however, as we look beyond this particular relationship, we necessarily find that all the other groups in the empire with whom the emperor had relations were formally structured bodies—primarily cities, but also provincial councils, and the 'oecumenical synods' of performers and athletes who took part in the festivals, games, and contests of the Greek world. Such bodies necessarily communicated with the emperor from a distance, and did so essentially by passing decrees and sending ambassadors to present them to the emperor with an appropriate oration. It is important to emphasize both the sheer volume of such embassies, which might concern anything from matters of pure diplomacy and formality to important local disputes and accusations, and the extent to which this pattern of communication simply disregarded problems of distance and time. It took no account either of whether the emperor was in Rome or somewhere in the provinces; as Severus and Caracalla replied in a *subscriptio*, 'Those who have served on an embassy

---

[21] On Octavian's speech in Alexandria see p. 9; for Germanicus', *P. Oxy.* 2435 *recto*.

[22] pp. 204, 430.

[23] Tacitus, *Hist.* II, 80, 2. Note that papyrus fragments preserve what seem to be the remains both of a speech addressed to Vespasian in Alexandria in the winter of 69/70 (*P. Fouad 8* = Musurillo, *Acts of the Pagan Martyrs*, VB) and of one by him addressed to the people (*SB* 9528).

[24] p. 37.

[25] Malalas, *Chron.* XII, p. 314 Bonn.

[26] pp. 424–5, 445.

are granted relief for two years; nor is it material whether the embassy was commissioned to go to us in the city or when busy in a province.'[27]

Moreover, the selection and despatch of ambassadors to the emperor was not only something which was among the significant corporate functions of cities, leagues and associations, or which was necessary in order to obtain from successive emperors the preservation of their rights and statuses. But rather the sending of embassies could itself be an implicit claim to, and expression of, a particular status. This is made clear above all in what Libanius says about the city of Emesa in Syria.[28] Few passages tell us so much about that local pride which was the essential element in the structure of the empire, or the pattern of diplomatic contacts which linked the cities to the emperor: 'Emesa still sends ambassadors and gold crowns to the kings, conscious indeed of her poverty, but ashamed none the less to drop out of the ranks of the cities.'

2. *The People of Rome and the Emperor*

In a well-known passage Cicero lists three types of occasion on which the judgment and wishes of the Roman people could best be assessed: in a *contio*—an informal meeting called and addressed by a magistrate—the assemblies, and when they gathered to see games (*ludi*) or gladiators.[1] Of these, the second at least played no significant role in the empire after the reign of Augustus. Though, as we saw, the electoral assemblies took place at least until the early third century,[2] from AD 14 onwards their business was purely formal, and it is unlikely either that many persons attended or that the emperor was often present in person. Trajan certainly presided as consul in 100, but the very emphasis which Pliny in the *Panegyric* places on his endurance of 'that long ritual of the elections' suggests that this was unusual.[3] Nor, though some laws may have been passed by the *comitia* up to the end of the first century, do such assemblies find a single reflection in our sources which would suggest that they were events of any significance.[4]

Contiones may perhaps be another matter, for as we saw, Fronto gives them a surprising prominence among the occasions on which imperial *eloquentia* was required—'to address the people on very many matters in public meetings'.[5] It must be confessed that the evidence for orations addressed by emperors to the people of Rome is slight; yet they continued

---

[27] *Dig.* L, 7, 9, 1.

[28] *Ep.* 846 Foerster (AD 388): ἔτι πρέσβεις Ἔμεσα πέμπει καὶ στεφάνους βασιλεῦσιν, εἰδυῖα μὲν τὴν ἑαυτῆς πενίαν, αἰσχυνομένη δὲ ὅμως τοῦ τῶν πόλεων ἐκπεσεῖν ἀριθμοῦ. See H. Seyrig, 'Caractères de l'histoire d'Émèse', *Syria* XXXVI (1959), 184. On the despatch of gold crowns to the emperor, see pp. 140–2.

[1] *Pro Sestio* 50/106, cf. 58/124.

[2] p. 302.

[3] *Pan.* 63, 2: 'perpessus es longum illud carmen comitiorum'; cf. 92, 3.

[4] Note however that Josephus, *Ant.* XIX, 1, 20 (158), states that after the murder of Gaius the people assembled in the forum where they were accustomed to meet—καὶ ὁ δῆμος ᾗπερ καὶ εἰώθασιν ἐκκλησιάζειν ἐπὶ τῆς ἀγορᾶς καταστάς.

[5] p. 203.

even after our period, for when Constantius made his famous visit to Rome in 357 he 'addressed the *nobilitas* in the senate-house and the populace from the tribunal'.[6] From our period, if we except funeral orations such as that of Tiberius for Augustus, Gaius for Tiberius, or Severus for Pertinax,[7] the recorded orations took place either on an emperor's first arrival in Rome, as with Vitellius in 69,[8] or on his return after a long absence, as with Marcus Aurelius in 176,[9] or in an extreme crisis, as with the speech which Nero prepared in 68 and had ready in his *scrinium* but had not the courage to deliver.[10] The routine addresses to the people to which Fronto seems to be referring are not clearly attested.[11]

With the confrontation of the emperor and the people as assembled in the Circus Maximus for chariot- or horse-races, in the amphitheatre (Colosseum) for gladiatorial shows, or wild-beast hunts, or in the theatres, the case is of course quite different, as it is also with the Greek-style athletic, literary and musical contests introduced in the imperial period, beginning with the short-lived *Neroneia* and developing from Domitian's *certamen Capitolinum*.[12] The construction of buildings for these various types of public shows, the maintenance of schools of gladiators and of *pantomimi*, the acquisition and display of exotic beasts all counted among the most prominent forms of imperial *liberalitas*.[13] We need only think of the long list of his shows which Augustus gives in the *Res Gestae*—gladiatorial displays involving some 10,000 men in all, two athletic contests, *ludi*, and especially the *ludi saeculares* of 17 BC, wild-beast hunts (*venationes*) in which some 3,500 animals were killed, and a mock naval battle with thirty ships and 3,000 men.[14]

The use made of these occasions for mass demonstrations and the expression of popular demands is also a familiar feature of imperial history.[15] That being so, we can concentrate on a specific aspect, the actual forms of communication between the people—or those of them who were present in the Circus Maximus, amphitheatre or theatres[16]—and the emperor who was present with them. Popular feelings could naturally be expressed and felt on other, less formal occasions, in particular when an emperor entered

---

[6] Ammianus XVI, 10, 13.

[7] Dio LVI, 34, 4–41, 9; Suetonius, *Cal.* 15, 1; Dio LXXIV, 5, 1 (328).

[8] Tacitus, *Hist.* II, 90.

[9] p. 15.

[10] Suetonius, *Nero* 47, 2; it was to be delivered 'pro rostris'. Cf. p. 204.

[11] Note however *HA, Sev. Alex.* 25, 11: 'contiones in urbe multas habuit more veterum tribunorum et consulum.'

[12] The fullest account is still that of L. Friedländer, *Darstellungen aus der Sittengeschichte Roms*[9] II (1920), ed. G. Wissowa, 1–160, and ibid., IV[9–10], 276–80. For the *Capitolia* and other Greek contests introduced subsequently in Rome see the brilliant study by L. Robert, 'Deux concours grecs à Rome', *CRAI* 1970, 6.

[13] See in particular H. Kloft, *Liberalitas Principis* (1970), chs. iii–iv.

[14] *RG* 22–3.

[15] See now especially Z. Yavetz, *Plebs and Princeps* (1969); T. Bollinger, *Theatralis Licentia: die Publikumsdemonstrationen an den öffentlichen Spielen im Rom der früheren Kaiserzeit und ihre Bedeutung im politischen Leben* (1969).

[16] J. P. V. D. Balsdon, 'Panem et Circenses', *Mélanges Renard* II (1969), 57 points out that the Circus Maximus held perhaps 200,000 spectators, the theatre of Marcellus 10,000, that of Balbus 6–7,000, that of Pompey some figure in between, and the Colosseum less than 50,000.

13

the city for the first time,[17] or for instance when an angry mob complaining about the cost of food attacked Claudius as he was giving justice in the Forum in 51.[18] The most striking of all such demonstrations occurred very early in the empire, when in 22 BC a mob, alarmed by famine and disease and the fact that Augustus had given up holding the consulship, shut the senate in the senate-house and forced them to vote Augustus the dictatorship; furthermore, they seized the twenty-four *fasces* of the consuls and went to Augustus, demanding that he accept the dictatorship and the charge of the corn-supply. Augustus avoided the invidious title of dictator only by addressing the people in imploring terms, and finally tearing his clothes before them.[19]

Demonstrations could also take place at public shows in the emperor's absence;[20] and it is noticeable in Dio's account of events in 193 that the Circus Maximus was now the normal place for the people to express their will, so that they went there spontaneously to demonstrate in favour of Pescennius Niger.[21] But the particular character of the distinctive exchanges which took place between people and emperor at the public shows derived from the facts that these were official events announced in advance, and possessing their own rituals and associations; that the structures in which they were held naturally allowed the participation in whatever occurred of large numbers of persons; and that the emperor made a formal entry,[22] and then sat—or at least was expected to sit—in a position in which his reactions were visible to all.[23]

If the emperor wished to court popularity, it was necessary for him not merely to be present at public shows,[24] but to be seen to be attending to and enjoying the proceedings, and not to be distracted by other concerns. As we saw earlier, Julius Caesar had incurred popular resentment by being observed to busy himself with *libelli* and *epistulae* while attending shows; Augustus did not allow himself to be similarly distracted, either (Suetonius says) to avoid criticism or because of the genuine pleasure which he gained from them.

[17] For example Suetonius, *Cal.* 13 (Gaius); Josephus, *BJ* VII, 4, 1 (64–74) (Vespasian in 70); Pliny, *Pan.* 22–4 (Trajan); *Pan.* VI(7), 8, 7 (Maximian, 298); *Pan.* IX(12), 19, 1–3; and Eusebius, *VC* I, 39 (Constantine, 312).

[18] p. 229.

[19] Dio LIV, 1, 2–5; cf. *RG* 5, 1; Velleius II, 89, 5; Suetonius, *Aug.* 52.

[20] e.g. Tacitus, *Ann.* VI, 13, 1; Dio LXXII, 13 (295), a demonstration in the circus, followed by an advance by the mob on the suburban villa where Commodus was; LXXV, 4, 3–6 (341–2); LXXVIII, 20, 1–2 (424–5).

[21] LXXIII, 13, 5 (317); cf. Herodian II, 7, 3. A similarly spontaneous occasion of resort to the Circus is briefly mentioned also by Dio LIX, 28, 11 (under Gaius).

[22] Cf. Nicolaus, *FGrH* 90 F. 127 (xxviii), the people applauding Octavian on his entering the theatre in 44 BC; for the emperor, Porphyrio on Horace, *Carm.* I, 1, 7; Martial, *Epig.* VI, 34, 5–6.

[23] For the placement of the emperor in the amphitheatre, theatre and Circus Maximus see Bollinger, o.c., 74–7. It is clear enough in all cases that the emperor had a specific and prominent position, but far less clear than is often supposed what the form or setting of his seat was. There does not seem to be any literary or archaeological evidence to support the statement of the *Chronicon Paschale* on the year 328 that the imperial box in the hippodrome of Constantinople to which the emperor gained access via a corridor leading from the palace was copied from a similar feature in Rome. Cf. p. 55.

[24] Note esp. Tacitus, *Ann.* I, 54, 2: Augustus 'civile rebatur misceri voluptatibus vulgi'; *Hist.* II, 91, 2: Vitellius 'omnem infimae plebis rumorem in theatro ut spectator, in circo ut fautor adfectavit'; cf. Dio LXIV, 8, 2² (107).

Marcus Aurelius, however, is said to have read, listened (to petitions, or to books read aloud to him?) and given his *subscriptiones* during games in the Circus—and to have been exposed to popular witticisms as a result.[25]

Given that the emperor took his seat in so formal and conspicuous a manner before large crowds, he could demonstrate favour to individuals simply by seating them with him, or by even more specific gestures, without the necessity of any verbal pronouncement. Thus Titus showed that he pardoned two conspirators by placing them next to himself at a gladiatorial show and handing them some gladiators' weapons to inspect.[26] At the beginning of his reign Claudius could commend his young son Britannicus to the people by holding him in his lap during public shows; but seven years later it was taken as a sign of what was to happen that Britannicus rode past at the circensian games in a mere civilian toga, while Claudius' adopted son Nero wore the triumphal dress.[27]

Many of the most specific exchanges between people and emperor concerned the shows themselves, namely their requests for items to be added, or for the granting of freedom to successful performers, and the emperor's responses to them. The relevance of the actual presence of the emperor is clear from the fact that Tiberius not only avoided giving shows of his own, but after being forced (as Suetonius puts it) to free an actor, kept away from shows given by others precisely to escape such demands; on one occasion when he was present he refused the crowd's demands for the manumission of a dancer until the man's owner agreed.[28] An emperor sometimes answered the demands of the people with his own voice, and it was precisely in response to expressions of a popular favour to performers which he did not share that Gaius uttered his famous threat, 'Would that the *populus Romanus* had only one neck!'[29]

Claudius also on occasion addressed the people at shows, and responded verbally or by gestures to requests for the freeing of gladiators; but he seems more commonly to have communicated with the people by having his messages written on boards, and carried round for the audience to read. This was his procedure for instance in the famous episode of Androclus and the lion. Androclus was personally interrogated by the emperor, and the story he told was written on a *tabula* which was taken round the amphitheatre. Androclus was then freed at the request of all, and the lion given to him by the *suffragia* of the people.[30] Dio makes clear that this means of communication was appreciated more than the use of a herald, which explains why Hadrian also used it in refusing demands for the freeing of a charioteer.[31] It was regarded as a sign of exceptional firmness that both Domitian and Hadrian used a herald to order the crowd to be quiet, and of Marcus Aurelius'

---

[25] Suetonius, *Aug.* 45, 1; *HA, Marc. Ant.* 15, 1. Cf. p. 214.

[26] Suetonius, *Tit.* 9, 2.

[27] *Claud.* 27, 2; Tacitus, *Ann.* XII, 41, 2.

[28] *Tib.* 47, 1; Dio LVII, 11, 6.

[29] *Cal.* 30, 2; Dio LIX, 13, 6; 30, 1c.

[30] *Claud.* 21, 5. Androclus: Aulus Gellius, *NA* v, 14, and (in slightly less detail) Aelian, *De nat. anim.* VII, 48.

[31] LX, 13, 5, and LXIX, 16, 3: ἀντεῖπε διὰ πινακίου γραφῆς.

distaste for such things that he answered through his herald demands for freedom for the trainer of a man-eating lion.³²

The most popular form of response was clearly that the emperor should speak himself, as Titus did on occasion, encouraging the people to make further requests, or making jokes 'by word or gesture' about his own preference for Thracian gladiators. Such a procedure had its dangers, as Suetonius makes clear in commenting that he did so without loss of dignity.³³ The emperor's concessions to the assembled people were a conscious and established part of his role,³⁴ and it is precisely to this that Fronto refers when, in writing to Marcus Aurelius, he urges on him the necessity of using oratory to gain public favour; 'And when you do so, remind yourself that you are but doing the same as you do when, at the people's request, you honour or enfranchise those who have slain beasts manfully in the arena; criminals they may be or felons, yet you release them at the people's request.'³⁵

The nature of the emperor's responses to the people could also serve to indicate his own conception of his position, as when Augustus was hailed in the theatre as *dominus*, and repressed the acclamation 'by gesture and expression', following this by issuing an edict on the next day; or when Otho at first showed no objection to being hailed in the theatres as 'Nero'.³⁶ But the crowd could also make demands over the wider issues of the food-supply or amenities of Rome. When the people complained of the scarcity and high price of wine, Augustus replied verbally that his son-in-law Agrippa had seen to it, by building aqueducts, that men would not go thirsty; and when they demanded a promised cash-distribution he replied, again verbally, that he was a man of good faith. When they turned to demanding one which had not been promised, he resorted once more to an *edictum* refusing it.³⁷

Again, when Tiberius removed to his bedroom a statue by Lysippus which Agrippa had set up at his baths, it was the shouts in the theatre which compelled him to restore it.³⁸ But popular demands and protests voiced in Rome were not limited to purely local issues. In 15 the people demanded the abolition of the sales tax, and were answered by an edict of Tiberius explaining the necessity for it.³⁹ In 58, however, 'repeated demands by the people' about the excesses of the *publicani* who collected the indirect taxes led to Nero's edict ordering that the relevant laws should be made public, and that the praetor in Rome and governors in the provinces should give precedence to cases against the *publicani*.⁴⁰

It is not clear in either of these instances in what context the demands were expressed, or whether they were made when the emperor was present in person. But it is evident, in the second case at least, that though they were certainly made in Rome, their results, or intended results, were to be felt

³² p. 68.
³³ *Tit.* 8, 2.
³⁴ See also e.g. Suetonius, *Dom.* 4, 1; Martial, *De spec.* 20; 29; Pliny, *Pan.* 33, 2.
³⁵ *Ad M. Caes.* 1, 8, 2, Loeb trans. (1, 9, 2, Van Den Hout).
³⁶ Suetonius, *Aug.* 53, 1; Plutarch, *Otho* 3, 1.
³⁷ *Aug.* 42, 1–2.
³⁸ Pliny, *NH* XXXIV, 19/62.
³⁹ Tacitus, *Ann.* 1, 78, 2.
⁴⁰ *Ann.* XIII, 50–1. Cf. p. 318.

generally throughout the empire. Moreover, Josephus both indicates the possible role of the populace in Rome in voicing wider discontents, and provides a much more detailed account of the context in which they did so on one occasion in describing an incident in the reign of Gaius:[41]

> Meanwhile there took place some horse-races, a type of spectacle to which the Romans are exceedingly devoted. They gather eagerly at the Circus, and coming together in the mass, petition the Emperor for whatever they need. Those emperors who regard these requests as not to be refused gain no small favour. So with earnest entreaty they bade Gaius to cut down the indirect taxes and to remove some of the burden [of the tributes]. He would not yield, and when they continued to shout, sent men hither and thither with orders to arrest those who were shouting, and lead them without delay to execution.

It is unfortunate that the words 'of the tributes' do not occur in all manuscripts of Josephus, for tribute was not levied in Italy, and if we could be sure that Josephus referred to it, it would indicate even more clearly how the populace in Rome at any one time not only contained large numbers of persons from the provinces but also could act as the mouthpiece of provincial grievances. But even as it is, we have a clear instance of protests about indirect taxation made in the Circus and directed to the emperor in person. How the emperor's refusal was conveyed is not stated, but it is evident from the narrative that it was known at once to the people.

Josephus' introduction to the scene implies that such episodes continued to be the rule when he was writing, namely not long before the completion of the *Antiquities* in 93/4. That is of some significance, for it has to be admitted that no reliable evidence from within our period for the use of the public shows for the expression of concrete demands on wider issues takes us beyond the end of the first century.[42] Eventually the increasingly frequent absences of the emperor from the city must in any case have led to the disuse of this particular form of petition-and-response in its Roman context. But given the much poorer narrative and biographical evidence for the second and third centuries we cannot state with any confidence how soon it ceased to be significant.

One form of concrete demand did continue to be expressed, that for the execution of individuals. This took two different forms, that for the putting-on of the execution of certain condemned criminals as a spectacle, and for the condemnation and execution of prominent individuals to whom the populace was hostile. Suetonius quotes Gaius' reply when a bandit named Tetrinius was 'demanded'—that is, to be thrown to the beasts.[43] Fronto, as we saw, regards it as a standard form of imperial concession to the people. At the end of the third century, however, Diocletian and Maximian took a different view. For a brief and enigmatic entry in the *Codex Justinianus* shows them first pronouncing in their council that the sons of town-councillors should not be thrown to the beasts: 'when there were shouts from

[41] *Ant.* XIX, 1, 4 (24–6).
[42] *HA, Sev. Alex.* 22, 7–8 recounts a dialogue between the emperor, via his herald, and the populace, evidently at a public show, over the price of meat.
[43] *Cal.* 30, 2.

the populace they again said, "The worthless voices of the people should not be listened to. Nor is it right to give credence to their voices when they demand either that the guilty should be acquitted or that the innocent should be condemned." ' No hint is preserved of the date or setting of this pronouncement, which does however seem to reflect the exposure of the emperors to popular demands in a provincial city.[44]

The populace might also use the occasion of public shows to demand executions, especially of imperial favourites and advisers. This is particularly clear during the rapidly-succeeding and relatively unstable reigns of 69.[45] But perhaps the best indication of the importance of such demands is Suetonius' report that Titus, when acting as praetorian prefect under Vespasian, would dispose of persons whom he suspected by sending agents to the theatres and the praetorian camp to demand their punishment. For whether the report is reliable or not, which we cannot tell, it presupposes that such demands would normally put in serious danger the life of anyone in a prominent position.[46]

The same is implied by Dio's account of the spectators in the Circus shouting at the praetorian prefect, Plautianus, some time before his fall, 'Why are you afraid, why are you white? You have gained more than the three [emperors]'.[47] It is clearly implied that he was present in person, presumably in attendance on the emperors; no explicit demand for his execution was made, but the implication was evident. Some years later, when Elagabal was killed in 222, the populace and soldiers lynched his *a rationibus* Aurelius Eubulus, who had previously been 'demanded (for execution) by the people'.[48]

The connection between popular reactions and the fortunes of imperial favourites is reflected in a weaker form in Eunapius' story of the fall of Sopater, the adviser of Constantine, The emperor, so he says, was dejected by the feebleness of the applause which greeted him in the theatre of Constantinople, and Sopater's enemies took the opportunity to suggest that it was he who by magic had 'fettered the winds' which brought the corn-ships to the city. Sopater was at once executed. Perhaps more significant are the introductory remarks which Eunapius attaches to the story, in which, as we saw earlier, he claims that Constantine transplanted a large population to Constantinople precisely in order to be applauded by them in the theatres.[49] The imputation is not wholly fanciful, for it is not an accident that the typical buildings for Roman public shows are attested in several of the new imperial centres of the tetrarchic and Constantinian period.[50] Without an urban centre with its concentrated population, and without the traditional mass entertainments at which the emperor would appear to receive

---

[44] *CJ* IX, 47, 12. The emperors are not recorded as ever having met in Rome. A possible setting is their meeting in Milan in 290/1, see p. 45. But the original text may in any case have referred to Diocletian alone, see Krueger ad loc.

[45] e.g. Tacitus, *Hist.* I, 72–3 (cf. III, 74–5); Suetonius, *Galba* 15, 2; Plutarch, *Galba* 17, 5.

[46] *Tit.* 6, 1.

[47] LXXVI, 2, 2 (358).

[48] Dio, LXXIX, 21, 1 (473).

[49] *Vit. Soph.* 462–3. Cf. pp. 54, 99–100.

[50] pp. 45–52.

the applause of the people and to answer their demands and complaints, a significant element would have been lost from the role and image of a Roman emperor.

These demands could even on occasion have some relevance for the empire at large. But episodic as they were, and largely dependent on the emperor's presence, they could not compare in importance with the communications endlessly addressed to the emperor in writing and in speech by the communities and associations of Italy and the provinces.

3. *Provincial Communities and the Emperor: Embassies*

We see how he meets the desires of the provinces and even the requests (*preces*) of individual cities. He makes no difficulty about giving them a hearing, or delay in replying. They come into his presence promptly, and are dismissed promptly, and at last the emperor's doors are no longer besieged by a mob of embassies which have been shut out.

So Pliny describes the return of Trajan to his regular imperial duties (*principales curae*) after holding the consulate in the first part of 100.[1] His emphasis on the rapidity with which the emperor heard the embassies is not without point or contrast, as we shall see.[2] The pressure of embassies did not cease when the emperor departed to the provinces, and the extent to which he acted as a focus for the attentions of the people is nowhere more clearly expressed than by Dio in describing the great earthquake which struck Antioch while Trajan was there in 114/15:[3]

While he was staying in Antioch an extraordinary earthquake occurred; many cities were affected by it but Antioch suffered the worst disaster. For as Trajan was wintering there, and many soldiers had collected there, and many civilians had come for law-suits or embassies, for trade or out of curiosity, there was not a province or a community which escaped unscathed. Thus in Antioch the whole world under Roman rule suffered loss.

Dio's account happens to relate to the established empire of the second century, and to the Greek east, the period and the area from which we have by far the largest concentration of documentary evidence for embassies to the emperor. But the same pattern can be found in other places and at other times. As an orator said before Constantine at Trier in 312, his purpose was to proclaim and acknowledge the emperor's benefits to Autun 'while there are present all the men from almost every city who have been sent on public missions or have come as suppliants on their own behalf'.[4]

It is important to emphasize that observers as well placed as Pliny in the early second, Dio in the early third and the orator in the early fourth century all envisaged the emperor as attracting crowds of ambassadors or litigants;

[1] *Pan.* 79, 6–7.
[2] p. 385.
[3] LXVIII, 24, 1–2. For the date see F. A. Lepper, *Trajan's Parthian War* (1948), Pt. I.
[4] *Pan.* VIII(5), 2, 1.

Dio, indeed, as we shall see, makes a proposal for reducing precisely this pressure.[5] But such references, though extremely valuable, still give no conception of the nature or frequency of contacts with the emperor on the part of any one community over a period. Although we now possess long series of imperial letters to the more favoured Greek cities, especially Delphi, Athens, Ephesus and Aphrodisias, such a conception of contacts over a period can be provided only by a literary source, and is provided by only one, namely Josephus.

Josephus' dual narrative, in the *Jewish War* and the *Jewish Antiquities*, of the history of Judaea as a province from AD 6 to 41 and 44 to 66 is of unique and inestimable importance for the understanding of the Roman empire. For it is not only the sole example of a continuous history of a province which we possess, but is the work of a man who was born into an aristocratic family in the province in the middle of the period concerned and who also took part personally in political events at the end of the period. It cannot of course be claimed that Judaea was typical, for it was a small province governed by an equestrian prefect, or later procurator, and dominated internally by a single council, the Sanhedrin in Jerusalem; the institutions of Jerusalem itself bore only a superficial resemblance to those of a Greek city proper.[6] Moreover, the presence of descendants of Herod significantly affected events, even though after AD 6 only Agrippa I in 41–4 ruled Judaea proper. None the less it is still possible, without going into the details of political history, to use Josephus' narrative as uniquely important evidence for the patterns of communication which could exist between subject community and emperor.[7]

The appearances of representatives of the Jewish people before the emperor had indeed begun a decade before the area became a province. For the death of Herod in 4 BC was followed by the hearing, referred to several times already, which Augustus held at the temple of Apollo on the Palatine; it was attended by the sons of Herod, making rival claims to the kingdom, by an embassy of no less than fifty persons from the Jewish community asking for an end to Herodian rule, and the attachment of the region to the province of Syria, and by embassies from the Greek cities asking for autonomy.[8] In the event Judaea proper went to Archelaus; but provincial status was achieved in AD 6, when delegations from the Jews and Samaritans went to Rome and accused him before Augustus.[9]

Josephus' narrative of the earlier part of the period is not so complete, and he omits an episode in AD 17 briefly mentioned by Tacitus, when 'the provinces of Syria and Judaea, exhausted by their burdens, petitioned for a deminution of tribute'; he does not state whether the appeal was made before

---

[5] p. 380.

[6] See V. A. Tcherikover, 'Was Jerusalem a "Polis"?', *IEJ* XIV (1964), 61.

[7] The relevant sections are *BJ* II, 7, 3 (111)–17, 1 (407); *Ant.* XVII, 13, 2 (342) to the end of XX (with long excursuses on events in Rome and Parthia). For full details it will be sufficient to refer to Schürer, *Jewish People* I, 357–98; 455–70. On Josephus, ibid., 43–63.

[8] *BJ* II, 6, 1–3 (80–100); *Ant.* XVII, 11, 1–5 (299–323); Nicolaus, *FGrH* 90 F. 136 (9); cf. pp. 19–20, 120, 230.

[9] *BJ* II, 7, 3 (111, 113); *Ant.* XVII, 13, 2 (342–4).

Tiberius or the senate.[10] Nor does Josephus mention what occurred when Pontius Pilate erected in the palace in Jerusalem gilded shields dedicated to Tiberius, which we know from a version of a letter of Agrippa I to Gaius, given by Philo. When Pilate refused demands for their removal, they asked permission to send an embassy to Tiberius. Pilate refused, fearing (so Agrippa says) what the embassy might report about his administration in general. So they wrote a letter instead (which must, though it is not stated, have been sent on by Pilate); when Tiberius, who was now settled on Capri, read it, he wrote angrily to Pilate telling him to remove the shields.[11]

Pilate eventually went the way of Archelaus when a Samaritan delegation accused him before Vitellius, the *legatus* of Syria, of bloodshed in quelling a popular movement, and Vitellius sent him to be tried by Tiberius.[12] On the next occasion also when popular feeling was aroused, with Gaius' attempt to place a statue of himself as Zeus in the temple, there were no direct representations to the emperor. But the contemporary narrative of Philo makes clear that the whole issue arose from conflicts between the Jewish and Gentile inhabitants of Jamnia and a report on them sent by the procurator, Herennius Capito.[13] Both his and Josephus' narratives of the following events show that the temporizing letters of Petronius, *legatus* of Syria, to Gaius were themselves a response to massive demonstrations by the Jewish population. Moreover, in Philo's account the Jewish elders specifically ask Petronius to delay while they select and despatch an embassy to the emperor; Petronius refuses precisely in order not to incur the danger of having the true situation made clear to Gaius, and writes himself instead.[14]

Both accounts record that the plan was finally abandoned at the intercession of Agrippa I, who subsequently regained the full kingdom of Herod from Claudius in 41. When direct rule returned after his death in 44, a further conflict arose over the demand by the new procurator, Cuspius Fadus, for the restoration of the high-priestly robes to his custody.[15] Once again the leaders of the community requested permission to send an embassy to the emperor. They were received by Claudius, who informed them that he was granting their request at the instance of the young Agrippa II, who was then in Rome. As we saw earlier, he also gave them a letter, addressed to the magistrates, council and people of Jerusalem, and the whole race of the Jews, which referred explicitly to the intercession of Agrippa, and his favour to Herod and Aristobulus (Agrippa's uncle and cousin), stated that he was writing also to Cuspius Fadus, and gave the names of the three ambassadors.[16] It is clear from the letter that the ambassadors had made a speech in appropriate style:[17]

[10] *Ann.* II, 42, 5.
[11] Philo, *Leg.* 38/299–305.
[12] *Ant.* XVIII, 4, 1–2 (85–9).
[13] *Leg.* 30/200–3; cf. pp. 321–2.
[14] *Leg.* 32/225–34/260; on the embassy, 32/239–42, 33/247–8; *BJ* II, 10, 1–5 (184–203); *Ant.* XVIII, 8, 2–6 (261–88).
[15] *Ant.* XX, 1, 1–2 (6–14); cf. XV, 11, 4 (406–7).
[16] cf. p. 219.
[17] XX, 1, 2 (12), Loeb trans.

My friend Agrippa, whom I have brought up and now have with me, a man of the greatest piety, brought your envoys before me. They gave thanks for the tender care I have shown your nation and earnestly and zealously requested that the holy vestments and the crown might be placed in your hands.

The next occasion on which the emperor was involved was of a different sort, when, following strife between the Jews and Samaritans, Ummidius Quadratus, the *legatus* of Syria, sent the leaders of both communities, along with the procurator and a tribune, to be tried by Claudius in about 52. But once again the matter was decided at a hearing by the emperor in person, in which speeches were made on behalf of all parties, and Agrippa again interceded successfully for the Jews, invoking the influence of Agrippina against the partiality for Cumanus on the part of the emperor's *amici* and *liberti*.[18]

About a decade later Agrippa II himself came into conflict with the Jewish leaders in Jerusalem, by building a palace which overlooked the Temple. When the procurator ordered them to pull down the wall which they erected to block this view, they again asked permission to send an embassy to the emperor. Twelve leading men were sent, and were heard by Nero, who ruled that the wall should stay; this he did at least partly as a concession to Poppaea, who interceded for the ambassadors, and also subsequently retained two of them, the High Priest himself and the keeper of the treasury, in her household.[19]

Before this a separate dispute had arisen between the Jewish and the Greek inhabitants of Caesarea over their respective rights in the city.[20] After violent conflicts, the procurator Felix, according to Josephus' version in the *Jewish War*, chose the leading men from both sides and sent them to argue their case before Nero. In the *Antiquities* he speaks instead of the leaders of the Jewish community in Caesarea going to Rome to accuse Felix, after the arrival of his successor, Festus. The difference is not profound, since accusations against Felix would undoubtedly have formed part of their case. Felix would have been condemned, Josephus says, but for the influence of his brother Pallas, an imperial freedman and formerly *a rationibus* under Claudius and at the beginning of Nero's reign.[21] A Greek delegation was certainly in Rome also, for they bribed Beryllus, the *ab epistulis* of Nero,[22] to ask for a letter to be written annulling the rights of the Jews in the city, and brought it back with them.

Finally, in 66 after a massacre in Jerusalem by the procurator, Florus, and when the revolt was about to break out, we find the people urging the High Priests and Agrippa II to send an embassy to Nero to accuse Florus and clear themselves of the blame for having rebelled without cause.[23] This was not done, although later the *legatus* of Syria, Cestius Gallus, was to send two

[18] *BJ* II, 12, 3–7 (232–46); *Ant.* xx, 6, 1–3 (118–36); cf. p. 231. The account of events in Judaea in Tacitus, *Ann.* XII, 54, is hopelessly confused.

[19] *Ant.* xx, 8, 11 (189–95).

[20] *BJ* II, 13, 7 (266–70); 14, 4 (284); *Ant.* xx, 8, 7 (173–8); 8, 9 (182–4).

[21] *Ant.* xx, 8, 9 (182), on Pallas, pp. 76–7.

[22] cf. p. 226.

[23] *BJ* II, 16, 3 (342).

members of the aristocracy of Jerusalem to Nero, who was then in Greece, to explain the situation and lay the blame on Florus.[24]

As was indicated earlier, the situation in Judaea was not typical; indeed, had it been so, the Roman empire could not have continued to exist. But more particularly, the evidence for Judaea may tend to give not too strong but too weak an impression of the readiness of the communities of the empire to address themselves to the emperor in person. For, first, it would tend to show—except in the case of the abortive embassy of 66—that embassies could only go with the concurrence of the governor. But we shall see later that while governors elsewhere could on occasion prevent embassies, there is nothing to suggest that their permission was normally asked. What applied in a small province to critical situations in which the governor was already involved, did not apply to the numerous cities of other, larger provinces, each of which the governor might visit rarely, or even not at all.[25] Secondly, the evidence from Judaea suggests nothing of the immense volume of formal and diplomatic embassies which appeared before the emperor on all significant occasions. For all the relevant evidence relates to important local crises. But that is precisely its most significant contribution, namely that although the crises were all purely local it was none the less the settled conviction, and frequently the practice, of the parties not only that these matters should be brought to the attention of the emperor, and settled by him in person, but that this should be done by the despatch of an embassy or embassies to speak before him. Where a letter from a community or a governor was sent instead, it was explicitly as a substitute for an embassy.

Just as important as the fact that embassies went so frequently to speak before the emperor is the fact which is the counterpart of this, that our uniquely full evidence for the history of the province does not include a single mention of any action or intervention there by the emperor which was not a response to direct or indirect initiatives by local communities, Jewish, Samaritan or pagan.

If we are to judge by the evidence from Judaea, therefore, the role of the emperor was essentially passive. It is not necessary or proper to conclude from this that he never issued positive pronouncements; and we have in any case seen that he did on occasion issue these in the form either of edicts or, more frequently at the end of the period, of letters to office-holders.[26] But it also serves to reinforce the implications of the structure of his immediate entourage, that his primary role was that of making responses, and issuing decisions on disputed points.[27]

The view of the emperor's function upon which the Jewish community in Jerusalem acted was merely the reflection of conceptions much more widely current in the Roman world. Without embarking on the many well-attested cases which we shall see later, it will be sufficient to give as illustration a few second-century instances: the freedman from Arelate who

---

[24] II, 20, 1 (558).
[25] pp. 380f.
[26] pp. 252–9, 318–21.
[27] pp. 270–2.

'made known' the grievance of some villagers in its territory to Antoninus Pius;[28] the decurion from Mediolanum who had undertaken at his own expense five embassies to Rome and the provinces for his city;[29] the office-holder from Sinope who had been on four embassies to Rome—one to Hadrian and three to Antoninus Pius;[30] and another from Tomi who had been to Antoninus Pius in Rome at his own expense.[31]

Even these few instances give some slight conception of the frequency of embassies, of the distances covered and the expenditure of time involved. It is not surprising, therefore, that we have some indications of efforts to check the flow, both to reduce expense to the cities, and to lift some of the burden from the emperor himself.[32] Dio makes Maecenas say in his speech of advice to Augustus, 'Do not allow them (the cities) to send any embassy to you, except if there is a matter involving a judicial decision, but let them explain whatever they require to their governor, and have such petitions as he approves sent on by him. Thus they will neither have any expenditure nor achieve their ends by improper means, but will receive proper responses without expense or trouble.'[33] This is of course, in reality, only a suggestion by Dio himself, and there is extremely little evidence to show any such procedure in general operation.

Inscriptional evidence reveals a number of cases where a city decree had been sent on to the emperor by a governor or other official, without in any instance making clear whether this was in accordance with a policy imposed from above.[34] Furthermore, Philo records that at the accession of Gaius in 37 the Jewish community of Alexandria passed a decree in honour of the new emperor, and since the prefect of Egypt, Avillius Flaccus, would not have granted a request to send an embassy, took the decree to him and asked him to send it on. He promised that he would do so, and add a testimony of his own to their orderly and loyal conduct, but in fact kept the decree back. It was finally sent on with an explanation by the future Agrippa I of Judaea.[35] This again is not likely to be a typical instance, for it was not usual for one section of a city to send an embassy, and in any case Alexandria was an anomaly in not being permitted the full normal constitution of a city, and being under the direct supervision of the prefect.[36]

Outside Alexandria and Judaea the only attested instance where a community is found asking permission from the governor to send an embassy to the emperor is that of the small town of Sala in Mauretania Tingitana, whose council in 144 passed a decree giving various honours to a *praefectus alae* who had been stationed in their territory; among the proposals was one

[28] *CIL* XII 594.

[29] *CIL* v 5894.

[30] *AE* 1916 120 = Abbott and Johnson, *Municipal Administration*, no. 126; revised text in *AE* 1969/70 592.

[31] *IGR* 1 608.

[32] For a discussion of such attempts see W. Williams, 'Antoninus Pius and the Control of Provincial Embassies', *Historia* XVI (1967), 470.

[33] LII, 30, 9.

[34] p. 217.

[35] *In Flacc.* 12/97-103.

[36] cf. pp. 384, 413.

that they should request the governor to allow them to erect a statue to the *praefectus*, and also 'that he should moreover permit them to proclaim through ambassadors before the most sacred emperor that Sulpicius Felix had acted as *praefectus* among us as was to be expected in the most august age (of the emperor) and under the most venerable discipline of Uttedius Honoratus (the governor)'.[37] It is thus very probable that one of the purposes of asking the governor's permission was to use the occasion to pay a diplomatic compliment to himself; whether his permission was strictly required is less certain.

A governor's action to prevent the sending of embassies is best attested in the well-known letter in which Pliny reports to Trajan that on examining the accounts of Byzantium he has found that each year the city sent an ambassador with a decree to greet the emperor himself, at a cost of 12,000 *sesterces*, and one to the governor of Moesia Inferior, at 3,000. Trajan agrees with Pliny's proposal to stop the sending of the ambassadors, and to pass on both decrees himself.[38] His action is thus closely in accordance with what Dio was to suggest a century later. But there is nothing to suggest that such a procedure became part of general imperial policy until, in perhaps 317, Constantine laid down that 'the decrees of the provincials' should not be brought to the *comitatus* without being checked and witnessed by the relevant governor.[39] In 324 he wrote similarly to the proconsul of Africa to say that town-councillors should not set off to go to the *comitatus*, either on their own or on public business, without first gaining permission from the governor.[40] There is nothing to indicate that either of these rules prevailed previously, and we cannot assume without proof that they were effective subsequently either.

The only general imperial pronouncement of the early part of our period which placed a restraint on embassies was the edict of Vespasian, mentioned by the jurist Marcianus, by which cities were ordered not to send more than three ambassadors each.[41] This does seem to have had some effect, for while we have no parallel to the fifty Jewish ambassadors who appeared before Augustus in 4 BC, the twelve who went to complain of Agrippa II's palace in Jerusalem are matched by the twelve from the Greek community of Alexandria who appeared before Claudius in 41;[42] and before Vespasian's reign cases of four or five ambassadors are quite common.[43] On the other hand even in this period some embassies consisted only of one man.[44] After this, however, one or two ambassadors seems to have been the norm. Only

[37] S. Gsell, J. Carcopino, 'La base de M. Sulpicius Felix et le décret des decurions de Sala', *MEFR* XLVIII (1931), 1; cf. J. Carcopino, *Le Maroc antique* (1943), 200–30.

[38] Pliny, *Ep.* X, 43–4.

[39] *CTh* I, 16, 2. The letter is stated to have been *proposita* at Caralis in Sardinia on 24 September 317. However the identity and post of the Bassus to whom it is addressed is obscure.

[40] *CTh* XII, 1, 9 = *CJ* X, 32, 16; *proposita* in Carthage.

[41] *Dig.* L, 7, 5, 6.

[42] pp. 376, 378; for the Alexandrian embassy, pp. 412–13

[43] e.g. P. Herrmann, *Ath. Mitt.* LXXV (1960), 70, no. 1b, at least six on an embassy from Samos to Augustus probably in 5 BC; *IGR* IV 251 = *Syll.*³ 797, five from Assos to Gaius in 37; O. Montevecchi, *Aegyptus* L (1970), 5, at least five from an Egyptian city to Nero; *IGR* IV 1123 = Abbott and Johnson, *Municipal Administration*, no. 52, about eight from Rhodes to Nero.

[44] e.g. the embassy from Gytheum to Tiberius and Livia, *AE* 1929 100 = *SEG* XI 922.

in the case of Septimius Severus' letter to Aezani of probably 196 do we find him referring to eight ambassadors, plus another who for some reason was disqualified from receiving his *viaticum*; it is noteworthy that the emperor records the names without adverting to Vespasian's edict.[45] Similarly the possibly fictional 'Acts of Hermaiscus', partially preserved on a papyrus, represents the Alexandrian Greeks as sending at least ten ambassadors plus an orator from Tyre to appear before Trajan, and the Jews selecting six, plus an orator from Antioch, to appear against them.[46]

The edict of Vespasian may thus have had some effect, though it should be emphasized that in all our abundant evidence about embassies it is referred to only in the single sentence of Marcianus mentioned above. The evidence for attempts to limit either the frequency or the expense of embassies is thus extremely slight, and is far outweighed not merely by the extensive documentary and literary evidence for the despatch of particular embassies, but perhaps more significantly by the large number of references in legal sources which discuss the consequences of a man's being absent from his native city while serving on an embassy to the emperor. The frequency of these references makes it quite clear that this was a familiar situation, which necessitated rulings for instance on such men's liability to *curae* or *tutelae* or to prosecution, and on what obligations could be imposed on them while in Rome.

The conduct of an embassy was naturally regarded as a burden, and much attention was given to the question of who was liable to it, and what circumstances gave exemption. Marcianus, for instance, lays down that men should be chosen in the order in which they were co-opted into their city council, and those co-opted later could not be compelled to go until those before them had served their turn; but if the embassy was one which required the leading men, and the order pointed to less important ones, then it need not be observed—and so Hadrian had replied, evidently as an answer to a dispute, in a letter to the city of Clazomenae. It is assumed that ambassadors will normally be city-councillors; persons of lower standing such as ex-gladiators, or debtors to the city (though not debtors of the *fiscus*) were debarred,[47] and an ambassador who deserted his embassy was normally removed from his council (*ordo*).[48] Once a man had completed an embassy, he was immune from further obligations for two years; and if, as was permitted, a father named his son as deputy (*vicarius*) for the embassy, the father but not the son kept the immunity (*vacatio*). Severus and Caracalla, however, made a slight concession in replying in a *subscriptio* to a man named Claudius Callistus: 'What you request, that on account of an embassy by your father you should have immunity from an embassy, is properly relevant to the intervals for holding offices (*honores*) which involve expenditure. As regards remission from embassies, which involve only the service performed itself, the case is different.'[49] As with every other privilege and immunity,

[45] *IGR* iv 566.
[46] Musurillo, *Acts of the Pagan Martyrs*, no. viii.
[47] *Dig.* L, 7, 5.
[48] L, 7, 1.
[49] L, 7, 7–9 (reading 'intercapedine' in 7, 7).

there was constant pressure to extend it to marginal cases. So Diocletian and Maximian reply sternly to someone named Mucianus: 'It is established that those who have travelled overseas to perform an embassy before us enjoy the two-year immunity from city obligations and offices, not those who have come from the immediate neighbourhood to express the loyalty of their town.'[50]

Ambassadors when appointed were voted their travelling-expenses (*viaticum*); it is precisely for this reason that imperial letters to cities often end by giving the name or names of the ambassador or ambassadors, and adding the clause, 'to whom the *viaticum* should be given unless he has [or they have] promised to go at his [their] own expense'.[51] Some expenses might be given to them before departure, for Paulus lays down that if a man dies in the course of an embassy, the expenses given to him when he set out could not be reclaimed by the city.[52] There was clearly social pressure to promise to go at one's own expense, and it is instructive that Arcadius Charisius, writing in the tetrarchic period, says that *legati* who are sent to the *sacrarium* of the emperor undertake what is strictly a personal rather than a financial obligation 'because they sometimes receive a *viaticum* which is called a *legativum*'.[53]

During the period of an embassy, Modestinus says, men could not be nominated as *tutores* or *curatores*, and if a provincial at Rome on an embassy were so nominated by the praetor, he should be released from the obligation.[54] Similarly, civil actions could not be instituted against an ambassador except under special circumstances,[55] and a ruling by Marcus Aurelius and Commodus allowed them an action for full restitution (*restitutio in integrum*) in respect of any proceedings which had taken place in their absence.[56] From the very existence of these rules it can be assumed that advantage was frequently taken of the absence of ambassadors. One particularly clear case is revealed by a *subscriptio* of Caracalla addressed in 212 to a man named Aemilianus:[57]

If you were condemned when genuinely absent on account of the duties of an embassy to me, and without being defended, you are entitled to ask for a re-hearing of your case, so that you may put forward your defence without prejudice. For it is accepted that those who are performing the duties of an embassy enjoy the same privilege as those who are absent on behalf of the state (*rei publicae causa*).

Nor could the ambassador be compelled to attend legal proceedings while

---

[50] *CJ* x, 65, 3.

[51] e.g. the letter of Hadrian to Stratonicea-Hadrianopolis, *IGR* IV 1156, i = *Syll.*[3] 837; revised by L. Robert, *Hellenica* VI, 80–4, ll. 17–18: ἐπρέσβευσεν Κλ. Κάνδιδος ᾧ τὸ ἐφόδι[ον] δοθήτω εἰ μὴ προῖκα ὑπέσχηται. Cf. *IG* VII 2870 = Abbott and Johnson, *Municipal Administration*, no. 104, ii and iii, and many other cases. Cf. *Dig.* L, 7, 3 (Ulpian): 'His, qui non gratuitam legationem susceperunt, legativum ex forma restituatur.'

[52] *Dig.* L, 7, 11, 1.

[53] L, 4, 18, 12.

[54] XXVI, 5, 21, 3–4.

[55] V, 1, 8; 24–8; cf. L, 7, 4; 6.

[56] IV, 6, 8.

[57] *CJ* II, 53, 1.

at Rome—unless, as Antoninus Pius ruled in a rescript, they stayed on there after the business of the embassy had been completed.[58] On the other hand they could not, except in certain special cases, initiate proceedings themselves while acting as ambassadors.[59] But according to Ulpian an ambassador could take the opportunity of being at court even to make a petition against the city of which he was the ambassador, provided that he did it through someone else; according to Modestinus, however, he could not present a *libellus* on matters unconnected with his embassy except with the specific permission of the emperor.[60] Given the number of occasions on which, as we shall see, ambassadors were personally rewarded by the emperor, it is not surprising that the possibility was envisaged that they might be more concerned with promoting their own interests than those of their city. Dio, for instance, had to make a speech in his native Prusa to refute exactly this charge, of having gained personal advantage from an embassy to Trajan, and says that he had had eyes only for the common good of the city.[61]

The question of sending an embassy might be debated in the assembly of a city—Philostratus describes the Athenian *ecclêsia* being dissuaded by the sophist Chrestus from voting an embassy to Marcus or Commodus to ask for the chair of Greek rhetoric in Rome for him.[62] But the ambassadors were normally selected by and from the councillors. Fronto indeed defends the claim of a client of his that he had long been a town-councillor (*decurio*) of Concordia partly by the fact that he had often been an ambassador of the town, and been voted his *viaticum*.[63] Similarly, a papyrus contains what is evidently part of the speech of an Alexandrian embassy before one of the early emperors asking that the city should be allowed a council like all fully-constituted cities, and giving the proper selection of embassies as one of the reasons for this: 'Moreover, if it were necessary to send an embassy to you, it would select suitable men. So no improper person would be sent off, nor would any appropriate person avoid the service of his native city.'[64] Embassies were in fact sent on occasion by Alexandria, though we do not know how they were selected; Josephus, however, describes a mass meeting of the Alexandrians in the amphitheatre in 66 debating a proposed embassy to Nero.[65]

The selection and despatch of embassies to the emperor was thus an established and familiar function of the cities of the empire as corporate entities. They could be viewed as burdens to be avoided, as when Plutarch gives as one of the compensations of exile the fact that a man did not find himself compelled by his city to make contributions, to go on embassies to

[58] *Dig.* V, I, 2, 4; XII, 2, 35, 2.

[59] L, 7, 9, 2; 10; 11 *pr.*; 12, 1.

[60] L, 7, 2 *pr.*; 16.

[61] *Or.* XLV, 3.

[62] *VS* II, 11.

[63] *Ad Amicos* II, 7. Compare also the provisions of the *Lex Ursonensis* (*ILS* 6087; *FIRA²* I, no. 21 = Abbott and Johnson, *Municipal Administration*, no. 26), para. xcii, for the selection of *legati* by the *decuriones*.

[64] *PSI* 1160, col. ii, ll. 11–14; cf. Musurillo, *Acts of the Pagan Martyrs*, no. i = Tcherikover and Fuks, *Corp. Pap. Jud.*, no. 150.

[65] *BJ* II, 18, 7 (490–1).

Rome, to give hospitality to the governor, or to accept liturgies. But else-where, speaking of the few opportunities left for distinction in city life, Plutarch says, 'there remain lawsuits on behalf of the city and embassies to the emperor, which require a man who is ardent, bold and intelligent'.[66]

The sheer volume of evidence for embassies from provincial communities to the emperor must make us realize that we are dealing with an essential aspect of the life of the empire. For the reasons which gave rise to so many lengthy and arduous journeys to Rome or other provinces cannot have seemed unimportant to those who undertook them. None the less the crucial ordeal was not that, but the fact that the success or failure of the embassy depended first on gaining and then on conducting a hearing before the emperor in person. Of all the emperors of our period only Augustus in old age is attested as delegating the hearing of embassies to others;[67] and while Trajan could be praised for the promptitude with which he heard embassies, Tiberius, so Josephus reports, deliberately delayed the reception of embassies in order to discourage the sending of others.[68]

Once the hearing was gained, all might depend on the favour with which the emperor greeted the oration; hence arose the well-attested role of the orators of the Second Sophistic on embassies before the emperor.[69] It is impossible to over-emphasize both the fact that these endlessly-repeated journeys to the emperor were the essential means by which the cities and other groups communicated with him, and that they required on the part of the ambassador a comportment, diction and choice of words in accordance with the exacting canons of Graeco-Roman culture. Few who had been to speak before the emperor would have disputed what an orator said about the reception by Constantine of the leading citizens of Autun in 311, when for once the emperor had come to them, and was established in the *palatium* of the city:[70]

> Nor is it any small matter to make a request on one's own behalf to the emperor of the whole world, to put on a brave face before the eyes of such majesty, to compose one's expression, to summon up one's courage, to choose the right words, to speak without fear, to stop at the right moment, and to await the reply.

4. *Provincial Leagues and Councils*

In 5 BC, when Gaius Caesar, the grandson of Augustus, assumed the *toga virilis*, the city of Sardis in Asia resolved to send an embassy to Rome to congratulate him and Augustus, to present him with the decree of the city and to address Augustus on the common interests of Asia and of the city. As regarded the interests of Sardis, a letter of Augustus duly acknowledged that the two ambassadors, Iollas and Menogenes, had carried out their

---

[66] *Mor.* 602 C; 805 A.
[67] Dio LV, 33, 5; LVI, 25, 7.
[68] *Ant.* XVIII, 6, 5 (170–1).
[69] e.g. pp. 234, 391–2, 434. Note also Philostratus, *VS* I, 24; II, 5; 20.
[70] *Pan.* VIII(5), 9, 3.

duties successfully. But Menogenes also had wider responsibilities, for he was at this time 'advocate of the Hellenes', that is of the common council (*koinon*) of the Greek cities of Asia, and in going to Rome he spoke also for the *koinon*. In the long inscription from Sardis which records his honours, the services of Menogenes on this occasion are acknowledged in two letters from High Priests to the *koinon* of the city of Sardis, and two decrees of the *koinon* from 3/2 and 2 BC. The second of these begins as follows:[1]

> It was voted by the Hellenes in Asia on the motion of M. Antonius Lepidus of Thyatira, the High Priest, and president for life of the Great Augustan Caesarean Games of the Goddess Roma and of Imperator Caesar Divi Filius Augustus, Pontifex Maximus, father of his country and of the whole human race: that since Menogenes, son of Isidorus, son of Menogenes, of Sardis, a member of a distinguished family which has performed many services in its native city through the offices and priesthoods entrusted to it, having been as ambassador to Augustus Caesar on behalf of the *koinon* of the Hellenes and of his city, and having carried out his duties successfully, as the replies show . . .

The *koinon* of the Hellenes in Asia existed already in the later republic, when, as an inscription shows, it met in Ephesus and chose two leading citizens of Aphrodisias to go as ambassadors to the senate and magistrates of Rome to complain of oppression by the tax-farmers.[2] It was also to the *koinon* that Marcus Antonius wrote as triumvir, perhaps in 42/1 BC, to confirm the privileges of the synod of sacred victors and crown-winners (probably athletes rather than actors).[3] We can thus be sure at least that a formal common council of the cities of Asia used to meet in the late republic and had some concern both with questions of status within the province, and the representation of its interests outside. Its association with the cults of emperors, however, began very early, when in 29 BC Augustus (or rather, as he still was, 'Imperator Caesar Divi Filius') allowed the Hellenes of Asia to establish a temple to him at Pergamum, and those of Bithynia one at Nicomedia. Dio's language clearly implies that the permission followed a request from them, which will certainly have been brought by an embassy.[4] He fails, however, to make clear that the temple was in fact dedicated to Roma and Augustus, a cult which replaced an existing one of Roma and Salus ('Safety' or 'Salvation').[5] When the temple was first dedicated, hymns were sung to Augustus by a chorus which assembled voluntarily and without pay; in recognition of this Augustus at some later stage ruled that the privileges voted to the hymnodes (presumably by the *koinon*) should be valid

---

[1] *Sardis* VII: *Greek and Latin Inscriptions* I, ed. W. H. Buckler and D. M. Robinson (1932), no. 8. The document partly translated is no. x. Cf. also pp. 217, 418.

[2] See the important inscription from Aphrodisias discussed by T. Drew-Bear, 'Deux décrets hellénistiques d'Asie Mineure', *BCH* XCVI (1972), 435, on pp. 443f. Note also the reference to a letter of a proconsul to the *koinon* in Sherk, *Roman Documents*, no. 52.

[3] p. 456.

[4] LI, 20, 7.

[5] Tacitus, *Ann.* IV, 37, 3: 'cum divus Augustus sibi atque urbi Romae templum apud Pergamum sisti non prohibuisset': cf. e.g. Chr. Habicht, *Altertümer von Pergamon* VIII.3: *die Inschriften des Asklepieions* (1969), no. 29, and p. 165, and in *Entretiens Hardt* XIX: *Le culte des souverains dans l'Empire romain* (1973), 83.

for their successors, and also ordered that the expenses should be borne not by Pergamum alone, but by the whole of Asia.[6] Once again it is probable that an embassy went to him to ask for his decisions on these matters.

It was thus that the cults and festivals dedicated to Augustus, and to some but not all later emperors, became one of the principal matters managed by the *koinon*, and thus that the annual presidents acquired the title of High Priest (*archiereus*), though what was perhaps their previous title, *Asiarchês*, continued in use as well. It was indeed the common feature of all the provincial councils of the imperial period, whether they had existed previously or emerged now, that their presidents had titles indicating priesthoods, *archiereus* in the Greek east, *flamen* or *sacerdos* in the west. That is significant, but does not imply that they were instituted by imperial initiative (except in the case of the Three Gauls, Britain, and briefly Germany) or that their activities were confined to cult or ritual functions.[7] One *koinon* indeed, that of Lycia, had been a genuine governing federation until the area was made a province by Claudius. Those of Thessaly and Greece had a continuous history from the classical period, the Greek ones eventually being for a short period combined in the 'Panachaean League' of Achaeans, Boeotians, Locrians, Phocians and Euboeans.[8]

The leagues, which united areas sometimes identical with that of a Roman province, sometimes larger and sometimes smaller, had thus very different backgrounds and histories, of which proper account cannot be taken here. But they all held meetings, probably annual, attended by representatives from their constituent cities, all eventually appointed priests for the cult of one or more emperors, and probably all conducted annual festivals. These institutions themselves necessitated arrangements between the cities on matters of mutual obligations and expenses which, like the question of the hymnodes at Pergamum, might themselves require rulings by the emperor. But the *koina*, or in the west *concilia* or *communia*, might also approach the emperor both on purely diplomatic occasions, such as accessions, victories, or Gaius' assumption of the *toga virilis*, and on matters of substance. As such, they resembled the *commune* (*koinon*) of Sicily, known from one of Cicero's orations against Verres, which had celebrated games (*Marcellia*) named after the conqueror of Syracuse in 212, and voted honorific statues for governors, but had also addressed complaints to the senate.[9]

We have already seen some instances where provinces brought either requests or accusations of governors before the senate in the early empire.[10] But from the beginning the councils also addressed themselves directly to the emperor. Even essentially diplomatic embassies might, like that from Asia in 5 BC, take the opportunity to speak to the emperor about matters which

[6] See F. K. Dörner, *Der Erlass des Statthalters von Asia Paullus Fabius Persicus* (1935), col. viii, ll. 11-19.

[7] See the thorough treatment by J. Deininger, *Die Provinziallandtage der römischen Kaiserzeit von Augustus bis zum Ende des dritten Jahrhunderts n. Chr.* (1965).

[8] p. 388. See J. A. O. Larsen, *Representative Government in Greek and Roman History* (1955), ch. vi, and for the earlier history of the leagues, *Greek Federal States: their Institutions and History* (1968).

[9] See Larsen, *Representative Government*, ch. vii, n. 2.

[10] pp. 345-9.

were of advantage to the council. Other diplomatic embassies might have to express themselves with some subtlety to avoid giving offence, and none more so than that from the Gallic provinces which came to Nero in 59 after his mother Agrippina had been murdered on his orders. Quintilian will hardly have been alone in admiring the words of the orator Julius Africanus from Saintes on that occasion: 'Your Gallic provinces, Caesar, implore you to bear your good fortune bravely.'[11]

Less testing was an imperial accession, when the choice of appropriate words would not present such difficulties. Even so, when in 37 the Panachaean League had met and taken the oath of loyalty to Gaius, and the question then arose of sending ambassadors to the new emperor, there was some reluctance to undertake it. A decree of the *koinon* honouring Epaminondas, son of Epaminondas, from Acraephia in Boeotia records that 'when an embassy to the new Augustus was sought for in the council of Achaeans and Pan-hellenes, and many rich and prominent men had assembled from the cities, but all refused and appealed, he entirely disregarded his own interests and eagerly accepted the embassy on behalf of the Boeotian people'. Epaminon-das went at his own expense, along with a number of other ambassadors, who presented to Gaius a decree offering him various honours; in his letter in reply the emperor accepts most of the honours, but modestly says that he would prefer statues of himself to be erected only at Olympia, Nemea, Delphi and the Isthmus of Corinth.[12]

In the same way it was probably in the first year of Nero that Cleophatus, son of Aristeus, from Messene went on an embassy to the emperor at his own expense 'on behalf of Hellas'.[13] Again in 126, so not at the moment of accession, fragmentary inscriptions from Athens and Olympia show that the *koinon* of the Achaeans (not the Panachaean League, if it still existed) voted honours to Hadrian, and received a letter from him acknowledging them.[14]

As we should expect, the record of such embassies to the emperor from councils, which were relatively few in number, and met only occasionally, is very slight compared to that of cities. We do, however, have indications that councils, like cities, began in the second century to communicate with the emperor on another type of purely diplomatic mission, that of testifying to the virtues and services of their more prominent citizens. So the immense inscription from Rhodiapolis in Lycia which provides a dossier of the honours voted to a local millionaire, Opramoas, contains two decrees in which the *koinon* of Lycia votes to send ambassadors to Antoninus Pius to give him a decree (*psêphisma*) and also inform him verbally about Opramoas' services; six containing votes for decrees to be sent by the governor; and five or six

---

[11] *Inst.* VIII, 5, 15: 'et insigniter Africanus apud Neronem de morte matris: "rogant te, Caesar, Galliae tuae, ut felicitatem tuam fortiter feras".' On Julius Africanus, *PIR*² I 120, and C. P. Jones in *HSCPh* LXXII (1967), 284f.

[12] *IG* VII 2711–12. The text translated is that of 2712, ll. 38–43. There are alternative descriptions of what happened in 2711, ll. 7–13, 61–5, 95–105. For a revised text of 2712 see J. H. Oliver, 'Epaminondas of Acraephia', *GRBS* XII (1971), 221. Gaius' letter is in 2711, ll. 21–42 = *ILS* 8792.

[13] *IG* V.1 1449. The date is suggested by the fact that in the relevant year Cleophatus was ὁ ἱερεὺς αὐτοῦ (Nero) πρῶτος.

[14] W. Dittenberger, K. Purgold, *Die Inschriften von Olympia* (1896), no. 57, with *IG* III 18.

letters of acknowledgment from Antoninus to the *koinon*.[15] These documents, which belong to the years 138–150, thus show a fair volume of diplomatic traffic between the *koinon* and the emperor—and are also accompanied on the inscription by six letters of Antoninus Pius in response to similar missives from individual Lycian cities.[16]

It was not the Lycian *koinon* alone which sent letters to the emperor testifying to the services of prominent citizens. For instance a fragmentary inscription from Ephesus contains a letter of Antoninus Pius in reply to one from 'the Hellenes in Asia' recording the benefits conferred by Vedius Antoninus.[17] Similarly, the new league of 'Panhellenes' instituted by Hadrian, and open to genuinely Greek cities from any province, testified to the services of M. Ulpius Eurycles of Aezani in Asia in letters to both the *koinon* of Hellenes in Asia and to Antoninus Pius, receiving a letter from him in reply.[18] The possibility of so regular an exchange of diplomatic or honorific communications between leagues and councils and the emperor has to be kept in mind as the background to those occasions when they made specific requests or complaints, brought accusations, or asked for decisions or rulings. In one instance, indeed, honours voted by the *koinon* of Lycia to one Jason son of Nicostratus were the subject of an accusation by a man named Moles. The matter was brought, possibly by the governor, before Antoninus Pius, who upheld the vote of the *koinon*—whereupon the *koinon* voted a decree of thanks which was taken to him, and presented by one of its members.[19]

There was no clear line between the honouring of individuals by a council and the acquisition by or for them of privileges, rights or ceremonial honours within the rituals and shows conducted by the council, for which imperial permission was required. So a man from Smyrna was 'honoured by the emperor (whose name is erased) with the charge of the conduct of the sacred contests of the most famous province of Asia';[20] and another from Ephesus gained from the emperor (perhaps Severus and Caracalla) the right to wear at his first ceremonial entry as Asiarch a gold crown and a purple robe.[21] We have already seen also that it came to be the emperors rather than the senate who gave permission for extra gladiatorial or other displays given by provincial high priests.[22]

---

[15] The standard text is now *TAM* II.3 905. Decrees for sending embassies: docs. 26, 53. Decrees to be sent on by the governor: docs. 32, 55, 59, 63, 66, 68. Letters of acknowledgment to the *koinon*: 40, 41?, 42, 44, 49, 51.

[16] p. 420.

[17] *IBM* III.2 493.

[18] Pius' letter: *OGIS* 506 = *IGR* IV 575; see J. H. Oliver, *Marcus Aurelius: Aspects of Civil and Cultural Policy in the East, Hesperia* Supp. XIII (1970), ch. iv, doc. 29; cf. 28 (*OGIS* 504 = *IGR* IV 573), letter of the Panhellenes to Aezani, and 30 (*OGIS* 507 = *IGR* IV 576), letter of the Panhellenes to the Hellenes in Asia. This chapter represents the fullest available account of the new Panhellenion.

[19] *IGR* III 704, ending with a letter of Antoninus Pius acknowledging the embassy.

[20] *IGR* IV 1441: τετειμημένον παρὰ τοῦ θειοτάτου αὐτοκράτορος [— — — — —] τῇ προστασίᾳ [τῆς] πράξεως τῶν ἱερῶν [ἀγών]ων τοῦ λαμπροτάτου [τ]ῆς Ἀσίας ἔθνους.

[21] p. 37, n. 66.

[22] p. 347, and cf. e.g. *Ins. Cret.* IV 305, a High Priest of Crete, μόνον Κρητῶν ἔχοντα κατὰ θείαν μεγαλοδωρίαν θεατροκυνηγεσίων ἡμέρας τρεῖς. μεγαλοδωρία refers to permission, not to imperial payment for the *venatio*.

The conduct of the affairs of a league or council involved both voting-rights and financial obligations (such as the upkeep of the hymnodes in Asia) on the part of the cities. Both areas were from the beginning subject to decisions by the emperors. For instance when Augustus commemorated his victory at Actium in 31 BC by founding a Greek city, Nicopolis, on the site, he ruled that it should be a member of the Amphictyonic League which met at Delphi, and should have six of the thirty votes in it.[23] Similarly, a newly-discovered inscription contains a perfectly-preserved letter of Commodus written in 190 to the city of Bubon in Lycia, in which he approves a decree of the *koinon* awarding Bubon three votes rather than its previous two; he does so in recognition of the city's success in killing and capturing bandits, grounds which were no doubt put forward by the ambassador from the city, whose name he gives in the usual way.[24]

It was probably also before the emperor (at some time in the early third century) that the jurist Licinius Rufinus from Thyatira acted as advocate for the council of Macedonia 'over the contribution of the Thessalians'—that is after Thessaly had been attached to Macedonia rather than Achaea.[25] The word used for 'contribution' here, *synteleia*, is exactly that which appears in the most specific imperial reply on this question, the letter which Valerian and Gallienus wrote from Antioch in 255 in reply to a one-man embassy from Philadelphia in Lydia.[26] The decree of Philadelphia and the speech of its ambassador had contained a request that the city should be freed from the *synteleia* made by the minor cities to the major ones (the *mêtropoleis*) towards the expenses of the high priesthoods and the official posts connected with festivals, on the grounds that Philadelphia itself had once been a *mêtropolis*. The emperors agree, while advising the city not to accept the privilege granted it in such a spirit as to cause offence.

Like magistracies and other offices within cities, the high priesthoods or other posts in the councils could be seen either as an honour, or as a burden to be avoided. It was inevitable therefore that questions of what circumstances gave exemption from high priesthoods should arise, and equally inevitable that some such cases should come before the emperor. So Septimius Severus on one occasion gave judgment in court (*decrevit*) that, although this was not a general ground for exemption, possession of five children exempted a man from being High Priest in Asia, and he later determined that this ruling should be valid for all provinces.[27] On the other hand it was possibly because any general exemption from public obligations also covered posts to be held in the provincial councils that it was to the *koinon* of Asia that Antoninus Pius wrote establishing the number of doctors, sophists and literature-teachers (*grammatici*) to whom minor cities, larger ones and the most important ones

---

[23] Pausanias x, 8, 3. See now G. Daux, 'Les empereurs romains et l'amphictionie pyléo-delphique', *CRAI* 1975, 348.

[24] F. Schindler, *Die Inschriften von Bubon (Nordlykien)*, S.-B. Öst. Akad. Wiss. CCLXXVII.3 (1972), 11, no. 2.

[25] *AE* 1946 180; see L. Robert, *Hellenica* v (1948), 29.

[26] J. Keil, F. Gschnitzer, 'Neue Inschriften aus Lydien', *Anz. Öst. Ak. Wien.* XCIII (1956), 219, on p. 226, no. 8; *SEG* XVII 528. Cf. C. P. Jones in *ZPE* XIV (1974), 294.

[27] *Dig.* L, 5, 8 *pr.* (Papinian).

could respectively give immunity. Modestinus, who records the provisions of this letter, says that the most important cities should be interpreted as those which were *mêtropoleis*—which often and perhaps always means those having a provincial temple of the imperial cult; and 'the larger ones' should be those which were assize-centres for the governors.[28]

It can be assumed that the letter was written in reply to an enquiry from the *koinon*, either brought by an embassy or sent on by the proconsul; and the issue could well have arisen in the *koinon* because of disputes over how many immunities from the obligations of provincial posts each city could grant. But if that is the most likely background, it is not the only possible one; for, as we have seen, the role of the councils was never confined to their own temples, cults and ceremonials; but on the contrary some, such as those of Sicily and Asia, are found representing the interests of the province in Rome even before the imperial period.[29] In the early empire provincial councils are found bringing requests and accusations before the senate, but they naturally turned also to the emperor himself. So for instance inscriptions reveal a man from Oenoanda who had been on embassy to Trajan at his own expense 'on behalf of the province of the Lycians';[30] one from Gortyn in Crete who was acting as ambassador 'on behalf of the province', to Trajan, perhaps shortly before the emperor's death in Cilicia;[31] another from Citium in Cyprus who was honoured by the *koinon* for going at his own expense to an unnamed emperor 'on behalf of the island';[32] and one from Dertosa in Spain honoured 'on account of embassies in the *concilium* of the province of Hispania Citerior successfully carried out before the emperor Antoninus'.[33]

In these cases we cannot discern the subject-matter of the embassies, any more than we can from the very fragmentary inscription from Larisa which seems to show an embassy from the Thessalian council to Gallienus at Sirmium.[34] But it is certainly the *koinon* of Asia to which Dio refers when he says that in 12 BC, 'when the province of Asia appealed urgently for help because of earthquakes, he paid its annual tribute from his own pocket into the *aerarium*';[35] in the same year it was in the temple dedicated to him by the *koinon*, at Pergamum, that Augustus had inscribed his edict preserving the rights of the Jews in Asia.[36]

In the Julio-Claudian period a number of prosecutions of proconsuls or procurators in Asia were brought before the senate, probably in most cases by the *koinon*.[37] Under Domitian the revival of Greek rhetoric in Asia was to achieve one of its earliest and greatest triumphs, in reversing an edict of

---

[28] *Dig.* XXVII, 1, 6, 2.
[29] pp. 386–7.
[30] *IGR* III 493, ll. 18–19.
[31] *AE* 1967 522; see L. Robert, *Documents de l'Asie méridionale* (1966), 80–1.
[32] *IGR* III 980.
[33] *CIL* II 4055. There may be a reference to an embassy to Trajan from the *concilium* of Africa in the inscription (*Ins. Lat. Afr.* 458) re-published more fully by P. Quoniam, 'Deux Notables de Bulla Regia', *Karthago* XI (1961/2), 1.
[34] p. 47.
[35] Dio LIV, 30, 3.
[36] Josephus, *Ant.* XVI, 6, 2 (165); cf. p. 257.
[37] For full references see P. A. Brunt in *Historia* X (1961), 224–7.

the emperor. Domitian, observing that two much wine and too little corn was being produced, ordered that no further planting of vines should take place in Italy, and that half of those in the provinces should be cut down.[38] The order represents one of the few attempts by a Roman emperor—or any ancient ruler or government—at any significant economic intervention, and was thereby inherently incapable of being enforced. None the less, it caused intense alarm in Asia, and the most famous sophist of the day, Scopelianus of Smyrna, was selected by the *koinon* to represent them before the emperor: 'an embassy from the *koinon* was needed, and a man who like an Orpheus or Thamyris would weave a spell on their behalf.' So effective was the oration, so Philostratus says, that the emperor was moved not merely to rescind his edict, but to threaten the punishment of those who failed to plant vines.[39]

In the second century, as we have seen, communications between the *koinon* of Asia and the emperor were a commonplace; for instance when Aelius Aristides delivered an oration *On Concord* at the meeting of the *koinon* at Pergamum in 167, he could allude to an imperial letter urging the cities to mutual harmony.[40] On one occasion at least a surprising degree of harmony seems to have been achieved, for it was in response to a request (*desideria*) of 'the Asians', which must mean the *koinon*, that Caracalla sent a rescript saying that the proconsul of Asia was obliged to arrive there by sea, and to visit Ephesus before the other *mêtropoleis*.[41]

Given the importance and prominence of the *koinon* of Asia, it is not entirely impossible that, if some Christians there appealed to Antoninus Pius or Marcus in about 161 against persecution, the emperor should have written to the *koinon* (though not in such positively favourable terms as our Christian sources represent), and that the letter should have been put up 'in Ephesus in [the sanctuary of] the *koinon* of Asia', just as Augustus' edict on behalf of the Jews had been at Pergamum. Even if the tradition is a fiction, it is one which made use of a significant element in the life of the empire.[42]

If our evidence is not misleading, the *koinon* of Asia was by far the most influential of the provincial councils, as the major cities of Asia were the most influential of provincial cities. But other councils, though again mainly Greek, could also approach the emperor. When for instance Dio describes 'the Bithynians' accusing a procurator of corruption before Claudius, this was no doubt an embassy from the *koinon*.[43] It was also to the '*koinon* of the Hellenes in Bithynia' that Severus Alexander wrote a letter, partially preserved both in the *Digest* and on a papyrus, evidently in response to

---

[38] Suetonius, *Dom.* 7, 2.

[39] *VS* I, 21; cf. *V. Ap. Ty.* VI, 42.

[40] Aristides, *Or.* XXIII Keil, 73; for the date and setting see C. A. Behr, *Aelius Aristides and the Sacred Tales* (1968), 104–5. I cannot follow his argument (p. 105, n. 30) that this will have been a letter of Antoninus Pius rather than Marcus.

[41] *Dig.* I, 16, 4, 5 (Ulpian, *De officio proconsulis*): 'ut imperator noster Antoninus Augustus ad desideria Asianorum rescripsit proconsuli necessitatem impositam per mare Asiam applicare καὶ τῶν μητροπόλεων Ἔφεσον primam attingere.' For the Ephesian inscription referring to the legal privileges of Ephesus as collected in Ulpian's *De officio proconsulis* see p. 342. Note also *IGR* IV 1236, an embassy from the *koinon* to the emperor 'about the twentieth' (the *vicesima libertatis?*).

[42] pp. 560–1.

[43] Dio LX, 33, 5 (13); cf. p. 224.

complaints that governors and procurators were physically preventing persons who had appealed from journeying to him.[44] In the nature of the case we can be certain that this complaint was brought by an embassy rather than sent on by the governor. Like most letters to Greek cities, this letter was sent in Greek.[45]

Of the other Greek provinces, Pliny mentions a letter of Titus to the Achaeans;[46] either Hadrian or Antoninus Pius sent a rescript in Greek to the *koinon* of Thessaly to rule that in a case where questions of criminal violence and possession of property were both involved, the former should be taken first;[47] and Antoninus Pius replied, also in Greek, to the *koinon* of the Thracians about the question of appeals against the rulings of imperial rescripts to individuals:[48]

> If anyone sends any communication to us, and we write anything back in reply, it is still open to those who wish to appeal against our ruling. For if they show that what was communicated to us was false or incorrect, it will be presumed that nothing has been prejudged by us, since our reply was based on information which was misleading.

Just as among provincial cities those of the Greek provinces predominate overwhelmingly in the surviving record of imperial correspondence, so the *koina* are far more fully represented than the *concilia* of the Latin provinces. However, Hadrian sent a rescript to the *concilium* of Baetica about what types of punishments were appropriate for cattle-rustlers under various circumstances.[49] Also a fragmentary inscription from Ain Zui in Numidia is clearly a response in some form by Severus Alexander to complaints about exactions by officials; the decree of the *concilium* is explicitly mentioned at one point.[50]

In the early fourth century, when there is very little evidence for the activities of the *koina* or *concilia*, Constantine is found issuing three pronouncements to 'the Africans', one of them explicitly a reply to a petition, and another formally addressed to 'the *concilium* of the province of Africa'. The first, of 315, which concerns abuses by officials, is described as an edict 'to the Africans' and was 'put up' in Carthage.[51] The second, also addressed 'to the Africans', is a letter issued from Serdica in May 327:[52]

[44] *Dig.* XLIX, 1, 25; *P. Oxy.* 2104. For a revised text and discussion see P. M. Meyer, 'Die *Epistula Severi Alexandri*: *Dig.* XLIX, 1, 25 = *P. Oxy.* XVII 2104', *Studi in onore di P. Bonfante* II (1929), 389. Apart from its contents, this text is extremely important in that in the version transmitted via the *Digest* the main text is effectively identical with that on the papyrus (which was originally published without the editors being aware of the *Digest* version). Cf. p. 514.

[45] cf. pp. 227–8.

[46] *Ep.* x, 65, 3.

[47] *Dig.* v, 1, 37 (Callistratus, attributing the rescript to Hadrian); XLVIII, 6, 5, 1 (Marcianus, attributing it to Antoninus Pius).

[48] *Dig.* XLIX, 1, 1, 1.

[49] *Coll.* XI, 7, 1–2; less fully in *Dig.* XLVII, 14, 1 *pr.* (both from Ulpian, *De officio proconsulis*).

[50] *CIL* VIII 17639 = Abbott and Johnson, *Municipal Administration*, no. 152; l. 20 mentions L. Apronius Pius, *leg. Aug.*, clearly L. Julius Apronius Maenius Pius Salamallianus, *PIR²* I 161, in office *c.* 224/6. Cf. Deininger, o.c., 135.

[51] *CJ* XII, 57, 1; cf. p. 258.

[52] *CTh* XI, 7, 4; note that the partial text in *CJ* x, 21, 1 begins in the middle with the provision about property, and therefore fails to indicate that the letter is a response; cf. p. 335.

Since in your protest (*subclamatio*) you have rightfully demanded that laxity in collecting overdue tribute should in no way be to the advantage of those who put off fiscal payments, we have specially ordered that it should be the rule that the property of those who contumaciously put off the payment of fiscal debts should be sold up, and the purchasers granted perpetual right of possession.

Finally, in his pronouncement addressed to the *concilium* of Africa, Constantine returns to precisely the issue about which Severus Alexander had sent his rescript to the *koinon* of Bithynia, laying down that governors should not take offence at appeals from their judgments, and must not imprison appellants or place a guard of soldiers over them. This document, which was put up in Carthage in July 329, was probably a letter written in response to a complaint from the *concilium*.[53] It is also probable from the subject-matter that it was brought by an embassy. The tradition of such addresses to the emperor still had a long life: Ammianus describes how in 364 or 365 the Tripolitanians, at the annual meeting of their *concilium*, chose two ambassadors to present gold statues of Victory to Valentinian to celebrate his accession, and also to complain of barbarian inroads and the refusal of protection by the *comes*. In the presence of the emperor they made a speech setting out their sufferings, and presented decrees containing the details.[54] Though in this case nothing but delay and further trouble resulted for the petitioners, the procedure as described illustrates with perfect clarity how the conventional form of approach to the monarch still survived after several centuries essentially unchanged.

The contacts of the *koina* and *concilia* with the emperor exhibit on a smaller scale many of the features of those on the part of the cities, which are illuminated by an incomparably greater volume of evidence. The background of recurrent formal and diplomatic addresses; the unquestioned involvement of the emperor in granting privileges and deciding disputes in a complex range of local ceremonials and cult-observances; the readiness to bring before him also both accusations and legal questions for decision; and above all the immense preponderance of evidence from the Greek east—all these features reappear in the relations of individual local communities and the emperor.

In spite of the real and significant role played by the *koina* and *concilia*, it is the relations of city and emperor which are the most essential to the nature of the empire as a social system. But first there remains a preliminary set of questions: what types and degrees of city-status existed, how were they acquired, and what was the role of the emperor in conferring them?

5. *Provincial Communities: the Acquisition of City Statuses*

It is twenty stades from Chaeronea to Panopeus, a city of the Phocians, if anyone would give the name of 'city' even to these people, who have no official building for magistrates, no gymnasium, no theatre, no market-place, no water

[53] *CTh* XI, 30, 15.
[54] XXVIII, 6, 7–9.

collected in a fountain, but live in hovels, which most resemble mountain huts, here on the edge of the ravine. But none the less they have territory marked by boundaries with their neighbours, and send representatives to the common council of the Phocians.

So writes Pausanias in his *Description of Greece*,[1] perfectly reflecting both the taste of the Graeco–Roman world for ordered and visible city life, and the fact that the definition of a city depended not on buildings but on its possession of certain legal rights. The city indeed provided the primary legal framework and the essential social context within which the lives of most inhabitants of the ancient world were conducted. As Pausanias' words show, it was hard to conceive of a city without an urban centre, and some at least of the normal range of public buildings; but what was more essential was its possession of the institutions of self-government, and a defined territory within which the jurisdiction of the city operated. In the nature of the case it is impossible to state precisely and with general application what conditions were required for recognition as a city. But one test will often have been the accepted right to send representatives to collective institutions; or, as we saw in the case of Emesa, to send ambassadors to the emperor.[2]

Under the empire the establishment of a new city as a constitutional entity was itself an act which depended on the emperor, and which might be petitioned from him. Both for this fact and for the expression by an emperor, or emperors, of a conscious ideology of the creation of cities, our best evidence is the Latin inscription of the later third or early fourth century containing an imperial reply to a request from the people of Tymanda in Pisidia, forwarded by an official, probably the provincial governor:[3]

... We have taken note, dearest Lepidus, of the fact that the Tymandeni hope with special longing, even with the greatest earnestness, to receive the right and dignity of a city (*civitas*) by our order. So since it is an established principle with us that throughout our world the honour and number of the cities should be increased, and since we see that they greatly desire to obtain the name and rank of a city, and also promise in the strongest terms that there will be a sufficient supply of town-councillors (*decuriones*) among them, we believe that the request should be granted ... In order, therefore, that this city may be able to carry out the same functions to which other cities are entitled, that is of assembling in the council-house, passing a decree and doing whatever else is permitted by law, they will have to elect magistrates, aediles, quaestors and whatever other posts need to be established ...

What the imperial letter, written in Latin because addressed to an official, calls a *civitas*, the people themselves would undoubtedly have called a *polis*. The creation of new Greek cities, sometimes by actual physical settlement, sometimes by granting of a city-constitution and sometimes by mere

[1] x, 4, 1.
[2] p. 368.
[3] *CIL* III 6866 = *ILS* 6090 = Abbott and Johnson, *Municipal Administration*, no. 151 = *MAMA* IV 236.

re-naming, had been a characteristic function of the Hellenistic kings,[4] was taken over by Roman pro-magistrates in the east in the last century of the republic, and continued by the emperors. The earliest foundation of a Greek *polis* by a Roman appears to be that established on the borders of Pontus by L. Licinius Murena in 83/2 BC, and duly named Licineia.[5] But it was of course with Pompey's foundations, Pompeiopolis, Neapolis, Megalopolis, Magnopolis, that the custom really took root. The imperial foundations or re-foundations often, though not always, bore the names of their founders, or of members of their families, followed by '-polis': Juliopolis, Claudiopolis, Flaviopolis, Philippopolis, Diocletianopolis, Constantinopolis.

Sometimes nothing more was involved than a change of name; Lucian records that the false prophet Alexander of Abonuteichus successfully petitioned Marcus Aurelius to have his native city renamed Ionopolis, and also for the right to mint coins; the coins are clearly attested, marked 'of the Ionopolites', and the town is still called Ineboli.[6] Where a new city came into existence, however, this must have involved the establishment of a constitution and laws. In almost all cases we have no evidence to illustrate this process, but various papyri tell us something of the constitution and privileges of Antinoopolis, the city which Hadrian founded in Egypt to commemorate his favourite Antinous, who was drowned in the Nile in 130. The city had the normal public buildings, including a theatre which was in the process of construction in 138, and a constitution based as usual on magistrates, council (*boulê*) and tribes. Its laws were adapted from those of Naucratis, the oldest of the few Greek *poleis* proper in Egypt, but with certain extra privileges: as a member of the *boulê* said in the course of a debate later in the second century, 'The right of legal marriage with the Egyptians was specially given to us by the Divine Hadrian. This the Naucratites, whose laws we use, do not have.' Hadrian also granted revenues for the upkeep of duly-registered children of citizens there, and freed the inhabitants from all obligations outside. Not surprisingly, these privileges subsequently required defence and reaffirmation, and the papyri contain letters to the city from Hadrian himself, Antoninus Pius, Marcus and Verus, and Gordian. That of Marcus and Verus, dating to 162, is a perfect instance of an imperial letter simultaneously acknowledging a city's greetings on accession and preserving privileges.[7] It is significant that Antinoopolis thus entered at once into the diplomatic relations with emperors which were characteristic of Greek cities.

[4] See the surveys in V. Tscherikower, *Die hellenistischen Städtegründungen von Alexander dem Grossen bis auf die Römerzeit*, Philologus, Supp. XIX. 1 (1927); A. H. M. Jones, *The Greek City* (1940), ch. i; *Cities of the Eastern Roman Provinces*[2] (1971).

[5] Memnon of Heraclea, *FGrH* 434 F. 26 (1): καὶ ἐπὶ ταῖς ἐσβολαῖς τῆς Μιθριδάτου βασιλείας κτίζει πόλιν Λικίνειαν. Cf. the community in Asia called Μουρηνιοι who appear on the new inscription from Ephesus published by Chr. Habicht, *JRS* LXV (1975), 64.

[6] Lucian, *Alex.* 58. See B. V. Head, *Historia Numorum*[2] (1911), 550.

[7] H. I. Bell, 'Antinoopolis: a Hadrianic Foundation in Egypt', *JRS* XXX (1940), 133; for the privileges granted by Hadrian and maintained by his successors see R. Taubenschlag, *Opera Minora* II (1959), 46–51; for the βουλή, A. K. Bowman, *The Town Councils of Roman Egypt* (1971), 14–15. The papyrus quoted is Wilcken, *Chrestomathie* I, no. 27. The second-century imperial letters are in *P. Würzburg.* 9, ll. 28–52, and *P. Strassburg* 130; Gordian's is *P. Antinoopolis* 191; for a reference to another, possibly the same, letter, see *BASP* V (1968), 48.

The vast majority of Greek *poleis* in the empire of course did not owe their existence as cities to Roman enactment, or still less to one of the emperors. But even in the case of already existing cities it was a common practice in the republic, though not formally attested in every area, for a Roman pro-magistrate, assisted by a commission of ten *legati*, to establish a general set of laws (the *lex provinciae*) on the constitutions of the cities; these provisions would then be ratified by the senate, and on occasion by the people in a *lex*. So for instance envoys from Narthacium in Thessaly, speaking in the senate in about 140 BC, referred to 'the laws of the Thessalians, which they observe up to this time, which laws Titus Quinctius (Flamininus) the consul gave on the advice of the ten *legati*, and in accordance with a *senatus consultum*'; Livy records in fact that the senate had subsequently confirmed Flamininus' measures.[8]

The same confirmation was required for Pompey's arrangements in Asia Minor, many of which, Dio says, were still in force in the early third century.[9] In the case of Pontus and Bithynia, Pliny's letters, dating from the early second century, reveal a few of the provisions of the *Lex Pompeia*;[10] it had laid down that magistracies in the cities should not be held before the age of 30, arranged for the co-optation of councillors by city censors, and permitted the Bithynian cities to enrol new citizens provided that they were not already citizens of another Bithynian city. However, the first of these had already been out-dated by an edict of Augustus, apparently of general reference, establishing 25 as the minimum age. As regards the second, reference is made to the *indulgentia* by which Trajan had already permitted certain cities to enrol councillors above the legal number—which, as we shall see, will certainly have been granted as a result of requests by embassies.[11] Moreover all three references arise because Trajan is being asked to make concessions as against the strict letter of the law, to remove anomalies created by previous imperial rulings or by custom. The process is a clear instance of the way in which the effective right to make law, which in the republic had always rested, even in the case of Pompey, with the organs of the *res publica*, had passed to the emperor in person. Even in this limited area, indeed, it is visible that it had done so from the beginning. Not only had Augustus' *edictum* superseded a provision of the *Lex Pompeia*, but elsewhere in the correspondence Trajan refers to a *libellus* from Nicaea claiming that Augustus had 'conceded' to the city the right to claim the property of any of its citizens who died intestate.[12] The expression makes perfectly clear that they had taken the initiative in requesting this privilege from the emperor.

Paradoxical as it may seem, it is necessary to begin with enactments, republican and imperial, relating to the foundation of new Greek cities or the regulation of the constitutions of existing ones, rather than with similar

---

[8] *Syll.*[3] 674 = Sherk, *Roman Documents*, no. 9, ll. 50–3; see Livy, XXXIV, 51, 4–6; 57, 1.
[9] XXXVII, 20, 2.
[10] *Ep.* X, 79–80; 112–13; 114–15. See A. J. Marshall, 'Pompey's Organization of Bithynia-Pontus: Two Neglected Texts', *JRS* LVIII (1968), 103.
[11] p. 427.
[12] *Ep.* X, 84; cf. pp. 159–60.

enactments relating to Italy or the Latin provinces of the west. For, first, the procedures in the Greek east reveal that it was possible to establish new cities, to give general laws or regulations for a whole range of cities, or specific laws for individual cities, and to grant or permit a city a new title, all without conferring any specifically Roman status. The cities concerned all became, or remained, Greek *poleis*. Secondly, the concept of a *polis*, if not perfectly definable, is in general terms clear and intelligible. The same does not apply to the definition of the characteristic terms used of urban communities in the west, *civitas, oppidum, municipium, colonia. Municipium* is the most troublesome, and indeed it remains impossible to offer a definition of the conditions necessary (in the imperial period) for the term to be applied—or even to prove that there were any such conditions. But even in the case of *colonia*, which is the least difficult, acute problems remain over the definition of the 'Latin right' (*Latium, ius Latinum* or *Latii*, or *Latinitas*) which some *coloniae*, many *municipia* and (as it now appears) some *civitates* possessed.[13] A further problem arises over whether communities in the provinces could be granted the Roman citizenship collectively, and if so, whether such a grant was necessarily linked with the adoption or conferment of any particular form of city constitution. All these questions are naturally relevant to our assessment of the role of emperors in relation to cities; but at the same time they may themselves be illuminated if we pay close attention to exactly what rights, statuses and privileges are clearly attested as being granted by the emperors, or requested from them. If a survey of these issues from this point of view turns out to suggest quite unorthodox conclusions, these may still be offered as a contribution to a continuing debate.

In Italy at any rate the complicating factors of grants of citizenship or 'Latin rights' do not arise in the imperial period, for since the Social War all the communities which had not possessed it previously had accepted full citizenship; the vast majority retained the designation of either *colonia* or *municipium*. Even in Italy, however, new cities could be created in the late republic, at least within the terms of agrarian laws for the settlement of civilians or discharged soldiers on the land. The unsuccessful agrarian law of 63 BC would have given the commissioners power to establish *coloniae*.[14] Caesar's law of 59 led among other things to the establishment of a *colonia* at Capua, whose citizens included some of the existing inhabitants, and new settlers who were still in the process of building themselves houses a few months before Caesar's murder in March 44 BC.[15] The settlement of soldiers in the triumviral period and by Augustus also involved the establishment of a significant number of new *coloniae* in Italy, most of which, however, replaced existing *municipia*.[16] Such a process involved not only the acquisition

[13] For the history of these terms and for full discussion of the problems see A. N. Sherwin-White, *The Roman Citizenship*[2] (1973).

[14] Cicero, *De lege ag.* II, 12/31; 13/34.

[15] Existing inhabitants, Cicero, *Pro Sestio* 4/9; *coloni*, Suetonius, *Jul.* 81, 1. See P. A. Brunt, *Italian Manpower 225BC–AD 14* (1971), 315f.

[16] See Brunt, o.c., 326–42, and App. 17. On the establishment of the constitution of a *colonia* in the late republic the best evidence is of course the bronze tablet with the *lex* of the Colonia Genetiva Iulia at Urso in Baetica, *FIRA*[2] I, no. 21.

of land, and its allotment to individuals brought to the spot, but the bringing into existence of the *colonia* as a constitutional entity, with a council and magistrates. In this Augustus himself will have been closely involved: as we saw, records of land distributed were kept in the imperial archive;[17] and Domitian, in giving judgment between Falerii and Firmum, refers to a letter which Augustus wrote to the soldiers of the fourth legion settled as *coloni* at Firmum, instructing them to sell all those portions of land granted to the *colonia* which had not been allotted to individuals.[18]

Aulus Gellius, as we shall see in more detail later, makes it precisely the essential difference between a *colonia* and a *municipium* that the latter enjoyed its own institutions, while the former owed both its existence and its constitution to Rome.[19] None the less, the text of what is probably an agrarian law passed by five tribunes in 55 BC speaks of 'whatever *colonia* is *deducta* under this law, and whatever *municipium, praefectura, forum* or *conciliabulum* is established', and thus may imply that *municipia* (as well as these other lesser, and little-known, urban institutions) could under certain circumstances be established as a legal act.[20] But of the two references in this period to men 'constituting' individual towns, one refers to some arrangement of affairs in an already long-existing *municipium*, Arpinum;[21] and the other is Caesar's reference to the fact that before 49 BC Labienus had 'constituted' the *oppidum* of Cingulum, and had built it up at his own expense;[22] the place is indeed not securely attested previously, but what, if any, constitutional act was involved still remains obscure.

Moreover, the only *municipium* in late-republican Italy for which a part of its laws survive in documentary form is Tarentum, which as the Greek city of Taras had been in existence since the late eighth century. In spite of the attachment of a Gracchan *colonia*, it was still recognizably a Greek city in the late republic.[23] It is clear that the bronze tablet which contains the constitution of Tarentum as a *municipium*, and which was found there, was also inscribed locally.[24] But the date, occasion, authorship and origin of the law are all entirely obscure. However, given that it clearly represents the giving of a new set of laws to an existing city, the circumstances may not have been entirely unlike those under which Halaesa in Sicily, after internal disputes, approached the senate to ask for 'laws' in 95 BC: the praetor, Claudius Pulcher, was appointed, and established rules for the co-optation of their senate (including the age-qualification of 30 which Pompey was later to apply

---

[17] pp. 263–4. On the granting of lands to *coloniae* by Augustus see also *Corpus Agrimensorum Romanorum*, 82–3, cf. 40.

[18] *CIL* IX 5420 = Abbot and Johnson, *Municipal Administration*, no. 63 = *FIRA²* I, no. 75. Cf. pp. 218–19.

[19] pp. 400, 408.

[20] For the text of the *lex Mamilia Roscia Peducaea Alliena Fabia* see *FIRA²* I, no. 12; for the probable date and circumstances see L. R. Taylor, 'Caesar's Agrarian Legislation and his Municipal Policy', *Studies in Roman Economic and Social History in Honor of A. C. Johnson* (1951), 68.

[21] Cicero, *Ad fam.* XIII, 11, 3.

[22] *BC* I, 15, 2.

[23] Gracchan *colonia*: Strabo VI, 3, 4 (281); Velleius I, 15, 4; Pliny, *NH* III, 11/99. Greek city: Cicero, *Pro Archia* 3/5; 5/10; Strabo VI, 1, 2 (253).

[24] *FIRA²* I, no. 18. See M. W. Frederiksen, 'The Republican Municipal Laws: Errors and Drafts', *JRS* LV (1965), 183, which is also basic to all the questions discussed in this section.

in Bithynia) conditions of disqualification, and a minimum census-rating.[25]

Halaesa did not thereby become a *municipium*, though it appears with this designation in the imperial period,[26] and it is not in the least certain that it was the 'giving of laws' to Tarentum which 'made' it a *municipium*—if indeed such an expression can properly be used at all. Moreover, the other much-quoted 'municipal' document from the late republic, the bronze tablet from Heraclea, was also inscribed locally and also comes from an old Greek city.[27] But the relevant part of it is not a law specifically for Heraclea but a copy of a general law laying down rules for the holding of office (including the age-qualification of 30), membership of the town-council and the conduct of the census in Italian towns of all descriptions—*coloniae, municipia, praefecturae* (and in some clauses *fora* and *conciliabula*).[28] It too contains no indication of date or circumstances; but it may be significant that in 45 BC Cicero enquired of Balbus as to 'what was in the law'—evidently a projected law of Caesar's; he replied that persons currently acting as auctioneers would be disqualified from being town-councillors, but former auctioneers would not. Precisely this provision appears in the document from Heraclea.[29]

Thus in the late republic general rules could be laid down for the various types of town in Italy, just as they could for the *poleis* of the Greek east. Under particular circumstances laws could also be given to individual towns; but it is quite uncertain whether this either would necessarily, or could, be connected with conferring upon them a particular status-designation, such as *municipium*. It was only with the establishment of a *colonia* that a particular form of constitution was regularly imposed, whether there was already an organized community on the site or not.

If the fundamental distinction which Aulus Gellius makes between *coloniae* and *municipia* is correct, the foundation of a *municipium* from Rome ought to be a contradiction in terms: for he claims that *municipia* were bound by no Roman laws except those which they voluntarily accepted, whereas *coloniae* 'do not come from outside into the (Roman) *civitas*, nor are based on their own roots, but are, as it were, propagated from the *civitas* (of Rome), and have laws and institutions which are all not of their own choosing but are those of the *populus Romanus*'.[30] The passing of general laws affecting *municipia* like all other types of town shows that this is not strictly correct. But it does correspond to a genuine historical distinction; and moreover it must be emphasized that it is coherent with the fact that—with one exception which proves the rule—there is not a single concrete and unambiguous case in the entire literary and documentary evidence for the empire which shows a town being specifically granted the status of *municipium*.

The exception is the instance which Aulus Gellius in the same passage quotes from an oration by Hadrian in the senate; the Praenestines, he recalled,

[25] Cicero, II *Verr.* 2, 49/122.

[26] See *RE* s.v. 'Alaisa'.

[27] See Frederiksen, o.c., 194f.

[28] *CIL* I² 593 = *ILS* 6085 = *FIRA²* I, no. 13, ll. 83f. (the first part contains regulations relating to the city of Rome, the reasons for inscribing which remain entirely obscure).

[29] *Ad fam.* VI, 18, 1, cf. *Tab. Herac.* ll. 104f.

[30] *NA* XVI 13.

had once urgently sought from Tiberius permission to revert from being a *colonia* to the status of *municipium*. Tiberius had granted the request in recognition of the fact that outside Praeneste he had once convalesced from a dangerous illness. Such a change was clearly regarded as a demotion, and a request for it as illogical; as Hadrian mentioned, it was more usually *municipia* which petitioned to be made *coloniae*. But he approved precisely because it would have restored to them (at least in principle) the right to use their own laws.

It is for this reason, because in the empire the change from *coloniae* to *municipium* was regarded as an anomaly, that the case of Praeneste is the exception which proves the rule. For what we lack is any certain instance whereby any community of lower status either sought or was granted promotion to the rank of *municipium*. What is in fact attested is not that, but the granting on the one hand of the privilege called *Latinitas* or *ius Latii*, or the full Roman citizenship, and on the other of the status of *colonia*. The latter, which developed in the first century AD out of the sending of genuine *coloniae*, may be considered later, for it affected both the Latin and the Greek provinces. The former grants were confined to the Latin-speaking areas, and are closely bound up with the complex and obscure history of the Romanization of Africa and western Europe.

No communal grants of full citizenship were made outside Italy until the Caesarian period. But in Cisalpine Gaul, not yet regarded as part of Italy proper, we find that Pompeius Strabo in 89 BC 'settled Transpadane colonies [that is north of the Po]. For he did not establish them with new *coloni* but gave to the former inhabitants, who remained on the spot, the *ius Latii*, so that they would have the same right as other Latin colonies, namely that by [sucessfully] seeking magistracies they would gain the Roman citizenship.'[31] The passage is extremely important, both for its clarity—in that it seems to define *ius Latii* by the privilege it offered to individuals who held magistracies —and because it exhibits a characteristic evolution of terms out of their original historical context. For there now existed communities which were called *coloniae* though they were not actually colonies, and were described as 'Latin' though their inhabitants had no connection with the geographical area of Latium.

In 65 the *coloniae Latinae* (whose identity, along with all the other problems of the history and organization of Cisalpine Gaul, cannot be discussed here)[32] are found making unsuccessful demands for the full citizenship;[33] but no general change took place until Caesar as dictator in 49, on the grounds of having been their governor, 'gave the citizenship to the Gauls living between the Alps and the Po'. Dio at least saw the act as a personal *beneficium*.[34]

Even before this, at some stage during his governorship of Gaul and before 51, Caesar, under the terms of the *Lex Vatinia* which appointed him, had established a new Latin colony at Novum Comum with 5,000 settlers added

[31] Asconius, *In Pis.* 2–3 (p. 3C).
[32] See U. Ewins, 'The Enfranchisement of Cisalpine Gaul', *PBSR* XXIII, n.s. X (1955), 73.
[33] Suetonius, *Jul.* 8: 'colonias Latinas de petenda civitate agitantes'; cf. Dio XXXVII, 9, 3.
[34] XLI, 36, 3.

14

to the existing inhabitants. Appian refers specifically to the Latin right and in exactly the same terms as Asconius—'of whom those who held annual office became Roman citizens; for this is the meaning of the Latin right'. It was precisely as a test-case of the legality of Caesar's foundation that the consul of 51 flogged an ex-magistrate of Comum, to demonstrate that he was not properly a citizen. Cicero was shocked—'Even if the man had not held a magistracy, he was still a Transpadane.'[35] Shocking or not, the action was one of the last occasions when the conferment by a Roman Imperator of any privilege on a provincial community was challenged by any representative of the *res publica*.

Novum Comum was at least a genuine colonial settlement. But Caesar went beyond this, and according to Strabo enrolled as citizens of it 500 Greeks to whom he also gave the full Roman citizenship, and who did not even settle there. We might find this hard to credit, if it were not for the fact that Cicero in 46 recommends to the proconsul of Sicily a Greek named C. Avianius Philoxenus, 'whom Caesar, as a *beneficium* to me, enrolled in the Novocomenses', and who had acquired the citizenship.[36] Once again we see that same progressive separation of status and function which is so marked a feature also of office-holding in the empire, and is a direct reflection of the emergence of monarchical characteristics in government.[37]

In 51 also two letters of Cicero refer in passing to rumours about the Transpadani 'that they had been ordered to elect *quattuorviri*', and 'about the elections of the Transpadani'.[38] Though nothing more is heard of this, the fact that the characteristic chief magistracy of *municipia* was a board of four might imply that it was supposed that Caesar was ordering the general establishment of *municipia*. But the deduction is highly uncertain, and even after 49 the fragments of a law or laws regulating jurisdiction in the area show that towns of various descriptions remained—*oppida, municipia, praefecturae, coloniae, fora, vici, conciliabula, castella*.[39]

Cisalpine Gaul ceased to be a province in 42 BC, and became part of Italy.[40] But already before this we have examples of communal grants of citizenship or *Latinitas* in provinces outside the Italian peninsula. The earliest case is Gades (Cádiz) to which Caesar gave the citizenship in 49 BC; according to Dio the grant was later confirmed by a vote of the people.[41] In 45 BC, when Caesar was in Spain again, Dio records that he gave land and immunity from taxation to those cities which favoured him, with

---

[35] Appian, *BC* II, 26/98; Cicero, *Ad Att.* V, II, 2.

[36] The evidence is conveniently collected by E. G. Hardy, *Some Problems in Roman History* (1924), 127–8. See esp. Strabo V, I, 6 (213); Cicero, *Ad fam.* XIII, 35.

[37] pp. 289–90, 293–4.

[38] *Ad Att.* V, 2, 3; *Ad fam.* VIII, I, 2.

[39] The Veleia tablet (*Lex Rubria*?): *FIRA*² I, no. 19; Fragmentum Atestinum: no. 20. See M. W. Frederiksen, 'The Lex Rubria: Reconsiderations', *JRS* LIV (1964), 129; and F. J. Bruna, *Lex Rubria* (1972).

[40] Dio XLVIII, 12, 5.

[41] Livy, *Per.* 110: 'Gaditanis civitatem dedit'; Dio XLI, 24, I. Pliny, *NH* IV, 22/119, describes it as an 'oppidum civium Romanorum qui appellantur Augustani urbe (urbs?) Iulia Augustana'. *CIL* II 1313 has 'mun(icipium) Aug(ustum) Gad(es)'. See H. Galsterer, *Untersuchungen zum römischen Städtewesen auf der iberischen Halbinsel* (1971), 17f.

citizenship for some and the title of *colonia* for others.[42] From a letter of Cicero's written after Caesar's death it appears that he had also conferred *Latinitas* on the Sicilians, and according to the same letter Antonius had now produced a spurious law supposedly passed through the assembly by Caesar, granting them the citizenship.[43] It is perhaps worth noting that this apparently non-existent law constitutes the last datable occasion on which the organs of the *res publica* are represented as having conferred the citizenship on a foreign community. All subsequent grants of citizenship or *Latinitas* are portrayed as actions of the emperor himself. So when Gaius says of *Latinitas* 'which right has been given to certain foreign *civitates* either by the people of Rome or by the senate or by Caesar',[44] it will have been from 'Caesar' that all the more recent grants will have come.

It is thus in the context of benefactions of various kinds to cities—relief from debt or refoundation after earthquakes—that Suetonius records that Augustus granted *civitas* or *Latinitas* to communities which claimed that they had deserved well of the Roman people.[45] The reference to communities claiming their *merita* may suggest, though cannot prove, that such grants were typically made in response to requests from the beneficiaries. Strabo's *Geography*, reflecting the situation under Augustus, shows that Latin rights were widespread in Baetica, had been granted by 'the Romans' to some communities in Aquitania, and were enjoyed by Nemausus. The definition given here is the same as elsewhere—'so that those elected to aedileships or quaestorships in Nemausus are thereby Roman citizens'.[46] From this time on the place of *civitas* and *Latinitas* among the benefits distributed by emperors is well established. 'What if the emperor gave the citizenship to all the Gauls, or immunity to the Spaniards?', Seneca wrote.[47] Pliny, describing the communities of Mauretania, lists in a single passage Oppidum Novum where Claudius settled veterans, Tipasa to which he gave *Latium*, Icosium to which Vespasian gave the same right, and Rusucurrium 'honoured with the citizenship by Claudius';[48] and Tacitus mentions in passing that Nero in 63 transferred the *nationes* of the Maritime Alps to the *ius Latii*.[49]

It has to be emphasized that the benefits which are granted are described as citizenship or Latin rights; it is never stated that a change of the local constitution followed, or still less that any community was 'made' a *municipium*; in the Celtic provinces indeed it can be shown that Latin rights were

[42] XLIII, 39, 5.

[43] *Ad Att.* XIV, 12, 1 (April 44 BC). A grant of citizenship to the whole island is recorded by Diodorus XIII, 35, 3, and XVI, 70, 6.

[44] *Inst.* I, 95; see pp. 405, 485.

[45] *Aug.* 47: 'urbium quasdam ... aut merita erga populum Romanum adlegantes Latinitate vel civitate donavit.' The reference may embrace two communities, Tingis (Dio XLVIII, 45, 3) and Utica (XLIX, 16, 1), which were given the citizenship in the triumviral period.

[46] III, 2, 15 (151), Baetica; IV, 1, 12 (187), Nemausus; IV, 2, 2 (191), Aquitania. Cf. also App. 4.

[47] *De benef.* VI, 19, 1.

[48] *NH* V, 1/20. The case of Rusucurrium, along with that of Volubilis, is decisive against the view of C. Saumagne, *Le droit latin et les cités romaines sous l'Empire* (1965), that the citizenship as such was never given to communities. See J. Desanges, 'Le statut des municipes d'après les données africaines', *Rev. Hist. du Droit* L (1972), 353, and H. Galsterer, 'Zu den römischen Bürgermunicipien in den Provinzen', *Epig. Stud.* IX (1972), 37.

[49] *Ann.* XV, 32. For this region note also Pliny, *NH* III, 20/135, a list of 'Latio donati incolae'.

enjoyed by communities with a variety of designations, *colonia, municipium, civitas* or *oppidum*.[50] These facts have to be remembered when we approach the well-known inscriptions from Volubilis in Mauretania which record the benefits which the community gained from Claudius. The most important inscription is the dedication in honour of M. Valerius Severus, son of Bostar, 'aedile, *sufes* (a Punic magistracy), *decemvir*, first *flamen* in his *municipium* . . .' It was set up by the council of the *municipium* of the Volubilitani, 'on account of his services to the community, and the successful embassy by which he gained for his own people from the Divine Claudius the *civitas Romana*, the right of legal marriage with foreign women, immunity from taxation for ten years, new settlers, and the right to the property of citizens killed in the war, and for whom there were no extant heirs'.[51]

The document is highly significant, firstly, in showing how the benefits were obtained. Like every other ambassador, Valerius Severus must have travelled to the emperor and made an appropriate oration before him. Secondly, it lists the citizenship along with a number of other privileges (one of which closely resembles the right gained by Nicaea from Augustus);[52] and thirdly it in no way implies that it had been Claudius who made the place a *municipium*. This in its turn has to be remembered when, passing over various grants made by the emperors of 68–9,[53] we come to the obscurely-worded statement of Pliny that Vespasian gave Latin rights to the whole of Spain. He may indeed have meant that Vespasian too made his concession under the pressures of civil war: 'To all of Spain Vespasianus Imperator Augustus, tossed by the storms of the state, gave [or yielded] the Latin right.'[54] If this speculation is not correct, however, then we have no evidence for the date or circumstances of the grant. But of its reality there is no doubt, for a few Spanish inscriptions refer explicitly to persons gaining the Roman citizenship *per honorem* (by holding a magistracy), by the *beneficium* of Vespasian.[55]

The right to the citizenship by holding office is clearly referred to in the municipal law of Salpensa in Baetica dating to the reign of Domitian, probably to its first two years.[56] The fact that this law, like its companion

---

[50] See the excellent paper by B. Galsterer-Kröll, 'Zum *ius Latii* in den keltischen Provinzen des Imperium Romanum', *Chiron* III (1973), 277.

[51] *Ins. Lat. Maroc* 116; cf. 56, a dedication to Claudius by the 'munic(ipium) Volub(ilitanorum), impetrata c(ivitate) r(omana) et conubio, et oneribus remissis'; and 57: 'divo Claudio, Volubilitani civitate Romana ab eo donati.'

[52] p. 397.

[53] Galba: Tacitus, *Hist.* I, 8, 1 (cf. 51, 4); Plutarch, *Galba* 18, 1–2 (the latter passage implying that the Gauls took the initiative in gaining citizenship and remission of tribute from Galba). Otho: *Hist.* I, 78, 1. Vitellius: III, 55, 2.

[54] *NH* III, 3/30, reading 'Universae Hispaniae Vespasianus imperator Augustus iactatus (rather than 'iactatum', agreeing with 'Latium') procellis rei publicae Latium tribuit'. Cf. Galsterer, *Städtewesen*, 37, n. 3; A. B. Bosworth, *Athenaeum*, n.s. LI (1973), 51–5. The sentence is given, devoid of all context, between details of the mines in Spain, and of its Pyrenean frontier.

[55] See Galsterer, *Städtewesen*, 43, n. 53.

[56] *FIRA*² I, no. 23. The provisions of the *ius Latii* appear clearly in para. xxv, but also (with some restoration) in xxi and probably by implication in xxii. Domitian is mentioned in paras. xxii–vi; the fact that the *cognomen* 'Germanicus', which he received in 83–4 (*RE* VI, col. 2550) is not used suggests (but does *not* prove) that the *lex* is previous to this. See Galsterer, o.c., 38, n. 13.

at Malaca,[57] was 'given' under Domitian, together with the fact that both towns have the designation *municipium Flavium*, has naturally led to the common assumption that both *leges* are necessary consequences of Vespasian's grant; that they represent the establishment of new *municipia*; and that they were 'given' by the emperor. But, as has been observed elsewhere, there are considerable objections.[58] Firstly, the acquisition of the title 'Flavium' need have no connection with a new constitution, In 77, for instance, Vespasian sent a letter in response to an embassy from Sabora in Spain, addressed to 'the *quattuorviri* and *decuriones* of the Saborenses' allowing them, among other things, to build a new *oppidum* 'named after me'.[59] It is unclear whether the place called itself a *municipium* or not, but in any case there is no question here of any grant of a constitution.

Secondly, on any interpretation there was a gap of several years between Vespasian's pronouncement and these two *leges*. Moreover the *lex* of Salpensa refers twice to persons of both sexes gaining citizenship either on the basis of this law, or by edict of Vespasian, Titus or Domitian.[60] It is also quite explicit in the *lex* of Salpensa that *duoviri*, *aediles* and *quaestores* were already in office in the *municipium* at the moment when the *lex* was given.[61] Perhaps then the reorganization took place spontaneously, and was officially approved by a 'charter' issued by the emperor?[62] But, as we have seen, while the *lex* of Salpensa speaks explicitly of *edicta* of Vespasian, Titus and Domitian, it contains no attribution of itself to Domitian. Indeed it cannot have been given directly by the emperor in Rome, for the magistrates in office are obliged to take an oath within five days 'after this law has been given'.[63] In other words the *lex* was given on the spot; by whom, on whose initiative, and whether the emperor had at any stage been involved, we do not know.

In spite of these problems it is clear that at the end of the first century Latin rights represented one of the two standard ways by which men gained the citizenship: Pliny, addressing Trajan, speaks of 'new (citizens) whether they had come into the citizenship by *Latium* or by the *beneficium* of the emperor'.[64] But in the second century, and only then, we hear of an extended form of Latin rights (*Latium maius*): Gaius defines it as the right not only of office-holders, but of those enrolled as town-councillors, to acquire the citizenship—'and that is indicated in several letters of emperors'.[65] It is reasonable to suppose that the letters were written in reply to approaches from cities, for the only explicit documentary reference to *Latium maius* which we have shows precisely this. It is a dedication put up by the people of Gigthis

---

[57] *FIRA*[2] I, no. 24. Domitian is mentioned, as a living emperor (and again without 'Germanicus') only in the oath formula in para. lix.

[58] For these points see H. Braunert, '*Ius Latii* in den Stadtrechten von Salpensa und Malaca', *Corolla Memoriae Erich Swoboda Dedicata* (1966), 68.

[59] *CIL* II 1423 = *ILS* 6092 = *FIRA*[2] I, no. 74: 'sub nomine meo'.

[60] Paras. xxii–iii. The edict of Vespasian seems to be his general pronouncement on *ius Latii*; the content of those of Titus and Domitian is unknown. Perhaps general edicts confirming *beneficia*? See p. 414.

[61] Para. xxvi.

[62] So Braunert, o.c.

[63] Para. xxvi. For this point see Galsterer, o.c., 44–5.

[64] *Pan.* 37, 3: 'novi, seu per Latium in civitatem seu beneficio principis venissent.' Cf. p. 484.

[65] *Inst.* I, 96.

in Africa to a local office-holder 'because over and above his many services to the city and his most abundant and willing generosity he undertook two embassies at his own expense to the city of Rome to obtain *Latium maius*, and at last reported success'. The privilege was thus achieved by the initiative of the town, and not without difficulty. The date is perhaps indicated by the dedication at Gigthis to Antoninus Pius, apparently described as 'founder of the *municipium*'.[66] In spite of appearances, this does not necessarily imply that Pius founded the town as a *municipium*. For 'Founder' was one of the appellations which existing towns or cities often addressed to benefactors.[67]

It cannot of course be *proved* that the expression *conditor municipii*, which is occasionally used elsewhere in Africa and Mauretania, always of emperors,[68] does not imply that the emperor in question formally conferred the title of *municipium*, or granted an appropriate local constitution. But it must be emphasized again that the only unambiguous instance of an emperor granting the status of *municipium* is the exceptional case of Praeneste, which was already a *colonia*. In the western provinces we cannot attest any positive introduction of urban institutions by any emperor other than the foundation of *coloniae*.[69] What is attested is the granting of *civitas* and *Latinitas* to communities, sometimes but not always in response to requests or claims by the beneficiaries. *Latinitas* is invariably defined strictly and solely in terms of the rights of citizenship for magistrates (or, for *Latium maius*, town-councillors also). It cannot be shown that any particular local constitution was either a precondition or a consequence of the grant. Nor have we yet seen any indication that the right brought any change in the condition of those members of these communities who did not gain magistracies; the question is one to which we shall have to return later.[70]

Communal grants of *Latinitas* persisted, as we have seen, into the second century. Similar grants of the full citizenship are, however, rarely, if ever, attested after the civil wars of 68–9. The one apparent allusion to such a grant is in the inscription from Lepcis dedicated to the memory of L. Septimius Severus, the grandfather of the emperor; according to this he

---

[66] *ILS* 6780; cf. 6779, '[C]onditori munic[ipi], Gigthenses pu[blice]' (or 'conditori, munic[ipes] Gigthenses publice'?). The reference to 'decuriones c.R.' in *ILS* 6781 (Thisiduo) may also be an implicit reference to *Latium maius*. It is not clear which type was the 'Lati[o] uno tempore impetrat[o]' by Lambaesis and Gemellae, *ILS* 6848. Note also *HA*, *Had*. 21, 6: 'Latium multis civitatibus dedit.'

[67] This is explicitly expressed, for instance, in *Pan.* VIII(5), 1, 1, addressed to Constantine. For Gordian III (238–44) as the Founder' (κτίστης) of Rhodes, see J. F. Oates, 'A Rhodian Auction Sale of a Slave Girl', *JEA* LV (169), 191, col. i, line 1, and see p. 200. For Hadrian as the 'conditor' of the already existing *colonia Gemella Julia Pariana* at Parium see *CIL* III 374; 'Hadriana' is now added. See B. Galsterer-Kröll, 'Untersuchungen zu den Beinamen der Städte des Imperium Romanum', *Epig. Stud.* IX (1972), 44, on p. 131. Note also *AE* 1969/70 592, a local figure as 'conditor' of his *colonia* (Sinope).

[68] See *CIL* VIII 799, Hadrian as '[condito]ri (?) munic[ipi]' of the *municipium Aelium Avitta Bibba*; VIII 27775 a–d, Hadrian as 'conditor' of the *municipium Aelium Hadrianum Augustum Althiburitanum*; *ILAfr.* 525, Severus and Caracalla as '[conditori]bus municipii Septimii Aure[l]ii Liberi Thug[ge]nsis'; *AE* 1949 55, Hadrian as 'conditori municipii' of the *Municipium Aelium Choba* (Mauretania Caesariensis).

[69] Contrast, however, Tacitus' report that Corbulo in 47 settled the Frisii on territory marked out by himself, and 'senatum, magistratus, leges imposuit', *Ann.* XI, 19, 1.

[70] pp. 485–6, and App. 4.

held the post of *sufes* at Lepcis (which towards the end of the first century is found with the designation *municipium*), and then was 'publicly elected *praefectus* when the Roman citizenship was first conferred'.[71] This must, however, be a reference to the fact that by 109–10 the town had become the *Colonia Ulpia Traiana Fidelis Lepcis Magna*.[72] For becoming a *colonia* did (as Aulus Gellius makes clear) imply a new constitution, normally headed by *duoviri*; and a *praefectus* would be appointed if one of the two duovirates was notionally held by the emperor.[73]

What the inscription refers to explicitly, however, is another invariable consequence of acquiring the rank of *colonia* in the imperial period, namely that all the citizens of the town became Roman citizens. There were other advantages as well, to which we shall come later. But for the moment it is important to stress that the rank of *colonia* is often explicitly attested as being conferred by emperors (and requested from them); that in the established empire it was the principal means by which the emperor gave the citizenship to communities; and as regards Greek cities it seems to have been the only means.

There seems indeed to be no obvious and immediate reason why an emperor could not have conferred the citizenship (or even *Latinitas*?) on a Greek *polis*. Philo in fact represents Agrippa I as saying in a letter to Gaius that in view of the favour in which he stood he might have dared to ask on behalf of his native city (Jerusalem), if not for the Roman citizenship, then at least freedom, or relief from taxes.[74] But for a full Greek *polis* it was, it seems, only the status of *colonia*—with the substantial privileges which normally attached to it—which carried sufficient prestige to be added to its existing standing as a city.

The custom of conferring the titular rank of *colonia* emerged, it seems, in the middle of the first century. The establishment of a genuine citizen *colonia* involved the settlement of colonists, the division of land, the imposition of a fixed form of local constitution, and might also bring with it the acquisition (if the site were in the provinces) of what lawyers of the imperial period called *ius Italicum*, whereby the land was subject to full legal ownership, as opposed to mere 'possession', and freedom from direct tribute on land or persons.[75] Some or all of a population already settled on the site could also be incorporated as *coloni* with the same rights, including the Roman citizenship, and this could be the case even with a long-established city. For instance the veterans of two legions were settled, probably in 15 BC, at

[71] *IRT* 412, and cf. *HA, Sept. Sev.* 1, 2. Municipium—*IRT* 342; 346.

[72] *IRT* 353. It is a pure assumption however that this inscription on the Arch of Trajan records the actual moment when the title was conferred. For the prefecture in this context see e.g. A. R. Birley, *Septimius Severus* (1971), 42–3, and H. E. Herzig, 'Die Laufbahn des Lucius Septimius Severus, Sufes, und das Stadtrecht von Lepcis Magna', *Chiron* II (1972), 393.

[73] Some *coloniae* developed from *municipia* did however retain *quattuorviri*, see A. Degrassi, *Scritta Vari di Antichità* I (1962), 99.

[74] *Leg.* 36/287: θαρρήσας ἂν ἴσως αἰτήσασθαι τῇ πατρίδι καὶ αὐτός, εἰ καὶ μὴ τὴν Ῥωμαϊκὴν πολιτείαν, ἐλευθερίαν γοῦν ἢ φόρων ἄφεσιν.

[75] See E. Kornemann, *RE* s.v. 'coloniae'; F. Vittinghoff, *Römische Kolonisation und Bürgerrechtspolitik unter Caesar und Augustus* (1952); note also B. M. Levick, *Roman Colonies in Southern Asia Minor* (1967), ch. i.

Berytus, which became the *Colonia Julia Augusta Felix Berytus*, and possessed the *ius Italicum*.[76]

Such a process may have provided a half-way stage to the conferment of the mere title of *colonia*, which could be accompanied by some, but not necessarily all, of these practical benefits. The development of this custom—once again typical of the empire in dissociating a title and privilege from its original context—is impossible to trace in detail; for of the several hundred cities, of which some are found in nearly all provinces, which had or acquired the title of *colonia* in the imperial period, most cannot be proved either to have received, or not to have received, an actual settlement of colonists. A few cases of titular grants, however, are relatively clear. As we saw, when Pliny lists the cities of Mauretania, he both mentions actual settlements of veterans and in the same paragraph calls Iol 'the capital of Juba, granted the right of a *colonia* by Claudius'.[77] Under 60 Tacitus mentions that 'the old *oppidum* of Puteoli received the right and title of *colonia* from Nero'; as an Italian city it had nothing but the status to gain, along with the appellation *Colonia Claudia Neronensis*.[78] The best evidence for the process by which the rank might be acquired is again the passage in Aulus Gellius where he discusses Hadrian's *oratio* in the senate. Most people were ignorant of the difference between *municipium* and *colonia*, and thought that the status of the latter was superior:[79]

> On the errors contained in this so widespread opinion, the divine Hadrian, in the speech *On the Italicenses* [his own place of origin] which he delivered in the Senate, discoursed with great learning, and expressed himself surprised that the Italicenses themselves and also certain other ancient *municipia*, among whom he mentions the Uticenses, although they could use their own customs and laws, had petitioned to be transferred to the status of a *colonia*.

In fact both Italica in Spain and Utica in Africa became *coloniae* named after Hadrian. Considerations of history evidently did not weigh sufficiently against the now conventional status-order. Their inhabitants may have been influenced also by the hope of more substantial benefits. But if so they were disappointed, for in Paulus' list of the *coloniae* which either had *ius Italicum*, or at least were immune from tribute, Italica does not appear; and Utica is described as having been granted the *ius Italicum* by Severus and Caracalla, along with two other African colonies, Carthage and Lepcis Magna.[80]

Hadrian's speech is also important for making clear that the initiative in seeking the status of *colonia* had come from the *municipia* themselves, though not whether they had addressed themselves to Hadrian or, as was still not unknown, to the senate.[81] The former is more likely—Ulpian mentions

---

[76] For details see Schürer, *Jewish People* I, 323, n. 150.

[77] Pliny, *NH* v, 1/20; cf. p. 403.

[78] *Ann.* XIV, 27, 1. The grant seems to have applied to a *municipium* surviving alongside an Augustan *colonia*. Up till recently the latter was not reliably attested, see *RE* s.v. 'Puteoli', XXIII.2, 2041–2; but see now *Rend. Acc. Naz. Napoli* XLV (1971), 219.

[79] *NA* XVI, 13, 4–5. See R. Syme, 'Hadrian and Italica', *JRS* LIV (1964), 142, and for discussion and bibliography F. Grelle, *L'autonomia cittadina fra Traiano e Adriano* (1970), ch. ii.

[80] *Dig.* L, 15, 8; African *coloniae* in 8, 11.

[81] pp. 343–50.

even a village (*vicus*) in Dacia which gained the status of *colonia* by request to Septimius Severus.[82] Ulpian's survey of *coloniae*, in his *On the Censuses*, is concerned with whether various *coloniae* in the Syrian region, Asia Minor and Dacia had or had not the *ius Italicum*; Paulus' survey notes also whether the places, even if without *ius Italicum*, had the privilege of immunity from tribute. Both of them regard both the making of *coloniae* and the conferment of these optional and additional privileges as the work of different individual emperors. So for instance Paulus writes:[83]

> The Divine Antoninus [Pius] made the Antiochenses *coloni*, but without relief from tribute. Our Emperor Antoninus [Caracalla] made the city of Emesa a *colonia* with the *ius Italicum*. The Divine Vespasian made the Caesarienses [in Judaea] *coloni*, without adding the *ius Italicum*, but remitting the poll-tax: but the Divine Titus gave the ruling (*interpretatus est*) that the soil had been made immune also.

Thus yet another act which had once been carried out by a law of the Roman people had become a *beneficium* to be conferred at will, and on terms of his choice, by the emperor. In the case of Caesarea, moreover, we can be reasonably sure that when Titus 'interpreted' Vespasian's conferment in a wider sense, this was either a response to a request from the city, or a decision in a dispute about tribute.

That marginal case apart, there is no concrete evidence of any Greek city formally requesting the rank of *colonia*.[84] They may none the less have done so, but our evidence suggests that to the Greek cities what was more important was freedom and immunity, and if they sought a particular status, it was a local one, which would alter the relative prestige of a city and its neighbours. So for instance a Byzantine encyclopaedia preserves for us the name of 'Paulus, a Tyrian, a rhetor . . . who by an embassy to Hadrian had his city made a *mêtropolis*'.[85] For those communities which did not have it already, it was the status of *polis* which was sought, as when the historian Julius Africanus from Jerusalem went on an embassy for Emmaus, and gained permission for it to become the city of Nicopolis.[86] It is paradoxical in view of the immense historical importance of the development of urban institutions in the Latin west under the Roman empire that the most explicit and detailed evidence for the conferment of city status by emperors should come from the Greek east. But it was there that the concept of a city had the strongest hold, and the need for that status most keenly felt. So for that very reason, because local communities did bring such requests to the

[82] *Dig.* L, 15, 1, 8–9: 'In Dacia . . . et Patavissensium vicus, qui a divo Severo ius coloniae impetravit.'

[83] *Dig.* L, 15, 8, 5–7.

[84] Though note that Ulpian (*Dig.* L, 15, 1, 3) says that Severus 'ius Italicum ob belli civilis merita concessit' to Laodicea, which could imply a request.

[85] Suda s.v. Παῦλος (ed. Adler IV, 69).

[86] Eusebius, *Chron.* ed. Schoene II, 178–9; Jerome, *Chron.* ad AD 221 (ed. Helm, p. 214): 'In Palaestina Nicopolis, quae prius Emmaus vocabatur, urbs condita est, legationis industriam pro ea suscipiente Iulio Africano scriptore temporum.' Other late Christian sources give 223, see *PIR*² I 124. For the problems connected with the status of Emmaus-Nicopolis see Jones, *Cities of the Eastern Roman Provinces*² (1971), ch. x, n. 72.

14*

emperor, it may be that our evidence on the role of the emperor in east and west is not wholly misleading.

At any rate it is nowhere clearer or more explicit than in Constantine's letter of 324–6 to Flavius Ablabius as *vicarius* of Asiana, recording his assent to the request for city status made by the people of Orcistus on the borders of Phrygia and Galatia:[87]

> To those who are eager either to found new cities or to adorn ancient ones or to revive decayed ones, what was requested was particularly welcome. For they claimed that their village over long previous ages enjoyed the splendour of a town, being adorned by the symbols of office of annual magistrates, having a large number of town-councillors, and being filled with a population of citizens ... It is unworthy of Our times that so appropriate a place should lose the name of city ... To all these considerations it comes as it were as the culminating argument that all the inhabitants are said to be devotees of the most holy religion.

In spite of the novel element introduced by the adherence of the Orcistans to Christianity,[88] the situation was essentially a traditional one, the assertion of a status of which they had been deprived by the efforts of a neighbouring city. It is even more typical that in 331 they had to petition Constantine again to protect their status and independence against the claims of the other city, Nacolea, that they should continue to make contributions for the upkeep of its cults. For it was precisely in order to protect their rights and privileges that for centuries previously the cities of the Greek east had most commonly addressed themselves to the Roman emperors.

6. The Cities: Diplomacy and the Retention of Privileges

In the autumn of 31 BC, when Octavian was briefly in Asia after the battle of Actium, an embassy from the city of Rhosus appeared before him at Ephesus. His reply was inscribed at Rhosus, probably in the following spring:[1]

> Imperator Caesar, *divi filius*, hailed as *Imperator* for the sixth time, consul for the third time, consul-designate for the fourth, to the magistrates, council and people of the sacred, inviolate and autonomous city of Rhosus, greetings. If you are well, it is well. I and the army are well. The ambassadors sent by you, Seleucus my naval commander, Heras Calli[.....]eros, Symmachus, good men from a good people, our friend and ally, having come to me at Ephesus, addressed me on the matters on which they had instructions. On receiving them I found

---

[87] *MAMA* VII 305; cf. p. 131. The letter to Ablabius is Panel I, l. 8–11, l. 16. The letter of 331 to the *ordo civitatis Orcistanorum* is III, 4–32. Cf p. 438.

[88] Note also that Maiuma, the harbour of Gaza, as a reward for abolishing its pagan cults and embracing Christianity, gained from Constantine the status of *polis*, with the name 'Constantia', Eusebius, *VC* IV, 38–9; cf. Sozomenus, *HE* V, 3, 6–8 (on the successful action which Gaza brought before Julian in person to have the old status of Constantia restored).

[1] *IGLS* III 718 = Sherk, *Roman Documents*, no. 58, doc. iii; see *JRS* LXIII (1973), 58. On the presentation of gold crowns (*aurum coronarium*, στέφανος) see pp. 140–2.

them to be patriotic and good men, and accepted the honours and the gold crown. When I come to those parts I will do my best to be of service to you and to preserve the privileges of the city; and I will do this the more gladly because of Seleucus my naval commander who served with me throughout the war, distinguished himself on all occasions and gave every evidence of goodwill and loyalty. He has lost no opportunity of interceding on your behalf and of giving enthusiastic support to your interests.

The procedure exhibited here follows a pattern which was already clearly established, and was never significantly altered in the following centuries. The cities of the Greek east knew that the occasion of Octavian's decisive defeat of Antonius and Cleopatra required the voting of honours to the victor and the despatch to him of an embassy to announce these honours, present a gold crown and make a suitable speech. Octavian for his part knew that the ambassadors must be received and heard, and their communications acknowledged in letters to the cities; and that something must be said to reassure those cities with privileged statuses that their rights would be maintained.

We can presume indeed that the embassy from Rhosus had formally requested that Octavian should make a pronouncement to this effect. Moreover, both they and he seem to have presumed that nothing beyond such a pronouncement was required; Octavian is unusual only in putting off such a statement until he reaches Syria (as he did in the following year). The initiative thus came, as was the rule, from the city; and in taking it they naturally chose as an ambassador a man who would have the best claim on Octavian's affection and goodwill.

In 30 BC, as we saw earlier, Octavian was to write again to Rhosus, recommending Seleucus and expressing his willingness to hear requests from the city.[2] In this case it was he who took the initiative. But while such an act was to prove rare on the part of any emperor, it was most common precisely, in this context, in letters recommending individuals, or testifying to their services. Such letters were however sent not only to cities from the emperor, but also from them to him, just as they were by *koina*.[3]

The diplomatic contacts between the cities and the emperor, which consisted essentially of deferential approaches from them to him, and of his responses, were an essential part of the social and governmental system of the empire. The occasions—primarily accessions, victories and formal events such as the assumption of the *toga virilis* by Gaius[4]—required primarily formal exhibitions of loyalty. But they were also commonly used, especially in the case of accessions, as the moment to ask for the preservation of existing privileges. Not surprisingly, the orations delivered before the emperor did not always stop at that, and the occasion might be taken to ask for new rights or privileges, or to ask for a favourable ruling on some local dispute. In subject-matter therefore, such approaches were not always wholly distinguishable from those of embassies sent in the first instance to ask for

[2] p. 7.
[3] pp. 388–9 (*koina*); pp. 419–20 (cities).
[4] cf. pp. 385–6.

help, represent a city in a dispute, or bring accusations. But the distinction is still sufficiently clear to allow us to treat as a separate, and highly significant and characteristic, group those approaches whose purpose was primarily diplomatic.

The moment of the accession of a new emperor was of course the crucial occasion, and all the more so if it came through victory in a civil war, when suspicions of non-adherence particularly needed to be dispelled. But something was also required when a man was clearly marked out as his successor, or taken as his colleague, by the reigning emperor. So in AD 4, when Tiberius was adopted by Augustus and given the *tribunicia potestas*, the city of Aezani in Asia sent an embassy with a congratulatory decree; he had gone straight off on military service, however, and they seem to have caught up with him only at Boulogne, from where he sent his formal letter of acknowledgment to the city.[5] When he acceded in 14, an embassy came from Cos to hand over a decree and express the city's loyalty; as frequently happened, there was some delay, and Tiberius' reply was written after mid-summer of 15.[6]

When Gaius became emperor in 37, our sources agree that there was general rejoicing, however shortlived. Philo clearly implies that all communities were expected to despatch decrees, for he describes how the prefect of Egypt held up that of the Alexandrian Jewish community, 'so that we alone of all men under the Sun would be regarded as hostile'.[7] One community which did send an embassy at this time was the city of Assos in the Troad, and the inscription recording what took place confirms the implication of Philo's words:

> Since the rule of Gaius Caesar Germanicus Augustus, the hope of the prayers of all mankind, has been proclaimed, and the joy of the world knows no bounds, and every city and every province has hastened to set eyes on the god, as the happiest of ages in now dawning for men: it was voted by the council and the Romans in business among us and the people of Assos to appoint an embassy of the foremost and best Romans and Greeks to address and congratulate him, and to beg him to remember and care for the city . . .

An oath of loyalty was taken at the same time, and an embassy of one Roman citizen and four Greeks went to Rome, and while there sacrificed on the Capitol for the safety of Gaius.[8] In all these cases there are clear indications both that the embassies were meant to gain the new emperor's goodwill, and that the apparent failure to send even an honorific decree could arouse fears of the opposite effect; but there is no evidence that other specific requests were addressed to the emperor at this moment.

When Claudius was proclaimed by the Praetorian cohorts on 24 January 41, however, two at least of the embassies which arrived came not only with honours but with pressing demands. By 10 November in that year the

[5] *IGR* IV 1693 = *ILS* 9463. Cf. Velleius II, 104, 4, and *ILS* 8898 (Bavai): 'Ti. Caesari, Augusti f., divi nepoti: adventui eius sacrum.'
[6] *IGR* IV 1042. He is *trib. pot.* xvii, probably from 26 June 15.
[7] *In Flacc.* 12/101.
[8] *IGR* IV 251 = *Syll.*[3] 797 = Abbott and Johnson, *Municipal Administration*, no. 48.

Alexandrians had passed a decree offering various honours to the new emperor, and making various requests of him; an embassy of twelve had been to Rome and returned, and the letter had been read out in the city. For on that date 'since at the reading of the most sacred letter, and most beneficial to the city the whole population could not be present owing to its numbers', the prefect of Egypt had it posted up for everyone to read.[9] Furthermore, if we adopt the hypothesis that the order of the topics referred to in Claudius' long letter follows that in which the matters were presented to him, it will emerge that they began with expressions of loyalty: 'Your ambassadors presented me with the decree and spoke at length about the city, directing my attention to your goodwill towards us, which you may be sure has long been stored in my memory.'[10] Then there were offers of various honours: the celebration of Claudius' birthday as a sacred festival; statues in Rome and Alexandria; the naming of a tribe after the emperor, and so forth. One is declined, the institution of a high priest and temple of Claudius himself.

Then came a number of requests relating to the public life of the city: the rules for citizenship of Alexandria; the choice of temple-wardens for the temple of Augustus; the term of office of magistrates. A decision on one point is deferred, namely whether Alexandria could be permitted a council (*boulê*) like normal *poleis*.[11]

These were requests for approval of new arrangements, which required imperial approval and might be accepted or rejected, but were not in any significant sense contentious. But what comes last, the question of the recent violent conflicts with the Jewish community, was a different matter, on which there had evidently been a disputation before Claudius between the Alexandrian embassy and a Jewish one (or possibly two Jewish embassies). Claudius declines to apportion blame, but sternly warns both sides to keep the peace and observe the *status quo*.

A closely comparable progression can be observed in the letter written by Claudius to the city of Thasos in 42.[12] He acknowledges the evidence of their enthusiasm and piety towards himself, communicated by more than one embassy; refuses a temple on the grounds that such a thing is appropriate only to gods, while accepting those honours suitable to the best of rulers; preserves the privileges granted them by Augustus; and in a very fragmentary part of the inscription appears to decide in their favour some issues about revenues, and the export of corn. At the end there survives a list of the ambassadors who 'handed over the decree'.

Similarly, just enough remains of a letter of Claudius to Samos in 41 to show that this too preserved their existing rights.[13] A papyrus also preserves part of a letter from Nero to an Egyptian city, probably Ptolemais, and the

[9] Tcherikover and Fuks, *Corp. Pap. Jud.* 153 (with previous publications and bibliography).
[10] ll. 20–3, trans. Tcherikover and Fuks; cf. p. 218.
[11] On the abnormal constitution of Alexandria and the relatively close control exercised by the prefect (shown here also by his being concerned with posting up the letter to the city), cf. pp. 380, 384.
[12] C. Dunant, J. Pouilloux, *Recherches sur l'histoire et les cultes de Thasos* II (1958), 66, no. 179.
[13] P. Herrmann, 'Die Inschriften römischer Zeit aus dem Heraion von Samos', *Ath. Mitt.* LXXV (1960), 68, on p. 94, no. 6; an ambassador to Claudius is honoured in no. 54, p. 157.

6475 Greeks settled in Arsinoe, in which he declines a temple, returns as a favour the gold crown which they had sent, and maintains their rights, including those granted by 'my divine father'.[14] But the established institution of approaching an emperor in his accession was, as was mentioned earlier, all the more urgent when he was proclaimed in a situation of civil war. So Josephus describes how Vespasian, after being proclaimed in Caesarea in 69, moved to Berytus, 'where many embassies from Syria, and many from the other provinces, met him, bringing crowns and congratulatory decrees from each city'. When he reached Alexandria in the winter, he was greeted 'by embassies of congratulations from every quarter of the world, now his own; and that city, though second only to Rome in magnitude, proved too confined for the throng'.[15]

Titus, followed certainly by Domitian, Nerva and Hadrian, and probably by all subsequent emperors as a matter of form, issued an edict at his accession confirming the *beneficia* granted by his predecessors.[16] The purpose was precisely to obviate the need to request re-affirmation of privileges whenever a new emperor acceded; and it seems to have applied in principle to communities as well as to individuals. But, as the dossier of imperial documents from Aphrodisias alone would show without other evidence,[17] such pronouncements were not sufficient in practice to upset long-established diplomatic forms.

It is quite clear that embassies bringing congratulations continued to be sent to a new emperor from all quarters. The atmosphere and after-effects of such a situation are nowhere more clearly portrayed than in the oration of Dio of Prusa, who had been a member of the embassy which the city sent to Trajan after his accession in 98. Rumours circulated in Prusa that their embassy had not been well received by the emperor: 'As if', Dio says, 'it were incumbent upon him to meet at the gate and there embrace all arrivals, or to speak the names of those who had not yet arrived, or to enquire about this one or that one, wanting to know how they were or why they had not all come.' Others spread the tale that the ambassadors from Smyrna in Asia had received lavish gifts, and that another city had been given both money and permission for a large increase in the number of its city-councillors. But why should they have demanded that imperial favour be shown only to them? Trajan had behaved as he was required to do: 'Being at once the most benevolent and sagacious of all men, the emperor not only gave me what I asked, but also gave others what they asked.' Dio will have delivered the

---

[14] O. Montevecchi, 'Nerone a una polis e ai 6475', *Aegyptus* L (1970), 5.

[15] *BJ* IV, 10, 6 (620); 11, 5 (656), Loeb trans. For Vespasian receiving embassies in Alexandria compare also the references in Philostratus, *V. Ap. Ty.* v, 28, and VII, 18.

[16] Suetonius, *Tit.* 8: 'primus praeterita omnia (beneficia) uno confirmavit edicto nec a se peti passus est'; cf. Dio LXVI, 19, 3. Domitian: LXVII, 2, 1. Nerva: Pliny, *Ep.* x, 58, 3 and 7–9. Hadrian: *Dig.* XXVII, 1, 6, 8 (Antoninus Pius, quoted by Modestinus): τούτοις ἅπασιν ὁ θειότατος πατήρ μου παρελθὼν εὐθὺς ἐπὶ τὴν ἀρχὴν διατάγματι τὰς ὑπαρχούσας τιμὰς καὶ ἀτελείας ἐβεβαίωσεν. See Mommsen, *Staatsrecht*[3] II, 1126–9.

[17] On the Aphrodisias dossier see p. xiii. The letter from Hadrian may well refer to the general edict issued by him—τὴν μὲν ἐλευθερίαν καὶ αὐτονομίαν καὶ τὰ ἄλλα τὰ ὑπάρχοντα ὑμεῖν παρὰ τῆς συγκλήτου καὶ τῶν πρὸ ἐμοῦ Αὐτοκρατόρων ἐβεβαίωσα πρόσθεν. But the unpublished letter of Gordian confirming the rights of the city is explicitly a response to an embassy congratulating him on his accession, as is that of Decius and Herennius (see pp. 343, 417).

oration which accompanied delivery of the decree; Prusa too had then
requested, and gained, an increase of 100 in the permitted number of its
councillors.[18]

It is thus perfectly clear that in 98 a general concourse of embassies from
Greek cities came before Trajan, and that they used the occasion to gain
extra rights, and imperial largesse. From the same moment a letter of Trajan
to Alexandria, preserved on a papyrus, shows him acknowledging the city's
goodwill, referring to the benefits conferred by Nerva and to certain rights
(*dikaia*) of theirs, and saying that he will write to the prefect of Egypt, his
amicus Pompeius Planta, to see that he takes care for their public order, corn-
supply and communal rights.[19] The surviving text of the letter breaks off
before it is indicated whether or not an embassy had come from Alexandria
also.

His letter to Delphi, however, also written in 98, refers to their embassy,
and confirms their freedom, autonomy and privileges granted by earlier
emperors; here too he says that he has written, or will write, to the governor,
this time about an accusation which they had made against one Pythodorus.[20]
Similarly Hadrian in 118, the year after his accession, writes to the magistrates, council and people of the island of Astypalaea: 'Both from your
ambassador Petronius, son of Heracon, and from your decree I have learnt
how you rejoiced at my succession to my father's rule, so giving you my
approval and [. . .] your freedom.'[21] In 118 also Hadrian replied to an
embassy from Delphi, confirming the freedom and immunity and other
beneficia granted to the city.[22] An ambassador from the *synodos* of *neoi*
(young men) at Pergamum had reached the new emperor even earlier, for
it was from Juliopolis in Bithynia, on his way from Syria to the Danube and
thence to Rome, that he wrote early in November 117 to acknowledge their
congratulations. From his letter it seems that this was a purely diplomatic
embassy, for he refers to no request on their part, but writes simply: 'Having
learnt from the letter and from the ambassador, Claudius Cyrus, of the joy
which you profess to having felt on our behalf, I regard this as a characteristic
of good men. Farewell.'[23] The persistence, in spite of general imperial edicts,
of specific requests for confirmation of rights should be seen in the context
of purely congratulatory embassies such as this.

When L. Aelius Caesar was adopted as his successor by Hadrian in 136
embassies went to him in Pannonia: examples are known from inscriptions
at Laodicea on the Lycus, Sparta, and possibly Magnesia.[24] When he died

---

[18] *Or.* XL, 13–15 (περὶ τῆς πρεσβείας ἣν ἐπέμψατε εὐχαριστοῦντες), Loeb trans. The 100
councillors, *Or.* XLV, 7; cf. 3–4 (comparison with Trajan's favour to a prominent city of Asia,
probably again Smyrna).

[19] *P. Oxy.* 3022.

[20] Plassart, *Fouilles de Delphes* III. 4 (1970), no. 287.

[21] *IGR* IV 1031C = *Syll.*[3] 832 = Abbott and Johnson, *Municipal Administration*, no. 75 (where
the heading, though not the restoration of the emperor's name, inadvertently ascribes it to Trajan).
Note that this is one of four letters addressed by Hadrian to this modest Aegean island.

[22] Plassart, o.c., no. 301.

[23] *IGR* IV 349 (another fragmentary copy in IV 351, ll. 13–15) = *Syll.*[3] 831.

[24] Laodicea: *IGR* IV 862 = *MAMA* VI 3, see J. Robert in J. des Gagniers *et al.*, *Laodicée du
Lycos: le nymphée* (1969), 358–9. Sparta: *IG* V. 1, 37. Magnesia: *Inschriften von Magnesia* (1900),
no. 180.

in 138, and Hadrian adopted Antoninus Pius and then died also, the established pattern is revealed again. It is not, however, till 140, that we find Antoninus Pius replying to an embassy from Coronea in Boeotia: 'In appropriately recalling my divine father, in suitably celebrating my accession and in rejoicing enthusiastically over my son, you have acted in a way proper to Hellenic men.'[25] At about the same time a dedication was put up in Rome to Antoninus by the city of Mopsuestia in Cilicia, 'which by his divine judgment had retained securely its ancient rights'.[26]

In 193, which like 69 saw a series of proclamations and counter-proclamations of emperors, Herodian describes embassies coming from all parts to congratulate Pertinax, and later others gathering from the eastern provinces to acknowledge Pescennius Niger after his proclamation at Antioch. In the next year, after Severus' forces had defeated Niger at Cyzicus, the Nicomedians were careful to send an embassy to him with promises of supplies for the army. Their rival city of Nicaea made the mistake of neglecting to do so.[27] The following years which saw the ending of civil wars, victories against Parthia and the elevation of Caracalla first as 'Caesar' and then as joint Augustus with his father, produce a whole series of imperial letters in response to manifestations of loyalty, which we may take as reflections of an unusually prolonged period of uncertainty in the establishment of a new regime.[28]

Probably in the winter of 195/6 Severus writes in reply to an embassy from Aezani in Asia acknowledging their pleasure at his successes, and at the entry of Caracalla on hopes of imperial rule along with himself; as the embassy had duly reported, the city had instituted a public festival and carried out sacrifices of thanksgiving.[29] In 197 Severus, evidently on his way to the east, wrote from Capua in response to an embassy from Delphi, and duly confirmed the privileges of the city 'and all the Pythian rights'.[30] In 199 he acknowledged the celebration of a festival at Aphrodisias in recognition of his victory over the 'barbarians' and also seems to have confirmed their rights, as he does also (for some unknown reason) in another letter of uncertain date.[31]

In 198/9 the *legatus* of Moesia Inferior, Ovinius Tertullus, sent on to Severus and Caracalla a decree of the city of Nicopolis, situated near the mouth of the Danube. Their elaborate reply aptly characterizes both many of the features of such diplomatic exchanges in general, and the particular overtones of this period:[32]

[25] *IG* VII 2870, ii = Abbott and Johnson, *Municipal Administration*, no. 104.

[26] *IGR* I 121 = *IGUR* I 24. *IGR* IV 1010 = Abbott and Johnson, *Municipal Administration*, no. 108, a fragmentary imperial letter preserving the freedom and immunity of Minoa, probably also belongs to Antoninus.

[27] Herodian II, 4, 3; 8, 7; III, 2, 9.

[28] This period is discussed in detail by Z. Rubin, *Supernatural and Religious Sanctions of the Emperor's Rule in the Severan Period (AD 193–217)* (unpublished Oxford D.Phil. thesis, 1971).

[29] *IGR* IV 566. There is considerable uncertainty both about the date of the letter and the circumstances to which it alludes.

[30] Plassart, *Fouilles de Delphes* III. 4 (1970), no. 329.

[31] Unpublished documents from the theatre at Aphrodisias; cf. p. xiii.

[32] *IGBulg*. 659. On Ovinius Tertullus' despatch of other communications to Severus, see pp. 331–2. On the contribution of money, p. 142.

We have been made aware of your most evident enthusiasm by the decree. For that you are men of goodwill and reverence, who are eager that we should have formed a favourable judgment of you, you have shown by your rejoicing at present events and the introduction of a public festival at the news of our successes, now that peace reigns among all men by virtue of the defeat of the barbarians who are ever challenging our rule, while we are yoked in a just partnership, having a Caesar [Geta] who is of our own true stock. So we have read the decree with the appropriate feelings of respect towards you, and have accepted the contribution of 700,000 as coming from men of goodwill.

When Maximinus the Thracian was killed by his army in 238 while besieging Aquileia, the moment came for the Italian cities of Italy to acknowledge the emperors, Pupienus Maximus and Balbinus, chosen by the senate. Maximus was in the field, and when he came to Aquileia, 'the Italian cities sent delegations of their prominent citizens dressed in white, wearing laurel wreaths and all bringing with them the statues of their local gods and any gold crowns that were among their dedications'.[33] In the following year we find the young Gordian III replying to Aphrodisias in words which perfectly echo the claims which the ambassador of a Greek city would make before the emperor:[34]

It was appropriate, Aphrodisians, to the antiquity of your city, to its goodwill and friendship towards the Romans, for you to be disposed towards my kingship as you have shown in the decree addressed to me. In return for which, and in response to your loyal disposition, I maintain securely the enjoyment of all your existing rights which have been preserved up to the time of my kingship.

Eleven years later Aphrodisias sent another embassy on the same mission, this time to Decius and Herennius, and were answered in very similar terms. The wording is not, however, identical; the mechanical repetition of expressions which we might have expected in such formal exchanges is never in fact in evidence:[35]

It was natural for you in view of the goddess after whom your city is named and of your friendship and good faith to the Romans, to rejoice at the establishment of our kingship, and to offer the proper sacrifices and prayers. We preserve your existing freedom and all the other privileges which you have gained from the emperors before us, being willing to reward your hopes in the future also.

The record of these diplomatic exchanges as preserved on inscriptions stops there. But we can see its counterpart in the west reflected very clearly in the words of an orator addressing Constantine in 313, and referring back to the moment of his victory at Turin during his invasion of Italy in 312: 'Embassies were sent by all, supplies offered from all sides, in order that it

---

[33] Herodian VIII, 7, 2 (Loeb trans.). For the carrying of images of a city's gods by an embassy cf. Diodorus XXXIII, 5, 2–3 (embassy from Marathus at Aradus, mid-second century BC); Musurillo, *Acts of the Pagan Martyrs*, no. viii (Alexandrian embassy before Trajan carrying a bust of Serapis).
[34] Aphrodisias dossier, see p. xiii.
[35] Abbott and Johnson, *Municipal Administration*, no. 145 = *MAMA* VIII 424; cf. p. 343.

should be apparent how long they had hoped for him to whom they so eagerly committed themselves, although the war was still in progress.'[36] We would certainly be wrong to detect any hint of irony here.

It is thus possible to trace a remarkable continuity of diplomatic forms through the best part of four centuries. It must of course be admitted that the essential evidence is provided almost entirely by inscriptions from Greek cities. Only occasional literary references show as comparable processes taking place in the west, and then (as regards imperial accessions) only in Italy. But a few items of evidence, for instance for the offering of gold crowns from Spain and Gaul, or formal embassies on other occasions from Gaul or Italian cities, prevent us from excluding the possibility that such exchanges were customary there also.[37] The Greek evidence, on the other hand, quite extensive though it is, can give only the faintest impression of what must have occurred at every accession: the passing of honorific decrees in cities all over the Greek east; the despatch of ambassadors, numbering hundreds in all; their reception by the emperor; and the composition of replies whose text was suited to the circumstances and status of each city. If we are tempted to think that these replies were empty formulae of no practical significance, it is only if we forget that the rights and duties of cities were liable to constant challenge by their neighbours, in which the evidence of an up-to-date imperial reaffirmation could be of crucial importance.

That said, it is not necessary to survey in the same detail the evidence for other formal exchanges. They included for instance embassies of congratulation on occasions such as Gaius' assumption of the *toga virilis* in 5 BC, when Sardis, as we saw, sent two ambassadors; it was then too, as it seems, that Samos sent an embassy to congratulate Augustus on his assumption of the consulate.[38] By contrast the city of Pisa sent embassies to Augustus in AD 2 after the death of Lucius Caesar and in 4 after that of Gaius. In the first case they were to ask his approval of the steps they had taken to commemorate Lucius' memory; in the second to present a *libellus* and explain the difficulties caused to the *colonia* by having no magistrates in office owing to electoral dissensions.[39]

Occasionally embassies arrived on very trivial pretexts, as when one from Tarraco reported to Augustus that a palm-tree had begun to grow on the altar to him there, or from the Olisiponenses in Lusitania to report the appearance of a Triton to Tiberius.[40] Alternatively, Astypalaea sent an

---

[36] *Pan.* IX(12), 7, 4.

[37] Gold crowns, see p. 141. Embassy from Gaul on the occasion of Agrippina's death, p. 388; for Italian *civitates*, see below.

[38] Sardis: p. 386. Samos: P. Herrmann, 'Inschriften römischer Zeit aus dem Heraion von Samos', *Ath. Mitt.* LXXV (1960), 68, no. 1 (pp. 70–82).

[39] *ILS* 139–40; for consolatory embassies cf. that of Ilium to Tiberius, p. 217, and perhaps one from Eresus to Augustus on the death of Agrippa, *IG* XII, 2, 531 = *IGR* IV 7.

[40] Quintilian, *Inst.* VI, 3, 77; Pliny, *NH* IX, 4/9. Note also the remarkable story in Phlegon of Tralles, *FGrH* 257 F. 36 (XIV). After an earthquake in the region of Sicily and Rhegium bones of superhuman size were revealed in the earth. An embassy came to Tiberius to show him one of the teeth and ask if he wished the 'hero' to be brought to him. He contented himself, however, with sending for a *mensor* to measure it, after which it was sent back.

embassy to Hadrian the purpose of which seems to have been to greet him on his arrival in Caria in 129;[41] and Autun sent one to Constantine at Trier in 312 to thank him for his visit to the city in the previous year, and the benefits which he had then conferred.[42]

Perhaps more frequently diplomatic embassies arrived to ask the emperor to accept newly voted honours (which, even if refused, would earn them goodwill). So for instance the well-known letter of Tiberius to Gytheum in Laconia is a response to proposals for divine honours to Augustus and himself embodied in a letter handed over by an ambassador from the city.[43] By comparison Vespasian, when some ambassadors announced that a colossal statue costing a large sum had been voted to him, stretched out his cupped hand and told them to place it (the money) there at once, as the base was ready.[44] The episode is significant, not so much in illustrating the emperor's miserliness as in showing once again that such formal offers were necessarily made verbally before the emperor in person.

On occasion cities sent to the emperor their testimony to the services or merits of individuals. These might be Roman officials, like the *praefectus* whom Sala in Mauretania wished to honour to Antoninus Pius,[45] or a provincial governor. For instance Hadrian wrote to the city of Stratonicea-Hadrianopolis in 127: 'On reading the letter sent by you I learn that you have expressed gratitude to Avidius Quietus, *vir clarissimus*, as having done you good service in the period of his proconsulship.' But more commonly such embassies related to prominent local persons; and indeed at exactly the same time Stratonicea-Hadrianopolis sent another ambassador to testify to the services of the very ambassador who had brought the testimony to Avidius Quietus. Both imperial replies were handed over to the *archôn* of the city in the assembly on the last day of April.[46]

With that exception all the inscriptional evidence for the despatch of *testimonia* to the emperor by cities relates to the following reign, of Antoninus Pius. Why that is so is quite unclear. It may indeed be an accident, for Dio of Prusa, speaking under Trajan, mentions that the city had honoured one of its citizens with portraits, statues and embassies to other cities and to the emperor; and he also recalls that some cities had sent embassies to the emperor to thank him for his fairness to Dio himself.[47] But it is under Antoninus Pius that we find not only the *koinon* of Lycia testifying to the

---

[41] *IG* XII. 3 177 = *IGR* IV 1033.

[42] *Pan.* VIII(5), I, 1–2.

[43] *AE* 1929 100 = *SEG* XI 922. The ambassador went also to Livia, who Tiberius says will answer for herself. The date is unclear, but must be between Tiberius' election as Pontifex Maximus in March 15 and Livia's death in 29.

[44] Suetonius, *Vesp.* 23, 3.

[45] pp. 380–1. Cf. also *CIL* V 5127 (Bergomum, probably second century) which also seems to show a testificatory embassy to a *praefectus cohortis* who is about to leave his present posting.

[46] *IGR* IV 1156, ii–iii; revised text by L. Robert, *Hellenica* VI (1948), 80–4. Doc. i shows that the first ambassador, Cl. Candidus Julianus, had simultaneously been making various requests of Hadrian, on which p. 426. This letter too was handed over on the same day. The *testimonia* were perhaps put forward first, for the two imperial letters relating to them (ii–iii) were issued in Rome on 11 February, but that answering requests is dated 1 March (or, alternatively, it took longer when a decision was required).

[47] *Or.* LI, 9; XLIV, 6.

emperor about the services of the millionaire, Opramoas, but two Lycian cities sending embassies, and four others having decrees sent on by the governor, all to the same purpose and all answered by imperial letters.[48] The custom was not entirely unknown in the west either, for when in the same reign the town-council of Tergeste passed a motion in honour of a senator from there, L. Fabius Severus, who had represented them before the emperor, they said that 'it would have been appropriate—if it had been possible, and if the modesty of the *clarissimus vir* permitted—to go in a body and express our thanks to him before the best of emperors'.[49]

It may have been in response to such initiatives that for instance a prominent Palmyrene was 'testified to' in a letter of Hadrian and Antoninus Pius.[50] But in very rare instances emperors seem to have written spontaneously to cities to recommend individuals. As we have seen, Octavian wrote in 30 BC to commend Seleucus to his native city of Rhosus;[51] and a fictional example is provided by a letter of Claudius recommending Apollonius to his native city of Tyana.[52] But the only clear case from the established empire is the letter of Hadrian to Ephesus recommending one L. Erastus as a member of the council on the grounds of his services as a ship-captain both in carrying proconsuls of Asia across the Aegean, and taking Hadrian himself previously from Ephesus to Rhodes, and now from Eleusis to Ephesus. Here too the request came in fact from the man himself: 'He wishes to be a councillor. For my part I leave the examination of his qualifications to you, but if there is no objection and he proves worthy of the honour, I will pay the sum which councillors give on entry.'[53]

Such letters cannot be regarded as an essential feature of the diplomatic relations of city and emperor, which were shaped fundamentally by embassies and letters from the cities. Whether or not their example was followed to any significant extent by urban communities in the west (which is an unanswerable question), the evidence from the Greek cities shows incontrovertibly how successful they were in imposing on the emperors the devotion to them of a large amount of time and attention, and a significant degree of assent to their claims. But in the nature of the case such a degree of assent, however essential to the role of the emperor as benefactor, could not be so fully maintained when the cities made substantial new demands, brought accusations or disputed with each other before him.

7. *The Cities: Requests and* Beneficia

In the reign of Hadrian a list was inscribed at Smyrna of the promises made by local magnates of contributions which they would make to the city: some

---

[48] *IGR* III 739 = *TAM* II 3905, paras. 37–8 (embassies); 46–8; 50 (decrees sent on). For the *koinon* cf. pp. 388–9.

[49] *ILS* 6680. On the matter in question cf. pp. 433–4.

[50] *AE* 1931 54 = *SEG* VII 135: [ἐπισ]τολ[ᾷ] θεοῦ ['Α]δριανοῦ καὶ τοῦ θειοτάτου Α[ὐ]τοκράτορος Ἀντωνείνου υἱοῦ αὐτοῦ μαρτυρηθέντα.

[51] p. 7.

[52] *Apollonii Ep.* 53 (Philostratus ed. Kayser, pt. ii, p. 62).

[53] *Syll.*[3] 838. These lines depend on some restoration, but the sense seems secure.

promised building works, others to give gardens or a temple, others sums of money. At the end comes an entry of a different sort:[1]

> The things which we obtained from the lord Caesar Hadrian through Antonius Polemo: a second *senatus consultum*, by which we gained a second title of Temple-Warden; a sacred festival; immunity from taxes; official panegyrists of the gods, and hymnodes; 1,500,000 (*sesterces?*); 72 columns of Synnadan marble, 20 of Numidian and 7 of Porphyrite for the anointing-room.

The implied mention of two *senatus consulta* indicates, like other evidence which we saw earlier, that the senate still played a role in determining the rights of provincial cities, but also—and much more significantly—reveals how its decisions could be seen from the provinces as being in the gift of the emperor in a way not entirely different from other *beneficia*. It is not surprising that within half a century provincial embassies seem to have ceased altogether to go before the senate.[2]

The columns of marble from Synnada, Numidia and Egypt may represent a relatively rare example of gift made by the emperor from the direct products of imperial properties.[3] The grant of a sum in cash follows a more normal pattern, one of the standard features of imperial liberality. It is perhaps to be identified with the 250,000 *drachmae* which, according to Philostratus, Polemo successfully demanded from Hadrian when in Rome. This sum was evidently intended for the use of the city, for Polemo was accused of having spent it on himself; he was saved by a letter which Hadrian wrote, evidently to the city, saying that Polemo had given him an account of the money spent.[4] The making of grants of money to cities, often in response to direct requests, was an integral part of the imperial role. Hadrian, for instance, as Dio says, 'aided the allied and subject cities most munificently. For he visited more of them than any other emperor, and assisted them all, so to speak, giving some aqueducts, others harbours, corn, public works, money or various honours.'[5] As we have already seen, it is only at best in relation to a short period at the beginning of the empire that we can make a valid distinction between the wealth of the emperor and the public wealth; but the social forms relevant to personal largesse and liberality continued to be employed and that the appropriate vocabulary continued to be applied to them.[6] When a supply of corn was granted to Hermopolis in Egypt 'out of the munificence (*megalodôria*) of the emperors Macrianus and Quietus',[7] or the walls of Adraa in Arabia 'from the gift (*dôrea*) of the emperor (Gallienus)' in 262/3,[8] we may well presume an order or permission

---

[1] *IGR* IV 1431.

[2] p. 343.

[3] p. 184.

[4] *VS* I, 25. Cf. *PIR*² A 862.

[5] LXIX, 5, 2-3; cf. *HA, Had.* 9, 6; 10, 1.

[6] ch. iii.

[7] Wilcken, *Chrestomathie*, no. 425.

[8] *IGR* III 1287. The work began earlier and continued later, see H.-G. Pflaum, 'La fortification de la ville d'Adraha d'Arabie (259-60 à 274-5) d'après des inscriptions récemment découvertes', *Syria* XXIX (1952), 307. Cf. also the payment by Marcus Aurelius for the walls of Philippopolis (*ILS* 5337), and possibly of Serdica (*IGBulg.* 1902).

from the emperor in person, but not a payment from funds specifically in his private possession. Moreover the vocabulary of 'gifts' is extended not merely to the very frequently conceded (and even more frequently requested) grants of exemption from what were certainly regular taxes, but to the whole range of privileges and rights which the emperor could confer.

Imperial 'gifts' of corn to provincial cities are quite widely attested. Dio records that Hadrian 'granted as a favour' to Athens a large amount of money, an annual supply of corn and the whole of Cephallenia—that is as part of the territory of Athens.[9] As we know from an oration of Julian, Constantine also 'gave as a gift' to Athens 'many myriads of bushels of corn each year, which provided the city with abundance, and the emperor with praise and honour from the leading citizens'.[10] But the imperial liberality will in fact have consisted of the diversion of corn from Egypt, as is indeed explicitly stated on a coin of Tarsus, one of a number which commemorate such grants to Greek cities.[11] In one instance at least, that of Tralles, the 'concession' (*synchôrêsis*)—which implies a previous request—of corn meant no more than permission to buy corn from Egypt.[12] This is probably not the case with the 'supplies of corn from Egypt' provided by Hadrian, which an inscription from Ephesus lists among the 'gifts' (*dôreai*) of the emperor.[13] If so, it was on some other occasion that an emperor wrote to Ephesus, encouraging them to use with moderation the 'concession' (again *synchôrêsis*) of importing corn from Egypt; for it is clear that the reference is to permission to buy corn, and not to the gift of a specific shipment.[14] It can however be assumed that the letter, of which only part survives, is a response to an approach from the city.

A gift of 'corn-money' by Severus to Laodicea also appears as one of the long series of imperial benefactions, both to Antioch itself and to other cities, given in the sixth-century *Chronicle* of Malalas, and including grants of cash, and the construction of buildings of all sorts; many of these reports may be essentially correct, but cannot be regarded as reliable evidence in themselves.[15] However in giving a prominent place to imperial generosity in restoring cities after earthquakes, they are certainly not misleading. The first such occasion occurred almost immediately after the establishment of Augustus' regime, when following an earthquake in about 27–6 the poet Chaeremon travelled to the emperor, then in Spain, to appeal for help for

---

[9] LXIX, 16, 2.

[10] *Or.* I, 6/8d.

[11] See H. Seyrig, *Syria* XXIX (1952), 56–9: δωρεὰ σείτου ἀπὸ Ἐγύ(πτου) Τάρσῳ.

[12] *CIG* 2927: A. Fabricius Priscianus, σειτωνήσαντα δὲ καὶ τὸν ἀπὸ Αἰγύπτου σεῖτον συγχωρηθέντα τῇ πατρίδι αὐτοῦ ὑπὸ τοῦ κυρίου Καίσαρος Τραϊανοῦ Ἀδριανοῦ Σεβαστοῦ, μοδίων μυριάδας ἕξ, καὶ προχρήσαντα ἐκ τῶν ἰδίων τὴν τειμὴν τοῦ σείτου.

[13] *Syll.*[3] 839; cf. p. 447.

[14] *AE* 1968 478, discussed by M. Wörrle, 'Ägyptisches Getreide für Ephesos', *Chiron* I (1971), 325.

[15] e.g. *Chron.* 243 Bonn, 15f. (Gaius—Antioch); 246, 11f. (Claudius—Ephesus, Smyrna, Antioch); 250, 1f. (Claudius—Crete); 259, 8f. (Vitellius—Nicomedia); 260, 12f. (Vespasian—Antioch, Caesarea, Corinth); 263, 11f. (Domitian—Antioch); 267, 14f. (Nerva—Cilician cities); 279, 3f. (Hadrian—Cyzicus); 289, 8f. (Commodus—Nicomedia); 290, 14f. (Didius Julianus—Antioch); 294, 1f. (Severus—Laodicea); 299, 1f. (Claudius Gothicus—Nicomedia). See A. Schenk Graf von Stauffenberg, *Die römische Kaisergeschichte bei Malalas* (1931), ad loc.

Tralles; Augustus gave money for both Tralles and Laodicea.[16] When earth-quakes damaged Sardis and other cities of Asia in AD 17, Tiberius promised a large sum, and remitted debts to the *aerarium* (namely tribute) and the *fiscus*. The references to his action in Strabo, Phlegon of Tralles and Dio, make quite clear that Tiberius both remitted tribute and gave money from what could still be clearly distinguished as his own funds.[17] From Tacitus' account a debate may well have taken place in the senate, as it did on some other such occasions;[18] but as an inscription from Asia shows, it was Tiberius who was regarded as 'the founder of twelve cities at once'.[19]

The aftermath of great natural disasters was inevitably the most prominent occasion for imperial liberality. Even Nero restored to Lugdunum, after it had been damaged, probably by fire, the 4,000,000 *sesterces* which it had earlier contributed for the rebuilding of Rome;[20] and Titus after the eruption of Vesuvius in 79 gave the inhabitants both grants of money and the right to the property of persons there who had died without heirs.[21] Similarly, Pausanias notes that Antoninus Pius gave large sums for the restoration of cities in Caria, Lycia, Cos and Rhodes after an earthquake.[22] But the best-attested occasion of restitution of a city by an emperor, and the processes which brought this about, is the rebuilding of Smyrna by Marcus Aurelius and Commodus after an earthquake, probably in 177: as Dio says, Marcus 'gave money to many cities, among them Smyrna which had been terribly damaged by an earthquake'. It was then that Aelius Aristides (without, as he says, waiting for an embassy to be arranged) sent a letter couched in emotive and rhetorical terms to the emperors, who were absent from Rome on the Danubian campaigns of 177–80. As we saw earlier, Philostratus describes Marcus as bursting into tears as he read it. In consequence, so Aristides recalls in a later speech, the emperors did not wait for an embassy from Smyrna to arrive but sent 'ambassadors' of their own to the senate in Rome to ask them to vote money for restoration.[23]

The letter is an invaluable document for supplying one example of what is normally lacking in our picture of the relations of city and emperor, the actual text of an appeal to the emperor on a specific occasion. Paradoxically, while we have the texts of a number of *libelli* from individuals or groups of individuals,[24] for the content of addresses by city ambassadors to the emperor

[16] Augustus' help is referred to briefly by Strabo XII, 8, 18 (579); for the (approximate) date, Eusebius, *Chron.* ed. Schoene, II, pp. 140–1; Jerome, *Chron.*, ed. Helm, p. 164; for Chaeremon, and an extract from his poem on the embassy, Agathias II, 17.

[17] Strabo, loc. cit., and XIII, 4, 8 (627); Tacitus, *Ann.* II, 47; Phlegon, *FGrH* 257 F. 36 (xiii): οἰκείᾳ δαπάνῃ πάλιν ἀνώρθωσεν; Dio LVII, 17, 7; cf. Pliny, *NH* II, 86/200.

[18] pp. 343–50.

[19] *OGIS* 471. On 'founder' meaning 'benefactor' or 'restorer', see p. 406.

[20] Tacitus, *Ann.* XVI, 13, 3.

[21] Dio LXVI, 24, 3; cf. p. 161.

[22] VIII, 43, 4.

[23] Dio LXXI, 32, 3 (272–3); Philostratus, *VS* II, 9. Aristides, *Or.* XIX Keil begins with the conventional form of address for a letter from a private person to the emperor(s): Αὐτοκράτορι Καίσαρι Μάρκῳ Αὐρηλίῳ Ἀντωνίνῳ Σεβαστῷ καὶ Αὐτοκράτορι Καίσαρι Αὐρηλίῳ Κομόδῳ Σεβαστῷ Αἴλιος Ἀριστείδης χαίρειν. For the reference to his not waiting for an embassy, see para. 6; cf. *Or.* XX Keil, 10. For the date see C. A. Behr, *Aelius Aristides and the Sacred Tales* (1968), 112–13. Cf. p. 10.

[24] pp. 537, 542–4.

we normally have to rely either on the general rules set out by 'Menander',[25] or on reconstructing the main points from the imperial replies. Even Aristides' composition is not actually a speech, but being a substitute for one, will still be indicative of their nature.

Aristides recalls Marcus' recent visit to the city, in 176, describes the destruction, and moves on to suggest that the occasion will give the emperors an opportunity to surpass the benefactions of Alexander and Lysimachus. After justifying his own intervention, he recalls the story of Domitian who had caused the annihilation of a Libyan tribe by saying, 'I do not wish the Nasamones to exist', and says that the emperors can now fulfil their very different characters by saying that they wish Smyrna to exist: they had recently restored some Italian cities after long decay, and could now re-create Smyrna, which had flourished up to the moment of its destruction. He then turns, as was obligatory, to the long loyalty (*eunoia*) of Smyrna to Rome (going back to the war against Aristonicus three centuries before), to the services of Smyrna to the other cities of Asia, and to its preeminence among them. He concludes with an apology:

> When I consider the magnitude of the disaster, it seems to me that no speech would be adequate, but that all possible words would fall short of what is appropriate; but when I consider your virtue and character and readiness to grant benefactions (*euergesiai*), it occurs to me to be afraid lest I seem to have gone on too long.

Philostratus had no doubt that the rebuilding of Smyrna was due to Aristides, and in expressing his view manages to embody some of the fundamental concepts in terms of which the Greek world saw the Roman emperors:[26]

> In saying this I do not mean to imply that the king would not have rebuilt after its destruction the city which he had admired while it was still standing; but rather that kingly and divine natures, if aroused by advice and speech, shine forth all the more, and are borne with greater impetus towards beneficent acts.

The Greeks were of course not alone in their conviction of the power of oratory in eliciting imperial munificence. The Gallic orator who in 310 invited Constantine to visit Autun expressed quite openly the claims and expectations of the city: 'This city, with its ancient eminence, once adorned with the title of ally of the Roman people, awaits the aid of your majesty, so that there too the public places and the most beautiful temples may be repaired by your *liberalitas*.' In fact, however, as his oration of 312 makes clear, when Constantine visited Autun in 311, received the representations of the city and heard their requests, his *beneficia* consisted essentially not of gifts of money, but of a reduction of taxation and remission of the taxes owed

[25] p. 8.
[26] *VS* II, 9.

for the past five years.[27] As we have seen, the distinction between the personal wealth of the emperor and that of the state had long since ceased to be discernible, and it was a matter of choice whether the emperor 'gave' money, or a remission of taxation. But the language of private liberality could on occasion still be used quite explicitly: as an inscription from Campania records, Constantine and his sons ordered an aqueduct to be restored 'with their own money, in accordance with the accustomed *munificentia* of their *liberalitas*'.[28]

A straightforward grant of freedom and immunity from Roman taxation was clearly the greatest gift which an emperor could bestow. But it is important to emphasize not only that cities could bring to the emperor requests for partial or temporary immunity from taxation, or specific taxes, but also that they might depend on him for a wide range of decisions and actions relating to their own internal revenues. Most of such decisions will have related to disputes between the city as an institution and either some of its inhabitants or its neighbours; but they may still be considered here, except for those cases where the imperial ruling was explicitly a decision between two parties. The most basic thing was necessarily the definition of the city's territory. We may note for instance a man from the Cures Sabini who went on an embassy to Antoninus Pius, apparently 'on account of the public boundaries'.[29] Antoninus also established the boundaries of the territory of Palmyra on the basis of a verdict by Hadrian; the procedure was carried out by a *legatus* of Pius in 153, fifteen years after Hadrian's death.[30] We shall see later several instances where boundary disputes between cities were heard or delegated by the emperor, or referred to him.[31]

Equally important was the question of the delimitation and renting out of the public lands of a city or of its temples, and the recovery of them from illicit private occupation; one such case was that of the territories of the temple of Zeus at Aezani, which the proconsul Avidius Quietus referred to Hadrian.[32] We find for instance the proconsul of Crete and Cyrene in 63 restoring the public lands of Gortyn on the authority of Nero;[33] under Vespasian such processes are widely attested: at *coloniae* such as Arausio (Orange) and Cirta;[34] at Pompeii, where on the emperor's authority a praetorian tribune heard cases and restored public places occupied by private persons;[35] and at Apollonia in Cyrenaica where the proconsul, again on the emperor's authority, leased out the public lands of the city.[36] The coincidence of examples naturally suggests some general imperial initiative at this time,

---

[27] *Pan.* VII(6), 22, 4; cf. VIII(5) passim; 4, 4, however, records that Constantius had given money for the restoration of the baths at Autun.

[28] *AE* 1939 151.

[29] *CIL* IX 4976: 'legato aput divum Piu[m ob fi]nes publicos'.

[30] *IGLS* V 2550.

[31] pp. 435-6.

[32] pp. 328-9.

[33] *Ins. Cret.* I. xxvi, 2.

[34] For Orange see A. Piganiol, *Les documents cadastraux de la colonie romaine d'Orange* (1962), 79f. For Cirta, *AE* 1957 175 and 1969/70 696.

[35] *ILS* 5942.

[36] *AE* 1967 531.

but there is no direct evidence for it. A specific request to the emperor is however more probable in the case of the lands in the territory of Pessinus, which were measured on the orders of Caracalla in 216.[37]

It cannot be pretended that we have any explicit evidence for the processes which led to an emperor giving his authority, or a direct order, for steps concerned with the public lands of cities. With other sources of city revenue the situation is clearer. For instance, when an embassy came to Vespasian from Sabora in Spain, they asked not only for permission to build a new *oppidum* named after him but for the retention of revenues granted to them by Augustus, to which the emperor assented, and for the addition of new ones, as to which he instructed them to approach the proconsul.[38] Vespasian's letter is notable firstly for giving both the date on which he received their decree and that, four days later, on which he dismissed the ambassadors. It can be presumed that this is mentioned because the period was exceptionally short. Secondly, it is one of the very few imperial letters preserved on inscriptions which contain even a partial refusal of the requests made (if we except refusals of divine honours, whose character is different). Though it is clear that emperor's normally assented to requests whenever they could, the reason for this rarity of negative replies is not so much the universality of their benevolence as the fact that in the case of refusal a city had no motive for going to the expense of inscription.[39]

The first letter which Hadrian wrote in 127 to Stratonicea, newly re-named Hadrianopolis, was in comparison more favourable: 'I regard your requests as proper, and necessary for a newly-formed city. I give you therefore the revenues from the *chôra* (the territory of the city); and as for the house of Tiberius Claudius Socrates which is situated in the city, let him either repair it or sell it to one of the inhabitants, so that it does not fall down through age and neglect.'[40] It is probable that the request was for the right to raise certain indirect taxes in the *chôra*; but the phrase could (though it is less likely) be a reference to a remission, or even diversion, of Roman indirect taxes. That it was necessary to ask for an imperial ruling in order to compel a citizen to repair or sell his house is a striking, but not uncharacteristic, example of the lack of powers of enforcement on the part of provincial cities.

According to the *Chronicle* of Eusebius, in 121 or 122 the Athenians petitioned Hadrian for 'laws', which he gave. There is no reason to suppose that these were to be solely concerned with revenues, but inscriptions preserve firstly a regulation (*nomothesia*) of his on the compulsory sale of a proportion of the olive-crop to the city, and a letter, probably from him, concerned with the sale of fish, and the tax payable on it. The writer lays

[37] J. Devreker, 'Une inscription inédite de Caracalla à Pessinonte', *Latomus* xxx (1971), 352; cf. *BE* 1972 482. There is no reason to suppose that such a measure had any connection with Roman taxation.

[38] *ILS* 6092 = *FIRA*² I, no. 74 = Abbott and Johnson, *Municipal Administration*, no. 61. Cf. pp. 235–6, 405.

[39] On the inscription of imperial replies which embodied decisions between rival parties see p. 436.

[40] *IGR* IV 1156 = *Syll.*³ 837; revised by L. Robert, *Hellenica* VI (1948), 80–4 = *AE* 1949 253; cf. p. 419.

down that the letter is to be inscribed on a pillar placed in the Peiraeus.[41]

The fact of a city's request to be permitted to raise certain internal revenues, and of an emperor's assent, is perfectly clear from a letter of Antoninus Pius to a city in Macedonia, possibly called Parthicopolis.[42] The two ambassadors sent by the city had asked permission for the imposition of some tax whose precise nature is unclear; for a poll-tax on free inhabitants—a unique feature, which is nevertheless granted; for an increase of the *boulê* to 80, each paying an entry-fee of 500 Attic *drachmae* (which would serve to increase both the prestige—*axiôma*—and income of the city); and finally that inhabitants who did not have the local citizenship should be subject to the jurisdiction of the magistrates in cases involving up to 250 *denarii*. The connection between imperial *beneficia* allowing extra councillors and the payment of entry-fees by these councillors is first clearly visible in Bithynia under Trajan.[43] Like all such customs it could be extended further, and an inscription from Lanuvium records that baths had been built in part 'from the sums gained, by the *indulgentia* of our lords the emperors (Severus and Caracalla), from the *summae honorariae* of the priesthoods'.[44]

The terminology used here implies a request to the emperors, as does the mention on an inscription from Milev in Numidia of the fact that a road had been paved by the authority of Antoninus Pius, and paid for by his *indulgentia* from what seems to be a toll on wheeled traffic.[45] In a very similar case the council of Tuficum in Umbria voted to erect a statue to a native of the place who had recently been promoted to the centurionate by Antoninus Pius, on the grounds that by his efforts he had secured the prompt assent of the emperor to the town's petition for a toll on a road paved with flint-stone.[46]

The ability of a city to acquire property or capital was also important. Apart from the instances of requests for or grants of the right to *bona vacantia*, mentioned earlier,[47] we find a man from Stratonicea going on an embassy to Rome in the first century to secure money left to the city by one Julius Pelago,[48] or the community of Thugga in Africa (described here as a mere *pagus*, village) recording that by the 'celestial *beneficium*' of Marcus Aurelius and Verus it had been 'endowed with the right of accepting legacies'.[49] In Roman law a community could in principle be neither an heir nor a legatee.

[41] For the request and the oil law see J. H. Oliver, *The Ruling Power* (1953), 958f.; for the letter on sales of fish, *IG²* II 1103; cf. H. W. Pleket, *Epigraphica* 1: *Texts on the Economic History of the Greek World* (1964), nos. 15–16.

[42] *IGBulg.* 2263 = *SEG* XXIV 619.

[43] Dio of Prusa, *Or.* XLV, 7 (cf. p. 414); see Pliny, *Ep.* X, 39, 5. See P. Garnsey, 'Honorarium decurionatus', *Historia* XX (1971), 309.

[44] *ILS* 5686.

[45] *CIL* VIII 10327/8: 'ex auctoritate Imp. Caes. T. Aeli Hadriani Antonini Aug. Pii p.p. via a Milevitanis munita ex indulgentia eius de vectigali [*sic*] rotari.'

[46] *ILS* 2666/2666a, cf. p. 64.

[47] pp. 160, 397, 404.

[48] L. Robert, *Études Anatoliennes* (1937), 538 = *AE* 1938 161. The man may be an imperial freedman of the Julio-Claudian period, so *PIR²* I 455, but the identities assumed there seem far from certain.

[49] *ILS* 9399.

It is impossible to give here (or indeed anywhere) any clear conception of the normal patterns of city finance under the empire. But it can on the one hand be said that direct taxation by cities was unusual, and on the other that they relied very heavily on the imposition of functions on the richer inhabitants, and on the extraction of promises by such individuals to pay for, or contribute to, specific projects. Hence there arose a vast case-law on the question of who was exempt under what circumstances from what obligations (*munera* or *leitourgiai*), and also (as we saw in the case of Pliny's governorship of Pontus and Bithynia) over the exaction of money promised by individuals or of other public funds held by them.[50] Nearly all our evidence of communications between cities and the emperors on this subject relates to specific disputes, many of which were actions brought by cities against individuals to compel them either to serve or to make payments.[51] But for instance a letter written in Greek by Marcus Aurelius and Verus on the immunity enjoyed by shippers must have been addressed to a Greek city, and does express a general rule:[52]

There have been others who on the pretext of being shippers and of trading in corn and oil to the market of the Roman people, and hence being immune, have claimed to avoid *leitourgiai*, although they neither sail themselves nor have the majority of their property in shipping and trade. Let their immunity be removed from them.

Similarly an emperor wrote, probably in the second century, in answer to an embassy from Ephesus to lay down rules for the exaction of debts to the city on the part of past office-holders, including claims on their estates if they had subsequently died.[53] But it was naturally for relief, whether complete, partial or temporary, from Roman taxation for which communities most typically addressed requests to the emperor. As we saw much earlier, the small Aegean island of Gyarus could send a single ambassador to ask Octavian for such relief as early as 29 BC, two years after Actium.[54]

In 15 BC similarly the Gauls took the opportunity of Augustus' presence there to appeal, unsuccessfully, against excessive exactions of tribute by his freedman Licinus.[55] For a Greek city the emperor's presence, though useful, was not necessary, and for instance an inscription from Cibyra honours a man 'who had been on four embassies to the emperors at Rome at his own expense'; his most important achievement on the embassies was that of having 'requested from Tiberius Claudius Caesar the removal from office of Tiberius Nicephorus, who has been exacting 3000 *denarii* from the city each year, and pocketing it, and to have it laid down that the exaction of grain should take place in the market place, at a rate of 75 *modii* per *iugerum*

---

[50] p. 326. Cf. P. Garnsey, '*Taxatio* and *Pollicitatio* in Roman Africa', *JRS* LXI (1971), 116.
[51] pp. 438–41.
[52] *Dig.* L, 6, 6, 6. Callistratus uses the word 'rescripserunt'. 6, 3 and 7, shows that the context is specifically that of city obligations. Cf. *Dig.* L, 5, 3.
[53] J. Keil, *JÖAI* XXVII (1931), Beiblatt, cols. 18–25.
[54] p. 11.
[55] Dio LIV, 21, 6–8; cf. p. 71.

from the whole *chôra*'.[56] We do not know the status of the official concerned, and have very little evidence of a tax in grain from Asia Minor. But it seems clear that the city was able to obtain from Claudius a ruling both on the rate of exaction and on its taking place in public, to prevent peculation or oppression.[57]

Similarly we find Hadrian writing to Astypalaea in 118, 'On reading your decree I have learnt that you are unable to pay the promised sum; but neither how much it is, nor when you began to incur it [text breaks off].'[58] In one of the new letters from Aphrodisias Hadrian also writes:[59]

> Having been requested by an embassy concerning the exploitation of iron and the tax on nails, although the matter is disputable, since it is not now for the first time that the *publicani* attempt to raise it from you, nevertheless knowing that city both otherwise deserves honour and has been removed from the framework of the province, I exempt it from the tax, and have written to my procurator, Claudius Agrippinus, to instruct the man who has contracted for the tax in Asia to exempt your city.

A comparable issue is the subject of the long but much-damaged dossier of documents in Greek and Latin from Chersonesus in the Crimea, concerning the tax on prostitutes. So far as can be determined, the city sent to the emperor, probably Commodus, a decree claiming that it had previously been exempt. The emperor writes briefly in Greek to the city, with instructions for his reply to be posted up, and also in Latin to the tribune of the unit posted at Chersonesus, and to its centurion; whether he accepted the exemption of the city is unclear, but he certainly ordered that the tax should be raised without injury or insult to the villagers.[60] Then, as we saw earlier, Caracalla used the *edictum* form anomalously in making certain concessions to the people of Banasa in Mauretania: 'Rewarding your obedience and loyalty, I remit you all fiscal debts of whatever kind, whether in corn or money . . . In granting this *beneficium* I presume that you will make all future payments either in corn or in money all the more promptly if you reflect that I do not anticipate making future grants, while you should neither request nor expect renewed assistance or munificent indulgence'.[61] It is therefore perfectly clear that the Banasitans had requested a remission

---

[56] *IGR* IV 914; reading πρᾶξιν for πρᾶσιν with D. Magie, 'A Reform in the Exaction of Grain at Cibyra under Claudius', *Studies in Roman Economic and Social History presented to A. C. Johnson* (1951), 152; accepted by L. Robert, *BE* 1953, no. 189.

[57] Compare the Alexandrian claim in the '*Boulé*-papyrus' that a *boulé*, if granted, would be able to check on both oppression and peculation in relation to taxes; *PSI* 1160 = Musurillo, *Acts of the Pagan Martyrs*, no. i = *Corp. Pap. Jud.* 150.

[58] *IG* XII.3 176 = *IGR* IV 1032 = *Syll.*³ 832 = Abbott and Johnson, *Municipal Administration*, no. 76. I am not convinced by the view that τὸ ἐπαγγελτικὸν ἀργύριον is a reference to *aurum coronarium*. Relief from taxation (see *Frag.* ii, l. 4 ἄφεσιν τῶν [. .) may be the subject of another, fragmentary, letter of Hadrian to Astypalaea, W. Peek, *Inschriften von den dorischen Inseln* (1969), 36, no. 84, supplementing even slighter fragments in *IG* XII.3 206.

[59] See p. xiii and App. 2. A tax on nails is not otherwise attested.

[60] *CIL* III 13750 = Latyschev, *IOSPE* IV 81 = Abbott and Johnson, *Municipal Administration*, no. 112.

[61] *AE* 1948 109; cf. p. 256.

of fiscal debts in corn and money, and that the emperor grants this, but not any remission of their standing obligations.

Grants of permanent exemption from direct Roman taxation were in fact almost unknown, except in the context of the acquisition of the status of *colonia*—and, as we have seen, were not universal even there. When Philo represents Agrippa I as rejecting the idea of requesting from Gaius 'if not the Roman citizenship, then at least freedom or relief from taxation', he ought on our evidence to have been thinking of temporary relief.[62] But Dio, on the other hand, records that Marcus Aurelius 'received those who came on embassies from the provinces not all on the same basis, but according to whether each was worthy to receive either the citizenship or immunity or some permanent or temporary reduction of tribute, or even to have permanent financial support'.[63] Even here the reference seems to be to exemption from indirect taxes (*ateleia*) on the one hand, and a reduction, rather than formal exemption, from direct tribute on the other. But two cases are clear, the first being the concession by Claudius in 53 of perpetual freedom from tribute for Ilium (Troy). The young Nero delivered an oration on their behalf, with appropriate reference to the Trojan origins of Rome; and a letter (whether genuine or not) was cited, in which senate and people obliged one of the Seleucids to grant immunity to the city.[64] The second is the grant of freedom and of immunity from tribute made to Greece by Nero, and proclaimed by himself at Corinth in 67. It deserves attention not only as the only speech of a Roman emperor preserved entire in documentary form, but for the vocabulary of imperial generosity, and its clear implication that it was exceptional for any privilege to be granted without being asked for:[65]

An unexpected gift (*dôrea*), Hellenes,—though indeed there is nothing which cannot be hoped for from my munificence (*megalophrosynê*)—I grant to you, so great that you would not have dared to ask for it. All you Hellenes who inhabit Achaea and what has up to now been called the Peloponnese, receive freedom and exemption from tribute (*aneisphoria*), which you did not all enjoy even in the period of your good fortune; for you were subject either to others or to each other. Would that I had been able to provide this gift when Greece was flourishing, so that more people might have enjoyed my favour (*charis*); for that I blame the passage of time for having reduced in advance the magnitude of my favour. And now I do you a service not through pity but through goodwill, and I give thanks to your gods, of whose care for me I have had proof on land and sea, for enabling me to confer so great a benefit. For other rulers have freed cities, [but only Nero] a province.

The freedom (and presumably also the immunity from tribute) which Nero granted was revoked a few years later by Vespasian.[66] But however abortive his own gesture was, Nero was correct in implying that freedom was not uncommonly granted to cities in the early empire. In the republic such

[62] p. 407.
[63] LXXI, 19, 1 (274).
[64] Tacitus, *Ann.* XII, 58, 1; Suetonius, *Claud.* 25, 3; *Nero* 7, 2.
[65] For the text *Syll.*³ 814; cf. p. 204. For the date see P. A. Gallivan, *Hermes* CI (1973), 230.
[66] Suetonius, *Vesp.* 8, 4.

a status had been conferred, as a recognition of services rendered, by senate and people;[67] and under the empire the senate still on occasion heard such requests, as it might those for remission of tribute.[68] Even in the third century reference could still be made to such enactments by the institutions of the *res publica*; under Severus Alexander a proconsul of Asia writes to Aphrodisias that he will visit them 'if neither a law of your city, nor a *senatus consultum*, nor a *constitutio*, nor a divine (i.e. imperial) letter forbids the proconsul to stay in [your] city'.[69] Such an exemption from the visits and jurisdiction of the governor was all that the precarious and revocable privileges of freedom amounted to under the empire; its formal character is shown by the fact that, as one of the new imperial letters from Aphrodisias shows. Commodus had already acceded to their request that the proconsul should in fact visit the city, but without prejudice to its rights (*dikaia*) of freedom.[70]

It was perhaps precisely because it had so formal a character, that 'freedom' had been granted already by Sulla[71] and Julius Caesar[72] as a favour to Greek cities, as it was subsequently by Augustus and later emperors. Nicolaus, for instance, relates that when Octavian was about to sail to Italy after hearing of the assassination of Caesar, the people of Apollonia begged him to stay safely with them; so when he came to power, he granted them freedom and *ateleia* and many other favours.[73] In one instance indeed we now know that a request for freedom (*eleutheria*) was at first refused by Augustus. As was noted earlier, imperial letters refusing privileges were not inscribed by the city concerned, and are therefore very rare in our evidence. But when the Samians sent a petition to Augustus asking for freedom, and he wrote a *subscriptio* refusing it, the text was inscribed not by them but by the Aphrodisians:[74]

You can see for yourselves that I have given the privilege (*philanthrôpon*) of freedom to no people except the Aphrodisians, who took my side in the war and suffered capture through their loyalty to us. For it is not appropriate for the greatest privilege of all to be granted at random and without cause. I am well disposed towards you and would like to grant this favour to my wife, who is

---

[67] The most formal evidence in the *Lex Antonia de Termessibus*, *ILS* 38 = *FIRA*² I, no. 11; cf. also the case of Aphrodisias, pp. 342–3. For a full survey of the evidence R. Bernhardt, *Imperium und Eleutheria* (Diss. Hamburg, 1971).

[68] pp. 346–7.

[69] Abbott and Johnson, *Municipal Administration*, no. 137.

[70] On the Aphrodisias dossier see p. xiii.

[71] Appian, *Mith.* 61/250: Ἰλιέας μὲν καὶ Χίους καὶ Λυκίους καὶ Ῥοδίους καὶ Μαγνησίαν... ἐλευθέρους ἠφίει καὶ Ῥωμαίων ἀνέγραφε φίλους. The freedom of Ilium is not to be identified with the exemption from tribute mentioned above. Sulla's grants of freedom were made while he was in Asia in 85, but it can be assumed by analogy with Sherk, *Roman Documents*, nos. 17–18, that they were subsequently confirmed by the senate.

[72] Plutarch, *Caes.* 48, 1 (Thessaly and Cnidus); Appian, *BC* II, 88/368 (Thessaly), both after Pharsalus. For Cnidus cf. p. 84 above. Cf. Dio XLII, 48, 4 (Amisus). Strabo XIII, 1, 27 (595) also reports that he preserved the ἐλευθερία and ἀλειτουργησία of Ilium. The latter was confirmed in a rescript of Antoninus Pius, *Dig.* XXVII, 1, 17, 1.

[73] *FGrH* 90 F. 130 (xvii).

[74] For the Aphrodisias dossier cf. p. xiii above; for this as a *subscriptio*, p. 243; for the Aphrodisian inscription of a letter of refusal to Smyrna from Trajan, pp. 438–9.

eager on your behalf, but not to the extent of breaking my established rule. It is not that I am concerned about the money which you pay in tribute, but that I would not wish the most valued privileges to be granted to anyone without good cause.

The motive of the Aphrodisians in including this among the documents of their own privileges is clear enough. The Samians had evidently asked for freedom and immunity from taxation, and been refused both. Subsequently freedom was both granted and removed by emperors, on less solid and well-grounded principles; Samos itself was to gain its freedom as a reward for being Augustus' residence over the winter of 20/19 BC.[75] In 53 the young Nero, as well as delivering his oration on the exemption of Ilium from tribute, also spoke in Greek before Claudius for the restoration to Rhodes of the freedom of which the emperor had deprived it nine years earlier, for crucifying Roman citizens; but this too was removed again by Vespasian.[76]

Perhaps surprisingly, the list of free cities does not seem to have been greatly increased in the course of the empire. But, for instance, Stratonicea in Caria regained its freedom under Nerva, and an inscription honours a man who often went on embassies to the emperor, and obtained the freedom.[77] It was probably to Hadrian or Antoninus Pius that a man from Chersonesus in the Crimea went over a period of six years 'for the sake of the freedom' (of the city), and was finally successful; the most likely date is indicated by the significant fact that the same man twice acted as ambassador to King Rhoemetalces, probably the Bosporan king of 131/3–154.[78] Our evidence suggests that Greek cities were more concerned with titles which affected their mutual precedence, such as the second title of 'Temple-Warden' (*neôkoros*) which Polemo gained for Smyrna, or *mêtropolis*, which as we saw, the rhetor Paulus gained for Tyre from Hadrian.[79] Both titles appear in an inscription from Beroea in Macedonia which perfectly typifies many of the institutions, values and aspirations of Greek provincial life under the empire.[80]

> The High Priest for life of the Augusti and *agonothetês* (president of games) of the *koinon* of Macedonians, Q. Popillius Python, who went as ambassador on behalf of his native city of Beroea to the Divine Nerva in order that it alone should have the wardenship of the temple of the Augusti and the rank of *mêtropolis* . . .

As a related inscription shows, these rights were 'preserved' by Nerva, and

[75] Dio LIV, 9, 7.

[76] Tacitus, *Ann.* XII, 58, 2; Suetonius, *Claud.* 25, 3; *Nero* 7, 2. *IGR* IV 1123 = Abbott and Johnson, *Municipal Administration*, no. 52, possibly refers to this occasion. See Suetonius, *Vesp.* 8, 4.

[77] *BCH* LI (1927), 98, no. 65.

[78] *IGR* I 865 = *IOSPE*² I 423; as noted there, the Rhoemetalces in question could be the Thracian king who died in AD 12; if so, πρὸς τὸν θεὸν Σεβάστον would be a reference to Augustus.

[79] pp. 409, 421.

[80] See J. M. R. Cormack, 'The Nerva Inscription in Beroea', *JRS* XXX (1940), 50.

not granted by him for the first time. But the wording of the inscription makes clear that the titles were at least potentially a subject of dispute and rivalry, and may already have been so. Such rivalries, as is notorious, were indeed a typical feature of the public life of the Greek provinces, especially Asia, under the empire. We shall return to them in more detail in the context of other disputes between cities or communities, which came before the emperor.[81]

In Italy and the Latin west our evidence does not provide us with anything like so complex a picture of the values of local life and the degree to which these gave rise to demands upon the emperor. But even quite unimportant or remote communities could on occasion address themsleves to him. So for instance we owe to Pliny's *Natural History* the pleasing information that the inhabitants of the Balearic Islands once petitioned Augustus for military assistance against a plague of rabbits.[82] Tacitus describes how the Frisians, under pressure from the Roman governor, sent an embassy of two to ask Nero to grant them permission to settle in a new area. The request was refused, but both men were granted the Roman citizenship by the emperor.[83] In the second or third century, as an isolated inscription records, a local office-holder in Aquitania went on an embassy to the emperor and success-fully requested a separation (in some form) of the communities of Novem-populana from the rest of the province.[84]

In Italy, for instance, the Marsi had assiduously petitioned Augustus to carry out the draining of L. Fucino, as Claudius finally did.[85] The city-council of Aquileia voted to erect a bronze statue of Minicius Italus, prefect of Egypt, because at his request Trajan had ruled that *incolae* there should be liable to local impositions along with those who possessed the full local citizenship.[86] Another equestrian office-holder, who had acted as host (*hospes*) to Hadrian and was the father of a senator, was honoured by some villagers in the territory of Camerinum because from the *indulgentia* of Antoninus Pius and by the *beneficium* of the man's exposition (presumably to the emperor) they had acquired privileges 'by which they had gained honour and security in perpetuity'.[87]

But our most vivid evidence comes from the decree which the city-council of Tergeste passed in the reign of Antoninus Pius to honour L. Fabius Severus, a senator from there, who had often acted as the city's advocate in cases either before judges given by the emperor or before the emperor himself, and always successfully, partly through the justice of the emperor, and partly by the excellence and learning of his *oratio*. Most recently, as was shown by the 'celestial letter' of Antoninus Pius, he had successfully put forward the request of the city that qualified persons from

[81] pp. 438-9.
[82] *NH* VIII, 55/218; cf. Strabo III, 2, 6 (144).
[83] *Ann.* XIII, 54.
[84] *ILS* 6961; cf. *RE* s.v. 'Novempopulana',
[85] Suetonius, *Claud.* 20, 1.
[86] *ILS* 1374; cf. p. 102.
[87] *ILS* 2735; cf. p. 40. Cf. 6183 (Laurentum): 'Divo Antonino Aug. senatus populusque Laurens quod privilegia eorum non modo custodierit sed etiam ampliaverit'.

15

the Carni and Catuli—tribes 'attributed' to the city by Augustus—should be allowed to hold the aedileship and enter the town-council.[88] In this way the treasury of the city had been enriched (for payment of an entry-fee appears to be assumed), a larger supply of rich men was available to share the burdens of local functions, and the persons themselves gained the Roman citizenship. Tergeste was a *colonia* and lay just within the borders of Italy; the exact location of the Carni and Catuli is unknown, but it is clear that as groups they did not enjoy the citizenship. They therefore received at this moment, as well as new potential obligations, a privilege which bore some resemblance to Latin rights.[89]

For our purposes the complex social relations of this border region are less significant than the implications of the inscription that cases before the emperor were frequent, and that success in them or in requesting *beneficia* depended on the quality of orations addressed to him by a patron of good standing. Rhetoric was crucial, whether it related to a new privilege or to the retention of an old one, or even more if rights were contested by a rival party. This unquestioned assumption is perhaps nowhere more clearly underlined than in Philostratus' story of the last triumph of Polemo, achieved after his death.[90] When Smyrna had to send an embassy to defend the rights of its temples, Polemo was chosen, but died before setting out. When the other ambassadors of the city presented their case badly in the imperial court-room (*dikastêrion*), Antoninus Pius asked if Polemo had not written a speech for the occasion; the court was then adjourned while the speech was brought, and after it had been read out before him the emperor decided in favour of Smyrna.

Between the granting of privileges by the emperor and his giving of verdicts in cases relating to them we can make only the formal distinction that in the latter instance at least two parties would actually appear before him. In a more general sense the two processes are continuous and indistinguishable. Which is to say that, in relation to communities as to individuals, we cannot rigidly distinguish between the emperor as benefactor and as judge.

8. *The Cities: Disputes, Accusations and Protests*

When in the second century a man set up a honorific inscription in Attalea to a friend who had held many local offices, and had been honoured with the 'public horse' and a place among the *iudices* by the emperor, he also referred to his services as advocate for his own and other cities—'having delivered many speeches on behalf of his native city and very many others, before both the emperors and the governors'.[1] Similar assumptions lie behind a compar-

---

[88] *CIL* v 532 = *ILS* 6680. For *attributio* see U. Laffi, *Adtributio e contributio* (1966), and for the problem of the location of boundaries in this region A. Degrassi, *Il confine nord-orientale dell'Italia romana* (1954).

[89] cf. pp. 401–6.

[90] *VS* I, 25.

[1] *IGR* III 778 = *OGIS* 567: πολλοὺς ὑπὲρ τῆς πατρίδος καὶ πόλεων πλείστων ἀγῶνας εἰρηκότα ἐπί τε τῶν Σεβαστῶν καὶ τῶν ἡγε[μόν]ων. Cf. p. 282.

able inscription to a local office-holder in Side 'in whose time the city was victorious in all the cases before the most divine emperor'.[2] The language used reflects the fact that disputes between cities which came to an emperor, or a governor, were in fact decided by a verbal contest in which both sides spoke and a decision was then rendered. It also reveals, as does much other evidence, the casual assumption of the frequency of such cases before the emperor, even in communities of no exceptional prestige or prominence.

The first and most essential issue which might arise between communities was the definition of their mutual boundaries. In the nature of the case this was a type of dispute which could not easily be finally decided except on the spot; though an inscription from Lydia contains what seems to be a decision of a Roman official in a boundary dispute between Thyatira and Hierocaesarea with a reference to a *decretum* of 'the emperor while present'. The issue may (for instance) have come before Caracalla on his journey through Asia Minor in 215.[3] More often the emperor appointed someone to hear the issue. So Claudius refers in his edict posted at Baiae to the old controversies between the Comenses and the Bergalei, which Tiberius had sent someone to settle, which had suffered neglect under Gaius, and which he now—having heard that some of the land was legally imperial property—appoints his *amicus* and *comes*, Julius Planta, to settle with the aid of the imperial procurators in the neighbourhood.[4]

In this document it is not clear how the issue reached Tiberius in the first place. But when for instance the Vanacini in Corsica had a dispute over boundaries with their neighbours, the Mariani (a *colonia* founded by Marius), over land, presumably imperial property, which they had bought from an imperial procurator, they sent an embassy to Vespasian. As his reply shows, they prefaced their request with a *testimonium* to the good government of a previous procurator; having acknowledged this, Vespasian says that he has written to another procurator to have the land measured, and has sent him a *mensor* to carry it out. Thirdly, the two ambassadors, both priests of Augustus, took the opportunity to ask, successfully, for the confirmation of the *beneficia* granted to the community by Augustus, and retained ever since.[5] Vespasian clearly received and heard the ambassadors, but did not actually decide the case. But, as we saw earlier, Domitian himself heard at his Alban villa in 82 the long-lasting dispute between the Firmum and Falerii;[6] this could be decided by him, for the issue was not one of the exact location of boundaries, but of whether the Firmani still had a claim to the lots which they ought to have sold off after the *colonia* had been established by Augustus. The emperor, after giving his verdict,

---

[2] G. E. Bean, *The Inscriptions of Side* (1965), no. 127.

[3] So J. Keil, A. von Premerstein, *Berichte über eine zweite Reise in Lydien* (1911), no. 18.

[4] *ILS* 206 = Abbott and Johnson, *Municipal Administration*, no. 49 = *FIRA*[2] I, no. 71; cf. pp. 32, 254, 256.

[5] *CIL* x 8038 = Abbott and Johnson, *Municipal Administration*, no. 59 = *FIRA*[2] I, no. 72. In relation to the question of city statuses, pp. 394–410, note that the Vanacini had a communal organization with magistrates and senate, but were not a *municipium*, and were not citizens (the two ambassadors were both *peregrini*, which *a fortiori* implies the same for the rest of the community).

[6] pp. 26, 218–19.

presumably wrote to both parties; but the letter which was preserved on an inscription was that brought back by the ambassadors of the victorious side, Falerii. It is for this reason, that only the party which was successful had a motive for inscribing the imperial reply, that our evidence presents us with a display of imperial benevolence even more one-sided than the most munificent of emperors can have hoped. It is only when cities chose to reinforce their point by inscribing also unfavourable imperial replies to their opponents or rivals that we gain any documentary evidence of the other side of imperial decision-making.

We do not know what led to the delimitation in 101 of the boundary between the Thracians and the Thasians on the authority of Trajan;[7] but when at the end of Trajan's reign, in 116–17, Avidius Nigrinus judged a boundary dispute between the Delphians and their neighbours, Anticyra, Ambryssus, Amphissa and Myania, the vast dossier of documents on the issue included his statement that Trajan 'ordered me to give judgment (*cognoscere*) about the boundaries', and a description of him as a 'judge given by the emperor' (*iudex datus a Principe*).[8] We may presume that an embassy from Delphi had presented the issue to Trajan, for the emperor had laid down the general principle that the delimitation was to follow the decision taken in the second century BC by the *hieromnêmones* at Delphi, itself based on an earlier ruling by M.' Acilius Glabrio and a *senatus consultum*. Such evidence could only have been put before him by the Delphians. Similar local initiatives will lie behind the judicial decision of a proconsul of Achaea under Hadrian, in which he says that the emperor has written to instruct him to decide the dispute over boundaries between Lamia and Hypata.[9]

In the case of a dispute over land between the cities of Coronea and Thisbe Antoninus Pius gave a judgment (*apophasis*) which was firmly in favour of the Coroneans—and it was again they who inscribed the letter which he wrote to them.[10] What is more, they also inscribed the unfavourable letter which he wrote to Thisbe, saying that they would either have to pay to Coronea a rent for the land they had occupied, or lose the pledges which they had given. The precise sums were to be determined by Mestrius Aristonymus, who the letter to Coronea says would also measure the disputed land. This letter also makes clear that the issue had previously been before Hadrian, who had ruled that certain land should be allotted to Thisbe, and that they should pay a rent for any beyond that which they cultivated. As in similar cases, two ambassadors from Coronea had been to the emperor and brought back his letter

In the established empire it was clearly a common pattern that the cities should send representatives to conduct cases on their behalf before the emperor: for instance a man from Oxyrhynchus in Egypt, in a letter to

---

[7] *AE* 1968 469.

[8] See now for a full edition of the fragments, with extensive commentary, A. Plassart, *Fouilles de Delphes* III. 4 (1970), nos. 290–9: for the phrases quoted, 292 = 293 (Greek text); 294 = 295 (fragmentary Greek text).

[9] *ILS* 5947a; cf. p. 328.

[10] *IG* VII 2870 = Abbott and Johnson, *Municipal Administration*, no. 104, i and iii (ii is the reply to the diplomatic embassy from Coronea of 140, p. 416

Severus and Caracalla, writes: 'When you were visiting the province, you honoured them (the Oxyrhynchites) by granting them admission to your *dikastêrion* first after the Pelusians.'[11] It cannot always have been clear in advance whether the admission of an embassy bringing claims, accusations or disputes would or would not lead to a two (or more)-sided contest before the emperor, for the other party or parties might either be as yet unaware of what was happening, or might be unable or unwilling to offer any opposition. Thus for instance Antoninus Pius' letter to Thisbe, mentioned above, does not give the name of any ambassador from there, and they may have failed to contest the representations from Coronea.

For example, it is clear that no representatives of neighbouring cities appeared when three ambassadors from Hyrcanus and the Jewish people had met Antonius at Ephesus after Philippi, presented a gold crown and asked both for the release of Jews taken prisoner in the regime of Cassius, and for the restoration of territory which they had lost. In reply to them Antonius names the ambassadors, as was usual; but in his letters to Tyre, which Josephus quotes (and presumably in those to Sidon, Antioch and Aradus, which he mentions), Antonius baldly instructs them to comply (saying that if they have a case he will hear it when he comes), and to post up his edict requiring restoration.[12] But, even leaving aside cases from the history of the Judaea as a province,[13] Josephus' narrative of the reign of Augustus contain one classic instance of a contest before the emperor himself; and one case before Agrippa, when acting as his deputy in the east, where a contest might have been expected but did not occur. On the first occasion, when Augustus was in the east in 20 BC, an embassy came from Gadara to request that their city be detached from Herod's kingdom, and to support their claim accused him of violence, robbery and destruction of temples. Herod defended himself (or resisted their claim—here as elsewhere we cannot distinguish a criminal trial from the resolution of a dispute), and speeches were made on both sides. It was then that the Gadarenes, as we saw earlier, committed suicide on seeing that Augustus and his assessors had maintained their friendly attitude to Herod.[14]

Later, when describing how Herod accompanied Agrippa on his journey through Asia Minor in 14 BC, Josephus relates how the Jews of Asia complained that their rights were not being observed, and Herod assigned Nicolaus of Damascus to make an oration on their behalf before Agrippa and a council of Roman office-holders, kings and dynasts. When he had finished, Josephus says, 'there was no counter-claim (*antikatastasis*) from the Greeks; for they [the Jews] were not setting out the matters concerned as if in a *dikastêrion*, but it was rather a petition (*enteuxis*) about the violence they had suffered'. So as a result of the oration Agrippa confirmed the rights of the Jewish communities.[15]

---

[11] *P. Oxy.* 705 = Wilcken, *Chrestomathie*, no. 153; cf. p. 452.

[12] Josephus, *Ant.* XIV, 12, 2–6 (304–23); cf. *JRS* LIII (1973), 54–5.

[13] pp. 376–9.

[14] *Ant.* XV, 10, 3 (354–9); more briefly on p. 9.

[15] XVI, 2, 3–5 (27–61), with an extended version of the speech (derived from Nicolaus himself); the undated letter of Agrippa to Ephesus, XVI, 6, 4 (167–8), may be a result of this occasion.

Explicit evidence of disputes between provincial communities or cities coming to the emperor is relatively rare, apart from boundary-disputes and the representations in the 'Acts of the Pagan Martyrs' preserved on papyrus of rival Alexandrian Jewish and Greek embassies appearing before various emperors.[16] But we may note the man from Sparta who went on a successful embassy to Antoninus Pius in Rome 'over the case against the Free Laconians';[17] the appeal addressed by Philadelphia to Valerian and Gallienus against the claims of the major cities of Asia;[18] or the petition to Constantine in 331 by the newly re-founded city of Orcistus against the claims of Nacolea.[19] Constantine and his two sons, Constantine and Constantius, write from Constantinople to affirm that the privilege granted to them involved their freedom (from obligations to other cities): 'So by the present rescript we forbid the injury done to you by the Nacoleans in defiance of the *beneficia* of our *indulgentia*, and yield to your request and petition that the money which you used to pay for the cults should in future definitely not be payable.' They have also, they say, written to the *rationales* of Asia to see that payment is not demanded.

Cities, or other communities or bodies, are perhaps more often found in overt disputes with individuals, usually over their liability to perform local services, or over specific sums due from them. One rare example of a boundary-dispute, involving the emperor, between an individual and a community is provided by an inscription from near Cnossus which shows that in 84 an imperial procurator, on the basis of a *sententia* by Titus (who had died three years earlier), established the boundaries between the property of an individual and that which the city of Capua owned in Crete; the word *sententia* should mean a verdict given by Titus in a case heard by him.[20] But, as regards local obligations, as early as the third Cyrene edict we find Augustus laying down that persons granted the Roman citizenship were not exempt from liturgies, unless by a *lex*, *senatus consultum* or *decretum* of himself or Julius Caesar they had also been given immunity from tribute (*aneisphoria*)—which he apparently holds, by analogy, to confer immunity from the local burdens, though only in respect of property owned at the time of the grant. Though no indication of the circumstances is given, it is clear that the contrary had been claimed by some persons.[21]

Disputes over obligations naturally arose most often between a man and his own native city. But Aphrodisias once again provides the exception, for among the documents of their privileges there appears a pronouncement from Trajan informing the city of Smyrna that it cannot lay claim to the services of a citizen of Aphrodisias for a temple of its own:[22]

I wish no one from any of the free cities to be forced to undertake a liturgy of

---

[16] cf. p. 234.
[17] *IG* v. 1 37.
[18] p. 390.
[19] *MAMA* VII 305, Panel iii; cf. p. 410.
[20] *AE* 1969/70 635.
[21] *SEG* IX 8 = *FIRA*² I, no. 68, iii.
[22] For the Aphrodisias dossier, see p. xiii.

yours, and especially no one from Aphrodisias, since the city is excepted from the framework of the province also, and therefore has no obligations either to the common liturgies of Asia or to those of the other cities. I release Tiberius Julianus Attalus from [service to] the temple in Smyrna, and especially because he has been testified to by his own city. I have also written about these matters to Julius Balbus, my friend and proconsul.

Under Hadrian a more typical case was heard in the emperor's court. Favorinus, who, though a well-known Greek sophist, came from Arelate, was summoned to take the position of high priest 'at home' (probably in the city rather than in the *concilium* of Narbonensis). In the imperial *dikastêrion*, where we may presume that representatives from Arelate were appearing against him, he realised that the emperor was unfavourable to his plea for exemption as a 'philosopher'; so he announced that his teacher, Dio of Prusa, had appeared to him in a dream and commanded him to serve.[23] Nearly a century later another sophist, Philiscus, was compelled, as we saw earlier, to come to Rome in 212–13 to answer in Caracalla's court the claim by the Heordaeans in Thessaly that he was liable to liturgies there. In this instance also the emperor's attitude was decisive, for he was offended by the sophist's effeminate voice, lazy manner and wandering discourse:[24]

> All this made the emperor hostile to Philiscus, so that he kept pulling him up throughout the whole speech, both by interjecting his own remarks in the others' allotted time and by interrupting with abrupt questions. And since the replies of Philiscus were beside the mark, the emperor exclaimed: 'His hair shows what sort of man he is, his voice what sort of orator!' And after cutting him short like this many times, he ranged himself on the side of the Heordaeans. And when Philiscus said: 'You have given me exemption from public service by giving me the chair at Athens', the emperor cried at the top of his voice: 'Neither you nor any other teacher is exempt! Never would I, for the sake of a few miserable speeches, rob the cities of men who ought to perform public services.'

This dialogue, which may have gained something in the telling, but which comes from Philostratus, who himself attended the court of Caracalla, and therefore cannot be rejected as unhistorical, is one of the prime examples of the personal exchanges through which imperial verdicts were reached. We can once again presume that a delegation for the Heordaeans, who were the petitioners, was present, will have spoken before Philiscus, and went away victorious. Their action illustrates the difficulties to which the cities were reduced in compelling the services of their more prominent citizens, especially those who like Philiscus had been drawn off to major centres like Athens, or on whom they had only an uncertain claim (which in this instance rested on the local law that citizenship passed by maternal descent).

The complexities of the cities' relations to their citizens, expecially those of some importance and influence, are nowhere clearer than in a letter written by Severus and Caracalla a few years before this episode, and concerning another sophist mentioned by Philostratus, Claudius Rufinus of

[23] Philostratus, *VS* I, 8; Dio LXIX, 3, 6.
[24] *VS* II, 30, Loeb trans.; cf. pp. 231–2 above, and note *AE* 1951 58.

Smyrna.[25] In this case two ambassadors had come from Smyrna to request that the immunity which Rufinus enjoyed in accordance with imperial constitutions relating to sophists engaged wholly in rhetoric should be preserved, even notwithstanding the fact that at the request of his fellow-citizens he had voluntarily undertaken office there. The emperors agree, 'especially since you request this favour (*charis*) on his behalf'. The reactions of all three parties could easily have been different. But the effect, whether consciously intended or not, was that Rufinus, having performed a service for Smyrna, still retained his exemption from services elsewhere, such as in the *koinon* at Asia.

On the other hand if an office were essentially honorific, a man might engage in a dispute in order to obtain it. This was the case with the rich landowner who passed through Nicopolis in about 107 or 108 on his way to appear before the emperor in Rome, and had a discussion with Epictetus. The issue at stake was his election, or recognition, as *patronus* of Cnossus, and the conversation reveals that he was to have an adversary (*antidikos*) and, as usual, that all would depend on the emperor's view of him. It is also one of the few places in our evidence where allusion is made to the difficulties posed by the journey itself for those who went to the emperor. 'What is it,' Epictetus says, 'for which you are now on your way to Rome? Mere opinion. And in winter, and with attendant danger and expense?'[26]

Disputes could also arise over the exercise of their powers, or handling of public funds, by those who did take local office, and more widely in the recovery of debts or other sums which were due. Pliny, for instance, was one of Trajan's assessors when the emperor heard the claim by, or on behalf of, Vienne that a *duovir* there had acted without authority in abolishing an athletic contest in the Greek style, which had previously been celebrated with funds left in someone's will. The man (who happened to be a friend of Pliny) made a speech marked by learning and gravity on his own behalf. It is not indicated who spoke for the Viennenses, but when the opinions of the *consilium* were asked for, it was agreed that the contest should be abolished.[27]

From Bithynia Pliny later consulted Trajan about accusations against Dio of Prusa claiming that he should be required to submit accounts of a public building carried out by him; Trajan rejects certain subsidiary charges, but states firmly that the interests of the city required that Dio should produce the accounts.[28] Some years later, in 120, the *gerousia* of Ephesus (a board for controlling temple funds) sent an ambassador to Hadrian over the question of debts due to it. Their decree referred to a judgment in their favour by a previous proconsul, Mettius Modestus, which Hadrian approves; 'and', his letter continues, 'since you have shown that many people have appropriated money belonging to you, inasmuch as holding estates of those who had borrowed from you, they deny that they are the heirs and assert that they themselves are also creditors'—so he has

---

[25] *IGR* IV 1402 = *Syll.*[3] 876 = Abbott and Johnson, *Municipal Administration*, no. 127; he is mentioned as a minor figure in Philostratus, *VS* II, 25.

[26] Epictetus, *Diss.* III, 9; cf. *JRS* LV (1965), 146.

[27] *Ep.* IV, 22, 1–3.

[28] *Ep.* X, 81–2.

sent a copy of their decree to the present proconsul, who will appoint someone to judge the matter and collect the sums due.[29]

On occasion both sides in such an issue would approach the emperor. Lucian relates how the Cynic Peregrinus, having given all his property to his native city of Parium, later changed his mind and presented a *libellus* asking for the emperor's order for its restoration; but the city sent an embassy to counter his claim, and it was refused.[30] The casual way in which this process is alluded to is itself an indication that such things were an accepted part of the life of the Greek east in the second century.

Similar issues could arise in western cities also, though inevitably we have far less evidence about them. But the *Digest* preserves for instance a letter, probably addressed to the *legatus* of Numidia, in which Severus and Caracalla deal in great detail with a case in which the heirs of a deceased man tried to reclaim a legacy which he had left to the city of Cirta for the building of an aqueduct. At the moment of the testator's death they had failed to appeal to the provisions of the *Lex Falcidia* on legacies, and the emperors reject their claim. Since the parties are referred to in the third person it can be presumed that the case had come before the governor, who had referred it to the emperors.[31] Severus Alexander by contrast writes directly to the *quattuorviri* and *decuriones* of Fabrateria in Latium, in answer to a complex enquiry relating to obligations made by, and payments made to, a public slave.[32]

Had such an issue arisen in a provincial town, it might well, though would not necessarily, have gone first to the governor, and have reached the emperor only by way of consultation or appeal. That was the case for instance with the only letter of Titus we possess, 'given' (*data*) on 7 September 79 to the *quattuorviri* and *decuriones* of Munigua in Baetica.[33] A previous proconsul of Baetica had given judgment that the city owed a certain sum to a man named Servillius Pollio, whereupon the city appealed to the emperor. Titus rejects the appeal, but remits part of the sum all the same: 'The penalty for improper appeal ought to have been exacted from you. But I have preferred to speak with my accustomed *indulgentia* rather than your temerity, and have remitted 50,000 *sesterces* in view of the poverty which you have claimed on the part of your *res publica*.' He says that he has written to the proconsul, his *amicus* Gallicanus, that the balance should be paid, but without the interest which would normally have been due from the day of the original judgment. He further agrees that the profits on the local revenues, which, as they had said, were leased by Pollio, should be taken into account.

It is not stated which if any of the parties travelled to Rome to appear

[29] *Syll.*³ 833 = Abbott and Johnson, *Municipal Administration*, no. 78 = J. H. Oliver, *The Sacred Gerusia, Hesperia*, Supp. VI (1941), 89, no. 7, whose translation is used here.

[30] Lucian, *Pereg.* 16: καὶ γραμματεῖον ἐπιδοὺς ἠξίου ταῦτα κομίσασθαι κελεύσαντος βασιλέως. εἶτα τῆς πόλεως ἀντιπρεσβευσαμένης οὐδὲν ἐπράχθη, ἀλλ' ἐμμένειν ἐκελεύσθη οἷς ἅπαξ διέγνω μηδενὸς καταναγκάσαντος.

[31] *Dig.* XXII, 6, 9, 5.

[32] *CJ* XI, 40, 1.

[33] H. Nesselhauf, 'Zwei Bronzeurkunden aus Munigua', *Madrider Mitteilungen* I (1960), 142, esp. pp. 148f.; *AE* 1962 288. The *poena iniustae appellationis* was known previously only from Tacitus, *Ann.* XIV, 28, 1.

before Titus; it is probable, however, that the letter was, as was usual, literally 'given' to an embassy in Rome. But the inscription has considerable significance as being a classic instance of an exception proving a rule. For the reason why the city inscribed Titus' letter containing his judgment, is clearly that, although it was basically a rejection of their appeal, he not only required no penalty but made three separate deductions from the sum due. In practical terms, therefore, the appeal was largely successful.

It was perhaps also to a city in Africa (or possibly to the *concilium* of the province) that at some time before 186 an emperor or emperors wrote to lay down appropriate punishments for free men or their slaves who pastured flocks of sheep on other people's land. The fragmentary inscription which provides our evidence mentions the 'sacred letter' and quotes what is evidently part of it: the writer in this part refers to 'your request' (*desiderium vestrum*) and, as he lays down what the proconsul should do, can only be the emperor.[34] It may on the other hand have been to a governor, the *legatus* of Noricum, that Severus and Caracalla replied in 205 on the question of the privileges of the corporation of *centonarii* (firemen) at Solva. But as the name of the addressee and the greeting (if any) are missing, the rescript could be either an *epistula* to a governor or a *subscriptio* to an interested party. It is evident at least that the addressee had reported that some persons of substantial means were enjoying the privileges of the *collegium*, that is exemption from other public duties, without performing the relevant functions. The emperors preserve the *beneficia* granted to such *collegia* by the senate or earlier emperors, but say 'let those who you say are enjoying their wealth without undertaking any burden, be compelled to undergo public functions'. A list of all the members of the *collegium*, as on 14 October 205, is attached to the rescript on the inscription.[35]

Thus, though the precise chain of communication is unclear, it is certain that the rescript, even though part of it enunciates general principles, is a response to a local dispute; the issue is indeed precisely comparable to that of the spurious shippers in some Greek city, mentioned earlier.[36] In both of these cases the issue at stake is liability to public functions. But though this was a very common occasion for reference to the emperor, it was not the only one which might concern professional groups: for we may note in passing that Antoninus Pius replied to the fishermen of Formiae and Caieta that they were permitted free access to the shore, provided that they kept away from villas, buildings and tombs there; and in Greek to a group of bird-catchers that it was not reasonable for them to pursue their calling on other people's land, if the owners were unwilling.[37] Where the bird-catchers

---

[34] *CIL* VIII 23956 = Abbott and Johnson, *Municipal Administration*, no. 146 (dated to 256). The letter quoted *may* be one of Commodus (so F. Grosso, *La lotta politica al tempo di Commodo* (1964), 623), but there is no certainty that it is.

[35] Earlier references in *FIRA²* I, no. 87; a revised text with photograph in E. Weber, *Die römerzeitliche Inschriften der Steiermark* (1969), no. 149; see G. Alföldy in *Historia* XV (1966), 433, and E. Weber in *Historia* XVII (1968), 106.

[36] p. 428.

[37] *Dig.* I, 8, 4: 'Divus Pius piscatoribus Formianis et Caietanis (a necessary correction for 'Capenatis') rescripsit'; VIII, 3, 16: 'Divus Pius aucupibus ita rescripsit: οὐκ ἔστιν εὔλογον ἀκόντων τῶν δεσποτῶν ὑμᾶς ἐν ἀλλοτρίοις χωρίοις ἰξεύειν.

were and what type of associations they formed, is quite unknown; but it is clear once again that their application to the emperor could only have arisen from some local dispute.

Communities might also bring before the emperor criminal accusations both against local persons and against Roman office-holders. Two well-known examples of the former occurred for instance under Augustus. In 6 BC an embassy from the free city of Cnidus presented itself to Augustus in Rome with a decree, and made accusations over the death of one of their citizens named Eubulus against another Eubulus who was now dead, and his wife Tryphaena, who was present in Rome. It was on this occasion, as we saw earlier, that Augustus gave Asinius Gallus the task of making an examination, on the basis of which he declares that the accused had suffered prolonged harassment and were not guilty of murder. Tryphaena had fled the jurisdiction of the Cnidian court; and, though it is not directly stated, it is probable that she had gone to Augustus, and been followed by the embassy. Though Augustus advises them to make their public records agree with his verdict, he does not order its public display; but since the inscription comes not from Cnidus but from the island of Astypalaea, some forty miles away, the reason for its existence is in any case quite obscure.[38]

In the same year ambassadors from the cities of Cyrene, evidently the same ones who had brought more general complaints about malpractices in jurisdiction there, accused a man named Aulus Stlaccius Maximus (who had also been sent in chains to Augustus by the governor over another matter) of removing statues from public places, including one of Augustus himself. Augustus says that the man must not leave until he has investigated the matter, and we hear no more of it.[39] Thereafter clear cases of criminal accusations brought specifically by cities or communities against private individuals, and heard before the emperor, are not common in our sources.[40] Hadrian's regulations on the sale of oil at Athens, however, envisage that people will appeal against condemnation either to the proconsul or himself, and lay down that in that case the city should elect advocates.[41] Even accusations against Roman office-holders were often brought, up to the early second century at least, before the senate, and frequently emanated from provincial councils rather than individual cities.[42] None the less, Philo, for instance, makes a particular point of emphasizing that Augustus and Tiberius (by contrast with Gaius) had kept a careful check on governors, particularly when cities which had suffered wrong sent ambassadors:[43]

On such occasions they played the role of judges for all, giving an equal hearing

---

[38] Sherk, *Roman Documents*, no. 67; cf. pp. 115, 217.

[39] *SEG* IX, 8, ii = *FIRA*[2] I, no. 68; cf. pp. 344–5.

[40] One example is the mutual accusations of Herodes Atticus and the Athenians before Marcus Aurelius at Sirmium, pp. 4–5. We do not know the subject of the accusation brought *apud Caesarem* (Augustus or Tiberius) against the orator, Vatienus Montanus, by his native city of Narbo, Seneca, *Controv.* VII, 5, 12; see *PIR*[1] v 674, and *RE* s.v. 'Vatienus Montanus'.

[41] *IG*[2] II 1100, ll. 54–7 (note also ll. 44–6, laying down that if someone sails off without paying the tax letters should be sent both to his native city 'and to me'). Cf. p. 426.

[42] pp. 345–50, 391–2.

[43] Philo, *In Flaccum* 12/105–6; 13/108–18/151.

to accusers and accused, thinking it wrong that anyone should be condemned unheard, and inclined neither to prejudice nor favour.

Philo's remarks serve as an introduction to the fall of the prefect of Egypt, Avillius Flaccus, who—as was virtually unknown—was arrested by emissaries of Gaius during his tenure, and when brought to Rome found himself accused by two leading Alexandrians, Isidorus and Lampo. They must have gone previously to Gaius, and probably though not certainly as ambassadors of the city.

After the Julio-Claudian period it is not easy to document instances where it is clear both that it was a city or community (rather than a provincial council) which brought an accusation against a governor and that it came to the emperor in person.[44] But in any case, as an example of the initiatives open to the cities and their ability to exact influence on the emperor, perhaps rather more significance attaches to those cases where they succeeded in reversing acts of imperial policy. Perhaps the clearest instance is that of certain steps which Vespasian took to raise extra capital:[45]

> The Emperor Vespasian also exacted money from certain *coloniae* to which the right to *subseciva* [plots of land not distributed to any individual by the founder] had not been conceded. For it could not be the case that that land which had been assigned to no one, belonged to anyone other than him who could have assigned it. So he collected no small amount of money for the *fiscus* by selling the *subseciva*. But after he had been moved by the complaints of embassies to the effect that every occupant of land in Italy was being disturbed, he gave up, without making any formal concession. Similarly Titus reclaimed some *subseciva* in Italy. But then the most excellent Domitian seized this opportunity to confer a *beneficium*, and in a single edict freed the whole of Italy from fear.

Though it is not clearly stated, the claim may perhaps have rested on the fact that Augustus had bought with his own money the land for all his numerous colonies in Italy;[46] only a few *coloniae* had been established there since then. Furthermore an alternative description of the same sequence of events describes Vespasian as taking the money for himself (*sibi*), rather than for the *fiscus*.[47] The confusion illustrates both the rapid blurring of any distinction between imperial funds as such, and the private wealth of the emperor as an individual.[48] But more important the account reveals firstly

---

[44] The speech preserved in Musurillo, *Acts of the Pagan Martyrs*, no. vii, seems fairly certainly to be that of an embassy, presumably from Alexandria, accusing the prefect of 103–7, C. Vibius Maximus, before Trajan; cf. R. Syme, *Historia* VI (1957), 480. Similarly Septimius Severus condemned a prefect of Egypt for *falsa instrumenta*, Dig. XLVIII, 10, 1, 4, but we do not know by whom the accusation was brought.

[45] *Corpus Agrimensorum Romanorum* I. 1 (ed. Thulin), p. 41 (Agennius Urbicus, *de controversiis agrorum*).

[46] p. 196.

[47] *Corpus Agrimensorum Romanorum*, pp. 96–7 (Hyginus, *de generibus controversiarum*); Domitian's measure is also referred to briefly on p. 128 (Siculus Flaccus, *de condicionibus agrorum*).

[48] cf. pp. 189–201.

that, as in the case of Domitian's own edict on vine-cultivation,[49] an emperor might simply be unable to carry out a policy to which there was widespread resistance; and secondly that the primary means of resistance was the despatch of embassies to make speeches appealing to his emotions (Vespasian was *commotus* by the *miseratio* of the *legationes*).

Naturally not all protests against official procedures were so effective, especially if they emanated from a single city—and there were, as we shall see, even slighter chances of success for *libelli* presented by groups of less than city status.[50] When for instance the city of Euhippe in Asia appealed to Caracalla, presumably through an embassy, over the misdeeds of official travellers, he merely referred them to the proconsul. An inscription preserves the beginning of the latter's *edictum*:[51]

> Gaius Gabinius Barbarus Pompeianus, proconsul, says. Since when the city of the Euhippeans, taking refuge at the great Fortune of our lord the Emperor Antoninus, over what they have suffered from soldiers and *officiales* turning off the royal trunk roads, were sent back to the governor of the province . . .

But it was precisely the influence of embassies from the cities which held up for almost a couple of years the steady retreat of the emperors from the great persecutions of the tetrarchic period. As we shall see in more detail later, when Galerius died in May 311 after the issue in the name of himself, Constantine and Licinius of the first proclamation of toleration, Maximin took over Asia Minor, and also obliquely subscribed to toleration. No positive measures of restoration were taken at this stage (except that a number of Christians were released from prison), but persecution ceased.[52] In the autumn of 311, however, popular reactions were felt. Maximin himself, in a letter of 312, describes one of the approaches made to him:[53]

> After that, when last year I arrived auspiciously in Nicomedia and took up residence there, citizens of the same city appeared before me, bearing images of the gods and earnestly requesting that I should by every means prevent such people [Christians] from dwelling in their native city. But when I realised that very many people of that religion inhabit those regions, I gave them the answers (*apokriseis*) that I viewed their request with joy and favour, but did not consider that it corresponded to a universal wish . . . Nevertheless I was compelled to give an amicable response both to the Nicomedians and to the other cities which also made the same request of me with such urgency . . . So it pleased me to confirm the most important request which they brought on behalf of their divine cults.

Both Eusebius and Lactantius believed that the embassies were in fact instigated by Maximin himself to afford a pretext for his reversal of the new

---

[49] pp. 391–2
[50] pp. 541–4.
[51] L. Robert, 'La ville d'Euhippè en Carie', *CRAI* 1952, 589, whence *AE* 1953 90 and *SEG* XIII 492.
[52] pp. 578–80.
[53] Eusebius, *HE* IX, 9a, 4–6. For embassies bearing images of their gods see p. 417.

policy of toleration.[54] If they were correct (which we cannot judge), it would only serve to confirm perhaps more clearly than any other item of evidence, the established relationship between city embassies and imperial reactions. But in either case the embassies themselves were a reality. From Antioch an embassy led by one Theotecnus came to request as a great gift (*dôrea*) that Christians should not be permitted to live there; speaking before the emperor, Theotecnus quoted oracles against the Christians, and claimed that the gods bade him expel them as being his enemies.[55]

Many other places followed suit, and, as Eusebius says, the decrees (*psêphismata*) against the Christians, and copies of the imperial decisions in reply were inscribed on bronze and affixed to *stêlai* in the middle of the cities. To illustrate this he gives two substantial extracts from the rescript of Maximin to Tyre, copied from the *stêlê* there. The text not only contains a remarkable statement of pagan belief, but makes explicit that the Tyrians also had demanded the expulsion of the Christians, and goes on to invite them to ask for further favours:[56]

> So that you may know how welcome to us has been your request (*axiôsis*) in this matter, in future, even in the absence of decrees or petition, we, whose spirit is most eager in conferring benefits, by our spontaneous wish permit your Devotion, in recognition of your devout dispositions, to ask for any munificence (*megalodôrea*) which you wish.

Stripped of the accretion of diplomatic verbiage which had developed under the empire, the promise is precisely that which another Syrian city, Rhosus, had received from Octavian 342 years before.[57] Eusebius' statement that the decrees and imperial replies were inscribed is confirmed by the document from Arycanda containing the 'petition and supplication' formally addressed to Maximin, Licinius and Constantine by the province (*ethnos*) of the Lycians and Pamphylians.[58] Exactly as in the instances given by Eusebius, the petitioners describe themselves as fleeing for aid to the emperors, advocate the abolition of Christianity, and allude to the benefits to be gained from the favour of the gods. Above the Greek petition there survive parts of a few lines of the emperors' evidently favourable reply in Latin, with references to the gods, the deserved rewards (of the petitioners) and the *clementia* of the emperors themselves.

This movement was temporarily successful, until the pressures resulting from the conversion of Constantine made themselves felt in 312–13.[59] Its

---

[54] Eusebius, *HE* IX, 2; Lactantius, *De mort. pers.* 36, 3.

[55] *HE* IX, 3.

[56] *HE* IX, 7. Para. 7, 3 gives the document as ἀντίγραφον ἑρμηνείας τῆς Μαξιμίνου πρὸς τὰ καθ' ἡμῶν ψηφίσματα ἀντιγραφῆς, ἀπὸ τῆς ἐν Τύρῳ στήλης μεταληφθείσης. If Eusebius means, as he seems to, that the original was in Latin, this is to be explained by the fact that Tyre was a *colonia* (see p. 96) and will have used Latin in its public documents. Eusebius' text then omits the imperial titles and formula of address and moves straight to the main contents.

[57] p. 7.

[58] *OGIS* 569 = H. Grégoire, *Recueil des inscriptions grecques chrétiennes d'Asie Mineure* I (1922), no. 281 = *TAM* II. 3, 785 (all texts necessarily contain conjectural restorations).

[59] pp. 580f.

significance lies, however, not merely in its being an example of the effectiveness of embassies from cities and *koina* in presenting demands to the
emperor for the removal of specifically promulgated imperial policies, but
in its content and presuppositions. For it is not only that applications to the
emperors were of remarkable frequency—so that inscriptions can record
individuals from Greek cities who had 'often' been on embassies to the
emperor[60]—but that their subject-matter extended to every significant aspect
of the civilization and communal existence of the cities. Within that civilization and communal life, the temples and their lands and incomes, their
priesthoods, cults, ceremonials and festivals had an integral place, both at
city and at provincial level. It was thus inevitable both that they would
afford an important area for imperial munificence, and that a wide range of
questions relating to these matters would come to the emperors for decision.
Precisely because of this integration it is in a sense artificial and misleading
to isolate some instances of imperial involvement in these areas. Yet this
element in the role of the emperors needs special emphasis specifically
because of its relation to the role which they came to play with regard to the
church. When Maximin, as both Eusebius and Lactantius record, tried to
reinforce his renewed persecution by appointing leading men from the cities
to special priesthoods, to carry out sacrifices and abolish the Christian
congregations,[61] his initiative was a product of exceptional circumstances.
But for centuries previously the communities of the empire had been
coming to request the emperor to grant new rights for temples, or preserve
old ones, to permit the establishment or expansion of ceremonials and
festivals, or to award priesthoods which were in dispute.

9. *Provincial Communities: Temples, Priesthoods and Festivals*

In 129 the council and people of Ephesus honoured Hadrian, 'their own
Founder and Saviour, for the unsurpassed gifts to Artemis, in that he gave
to the goddess the rights of accepting legacies and vacant estates, and her
laws, provided shipments of corn from Egypt, made the harbours navigable,
and diverted the river Cayster which was damaging the harbours . . .'[1] The
inscription is typical of the empire in describing as gifts (*dôreai*) both actual
contributions, in this case of corn,[2] the granting of privileges and the carrying
out of public works; the question of the harbour was to be of continuing
concern, and the proconsul of 161–2 was later to write that the emperor was
'constantly sending (letters)' about its maintenance.[3] But it is representative
also in regarding the rights and privileges of the main temple of the city as
an extension or expression of those of the city itself. Ulpian notes that it was

---

[60] e.g. *ILS* 8860 = *OGIS* 494, Claudius Chionis from Miletus, πεπρεσβευκὼς ὑπ[ὲρ τῆς
π]ατρίδος πολλά[κις πρὸς] τοὺς αὐτοκράτορας. Cf. *IGR* III 628 (Xanthus); 982 (Citium);
CIG 2786 (Aphrodisias), [πλε]ονάκις.

[61] Eusebius, *HE* IX, 4, 2; Lactantius, *De mort. pers.* 36, 4.

[1] *Syll.*[3] 839. On 'founder' meaning 'benefactor' see p. 406.

[2] cf. p. 422.

[3] *SEG* XIX 684; cf. G. W. Bowersock, 'The Proconsulate of Albus', *HSCPh* LXXII (1968), 289.

in principle impossible to leave legacies to gods except those to whom this right had been conceded by a *senatus consultum* or *constitutiones* of the emperors, and gives as examples Juppiter Tarpeius (Capitolinus), Apollo Didymaeus at Miletus, Mars in Gaul, Minerva at Ilium, Hercules at Gades, Diana (Artemis) at Ephesus, the Mother of the Gods on Mt Sipylus, Nemesis at Smyrna and Caelestis at Carthage.[4] The passage may remind us that, as we saw in the case of the embassies over rights of asylum,[5] in the early empire the senate could still rule on issues relating to city-temples; and also that, although in this area as in most others nearly all our evidence comes from the Greek east, processes which cannot have been entirely dissimilar took place in the Latin west also. In the east we can see, and in the west must surely presume, that the predominant role in issuing rulings on all such matters soon passed to the emperor.

In the east it will have done so all the more naturally because cities and temples had previously looked to the kings for the granting, extension and preservation of rights. So Strabo records that Alexander had extended the area of asylum associated with the temple of Artemis at Ephesus to a stade, Mithridates had increased it a little further, and Antonius doubled it, so that it incorporated part of the city; but this step gave protection to wrong-doers, and was cancelled by Augustus.[6] It was Augustus, however, who, as a bilingual inscription from Ephesus records, granted to Artemis revenues from certain sacred lands;[7] and he also, when warned by a dream, returned to the Ephesians the statue of Apollo by Myron which Antonius had taken.[8] The restoration of revenues to Artemis by Augustus is referred to in the long pronouncement by Paullus Fabius Persicus as proconsul of Asia under Claudius, as is the fact that Augustus had preserved a *diataxis* of Vedius Pollio (which may mean either some arrangement, or an endowment of money), which gave certain revenues to the goddess. Persicus' pronouncement itself relates, in a way which is not clear, to an *epikrima* (judgment?) of Claudius, and is concerned with the priesthoods of the temple and the handling of its funds.[9]

The cult of Artemis was not the only one at Ephesus which depended on the imperial will. In a letter to L. Mestrius Florus, the proconsul of Asia of about 88–9, an Ephesian explained that mysteries and sacrifices were carried out annually there for Demeter Carpophorus and Thesmophorus, and had been 'preserved over very many years by kings and emperors and the annual proconsuls, as the attached letters of theirs show'.[10] We do not know whose

---

[4] Ulpian, *Fr.* xxii, 6.

[5] p. 346.

[6] Strabo xiv, 1, 23 (641).

[7] *JÖAI* xlv (1960), Beiblatt, col. 42. Compare *Ins. Cret.* i, viii 49 (Cnossus): '[Nero] Claudiu[s] Caesar Aug. Germanicus Aesculapio iugera quinque, data a divo Aug. confirmata a divo Clau[dio] restituit C. I. N. Cnos(so) P. Licinium Secundum proc.'

[8] Pliny, *NH* xxxiv, 19/58.

[9] F. K. Dörner, *Der Erlass des Statthalters von Asia Paullus Fabius Persicus* (1935), iv, 5–9 (restoration of revenues); vi, 10–11; vii, 3–4; viii, 4 (διάταξις of Vedius Pollio); ii, 2 (ἐπίκριμα of Claudius); cf. *JRS* lvi (1966), 162–3.

[10] *Syll.*[3] 820, depending on a copy by Cyriac of Ancona. On the date see W. Eck, *Senatoren von Vespasian bis Hadrian* (1970), 85f.

letters are referred to, but can assume again that they would only have been written in response to applications from the city. Such applications could of course refer also to new ceremonials, as when Vespasian, on the intercession of an astrologer named Barbillus, permitted Ephesus to institute a 'sacred contest', a thing to which, according to Dio, he did not assent in the case of any other city; the athletic contest, known as Balbilleia or Barbilleia, is first attested in a long list of the victories won by an all-in wrestler (pankratiast) towards the end of the first century.[11] Later, under Hadrian, a similar contest called the *Hadrianeia* was instituted. In recognition of his *liberalitas* a man from Antioch in Pisidia was appointed as perpetual *agonothetês* of this 'sacred contest' by Marcus Aurelius.[12] The same man was 'Asiarch' of the temple of Ephesus, but it remains obscure how he came to be appointed by the emperor. It was not unknown however for other positions in relation to Greek athletic contests to be granted as a favour by the emperor. A pankratiast from Smyrna is honoured by the people of Smyrna for, among other things, 'having gained through his acquaintance with the emperors the hereditary xystarchy (presidency of the association of athletes) of all the contents held in Smyrna'.[13] Another athletic victor, from Sardis, 'requested and obtained from our lords the most divine Emperors Severus and Antoninus the high priesthood and the athletic presidencies with succession to his sons'. As a later part of the inscription makes clear, the two xystarchies which he gained from Severus and Caracalla were only an addition to a long list, relating to games in Rome, Greece, Asia and Egypt, which he had already received from Marcus Aurelius and Commodus.[14]

It is thus possible that when a man became *agonothetês* of games at Ephesus by the appointment of the emperor, it was at his own request, or perhaps that of the city. At any rate, even if we ignore the institutions of the provincial imperial cults, whose temples, even though located in different cities, were essentially a matter for the *koinon*, and where it is not surprising that applications were made to senate or emperor,[15] it is clear that much in the religious life of the cities depended on the emperors and was liable to be referred to them.

This was especially true of Athens and Delphi. It is not necessary to dwell in any detail on the relations between the emperors and these two places, which occupied so exceptional a place in the culture of the Graeco-Roman world. But we may note for instance that at some time after he had been initiated in the Eleusinian mysteries in 31 BC Augustus heard a case in Rome over the privileges of the priests at Eleusis; when some matters had to be put forward which were private to initiates, he dismissed his *consilium* and the circle of bystanders, and heard the disputing parties alone.[16] In the second century Hadrian, Lucius Verus, Marcus Aurelius and Commodus were all

[11] Dio LXVI, 9, 2 (142); see L. Moretti, *Iscrizioni agonistiche greche* (1953), no. 67.
[12] *ILS* 5081; see B. M. Levick, *Roman Colonies in Southern Asia Minor* (1967), 127.
[13] *Syll.*³ 1073; see now *ZPE* XIV (1974), 49.
[14] *Sardis* VII, no. 79, trans. Buckler and Robinson; Moretti, o.c., no. 84.
[15] See pp. 345, 386–7, 390, and note the discussion by L. Robert, *Rev. de Phil.* XLI (1967), 44f.
[16] Suetonius, *Aug.* 93. See Dio LI, 4, 1, and P. Graindor, *Athènes sous Auguste* (1927), 14f.

initiates,[17] as, perhaps, was Gallienus in the third.[18] But even before his initiation in 176 we find Marcus, during his Danubian campaigns, deciding cases concerning the rights of the priests. The Eleusinian priesthoods occupied a special position at Athens, in that they were confined to two families, the Eumolpids and Ceryces, and were held for life; but they otherwise fell, like the others, within the supervision and control of the city institutions. Several issues relating to them were referred to Marcus, whose verdict in one instance runs:[19]

> The appeals which Sentius Attalus, Clemens the son of Clemens, and Claudius Chrysippus made from the court and the king archon, Claudius Eupraxides, against Valerius Mamertinus shall be referred back. Now Mamertinus, since he is a Eumolpid and neither of his parents is of the family of the Ceryces, lacks the only means by which it is permitted to a member of one of these two families to transfer to the other: he will refrain from seeking the office of sacred herald, and the elections will be resumed according to the laws of the Athenians between the others who have already gone to law and those who now choose to stand.

Marcus thus enters into considerable detail on the question of qualification by birth for the Eleusinian priesthoods, as he does in his verdicts on other matters from the internal life of Athens which appear on the same inscription.[20] Commodus, as a letter of his inscribed at Eleusis shows, was actually enrolled in the family of the Eumolpids and accepted election as its *archôn*, or president.[21]

At Delphi a long list of imperial letters attests the claims on the emperors' attention which the city owed entirely to the oracle and to the games held there.[22] Many of these explicitly mention embassies, and we also have two examples, both very fragmentary, of letters addressed by the city to Hadrian. Domitian, for instance, restored the temple of Apollo at his own expense in 84, and in 90 replied favourably to an embassy from Delphi which complained of some proposal by the Amphictyonic league to change the procedure at the Pythian games; he also wrote to the proconsul of Achaea to

[17] Hadrian: P. Graindor, *Athènes sous Hadrien* (1934), 5f. Verus and Marcus: pp. 4–5. Commodus: G. E. Mylonas, *Eleusis and the Eleusinian Mysteries* (1961), 231, 233.

[18] The evidence is only *HA, Gall.* 11, 3: 'Gallienus apud Athenas archon erat, id est summus magistratus, vanitate illa, qua et civis adscribi desiderabat et sacris omnibus interesse'; cf. A. Alföldi, *Studien zur Geschichte der Weltkrise des 3. Jahrhunderts nach Christus* (1967), 44.

[19] J. H. Oliver, *Marcus Aurelius: Aspects of Civic and Cultural Policy in the East, Hesperia*, Supp. XIII (1970), Plaque E, ll. 7–15, trans. C. P. Jones from his revised text *ZPE* VIII (1971), 161, on pp. 163–7.

[20] cf. p. 512.

[21] *Syll.*³ 873 with additions by A. E. Raubitschek in *Hesperia*, Supp. VIII (1949), 285. It does not seem to me certain, however, that the letter was addressed to the Eumolpids rather than to Athens.

[22] Most of the letters edited by E. Bourguet, *De rebus Delphicis imperatoriae aetatis* (1905), have been re-edited with extensive commentary by A. Plassart, *Fouilles de Delphes* III. 4 (1970), which contains letters of Claudius (no. 286); Trajan (287–8); Hadrian (300–3, 305); Marcus Aurelius and Verus (313–14, 316, 318?); Marcus Aurelius alone? (two fragments, apparently of letters sent from Viminacium, 323–4; more clearly, 326); Marcus and Commodus (327); Severus and Caracalla (329); Elagabal and Severus Alexander (332). The letters of the Delphians to Hadrian are 304 and 308.

say that the ancient procedures should be observed, and the proconsul in his turn wrote to both the league and the city of Delphi.[23]

In 125 a long and fragmentary letter of Hadrian to Delphi shows him dealing with a complex set of disputes between the city and the Amphictyonic league: giving rulings relating to the invalidation of victories in the games; arranging to be supplied with accounts of the sacred funds of Apollo (as to which the Amphictyons had accused the Delphians of malpractices); and saying that he will judge a dispute about a harbour after he has been supplied with copies of decrees of the league.[24] The precise situation here is very obscure, as it is in the partially preserved letter in which Antoninus Pius makes some regulations about the Pythian games, apparently in reply to an embassy.[25]

We are at least clearer about the circumstances under which an appeal over the prize for actors in the Amphictyonic games reached Septimius Severus. Philostratus records that during the siege of Byzantium in the civil war of 193–6 an actor from there was awarded the prize, after some hesitation on the part of the judges. Another actor appealed to the emperor against their verdict, but 'the Byzantine was victorious in Rome also'.[26] We might explain such an appeal to the emperor in terms of the political situation. But it is not necessary to do so, for Philostratus also describes how an actor appealed to Antoninus Pius against being debarred by the sophist Polemo when presiding at the 'Olympic' games in Asia—and in the subsequent hearing was questioned, as was normal, by the emperor himself.[27]

Although, as is to be expected, the involvement of the emperor is best attested for the great centres, it was not confined to them, for other places could also take the initiative in approaching him. So for instance a famous pankratiast from Thyatira went on behalf of his city as ambassador to Elagabal, and 'gained from his divine fortune a sacred contest which was *eisêlastikos* (meaning that victors should be driven in triumph into their own cities), Augustan, and equal to the Pythian games for all the world'.[28] Similarly the 'Sacred Oecumenical Apollonian Gordianian Antoninian, Isopythian, Truce-bringing, Iselastic for all the world', games at Side were first celebrated under Gordian 'by divine gift' (*dôrea*).[29] Since all forms of contest involved expenditure either from public funds or from the pockets of rich local office-holders, there existed practical motives for the emperors to reserve permission for them to themselves. Also, as with the apparently trivial question of the number of pairs of gladiators which provincial high priests might put on,[30] it was necessary to keep within limits the means by

[23] Bourguet, o.c., 65 = *Syll.*³ 821; cf. *ILS* 8905. Cf. p. 322.

[24] Plassart, o.c., no. 302.

[25] Bourguet, o.c., 89.

[26] *VS* II, 27.

[27] I, 25.

[28] L. Robert, *Études Anatoliennes* (1937), 119f.

[29] G. E. Bean and T. B. Mitford, *Journeys in Rough Cilicia 1964–1968* (1970), no. 21; cf. e.g. *IGR* III 785 (Attalea), games established κατὰ τὸ θεῖον θέσπισμα, cf. III 319 = *MAMA* IV 154 (Apollonia). Note also the report in Malalas x, 248, 5f., of a request to Claudius for 'Olympic' games at Antioch, and, for their restoration, to Commodus, XII, 284, 1f.

[30] p. 347.

which local magnates sought to carry popular favour. So for instance a man from Apamea in Asia in the second century had to go on an embassy to the emperors to secure 'the liberalities (*philodosiai*) from the high priests', meaning the right for the high priests of the city to give shows, perhaps of gladiators.[31]

Alternatively, in establishing a contest the founders themselves might wish to have the regulation of the funds confirmed by an imperial reply. In the letter which Aurelius Horion, a former office-holder in Alexandria, writes to Severus and Caracalla to ask permission to establish a contest for ephebes in Oxyrhynchus, where he has estates, he ends, after recommending the town, by saying: 'And I request you to order that no one should be permitted to spend this money on any other purpose.'[32] It is significant that although the money was entirely provided by Horion, a document of a few years later refers to the contest as the 'gift' of the emperors.[33] Such requests can be found in the west also; for instance a man died at Aeclanum in Italy just at the moment when he gave a show, 'having requested the right to give it from the Emperor Antoninus Augustus Pius'.[34]

Since we have seen earlier many examples of issues brought before emperors by communities, which concerned their religious institutions, it is hardly necessary to stress again that these must be seen as integrated with other aspects of communal life. The conjunction is particularly clear for instance in the edict of an emperor of perhaps the late second or early third century, dealing with the allowable limits of time in appeals to himself: 'Those appeals, however, which relate to magistracies or priesthoods or other posts, let them take their course in accordance with the relevant period of tenure.'[35] It is significant that the emperor envisages such appeals as a normal occurrence, and exactly such a case is in fact mentioned in the speech of a senator on the measure of Marcus Aurelius and Commodus to reduce the price of gladiators. After referring to the joy expressed by the priests (*sacerdotes*) of the Gallic provinces, he continues directly:[36]

> There was one who upon being appointed priest had given up his fortune for lost, had named a council to help him in an appeal addressed to the emperors. But at that very gathering, he himself, before and after consulting his friends, exclaimed, 'What do I want with an appeal now? Their most sacred majesties the emperors have released the whole burden which crushed my patrimony. Now I desire and look forward to being a priest, and as for the duty of putting on a spectacle, of which we once were solemnly asking to be relieved, I welcome it.' And so permission to withdraw the appeal was sought not only by him but

[31] *IGR* IV 791; see L. Robert, *Les gladiateurs dans l'Orient grec* (1940), 276, n. 1. Cf. e.g. *IGR* III 362 = Robert, o.c., no. 98 (Sagalassos).

[32] *P. Oxy.* 705 = Wilcken, *Chrestomathie*, no. 153.

[33] *P. Oxy.* 1202, ll. 5–7: ἀφ' οὗ ἠὐτυχήσαμεν ἐκ τῆς τῶν [κυρί]ων Σεουήρου καὶ μεγάλου Ἀντωνίνου [δω]ρέας τοῦ τῶν ἐφήβων ἀγῶνος.

[34] *ILS* 5878.

[35] *BGU* II 628 *recto* = Cavenaille, *Corp. Pap. Lat.*, no. 237, col. ii, ll. 14–16: 'Appella[ti]ones vero quae ad magistratus et sacerdotia et alios honores pertinebant habe[ant] formam tem[po]ris sui.' For the date of this edict, and its other provisions see pp. 512–13.

[36] *Aes Italicense* 16–20, trans. Oliver and Palmer, *Hesperia* XXIV (1955), 320; cf. pp. 195, 349–50.

by all the others, and how much more numerous petitions to withdraw them will be. Now this class of case will assume a new form in which those will appeal who have *not* been made priests, in fact even those who do not qualify as members of an order.

In a very similar way, imperial generosity to cities could benefit their temples just as it did other public works and buildings. When Polemo persuaded Hadrian to give 250,000 *drachmae* to Smyrna, the money was used, according to Philostratus, to build a corn-market, the most magnificent gymnasium in Asia and a temple prominently placed on a headland.[37] So too the orator who in 310 invited Constantine to visit Autun openly states that the public buildings and the temples of the city await his liberality in repairing them; immediately before this he has recalled that Constantine had recently made rich offerings to a temple of Apollo in Gaul. He could not have predicted that within a few years the emperor was to make gifts to the churches of Rome, and later elsewhere.[38]

The involvement of the emperors with the pagan cults and their ceremonial institutions persisted even after the conversion of Constantine. The well-known inscription from Hispellum in Umbria contains what must be a letter (rather than a *subscriptio*) of Constantine and his sons written in 333/7 in answer to a request from the town. By what means this missive had been brought to Constantine, who came no further west than Pannonia in these years, is not clear. The Hispellates had explained, however, that they were obliged to supply priests (*sacerdotes*) in alternate years, with the obligation of putting on theatrical and gladiatorial shows in Volsinii, and asked to be released on account of the arduousness of the route, and the expense involved. They also reported that a temple of the Flavian family (to which Constantine belonged) was being built at Hispellum, and asked that their *sacerdos* should give his games there. They also, in familiar diplomatic style, requested that their town should have a name drawn from the emperors' names.[39]

The emperors agree that the town should be called 'Flavia Constans'; that the temple should be completed—provided that it should not be polluted by the contagion or deceptions of paganism (whatever that may have meant in practice); and that the shows should be given there, provided that this did not mean the collapse of those at Volsinii. The letter begins with a statement of the emperors' commitment to preserving and enhancing the splendour and dignity of the cities, in a style very close to that of the imperial pronouncements from Tymandus and Orcistus;[40] and it is significant that the emperors not only permit the new temple and associated shows at Hispellum, but make the condition that those at Volsinii should not suffer.

It was precisely because the temples with their priesthoods, rights and

[37] *VS* I, 25; cf. p. 421.

[38] *Pan.* VII(6), 22, 4; cf. p. 424. Gifts to the temple of Apollo, ibid., 21, 4–7. For Constantine's gifts to churches see pp. 147–8, 186–7, 590–3.

[39] *CIL* XI 5265 = *ILS* 705 = Abbott and Johnson, *Municipal Administration*, no. 155; see now J. Gascou, 'Le rescrit d'Hispellum', *MEFR* LXXIX (1967), 609.

[40] pp. 395, 410.

ceremonials were essential to the fabric of local society, that concerns relating to them had always been placed before the emperors, or before that to Roman generals. For instance, when Julius Caesar conducted his rapid campaigns in Asia Minor in 47 BC he still had time to hear a dispute over the powerful priesthood of the goddess Ma at Comana, and awarded (*adiudicavit*) it to a descendant of the Cappadocian royal family.[41] It is evident that advantage was taken of his presence to bring the issue before him. Sometimes on the other hand, the same issues could be brought back to kings or emperors over a period of centuries. The clearest example is the famous dossier of the privileges of the temple and sanctuary of Zeus at Baetocaece in Phoenicia.[42] The rights of the sanctuary were based on a memorandum (*hypomnêmatismos*) issued by a King Antiochus, probably Antiochus I of 293–261 BC, after a report had been presented to him on the powers (*energeia*) of the Zeus worshipped there: the temple was to enjoy all the revenues of the village near it; a fair immune from taxation should be held twice each month; the temple was to have the right of asylum, and the village to be exempt from quartering troops or official travellers.

Then, in chronological order, there is 'the decree of the city sent to Divus Augustus'. The city must be Aradus, situated on an island off the coast, for the subject-matter concerns goods 'going up' to the sanctuary (which lay in the hills between the coast and the Orontes valley) for the use of worshippers. Nothing is indicated about the circumstances, but, as we have seen from a wide range of other evidence, we should presume that such a decree embodied a request or complaint from the city and was taken to Augustus by an embassy. What was inscribed is clearly only an extract from the decree, laying down that the market-officials of the city should be obliged to assist the transport of goods up to the temple and should not make any exactions on them. We may presume that the original decree embodied an explanation of the circumstances, was provoked by complaints from the devotees of the sanctuary, or from the villagers, and received the assent of Augustus.[43]

In 258/9 some persons attached to the temple found their rights threatened again (though which and by whom is not stated) and presented a *libellus* to Valerian. We can deduce that their application was in this form because the reply is a classic instance of a *subscriptio*, brief and without formulae of address or farewell; as we shall see later, this form was used in reply to groups of persons who did not have a recognized status as a community or organization, and therefore presented *libelli* rather than *epistulae*.[44] The *subscriptio* begins with the names of Valerian, Gallienus and Saloninus, but

[41] *Bell. Alex.* 66, 4; cf. Strabo XII, 2, 3 (535). Augustus was later to award it to Cleon of Gordiokome, who deserted to him in the war of Actium, Strabo XII, 8, 9 (574).

[42] The older editions, *CIL* III 184 (cf. p. 972); *IGR* III 1020; *OGIS* 262 (Greek text only); Abbott and Johnson, *Municipal Administration*, no. 147, are now replaced by *IGLS* VII 4028, with extensive commentary. See also the important article by H. Seyrig, 'Aradus et Baetocaecé', *Syria* XXVIII (1951), 191.

[43] Seyrig, o.c., 197, suggests that, following complaints, Augustus required the city to pass this decree, and send a copy to him, a procedure which is perhaps possible, but is not so well supported by other parallels.

[44] pp. 541–4.

we can reasonably assume that it emanated from Valerian, who was probably now in Syria, and only nominally from his son and grandson, who were in Gaul. After the names of the emperors it continues: 'To Aurelius Mareas and others. As for the ancient *beneficia* of the kings, approved also by the customs of subsequent times, he who governs the province will suppress the violence of the opposite party and see that you retain them inviolate.'[45] As the last part of the inscription records, this positive but not especially helpful reply was 'worshipped by all, and put up by the '*katochoi* (devotees?) of the sacred heavenly Zeus'.

This was not the first occasion on which questions relating to a local temple had come before an emperor in Syria. For, as we have seen, it was in May 216 in Antioch that Caracalla heard the case which some villagers called the Goharieni brought against a man who, they alleged, had usurped the priesthood of their local temple.[46] The temple itself, where the text of the proceedings was inscribed, is situated some 40 km east of Damascus, on the edge of what is now desert. The earlier part of the proceedings is taken up with disagreements between the advocates as to whether the case was admissible; for, as is made clear, it was not a regular appeal from the governor, but had been the subject of a supplication presented, along with other petitions, by the peasants. Caracalla finally intervenes to say, in effect, that he could rule the case out of order if he chose, but prefers to hear it. At this point the advocate for the villagers begins his speech.

> To the peasants, the case is over matters of piety, to you nothing is more important than piety. So now they have confidence in the present instance in engaging in a case before a most pious king and judge. There is a famous temple of Zeus in their territory, which is visited by people from all the neighbouring regions. They go there, and arrange processions to it. Here is the first wrong committed by our adversary. He enjoys [immunity from taxation and] exemption from liturgies, wears a gold crown, enjoys [precedence], has taken the sceptre in his hand and has proclaimed himself the priest of Zeus.

As is evident from what is said earlier in the proceedings, Caracalla could easily have declined to take the case, but did in fact hear it. The rest of the text is missing, but it can be presumed, from the fact that it was inscribed, that the community of peasants was successful in its case. The description which their advocate gave of Caracalla as a 'most pious king and judge' was of course flattery designed to secure a benevolent hearing. But it was flattery which rested both on the general and fundamental conception of the giving of justice as an attribute of a good king, and on the more specific preconception that his dispensation of justice would extend to the temples, cults and priesthoods of his subjects, and to questions of rights, duties, property

[45] 'Aurelio Marea et aliis. Regum antiqua beneficia, consuetudine etiam insecuti temporis adprobata, is qui provinciam regit, remota violentia partis adversae, incolumia vobis manere curabit.'

[46] P. Roussel, F. de Visscher, 'Les inscriptions du temple de Dmeir', *Syria* XXIII (1942/3), 173; see *AE* 1947 182 and for later readings and references *SEG* XVII 759; the restorations on which the translation offered here depends are those of N. Lewis, 'Cognitio Caracallae de Goharienis', *TAPhA* XCIX (1968), 255. Cf. pp. 38, 121, 233, 535.

and qualifications for office which arose in relation to them. The fact is of more than merely antiquarian significance: for it was to be precisely in connection with claims to property, and disputes over the validity of episcopal elections, that the emperor was first brought in to play a role in the life of the church.

The church of course differed fundamentally from the typical institutions of paganism in not being embodied in essentially local cults. But the 'sacred contests' held ever more widely in the cities of the Greek east in the Hellenistic and Roman periods, in close association with their cults, did give rise to universal institutions of a sort, the 'oecumenical synods' of performers and athletes; and these associations also laid a firm claim on the attention of emperors.

10. *The Synods of Athletes and Performers*

On a former occasion also I was petitioned in Ephesus by my friend and gymnastic trainer, along with the eponymous priest of the synod of sacred victors and crown-winners from the inhabited world (*oikoumenê*), Charopinus of Ephesus, to ensure that the existing (privileges) of the synod should remain untouched, and to request, concerning the other honours and privileges which they asked from me, exemption from military service, all liturgies and from providing lodgings, as well as the rights of truce, asylum and the wearing of the purple in relation to the festival, that I should agree to write at once to you.

So Antonius, after a second petition, writes to the *koinon* of Asia; the first probably took place when he was in Ephesus after the victory of Philippi, in the winter of 42/1 BC.[1] The reference to his trainer strongly suggests, but cannot quite prove, that the world-wide synod was composed of athletes rather than actors or musicians.[2] But the essential point is that demands for preservation and extension of privileges came to Antonius from a non-territorial professional association, with its own structure and posts, in a way closely comparable to that in which they came from cities or provincial leagues.

Thereafter, it becomes acutely difficult to distinguish from the elaborate titles of the *synodoi* which appear on numerous inscriptions, whether we are dealing with separate associations, branches (in some sense) of the same association, or the same one using a variety of honorific titles. The precise title of the *synodos* whose representatives approached Antonius is not found again. But a papyrus of 194 (relating to the membership-qualifications of a boxer from Hermopolis in Egypt) reproduces two letters of Claudius and one of Vespasian, addressed (to give the fullest title) to the 'Sacred Gymnastic Travelling Synodos of those devoted to Heracles'. In the first letter, from 46, Claudius writes, exactly as he might to a city, that he has accepted the gold crown sent to him in respect of the British victory, as a

---

[1] Sherk, *Roman Documents*, no. 57; cf. p. 386.

[2] So H. W. Pleket, 'Some Aspects of the History of the Athletic Guilds', *ZPE* x (1973), 197 (on pp. 200–1), to which the following pages owe much. See also C. A. Forbes, 'The Ancient Athletic Guilds', *CPh* L (1955), 238.

sign of their loyalty. In the second, he receives two decrees from the synod, and also acknowledges the recommendations made to him on its behalf by two kings, Julius Antiochus of Commagene and Julius Polemo of Pontus. Vespasian writes a letter of classic brevity confirming their privileges: 'Knowing the reputation and distinction of your athletes, I choose also to preserve all the rights which Claudius conceded to you at your request.'[3]

In 134 Hadrian wrote from Rome to an athletic association with a rather different title 'the Gymnastic (*xystikê*) Synodos of Athletes, Sacred Victors [and] Crown-wearers, devoted to Heracles', granting them at their request a site and building for archives. The place concerned is evidently Rome, where the inscription was put up, but the person who brought the request is still duly described as an ambassador. He is described here as high priest of the whole *xystos* (gymnasium), and in charge of the imperial baths.[4] Nine years later the same man went again as 'ambassador' to Antoninus Pius, also in Rome, and was granted a site where they could deposit their cult-objects and archives, near the baths of Trajan 'where you gather for the *Capitolia*' (the Greek-style contest introduced by Domitian).[5] The relation of this to the previous request is not clear.[6]

Thereafter, we have no evidence of relations of the emperors with associations of athletes as such. But we may note, for instance, that an athlete from Aphrodisias was 'crowned with his own hands by the divine Antoninus (Pius)', presumably at the *Capitolia* or at games in Naples or Puteoli, and was also given exceptional honours by him. The Greek decree in his honour put up at Aphrodisias by the colony of Antioch in Pisidia also mentions that they had often sent to the emperors decrees acknowledging his services.[7]

The immunity from liturgies which the world-wide association of victors had requested from Antonius was still enjoyed in the late third century. But, as Diocletian and Maximian replied to a man named Hermogenes, it was confined to those who had both taken part in contests continually, and had won at least three victories, of which one had to have been either in Rome or 'ancient Greece'—and they had to have been gained without bribery of opponents.[8] The reasons for such a provision are perfectly illustrated by a letter of Gallienus to Aurelius Plution, a *ducenarius* and landowner

---

[3] *P. Lond.* 1178 = Wilcken, *Chrestomathie*, no. 156. The full version appears in the letter of Vespasian, ἱερᾷ ξυστικῇ περιπολιστικῇ συ[νόδ]ῳ τῶν περὶ τὸν Ἡρακλέα. On the presentation of gold crowns cf. p. 141.

[4] *IG* XIV 1054 = *IGR* I 149 = Moretti, *IGUR* I 235. The title is συνόδῳ ξυστικῇ τῶν περὶ τὸν Ἡρακλέα ἀθλητῶν ἱερονεικῶν στεφανειτῶν.

[5] *IG* XIV 1055 = *IGR* I 146 = Moretti, *IGUR* I 236. The association concerned is not necessarily the same as the ἱερὰ ξυστικὴ σύνοδος τῶν περὶ τὸν Ἡρακλέα ἀπὸ καταλύσεως ἐν τῇ βασιλίδι Ῥώμῃ κατοικούντων (*IGUR* I 237), which also honours Ulpius Domesticus. ἀπὸ καταλύσεως is probably a reference to retirement on the part of individuals, as argued by Pleket, o.c., 214f. It does not follow that the body which approached Hadrian and Antoninus was composed of retired athletes settled in Rome.

[6] It may be, as Pleket argues, o.c., pp. 220f., that these letters represent the actual process whereby a world-wide association of athletes established 'headquarters' in Rome. But both the recurrent difficulties of titulature, and the absence of later evidence, must make the conclusion uncertain.

[7] *CIG* 2811b (vol. II, 1113–14) on which the text in *MAMA* VIII 421 almost entirely depends.

[8] *CJ* x, 54, 1. A restriction of exemption to those crowned in *sacra certamina* is mentioned earlier, by Ulpian in *Dig.* XXVII, 1, 6, 13.

at Hermopolis in Egypt.[9] The man, being of relatively high rank, has evidently written a letter to the emperor, and receives one in return. In it Gallienus acknowledges his report of having cared for an orphan who is descended from a line of distinguished athletes, and readily agrees in response to the man's request, that the boy should be exempt from offices and liturgies, 'so that in view of the distinction of his ancestors he may enjoy my benevolence (*philanthrôpia*)'. Once again we see the tendency to divorce status and function which is so typical of the empire.

Another papyrus shows, as we shall see, that Diocletian and Maximian attempted to resist this tendency not merely in their reply to Hermogenes but in one addressed to a synod apparently composed both of athletes and of stage-performers.[10] The latter group, who normally described themselves as in some way devoted to Dionysus, and who included actors, instrumentalists, singers and dancers, had an even longer history of organized synods, going back to the third century BC.[11] In the Hellenistic period regional synods developed, and entered into relations with the kings. By the late second century a dispute between the Isthmian and Athenian synods came before the proconsul of Macedonia, and was finally settled by a *senatus consultum* of 112 BC. From some indeterminable time in this period we also have on a fragmentary inscription the pronouncement of a Roman office-holder on the immunity from taxation, liturgies and provision of lodgings for troops or official travellers of the association of *technitai* (performers) devoted to Dionysus.[12] Then while Sulla was still in Asia, perhaps in 84 BC, he wrote to state that, following the opinion of his *consilium*, he confirmed these same privileges as given then by the senate, magistrates and promagistrates; and later as dictator, probably in 81, he writes to the city of Cos to say that he has granted permission to Alexander of Laodicea, 'a lyre-player, a fine and good man and our friend, ambassador of the *koinon* of the performers devoted to Dionysus in Ionia and the Hellespont, and those devoted to Dionysus 'Kathêgemôn' ', to put up an inscription there recording their privileges. A *senatus consultum* was also passed on the occasion of the embassy.[13]

In the imperial period we have occasional items of evidence for the relations of the emperors with local associations of performers, for instance a letter of Claudius in response to a decree passed by the hymn-singers who performed at the festivals in Asia.[14] A set of now very fragmentary inscriptions from Athens appears to contain the remains of no less than eight letters of Hadrian to the synod of *technitai* devoted to Dionysus 'Choreus' there.[15]

---

[9] Wilcken, *Chrestomathie*, no. 158; cf. p. 470.

[10] pp. 461–2.

[11] For an excellent survey see A. Pickard-Cambridge, *The Dramatic Festivals of Athens*[2], ed. J. Gould and D. M. Lewis (1968), ch. vii, and Appendix of inscriptions (pp. 306–21), to which again what follows owes much.

[12] Sherk, *Roman Documents*, no. 44.

[13] Sherk, o.c., no. 49. Note C. Garton, 'The Theatrical Interests of Sulla', *Personal Aspects of the Roman Theatre* (1972), 141.

[14] *IGR* IV 1608.

[15] *IG*[2] II 1105, re-edited with additions by D. J. Geagan, 'Hadrian and the Athenian Dionysiac Technitai', *TAPhA* CIII (1972), 133.

Then we have three imperial letters of the second century to the *synodos* of the *mystai* devoted to Dionysus 'Briseus' in Smyrna, which seems to have been a comparable type of association, since it appears elsewhere as the *synodos* of *mystai* and *technitai*. The letter of Marcus Aurelius and Verus, and that of Antoninus Pius in 158 are too fragmentary to reveal anything, but that of Marcus Aurelius in 147 is an acknowledgment of their congratulations on the birth of a son.[16]

The existence of these letters to local 'synods' is quite significant in extending the range of diplomatic and other relations in which the emperors engaged. But there is much more to be learned from the extensive documents of the world-wide synod of performers, which certainly existed under Claudius and from what he says in a letter must have emerged in some comparable form already by the time of Augustus.

An inscription from Miletus shows Claudius in 48 writing 'to the sacred victors and performers devoted to Dionysus', referring to their acknowledgment of his preservation of the rights given by previous emperors and the senate, and saying that in view of their loyalty he will try to increase them.[17] If we confine ourselves to strictly contemporary documents however, it is in the second century that we find the full title, 'the Sacred Synod of the Performers, Sacred Victors and Crown-winners from all the world (*oikoumenê*), devoted to Dionysus and (name of reigning emperor), and their fellow-competitors', at places as far apart as Jerash and Nîmes.[18] Those meeting at Ancyra in 128 to celebrate a contest, including the performance of mysteries, recently 'given' to the city by Hadrian voted among other things to send decrees testifying to the services of their *agonothetês* both to the governor and to the emperor. Similarly 'the Performers, Sacred Victors and Crown-Winners from the *oikoumenê* devoted to Dionysus and Imperator Caesar T. Aelius Hadrianus Antoninus Augustus Pius', meeting for the quinquennial contest called the 'Great Ephesia' in about 142, passed various motions in honour of one Aelius Alcibiades, including one for the sending of an embassy to express their gratitude for the actions of their benefactor both to the *synodos* in Rome and to the emperor.[19] In both cases the despatch of a communication to the emperor is mentioned briefly, as if it were a relatively routine aspect of any significant vote of honours. We may or may not be seeing another aspect of an emperor's relations with this synod in an inscription from Rhodes recording that a sophist, T. Aurelianus Nicostratus (who had often been on embassies for his native city), had been 'honoured by the emperor with the presidency and curatorship of the sacred stage (*thumelikê*) *synodos*'.[20]

But our most substantial evidence for the contacts of the synod with the

[16] The letters of 147 and 158: *Syll.*³ 851 = *IGR* IV 1399 (for that of Marcus cf. p. 27 above); that of Marcus Aurelius and Verus: *CIG* 3177; the fuller title, ἡ ἱερὰ σύνοδος τῶν περὶ τὸν Βρεισέα Διόνυσον τεχνειτῶν καὶ μυστῶν in *CIG* 3190.

[17] *Milet* 1.3 (1914), 381, no. 156: τοῖς περὶ τὸν Διόνυσον ἱερονείκαις καὶ τεχνείταις.

[18] Pickard-Cambridge, o.c., 297f.

[19] *SEG* VI 59 = Pickard-Cambridge, o.c., 318, no. 14; *SEG* IV 418 = Pickard-Cambridge, 319, no. 15.

[20] For a revised text, replacing *IG* XII, 1 83 = *IGR* IV 1134, see *Lindos* II (1941), under no. 492. Cf. *PIR*² A 1427.

emperors comes from three papyri of the late third century, from Oxyrhynchus in Egypt. All three, of which one dates to 275, another to 289 and the other is undated, form part of dossiers submitted to the town-council of Oxyrhynchus in support of claims for immunity from taxation and liturgies on behalf of individual performers.[21] In the dossier of 275, 'the Sacred Artistic Travelling Aurelian Great Synodos' addresses a document to the 'performers, sacred victors and crown-winners devoted to Dionysus'— perhaps to be envisaged as a local branch; other documents are attestations sealed by officials of the 'Sacred Artistic Travelling Aurelian Oecumenical Great Synodos'.[22] In that of 289 we find a document addressed by 'the [performers devoted to Dionysus] from the *oikoumenê* and the Sacred Artistic Travelling Oecumenical [Diocletianic] Maximianic Pious Fortunate Augustan Great [Synodos] of the Performers, Sacred Victors and Crown-Winners [devoted to Dionysus] to the Performers, Sacred Victors and Crown-Winners from the [same Synods]'.[23] If we cannot pretend to grasp the structure and relations of these bodies, it is clear at least that behind the ever more elaborate verbiage and titulature typical of the institutions of the empire, there did lie a definite organization with its own funds and bureaucratic structure, which controlled the entry of new members, and protected their privileges once they were enrolled.

More important for our purposes is the fact that all these documents contain very similar texts of a series of imperial pronouncements guaranteeing the privileges of the synod, which can be compared with the inscribed dossiers of imperial letters from the cities of Delphi and Aphrodisias. Since the papyrus copies have the advantage of brevity, it is possible to set out a composite text, reconstructed from these three versions, as an example of the forms and types of imperial pronouncement on which a non-local association depended:[24]

(Claudius, 43)
Tiberius Claudius Caesar Augustus Germanicus, Pontifex Maximus, *tribunicia potestate* II, consul III, Imperator IV, Pater Patriae, to the Performers, Sacred Victors, and Crown-Winners from the *oikoumenê* devoted to Dionysus, greeting: I permit the statues to be erected, so that your piety to us may be shown in a fitting manner. I preserve the rights and privileges granted by the Divine Augustus. The ambassadors were Claudius Ph[. . .]us, Claudius Epagathus, Claudius Dionysius, Claudius Thamyris.[25]

(Hadrian)
Summary of an Edict of the Divine Hadrian, concerning the grants (*dôreai*) given to the synodos, namely inviolability, precedence, exemption from military

---

[21] The undated document is *P. Oxy.* 2610; that of 275, *BGU* 1074 = *SB* 5225; that of 289, *P. Oxy.* 2476 (cf. 2475 and 2477). For the *boulê* of Oxyrhynchus in this connection, A. K. Bowman, *The Town Councils of Roman Egypt* (1971), 85–6.

[22] *BGU* 1074 = *SB* 5225, e.g. l. 19: [ἄρ]χων τῆς ἱερᾶς μουσικῆ[ς] περιπολεισ[τ]ικῆς Αὐρηλιανῆς οἰκουμενικῆς μεγάλης συνόδου.

[23] *P. Oxy.* 2475, ll. 12–14.

[24] *BGU* 1074 = *SB* 5225, ll. 1–9; *P. Oxy.* 2476, ll. 1–12; 2610, ll. 1–8. The composite translation is given *exempli gratia*, and does not attempt to indicate all the variants between the texts.

[25] The list of names is almost entirely different in *P. Oxy.* 2476, l. 3.

service, public liturgies, and taxation, exemption from tolls for whatever they carry with them for private use or for the sacred contests, [not to be appointed as?] judges, not to appoint guarantors, exemption from tribute and communal sacrifices, not to be obliged to receive official travellers, nor be prevented by any military guard (?)...[26]

(Septimius Severus)

Letter of the Divine Severus. That you who are members of the Sacred Synod in my native city rejoiced, when the care and kingship of all the world devolved upon me, to make clear your opinion through a decree... wishing to increase whatever rights and privileges granted by emperors before me which you have initially, and to hold in honour men of artistic training and devoted to the service of Dionysus. Farewell.

(Severus and Caracalla. Not in the copy of 289)

(Letter) of the Divine Severus and Antoninus. We have read your decrees with especial care, so that you shall not lack any of the existing rights... (nor?) of the privileges laid down of old.

(Severus Alexander)

(Letter) of the Divine Alexander. Whatever was decreed concerning you by the Divine Antoninus, my father, and by the Divine Severus, my grandfather, and by more distant ancestors... I have (often) declared to be valid. Those taking part in every festival shall obey.

Thus the association of performers devoted to Dionysus, however obscure many aspects of its history and organization may be to us, regarded itself as having a relationship to the emperors, and dependence on their grants, which stretched back in unbroken continuity from the reign of Diocletian to that of Augustus three centuries earlier. Though our evidence on the precise forms in which the synod made applications to the emperor is slight, it is evident at least that under Claudius both they and the society of athletes sent embassies to him, exactly as cities or *koina* did. The later imperial letters are also likely to have been in response to embassies, though that cannot be proved.

In responding to such applications and in preserving the rights of the societies, the emperors were playing a role in a central feature of both the social and the religious life of the Greek world. Not only were the two societies attached to the names of their respective deities, Heracles and Dionysus, but all the innumerable festivals and contests round which they travelled were part of the observance of local cults. One of the documents of 289, for instance, was executed at Panopolis 'during the Sacred, Eiselastic, Oecumenical, Theatrical and Athletic Pythian Contest of Perseus 'Uranios', at the great festival of Pan'.[27] That title may also remind us that the same festivals contained both theatrical (including musical) and athletic contests, that the roles and functions of the two societies were very similar, and that it is therefore not always easy to distinguish them. In consequence, it is not surprising that a joint association of the two groups is sometimes attested, as it is, for instance, in a pronouncement of Diocletian and Maximian, along

[26] The general bearing of the privileges is clear, but even with two copies (both damaged) the meaning of the precise terms, and their interpretation, remains obscure.

[27] *P. Oxy.* 2476, l. 18.

with Constantius and Galerius as 'Caesars' (so 293–305), addressed 'to the Synod of Gymnasts and Stage-Performers etc.'.[28] Though it is impossible to be certain on the basis of a single private copy, the document, given in answer to a petition (*preces*), appears to be a *subscriptio* rather than a letter. Once again the petition had concerned in some way the definition of which persons were entitled to exemption from city obligations. The emperors write that it is their custom to preserve intact all the privileges granted by their predecessors but that the winning of crowns cannot be used as an excuse for avoiding *munera*. Only those persons should be exempt who have won no less than three(?) victories in Rome or ancient Greece; here they seem to repeat what they wrote in their *subscriptio* to Hermogenes.[29]

The significance of the relations of the emperors with the associations of athletes and performers goes far beyond the routine diplomatic forms and missives in which it was expressed. First, the third-century evidence is a prime case of the tension between the pressure to confer *beneficia* ever more widely, and the need to confine such privileges to those properly qualified for them. But, more generally, the exchanges illustrate something more than a mere passive acceptance by the emperors of the social, cultural and religious values of the Greek world; and they also show that bodies which seem to have had a developed formal structure, but were neither cities, leagues nor any other type of local grouping, could address themselves to emperors just as cities or leagues did.

These relations are also not without relevance to the history of the contacts of church and emperor.[30] For those contacts themselves have to be considered in the light of the fact that for centuries the emperors had been granting rights, privileges and exemptions to the world-wide, 'oecumenical' associations of athletes and performers, which had their own officers and priests, and whose members took part in the religious festivals, great and small, of the Greek world; and more recently at least, had been laying down the rules as to who qualified for membership, and responding to individual petitions on this question.

These facts are in themselves only minor facets of that wider pattern by which the communities, cities and leagues of the empire had from the beginning employed certain established modes of diplomatic contact with the emperor, depended increasingly on him alone for their rights and privileges, and appear to have assumed without question that their demands, disputes and grievances could and should be brought to his attention. It is necessary to stress once again that neither the barriers of distance or expense, nor the considerations of the emperor's time or the need (which we might be tempted to presume *a priori*) for him to concentrate his attention on more

---

[28] Mitteis, *Chrestomathie*, no. 381 = Cavenaile, *Corp. Pap. Lat.*, no. 241; cf. Pickard-Cambridge, o.c., 321, no. 17: 'Ad synodum xysticorum et thymelicorum et ividem.' Cf. *OGIS* 713: ἀπὸ τῆς ἱερᾶς θυμελικῆς καὶ ξυστικῆς συνόδου, probably from Alexandria and perhaps late third century.

[29] p. 457.

[30] Certain aspects of this analogy, primarily the prevalence of the term 'oecumenical synod' itself in this context, are examined in the illuminating note by H. Chadwick, 'The Origin of the Title "Oecumenical Council" ', *JThSt* XXIII (1972), 132.

general and important matters, seem to have done anything to prevent the presentation to the emperor in person, verbally or in writing, of the affairs and concerns of his subjects as organized in territorial groups, or even, as we have seen, in non-territorial associations. It remains to ask how far comparable patterns are visible in the relation of individual subjects to the emperor.

VIII

Private Persons

1. *Introduction: Imperial Benevolence and Individual Access*

In a passage preserved in the *Digest* Paulus quotes a jurist of the middle of the first century for the words of a letter written by 'Caesar':[1]

> Aticilinus says that Caesar wrote back to Statilius Taurus in these words: 'Those who have been accustomed to draw water from the *fundus Sutrinus* have approached me and explained that they have not been able to draw the water which for some years they have taken from the spring which is situated in the *fundus Sutrinus*, because the spring had dried up, and then water had begun to flow from it again. They have petitioned from me that because they had not lost the right through their own fault or negligence, but because it was impossible to draw water, it should be restored to them. Since this request seems not unreasonable to me, I have concluded that they should be helped. So it pleases me that the right which they enjoyed at the moment when the water ceased to be available to them, should be restored.'

The date and setting of this letter are far from certain. But it is probable that it was addressed to the Statilius Taurus to whom Augustus entrusted 'the city and the rest of Italy' on his departure to Gaul in 16 BC;[2] alternatively, this man and various other Statilii Tauri held the consulship on at least five occasions between 37 BC and AD 45. Nor, although 'Caesar' is said to have 'written back' (*rescripsisse*), is it at all clear from the contents that this is actually a rescript, since there is no indication that Taurus had previously been involved in the matter, or that he had consulted the emperor.

Such difficulties need not, however, obscure the immense importance of the document—which is certainly from an early emperor, and probably from Augustus himself—for the nature and ideology of the relations of subject and emperor. First, the matter concerned is of purely local importance; the 'Sutrine farm' presumably lay in the territory of Sutrium in Etruria.[3] Secondly, the persons who had traditionally had the right to draw water from the spring there approached the emperor directly (*adierunt me*), explained the circumstances and petitioned (*petieruntque*) for the restoration of the right. The emperor regards this request (*postulatio*) as reasonable, and his own response to it as taking the form of coming to their aid (*succurrendum*

---

[1] *Dig.* VIII, 3, 35.

[2] Dio LIV, 19, 6, cf. Tacitus, *Ann.* VI, 11, 3. See *PIR*[1] s 615, where this identification is mentioned as possible, though no more than that.

[3] For this presumption see *CIL* XI, p. 489.

his putavi). His decision, however, is given as such (*id eis restitui placet*), and not as a mere opinion or recommendation.

As we shall see, the workings of imperial jurisdiction in the earliest period are attended by obscurities which are exceeded only by those relating to jurisdiction in the late republic, against which we should naturally wish to trace its development.[4] But it is possible to discern the essential fact that at least a large area of the emperor's jurisdiction was seen as a form of granting aid and succour to individuals and groups, and to take this as continuous with the related activities of hearing complaints, solving problems, conferring or affirming rights or privileges or making actual gifts. In this instance, had the owner of the *fundus Sutrinus* appeared also, there would presumably have been an actual hearing before the emperor; but since he did not, what the emperor pronounces is not a verdict between two parties but a ruling in aid of the aggrieved party.

That it was a primary characteristic of a good king to give justice was, as we saw, an established conception in the Greek east.[5] Moreover, it was still current in practice in the Roman period; Josephus, for instance, notes that Philip the tetrarch always took with him the throne from which he gave judgment, and had it set down whenever someone approached him who was in need of his assistance.[6] So prevalent a Greek conception was of course also familiar in Rome, and Cicero's *De re publica* touches on the notion that 'nothing is so regal as the exposition of justice', of which part consisted in the interpretation of the law: 'and to me indeed it is Numa above all who kept this ancient custom of the kings of Greece'.[7] But more specifically than that, we can see that in practice in the west also, as soon as individuals came to be marked out as sole rulers, individuals and communities would spontaneously come to them for justice. So Sertorius in Spain in the 80s is found taking his seat on the tribunal in order to give a hearing to petitioners.[8] Furthermore, Nicolaus gives a graphic portrayal of the dispensation of justice and *beneficia* by Julius Caesar at Nova Carthago in 45, and the role of the young Octavian as *patronus* there, which is all the more significant for the ideology of monarchy because of its strongly idealizing tone:[9]

> Caesar came to Carthago to make himself available to those who needed something. A large number had gathered, some to get justice, some about disputes which they had against someone, others about the arrangement of the affairs of their cities, others to gain the rewards of valour . . . The Saguntines also came for refuge to Caesar, being under serious accusations and needing his succour. He [Octavian] acted as their *patronus*, spoke most successfully on their behalf at a hearing before Caesar, cleared them of the charges and sent them off home rejoicing, lauding him to all and calling him their saviour. Hence many people flocked to him for patronage, for most of whom he was able to perform

---

[4] pp. 507f. passim.

[5] pp. 3–4.

[6] *Ant.* XVIII, 4, 6 (107): ὁπότε τις ὑπαντιάσας ἐν χρείᾳ γένοιτο αὐτῷ ἐπιβοηθεῖν.

[7] v, 2/3.

[8] Plutarch, *Sert.* 20, 3: εἶτ᾽ ἀναβὰς ἐπὶ τὸ βῆμα τοῖς ἐντυγχάνουσιν ἐχρημάτιζεν.

[9] Nicolaus, *FGrH* 90 F. 127 (XII). The Saguntines are described as προσφεύγουσί ⟨τε⟩ τῷ Καίσαρι.

services, freeing them of charges, asking for gifts or getting promotion for them.

Once again we see the conjunction of communal and individual affairs brought before the monarch, and the indivisibility of the giving of justice and of *beneficia*. Nicolaus' portrayal is matched almost exactly by the words of a Gallic orator addressing Constantine in 307: 'You imitate and follow the justice and dutifulness of your father, in such a way that to all who come to you for refuge you give help in various forms, whether against wrongs inflicted by others or in answer to requests for benefits to themselves, so that you seem as it were to be paying legacies left by your father.'[10]

When it was so firmly and so long established that one important function of the emperor was to give ear to his subjects, it was natural that he should be judged partly on how approachable he was, and how graciously he heard people.[11] But perhaps more significant and more surprising is the recurrent motif, in descriptions of the relations of favoured persons with the emperor, of his granting the right to ask for a favour at will. Fictional or absurd as it may seem, the theme reappears too often not to have some foothold in reality. We have indeed already seen it in documentary form in relation to cities, Rhosus in 30 BC and Tyre in 312, and also in a number of anecdotes relating to individuals.[12] Some such anecdotes may indeed be wholly or partly fictional. Josephus, for instance, relates that Gaius' change of mind about his plan to desecrate the Temple in Jerusalem came about because, as a reward for an especially lavish dinner, he gave Agrippa I the right to ask for what he wished—and the latter asked not for further *dôreai*, such as territories or revenues, but for cancellation of the plan. But Philo, who was in Rome at the time, describes Agrippa as writing spontaneously to Gaius (though mentioning in the letter that he might have asked for other benefits for Jerusalem).[13] Similarly, the *Life* of Oppian represents him as winning the favour of Caracalla by his poems, being granted the right to ask for whatever he wanted, and successfully requesting the restoration of his father from exile.[14] Yet we should beware of concluding too quickly that such a tale is fictional, for abundant evidence shows that release from exile, or amelioration of its conditions, was one of the characteristic fields for the deployment of imperial *indulgentia*.[15]

Again, Lucian relates how a man from the Black Sea region, apparently from the Bosporan kingdom, was granted by Nero the right to make whatever request he wished—and asked for a dancer whose mimes would serve as a means of communication with the barbarians.[16] Josephus himself was granted by Titus the right to take anything he wanted from the ruins of

[10] *Pan.* VI(7), 5, 1: 'ut omnibus ad te confugientibus diversamque opem aut contra aliorum iniuriis aut pro suis commodis postulantibus quasi legata patris videaris exsolvere.'

[11] See e.g. Dio LXVIII, 11, 3 (Trajan); Aelius Aristides, *Or.* XXXV Keil, 23 (Antoninus Pius?); *Pan.* X(4), 34, 4 (Constantine).

[12] pp. 7, 118, 138, 212, 446.

[13] Josephus, *Ant.* XVIII, 8, 7–8 (289–301); Philo, *Leg.* 36/276–42/333 (cf. p. 407).

[14] A. Westermann, *Biographi Graeci Minores* (1845), 63–4 (*Vita* A); 65–6 (*Vita* B); cf. p. 31.

[15] pp. 539–41.

[16] *De salt.* 64.

Jerusalem, and in fact asked for the liberation of some of his countrymen, and the right to salvage some sacred books.[17] The interchangeability of actual and metaphorical gifts is evident here, as it is in Philostratus' classic account of how Septimius Severus gave the sophist Hermocrates of Phocaea the right to ask for 'gifts' (*dôreai*). Hermocrates replied:[18]

> Crowns, immunities, public maintenance, the purple, the high-priesthood were transmitted by my great-grandfather to us who descended from him, and why should I ask from you today what I have so long possessed? But since I have been ordered by Asclepius at Pergamum to eat a partridge scented with frankincense . . . I ask for fifty talents worth of frankincense, so that I may serve the gods, and be served myself.

The story, told by a well-placed contemporary, recalls that of the Scythian who in precisely the same situation asked Claudius Gothicus for wine, and also the fact that imperial stores of valuable commodities are well attested.[19] The great-grandfather to whom Hermocrates referred was Antonius Polemo, who, as Philostratus had recorded earlier, had received from Trajan the right to immunity from tolls when travelling, and from Hadrian the extension of this to all his descendants. The free meals were those enjoyed by those enrolled in the Museum in Alexandria, another privilege which the emperor conferred, and which Hadrian had granted to Polemo.[20]

Very few persons could address an emperor with the arrogance and confidence shown by the great sophists of Asia. To others, the emperor's pronouncements, with their unpredictable and uncontrollable character, and their dramatic effects for good or ill on those who received them, more resembled the oracular responses which emerged mysteriously from the inner recesses of the temples. At least one god indeed, Zeus at Heliopolis, actually replied in rescripts to written consultations sent in on sealed *diplomata* or *codicilli*.[21] It is not surprising therefore that the analogy between divine and imperial pronouncements was quite frequently expressed,[22] and not least in the context of personal petitions.

The earliest specific example is remarkably early, namely one of Ovid's *Letters from the Pontus* asking his wife to intercede with Livia to obtain his release from exile. She should choose the right moment to make her request: 'The oracles do not at all times give out their sacred responses, and the temples themselves are not open always . . . when the house of Augustus, to be worshipped like the Capitolium, is content—as it is and may it remain—and full of peace, then may you take the opportunity of approaching the god, and may expect that your words will meet with some success.'[23] A very

---

[17] *Vita* 75/417–21.
[18] *VS* II, 25.
[19] pp. 138, 144–5.
[20] *VS* I, 25. On the Museum see further pp. 504–6.
[21] Macrobius, *Sat.* I, 23, 14–16, referring to Trajan's consultation of this deity before embarking on his Parthian campaign.
[22] For examples see pp. 98, 100.
[23] *Ep. ex Ponto* III, 1, 131–8.

similar metaphor is employed by Martial in asking Parthenius, the *a cubiculo* of Domitian, to present a volume of epigrams to his master: 'May you admit this slight and timid book across the threshold of the sacred court. You know the moment when Jupiter is serene, when his countenance is bathed in its true calm, and when he will not deny anything to suppliants.'[24]

Both passages of course embody literary affectations, ultimately for the purpose of flattery. But they also reflect real anxieties about the success of approaches to the emperor, and the realization that all would depend, like everything else, on his attitude at the time. In that they offer a necessary contrast to the well-known statement of Titus, when reproached by his attendants for promising too much, 'that no one should leave an interview with the emperor disappointed', and his remark on realizing at dinner that he had passed a day without granting anything to anyone, '*Amici*, I have wasted a day.'[25] The existence of a conscious ideology by which it was part of the functions of a good emperor to respond favourably to requests is undeniable, and it is reflected again in Eusebius' account of how Constantine would compensate with gifts those who lost cases before him.[26]

The existence of such a pattern of expectations, and of actual conduct on the part of the emperor himself, is of considerable significance in its own right. For the activities of a monarch could of course have been formed by quite different preconceptions. But naturally the extent of the significance of this pattern depends on wider considerations of the forms in which individuals communicated with the emperor and of what barriers were imposed by questions of social standing, or by sheer distance and the difficulties of travel. From the fact that distance was surmounted by the established institution of the despatch of embassies by cities, leagues and synods, it does not necessarily follow that it did not pose more serious problems to the private petitioner or litigant. It is significant that according to Modestinus a man serving on an embassy had to ask the permission of the emperor before submitting a *libellus* on private business of his own; for many men such an occasion must have provided a rare opportunity.[27]

Most of the evidence on these questions must necessarily be considered in the context of the different types of issue or demand which private persons brought before the emperor. But as a preliminary it can be emphasized that, with certain exceptions, all the forms of contact with the emperor open to private persons involved their travelling in person to where he was. We may recall that the earthquake at Antioch in 115 caused the deaths of persons from all parts who had come about lawsuits as well as on embassies.[28] The exceptions were, first, if a man were of sufficient standing to communicate with the emperor by letters (carried by slaves), as for instance did Herodes Atticus.[29] We would probably be correct to assume that this applied to all

[24] *Epig.* V, 6, 7–11.
[25] Suetonius, *Tit.* 8, 1. For the vocabulary in which Byzantine writers clothed this story see Dio ed. Boissevain III, 162–3.
[26] p. 10.
[27] *Dig.* L, 7, 16 (15).
[28] p. 375.
[29] p. 5.

senators, and to the more prominent *equites*. Emperors might also correspond by letter with prominent literary figures, as Augustus did with Vergil,[30] or with persons with whom they shared intellectual interests, as Hadrian with the grammarian Velius Celer.[31] For others it was clearly an exceptional honour to engage in correspondence with the emperor: so the honorific inscription to an office-holder in Rhodes includes a mention of the fact that 'in the period of his *prytaneia* he received the most noble letters from the Divine Augustus (Vespasian)';[32] and that of a very prominent Thessalonian of about 200 that he 'had written throughout his life to the emperors'.[33]

Most, though not quite all, of the persons whom we find corresponding with the emperor can be seen independently to have had some particular claim of rank or personal prominence, and most, like Aurelius Horion under Severus or Aurelius Plution under Gallienus,[34] are found using their position on behalf of themselves or dependants. Occasionally the context remains obscure. We do not know anything more of the Menophilus from Aezani, to whom Nero wrote to say that his two sons had arrived in Rome and had testified to his fervent loyalty to the emperor.[35] Again, the Julius Tiro, some codicils of whose will were alleged to have been forged by an *eques* and an imperial *libertus*, was certainly a senator; but it is still significant that his heirs should have written a joint letter to Trajan, while he was absent on the Dacian campaign of 105–6, asking him to hear the case in person, as he did on his return.[36]

Tiberius Claudius Atticus Herodes, the father of the famous sophist, may or may not have been already a senator when he wrote a letter asking Nerva if he was entitled to keep a vast treasure discovered on his property in Athens; but he was certainly from a very prominent Athenian family, which is sufficient to explain his doing so.[37] Equally, it was not every inhabitant of Prusa who could have proclaimed confidently, as Dio the orator did in the assembly there, that 'if you had not attended to the matter and if it had not been taken up by the governors, it would not have been difficult to send a letter to the emperor'. On an earlier occasion he had read out in the assembly his answer to an invitation from the emperor, probably Nerva, and the letter which the emperor had sent in reply.[38]

Similarly in 152, long before his letter to Marcus Aurelius about the earthquake at Smyrna, Aelius Aristides appealed 'to Rome' over his appointment

---

[30] Donatus, *Vita Vergilii* 31 (OCT, *Vitae Vergilianae*, p. 12).

[31] Priscian, *Inst.* x, 57 (Keil, *Gram. Lat.* II, 547).

[32] *IGR* IV 1129: καὶ τυχόντα τῶν καλλίστων γραμμάτων ἀπὸ τοῦ θεοῦ Σεβαστοῦ ἐν τῷ τᾶς πρυτανείας καιρῷ.

[33] *AE* 1923 47 = *SEG* II 410 = *IG* x. 2 (1) 181. Note also Artemidorus, *Oneir.* IV, 31: ὁ Ζήνων ἔδοξεν (in a dream) ἑκατόνταρχος γεγονέναι. προελθὼν ἔλαβεν ἑκατὸν βασιλικὰς ἐπιστολάς.

[34] pp. 452 (Aurelius Horion); 457–8 (Aurelius Plution).

[35] *IGR* IV 561 = *OGIS* 475. Compare the fragmentary letters of Trajan to a man named Claudianus at Pessinus, W. H. Buckler, 'Les lettres impériales de Pessinonte', *Rev. Phil.* XI (1937), 105. Two of them seem to be acknowledging gifts.

[36] Pliny, *Ep.* VI, 31, 7–12; see *PIR²* I 603, and now J.-P. Rey-Coquais, *MUSJ* XLVI (1970), 243.

[37] Philostratus, *VS* II, 1. See *PIR²* C 801. On the emperor's claims to treasure-trove see *JRS* LIII (1963), 36.

[38] *Or.* XLV, 8; XLIV, 12. Compare the letter of Caracalla to Aurelius Julianus, read out in the theatre at Philadelphia, p. 115.

as collector of taxes there. The step must in fact have consisted of a letter to Antoninus Pius, for in the following year 'letters arrived for me from Italy from the kings, the emperor himself and his son (Pius and Marcus), both containing other greetings and setting their seal on my immunity in respect of my oratory, on the assumption that I was practising it'; the letters were just in time to prevent his being appointed to another post, as *eirênarch* (guardian of the peace) at Hadriani, though not in fact without complex further proceedings.[39] Questions of immunities and exemptions were standard features of such letters from private persons as reached the emperor. Marcus and Verus, for instance, replied to the *litterae* of a man named Sentius Potitus, who is evidently in Rome and possibly a senator, that individually the reasons he had put forward for *excusatio* from a *tutela* were invalid, but that together they were adequate;[40] and a 'sacred letter' of 204, necessarily from Severus, informed a man in Paros, evidently a senator, that he seemed to be ignorant of the fact that a *senatus consultum* had laid down that senators could not be obliged to receive official travellers.[41]

From the middle decades of the third century, when our evidence in general is relatively slight, we have four imperial letters to individuals, as well as that to Aurelius Plution. Gordian III replies to a letter of Aurelius Epaphras of Aphrodisias, to say that his *amicus*, the *praefectus urbi*, if approached, will in accordance with precedent allow a case to revert to the jurisdiction of the city.[42] Philip replies in 249 to 'Agilius Cosmianus', almost certainly the senator, Atilius Cosminus, who by the following year was in office as governor of Syria Coele. It is significant that although the man had enquired about a legal point (the status of gifts of property which he had made to one of his freedmen) which was very similar to many which emperors answered regularly by *subscriptiones*, courtesy demanded that the imperial reply be in the form of an *epistula* with the normal opening formula, 'the emperor Philippus to his Agilius Cosmianus, greetings'.[43] Similarly the letter in the names of Valerian, Gallienus and Saloninus, addressed to Julius Apellas, the descendant of a distinguished family of senatorial rank in Smyrna, begins with the same formula of address and ends, 'Farewell, Apellas, dearest to us.' It too is a reply, and appears to be concerned with protecting Apellas' rights as a senator.[44]

---

[39] Aristides, *Or.* L Keil, 95–6; 75 (on the whole issue of the *eirênarchia*, see 71–93). See C. A. Behr, *Aelius Aristides and the Sacred Tales* (1968), 77–86.

[40] *Frag. Vat.* 245 (from Paulus, *de officio praetoris tutelaris*).

[41] *CIL* III 14203[8–9] = *IG* XII. 5 132 = *Syll.*[3] 881 = Abbott and Johnson, *Municipal Administration*, no. 132. The document, which lacks opening and concluding formulae, could be a *subscriptio*, but it is described as *sacra[e litt]erae*; and the indication *dat(a)* followed by place and date, suggests (though does not prove) that it is an *epistula*.

[42] K. Erim, J. M. Reynolds, *JRS* LIX (1969), 56; *AE* 1969/70 599; see *BE* 1970 536 and 1971 612.

[43] The letter is preserved in *CJ* VIII, 55, 1 (which retains the indication that it was *D(ata)* in 249) and *Frag. Vat.* 272 (which has the greeting formula 'Imp. Philippus Agilio Co[s]mi[an]o salutem'). For Atilius Cosminus see *P. Dura* 95b; 97.

[44] *CIL* III 412 = *IGR* IV 1404. The inscription (now lost) contained the last part of the (original) Latin text, ending 'Vale, Apella carissime nobis. data V Kal. Jun.', and then a Greek translation with the address Ἰουλίῳ Ἀπελλᾷ ἰδίῳ χαίρειν. Like the *subscriptio* to the villagers of Baetocaece, p. 454, it is likely in fact to be the work of Valerian alone. On Apellas' family see *PIR*[2] I 155; 156 = A 905; I 326; I 507 and A 906 (cf. p. 300).

A year or two previously, Valerian, Gallienus and Valerian (Gallienus' elder son, killed early in 258) had written in the same style to 'their' Avinius Octavianus. Whether the latter was a senator is not known. But the matter about which he had written to them related to upper-class society in Rome:[45]

> Your petition (*preces*) has the support both of the authority of the law and of equity . . . So whatever Julius Agrippinus, *vir clarissimus*, gave to your daughter Avinia as his fiancée, he can in no way reclaim. And if he tries to do this Ju(n)ius Donatus, *vir clarissimus*, the *Praefectus urbi* and our *amicus*, will interpose his authority to reject so improper a request.

If we can regard as genuine the letter with which the senator and poet, Publilius Optatianus Porphyrius, secured his release from exile from Constantine, probably on the occasion of the *vicennalia* in 325, and the emperor's equally mannered reply, then we have a clear example of the advantages conferred by social and by literary eminence, and the uses to which they could be put.[46] But even without that, the examples given are sufficient to suggest how exceptional had to be the position of anyone who could correspond by letter with the emperor; and thereby we can see in its proper relief the significance of Constantine's quite frequent correspondence with bishops from 313 onwards.[47]

Correspondence by letter presupposed at least some comparability of status, and normally indicated some personal acquaintance. In the nature of the case the proportion of the population which could claim acquaintance with the emperor was minute. But it is not untypical of Greek society under the empire that some of those who could did so, and *sebastognôstos*—'known to the emperor'—is used on occasion to describe men in places as distant as Olbia and Panticapaeum;[48] a man at Panticapaeum, for instance, was both *sebastognôstos* and 'honoured by Diocletian and Maximian'.[49] But for our purposes perhaps the more significant aspect of the ability to exchange letters with the emperor is, as mentioned earlier, that it was one of the few means by which an approach could be made to him without the person travelling to the emperor himself (it is to be noted that in every one of the specific instances mentioned the initiative is taken by the other person, and not by the emperor).

The other possible means of approach without physical presence were

---

[45] *Epit. Cod. Gregoriani* II, I, I–3. The letter is stated to have been 'data prid. Id. Iun. Aemiliano et Basso conss.', i.e. 259, but both the name of Valerianus (for whose death in the first part of 258 see *PIR*² L 184) and the mention of 'Julius Donatus', as *Praefectus urbi*, who must be C. Junius Donatus, prefect in 257 (*PIR*² I 749) show that this must be incorrect.

[46] For the text of the letters see now *Publilii Optatiani Porphyrii Carmina*, ed. I. Polara (1973), I, I–6. The editor's arguments against authenticity (I, xxxi–ii; II, 19–27) seem to me wholly unconvincing. But a doubt must persist. This release from exile 'misso . . . insigni volumine' is mentioned by Jerome, *Chron.* ed. Helm, p. 232 under 329. But the poems sent contain references to the *vicennalia*, *PLRE* Optatianus 3. For a different dating of the letter see T. D. Barnes, 'Publilius Optatianus Porfyrius', *AJPh* LXXXXVI (1975), 173.

[47] pp. 583f.

[48] See L. Robert, *Études anatoliennes* (1937), 227–8; cf. B. Nadel, 'A Note about Σεβαστόγνωστος', *Eos* LII (1962), 295.

[49] *IGR* I 873 = Struve, *Corpus Inscriptionum Regni Bosporani*, no. 64.

ones which we have already noted in different contexts: the submission to the emperor of requests on behalf of protégés by well-placed persons not actually holding office, as by Pliny before his governorship of Pontus and Bithynia,[50] or the similar process by which a Roman office-holder might send to the emperor *libelli* from individuals, with a covering *epistula* of his own. This latter procedure is in fact attested only rarely.[51] Pliny, for instance, sent to Trajan the *libellus* of an auxiliary centurion asking for the citizenship for his daughter:

> When requested, lord, by P. Accius Aquila, centurion of the sixth *cohors equestris*, to send you a *libellus* by which he implores your *indulgentia* in relation to the status of his daughter, I thought it harsh to refuse, since I knew with how much tolerance and humanity you are accustomed to treat the petitions (*preces*) of the soldiers.

Trajan, as we saw earlier, replied that he had read the *libellus*, been moved by the *preces*, and had granted the request.[52] Similarly, both Marcus and Verus and later Marcus and Commodus received *libelli* from a chief, or chiefs, of the Zegrenses, with supporting letters from the then procurators of Mauretania Tingitana, asking for the citizenship for his (or their) families.[53] These instances, none of which can be taken as suggesting an opportunity which was open generally, or even widely, to the inhabitants of the provinces, seem to be the only specific cases of *libelli* embodying petitions sent on by a governor until we come to the two *libelli* from the Donatist faction of the African church, which Anullinus, the proconsul of Africa, despatched to Constantine in April 313.[54]

In this instance, however, the two parties in the African church were already involved in a dispute; and in the area of actual legal cases, whether civil or criminal, we have already observed many occasions when governors transmitted to the emperor detailed accounts of the circumstances of individuals; some of these were in fact petitions for *indulgentia* sent at the request of the party concerned.[55] According to Ulpian, moreover, a governor might refuse the appeal of a condemned criminal, but put off execution of the sentence until the emperor had replied to his letter 'and the *libellus* of the accused sent with the letter'.[56]

Such an appeal, for a reduction in the severity of the sentence, can be regarded as an extreme instance of the way in which petitions for the *indulgentia* of the emperor could be channelled through a governor. But the emperor might also be involved at an earlier stage in legal proceedings in the provinces, and Pliny's letters from Bithynia provide a classic instance of

---

[50] pp. 114–15.

[51] This point is rightly emphasized by W. Williams, 'The *Libellus* Procedure and the Severan Papyri', *JRS* LXIV (1974), 86, esp. 93f.

[52] Pliny, *Ep.* x, 106–7; cf. p. 216.

[53] For the *Tabula Banasitana*, see pp. 130, 216, 261–2. It still seems to me an open question whether the document relates to two successive Juliani and their families, or to two successive families of one Julianus.

[54] Augustine, *Ep.* 88, 2; p. 586.

[55] pp. 329–36.

[56] *Dig.* XXVIII, 3, 6, 9.

16*

such a case, where questions of criminal liability, exemption from public burdens, and imperial favour could be inextricably intermingled.[57] Flavius Archippus also provides exceptionally vivid evidence of the various means of approach to a succession of emperors which were open to a well-placed provincial, and of the most favoured starting-point for such an approach, namely the practice of some intellectual profession.

When Pliny was enrolling jurymen before holding assizes, Flavius Archippus claimed exemption as being a philosopher. But simultaneously others alleged that an earlier proconsul had condemned him to *metallum* for forgery, and that he had escaped from his hard labour. In reply Archippus produced no evidence to show that he had been restored to liberty, but instead submitted various documents demonstrating his social prestige, and in particular his favour from successive emperors. The first was a *libellus* which he had given to Domitian. Here, as in other cases where *libelli* are described as being 'given' to emperors, we must presume either that he had already been in Rome at the time, or that he had travelled to present it in person;[58] Domitian never visited the Greek provinces in the course of his reign. The *libellus* is not quoted, but its content is clear from the first of the two 'letters of his [Domitian's] relevant to his honourable status' which are quoted in part. It is addressed to Terentius Maximus, probably a procurator:

> Flavius Archippus, a philosopher, has asked (*impetravit*) of me, that I should give instructions for landed property to a value of 100,000 *sesterces* near Prusias, his native city, to be bought for him to provide a revenue for the upkeep of his family. I wish this to be granted to him. You may charge the sum expended to my *liberalitas*.

The second letter was addressed to Lappius Maximus, proconsul of Pontus and Bithynia in perhaps 83/4,[59] and anticipates further requests to be made by Archippus:

> Archippus, a philosopher, a good man whose conduct is in accordance with his profession, I wish you, my Maximus, to treat as having my commendation, and to show him ample benevolence in those things which he may with due respect ask of you.

Archippus further quoted not only Nerva's general *edictum* confirming the *beneficia* of Domitian, and a letter of his to the same effect, but also a honorific decree passed by the council of Prusias and a letter or letters written to himself by Trajan. He was thus within the favoured category of persons who might correspond with emperors—but Pliny does not reproduce any letter by Trajan.

Subsequently Pliny sent a second letter enclosing, at his request, a *libellus* from Archippus, and also one from his accuser, 'so that you, having as it were heard both parties, may more easily consider what decision should be

---

[57] *Ep.* x, 58–9.

[58] See p. 248; and for other examples of emperors referring to *libelli* as being 'given' (*dare*) to them: *CJ* x, 4, 1; *Coll.* i, 9, 1.

[59] See Sherwin-White, ad loc.; W. Eck, *Senatoran von Vespasian bis Hadrian* (1970), 133.

given'. Trajan read both, but made his decision on the basis that the imperial letters should be regarded as amounting to a pardon for Archippus.

For a provincial of sufficient status or prestige, therefore, it was possible to invoke the indulgence and protection of the emperor both within the context of a case before the governor and outside it. Such a man might even be able to present a dossier of written communications to or from the emperor, including ones sent to others on his behalf. But even Archippus had earlier had to 'give' his *libellus* to Domitian, and the necessity of presenting oneself where the emperor was must have been the crucial factor which for the ordinary inhabitant of the empire limited access to him. It cannot be proved that every *libellus* had to be presented to the emperor in person, though we have seen evidence of this being done in the early empire, under Hadrian, and under Constantine. But it is quite clear that in the second and third centuries *libelli* were answered by posting up the *subscriptiones* at the emperor's place of residence, and there is no indication that the petitioner himself, or herself, received any answer other than the copy which he or she could then make.[60] The petitioners thus had either to take advantage of the emperor's presence in their vicinity or to travel to where he was. That some at least did in fact do so, and not merely within a limited area, is suggested by a couple of imperial letters apparently addressed to provincial governors and referring to the contents of *libelli* given to them by persons from the province concerned.[61] It is perhaps more indicative that as early as Antoninus Pius the *subscriptio*, 'You may approach the governor of the province', was a standard form of reply;[62] and both literary and documentary evidence provides numerous examples of the same reply in a variety of forms. These vary from what is in effect a rejection of the petition by the emperor to a fairly specific oblique instruction to the governor to follow a certain course of action.[63] In most of the instances neither the name of the province concerned nor the current location of the emperor is indicated. But, for instance, the unhelpful reply of Gordian III to the villagers of Scaptopara in Thrace was put up in 238 in Rome, where the *libellus* had been presented by a fellow-villager who was serving in the praetorian cohorts.[64] Similarly, Diocletian replied to a petitioner in Sirmium in 294, after stating the principle at stake, 'So, having heard the propositions put forward by the parties, the *vir clarissimus*, proconsul of Africa, our *amicus*, will in pronouncing his verdict, follow the terms of the law.'[65]

---

[60] pp. 240–52, and note the valuable demonstration by W. Williams, *JRS* LXIV (1974), 86.

[61] The less uncertain case is *Dig.* XLVIII, 6, 6, from Ulpian's *De officio proconsulis* and sent by Antoninus Pius (who never left Italy while emperor) to someone addressed as 'Gemine carissime': 'Exemplum libelli dati mihi a Domitio Silvano nomine Domitii Silvani patrui subici iussi, motus querella eius . . .' (cf. p. 248). Less clearly to a governor is *Dig.* XLII, 1, 33 (Hadrian), 'Exemplum libelli dati mihi a Iulio Tarentino mitti tibi iussi . . .'.

[62] *Dig.* I, 18, 8 (cf. p. 220, n. 53).

[63] e.g. *Dig.* XXII, 1, 17 *pr.* (Marcus Aurelius): 'Praesidem provinciae adi, qui stipulationem, de cuius iniquitate questus es, ad modum iustae exactionis rediget'; *P. Oxy.* 1020 = Meyer, *Juristischer Papyri*, no. 17 (Severus and Caracalla, cf. p. 245); *CJ* IV, 62, 1 (Severus and Caracalla); *Lex Rom. Wisig.* II, 6 (Severus Alexander, 227); *CJ* IV, 14, 6 (Diocletian and Maximian, 293); VIII, 6, 1 (*eidem*, 294). Cf. *Coll.* III, 3, 5–6 (Antoninus Pius).

[64] See pp. 64, 543.

[65] *Epit. Cod. Herm.* II, 1.

It is thus clear that, while distance must have been an important factor in determining from which sources petitions were presented to an emperor at any one time, it was not necessarily an overriding factor. People could and did travel to the emperor, whether in Rome or elsewhere. Again it must have been the case that considerations of wealth, social class and prestige fundamentally affected the issues both of who presented petitions and what answer they received. Yet the abrupt answer which the Scaptopareni received, telling them to take their complaint to the governor, is perhaps not as significant as the fact that they, like several village communities in Asia Minor, did address themselves to the emperor.[66] If we turn to *subscriptiones* addressed to individuals, it is conspicuous that many of the recipients are women, who may in certain cases have been of high social status, but who necessarily did not and could not occupy any public position, other than certain local priesthoods.[67] Others are addressed to freedmen or even to persons whom others claimed were still slaves, but who themselves alleged that they had been freed, or that they ought to have been freed. Thus, for instance, the tetrarchs (that is, in effect, Diocletian) replied to a woman named Pythagoridas in December 294.[68]

> If he [your master] gave you to his wife before marriage, and afterwards having left her a legacy, expressed a wish in his will or codicils that you should be freed by his heirs, then there is no doubt that they were obliged to purchase and manumit you (as they were, by virtue of accepting the inheritance to whatever was in accordance with the wish of the deceased), and that a fideicommissary freedom is due to you.

We know nothing of the circumstances under which the woman was able to approach Diocletian, who was then at Nicomedia. But it is noticeable that nothing in the text of the *subscriptio* suggests that the emperor found anything unusual in replying to a woman of freed or slave status. Similarly, Paulus at the beginning of the third century refers to the possibility of a freedman giving a *libellus*, with a complaint against his *patronus*, to a governor or emperor, and rules that this did not fall under the rule which prevented a freedman bringing legal action against his *patronus*.[69]

It need not be denied that the whole nature of the assumptions within which the government of the empire worked gave an advantage to individuals from those provincial aristocracies whom a network of ties bound to the emperor and his circle. The fact is perfectly clear for instance in the letter which Fronto wrote to Antoninus Pius about his preparations for his prospective proconsulship of Asia: 'I have encouraged distinguished men to come from Cilicia also, in view of the fact that I have a host of *amici* in that province, since I have always acted as advocate before you on behalf of the Cilicians, both communally and individually.'[70] Fronto's friends from Cilicia,

[66] On the complaints of village communities see further pp. 541–4.
[67] For examples see pp. 546–9.
[68] *CJ* VII, 4, 13.
[69] *Dig.* II, 4, 15.
[70] *Ad Ant. Pium* 8.

who might be sent on public embassies to the emperor, and could have found themselves on Fronto's staff in Asia if illness had not prevented him from going, could clearly face proceedings which came before the emperor with more confidence than men of lesser rank.

The passage also, however, reflects the assumption, found very widely in our evidence, that the hearing of cases by the emperor was something normal and unexceptional, and that cases from a province will quite frequently have reached the emperor in Rome. The many questions relating to the emperor's jurisdiction, its origins, legal basis, function and the routes by which cases were brought to him, must be considered later, as being an essential manifestation of the role of the emperor as monarch within Graeco-Roman society. But its significance is best seen against a wider background, in which the emperor was the object of petitions and requests on a whole variety of matters from individuals whose social and geographical range cannot at any stage be accurately defined, but from whose numbers neither imperial policy nor social prejudice nor distance categorically excluded anyone.

2. *Personal Status: Citizenship and Freedom*

Defending the Greek poet Archias in 62 BC against a charge that he was enjoying the Roman citizenship illegally, Cicero claimed firmly that his client would have become a citizen even if he had not gained it along with the citizens of Heraclea, among whom he had been enrolled, when they accepted it communally after the Social War. For other avenues to the citizenship were open:[1]

> So, I suppose, if Archias had not been a citizen as a result of the laws passed, he could not have seen to it that he was granted the citizenship by some *imperator*? And Sulla, I suppose, although he gave it to Spaniards and Gauls, would have refused this man when he requested it? . . . Or indeed, could he not have gained it on request from Q. Metellus Pius, his close friend, who has granted the citizenship to many, either on his own behalf or through the Luculli?

Cicero's words perfectly reflect the transitional nature of the assumptions which at that moment governed the granting of the Roman citizenship to foreigners. In the earlier republic such a grant could be made to individuals, as to communities, only by a formal act of senate or people. When Marius, apparently towards the end of the Cimbric War, in 102 or 101, granted the citizenship as a reward for valour to a troop of horsemen from Camerinum, the award was claimed to be illegal; but the consul replied that amid the clash of arms he had not heard the words of the law.[2]

Soon after this the inevitable step was taken of passing laws granting at least to some and possibly to all, holders of *imperium*, the right to confer

---

[1] *Pro Archia*, 10/25–6.

[2] Cicero, *Pro Balbo* 22/50 (where the question of legality is suppressed); Valerius Maximus v, 2, 8; Plutarch, *Mar.* 28, 3.

the citizenship. Even if granted in fact to all, which remains uncertain, it was still, however, voted by a *lex* passed for each commander individually and by name. The right was at least in some cases specifically related to awards for valour, and the powers of senate and people were thus in theory still maintained. But, though many such grants were in fact made for services in the field, Cicero's words demonstrate that it was already an accepted fact that they could be, and were, petitioned for by persons who had never heard the clash of arms.[3] If necessary, as Cicero states, influential friends—in this case his patrons the Luculli, whose *nomen*, Licinius, he had taken to form his full Roman name, Aulus Licinius Archias—could intercede for a petitioner; an exactly similar case appears in Cicero's *Verrines*, a Sicilian named Q. Lutatius Diodorus, 'who by the *beneficium* of Q. (Lutatius) Catulus was made a Roman citizen by L. Sulla'.[4]

The other common practice was for the beneficiary to take the *nomen* of the commander who actually bestowed the citizenship. As Cicero had just mentioned in the *Pro Archia*, Pompey awarded the citizenship at an assembly of his soldiers to Theophanes of Mytilene, 'the historian of his campaigns'; as a citizen, Theophanes' name was to be Cn. Pompeius Theophanes.[5] In this case the context was military, but Cicero makes quite clear that the services which Theophanes performed with Pompey in the east were essentially literary.

There is no specific evidence that Julius Caesar either as proconsul in Gaul or subsequently as dictator and consul, was voted the right to confer the citizenship, though it is quite probable that he was. But he certainly granted citizenships, most notably to Antipater, the father of Herod, who as the agent of the High Priest, Hyrcanus, gave him military assistance at a crucial juncture in 47 BC.[6] He also, according to Suetonius, gave it to all doctors practising at Rome and all who taught literature there, in order to retain them and attract others.[7] It can be assumed that both professions were occupied typically by immigrants from the Greek cities. Other Greeks benefited by more individual measures. Antonius in 43 reproached the senate with approving the execution of Petraeus and Menedemus, 'men who had been granted the citizenship and had been hosts to Caesar'; they were in fact leading citizens of Thessaly and Macedonia, who had aided Caesar in the campaign of Pharsalus.[8] Cicero himself obtained the citizenship from Caesar for the leading Peripatetic philosopher, Cratippus of Pergamum; the latter took Cicero's *nomen*, for an inscription from Pergamum records one M. Tullius Cratippus, *sacerdos* of Roma and Salus, certainly a descendant and

---

[3] The development of personal grants of citizenship in the late republic is a much-discussed subject which it is unnecessary to rehearse in detail here; see C. E. Goodfellow, *Roman Citizenship* (1935), esp. ch. iii; E. Badian, *Foreign Clientelae* (1958), esp. ch. xi and App. B; A. N. Sherwin-White, *The Roman Citizenship*[2] (1973), esp. ch. xiii.

[4] *Verr.* II. iv, 17/37.

[5] *Pro Archia* 10/24; the same scene in Valerius Maximus VIII, 14, 3. For the name see e.g. *Syll.*[3] 755. Cf. pp. 83–4, 611–12, 620.

[6] Josephus, *BJ* I, 9, 5 (194); *Ant.* XIV, 8, 3 (137).

[7] *Jul.* 42, 1.

[8] Cicero, *Phil.* XIII, 16/33; see Caesar, *BC* III, 34–5.

probably his son.[9] The complex relations which might be involved in the acquisition and defence of a grant of citizenship for a Greek are best revealed in a letter of Cicero's written in 45 BC:[10]

> With Demetrius Megas I have a long-established relation of mutual hospitality, and a friendship such as I have with no other Sicilian. For him Dolabella at my request asked for the citizenship from Caesar, in which matter I also was involved. So now he is called P. Cornelius [the *nomen* of Dolabella]. But since on account of certain venal characters who were selling the *beneficia* of Caesar, he ordered the tablet on which the names of those granted citizenship were inscribed to be broken up, Caesar affirmed to Dolabella in my hearing that Megas had no reason to fear, and that the *beneficium* granted to him was unaffected.

Nothing could show more clearly the introduction of typically monarchic social patterns, the acquisition of benefits for their protégés by well-placed intermediaries, the activities of hangers-on of the monarch, and the ultimate dependence of the distribution of favours on the will of the monarch himself.

In such instances all trace of the original principle that citizenship should be granted as a reward for military services has disappeared. None the less the passing of a law to give authority to such grants by a commander is still attested in the dossier of Seleucus of Rhosus, who served in Octavian's naval operations as triumvir.[11] The main document of the dossier is the pronouncement by which Octavian, or rather originally, as is probable, the three triumvirs acting together, awarded citizenship and immunity from tribute to Seleucus and his wife and children as a reward for services; he, or they, did so on the basis of a *Lex Munatia Aemilia*, evidently passed by Munatius Plancus and Aemilius Lepidus as consuls of 42 BC. Even though the latter was himself a member of the triumvirate and the former a close follower, it is still significant that it was felt necessary to pass a law authorizing such grants.

With that, however, the institutions of the *res publica* make their last appearance in relation to the granting of citizenship to individuals, except for Augustus' statement in the third Cyrene edict of 7/6 BC, that immunity from local burdens was enjoyed by persons honoured with the Roman citizenship only if at the same moment they had also been given immunity from tribute 'in accordance with a law or *senatus consultum* or by the *decretum* (*epikrima*) of my father [Julius Caesar] or myself'.[12] The reference at least includes grants made up to four decades earlier, and all actual cases from Augustus' reign show the citizenship as the personal gift of the emperor. Such grants could, for instance, be used to secure the loyalty of persons on

[9] Plutarch, *Cic.* 24, 7. See A. O'Brien-Moore, 'M. Tullius Cratippus, Priest of Rome,' *YCS* VIII (1942), 25; Chr. Habicht, *Altertümer von Pergamon* VIII.3: *die Inschriften des Asklepieions* (1969), 163–4.

[10] *Ad fam.* XIII, 36, 1.

[11] *IGLS* III 718 = Sherk, *Roman Documents*, no. 58. See *JRS* LXIII (1973), 55. Since the subject of this section is the modes of acquisition of the citizenship and not the citizenship itself, it is not necessary to discuss the complex and poorly preserved conditions attached to this grant in the pronouncement which forms document ii.

[12] *FIRA*[2] I, no. 68, iii; cf. p. 344.

the fringe of the empire. One C. Julius Vepo records on his marble tomb at Celeia in Noricum that he had been 'granted the Roman citizenship individually, and immunity, by the Divine Augustus'. Noricum became a province in 15 BC, in the middle of Augustus' reign.[13] But even outside the provincial area we find the Cheruscan chief Segestes in Tacitus' narrative of AD 15 speaking of his unbroken loyalty 'since the day on which I was granted the citizenship by the Divine Augustus'.[14]

In such cases a political motive for the grant may be surmised with more or less certainty. But in accordance with already established custom requests were made to Augustus purely on a basis of patronage or influence. Suetonius records two such petitions on behalf of protégés, one by Tiberius and one by Livia. When Tiberius petitioned, apparently in writing, for the citizenship for a Greek *cliens* of his, the emperor wrote back 'that he would not give it unless the man (or Tiberius?) appeared in his presence and persuaded him that he had proper grounds for the petition'.[15] The passage is a classic instance of the ultimate dependence on verbal exposition in ancient society, closely comparable to Hadrian's often-expressed preference for examining witnesses verbally rather than relying on written depositions (*testimonia*).[16] When Livia petitioned for citizenship for a Gaul who was liable to tribute, he again refused, but offered immunity from tribute instead; the exchange was evidently verbal, for he is recorded to have declared (*affirmans*) that he would rather incur some loss to the *fiscus* than cheapen the prestige of the Roman citizenship. His words are strikingly similar to those which the inscription from Aphrodisias records his having 'written under' a petition for freedom and immunity from the Samians, which had also been supported by Livia.[17] The similarity of wording in verbal and written pronouncements is of some significance in suggesting that the latter also emanated from the emperor in person.

Both these anecdotes are retailed by Suetonius as illustrations of the general statement that Augustus gave citizenships very sparingly. It is however assumed that they were in his gift, and later in Suetonius' *Lives* we find Gaius perversely denying that persons were legally in possession of the citizenship although their ancestors had secured it for themselves and their descendants, and ruling that 'descendants' did not apply to any except sons: 'when *diplomata* of the Deified Julius and Augustus were submitted, he would brush them aside as being old and obsolete'.[18] The reference does not seem to be to the *diplomata*, giving the citizenship and the right of *conubium* with foreign women, which were issued to auxiliary soldiers on discharge, and are familiar from many examples from the reign of Claudius onwards; but

[13] *ILS* 1977. See G. Alföldy, *Noricum* (1974), 52f. (annexation); 76 and Pl. 16 (Julius Vepo).

[14] *Ann.* 1, 58, 1. Arminius, whom Velleius II, 118, 2, describes as 'iure etiam civitatis Romanae decus equestris consequens gradus' will certainly have gained his citizenship from Augustus. But it is necessary to keep strictly to those cases where the grant is actually described.

[15] *Aug.* 40, 3: 'Tiberio pro cliente Graeco petenti rescripsit, non aliter se daturum, quam si praesens sibi persuasisset, quam iustas petendi causas haberet.'

[16] p. 236.

[17] Suetonius, loc. cit. For the problems raised by the use of *fiscus* here, see p. 623. For the *subscriptio* to the Samians, pp. 243, 431–2.

[18] *Cal.* 38, 1.

rather to some form of civilian *diploma* of citizenship, a thing attested only
once elsewhere, when Suetonius describes Nero giving them individually to
ephebes from the Greek cities who danced in shows put on by him.[19] These
two instances apart, there is no indication that civilians who were granted
the citizenship normally received any individual documents to prove it.[20]
The possession of the citizenship, however, spread very widely in the course
of the first and second centuries and with it the use of the *nomina* of successive imperial dynasties, 'Julius', 'Claudius', 'Flavius', 'Ulpius', 'Aelius',
'Aurelius', 'Septimius', as well as other *nomina* which will often denote
patrons or intermediaries.[21] Many of these acquisitions of imperial or
other Roman names will undoubtedly go back to actual grants by emperors;
but it does not follow that they all do, for we must allow both for simple
usurpation of Roman names and the implied status as a Roman citizen, for
genuine confusion and for corrupt acquisition from members of the imperial
entourage.

All these modes of acquiring the citizenship, as well as genuine individual
grants, are attested for instance in the reign of Claudius. The emperor is
stated to have forbidden non-citizens to adopt Roman *nomina* and to have
had some who usurped the citizenship executed; he also removed not only
from the *album* of *iudices*, but from the citizenship, a prominent man from
Greece who turned out to know no Latin.[22] But when men from the Alpine
tribes of the Anauni, Tulliasses and Sinduni were shown to have been
wrongly under the impression that they were citizens, he confirmed their
right to it by a *beneficium*, not least on the grounds that some had served in
the praetorian cohorts, some even as centurions, and others had been enrolled in the *decuriae* of *iudices* in Rome.[23] All the persons in these latter
categories must have been using Roman names, and it was only by the accident of an accusation that any public doubt was raised about their status.

Dio also reports that Claudius gave the citizenship very liberally both to
individuals and groups; some people requested it from him, and others
obtained it by purchase from Messalina and the imperial freedmen. Claudius
was blamed for the fact that it could be bought cheaply, but praised for
refusing to hear accusations against new citizens either for not taking the
name 'Claudius' or for not leaving him anything in their wills.[24] One man
who gained the citizenship individually from Claudius, and who did not
take the *nomen* 'Claudius' was P. Cornelius Macer, a local office-holder in
Lusitania.[25] Another, perhaps, from almost the opposite end of the empire,
was the maternal grandfather of Dio of Prusa; addressing the people of the

---

[19] *Nero* 12, 1.

[20] On this point see A. N. Sherwin-White, *Roman Society and Roman Law in the New Testament*
(1963), 146f. As the *Tabula Banasitana* shows, however, it was possible to produce a copy of the
relevant extract from the *commentarius civitate romana donatorum*, see pp. 261–2, and Sherwin-
White, *JRS* LXIII (1973), 90–1.

[21] For a survey see G. Alföldy, 'Notes sur la relation entre le droit de cité et la nomenclature
dans l'Empire romain', *Latomus* XXV (1966), 37.

[22] Suetonius, *Claud.* 25, 3; 16, 2.

[23] *CIL* v 5050 = *ILS* 206; cf. p. 64.

[24] LX, 17, 5–7.

[25] *ILS* 1978.

colonia of Apameia in Bithynia, Dio says, 'My grandfather, along with my
mother, acquired from the emperor of that day, who was his friend, not only
Roman citizenship but along with it citizenship in Apameia too.'[26] The
emperor must have been either Claudius or one not far from him in time;
but the grandfather's favour from emperors apparently stretched over more
than one reign, for elsewhere Dio says that he spent his whole fortune on
local benefactions, and gained another one 'from his learning and from the
emperors'.[27] Adlection into a Roman *colonia* was a separate imperial
beneficium, attested on several occasions in the second century.[28]

If the identity of the emperor concerned is uncertain in this instance, there
is at least no doubt about the letter of Claudius to the synod of athletes in
which he refers to Diogenes of Antioch, an ex-high priest of the synod 'whom
I have thought worthy of the Roman citizenship along with his two
daughters'.[29] Diogenes' name, it seems, had merely appeared on decrees
of the synod, and there is no indication that he had gone to Rome as ambassador. For those who did so, there was of course an extra chance of reward,
as for the two Frisians who went as ambassadors to Nero in 58, failed to gain
their request, but were still rewarded with the citizenship by the emperor.[30]
The same connection is visible in the inscription put up by the *Gerousia* in
Athens in honour of M. Aurelius Prosdectus, 'who went on an embassy at
his own expense, and who was honoured with the Roman citizenship by the
Divine Commodus'.[31]

Our evidence from the first century consists almost entirely of sporadic
individual instances of grants of citizenship by emperors. But the very ran-
domness of the examples is some indication of how general a form of *beneficium* this was. Tacitus for instance mentions in passing an auxiliary soldier
from the British cohorts who had recently been given the citizenship by
Galba.[32] But, much more substantially, we have the evidence of Josephus
himself for the citizenship and other benefits which he received from Vespasian and his sons. Even before he left Judaea with Titus, he had received
from him land in the plain, in place of that which he had owned near
Jerusalem. When he reached Rome, he received from Vespasian accommodation in the house which the emperor had owned before assuming
power, the citizenship (hence his name, Flavius Josephus), an annual income,
and more land in Judaea; later Domitian granted him *ateleia* in respect of
his property there.[33] Josephus is thus a perfect example of how the

[26] *Or.* XLI, 6, Loeb trans.; see *JRS* LVIII (1968), 222.
[27] *Or.* XLVI, 3, spoken in Prusa.
[28] *ILS* 6933; 6943.
[29] Wilcken, *Chrestomathie*, no. 156. Cf. p. 456–7.
[30] Tacitus, *Ann.* XIII, 54; cf. p. 433. Note also the tale in the *Prologus* of Dictys Cretensis (ed.
Eisenhut, pp. 1–3) of how Eupraxides, the Cretan landowner on whose land the text was found,
was sent to Nero with it, and came back 'muneribus et Romana civitate donatum'. Like other
tales of dubious authenticity, it may still be significant in revealing patterns and assumptions.
[31] *IG*² II 3658 = J. H. Oliver, *The Sacred Gerusia*, *Hesperia* Supp. VI (1941), no. 27. Compare
the pankratiast from Magnesia who gained the citizenship for himself, and his father, mother and
brothers, from Hadrian, and also served on several embassies to the emperors, L. Moretti,
Iscrizioni agonistiche, no. 71.
[32] *Hist.* I, 43, 2.
[33] *Vita* 76/422–3, 425, 429.

emperor's benevolence could be expressed in actual gifts, in cash or property, in financial benefits in the form of exemption from taxation or local obligations (for we cannot tell in which context the *ateleia* of his land applied) and in grants of status.

From the second century we again have random evidence of specific grants; and it is noticeable here that most of the instances show quite explicitly that the citizenship had been petitioned for. For instance the epitaph of a doctor, who came from Prusa in Bithynia and settled in Italy, records that he obtained from Trajan the citizenship for his parents, himself and his brothers, seven persons in all. The inscription makes clear that he was a well-established person who had acted as *assessor* to Roman senatorial officials both in Rome and the provinces; his request seems to have been made by himself and not through any intermediary.[34] In the same reign, as we saw briefly earlier, Pliny wrote to the emperor to ask for the citizenship for a therapist (*iatroliptês*) who had attended him. Discovering in the process that according to custom the man, being an Egyptian, could not be given Roman citizenship without having that of Alexandria, he simply asked for that as well, which Trajan granted. Pliny justifies his request solely on the grounds of his personal obligation to the doctor 'whose care and concern I can repay with adequate gratitude only by the *beneficium* of your *indulgentia*'; neither party finds anything unusual in the citizenship of Alexandria also being in the gift of the emperor.[35] Later Pliny wrote again, when another illness had obliged him to a different doctor; in this case the man himself already enjoyed the citizenship, so Pliny asked on behalf of various of his relatives, a man, his wife and their three children 'on the terms that they should be in *patria potestas* and their rights as patrons should be retained in relation to their *liberti*'.[36]

That brings us to a set of problems which evidently caused considerable difficulty in this period, namely the effects of individual grants or acquisitions of citizenship on the existing family and social relationships of the beneficiaries. For our purposes it is not necessary to examine these problems themselves in any detail, but rather to stress that the terms in which they are referred to show more clearly than any accumulation of specific instances how common and accepted it was to gain the citizenship by the *beneficium* of the emperor, and usually by request to him. This evidence has the same bearing as the *commentarius*, or record, of persons granted the Roman citizenship by the emperors from Augustus onwards, which the *Tabula Banasitana* shows to have been kept up at least until the reign of Marcus Aurelius and Commodus.[37] It is no doubt an accident that this is thus the most explicitly attested of all imperial archives; but it unambiguously shows that the granting of the citizenship was, and always had been, an established imperial function.

One consequence of such grants was discussed by Pliny in his *Panegyric* addressed to Trajan. The 5% tax on inheritances applied to all except

[34] *ILS* 7789 (from the Ager Capenas).
[35] *Ep.* x, 5–7, 10. Cf. p. 114.
[36] x, 11.
[37] pp. 261–2.

sums left by close relatives. But if one member of a family became a Roman citizen, he became liable to pay the tax on inheritances from other members who had not so benefited: 'New citizens, whether they had come into the citizenship by *Latium* or by *beneficium* of the emperor, unless they had asked at the same time for the rights of relationship, were regarded as complete strangers to those to whom they had been most closely related.' Nerva had removed this restriction as regarded inheritance by children from their mother and *vice versa*, and by a son from the father, provided that he had been placed in *patria potestas*. He thus left some 'material for beneficence' to Trajan, whose *liberalitas* allowed father to inherit from son and son from father, while removing the necessity of *patria potestas*. He also went further and extended the relationships within which the inheritance-tax was not payable by new citizens to include grandparents and grandchildren: 'These also, to whom citizenship had been made available by *Latium*, he indulged, and granted them all at the same moment, equally and in accordance with nature, those rights of relationship which previous emperors had insisted should be petitioned for from them, and in a spirit of denial rather than generosity.' He thus gave to all what often individuals had not even asked: 'and finally deprived himself of so many occasions for *beneficia*, so extensive a source of obligation and gaining credit'.[38] The literature of the empire offers few better examples of how all rules, legal and otherwise, could be used as a framework against which to confer benefits and exceptions on individuals; and few better indications of what the emperor himself gained from exercising this role in response to petitions. But it also makes clear that along with *Latium*—that is by holding a magistracy in a town with Latin rights[39]— the other standard means of gaining the citizenship was by *beneficium principis*.

Precisely the same patterns are visible in what Gaius says in the first book of his *Institutes* about the various civil statuses which existed in the empire. First he lays down that *patria potestas* was a purely Roman institution, and supports this with the statement: 'And this Hadrian indicated in the *edictum* which he put up (*proposuit*) concerning those who asked him for the Roman citizenship for themselves and their children.'[40] What Hadrian said about such petitioners in his edict is not made clear here. But a little later Gaius returns to the topic, revealing something of the content of the edict and much more about the customary forms of procedure:[41]

> If a non-citizen has petitioned for the Roman citizenship for himself and his children, his sons do not come under his *patria potestas*, unless the emperor has placed them in it, which he does if, having examined the case, he concludes that this is of advantage to the sons. He examines the case (*causam cognoscit*) even more diligently and strictly with respect to those who are below adult age, or absent. These points are stated in this form in the *edictum* of the Divine Hadrian.

---

[38] Pliny, *Pan.* 37–40. The passages quoted are 37, 3 and 39, 2–3. Note the comparable concession attributed to Antoninus Pius by Pausanias VIII, 43, 5.

[39] See pp. 401–6, 485–6, and App. 4.

[40] *Inst.* I, 55.

[41] I, 93–4; cf. also III, 20, referring to cases where the emperor does not grant *patria potestas*.

Similarly, if anyone is granted Roman citizenship while his wife is pregnant, although the child when born is, as we said above, a Roman citizen, nevertheless he does not fall under *patria potestas*. That is stated in a *subscriptio* of Hadrian. For this reason, anyone who realises that his wife is pregnant, must, while asking the emperor for the citizenship for himself and his wife, at the same time petition him for the right to have the child who will be born in his *potestas*.

This passage makes perfectly clear that it was customary not only for requests for the citizenship to be directed to the emperor, but for the emperor to enter into some detail as regarded the consequential legal position in individual instances. For the emperor to 'examine the case' (*causam cognoscere*) probably means that he conducted a verbal hearing, and at least implies that he had relevant documents submitted to him. We may, if we choose, treat passing references in literary authorities to the emperor giving the citizenship as not necessarily proving any action on the part of the emperor himself,[42] but we can hardly do the same for the explicit statement of Hadrian, as paraphrased in the best-preserved legal writer of the second century.

So we cannot but accept that in the period before Caracalla issued his edict making a general grant of citizenship, individual grants were a standard form of *beneficium* by the emperor, which could be bestowed as a reward, or petitioned for from him. What is more, Gaius tends to confirm that, in the second century at least, Latin rights and imperial *beneficium* were the two normal paths by which individual civilians gained the citizenship. For immediately after the passage quoted he goes on to say that by contrast those who came to the citizenship with their children 'by the right of *Latium*' automatically acquired *patria potestas*, and follows this with the definition of the two forms of Latin right which we saw earlier.[43]

If Gaius is correct in stating that those who came 'by right of Latium' all gained *patria potestas*—and what he says is not quite what Pliny says in the *Panegyric*—does he also imply a pre-existing difference of status between them and ordinary non-citizens? The question is of some importance, for it has been widely assumed that all the citizens of towns with the Latin right were thereby 'Latins', and enjoyed some status intermediate between that of non-citizens and citizens. But, first, as we saw earlier, the definitions of 'Latin rights' given in sources of the late republic and empire are unanimous in describing them as consisting of the right to the citizenship on the part of magistrates (or, with *Latium maius*, of councillors also).[44] Secondly, if so wide a category of persons existed, it is remarkable that we cannot state what civil rights they enjoyed in this period, what form of nomenclature they used, or whether they served in the legions or the *auxilia*. In short, while there are complex problems, mainly relating to the question of whether any 'Latins' can be detected who are provably distinct from the category of freed slaves known as *Latini Juniani*, which need to be discussed elsewhere,[45] and while

[42] For example the Athenian in Lucian, *Demonax* 40, who says 'ὁ βασιλεύς με τῇ Ῥωμαίων πολιτείᾳ τετίμηκεν'.

[43] *Inst.* I, 95–6; cf. p. 405.

[44] pp. 401–6.

[45] App. 4.

negative generalizations in such an area can never be secure, it may be tentatively suggested that no such category existed, and that the ordinary inhabitants of provincial towns with 'Latin rights' were simply non-citizens. The range of private problems which were put before the emperor was so wide that had such a category of 'Latins' existed, it is scarcely credible that some of them would not have petitioned the emperor over matters relating to their status, and some trace, however slight, of such issues have survived to us. No such evidence can be presented.

In any case such a category, if it ever existed under the empire, disappeared when Caracalla, perhaps in 213, issued his famous edict, the so-called *constitutio Antoniniana*, by which he granted the Roman citizenship to all the inhabitants of the empire, with some exceptions which are notoriously hard to define.[46] The context and motives of this edict are very uncertain, and the consequences too complex and indeterminate to discuss here. But, as regards the relations of subject and emperor, it naturally meant that the citizenship disappeared from the range of matters on which men of free birth petitioned the emperor, and from the *beneficia* which he had at his disposal to confer on them.

There were, however, questions of personal status of a different sort, namely those which affected people who either were, or claimed to be, freed slaves. First, there were direct petitions, either from them or on their behalf, for full citizen status; secondly we find them approaching the emperor, as we saw the woman Pythagoridas approach Diocletian, for rulings on disputed questions as to whether they had been legally freed or not. The direct petitions related mainly to *Latini Juniani*, persons who under the terms of legislation of the early imperial period were not fully manumitted, either because of the informality of the procedure or the incomplete rights of the *patronus*. Unlike full *liberti* they could neither inherit nor make a will, and on their death their entire property reverted to the *patronus*.[47]

Claudius, Nero and Trajan are all recorded as defining services to the city of Rome, by performing which a *Latinus Junianus* could acquire the full civil rights of a citizen (*ius Quiritium*).[48] But, as usual, to these actual functions, and other possible avenues to full rights, a procedure of another sort was added. Ulpian writes: '*Latini* gain the *ius Quiritium* in the following ways —by *beneficium* of the emperor, having children, repetition (of the informal manumission), military service (in the *vigiles*), building a ship (for use in the corn-supply of Rome), building a house (in Rome), operating a bakery (in

---

[46] The expression *constitutio* (a general expression for any form of imperial ruling) is used of it by Ulpian, *Dig.* I, 5, 17; *constitutio Antoniniana* is a modern title. The pronouncement in *P. Giessen* 40 which appears to embody the general grant of citizenship is in *edictum* form, using λέγει (*dicit*). For literature and discussion, see Chr. Sasse, *Die Constitutio Antoniniana* (1958); note also Em. Condurachi, 'La costituzione Antoniniana e la sua applicazione nell'Impero Romano', *Dacia* II (1958), 281, and especially A. N. Sherwin-White, 'The *Tabula* of Banasa and the *Constitutio Antoniniana*,' *JRS* LXIII (1973), 86, esp. 95-8. For the dating question, and the arguments for 213, see Z. Rubin, 'Further to the Dating of the *Constitutio Antoniniana*', *Latomus* XXXIV (1975), 430.

[47] On the *Latini Junianai* see also App. 4, and for full discussion A. M. Duff, *Freedmen in the Early Roman Empire* (1928), 75f.; H. M. Last in *CAH* x (1934), 429f.; A. N. Sherwin-White, *The Roman Citizenship*[2] (1973), 328f.

[48] Gaius, *Inst.* I, 32c-34.

Rome) . . . A *Latinus* receives the Roman citizenship by imperial *beneficium*, if he has requested the emperor for the *ius Quiritium*.'[49] It is clearly implied that such requests to the emperor were an established institution, and were made by the *Latinus* himself. A century earlier we find Pliny making such requests for *Latini* in letters to Trajan; whether the intervention of so well-placed an intermediary was still a necessity is uncertain, but it is noticeable that Pliny makes his requests without much detail or elaborate justification, as if they were almost matters of routine. At the end of his letter requesting the citizenship for his *iatroliptês*, for instance, he adds simply, 'I also ask for the *ius Quiritium* for the freedwomen of Antonia Maximilla, a woman of excellent standing, namely Hedia and Antonia Harmeris; I make the request at the request of their *patrona*.'[50] This latter proviso evidently presupposes the *edictum* of Trajan by which a *Latinus* who gained the citizenship by imperial *beneficium* either without the knowledge or against the will of his *patronus* kept his citizen status during his lifetime, but reverted to Latin status (that is in respect of his property) on death.[51] In exactly the same way Pliny attaches to his second request for citizenship for a doctor a single sentence asking for the *ius Quiritium* for three freedmen, 'which I ask for with the concurrence of their *patroni*'.[52]

In neither of these two cases does he explicitly describe the freedwomen or freedmen as Latins, and the fact that they were has to be deduced from the context. But later, from Bithynia, Pliny writes to say that a friend has left him the rights over his *Latini*, and asks the emperor to grant him as an interim measure the *ius Quiritium* for three of them, whose names he gives; to ask on behalf of all at once would be to presume too far on the emperor's *indulgentia*. Trajan replies briefly but in generous terms:[53]

> Since it is entirely proper that you should wish that the interests of those left to your care by Valerius Paulinus should be protected through me, I have ordered it to be recorded in my *commentarii* that I have given them the *ius Quiritium*, being ready to do the same for the others when you make the same request on their behalf.

A few years later Hadrian promoted a *senatus consultum* to cover the case of a *Latinus* 'who without the knowledge or against the will of his *patronus* gained the *ius Quiritium* from the emperor', to the effect that, if they afterwards fulfilled any of the other conditions by which they could gain full rights, they should not revert on death to Latin status.[54]

All these references make quite clear that by the early second century the imperial *beneficium* (*beneficium principale*) was an established institution of Roman law, and in this area was put into effect by the request either of the beneficiary or of some intermediary. The status of *Latinus Junianus* in fact survived until formally abolished by Justinian; but, perhaps surprisingly,

[49] *Tit. Ulp.* III, 1–2; cf. 3–6.
[50] *Ep.* X, 5, 2.
[51] Gaius, *Inst.* III, 72; Justinian, *Inst.* III, 7, 4.
[52] *Ep.* X, 11, 2.
[53] *Ep.* X, 104–5; for the *commentarii* cf. pp. 261–2.
[54] Gaius, *Inst.* III, 73.

there does not seem to be any later reference to imperial *beneficia* in regard to it within our period except for the brief statement preserved in the name of Ulpian. It was perhaps a matter of so routine and formal a character that no occasion to mention it arose.

One of the standard means of formally manumitting a slave was to make the necessary declaration before a magistrate in Rome, or governor with *imperium* in the provinces, and a few items of evidence indicate that this could also be done before the emperor. For instance an inscription, now lost, shows someone manumitted before Domitian in his second consulate, held under Vespasian in 73,[55] which we can regard as a marginal case. It is more significant that Constantine refers in 319 to the case where a man manumitted a slave 'in our sight', but where it afterwards appeared that he was not the legal owner.[56] Later, speaking of cases where freed slaves behaved ungratefully to their masters, and were judged to have lost their freedom, he writes:[57]

> But if a man who has been freed 'by the rod' [the normal ceremony] before our *consilium*, after punishment shows himself by his penitence worthy to have the Roman citizenship restored to him, he will not enjoy the *beneficium* of freedom, until his *patronus* offers a petition (*preces*) and requests this.

It is striking to find Constantine, already settled in the east, still presiding over a symbolic ritual which had been performed before magistrates in the republic. But the emperor could not only grant freedom to slaves, but confer on *liberti* grants which amounted, in differing degrees, to a fictional assertion that they were freeborn. The first of these forms was the grant of the right to wear a gold ring. The known recipients of the late republic and early empire begin with the actor, Sextus Roscius, who gained it from Sulla, but who seems to have been of free birth.[58] Subsequently, however, the grant of the gold ring seems to have been confined to freedmen, and to have brought not merely freeborn but equestrian status; but exactly what consequences its conferment entailed, we do not know.[59] In the empire it is clear that the right to a gold ring was yet another privilege which could be petitioned for from the emperor. Ulpian implies that the custom went back at least to Hadrian: 'If a freedman has asked for the *ius anulorum*, although the rights of free birth (*ingenuitas*) which he has gained are without prejudice to the claims of his *patronus*, nevertheless he is understood to be an *ingenuus*. So the Divine Hadrian wrote in a rescript.'[60] It was certainly known under Commodus, for an inscription records a freedman who gained the right from him; and Marcianus states that he removed it again from those who had accepted it without the knowledge or against the will of their

---

[55] *ILS* 1910, which depends on a copy made in the fifteenth century.
[56] *CTh* IV, 9, 1 = *CJ* VII, 10, 7. Cf. *CJ* VII, 1, 4 (Constantine).
[57] *CJ* VI, 7, 2, 1. On the use of the rod (*vindicta*) in the ceremony before a magistrate see e.g. A. M. Duff, o.c., 23; S. Treggiari, *Roman Freedmen during the Late Republic* (1969), 20f.
[58] See C. Nicolet, *L'ordre équestre* II (1974), no. 300.
[59] See Duff, o.c., 85–6; A. Stein, *Der römische Ritterstand* (1927), 30f.
[60] *Dig.* XL, 10, 6.

patroni.[61] The position remained throughout that a *libertus* who had gained the *ius anulorum* had during his lifetime a status as if he were freeborn, except in relation to his *patronus*. But the obligations of the *patronus* to him remained —as Papinian says, 'a pension (*alimenta*) left to a freedman does not cease to be due just because the freedman has gained the *ius anulorum* from the emperor';[62] and, more important, his *ingenuitas* was, as Diocletain and Maximian twice express it, an *imago* which lasted only until death, after which his *patronus* had the same claims on his property as he did on that of other freedmen.[63]

It was precisely this which distinguished the grant of the 'right of gold rings' from the 'restitution of [free] birth'. The distinction is clearly expressed by Ulpian early in the third century: 'But if a man accepts the *ius anulorum*, I hold that he should still show reverence to his *patronus*, even though he has all the privileges of free birth. It is otherwise if he has been restored to free birth; for the emperor makes him freeborn.'[64] It is propounded in even more definite form by Diocletian and Maximian in 294:[65]

> The use of the gold rings granted to freedmen by imperial *beneficium* provides them during their lives with the *imago* of free birth, not the actual status. But men restored to their original free birth are established as freeborn by our *beneficium*.

The notion of an imperial *beneficium* in such a case was a derivation, typical of the empire, from a class of actions in which persons who actually were of free birth but had subsequently been enslaved and freed, could bring evidence on the point, and claim restitution of their original rights. Such actions also could indeed be brought before the emperor, and Ulpian lays down firmly that a grant of restitution made to a man who affirmed (*adfirmavit*) to the emperor that he was of free birth was void if it turned out subsequently that he was the son of a slave-woman.[66] These claims had normally to be made before a magistrate or governor within five years of manumission; a man who claimed after this to have found the evidence of his free birth had to approach the emperor, who would examine the case.[67]

In the early empire the known beneficiaries were again imperial favourites, and in any case some evidence of free birth, genuine or otherwise, was often produced on their behalf.[68] But by the end of the second century it is clear that the true imperial *beneficium* consisted of a fictitious 'restoration' of free birth, an institution which Marcianus does his best to justify as a restoration

---

[61] *ILS* 1899 (cf. also the fragmentary *ILS* 5631); *Dig.* XL, 10, 3.

[62] *Dig.* XL, 10, 1 *pr.* He also retained, according to a rescript of Caracalla, the freedman's *excusatio* from *tutela*, *Dig.* XXVII, 1, 14, 2. Cf. also XXVII, 1, 44.

[63] *CJ* IX, 21, 1 (300?): 'iure aureorum anulorum impetrato a principe . . . tunc enim quoad vivunt imaginem, non statum ingenuitatis obtinent'; for the rights of the *patronus* (and the term *imago*), cf. *Frag. Vat.* 226. See also *Dig.* XXXVIII, 2, 3 *pr.* (Ulpian).

[64] *Dig.* II, 4, 10, 3.

[65] *CJ* VI, 8, 2.

[66] *Dig.* XL, 11, 1.

[67] *Dig.* XL, 14, 2, 2.

[68] Duff, o.c., 86–8.

to the condition in which all men originally were. By it the *patronus* lost all his rights—'and so the emperor does not readily restore anyone to free birth, unless the *patronus* agrees'.[69] Once again we cannot tell to how wide a range of persons such 'restorations' were available, but the essential thing is that they are referred to in such a way as to make clear that they represented an accepted function of the emperor. Thus Diocletian and Maximian state firmly in reply to a freedman named Philadelphus: 'Your original free birth and right of *ingenuitas* could not have been legally bestowed by a city-council, but could have been petitioned for from us.'[70]

Such were the formal means by which the emperors, usually in response to requests, granted the status of a citizen, of a freedman with full rights, or, fictitiously, of a freeborn man. But it is important to stress again that the wide range of petitions on legal matters addressed to the emperors also included a significant number from individuals, male and female, requesting rulings on whether they had or had not been legally freed.[71] A positive answer to such a request was therefore in effect a declaration of the person's freedom, or at least a statement that he or she had a ground for seeking it in some other court. *Subscriptiones* addressed to persons of freedman status, or of indeterminate status between slave and freed, are not attested before the middle of the second century, but are common thereafter up to the reign of Diocletian.[72] Not all the responses are favourable: in 205 Severus tells a man that, as he has been given as a pledge by a husband to his wife, it is beyond doubt that he cannot be manumitted without her consent. But if he could prove that his manumission had been with her knowledge and consent, an action by her heir to regain him as a slave could not stand.[73] In Severus' view, therefore, the man's status was still in doubt. From the vast variety of pressing personal concerns which the *subscriptiones* reveal, we may conclude with one addressed by Valerian, Gallienus and the younger Valerian (so probably in 254–7) to a man named Vausumetius, which illustrates as well as any other how the system of *libellus* and *subscriptio*, however partial or erratic its operation may have been, still meant that the emperor could give aid to his subjects in matters of urgency to them:[74]

> Not even if you had voluntarily stated in writing that you were a slave, rather than a free man, would you have incurred any prejudice to your status. How much more is this the case in this instance, in that you affirm that it was under compulsion that you made this written statement.

[69] *Dig.* XL, 11, 2; for the emperor's role, and this condition, see also ibid., 3 (Scaevola, the earliest reference to the established custom of fictional restoration by the emperor) and 5.

[70] *CJ* VI, 8, 1. The fact that the man was a freedman is shown by *CJ* VII, 9, 3 which is another part of the same reply.

[71] Examples of *subscriptiones* addressed to the persons whose slave or freedman status was in doubt are *CJ* VII, 2, 6 (Gordian); 2, 12 (Diocletian and Maximian); 4, 1 (Septimius Severus, 197); 4, 8 (Severus Alexander); 4, 11 (Diocletian and Maximian); 9, 1 (Gordian). Others are addressed to relatives or descendants of such persons, e.g. VII, 9, 2; 14, 3; 14, 4 (Diocletian and Maximian to a man whose relative had been enslaved in the 'Palmyrenae factionis dominatio').

[72] See A. Piganiol, 'Les Empereurs parlent aux esclaves', *Romanitas* I (1958), 7 = *Scripta Varia* III (1973), 202.

[73] *CJ* VII, 5, 1 and VIII, 5, 1.

[74] *CJ* VII, 16, 6.

3. *Gifts, Immunities and Positions: the Predominance of the Learned Professions*

In 23 BC, when his regime of cold baths and drinking cold water cured Augustus of a serious illness, the doctor Antonius Musa was richly rewarded; he received large sums from the emperor and the senate, as well as the right to gold rings (for he was a freedman, presumably of Antonius), and *ateleia* for himself and his fellow-practitioners both present and future. As a successful imperial doctor—whose brother Euphorbus was doctor to King Juba of Mauretania—he was a public figure, known for instance to Horace; a statue of him was erected by public subscription next to that of Asclepius. Moreover an inscription now shows the people of Samos honouring him for his goodwill towards them, perhaps during Augustus' winters there in 21/20 and 20/19.[1]

In this period the grant of gold rings was, as we saw, confined to freedmen who were personal favourites, and its precise implications are not clear.[2] The position of imperial doctor cannot be clearly separated from those 'secretarial' positions in which men assisted the emperor directly in his work, and like them was soon open to men of free birth; both facts are clearly exemplified in the career of Stertinius Xenophon of Cos, who combined being Claudius' chief doctor at a salary of 500,000 *sesterces* with being in charge of imperial responses in Greek.[3] But medicine was only one of a linked series of intellectual accomplishments, philosophy, rhetoric, literature, history or law, where again we cannot draw a clear line between regular service with the emperor, *ad hoc* rewards in the form of cash or privileges, positions not connected with the court for individuals who earned imperial favour, and immunities and privileges for whole classes of persons practising their professions in Rome, Italy or the provinces. We can indeed see precisely this process of generalization at work in the case of Antonius Musa and his fellow-doctors. Dio does not define exactly in what the *ateleia* given to Musa, and extended to present and future practitioners of medicine, consisted; and as usual we cannot state whether it related to local personal and financial obligations, to Roman indirect taxes or to all Roman taxes. It is only a century later, in the Flavian period, that we begin to have clearer evidence of the immunities which imperial pronouncements conferred on *grammatici*, rhetors and doctors.[4]

Such rights and privileges naturally affected both the internal workings and the mutual relations of the cities, and we have already seen how various issues of this sort were the subject of communications between cities, and even *koina*, and the emperor;[5] to a large extent it is a matter of choice whether one sees any one such matter as part of the relations of communities or of

---

[1] See Dio LIII, 30, 3; cf. Suetonius, *Aug.* 59; 81, 1; *PIR*[2] A 853; and for the Samian inscription, P. Herrmann, *Ath. Mitt.* LXXV (1960), 141, no. 35.
[2] pp. 488–9.
[3] pp. 85–6.
[4] pp. 501–2.
[5] pp. 390–1, 438–40.

individuals with him. But they were questions of personal privilege also, and in the second and third centuries at least could be petitioned for like any other *beneficium* which was at the emperor's disposal. This is nowhere more clearly visible than in a papyrus from Oxyrhynchus, containing two drafts of a *libellus* addressed by a 'public *grammaticus*' there to Valerian and Gallienus. With them there is a covering letter to an influential friend who appears to be in Rome (since it is mentioned that he knows the consuls) and who will be able to despatch letters to be carried 'by those coming in to Alexandria from the *comitatus*'. The *grammaticus*' own letter and draft petition seem to have been carried by slaves. If that is so, the presence of a friend with access to the court seems to have enabled him to anticipate being able to submit a *libellus* from a distance, in the manner of a letter. The text of the fuller version of the *libellus* is of great value both for the diplomatic vocabulary of the time and for its presumptions about the interest of the emperors in education and culture:[6]

> To the [masters] of land and sea and every nation of men, Imperatores Publius Licinius Valerianus and Publius Licinius Valerianus Gallienus, Pii Felices Augusti, from Lollianus also called Homoeus: Your heavenly magnanimity, great Emperors, which has extended its benevolence (*philanthrôpia*) to the whole of your domain, the civilised world, and sent it forth to every corner, has given me too confidence to offer your heavenly genius a petition (*axiôsis*) closely connected with both reason and justice. It is this. Your deified ancestors who have ruled at different times, rulers who irradiated their domain, the world, in virtue and culture, fixed, in proportion to the size of the cities, a number of public *grammatici* as well, ordering . . .

At this point, where there is a break in the longer draft, the shorter one states specifically that the emperors had ordered that incomes (*syntaxeis*) should be given to the *grammatici*. The longer draft continues on this assumption, requesting that, as the payments made by the city were inadequate, the emperors should order that a garden should be given by the city to Lollianus to provide him with an income. As we shall see, it is more than doubtful whether any earlier emperors had actually ordered the payment of a salary to a fixed number of rhetors, as opposed to laying down a maximum who could be granted immunity from other obligations.[7] Lollianus is probably attempting, consciously or unconsciously, to stretch the terms of the imperial rulings.

None the less, it is the case not only that literary men and intellectuals of various specialities were among the most frequent recipients of imperial benefactions, but that a whole series of imperial rulings had concerned itself with their status and privileges, and would continue to do so. Moreover, one institution of higher learning in particular, the Museum in Alexandria,

---

[6] P. J. Parsons, 'The Grammarian's Complaint', to be published in A. E. Hanson (ed.), *Collectanea Papyrologica: Texts Published in Honour of H. C. Youtie* II (1976). I am most grateful to Mr Parsons for allowing me to see the text and article in advance of publication. The section which follows has also benefited from the collection of material made there. The translation given is that of Mr Parsons.

[7] pp. 501–2.

provides the most specific and concrete of all instances of a direct transfer of functions from Hellenistic kings to Roman emperors. Strabo, who visited Egypt within about five years of its conquest, includes the Museum in his description of Alexandria:[8]

> Within the palace area is the Museum, which has a cloister and hall, and a large house for the common meals of the learned men who are members of the Museum. This body (*synodos*) also has common funds and a priest 'in charge of the Museum', appointed formerly by the Kings and now by Caesar.

We shall return later to the evidence for the emperor's connections with the Museum, and his nominations to membership, with its attendant privileges.[9] For the moment it will be sufficient to note that a Museum was in origin a shrine dedicated to the Muses,[10] and that in nominating its presiding priest (*hiereus*), Augustus was assuming a role in religious life no less significant than his hearing, as an initiate, the case of the priests of Eleusis.[11] He was also, of course, assuming a role in intellectual life, and one whose beneficiaries on occasion received posts at court as well as in Alexandria.[12]

It need not be claimed that those private individuals in the empire who succeeded in being granted sums of money, immunities or positions by the emperor consisted exclusively of literary men, scholars, orators, and doctors. But, unless our evidence is grossly misleading, it is the case that apart from senators or leading *equites* and from the different category of soldiers and veterans, literary and scholastic pursuits provided by far the best and most direct means of access to imperial favours; and until in the reign of Constantine very similar benefits became available to the *clerici* of the Christian church, it was these groups alone (along with performers and athletes) on whom any general immunity from local obligations was conferred by the emperors. In this respect, as in so many others, the pattern of the *beneficia* which the emperors distributed accurately reflects the values of the society over which they ruled.

These values were, as we saw, expressed with particular clarity in the qualifications which brought persons of free birth into 'secretarial' positions in the immediate entourage of the emperor.[13] Only the purely formal criterion that such men were specifically concerned with imperial pronouncements partially separates them from the doctors and teachers of various kinds who also attended the emperor and his family. All these positions were certainly paid, though no doubt normally less than the 500,000 *sesterces* which Xenophon finally condescended to accept from Claudius. Herodian notes that Marcus Aurelius 'summoned from all parts those men who in the

---

[8] XVII, 1, 8 (794). See G. W. Bowersock, *Augustus and the Greek World* (1965), 128–9; for the date, perhaps about 26 BC, see S. Jameson, 'The Chronology of the Campaigns of Aelius Gallus and C. Petronius', *JRS* LVIII (1968), 71, esp. 78–9.

[9] pp. 504–6.

[10] For the origin and background of the Alexandrian Museum see P. M. Fraser, *Ptolemaic Alexandria* (1972), 312f.

[11] p. 449.

[12] pp. 87–8.

[13] pp. 83–101.

provinces were most distinguished for learning, and appointed them at not inconsiderable salaries (*syntaxeis*) to be in permanent attendance and educate his son (Commodus)'.[14] In the fourth century Exuperius, a rhetor from Tolosa (Toulouse), moved to Narbo 'at a high fee' to educate the sons of Dalmatius, the half-brother of Constantine.[15]

Ausonius, who relates this, also records that in the 330s his maternal uncle, Aemilius Magnus Arborius, died in Constantinople, 'wealthy and honoured as the teacher of a Caesar'.[16] The honour and prominence of such persons is easily attested. Even among the freedmen, Antonius Musa was not the only one to earn an honorific inscription in a Greek city.[17] An imperial doctor of free birth like Ti. Claudius Menecrates might be 'honoured by famous cities with fulsome decrees' in recognition of the 157 books in which he had set out his own system of medicine;[18] while T. Statilius Criton, the doctor of Trajan as well as his *amicus*, procurator and historian of the Dacian wars, was honoured by a society of doctors at Ephesus, and left money in his will for a statue of Trajan at his native city of Heraclea Salbace in Caria.[19] Inevitably, imperial influence was mediated through these men, as it was through all other close associates of the emperor; it is not surprising for instance that, as an inscription from Cos records, the brother of Stertinius Xenophon had 'often' been as ambassador for his city to the emperors.[20] More clearly still, Marcus Aurelius himself, when 'Caesar' in the late 150s, writes to Fronto before the latter's expected proconsulate of Asia, exactly as Cicero had done to a whole series of friends and acquaintances:[21]

> If while you are in the province, my master, you are approached by a certain Themistocles who says that he is acquainted with my teacher in philosophy, Apollonius, you should know that he is a man who came to Rome this winter and at the wish of my teacher was brought before me by the younger Apollonius. I would wish you, my master, to grant him whatever favours and good advice you can.

The delicate phrases with which Marcus goes on to emphasize that such help will naturally not be in contravention of Fronto's duty as proconsul, cannot conceal the clear implication that Apollonius was well-placed to confer *beneficia* on his friends. The same pattern is even clearer from what Aelius Aristides says in the letter which he wrote to the council and people

---

[14] Herodian, I, 2, 1.

[15] Ausonius, *Prof.* XVII, 9-11: 'illic Dalmatio genitos, fatalia regum / nomina, tum pueros, grandi mercede docendi / formasti rhetor.'

[16] ibid., XVI; see *PLRE* Arborius 4.

[17] e.g. *Syll.*[3] 807 (Magnesia on the Maeander), honouring an imperial freedman, Ti. Claudius Tyrannus, 'approved by the divine judgments of the emperors, for his medical skill and the propriety of his character', who had behaved with pleasing condescension on his return to his native city.

[18] *Syll.*[3] 803.

[19] See W. H. Buckler, 'T. Statilius Crito, Traiani Aug. medicus', *JÖAI* XXX (1937), Beiblatt, 5; Jacoby, *FGrH* 200; L. Robert, *La Carie* II (1954), 167, no. 49.

[20] *Syll.*[3] 805.

[21] Fronto, *Ad M. Caes.* V, 36. Cicero's letters of this type are of course collected in *Ad fam.* XIII.

of the city of Cottiaeum to console them on the death of their famous citizen, Alexander the grammarian, a teacher of Marcus Aurelius and Verus. Alexander's fame, he says, had spread throughout the Greek world until it finally reached the court. Later in a letter Aristides emphasizes Alexander's generosity to his native city, the fame he brought to it, and the advantages which his association with the emperors brought to the Greeks in general. But he is also quite specific about what Alexander's role was, and what it might have been:[22]

> It was the same in his association with the emperors. He never caused any pain to anyone, but throughout never stopped doing good for relatives, friends, his homeland and other cities. In the myriad benefits which he conferred on myriads of persons he never asked for any payment; but for the practice of his professional skill he did not disdain to take it.

From the concluding remark it can be assumed that Alexander was paid as an imperial teacher, which would not have excluded payment from others. But it is clear also that such regular pay was only part of the financial benefits open to anyone with access to the emperor, if he were prepared to take them. The letter also illustrates how a man's reputation in any intellectual pursuit would finally bring him to the notice of the emperor; Galen describes exactly such a process in his own case, which led to his being summoned to attend Marcus and Verus at Aquileia, just before the latter's death.[23] In view of this network of personal relationships it is not surprising that later Aristides was to dream 'that I was coming before the emperor with my teacher, Alexander'.[24]

Medicine, though in its theoretical aspect it counted as a form of 'philosophy', was also of course a practical art, and we have occasional indications that other technical experts found positions with the emperor. Vitruvius was paid, as we saw earlier, for his functions in relation to preparing siege-engines for Augustus,[25] and Apollodorus from Damascus, the architect of Trajan's bridge over the Danube, is also found in association with him over his building-programme in Rome, criticizing Hadrian's plans for the temple of Venus and Roma, and writing to him about the construction of military engines.[26] Similarly, the Christian chronographer, Julius Africanus, whose embassy on behalf of Emmaus-Nicopolis we noted earlier, was Severus Alexander's architect for the library of the Pantheon, and is also alleged to have addressed to the emperor the vast array of variegated practical learning which he entitled *Kestoi*.[27]

[22] The letter is preserved as *Or.* XXXII Keil. See *PIR*[2] A 502 and C. A. Behr, *Aelius Aristides and the Sacred Tales* (1968), 10f. The passage quoted is 15–16.

[23] Galen XIV, 647–50 Kühn. See V. Nutton, 'Galen and Medical Autobiography', *PCPhS* CXCVIII, n.s. XVIII (1972), 50.

[24] *Or.* XLVII Keil, 23; see Behr, o.c., 219.

[25] p. 200.

[26] For the evidence see Millar, *A Study of Cassius Dio* (1964), 65–6.

[27] For the embassy see p. 409. See *PIR*[2] I 124. His own testimony to his role as architect is in *P. Oxy.* 412 and for the address see Syncellus, *Chron.* 676 Dindorf. For the text and French translation, and a discussion, see now J.-R. Vieillefond, *Les 'Cestes' de Julius Africanus* (1970).

Whether Africanus gained any established and salaried post is unclear, but the claim that he addressed his learned work to the emperor may serve to emphasize the fact that the presentation of works, whether literary, rhetorical, philosophical or technical, to the emperor afforded at all times a privileged form of access, and a promising (if not always successful) means of securing gifts, privileges and exemptions. So for instance at the very beginning of the empire L. Varius Rufus earned 1,000,000 *sesterces* for his tragedy *Thyestes*, which was performed at the games to celebrate the victory of Actium;[28] Horace was enriched by two *liberalitates* from Augustus;[29] and Tiberius gave Asellius Sabinus 200,000 *sesterces* for a dialogue containing the strained conceit of a contest between a mushroom, a fig-pecker, an oyster and a thrush.[30] There is no need for a further catalogue of similar gifts, but it should be emphasized that these are substantial sums, equivalent respectively to the census-valuation of a senator, and half that of an *eques*; the *liberalitas* of 500,000 *sesterces* which Vespasian granted to the poet, Saleius Bassus, was of the same order of magnitude.[31]

Just as gifts, ranks and privileges, were the common currency of exchange between the emperors and the sophists who spoke before them,[32] so Philostratus can represent a discussion between Vespasian and three philosophers in Alexandria in 69 as ending with an offer, nobly declined, of gifts to Apollonius; a request for release from military service for a third party by Dio of Prusa; and a written demand for presents in cash and kind, for himself and others, from Euphrates.[33] Statius acquired from Domitian the right to draw water from an aqueduct for his Alban property, a right which, as we saw, was an established imperial *beneficium*; and from the publication of Martial's poem embodying the same request we can probably deduce that he too was successful.[34] Martial also requested and gained from Domitian, and apparently earlier from Titus, the privileges of those with three children, resting his claim explicitly on his poems; the fact that these privileges could be gained on petition by or for persons who were childless illustrates once again the separation of status and function under the empire.[35] He claims also to have obtained from the emperor the citizenship for a large number of others.[36] But one poem reflects his anxiety at the outcome of a request for money from Domitian, which he does not seem to have obtained. He still hoped, however, for 'how unforbidding he was, how unclouded with anger, with how calm a countenance he read our *preces*!'[37] Martial's wording clearly implies that he had presented the petition (in verse?) himself, and had

---

[28] *RE* s.v. 'Varius' (23).

[29] Suetonius, *De poetis* (ed. Reifferscheid, p. 46).

[30] Suetonius, *Tib.* 42, 2.

[31] Tacitus, *Dial.* 9, 5.

[32] pp. 91–2, 138, 281, 468.

[33] Philostratus, *V. Ap. Ty.* v, 38.

[34] Statius, *Silvae* III, 1, 61–4; Martial, *Epig.* IX, 18. Cf. p. 193.

[35] Martial, *Epig.* II, 91–2; III, 95, 5–6; IX, 97, 5–6. Cf. p. 114, the same right gained for Pliny by Julius Servianus; Pliny gained it for Voconius Romanus (*Ep.* II, 1, 38) and Suetonius (x, 94–5). See also *ILS* 1910, Ulpian, *Tit.* XVI, 1a; *Frag. Vat.* 170.

[36] *Epig.* III, 95, 11.

[37] VI, 10.

observed the emperor's reaction as he read it. But all depended on the unpredictable workings of the emperor's will. Even if this request was rejected, however, it does not reduce the importance of Divum Martial's evidence as to the range of matters on which petitions could be made, or the relevance of his poetry to them.

It should be emphasized briefly that the works addressed to emperors included not only those embodying specific requests,[38] nor merely literary works in prose or verse for his pleasure,[39] but also collections of improving *exempla* like that of Valerius Maximus, addressed to Tiberius; detailed works of general information, like the *Natural History* of Pliny, addressed to Titus; various works on medicine;[40] or the work *On Fate* addressed by Alexander of Aphrodisias to Severus and Caracalla, whose preface and conclusion make explicit that it is intended as a practical guide to conduct.[41] With the immense importance attached to correct Greek vocabulary and grammar in the second century, works on this topic too were addressed to emperors. For instance each book of the *Onomastikon* of 'Pollux' (Julius Polydeuces) begins with an address to Commodus as Caesar, cast in the form of a letter, urging on him the importance of this branch of study; whether this service had any connection with the fact that later, as emperor, Commodus appointed him to the chair of Greek rhetoric at Athens cannot be determined.[42] Works of military science were naturally also included, such as the *Strategemata* addressed by Polyaenus to Marcus and Verus; the examples of stratagems which he collected were explicitly intended to be of practical use in their wars.[43]

The list could be greatly extended. Its significance is that literary productions, whether sent to the emperor (as Alexander's *On Fate* explicitly was, as was also that on the emperor's prophetic dreams which Cassius Dio sent to Septimius Severus),[44] or handed to him, or recited before him, afforded a privileged means of access, which could be used both to secure benefits and, in intention at least, to influence his conduct more widely than this. Works actually read or delivered before emperors, apart from the innumerable orations on immediate issues mentioned earlier, ranged from the contest in declamation before Severus, as a result of which the sophist Apollonius lost his *ateleia*, and Heraclides the Lycian was rewarded with gifts,[45] to general

---

[38] A nice example is *Anth. Pal.* IX, 137, the poem of a *grammaticus* addressed to Hadrian: Ἥμισύ μου τέθνηκε, τὸ δ' ἥμισυ λιμὸς ἐλέγχει· σῶσόν μου, βασιλεῦ, μουσικὸν ἡμίτονον, heartlessly answered with Ἀμφοτέρους ἀδικεῖς, καὶ Πλουτέα καὶ Φαέθοντα, / τὸν μὲν ἔτ' εἰσορόων, τοῦ δ' ἀπολειπόμενος.

[39] A relatively late example in our period is the *Cynegetica* of M. Aurelius Olympius Nemesianus addressed, at least notionally (ll. 63-85), to Carinus and Numerianus.

[40] Pliny, *NH* XXV, 2/4, a work on medicine by Gaius Valgius, 'ad Divum Augustum' (with a suitable preface to the effect that Augustus would cure all human ills); Scribonius Largus, *Compositiones, praef.* (his *scripta latina medicinalia* passed to Claudius by Callistus); Galen XIV, 32f. Kühn, a poem Γαλήνη, on the recipe for an antidote, addressed to Nero by his doctor Andromachus.

[41] *Comm. in Arist. gr.*, Supp. II.2, 164, 212; cf. p. 275.

[42] Philostratus, *VS* II, 12, see p. 503. Compare also the grammarian Aelius Herodianus from Alexandria who came to Rome under Marcus, gained his favour, and wrote at his request his two works on prosody, the latter with a preface addressed to the emperor, *Gram. Graec.* III. 1, vi f.; see *PIR*² A 189.

[43] *Strat.* I, 1-4; II-VIII *pr.*

[44] Dio LXXII, 23, 1-2 (305).

[45] Philostratus, *VS* II, 20.

17

orations *To the King* or *On Kingship* which held up an ideal of conduct for the emperor to follow. Of the four discourses of Dio of Prusa *On Kingship*, two have the form of addresses to Trajan, and will surely either have been delivered before him or sent to him.[46] The same may apply to the Christian apologies of the second century, which cannot be fully understood unless set against the background of those exhortatory or informative works so commonly addressed to emperors in this period. At the very least they owe their literary form to this custom; and we must be open to the possibility that some were actually sent, or even read, to emperors.[47]

Throughout the empire the demonstration of some pre-eminence in literature, rhetoric or philosophy opened the most direct route to rewards in cash or privileges from the emperor. Dio says sourly that Marcus Aurelius had as teachers of philosophy the Stoics, Junius Rusticus and Apollonius of Nicomedia, as a result of which many others affected to philosophize 'in order to be enriched by him'; and later that a Cynic philosopher named Antiochus demonstrated his indifference to suffering by rolling in the snow, 'by which he gained both money and honours from Severus and Antoninus [Caracalla]'.[48] Generosity was also called for in relation to actors and musicians, and other performers who appeared before the emperor. But this was essentially an aspect of the 'liberality' required of the ruler, which should be on a scale neither so slight as to seem niggardly nor so extravagant as to be improper.[49] Though the sums might in fact be large, they clearly did not represent an important feature of the emperor's relations with his subjects.

Gifts of money were in any case necessarily confined to those who come into direct contact with the emperor, except in circumstances of disturbance or civil war, where the emperor might offer a reward for the death or capture of an individual, or for other services. Thus Augustus offered 250,000 *sesterces* for the capture of a Spanish bandit; but when the man appeared in person he received the reward himself.[50] Similarly, Nero rewarded the informer who revealed the conspiracy of 65, and offered 2,500,000 *sesterces* for the head of Vindex when he led the revolt of 68.[51] In the following year, after Galba had been murdered in Rome, no less than 120 people are stated to have presented to Otho *libelli* claiming a reward for taking part; these were found subsequently by Vitellius, and their authors were all sought out and executed.[52] On the other hand a man who had prophesied the day of Domitian's death received a reward of 400,000 *sesterces* from Nerva;[53] by

[46] *Or.* I–IV; I and III are addressed to the emperor (Trajan, though he is never actually named).

[47] pp. 561–6. Compare Aelius Aristides' opening remark in his letter about Smyrna, *Or.* XIX Keil, 1: πρότερον μὲν, ὦ μέγιστοι βασιλεῖς, ἀγωνίσματα καὶ λόγους ἐκ διατριβῶν καὶ τοιαῦθ' ὑμῖν ἀπέστελλον. Cf. p. 423.

[48] LXXI, 35, 1–2 (277); on Apollonius see p. 494; LXXVII, 19, 1–2 (398).

[49] Suetonius, *Aug.* 45, 2; Porphyrion, Σ Horace, *Serm.* 1, 2 *pr.*; Suetonius, *Cal.* 55, 2; *Nero* 20, 3; 30, 2; Dio LXI, 6, 3; Suetonius, *Vesp.* 19, 1. Cf. also pp. 135–9.

[50] Dio LVI, 43, 3.

[51] Tacitus, *Ann.* XV, 71, 1; Dio LXIII, 26, 2/23, 2 (89–90).

[52] Tacitus, *Hist.* 1, 44, 2; Suetonius, *Vit.* 10, 1; Plutarch, *Galba* 27, 9–10. Suetonius' account seems to suggest that the *libelli* were in the train of Otho at the time of his death at Bedriacum.

[53] Dio LXVII, 16, 2.

comparison a *grammaticus* who spontaneously raised forces for Severus in the war against his rival Albinus, while pretending to be a senator, 'did not ask to be made a real senator, and although he could have been loaded with great honours and wealth did not seek it, but lived out his life on a small property, receiving a small daily allowance from him'.[54]

In the nature of the case such opportunities did not present themselves very widely. But it is significant that three pronouncements of Constantine concern themselves with the affirmation and preservation of the subsequent property-rights of persons to whom the emperor has made gifts. In 313 he writes to a *rationalis* that if an imperial *adnotatio* stated that a house had been given 'in its integral state', this has the same force as when 'we previously used to write' that it was given 'with the attached slaves, flocks, products and all its rights'.[55] Perhaps a couple of years later he writes that if any persons have gained a just gift from 'our *clementia*' and one of them dies without heirs, his partner can inherit.[56] Only in a letter of 326 to the prefect of Rome does he envisage the recipients as being specifically those 'to whom on account of their efforts or deserts we have granted something'; if any third party could prove that they had been wronged thereby, the fact was to be reported to *nostra scientia*, so that it could be considered 'in what manner . . . they should be assisted by the *beneficium* of our gentleness'.[57]

It is clear that grants of cash and property by the emperor were a common phenomenon, though it is as impossible to estimate the number or social or geographical range of the beneficiaries here, as it is with less concrete grants of exemptions or immunities. As with cities and communities, however, the emperor could grant, not actual money or property, but exemption from some or all forms of Roman taxation, or immunity from the financial or personal obligations imposed by cities.[58] In the nature of the case such exemptions from taxation or local burdens were normally achieved only by the relatively prominent types of individual already discussed. But it was still possible to appeal to the emperor over specific impositions. One such case is recorded in the second-century *Oneirocritica* (*On the Interpretation of Dreams*) of Artemidorus of Daldis, a priceless source for the aspirations and realities of imperial society:[59]

A ship-captain dreamed that he was in the Isles of the Blessed and was detained by the Heroes, whereupon Agamemnon came and released him. Becoming liable to transport-service, he was detained by the procurators of the emperor, then petitioned the King, and was released from the transport-service.

The passage, which is notable for using both *autokrator* and *basileus* for the emperor in a single sentence, treats both the liability and the means of escaping from it as unsurprising. Similarly, a papyrus reveals the fragmentary

[54] Dio LXXV, 5, 1–3.
[55] *CTh* x, 8, 1 = *CJ* x, 10, 2. On *adnotationes* see p. 266.
[56] *CTh* x, 14, 1 (315?).
[57] *CTh* x, 8, 3; cf. p. 340.
[58] cf. esp. pp. 438–40.
[59] *Oneir.* v, 16.

text of a 'petition and supplication' addressed by a woman from the Leontopolite district in Egypt to 'the masters of land and sea and of all the race of men', Licinius, Constantine and their 'Caesars', some time between 317 and 324, and asking for relief from taxation on her land. There is no indication of how it was intended to transmit the document to Licinius (who would in practice have been the addressee).[60] Similar petitions over questions of liability to local obligations will have been even more frequent. It is impossible to deal in any detail with the immense range of legal issues involved, which fill substantial parts of the *Digest* and *Codex Justinianus*.[61] Nor did imperial replies to such petitions always grant the exemptions requested. But by way of example it may be sufficient to quote one favourable answer from a legal source and one unfavourable one from a papyrus. Pertinax, in one of the few *subscriptiones* preserved in Greek in a legal source, replies as follows to a man named Silvius Candidus:[62]

> Even granted that the number of their children does not afford to fathers exemption from all liturgies, as you have declared in your *libellus* that you have sixteen children, it is not unreasonable to permit you to devote yourself to their upbringing, and to release you from the liturgies.

Severus on the other hand replies as follows in one of the *subscriptiones* posted in Alexandria in March 200 and preserved on a papyrus:[63]

> Temporary illnesses on the part of citizens [of a town] do not exempt them from liturgies; and those who have bodily ailments incur liturgies so long as they are fit to manage their own affairs.

It is more important to examine briefly which were the categories of persons who received from the emperor some general immunity from local obligations. The list includes Roman senators, and eventually the higher grades of *equites*,[64] veterans (and of course serving soldiers), some *collegia*, such as *fabri*, and shippers engaged in transport for the food-supply of Rome.[65] At the very end of his life Constantine also granted exemption to all types of *artifices*, from architects to silversmiths, provided that they would teach their skills to others.[66] With that exception the only professional groups who benefited from a general exemption were the synods of athletes

---

[60] *P. Ryl.* IV, 617. Note the further fragmentary petitions to the emperors, 618f. For the archive from which the petitions came, ibid., pp. 104f., and cf. B. R. Rees, 'Theophanes of Hermopolis Magna', *Bull. J. Rylands Lib.* LI (1968), 164.

[61] See e.g. *Dig.* XXVII, 1 *de excusationibus* (essentially on exemption from *curae* and *tutelae*, but the same persons benefited in relation to public *munera*); L, 1–7, 10, 12; *CJ* X, 39–70.

[62] *Dig.* L, 6, 6, 2; cf. p. 246. For a Greek *subscriptio*, addressed to a group of Jews, see *CJ* I, 9, 2 (allowing them exemption from *munera personalia* on the Sabbath).

[63] *SB* 9526, no. 9; cf. p. 244. *P. Oxy.* 1405, from the same period, also concerns the performance of local office.

[64] pp. 289–90.

[65] *Dig.* L, 5, 3; 6, 6, 3–9 and 12. For the passage on nominal shippers see p. 428. For the immunities of the *collegium fabrorum* at Solva see p. 442.

[66] *CTh* XIII, 4, 2 = *CJ* X, 66, 1. The pronouncement is in Constantine's name, but is actually dated after his death.

and stage-performers;[67] and doctors, *grammatici*, rhetors and, in exceptional
cases, philosophers. In the system as it had developed by the middle of the
second century each city was allowed specific numbers of exempt doctors,
grammatici and rhetors according to its size. The appointments were made
by the city councils, and maintenance of the exemption depended on satisfactory practice or teaching. Those of exceptional learning could (it seems)
be exempt without these conditions; and those who taught in Rome itself
were automatically exempt.[68] Rather remarkably, there was no provision
for exemption for provincial teachers of law; but they did benefit if they
taught in Rome.[69] Nothing could show more clearly that the values which
informed this system of exemptions were not based on practical considerations of service to the state, but on the prestige within contemporary culture
of the various branches of learning. Poetry for instance was not so highly
regarded, at least as practised by contemporaries. So Philip and his son
replied sharply to a man named Ulpianus: 'Poets do not benefit from any
privilege of immunity.'[70]

This reply and the request which will have prompted it reflect a typical
process whereby potential beneficiaries attempted to extend the application
of any imperial *beneficium*. In our sources philosophers are sometimes included in the exempt categories. But Antoninus Pius' well-known witticism,
that if a man were concerned about his property that showed that he was not
a true philosopher, could always be brought into play. Purely financial
burdens (as opposed to those involving some personal responsibility) were
also another matter. So Diocletian and Maximian reply to a man named
Polymnestus:[71]

> Your profession and your request do not accord with each other. For while you
> declare that you are a philosopher, you are blinkered by avarice, and alone
> attempt to refuse the burdens which are imposed on your property. That you
> do so in vain you could have learnt from the example of others.

Thus in the case of city doctors and higher teachers the emperors fixed
general rules for immunity. But in the individual rulings for which
approaches were made to them they seem to have been at least as likely to
deny immunity as to grant it; while they might protect that of a Flavius
Archippus or an Aelius Aristides, they might also remove that of well-known
sophists like Favorinus or Philiscus.[72] None the less, the special status of
doctors and those who professed *liberalia studia* is shown by the fact that

---

[67] pp. 456–63.

[68] For recent discussions of these privileges see G. W. Bowersock, *Greek Sophists in the Roman
Empire* (1969), ch. iii; V. Nutton, 'Two Notes on Immunities: *Digest* 27, 1, 6, 10 and 11', *JRS*
LXI (1971), 52; Parsons, o.c. (p. 492). The basic document is Antoninus Pius' letter to the *koinon*
of Asia, *Dig.* XXVII, 1, 6, 2, cf. pp. 390–1.

[69] *Dig.* XXVII, 1, 6, 12.

[70] *CJ* X, 53, 3.

[71] *CJ* X, 42, 6. For Antoninus Pius' witticism, in his letter, see *Dig.* XXVII, 1, 6, 7. It is repeated
also by Papinian, *Dig.* L, 5, 8, 4. Philosophers are included in the exempt category in *Dig.* L, 4, 18, 3,
and *Frag. Vat.* 149.

[72] pp. 439, 470–5.

according to a ruling of Diocletian and Maximian these were the only categories to which city councils were entitled to grant immunity.[73] So far, however, we have seen nothing to indicate that cities were obliged to pay an actual salary to the doctors or teachers whom they appointed. The claim which Lollianus made to Valerian and Gallienus receives no support in our sources except a vague and dubious sentence of the *Historia Augusta* about Antoninus Pius.[74] It is only Constantine, once again, who proclaims 'to the people' that *medici*, and especially *archiatri* (and even ex-*archiatri*) and other *professores litterarum*, and their wives and children, should be entirely exempt from local burdens and other vexations, and also that payment should be made to them.[75]

It was a different matter again when the emperors began to pay teachers who were not attached to their own households. Such payments developed slowly, and their application was almost entirely confined to Rome and Athens. But limited as they were, these posts by their very existence serve to emphasize the immense importance of *liberalia studia* in ancient society; for they were in fact the only posts outside their households, the equestrian 'career' and senatorial governorships for which the emperors paid on a regular basis. The earliest case was indeed at least partly a household one; when the grammarian, Verrius Flaccus, was appointed by Augustus as the teacher of his grandsons, he moved 'with his whole school' to the Palatium, and was paid 100,000 *sesterces* a year.[76] Genuinely public teachers of Greek and Latin rhetoric were first appointed in Rome, at the same salary, by Vespasian; Suetonius lists this as an example of the emperor's liberality, and says that they were paid from the *fiscus*, as does Jerome who states that Quintilian was the first beneficiary (under Domitian).[77] The next step was due to Marcus, and it too is treated by Dio as a benefaction, made by the emperor when he visited Athens in 176: 'On arrival at Athens and after being initiated [in the Eleusinian mysteries], he granted honours to the Athenians, and, for the benefit of all men, teachers in Athens of all branches of learning, with an annual salary.' If passing references in contemporary writers are correct, the posts included all four of the main schools of philosophy, Stoics, Platonists, Epicureans and Peripatetics, and were paid at 60,000 *sesterces* per year.[78] There was also a chair of Greek rhetoric, and from Philostratus' *Lives of the Sophists* we know something of the men who held it, and how they came to do so. Indeed there had been a chair already, but not paid by the emperor, which Lollianus of Ephesus had held earlier in the second

---

[73] *CJ* x, 47, 1.

[74] *Ant. Pius* 11, 3: 'rhetoribus et philosophis per omnes provincias et honores et salaria detulit. Even this does not make clear what the author supposed the source of the *salaria* to have been. For Lollianus' petition, p. 492.

[75] *CTh* xiii, 3, 1 (321 or 324); 2 (326); 3 (333). A composite version, dated to 333, in *CJ* x, 53, 6.

[76] Suetonius, *De gram. et rhet.* 17; cf. p. 20.

[77] Suetonius, *Vesp.* 18; Jerome, *Chron.* ad. AD 88 (ed. Helm, p. 190): 'primus Romae publicam scholam et salarium e fisco accepit', cf. Dio (Zonaras) LXVI, 12, 1a (146): διδασκάλους ἐν τῇ Ῥώμῃ καὶ τῆς Λατίνων καὶ τῆς Ἑλληνικῆς παιδείας κατέστησε, μισθὸν ἐκ τοῦ δημοσίου φέροντας.

[78] Dio LXXI, 31, 3 (272); Lucian, *Eun.* 3, and Philostratus, *VS* 11, 2 (the four branches of philosophy); Tatian, *Adv. Graecos* 19 (600 *aurei* = 60,000 *sesterces*).

century;[79] and it may have been this which Hadrian of Tyre was holding when Marcus arrived. The evidence is confused, for Philostratus says both that Hadrian had been appointed by Marcus, and that Theodotus was the first 'to be in charge of the youth at Athens at the salary of 10,000 *drachmae* (40,000 *sesterces*) from the emperor', and indicates a date in the mid-170s. At any rate Marcus heard Hadrian declaim in Athens, gave him extravagant rewards, including *ateleia*, and then or later promoted him to 'the upper chair' in Rome.[80] At that moment the Athenians voted to send an embassy to ask for their chair to be filled by Chrestus of Byzantium. But he came before the assembly and persuaded them not to.[81] Thereafter Philostratus notes that it was by the charm of his voice that Pollux of Naucratis gained the chair in Rome from Commodus (so he must have declaimed before him on some previous occasion);[82] that Philiscus the Thessalian had been given the chair at Athens by Caracalla;[83] and that Aspasius of Ravenna, who held that at Rome, travelled widely with the emperor, and like Hadrian of Tyre, became *ab epistulis Graecis*.[84]

The chairs at Athens and Rome were thus central elements in the contacts between the emperor and the leading representatives of the Greek Renaissance, as we can dimly perceive for the mid-third century also, when a prominent Athenian, Nicagoras, wrote an ambassadorial speech to Philip, and was also 'holder of the chair' in Athens.[85] Thereafter we lose all sight of the process of imperial nomination of the professors, but should certainly assume that it continued. For we find that when the post of teacher of rhetoric at Autun fell vacant, probably in 297, Constantius appointed his own *magister memoriae*, Eumenius, and laid down what salary he should receive. Our evidence comes from Eumenius himself, in his oration of 298 in which he quotes the letter of appointment, which is a fine example of the courtesies of imperial diplomacy, accentuated by the fact that the appointment was an apparent (and perhaps real) demotion. It concludes as follows:[86]

Therefore without prejudice to your privileged status, we urge you to resume the profession of rhetoric, and in the above-mentioned city, which you are aware we are restoring to its former glory, to train the minds of the young men towards the pursuit of a better life, and not to regard this duty as a slight on your former honours, since an honourable profession adorns rather than detracts from any *dignitas* which a man possesses. Finally, we also wish you to receive from public funds a payment of 600,000 *sesterces*, so that you may

[79] Philostratus, *VS* I, 23; presumably the πολιτικὸς θρόνος mentioned in II, 20.
[80] Hadrian: *VS* II, 10 (cf. p. 91–2); Theodotus, II, 2. The '10,000' mentioned here (and also in II, 11) as the pay of the holder of the chair of rhetoric would, if *drachmae* equal *denarii*, give a salary of 40,000 *sesterces* rather than 60,000.
[81] II, 11.
[82] II, 12; cf. p. 497.
[83] II, 30; cf. p. 439.
[84] II, 33; cf. p. 93. Philostratus mentions also Pausanias of Caesarea in Cappadocia, promoted from Athens to Rome (II, 13); Euodianus of Smyrna, appointed to the chair at Rome (II, 16); Heraclides of Lycia, holder of that at Athens, which he lost (II, 20, 26); and Hippodromus of Thessaly, holder at Athens (II, 27).
[85] *Syll.*³ 845; Suda N 373; see *JRS* LIX (1969), 16–17.
[86] *Pan.* v(9), 14, 4–5; cf. p. 99.

understand that our *clementia* also has recognised your deserts. Farewell, Eumenius, dearest to us.

The letter is especially valuable since we happen to have no other example of an imperial letter of appointment to a professional position. Nor do we have any formal letters of the sort addressed to the associations of performers or athletes, for sophists, philosophers and doctors did not form organized associations of this type. If matters affecting a group of such persons arose, they were probably presented to the emperor in a *libellus*, and were answered in a *subscriptio*, such as the reply of Diocletian and Maximian to 'Severinus and other *scholastici* from Arabia':[87]

> Since you affirm that you are engaged in *liberalia studia*, and especially with regard to the profession of the law, and are established for the purpose in the city of Berytus in the province of Phoenicia, we have determined that it is in the public interest and to your advantage, that each of you should not be called away from his studies before his twenty-fifth year.

These were mere students, who none the less received a temporary immunity from local obligations. But even when Hadrian, at the request of Plotina, the widow of Trajan, permits the head of the Epicurean sect in Athens to use Greek in his will nominating his successor, and to nominate a non-citizen, he does so in what seems clearly to be a *subscriptio*, directed without formulae of address or farewell, to the man as an individual.[88] What remains obscure is by what agency (an emperor?) the original rule had been laid down that the succession could pass only to a Roman citizen; at all events it was now relaxed as a concession.[89]

But if imperial relations with the philosophical sects of Athens before Marcus' measure are obscure, there was, as we saw earlier, one institution which was central to the culture of the Greek world and in which the emperors had a role from the beginning, namely the Museum in Alexandria.[90] Moreover, when Hadrian visited Alexandria in 130 he put many problems, so the *Historia Augusta* relates, to the *professores* in the Museum, and then answered them himself.[91] During the same visit a poet named Pancrates presented or recited to him an elaborate poem on the lion which the emperor had just killed in Libya; as a reward Hadrian granted him maintenance in the Museum.[92] In the same reign L. Julius Vestinus was

---

[87] *CJ* x, 50, 1.

[88] For the full text of the dossier, *CIL* III 12283; *IG²* II 1099. What survives is (a) remains of a line of Greek letters; (b) date (121); (c) Plotina's request to Hadrian (a *libellus*?); (d) Hadrian's brief reply: '[I]mp. Caesar Traianus Hadrianus Aug. Popillio Theotimo: permitto Graece testari de eis quae pertinent ad diadochen sectae Epicureae. Set cum et facilius successorem [el]ecturus sit, si ex peregrinis quoque substituendi facultatem [h]abuerit, hoc etiam praesto e[i et] deinceps ceteris [qui] diadochen habuerint: licebit vel in pe(re)greinum vel in civem Romanum ius hoc transferri'; (e) Plotina's letter in Greek 'to all her friends' about the decision.

[89] It may be that there was no specific ruling, but that as soon as one *diadochus* became a Roman citizen (as was Popillius Theotimus) he was automatically compelled to make his will in Latin, and to make testamentary dispositions (including the succession) only in favour of Roman citizens.

[90] pp. 87, 492–3.

[91] *HA, Had.* 20, 2.

[92] Athenaeus, *Deipn.* 677 D–F; for a papyrus text of part of the poem E. Heitsch, *Die griechischen Dichterfragmente der römischen Kaiserzeit* (1961), no. xv.

a studiis and *ab epistulis* after (it seems) being *epistatês* of the Museum.[93] The same term had been used for the overseer of the Museum in the Ptolemaic period, and it is possible that the post was the same as that of the priest 'in charge of the Museum' whom Strabo mentions.[94] Furthermore, the Byzantine lexicon called the 'Suda' records that Chaeremon, the teacher of Nero, was 'succeeded' in Alexandria by Dionysius, who was in charge of imperial letters, embassies and *apokrimata*.[95] It is no more than probable that the succession was as head of the Museum; but Ti. Claudius Balbillus was certainly both *supra Museum* and in charge of embassies and of rescripts or responses in Greek under Claudius.[96]

From Hadrian's reign also there is evidence that imperial patronage extended not merely to the head of the Museum but to its other members. The famous sophist Polemo was, as we saw, enrolled in the Museum by the emperor, gaining the 'upkeep' (*sitêsis*) which went with it.[97] He also gave this and other rights to Dionysius of Miletus: 'Hadrian appointed him governor of some prominent peoples, and enrolled him among holders of the "public horse" and among those who receive upkeep in the Museum (the Museum is a dining-table in Egypt to which are summoned the distinguished men from every land).'[98] There is nothing to suggest that either of those sophists took up residence in Alexandria; what was conferred by the emperor must have been the honour, the *ateleia* which went with it and perhaps an actual annual payment. The appellation 'belonging to the immune philosophers who receive upkeep in the Museum' is attached on documents to the names of prominent Egyptian citizens from 38 to the later third century;[99] and it appears also on the inscription of a man from Lydia in the early third century,[100] and on that from Rome of a famous pancratiast, M. Aurelius Asclepiades, who was also high priest for life of an association of athletes and (a post which often accompanied it) 'in charge of the imperial baths'.[101] In none of these cases is it stated that the privilege was granted by the emperor, but it is highly probable that it was—just as Dio states that Caracalla abolished the communal dinners of the Aristotelian philosophers in Alexandria, and removed their other privileges, on the supposition that Aristotle had been hostile to his model, Alexander.[102]

It was probably also from the emperor that various other persons, often of procuratorial rank, received the appellation 'belonging to those receiving

[93] p. 88.

[94] See P. M. Fraser, *Ptolemaic Alexandria* (1972), 316 (suggesting however that the two offices should be regarded as separate).

[95] Suda Δ 1173; cf. p. 87.

[96] cf. pp. 86–7.

[97] Philostratus, *VS* I, 25; cf. p. 468. His great-grandson Hermocrates seems to imply that he could have been granted it by Severus, if he had not inherited it.

[98] *VS* I, 22; on the 'public horse' see pp. 280–2.

[99] For the papyrus evidence (to which add now *P. Oxy.* 2978) see N. Lewis, 'The Non-Scholar Members of the Alexandrian Museum', *Mnemosyne* xvi (1963), 257; see also the inscription, *SB* 6012 (a *bouleutês* of Antinoopolis, who also describes himself as a 'Platonic philosopher'); A. and E. Bernard, *Les inscriptions grecques et latines du Colosse de Memnon* (1960), no. 20.

[100] J. Keil, A. von Premerstein, *Bericht über eine zweite Reise in Lydien* (1911), 107, no. 210.

[101] *OGIS* 714 = *IGR* I 154 = Moretti, *IGUR* I 241 (see also 239, 240, 250).

[102] LXXVII, 7, 3 (380).

17*

upkeep in the Museum',[103] or simply 'from the Museum'. Among the latter we may note a man who held local priesthoods in Panamara in Caria under Maximin, so between 305 and 313, and who was a 'philosopher from [the] Museum';[104] and an imperial doctor and *ducenarius* from Antioch in Pisidia in the late second or early third century, L. Gellius Maximus.[105] Exactly what is meant by 'from (the) Museum' is not clear. But there is no such doubt about another office-holder at the imperial court, M. Aurelius Hermogenes, a *patronus* of Ostia who was *a studiis* at 60,000 and then at 100,000 *sesterces* some time after the middle of the third century, and was 'sustained by the immunity of the Museum'.[106] In this context it cannot be doubted that the immunity had been granted by the emperor.

However scattered, disparate and enigmatic the evidence may be, there is enough to suggest that the Museum in Alexandria was yet another institution where the effect of monarchy, and its attendant distribution of *beneficia*, was to separate status and privilege from its original function. Yet none the less the role adopted by the emperors in relation to the Museum was an aspect of their attachment to the cultural and religious values and institutions of the Greek world. When we come to consider Constantine sitting with the bishops at Nicaea, it may not be wholly irrelevant to recall Hadrian putting problems to the scholars in the Museum, and answering them himself.

The acquisition of privileges by prominent individuals, by lesser persons who depended on them, and by communities associated with them, was an indivisible process. The landowner from Hermopolis, Aurelius Plution, whom we saw earlier writing to Gallienus and obtaining immunity for a boy who, merely descended from athletes, was himself a *ducenarius* and 'from (the) Museum'.[107] The latter distinction, like the former, will have been granted by the emperor. Moreover, in another papyrus the magistrates and council of Hermopolis write to welcome him on his return from Rome, saying, 'While you were staying in the ruling [city] you achieved the greatest success on behalf of your native city by appealing to the Fortune of our Lord Gallienus Augustus', and adorning their letter with a suitable quotation from the *Ion* of Euripides. Nothing could be more typical of the values which marked the diplomatic forms with which cities, groups and individuals clothed their contacts, direct and indirect, with the emperor, and their dependence on him not only for privileges, but for protection and succour in innumerable situations of ordinary life.

---

[103] See P. Lemerle, *BCH* LIX (1935), 131, no. 39 (Philippi) and following discussion; *AE* 1936 44.
[104] *Syll.*³ 900.
[105] See V. Nutton, 'L. Gellius Maximus, Physician and Procurator', *CQ* n.s. XXI (1971), 262, to which this section owes much.
[106] *CIL* XIV 5340; see *PIR*² A 1528; Pflaum, *Carrières*, no. 352, cf. pp. 97–8.
[107] *PIR*² A 1576; *PLRE* Plution 2. *Ducenarius* in Wilcken, *Chrestomathie*, no. 39; for ἀπὸ Μουσίου, see no. 151 (and restored with certainty in no. 39); the letter of the magistrates and council, ibid., no. 40. For his correspondence with Gallienus (ibid., no. 158), see pp. 457–8.

4. Appeals to the Emperor

> You will say to me, 'Why do you not worship the emperor?' Because he was made not to be worshipped but to be honoured with legitimate honour. He is not God, but a man appointed by God, not to be worshipped but to judge justly.

Few passages in our evidence mark out more clearly than do these words of Theophilus, bishop of Antioch, writing under Commodus, the prominence of jurisdiction in popular conceptions of the emperor's role.[1] For the reference to jurisdiction is quite explicit (*dikaiôs krinein*), is not specifically required by anything in the context, and is not supplied by any of the echoes of the New Testament with which this chapter is full. Had any better brief characterization of the essential function of the emperor seemed more apposite, it could have been used instead.

The fact that Christians came (as was natural) to share this general conception of the emperor's function is of fundamental importance for the history of the church.[2] But before we approach that topic, it is necessary to examine the various different contexts in which the emperor gave judgment; or, to view the matter from the standpoint of the parties concerned, the different routes by which cases or legal points came before him. We have already considered one, namely consultations of him by office-holders or governors, which themselves very often represented petitions or queries emanating from persons appearing before them.[3] A second, and so far as our evidence goes, much smaller category, was that of prisoners spontaneously sent by provincial governors to be judged by the emperor.[4] But the important patterns which remain to be considered are those of appeals from the courts of provincial governors, or of office-holders in Rome; requests for legal rulings or petitions for restitution of rights given to the emperor in the form of *libelli*; and cases in which he was approached (*aditus*) directly and which he heard and decided himself, as the judge of first instance.

The emperor's *subscriptiones* in response to queries or petitions are (if our evidence is not misleading) a feature of the established empire, primarily of the mid-second century and after.[5] But the emperor's role as judge, on appeal or in the first instance, takes us back to the very beginning of the empire and raises the most acute problems about its origin, legal basis (if any) and

---

[1] Theophilus, *Ad Autolycum* I, 11, trans. R. M. Grant (1970). The last sentence reads: θεὸς γὰρ οὐκ ἔστιν, ἀλλὰ ἄνθρωπος, ὑπὸ θεοῦ τεταγμένος, οὐκ εἰς τὸ προσκυνεῖσθαι, ἀλλὰ εἰς τὸ δικαίως κρίνειν.

[2] ch. ix passim.

[3] pp. 328–41.

[4] For prisoners sent by proconsuls in the first century see p. 323. For such prisoners sent from the provinces by imperial appointees see Josephus, *BJ* II, 5, 3 (77–8); *Ant.* XVII, 9, 10 (297–8), Quinctilius Varus as *legatus* of Syria, 4 BC; Dio LIX, 29, 4, a prophet of Gaius' death sent from Egypt; Tacitus, *Hist.* IV, 13, 1, Julius Civilis sent on a charge of rebellion to Nero, and *absolutus* by Galba; *BJ* III, 8, 8 (398), Vespasian intending to send Josephus to Nero; Suetonius, *Dom.* 16, 1, cf. Dio LXVII, 16, 2, a prophet of his death sent from Germany to Domitian. Compare the analogous case sent from Rome to Caracalla in Syria in 217, Dio LXXVIII, 7, 4–5 (410).

[5] p. 244.

relation to late-republican practice. His role as judge on appeal may be taken first since it alone is the subject of some statements in our sources about its origins; because it relates closely to the emperor's communications with governors and office-holders; and because it is the subject of fairly detailed and explicit evidence from the second and early third centuries, and from the tetrarchic and Constantinian periods.

The background of imperial jurisdiction on appeal is extremely obscure. In the late republic we can find, for instance, precisely one instance of a provincial appeal, a man bringing an action before Verres in Sicily and asking him (in vain) to remit the case to Rome.[6] The petitioner was not appealing against judgment, but was attempting to find an alternative to the corrupt judges whom the governor proposes to appoint. But since Verres refused the request, we do not even know whether the case would have gone to the praetor in Rome; another of Verres' victims simply fled to Rome and obtained a *senatus consultum* to the effect that he should not be condemned in his absence.[7] Alternatively, there is some slight evidence that in the city of Rome a higher or equal magistrate could be approached to nullify proceedings before another; thus when in 77 BC a eunuch applied to the praetor to be granted possession of some property, the consul was appealed to (*appellatus*) to rule that such a person had no standing in bringing an action.[8] It is to this principle, as applied to criminal jurisdiction, to which Cicero seems to be referring when he proposes in his *De legibus*: 'Let a magistrate be able to punish a disobedient and disorderly citizen by fining, chaining or beating, unless prohibited by another magistrate of equal or greater power, or by the *populus*, to whom let there be *provocatio*.'[9]

We simply do not have adequate evidence about concrete cases to know whether it was common in the late republic for a consul to be appealed to to overrule proceedings or decisions in the jurisdiction of the praetor. If it was, that may provide one element in the origins of imperial jurisdiction on appeal; for the regime of Augustus began with his holding the consulate continuously, and thereafter he and other emperors had some consular rights even apart from those years when they actually held the consulate. Our sources, however, relate such jurisdiction to other elements in the republican system, namely *provocatio* to the *populus*, and the powers of the tribunes. In the earlier republic a citizen could literally call (*provocare*) on the people, and his doing so might often result in the tribunes putting to the people a vote which might override or annul the actions of a magistrate;[10] but of this too we have no specific instances from the last century of the republic. Either by law or custom it was not used against verdicts of the permanent courts (*quaestiones perpetuae*) which existed in this period; Cicero

---

[6] II *Verr.* III, 58–6/135–40. For this episode see P. Garnsey, 'The *Lex Iulia* and Appeal under the Empire', *JRS* LVI (1966), 167, on p. 183. Cicero, *Ad fam.* XIII, 26, 3, also contains a puzzling suggestion to a governor that he should return a case 'to Rome'.

[7] II *Verr.* II, 36/88f. See E. Badian, *Foreign Clientelae* (1958), 282.

[8] Valerius Maximus, VII, 7, 6. See A. H. J. Greenidge, *The Legal Procedure of Cicero's Time* (1901), 29; see pp. 518–19.

[9] *De leg.* III, 3/6.

[10] See the very clear discussion by A. W. Lintott, 'Provocatio. From the Struggle of the Orders to the Principate', *Aufstieg und Niedergang der römischen Welt* I. 2 (1972), 226.

protested vigorously when Marcus Antonius as consul in 44 BC proposed a law by which appeal would have been possible for those condemned in these courts for violence or treason.[11]

Thus when Ulpian paraphrases the *Lex Julia de vi publica* (passed by Julius Caesar or Augustus) as forbidding office-holders to execute or punish a Roman citizen 'in the face of a *provocatio*', and when a legal source of the later third century applies it to a citizen 'appealing (*appellantem*) formerly to the *populus* and now to the emperor',[12] we cannot demonstrate that this refers to any precise transference of functions which took place at the beginning of the empire.

Our nearest approach to such an item of evidence is the notoriously enigmatic passage of Dio referring to a vote of powers to Octavian made in 30 BC: 'They also decreed that Caesar should hold the tribunician power for life, that he should aid those who called upon him for help both within the *pomerium* [the notional boundary of Rome] and outside for a distance of one mile—a privilege possessed by none of the tribunes—also that he should judge appealed cases, and that in all the courts his vote was to be cast as Athena's vote.'[13] The passage raises many problems: Augustus was to date his tribunician power from 23 BC, not 30; the tribunes could in fact exercise their powers up to a mile outside the *pomerium*; and the 'vote of Athena' (a casting vote for acquittal in the case of tied vote) could hardly have had much application in practice, and is never referred to again in connection with the emperor until an oration of Julian almost four centuries later.[14] None the less it can be accepted that a vote was passed at this time which gave Octavian the right to grant assistance (*auxilium*) in the manner of a tribune to those who requested it, and to hear cases on appeal; the reference is quite specific—'to judge when appealed to (*ekklêtos dikazein*)'.

There is of course nothing in this to indicate whether or not both criminal and civil appeals were to be entertained by him, or from which office-holders they could be made. Nor is it clear whether appeal could be against the actual jurisdiction of another, or only against his verdict, or whether the privilege applied also to the public jury-courts in Rome. To make matters worse, none of the quite numerous cases attested for Augustus' reign can be specifically identified as an appeal; though the persons whom an embassy from the free city of Cnidus accused unsuccessfully before Augustus in 6 BC may well have come spontaneously to him to avoid the prejudiced courts of their native city.[15] None the less, various general references from the

---

[11] *Phil.* I, 9/21.

[12] *Dig.* XLVIII, 6, 7; *Pauli Sent.* V, 26, 1–2. See the invaluable discussion of Garnsey, o.c., 168f., who however slips in referring to *Pauli Sententiae* as a 'mid-fourth-century compilation'. The parchment fragment of it dates to around the turn of the third and fourth centuries, see G. G. Archi, M. David, E. Levy, R. Marichal, H. L. W. Nelson, *Pauli Sententiarum Fragmentum Leidense* (*Cod. Leid. B.P.L. 2589*) (1956), esp. 57.

[13] LI, 19, 6–7, Loeb trans.

[14] *Or.* III, 114D–115A, explains the application of the custom in Athens (whereby the accuser was also freed of the charge of false accusation), and adds τοῦτον δὴ φιλάνθρωπον ὄντα καὶ χαρίεντα τὸν νόμον ἐπὶ τῶν δικῶν, ἃς βασιλεὺς κρίνει, σωζόμενον πρᾴότερον αὕτη (the Empress Eusebia) καθίστησιν.

[15] p. 443.

first few reigns make clear that *appellationes* were an established procedure. Suetonius states briefly, after mentioning other features of Augustus' conduct of his jurisdiction, that each year he delegated the appeals of litigants from Rome to the praetor and those of provincials to *consulares*, of whom one was appointed for each province.[16] If *litigatores* is intended precisely, the reference is to civil suits; but nothing more is heard of such a system of delegation until we find senators exercising jurisdiction *vice sacra*, 'in place of the emperor' from the early third century onwards.[17] Again Tiberius is stated to have held M. Junius Silanus in such high regard that he refused cases appealed from him. The only position he is known to have held in Tiberius' reign is that of suffect consul in 15; the reference *may* therefore be to his decisions as a private *iudex* appointed by the emperor to hear a case.[18] Of Gaius it is reported on the one hand that the magistrates (of Rome) were allowed to give judgment freely, without appeal to the emperor; and on the other that there were appeals to him from the senate's jurisdiction.[19] Under Claudius civil suits which had been heard by private *iudices* might also come (on appeal?) to the emperor; for he is reported to have restored the right of action to those who had lost it by claiming more than what the *formula* given to the *iudex* had stated.[20]

To list these items of evidence is to show at once that, while there certainly existed a nexus of procedures which we may reasonably label 'appeal to the emperor', we have so far not the slightest basis for statements about its conditions, limits or modes of operation. Under Nero the established nature of such appeals becomes even clearer; for he 'increased the dignity of the senators by laying down that those who appealed (*provocavissent*) from private *iudices* to the senate should be liable to a penalty of the same amount as those who appealed (*appellarent*) to the emperor'. The penalty evidently applied to civil suits; our only documentary evidence for such a thing comes from the letter of Titus to the town of Munigua, referring to a civil suit originally heard by a proconsul of Baetica.[21]

From Nero's reign, however, we have two actual instances of appeal to the emperor in criminal cases. One was heard in the senate, an accusation of incest and black magic against members of a senatorial family and others; by appealing to Nero they escaped immediate condemnation, and appear never to have been heard by him, as he was preoccupied elsewhere.[22] The other example forms a complete contrast, though its result is even more uncertain, namely the appeal of Paul when tried before Festus, the procurator of Judaea. Here at last we have a concrete case of someone who 'calls on' the emperor, and is thereby involved in a journey to Rome to appear before him. Whether the narrative of Acts tells us anything about the legal basis of such an appeal is less clear. For it is not in this connection but

[16] *Aug.* 33, 3.
[17] pp. 514–15.
[18] Dio LIX, 8, 5; see *PIR*² I 832. On emperors appointing *iudices* see pp. 512, 514–15, 525, 535.
[19] Suetonius, *Cal.* 16, 2; Dio LIX, 18, 2.
[20] Suetonius, *Claud.* 14.
[21] Tacitus, *Ann.* XIV, 28, 1; for the letter to Munigua see p. 441. Cf. also p. 512.
[22] *Ann.* XVI, 8, 2–3.

earlier, under Felix, when he is about to be beaten in Jerusalem, that Paul lays claim to the protection afforded by his Roman citizenship.[23] His subsequent appeal to Caesar is a reaction to the proposal of Festus, 'wishing to do the Jews a favour', that Paul should be judged before him in Jerusalem: 'I am standing at the tribunal of Caesar . . . I appeal to Caesar.' Even though the appeal is made and accepted (after Festus has consulted his *consilium*), when proceedings have already started, it has the character of a rejection of one court in favour of another one rather than of an appeal from a verdict— 'as Paul has appealed that he should be reserved for the judgment (*diagnôsis*) of Caesar.'[24] No adequate criterion exists for checking the historicity of the narrative of Acts; as it stands, it will tell us nothing about any precise rules of Roman law which may have been applicable in this area, but a lot about the power of the name of Caesar in the minds both of his subjects and of his appointees. It also reflects of course the presumption that, if called upon to do so, the emperor would hear in person the cases of even relatively unimportant provincials; it is unfortunate only that the narrative stops before that point is reached—and quite remarkable that so far as we know the rich imagination of the authors of apocryphal Acts did so little to fill the gap.[25]

The same expectation, as well as the ease with which it could be frustrated under a weak emperor, appears in an anecdote retailed by Dio to illustrate the power of Fonteius Capito, *legatus* of Lower Germany under Galba in 68: when a man appealed from him as he was giving justice (so again in the middle of a case?) he mounted a high tribunal, said 'Present your case before Caesar', and condemned the man to death.[26] The charade clearly reflects an established practice of appeal, which again appears to be from the jurisdiction, rather than from an actual verdict, of a provincial governor. But the emperor could also reverse verdicts, as Domitian is reported to have done with corrupt verdicts of the centumviral court in Rome.[27] He could act similarly over verdicts of the senate itself, until Hadrian in an *oratio* pronounced there laid down that appeals from senate to emperor were not permitted.[28] In the second century, however, an incomparably greater volume of evidence illustrates appeals to the emperor sometimes from local courts, sometimes from magistrates in Rome, but above all from provincial governors. The real confusion which resulted from the consequent delays in time, the necessity of journeys to Rome (or wherever the emperor was) and the mutual effects of the presentation of *libelli* by interested parties, appeals against verdicts and *consultationes* of the emperor by governors, whether spontaneous or in one of the obligatory categories,[29] gave rise to a considerable literature, whose remains in the *Digest* do not present any coherent and orderly system.[30]

[23] Acts 22, 25–6; 23, 27.
[24] Acts 25, 6–22; see Garnsey, o.c., 182–5.
[25] The Acts of Paul, however, contain a brief representation of his appearance before Nero and execution, see E. Hennecke, W. Scheemelcher, *Neutestamentliche Apokryphen*[3] II (1964), 263–7.
[26] LXIV, 2, 3 (101).
[27] Suetonius, *Dom.* 8, 1: 'ambitiosas centumvirorum sententias rescidit.'
[28] *Dig.* XLIX, 2, 1, 2.
[29] pp. 330–1.
[30] See esp. *Dig.* XLIX, 1–13.

Just how extensive and varied might be the range of cases brought on appeal to the emperor is shown by the long inscription of verdicts of Marcus Aurelius on 'appealed suits' (*ekklêtoi dikai*) from Athens.[31] The subject-matter relates to priesthoods and other offices in Athens, membership of the ancient council of the Areopagus there, membership of the Panhellenic council founded by Hadrian, possession of Athenian citizenship, and disputes about property. The courts from which appeals have been made include those of the Athenian magistrate called the *basileus* (king), the president of the *Panhellenion*, the Areopagus, and a man apparently named Gavinius Saturninus, whose status is not clear. Thus both in subject-matter and context the matters heard by the emperor on appeal have moved right outside the setting of Roman private or criminal law; none the less we find Marcus referring to the requirement of 'pledges for appealed suits in relation to the suits pleaded before me',[32] which may be related to the penalty attested under Nero and Titus. We also find him apparently appointing *iudices* (*dikastai*) to hear particular cases, or groups of future cases, primarily the two senatorial brothers whom he refers to as 'my Quintilii'.[33] If this is correct, then a large range of matters of essentially local interest and importance have been brought before the emperor, and to some extent integrated in the established procedures by which he gave justice.

These detailed judgments of Marcus on matters brought before him on appeal from Athens are a matter of documentary record, and cannot be ignored in any picture of the range of contacts which might develop between his subjects and the emperor. But just because the city was Athens and the emperor Marcus Aurelius, we cannot assume that such a pattern was typical. For a conception of what was typical we have to rely on imperial pronouncements of more general bearing. The most important of these is an imperial edict which is partially preserved on papyrus, and whose terminology and contents suggest a date in the late second or early third century.[34] In it the unnamed emperor refers to a measure 'of my divine parent' setting time-limits for cases 'sent on appeal or remission to the imperial attention', and warning interested parties to appear on time and not to depart before the verdict, otherwise cases would be decided in favour of those who were present. After a gap in the text the emperor refers to a limit of six months for cases from Italy and a year for those from beyond the Alps; 'but since capital cases permit of the help offered by [longer] delay' he will set limits of nine and eighteen months for those from across the Alps or the sea. After some advice as to the necessity of making an appearance, he seems to turn

---

[31] Edited by J. H. Oliver, *Hesperia*, Supp. XIII (1970), with emendments by C. P. Jones, *ZPE* VIII (1971), 161. Cf. pp. 5, 7, 239, 450.

[32] Plaque E, 48–52; cf. p. 510.

[33] Quintilii: e.g. E 20–3, 25–6, 39–40, 42–3, 83–4. For the puzzling evidence on the Quintilii (whom Philostratus, *VS* II, 1, describes as jointly 'ruling' Greece at this time) see Oliver, o.c., 66–72. It is not possible to state what formal position, if any, they occupied in Greece. Note also E 43: περὶ τῶν καρπῶν Ἰνγένουος δικάσει. Cf. 53–7, 81–3, 85–7.

[34] *FIRA*² I, no. 91 = Cavenaile, *Corp. Pap. Lat.*, no. 237; for a discussion of the date see A. A. Schiller, 'The First Edict of *BGU* II 628 Recto', *The Classical Tradition: Literary and Historical Studies in Honor of Harry Caplan*, ed. L. Wallach (1966), 293.

to civil cases, mentioning *appellationes* concerned with magistracies, priesthoods and other *honores*, which have inherent time-limits.[35]

The edict envisages cases coming on appeal to the emperor from the provinces as a regular occurrence, and also accepts substantial delays in time before the parties make their appearance, even without allowing for the period of the hearing itself, or for the return home of those involved. It is not surprising therefore that Papinian includes among those exempt from local obligations anyone 'who has appealed to the greatest emperors and in order to conduct his case has set off for Rome'; his immunity lasted until the *cognitio* was finished.[36]

Though in this period it was still convenient to refer to Rome as the emperor's normal domicile, the same procedures applied wherever he was. So for instance the *Codex Justinianus* preserves the verdict (*sententia*) which Septimius Severus pronounced (*dixit*) in January 209, when he will already have been in Britain:[37]

> The governor of the province ought to have given judgment first on the issue of possession and then dealt with the accusation of violence. Since he did not do so, the appeal is justified.

In this case both civil and criminal judgments were involved. On occasion it might be because of exceptional acts of violence that a case went on appeal to the emperor, as Dio implies in describing an advocate making such accusations against a man called Alexander in an appeal-case before Caracalla; the emperor was obsessed with the memory of Alexander the Great, and when the advocate spoke of 'the bloodthirsty Alexander, Alexander the enemy of the gods', he retorted angrily.[38] But even though it is evident that Caracalla was hearing the case in person, it would be a fundamental error to suppose that his doing so was itself evidence that the case was of some especial importance. Equally typical is the highly complicated issue about a will which Paulus included in his *Imperial Sententiae Issued in Cognitiones* and which will have been heard by Septimius Severus. A man named Polycrates claimed a *fideicommissum* on the basis of his father's will from his half-brother, and was successful before the proconsul of Achaea; when an appeal was made, it was rejected on the grounds that the action had been brought by only one of the half-brothers.[39] There is no indication that anything was involved other than a typical family dispute. In his *Decreta* Paulus also records a similar case from Rome where a woman sued for restitution of some property, lost her case successively before the praetor and the *praefectus urbi*, and appealed to the emperor. Paulus as *assessor* argued for a contrary verdict, but the emperor (Severus) was 'moved' by other considerations.[40] Severus is clearly hearing (and deciding) the case himself, just

[35] cf. p. 452.
[36] *Dig.* L, 5, 8, 5.
[37] VII, 62, 1.
[38] LXXVII, 8, 3 (381).
[39] *Dig.* XXXVI, 1, 83; cf. XXXII, 97, another appeal against the verdict of a governor, heard in person by the emperor.
[40] *Dig.* IV, 4, 38; cf. p. 238.

as a few years later in the 'speech of Maecenas' Dio advises the emperor to hear in person cases appealed from or referred by governors, procurators, the *praefectus urbi* and other officials in Rome.[41]

An appeal was normally lodged by presenting a *libellus* or *libelli* to the provincial governor, or other person hearing the case, a procedure which had obvious dangers if the judge were prejudiced or if the appeal implied some criticism of himself. Thus Severus pardoned one individual who because of the violence of the judge did not give the *libelli* to him but posted them publicly, and allowed him to pursue his appeal.[42] Even more explicit attempts to repress appeals were the subject of Severus Alexander's letter to the *koinon* of Bithynia, preserved both in the *Digest* and on two contemporary papyrus copies:[43]

> How anyone could be prevented by those exercising jurisdiction from appealing I do not see, since it is possible to achieve the same result by taking a different course, and to come to me instead. I forbid procurators and provincial governors to treat with insolence and violence those who make appeals, to put a guard of soldiers on them and literally to bar their road hither. They will obey this pronouncement of mine knowing that the freedom of my subjects is of as much concern to me as is their loyalty and obedience. Those however who have been condemned or have appealed against capital charges . . . [text becomes fragmentary].

Here the emperor offers himself quite explicitly as the object of appeals from his subjects, whether allowed by lesser office-holders or not. It is noticeable that for the ordinary subject the alternative was not a letter to the emperor but a journey to his presence to deliver his appeal verbally, or perhaps by *libellus*. A century later, Constantine was to warn judges in very similar terms against imprisoning appellants or setting a guard of soldiers on them, and also promises to hear in person, and to reward with dignities and wealth, any person who comes to him with justified complaints against officials.[44]

None the less it was inevitable that some steps should be taken to limit and control appeals.[45] Marcus Aurelius and Verus stated in a rescript that appeals from lower courts which were taken straight to the emperor should be referred back to the provincial governor, and that an appeal from a *iudex* appointed by a governor should go to him and not to the emperor.[46] Ulpian notes further that it was customary for the emperor to appoint a *iudex* to

---

[41] Dio LII, 33, 1; for a case appealed to Severus from a procurator see *Dig.* XLVIII, 18, 20; from the *Praefectus annonae*, XIV, 5, 8.

[42] *Dig.* XLIX, 1, 7.

[43] *Dig.* XLIX, 1, 25 = *P. Oxy.* 2104. See also 3106, and pp. 392–3.

[44] *CTh* XI, 30, 15, to the *consilium* of Africa (cf. p. 394); cf. also *CTh* XI, 30, 2 = *CJ* VII, 62, 12; *CTh* XI, 30, 4. His promise to hear complaints against officials, *CTh* IX, 1, 4 (cf. pp. 526–7).

[45] It does not seem to me certain that *IG* V 21 = Abbott and Johnson, *Municipal Administration*, no. 121, referring to appeals, emanates from an emperor; *contra*, J. H. Oliver, 'Hadrian's Reform of the Appeal Procedure in Greece', *Hesperia* XXXIX (1970), 332.

[46] *Dig.* XLIX, 1, 21, *pr.* –1. Note also the fragmentary *IGR* IV 1044 = Abbott and Johnson, *Municipal Administration*, no. 119 (Cos), asserting that appeals to the emperor should first be examined by the proconsul. A fuller text, M. Segrè and R. Herzog, *Parola del Passato* CLX (1975), 102, now shows that this was a letter to Cos from Cn. Domitius Corbulo as proconsul of Asia under Claudius.

hear a case on the condition that there should be no appeal from him—'on which condition I know that *iudices* were very often given by Divus Marcus'.[47] Again, according to Arcadius Charisius, it had previously been a matter of dispute whether there could be an appeal from the *praefectus praetorio* to the emperor, but subsequently an imperial *sententia* was read out which forbade this; the date of this change is uncertain.[48] The principle is probably not affirmed for the first time in Constantine's proclamation of 331 'to all the provincials' in which he states that appeals are allowed from other office-holders: 'From the *praefecti praetorio*, however, who alone should be described as judging "in place of the emperor" (*vice sacra*) we do not allow appeals to be made (*provocari*), lest the veneration due to us might appear to be impaired.'[49] These words might, however, serve to explain the various expressions which begin to be used of some senatorial office-holders at the beginning of the third century, and are later used of equestrian ones also, and which suggest in various ways that the persons concerned are representing the emperor in jurisdiction.[50] Sometimes it is indicated that this meant, as Constantine implies, that there could be no appeal, even to the emperor, from the verdicts of such persons; but Philip and his son, in a *subscriptio* addressed to a woman in 245, state that only the emperor could give restitution 'against the *sententia* of him who then gave judgment *vice principis*'.[51] On the other hand their role might have been to hear appeals in place of the emperor, as Constantine writes to the proconsul of Africa in 315: 'The cases on appeal, which are decided in our *auditorium* by you, to whom we delegate our judgment, you should hear in the following manner . . .'[52] As this instance shows, the function of judging *vice principis* was now often granted to regular office-holders. Constantine expresses this also in writing to the *praefectus urbi* in 321, 'your Sublimity, who takes our place in *cognitiones*'; this letter shows clearly that these, like other office-holders, could address to the emperor *consultationes* containing the representations of parties to a case, and that if this were not done properly the injured parties would resort to *querimonia* and supplication, namely to the emperor.[53]

Thus, though the appointment of persons judging *vice sacra* seems to have been an attempt to put some barriers in the way of appeals direct to the Emperor the practice of *consultationes* by officials on the one hand and the persistence of litigants on the other meant that a wide range of cases still

[47] *Dig.* XLIX, 2, 1, 4.
[48] *Dig.* I, 11, 1, 1; cf. IV, 4, 17 (Hermogenianus). See Jones, *Later Roman Empire*, ch. ii, n. 1.
[49] *CTh* XI, 30, 16; most of the relevant words are omitted from the version in *CJ* VII, 62, 19.
[50] e.g. *ILS* 8841 = *TAM* II.1 278: Pollenius Auspex (Barbieri, *Albo senatorio*, no. 412), ἐν χώρᾳ Σεβαστῶν διαγνό[ν]τος, and his son (*Albo*, no. 413), ἐν χώρᾳ Σεβασ[τ]οῦ δικάσαντος; *ILS* 1159: C. Octavius Appius Suetrius Sabinus (*cos.* 214), 'iudici ex dele[g]. cognition. Caesarian.'; *ILS* 1186: L. Caesonius Lucillus Macer Rufinianus, 'electus ad cognoscendas vice Caesaris cognitiones' (after 238); *AE* 1964 223: his son, L. Caesonius Ovinius Manlius Rufinianus Bassus, 'iudici sacrarum cognitionum vice Caesaris sine appellatione(m) cognoscendi inter fiscum et privat(o)s, item inter privatos Roma et in provinc. Africa'. See also *ILS* 716, 1190–1, 1210–11, 1213–14, 1220–1, 1227–8, 1240–1, 2941.
[51] See *AE* 1964 223 (previous note); *CJ* II, 26, 3.
[52] *CTh* XI, 30, 3.
[53] *CTh* XI, 30, 11; a small extract in *CJ* VII, 62, 16.

presented themselves in various forms for his personal attention. For no period of the empire is it possible to state clearly either the legal basis or the procedural limits of the hearing of individual cases on appeal by the emperor; and it is better merely to accept the evident, if not delimitable, facts and to see this as part of a wider social process whereby individual concerns were also passed to him by officials in the form of *consultationes*, delivered in the form of *libelli*, or brought for his personal judgment in a verbal hearing—in short to see it as one facet of the popular conception of the emperor as judge.

To be effective such a conception had of course to be shared by the emperor himself, in spite of the delays caused,[54] the journeys involved, and the amount of his own time which the giving of justice in all these forms occupied.[55] The potential conflicts between an emperor's conception of his own role as the ultimate source of justice on the one hand, and on the other the uses to which such procedures could be put by interested parties (and the strains imposed by travel to the *comitatus*), are clearly reflected in the letter by Constantine from Constantinople in 334 to an office-holder named Andronicus:[56]

> If a judgment by our Clemency is requested by anyone in a case against wards, widows, or [permanently] sick or disabled persons, such persons may not be compelled by any of our *iudices* to make themselves available at our *comitatus* . . . But if wards, widows or other persons who have suffered from the blows of fortune have begged for a judgment by our Serenity, especially if they are in terror of anyone's power, let their adversaries be compelled to make themselves available for our consideration.

5. *The Emperor as Judge of First Instance:* *Origins and Criminal Cases*

> When he was approached (*aditus*) by the parents of a girl who had been carried off, and when the man who had violated her had been found guilty, he gave as his verdict (*decrevit*) that he should be relegated. When they complained that they were being unfairly treated because the man had not been punished by death, he replied, 'Let the laws find fault with my *clementia*, but it is right that an emperor of indulgent disposition should be superior to all laws'.

This illustration which Ammianus gives of the virtues of Julian as 'Caesar' in the 350s shows how the possibility of a direct approach to the emperor for justice remained even beyond our period.[1] The conceptions of the emperor as the dispenser of justice and as the source of indulgence and

---

[54] See *CTh* XI, 30, 14 (327), for fiscal debtors causing delays by pretending to appeal.

[55] For a rare mention of this last factor note *CTh* XI, 29, 1 (Constantine to a *corrector*): 'Super paucis, quae iuridica sententia decidi non possunt, nostram debes consulere maiestatem, ne occupationes nostras interrumpas, cum litigatoribus legitimum remaneat arbitrium a sententia provocandi.'

[56] *CTh* I, 22, 2 = *CJ* III, 14, 1.

[1] XVI, 5, 12.

clementia inevitably conflicted; for, as in this instance, what was *clementia* for one party was seen as an inadequate response by the other. The conflict was even clearer in innumerable private suits over rights and properties.

Moreover, whether the emperor allowed himself to be guided strictly by the laws, or applied greater indulgence (or severity), was a matter of his choice. We could of course hardly expect that in the fourth century any laws could have bound the emperor, for he had long been able to promulgate law himself,[2] and by the early third century the doctrine was current that the emperor was 'above the laws'—though it was agreed by both emperors and others that it was proper for him to observe them.[3] But as regards the origins and basis of both criminal and civil jurisdiction of first instance, which can be easily attested, even for the very beginning of the period, we lack even those unreliable traces of measures giving a legal justification for this which we possess for his appellate jurisdiction.[4]

The problem must be stated, even though it cannot be solved. According to the accepted view, in late-republican Rome criminal cases were judged by a jury-court, presided over by a praetor or by a *quaesitor* appointed for the purpose. Civil cases came to a praetor who gave a *formula* establishing the point at issue and then passed it to a private *iudex* who actually gave judgment between the parties.[5] In consequence there was no office-holder in the city who himself heard any criminal or civil case throughout, and himself delivered a verdict or judgment on it. The fact that the emperor did precisely this therefore appears to mark a fundamental and inexplicable break with republican forms. For even if it is an illusion that anyone supposed, when Augustus had attained sole power, that 'the republic had been restored',[6] we should still expect that the procedures which he followed in ordinary business were at least closely related to those of republican magistrates. Can any such relations be found in the area of jurisdiction?

The procedure by *cognitio* (literally 'enquiry', in Greek *diagnôsis*) which the emperor used, had however been employed in criminal cases by provincial governors in the late republic,[7] as it was also, for instance, by Pompey in Sicily in 82 even though he held no pro-magistracy.[8] Cicero's *Verrines* also show that on occasion, rather than appoint a *iudex*, Verres, as governor

---

[2] For the various forms of pronouncement in which he did so see p. 206.

[3] The principle is, however, applied primarily to their own affairs: *Dig.* I, 3, 31 (Ulpian, *ad legem Juliam et Papiam*): 'Princeps legibus solutus est: Augusta autem licet legibus soluta non est, principes tamen eadem illi privilegia tribuunt, quae ipsi habent'; Dio LIII, 18, 1 (and LIII, 28, 1–2, erroneously generalizing a grant to Augustus in 24 BC); *Dig.* XXXII, 23 (Paulus); Justinian, *Inst.* II, 17, 8 (Severus and Caracalla); *CJ* VI, 23, 3 (Severus Alexander).

[4] p. 509.

[5] This is of course a grossly over-simplified summary. For the basic discussion, A. H. J. Greenidge, *The Legal Procedure of Cicero's Time* (1901).

[6] For the argument (not universally accepted) see 'Triumvirate and Principate', *JRS* LXIII (1973), 50.

[7] See e.g. Cicero, II *Verr.* I, 28/71–30/76 (C. Claudius Nero, in Asia 80 BC); II *Verr.* II, 28/68–30/75; 37/91f. (Verres); cf. Valerius Maximus VIII, 7, 6: P. Licinius Crassus *decreta reddens* from his tribunal in Asia in 132/1 BC; Diodorus XXXVII, 5, 2–3: Q. Mucius Scaevola delivering sentences in Asia in 97 BC; perhaps also Valerius Maximus VIII, 1, *amb.* 2.

[8] See II *Verr.* II, 46/113: Sthenius *accusatus* before Pompey, and *absolutus* by him; cf. Diodorus XXXVIII/IX, 20.

of Sicily, would hear civil cases himself.[9] The steps by which similar procedures came to be used in Rome and Italy are far from clear. In the first
place we cannot make too confident a distinction between the role of a
consul and *pro consule*, for it was still possible in the late republic up to
52 BC for a man to have his *provincia* during his year as consul, and to
proceed to it before the end of the year.[10] In exceptional circumstances
Pompey could be consul in 52, remaining near Rome, while still retaining
the Spanish provinces. Moreover, as the example of Cicero on his way to
Cilicia shows, a governor could be approached by embassies and private
persons from his province even before he reached its borders.[11]

More suggestive than such possibilities however is the brief reference in
the Epitome of Livy to Sulla during his campaign in 83 being approached by
litigants, whom he ordered to give a guarantee (*vadimonium*) to appear in
Rome, which was still held by his enemies.[12] His formal status was (at best)
that of proconsul of Asia,[13] and no one could have known what position he
would occupy in Rome when and if finally victorious. None the less *litigatores* pursuing private suits approached him, and were not repulsed. There
seems to be no way in which this report can be related to the received patterns
of republican jurisdiction.

A different set of problems is presented by the jurisdiction of Julius Caesar
in 49–44. Even if we set aside for the moment his semi-judicial hearings and
decisions in relation to his political enemies, we can see various instances of
his giving judgment both in the provinces and in Rome. In the circumstances
it is perhaps meaningless to ask whether he did so *qua* consul, as he was in 48,
and from 46 until the end of September 45, and in 44, or as dictator, as he
was briefly in 49, from autumn 48 to autumn 47, and from the late spring of
46 onwards. In Asia Minor in 47 he is twice explicitly described as exercising jurisdiction, and we have already noted Nicolaus' description of his
jurisdiction (*dikaiodosia*) at Carthago Nova in Spain in 45.[14] He also gave
judgment in Rome. Valerius Maximus relates an incident which took place
'when his victories were complete' (so after the spring of 45), and when he was
giving judgment (*ius dicentem*) in the Forum from a tribunal.[15] From the
same period and probably the same place, Seneca tells a story of a veteran of
the last Spanish campaign appearing before Caesar in a case relating to a
dispute over property with his neighbours, in which he was alleged to have
used violence. It is not clear whether the issue was purely a civil one relating
to ownership, or involved also a criminal charge; in the later *cognitiones* by

[9] II *Verr*.1, 10/27; II, 9/25; 25/60–1. He also annulled the decisions of *iudices* appointed by himself, 13/33 ('si quis perperam iudicasset, se cogniturum'); 27–66.
[10] See J. P. V. D. Balsdon, 'Consular Provinces under the Late Republic', *JRS* XXIX (1939), 57.
[11] Cicero, *Ad Att*. V, 13, 1; VI, 1, 6; 2, 9.
[12] *Epit*. 86: 'Itemque ex fiducia iam certae victoriae litigatores, a quibus adibatur, vadimonia
Romam deferre iussit, cum a parte diversa urbs adhuc teneretur.'
[13] No source formally states that he had been deprived of his *imperium*; but Appian, *BC* I,
73/340, records more than this, that his house was destroyed, his property confiscated, and he
himself declared a *hostis*.
[14] *Bell. Alex.* 65, 4: 'Commoratus fere in omnibus civitatibus ... de controversiis veteribus
cognoscit ac statuit'; 78, 1: 'Ita per Gallograeciam Bithyniamque in Asiam iter facit omniumque
earum provinciarum de controversiis cognoscit et statuit.' See p. 466.
[15] VI, 2, 11. See *JRS* LXIII (1973), 60.

emperors or governors both could have been heard. This too is described as a *cognitio*, and the verdict is issued by Caesar. For when the man finally establishes his identity as a veteran who had done a personal service to him, Caesar orders that the action against him shall not proceed, and awards the fields in dispute to him.[16]

From the same few months also Valerius Maximus briefly relates how a man who pretended to be the son of Marius, and held a *salutatio* rivalling that of Caesar, was relegated from Italy by the *decretum* of Caesar.[17] Whether *decretum* here implies a formal verdict (as it would have done later) must remain in doubt. It is far more significant that Caesar appears to have exercised some regular jurisdiction—'he gave judgment very conscientiously and very severely', as Suetonius notes[18]—and *not* merely in relation to political issues. Could he perhaps have done so *qua* consul? It is normally assumed that the consuls did not exercise a regular jurisdiction in the late republic.[19] But they perhaps began to usurp semi-judicial power, for Cicero mentions a man who had been relegated by Gabinius as consul in 58 BC— 'which before that time never happened to a Roman citizen in Rome'.[20] Moreover, the consuls could still on occasion be entrusted with carrying out a *cognitio* on a particular topic, as for instance in the law of June 44 BC empowering them to enquire into all the individual measures of Caesar. Under this heading they held a hearing over whether the land of the Buthrotians in Epirus had been duly distributed to veterans. Documents were produced, and the proceedings concluded by the consuls giving a verdict 'on the advice of their *consilium*' in favour of the Buthrotians.[21] But Nicolaus also describes how, when the consuls were out of Rome for the *Feriae Latinae* of 47 BC, the young Octavian acted as their deputy 'for jurisdiction' (that is as *praefectus urbi*); 'Caesar took his seat on the tribunal in the middle of the Forum, immense numbers approached him for justice . . .'[22] An anecdote in Appian referring to 31 or 30 BC may also be relevant, for in it he refers to a consul both as giving judgment and as attempting to demand a *vadimonium* from the mother of a conspirator, the younger Lepidus, for her appearance before Octavian.[23]

The evidence is thus poor, varied and inconclusive, but it *may* be that people approached the consuls for justice more regularly than has been

[16] *De ben.* v, 24.

[17] IX, 15, 1.

[18] *Jul.* 43, 1.

[19] See Mommsen, *Staatsrecht*[3] II, 101f.; for the hypothesis of a law of the Augustan period granting 'exercitio iudicii publici' to the emperor, consuls and perhaps others see A. H. M. Jones, *Studies in Roman Government and Law* (1960), 67f., esp. 90f. (applied to primary criminal jurisdiction only).

[20] *Ad fam.* XI, 16, 2.

[21] Cicero, *Ad Att.* XVI, 16, 11 (16c, 2): 'Quae lex earum rerum quas Caesar statuisset, decrevisset, egisset, consulibus cognitionem dedit. Causa Buthrotium delata est ad consules. Decretum Caesaris recitatum est et multi praeterea libelli Caesaris prolati. Consules de consilii sententia decreverunt secundum Buthrotios.' Cf. p. 241.

[22] *FGrH* 90 F. 127, V (13).

[23] *BC* IV, 49–50/215–19. The consul 'Balbinus' is not known from any other evidence, but *may*, as suggested in *RE* s.v. 'Balbinus' (2), be identical with L. Saenius, *suffectus* in 30 BC. The anecdote forms part of Appian's set of illustrations of the varied turns of fortune in the proscriptions, and errors could easily have crept in.

realized, and it *may* even be that it was as consul that Caesar gave judgment in the Forum in the last months of his life. But the evidence, slight as it is, for his jurisdiction in the provinces, and even more the story of the *litigatores* who approached Sulla in 83, may suggest that people tended now to turn for justice to anyone wielding exceptional power, without regard to the formalities of their position.

Appian's anecdote, however, also relates to a different pattern of jurisdiction (or something roughly resembling it), namely the judgments over life or death, rights and property carried out in relation to their political enemies by Caesar and the triumvirs. These political judgments, like those of the emperors themselves in relation to persons accused of treason or conspiracy, are not central to our essential theme here, namely the role of the emperor as the source of justice for his subjects. But they do present a number of relevant aspects. First, they were on occasion carried out in the form of public verbal hearings in which speeches might be made by or on behalf of the person concerned. The classic instance of such a speech is Cicero's *For Ligarius*, spoken before Caesar in the Forum in 46 BC. The occasion had to a large extent the character of a judicial hearing, for a speech accusing Ligarius was made first by Aelius Tubero, and answered by that of Cicero, pleading for permission for Ligarius to return to Italy.[24] But as Quintilian saw, the function of a speech of this type was not really to answer an accuser, but to appeal to the clemency of the judge:[25]

> A *deprecatio*, which is devoid of any semblance of defence, is indeed relatively rare, and is used only before those *iudices* who are not bound to any fixed form of verdict. Moreover, even those speeches made before Caesar and the Triumvirs on behalf of men of the opposite party, even if they employ *preces*, involve some element of defence—unless it is not the mark of a man making a very bold defence to say, 'What else have we done, Tubero, except in order that we should be able to do what this man can do?' So if we have to say before the emperor (or anyone else who is free to choose his response) that the man for whom we are appearing is worthy of death but should none the less be preserved, as a mark of clemency, or something of the sort, we are addressing ourselves above all not to our adversary but to the judge ...

Caesar, after the victories of Pharsalus and Thapsus, and Octavian, after Actium and then after the capture of Alexandria, appear to have held regular sessions at which they decided on the punishment or release of the leading men among the captives.[26] Such sessions in particular, and the whole period of the civil wars and proscriptions in general, provided the context for the second significant feature of the proceedings, the role played by petitions from third parties in securing the release or restoration of their friends. Cicero's letters from the period of Caesar's dictatorship return

[24] See Quintilian, *Inst.* XI, 1, 78f. (Tubero's speech); Plutarch, *Cic.* 39, 7 (Caesar's reaction to Cicero's speech); *Dig.* 1, 2, 2 46.

[25] *Inst.* V, 13, 5–6 (quotation from *Pro Lig.* 4/10).

[26] e.g. Dio XLI, 62, 2–3 (Pharsalus); XLIII, 13, 2–3 (Thapsus); LI, 2, 4 (Actium); LI, 16, 1 (Alexandria).

constantly to his activities in this connection,[27] and similar efforts, with varying success are recorded after the final victories of Octavian.[28] The third feature is very clearly revealed by a letter of Cicero, namely that one consequence of the power of life and death wielded by individuals without any effective restraint of law was that it could fall to those individuals to make consequential decisions on matters of civil law. In 46 Cicero wrote in very formal style to L. Munatius Plancus, asking him to intercede with Caesar in the matter of the will of one T. Antistius who had been in the wrong place during the civil war, but had been careful to do nothing. When he died, leaving C. Ateius Capito as heir to most of his property, there was nothing concrete against him, but it still required Caesar's confirmation before the inheritance could pass: 'I ask and beseech you . . . to strive to bring it about that by my commendation, your support, and the *beneficium* of Caesar, C. Capito may secure his inheritance from his relative.'[29]

Though even these cases could thus involve what were effectively decisions on matters of civil law, the judgments which an emperor passed on those who had fought or conspired against him (or were alleged to have done so) were necessarily something rather different from the rest of his jurisdiction, since his own interests and safety were directly involved. Such jurisdiction grew directly out of the irregular hearings and executions of the civil war period, and so, probably, did the equally invidious practice of confiscating the property of the condemned (*bona damnatorum*) for the benefit of the emperor.[30] As is well known, however, many such accusations, of conspiracy or the wider range of offences classified as *maiestas* (treason) were heard in the senate, at least up to the third century.[31] Moreover, many of the emperors from the late first to early third century are recorded to have sworn on accession not to execute any senators (though not all kept the oath).[32] Dio is clearly reflecting a long-established view when he makes 'Maecenas' advise Augustus to ignore reports of slanders against him, but to bring accusations of actual conspiracy before the senate.[33] In the case of the revolt of Avidius Cassius in 175 Marcus Aurelius had sent the senatorial participants for trial to the senate, but judged the others in his own court.[34]

We do, however, find quite frequent instances of emperors judging real or

[27] e.g. *Ad fam.* IX, 9, 3; *Ad Att.* XI, 20; *Ad fam.* XIII, 19; VI, 6, 10, 12. See also Nicolaus, *FGrH* 90 F. 127 (vii); Cornelius Nepos, *v. Attici* 7, 3 (12, 2–4); Dio XLI, 62 2: πλὴν εἴ τινας οἱ φίλοι αὐτῶν ἐξητήσαντο.

[28] e.g. Dio LI, 2, 5; Plutarch, *Ant.* 72, 3–4, with Josephus, *BJ* I, 20, 3 (393–4); *Ant.* XV, 6, 7 (197); Plutarch, *Ant.* 80, 3–4.

[29] *Ad fam.* XIII, 29.

[30] pp. 163–74.

[31] For the origins of the senate's jurisdiction see J. Bleicken, *Senatsgericht und Kaisergericht* (1962); for *maiestas*, R. H. Bauman, *The Crimen Maiestatis in the Roman Republic and Augustan Principate* (1967); *Impietas in Principem* (1974). Dio LXXVI, 8–9, describes a *maiestas* case heard in the senate in about 205. The senate could still impose criminal penalties in the early fourth century, see Firmicus Maternus, *Math.* II, 29, 13, and T. D. Barnes, *JRS* LXV (1975), 47.

[32] For a discussion see A. R. Birley, 'The Oath Not to Put Senators to Death', *CR* n.s. XII (1962), 197.

[33] LII, 31, 5–10.

[34] Dio LXXI, 28, 2–3 (268); for a *vaticinator* involved in the revolt, whom Marcus relegated, see *Coll.* XV, 2, 5.

supposed conspirators in person, interrogating them, on occasion being present when they were put to the torture, and determining the penalty.[35] Thus Dio reports the speech of a senator who was tried before Severus as an adherent of Pescennius Niger, and who so far succeeded in justifying his action that the emperor confiscated only half his property.[36] Such trials would normally involve a formal speech by an orator setting out the charges. Dio describes how a man was accused of taking down statues of the praetorian prefect, Plautianus, while governor of Sardinia. The orator declared that the heavens would fall before Plautianus suffered anything from Severus, and the emperor confirmed this in an aside to his *assessores*, among whom was Dio himself.[37]

Although in certain circumstances persons might be examined and punished without a formal accusation, this was clearly exceptional.[38] Tacitus, for instance, records how an informer tried to gain access (*aditus*) to Tiberius to lay information against Libo Drusus.[39] This being so, the way was open for private persons to use accusations of conspiracy or *maiestas* as a means of damaging or removing personal enemies, and furthering their own interests. Thus under certain circumstances even charges relating to the emperor himself could reflect private initiatives for private purposes. We see an extreme instance of this in the accusation brought by his enemies in Bithynia against Dio of Prusa, in which they added to the original charge of peculation another of *maiestas*, alleging that a statue of Trajan had been placed in conjunction with the tombs of Dio's wife and son. This particular charge only reached Trajan because Pliny consulted him about it, and it was immediately ruled out.[40] But it renders the possible uses of *maiestas* charges, even in provincial society, clearly comprehensible.

Except perhaps for those cases where Augustus seems to have imposed semi-judicial penalties on individuals as a matter of public order,[41] the same necessity of formal accusation applied normally to all of the wide range of criminal charges which emperors could hear if they wished. Ulpian notes as an exception that when a senator was found to have kept his wife although she had been detected in adultery, Severus condemned him 'even without

[35] e.g. Strabo, XIV, 5, 4 (670), Athenaeus of Seleucia, an associate of Murena, acquitted by Augustus; Dio LIV, 15, 4; Seneca, *De clem.* I, 9 (Augustus intending to call a *consilium amicorum* to try Cn. Pompeius Cinna Magnus); I, 10, 3 (Augustus condemning adulterers of Julia); Josephus, *Ant.* XIX, 4, 5 (268), Claudius and the assassins of Gaius; Tacitus, *Ann.* XI, 2, Valerius Asiaticus before Claudius, cf. Dio LX, 29, 4–6; *Ann.* XI, 34–5, Claudius trying Messalina and Silius; XV, 58, Nero and conspirators of 65; Dio LXXVIII, 35, 3 (444), Elagabal executing Basilianus at Nicomedia; Zosimus, I, 56, Aurelian trying Zenobia and her adherents at Emesa; Firmicus, *Math.* II, 29, 14 and 17–18, Ceionius Rufius Albinus exiled by Constantine for adultery and *absconsae litterae*.
[36] LXXIV, 9 (333); cf. p. 237.
[37] LXXV, 16, 3–4 (355–6). Compare Quintilian's references (*Inst.* VIII, 5, 16; IX, 2, 20; 3, 66; 4, 31) to the speech with which Domitius Afer defended Cloatilla before Claudius.
[38] In the speech of 'Maecenas' Dio LII, 31, 10, recommends this in the case of an army commander who has rebelled openly.
[39] *Ann.* II, 28, 1–2. Cf. Dio LXI, 16, 3, accusations against people who said that Nero had murdered Agrippina, not accepted by the emperor.
[40] *Ep.* X, 81–2.
[41] Suetonius, *Aug.* 45, 4; Jerome, *Chron.* on 28 BC (ed. Helm, pp. 163/4); perhaps also Valerius Maximus IX, 15, 2 (a man pretending to be the son of Octavia sent to the galleys).

an accuser'.[42] To make clear the significance of this, it is essential to emphasize that it is impossible to demonstrate that there was any category of criminal accusation which by law or custom, could only be brought before the emperor. In all instances alternative courts existed, and for a case to come to the emperor required a positive choice, normally on the part of the accuser—as it did, when an appeal was made, on the part of the defendant. Moreover it also required a willingness on the part of the emperor to hear it, since it was invariably open to him to refuse, if he so wished.

That the court of the emperor functioned as an alternative to other courts is particularly clear from two items of evidence from the reign of Augustus. As is notorious, we have no evidence to make clear by whom Ovid was accused nor even precisely of what crime. But, looking back on the process from his exile on Tomi, Ovid was able to draw some slight consolation from his condemnation by Augustus:[43]

> You did not have my misdeeds condemned by a decree of the senate, nor was my exile ordered by a *iudex selectus*. Having reproached me with regretful words, as was appropriate for the Princeps, you took revenge yourself, as was suitable, for the offences against you. Add that the *edictum*, unrelenting and stern though it was, was mild as regards the name of the penalty, since in it I am called a *relegatus*, not an exile . . .

The poem is intelligible only if it had been Augustus' own choice to hear the case himself. The same implication is perfectly clear in a story narrated by Dio under the year AD 10. Since the popular Germanicus was about to defend a quaestor on a charge of murder, the accuser was afraid that he would fail if the case were brought before the ordinary *quaestio*; so he asked, successfully, for it to come before Augustus himself; but in vain, for the man was acquitted.[44] Similarly, after the death of Germanicus in Syria in AD 20, his friends requested that Tiberius should agree to hold the *cognitio* to hear the accusation that he had been murdered. The emperor, with a few *amici* to assist him, heard 'the threats of the accusers and the *preces* (of the accused)' and referred the case back to the senate.[45] He did the same a few years later, when a praetor who had murdered his wife was 'brought before Caesar' by his brother-in-law.[46] By contrast, as we saw, an embassy from Bithynia under Trajan was to request that the question of accusations against a proconsul should be dropped by the senate, so that the matter could be reserved for the *cognitio* of Caesar.[47] So also, when Herodes Atticus was intending to accuse his Athenian opponents before the proconsul of Achaea, they went directly to Marcus Aurelius at Sirmium; he duly heard the

---

[42] *Dig.* XLVIII, 5, 2, 6. From the context it appears that this occurred when Severus was hearing the original case of adultery.

[43] *Tristia* II, 131–7; for other references to his condemnation and relegation, see I, 2, 95–6; IV, 9, 11–12; V, 2b, 11–14; II, 15 and 21–3. We should have expected Augustus' pronouncement to be called *decretum*. Whether the use of *edictum* here is significant is not clear.

[44] LVI, 24, 7.

[45] Tacitus, *Ann.* III, 10.

[46] *Ann.* IV, 22, 1–2.

[47] p. 349.

case, which evidently consisted of mutual accusations by the two sides.[48]

More than a century and a half earlier, under Augustus, the opponents of Julius Eurycles, the dynast of Sparta, had twice accused him before the emperor of violence and disorder in Achaea. They too could presumably have gone to the proconsul. If they did not do so, it will have been because the power and favour of Eurycles meant that only a verdict from the emperor would be effective. That one of the accusers was a descendant of the great Spartan general of the fifth century, Brasidas, and was not averse to reminding the emperor of the fact, may also have contributed to their confidence in bringing the case, and (on the second occasion) securing Eurycles' exile.[49] We may contrast with this Pliny's brief report of one of the *cognitiones* of Trajan in which he took part at Centumcellae: 'There stood trial Claudius Aristion, *princeps* of the Ephesians, a man munificent and popular, but not in a harmful way. Hence an accuser was put up, out of envy and by persons very different from himself. So he was acquitted and freed.'[50]

If he were not aware of the prosecution from the beginning, and had not gone spontaneously to make his defence, a provincial might find himself being summoned to the emperor in order to do so. Thus Philostratus represents Apollonius as being summoned from Asia to appear before Domitian in Rome,[51] and Arrian's record of Epictetus' discourses at Nicopolis represents him as saying to someone:

> And if Caesar sends for you when you are under accusation, remember to make the proper distinctions. And similarly if anyone comes up to you as you are pale with terror before going in, and says, 'Why are you afraid, fellow? What issues will be at stake for you? Surely it is not that Caesar can give virtue or vice to those who come before him?'

The situation is probably the same with the man whom he addresses earlier, who is about to sail across the Adriatic to be judged by Caesar, and is in danger of being sent into exile.[52]

Mere distance must have had some influence in reducing the volume of accusations of provincials made directly before the emperor, and social considerations also will have affected access to his judgment. This is visible for instance in Josephus' story of how a senator brought to Tiberius the issue of how his wife had been tricked into having intercourse with an *eques*, whereupon the *eques* was exiled, and other participants crucified.[53] In the first and early second centuries at least, we have sufficient evidence to show that social or family crimes in upper-class Roman society readily attracted the emperor's notice. Suetonius records the case of an *eques* against whom powerful enemies produced a false charge of corrupting women. The case

---

[48] Philostratus, *VS* II, 1; cf. p. 4.

[49] Strabo VIII, 5, 5 (366); Josephus, *BJ* I, 26, 4 (531); Plutarch, *Mor.* 207 F (Brasidas' descendant). See G. W. Bowersock, 'Eurycles of Sparta', *JRS* LI (1961), 112. Cf. p. 236.

[50] *Ep.* VI, 31, 3. For the extensive epigraphical evidence for Aristion's role in Ephesus see Sherwin-White, ad loc.; *AE* 1967 467, 472; *JÖAI* XLIX (1968–71), Beibl. 35f., nos. 9–10.

[51] *V. Ap. Ty.* VII, 10.

[52] Epictetus, *Diss.* II, 19, 17; 6, 20–7; cf. *JRS* LV (1965), 146.

[53] *Ant.* XVIII, 3, 4 (65–80).

was heard by Claudius in person, and when the man found prostitutes being called to give evidence against him, he threw the pen and *libelli* which he was holding in his hand at the emperor's face.[54] How this case reached the emperor is unclear, as it is in Statius' brief reference to Domitian's condemnation of the wife of Vettius Bolanus for poisoning, and the report that Hadrian relegated a *matrona* for cruelty to her slave-girls.[55] But Pliny's letters illustrate several possible procedures for bringing criminal cases to the emperor's attention. In one instance a mother, after the death of her son, brought to Trajan an accusation that his freedmen, who were co-heirs with herself, were guilty of forgery and poisoning. Moreover she asked for, and obtained, the ex-consul Julius Servianus as *iudex*, after whose *cognitio* the case appears to have been referred to an ordinary jury-court. When this acquitted the accused, the woman approached (*adiit*) the emperor again, saying that she had new evidence, whereupon Sex. Attius Suburanus was detailed to hold a further hearing. There are many problems about the legal background and unparalleled procedure in this case,[56] but what is clear is the availability of the emperor to approach by anyone who was sufficiently persistent, the flexibility of the possible procedures and the degree to which they might depend on the suggestion of an interested party.

The unnamed woman had apparently approached Trajan in person. But, as we saw, it was possible for office-holders or other persons of sufficient prominence to address the emperor by letter,[57] and this means of approach could also be used for bringing accusations. Pliny was in the *consilium*, for instance, on one occasion when Trajan heard charges which a provincial governor had originally made by letter against one of his *comites*; in this instance too mutual accusations were made, and the emperor was free to choose which of the parties he would regard as the accused, and thus on whose guilt or innocence he would seek the opinions of his advisers.[58] Cases of this origin were also heard by Trajan on the second and third days of Pliny's participation in the *cognitiones* at Centumcellae. On the second, there was that of a military tribune's wife who had committed adultery with a centurion. The tribune had written to the consular *legatus* of the unnamed province and he to Trajan. There is nothing to indicate that any proceedings had begun before the *legatus*, and it was presumably at his request that the emperor heard the case. The centurion was dismissed and relegated without further proof, while the husband had to be compelled (under the Augustan adultery-law) to carry through an accusation of his wife. Pliny's report ends with a significant indication of the tendency of cases to gravitate towards the emperor, unless counter-measures were taken: 'Caesar added the name of the centurion and an allusion to military discipline to his *sententia*, in order that he should not seem to be reserving (*revocare*) all such cases to

---

[54] *Claud.* 15, 4.
[55] Statius, *Silvae* v, 2, 75–97, esp. 91–3; *Dig.* I, 6, 2 = *Coll.* III, 3, 4. Cf. also *Dig.* XXIV, 2, 8, and XLVIII, 9, 5.
[56] *Ep.* VII, 6, 8–13. For the problems see the valuable discusion by Sherwin-White, ad hoc.
[57] pp. 215–16, 469–72.
[58] *Ep.* VI, 22, 1–6.

himself.'[59] None the less, it may be noted, Papinian makes clear that Marcus Aurelius and subsequent emperors regularly heard adultery cases.[60]

On the third day came the case over the alleged forgery of part of the will of a senator, Julius Tiro. Perhaps because the two accused were an *eques* and an imperial *libertus* and procurator, the heirs had written to Trajan when in Dacia and asked him to take the case, which he did. It is quite clear here, as elsewhere, that he was free to decline. As Trajan's conduct of the case was to show, he took it precisely because one of his own freedmen was involved, and he wished to demonstrate that justice could be done.[61] In a rather different way, when a senator, Fabricius Veiento was accused in 62 of slanderous writings about prominent senators, the accuser added the charge that he had sold 'the gifts of the emperor and the right of seeking office' (that is his influence in obtaining these from the emperor): 'This was the reason for Nero's acceptance of the case,' Tacitus says, and Veiento was banished, only to resume a successful and notorious career in the Flavian period.[62]

It was naturally common to go before the emperor in order to accuse his freedmen or appointees. A sympathetic hearing could not of course be guaranteed: Tacitus describes how when 'Asia' (the *koinon*?) accused Publius Celer, Nero's procurator of the province, in 57, the emperor, while unable to acquit him, dragged out the case until the man died of old age.[63] It could also be an honour for an orator, and no doubt a source of favour, 'to shield and defend those *liberti* and procurators themselves before the emperor'.[64] On the other hand an emperor might be regarded as positively eager to hear accusations of governors, and carry out sentences on them: Herodian describes accusations being laid against governors and commanders before Maximinus the Thracian, and the men thsemselves being forced to travel to the emperor in Pannonia, to be condemned by him to death or exile.[65] By contrast Eusebius expresses the most profound satisfaction in describing how, when the tetrarch Maximin visited Caesarea in about 307, he condemned to death Urbanus, the *praeses* of Palaestina.[66]

Eusebius does not say what accusations were brought against Urbanus or by whom. But what he saw as the operation of divine justice against a persecutor, others will have seen as an example of the cruelty of a tyrant. The emperor's readiness to hear accusations against office-holders could of course be seen as part of his function of dispensing justice to his people, and is expressed as such most clearly of all in the proclamation which Constantine addressed 'to all the provincials' from Nicomedia in 325:[67]

---

[59] VI, 31, 4–6. For a comparable issue relating to civil cases about wills see pp. 532–3. For Gaius condemning the *comes* of a *legatus* for having a woman in the *principia*, Plutarch, *Galba* 12, 2–3.
[60] *Dig.* XLVIII, 18, 17, *pr.*
[61] *Ep.* VI, 31, 7–12. Cf. pp. 77, 470.
[62] Tacitus, *Ann.* XIV, 50; cf. *PIR²* F 91.
[63] *Ann.* XIII, 33, 1.
[64] Tacitus, *Dial.* 7, 1.
[65] VII, 3, 3–4.
[66] *Mart. Pal.* 7, 7: ἡ θεία . . . δίκη . . . δικαστὴν ἀπηνῆ καὶ ὠμότατον ἐπ' αὐτῆς τῆς Καισαρείας καταστήσασα, ὡς καὶ τὴν ἐπὶ θανάτῳ κατ' αὐτοῦ ψῆφον ἐξενεγκεῖν.
[67] *CTh* IX, 1, 4. The key words are 'intrepidus et securus accedat, interpellet me: ipse audiam omnia. ipse cognoscam et si fuerit comprobatum ipse me vindicabo.'

If there is anyone belonging to any place, order or dignity who is confident that he can truthfully and clearly prove against any of my *iudices, comites, amici* or *palatini* anything which appears to have been done corruptly or unjustly, let him approach without fear or anxiety, and let him petition me. I shall hear the whole matter myself, I shall judge it myself and if it is proved I will exact retribution myself.

The criminal justice of the emperor could be seen in less elevated terms: according to Firmicus Maternus, writing under Constantine, whoever was born in the eighteenth section of Libra 'will be put on the cross by order of the emperor, or tortured in his presence or hanged by imperial command'.[68] Whatever its legal justification, if any, the emperor's power to inflict death, confiscation or exile was from the beginning an integral part of his role, an inheritance it seems from the summary hearings, punishments and confiscations of the civil war period. So was the informal and untrammelled procedure by which it was exercised, and (as Firmicus Maternus reflects) the immediate and drastic cruelties which could accompany it. We may recall Suetonius' story of Tiberius on Capri being so intent on the examination by torture of suspects that when a former host of his from Rhodes arrived, 'summoned by letter as a friend', he automatically ordered him to be tortured, and when the mistake became evident, had him killed.[69] But the essential fact from the beginning was that now capital punishments could be inflicted by one man, influenced but not bound by the opinions of his *consilium*. Dio describes how Maecenas, attending Augustus at a capital trial, saw that the emperor intended to pass a large number of death penalties, and, being unable to push through the crowd to dissuade him, threw a note into his lap with the words, 'Rise for once, executioner!'[70]

The ability of the emperor to inflict punishments by his personal decision is perhaps the most concrete and specific of all the features of monarchy which were established from the beginning. It was recognized both in the despatch of men to him for judgment,[71] and in the bringing of criminal accusations before him. The motives of the accusers were various, but among them we must give a certain place to the conception which saw the emperor as the ultimate source of justice. For instance, we find Caracalla in 216 (and hence while he was in Syria), having given a hearing 'in the manner of a *cognitio*' (*cognitionaliter*), issuing a verbal ruling on the procedure to be adopted in a case where a woman was alleged to have poisoned her husband.[72] No political issues nor interests of the emperor himself were involved, and it may be presumed that a party to the case brought it to him in order to obtain such a ruling. Nevertheless, it is essentially not in his criminal jurisdiction but in his decisions on matters of private law that we see most clearly how important the giving of justice was among the emperor's responses to his subjects.

[68] *Math.* VIII, 25, 6.
[69] *Tib.* 61, 1.
[70] LV, 7, 2. It cannot be *assumed*, as by Bleicken, *Senatsgericht und Kaisergericht*, 77, that the episode belongs to the triumviral period.
[71] pp. 323, 507.
[72] *CJ* IX, 41, 3.

6. *The Routine of Jurisdiction: Civil Cases*

Nothing could be easier than to show that in the established empire of the second and third centuries the giving of justice had a central place in popular conceptions of the imperial role. The evidence is, as always, partial and fragmentary, but in sum entirely conclusive. Appian, from Alexandria, and Polyaenus from Macedonia both mention that they themselves had appeared as advocates before the emperors.[1] Similarly Censorinus, addressing his *De die natali* in 238 to Q. Caerellius, a local senator and *sacerdos* of equestrian rank, says: 'I say nothing also of your *eloquentia*, which all the tribunals of our provinces and all the governors have known, and which finally the city of Rome and the sacred [imperial] *auditoria* have admired.'[2] 'Our provinces' here are certainly in the Latin west, though whether African, Spanish or Gallic remains unclear; but sixty years later, as we saw, Eumenius portrays the youth of Autun as being brought up to do service in the *sacrae cognitiones*, whence they might even rise to the *magisteria palatii* themselves.[3]

Moreover, when Artemidorus of Daldis in his *Oneirocrita* collects instances of dreams, how they were interpreted at first and what their meaning turned out to be, he includes several on the part of persons engaged in cases before the emperor: a Corinthian named Chrysippus who dreamed that he received two teeth from the mouth of the emperor, and was successful in two cases before him on the same day; a Cilician who was petitioning for his brother's estate from the emperor, dreamed that he sheared half a sheep, and got not half but nothing; and Paulus, the jurist (*nomikos*), who, when he had a case before the emperor, dreamed that the advocate on the other side was called Nikon, the name of a man who had formerly lost a case before the emperor —but it was the name (which meant 'winner') which was significant.[4]

Artemidorus thus accepts appearances in court before the emperor simply as one out of many categories of crucial events in which men's anticipations of success or failure might be keenly aroused. Similarly another provincial writer, Herodian, when he refers to imperial business, usually specifies only jurisdiction: after a plot Commodus 'spent most of his time in suburban villas, or imperial properties more distant from Rome, and abstained from jurisdiction and imperial business'; Severus passed the middle part of his reign in Rome 'judging continuously and managing the affairs of state'; and his mother Mammaea urged the young Severus Alexander 'to give justice continuously and throughout most of the day, so that by being busy with weightier matters which were essential to his rule, he should not have time to acquire any faults'.[5] Similarly, in the oration *To a King*, probably

---

[1] Appian, *BC, praef.* 15/62: δίκαις ἐν Ῥώμῃ συναγορεύσας ἐπὶ τῶν βασιλέων (cf. p. 276); Polyaenus, *Strat.* II, *praef.*: καὶ ταῦτα σχολὴν οὐκ ἄγων, ἀλλὰ καὶ δίκας ἐφ' ὑμῶν λέγων (addressed to Marcus Aurelius and Verus).

[2] *De die natali* 15, 6.

[3] *Pan.* v(9), 5, 4, cf. p. 99.

[4] *Oneir.* IV, 31, 51, 80.

[5] Herodian I, 11, 5; III, 10, 2; VI, 1, 6. Compare the portrayal in *HA, Veri* 8, 8, of Aurelius coming to Verus' villa on the via Clodia, the scene of many debaucheries, and showing him his duty by spending five days there giving judgment continuously.

by Aelius Aristides and relating to Antoninus Pius, the giving of justice by
the emperor takes second place among his virtues only to his moderation in
taxation, and is explained in much greater detail. The emperor combined
justice with *philanthrôpia*, and was able to do so because he knew the laws
himself, and did not have to depend on others.[6]

Although it is in the literature of the second and third centuries that such
conceptions are most clearly and vividly expressed, the fact of the emperor's
established role as judge is firmly attested as early as the reign of Augustus
himself. Moreover our evidence shows quite clearly that it was already a
matter of routine. Suetonius records that Augustus gave justice assiduously,
sometimes continuing into the night, and if he were ill would have his litter
placed on the tribunal, or if necessary would continue while lying at home;
Dio similarly notes under AD 8 that in old age Augustus continued to examine
matters and judge cases with assessors from a tribunal in the Palatium. When
out of Rome he might, as we saw earlier, take his seat to give justice in the
porticoes of the temple of Hercules at Tibur; and shortly before his death,
when he was intending to accompany Tiberius as far as Beneventum, he
found himself delayed by applicants (*interpellatores*) detaining him with case
after case as he gave justice.[7] The initiative of the parties to the cases is
particularly evident here.

Justice remained part of his functions when he visited the provinces.
When he reached Narbo in 27 BC he 'conducted the *conventus*', which can
only mean that he exercised jurisdiction.[8] Narbonensis was then briefly an
imperial province, and it may be that when there he acted in place of his
legatus. At any rate an anecdote preserved by the elder Seneca shows him
hearing a series of cases in Tarraco, and paying a compliment to the
eloquence of the advocate who presented them.[9] This must have been in
26–4 BC, and again in an imperial province. It may also have been in the
context of a similar session that envoys from Gadara presented before him
complaints against Herod in 20 BC, apparently at Antioch and certainly in
Syria, an imperial province.[10]

Whatever the explanation in terms of Augustus' constitutional role, or
roles, the evidence is distributed sufficiently widely in time and place to
make clear that jurisdiction was an established part of his functions. Cases
sent to him, or judged on appeal, have already been mentioned, as have
criminal charges brought before him in the first instance. There remains
the question of whether civil cases will also have been among those which
interpellatores pressed upon him. The case over the drawing of water from
the *fundus Sutrinus* over which he was approached (*aditus*) implies that they

[6] Aristides, *Or.* xxxv Keil, 16 (moderation in raising money); 17–18 (justice and knowledge of
the law); 19 refers explicitly to criminal jurisdiction. For the question of authorship, see C. P.
Jones in *JRS* LXII (1972), 134.

[7] Suetonius, *Aug.* 33, 1; 72, 2–3; 97, 3; Dio LV, 33, 5.

[8] Livy, *Epit.* 134: 'cum ille conventum Narbone egit, censum a tribus Galliis, quas Caesar
pater vicerat, actus'; for the occasion, Dio I.III, 22, 5.

[9] *Controv.* 10, *praef.* 14.

[10] p. 437.

18

could be[11]—though in that instance he based his decision not on a hearing of both parties, but on the facts as presented by one side. He was similarly approached (*aditus*) by the sons of a woman from Ariminum who had subsequently married an elderly second husband, and passed them over in her will. Augustus ruled that both the marriage and the will were invalid, giving the sons possession of their mother's inheritance and not allowing the husband to retain the dowry, on the grounds that the marriage had not been contracted for the purpose of producing children. There is nothing in the brief account of the issue to suggest that this involved a formal hearing and verdict, except perhaps Valerius Maximus' laudatory comment, 'If Equity herself had examined this matter, could she have pronounced a more just or well-founded verdict?'[12] Similarly, we can discern what seems to be the reflection of an actual case in Valerius' report about a woman who impersonated someone named Rubria from Milan, and laid claim to her property: she did not lack witnesses of high standing nor favour on the part of the imperial entourage, but by the invincible constancy of Caesar she failed to achieve her object.[13] The words suggest, but do not prove, a regular hearing of the normal type, with witnesses and a *consilium*, but with the final verdict at the discretion of the emperor. Augustus also issued a *decretum* by which one Tettius, though passed over in his father's will, was given possession of his property; the term is the normal one for a verdict, but might apply to any decision in an individual case, and nothing more is revealed of the procedure or circumstances.[14]

It thus seems probable that when Augustus regularly took his seat to give justice, he was 'approached' directly with civil cases as well as with criminal accusations. For the rest of the first century we have ample evidence of the routine nature of imperial jurisdiction,[15] the extent of which however depended on the individual emperor's inclinations. Seneca's *Apocolocyntosis*, for instance puts particular emphasis on the avidity with which Claudius listened to cases, and makes him recall giving justice for days at a time at the temple of Hercules at Tibur.[16] Our evidence for the period up to Hadrian also shows that the emperor normally gave justice as emperor but, if holding the consulate, did so as consul. For, whatever may have been the situation previously, it is clear that from the early empire onwards the consuls gave justice in their own, and might appoint *iudices* to hear private suits.[17] It is not clear whether there was any difference in the subject-matter or procedure between the jurisdiction which the emperor exercised when holding the consulship himself, and that which he exercised otherwise.[18] If there was,

---

[11] p. 465.

[12] VII, 7, 4: 'Si ipsa Aequitas hac de re cognosceret, potuitne iustius aut gravius pronuntiare?'

[13] IX, 15, *ext*. I.

[14] VII, 7, 3; for *decretum*, p. 239.

[15] pp. 228–9, and also, for example, Dio LIX, 18, 1; Athenaeus 148D (Gaius); Suetonius, *Claud.* 46; Dio LX, 28, 6 (Claudius).

[16] *Apoc.* 7, 4–5 (cf. p. 25), cf. 12 and 15.

[17] Mommsen, *Staatsrecht*[3] II, 104–5; cf. pp. 518–20.

[18] Suetonius, *Claud.* 14: 'ius et consul et extra honorem laboriosissime dixit'; *HA, Had.* 8, 5: 'ipsum autem tertium consulatum et quattuor mensibus tantum egit et in eo saepe ius dixit.'

his subjects were evidently unaware of the fact, as Pliny's description of Trajan's consulate in 100 shows:[19]

> The remaining part of the day was devoted to the tribunal. There indeed what devotion to equity there was, what reverence for the laws! Someone would approach him (*adibat*) as emperor; he would reply that he was consul. He did not diminish the right or authority of any magistracy, but even increased it; in particular he remitted most matters to the praetors, and in doing so referred to them as his colleagues, not because it was popular or welcome to his hearers, but because that was how he considered it.

Once again the nature of the proceedings was that the emperor took his seat in public or at least in some formal, semi-public setting, and was approached by interested parties, who are represented as not having known, until he replied, that he was doing so *qua* consul. Pliny's account does not make clear whether the cases brought to him were typically criminal or civil. But when he goes on directly to describe the ordinary imperial duties, to which Trajan returned after his two-month tenure of the consulship, he mentions first the reception of embassies[20] and then jurisdiction, at least part of which explicitly related to civil litigants (*litigatores*):[21]

> Indeed, in all the *cognitiones* how mild a severity, how controlled a *clementia*! You do not take your seat for the purpose of enriching the *fiscus*, nor do you seek any reward for your *sententia* except that of having judged well. The *litigatores* stand before you anxious not about their wealth, but about your opinion; nor do they so fear your judgment about the case so much as that about their character.

So far we have seen that the emperor was available to be 'approached' by civil litigants as well as persons making accusations, and was so in a way which was not obviously different whether he was holding the consulship or not. The initiative clearly had to be taken by the parties concerned, as is visible also in Suetonius' report that, when Claudius decided to leave the tribunal, the advocates (*causidici*) would not only urge him verbally to remain, but might even try to retain him by grasping his toga or foot.[22] None the less, although we can thus gain some slight conception of the process of approach to the emperor, we have very little evidence from this period as to what types of civil cases were brought to him, or by whom. A Greek *litigator* is briefly attested making an offensive remark to Claudius, who is also found deciding a case where a mother refused to acknowledge her son; and the *postulatores*, to whom in giving judgment Nero would not give answers except on the following day and in the form of written *libelli*, were probably civil litigants asking for a case to be taken, rather than accusers.[23] But, for instance, all the *cognitiones* of Trajan in which Pliny took part involved

[19] *Pan.* 77, 3–4.
[20] p. 375.
[21] 80, 1–2. The reference to the *fiscus* here presumably relates to properties which might be judged to fall to it as *bona vacantia* or *caduca* (pp. 158–63).
[22] *Claud.* 15, 3.
[23] *Claud.* 15, 4; 15, 2; *Nero* 15, 1.

criminal accusations. The only probable instance of a civil suit decided by him is that when he compelled a father who had maltreated his son to emancipate him; after the son's death the father claimed possession of his property, but this was denied him (evidently by Trajan again) 'on the advice of Neratius Priscus and Aristo'.[24]

It is in the following period, from the reign of Hadrian into the first half of the third century, that we have the clearest evidence of the civil jurisdiction of the emperor. We saw earlier that Hadrian 'having heard the case' gave his verdict (*causa cognita decrevisse*) that a baby born in the eleventh month after the husband's death could be legitimate; and he also gave the verdict (*decrevit*) in a case where a mother made a new will on the false report of her son's death.[25] In neither of these cases, however, do we gain any information as to what steps led to the cases being heard by the emperor. A rough impression of such processes is obtainable from the text called *Sententiae et Epistulae Divi Hadriani*, pronouncements of Hadrian preserved in parallel in Greek and Latin in an early third-century collection designed as an aid to learning Latin. Here we find people presenting civil-law issues to Hadrian verbally (when he had taken his seat in the Forum or elsewhere to give justice?), and the emperor either giving a ruling directly, referring it to someone else, or conducting a further interrogation.[26] Thus, following a complaint of neglect, he warns a son to care for his father, and refers a report about excessive interest to the Praetorian Prefect. In a more complex case a woman alleges that the *curator* of her son has made no payments for his upkeep for three years, and has now stolen his *congiarium*. Hadrian interrogates the *curator*, who defends himself on the grounds that his partner as *curator* has been absent, and orders him to pay as much as his means allow. We cannot place too much weight on these disjointed and not readily intelligible exchanges; but it would be reasonable to regard them as reflecting a custom whereby, at least on relatively simple issues, one or both parties could address the emperor directly and receive answers from him.

From the reign of Antoninus Pius the *Digest* preserves a number of references to *decreta* by the emperor on civil cases, but in none of them is there any indication of how the matter came before him.[27] A letter of Marcus Aurelius, however, quotes part of a speech which Fronto had addressed to Antoninus Pius on the undesirability of having all cases about wills brought before himself:[28]

> In those matters and cases which are judged by private *iudices*, there is no danger, since their *sententiae* are valid only for the cases in question; but by your *decreta*, Emperor, models are established publicly which will be valid in perpetuity . . . So if you approve the *decretum* of this proconsul, you will have given a rule for all the governors of all provinces as to what verdicts they should

---

[24] *Dig.* XXXVII, 12, 5 (Papinian). For these two jurists see W. Kunkel, *Herkunft und soziale Stellung der römischen Juristen*[2] (1967), nos. 25 and 26. Their prominence under Trajan is well-attested, but there is no specific evidence beyond this passage for their part as his advisers.

[25] Aulus Gellius, *NA* III, 16, 12 (p. 239); *Dig.* V, 2, 28.

[26] *Corp. Gloss. Lat.* III, 31–7.

[27] e.g. *Dig.* XXXII, 11, 1; XXXIV, 9, 3; XXXVI, 1, 36; XXXVIII, 17, 2, 9; XLIII, 30, 1, 3.

[28] *Ad M. Caes.* I, 6.

give in such cases. So what will be the result—namely that all wills from distant overseas provinces will be brought to Rome for your *cognitio*.

It is impossible to discern exactly what the proconsul had done, though it is probable that he had either allowed an appeal to the emperor, or had sent the case spontaneously. The province concerned was Asia, and the *cognitio* had twice been postponed because one party to the case had not yet arrived. Fronto expatiates on the consequences in future if relatives were able to prevent the opening of wills which they suspected to be unfavourable by asking for them to be brought to Rome; delays would be inevitable, and the wills themselves might well be lost by shipwreck.

This particular case seems to have been one of remission or appeal rather than primary jurisdiction. But the future which Fronto imagined, or pretended for the purposes of his argument to imagine, was one where the *cognitio* of the emperor would actually be substituted for that of proconsuls. In portraying the consequences, he is one of the remarkably few writers of the imperial period to dwell even in passing on the distances and difficulties of travel which separated the vast majority of the population from the emperor and his court.[29]

Such a view did not entail that no cases relating to wills would be heard by the emperor. We have earlier, for instance, seen part of Marcellus' verbatim report of a case which Marcus Aurelius heard in 166, and which was concerned with whether legacies in someone's will should fall with the rest of his property to the *fiscus*; the case was conducted by verbal exchanges between the emperor and the *advocati*, and decided by the emperor after deliberation in private.[30] Similarly, Scaevola reported the judgment which Marcus gave in his *auditorium* in a case where the divorced wife of a senator from Sparta named Brasidas had left a *fideicommissum* to their sons, provided that they had in the meantime become *sui iuris* after his death. But he emancipated them, and they claimed the *fideicommissum* on that basis. Marcus gave as his *decretum* that the *fideicommissum* should be paid, since this represented the deceased woman's intentions.[31] The fact that the case arose in a senatorial family (whether resident in Rome or in Sparta) may well have been relevant to the fact that Marcus heard the case; whether similar considerations applied to three other cases concerning wills which he heard, is quite unclear.[32]

With the reign of Severus the acute limitations of our evidence for other periods become particularly obvious, for we have a long list of civil cases heard by the emperor, by himself or with Caracalla, most of which are preserved either in Paulus' three books of *Decreta* or six books of *Imperial Sententiae Pronounced in Cognitiones*,[33] while others are recorded by other

[29] pp. 364, 440.
[30] pp. 163, 237.
[31] *Dig.* xxxvi, 1, 23 *pr.* It is more than probable that the man descended from that descendant of the fifth-century Brasidas who had appeared before Augustus, pp. 236, 524.
[32] *Dig.* v, 3, 25, 16; xxxv, 2, 11, 2; xxxvi, 1, 19, 3.
[33] The fact that some cases are described as having been recorded in both works (see e.g. *Dig.* xxxvi, 1, 83, cf. p. 513) does not seem to be a sufficient reason for denying that these were two separate works, see O. Lenel, *Palingenesia Iuris Civilis* 1 (1889), 959, n. 1; *RE* x, 722–3, 725–6.

contemporaries, Papinian and Ulpian. Three of these also concerned the property of senatorial families. Papinian relates that 'our best and greatest emperors' judged (*iudicaverunt*) a case concerning the will of a senator named Cocceius Cassianus.[34] More clearly, Ulpian records how the emperors, after they had given their *sententia* in their *auditorium* in a case brought by Acilius Glabrio against his brother, refused to 'hear' his claim for restitution on the grounds that he had been deceived, being under the age of twenty-five; they did however allow this, after two previous hearings, to one Percennius Severus.[35] Another issue which Severus and Caracalla heard went back to the executions of the last years of Commodus' reign.[36] One Pactumeius Androsthenes named as heir to all of his property Pactumeia Magna, and as substitute heir her father, Pactumeius Magnus. He was the suffect consul of 183, and in about 190 was executed on the orders of Commodus. On the news of this, accompanied by the rumour that Pactumeia had also been killed, Pactumeius Androsthenes changed his will and named another heir, 'since I cannot have the heirs whom I wished'. Pactumeia subsequently petitioned (*supplicavit*) Severus and Caracalla, the *cognitio* was accepted, and Severus pronounced his verdict that she should inherit, provided that she paid the legacies due under the previous will. These two instances clearly suggest that persons of senatorial standing made good use of their position, and what will have been normally their physical propinquity to the emperor, to gain a hearing from him in relation to their private affairs.[37]

Another recognizable group of cases heard by Severus is that of cases in which the *fiscus* was involved. Some of these derived (like that heard by Marcus in 166) from the claims to property, *bona vacantia* or *caduca*, which the *fiscus* could make, if either a will were invalid or legally entitled heirs not available.[38] But others concern issues where property had been purchased from the *fiscus*,[39] where a procurator claimed as a slave a freedwoman who had been manumitted by a debtor to the *fiscus*,[40] or particularly over claims on persons who had leased revenues or properties from the *fiscus*.[41] In none of these instances, however, is there any indication of the origin or standing of the persons concerned, or the steps by which their cases were brought before the emperor. The same is also unfortunately true of a number of cases

---

[34] *Dig.* xxxiv, 9, 16, 1. Could 'Cocceius Cassianus' have been a relative of Cassius Dio Cocceianus?

[35] *Dig.* iv, 4, 18, 1–2. For the Acilii Glabriones, probably the oldest senatorial family of the period, see *PIR*² A 59–73 and *stemma* p. 12. The brothers were probably the sons of the *cos.* II of 186. The status of Percennius Severus is not known.

[36] *Dig.* xxviii, 5, 93; see *RE* s.v. 'Pactumeius' (5).

[37] The case which Severus heard, *Dig.* xxxvi, 1, 38, 1, about the mutual rights of *tutores* and *pupilli* was probably another instance, for the uncle and *tutor*, Arrius Antoninus, is almost certainly C. Arrius Antoninus (Barbieri, *Albo senatorio*, no. 50), and the nephew and *pupillus*, Arrius Honoratus, identical with C. Arrius Calpurnius Frontinus Honoratus (*Albo*, no. 52).

[38] e.g. *Dig.* xxxii, 27, 1 (the Pompeius Hermippus here *could* be the senatorial Cn. Pompeius Hermippus Aelianus from Ephesus, Barbieri, *Albo*, no. 419); xxxii, 27, 2; xlix, 14, 48, *pr.* (in this case the emperors were first consulted by their procurators; whether an actual *cognitio* later followed is not quite clear). The interests of the *fiscus* are present implicitly in xxix, 2, 97, in which Paulus gave an opinion (*dicebam*), but Severus 'pronuntiavit' otherwise.

[39] *Dig.* xxii, 1, 16, 1.

[40] *Dig.* xl, 1, 10.

[41] *Dig.* xlvi, 1, 68; xlix, 14, 37 (two separate cases).

on which Severus gave a verdict, apparently in the first instance, and which concerned issues purely of private law or local obligations.[42] Yet they are sufficient to suggest very strongly that primary jurisdiction by the emperor in civil cases was common, as does Ulpian's reference to the fact that restitution after a verdict by a *iudex* 'given' by the emperor could be granted by no one except the emperor.[43]

The mere fact that the emperor spent any significant proportion of his working life deciding cases in civil law is of considerable importance in itself, even if, as has to be admitted, we cannot map the social or geographical origins of those who appeared before him, nor assess the claims which had to be made before such an appearance was granted. Nor is there anything to contradict the natural assumption that both social standing and geographical proximity had some bearing on the question of which persons would finally achieve the hearing of their case by the emperor. Both are certainly relevant to the only case heard by an emperor which happened to be recorded in documentary form, that of the Goharieni from east of Damascus, which Caracalla heard at Antioch in May 216. We have seen the importance of this document both for the entourage of the emperor and for the arguments relating to the temple there which were put before him.[44] But it remains to consider the relevance of the first part of the hearing to the question of how this apparently civil suit (not involving Roman law proper) came to the emperor. The opening exchange between the *advocati* makes quite clear why the case is described as one 'which the emperor deigned to accept'. All the parties including the emperor speak in Greek, though the protocol of the proceedings is given in Latin. As always, the *advocati* address themselves directly to the emperor, here using the singular:

> Aristaenetus: I object.
>
> Lollianus: You have ordered that the *cognitio* should proceed.
>
> Aristaenetus: Cases on appeal are determined by law. Either the governor accepts the appeal and it comes to your *dikastêrion*, or if he does not accept it, how can the case be admissible? After many hearings and verdicts you were approached with petitions from the Goharieni. A man who was neither an *advocatus* nor an ambassador [but . . .] a private person entered a petition that you should be the judge rather than the governor. You said to him, 'If you wish me to hear it, I will hear it.' [We], having objected [from the beginning to this], now that we enter under the rules of the court [object to the case], on the grounds that they neither have a case on appeal nor can have [access to your *dikastêrion*].
>
> Lollianus: Your peasants have, along with other requests, brought you this supplication . . . [fragmentary exchanges]

After this the emperor intervenes to make clear that he has his own opinion

---

[42] e.g. *Dig.* XXVI, 7, 7, 4; XXVI, 7, 53; XXVII, 3, 1, 3; XXXVI, 27, *pr.*; XXXIV, 9, 5, 10; XXXVI, 1, 1, 13; XXXVI, 1, 76, *pr.* (a *testamentum* in Greek); XL, 5, 38; L, 16, 240.

[43] *Dig.* IV, 4, 18, 4.

[44] *SEG* XVII 759; see pp. 38, 121, 233, 455.

on the matter, accepts in principle the force of the objection and says that he would have allowed it, if he had been in a hurry to leave. But after Lollianus, the advocate for the Goharieni, has said that he will need only half a day, the case proceeds.

It is evident from the exchange that cases from Syria did not normally reach the emperor except on appeal. The opportunity for a different form of access to his court was created by his presence there, and an agreement in principle to hear the court is secured by an individual petition from a representative of the villagers. Even after this, when the case has been set down for hearing, whether it proceeds is entirely a matter of the discretion, and the convenience, of the emperor. It would not be in the least surprising if similar petitions or cases were rejected at one stage or another. None the less, as we saw, the fact that the text of the proceedings was inscribed on the wall of the temple clearly implies that it was heard to the end, and that the suit over the usurpation of the priesthood was successful.[45]

The subsequent evidence for private suits heard by the emperor is very slight. In 238, for instance, Gordian in a *subscriptio* makes a rather puzzling reference to *iudices* 'given' by the emperor.[46] Then Philip, 'having spoken with his *consilium*' pronounced a verdict on a standard issue of private law: 'Since it has been proved that the object was offered as a pledge and afterwards [improperly] sold by the debtor, ownership of it could not, since it was stolen property, pass by right of continued possession (*usucapio*).'[47] Thereafter, nothing seems to be recorded until we come to the case where Constantine interrogates in Latin a woman who speaks Greek and who is claiming ownership of an object which the vendor had acquired improperly while holding office.[48] Again we do not know how the case came before him, or when, or whether the fact that the interests of the *fiscus* were involved had any relevance. None the less the case may just be enough to suggest that our ignorance of such cases in this period may be an effect of the pattern of our evidence. In the affairs of the Christian church, for which we do have substantial evidence from the Constantinian period, we shall see reflected almost every feature of imperial jurisdiction, petitions to the emperor to appoint *iudices*, or hear a dispute himself, accusations leading to criminal penalties, appeals from other courts, flight from other courts to petition the emperor.[49] It would be hard to believe that such patterns of approach and of imperial judgment were in fact deployed in that period solely in the affairs of the church. Moreover, when Eusebius records that Constantine compensated with gifts those who lost cases before him, he must surely be referring to civil litigants.[50]

None the less there is no doubt that the existence of other courts, combined with the effects of distance and the necessity of employing advocates and

[45] p. 436.
[46] *CJ* III, 1, 5: 'A iudice (meaning a governor?) iudex delegatus iudicis dandi non habet potestatem, cum ipse iudiciario munere fungatur, nisi a principe iudex datus fuerit.'
[47] *CJ* VII, 26, 6.
[48] *CTh* VIII, 15, 1; cf. p. 237.
[49] pp. 584–607.
[50] p. 10.

bringing witnesses to the imperial court, must in practice have greatly limited the availability to his subjects of formal legal hearings before the emperor. Not all of these limitations, however, applied to the most distinctive of all the means of approach to him, and the most distinctive of his functions as 'judge' the presentation of petitions, usually in the form of *libelli*, and the giving of justice through the written replies which he made.

7. Petition and Response

Of all the forms in which the population of the empire could address the emperor and receive responses from him, by far the most fully attested is the presentation of *libelli* on legal matters and the promulgation of *sub-scriptiones* in answer to them; as we have seen, the evidence of the *Codex Justinianus*, the *Digest* and minor legal collections, is now substantially supplemented by papyri. But it is important to recall that a principle of selection has necessarily been at work, and that *subscriptiones* on strictly legal matters were only a part of all those that were requested and given. Furthermore, what the legal sources give us is the imperial *subscriptiones* themselves, but not the *libelli* which prompted them; though the contents and circumstances of the *libelli* are often quite clearly reflected in the *subscriptiones*, this is not a substitute for the actual tone and wording of a petition as addressed by an individual to the emperor.

To restore the balance it is therefore necessary to pay particular attention to those inscriptions or papyri where the actual text of a petition to the emperor is preserved. A particularly fine example, for instance, largely survives on a third-century papyrus, in which a retired athlete petitions the emperor for the post of herald on the staff of the *epistrategus* of the Hep-tanomia district of Egypt. It would be difficult to imagine a less exalted position in the imperial service or one more remote from what we would suppose to be the interests of the emperor. But the petitioner had no doubt that he had claims which merited attention. After a few fragmentary lines which cannot be restored, he continues:[1]

> I have hastened to the feet of you, the lords of the whole inhabited world, and saviours of myself, a man of modest rank who has endured much. For twenty-eight years until now I have been making the rounds as a competitor in the contests which are held for your victory and the eternity of your rule, and, while making my living in these, have been offering incessant prayers to Olympian Zeus to preserve and increase your rule for long ages, and to grant me benevolence from you [the emperors]. Since I am already passing the age of fifty and turning to old age, I approach you with this petition of mine requesting, if it please your heavenly Fortune, to bestow upon me the position of Greek herald in the administration of the Heptanomia . . . It has long been laid down by your [divine] forebears that no one should serve in this position except those who have trained and endured as competitors . . .

---

[1] *PSI* 1422.

18*

There is nothing to indicate that the unnamed emperors were in Egypt at the time, nor to show how the petition was to have been presented to them. But even if it is merely a draft, we cannot doubt the seriousness of the petitioner's intentions nor his conception of how his objective was to be attained.

The main bulk of legal *subscriptiones* has to be seen against the background not only of contemporary *libelli* on other subjects, but also as a development from an earlier stage when petitions on various topics could be presented to the emperor in various ways, including *libelli*, but when the regular system of 'posting-up' *subscriptiones* had not yet developed; for if our evidence is reliable, the *libellus-* and *-subscriptio* system is primarily a feature of the mid-second to early fourth centuries.[2] It is therefore a matter of some significance to discover whether, and if so how and in what form, written or verbal petitions were addressed to the emperor in the earlier period.

There is some evidence to suggest that in this period, though *libelli* could be presented, petitions were normally addressed verbally to the emperor. In consequence the person concerned either had to have sufficient standing to gain access to the emperor either privately or at his *salutatio*, or had to find an intermediary; or alternatively he could try to use the occasion of a public appearance of the emperor. So, for instance, a man who had made an incautious remark about Augustus at dinner, next morning took the opportunity of approaching the emperor as he came down from the Palatium.[3] Alternatively, an *eques* who had written an abusive poem about Tiberius was saved by the *preces* offered on his behalf by his brother, who was a senator.[4] Not all those who had access to the emperor necessarily improved their position by using it; another senator, Q. Haterius, entered the Palatium to implore Tiberius whom he had offended, clasped his knees and succeeded only in throwing him down, nearly losing his life as a result.[5]

Haterius escaped ultimately only by gaining the intercession of Livia, just as we saw Ovid, from his exile in Tomi, advise his wife to attempt to do.[6] Ovid's *Epistulae* from the Pontus provide indeed some of our most vivid testimony for the conception that the most effective approach to the emperor was by the verbal intercession of a well-placed intermediary. The option of imploring the emperor's mercy in person was of course not open to him, but while he once addresses Augustus directly, in a poem requesting a less arduous place of exile, and once Germanicus, to celebrate his triumph, his normal means of approach was to request others to intercede verbally for him.[7] So he writes to Paullus Fabius Maximus, formerly consul in 11 BC:[8]

---

[2] pp. 243–4.

[3] Seneca, *De ben.* III, 27; see p. 135.

[4] Tacitus, *Ann.* IV, 31, 1.

[5] *Ann.* I, 13, 6.

[6] p. 468.

[7] *Tristia* II (Augustus); *Ep. ex Ponto* II, 1 (Germanicus). For his exile and works sent from there, L. P. Wilkinson, *Ovid Recalled* (1955), chs. ix–x; R. J. Dickinson, 'The *Tristia*: Poetry in Exile', *Ovid*, ed. J. W. Binns (1973), 154.

[8] *Ep. ex Ponto* I, 2, see 115f. Cf. IV, 6, 9–10: 'certus eras pro me, Fabiae laus, Maxime, gentis, / numen ad Augustum supplice voce loqui.' Paullus Fabius Maximus was in fact a renowned orator, see *PIR*² F 47.

Your voice, I pray, will mollify the ears of Augustus, just as it is accustomed to aid terrified defendants, and with the accustomed sweetness of your learned tongue, incline the heart of the man whom we must equate with the gods.

To M. Valerius Messalla Messalinus, consul of 3 BC, he addresses himself in very similar terms:[9]

Adore that divinity which is merciful, but rightly angered against me, so that I may be removed from this fearsome Scythian place. It is hard, I admit; but courage seeks a challenge, and the *gratia* of such a service will be all the greater. Nor will it be a Polyphemus in his vast Aetnan cave, nor an Antiphates, who will receive your words, but a mild and approachable father, open to mercy, who often thunders without unleashing a fiery bolt.

Here, as in his letter to his wife, we find a perfectly explicit metaphor comparing Augustus to a god, and approaches to him or members of his household to supplications to the gods.[10] In the latter case there is also visible the familiar motif that the credit of a well-established senator depended in part on his ability to gain from the emperor favours for his protégés.[11]

Rather different conceptions applied for instance when Ovid asked for the intercession of Salanus, the teacher of Germanicus.[12] But throughout there is an acceptance of the fact that all depended on the will of the emperor, who was perfectly free to modify his sentence as he wished; and that the way to achieve the desired modification was for him to be addressed verbally by someone to whom he would be inclined to listen. The fact that Ovid's pleas were unsuccessful is not so significant as the assumptions on which they were based. The same assumptions clearly underlie the *Consolatio* which Seneca addressed from exile to Claudius' freedman, Polybius, on the occasion of his brother's death; the necessities of the literary form precluded an explicit request for intercession, but a firm expectation of Claudius' *clementia* is expressed in the middle, and an apology for inadequacy of a *Consolatio* written in such circumstances added at the end.[13] Seneca was not to be restored, however, until Agrippina marked her marriage to Claudius in 49 by requesting simultaneously a pardon for him and a praetorship.[14]

The emperor retained throughout the effective power to remit or increase sentences already passed, or to vary their conditions or consequences. Moreover, though the evidence is, as usual, scattered and disparate, this gradually extended beyond sentences passed by himself or a previous emperor,[15] to any sentence passed by any judge; concurrent with this was inevitably the extension of petitioning for the abolition or variation of penalties beyond

[9] *Ep.* II, 2, 109f. On the addressee *RE* s.v. 'Valerius' (264).
[10] p. 468.
[11] For the same theme in relation to Pliny see p. 286.
[12] *Ep.* II, 5.
[13] *Ad Polybium de consolatione* 13; 18, 9.
[14] Tacitus, *Ann.* XII, 8, 2; cf. p. 306.
[15] For example *Dig.* I, 2, 2, 51–2 on C. Cassius Longinus: 'plurimum in civitate auctoritatis habuit eo usque, donec eum Caesar civitate pelleret. expulsus ab eo in Sardiniam, revocatus a Vespasiano . . .'; Pliny, *Ep.* IV, 9, 2: Julius Bassus, 'a Domitiano relegatus; revocatus a Nerva . . .'

upper-class circles in Rome to lower, if undefinable, levels of society. The original pattern of course persisted also. Claudius Etruscus was able for instance to secure from Domitian a remission of the exile to which the emperor had condemned his father, at the end of a long career as an imperial freedman.[16] Similarly the future emperor Macrinus was saved, when his patron, the praetorian prefect Plautianus fell, by the intercession of Septimius Severus' most prominent senatorial friend, L. Fabius Cilo.[17]

But much earlier than this we can see less prominent individuals coming to petition the emperor on this topic. The earlier cases still seem however to relate to condemnations by emperors; when someone petitioned Hadrian for the restoration of his father from exile, the emperor told him to allow time for him to consult the (imperial) *commentarii* and then return.[18] Apuleius describes in the *Metamorphoses* how the wife of an exiled *ducenarius* first accompanied him and then 'by directing *preces* to the *numen* [divinity] of Caesar' secured his restoration.[19] The significance of the story is if anything increased by the fact that it is fictional, for it can thereby be taken as something typical of the period. At about the same time Gaius provides evidence of a general expectation that third parties might petition for the restoration of a man who had been relegated; for he discusses the case of such a man who left in his will a sum to be given by his heirs, 'if any one of the heirs, or other friends whom I have mentioned in this will, or anyone else, has requested my restoration from the emperor, and I die before being able to express my gratitude to him'.[20] In this period also Antoninus Pius is attested as replying favourably to the petition of one Ulpianus Damascenus (or from Damascus?) who had asked permission to leave to his mother, who had been deported, a sum sufficient for her upkeep; the emperor makes an exception in this instance, while retaining the rule that such persons (unlike *relegati*, who could also make a will) could not receive inheritances, legacies or *fideicommissa*.[21] The emperor's discretion applied even to the bodies of those who had died while deported or relegated, for they could not be taken elsewhere for burial without consultation of the emperor, 'as Severus and Antoninus have very often written back, and have conceded this very right to many who sought it'.[22]

In replies to individuals the exercise of *indulgentia* and of interpretation of the laws were necessarily closely interwoven. If nothing else, it was endlessly necessary to set, and repeat, the limits of what was granted. For instance Caracalla replies to a man named Quietus:[23]

As you state that your father was condemned to *metallum*, and his property rightly occupied by the *fiscus*, it is not the case that, because by my *indulgentia* he

[16] For Claudius Etruscus' intercession see Martial, *Epig.* VI, 83. On the father's career see p. 73.
[17] Dio LXXVIII, 11, 2 (413).
[18] p. 261.
[19] *Met.* VII, 6–7.
[20] *Dig.* XXXIV, 5, 5, *pr.* (Gaius, *liber 1 fideicommissorum*).
[21] *Dig.* XLVIII, 22, 16. The text of this section is restored from the *Basilica*.
[22] *Dig.* XLVIII, 24, 2 (Marcianus): 'ut saepissime Severus et Antoninus rescripserunt et multis petentibus hoc ipsum indulserunt.'
[23] *CJ* IX, 51, 2.

was freed from the penalty as far as regards *metallum*, he also gained restitution of his property, unless a special *beneficium* was gained on this point.

Such interpretations might also be a necessary consequence of general indulgences proclaimed by emperors, which are attested for emperors from the early third century to Constantine. As we know from Dio, Caracalla announced the release of all exiles to the senate immediately after the murder of his brother, probably in December 211.[24] There was also an *edictum*, for a phrase from it is quoted in the supplementary edict which he issued in Rome in the following July, to emphasize that his indulgence (*charis* in Greek) meant that the restored exiles re-gained their full former status.[25] Thereafter Severus Alexander, Philip, and Diocletian and Maximian all send *subscriptiones* to answer problems raised by a *generalis indulgentia*;[26] and Constantine wrote in 322 to the praetorian prefect, 'On account of the birth of a child to Crispus and Helena I grant indulgence to all except poisoners, murderers and adulterers.'[27]

Such general indulgences, which began with Caracalla, and may well have owed their origin to his passionate imitation of Alexander the Great,[28] did not of course exclude individual indulgences whether in response to petitions,[29] granted to a condemned criminal before an applauding crowd in the amphitheatre[30] or as a concession to favoured persons. One such was the Christian hermit Eutychianus who lived on Mt Olympus in Bithynia and was greatly honoured by Constantine; when an officer in the emperor's escort was under accusation, his friends persuaded the hermit to come to Constantinople and request the emperor for an indulgence.[31]

Such petitions to the emperor for indulgence to those condemned or under accusation are matched by the well-attested series of *libelli* from communities of below city status requesting aid against oppression by imperial or local officials. Their significance, as mentioned earlier, lies first of all in the fact that they provide what is lacking in the case of *libelli* on legal matters addressed by individuals to the emperor, their actual texts, which show a remarkable similarity of form in examples which come from Africa, Thrace and Asia. Their limitation as evidence for the nature of the imperial system is that we do not have any examples from earlier than the second half of the second century. Perhaps the earliest known case is a fragmentary inscription

[24] Dio LXXVII, 3, 3 (375–6). For the date, T. D. Barnes in *JThS* n.s. XIX (1968), 523–4.

[25] *P. Giessen* I, 40, col. ii, ll. 1–14 (cf. p. 254); cf. F. M. Heichelheim, *JEA* XXVI (1940), 19–21.

[26] *CJ* IX, 51, 4 and 5 (Severus Alexander; in 6 Gordian refers to the 'indulgentia divi Alexandri'); 7 (Philip: 'generalis indulgentia nostra reditum exsulibus seu deportatis tribuit . . .'); 9 (Diocletian and Maximian: 'si pater vester in insulam deportatus generali indulgentia restitutus est . . .'); cf. IX, 43, 2; and Eusebius, *Mart. Pal.* 2, 4, referring to a general release of prisoners to celebrate the *vicennalia* of 303.

[27] *CTh* IX, 38, 1.

[28] Alexander's proclamation of the return of all exiles except those guilty of sacrilege or murder is attested by Diodorus XVII, 109, 1; XVIII, 8, 2–7; Justin XIII, 5, 2–5; Curtius X, 2, 4–7.

[29] *CJ* IX, 51, 2 (Caracalla; see p. 331) and 3 (Severus Alexander) both seem to refer to cases of individual *indulgentia* and release from penalties.

[30] See Eusebius, *Mart. Pal.* 6, 5 for Maximin in the amphitheatre at Caesarea freeing a condemned murderer.

[31] Sozomenus, *HE* I, 13, 9–11.

from near Vaga in Africa, which seems to date to 181, and thus to be addressed to Commodus; the petitioners are peasants who are complaining of excessive demands on them for days of labour in ploughing, sowing and reaping, and of the contributions in kind which they have to make to an inn used by official travellers—'We request you, lord, by your *Salus* to come to our aid.'[32] As has long been recognized, the document closely resembles the well-known *libellus* addressed to Commodus by the tenants on an African imperial estate, the *saltus Burunitanus*; it does not necessarily follow, however, that these peasants were also on such an estate.

Those of the *saltus Burunitanus* certainly were imperial tenants, and, as we saw earlier, made as much use as they could of the fact in their *libellus*. The issue was the same, the question of the level of services required, but was complicated by bribery by the lessees (*conductores*) and violence by the procurators; it had been going on already for years and there had already been at least one imperial *subscriptio*, which they refer to as 'yours' in the plural (*vestra*), and which will therefore have been issued by Marcus and Commodus. Even though our text is far from complete, it still covers 60 lines, and its urgent and detailed nature contrasts forcefully with Commodus' brief and formal *subscriptio*.[33]

These peasants, like some from Lydia in the early third century, could urge on the emperor or emperors the consideration of loss to their own revenues, if oppression continued.[34] But this was not a necessary condition for peasants to be able to appeal to the emperor. One such petition was addressed to some early third-century emperors (perhaps Severus and Caracalla) by an individual on behalf of the villagers at a place now called Mendechora in Lydia, to protest against exactions by imperial officials:[35]

> In this state of fear [this was] the remedy which the above-mentioned village thought of, namely to petition through me to your great, heavenly and [most sacred] kingship, choosing me to do this and to bring the [supplication]. And thus we implore you, greatest and most divine of Emperors ever, to consider your laws and those of your ancestors and your peace-giving justice to all, and to shun, as you and all your royal ancestors have always shunned, *collêtiônes* who act in this way . . .

The inscription continues for as long again without preserving the full text of the petition, or the emperors' reply. We may, however, presume from the fact that it was inscribed at all, that the reply was not actually hostile. The precise nature of the oppression complained of is not clear; but the *libellus* is in any case most significant for its conception of 'the laws' and justice as emanations of the emperors and their ancestors.

Exactly what *collêtiônes* were is not known, for the word appears only here and in another, more fragmentary, *libellus* from the same region.[36] This

---

[32] *CIL* VIII 14428 A (B, which may be connected, may have the dates 139 and 149).
[33] Cf. p. 181 (imperial estates); 246 (on the form of the *subscriptio*).
[34] p. 181.
[35] J. Keil, A. von Premerstein, *Bericht über eine dritte Reise in Lydien* (1914), 24, no. 28 = Abbott and Johnson, *Municipal Administration*, no. 143.
[36] P. Herrmann, *Ergebnisse einer Reise in Nordostlydien*, Öst. Ak. Wiss., *Denkschr.* LXXX (1962), no. 19 = *AE* 1964 231.

seems to date to 247/8, refers to Severus Alexander and Gordian, and speaks of 'your *philanthrôpia*' and 'your most blessed [times]'. It must have been addressed to Philip and his son, and evidently also contained complaints about official oppression. Seven lines with very slight traces of a Latin inscription following this text are just sufficient to indicate that it did receive an imperial *subscriptio*, presumably again at least notionally favourable.

We have already noted the Greek *libellus* addressed to Philip by the villagers of Aragua in Pisidia, answered also by a brief *subscriptio* in Latin.[37] But our fullest and best-preserved example of a Greek *libellus* protesting against oppression is that which the villagers of Scaptopara in Thrace 'gave' to Gordian III in 238 through their fellow villager, Aurelius Pyrrhus, a soldier in the tenth praetorian cohort.[38] It is important to emphasize that the *libellus* could only have been 'given' to the emperor as a result of someone (either Pyrrhus himself, another villager or some intermediary) travelling to Rome with it. It was certainly not sent on by the governor, for the brief Latin *subscriptio* consists of a rather abrupt instruction to take the petition to him. Someone must also have copied the *subscriptio* and brought the text back to Scaptopara. The procedure was thus arduous and lengthy, involving in this instance at the very least a delay of several weeks and probably substantially more—but the option was open, and could be used by those who felt it to be required.

The first necessity, however, was to compose a *libellus* in suitably obsequious and appealing language, and it is interesting to note that these villagers from a remote district in western Thrace near the borders of Macedonia and Moesia, could employ the conventional forms to express their request:[39]

> To Imperator Caesar M. Antonius Gordianus Pius Felix Augustus, a petition from the Scaptoparan, also called Greseitan, villagers. In your most fortunate and never-ending times you have often sent rescripts to the effect that the villages should be settled and improved rather than that the inhabitants should be uprooted. Such a thing is relevant both to the safety of mankind and the interests of the most sacred treasury [the *fiscus*?]. So we too bring a lawful supplication to your divinity, praying that you will graciously assent to our petition which follows . . .

They go on to describe in great detail how both persons attending a fair or market held near their village, and soldiers, would descend on them and demand hospitality and services. Complaints to the governors of Thrace had been of no avail, and there was a danger that such inhabitants of the village as remained would be forced to leave. They ask for a rescript to prevent this— 'so that having received pity through your divine forethought, and remaining in our homes, we will be able to pay the sacred tributes and other taxes. This will be possible for us in your most fortunate times, if you order your divine rescript to be put up publicly on a *stêlê*, so that having been granted this we

[37] p. 247.
[38] *IGBulg.* 2236. Cf. pp. 64, 247.
[39] The passages translated are ll. 8–21 and 94–107.

shall be able to render thanks to your Fortune, as we do now in [beseeching?] you.'

From the Constantinian period we have on a long inscription the first part of the petition (*preces*) which the people of Orcistus addressed to the emperor to request from him the status of a city. The formula of address is unusual, as is the fact that this Phrygian community writes in Latin: 'We have fled to seek the aid of your piety, Lord Emperors Constantinus Maximus Victor, Augustus for ever, and Crispus and Constantinus and Constans, *nobilissimi Caesares . . .*' But it is certainly a *libellus* rather than a letter, as befitted a community which was not yet a city, just as the emperor's reply, of which the last part is preserved, seems to be a *subscriptio*.[40] It is, however, precisely because *libelli* from communities of less than city status performed a function very like that of the decrees which the ambassadors of cities, associations or provincial councils presented to the emperor that they had some chance of being inscribed at communal expense, and hence of being preserved for us along with the imperial response.[41] Otherwise we know the texts of *libelli* addressed by individuals to the emperor only from occasional copies preserved on papyrus; these usually seem to be drafts, and, even if they were ever taken to the emperor, are not accompanied by the replies.[42]

Such evidence apart, we are left with the imperial *subscriptiones* themselves, known in very large numbers from the mid-second to early fourth centuries. As we have seen, we have no adequate evidence with which to trace the origins of the system.[43] But it may be that in the first half of the second century written *libelli*, which are attested from the beginning came to preponderate over spoken petitions as a means of approaching the emperor. If this is so, the earlier pattern is still visible in the anecdote of a woman calling out to Hadrian as he was distributing a *congiarium*, 'I beseech you, lord, to order my son to provide for me, for he neglects me.'[44] The later one is certainly already evident in a *subscriptio* of Antoninus Pius: 'If you approach the relevant *iudices*, they will give orders that you should receive upkeep from your father, provided that, since you say that you are a workman, you are in such ill-health that you cannot sustain your work.'[45] Here even a petitioner of low social standing has presented his request in writing. On the other hand Volusius Maecianus in his work *On the Rhodian Sea-Law* (apparently in Greek) quotes Pius as replying verbally to the complaint of a

[40] *MAMA* VII 305, Panel ii, ll. 18f. (*preces*); i, ll. 1–7 (end of reply). For this see also pp. 131, 410. Note that by contrast Constantine's reply to this complaint about violation of their rights after they had gained city status (p. 438) is a letter.

[41] Note also the two fragmentarily-preserved petitions in Greek, with *subscriptiones* in Latin, of the *collegium* of Paeanistae in Rome, addressed to Severus and then Caracalla, *IG* XIV 1059 = *IGR* I 145 = Moretti, *IGUR* I 35; p. 246.

[42] pp. 492, 500, 537. In *P. Rendel Harris* 67 an emperor named Antoninus writes that he has ordered to be appended a copy both of a *libellus* (βιβλίδιον) given to him and of his *subscriptio* (ὑπογραφή, cf. p. 243) but the text breaks off thereafter, and the context is in any case obscure,

[43] pp. 240f.

[44] *Corp. Gloss. Lat.* III, 36, ll. 49f. For verbal replies to petitioners note also ibid., 32, ll. 13f. and the engaging story in *HA, Had.* 20, 8.

[45] *Dig.* XXV, 3, 5, 7, reading 'ut operi [for 'operis'] sufficere non possis' I can see no reason why the words 'competentes iudices' should be regarded as interpolated.

shipper that his ship after being wrecked had been ransacked by the
publicani.[46]

From the immense volume of historical evidence presented by the imperial
subscriptiones it is only possible to select a few further themes. We have seen
for instance that it was common for persons from the provinces to give
libelli to the emperor, receiving sometimes a refusal, very often a bare
instruction to approach the governor, but on occasion also what were in
effect indirect instructions to the governor as to how he should proceed.[47]
The *libellus*, if successful, could thus function as a means of bringing pressure, or even compulsion, on the governor in accordance with the wishes of
the petitioner. The same was also true of the office-holders in the city of
Rome, not merely imperial appointees but the praetors and consuls themselves. So for instance Antoninus Pius replied to 'a certain Telesphorus',
who evidently represented a group of freedmen:[48]

> The consuls, having summoned those from whom it is established that upkeep
> is owed to you [plural] on the basis of a *fideicommissum*, will decide as to whether
> you should all receive the upkeep from one person, or dividing the obligation
> proportionately, will decide who should receive it from whom.

Equally explicitly Marcus Aurelius and Verus 'wrote back' to a man named
L. Apronius Saturninus:[49]

> If you prove by documents that you have three legitimate children, the praetor,
> Manilius Carbo, *vir clarissimus*, will accept your *excusatio* [from *tutela*]. But the
> reference to 'legitimate children' is to be taken as meaning that they have been
> acquired in accordance with the civil law.

On occasion a litigant, showing that persistence to which the entire judicial
system of the empire was so vulnerable, would come more than once to the
emperor in the course of a single case, each time succeeding in putting some
compulsion on the officials of the city. Thus Marcus and Verus wrote again:[50]

> Since you say that it was as the result of an error that from the *iudex* whom you
> had received from the most honourable consuls in accordance with our *rescriptum*
> you appealed to Junius Rusticus, our *amicus*, prefect of the city, the most noble
> consuls will hear the case exactly as if the appeal had been made to them.

Similarly, Severus Alexander replied to a man named Socrates to the effect
that the prefect of the city would send before the relevant praetor the case
of a slave-girl whose eventual purchaser had improperly used her as a pros-
titute.[51] Replies directing the petitioner to go before a magistrate of Rome
are rare after the first part of the third century (perhaps one small reflection

---

[46] *Dig.* XIV, 2, 9. For a defence of the authenticity of the passage see J. Rougé, *Rev. Phil.* XLIII
(1969), 83.

[47] p. 475.

[48] *Dig.* XXXIV, 1, 3. Compare the rescript of Pius, *Dig.* XXXV, 1, 50: 'aditi a vobis amplissimi consules arbitrum dabunt.'

[49] *Frag. Vat.* 168.

[50] *Dig.* XLIX, 1, 1, 2.

[51] *CJ* IV, 56, 1.

of the increasing absence of the emperor from Rome); but in 293 the tetrarchs, in practice probably Maximian, told one Julianus that he could go before the praetor to reclaim money from his estate which had been retained by his former guardian.[52] In October 315 Constantine replied from Milan to an unnamed petitioner, emphasizing the invalidity of presents between husband and wife:[53]

> So you are not debarred from approaching Vettius Rufinus, *clarissimus vir*, prefect of the city, our *amicus*, who has jurisdiction in the matter, and who will examine the depositions of the parties and deal with your petition according to the justice of the law.

This reply, which must be regarded as a direction to the prefect of the city to take the case, is preserved by the *Fragmenta Vaticana*, one of a small group of late collections of legal material which perform the important function of making clear that replies to individuals did not cease in the first years of the fourth century, as the *Codex Justinianus* might suggest.[54] For instance the next entry in the *Fragmenta Vaticana* shows Constantine replying in very similar terms (from Rome in August of the same year, 315) to a petition from a woman named Aurelia Sabina or Gaudiosa She too is directed to the prefect of the city, 'who having duly considered all those things which you have thought fit to include in your *preces*, will see that they are properly decided in the light of his experience'.[55]

The insistent lady who according to Dio's story addressed a verbal petition to Hadrian, and who herself seems to be a literary fiction based on Hellenistic stories,[56] none the less finds innumerable real-life counterparts in imperial replies from the middle of the second century to the end of our period, and beyond it.[57] Calpurnia Aristaeneta indeed, to whom Diocletian and Maximian replied in 286, showed a determination worthy of her mythical predecessor, provoking the emperors into beginning their *subscriptio* as follows:[58]

> Since, not content with the *rescriptum* which you had received in answer to your previous *preces*, you have wished to petition (*supplicare*) a second time, you will take back a *rescriptum* based on strict law.

Few texts reveal more clearly how far both the acquisition of the

---

[52] *CJ* v, 51, 9; but note v, 62, 23, sent from Sirmium in 294, and hence by Diocletian, also telling a man that he should approach the praetor.

[53] *Frag. Vat.* 273. The reply is described as having been *data*, which may suggest (though cannot prove) an *epistula*, and hence a petitioner of good standing. It is dated 'XIIII Kal. Nov. Mediolano Constantino et Licinio conss.', which together with the name of the prefect makes the year 315 certain.

[54] The latest reply to an individual in *CJ* seems to be ix, 1, 18, of 304.

[55] *Frag. Vat.* 274: 'Data idibus Augustis Romae Constantino et Licinio Augg. conss.' This could be 312, 313 or 315, but we know that Constantine moved from Rome to Milan in a year which is almost certainly 315 rather than 316, Augustine, *Ep.* XLIII, 7/20, see p. 588.

[56] p. 3.

[57] *Consultatio* IX, 5 and 6, shows Valens and Valentinian replying from Mediolanum in 365 to a litigant named Aelia Bavonia, and from Sirmium in 364 to one named Ampelia, who is advised that possession will be granted by the proconsul of Africa.

[58] *Frag. Vat.* 282. A brief extract in *CJ* VIII, 53, 6, and a longer one in III, 29, 4 (both without the opening sentence).

rescriptum and the use to be made of it depended on the petitioner. If the emperors are correct in envisaging her as going subsequently to 'the governor of the province', she will literally have been 'taking it back' to some other part of the empire, and once there will have been free to make whatever use of it she could. But the text is perhaps more significant as one of the long series of *subscriptiones* in reply to women. At a more profound level it would be possible to use these as a means of enquiry into the steadily evolving position of women in law, and in particular their position as parties to legal proceedings. But it may be sufficient to consider some cases from a different point of view, namely as replies to petitions which by the nature of the position of women in Roman society could normally be related only to private matters of inheritance, property, marriage-law, dowries and so forth. As Diocletian and Maximian replied to a woman named Corinthia, a woman could not bring a criminal action unless it related to an *iniuria* done to herself or her family.[59] Nor would replies to women be concerned with questions of public office or privileges, or that vast borderland of public obligations, exceptions and excuses to which so much attention was directed. But even for women questions of status might be involved. Severus Alexander wrote for instance to a woman named Severiana: 'If, as you state, you had a grandfather of consular and a father of praetorian rank and have been married to men (?) not of private station but *clarissimi*, you retain your *claritas* of birth.' But Diocletian and Maximian had to point out to a woman who was not of senatorial birth that she owed her *claritas* to her senatorial husband, and that as she had subsequently married an *eques*, she had lost her status.[60]

But ordinarily the petitions concerned urgent matters of family or property, and thus exhibit as clearly as any other evidence the role of the emperor in redressing the rigour of the law, making allowances for ignorance of it and giving guidance on procedure. Replies to women begin very early, under Antoninus Pius.[61] Thereafter they are common,[62] and on occasion give insights into the private life of the population comparable to those provided by the *consultationes* of provincial governors.[63] Like other rescripts they may also reveal that the interested parties have in fact been acting in accordance with customs other than those of Roman law, and are thus primary evidence both for the imposition of Roman law and its modification in the face of prevailing local law, especially, but not only, Greek law.[64] A

[59] *CJ* IX, 1, 12. For instances see IX, 1, 4 (222), and 14 (294), but cf. 5 (222); also IX, 46, 2 (224).

[60] *CJ* XII, 1, 1; V, 4, 10.

[61] *Dig.* XXXVI, 4, 3, 3: 'hoc enim divus Pius rescripsit Pacuviae Licinianae.'

[62] Apart from those cases mentioned individually below, note *exempli gratia CJ* II, 12, 2; V, 25, 3; *Dig.* XXXV, 3, 3, 4 (Marcus and Verus to a freedwoman); *Frag. Vat.* 267 (Severus and Caracalla); *CJ* X, 3, 1; *Consultatio* I, 7 (Caracalla); *CJ* V, 4, 2 (283); *Frag. Vat.* 279, 297 (285); 315 (291); *Coll.* X, 6 (294); *Frag. Vat.* 41 (298). For a survey of the female addressees of rescripts in the *Codex Justinianus* (only), see L. Huchthausen in *Klio* LVI (1974), 199; LVIII (1976), 55.

[63] pp. 329ff.

[64] For this fundamental historical theme, far too large to be considered here, see the classic work of L. Mitteis, *Reichsrecht und Volksrecht in den östlichen Provinzen des römischen Kaiserreichs* (1891); for examples of rescripts to parties who have been acting in accordance with something comparable to Talmudic law see R. Yaron, 'Reichsrecht, Volksrecht and Talmud', *RIDA* XI (1964), 281.

classic example of family life conducted by Roman citizens in ignorance of the principles of Roman law is provided by the *subscriptio* of Marcus Aurelius and Verus to a woman named Flavia Tertulla, who had presented her petition through her *libertus*:[65]

> We are moved both by the length of time during which, in ignorance of the law, you have been married to your uncle, and the fact that you were placed in matrimony by your grandmother, and by the number of your children. So, as all these considerations come together, we confirm that the status of your children who result from this marriage, which was contracted forty years ago, shall be as if they had been conceived legitimately.

This is a clear instance where what the emperors granted was a *beneficium* as against the strict provisions of the law. Elsewhere they might come to the aid of a woman precisely by re-enunciating those provisions, as Diocletian and Maximian did in 285 in reply to a woman named Sebastiana:[66]

> It is generally known that no one under the rule of the Roman name may have two wives, since even in the praetor's edict such men are marked by *infamia*. The appropriate *iudex* will not allow this offence to go unpunished.

We can be quite certain that the woman had reported a particular case, probably involving herself as one of the wives. The detailed presentation of a family dispute is, however, clearer in another reply of the same emperors, to Ulpia Marcellina:[67]

> If the governor of the province finds on enquiry that your ignorance has been deceived by a fraudulent transaction and the skilful wiles of your son-in-law . . .

It is visible also in the *subscriptio* of Diocletian (and notionally Maximian) which was *proposita* in 286 at Heraclea-Perinthus, a frequent imperial stopping-place on the road from Pannonia to Byzantium and Asia Minor; they reassure her that the governor of the province will protect her rights to whatever her mother-in-law had given her as a gift, and state that she is free to decide whether to stay *in matrimonio* or to persist in her intention to end the marriage.[68] We can easily perceive that her husband had claimed that she was not free to do so, and that her mother-in-law had threatened to take back the gifts if she left. It is not surprising, therefore, that she felt the need of some outside support and advice. How far she had to travel to intercept Diocletian on his journeys and present her *libellus* is not known, but there is no reason to presume that the governor in question was that of the province in which Heraclea lay. But however clear her need was, we should not lose sight of the significance of the fact that she both had open to her, and actually employed, a means of satisfying it which consisted of going to where

[65] *Dig.* XXIII, 2, 57a.
[66] *CJ* V, 5, 2.
[67] *Consultatio* IX, 9.
[68] *Frag. Vat.* 284; on Heraclea-Perinthus as a stopping-place on this road, p. 47.

the emperor was, presenting a *libellus* which related to nothing more than the internal dissensions of her family, and awaiting the 'putting-up' of the emperor's reply.

It is indeed precisely the triviality of the issues concerned which is the most important fact about many of the *libelli* which his subjects presented to the emperor, and the *subscriptiones* which were issued in response to them. From these written exchanges, of which immense numbers survive from this period, we cannot of course prove more than that they had to take place wherever the emperor was. But even if it could be shown—which it cannot— that the replies were composed and issued by his staff in his name without his personal involvement, it would hardly decrease the significance of his symbolic role as the source of justice for individual subjects. Moreover our presumptions about his responsibility for written responses issued in his name have to be formed in the light of the fact that he continued for instance to receive embassies, to hear cases and to pronounce verdicts in person. In any case, the words of Constantine himself show that in one area at least, the endlessly contentious question of relief from public obligations, peti- tioners might still present themselves personally before the emperor:[69]

> Since we have learned that some have obtained from us exemption from personal burdens by offering to our sight the children of others as if they were their own, we order that, in cases where this is proved, they should be deprived of the *beneficium* which has been granted to them.

Constantine's words are not metaphorical, for in petitions presented on paper purely fictional children would have sufficed. It was only when the required number of five children was needed in order to be displayed before the emperor and attract his indulgence that it will have been necessary to borrow those of others.

It is perhaps not inappropriate that this testimony of Constantine to the petitions which his subjects might present in person to him, and the means which they might employ, dates from June 324. It was thus written shortly before the final victory whose most momentous consequence was that the affairs of the church in the Greek east would be pressed upon him with a vigour and resource which surpassed even that of its counterpart in the west.

---

[69] *CTh* XII, 17, 1: 'Quoniam cognovimus nonnullos vacationem a nobis personalium munerum impetrasse, alienos pro suis liberis nostris conspectibus offerentes, iubemus eos, cum hoc probatum sit, indulto beneficio privari.' A partial text, not including these words, in *CJ* X, 52, 6.

IX

Church and Emperor

1. *Introduction*

When Constantine died in 337 and was buried in the Church of the Holy Apostles in Constantinople, in the tomb which he had prepared in advance, flanked on each side by six symbolic tombs of the Apostles,[1] there had occurred within a few decades a revolution of a significance hardly paralleled in the history of the world. Yet, we may wonder what thoughts can have passed through the mind of any onlooker who happened to have read how, at Aegae 673 years before, Philip II of Macedon had had his statue carried with those of the twelve Olympian gods;[2] and so too the Constantinian revolution itself cannot be understood without considering the patterns of contact and exchange which constituted it, which themselves were products of those values and expectations within Graeco-Roman culture which finally transformed a Roman emperor into a *basileus*.

If we look back from the end of Constantine's reign over the relations of church and emperor, we can see mirrored in them almost every one of the distinctive features of the imperial monarchy which we have observed in operation in other contexts: the emperor's personal pronouncement of decisions and verdicts; the addressing of accusations and petitions to him; his conferment of privileges, and his decisions on the exclusion or inclusion or marginal cases; gifts in cash and kind; confiscation and restoration of property; the issuing of *edicta* and general *epistulae*, and before that, for a long period, only of *rescripta* in answer to *consultationes* by governors, or to letters from *koina* or cities.

To examine these channels of communication to the emperor, and the pattern of his pronouncements and decisions as they affected the church over three centuries, is not of course to write a history of the church itself. It is, on the one hand, to use evidence which relates not to settled institutions, social expectations and diplomatic forms, but to a new development with momentous consequences, in order to test both the reality and the significance of the patterns considered so far. On the other, it is to bring to bear on the history of the church an awareness of how its contacts with the emperor not merely resembled those characteristic of other groups and persons, but were fundamentally shaped by them. At the same time such

---

[1] Eusebius, *VC* IV, 58–60, 70–1; cf. Socrates, *HE* I, 40; Sozomenus, *HE* II, 34, 5.
[2] Diodorus XVI, 92, 5, cf. 95, 1.

an analysis—and it alone—can determine exactly what was distinctive about the emperor's relation to the church.

So far as our evidence goes, such a relation did not exist in any established form until the early second century. This was not, however, because Christianity remained even for this period an obscure phenomenon, remote from all possible contact with the emperor. On the contrary the early church remained, until the revolt of 66–70, attached to Jerusalem, 'by far the most famous city of the East',[3] from which, as we have seen, a succession of embassies, accusations and disputes went to Rome between the governorship of Pontius Pilatus and the early 60s.[4] As a man who had studied with Gamaliel, and who (if we may believe the author of Acts) told Agrippa II that he had earlier arrested Christians on the authority of the high priests and had voted (in the Sanhedrin?) for their execution,[5] Paul cannot have failed to know men who had been to appear before the emperor, long before his own appeal. Moreover, when he went, he was only one of a group of prisoners being sent to Rome at the same time;[6] whether any of the others had appealed, and whether all of them were due to be tried by Nero, must naturally remain in doubt.

To the factual evidence of Josephus as to issues and persons from Judaea coming before the emperor in these decades we can add the less tangible testimony of the Gospels. For in spite of the fact that no one can state with certainty by whom, when, where or with what purpose any one of them was written, they bear all the marks of deriving in some sense from the environment of Galilee and Judaea.[7] As such they remain, in spite of all the unanswered questions which hang over them, authentic testimony to popular conceptions and attitudes in one part of the empire. One parable even reflects with perfect clarity Archelaus' mission to Rome in 4 BC, and the Jewish embassy which went at the same time to ask Augustus for an end to Herodian rule:[8]

> A nobleman went on a journey to a distant land to acquire for himself a kingdom and return . . . But his fellow-citizens hated him and sent an embassy after him, saying, 'We do not wish this man to be king over us.'

In this instance the emperor himself is not explicitly mentioned. But in general the mentions of the emperor in the Gospels tend to portray him as even more ever-present to the minds of his subjects than we might expect, and as acting more positively than other evidence would suggest. So in Luke the well-known census of AD 6/7 in Syria and Judaea, which caused such turmoil in Jewish society, is seen as resulting from an edict of Augustus 'that the whole *oikoumenê* should be registered'. No other evidence suggests

---

[3] Pliny, *NH* v, 15/70.

[4] pp. 376–9.

[5] Acts 26, 10: καὶ πολλούς τε τῶν ἁγίων ἐγὼ ἐν φυλακαῖς κατέκλεισα, τὴν παρὰ τῶν ἀρχιερέων ἐξουσίαν λαβών, ἀναιρουμένων τε αὐτῶν κατήνεγκα ψῆφον. Cf. 22, 4.

[6] Acts 27, 1.

[7] For the best analysis of the Jewish substratum of the Gospel tradition see G. Vermes, *Jesus the Jew* (1973).

[8] Luke 19, 12–14; cf. pp. 19–20, 230, 376.

that there was such an edict, or a universal census, at this moment.[9] Then, as we saw briefly earlier, the famous discussion between Jesus and the Pharisees about the propriety of paying tribute (which takes place in Jerusalem, which was subject to Roman tribute, not in Galilee which lay in the tetrarchy of Herod Antipas) concludes with the deduction that because the 'coin of the census' bore Caesar's name and image, the tribute was due to be paid to him.[10] More significantly still, John's Gospel represents the crowd in Jerusalem as shouting to Pilate, 'If you release this man, you are not a friend of Caesar; anyone who claims to be a king opposes Caesar'; and when Pilate asks if he should crucify their king, they reply, 'We have no king except Caesar.'[11] Jerusalem had been ruled by a king until 4 BC, and by an ethnarch until AD 6. But the words imply more than the fact these titles could be conferred or removed by the emperor. For to the people the emperor himself was another king.

Outside Judaea the spread of Christianity necessarily depended on that same evident fact of intensive travel and intercommunication in the Mediterranean area which was one of the conditions which allowed the role of the emperor to be what it was. It is a too familiar and unsurprising fact that within three decades of the Crucifixion there should have been Christian communities over large parts of Syria, Asia Minor, Macedonia and Greece, and at least at Puteoli and in Rome in Italy. Here too we encounter very similar conceptions of the emperor. In Thessalonica the hostile crowd of Jews and Gentiles shouts, 'These men all act against the edicts of Caesar, saying that there is another king, Jesus.'[12] The population is represented as believing in 'edicts of Caesar' as the source of law, and specifically in edicts of a nature which we can be confident had never been promulgated. More important still, they too see the emperor as a 'king', to whom another king would be a rival.

In fact of course the surviving letters written for internal use in the early church are, as is well known, united in their acceptance of the prevailing order, and their conviction that authority within it was delegated by God.[13] Specifically, the first letter ascribed to Peter, and addressed to the Christians of Pontus, Galatia, Cappadocia, Asia and Bithynia, says: 'Be obedient to every human institution for the Lord's sake, whether to the king, as being above all, or the governors, as being sent out by him to punish wrongdoers and reward the meritorious.'[14] Here too the emperor is a king, and what is more all the governors are seen as being 'sent' by him; yet Asia was ruled by proconsuls at all times, as was the province of Pontus and Bithynia up to 109, when Pliny was sent by Trajan. Once again, if these passing references are any guide, Christians in the east, like Jews and pagans, not only saw the

---

[9] Luke 2, 1. For the census and Josephus' evidence about it see Schürer, *Jewish People* I, 399–427.

[10] Mark 12, 13–17; Matthew 22, 17–22; Luke 20, 21–6; cf. p. 199.

[11] John 19, 12–16.

[12] Acts 17, 7: καὶ οὗτοι πάντες ἀπέναντι τῶν δογμάτων Καίσαρος πράττουσι, βασιλέα λέγοντες ἕτερον εἶναι, Ἰησοῦν.

[13] esp. Rom. 13, 1: οὐ γὰρ ἔστιν ἐξουσία εἰ μὴ ὑπὸ θεοῦ, αἱ δὲ οὖσαι ὑπὸ θεοῦ τεταγμέναι εἰσίν, and 13, 7 (on the payment of tribute and other dues); I Tim. 2, 1–2 (prayers for kings and those in authority); Titus 3, 1.

[14] I Peter 2, 13–14. cf. 17.

emperor as a king, but attributed to him an authority even more general than that which he actually exercised. Christian writings provide what is far from the least significant evidence for those attitudes on the part of the population, as a result of which they tended to approach the emperor in a way which contributed to detaching him from the institutions of the *res publica*.

In practice, however, it was of course the emperor's role as judge of criminal cases which first affected Christians directly, though our evidence for both the occasions and the proceedings is of quite remarkable obscurity and fragility. For instance, the fact of the martyrdom of Peter and Paul is alluded to by the first letter of Clement at the end of the first century.[15] But what Eusebius can collect about the manner of their death depends partly on passing references in Christian sources of the late second and early third centuries,[16] and partly on the references in II Timothy to escaping 'from the mouth of the lion', which he takes as being probably a reference to Nero, before whom Paul will first have been acquitted before his second trial and martyrdom; but it is more than dubious whether the letter was in fact written by Paul.[17]

That Nero did in fact preside at the trials of a number of Christians in Rome in 64 is of course attested in the well-known account by Tacitus;[18] but brief, allusive and rhetorical as it is, it reveals no more than that Nero 'put up the accused' (*subdidit reos*), that they were convicted, and that Nero was responsible for subjecting them to gruesome forms of execution. We are left wholly in the dark as to whether accusers came forward spontaneously, or supposedly so, whether anything resembling a formal trial was held, and if so whether solely before the emperor, or in other courts also.

Even greater difficulties attach to other possible cases of imperial *cognitio* in relation to Christians in this period. According to Eusebius, for instance, under Domitian Flavia Domitilla, niece of a consul Flavius Clemens, was exiled to the island of Pontia, along with many others, for confessing Christianity. But Cassius Dio a century earlier had recorded that Domitian executed his nephew, Flavius Clemens, and exiled to Pandateria the latter's wife, Flavia Domitilla, on a charge of impiety, brought because they both inclined to Judaism.[19] This episode is a good example of the emperor's criminal jurisdiction, and its exercise in relation to leading circles in Rome;[20] the later Christian version is merely an inaccurate attempt to absorb an item from pagan historiography into the tradition of martyrdom.

The conception of the emperor as judge did indeed exercise a powerful influence, and as early as the middle of the second century Hegesippus had evolved a tale of certain impoverished persons who were denounced to

---

[15] I Clement 5.

[16] *HE* II, 25, 5–8. The tradition that Paul was beheaded and Peter crucified is reflected also in Tertullian, *Scorpiace* 15, 3, and *De Praescr. her.* 36, 3.

[17] *HE* II, 22, 2–6 (II Timothy 4, 16–17). For a survey of the question of II Timothy see for example A. Wikenhauser, J. Schmid, *Einleitung in das Neue Testament*[6] (1973), 309–38.

[18] *Ann.* xv, 44; no light is thrown on these questions by the brief allusion in Suetonius, *Nero* 16, 2.

[19] Eusebius, *HE* III, 18, 4; Dio LXVII, 14, 1–2.

[20] cf. pp. 524–6.

Domitian as belonging to the race of David, and to the family of Jesus. Brought before the emperor by an *evocatus*, they demonstrated both that they lived in poverty, and expected only a heavenly kingdom. In response, the emperor freed them and 'ended by an edict the persecution of the church'.[21] Persons from the provinces might indeed, as we saw earlier, be summoned to Rome to stand trial before the emperor,[22] and it cannot be proved that such a summons and examination could not have taken place in this instance. But the story, with its explicit comparison of Domitian to Herod, bears all the marks of legend.

If so, it is all the more significant that Domitian's supposed edict ending persecution is the only general pronouncement relating to Christianity which any source earlier than Sulpicius Severus at the beginning of the fifth century specifically attributes to any first-century emperor.[23] Neither Tacitus nor Suetonius reports any such pronouncement by Nero, and in their well-known exchange about the Christians in Pontus, neither Pliny nor Trajan shows any awareness of a pronouncement in any form by any previous emperor. The evidence from which a belief in such a pronouncement has traditionally been derived is of a quite different, and highly significant nature. For it was in the *Apology* which Melito, the learned bishop of Sardis, addressed to Marcus Aurelius to petition him on behalf of the Christians that the argument was first used that persecution was an unworthy aberration, characteristic only of emperors such as Nero and Domitian: 'Alone of all, under the persuasion of certain evil men, Nero and Domitian were willing to place our doctrine under accusation; since their time, by an irrational custom, the bringing of false accusation has come to extend to such persons.' From the 'irrational custom' of Melito derives the 'Neronian institution' (*institutum Neronianum*) of Tertullian, not a pronouncement but a proceeding, 'Neronian' and hence (it was to be hoped) to be regarded as disreputable.[24]

The *Apologies* addressed to the emperors are a crucial feature of the second century, to which it will be neccessary to return. For the moment it will be sufficient to emphasize that, once we understand the nature of this persuasive description of persecution expressed in one of these, we lose all the supposed evidence for a general imperial pronouncement (an *edictum* or some other legislative act) directed against the Christians. Instead we have condemnations by Nero, following proceedings whose nature Tacitus leaves obscure, and perhaps by Domitian. Whether such condemnations provided the model and justification for prosecutions of Christians before other judges—or whether indeed such a model was required—we do not know. All that is certain is that trials (*cognitiones*) of Christians had taken place before Pliny

---

[21] Eusebius, *HE* III, 19–20.

[22] p. 524.

[23] Sulpicius, *Chron.* II, 29, 3, attributes to Nero *leges* and *edicta* forbidding Christianity. I ignore here Tertullian's legend of a report about Christianity sent by Tiberius to the senate, sufficiently dealt with by T. D. Barnes, 'Legislation against the Christians', *JRS* LVIII (1968), 32. It will be patent that in what follows I owe a fundamental debt to this paper.

[24] Melito, *ap.* Eusebius, *HE* IV, 26, 9; Tertullian, *Ad Nat.* I, 7, 8–9, cf. *Apol.* 5, 3–4. See, essentially, Barnes, o.c., 34–5.

wrote to Trajan about those accused before him in Pontus. Since Pliny had
not been present at any of these, this topic became one of the many on which
he consulted Trajan and received *rescripta* in return.[25] It was entirely
characteristic of the period that *rescripta* to consultations by provincial
governors became perhaps the primary form in which emperors made specific
pronouncements about Christianity, as they did on so many other issues.
It was also characteristic that in the second century they should have written
on the same topic to various Greek cities, and perhaps to *koina* also; and
equally characteristic, and in the long run even more significant, that they
should have been addressed in petitions by individual Christians of suitable
literary ability, one of whom was to emphasize the coincidence of the birth
of Christ and the *basileia* of Augustus.

2. Consultation, Petition and Rescript

According to Lactantius, Ulpian in the seventh book of his *On the Office of
Proconsul* 'collected the disgraceful *rescripta* of the emperors, in order to
make clear what penalties should be applied to those who confessed themselves worshippers of God'.[1] If Lactantius is correct, and we have no reason
to suppose otherwise, it is of considerable significance that the type of
imperial pronouncement mentioned is *rescripta*, not *edicta*, or *orationes*
before the senate, or *leges*, or even *decreta*—verdicts in individual cases. For
even if it cannot be shown that these other types of pronouncement are
specifically intended to be excluded, it is very suggestive that it is *rescripta*
which are explicitly mentioned. For in that case it would show that the
characteristic, and perhaps the only, form in which emperors had made
legally valid pronouncements about the Christians was that of the reply,
whether to governors, cities, or individuals (pagan or Christian).[2]

Negative generalizations can never be proved, and it therefore cannot be
shown strictly that there were no positive and general imperial pronouncements about the Christians in the period before the persecution of Decius.
All that can be shown is that reliable evidence does not record any specific
pronouncements by named emperors other than *rescripta*. The most that
Eusebius can say of Septimius Severus, for instance, is that he 'stirred up a
persecution against the churches'.[3] On Maximinus the Thracian he is at
least more specific: 'Having raised a persecution, he ordered that the leaders
of the Church only should be put to death, as being responsible for the

---

[25] Pliny, *Ep.* x, 96–7; on his correspondence with Trajan from Pontus and Bithynia, and its
significance in the development of the emperor's role, see pp. 325–8.

[1] *Div. Inst.* v, 11, 19.

[2] The point was made briefly in 'The Imperial Cult and the Persecutions', *Entretiens Hardt* XIX.
Le culte des souverains dans l'Empire romain (1973), 145, on p. 159; and previously by G. E. M.
de Ste. Croix, 'Why were the Early Christians Persecuted?', *Past and Present* XXVI (1963), 6, on
p. 14 = M. I. Finley (ed.), *Studies in Ancient Society* (1974), 210, on p. 223.

[3] *HE* VI, 1, 1: ὡς δὲ καὶ Σευῆρος διωγμὸν κατὰ τῶν ἐκκλησιῶν ἐκίνει. For the refutation
of the notion of a general persecution instigated by Severus see K. M. Schwarte, 'Das angebliche
Christengesetz des Septimius Severus', *Historia* XII (1963), 185. I ignore here *HA, Sept. Sev.* 17, 1,
on which see the arguments of T. D. Barnes, *JRS* LVIII (1968), 40–1.

teaching according to the Gospel.'[4] If the statement is true, however, it must imply either an *edictum* or letters sent generally to office-holders or governors, for which we have no evidence; and in the only area for which we have good contemporary evidence for the course of persecution at this time, namely Cappadocia, the causes were purely local.[5]

Yet apart from various martyr-acts, whose historicity in detail provides notorious problems,[6] one text of the period, Hippolytus' *Commentary on Daniel*, does represent the prosecutions of Christians as being based on an imperial decree: when the Christians will not worship the gods 'they lead them to the tribunal and accuse them of acting against the decree of Caesar, and condemn them to death'.[7] The statement may well be true of what was actually said in the course of prosecuting Christians; but, as we saw in the case of the report in Acts (in very similar words) about the mob in Thessalonica, the people seem to have tended to imagine more positive and more general imperial commands than are reliably attested. The evidence against such general commands can never be conclusive; but the tenuous and fragile nature of the evidence for them in the period before Decius contrasts very clearly both with the specific and concrete evidence for the general *epistulae* and *edicta* of Decius, Valerian and the tetrarchs, and the equally specific and concrete evidence for imperial pronouncements of the earlier period which were responses to office-holders or subjects.

The first case is of course the famous letter of Pliny written from Pontus probably in 110/11, and Trajan's reply.[8] We cannot know if similar consultations had already been addressed to Trajan, or earlier emperors, by *legati*, and been answered in similar terms. But, so far as our evidence goes, it was in this exchange that the basic principles were first laid down, in accordance with which the Christians were treated up to the persecution of Decius. We could hardly ask for a clearer demonstration of the importance of consultation and rescript within the imperial system. Pliny did not need to consult Trajan about confessed Christians, whom he had already executed (except for citizens, whom he had set aside for despatch to Rome, for what reason is not clear);[9] he had also freed those who had denied ever having been Christians, and who had sacrificed to statues of the gods, and an image of Trajan, brought for the purpose. Pliny's questions related firstly to a general principle, whether accusations contained in an anonymous *libellus* were

---

[4] *HE* vi, 28.

[5] For a discussion of the evidence see G. W. Clarke, 'Some Victims of the Persecution of Maximinus Thrax', *Historia* xv (1966), 445. For Cappadocia the letter of Firmilian in Cyprian, *Ep.* 75, 10.

[6] See Barnes, o.c., 44–8.

[7] *In Dan.* I, 20, 3.

[8] *Ep.* x, 96–7; for the most probable date see the arguments of Sherwin-White, *The Letters of Pliny* (1966), 81; for the location, ibid., 693–4.

[9] They *may* have been sent, as other prisoners sometimes were (pp. 323, 507), for trial by the emperor. They had not appealed, however, and this can have no relevance to the supposed right of citizens to appeal to the emperors. They *may* even have already been *condemnati*, as the letters of Ignatius (*Ad Trall.* 3, 3; Rom. 4, 3) make clear that he was when sent, probably a few years earlier, from Antioch to Rome, in chains (Eph. 21, 2; *Trall.* 10, 1), and anticipating martyrdom in the arena.

admissible, which Trajan rejected.[10] His major question, however, related to
those who admitted having been Christians in the past, but claimed (and
proved by sacrificing and cursing Christ) that they had since lapsed. Pliny
retails their testimony that there had been nothing criminal in their activities
while Christians, and argues that allowance should be made for penitence,
especially as there were welcome signs of a return to pagan worship. Trajan
agrees—such a person 'should gain pardon by penitence'. The proposal was
thus Pliny's, and there is nothing in the exchange to suggest that it had ever
been made before; but might it even, like the contents of so many other
consultationes,[11] have originated in fact with the interested parties?

Whether that is so or not, Trajan's assent set the pattern for the peculiar
treatment of Christianity in the courts, on which Tertullian was later to
expend some of his considerable rhetorical powers:[12]

> You regard a Christian as guilty of every crime, the enemy of the gods, the
> emperors, the laws, morality and of all nature—and yet you try to force a denial
> in order to acquit him, from a man whom you could not have acquitted unless
> he had made a denial.

From this moment on, up to and including the persecution of Decius, and
on occasions later, the test of Christianity was whether a man performed an
act of pagan worship in court without regard to what he had done in the past,
or even (as Tertullian points out in the same passage) what he might do in
the future.

A few years later the proconsul of Asia in 121/2, Q. Licinius Silvanus
Granianus, consulted Hadrian (who was then visiting the western provinces,
including Britain) about accusations of Christians which had been made
before him. What situation he described, and what questions he asked, can
only be deduced from Hadrian's rescript, sent to his successor in office in
122/3, Minicius Fundanus:[13]

> I have received a letter written to me by Serenius [i.e. Silvanus] Granianus,
> *clarissimus vir*, whom you have succeeded. I do not think it right to leave the
> matter undecided, lest the people be disturbed and an opportunity for mischief
> provided for accusers. So assuredly, as regards this petition, if the provincials
> are able to make affirmations against the Christians, such that they can be
> defended in court, let them resort to that means, and not to mere petitions or
> shouts. For it is much more appropriate that if anyone wishes to make an
> accusation, you should hear the case. So if anyone makes an accusation and
> proves that they are acting against the laws, determine the verdict in accordance
> with the gravity of the offence. But by Hercules if anyone takes this course in

[10] Note now the reference in *P. Karanis* 522 to [τὸ δ]οθέν μοι βιβλίδιον χωρὶς ὀνόματος
(Valerius Eudaemon, prefect of Egypt, 142–3).

[11] pp. 332–6.

[12] *Apol.* II, 16.

[13] The text is given by Justin, *Apol.* I, 68; Eusebius, *HE* IV, 9, records that he found the letter
in Latin in Justin, and translated it into Greek (as it now appears in Justin also); it was referred to
also in the *Apology* of Melito, quoted by Eusebius, *HE* IV, 26, 10. For the parallel case of a *consultatio* by a praetor, answered in a rescript to his successor, see p. 338. For Q. Licinius Silvanus
Granianus, see *PIR²* L 247.

order to make a mischievous accusation, take cognisance of his wickedness and consider how to punish him.

We cannot of course be absolutely confident that the Greek text as we have it faithfully represents what Hadrian wrote. But it is even more unlikely that the Latin text which Justin attached to the *Apology* which he addressed to Antoninus Pius, could have been a deliberate forgery of a letter allegedly written by the emperor's immediate predecessor; and it is noticeable that what we have is a rescript about criminal procedure, not significantly dissimilar to various letters of Hadrian preserved in legal sources.[14] It was common also for governors to consult the emperor about forms of punishment, and this is exactly what is recorded in the letter sent by the Christian community of Lugdunum to those of Asia and Phrygia to record the martyrdoms which took place there in about 177. In this instance the pressure of popular initiative is described with particular vividness; it lead to the appearance of Christians first before the city magistrates and then before the *legatus* of Lugdunensis. It was indeed while the crowd was shouting against one of them named Attalus in the arena that the *legatus* learned that he was a Roman citizen and 'ordered him to be kept aside with the others who were in prison, about whom he sent to Caesar, and awaited the reply from him'. When Marcus Aurelius' reply came, it was to the effect that they should be flogged to death, but released if they made a denial. The reply, as reported, seems to relate to the other prisoners, for the letter subsequently records both that the Roman citizens were beheaded (rather than sent to the beasts), and that Attalus was after all sent to the beasts 'to please the crowd'.[15] The emperor's letter may indeed have included the provision that citizens should have the (relative) privilege of beheading. If so, this sequence of events is a clear illustration of the obvious but neglected fact that the emperor's words in a letter (or any other form of pronouncement) could not of themselves determine what was done in a province.

These letters of Trajan, Hadrian and Marcus Aurelius on the subject of the treatment of Christians were thus all replies to enquiries by provincial governors. Melito indeed, in his *Apology* addressed to Marcus, states that Hadrian wrote to many others (that is, governors) also, and furthermore that Antoninus Pius had written to Greek cities, and perhaps to a *koinon*. He comes on to this point immediately after his mention of Nero and Domitian, and in deliberate contrast to it:[16]

But their ignorance has been put right by your pious forebears, who have often chastised in writing many who had the temerity to act unlawfully against such people [Christians]. Among them, your grandfather Hadrian is shown to have written both to many others and to the proconsul Fundanus, governor of Asia; and your father, when you were directing affairs in concert with him, wrote to

---

[14] pp. 328–30.
[15] The letter is reproduced by Eusebius, *HE* v, 1; for the correspondence of the *legatus* and the emperor, paras. 44 and 47. For the various punishments mentioned, 47 and 50–2, and cf. p. 333.
[16] Eusebius, *HE* IV, 26, 10.

the cities to do nothing unlawful in relation to us, for instance to the people of Larisa, of Thessalonica and of Athens, and to all the Greeks.

Melito can thus mention three separate letters of Pius to Greek cities, and once again it is barely conceivable that he could have done so in addressing Marcus Aurelius if no such letters had ever been written. As we have seen, our evidence (primarily inscriptions) provides abundant testimony to imperial letters to Greek cities in this period. Moreover the natural assumption from the mass of documentary evidence must be that the imperial letters were replies to decrees passed by these cities, and either brought by embassies or sent on by the proconsul of Achaea or Macedonia. The alternative possibility, imperial letters sent spontaneously to these cities, is supported by almost no parallels except for occasional letters of recommendation.[17] We must therefore presume, though we cannot prove, that these cities had applied to the emperor in terms hostile to the Christians (as those of Asia Minor and Syria were to do to Maximin in 311/12),[18] but had received unfavourable or neutral replies.

The nature of the letter to 'all the Greeks' is more mysterious, but it is most likely that this is a reference to one addressed to the *koinon* of 'Hellenes' of some area outside Greece proper, most probably in Asia Minor.[19] As has been generally recognized, this reference will have provided the origin of a letter of Antoninus Pius or Marcus to the *koinon* of Asia, attested in differing forms in two Christian traditions. Eusebius quotes Melito in corroboration, but the letter which he gives has the titulature of Marcus Aurelius in 161, with one later element. A variant text, with a version of the titulature of Antoninus Pius, is preserved along with *Apologies* of Justin.[20] At least part of the text as it stands (in either form) must be a Christian forgery, but a reference to letters addressed by governors to 'my most divine father' and his rescripts to the effect that Christians should not be molested unless they were guilty of subversion, conceivably could be authentic.

Such a letter to a *koinon* would also normally have been in response to a decree of the *koinon* itself.[21] But Eusebius' introduction to it raises another possibility: 'The same king, when petitioned by others of the brothers [Christians] in Asia, who were suffering all manner of insults at the hands of the local peoples, saw fit to address the following pronouncement to the *koinon* of Asia.'[22] We have no indication of the source of Eusebius' statement, and he may well be entirely mistaken. But for instance the example of Antonius' letter to the *koinon* of Asia following an embassy from the *synodos* of athletes[23] shows that we cannot categorically rule out the possibility that

---

[17] p. 420.

[18] pp. 445–7.

[19] A *koinon* of Achaeans, with varying titulature, is however well-attested in Greece in this period, see U. Kahrstedt, *Symb. Osl.* XXVIII (1950), 70.

[20] Eusebius, *HE* IV, 13; *GCS* IX, 1, 328; see esp. T. D. Barnes, *JRS* LVIII (1968), 37–8.

[21] cf. pp. 385–94.

[22] *HE* IV, 13 *praef.*: ἐντευχθεὶς δὲ καὶ ὑφ' ἑτέρων ὁ αὐτὸς βασιλεὺς ἐπὶ τῆς 'Ασίας ἀδελφῶν παντοίαις ὕβρεσιν πρὸς τῶν ἐπιχωρίων δήμων καταπονουμένων, τοιαύτης ἠξίωσεν τὸ κοινὸν τῆς 'Ασίας διατάξεως. The last phrase is clearly incomplete, but the original sense is evident.

[23] p. 456.

Pius (if we follow Melito) wrote to the *koinon* following a petition from Asian Christians. This slight and tenuous possibility gains some small support from the fact that it is precisely from the middle part of the second century that Christian *Apologies*, among them ones addressed to emperors, are best attested.

It should be stated at once that in the nature of the case we cannot determine with certainty whether such a work actually was presented, or sent, to the emperor named, or merely has the literary form of a work so presented. Later Christian sources, mainly Eusebius, invariably speak as if they were describing a genuine presentation, but this could of course be dismissed as a deduction from the texts of the works themselves. Moreover, the very fact that these works passed into the Christian tradition shows that the emperor did not form their only intended readership, and that they were designed also for the edification and fortification of Christians—and perhaps for the instruction of educated pagans. None the less, we must recall not only that works addressed, for instance, by Martial to the emperor passed subsequently into the body of his works, but so also did prose works, similarly addressed to emperors by Greek writers of the second and early third century. What is more, such works include for instance Aristides' letter on Smyrna and Alexander of Aphrodisias' *On Fate*, both of which were sent to emperors in the first instance.[24] The existence of a substantial body of pagan works addressed in various forms to the emperors not only does much to explain the existence and literary form of the *Apologies*, but allows us to pose in different terms the question of their authenticity as works genuinely intended for the emperor: *could* such works have been given this form, headed by the name of the reigning emperor, *without* in fact ever being presented or sent to him?

The question must simply be posed, for no certain answer to it can be given. If we turn to the actual instances of *Apologies* addressed to emperors, the earliest of which we know was that of Quadratus to Hadrian: Eusebius reports, 'To him Quadratus gave a work which he addressed to him, having composed an apology for our faith, because some wicked men were attempting to harass our people.' He adds that copies were still kept by many Christians, including himself, and quotes a fragment defending the authenticity of the miracles of Jesus.[25] Eusebius says nothing more about the date or circumstances of the presentation; but Jerome claims to know that Quadratus was bishop of Athens, and that he presented his work to Hadrian when the latter was visiting Greece, and by being initiated at Eleusis (in 124) 'and almost all the mysteries in Greece' had given an occasion to those who believed that by persecuting the Christians they were following his command.[26] His only report of its contents, however, merely paraphrases Eusebius' quotation. There is in fact nothing implausible in what he reports, but it must remain more than dubious whether he had any independent evidence for doing so.

[24] pp. 423–4, 497.
[25] *HE* IV, 3, 1–2: τούτῳ Κοδρᾶτος λόγον προσφωνήσας ἀναδίδωσιν.
[26] *De vir. ill.* 19.

19

Eusebius also records briefly that a Christian named Aristides left an
Apology addressed to Hadrian, of which copies were still preserved (though
apparently not by Eusebius himself). Here too Jerome gives more detail,
namely that Aristides was an Athenian and 'a most eloquent philosopher'.[27]
This work is preserved, mainly in Syriac in a manuscript of the sixth or
seventh century, and also in fragments of Greek, some from later manuscripts but two from papyri of the fourth century.[28] The Syriac text unfortunately begins with a double address (presumably a combination of
openings from earlier texts), the latter of which calls the emperor 'Caesar
Titus Hadrianus Antoninus', which is the name of Antoninus Pius. Thereafter the text as preserved is a fairly brief and sober argument against various
pagan (and, even more briefly, Jewish) beliefs, and an exposition of the nature
of Christian beliefs and practices. Here, as in the Greek fragments, he
addresses the emperor as 'king' (*basileus*).

It is perhaps the most important feature of this *Apology* that its author
describes himself as a 'philosopher from among the Athenians', for it was a
necessary condition of any defence of Christianity that it should be expressed
in language and in a conceptual framework comprehensible to educated
pagans familiar with Greek philosophy. It is precisely this harmonization
which is the essential contribution of the *Apology*, or *Apologies*, which
Justin addressed to Antoninus Pius. More precisely, his address ran:[29]

> To the Emperor Titus Aelius Hadrianus Antoninus Pius Augustus Caesar and
> to his son Verissimus, a philosopher [Marcus Aurelius], and to Lucius, a
> philosopher [Lucius Verus], son of Caesar by birth, and of Pius by adoption,
> a lover of learning, to the sacred Senate and the whole *populus* of Romans, on
> behalf of those from all races of men who are wrongly hated and abused, I,
> Justin son of Priscus, son of Bacchius, belonging to the city of Flavia Neapolis
> in Palestine, have alone made this address and petition.

But in a way which distinguishes it entirely from the *Apology* of Aristides
it is also an attempt to describe and ameliorate the situation of the Christians
in the real world. He refers in the course of this to actual events, Hadrian's
letter to Silvanus Granianus, the presentation by a Christian to L. Munatius
Felix, prefect of Egypt (150–2?), of a *libellus* asking permission to be
castrated, which the prefect declined to 'subscribe';[30] a case before Q.
Lollius Urbicus, prefect of the city probably 146–60;[31] and in connection
with this the presentation to 'you, the emperor' (Antoninus Pius), of a

---

[27] Eusebius, o.c., IV, 3, 3; Jerome, o.c., 20; cf. Jerome, *Chron.* (ed. Helm, p. 199).
[28] For a full study, see C. Vona, *L'Apologia di Aristide: introduzione, versione del siriaco e
commento* (1950).
[29] *Apol.* I, 1 (ed. G. Krüger, 1915). The latter part, conventionally given (as here) as *Apol.* II,
may not in reality have been a separate work, and is not the second *Apology* of Justin, addressed
to Marcus Aurelius, referred to by Eusebius, *HE* IV, 18, 2 (16, 1?). Moreover, Eusebius, o.c., IV,
8, 5 and 17, cites passages from our *Apol.* II as coming from the first *Apol.* On the importance of
Justin in the intellectual history of Christianity see H. Chadwick, *Early Christian Thought and the
Classical Tradition* (1966), ch. i.
[30] *Apol.* I, 29, 2–3. On the background to this request, see Schürer, *Jewish People* I, 536–40.
[31] *Apol.* II, 1–2 (here and in what follows I treat *Apol.* I and II together); for Urbicus see *PIR*²
L 327.

libellus from a Christian woman asking permission to put her affairs in order before standing trial as a Christian, to which the emperor had agreed—'and you consented to this'.[32]

As with the instances of imperial letters given by Melito, these mentions of specific issues brought before the emperor or other judges must tend to support the genuineness of Justin's work as one actually presented to the emperor. What is more, at the end he describes his work as a *libellus* and asks for it to be 'subscribed' by the emperor in a way which would dispel false accusations, and to be 'put up'—that is in public, as we know *subscriptiones* now were.[33]

In his text Justin begins by appealing to the emperors as men of piety, philosophers, defenders of justice and lovers of learning, exactly as any pagan might have done. He continues by requesting that Christians should not be condemned for the 'name' alone, and later defends them against the charge that the kingdom (*basileia*) which they awaited was an earthly one, and emphasizes the law-abidingness of Christians and their long-established acceptance of the payment of tribute. Subsequently, he embarks on a defence of Christian doctrine and of the divinity of Christ, whose essential antiquity is demonstrated by its being the fulfilment of prophecy. After a description of Christian rituals he comes rather abruptly to Hadrian's letter to Silvanus Granianus. If our *Second Apology*, which has no formula of address, should be regarded as a continuation of the *First*, he then moves straight to the case before Lollius Urbicus and to expected accusations against himself by a philosopher named Crescens. Justin has already cross-questioned him and found him totally ignorant of Christianity; if the emperors were not aware of this, he would be happy to repeat the demonstration before them—'this too [such a hearing] would be a kingly task'. He concludes with a defence of the fact that Christians avoided suicide but were willing to face martyrdom, and with the claim that Christianity represented the full truth, of which Plato, the Stoics and other Greek writers had possessed only the seeds.

There cannot be any certainty that we either possess or can reconstruct the original form of Justin's *Apology* or *Apologies*. As a literary work it was substantially longer than any *libelli* known to us from inscriptions or papyri, but since he himself calls it a *libellus* (*biblidion* in Greek) it must owe something to the *libelli* which ordinarily were presented to the emperors. Moreover, it is at least as convincing, and far more economical, an explanation of its contents and its concrete references to events, to suggest that it actually was presented—or was intended to be presented—to the emperors, as that it is an elaborate literary fiction.

Under Marcus Aurelius we know of three *Apologies* addressed to the emperor: that of the bishop Apollinaris of Hierapolis, known only from a

[32] *Apol.* II, 2, 8: καὶ ἡ μὲν βιβλίδιόν σοι τῷ αὐτοκράτορι ἀνέδωκε, πρότερον συγχωρηθῆναι αὐτῇ διοικήσασθαι τὰ ἑαυτῆς ἀξιοῦσα, ἔπειτα ἀπολογήσασθαι περὶ τοῦ κατηγορήματος μετὰ τὴν τῶν πραγμάτων αὐτῆς διοίκησιν· καὶ συνεχώρησας τοῦτο.

[33] *Apol.* II, 14, 1: καὶ ὑμᾶς οὖν ἀξιοῦμεν ὑπογράψαντας τὸ ὑμῖν δοκοῦν προθεῖναι τουτὶ τὸ βιβλίδιον Cf. pp. 244-5.

reference in Eusebius;[34] that of Melito bishop of Sardis; and the only one
which is preserved complete, that of Athenagoras, addressed to Marcus
Aurelius and Commodus.[35] By entitling his work *Presbeia—Embassy—*he
unambiguously relates his work to the standard form in which communities
and organized bodies approached the emperors, namely by sending representatives to make a speech before them. Moreover, not only is the work cast
in the form of a speech (as opposed to that of an *epistula* or a *libellus*), but
in the middle of it he explicitly refers, in obsequious terms, to the attitudes of
those who came before the emperors with requests:[36]

> Nor do those of your subjects who come to you neglect to pay obeisance to you,
> their lords and masters, from whom they make and gain their requests, and
> turn rather to the splendour of your dwelling; but rather, while they admire
> the beautiful adornments of the royal palace as they happen to observe them,
> it is you who are in every way uppermost in their minds.

The joint rule of Marcus and Commodus began in 177, and in August 178
they left Rome to conduct campaigns on the Danube, where they remained
until Marcus' death in 180. As abundant parallel evidence shows, any number
of speeches by embassies from the Greek world will have been delivered
before them in this period, whenever the course of the fighting allowed.[37]
Lack of external evidence means that we have no confirmation that Athenagoras' *Presbeia* was among them (and if it were, it would mean that some
church or churches had assumed a status comparable to that of a *koinon*,
city, or *synodos* of athletes or performers). The alternative is to believe that
when he asks the emperors to listen fairly as he begins his defence of
Christian doctrine, he is indulging in a piece of literary fiction.[38] The work
is essentially a demonstration of the falsity of the three standard charges
against Christians, atheism, cannibalism and incest; and much the largest
part of it is devoted to proving that Christianity can be classified as worship
of a god (indeed a superior form of such worship) in pagan terms. Its
purpose is to persuade the emperors that, this being so, they should rule that
prosecution for the name of Christian alone is illegal:[39]

> It is your task, as the greatest, most benevolent and most devoted to learning
> of kings, to remove by a law this harassment of us, so that just as the whole
> world, both together and city by city, has enjoyed your beneficent acts (*euer-*

[34] *HE* IV, 26, 1.
[35] See the edition with introduction, notes and translation, by W. R. Schoedel, *Athenagoras:
Legatio and De Resurrectione* (1972). It is only unfortunate that the editor, by translating πρεσβεία
as 'plea', misses the point of the implied context.
[36] *Leg.* 16, 2.
[37] Compare, however, T. D. Barnes in *JThSt* XXVI (1975), 111, emphasizing the reference to
peace in 1, 3 and the fact that Commodus could have been addressed as joint emperor even earlier,
and suggesting that the address was delivered during, or intended for, the visit of Marcus and
Commodus to Athens in 176; cf. pp. 36, 502.
[38] 2, 6: ἀναγκαῖον δέ μοι ἀρχομένῳ ἀπολογεῖσθαι ὑπὲρ τοῦ λόγου δεηθῆναι ὑμῶν, μέγιστοι
αὐτοκράτορες, ἴσους ἡμῖν ἀκροατὰς γενέσθαι. Cf. 11, 3: ὡς ἐπὶ βασιλέων φιλοσόφων
ἀπολογούμενον.
[39] 2, 1.

gesiai), so we too may solemnly give thanks to you because we have ceased to be the object of false accusation.

Athenagoras' language is exactly that which a representative of a group of pagans might have addressed to the emperors. His conclusion is similar, and is also adapted specifically to the circumstances of Commodus' joint rule with his father:[40]

> You who are by nature and education in every respect good, moderate, beneficent and worthy of kingship, since I have dispelled the accusations and shown that we are god-fearing, reasonable and chastened in our spirits, grant me the assent of your kingly nod. For what men more deserve to receive what they request than we who pray for your rule, so that son may most justly inherit the kingship from father, and that your rule may receive increase and addition, with all men subject to it?

Thus Athenagoras' *Presbeia* has the form of those innumerable speeches delivered before emperors in order to gain requests—and we cannot dismiss categorically the possibility that it too actually was delivered, or was written for delivery. By contrast we can tell very little of the literary character of the work addressed by Melito of Sardis to Marcus Aurelius, perhaps in about 170.[41] It was occasioned by 'new edicts' which had led to persecutions throughout the province of Asia. Since Melito does not know whether this was at Marcus' command or not, they most probably emanated from the proconsul, whose *edicta* might or might not explicitly embody the *mandata* of the emperor:[42]

> If this is done at your order, so be it. For a just king would never have taken unjust counsel, and we gladly accept the honour of such a death. We bring this petition to you only so that you, having first taken cognisance of the authors of such strife, may judge rightly as to whether they are worthy of death and punishment, or peace and safety.

Later Melito emphasizes the coincidence in time between the rule of Augustus and the appearance of the 'philosophy' of the Christians, an essential conjunction disturbed only by the disreputable figures of Nero and Domitian, and reasserted in letters of Hadrian and Antoninus Pius.

Melito's work was probably a *libellus*, but whether it was actually conveyed to Marcus, or intended to be so, we do not know. His assertion of the conjunction between Christianity and the imperial *basileia* was to be of the utmost significance in the long run. For the present it glossed over the fact that no imperial rescript had yet disturbed the principle that Christians could be punished as such. Nor indeed, is there any evidence that any of

---

[40] 37, 1–2.

[41] It is known only from Eusebius, *HE* IV, 26, 1 and 5–11 (quotation), and a probable quotation in *Chron. Pasch.* (Migne, *PG* XCII, 632 A), see O. Perler, *Méliton de Sardes: Sur la Pâque et fragments, Sources Chr.* CXXIII (1966), 218f. The date 170 is provided by Jerome, *Chron.* (ed. Helm, p. 206). As it is addressed to Marcus alone, it should in any case date to between 169 and 176.

[42] See Barnes, *JRS* LVIII (1968), 39, and cf. p. 316.

these petitions or addresses to the emperors received any reply. In the early third century, it is true, Hippolytus addressed a work 'to a certain queen',[43] who cannot now be identified; Julius Africanus, the Christian chronographer, is said to have dedicated his *Kestoi* to Severus Alexander;[44] and Alexander's mother, Julia Mammaea, while at Antioch in the early 230s, sent an escort of soldiers to bring Origen from Caesarea, so that he could expound his teaching to her.[45] Subsequently, according to Eusebius, Origen wrote a letter to Philip (who was supposed to have been a Christian himself), and another to his wife Severa.[46] In the late second and early third centuries we also have some indisputable evidence of Christians in the imperial household. In particular Marcia, the Christian concubine of Commodus, was able to obtain from the bishop of Rome a list of the Christians condemned to hard labour in Sardinia, petition Commodus for their release, and obtain a letter of authorization, which a presbyter took to the procurator there.[47] Similarly, Tertullian recalls that Severus had summoned a Christian named Proculus to the *palatium* to assist in the education of Caracalla.[48]

As portents of the future, these instances of the encroachment of Christians on the imperial household have some significance in the long term, just as do the *Apologies*, in spite of their lack of immediate success, by virtue of the assumptions and expectations in the light of which they were written. In the shorter term, however, the continuing exposure of Christians to prosecution and condemnation is exhibited with even greater clarity by the fact that Origen's father, martyred in Alexandria early in the third century, was the first Christian of whom we know whose property was taken for the imperial *fiscus*.[49]

3. Edicta *and* Epistulae: *Persecution and Confiscation*

The period of the persecutions, of Decius, Valerian and the tetrarchy, is the first in which we have clear evidence of positive imperial initiatives relating to the church, whether in *edicta* or in *epistulae* to provincial governors. It is also now that we have occasional evidence of emperors personally sitting in judgment on Christians. More important perhaps, it is from the persecutions that we see in some detail the confiscation of the property not only of individual Christians but of the churches themselves. This evidence is of some significance precisely because it serves to indicate how far the church had developed as a settled and visible institution. But for our purposes it is

---

[43] *GCS* I. 2, 249f.

[44] p. 495.

[45] Eusebius, *HE* VI, 21, 3-4.

[46] For Origen's letters, Eusebius, *HE* VI, 36, 3. For the tradition about Philip, see VI, 34 (also apparently referred to by Dionysius of Alexandria, quoted in VII, 10, 3).

[47] Hippolytus, *Ref. omn. haer.* IX, 12.

[48] *Ad Scap.* 4, 5. For inscriptional evidence note for instance, M. Aurelius Prosenes, *a cubiculo* of Caracalla, *ILS* 1738; see H. U. Instinsky, *Marcus Aurelius Prosenes: Freigelassener und Christ am Kaiserhof* (1964); G. W. Clarke, 'Two Christians in the *Familia Caesaris*', *HThR* LXIV(1971), 121.

[49] p. 170.

more relevant still that the previous confiscations determined the precise form and content of the restitution of the church granted by Constantine and Licinius.

To Eusebius the edict of Decius was issued because of his hatred of Philip, an unconvincing explanation which is none the less shared by an illuminating work written soon after the middle of the century, the thirteenth *Sibylline Oracle*.[1] We cannot indeed provide any better explanation, though we may speculate on the fact, attested by the then bishop of Alexandria, Dionysius, that mob violence against the Christians had begun there a full year before the order of Decius arrived;[2] it *may* be that popular pressure lay behind the edict, but there is nothing positive to suggest it. Moreover the evidence as to the edict itself, and its promulgation through the provinces, is very slight. Eusebius states that Decius 'raised a persecution against the churches' in which Fabian the bishop of Rome was martyred, which we know took place on 20 January 250.[3] Dionysius explicitly mentions the arrival of the imperial *prostagma* in Alexandria, and its being put up there (as was normal for *edicta*), after which he himself was arrested on the orders of the prefect, Aurelius Appius Sabinus.[4] As is well known, the essential command conveyed by the edict was simply the general enforcement of the test of sacrifice which had previously been used when accusations were brought against Christians.[5] The *libelli*, or certificates, of sacrifice which people in Egypt acquired, state explicitly that they had acted 'in accordance with what has been ordered' (or in one case 'according to what has been ordered by the divine—i.e. imperial—judgment'), and date to between 2 June and 14 July 250.[6] On comparative evidence, this is approximately the date which we should expect, if the *edictum* had first been 'put up' in Rome in the winter of 249/50.[7]

Similar precision cannot be derived from the extensive correspondence of Cyprian, which otherwise illuminates in great detail the effects of persecution in Carthage, elsewhere in Africa, and in Rome itself. Cyprian himself made a prudent withdrawal for a period of fifteen months; in his absence his property seems to have been confiscated, as was that of others who 'were

---

[1] *HE* VI, 39, 1; *Or. Sib.* XIII, 87–8: αὐτίκα δ' αὖ πιστῶν τε λεηλασίαι τε φόνοι τε / ἔσσοντ' ἐξαπίνης [γε] διὰ πρότερον βασιλῆα. See A. T. Olmstead, 'The Mid-Third Century of the Christian Era', *CPh* XXXVII (1942), 241 and 398, on p. 398.

[2] Dionysius, quoted in Eusebius, *HE* VI, 41, 1.

[3] *HE* VI, 39, 1; *Liber Pontificalis*, ed. Duchesne, I, 148.

[4] *HE* VI, 41, 10: καὶ δὴ καὶ παρῆν τὸ πρόσταγμα, and 40, 2: τοῦ κατὰ Δέκιον προτεθέντος διωγμοῦ (presumably to be understood as an elliptical expression for the *edict* of persecution having been 'put up').

[5] In consequence it can be argued, as by J. Molthagen, *Der römische Staat und die Christen im zweiten und dritten Jahrhundert* (1970), 81f., that the performance of sacrifices itself was the object of Decius' measure, rather than specifically a repression of Christianity.

[6] See the standard article by H. Knipfing, 'The Libelli of the Decian Persecution', *HThR* XVI (1923), 345. *P. Oxy.* 1464 has [κατ]ὰ τὰ κελευσθέντα ὑπὸ τῆς θείας κρίσεως. Cf. *Mart. Pionii* 3, 2: οἴδατε πάντως τὸ διάταγμα τοῦ αὐτοκράτορος ὡς κελεύει ὑμᾶς ἐπιθύειν τοῖς θεοῖς. For other references to the imperial order, in sources of more or less probable authenticity, see *Acta Carpi, Papyli et Agathonicae* 4, *Acta Maximi* 1, and Gregory of Nyssa, *v. Greg. Thaum.* (*PG* XLVI, col. 944).

[7] p. 254.

made exiles and abandoned their property, which the *fiscus* now holds'.[8]
Two letters in his correspondence also seem to reveal an important aspect
of the persecution in Rome, namely that one Christian at least stood trial
before Decius in person. The language used to describe the event is metaphorical, and the reference to the emperor is not beyond doubt. The man in
question was a Roman named Celerinus, to whom another *confessor* named
Lucianus writes in 250, and compares Celerinus with himself who had
'confessed the name and fear of God before more insignificant judges';
but, he says, 'You, by the grace of God, not only confessed before the great
serpent himself, the forerunner of Antichrist, but struck fear into him with
that voice and those godly words which I know.'[9] Then, writing in 251 to
recommend Celerinus as a *lector* in the church of Carthage, Cyprian says,
'This man, when the persecution first blazed forth, encountered the chief
and author of the attack in person, and not only overcome his adversary by
his resolute firmness, but by doing so opened a way for others to overcome.'[10]
There is no reason in principle why some Christians should not have been
accused before the emperor, among whose functions jurisdiction played so
important a part; and we shall see that Diocletian and Maximin later
condemned Christians in person. Such trials may even have occurred earlier.
But it is perhaps significant that they are not attested before the persecution
of Decius.

Cyprian's correspondence happens not to mark specifically either the
beginning of the persecution in Carthage (that is, the arrival of the *edictum*),
nor its end, if indeed it had any definite end.[11] In 252, however, under
Gallus, he not only writes to say that he anticipates a new persecution,[12] but
soon after describes himself as being 'in these very days in which I write this
letter to you, once again the subject of the clamour of the populace, demanding that I be sent to the lions, because of the sacrifices which the edict
posted up has commanded the people to carry out'.[13] The reference may be
to some local celebration; but a letter of Dionysius also seems to allude to
persecution by Gallus in his brief reign (251–3).[14]

By comparison we are very well informed about both the form and the
content of the orders for persecution issued by Valerian in 257 and 258. The
most specific evidence is provided by the *Acta* of the two trials of Cyprian,
held in these two years, and by letters of his from the latter year. In 257
Cyprian appeared before the proconsul of Africa, who said: 'The most
sacred emperors Valerianus and Gallienus have sent a letter [or letters] to
me, in which they have ordered that those who do not follow the Roman

---

[8] *Ep.* 24, 1, 1. Cf. 66, 4, 1: 'Persecutio . . . me autem proscriptionis onere depressit, cum publice
legeretur: "Si quis tenet possidet de bonis Caecili Cypriani episcopi Christianorum".'

[9] *Ep.* 22, 1, 1: 'Nam tu Deo volente ipsam anguem maiorem, metatorem Antichristi, non tantum
confessus es, sed et terruisti . . .' See G. W. Clarke, 'Some Observations on the Persecution of
Decius', *Antichthon* III (1969), 63.

[10] *Ep.* 39, 2, 1.

[11] See Clarke, o.c., 63.

[12] *Ep.* 57, 1, 2.

[13] *Ep.* 59, 6, 1.

[14] Eusebius, *HE* VII, 1.

religion, ought to observe Roman rituals.'[15] However puzzling the particular terminology may be, it is clear that the imperial order was once again for sacrifice, but the vehicle of it was this time not an *edictum*, but *epistulae* to provincial governors.[16] Moreover its contents were evidently specifically related to the church as such, in a way which is not attested for any previous imperial pronouncement, for the proconsul goes on to say that the letter concerned presbyters as well as bishops, and that it ordered that Christians should not, on pain of execution, hold meetings or enter their cemeteries.

These provisions of the imperial order are also recorded in the account which Dionysius of Alexandria gives, complete with documentary extracts from the proceedings of his trial before L. Mussius Aemilianus, who is attested as occupying the position of prefect of Egypt in 258–61.[17] Though Dionysius makes some allegations about the personal influences which diverted Valerian from his previous benevolence towards Christians (who were even common in his household),[18] the surviving extracts from his letters do not refer to the imperial letter itself. But Aemilianus is recorded as referring to the imperial order for sacrifice, and to the ban on Christian meetings and on entry to the cemeteries. As with Cyprian, the penalty imposed on Dionysius by Aemilianus ('in accordance with the order of the emperors', as he says) was no more than relegation to a different part of the province. In the same period however, Cyprian is found corresponding with Christians who had been condemned to the harsher penalty of *metallum*.[19]

The proceedings against Dionysius, which are not dated, thus seem to correspond to those against Cyprian in 257, and to fall before the further imperial pronouncement which Cyprian's evidence clearly attests for 258. The date is provided in the first instance by his reference to the martyrdom of Xystus, the bishop of Rome, on 6 August 258, also described by the *Liber Pontificalis*: 'He was arrested by Valerianus and led to sacrifice to demons. He ignored the orders of Valerianus, and was decapitated.'[20] Various others were executed at the same time, and three days later another group including the archdeacon Laurentius, who was buried in the cemetery of Cyriace—clearly the devout woman, whose property 'which the *fiscus* had occupied at a time of persecution', was to be granted to the *basilica* of St Laurentius by Constantine.[21]

The letter of Cyprian which mentions the execution of Xystus belongs in a period when the imperial orders had been promulgated in Rome but had not yet reached Africa.[22] The slowness of official communications is clearly

[15] *Acta Cypriani* (Knopf-Krüger-Ruhbach, *Ausgewählte Martyrakten*[4], no. 13; Musurillo, *Acts of the Christian Martyrs*, no. 11), 1, 1.

[16] cf. p. 319.

[17] Eusebius, *HE* VII, 11, 1–11; for the tenure of L. Mussius Aemilianus see O. W. Reinmuth, *Bull. Am. Soc. Pap.* IV (1967), 119–20. The expression διέπων τὴν ἡγεμονίαν, used in VII, 11, 6 and 10 (extracts from the proceedings) is paralleled in *P. Oxy.* 1201; its precise meaning is uncertain.

[18] *HE* VII, 10.

[19] *Ep.* 76, 79. On the use of the imperial *metalla* (mines or quarries) as places of hard labour see pp. 182–3.

[20] *Ep.* 80, 1, 4; *Liber Pontificalis* xxv (ed. Duchesne I, p. 155).

[21] p. 172.

[22] *Ep.* 80, 1, 1–3.

19*

revealed in this instance by the fact that Cyprian had had time to send emissaries to Rome to discover 'in what terms a rescript had been sent about us', and these had already returned with the information, before anything reached the proconsul. As we saw earlier, the imperial pronouncement was in fact a rescript, also described as an *oratio*, addressed to the senate, which may imply that the senate had taken the initiative in requesting action against the Christians.[23] The delay would be more intelligible if, as is almost certain, Valerian was already in Syria in the summer of 258.[24] Under such circumstances, if Cyprian's emissaries had been sent off when news of the senate's motion was received, they could well have been in Rome in time for the arrival of the imperial reply. It laid down that bishops, presbyters and deacons should be executed, that senators and *equites* should lose their *dignitas* and property, and if they persisted in their faith, be executed also; while *matronae* should have their property removed and go into exile. Members of the imperial household were to suffer confiscation, and be despatched in chains to imperial properties.[25] It was reported that the prefects (those of the praetorian cohorts and the city?) were carrying on vigorously with the persecution in Rome—perhaps another hint that the emperors were elsewhere—executing those brought before them, and taking their property for the *fiscus*.

Valerian had attached to his *rescriptum* or *oratio* copies of the letter which he had written to provincial governors—'which letter we daily expect to arrive' as Cyprian writes. Events evidently moved swiftly thereafter, for, according to the *Acta*, on 13 September officers were sent to bring him to the proconsul, and the hearing took place on the following day.[26] Even after the imperial order for execution the proconsul still put to Cyprian the proposition that 'the most sacred emperors have ordered you to carry out a sacrifice', and only after his refusal ordered his decapitation. The same sequence is visible in the *acta* of the martyrdom of Fructuosus and others in the following year, probably in Tarraco.[27]

These imperial orders of the mid-third century thus provide for the first time a substantial body of evidence for the confiscation of the property of condemned or executed Christians, for detailed attention to the various ranks of the clergy, and for orders relating to Christian meetings and to their cemeteries. It is significant that the emperors seem to have used the specifically Christian term *coemeteria*—derived from the Greek word for 'to sleep', and to have attempted to prevent the congregations from using them. What

---

[23] p. 277.

[24] This cannot be deduced with absolute certainty from *CJ* v, 3, 5 = IX, 9, 18, a *subscriptio* (or *epistula*?) *accepta* by a female petitioner in Antioch in May of that year; for later cases distinguishing the place where an *epistula* was *data* (i.e., where the emperor was) from where it was *accepta*, see p. 39. But if this document is a *subscriptio* this ought not to apply. Cf. *CJ* II, 12, 2, also a *subscriptio*, 'accepta' by a female petitioner. Cf. also pp. 454–5.

[25] cf. pp. 182–3.

[26] *Acta* 2, 3 and 3, 1. There seems in fact to have been an earlier stage, for his *Ep.* 81 records that when he heard that officers had been sent to his *horti*, suburban villa, in order to take him to the proconsul at Utica, he hid elsewhere, in order that the trial should take place, appropriately, when the proconsul had reached Carthage itself.

[27] See Musurillo, *Acts of the Christian Martyrs* (1972), no. 12, which mentions the date, 259, but not the place, supplied by Prudentius, *Peristephanon* VI.

is not clear is what actual process of expropriation, or confiscation, of these or other communal properties of Christian congregations accompanied these measures.

It is not surprising, therefore, that it is precisely in the following two decades that we find the first evidence of the churches as such, or their bishops, addressing petitions to the emperor on concrete matters relating to church property. For even though some of the apologists of the second century had in fact been bishops, the works which they addressed to emperors were essentially philosophical or intellectual justifications of Christianity, designed indeed to persuade the emperors to intervene in order to prevent persecution, but not (so far as we know) written in the interests of particular congregations. The essential condition for this new stage, which in a sense marks the moment when direct relations between church and emperor come into being, was the abandonment of persecution by Gallienus, which he apparently proclaimed soon after the capture of Valerian by the Persians, probably in 260.[28] Of this measure Eusebius reports only that it was promulgated by *programmata*—probably again *edicta* posted up in the provinces—and says nothing specific about its contents. For illustration of its effects he seems to be entirely dependent on Dionysius of Alexandria, and it is therefore relevant that for the Egyptian years 260/1 and for some of 261/2, Egypt was subject to the usurpers Macrianus and Quietus; there are no datings by Gallienus' rule in papyri until March 262.[29]

It was therefore almost certainly after this usurpation that Gallienus replied to a petition from the bishops of Egypt; it was in his ninth year, 261/2, and apparently at Easter 262, that Dionysius wrote of him as being 'more holy and more beloved of God' than his predecessors.[30] Eusebius continues directly from his mention of the cessation of persecution to reproduce a rescript (*antigraphê*) of Gallienus addressed to Dionysius and other bishops. From its form, with the absence of formulae of address or farewell, it is probably a *subscriptio* granted to the bishops as a group of individuals, rather than an *epistula*. It is likely, therefore, that they had presented a *libellus* to him rather than sent a formal delegation.[31] But in either case at least one of them would have had to travel to where Gallienus was, and there is no reason to suppose that he ever visited Egypt.

Even if it were not for its historic significance as the earliest reply of an emperor to representatives of the Christian church, Gallienus' rescript would deserve quotation as a fine and typical example of the grandiloquent vocabulary of imperial beneficence:[32]

[28] Eusebius, *HE* VII, 13. The date has been much debated. *PIR²* L 258 favours 259. Dating by the joint reign of Valerian and Gallienus continues on papyri until year 7, 29 Aug. 259–29 Aug. 260, but on Alexandrian coins to year 8, J. Vogt, *Die alexandrinischen Münzen* II (1924), 204.

[29] For datings by Macrianus and Quietus see P. Bureth, *Les Titulatures impériales dans les papyrus, les ostraca et les inscriptions d'Égypte (30 a.C.–284 p.C.)* (1964), 119–20; add *P. Oxy.* 2710 (May 261) and *P. Strassb.* 6, iv, 37, year 2 (261/2). For the dating by Gallienus in March 262, *P. Strassb.* 7. For the regime of Macrianus and Quietus, D. Magie, *Roman Rule in Asia Minor* (1950), 709–10. Macrianus' brief appearance and disappearance is scornfully alluded to by Dionysius in Eusebius, *HE* VII, 23, 1.

[30] Eusebius, *HE* VII, 23, 4.

[31] The latter was suggested in *JRS* LXI (1971), 15.

[32] Eusebius, *HE* VII, 13.

Imperator Caesar Publius Licinius Gallienus Pius Felix Augustus to Diony-sius and Pinnas and Demetrius and the other bishops. I have ordered that the benefits conferred by my gift [*dôrea*] should be spread throughout all the world, namely that [other] people should retire from the [Christian] places of worship. Therefore you too are entitled to make use of the provisions of my rescript, to the end that no-one should harass you. This has already been granted by me long since, as far as it is within your powers to fulfil it. Therefore Aurelius Quirinius, the *procurator summae rei* (?), will observe the provisions laid down by me.

Neither the circumstances referred to, nor the functions of Aurelius Quirinius are at all clear, but it seems likely that the bishops' petition arose from non-fulfilment of the provisions of the edict by officials in Egypt. Similar circumstances may have lain behind the *constitutio* (*diataxis*) of Gallienus addressed to other unidentified bishops, allowing them to resume possession of cemeteries, to which Eusebius refers in the same chapter. In spite of the brevity of the report, the mention of cemeteries is significant, since it shows how the measures of restitution were conditioned by the nature of the anti-Christian measures of the previous reign. Indeed it is clear that it was precisely the balanced process of deprivation and restitution which brought the representatives of the church to petition the emperor and obtain his response, and thus to establish their first direct communication with him.

It is against this background that we should understand the next stage in this communication, when the church of Antioch petitioned Aurelian for a judgment on an internal dispute.[33] In brief, the sequence of events was that Paul of Samosata, a heretical bishop of Antioch, was removed from his see by a council which met in 268/9. When he declined to leave the church house there, Aurelian was petitioned, and ruled that it should be adjudged to those to whom the bishops of Rome and Italy would communicate. We can now rule out the long-held theory that Paul's role as bishop was that of a protégé of the Palmyrenes, whose brief rule over northern Syria probably did not begin until 270. It is not equally certain whether Aurelian, who seems to have assumed power in the summer of 270,[34] was petitioned by representa-tives of the Antiochene church who had gone to Europe to find him (or his predecessor, Claudius?); or whether, as has normally been supposed, the petition was presented when Aurelian re-took Antioch from the Palmyrenes in 272. In either case the question of rival political loyalties *may* have been relevant; and various confused, and mutually contradictory, remarks in later Christian writers recall some connection between Paul and Zenobia. But such a hypothesis is unnecessary, for there was now no reason why Aurelian should not have decided the question of the rights to the church-house at Antioch, just as Caracalla in 216 had decided that of the priesthood of Zeus in the territory of the Goharieni.[35] As the church became an

---

[33] For what follows see 'Paul of Samosata, Zenobia and Aurelian: the Church, Local Culture and Political Allegiance in Third-Century Syria', *JRS* LXI (1971), 1. The main evidence is Eusebius, *HE* VII, 27–30.

[34] For the evidence of Oxyrhynchus papyri, briefly summarized in *JRS* LXI (1971), 16, n. 164, see now J. R. Rea in *Oxyrhynchus Papyri* XL (1972), 15–26.

[35] p. 455.

established institution, it was only to be expected that an emperor might be called upon on occasion to decide a dispute over rights within it. The petition to Aurelian and his response was thus a foretaste of that progression by which Constantine became involved in a dispute over the rightful tenure of the see of Carthage more than a decade before he entered the more treacherous area of doctrinal differences.

For some four decades after Gallienus' edict persecution was in abeyance (though Eusebius alleges that Aurelian died when about to put his *subscriptio* to letters ordering measures against the Christians; and Lactantius that such letters were actually on the way to the more distant provinces).[36] When it began again in perhaps 301, with imperial letters to provincial governors, there also began a period of intense involvement, first negative and then positive, of emperor and church, which was to last as long as the Byzantine empire itself. Once again it may be necessary to emphasize that what follows is in no sense a history, still less a full analysis, of these events, but an examination of them as providing a uniquely-documented example of communication between subject and emperor. For the earlier part of this process it is important to keep in mind that of our two main sources one, Eusebius, was in Caesarea and is a witness to imperial pronouncements as and when they arrived there or in that region; while the other, Lactantius, was in Diocletian's 'capital', Nicomedia.[37]

Lactantius had been summoned, one may assume by the emperor, to teach Latin rhetoric in Nicomedia, and is the only witness to the intellectual background of the persecutions.[38] He describes two anti-Christian propagandists, one a philosopher, 'an advocate of parsimony and poverty who ate less well in the *palatium* than at home', who proclaimed that the chief function of philosophy was to recall men to the worship of the gods; he addressed the emperors in flattering terms, calling on them to show their *pietas* and *providentia* by repressing Christianity. The other, Hierocles, the *praeses* of Bithynia, 'among the leading authors of the persecution', wrote two books with the overt object of recalling Christians from their errors, attacking the Gospels and their authors, and apparently proposing a form of higher pagan monotheism.[39] These men, who wrote in Greek, were not the only pagan Greek intellectuals attracted to Nicomedia at this time;[40] it would be rash to discount too readily the possible influence of intellectual factors on the great persecution. As was suggested earlier, it may not be an accident that

[36] Eusebius, *HE* VII, 30, 20–1; Lactantius, *De mort. pers.* 6, 2.

[37] For Eusebius see the convenient survey by D. S. Wallace-Hadrill, *Eusebius of Caesarea* (1960); for Lactantius' angle of vision on these events T. D. Barnes, 'Lactantius and Constantine', *JRS* LXIII (1973), 29.

[38] *Div. Inst.* V, 2,1–4,2; 2, 2: 'ego cum in Bithynia oratorias litteras accitus docerem', cf. Jerome, *De vir. ill.* 80. This autobiographical reference introduces his account of the two anti-Christian writers.

[39] The 'alius . . . qui erat tum e numero iudicum et qui auctor in primis faciendae persecutionis fuit' of *Div. Inst.* V, 2, 12, is normally, and reasonably, identified with the 'Hieroclem ex vicario praesidem, qui auctor et consiliarius ad faciendam persecutionem fuit', of *De mort. pers.* 16, 4. For the further evidence on his career see *PLRE* Hierocles 4.

[40] That they wrote in Greek is clear from *Div. Inst.* V, 4, 1–2; see also Themistius, *Or.* V, 63d (the influence of his grandfather, a philosopher, with Diocletian); Suda s.v. Ἀνδρόμαχος (ed. Adler I, 197), a sophist from Neapolis in Syria who taught at Nicomedia under Diocletian.

it took place when the court was for the first time firmly established in a Greek city.[41]

It is Lactantius also who describes a preliminary stage before the proclamation of persecution in 303. On this account, when Diocletian was performing sacrifices, and the entrails of the beast repeatedly failed to give the expected signs, a *haruspex* announced that this was due to the malign influence of Christians in the entourage. As a result, Diocletian ordered sacrifices on the part of all serving in the *palatium*, and sent letters to provincial governors requiring soldiers to do the same or leave the service. The date was perhaps 301.[42]

Lactantius also attributes the outbreak of the great persecution to the influence on Diocletian of his junior colleague Galerius, when both were resident in Nicomedia over the winter of 302–3; so also did Eusebius in an earlier edition of his *Ecclesiastical History*.[43] This view was not shared by a witness of even better credentials, namely Constantine, who was now at Nicomedia, and whose later references attribute the blame to Diocletian.[44] Constantine does, however, confirm Lactantius' report that before the first *edictum* was published the oracle of Apollo at Didyma was consulted, and gave a response hostile to the Christians.[45]

As we saw earlier, we can observe the diffusion of the first edict from its posting-up at Nicomedia on 24 February 303 to its appearance in the Palestine region (where Eusebius was) in about March, and in a town in Africa on 5 June.[46] Its provisions represented a more fundamental assault on the existence of the church than any previous measures: the churches themselves were to be destroyed; the scriptures handed over for burning; Christians were to lose ranks and dignities and to be banned from courts of law; freedmen, perhaps only imperial freedmen, who persisted in Christianity were to lose their freedom; and services were prohibited.[47] The innumerable problems of the persecution and its application and effects in different areas cannot be treated here.[48] But certain points may be selected.

First, there is no mention of a universal order for sacrifice until the fourth edict of 304/5;[49] but an earlier edict had commanded the application of the

[41] p. 9.

[42] *Div. Inst.* IV, 27, 4–5; *De mort. pers.* 10, 1–5; cf. Eusebius, *HE* VIII, 1, 7; 4, 2–3. Jerome, *Chron.* ed. Helm, p. 227, dates the persecution of the Christians in the army to 301.

[43] Lactantius, *De mort. pers.* 10, 6–11, 8; Eusebius, *HE* VIII, App. 1 and 4. On the complex question of the successive editions of Eusebius' *HE*, see G. Bardy, *Eusèbe de Césarée: Histoire Ecclésiastique* IV (1960), 121f.

[44] See Constantine's letter of 324, quoted in Eusebius, *VC* II, 50–1, and the *Oratio ad Coetum Sanctorum* 25.

[45] Lactantius, *De mort. pers.* 11, 7–8; Eusebius, *VC* II, 50. The fragmentary inscription, *Inschr. von Didyma* 306, may be connected with this event.

[46] p. 254.

[47] Lactantius, *De mort. pers.* 13; Eusebius, *HE* VIII, 2, 4; *Mart. Pal., praef.* 1.

[48] For the most thorough account see G. E. M. de Ste. Croix, 'Aspects of the "Great" Persecution', *HThR* XLVII (1954), 75; see also W. H. C. Frend, *Martyrdom and Persecution in the Early Church* (1965), ch. 15.

[49] The fourth edict is recorded only in *Mart. Pal.* 3, 1. It may be implicit in Lactantius, *De mort. pers.* 15, 4: 'iudices per omnia templa dispersi universos ad sacrificia cogebant'; and seems to be alluded to clearly in *Mart. Crispinae* 1, 2–3 (Musurillo, *Acts of the Christian Martyrs*, no. 24), in Theveste in Africa on 5 December 304: 'Praecepti sacri cognovisti sententiam? . . . ut omnibus diis nostris pro salute principum sacrifices.'

test of sacrifice to individual Christians.[50] Moreover a papyrus now illustrates perfectly Lactantius' statement that litigants were required to sacrifice before being allowed to plead—and how this could be circumvented by having an agent do it for one.[51]

Secondly it is essential to the understanding of the measures of restitution undertaken by Constantine and Licinius that the churches were now substantial institutions, with identifiable buildings (like that at Nicomedia which until its destruction on the day before the first edict stood within sight of the *palatium*),[52] and possessing valuable property and fittings, which were to be handed over along with the scriptures. At Cirta in 303 the list of valuables in the church included gold and silver vessels, silver and bronze candlesticks, and stores of male and female clothing.[53] But much more significant both for the assumptions made about the possible wealth of churches, even in small and obscure places, and its confiscation in the persecution, is the papyrus of 5 February 304, containing a declaration of church property at Oxyrhynchus in Egypt; it is also an important document of the role in confiscation now played by the (*ratio*) *privata*. The declaration is made by a reader in the church, and its central part runs as follows:[54]

> Whereas you gave me orders in accordance with what was written by Aurelius Athanasius, *procurator privatae*, in virtue of a command of the most illustrious *magister privatae*, Neratius Apollonides, concerning the surrender of all the goods in the said former church and whereas I reported that the said church had neither gold, ⟨coined⟩ or uncoined, nor silver nor clothes [vestments?] nor beasts nor slaves nor lands nor property either from grants or bequests, excepting only the bronze gate which was found and delivered to the *logistês* to be carried down to the most glorious Alexandria . . .

Thirdly we have some evidence from the period of persecution of the personal activity of the emperors. Lactantius describes how after a fire in the *palatium* at Nicomedia, Diocletian 'sat (in justice) himself' and had people tortured by burning, and also forced his own wife and daughter to sacrifice; Eusebius describes in detail how a member of the household was tortured to death in the presence of Diocletian and Galerius, without abandoning his refusal to sacrifice.[55] Later, when Diocletian was in Antioch, an exorcist from Caesarea, who protested aloud at seeing that many Christians sacrificed, had his tongue cut out by the order of the emperor.[56]

From the period after the retirement of Diocletian and Maximian in 305, most of our evidence on the course of persecution comes from Eusebius,

---

[50] The second and third edicts (for the arrest of the leaders of the churches, and their release if they sacrificed) are mentioned, briefly, only by Eusebius, *HE* VIII, 2, 5 and 6, 8–10, and *Mart. Pal., praef.* 2.

[51] *P. Oxy.* 2601; Lactantius, *De mort. pers.* 13, 1; 15, 5.

[52] Lactantius, *De mort. pers.* 12, 2–3.

[53] See *Gesta apud Zenophilum* (Optatus, App. 1), *CSEL* XXVI, 187.

[54] *P. Oxy.* 2673, trans. J. R. Rea (with slight amendments); for the (*ratio*) *privata* and confiscation, see pp. 171–4, and App. 3.

[55] Lactantius, *De mort. pers.* 14, 4; 15, 1; Eusebius, *HE* VIII, 6, 2–4.

[56] *Mart. Pal.* 2, with greater detail in the long (Syriac) recension. See Lawlor and Oulton, *Eusebius, Bishop of Caesarea: The Ecclesiastical History of the Martyrs of Palestine* I (1927), 336–8.

and hence relates to the area controlled by Maximin, who ruled mainly from Antioch up to 311, as 'Caesar' and then 'Augustus'.[57] In the third year of the persecution, presumably 305/6, he sent round instructions that the magistrates of each city should compel people to sacrifice.[58] At a later date, by the exercise of what Eusebius ironically calls imperial beneficence and philanthropy, death was replaced by the gouging of one eye and despatch to the copper mines as a punishment for recalcitrant Christians.[59] Then in about 309 letters of Maximin went round all the area controlled by him to institute an organized renewal of pagan worship: the temples were to be rebuilt, priests and high-priests appointed, everyone was obliged to sacrifice, to eat meat which had been offered for sacrifice, and so forth. Yet these orders, which represent one of the most positive of attested efforts by Roman emperors to impose their will on the populace, at the same time illustrate how limited and indirect were the means which an emperor had at his disposal. In this instance he sent letters to governors and *duces* ordering them to give instructions, by means of edicts and letters, to city officials.[60]

It was more typical of the normal pattern of imperial decision-making when the *praeses* of Palestine consulted Maximin over the discovery that the Christians in the copper-mines had organized their own churches there, whereupon the procurator of the mines was ordered to disperse them to other areas;[61] or when other Christian prisoners refused the training and upkeep from the *fiscus* preparatory to their performing as gladiators, and in consequence suffered 'not before procurators or governors but before Maximin himself', apparently at Caesarea;[62] and when Maximin, celebrating his birthday at Caesarea on 20 November 306, by sending convicts to the beasts, released a murderer in response to the shouts of the crowd, personally asked a Christian to recant, and on his refusal watched his exposure to a wild boar.[63]

We cannot understand the nature of the role of emperor without keeping in mind on the one hand the importance of the succession of ad hoc decisions which he pronounced verbally in public or in semi-public sessions, and on the other the limits of his communication and control beyond his own immediate environment. But at the same time the example of the persecutions themselves shows that the personal preferences of the emperor could influence the conduct of affairs over a wide area. Diocletian and Galerius had written in 303 to their counterparts in the west, Maximian and Constantius, telling them to carry out the measures of the first edict. While Maximian had done

[57] See H. Castritius, *Studien zu Maximinus Daia* (1969).

[58] *Mart. Pal.* 4, 8. The inscription *MAMA* I 170 should refer to this order. The reasons given in *PLRE* Diogenes 8 for dating the order to sacrifice mentioned in it to 310–11 are not compelling.

[59] *HE* VIII, 12, 8–10: δεῖν δὲ μᾶλλον τῆς φιλανθρώπου καὶ βασιλικῆς ἐξουσίας εἰς πάντας ἐκτείνεσθαι τὴν εὐεργεσίαν. An instance in *Mart. Pal.* 7, 2 (307/8).

[60] *HE* VIII, 14, 9–10; *Mart. Pal.* 9, 2. The same process is reported by Lactantius, *De mort. pers.* 36, 4, but only in the context of Maximin's seizure of Asia Minor (including Nicomedia) after the death of Galerius in 311—a clear example of the operation of a localized viewpoint in our sources for these events.

[61] *Mart. Pal.* 13, 1–2.

[62] *Mart. Pal.* 8, 2–3; cf. pp. 194–5.

[63] *Mart. Pal.* 6, 3–7; in more detail in the long, Syriac, recension.

so, Constantius had at the most fulfilled the provision about the destruction of churches; and when he succeeded Maximian as 'Augustus' in 305, active persecution ceased in the west.[64] When he died in 306, his son Constantine usurped his place, and (according to Lactantius) his first act was to restore freedom of worship to the Christians.[65] But he was not yet a Christian; as late as 310 an orator speaking before him could expatiate on his recent vision of Apollo—and his lavish gifts to his temple.[66] Mere toleration was only the first stage. In most, and perhaps all, areas of the empire there remained a further and more fundamental issue, the restitution of property. It was to be this, accompanied by imperial generosity in its typical forms of immunities and grants of cash, which was to lay the foundations of a permanent relationship between church and emperor.

4. Edicta *and* Epistulae: *Toleration, Restitution and* Beneficia

The extension of toleration and then of actual restitution of the church was an erratic and fitful process covering the years 305 to 313, very different in different regions of the empire, and much more clearly attested in the east than in the west. There even the question of which regions were controlled at any time by which emperor is not always clear. But we can be sure at least that Constantine controlled Gaul and Britain from 306, and that toleration applied there; whether restitution was needed—and if so whether it took place—is not clear, since Eusebius and Lactantius contradict each other as to whether Constantius had or had not destroyed the churches.[1] In Rome and Italy, Maxentius, the son of Maximian, had usurped power in 306 and ruled until his defeat by Constantine in 312; even Eusebius, who gives two powerful descriptions of his tyrannical rule, concedes that to win favour he ordered an end to persecution;[2] two contradictory later traditions however report that the bishop of Rome, Marcellus (308–9), was either martyred on his orders, or (more probably) exiled by him on an accusation brought by a lapsed Christian.[3] If it is indeed the case that another Christian, even one who had lapsed, brought before Maxentius an accusation against Marcellus which led to his exile, we have a clear foretaste of the new element which was to enter the life of the church in the next few years.

[64] For the letter, Maximian's compliance and Constantius' limitation to the destruction of churches, Lactantius, *De mort. pers.* 15, 6–7; 16, 1 (and for the cessation of persecution in the west in 305, Eusebius, *Mart. Pal.* 13, 12). For the martyrdom of the bishop of Rome, Marcellinus, in 304, *Liber Pontificalis* xxx (ed. Duchesne I, 162); cf. also Augustine, *De unico baptismo* 16/27. Eusebius denies even the destruction of churches under Constantius, *HE* VIII, 13, 12–13; *VC* I, 13. Cf. I, 16–17 (retention of Christians at court).

[65] *De mort. pers.* 24, 9; cf. Eusebius, *HE* VIII, 13, 14.

[66] *Pan.* VII(6), 21, 4–7.

[1] n. 64 above.

[2] *HE* VIII, 14; *VC* I, 33–7.

[3] Martyrdom: *Liber Pontificalis* xxxi (ed. Duchesne I, 164). For his exile on accusation before Maxentius, Diehl, *ILCV* I, 962, one of the *epigrammata* put up by Pope Damasus (366–84): 'Crimen ob alterius, Christum qui in pace negavit, / finibus expulsus patriae est feritate tyranni.' For the background see H. von Schoenebeck, *Beiträge zur Religionspolitik des Maxentius und Constantin, Klio* Supp. XLIII (1939), Pt. I.

It is also to Maxentius that our evidence for the first restitutions of church property relates. The sequence of events is obscure, because the only viewpoint available to us is that of the African church, and Maxentius' control over Africa was interrupted in (probably) about 308 to 310/11 by the usurpation of the *vicarius*, Domitius Alexander.[4] The churches in Africa had been duly expropriated in the Diocletianic persecution, for Optatus describes the synod which met at Cirta on 5 March 305 as happening when 'the basilicas had not yet been restored'.[5] Such a restoration did not indeed occur until the last year or so of Maxentius' rule, after the re-establishment of his rule in Africa. When Optatus describes how a deacon named Felix was accused of writing an abusive letter about a tyrant emperor (a usurper?), took refuge with Mensurius, bishop of Carthage, and was the subject of a *relatio*, answered by a rescript summoning Mensurius to the *palatium* if he did not give him up, the reference *may* be to Domitius Alexander;[6] if so, it was before him that Mensurius gave his defence, apparently successfully, but died before he could return. For immediately afterwards Optatus records: 'The storm of persecution was over and finished; by God's command Maxentius sent an *indulgentia*, and *libertas* was restored to the Christians.'[7] What actually happened is recorded in more detail by Augustine.[8] Miltiades, the bishop of Rome (311–14), sent to Africa deacons with copies of letters of Maxentius and his praetorian prefect to the prefect of Rome, ordering the restoration of the properties which had been taken from Christians during the persecutions. Thus the pronouncement took the form of letters to the official in charge of one area, and if our evidence is correct, its further diffusion was left to interested parties, who took care to distribute it in other areas under Maxentius' control.

We know nothing further of the process of restitution under Maxentius,[9] and can only speculate as to what connection, if any, this step of his had with the roughly contemporary proclamation of toleration (but not specifically restitution) by Galerius, Constantine and Licinius. This proclamation, recorded by Lactantius and Eusebius, is that sometimes labelled the 'Edict of Serdica', because it was issued a few days before Galerius' death at Serdica in early May 311.[10] Lactantius calls it an *edictum* and says that it was put up

[4] For the chronology see *PLRE* Alexander 17. Cf. R. Andreotti, 'Problemi di epigrafia constantiniana I: la presunta alleanza con l'usurpatore Lucio Domizio Alessandro', *Epigraphica* XXXI (1969), 144.

[5] *Contra Parmenianum donatistam* I, 14. Cf. the verbatim record of the synod in Augustine, *Contra Cresconium* III, 27/30. For the ecclesiastical history of Africa in these years see Frend, *The Donatist Church* (1952), ch. i, and cf. now T. D. Barnes, 'The Beginnings of Donatism', *JThSt* XXVI (1975), 13.

[6] I, 17. Cf. p. 335. Frend, o.c., 15–16, assumes that these events took place in the second period of Maxentius' rule, and could be correct. Alternatively, T. D. Barnes, o.c., 18–20, argues that 'tyrannus imperator' means 'persecuting emperor' and that the reference is to Maximian. I prefer to rely on the well-attested usage of 'tyrannus' as usurper, see J. Béranger in *Bonner Historia-Augusta Colloquium 1971* (1974), 29–31.

[7] I, 18.

[8] *Gesta Coll. cum Don.* 13/17 (*CSEL* LIII, 113–14); *Brev. Coll. cum Don.* III, 18/34 (*CSEL* LIII, 84).

[9] Eusebius, *HE* X, 5, 16 (Constantine's letter to Anullinus, see p. 581), implies, however, that some church property in Africa may not have been restored by 313.

[10] For the place see *Origo Constantini Imperatoris* (*Anon. Vales.* I), 3/8.

at Nicomedia, Galerius' 'capital', on 30 April 311.[11] Both he and Eusebius
see the proclamation as having its origin in the illness of Galerius, whose
agonies at last caused him to repent. But Eusebius' text shows that it was
issued by Galerius, Constantine and (except in the last edition) Licinius;
and the earlier edition also seems to show that it was cast in the form of a
general letter, since the address ends 'to their own provincials, greeting'.[12]
If that is correct, it reflects a development typical of the period, whereby
the *epistula* form, whether addressed to office-holders or to the populace at
large, came to be used to convey general pronouncements of a type previously
typical of *edicta*.[13]

At any rate Eusebius, as usual, reflects the wider diffusion of the pronouncement, saying that imperial *dogmata* were put up city by city. Moreover, he seems to claim that Galerius actually ordered the building of
churches. But the words of the pronouncement, as given both by Lactantius
in Latin and himself in Greek, do not go quite as far as this. What the
emperors do is to defend their previous attempt to recall men to the ancient
disciplina; to announce the exercise of their *clementia* and *indulgentia* in the
face of the obstinacy of the Christians, so that they might be permitted to
'put together' their meetings, or meeting-places; and finally to state that
the Christians should pray to their god for the safety of the empire.[14]

Exactly what the Christians were permitted is obscure, for Lactantius'
word (*conventicula*) could refer either to meetings or to the places where
they were held, while Eusebius' version speaks explicitly of 'the houses in
which they met'. In either case there is no mention of any specific arrangements for the restoration of church properties such as are found in the
measures of Constantine and Licinius two years later; such instructions
might, none the less, have been contained in the 'other letter' which the
emperors say they are about to write to provincial governors to tell them how
to proceed.[15]

However, our evidence on what such letters might have contained again
relates only to Maximin, who on the news of Galerius' death hastily moved
from Syria and established himself at Nicomedia, thus controlling the whole
area east of the Bosporus. Eusebius believed that he did not fully subscribe
to the proclamation of the three emperors, and deliberately avoided commit-
ting himself to toleration by giving only oral instructions to his subordinates.
Eusebius' only documentary evidence for this stage is a letter written by
Sabinus, apparently Maximin's praetorian prefect, to a provincial governor,

---

[11] *De mort. pers.* 33, 11; 35, 1: 'Hoc edictum proponitur Nicomediae pridie Kalendas Maias
ipso octies et Maximino iterum consulibus.'

[12] Illness of Galerius: Lactantius, o.c., 33; Eusebius, *HE* VIII, 16, 2–5. Names of emperors and
address: *HE* VIII, 17, 3–4 (Galerius and Constantine); [5], in the MSS of the earlier edition only,
has Licinius and ἐπαρχιώταις ἰδίοις χαίρειν.

[13] pp. 319–21.

[14] *De mort. pers.* 34. The key phrase, 34, 4, is 'ut denuo sint Christiani, et conventicula sua com-
ponant'; cf. *HE* VIII, 17, 3–10, esp. 9: ἵνα αὖθις ὦσιν Χριστιανοὶ καὶ τοὺς οἴκους ἐν οἷς
συνήγοντο συνθῶσιν.

[15] *De mort. pers.* 34, 5: '⟨Per⟩ aliam autem epistulam iudicibus significaturi sumus, quid debeant
observare'; *HE* VIII, 17, 9; cf. p. 320. This is another indication that the main proclamation itself
was an *epistula*.

ordering the release of detained Christians and the prevention of the harassment of others; the governor is to write to this effect to local officials. The prefect, however, states that he is following the orders of all the emperors —'The divinity of our masters the most powerful emperors . . . has ordered it to be made known to your Sagacity through my Sanctity'—and there is no explicit evidence that any of them took any more positive steps at this stage.[16] The release of prisoners, however, was a reality, as both Lactantius and Eusebius attest.[17]

In the east the proclamation of toleration was followed by a reaction, manifested first by an attempt, whose form is unknown, on the part of Maximin to prevent Christians assembling in their cemeteries,[18] and then by the succession of embassies to him from cities and *koina*—among them Nicomedia, Antioch, Tyre and Lycia-Pamphylia—which we observed earlier, and which requested the prohibition of Christians from their territories.[19] The emperor's *rescripta* consented to these demands, and he seems now to have continued further with the installation of pagan priests in the cities.[20] In the same period a *dux* extracted by torture from some women at Damascus a confession of Christian malpractices which he sent in a report to the emperor, who ordered that the text should be published in the cities.[21] One Christian at least seems to have been tried by the emperor in person: the great biblical scholar, Lucian of Antioch, was taken to Nicomedia 'where the king happened to be resident, and having delivered before the ruler a defence of the teaching over which he presided, was committed to prison and killed'. The 'ruler' must be indeed Maximin, for Eusebius has noted earlier in his narrative that Lucian proclaimed his faith both by word and deed (namely his death) 'in the presence of the king'.[22]

This stage lasted until towards the end of 312, during which time Constantine had invaded Italy from Gaul, defeated Maxentius at the battle of the Milvian Bridge, and occupied Rome. Our viewpoints remain eastern, Lactantius and Eusebius, and we cannot say exactly when or in what form Constantine first proclaimed his adherence to Christianity; but perfectly clear evidence shows that he had done so at least by the first part of 313.[23] As we see the sequence of measures unfolding through the testimony of Eusebius, Constantine and Licinius took concerted action soon after Constantine's victory (24 October 312), composed 'a most complete law' in favour of the Christians, and sent it along with a report of the victory to

---

[16] *HE* IX, 1, 1–6; cf. p. 320.

[17] *De mort. pers.* 35, 2 (Donatus, Lactantius' addressee); *HE* IX, 1, 7–11.

[18] *HE* IX, 2.

[19] pp. 445–7.

[20] *HE* IX, 4, 2–3; 7, 12 (from the *rescriptum* to Tyre). Cf. p. 576.

[21] *HE* IX, 5, 2.

[22] *HE* IX, 6, 3; VIII, 13, 2; for a general reference to Christians executed in Maximin's presence see IX, 10, 12.

[23] It is to be hoped that it is no longer necessary to enter into debate on the authenticity of Constantine's conversion. Neither the fact that what Lactantius, writing probably still from Nicomedia in about 314/15, says of it (*De mort. pers.* 44) differs somewhat in context and content from what Constantine himself retailed to Eusebius years later (*VC* I, 28), nor the fact that his conception of Christianity may not always have attained the highest theological levels, is sufficient to deny an evident and public fact of the greatest historical importance.

Maximin; they called on him to allow Christian meetings and the re-building of churches, and allowed these things to their own subjects by 'edicts and laws'.[24]

That is all that Eusebius can report so far, since these measures were not yet published in the east. Instead, he can reproduce the letter which Maximin wrote to Sabinus at the end of 312 justifying both his previous toleration and his renewed persecution (in terms of the demands from the cities), and now proclaiming a bare toleration once again; Sabinus was to make it public by an *edictum* of his own.[25] There seems no good reason to disbelieve Eusebius' view that Maximin did so as a reluctant and partial concession to the more positive measures of Constantine and Licinius. For in the meantime two documents, preserved in isolation by Eusebius, show Constantine writing to the proconsul of Africa, Anullinus, first to have church property restored, and then to have *clerici* exempted from obligations in the cities. The letter about church property probably dates to the first three months of 313, and is a fine example of the later Roman diplomatic and administrative style:[26]

> Hail, Anullinus, most honoured by us. It is in the nature of our love of doing good, to wish that those things which rightfully belong to anyone should not only not be disturbed by another, but should be restored, dearest Anullinus. So we wish that when this letter arrives, if anything belonging to the Catholic church of the Christians, in any of the cities or other places, is in the possession of citizens or any others, you should have it restored at once to those same churches, since we have decided that those things which the churches formerly possessed should be restored to their ownership. Since your Devotion observes how perfectly clear is the burden of our command, make haste to see that everything, whether gardens, houses or anything else which is the lawful property of the churches, is restored to them as soon as possible, so that we may learn that you have applied the most conscientious obedience to this order of ours. Farewell, Anullinus, most honoured and longed-for by us.

In March or early April 313 Constantine wrote again to Anullinus laying down that those, 'whom it is customary to call *clerici*', provided that they belonged to the Catholic church headed by Caecilian (the then bishop of Carthage), should be exempt from all city obligations; thus liberated, they could apply themselves to their devotions, which were essential for the safety of the state.[27] It will have been to this letter that Anullinus replied in highly formal and diplomatic terms, saying that it had been received with due reverence by Caecilian and the *clerici*, whom 'my Insignificance' had urged to unity and obedience 'now that it appears that they have been liberated from every obligation by the *indulgentia* of your *maiestas*'.[28] The privilege was precisely that given long since, under various conditions, to athletes, doctors,

---

[24] *HE* IX, 9, 12; 9a, 11–12.
[25] *HE* IX, 9a, 1–9. Referred to in IX, 10, 8. Cf. p. 445.
[26] *HE* X, 5, 15–17. These two letters are not dated, but X, 7 (below) is clearly presupposed by the letter of Anullinus, Augustine, *Ep.* 88, 2 (below), dated to soon after 15 April 313; and this one, restoring church property, is likely to precede X, 7, giving exemption from *munera*.
[27] *HE* X, 7.
[28] Augustine, *Ep.* 88, 2. Cf. p. 320.

grammatici and rhetors; but the problems and disputes as to the relevant qualifications for it, serious enough in all these cases, were to be easily surpassed in intensity by the question of which body of persons represented the true Catholic church; and Anullinus' reply itself contained two *libelli* from a branch of the church which claimed the designation of 'Catholic' for itself, and had charges to bring against Caecilian.[29]

Meanwhile war had broken out between Maximin and Licinius. Maximin was defeated in an attempt to seize Licinius' possessions in Europe, and was driven back to Asia Minor. Early in May 313 he finally issued a proclamation of full restitution for the Christians, of which Eusebius gives a Greek translation. Here, as before, Maximin rehearses the previous history of the measures relating to Christians, and then states emphatically that 'by this gift (*dôrea*) of ours' Christians had full freedom of worship, and might rebuild their churches. More important still, it is here that Maximin orders the restoration of houses or lands formerly owned by the church, and now fallen to the *fiscus*, taken by a city, sold up, or given to anyone as a favour (*charisma*).[30]

If we may believe Eusebius, this edict was no more than a final despairing gesture to court popularity. The victory of Licinius was already inevitable; in June he entered Nicomedia and on the 15th ordered the posting-up of the proclamation often called the 'Edict of Milan'. In form indeed it was not an *edictum* but the text of a letter addressed individually to provincial governors in the east; in it, however, the emperors do refer to their meeting at Milan, which had taken place in the previous winter, when we have every reason to think that they had in fact proclaimed restitution for the church in the area which they then controlled.[31]

Both Lactantius' Latin and Eusebius' Greek texts represent a letter to a governor, who is addressed in the second person singular throughout. Each governor was to post up the imperial letter, followed by an edict of his own; 'But in order that the contents of the command of our benevolence should come to the notice of all, it will be appropriate for you to post up this letter everywhere, placed before your edict . . .'[32] The significant novelty of the imperial letter is not the proclamation of toleration, but the detailed instructions for the recovery of the property both of individual Christians and of the churches as corporations; and, what is more, the arrangements for the compensation of those who had in the meantime acquired it. Christian meeting-places owned by individuals, which had subsequently been bought from the *fiscus* or from anyone else, were to be given back without payment, as were any which had been acquired as a gift; but those who had acquired

---

[29] See p. 586.

[30] *HE* IX, 10, 6–12. It was evidently an *edictum* – τοῦτο τὸ διάταγμα προτεθῆναι ἐνομοθετήσαμεν (10). For the reference to confiscated property and the *fiscus* cf. p. 174.

[31] Lactantius, *De mort. pers.* 48, 1: 'de restituenda ecclesia huius modi litteras ad praesidem datas proponi iussit' (cf. 48, 13: 'his litteris propositis'); text in 44, 2–12, cf. *HE* x, 5, 1–14. The reference to Milan is 48, 2, and *HE* x, 5, 4; the meeting is described separately by Lactantius (45, 1): 'Constantinus rebus in urbe compositis hieme proxima Mediolanum concessit. Eodem Licinius advenit ut acciperet uxorem.' Cf. for discussion and bibliography, M. Anastos, 'The Edict of Milan (313): a Defence of the Traditional Authorship and Designation', *Rev. Ét. Byz.* XXV (1967), 13.

[32] *De mort. pers.* 48, 12; cf. *HE* x, 5, 14; cf. Crawford and Reynolds, *JRS* LXV (1975), 161.

the properties by purchase or gift (that is, 'if they had petitioned for any property from our Benevolence'), should address a request to the *vicarius*, 'in order that their interests too may be served by our *clementia*'. The same applied to properties owned by the Christian congregations, and under the same condition: 'that those who make restitution without payment, as we have said, should hope for compensation from our *benevolentia*'.[33]

The emperors thus set out to reverse a complex process of the transfer of wealth from the church to the *fiscus* and to private persons in the only way open to them, namely by offering compensation from imperial funds to those obliged to make restitution. Moreover, in this new situation, when the church now benefited from positive imperial favour, it was not likely that the imperial generosity would stop there. It is not surprising that what seems to be the earliest letter of an emperor to a bishop, that of Constantine to Caecilian of Carthage, should be on just this topic. As we have seen, the very fact that bishops could now be addressed in *epistulae* by emperors it itself an indication of their new standing,[34] and all the more in this instance, as Constantine's letter seems to be spontaneous, and not to be a response to any initiative by Caecilian. The letter seems to belong in the first half of 313:[35]

> Constantinus Augustus to Caecilian, bishop of Carthage, [greetings?]. Since it has pleased me that throughout the provinces of Africa, Numidia and Mauretania something should be provided for their expenses for certain servants of the lawful and most sacred Catholic religion, I have given letters to Ursus, *vir perfectissimus*, *rationalis* of Africa, and instructed him to have 3000 *folles* paid to your Integrity. You, however, when you have received the afore-mentioned sum of money, must order it to be distributed to all the afore-mentioned persons according to the schedule sent to you by Ossius. But if you find that it is at all insufficient to fulfil my intention with regard to all of them, you should without question ask for whatever you find to be necessary from Heraclides, the procurator of our properties. For when he was here in person, I gave him instructions that if your Integrity asked for any money from him, he should be sure to pay it without hesitation . . .

The letter marks the first appearance at the side of Constantine of the bishop Ossius of Corduba, who was to play so important a role in the ecclesiastical politics of the following decades.[36] But more significant is its demonstration of the entirely new resources which were opening to the church—resources which, as we have seen, it is perhaps better to characterize as an institutionalized development and extension of the private wealth in the hands of the emperor, rather than as that of the 'State'. Here, as in the immense donations of Constantine to the churches of Rome, recorded in the *Liber Pontificalis*, such wealth is at the emperor's free disposal, to grant as he

---

[33] 48, 7–9; *HE* x, 5, 9–11.
[34] p. 472.
[35] *HE* x, 6. That the opening formula is incomplete and should be restored as that of a letter is suggested by the presence of an elaborate closing formula, 6, 5: ἡ θειότης τοῦ μεγάλου θεοῦ σε διαφυλάξει ἐπὶ πολλοῖς ἔτεσιν.
[36] See V. C. De Clercq, *Ossius of Cordova* (1954), and pp. 591, 594–5.

wishes.[37] But already there were problems, and in the conclusion of this same letter Constantine says that he has learned that there were some who wished to divert the Christian laity to base doctrines, and tells Caecilian to accuse them before the proconsul or the *vicarius*. The persons referred to were the schismatics soon to be known as the Donatists after their most prominent leader; and in fact it was they who took the initiative in accusing Caecilian and the Catholics, and the judge on whom they insisted was the emperor himself.

5. *Petitions, Disputes and Accusations: the Donatist Controversy*

The social and religious background of the Donatist schism, which was to divide the African church for more than a century, and to linger on even after that, is a matter of acute controversy, and cannot be discussed here. But its formal origins can be briefly and inadequately summarized.[1] In 311, immediately after the restoration of the church by Maxentius, Caecilian was elected as bishop of Carthage. But another party claimed that one of the bishops who ordained him, Felix of Aphthungi, was a *traditor*—one who had handed over the scriptures in the great persecution. Consequently they held his election to be invalid and elected a rival bishop, Maiorinus; Caecilian's party claimed, apparently correctly, that one of his *ordinatores* was also a *traditor*. But his schismatic church persisted and gained its name from Donatus, who succeeded Maiorinus at Carthage in perhaps 313.

It is important to emphasize that the schism was itself created by the provisions of the great persecution, and that, whatever its social or spiritual background, it was about the validity of rival ordinations, and not about matters of doctrine. That made it all the easier and more natural for the judgment of the emperor to be invoked; and it was invoked all the more readily because both sides claimed the designation of 'Catholic', and because it was the Catholic clergy on whom grants of cash and immunities were now bestowed by the emperor. But was it in fact at this stage, the first part of 313, that the issue first came to Constantine? The issue is complicated, but of considerable significance; for if it could be shown that the schismatic party first approached Constantine before he had become a Christian, or at least before they knew of it, it would illustrate with even greater clarity than the petition against Paul of Samosata which the church of Antioch addressed to Aurelian, who was indisputably a pagan, how the relations of church and emperor had their origins in conceptions of the emperor's role already long established in the Graeco-Roman world.

Unfortunately our crucial evidence is provided by the vivid and important,

---

[37] See *Liber Pontificalis* xxxiv (ed. Duchesne I, 170–87) relating to the tenure of Silvester (314–35), and pp. 186–7.

[1] See W. H. C. Frend, *The Donatist Church* (1952), with subsequent bibliography mentioned in second impression (1973); cf. P. Brown, *Religion and Society in the Age of Saint Augustine* (1972), pt. iii. For a different chronology see T. D. Barnes, 'The Beginnings of Donatism', *JThSt* xxvi (1975), 13.

but episodic and incomplete, narrative given by Optatus in his anti-Donatist work written in the middle of the fourth century. After describing the ordinations of Caecilian and Maiorinus, and devoting a chapter to expostulations on the enormity of the schism, he comes at once to the demonstration of the irrefutable fact that it was the schismatics who had invoked the intervention of the emperor:[2]

> For your predecessors, Lucianus, Dignus, Nasutius, Capito, Fidentius and the others made a request to the emperor Constantine, who was still unaware of these matters, in the petition (*preces*) of which a copy is given below:
> 'We address our request to you, Constantine, best of emperors—since you come from a just race, and your father (alone) among the other emperors did not carry out the persecution, and Gaul is immune from this crime—as in Africa there are disputes between us and the other bishops, we ask that your *pietas* should order that *iudices* should be granted to us from Gaul. Given by Lucianus, Dignus, Nasutius, Capito, Fedentius, and the other bishops of the party of Donatus'.

The last phrase is clearly not original, since the schismatic bishops had not yet become 'the party of Donatus'. Nor can we be certain that the main part of the text is complete. None the less we must deal with what we have, and several features stand out at once. Firstly, the petitioners not only make no mention of the Christianity of Constantine, but rest their claim to his benevolence on his *pietas* to his father, who had not been a persecutor. Secondly, they ask for *iudices* from Gaul, Constantine's chief region until the campaign of 312. Thirdly, they make no specific accusation against anyone, but state no more than that they have disputes against other bishops. Could it be therefore that they sent someone to carry these *preces* to Constantine at a time when, so far as they know, he was still a pagan—even if benevolently disposed—and still in Gaul? Such a petition could have been written at any time from the late summer of 311 to the spring of 312. It is even possible to suggest that they hit inadvertently on the moment of his conversion, for Optatus continues by describing his reaction in the following terms:[3]

> When he had read these words, Constantine replied full of anger. In this response he exposed the nature of their *preces* also, in saying: 'You ask from me a court in this world, although I myself look forward to the court of Christ.'

However attractive such a hypothesis may be, many difficulties remain. Optatus continues directly to the eventual result of the petition, when Constantine appointed as *iudices* three bishops from Gaul and fifteen from Italy, who met in the house of Fausta on the Lateran under the presidency

---

[2] *Contra Parmenianum Donatistam* I, 22. The petition runs: 'Rogamus te, Constantine optime imperator—quoniam de genere iusto es, cuius pater inter ceteros imperatores persecutionem non exercuit et ab hoc facinore immunis est Gallia. nam in Africa inter nos et ceteros episcopos contentiones sunt—petimus, ut de Gallia nobis iudices dari praecipiat pietas tua.' In spite of the arguments of T. D. Barnes, *JRS* LXIII (1973), 45, and *JThSt* XXVI (1975), 20–1. I cannot take 'hoc facinore' as other than referring back to 'persecutionem'.

[3] I, 23.

of Miltiades, bishop of Rome, in October 313. There was thus, on this view, a long interval before Constantine acted; but what he then did was in any case very different from what they had requested, for on our evidence they had not even specified bishops as *iudices*. Moreover, the nineteen bishops met to consider actual accusations against Caecilian (and counter-accusations against Donatus),[4] of which there is no word in the *preces*. If we come to 313, there is no explicit mention of disputes in the African church in either of Constantine's letters to Anullinus, on the restoration of church property and the immunity of *clerici*, though the letter defines the 'Catholic church' as that headed by Caecilian. Moreover, in his letter to Caecilian about grants of money to the clergy, he knows of dissension in the church, but thinks of accusations which Caecilian might in future bring before the proconsul or *vicarius* of Africa.[5] Actual accusations appear for the first time in Anullinus' letter of acknowledgement, which also happens to contain the only surviving description of *libelli* on their way to the emperor. After describing the reception of Constantine's *indulgentia* by Caecilian and the Catholics, he continues:[6]

> But after a few days, certain persons appeared, accompanied by a crowd of people, who saw fit to oppose Caecilian, and who presented to my Reverence a packet sealed on the leather covering and a *libellus* without a seal, and urgently requested that I despatch them to the sacred and worshipful *comitatus* of your Divinity. These my Insignificance has taken care to despatch, while Caecilian retains his status notwithstanding their proceedings, in order that your *maiestas* might be able to consider the whole matter. Two *libelli* are sent herewith, one addressed on the covering as follows, '*Libellus* of the Catholic Church containing accusations against Caecilian, presented by the party of Maiorinus', and also another without seal attached to the same covering, given on 15 April at Carthage in the third consulship of our lord Constantinus Augustus.

According to the letter of some Catholic *clerici* included in the correspondence of Augustine, it was in response to this *relatio* by the proconsul that Constantine summoned the episcopal court to Rome; and this is supported by Constantine's letter to Miltiades, bishop of Rome (the second *epistula* to a bishop of which we know), which is quoted in isolation by Eusebius, and in which the emperor refers to reports from Anullinus (of which he encloses copies) and gives instructions for the establishment of the episcopal court.[7] It is thus certain that it was these *libelli* transmitted through the proconsul which caused Constantine to make the first of his successive attempts to solve the schism. It *may* be that the petition which Optatus quotes was identical with one of the two *libelli*, or belonged in the same period; but it may still be suggested that its words imply an earlier stage, when the dissident bishops thought that they were approaching a pagan emperor. If so, the

---

[4] 1, 23–4. We have to presume from this that Donatus had succeeded Maiorinus in the summer of 313.

[5] p. 583.

[6] Augustine, *Ep.* 88, 2.

[7] Augustine, *Ep.* 88, 3; Eusebius, *HE* x, 5, 18–20.

fact that their approach was for the time being abortive hardly lessens its significance for the developing relations of church and emperor.

The rest of the Donatist affair as it developed under Constantine can be surveyed more briefly. Indeed it is perfectly summarized in a letter included in the correspondence of Augustine, mentioned above.[8] After the court of bishops in Rome had found in favour of Caecilian, all strife ought to have ended:

> But again your predecessors went back to the emperor, complaining that the judgment was incorrect, and that the whole case had not been heard. So he appointed another episcopal court to be held in the city of Arelate in Gaul (314), when many of your side, after the vain and Satanic dissension had been condemned, returned to concord with Caecilian; but others, the most obstinate and litigious, appealed to the same emperor. Afterwards he too was forced to hold a hearing between the parties on this episcopal case and to bring it to an end (315); he was also the first to lay down against your party a law by which your meeting-places were claimed for the *fiscus*.

It was in connection with the synod at Arelate (which also decided various quite separate and general questions of ecclesiastical law)[9] that bishops first enjoyed the privilege of using the vehicles of the public transport-service; Constantine is found giving instructions on this point both to Aelafius (apparently *vicarius* of Africa), and to Chrestus, bishop of Syracuse—who was to request a public vehicle from the *corrector* of Sicily, and to travel with two priests and three slaves.[10]

It was perhaps, as is normally assumed, to the bishops at Arelate, but possibly later, to the Catholic bishops of Africa, that Constantine wrote a letter which perfectly exemplifies the current intrusion of secular patterns into the church, by expostulating at the wickedness of those who imitated pagans by appealing to higher courts—'Just as is usual in cases among pagans, they have interposed an appeal. Pagans indeed sometimes shun the lower courts, where justice will quickly overtake them . . . and make a habit of seeking refuge in higher courts. What of these deniers of the law, who have refused a divine court and seen fit to demand mine?' The emperor states that he has written to the *vicarius* of Africa to have the guilty men brought to his *comitatus* for suitable chastisement.[11] By the spring of 315 a number of Donatist bishops, Lucianus, Capito, Fidentius and Nasutius, and others of the same party, had indeed been summoned by 'celestial order' to the *comitatus*. But they departed unharmed, for the praetorian prefects issued a

---

[8] Augustine, *Ep.* 88, 3; cf. 43, 2/4; 7/20.

[9] See the *acta* of the council, e.g. in E. J. Jonkers, *Acta et Symbola Conciliorum quae saeculo quarto habita sunt* (1954), 23f.

[10] Optatus, App. III; Eusebius, *HE* X, 5, 21–4.

[11] Optatus, App. V. For the assumption that the letter is addressed to the synod of Arles see e.g. H. Dörries, *Das Selbstzeugnis Kaiser Konstantins* (1954), 28f.; this is nowhere explicit, however, and the reference to the despatch of Donatists from Africa to the *comitatus* may suggest a later date. A paraphrase of Constantine's remarks about appeal appears in Optatus I, 25, followed (26) by an episode of uncertain date in 313–15 in which, at the suggestion of Filumenus, the *suffragator* of Donatus, Caecilian was retained at Brixia, and an abortive mission of two bishops was sent to Africa.

letter to the *vicarius* of Africa from Trier on 28 April, to arrange for their safe return by official transport.[12]

Moreover, in spite of his brave words about the impropriety of secular jurisdiction in such cases, Constantine wrote in 314 or 315 to Aelianus, the proconsul of Africa, instructing him to hold an enquiry as to whether Felix (one of the *ordinatores* of Caecilian) had in fact been a *traditor*.[13] The hearing held by Aelianus, preserved verbatim by Optatus,[14] showed that Felix was innocent and that a letter purporting to prove the contrary had been forged by one Ingentius. The proceedings were reported to Constantine, and probably later in 315, he wrote to Aelianus' successor, Probianus, to send Ingentius to the *comitatus*—'in order that those who are present at court, and day after day never cease from presenting petitions, should by being present and hearing in person be made to realise that it is in vain that they have tried to defame the bishop Caecilian and have thought fit to make violent attacks on him'.[15] The Donatists, in other words, had not yet given up their attempts to have the issue heard by Constantine himself, and they were finally successful. For Constantine wrote in the summer of 315 to some Donatist bishops who were themselves evidently at the *comitatus*, to say that a few days previously he had decided that they should return to Africa, for the case against Caecilian to be heard by *amici* of his whom he would choose; but now he had changed his mind and was sending for Caecilian. Moreover, if they could prove before him even one charge against Caecilian, it would be as if he were guilty of all.[16] According to the narrative of these events given in a letter of Augustine, the parties were due to be heard in Rome (hence between July and September 315), but Caecilian failed to arrive. Following a further petition by the Donatists, he ordered them to follow him to Milan (whereupon some tried to abscond, and were brought under guard). There the case was heard, and Caecilian declared innocent.[17]

Thus the issue had been presented to Constantine in one form or another over a period of at least two and a half years, and possibly longer. At all times the initiative in bringing the case before him was kept by the Donatists, who insisted relentlessly on having it judged by the emperor in person; not only did Constantine not seek to hear the case or to exert a positive control over the church, but he did so in the end only against his own conviction of the primacy of episcopal decisions. As an illustration of the workings of petitions to the emperor and of his jurisdiction, the issue rivals in bulk and range of evidence anything known to us from the previous period; and it also graphically illuminates how the parties, voluntarily and involuntarily, had to pursue the emperor and his now peregrinatory court, perhaps to Gaul in 311/12, and certainly to Trier in 314/15, and Rome and Milan in 315.

---

[12] Optatus, App. VIII. For the fact that the document belongs to 315, not 316, see *PLRE* Celsus 8, and Barnes, *JRS* LXIII (1973), 37–8.

[13] Optatus I, 27.

[14] App. II. On the date of the hearing, probably 15 February 315 rather than 314, *PLRE* Aelianus 2.

[15] Augustine, *Ep.* 88, 4; *Contra Cresconium* III, 70/80.

[16] Optatus, App. VI.

[17] *Ep.* 43, 7/20. For the chronology see Barnes, *JRS* LXIII (1973), 38. Cf. *Frag. Vat.* 273, p. 546 above.

Above all it represents a total failure of the emperor to impose a decision on the dissident party.

Moreover, active dissension was by no means over. Not long after his judgment between Caecilian and his opponents he received a report from Celsus, the *vicarius* of Africa about further troubles ('the latest letter from your Gravity has borne witness . . .'). He instructed Celsus to inform both parties that with God's favour he would come himself to Africa, would search out the truth and would show them in what manner reverence ought to be shown to God. His tone had already changed markedly: 'What else should be done by me, in the light of my principles and the very function of emperor, than that by dispelling errors and pruning all excesses I should cause all men to present to the omnipotent God a true devotion, a simplicity in concord and a proper worship?'[18] In fact, it seems clear that Constantine never went to Africa; it may well be relevant that he fought a war against Licinius in 316/17. But if we follow the letter preserved in Augustine's correspondence, it was about now that Constantine applied to the Donatists the very measure which the tetrarchs had applied to the church as a whole, and expropriated their churches for the *fiscus*; they were later to regain them by petition to Julian.[19]

It may also have been now that there began a period of violent repression of Donatism in Africa.[20] But as regards the emperor, we know only of a letter of 10 November 316, to the *vicarius* Eumelius, attesting to Caecilian's innocence.[21] In the meantime some Donatists had evidently been exiled, for on 5 May 321 Constantine is stated to have written to the *vicarius* of Africa, ordering their release, and saying that they should be left to the judgment of God;[22] it is likely to have been at about the same time that he wrote to the bishops and laity of the Catholic church in Africa recommending tolerance and, again, faith in God's judgment.[23]

The emperor was thus plainly unable to impose concord, a fact barely concealed by Eusebius' brief reference to his treating with smiling contempt the ravings of schismatics in Africa.[24] Moreover, there were other ways in which local dissensions could impose themselves on him. The immunity of *clerici* from city obligations (*munera*) had been proclaimed, as we saw, in the spring of 313. By October of that year we find Constantine writing to an unidentified office-holder (perhaps, indeed, the proconsul of Africa) to say that he has learned that heretics are nominating Catholic clerics for such

[18] Optatus, App. VII. The letter is subsequent to the trial which Constantine held—'cum statuissem inter ipsos atque Caecilianum plenissime super allegationibus diversis requirere, praesentiae meae susceptam fugam subtrahere laborarunt'—and Caecilian and his opponents are already back in Africa. But Celsus' successor, Eumelius, was already in office in March 316, see *PLRE* Celsus 8.

[19] Augustine, *Ep.* 88, 3 (cf. p. 587); petition to Julian, Augustine, *Contra litteras Petiliani* II, 92/205; cf. *Ep.* 105, 9.

[20] See Frend, *Donatist Church*, 159f., relying essentially on a presumed dating of the events recorded in the *Passio Donati*.

[21] A fragment quoted in Augustine, *Contra Cresconium* III, 71/82; referred to in *Post Collationem* 33/56 (giving the date).

[22] Augustine, *Post Collationem* 33/56.

[23] Optatus, App. IX.

[24] *VC* I, 45.

functions, and instructing him to intervene.[25] On the other hand, in 320 and 326 we find him having to write ordering measures to prevent rich men from avoiding public duties by entering the ranks of the clergy;[26] and in 326 he writes (in response to a particular issue?) to affirm that the privileges of *clerici* are confined to those of the Catholic church—heretical and schismatic clergy were not only not immune, but should be subject to extra obligations.[27] In 330 he again had to protect the rights of Catholic clergy from specific attack by heretics, writing as follows to the *consularis* of Numidia from Serdica on 5 February:[28]

> Let the readers of the divine scriptures, the sub-deacons and the other *clerici*, who by the malice of the heretics have been called to membership of town-councils, be released; and for the rest they should, as is the custom in the east, by no means be summoned to the councils, but enjoy the most complete immunity.

As has long been recognized, it cannot be an accident that it was also from Serdica on 5 February that Constantine replied to a number of Numidian bishops who had complained of the activities of heretics and schismatics. The letter to the *consularis* must have been a result of their complaint, for Constantine, in his letter to the bishops, explicitly refers to the same categories of clergy, and states that he has given orders for their release from city obligations. What is more, as we saw much earlier, the Catholics had also asked for a basilica to replace that occupied by the schismatics, and Constantine offers them a site 'from among our properties' on which a new one will be built at fiscal expense.[29] There are few clearer examples of how interested parties could take the initiative in approaching the emperor, of what he had within his power to grant—above all privileges and money—and at the same time of the inevitable limits of his power to control events in other parts of the empire. The same features were already becoming more than clear in his dealings with the churches of the Greek east.

6. *Disputes, Councils and Accusations: the Arian Controversy*

When Constantine won his final victory over Licinius at the battle of Chrysopolis on 18 September 324, it was already more than a decade since he had spoken publicly as a Christian, had conferred privileges and money on the church, and had begun to build, adorn and endow churches in Rome at immense expense to the imperial wealth.[1] We also find him, in further

[25] *CTh* XVI, 2, 1.

[26] *CTh* XVI, 2, 3 and 6 (both to praetorian prefects).

[27] *CTh* XVI, 5, 1 = *CJ* I, 5, 1 (omitting 'autem atque schismaticos'). Dracilianus is apparently acting as vice praetorian prefect in Oriens, see *PLRE* Dracilianus.

[28] *CTh* XVI, 2, 7.

[29] Optatus, App. X; cf. p. 133.

[1] Precise dates are lacking for the building of churches in Rome, and it is not clear, for instance, whether the fact that the *episcopale iudicium* of 313 met 'in domum Faustae in Laterano' (Optatus, *Contra Parmenianum* I, 23, cf. p. 586) means that the site had already been granted to the Church;

letters to individual bishops, allowing concessions to Christians in respect of
legal formalities. In 316 for instance he wrote to the bishop Protogenes
(presumably the bishop of Serdica who was later to take part in the Council of
Nicaea), re-affirming the right of Christians to carry out a legal manumission
of slaves by a formal procedure in church and before the congregation and
clergy. He then continues: 'Hence it is not undeserved that you (the clergy?)
should be able to grant freedom to slaves, or leave it by testament, in any
form which you may wish, provided that there is clear evidence of your
intention.'[2] Both the fact that this is a letter to a named individual bishop and
the form of the wording strongly suggest that this concession was granted
in response to a particular petition or enquiry. The same is true of a letter
written in 321 to bishop 'Hosius' (evidently Ossius of Corduba), rehearsing
the same general principle and conceding, first, that Christians could
legally manumit in the presence of clergy alone, and secondly, again, that
clerici could do so by will, without being subject to the strict forms of the
law.[3] Though these two letters belong in a sense to Constantine's 'legislation',
by their occasion and nature they are distinct from measures embodied
in *edicta*, or even in *epistulae* to office-holders, and it is not in the least
surprising that they partially repeat each other. It is also relevant that
earlier emperors had made comparable concessions to soldiers, to the effect
that their testamentary dispositions would be valid, provided only that
there was some minimal evidence of intent.[4]

Similarly, when in 321 Constantine granted churches the right to acquire
ownership on the basis of testamentary dispositions, he was conferring
something which had quite frequently been conceded as a privilege to
temples, and which the papyrus of 304 suggests that churches too had
enjoyed by custom anyway.[5] But this does seem to have been a positive piece
of legislation, addressed, 'to the people' and posted up in Rome in July 321
(when Constantine was in Sirmium).[6] It may also have been in this period that
Constantine issued an *edictum* granting legally valid judicial powers to
bishops, as to which he answered an enquiry from his praetorian prefect,
Flavius Ablabius, in May 333.[7] Whenever it was promulgated, this was

---

cf. G. Pelliccioni, *Le nuove scoperte sulle origini del Battistero Lateranense, Mem. Pont. Acc. Rom.
Arch.* III, xii, 1 (1973). But, as is well known, the endowments of the *titulus Equitii* and the Lateran
basilica and baptistery in Rome, *Liber Pontificalis* XXXIV (ed. Duchesne I, 170–7) reflect a period
when Constantine did not yet control the eastern provinces. For an illuminating survey see
R. Krautheimer, 'The Constantinian Basilica', *DOP* XXI (1967), 115.

[2] *CJ* I, 13, 1; see *RE* s.v. 'Protogenes' (5), not using this item.

[3] *CTh* IV, 7, 1 = *CJ* I, 13, 1 (omitting 'episcopo'), Cf. Sozomenus, *HE* I, 9, 6–7.

[4] See the abundant evidence collected in *Dig.* XXIX, 1 (*de testamento militis*).

[5] *CTh* XVI, 2, 4 = *CJ* I, 2, 1. For concession to temples of the right to receive legacies, see pp.
447–8. For *P. Oxy.* 2673, see p. 575

[6] For the significance of this novel form of legislative act see C. Dupont, 'Les constitutions
ad populum', *Rev. hist. droit fr.* XLIX (1973), 586.

[7] The reply to Ablabius (cf. p. 337) is clearly attested, *Const. Sirmond.* 1. But the pronouncement
in *CTh* I, 27, 1 is fragmentary and of uncertain form and date. It is described as 'data (which should
indicate an *epistula*) IX Kal. Iulias Constantinopoli [Licinio?] A(ug). et Crispo Caes. conss.'
The only possible restoration gives June 318. 'Constantinopolis' is sometimes found by retrojection
for 'Byzantium'—but Constantine was now in Aquileia (Seeck, *Regesten*, 166). Could it even have
been issued by Licinius?

indeed a step which went beyond the normal range of privileges or rights conferred by the emperors. Yet the measure was confined to civil suits, and its exercise depended on the choice of at least one of the parties.

Thus when Constantine reached Nicomedia in September 324 he had imposed some of the consequences of his Christian convictions on Graeco-Roman society; but in doing so had also, inevitably, found himself forced to respond to initiatives from within the Catholic church, from schismatics, and from pagans: in 323 for instance he had written from Sirmium to Helpidius, *vicarius* of Rome, to say 'we have learnt that certain *ecclesiastici* and other followers of the Catholic sect are being forced by men of various cults to take part in sacrifices of purification', and ordering him to mete out punishment.[8] Moreover, his campaign itself was at least claimed to be, and his immediate measures after its conclusion inevitably were, a reaction to a brief period of renewed persecution, imposed by Licinius in the east. From perhaps 320 soldiers and persons serving in the *palatium* had been forced to sacrifice or leave the service;[9] afterwards he proceeded to executions of bishops and destruction of churches,[10] and to a prohibition on meetings of councils of bishops.[11] But, as with the great persecution of the tetrarchic period, our best evidence for the effects on individuals comes from the pronouncements made immediately after his victory by Constantine, concerning the restoration of the status and property of those who had suffered.

Eusebius briefly summarizes these steps in his *On the Life of the Blessed King Constantine*, but his most valuable service is to reproduce the full text of the proclamation in letter form which Constantine addressed to the inhabitants of all the eastern provinces; Eusebius used, as was natural, the version addressed to the population of Palestine, and affirmed, as we saw earlier, that its authenticity was guaranteed by the *subscriptio* in the emperor's own hand.[12] Moreover, it is crucial to the whole question of the historicity of the Constantinian documents given by Eusebius that a fragmentary text of some of the earlier part of the letter (where Constantine describes and justifies his previous career in the light of his Christian convictions) is preserved on a papyrus of about 330–50.[13] We can thus be certain that such a letter, performing the functions of an *edictum*, was actually issued. Its essential purpose was very similar to that of the proclamations issued by

---

[8] *CTh* XVI, 2, 5. For Helpidius' office, *PLRE* Helpidius 1.

[9] The date 320 (not necessarily reliable) is given by Jerome, *Chron.* ed. Helm, p. 230; see Eusebius, *HE* X, 8, 10; *VC* I, 52, 54; *ILS* 8940, and for the anecdote of Auxentius, p. 52; cf. also Sozomenus, *HE* IV, 16, 6. For the best account of Licinius, see R. Andreotti in *Diz. Epig.* s.v.

[10] Eusebius, *HE* X, 8, 14–19; *VC* I, 56; II, 1–2.

[11] Eusebius, *VC* I, 51, confirmed by II, 66 (Constantine's letter of late 324) and the explicit reference in the letter of the synod held at Antioch early in 325, preserved in Syriac; see E. Schwartz, 'Zur Geschichte des Athanasius', *Ges. Schr.* III (1959), 136f., on p. 138 = Opitz, *Urkunden zur Geschichte des arianischen Streites 318–333* I–II (1934–5), no. 18.

[12] Eusebius' summary, *VC* II, 20–1; introduction of letter, 23; text, 24–42. On the *subscriptio* see p. 222.

[13] *P. Lond.* 878, demonstrated in the historic article by A. H. M. Jones and T. C. Skeat, 'Notes on the Genuineness of the Constantinian Documents in Eusebius' Life of Constantine', *JEH* V (1954), 196 = A. H. M. Jones, *The Roman Economy* (1974), 257. The papyrus preserves parts of *VC* II. 26–9.

Constantine and Licinius in 312/13: to restore the status and property of
Christians who had been condemned; and to grant the property of those
executed to their relatives, or failing such to the nearest church. Such
property was to be restored both by the *fiscus* and by private persons who had
subsequently acquired it. The same applied to shrines of martyrs or other
property belonging to the churches. It is noteworthy that Constantine
specifically grants exemption to those (evidently *clerici*) who had been
enrolled in town-councils; restores their ranks to those compelled to leave
the army; and releases those who had been condemned to hard labour 'so as
to be considered slaves of the *fiscus*'.[14] At the end he appears to indicate that
there might be imperial compensation for those who had acquired former
church property from the *fiscus*, though in much less explicit terms than in
the former proclamations of himself and Licinius:[15]

> Whichever persons have bought anything from the *fiscus* by a legal process of
> sale, or possess anything conceded to them as a gift, vainly extending their
> insatiable avarice to such things, let them be aware that by the very audacity of
> such purchases such men have done their utmost to alienate our generosity
> (*philanthrôpia*) from them; none the less they will not—as far as is possible and
> appropriate—fail to gain it.

These measures of restitution, combined with what seems to be a promise
of compensation in response to petitions from deserving cases, were a
necessity imposed on Constantine by the complex effects of even a brief
period of persecution and confiscation in the preceding few years. Now, as
in 313, the proclamation of restitution was followed by a positive exercise
of the imperial largesse, in letters to bishops commanding the repair and
extension of churches and empowering them to ask governors and praetorian
prefects for funds from the 'royal treasuries'.[16] This modest initial measure
was of course to be followed later by a vast programme of new church-
building in the east, in Jerusalem, Bethlehem and Mambre, and in the
imperial centres, Antioch, Nicomedia and Constantinople itself, of which
the details cannot be followed here.[17]

Writing to Macarius, bishop of Jerusalem, Constantine expressed the
hope that the Church of the Holy Sepulchre would surpass all the beautiful
buildings in all other cities; and the Bordeaux pilgrim who visited the Holy
Land in 333 duly registers basilicas 'of wonderful beauty' built by Constantine's order at the Sepulchre and at the terebinth (Mambre) near Hebron,
as well as others on the Mount of Olives and at Bethlehem.[18] Indeed, if the
expenditure of imperial wealth, and the application of organizational, artistic

[14] *VC* II, 30, 33, 34 (on *servi poenae* or *fisci* see p. 183).
[15] *VC* II, 41.
[16] *VC* II, 43–6 (where Eusebius quotes the letter addressed to himself as bishop of Caesarea).
[17] See the survey by R. Krautheimer, *DOP* XXI (1967), 115; for the question of Constantine's
foundations in Constantinople see now G. Dagron, *Naissance d'une capitale: Constantinople et ses
institutions de 330 à 451* (1974), 388f.; see also C. Coüasnon, *The Church of the Holy Sepulchre in
Jerusalem* (1974) and G. Downey, *History of Antioch in Syria* (1961), 342f.
[18] Constantine's letter to Macarius (*c.* 326?), *VC* III, 30–2; Bordeaux Pilgrim, *Corpus Christianorum* clxxv, *Itineraria et Alia Geographica*, pp. 17, 18, 20.

and material resources to the glorification of the church, had been the only
imperial function which his Christian beliefs required Constantine to
exercise, his task would have been simple. But within what must have been
no more than a matter of weeks after the victory of Chrysopolis, he was
confronted for the first time not with a mere schism over the validity of
episcopal ordinations, but with a fundamental doctrinal debate, the Arian
controversy.

Here again it must be emphasized that our concern is solely with the pattern
of relations between the emperor and various elements in the church which
the controversy called into being; the controversy itself, with its profound
intellectual roots and its complex personal and political ramifications
throughout the Greek church, must be given only cursory treatment, and
an understanding even more superficial than it received from Constantine
himself.[19] In brief, the Arian heresy rested on the teaching of Arius, a
presbyter in Alexandria, to the effect that the Son was not co-eternal with
the Father, and had been created by him in time. In a period probably of
a few years, perhaps only of a few months, before Constantine's victory his
teaching had gained wide support in the east, including that of Eusebius of
Caesarea, and his namesake Eusebius of Nicomedia. The latter, as we saw
earlier, had already been accused by Alexander, the bishop of Alexandria, of
moving from Berytus to Nicomedia, an imperial centre, in order to increase
his power in the church.[20] How he survived the persecutions under Licinius
is not known; but when Constantine wrote to the congregation of Nicomedia
after the council of Nicaea, he alleged that Eusebius had actively assisted in
the persecution, and had also sent agents to spy on himself.[21] There may
thus have been some slight political overtones even before Constantine's
involvement. But essentially it was a matter of theological debate, and had
already been the subject of rival synods, and of a vast correspondence
between the bishops.

Since the controversy and the council of Nicaea marked another major
stage in the relations of church and emperor, it is all-important to determine
how the issue first reached Constantine. Most of our sources say no more than
that Constantine heard of it, and sent a letter to Alexandria carried by an
emissary, whom some name as Ossius (who, if so, was in his entourage).[22]
One source, Epiphanius, goes further and says explicitly that Alexander,
the bishop of Alexandria, wrote to Constantine,[23] which would be of vital
significance if only his whole conception of the sequence of events in the

[19] For a clear account of the controversy see J.-R. Palanque, G. Bardy, P. de Labriolle, *Histoire
de l'Eglise* III: *de la paix constantinienne à la mort de Théodose* (1947), 69f.; for the council of
Nicaea, I. Ortiz de Urbina, *Histoire des conciles oecuméniques* I: *Nicée et Constantinople* (1963).
For the background see now H.-I. Marrou, 'L'arianisme comme phénomène alexandrin', *CRAI*
1973, 533. For the documents see Opitz, *Urkunden* (see p. 592, n. 11).

[20] The letter of Alexander in Socrates, *HE* I, 6 = Opitz, *Urkunden*, no. 4b. Cf. p. 52.

[21] Gelasius, *HE* III, Supp. i = Optiz, *Urkunden*, no. 27.

[22] Eusebius, *VC* II, 63; Rufinus, *HE* X, 1; Theodoret, *HE* I, 7, 1; Sozomenus, *HE* I, 16, 1 and 5;
Socrates, *HE* I, 7, 1; Gelasius, *HE* II, 3, 22. The mention of Hosius by the latter three *may* be con-
firmed by the reference in Athanasius, *Apol. c. Arian.* 76 (a letter of 335) to a synod including
Hosius which deposed a supposed presbyter in Alexandria named Colluthus.

[23] *Panarion* 69, 9, and cf. 68, 4: Ἀλεξάνδρου ... κινήσαντος τὸν μακάριον Κωνσταντῖνον,
συνεκρότησε σύνοδον ἐν τῇ Νικαίᾳ τῇ πόλει.

controversy were not hopelessly confused. However, we have a better source which at least reveals the context, namely Constantine's letter to Alexander and Arius. Here he states emphatically his commitment to unity and concord, and says that he had hoped to invoke the aid of the eastern church in ending the Donatist schism; but when he was actually on his way from Nicomedia to the eastern provinces, he had heard of their divisions and turned back.[24] It does not appear from the letter that he is replying to an actual communication from either of his addressees; but it is clear that some third party had informed him of the situation when he had visited Nicomedia after the victory, and was beginning his journey eastwards.

The next stages are obscure, and do not seem to have involved the emperor directly.[25] But from texts now preserved in Syriac it appears that early in 325 there was a synod at Antioch at which Ossius presided, and at which three Arianist bishops, Theodotus of Laodicea, Narcissus of Neronias and Eusebius of Caesarea, were given until an expected synod at Ancyra to repent.[26] But the synod was summoned from Ancyra to Nicaea by Constantine, who gave three reasons: its convenience for bishops from the west, its agreeable climate, and the opportunity for himself to be present.[27]

The authenticity of his letter, as preserved in differing forms, cannot be firmly determined. But the summons itself was a reality, recalling his establishment of a court of bishops in Rome in 313, and of an actual synod at Arelate in 314. The former seems to have been a response, perhaps significantly delayed, to the schismatics' petition for *iudices* from Gaul; but though the *iudices* appointed were three bishops from Gaul, joined by sixteen from Rome and Italy, this did not make the body a synod. Synods of varying sizes had been meeting in different parts of the empire since the second century; but that at Arelate (which, as we saw, also determined matters other than the case of Caecilian and Donatus) was the first to be summoned by the emperor. Like their predecessors eleven years before, the bishops summoned to Nicaea were provided with official transport: a letter couched in polite terms went to each bishop 'providing some with authority to use the *cursus publicus* (*diplomata*, in other words) and some with an ample supply of beasts of burden'.[28] In addition, the bishops received their daily upkeep during the course of the synod, were invited to dinner at the end of it to celebrate the emperor's *vicennalia* ('so that one would think that an image of the Kingdom of Christ was being conjured up') and on departure were given gifts (*xenia*), as appropriate to each one's rank.[29] The conventions

[24] Eusebius, *VC* II, 64–72; for the reference to Africa, 66–7; for his receipt of the news, 68, and more specifically, 72.

[25] Philostorgius, *HE* I, 7a, ed. Bidez (from the *Vita Constantini Cod. Angelic.*) alleges, however, that Arius and his supporters went to Nicomedia to put their case to Constantine, and were followed by Alexander and his.

[26] For the evidence see n. 11 above, and H. Chadwick, 'Ossius of Cordova and the Presidency of the Council of Antioch, 325', *JThSt* n.s. IX (1958), 292.

[27] For the Syriac text of Constantine's letter (preserved also in Arabic), and a re-translation into Greek, Optiz, *Urkunden*, no. 20. For an English translation with notes, P. R. Coleman-Norton, *Roman State and Christian Church* (1966), no. 48.

[28] Eusebius, *VC* III, 6, 1. Cf. p. 327.

[29] *VC* III, 9; 15, 2; 16.

were thus not entirely dissimilar to those which had applied, on a more
intimate scale, when Pliny took part in the *consilium* of Trajan in his villa
at Centumcellae some two centuries earlier.[30]

At least one session of the council met 'in the very innermost building of
the *basileia*' at Nicaea.[31] As we have seen, the terms *basileia* and *palatium*
had come by this period to be applicable to buildings which were not
necessarily specifically for the use of the emperors themselves.[32] But if, as
it seems from the tone of Eusebius' reference, the building was an imperial
'palace', this too was a novel element in the history of synods (though the
'house of Fausta' in which the court of bishops had met in 313 was evidently
imperial property, presumably granted to Fausta, the daughter of Maximian,
before her marriage to Constantine in 307).

But the true innovation was that the synod met for the first (and, in our
period, the only) time in the presence of the emperor himself.[33] For lack of
reliable evidence we cannot determine how extensive or continuous was
Constantine's involvement, nor *a fortiori* state what formal description
would have been given to his role there. Eusebius' deliberately superficial
account does, however, record, in suitably elevated terms, the genuinely
historic moment on 'the day on which a solution was due to be applied to
the disputes', when Constantine entered without a military escort, and took
his seat on a golden throne along with the synod. A speech was addressed to
him by one of the bishops, and in reply he delivered an oration in Latin
urging harmony, which was then repeated in Greek.[34] Thus far the pattern
of exchange cannot have been very different from that in which emperors
were involved on countless occasions, from receiving embassies to being
welcomed on arriving at a city. The distinctive feature was that the other
persons present were there in order to vote among themselves on disputed
questions, an element which (so far as can be discerned) emperors could not
have encountered elsewhere except in the senate, and perhaps, on a much
smaller scale of numbers, within the priestly colleges in Rome.[35]

Eusebius also describes in flattering terms how Constantine, now using
Greek, took part in at least some actual discussions in the synod; and his
letter to his congregation at Caesarea records that his proposed draft for a
creed was read out in the presence of Constantine, and approved by him.[36]
There is nothing to suggest, however, that Constantine formally subscribed
to the creed as a member of the synod, or voted himself on any of the other

[30] p. 27.

[31] *VC* III, 10, 1: ἐν αὐτῷ δὴ τῷ μεσαιτάτῳ οἴκῳ τῶν βασιλείων.

[32] pp. 41–2.

[33] Nothing in the accounts of Arelate suggests that Constantine was present in person, though
the sentence 'Tunc taedians iussit omnes ad suas sedes redire', at the end of the letter of the
council to Silvester, bishop of Rome (Routh, *Reliquiae Sacrae* IV, 306) *may* refer to him. The
general issue is suggestively discussed by F. Dvornik, 'Emperors, Popes and General Councils',
DOP VI (1951), 1, which is however marked by errors, e.g. (p. 9), 'The emperor never had the
right to vote in the senate.'

[34] *VC* III, 10–12; cf. p. 206.

[35] cf. pp. 355–61.

[36] *VC* III, 13; letter to Caesarea, Socrates, *HE* I, 8; Theodoret, *HE* I, 12; Gelasius, *HE* II, 35
(Opitz, *Urkunden*, no. 22). Constantine's presence at the Arian debate (but not specifically the
others) is also emphasized in the letter of the synod to the churches of Egypt (n. 40 below).

matters which it discussed. Nor can it be strictly proved that he attended the debates on these other matters—the date of Easter, the Meletian schism in Egypt,[37] and the evolution of a further set of canons—though he may in fact have done so. What is explicitly attested is activities of a more traditional type, his public reception of *libelli* of accusation against each other by the bishops (and perhaps also by laymen present against bishops), all of which he then had burnt;[38] or his personal interrogation of the Novatianist schismatic, Acesius.[39]

It is noteworthy that the synod wrote a letter collectively, announcing the results of their deliberations on the Arian and Meletian questions and the date of Easter, in which they refer to the emperor in the third person;[40] while Constantine wrote separately to all churches urging conformity to the procedure for determining the date of Easter;[41] and to the Alexandrian church warning them to conform to 'what was decided by the three hundred bishops'.[42] In this respect therefore the synod and the emperor maintained in essence their distinctive roles. So far as our evidence goes, the emperor's relation to the decisions of the synod was not even as formal as when earlier emperors had for instance approved votes or decisions by provincial *koina*,[43] or as in the wide range of verdicts or rescripts which emperors (including Constantine himself) had for centuries issued in relation to the affairs of pagan temples and religious festivals.[44]

Moreover, most of the matters debated at Nicaea were essentially concerned with the internal rules of the church, whether it was the conditions of tenure of different offices, or the methods for calculating the proper date of Easter. The question of the creed, however, though it too had such a character in the sense that it became a question of finding a formula to which a formal subscription could be made, of course involved questions of a quite different order, relating to fundamental, and opposed, metaphysical beliefs. Neither side had shown, or was later to show, any inclination to follow Constantine's initial reaction, that speculation on such theological issues was essentially vain and fruitless.[45] Compared to a theological debate of such importance, the fact that the intellectual life of the empire had never been totally without impact on the emperors—who might judge contests of sophists, receive serious works on philosophy or debate with the scholars in the Museum at Alexandria[46]—is only of limited relevance. None the less, it

---

[37] See further pp. 600–1.

[38] For the public session see p. 252; Gelasius, *HE* II, 8, 5–6 (alone) adds that similar *libelli* were given in by laymen, and met the same fate.

[39] Socrates, *HE* I, 10 (affirming that he had the story from a private source); cf. Sozomenus, *HE* I, 22; Gelasius, *HE* II, 30.

[40] Socrates, *HE* I, 9, 1–14; Theodoret, *HE* I, 9, 2–13; Gelasius, *HE* II, 34, 2–14 (Opitz, *Urkunden*, no. 23).

[41] *VC* III, 17–20 (Opitz, *Urkunden*, no. 26).

[42] Socrates, *HE* I, 9, 17–25; Gelasius, *HE* II, 37, 1–9 (Opitz, *Urkunden*, no. 25). It is superfluous to give the details of the differing figures which various sources provide for the number of bishops attending.

[43] cf. pp. 385–94.

[44] pp. 447–56.

[45] In the letter to Alexander and Arius, see p. 595.

[46] p. 504.

would be interesting to know if the reports of several later church historians that pagan philosophers and dialecticians came to the synod are more than legend.[47]

However, one major contribution of Christianity to Graeco-Roman culture was precisely to conjoin metaphysical belief and religious practice, and, as one consequence of that, to make the tenure of a priesthood dependent on appropriate belief; for instance the synod of Antioch of 268/9 had already deposed a bishop, Paul of Samosata, for a combination of heresy and misconduct, and had also involved a pagan emperor in the enforcement of that decision.[48] One of the decisive extra elements in this pattern which appeared at Nicaea was the imposition by the emperor of criminal penalties on those bishops or presbyters who refused to subscribe to the creed. Eusebius of Nicomedia, Theognis of Nicaea and their followers, as well as Arius himself, were exiled by imperial command.[49] Constantine referred explicitly to the fact that he had exiled Eusebius and others in the letter which he wrote to the congregation of Nicomedia, explaining the circumstances and telling them to select a new bishop,[50] and obliquely in that in which he warned Theodotus of Laodicea of the consequences of nonconformity.[51] Moreover it was evidently not later than 326 that he issued a pronouncement, of *edictum* type but in *epistula* form, addressed to heretics of all denominations, in which he stated that their meeting-places would be confiscated, and some of them handed over to the Catholic church.[52] This proclamation is evidently presumed in the letter which he wrote on 25 September 326, to the praetorian prefect conceding that the Novatianists (who were not heretics proper, but belonged to a rigorist schism which had originated in the Decian persecustion) could retain their properties:[53]

> We have learnt that the Novatianists are not so clearly destined for damnation that we should refuse to grant to them those things for which they have petitioned. So we order that they may possess the houses of their church, and burial places, securely and without question—those, that is, that they have possessed for a long time, by purchase or some other means. But steps must be taken to ensure that they do not try to usurp any of those properties which are proved to have belonged to the ever-holy church before the schism.

The proclamation, the Novatianist petition and Constantine's letter perfectly symbolize the main features of the new relationship of emperor and

---

[47] Rufinus, *HE* x, 3; Sozomenus, *HE* I, 18, 1–4. Socrates, *HE* I, 8, speaks instead of lay Christians, skilled in dialectic, who came to represent the two sides.

[48] pp. 572–3.

[49] Socrates, *HE* I, 8; cf. Philostorgius, *HE* I, 9a; 9c; 10; Gelasius, *HE* II, 33, 5, mentioning Eusebius and Theognis 'and the *Ariani* with them'; Sozomenus, *HE* I, 21, 4–5 (Arius, Eusebius, Theognis).

[50] Gelasius, *HE* III, App. i, 16: ἁρπαγέντας γὰρ αὐτοὺς ἐκέλευσα ὡς πορρωτάτω ἐξορισθῆναι (Opitz, *Urkunden*, no. 27).

[51] ibid., App. ii (Opitz, *Urkunden*, no. 28).

[52] Eusebius, *VC* III, 64–5. It is described as an ἐπιστολή and addressed αἱρετικοῖς, but can of course have had no specific addressees. Furthermore, the final subscription, προτεθήτω, 'let it be posted up', is characteristic of an *edictum*.

[53] *CTh* XVI, 5, 2, written from Spoletium on his journey back from his visit to Rome in 326.

church; the attempt to impose unity by using the normal penalties of the criminal law, the vigorous and successful reaction of the interested parties, and the consequent efforts by the emperor to balance his remarkably flexible responses with the interests of the Catholic church. All these features appear with the utmost clarity in his subsequent attempts to deal with the Arian controversy.[54]

The pattern of events in the later stages of the controversy was set by three events: the restoration of Eusebius of Nicomedia and Arius; the death of Alexander, bishop of Alexandria, and his succession by Athanasius; and the emergent influence of the Meletian schismatics on ecclesiastical politics and on the emperor. If the letter of Constantine to Alexander urging him to re-admit Arius, which Gelasius quotes, is genuine,[55] then certain political machinations recorded by various church historians must be placed before the bishop's death on 17 February 328. It is only unfortunate that the story gains in circumstantial detail as told by successive historians, starting with Rufinus, who says that an unnamed Arian presbyter was received into the confidence of Constantine at the deathbed request of his sister Constantia, and in turn won Constantine's favour for Eusebius.[56] Socrates begins the story of the restoration with a pamphlet (*libellus*) demonstrating their change of heart, which was sent to their fellow-bishops by Eusebius and Theognis, and which *may* have been addressed to a hypothetical second council of Nicaea in 327;[57] when he comes to the story of Constantine and the presbyter, he makes the latter's influence effect not the recall of Eusebius but that of Arius, and adds Constantine's letter to Arius, which he may have placed in the wrong context but which is at any rate a fine example of late Roman administrative vocabulary:[58]

Constantinus Magnus Victor Augustus to Arius. Your Integrity was long since informed that you should come to my camp (*stratopedon*) so that you may have the pleasure of the sight of us. I am most surprised that this has not been done immediately. Therefore take a public *vehiculum* and make haste to come to our camp, so that by gaining our goodwill and consideration you may be able to return to your native city. May God preserve you, beloved one. Given on 27 November.

On this reconstruction the year was 327, and we know that the *comitatus*

---

[54] What follows largely ignores various side-issues, such as the dispute over the see of Antioch, and also represents only one of many possible solutions to the extremely complex problems of the sequence of events, confusingly and variously related by the various church historians. A firm chronological framework is provided only from 328 onwards by the Festal Letters of Athanasius preserved (for the relevant years) only in Syriac. English translation by A. Robertson, *Select Writings and Letters of Athanasius, Bishop of Alexandria* (1892), 500f.

[55] *HE* III, 15, 1–5 (Opitz, *Urkunden*, no. 32).

[56] *HE* X, 12–13. Sozomenus, *HE* II, 27, 1f., has the story about the presbyter and Constantine but places it in the context of the councils of Tyre and Jerusalem (335), see pp. 603–5.

[57] *HE* I, 14 (Opitz, *Urkunden*, no. 21). For the argument for a second council—based essentially on the reference in Athanasius, *Apol. c. Arian.* 59 to the death of Alexander as having occurred five months after Nicaea—see H. G. Opitz, 'Die Zeitfolge des Arianischen Streites von den Anfängen bis zum Jahre 328', *ZNW* XXXIII (1934), 131.

[58] *HE* I, 25.

(*stratopedon*) was in the area of Nicomedia over that winter.[59] Arius and a
follower named Euzoius then addressed to Constantine a *biblion* (*libellus*),
attesting their acceptance of the Nicene formula, and (in Socrates' version)
returned to Alexandria, where they were rejected by Athanasius.[60]

The most detailed (and latest) account is given by Gelasius.[61] He names
the presbyter as Eutocius, and says that he gained first the favour of
Constantia's servants then of herself, leading to her deathbed request to
Constantine to restore Arius and have confidence in Eutocius. The latter
thus gained 'freedom of speech' before the emperor (*parrhêsia*—a word now
used of addressing superiors), and as a result Eusebius and Theognis
indicated their change of heart to their fellow-bishops, came to the *comitatus*
and were favourably received by Constantine. Further persuasion from
Eutocius resulted in Constantine summoning Arius and Euzoius from
exile, interrogating them in person on the creed and sending them to
Alexandria, where they were rejected by Alexander. It is here that Gelasius
places Constantine's letter to Alexander (in which he describes his interrogation of them), and states that Alexander died not long after receiving it.

It need hardly be emphasized that we cannot assert with confidence exactly
what influences really led to the restoration of Eusebius and Theognis
and the attempted restoration of Arius. But a possible chronology can be
discerned, and the change of fortune itself was a reality, as was the essential
role in it of the change of mind by the emperor himself. The effects of
recourse to the emperor, and hence dependence on him, were beginning to be
felt; and it is not surprising that an explicit attempt to limit them was made
at the synod held at Antioch at about this time (itself a remarkable example
of contemporary ecclesiastical politics and imperial influence, into which we
cannot enter here).[62] The eleventh and twelfth canons passed by the synod
laid excommunication on a bishop or presbyter who, without the approval
of the metropolitan of his province, went to the emperor and 'dared to
disturb the hearing of our king most beloved by God'; or on a deacon or
presbyter deposed by a bishop, or a bishop deposed by a synod, who did
likewise.

If these measures served to spare the hearing of Constantine, the fact is
not evident in our sources. For from the period immediately after the restoration of Eusebius we have perhaps the most vivid of all narratives of a petition
from a section of the church to the emperor. The persons concerned were
members of the Meletian schism, which like the Donatist one was a product of
the great persecution; in brief a division had arisen in the Egyptian church
over the conditions of re-admission of those who had lapsed; Peter, the then

---

[59] See Opitz, o.c., 156; Seeck, *Regesten*, 178. For *comitatus/stratopedon* see p. 43.

[60] *HE* I, 26–7. Socrates had mentioned the death of Alexander and the succession of
Athanasius in I, 15, 1.

[61] *HE* III, 12–15.

[62] For some bland references to these proceedings Eusebius, *VC* III, 59–62; for more details
see e.g. Athanasius, *Hist. Arian.* 4, 1; Socrates, *HE* I, 24; Sozomenus II, 19; Theodoret I, 21;
Philostorgius II, 7; Gelasius III, 16, 8–20. For the canons see Mansi, *Sacrorum Conciliorum nova
et amplissima Collectio* II, 1305f., and Jonkers, *Acta et Symbola Conciliorum* (1954), 51–2 (still
attributed to 341). For a discussion of the date Schwartz, o.c. (p. 592, n. 11), 216–26.

bishop of Alexandria, represented a lenient view and Meletius, bishop of Lycopolis, a rigorist one.[63] The Council of Nicaea had attempted to impose an interim solution, but dissension continued between the Catholic church in Egypt and the now quite widespread Meletian congregations. It was these, now led by one John Archaph, who in about 328 sent representatives to Constantine to complain of harassment by the Catholics:[64]

> They were sent to the *comitatus* to make a petition, that is to ask for the right to hold their own meetings without being prevented ... When they had gone to present the petition to the king they were turned away and sent off. For those in the *palation*, hearing the name of Meletians, and having no knowledge of what it was, did not grant them access to the king. Thus in this period it resulted that Paphnutius, John and their companions were waiting about in the area of Constantinople and Nicomedia. Then they became acquainted with Eusebius, bishop of Nicomedia, and put their case before him. For they knew that he had the ear of the king Constantine (*parrhēsia*), and asked him to make them known to him.

Eusebius granted their request, on condition that they admitted Arius to communion with themselves, brought them before Constantine, and obtained for them his permission to meet without hindrance. The story presents a relatively rare example of petitioners being turned away by the imperial attendants; but also one of innumerable instances, from both within the history of the church and outside it, of how the fortunes of individuals and groups depended on the results of a personal verbal exchange with the emperor.

The Meletian petition seems to have been directed in the first instance against Alexander.[65] But after Athanasius was elected to succeed him in June 328,[66] they and the Arians combined against him; in the welter of accusations which mark the next few years the two groups cannot usually be clearly distinguished. The sequence of events began, however, with Constantine writing to Athanasius, as he had to Alexander, urging him to readmit Arius. Athanasius himself attributes the letter to the influence of Eusebius (whom he also describes as having bought the Meletians by promises) and quotes an extract from it, threatening himself with exile for non-compliance. He firmly refused, however, and the result was a succession

[63] For an invaluable account, with a good survey of the evidence, see H. I. Bell, *Jews and Christians in Egypt: the Jewish Troubles in Alexandria and the Athanasian Controversy* (1924), ch. ii.

[64] Epiphanius, *Panarion* 68, 5–6. Epiphanius regards this petition as having been directed against Alexander of Alexandria (died February 328) which is possible, though his chronology in what follows is hopelessly confused. But at any rate it must have occurred between the return of Eusebius (late 327?) and the accusations against Athanasius (below). As noted on p. 54, the reference to 'waiting about' (χρονοτριβῆσαι) in the area of Nicomedia and Constantinople fits perfectly with *c.* 328–30.

[65] The letter of the Egyptian synod of 338/9 in Athanasius, *Apol. c. Arian.* confirms (11, 3) that the Meletians had made such an accusation—'Αλεξάνδρου κατηγορήσαντες μέχρις αὐτοῦ τοῦ βασιλέως—which of course may not refer to the same occasion.

[66] Epiphanius, *Panarion* 68, 7, has the story that at the moment of Alexander's death Athanasius was absent, having been sent by him to the *comitatus*; and the tenth-century *Life* of Constantine (*Vita Constantini Codicis Angelici* 49) states that the *psephisma* of his election was sent to Constantine, and quotes his letter of confirmation. Either or both could be correct.

20*

of accusations brought against him by his enemies.[67] Not all the stages of this process can be clearly discerned, but one is perfectly reflected in the Index to the *Festal Letters* which Athanasius addressed to his congregation each Easter. Of the letter of Easter 331 the Index records:[68]

> He sent this letter while journeying on his return from the Imperial Court. For this year he went to the Imperial Court to the Emperor Constantine the Great, having been summoned before him, on account of an accusation his enemies made, that he had been appointed too young. He appeared, was thought worthy of favour and honour, and returned when the feast was half-finished.

In the following year he was at the *comitatus* agains, and from there wrote the letter which, as we saw earlier, was brought by a soldier supplied by the Christian praetorian prefect, Flavius Ablabius:[69]

> For I am at the Court, having been summoned by the emperor Constantine to to see him. But the Meletians, who were present there, being envious, sought our ruin before the emperor. But they were put to shame and driven away thence as calumniators, being confuted by many things. Those who were driven away were Callinicus, Ision, Eudaemon and Geloeus Hieracammon . . .'

The mention of these names serves to identify with this occasion, and hence to date securely, an episode which is described elsewhere by Athanasius himself, and subsequently by the later church historians. According to him, these same persons first accused him of laying a tax on linen vestments on the Egyptians, but were refuted in the hearing of the emperor by some Alexandrian presbyters. Athanasius himself was then summoned, and when he arrived, his presbyter Macarius was accused of breaking a chalice (in a Meletian church as it later appears), and Athanasius of sending a bribe for a purpose hostile to the emperor. Constantine heard the case in person at Psammathia, a suburb of Nicomedia, dismissed the charges, and wrote to the congregation of Alexandria in support of Athanasius.[70]

Thereafter, perhaps in 333, there were further accusations against Macarius (or, as appears from a letter of Constantine, Athanasius) of breaking the chalice, and against Athanasius of killing a Meletian bishop called Arsenius—whom however he was able to produce alive; Constantine, hearing of these charges, first delegated the case to Dalmatius at Antioch, and then suspended it. At this time also John Archaph begged the emperor's forgiveness, and like Arius earlier was empowered to take an official *vehiculum* and come to 'the camp (*stratopedon*) of my Clemency'; the essential element, as always, would be a personal interview with the emperor.[71]

---

[67] *Apol. c. Arian.* 59, 4–60, 2. This work, partisan as it inevitably is, is the most important source for the ecclesiastical politics of the period.

[68] Trans. Robertson, o.c., p. 503.

[69] *Festal Letter* IV, 5, trans. Robertson, p. 517; cf. p. 131.

[70] Athanasius, *Apol. c. Arian.* 60, 2–62, 7. For the later accounts see Socrates, *HE* I, 27; Sozomenus, *HE* II, 22, 6–9; Theodoret, *HE* I, 26, 4–27.

[71] The narrative is given in great detail in Athanasius, o.c., 63–70. In 65, 1, Dalmatius is described as τῷ κήνσωρι, a title otherwise unknown at this period. He was however consul in 333, *PLRE* Dalmatius 6. Constantine's letter to John Archaph in 70, 2.

Athanasius' narrative of his troubles passes over an abortive episode in 334, which the Index to the *Festal Letters* describes as follows: 'In (this year) he was summoned to a synod, his enemies having previously devised mischief against him in Caesarea of Palestine; but becoming aware of the conspiracy he excused himself from attending.'[72] The entry fails to allude to the fact that the holding of the synod had been ordered by Constantine, influenced, according to Sozomenus and Theodoret, by Eusebius and his followers.[73] But both the fact that it was called by the emperor's order, and the pragmatic acceptance of this by the church (less than a decade after Chrysopolis), are illustrated by documentary evidence in the form of a papyrus containing a letter written by an Egyptian presbyter on 19 March 334:[74]

> Whereas sacred imperial letters have been sent by the most pious emperor Constantine ordering certain persons from Egypt, both bishops and priests and many others and myself among them . . . to proceed to Caesarea in Palestinian Syria to come to a decision concerning the purgation of the holy Christian body . . .

The decisive steps in this period of the struggle between Athanasius and his opponents were postponed by his non-appearance at Caesarea until 335, when Constantine summoned a synod at Tyre. Once again the events are clearly summarized in the Index of the *Festal Letters*, this time with the addition of valuable evidence on the chronology.[75] Athanasius left for the 'synod of his enemies' on 11 July 335, but when he realized that a plot was being made against him, fled to Constantinople in an open boat, arriving there on 30 October. After eight days he appeared before Constantine and 'spoke plainly'. But his enemies brought influence to bear on the emperor, who suddenly condemned him to exile; he set out for Trier probably on 5 February 336. These events are also described in great detail by Athanasius himself, and by the letter of a synod of Egyptian bishops in 338/9, which he quotes, as well as by the later church historians.[76] By contrast, Eusebius' deliberately bland account refers only in passing to differences in the Egyptian church, describes how Constantine ordered the convocation of the synod and quotes his letter enjoining them to end dissension; from these he continues directly to the second imperial order which instructed them to proceed to Jerusalem to celebrate the dedication of the Church of the Holy Sepulchre, and to their lavish entertainment there by the imperial *notarius* Marianus.[77] The realities of the situation are hinted at only in Constantine's

[72] Trans. Robertson, p. 503.

[73] Sozomenus, *HE* II, 25, 1; Theodoret, *HE* I, 28, 2–3.

[74] *P. Lond.* 1913, published and trans. by Bell, o.c., 45f. The language of command is clear: ll. 3–4: γραμμάτων ἀναπεμ/φ[θέν]των ὑπὸ τοῦ εὐσεβεστάτου βασιλέως Κωνσταντίνου κελευ[ό]ντων.

[75] See Robertson, p. 503.

[76] Athanasius' account, *Apol. c. Arian.* 71–87; letter of synod, ibid., 3–19; cf. also Epiphanius, *Panarion* 68, 8–9; Rufinus, *HE* X, 17–18; Socrates, *HE* I, 28–35 (the clearest of the later accounts); Sozomenus, *HE* II, 25–8; Theodoret, *HE* I, 29–31.

[77] Eusebius, *VC* IV, 41–6; Constantine's letter is quoted in 42 (also Theodoret, *HE* I, 29); on Marianus, cf. p. 108.

reference to his despatch of a *consularis* (elsewhere called a *comes*), Dionysius, to maintain order, and his threat to exile anyone who disobeyed his commands. The synod thus met, as had that at Antioch a few years earlier, not in the presence of the emperor but under the supervision of his emissaries.[78] These still novel circumstances could not fail to have their impact on the church, as the letter of the Egyptian synod makes clear:[79]

> How do they dare to call it a synod, over which a *comes* presided and a *speculator* was present and a *commentariensis* led us in instead of deacons of the church?

The charges laid were the same, the breaking of the chalice and the murder of Arsenius (whom Athanasius again produced in person and alive). From the immensely complex proceedings, accompanied by a commission of enquiry in Egypt, we need retain only two details. First, the Catholics claimed that the building where the cup had been broken was not a church, and the local Meletian priest not a presbyter. So the Meletians in the meantime improved their position by calling him a bishop and petitioning Constantine to have a church built for him. The petition was successful, and in consequence we find the *rationalis* of Egypt writing in familiar style to a lower official in Mareotis: 'Ischyras the presbyter having petitioned the piety of our lords the Augusti and Caesares to have a church built in the village of Eirene Sekontarourou, their divinity has ordered that this should be done without delay'.[80] The exchange thus provides a clear parallel to the initiative by which a few years earlier the Catholics of Cirta had had a church built for them at imperial expense.[81]

Secondly, in the course of the proceedings the Catholic bishops of Egypt wrote formally to the *comes* to request that the hearing of the charges against them be reserved for the emperor,[82] thus revealing that reliance on the personal examination of disputes by the *basileus* which was so fundamental a characteristic of the period. It was when this was refused that Athanasius 'withdrew', and made his way to Constantinople. Alone of all the innumerable petitions which had been presented to emperors over the preceding centuries, Athanasius' approach and its reception is attested in a detailed description by its addressee, Constantine, in the letter which he then wrote calling the synod of Tyre to Constantinople:[83]

> When I was entering our eponymous and ever-blessed city of Constantinople (happening then to be riding on horseback), suddenly the bishop Athanasius, with several others whom he had with him, approached so unexpectedly in the middle of the road as to give rise to alarm. The all-seeing God is my witness that on first seeing him I would not have recognised who he was, had not some

---

[78] On the imperial emissaries sent to both occasions see p. 118; for a brief mention of the synod at Antioch, p. 600.

[79] Athanasius, *Apol. c. Arian.* 8, 3.

[80] *Apol.* 85, 7.

[81] p. 590.

[82] *Apol.* 79, 2: τηρῆσαι τὴν ἀκρόασιν τῶν καθ' ἡμᾶς πραγμάτων αὐτῷ τῷ εὐσεβεστάτῳ βασιλεῖ.

[83] *Apol.* 86. Cf. p. 43.

of our people enquired, as was natural, who he was and what wrong he had suffered, and informed me. For my part I did not speak to him at that moment nor grant him an interview. But when he demanded to be heard, and I refused and came near to ordering him to be driven off, he with greater boldness insisted that he demanded nothing for himself other than your coming here, so that he might in your presence be able to complain appropriately of what he had suffered. As this seemed reasonable to me and suitable to the times, I have gladly ordered this to be written to you, so that all of you who are taking part in the synod of Tyre may without fail hasten to the camp of my clemency in order to demonstrate by the facts the purity and reliability of your judgment, before myself whom you would not deny to be a true servant of God.

In the event only a few bishops from each side travelled to Constantinople, and no proper synod took place there. Moreover, the Arian party passed over the charges of which so much had been made in the previous years, and produced a different one, that Athanasius had threatened to hold back the corn which was sent from Alexandria to Constantinople; the emperor was immediately enraged, and exiled Athanasius to Trier. The personal quality of the exchange and the nature of the emperor's reaction appear all the more clearly in the letter written only some three years later by the bishops of Egypt. When the accusation about the corn was made, they report:[84]

Some of us were within with Athanasius, and heard the king's threats. Then when Athanasius lamented at the slander and affirmed that it was untrue (for how could he, a private person and of poor means, do such a thing?), Eusebius did not hesitate to repeat the charge publicly, and swore that Athanasius was rich and powerful and capable of anything, so that from this it might be credible that Athanasius had said such a thing. This was the accusation which the worthy bishops made. But the grace of God was stronger than their wickedness, turned the piety of the king to *philanthrôpia*, and afforded exile rather than death.

With that we may leave the details of the contacts of the church and Constantine. For even though we have considered only a few of the salient points from only one of the main sequences of such exchanges, enough has been said to reveal certain significant features. The impact of Constantine on the church begun in both west and east with restitution, largesse and privileges. It continued in both with initiatives being taken by parties in the church to invoke his personal decision in ecclesiastical disputes. Thus the long-debated question of how the church came to accept the 'intervention' of Constantine in its affairs is misconceived. For it was as a result of such initiatives that he came to summon synods and then to control their conduct through his emissaries. But all these synods, even Nicaea, formally at least arrived at their own decisions, just as earlier synods had done. At Nicaea alone the emperor personally participated in the debates on at least one of the topics; and at Nicaea alone the subject was the definition of metaphysical beliefs, rather than disputes over internal order. Moreover, with the personal imposition of criminal penalties by the emperor on

[84] *Apol.* 87, 9 (letter of bishops).

dissenters, the accusations which were pressed upon him steadily developed from ones of strictly ecclesiastical content to criminal and political charges.

Whether all the letters attributed by various sources to Constantine are authentic, and how much of the wording of those which were issued by him was truly his own are questions which do not admit of absolute answers. But we hardly need such answers, for abundant contemporary evidence shows that Christians of the time, like pagans of the preceding centuries, hoped for, demanded and quite frequently obtained hearings before the emperor in person, and his personal verdicts on their disputes. That they could and did do so was partly, as we have seen, a result of the underlying conception of the emperor as the source of justice and benefits, on the basis of which their predecessors had on occasion petitioned even pagan emperors. Moreover, it is highly relevant to the approaches made by Christians that the subject-matter of petitions and requests made by pagans had embraced almost all aspects of the social, cultural, intellectual and religious life of the Graeco-Roman, and especially the Greek, world, and could be presented on behalf of philosophical schools or temple-communities, as well as of cities or of provincial councils.

Such petitions, moreover, presumed something more on the part of the emperor than a mere duty to deal justly or make equitable decisions between conflicting parties; they rested on a presumption of the commitment of the emperor himself to the values of Graeco-Roman society. So the ambassadors of an ancient Greek city could appeal to its past fame, or the villagers of Dmeir invoke the piety of the emperor to protect the rights of their temple. In the same way the Apologists of the second century could hope (though in vain) to touch the philosophical interests of the emperors, and the cities of Asia Minor and Syria under Maximin demand and obtain from the emperor a commitment to the preservation of their cults uncontaminated by the presence of Christians.

With the conversion of Constantine new presumptions could be made, though not to the exclusion of others relating to the creation of cities or even the maintenance of a local pagan festival.[85] The full consequences and significance of those new presumptions cannot be discussed here; all that need be claimed is that the form of the emperor's exchanges with the church, and the presumptions which underlay them, cannot be understood without close reference to the long-established patterns of his contacts with other bodies and with individuals seeking justice or benefits. More specifically, it may be emphasized both that Constantine's conversion did produce a personal commitment of entirely novel content, and (on the other hand) that this commitment could not fail to express itself in forms which were essentially traditional.[86] Both facts are visible in Eusebius' account of how Constantine assented to his request to be allowed to deliver a speech on the Holy Sepulchre before him in the palace, and moreover insisted on remaining

---

[85] pp. 410, 453.

[86] It may be permitted to note in passing that the nuns whom Helena, the mother of Constantine, established, with a regular imperial income, in Jerusalem, were called Ἑστιάδες—Vestal Virgins, Suda E 3213 (ed. Adler, II, 429).

standing while hearing it to the end.[87] For what could have been more natural, or more typical of Graeco-Roman culture, than to mark the emperor's profound interest in the site by the delivery of a learned disquisition before him? Eusebius later returned to the topic in an elaborate account of the new church, which he delivered in Jerusalem in 335, and afterwards presented to the emperor. Celebrations of the completion of particularly grand or lavishly adorned buildings were an established branch of ancient rhetoric.[88]

Eusebius, however, was able to make the presentation because he was one of the group of bishops who, with Eusebius of Nicomedia, travelled to Constantinople in 335, and finally produced the accusation which sent Athanasius into exile.[89] That was one aspect of the role of the emperor as *basileus*, as a monarch who could decide any question by his personal pronouncement, and who would surely give a favourable verdict if only one found the right arguments to put before him. As such it was no less significant than the more elevated view of the same function which Eusebius offered on the same occasion, when he celebrated the thirtieth anniversary of Constantine's reign by delivering an oration before him in the palace in Constantinople.[90] Moreover, he could do in the course of it what no pagan panegyrist could have done in the same terms,[91] and represent the *basileia* of Constantine as the earthly reflection of the monarchy of God, as mediated by the Word: 'who, pervading all things, presenting himself everywhere, and abundantly distributing to all the favours of the Father, has vouchsafed. even to the rational beings on earth the image of the royal power.'[92]

[87] *VC* IV, 33.

[88] For Eusebius' discourse see *VC* IV, 45–6. It does not survive, but some idea of its nature can be gained from *VC* III, 25–40, or (by analogy) from the discourse on the basilica at Tyre in *HE* x, 4. I cannot see any conclusive reason for identifying ch. 11f. of the Tricennalian Oration as part of the speech. For an example of a speech celebrating the dedication of a temple see e.g. Aristides, *Or.* XXVII (panegyric on the Temple at Cyzicus), or that of Polemo following the completion of the temple of Olympian Zeus at Athens by Hadrian, Philostratus, *VS* I, 25.

[89] That 'the other Eusebius' was a member of the group is recorded by Athanasius, *Apol. c. Arian.* 87, 1.

[90] Eusebius, *VC* IV, 46. For the text see *GCS Eusebius* I, 193f. See also K. M. Setton, *The Christian Attitude towards the Emperor in the Fourth Century especially as shown in Addresses to the Emperor* (1941), and for a detailed collection and analysis of the evidence from Eusebius, R. Farina, *L'impero e l'imperatore cristiano in Eusebio di Cesarea: la prima teologia politica del cristianesimo* (1966). The oration was probably not delivered until some time in 336, see H. A. Drake, 'When was the 'De Laudibus Constantini' delivered?', *Historia* XXIV (1975), 345. I am grateful to Professor Drake for allowing me to see this in advance of publication.

[91] Pagan writers do, however, on occasion and in much less detail, portray the emperor as the earthly representative of Zeus/Jupiter, see E. Peterson, *Der Monotheismos als politisches Problem* (1935), 31.

[92] *Or. Tric.* III, 8.

PART FOUR

Epilogue

X

From Pompey to Constantine

'*Imperator*, Saviour, Benefactor, Founder of the City'—such are the terms
in which various dedications from Mytilene describe Pompey the Great.[1]
In themselves these expressions did no more than reflect the long-established
custom of applying to Roman commanders the honorific and semi-divine
appellations of Hellenistic kings.[2] On a notorious occasion a century earlier
one of the kings, Prusias II of Bithynia, had gone further and addressed the
senate collectively as 'Saviour Gods'.[3] But the dedications to Pompey will
mark a moment of particular significance, his visit to the city after the news
of Mithridates' death in 63 BC had signalled the end of the last serious military challenge to Rome in the Greek world. At this moment also Roman
rule had just been established in Syria for the first time. In consequence,
while vast conquests remained to be made in Europe before the empire
acquired its ultimate extent, it was already clear that the surviving Greek
kingdoms and independent territories possessed only a precarious freedom.
The stage was thus finally set for those innumerable and indefinable cultural,
historical, social and diplomatic influences from the Greek world which
were to contribute so much over the following centuries to the detachment
of the emperor from the collective institutions and traditions of the city of
Rome.

The recognition of the supremacy of Greek culture was of course perfectly conscious, and embodied in deliberate public acts. The fact is rarely
expressed more clearly than in Plutarch's description of Pompey's return
journey after hearing in Arabia of Mithridates' death:[4]

> After arranging and settling affairs in those parts, Pompey proceeded on his
> journey, and now with greater pomp and ceremony. For instance, when he
> came to Mitylene, he gave the city its freedom, for the sake of Theophanes,
> and witnessed the traditional contest of the poets there, who now took as their
> sole theme his own exploits. And being pleased with the theatre, he had sketches
> and plans of it made for him, that he might build one in Rome, only larger and

[1] *Syll.*³ 752–3; Ἀρχ. Δελτ. XXII.2 (1967), 461 = *BCH* XCIV (1970), 1090: Γναίῳ Πομπήῳ
μεγ[ά]λ[ῳ] αὐτοκράτορι σωτῆρι καὶ εὐεργέτᾳ καὶ κτίστᾳ τᾶς πόλεος.

[2] See A. D. Nock, '*Soter* and *Euergetes*', *Essays on Religion and the Ancient World*, ed. Z. Stewart
II (1972), 720, showing that while *soter* could be applied to a god, its application to a man did not
of itself imply that he was regarded as divine. For the application of *soter* and *euergetes* to Hellenistic
kings see Chr. Habicht, *Gottmenschentum und griechische Städte*² (1970), 156–7, who however
regards the appellation *sotêr* as invariably implying a cult.

[3] Polybius XXX, 18, 5; Diodorus XXXI, 15, 3: 'Χαίρετε θεοὶ σωτῆρες'.

[4] Plutarch, *Pomp.* 42, Loeb trans.

more splendid. And when he was in Rhodes he heard all the sophists there and made each of them a present of a talent. Poseidonius has actually described the discourse which he held before him on Investigation in General. At Athens too he not only treated the philosophers with like munificence, but also gave fifty talents to the city towards its restoration.

Pompey's grant of freedom to Mitylene, 'for the sake of Theophanes', his friend and the historian of his campaigns, was only one of a long series of benefits and concessions gained for themselves and their native cities by the leading intellectuals of the Greek world. Similarly the learned discourse by the great Poseidonius was to have innumerable counterparts on various topics over the following centuries, up to those on the Holy Sepulchre and on his *Tricennalia* which Eusebius was to deliver before Constantine.

Pompey's role as the decisive conqueror of the east had, however, exposed him to influences and contacts which seemed at the time to be more significant. It was not for nothing that Cicero would refer to him ironically as 'our Sampsiceramus' (the characteristic name of the dynasts of Emesa),[5] or Favonius say of a white bandage which he happened to have round his leg, that it did not matter on what part of the body his diadem was placed.[6] For contemporaries could not fail to suspect regal ambitions on the part of a man who had allotted and removed kingdoms, founded cities named after himself, and laid down the rights and laws of others;[7] and before whom kings had solemnly laid down the diadem which was the established symbol of royalty, to receive it back at his hands.[8]

In the same way, after Octavian's victory at Actium, Herod appeared before him at Rhodes without his diadem, made a speech in his own defence, and received it back from his hands.[9] Thereafter at least until the early third century, the granting of diadems to dependent kings was to be a recognized imperial function.[10] The fact that the diadem continued to have this quite specific use lends a greater significance to its eventual adoption by the emperors themselves, perhaps by Aurelian or Licinius, but definitively on the coinage of Constantine after the victory of 324.[11] When he lay in state in 337, his body was dressed in 'the royal ornaments, the purple robe and the diadem'.[12]

---

[5] *Ad Att.* II, 14, 1; cf. 16, 2; 17, 1–2; 23, 2–3. On the dynasts of Emesa see *IGLS* v 2212, and commentary.

[6] Valerius Maximus VI, 2, 7.

[7] See in general M. Gelzer in *RE* s.v. 'Pompeius' (31), XXI.2, 2107–18.

[8] For Tigranes of Armenia laying down his diadem before Pompey see Cicero, *Pro Sestio* 27/58; Valerius Maximus v, 1, 9; Plutarch, *Pomp.* 33, 4–5; Dio XXXVI, 52, 2–4. For Pompey granting the diadem of Ariobarzanes of Cappadocia to his son see Valerius Maximus v, 7 *ext.* 2. For the background see H.-W. Ritter, *Diadem und Königsherrschaft* (1965).

[9] Josephus, *BJ* I, 20, 1–3 (387–93); *Ant.* xv, 6, 6–7 (187–96).

[10] For the evidence see Ritter, o.c., 165–9.

[11] *Epit. de Caes.* 35, 5, and Malalas, *Chron.* p. 299, 20C, allege that Aurelian wore the diadem. P. Váczy, 'Helm und Diadem (Numismatische Beiträge zur Enstehung der byzantinischen Kaiserkrone)', *Acta Ant. Ac. Sc. Hung.* XX (1972), 169, defends the authenticity of a cameo showing Licinius with the diadem. For Constantine's coinage of 324 with it, A. Alföldi, *Die monarchische Repräsentation im römischen Kaiserreiche* (1970), 267; P. Bruun, *RIC* VII: *Constantine and Licinius AD 313–337* (1966), 53.

[12] Eusebius, *VC* IV, 66.

From the second century BC onwards the symbolic meaning of the diadem will have been emphasized within Roman society by the recurrent presence of allied kings or members of their families, contact with whom must have exercised some real, though entirely undefinable, influence on the outlook of senators, and on their views of each other's potential ambitions. Thus his enemies alleged of Tiberius Gracchus in 133 BC not only that he hoped to be crowned with a diadem but that the messenger who brought the news of the death of Attalus of Pergamum had actually presented him with a diadem and purple robe.[13] Later it was reported that Gaius, while entertaining a number of client kings at dinner, overheard them disputing over the nobility of their various lines, quoted the line of Homer 'Let there be one lord, one king'—and came near to assuming the diadem and converting his rule into a kingship.[14] Moreover, if we may believe Dio, people attributed the increasing ferocity of Gaius' rule to the influence of his 'teachers in tyranny', the kings Agrippa I of Judaea and Antiochus of Commagene.[15]

In a formal and concrete sense such fears and expectations never were fulfilled in our period. The traumatic scene of the offer of a diadem to Julius Caesar at the Lupercalia of 44 BC was never repeated in Rome; nor was it ever proposed in the senate that (as Cicero records of rumours in 44) 'the king whom in fact we had should also be given the title of king'.[16] No emperor ever used the title *rex*, or (we may confidently assume) seriously considered doing so. None the less it is a highly significant slip when Solinus, an unoriginal compiler from the imperial period, in retailing the famous story of how Scipio Africanus was hailed as king by the army in Spain in 209 BC, says instead that he was hailed as 'Caesar'.[17] For this is an example of the conceptions and presuppositions in terms of which people thought of the emperor as a monarch, and in effect a king.

The terminology which was used for the Roman emperors in the Greek east, and in particular the use of *basileus*, 'king', has never been studied in full detail, and cannot be so studied here.[18] But it may be noted that as early as the reign of Augustus a Greek poet could refer to him in an epigram as a *basileus*;[19] and that from the second century onwards, as we have seen from numerous examples, *basileus*, *basileia* and cognate terms were frequently used both in public documents and in literary works, including those

[13] Plutarch, *Tib. Gracch.* 14, 3. See S. Weinstock, *Divus Julius* (1971), 335.

[14] Suetonius, *Cal.* 22, 1.

[15] Dio LIX, 24, 1.

[16] *De Div.* II, 54/110: 'Quorum interpres nuper falsa quadam hominum fama dicturus in senatu putabatur eum, quem re vera regem habebamus, appellandum quoque esse regem.' See Weinstock, o.c., 331–41.

[17] Solinus, *Collectanea rerum memorabilium* I, 68: 'primus Romanorum Caesar dictus est.' For the episode itself Polybius X, 38, 3; 40, 2–9; Livy XXVII, 19, 3–6. Cf. A. Aymard, 'Polybe, Scipion l'Africain et le titre de "roi"', *Études d'histoire ancienne* (1967), 387.

[18] For some sketches of the use of *basileus* for the emperor see A. Wifstrand, 'Autokrator, Kaisar, Basileus', ΔΡΑΓΜΑ *M. P. Nilsson . . . dedicatum* (1939), 529; L. Wickert in *RE* s.v. 'Princeps', XXII. 2 (1954), 2108–18; cf. J. Modrzejewski, *RIDA* VIII (1961), 112; H. J. Mason, *Greek Terms for Roman Institutions: a Lexicon and Analysis* (1974), 117–21.

[19] *Anth. Pal.* X, 25, 5–6 (Antipater of Thessalonica): καὶ τὸν ἐμὸν βασιλῆα τὸν ἄλκιμον εὖ μὲν ἐκείνῳ / ἵλαον, εὖ δ' ὕμνοις ἄρτισον ἡμετέροις. The reference is to L. Calpurnius Piso (*PIR*² C 289), and the occasion will be his proconsulate of Asia in perhaps 9/8 BC, see R. Syme in *Akten VI. Int. Kong. Gr. u. Lat. Epig. 1972* (1973), 597.

addressed to him, to refer to the emperor and his rule. What is more, in the third century, in imperial letters to Greek cities, which we have every reason to believe were prepared in Greek at the court, emperors sometimes refer to their rule as *basileia*. Writing to Aphrodisias, Gordian speaks of what is appropriate 'in my *basileia*', as do Decius and Herennius of 'the establishment of our *basileia*'.[20]

Educated Greeks were of course perfectly aware that the emperors did not have the title of king. But Appian at least, writing in the middle of the second century, had no doubt of the realities: 'And the government has remained in the hands of one ruler up till now. They do not speak of them as kings, out of respect, I believe, for the ancient oath, but call them *Imperatores*, which used to be the title of those who held commands for limited periods. But they are in fact in every respect kings.'[21]

Appian does indeed frequently use *basileus* when referring to the Roman emperors, just as he naturally does in speaking of 'my kings', the Ptolemies.[22] More important, however, is the fact that we cannot regard Appian's view of what a Roman emperor really was as a mere personal attitude, or as the application to the present of an irrelevant historical concept. For, as we saw earlier, he represents in himself a perfect example of the class of men through whom the emperor's incessant exchanges with the cities of the Greek east were mediated: one of the leading men of Alexandria, he acted as advocate in cases 'before the kings', and was honoured with a procuratorship by them.[23]

But even in the Greek east, where a rich historical and literary tradition enabled men to be aware in detail of a past in which kings had been prominent, we cannot deduce with any precision from the mere use of words what they conceived a *basileus* to be. For one thing the Hellenistic monarchies themselves had been institutions of no simple or uniform character, but had embraced forms and traditions of many different origins, Macedonian, Persian, Iranian, Egyptian or Jewish. For another, from the late third century onwards they had begun to come under the influence of Rome, and to be affected by Roman customs, and the forms in which Roman magistrates and governors conducted their affairs. Our sources preserve only the extreme or scandalous instances, Antiochus Epiphanes putting on a toga and canvassing as if for senatorial office, and taking his seat on a tribunal in the market-place 'in the Roman fashion' to settle disputes;[24] or Prusias of Bithynia greeting a senatorial delegation in the dress of a Roman freedman.[25] None the less, it is an undeniable fact that with the extension of Roman rule through the Greek east Roman office-holders took over, or had imposed on them, some of the functions and forms of contact or exchange with cities or

---

[20] p. 417.

[21] *Hist.*, *praef.* 6/23. The same point is made in Dio LIII, ,17 2, and cf. Justin, *Epit. Pomp. Trog.* XLI, 5, 8.

[22] *Basileus* as applied by Appian to the emperors, see e.g. *Hist.*, *praef.* 7/26; *BC* I, 106/500; II, 86/362 (Hadrian); 'my kings', *Hist.*, *praef.* 10/39.

[23] p. 276.

[24] Polybius XXVI, 1, 5–6.

[25] Diodorus XXXI, 15, 2; Appian, *Mith.* 2/4–5.

individuals which characterized the kings. We have seen already a variety of instances of such transferences of roles, and the way in which these were transmitted in time to the emperors.[26] We cannot expect to be able to trace more than a small proportion of such developments in detail; but a careful study area by area would inevitably reveal more. For the moment we may recall that such mutual influences could take root in the popular imagination, and that when the leader of a slave revolt in Sicily set himself up as a *basileus* he in fact adopted many of the attributes of a Roman office-holder.[27]

From the Latin west we have no such developed literary, diplomatic or documentary tradition. We can trace no indigenous conceptions of government in general or of monarchy in particular which influenced attitudes to the emperor or affected the form of approaches to him.[28] At the level with which we are concerned, the culture and concepts of the Latin west, from Africa to central Europe, were derived from those of Rome (in so far as they did not depend directly on influences from the Greek world). So for instance the Gallic Panegyrics of the late third and early fourth century, one of them the work of the grandson of an orator who had immigrated from Athens, present us not with specifically Gallic concepts, but with highly literary derivatives of the Roman rhetorical tradition.[29] Thus, though the Panegyrics express as clearly as any other surviving statements the absolute nature of the imperial power, they never address or describe an emperor as *rex*, and nor indeed does any document or formal address of the entire period. Only the orator of 289 approaches this term, in speaking of the joint rule of Diocletian and Maximian:[30]

> You rule (*regitis*) the state with a single mind, and so great a distance in space does not prevent you from steering it as it were with linked hands. So by your double spirit you increase the royal majesty (*regia maiestas*), but by your harmony retain the effectiveness of a single rule.

Where literary sources employ *rex* or its cognates in relation to emperors past or present the intention is almost always abusive, joking or metaphorical.[31] Seneca's *De clementia* is alone in systematically using *rex* in a favourable sense, for the 'good king' held up as an ideal for Nero.[32] For the rest, the literary tradition of the expulsion of the kings, reinforced by the catastrophe of Julius Caesar, exercised an enduring influence.

[26] e.g. the offer of gold crowns (στέφανοι), pp. 140–2; the receipt of embassies and despatch of letters in return, p. 213.

[27] For a view of the mutual influences exerted by kings and republican senators, see now E. Rawson, 'Caesar's Heritage: Hellenistic Kings and their Roman Equals', *JRS* LXV (1975), 148.

[28] An exception must be made for the *devotio* to a leader known from Spain (an oath on the part of individuals or groups not to survive the leader), attested both in relation to Sertorius (Plutarch, *Sert.* 14, 5) and, on the part of an individual senator, to Augustus, Dio LIII, 20, 2–4 (whence, Dio says, the customary greeting to an emperor, σοι καθωσιώμεθα). See R. Étienne, *Le culte impériale dans le péninsule ibérique* (1958), 75f.; 359f.

[29] See the essay by F. Burdeau, 'L'Empereur dans les Panégyriques latins', *Aspects de l'Empire romain* (1964), 1.

[30] *Pan.* II(10), 11, 1–2.

[31] See the survey by Wickert, o.c. (n. 18 above).

[32] *De Clem.* I, 3, 3: 'regem aut principem decet'; cf. 3, 4; 4, 3; 5, 4: 'regia (domus)'; 5, 6; 7, 1: 7, 3: 'regnum'. For the Hellenistic background of the work see now T. Adam, *Clementia Principis* (1970).

The varying forms of description used (or avoided) in relation to the emperor naturally have to be recalled, and their varying historical associations taken into account, in any attempt to assess what a Roman emperor was. But any definition of the imperial power which was based essentially on deductions from the terminology used to describe emperors could have only a limited relevance to the real problem; for, even without attempting any more subtle distinctions, we can see that, at least from the second century onwards, the population of one part of the empire generally referred to the emperor by a word which can be translated 'king', and that of the other did not.

Throughout our period the official titles of the emperor remained those drawn from the vocabulary of republican office-holding. If we disregard the customary imperial names, 'Imperator', 'Caesar', 'Augustus', honorific appellations like 'Pater Patriae' or references to the consulates which emperors from time to time held, we are left with two elements which were both permanent and referred to an actual power or function, Pontifex Maximus and *tribunicia potestas*, and another used on occasion, proconsul, which did likewise. As we have seen, it is possible to discern certain specific and limited functions which the emperor performed as Pontifex Maximus.[33] A 'tribunician' role or function *may* also have had some genuine connection with his exercise of jurisdiction, at least that in response to appeals.[34] It is furthermore indisputable that the form of his public appearances and the style in which he exercised his role in public owed much to that of consuls or proconsuls; like them he was attended everywhere by lictors and other *apparitores*, and would give his decisions from a raised tribunal.

But once again no attempt to define what an emperor was in terms of the 'powers' of republican origin with which he was invested could possibly succeed. For, first, it was shown long since how fragile would be any deduction from the republican meanings of these terms to their supposed connotation in relation to the emperor.[35] But, more important, while our evidence from the early empire records a few isolated cases where the precise source of an emperor's power to take a particular step is indicated,[36] the entire period does not present a single instance where the emperor's right or power to take any particular action was specifically tested or challenged. The counterpart of this was that although emperors can be found quite frequently referring matters to the senate, making requests of it, or having legislation enacted in the form of *senatus consulta*,[37] it is never implied that their actions or pronouncements would lack validity unless confirmed by the senate, or *a fortiori* by any other organ of the *res publica*.

[33] pp. 359–61.

[34] p. 509.

[35] See the masterly work of J. Béranger, *Recherches sur l'aspect idéologique du Principat* (1953), ch. ii.

[36] e.g. *RG* 8, 3–4: censuses carried out by Augustus 'consulari cum imperio'; Tacitus, *Ann.* 1, 7, 3, and Suetonius, *Tib.* 23: Tiberius summoning the senate in 14 by virtue of his *tribunicia potestas* (and cf. *Ann.* 1, 13, 4, his non-use of the tribunician veto); note also 11, 3: Tiberius using the *trib. pot.*, anomalously, on Rhodes; for the censorships taken by emperors up to Domitian, see pp. 293–5. For their jurisdiction as consul and otherwise, pp. 530–1.

[37] pp. 341–55.

It is indeed precisely this characteristic which distinguishes the emperors from even the most prominent commanders of the late republic, or indeed from the triumvirs themselves.[38] To the cities, peoples and kings of the Greek east, for instance, Pompey played a role which more than resembled that of a king, and he was honoured accordingly. But, as is notorious, it was precisely 'the promises he had made to cities or the rewards for service',[39] or alternatively 'the many awards which he had made to kings, dynasts or cities',[40] for which his enemies were able to withhold confirmation by the senate until the consulate of Caesar in 59.

When Pompey founded cities called 'Pompeiopolis', or others like Magnopolis or Megalopolis, whose names reflected his appellation 'the Great'—a conscious echo of Alexander (just as the cloak which he wore at his triumph was rumoured to be the actual cloak of Alexander)[41]—this was, as we saw earlier, a portent of an established imperial role. But the imperial foundations, from Nicopolis, established to commemorate the victory of Actium, to Constantinople itself, are characterized by the crucial difference that our sources nowhere suggest that their legal existence depended, even retrospectively, on validation by any organs of the *res publica*.

The imperial regime simply cannot be adequately characterized in constitutional terms, for while the institutions of the *res publica* persisted, and while the emperor performed his functions partly within them (speaking, and originally even voting, in the senate, or having his nominees to office formally elected by the *comitia*), he also assumed from the beginning a direct relationship to cities, institutions and individuals in which his pronouncements and decisions were treated as being of automatic legal validity. As we saw, as early as the year after Actium Octavian is found formally proclaiming his readiness to confer benefits on a Syrian city.[42] The role was thus conscious and explicit, as it was to remain throughout the empire. But the essential fact is that the adoption of such a role could only have been of limited application and of relative insignificance if it had not answered to a conception of a ruler's function which was both widely held and widely acted upon by his subjects. It is perhaps not necessary to emphasize once again how the whole nature of the imperial entourage, with its remarkably limited resources and increasingly peregrinatory character, was shaped by the pressure to respond to initiatives from below, ranging from requests or consultations by senators, to formal embassies from cities or associations, and to *libelli* from individuals or groups of low status seeking protection, justice or rulings on points of law.

It need not be claimed, and is not claimed, that there are not many other elements which would need to be taken into account in any complete analysis even of the functions of an emperor, let alone of the entire cultural,

---

[38] See 'Triumvirate and Principate', *JRS* LXIII (1973), 50, esp. 53.

[39] Velleius II, 40, 5; cf. 44, 2.

[40] Appian, *BC* II, 9/31; cf. Dio XXXVII, 49; XXXVIII, 7, 5.

[41] Appian, *Mith.* 117/577. See O. Weippert, *Alexander-Imitatio und römische Politik in republikanischer Zeit* (Diss. Würzburg, 1972), 84.

[42] p. 7.

social and political system within which he lived. To mention only the most obvious, there is his role as a commander and in relation to the army, and his complex diplomatic relations with foreign powers and dependent kings. But it may be firmly claimed that we cannot begin to assess what an emperor was without taking into account the sheer volume of approaches to him, verbally and in writing, made by his subjects. Within the context of such approaches it is impossible to over-emphasize the primary role of verbal addresses, and the extent to which his subjects' judgment of him depended on the quality, in both style and content, of his verbal replies. The role and functions of an emperor present us, if examined closely, with the most complete exemplification of the predominance of rhetoric in the culture of the Graeco-Roman world.

Nor can it be emphasized too strongly that the emperor could have no exchanges with his subjects, as groups or individuals, except with those who already were where he was, travelled to there or (in the case of certain limited and privileged categories) sent employees to bring letters to him. The distance in space and time which inevitably separated the emperor from the overwhelming majority of his subjects is one of the fundamental categories within which the nature of 'government' in the Roman empire has to be assessed. It goes without saying that the necessity of travel to where the emperor was must have imposed crucial limitations on the ability of most of his subjects to make use of the possibility of presenting petitions to him. The delays involved also imposed similar limitations on the practical effectiveness of his replies. None the less, it remains far more significant that the possibility was open, and that many people did in fact travel from their own provinces to be judged by the emperor in person, or to await the posting-up of his replies to their petitions. It was precisely in the form of such judgments and replies, along with their answers to letters from office-holders, that the emperors of the mid-second century onwards made their fundamental contribution to the shaping of the body of Roman law as it has come down to us.

The limitations imposed by distance, and the difficulties and delays of travel, had even less effect—indeed seem hardly to have been taken into serious account—in the relations between cities and other formal bodies and the emperor. As we saw, the ritual of the passing of a decree, despatch of ambassadors, and presentation of the decree with an accompanying oration, was perhaps the most fundamental contribution of Hellenistic diplomacy to the shaping of the imperial rule, and survived effectively unchanged through and beyond our period. As such, it was the most specific and concrete of all the innumerable forms in which the values and expectations of the Greek east imposed themselves on the imperial court. Like the petitions of individuals, the endless traffic of embassies presupposed both that any one of innumerable local issues could be taken to the emperor and expounded to him, and that a response from him in person could be expected.

Against this background it was only to be expected that the establishment of the church as a social institution, with property, rules, and grades of membership, would lead to requests or disputes about its affairs being placed before emperors. So too the conversion of Constantine opened the way to a long series of rival approaches to him which demonstrated perhaps even more clearly than anything attested over the previous centuries the tenacity of men's claims to the emperor's personal judgment. Over more than two decades the affairs first of the Carthaginian and then of the Alexandrian church were brought before him by a succession of interested parties, without his visiting Africa or Egypt.

The exchanges between the church and Constantine may thus be regarded as one of the clearest expressions of a unique political system, to which there had accrued conceptions, associations and specific functions from various different sources: from the Hellenistic kingdoms, either directly or through the roles and functions assumed by, or imposed on, Roman governors and commanders in the east; the peregrinatory jurisdiction which was the basic function of a provincial governor; and the functions, powers and appurtenances of the magistracies of the city of Rome, whose titles continued to be reflected in his own. But the nature of the Roman emperor, while it can be partially explained, cannot be defined in terms of any of these. For the emperor was a unique product of the circumstance that the civil wars brought about a return to monarchic rule at a moment not long after the definitive absorption of the Greek world into the empire.

That the emperor could fulfil his role in detachment from the institutions of the *res publica* was immediately demonstrated by Augustus, who passed some eleven of the eighteen years after Actium in the provinces. The presumption on the part of Greek cities that they could approach him directly for decisions was also immediately in evidence. Both factors, a steadily increasing absence from Rome and the continued demand for the emperor's direct replies and decisions, were to be acutely relevant over the following centuries to the steady attenuation, though not yet the disappearance, of the emperor's relations to the city of Rome and its institutions.

The complex and undefinable nature of the developed monarchy was displayed most clearly of all in the foundation of Constantinople, which was many different things at once: a Christian centre with magnificent churches and its own bishop; a Greek city re-founded and re-named after himself, following a long tradition, by a Roman *Imperator*; and a reproduction of Rome, with many of its privileges, offices, and public buildings, including places of public entertainment where the emperor could appear before his people. One of these was the hippodrome, adorned with a long series of historic monuments and works of art looted from the Greek cities. In some cases the reason could be given that, as pagan cult-objects, these works could thus be robbed of their noxious influence by exposure in a secular setting. But the procedure was at least as much an extension of that by which Roman conquerors had for more than half a millennium paid an unwelcome tribute to the supremacy of Greek art and culture, in seeking the most famous works for the adornment of Rome. The counterpart of that process, however, was their willingness to listen to the intellectuals and orators of the Greek world, and to be moved by their words; a pattern which was never displayed more vividly than in Constantine's prolonged involvement in the affairs of the Greek church. Here too his truly revolutionary step was none the less instantly given expression in long-established forms. So it was entirely appropriate that among the statues brought to adorn the hippodrome of Constantinople there should have been one from Mytilene representing Theophanes, the confidant and historian of Pompey,[43] with an inscription recording that he had 'regained the city and its territory and its ancestral freedom from the common benefactors, the Romans'.

[43] L. Robert, 'Théophane de Mytilène à Constantinople', *CRAI* 1969, 42.

APPENDIX 1

The Emperor and Public Properties

It is argued above (ch. iv) that the imperial estates were typically acquired from private persons, by gift, inheritance, legacy, confiscation or lapsing as *caduca* or *vacantia*. It is however often assumed or asserted that the imperial properties at some stage absorbed the surviving *ager publicus* of the *res publica*.[1]

The evidence on this whole question is extremely sparse. But it may help to begin by distinguishing (a) public sites and buildings in Rome (b) *ager publicus* in Italy and (c) *ager publicus* (if any) in the provinces. As regards (a) we find *equites* as *subcuratores* or *adiutores* concerned with *opera publica* in Rome (Pflaum, *Carrières*, 1028–9), and imperial freedmen as for instance *tabularius oper(um) public(orum)* (*CIL* VI 8479); *a commentariis operum publicorum et rationis patrimoni* (XI 3860); cf. X 529: *dispensatoris rat(ionis) aed(ium) sacr(arum) et oper(um) publicor(um)*; VI 8478: *dis[p]. operum publicorum*; *AE* 1972 35: *adiutori tabulariorum operum publicorum*. As always, the mere titles of employees or officials can tell us very little. We catch a glimpse of the imperial freedmen at work in relation to buildings in Rome only in the well-known inscription (*ILS* 5920) which shows an imperial freedman named Adrastus, *procurator columnae divi Marci*, applying in 193 for permission to build himself a hut beside the column at his own expense, against payment of a ground-rent (*solarium*). The inscription includes letters of the *rationales* requesting the issue to Adrastus of the materials, including ten beams at the price which they had cost the *fiscus* (*quanti fisco constiterunt*). The site (*area*) is assigned by two men who are evidently the senatorial *curatores operum publicorum*, but the beams are to be issued by Aquilius Felix. This man (Pflaum, *Carrières*, no. 225) is described in one inscription as *proc(urator) oper(um) pub-(licorum)* and on another as *proc(urator) oper(um) publi(corum) et fiscal(ium) urb(is) sacrae*. Whether the column of Marcus Aurelius had been made public or whether it was in theory fiscal property, it is evident that both imperial freedmen and senatorial officials were concerned with it. The contrast between the two inscriptions shows that it was possible, but not invariable, to distinguish between *opera publica* and *opera fiscalia* in Rome. A similar distinction is made in this period by Callistratus, *de iure fisci* (*Dig.* XLIX, 14, 3, 10–11), who however goes on to introduce a further category, *Caesaris possessiones*. Yet a different distinction appears in *ILS* 3512 (dated to 88), *redemptor operum Caesar(is)* or (*-um*) or (*-ianorum*) *et puplicorum*[*sic*].[2]

In the case of public buildings and works in Rome, as in the specific instance of the aqueducts (pp. 192–3), we have to take into account the effects of vast imperial expenditure on such buildings. The role of imperial freedmen and procurators in this field does none the less provide a possible model for how *ager publicus* might have come *de facto* under imperial management, and ultimately have been seen as

---

[1] This is suggested for instance by Jones, *Later Roman Empire*, 415, who however offers no evidence on this point. See also Brunt, *JRS* LVI (1966), 82, who however talks, hesitantly, of the emperor 'administering' *agri publici* 'in his own provinces and ultimately in senatorial', and refers to Hirschfeld, *Verwaltungsbeamten*[2], 139f.

[2] See Hirschfeld, o.c., 265f.

imperial property. On the other hand it should be emphasized that in the fourth century the public buildings of Rome were still regarded as the public property of the city, and under the control of both imperial and senatorial officials.[3]

(b) *Ager publicus* in Italy. It is clear that significant areas of such land existed at the end of the first century. The alimentary table of Veleia (*CIL* XI 1147) gives *populus* (as opposed to *Imperator noster*, nearby towns, or private persons) as neighbouring owner over 100 times, and that of the Ligures Baebiani (IX 1455) five times. In the *Corpus Agrimensorum Romanorum*, ed. Thulin, we find:

p. 8 (Frontinus): 'aut silvas, quas ad populum Romanum multis locis pertinere ex veteribus instrumentis cognoscimus, ut ex proximo in Sabinis in monte Mutela.'

pp. 42–3 (Frontinus?): land left by change of course of R. Po—'negant illu[d] solum, quod solum p. R. coepit esse, ullo modo usu capi a⟨t⟩ quoquam mortalium posse.'

p. 48 (Frontinus?): 'in Italia autem densitas possessorum multum inprobe facit, et lucos sacros occupant, quorum solum indubitate p. R. est.'

p. 100 (Siculus Flaccus): 'a[li]i ita remanserunt, ut tamen p. R. [terri]toria essent; ut est in Piceno, in regione Reatina, in quibus regionibus montes Romani appellantur. nam sunt p. R. [terri]toria, quorum vectigal ad aerarium pertinet.'

Note also p. 77: *vectigalis ager virginum Vestae* (cf. pp. 80; 127).

It is thus clear enough that *ager publicus* was a common phenomenon in Italy well into the imperial period. What evidence is there of imperial intervention in relation to it? In the third century L. Didius Marinus (Pflaum, *Carrières*, no. 295) was at one stage *proc(urator) vectigalior(um) [p]opuli R. quae sunt citra Padum*. This could relate to *ager publicus*, or to indirect taxes (App. 2) There seems to be no other relevant evidence.

(c) *Ager publicus* in the provinces. In the *Corpus Agrimensorum* there is only one specific reference to property of the *populus Romanus* in a province: pp. 85–6, in Cyrene, 'agri sunt regii, id est illi quos Ptolomeus rex populo Romano reliquit . . . lapides vero inscripti nomine divi Vespasiani sub clausula tali, OCCUPATI A PRIVATIS FINES, P. R. ⟨P⟩RESTITUIT.' This is confirmed by *SEG* IX 166 (Cyrene): Vespasian 'per Q. Paconium Agrippeinum legatum suum populo R. Ptolemaeum restituit'. For the beginnings of the issue see Tacitus, *Ann* XIV, 18. Nothing is recorded of the later history of this property.

Otherwise evidence for he existence of *ager publicus* in any province under the Empire is almost non-existent.[4] There may, however, be such evidence in *ILS* 9017, recording a man who was *proc. Augg. nn. ad fu[nct. ? . . fru]menti et res populi per tr[actum] utriusque Numidiae*, see Pflaum, *Carrières*, no. 274. His precise role is not easily intelligible, but *may* have involved some control or supervision of public property.

Perhaps the most positive evidence is that which shows that a prominent Ephesian of Trajan's time, Vibius Salutaris, was *promagister frumenti mancipalis* in Sicily, which the Greek texts of his inscriptions give as ἀρχώνης σείτου δήμου Ῥωμαίων (*ILS* 7193–5). From Hyginus in *Corpus Agrimensorum*, pp. 79–80, referring to *mancipes* who rented *ager publicus*, it may well be that this is a reference to rent in kind from such *ager publicus* in Sicily.[5] But it still remains obscure whether Salutaris was a private contractor or an imperial official.

[3] See A. Chastagnol, *La Préfecture urbaine à Rome* (1960), pt. ii, ch. v.

[4] None is revealed in Asia in the detailed discussion by T. R. S. Broughton, 'Roman Landholding in Asia Minor', *TAPhA* LXV (1934), 207.

[5] See Hirschfeld, o.c., 139–43, quoting also *CIL* VI 8853 (Rome): *Aug. (servus) disp(ensator) frument(i) mancip(alis)* and *CIL* II 1197 (Hispalis): *Pius Aug. n. verna dispensator [frumen]t(i) mancip(alis)*. Note also the touching grave-epigram of a trader in the Sabine country (*ILS* 7542),

It thus has to be admitted that we do not know either how much *ager publicus* still existed at the beginning of the empire, or what happened to it. But it is at least as likely that most of it was successfully and definitively 'occupied' by private persons as that it became fused with the imperial estates.

APPENDIX 2

Imperial Agents, the *Fiscus* and the Public Revenues

As stated above (p. 199), it is clear that by the middle of the third century at the latest our sources cease to reflect any distinction between public and imperial revenues. As regards the earlier period, it may be useful to make a summary collection of those items of evidence which either show imperial agents concerned in some way with public revenues or imply that those revenues went to the *fiscus*.

1. Tribute

There are no good grounds for the belief that the division of the provinces in 27 BC meant that the tribute from the emperor's provinces became his property (p. 197). Such a view would in any case greatly exaggerate the significance of the division, see *JRS* LVI (1966), 56. But it is the case that from the beginning the tribute of imperial provinces was collected and dispensed by imperial procurators (see especially Dio LIV, 21, 2–8—Licinus, a *libertus*, collecting tribute in Gaul; Strabo III, 4, 20 (167), and in general Dio LIII, 15, 3). But we may deduce from Velleius II, 39, 4, that this was not an indication that the emperor owned these revenues.

None the less, Suetonius, *Aug.* 40, 3, writes, 'et Liviae pro quodam tributario Gallo roganti civitatum negavit, immunitatem optulit affirmans facilius se passurum fisco detrahi aliquid, quam civitatis Romanae vulgari honorem.' There is no obvious way of dismissing the implication of this passage that a loss of tribute was a loss to the *fiscus*. Pliny, *Pan.* 29, 4–5, apparently discussing provincial payments of corn as tribute, has 'nec novis indictionibus pressi ad vetera tributa deficiunt. emit fiscus quidquid videtur emere, inde copiae. inde annona . . .' The passage *may* imply some relationship of the *fiscus* to *tributa*.

A number of passages in legal writers of the third century also imply the payment of *tributa* on land to the *fiscus*: *Dig.* II, 14, 42 (Papinian); L, 15, 5, *pr.* (Papinian); XLIX, 14, 46, 5 (Hermogenianus); L, 4, 18, 26 (Arcadius); cf. VII, 1 ,27, 3 (Ulpian), *fructuarius* of land liable for *fusiones* to *fiscus*. In *Dig.* XXXIX, 4, 1, 1 (Ulpian) it is not clear whether the author is equating the collection of tribute by *publicani* and their payment of a *vectigal* (rent or indirect tax) to the *fiscus*, or distinguishing the two: 'publicani autem sunt qui publice fruuntur (nam inde nomen habent), sive fisco vectigal pendant vel tributum consequantur; et omnes qui quod a fisco conducunt

---

who records *int. al.* 'solvi semper fiscalia manceps'. It seems as likely as any other interpretation that among his interests were the leasing of public(?)—or imperial?—land.

recte appellantur publicani.' It seems clear that the author is recommending, rather than simply referring to, the description of those who contracted with the *fiscus* as *publicani*. The usage is on any basis curious, for it is quite certain that *publicani* had long since ceased to collect the direct *tributa*. The implications of the passage are therefore very unclear (for its relevance to *vectigalia* see below).

As regards documentary evidence, *IGR* III 488=*OGIS* 565 (Oenoanda, Lycia) shows a local magistrate πληρώσαντα καὶ [εἰς] τὸ ἱερώτατον ταμεῖον τοὺς ἱεροὺς φόρους καὶ τὴν πρᾶξιν ποιησάμενον ἐπεικῶς καὶ τειμητικῶς. There seems no reason to question that these φόροι were *tributa*, collected, as was normal in the empire, by city officials. *Tributa* may also be concerned in *IGR* IV 1637 (Philadelphia, Asia), πληρώσαντα δὲ καὶ τὸ ἱερώτατον ταμεῖον παρ' ἑαυτοῦ and also in *IGR* III 739 (Rhodiapolis, Lycia; the inscription of Opramoas), ii, 59f., [τ]ὰ δὲ ἀναλώματ[α] μεγαλοψύχως ὑφίστα[ται] τὴν πρὸς τὸν φί[σ]κον ὑπὲρ του ἔθνους ἐ[υ]σέβειαν ἐκπλρ[ῶ]ν .... τῇ δὲ ἀναπράξει με[τ]ὰ πάσης φιλανθρωπί[ας] [σ]υ[ν]αρχόμενος [π]ροσέρχεσθαι. The long inscription published by P. Herrmann, K. Z. Polatkan, *Das Testament des Epikrates, S-B. Öst. Akad. Wiss.* 265.1 (1969), shows a yearly payment for land to the *fiscus*, ll.23–4: δώσει ἐπ' ἐνιαυτῷ εἰς φίσκον ἁπλῆς οὐνκίας ὁ διακατέχων (cf. pp. 27–8, suggesting that the 'provincial' *fiscus* is meant).

Finally we may note the annual payments in cash and corn referred to by Caracalla in his edict preserved at Banasa in Mauretania (*AE* 1948 109). In l.5f. he says, 'omnia quaecumque sunt debita fiscalia frumentaria sive pecuniaria pendentium quoque causarum concedo vobis', and in l.14f., 'hoc beneficio meo praesumo omnes de cetero annuas pensitationes sive in frumento sev [*sic*] in pecunia eo promptius daturos . . .' It is quite possible that payments of tribute are in question, but it cannot be certain.

2. Indirect Taxes

From the Julio-Claudian period onwards we find imperial procurators, of equestrian and freedman status, whose posts related to indirect taxes in various areas; see Hirschfeld, *Verwaltungsbeamten*[2], 77–109; de Laet, *Portorium* (1949); Pflaum, *Carrières*, 1026–97 *passim*; G. Boulvert, *Esclaves et affranchis impériaux* (1970), 127–36, 276–82, 308–14, 321–3. The existence of such posts did not necessarily mean that the proceeds of these taxes went to the emperor (or the *fiscus*), and the contrary seems to be indicated, at least in principle, by the use of terms such as *procurator publici* xx *hereditatum Itali(a)e* (*CIL* XI 7487), or *procurator* IIII *publicorum Africae* (*ILS* 1408 etc.). These taxes seem to have continued to be contracted out to *publicani* (or *mancipes*) at least into the second century (see e.g. Pliny, *Pan.* 37–40, and *ILS* 1410: *procurator Aug inter mancipes* XL *Galliarum et negotiantis*). Moreover, a letter of Hadrian from the new dossier of imperial documents at Aphrodisias (see p. xiii) shows both that a tax on nails in Asia (otherwise totally unattested) was then contracted out to *publicani*, and that these *publicani* were subject to the orders of an imperial procurator.

On the other hand we find one *fisci advocatus* XL *Galliarum* (*ILS* 1411) in the first half of the third century. As usual we have no evidence as to the actual functions of the post, which *may* imply that the revenues of the tolls in Gaul went to the *fiscus*; but the man might also have had the task of protecting 'fiscal' (or 'patrimonial') goods from the attentions of the tax-collectors. That may be why certain portable goods are marked (VECTIGAL) PATRIMONI (see p. 627).

However Ulpian was in no doubt that indirect taxes went to the *fiscus*: 'publica vectigalia intellegere debemus, ex quibus vectigal fiscus capit; quale est vectigal portus vel venalium rerum, item salinarum et metallorum et picariarum' (*Dig.* L,

16, 17, 1). It is noticeable that, as in the passage quoted above, he is recommending a certain terminology (the effect of accepting which would have been to allow the application to those who contracted for 'fiscal' revenues of older legislation relating to *publicani* proper). It is also evident that he brings under the heading of *vectigalia* both taxes proper (the *portorium* and *centesima rerum venalium*) and income from properties. In consequence, when we have references elsewhere in legal texts to *conductores* or *redemptores* of the *vectigalia* of the *fiscus* (*Dig.* XLIV, 1, 68, 1; L, 5, 8, 1, *CJ* V, 41, 1 (213); *CJ* X, 57, 1 (Diocletian and Maximian): 'qui mancipatum suo nomine vectigal a fisco conducunt') we cannot tell whether property or taxation is involved. *Dig.* XXXIX, 4, 16, 12 (Marcianus), referring to the case 'si quis professus apud publicanum fuerit, non tamen vectigal solverit, hoc concedente publicano . . . fisco ex bonis publicanorum vel fideiussorum', probably does concern taxes.

In consequence 'fiscus' *may* be correctly restored in Ps.-Quintilian, *Declam.* 341 (of uncertain date): 'quanto illud iniustius videri potest, quo partem hereditatis ⟨fiscus⟩ sibi vindicat.'

Similarly a papyrus of 139, P.Amh. 77=Wilcken, *Chrestomathie*, no. 277=Hunt and Edgar, *Select Papyri*, no. 282, seems to show tolls at Socnopaiou Nesos in Egypt being paid to the *fiscus* (φίσκος or κυριακὸς λόγος); and the reference in Pliny, *NH* VI, 24/84, to Annius Plocamus, 'qui Maris Rubri vectigal a fisco redemerat' *can* be explained as an early example of a *publicanus* contracting with the *fiscus* for the collection of a toll—presumably the 25% customs duty at the Red Sea ports. See *JRS* LIII (1963), 40–1.

Thus as with all other aspects of the history of public or imperial finance under the empire, it is difficult and often impossible to distinguish between a development of vocabulary (or just a loose terminology) and an actual development of practice. It is clear that in the end the emperor absorbed all the revenues of the state; the steps by which he did so may be obscurely divined, but cannot be clearly set out.

APPENDIX 3

Patrimonium and *Ratio Privata*

The following summary collection of evidence does not set out to list every relevant use of these terms, but is designed as a guide to the pattern of ways in which they appear. Their exact connotations still remain obscure. For recent discussion see H. Nesselhauf, 'Patrimonium und res privata des römischen Kaisers', *Bonner Historia-Augusta-Colloquium 1963* (1964), 73; A. Kränzlein, 'Patrimonium', *RE* Supp. X (1965), 493f.; A. Masi, *Ricerche sulla 'Res Privata' del 'Princeps'* (1971).

1. *Patrimonium*

As noted above (p. 192), *patrimonium* appears as early as the *Res Gestae* (15, 1; 17, 2; 18), as the source of expenditure by Augustus; cf. Velleius II, 130, 2, a payment by Tiberius from the *patrimonium*.

Equestrian officials of the *patrimonium*: the earliest is Sex. Caesius Propertianus, *proc. imp. a patrimonio et hereditatibus* in 69 (*ILS* 1447). Examples of men as *procurator patrimonii* or *procurator a patrimonio* are attested up to the early third century, but not beyond (Pflaum, *Carrières*, p. 1025). M. Aquilius Felix (Pflaum, no. 225) appears with a variant terminology in two inscriptions:

> *ILS* 1387: *proc(urator) hered(itatium) patrim(onii) privati*, then *proc(urator) patrim(onii) bis*;
> *AE* 1945 80: *proc(urator) rat(ionis) patr(imonii)*, then *proc(urator) rat(ionis) patr(imoni) iterum*.

The occasional conjunction of *patrimonium* and *hereditates* may well be significant, and reappears in *ILS* 1489 (reign of Domitian): *Lemnus Aug. l. proc. patrimoni et hered.* For freedmen officials of the *patrimonium* (*tabularii, a commentariis, adiutores tabularii, custos ration.* etc.) see *CIL* VI 8498(=*ILS* 1738, Prosenes, *proc. patrimoni* under Caracalla)—8509. Note also *AE* 1945 134=1949 70; 1945 116.

From outside Rome, *CIL* II 1198 (Hispalis); XI 3885 (Capena); *AE* 1962 19= Wuilleumier, *Ins. lat. des Trois Gaules*, no. 237 (Lugdunum);?*AE* 1952 59=1956 12 (Aquileia)

Patrimonial officials whose titles relate to specific areas:

(a) freedmen: *EE* VIII, 366, no, 26: *tabul. provinc. Lusit. rat. pat.* (Emerita, 2nd— 3rd cent.); (?)*CIL* III 4828: Eutyches, *Aug. n. disp. P.R.N.*; *ILS* 4198: *Aug lib. tab. P.R.N.* (*patrimonium regni Norici*? —see G. Alföldy, 'Patrimonium regni Norici', *BJ* CLXX (1970), 163); *ILS* 1491: *qui proc(uravit) Alexandriae ad rat. patrim.* (reign of Hadrian).

(b) *equites*: (1) *AE* 1962 183: Q. Domitius Marsianus, promoted to *proc. Aug patrimoni provin(ciae) Narbonenis* by Marcus Aurelius. From the level of pay, 200,000 *sesterces*, it is certain that this post was that which normally appears as *proc. prov. Narbonensis* (and so for any other proconsular province). See p. 288, and H.-G. Pflaum, *BJ* CLXXI (1971), 349.

(2) *proc. Augg. nn. patrimonii reg. Leptiminensis.* Third century, see Pflaum, *Carrières*, p. 1094. Note that Pflaum nos. 245a and 302 were both also (simultaneously) procurators of the *ratio privata*.

(3) C. Furius Sabinus Aquila Timesitheus (Pflaum, n. 317), in 230s *proc(uratori) patrimon(i) provinciarum Belgic(ae) et duaram Germaniarum*, then *proc. prov. Bithyniae Ponti Paphlagon[iae] tam patrimoni quam rat(ionis) privata[e]* (*ILS* 1330).

(4) *fisci advocatus patrimoni tractus Karthaginiensis*, third century, Pflaum, *Carrières*, p. 1093-4.

Officials whose title relates to the *patrimonium* of certain regions are not found later than about the middle of the third century. It is noticeable that in (3) and (4) *patrimonium* appears as distinct from, but in close relation to, *ratio privata*.

Note, however, the one reference to the office of *procurator patrimonii* in the *Digest*, XXX, 39, 10 (Ulpian); 'ea praedia Caesaris quae in formam patrimonii redacta sub procuratore patrimonii sunt' (cf. p. 176).

Objects marked as belonging to the *patrimonium*:

(a) *Fistulae* from Rome and vicinity, *CIL* XV, 7294, 7303, 7312, 7315, 7318, 7341-4; see ibid. pp. 906-9. Cf. A. Ferrua, *Epigraphica* XXIX (1967), 77, no. 91.
(b) Sherds from the Monte Testaccio in Rome, *CIL* XV 4102 (dated 217), 4111, 4114, 4124-33 (FISCI RATIONIS PATRIMONI PROVINCIAE

BAETICAE); 4134–6 (FISCI RATIONIS PATRIMONI PROVINCIAE TARRACONE).

(c) Objects from places other than Rome:

AE 1914 292 (glass found at Chester): VECTIGAL (P)ATRIMONI; cf. *JRS* XLVI (1956), 149 (Colchester) and for other examples, R. MacMullen, *Aegyptus* XXXVIII (1958), 185, n. 1.

Patrimoniales fundi and comparable expressions in legal documents of the late third and fourth centuries:

CJ V, 71, 13 (293): 'etiam vectigale vel patrimoniale sive emphyteuticum praedium sine decreto praesidis distrahi non licet.'

CJ XI, 65, *de collatione fundorum patrimonialium et emphyteuticorum*, 2 (319, to *proconsul Africae*): 'patrimoniales fundos extraordinariis oneribus vel mediae vel tertiae portionis obsequiis fatigari non convenit . . .' (=*CTh* XI, 16, 1).

CJ XI, 62, *de fundis patrimonialibus et saltuensibus et emphyteuticis et eorum conductoribus*, 2: 'patrimonialis fundi pensitationem aurarium seu frumentariam intra tempus omissam . . .'

CTh XI, 19, 1 (321): 'quotiens plures fundum patrimonialem possident . . .' (both of these are addressed to Dracontius, given in *CTh* X, 1, 4 as *magister privatae rei* in Africa in 320).

CTh IV, 12, 3 (320): '. . . quod ius et in fiscalibus servis et in patrimoniorum fundorum originariis et ad emphyteuticaria praedia et qui ad privatarum rerum nostrarum corpora pertinent servari volumus'.

CTh XI, 16, 2 (323): (applying *CJ* XI, 65, 2 to Italy).

CTh II, 25, 1=*CJ* III, 38, 11 (325): 'In Sardinia fundis patrimonialibus vel enfyteuticariis . . .'

In the period up to 337, *patrimonium* and its cognates appear very rarely in the papyri: πατριμουνά[λια] twice in a tax-list of the first half of the third century, *P. Strassb.* 315, ll. 12, 14; then in the fourth century dubiously restored in *P. Ryl.* 655, l. 11; in an uncertain context in *P. Ryl.* 658, l. 6; σίτου πατριμουνα[λ]ίο[υ] in *P. Strassb.* 325, col. II, l. 5, probably of 321; πραιποσίτου μου ὄντος πατριμων‹ι›αλίων δεκάτου πάγου τοῦδε τοῦ νομοῦ in a petition of 322, *P. Oxy.* 900=Wilcken, *Chrestomathie*, no. 437; ἐξαργυρισμοῦ πατρεμουνίου in *P. Strassb.* 337 II. 4–5 (330 or 331). Cf. also *P. Vindob. Sijpesteijn* 2, col. I, 12. 32, both of 339.

2. *Ratio Privata*

The expression *ratio privata* is attested earlier and far more frequently than *res privata*, which in this period appears only retrospectively in the later legal sources (see below); *privata* alone, as in *procurator privatae*, or later *magister privatae*, is also very common. It seems difficult to assert that the use of *ratio privata* in Latin owes nothing to the term ἴδιος λόγος in Greek, whose meaning is identical. A rough resemblance, though not a precise continuity, of functions is perfectly evident (cf. pp. 166, 171–4).

Procurator rationis privatae. One is very dubiously attested on *CIL* VIII 8810 (Bordj Medjana, Mauretania Sitifensis), under Hadrian or Antoninus Pius; what remains is *procura*[ ] at the beginning of a line of quite uncertain length, with *privatae*[ ] at the beginning of the next line. The inscription provides no basis for the assertion that the 'res privata' was created in this period, and it is a further pure hypothesis to relate to this an inscription from Cimiez about the division of *praedia*, see P. Baldacci, *Centro Studi e doc. It. rom. Atti* II (1969/70), 127. The first secure attestation is *AE* 1961 280, T. Aius Sanctus, *proc. ration. privatae* at some time towards the end of the reign of Marcus Aurelius (Pflaum, *Carrières*, pp. 1002–7). The inscriptions of M. Aquillius Felix, (Pflaum, *Carrières*, no. 225) again present variants, *proc. hered. patrim. privat.* in *ILS* 1387; *proc. rat. privat.* in *AE* 1945 80. *Proc. rat. privat.* continues in the Severan period, Pflaum, p. 1020, and see now *AE* 1969/70 193, Q. Cerellius Apollinaris, *proc. rat. privat.* just before 212. By the middle of the third century a new title appears, *magister summae privatae* (C. Attius Alcimus Felicianus, Pflaum, no. 327).

In the mean time a different development had occurred, which offers a justification for the statement made by *HA, Sept. Sev.* 12, 4, immediately after describing confiscations by Severus: 'tuncque primum privatarum rerum procuratio constituta est'. This is the appearance, beginning in the first decade of the third century, first (it seems) in Italy, or separate regions of Italy, and then in some provinces, of local *procuratores* (*rationis*) *privatae* (listed in Pflaum, *Carrières*, 1036, 1038–40, 1057, 1073, 1077, 1079, ?1093, 1095); note also *JÖAI* XLIX (1968–71), Beibl. 78, no. 14. As noted above (p. 626), posts connected with the *ratio privata* sometimes appear held in apparent conjunction with those of the *patrimonium*. The two categories of land in a particular area *could* therefore be regarded as distinct, though on what principle is not clear. None of the evidence so far listed gives any indication of the nature of the property under the *ratio privata* or of the functions of its officials. But Ulpian's statement in *Dig*, XLIX, 14, 6, 1 'quodcumque privilegii fisco competit, hoc idem et Caesaris ratio et Augustae habere solet', *may* be a reference to the *ratio privata*.

One other legal reference of this period relates to the *ratio privata*. In *CJ* II, 1, 7 (225) Severus Alexander addresses a *subscriptio* to one Valens: 'Procurator privatae rationis instrumentorum, quae communia tibi esse dicis cum fisco, describendorum facultatem secundum morem fieri iubebit . . .' The question evidently relates to land (the *instrumenta* of a *fundus*); it is obscure what relationship between *ratio privata* and *fiscus* is implied.

A few inscriptions also relate to the *ratio privata*, notably *AE* 1908 154: *termines* [*sic*] *defensiones rationis privati* [*sic*] *dd. nn. Augg.* (Bahira, Algeria); *CIL* v 7752: *Lupercus disp. rationis privatae* (Genoa); VI 8510: *Aug. lib. aduit. tabular. rat. privatar.*; VI 29682: an *a cens. prov.* (or *agens pro*) *comm. summ. privatae* honoured by a city council (cf. XI 712, possibly the same man, T. Julius Eutychianus); XV 7236: lead pipes with RATIONIS PRIVATAE; 7333, another with STATIONIS PROPIAE [*sic*] PRIVATAE DOMINI N. ALEXANDRI AUG.

In the late third century and the first half of the fourth a few *rationales* (*summae*) *privatae* are attested (*PLRE*, p. 1062) and also a few diocesan *magistri privatae* and local *procuratores privatae* or *rerum privatarum* (*PLRE*, p. 1063). The expression *res privata*, or *privata res*, in the singular is attested in our period only in the headings or texts of imperial pronouncements preserved in *CTh* and *CJ*. There is *no* documentary attestation for it. So in legal texts, of which the earliest is *CJ* III, 22, 5 (294?), *res privata* may have replaced either *privata* or *ratio privata*. In III, 22, 5 itself we have the expression 'magistrum privatae rei', where the last word can very easily be intrusive.

Much more significant is the fact that papyri and legal sources give fairly extensive evidence of the functions of the *privata* in this period. First a summary table of the papyrus evidence:

298   *P. Beatty Panop.* 1 (letters of *strategus* of Panopolite nome)

120 f.: to Pomponius Domnus (*magister privatae*), on despatch of ships carrying matting.

149 f.: to Pomponius Domnus (*magister privatae*), on arrest of man and his despatch to Domnus.

160 f.: to us the *magister* (Pomponius Domnus), on despatch of ships.

192 f.: to Ammonius concerning arrests on the orders of the μαγίστρου τῆς πριουάτης (193). Note 200, a reference to the interests of τὸ ἱερώτατον ταμῖο[ν].

205 f.: public notice subsequent to enquiry by Pomponius Domnus, *magister privatae*, about wine included in confiscated goods (cf. p. 173).

225–9: to *proedros* of Panopolis on the despatch of a slave, formerly of a man now condemned and now [τοῦ ἱερ]ωτάτου ταμίου, on the orders of Domnus, *m. p.*

338 f.: to the nominators of the metropolis concerning arrests ordered by Domnus, *m.p.* κατὰ τὰ διαφέροντα τῷ ἱερω[τάτῳ] ταμίῳ.

365–73: to *boulê* of Panopolis and to Melas, ἐπίτροπος πριουάτης, concerning the latter's orders for the appointment of προνοηταὶ ταμιακῶν οὐσιῶν.

400–4: to the *boulê* on the same subject, ordering them to act ὑπὲρ λυσιτελείας τοῦ ἱερωτάτου ταμείου.

301/2   *P. Lond.* 1271 (edited by Skeat, *Two Papyri from Panopolis*, 156–7): letter from the [ἐπ]ίτρο[πος] πριου[ά]της Θηβαί[δος . . . .] apparently about the lease of confiscated land.

304   *P. Oxy.* 2673: surrender of church property on the orders of Aurelius Athanasius, ἐπίτροπος πριουάτης, under the superior orders of Neratius Apollonides, μαγίστερ τῆς πριουάτης. See p. 575.

305/6   *P. Oxy.* 2665: report on confiscated property, ordered by Aurelius Athanasius, ἐπίτροπος τῆς κατ' Αἴγυπτον πριουάτης in accordance with letters from Neratius Apollonides. See pp. 173–4.

306   *PSI* 310: fragment of receipt for uncoined silver, mentioning (l. 3) [τ]άξεως πριουάτης and (l. 11) the *magister*. For the date, J. R. Rea, *Chron. d'Eg.* XLIX (1974), 163.

309   Mitteis, *Chrestomathie*, no. 196: report on confiscated property (τὰ ὑπάρχοντα. . . ἐκδικηθῆναι τοῖς τοῦ ταμείου λογισμοῖς) on the orders of Valerius Asterius, ἐπίτροπος πριουάτης Αἰγύπτου.

319   *SB* 10264, re-edited by D. Hagedorn, *ZPE* XVII (1975), 91: a quantity of woad paid τῇ τάξι τῆς πριουάτης.

325   *P. Oxy.* 3125: delivery of documents to the *magister privatae*, Flavius Graphicianus.

Early fourth century: *SB* 9883 (N. Lewis, 'A New Document on the Magister Rei Privatae', *JJP* XV (1965), 157), a document mentioning (l. 2) μαγίστρου πριουάτης and concerning the sale of *ousiai tamiakai*.

Early fourth century: Wilcken, *Chrestomathie*, no. 178: a fragment referring to συντελεία and hypothetically restored [κατὰ] κέλευσιν τοῦ διασημοτάτου μαγίστρου [τῆς] πριουάτης (cf. the original, *BGU* 927).

The *privata* and its officials are also referred to in imperial pronouncements of the tetrarchic and Constantinian period preserved in *CTh* and *CJ* and on inscriptions:

CJ III, 22, 5 (?294 or 300 or 305): *causae libertatis* between *fiscus* and *privati* to be remitted 'ad rationalem vel magistrum privatae rei, hoc est unde mota est quaestio'.

?*CTh* X, 4, 1 (313—attributed to 326 by Seeck, *Regesten*, 51): 'si quis ab

actore rerum privatarum nostrarum sive a procuratore fuerit vexatus . . .'
(cf. *CJ* III, 26, 9, by Valentinian and Valens).
*FIRA*² I, no. 94 (314), from *CIL* V 2781 (Patavium); *CIL* III 12043=*Ins.
Cret.* I. xviii 188 (Lyttos); *CIL* III 12133 (Tlos, Lycia). Partial texts with
misleading headings in *CTh* IX, 5, 1 and *CJ* IX, 8, 3. Edict of Constantine
repressing accusations by informers, ll. 46–8 (Lyttos): '[S]uper i(s)tis
i[taque o]mnibus tum ad praefectos nostros quam eti[am ad p]raesides et
rationalem et magistrum privat[ae] scripta direximus . . .'
cf. *CIL* III 13569=*Ins. Cret.* I. xviii 189 (Lyttos): Constantinian (?) edict
of similar content, mentioning instructions sent to officials, including
pribate [*sic*] *magistro* (l. 44).
CTh XI, 27, 1 (315) on provision of *alimenta* for children in Italy (cf. p. 200):
'ad quam rem et fiscum nostrum et rem privatam indiscreta iussimus
praebere obsequia'.
CTh X, 1, 2 (319), on gifts of property and slaves *exempta fisci patrimonio*.
Rights of beneficiaries to be protected, and penalties laid on *rationales et
magistros privatae rei atque officiales* who interfere.
CTh IV, 12, 3 (320), see pp. 175–6.
CTh X, 1, 4 (320) to Dometius Dracontius, *mag(ist)rum privatae rei Afric(ae)*.
'cum fiscus litem patiatur aut inferat . . .' Cf. *CTh* XI, 19, 1 and *CJ* XI, 62, 2,
both addressed to Dracontius, and both referring to *patrimoniales fundi*
(see p. 627).
CTh I ,32, 1=*CJ* XI, 8, 2 (333): 'procuratores rei privatae (b)afii et gynaecei,
per quos et privata nostra substantia tenua(t)ur et species in gynaeceis
confectae conrumpuntur . . .'

It should thus be evident that no clear or definite statements can yet be made
about the juridical nature, origins or history of the *patrimonium* and *ratio privata*.
But it *may* be that (at least) one of the functions of the *ratio privata* was the handling
of confiscated property, and that it inherited this from the *idios logos*, which disappears not long after it appears. The *Historia Augusta* may then be correct
in apparently associating its origins with confiscations under Severus; its attribution
of the origin of the *rerum privatarum procuratio* to that reign also seems to be
justified by the contemporary appearance of regional or local *procuratores rationis
privatae*. If so, the properties which continued to be regarded as 'patrimonial' *may*
have been those which either had come, or continued to come, to the Emperor by
ordinary private-law means, notably inheritance and (perhaps) gift. The evidence
of the earlier fourth century could suggest that these were relatively less important,
and were handled, or at least could be handled, by officials of the *privata*.

APPENDIX 4

Freeborn Provincial *Latini* in the Imperial Period?

It is widely assumed (p. 485) that under the empire those inhabitants of communities possessing 'Latin rights' who did not possess the Roman citizenship (either

per magistratum, by *beneficium* of the emperor, birth or some other means) were *Latini*, and thus enjoyed some status in between that of *peregrini* and of full citizens. That was of course the case with the Latin communities of republican Italy before the Social War, both those belonging to the geographical area of Latium itself and *coloniae Latinae*. See *Diz. Epig.* s.v. 'Latium'; A. Alföldi, *Early Rome and the Latins* (1965); E. T. Salmon, *Roman Colonisation under the Republic* (1969); A. N. Sherwin-White, *The Roman Citizenship*[2] (1973), esp. ch. i and iii.

But is it correct to assume that the same applied to provincial communities of the late republican and imperial period which enjoyed what was then called *Latinum, ius Latii* or *Latinitas*? That is indeed implied by Strabo III, 22, 15 (151), speaking of Baetica in the Augustan period, Λατῖνοί τε οἱ πλεῖστοι γεγόνασι, and also by the designations of some towns in the western provinces, as listed by Pliny in the *Natural History*:

(Baetica)

III, 1/15: 'Gaditani conventus civium Romanorum Regina, Latinorum Laepia Regia, Carisa cognomine Aurelia, Urgia cognominata Castrum Iulium, item Caesaris Salutariensis';
3/18: 'oppida civium Romanorum XIII, Latinorum veterum XVIII;
3/20: 'Latinorum Lucentum';
(Hispania Citerior)
3/23: 'Latinorum Ausetani, Cerretani qui Iuliani cognominantur et qui Augustani, Edetani, Gerundenses, Gessorienses, Teari qui Iulienses';
3/24: 'Latinorum veterum Cascantenses';
(Narbonensis)
4/32: 'Ruscino Latinorum';
(Sicilia)
?8/91: 'Latinae condicionis Centuripini, Netini, Segestani';
(Alpes)
?20/133: 'Latini iuris Euganeae gentes';
(Mauretania)
V, 1/20: 'Arsennaria Latinorum'.

The relevance of these expressions is that they indicate, or appear to indicate, that the individual inhabitants of these places were called *Latini*. The basic sources from which Pliny obtained these lists are, however, regarded as early, whether Augustan, see e.g. M. I. Henderson, 'Julius Caesar and *Latium* in Spain', *JRS* XXXII (1942), 1, or late-republican, see e.g. L. Teutsch, *Das Städtewesen in Nordafrika* (1962), 27 f.; P. A. Brunt, *Italian Manpower* (1971), App. 13 and 14. Furthermore the extensive epigraphic documentation of the imperial period does not provide a single case where the expression 'Latinorum' is attached to the name of a town or locality. It therefore must remain an open question whether the use of this expression by Pliny has any relevance to personal statuses under the empire. The whole question therefore needs re-examination.

Various points need to be considered. (a) As we saw (pp. 401–6), all the explicit descriptions of 'Latin rights' from this period *define* these rights in terms of the fact that magistrates (or councillors also) in the communities which possessed them became Roman citizens, as did their descendants. None makes any explicit reference to the status of those inhabitants of such communities who did not attain to magistracies (or the council). (b) As we saw also (p. 485ff.), the imperial period did know an explicitly defined category of persons known as *Latini* (*Juniani*), namely ex-slaves manumitted by various processes or under various conditions which a

Lex Junia (of Augustan or Tiberian date, see Sherwin-White, o.c., 332f.) and also the *Lex Aelia Sentia* of AD 4, defined as incomplete or provisional, and who did not enjoy the full rights of citizens (*ius Quiritium*) possessed by fully manumitted *liberti* or *libertae*. These could be referred to simply as *Latini* even in official communications between a governor and the emperor (Pliny, *Ep.* X, 104).

Therefore, if we are to determine what categories of persons existed in the empire it is necessary to distinguish between (a) evidence relating explicitly to the known category of ex-slaves, the *Latini Juniani*; (b) evidence which does not make clear whether the 'Latin' is an ex-slave or a freeborn provincial of special status; (c) evidence which explicitly relates to the as yet hypothetical category of freeborn provincials enjoying 'Latin' rights.

(a) It can be stated at once that most references to *Latini* are concerned explicitly with ex-slaves. Our best evidence comes from the *Institutes* of Gaius, especially Book I. Discussing the *ius personarum*, he says that the term *dediticii* was applied to the inhabitants of communities which had fought against Rome and then surrendered (*se dediderunt*), and that slaves of this shameful origin could not become either *cives Romani* or *Latini*; he then describes the two forms of manumission, complete and incomplete (I, 14–17). Thereafter throughout the main part of Book I there are repeated references to *Latini* and *Latinae*, some of which individually make it explicit that they concern ex-slaves, namely 22–4; 28–41; 66; 68; 71; 80. Moreover, in one passage Gaius explicitly contrasts these ex-slave *Latini* with the communities of *Latini* which had once existed in the past, I, 79: '(*vacat*) . . . non solum exterae nationes et gentes, sed etiam qui Latini nominantur; sed ad alios Latinos pertinet, qui proprios populos propriasque civitates habebant, et erant peregrinorum numero'.

Other passages, taken individually, do not make this explicit (56–7; 67; 81); but as no category of *Latini* other than ex-slaves has so far been mentioned all of these can be taken as mentions of freed slaves, and it might be argued that they definitely should be so taken. In order not to prejudice the issue, however, they will be considered further below. It must be emphasized that it is only later, in I, 95–6, that Gaius mentions the *Latii ius*, as a right given to some *peregrinae civitates* (not persons) and defines *Latium minus* and *maius* (p. 405 above). He makes no reference to the status of the ordinary inhabitants of such *civitates*, but mentions the *ius* only in connection with the *patria potestas* enjoyed by those who gained the citizenship under it.

In the strict sense Gaius has already mentioned one other category of *Latini* for he says that the *Latii Juniani* gained part of their appellation 'quia adsimulati sunt Latinis coloniariis' (I, 22). Later he says, 'Olim quoque, quo tempore populus Romanus in Latinas regiones colonias deducebat, qui iussu parentium in coloniam Latinam nomen dedissent, desinebant in potestate parentis esse' (I, 131). Material from the two passages appears to be inaccurately conjoined in the *Fragmentum Dositheanum* 6: 'fiunt Latini Juniani, quoniam lex Junia, quae libertatem eis dedit exaequavit eos Latinis coloniariis, qui cum essent cives Romani liberti (?), nomen suum in colonias dedissent' (for the demonstration that this text is at least the remains of a legal work of the later second century, see A. M. Honoré, *RIDA* XII (1965), 301). These references are essentially antiquarian, and do not in themselves imply that any category of *Latini coloniarii* still existed. Whether anything in legal sources does imply this will be discussed further below.

In the rest of Gaius' *Institutes* most of the references to *Latini* or *Latinae* again explicitly concern ex-slaves (I, 167; II, 110; 195; 275; III, 55–73). The same is true of the other legal works which have survived in fragmentary form: *Tit. Ulp.* I, 10; 12; 16; III, 1; VII, 4; XVII, 1; XX, 8; 14; XXII, 3; 8; XXV, 7; *Frag. Vat.* 193; 221; *Sent. Pauli* IV, 12, 1; *Coll.* IV, 3, 3; *Frag. Dosith.* 4–17. See also *CTh* IV, 12, 3; IX, 24, 1, 4; *CJ* VII, 6, 1 (abolition of this status by Justinian).

Latini who are ex-slaves also appear in clause 22 of the *Gnomon* of the *Idios Logos* (ed. Riccobono, 1950), laying down that on their death their property reverted to their *patroni*.

The status of ex-slave *Latini* (*Juniani*) is thus attested in considerable detail. But very few actual individuals even of this status make an appearance in non-legal sources other than Pliny's letters. One who does is the wife of Vespasian, Suetonius, *Vesp.* 3: 'Inter haec Flaviam Domitillam duxit uxorem, Statili Capellae equitis R. Sabratensis ex Africa delicatam olim Latinaeque condicionis, sed mox ingenuam et civem Rom. reciperatorio iudicio pronuntiatam.' Before being declared *ingenua* she was clearly regarded as being a freedwoman.

(b) *Latini* whose origin is not immediately clear make an appearance in two groups of documentary sources, and quite widely in legal evidence: The most important documents are the *leges* of two Spanish towns, Malaca and Salpensa (cf. pp. 404–3).

Lex Salpensana (*ILS* 6088=*FIRA*[2] I, no. 23), ch. xxviii:
'Si quis municeps municipi Flavi Salpensani, qui Latinus erit, apud IIvir(os), qui iure dicundo praeerunt eius municipi, servom suom servamve suam ex servitute in libertate[m] manumiserit … qui ita manumissus liberve esse iussus erit, liber esto, quaeque ita manumissa liberave (esse) iussa erit, libera esto, uti qui optum[o] iure Latini libertini liberi sunt erunt.'

Does the expression 'municeps municipi Flavi Salpensani, qui Latinus erit' refer simply to any ordinary citizen of the *municipium* (which, as chs. xxi–ii and xxv show, enjoyed the *ius Latii*)? It may indeed do so. But it should be noted that the following paragraph (xxix) lays down the procedure for the appointment of a *tutor* for a 'municeps municipi Flavi Salpensani' (without the qualification), and concludes 'tam iustus tutor esto, quam si is c(ivis) R(omanus) et (ei) adgnatus proximus c(ivis) R(omanus) tutor esset'. Though no certainty can be, or is, claimed, the two chapters are compatible with the view that the ordinary *municipes* of Salpensa were neither *Latini* nor *cives Romani*. On the other hand, if the *municeps* 'qui Latinus erit', is a *Latinus Junianus* then the chapter shows such a person owning and manumitting slaves, as a full *libertus* in fact could. On this hypothesis the freed slave when duly manumitted, on becoming free 'uti qui optum[o] iure Latini libertini liberi sunt', is acquiring the same status as his master.

Lex Malacitana (*ILS* 6089=*FIRA*[2] I, no. 24):
Latini appear only in ch. liii, instructing whatever magistrate was presiding at the elections to draw by lot one *curia*, 'in qua incolae, qui cives R(omani) Latinive cives erant, suffragi[um] ferant.'

It is clear enough that out of those persons who were domiciled in Malaca but were not citizens of it (*incolae*) two special categories were reserved the right to vote in the town elections. They are Roman citizens and *Latini cives*. The latter expression is rare (though note Gaius, *Inst.* I, 15, 'cives Romanos aut Latinos', and 16, 'civem Romanum modo Latinum', both referring to freed slaves), and could of course refer to citizens of other 'Latin' towns who lived in Malaca. We cannot however exclude the possibility that the reference is to incompletely manumitted slaves of Roman citizens.

Cives Latini also seem to be attested in one very specialized group of military documents, namely dedications from Britain (only) put up by the *cohors II Tungrorum milliaria equitata c(ivium) L(atinorum)* (*RIB* 1981–3; 2092; 2104; 2110). All the inscriptions give only the initial letters, c.L., which are interpreted only by analogy with the quite common appellation for auxiliary units, *c(ivium) R(omanorum)*. This appellation persists after the *constitutio Antoniniana* (*RIB* 1983), and is unique, not even being shared by other units of Tungri. Both its significance and the reason for its being granted must remain uncertain. All that is clear is that it cannot help towards the solution of a problem which is potentially relevant to the whole of western society in the imperial period.

Latini, as mentioned above, are attested in a number of passages in legal works which do not make explicit whether they are dealing with ex-slaves or freeborn provincials. Gaius, *Inst.* I, 56–7 says that *patria potestas* followed if a Roman citizen married a woman who was a citizen 'vel etiam Latinas peregrinasve cum quibus conubium habeant' (cf. also *Tit. Ulp.* v, 4), and goes on to say that imperial *constitutiones* customarily gave veterans 'conubium cum his Latinis peregrinisve quae primas post missionem uxores duxerint'. He is hardly a safe guide here, since of the numerous preserved *diplomata* only those addressed to various categories of soldiers who were already citizens confine the grant of *conubium* to future marriages, and even these only refer to *peregrinae* (*CIL* XVI, p. 156). Those granted to non-citizen auxiliaries and others refer just to 'uxores' (present or future) without specifying their status (*CIL* XVI, pp. 158–9).

A couple of other passages in Gaius (*Inst.* I, 67; II, 142) refer to the consequences if a Roman citizen married a *Latina* or *peregrina* under the impression that she was a citizen. Similarly, *Sent. Pauli* II, 21A, 1 states that a 'mulier ingenua civisque Romana vel Latina' who formed a union with another's slave herself became a slave. The term *ingenua* may well qualify 'Latina' also here, for *Sent. Pauli* IV, 9, 8 has: 'Latina ingenua ius Quiritium consecuta si ter peperit, ad legitimam filii hereditatem admittitur: non est enim manumissa'. Along with the statement made by this source soon after, 'ad legitimam intestatae matris hereditatem filii cives Romani, non enim Latini admittuntur' (IV, 10, 3=*App. Leg. Wisig.* I, 19), the reference might seem to confirm the existence of a class of freeborn provincial *Latini*. But apart from the difficulty that the *Sententiae Pauli* is normally regarded as being a work of the second half of the third century, i.e. later than the *constitutio Antoniniana*, earlier evidence shows that the children of a mother who was a *Latina* themselves remained *Latini* (Gaius, *Inst.* I, 67; 81, etc.; *Tit. Ulp.* v, 9). A female of such origin could have been described as a *Latina ingenua*, though it cannot be proved that the expression was so used.

There is nothing explicit to indicate which status is presumed on the part of the *Latina* referred to in *Gnomon*, clause 26. But note that the preceding reference to *Latini* (22) is to ex-slaves (p. 633)

Thus the legal sources also do not provide any conclusive evidence of *Latini* who were neither ex-slaves, not descended from ex-slaves.

(c) There seems in fact to be no definitive and conclusive evidence for a whole class of freeborn provincial *Latini* under the empire. But it has to be stated that two passages in legal works appear to speak as if the class of *Latini coloniarii* still existed:

Gaius, *Inst.* I, 29: 'Statim enim ex lege Aelia Sentia minores triginta annorum manumissi et Latini facti si uxores duxerint vel cives Romanes vel Latinas coloniarias vel eiusdem condicionis cuive et ipsi essent . . .'

Tit. Ulp. XIX, 4: 'Mancipatio locum habet inter cives Romanos et Latinos coloniarios Latinosque Junianos eosque peregrinos, quibus commercium datum est.'

The inhabitants of the old *coloniae Latinae* in Italy had of course been Roman citizens since the Social War; in Gaul, it is true, a number of communities with Latin rights are attested as *coloniae* in the early Empire (see, independently, B. Galsterer-Kröll, *Chiron* III (1973), 290; Sherwin-White, o.c. 364f.). But this is still insufficient to suggest that a general category of *Latini coloniarii* existed in the provinces in the imperial period. Their inclusion in these passages must therefore either be of purely antiquarian interest, or the term must be intended as a reference, however inappropriate, to the hypothetical class of 'Latins' who inhabited provincial communities with the *ius Latii*.

The alternative hypothesis, that no such class existed, is put forward purely tentatively. It would however serve to explain why we cannot state whether 'Latins' served in the legions or the *auxilia*, or why even the most careful examination of the evidence cannot demonstrate whether they used the Roman *tria nomina*, or, if not, what type of nomenclature they employed (for such an attempt see G. Alföldy, 'Notes sur la relation entre le droit de cité et la nomenclature dans l'Empire romain', *Latomus* XXV (1966), 37, on pp. 47–55). It would also explain why the last freeborn individual of Latin status who appears in a literary source is the Latin actor who was performing in Picenum on the eve of the Social War (Diodorus XXXVII, 12). Had such a class of persons existed in the empire, it is unlikely (though not of course impossible) that our relatively rich anecdotal information should have revealed not a single one of them; and more unlikely still that no emperor should be attested as ruling on any question relating to their status, as they did with the manumission of slaves, the promotion of *Latini Juliani* and the conferment of citizenship on *peregrini*.

INDEX

In view of the large amount of material which is given merely by way of illustration this index is highly selective, and is intended as no more than a guide to the main topics, names and subjects in the book. The material in the Appendixes is not included. I am most grateful to Mr S. R. F. Price for preparing it.

1. *Names and Subjects*

ab epistulis:
  accompanied emperor, 6, 79, 90–3
  liberti as, 75–6, 79
  literary qualifications of, 85, 87–93
  equites as, 85, 88, 89–90, 103, 104, 107
  equites as *ab epistulis Graecis*, 88, 91–3, 102, 105
  equites as *ab epistulis Latinis*, 95, 97, 107
  role of in composition of letters, 93, 207, 224–225
  careers of, 104–5
  role of *ab epistulis Graecis*, 225–8
Ablabius, Flavius:
  praetorian prefect, 130–1
accensi:
  of emperor, 66, 68–9
a cognitionibus:
  lawyers as, 94
  equites as, 98, 106–7; careers of, 107, 232
  function of, 232, 235
Acts of Pagan Martyrs:
  evidence for imperial hearings, 234–5
adlection to senate:
  by emperor, 293–7
  policy in, 299
adnotatio:
  nature of, 265–6
adventus:
  of governor or senator, 29
  of emperor, 31–2
Aelius Antipater:
  rhetor and *ab epistulis Graecis*, 92–3
  composed imperial letters, 227
Aemilius Papinianus:
  see Papinian
Aerarium:
  lost *bona damnatorum* to *fiscus*, 167
  relation of to *fiscus*, 189–90, 197–200
Aezani:
  land dispute at, 328–9
Africa:
  imperial estates in, 179
Alba:
  imperial villa at, 25–6
Alexander:
  see Severus Alexander

Alexander of Seleucia:
  rhetor and *ab epistulis Graecis*, 6, 91
  pleaded before Antoninus Pius, 234
Alexander the grammarian:
  conferred *beneficia*, 494–5
Alexandria:
  embassies from to Augustus, 19, 120, 233
  Museum in, connected with imperial court, 86–7, 97–8, 468, 493, 504–6
  subscriptiones of Severus and Caracalla posted in, 244
  choice of ambassadors by, 384
  cf. Acts of the Pagan Martyrs, Egypt
a libellis:
  liberti as, 75, 77–9
  equites as, 89, 102–4
  lawyers as, 94–7, 103; careers of, 104–5
  role of, 207, 249–51
amici, imperial:
  instability of relationship, 110, 112–13
  different categories of ?, 111
  could confer benefits, 113–15
  public role of, 115–16
  advisors of emperor, 119–22
  consulted on correspondence, 223
  cf. *comes*, *consilium*
Antonius, Marcus:
  letters on privileges of athletes, 456
Antinoopolis:
  foundation of, 396
Antioch:
  imperial centre, 48–50
Antoninus Pius:
  subscriptio of on papyrus, 243
  subscriptio of on stone, 247
  on *libelli*, 248
  subscriptio of in *Digest*, 248
  rescript to proconsul, 332
  rescript to praetor, 337–8
  rescript to *koinon* of Thracians, 393
  granted imposition of taxes to city, 427
  judgment on land dispute, 436
  subscriptio of to workman, 544
  subscriptio of for consular enforcement, 545
  letters of on Christians, 559–61
  Apology of Justin addressed to, 562–3

2. *Literary Authorities*

3. *Inscriptions*

4. Papyri